1996 BASEBALL ALMANAC

Contributing Writers
Dan Schlossberg
Stuart Shea
Mike Tully
Michael Bradley
Pete Palmer
Jeff Kurowski
Bruce Herman

Publications International, Ltd.

Cover photo: Focus On Sports

All rights reserved under International and Pan American copyright conventions. Copyright © 1996 Publications International, Ltd. This book may not be reproduced or quoted in whole or in part by mimeograph or any other printed or electronic means, or for presentation on radio, television, videotape, or film without written permission from Louis Weber, C.E.O., Publications International, Ltd., 7373 North Cicero Avenue Lincolnwood, Illinois 60646. Permission is never granted for commercial purposes. Printed in U.S.A.

Dan Schlossberg is a baseball editor for the *American Encyclopedia Annual*, featured columnist for *Legends Sports Memorabilia*, and contributor to *Street & Smith's Official Baseball Yearbook* and *Bill Mazeroski's Baseball*. His 17 books inlcude *The Baseball Catalog*, *The Baseball Book of Why*, and *Total Braves*. The former Associated Press and United Press International sportswriter is a co-author of *Players of Cooperstown: Baseball's Hall of Fame*.

Stuart Shea is Director of Research with the Baseball Workshop and is the Associate Editor of *The Scouting Report: 1996*. He has written for the Associated Press, and his freelance work has appeared in *Baseball Legends of All Time*, *1001 Fascinating Baseball Facts*, and *1992 Fantasy League Baseball*.

Mike Tully is a former national baseball writer for United Press International. He has written six books, including *Leagues and Barons* and *1990-91 Baseball's Hottest Rookies*. His freelance work has appeared in *The National Sports Daily*, *Sports Illustrated*, and *The New York Times*. He was a co-author for the *1994-95 Hockey Almanac*.

Michael Bradley is a freelance writer and radio analyst whose written work has appeared in *The Sporting News*, *Sport Magazine*, *College Sports*, *Slam*, and the *Philadelphia Inquirer*. He is also a contributor to the One-On-One Radio Network.

Pete Palmer edited both *Total Baseball* and *The Hidden Game of Baseball* with John Thorn. Palmer was the statistician for *1994 Golf Almanac*, *1995-96 Basketball Almanac*, and *1001 Fascinating Baseball Facts*. He is a member of the Society for American Baseball Research.

Jeff Kurowski is a professional baseball and sports-card price guide coordinator for books and sports-card magazines, including *1996 Baseball Card Price Guide*, *1994-95 Basketball Almanac*, and *1995-96 Hockey Almanac*. He is the former editor of *Sports Card Price Guide Monthly* and *Sports Collector's Digest Baseball Card Price Guide*. He is also the editor of *The Standard Catalogue of Baseball Cards*.

Bruce Herman is a freelance sportswriter and a sports media consultant. He has contributed to such publications as *Sports Illustrated*, *Inside Sports*, and *USA Today Baseball Weekly*.

CONTENTS

Current Players and Rookie Prospects 11

Player Profiles 12
Jim Abbott 12
Kurt Abbott 12
Kyle Abbott 13
Juan Acevedo 13
Mark Acre 14
Rick Aguilera 14
Mike Aldrete 15
Manny Alexander 15
Edgardo Alfonzo 16
Luis Alicea 16
Roberto Alomar 17
Sandy Alomar 17
Moises Alou 18
Wilson Alvarez 18
Rich Amaral 19
Brady Anderson 19
Brian Anderson 20
Garret Anderson 20
Shane Andrews 21
Eric Anthony 21
Kevin Appier 22
Alex Arias 22
Rene Arocha 23
Andy Ashby 23
Billy Ashley 24
Paul Assenmacher ... 24
Pedro Astacio 25
Brad Ausmus 25
Steve Avery 26
Bobby Ayala 26
Carlos Baerga 27
Jeff Bagwell 27
Harold Baines 28
Bret Barberie............ 28
Kevin Bass 29
Jason Bates 29
Danny Bautista......... 30
Jose Bautista 30
Rod Beck 31

Rich Becker 31
Tim Belcher 32
Stan Belinda 32
Derek Bell 33
Jay Bell 33
Albert Belle 34
Rafael Belliard 34
Andy Benes............. 35
Armando Benitez 35
Mike Benjamin 36
Jason Bere 36
Sean Bergman 37
Geronimo Berroa 37
Sean Berry 38
Damon Berryhill........ 38
Andres Berumen 39
Dante Bichette 39
Mike Bielecki 40
Craig Biggio 40
Willie Blair 41
Jeff Blauser 41
Mike Blowers 42
Joe Boever 42
Tim Bogar 43
Wade Boggs 43
Brian Bohanon 44
Barry Bonds 44
Ricky Bones 45
Bobby Bonilla 45
Bret Boone.............. 46
Pedro Borbon 46
Pat Borders 47
Mike Bordick............ 47
Toby Borland 48
Chris Bosio 48
Shawn Boskie 49
Ricky Bottalico 49
Ryan Bowen 50
Darren Bragg 50
Jeff Branson 51
Jeff Brantley 51
Doug Brocail 52
Rico Brogna 52

Scott Brosius 53
Kevin Brown 53
Jerry Browne 54
Tom Browning 54
Jacob Brumfield....... 55
Damon Buford 55
Jay Buhner 56
Scott Bullett 56
Jim Bullinger 57
Dave Burba 57
John Burkett 58
Ellis Burks 58
Mike Butcher 59
Brett Butler 59
Edgar Caceres 60
Ken Caminiti 60
Tom Candiotti 61
John Cangelosi 61
Jose Canseco 62
Ramon Caraballo 62
Chuck Carr 63
Hector Carrasco 63
Mark Carreon 64
Joe Carter 64
Vinny Castilla............ 65
Frank Castillo 65
Tony Castillo 66
Andujar Cedeno 66
Domingo Cedeno 67
Norm Charlton 67
Jason Christiansen .. 68
Archi Cianfrocco 68
Jeff Cirillo 69
Dave Clark 69
Jerald Clark 70
Mark Clark 70
Phil Clark 71
Terry Clark 71
Will Clark 72
Royce Clayton 72
Roger Clemens 73
Brad Clontz 73
Greg Colbrunn 74

CONTENTS

Alex Cole 74	Cal Eldred 97	Brian Givens 120
Vince Coleman 75	John Ericks 98	Tom Glavine 121
Darnell Coles 75	Scott Erickson 98	Chris Gomez 121
David Cone 76	Vaughn Eshelman 99	Leo Gomez 122
Jeff Conine................. 76	Alvaro Espinoza 99	Alex Gonzalez........... 122
Steve Cooke 77	Tony Eusebio 100	Juan Gonzalez........... 123
Scott Cooper.............. 77	Carl Everett 100	Luis Gonzalez........... 123
Joey Cora................... 78	Jorge Fabregas 101	Dwight Gooden.......... 124
Wil Cordero 78	Rikkert Faneyte 101	Curtis Goodwin 124
Marty Cordova 79	Jeff Fassero 102	Tom Goodwin 125
Rheal Cormier............ 79	Felix Fermin 102	Tom Gordon 125
Tripp Cromer 80	Alex Fernandez 103	Jim Gott 126
John Cummings 80	Sid Fernandez 103	Mark Grace 126
Chad Curtis 81	Tony Fernandez......... 104	Joe Grahe 127
Milt Cuyler 81	Mike Fetters 104	Craig Grebeck 127
Ron Darling 82	Cecil Fielder 105	Shawn Green 128
Danny Darwin 82	Chuck Finley 105	Tyler Green 128
Darren Daulton 83	Steve Finley 106	Tommy Greene 129
Chili Davis 83	John Flaherty 106	Willie Greene 129
Russ Davis 84	Dave Fleming 107	Mike Greenwell 130
Andre Dawson 84	Darrin Fletcher 107	Rusty Greer 130
Steve Decker 85	Scott Fletcher 108	Ken Griffey Jr. 131
Jose DeLeon 85	Kevin Flora................ 108	Marquis Grissom 131
Carlos Delgado 86	Cliff Floyd 109	Kevin Gross 132
Rich DeLucia 86	Chad Fonville 109	Mark
Delino DeShields 87	Tony Fossas 110	Grudzielanek 132
Mike Devereaux 87	Kevin Foster 110	Eddie Guardado 133
Alex Diaz 88	John Franco 111	Mark Gubicza............ 133
Mario Diaz 88	Julio Franco 111	Ozzie Guillen 134
Rob Dibble 89	Lou Frazier 112	Mark Guthrie 134
Jerry DiPoto 89	Marvin Freeman........ 112	Ricky Gutierrez.......... 135
Gary DiSarcina 90	Jeff Frye 113	Jose Guzman 135
Glenn Dishman 90	Travis Fryman 113	Juan Guzman 136
John Doherty 91	Gary Gaetti 114	Chris Gwynn 136
Jim Dougherty 91	Greg Gagne 114	Tony Gwynn 137
Doug Drabek 92	Andres Galarraga 115	John Habyan 137
Darren Dreifort 92	Dave Gallagher 115	Chip Hale 138
Mariano Duncan 93	Mike Gallego 116	Darren Hall................ 138
Shawon Dunston 93	Ron Gant 116	Bob Hamelin 139
Ray Durham 94	Carlos Garcia 117	Darryl Hamilton 139
Mike Dyer 94	Mike Gardiner 117	Joey Hamilton............ 140
Lenny Dykstra 95	Mark Gardner 118	Chris Hammond......... 140
Damion Easley 95	Brent Gates 118	Jeffrey Hammonds . 141
Dennis Eckersley 96	Benji Gil 119	Mike Hampton 141
Jim Edmonds 96	Bernard Gilkey 119	Chris Haney 142
Jim Eisenreich 97	Joe Girardi 120	Dave Hansen............. 142

5

CONTENTS

Erik Hanson 143	Jason Jacome......... 165	Mark Leiter 188
Mike Harkey 143	John Jaha 166	Scott Leius............ 189
Pete Harnisch 144	Chris James 166	Mark Lemke 189
Gene Harris............. 144	Dion James 167	Curtis Leskanic 190
Lenny Harris 145	Stan Javier 167	Darren Lewis 190
Bryan Harvey 145	Gregg Jefferies 168	Mark Lewis 191
Charlie Hayes 146	Reggie Jefferson 168	Jim Leyritz............. 191
Scott Hemond......... 146	Charles Johnson..... 169	Jose Lima 192
Rickey Henderson 147	Howard Johnson 169	Felipe Lira 192
Tom Henke 147	Lance Johnson 170	Nelson Liriano 193
Mike Henneman...... 148	Mark Johnson......... 170	Pat Listach 193
Butch Henry............ 148	Randy Johnson....... 171	Scott Livingstone ... 194
Doug Henry 149	Bobby Jones 171	Graeme Lloyd 194
Pat Hentgen 149	Chipper Jones........ 172	Esteban Loaiza........ 195
Gil Heredia 150	Chris Jones 172	Keith Lockhart 195
Carlos Hernandez.... 150	Doug Jones 173	Kenny Lofton 196
Jeremy Hernandez .. 151	Todd Jones 173	Tony Longmire 196
Jose Hernandez 151	Brian Jordan 174	Javier Lopez 197
Roberto Hernandez. 152	Wally Joyner 174	John Mabry 197
Xavier Hernandez.... 152	Jeff Juden.............. 175	Mike Macfarlane 198
Orel Hershiser......... 153	David Justice 175	Greg Maddux 198
Greg Hibbard 153	Scott Kamieniecki ... 176	Mike Maddux 199
Bryan Hickerson 154	Ron Karkovice 176	Dave Magadan 199
Bob Higginson 154	Scott Karl 177	Pat Mahomes 200
Glenallen Hill........... 155	Eric Karros 177	Candy Maldonado ... 200
Ken Hill 155	Steve Karsay 178	Jeff Manto 201
Sterling Hitchcock .. 156	Mike Kelly 178	Kirt Manwaring 201
Trevor Hoffman....... 156	Pat Kelly 179	Tom Marsh 202
Chris Hoiles 157	Roberto Kelly 179	Al Martin 202
Todd Hollandsworth 157	Jeff Kent 180	Norberto Martin 203
Dave Hollins 158	Jimmy Key 180	Angel Martinez 203
Darren Holmes........ 158	Darryl Kile 181	Dave Martinez 204
Rick Honeycutt 159	Jeff King 181	Dennis Martinez..... 204
Dwayne Hosey 159	Mike Kingery 182	Edgar Martinez 205
Thomas Howard 160	Wayne Kirby 182	Pedro Martinez 205
Steve Howe 160	Ryan Klesko 183	Ramon Martinez 206
John Hudek 161	Chuck Knoblauch.... 183	Tino Martinez 206
Rex Hudler 161	Randy Knorr 184	Don Mattingly 207
Mike Huff 162	Tim Laker 184	Derrick May 207
Todd Hundley 162	Mark Langston........ 185	Brent Mayne 208
Brian Hunter 163	Ray Lankford 185	Kirk McCaskill......... 208
Brian Hunter 163	Mike Lansing 186	Ben McDonald 209
Jeff Huson 164	Barry Larkin 186	Jack McDowell........ 209
Danny Jackson 164	Mike LaValliere 187	Roger McDowell 210
Mike Jackson.......... 165	Phil Leftwich........... 187	Chuck McElroy 210
	Al Leiter 188	Willie McGee........... 211

CONTENTS

Fred McGriff 211	Melvin Nieves 234	Hipolito Pichardo 257
Mark McGwire 212	David Nilsson........... 235	Greg Pirkl................. 258
Mark McLemore 212	C.J. Nitkowski 235	Phil Plantier 258
Greg McMichael...... 213	Otis Nixon................ 236	Dan Plesac 259
Brian McRae 213	Hideo Nomo............. 236	Eric Plunk 259
Rusty Meacham 214	Jon Nunnally............ 237	Luis Polonia............. 260
Pat Meares.............. 214	Charlie O'Brien........ 237	Mark Portugal.......... 260
Roberto Mejia 215	Jose Offerman 238	Kirby Puckett 261
Orlando Merced 215	Chad Ogea 238	Tim Pugh 261
Kent Mercker 216	Troy O'Leary 239	Bill Pulsipher 262
Matt Merullo 216	John Olerud 239	Paul Quantrill 262
Jose Mesa 217	Jose Oliva 240	Scott Radinsky........ 263
Dan Miceli 217	Joe Oliver................ 240	Brad Radke 263
Matt Mieske 218	Paul O'Neill.............. 241	Tim Raines 264
Orlando Miller......... 218	Steve Ontiveros 241	Manny Ramirez....... 264
Michael Mimbs 219	Jose Oquendo......... 242	Pat Rapp 265
Angel Miranda 219	Joe Orsulak............. 242	Jeff Reboulet 265
Dave Mlicki 220	Donovan Osborne... 243	Jeff Reed 266
Paul Molitor 220	Spike Owen 243	Jody Reed................ 266
Raul Mondesi.......... 221	Mike Pagliarulo 244	Steve Reed.............. 267
Jeff Montgomery 221	Tom Pagnozzi 244	Carlos Reyes........... 267
Mike Moore 222	Rafael Palmeiro 245	Shane Reynolds...... 268
Mickey Morandini ... 222	Dean Palmer 245	Armando
Mike Morgan 223	Craig Paquette 246	Reynoso ....: 268
Hal Morris................ 223	Mark Parent 246	Arthur Rhodes 269
James Mouton 224	Jeff Parrett............... 247	Jose Rijo.................. 269
Lyle Mouton 224	Lance Parrish.......... 247	Cal Ripken 270
Jamie Moyer........... 225	Bob Patterson 248	Bill Risley................. 270
Terry Mulholland..... 225	John Patterson 248	Kevin Ritz................. 271
Bobby Munoz.......... 226	Roger Pavlik 249	Sid Roberson........... 271
Mike Munoz 226	Steve Pegues 249	Bip Roberts 272
Pedro Munoz 227	Geronimo Pena....... 250	Frank Rodriguez...... 272
Eddie Murray 227	Tony Pena................ 250	Henry Rodriguez..... 273
Mike Mussina 228	Terry Pendleton 251	Ivan Rodriguez........ 273
Greg Myers 228	Troy Percival 251	Kenny Rogers 274
Randy Myers 229	Carlos Perez............ 252	Mel Rojas................. 274
Tim Naehring 229	Eduardo Perez 252	John Roper 275
Charles Nagy 230	Melido Perez 253	Scott Ruffcorn 275
Jaime Navarro 230	Mike Perez 253	Bruce Ruffin............. 276
Denny Neagle.......... 231	Yorkis Perez 254	Jeff Russell.............. 276
Jeff Nelson.............. 231	Herb Perry 254	Ken Ryan 277
Robb Nen................ 232	Roberto Petagine 255	Bret Saberhagen 277
Phil Nevin 232	Andy Pettitte 255	Tim Salmon 278
Marc Newfield......... 233	J.R. Phillips 256	Juan Samuel 278
Warren Newson 233	Tony Phillips 256	Rey Sanchez 279
David Nied 234	Mike Piazza............. 257	Ryne Sandberg 279

7

CONTENTS

Deion Sanders 280
Reggie Sanders 280
Scott Sanders 281
Benito Santiago 281
Steve Scarsone 282
Curt Schilling 282
Pete Schourek 283
Tim Scott 283
David Segui 284
Kevin Seitzer 284
Aaron Sele 285
Scott Servais 285
Jeff Shaw 286
Danny Sheaffer 286
Gary Sheffield 287
Craig Shipley 287
Ruben Sierra........... 288
Mike Simms............ 288
Don Slaught 289
Heathcliff
Slocumb 289
John Smiley 290
Dwight Smith 290
Lee Smith 291
Mark Smith 291
Ozzie Smith............. 292
Zane Smith 292
John Smoltz............ 293
J.T. Snow 293
Luis Sojo 294
Paul Sorrento........... 294
Sammy Sosa 295
Steve Sparks 295
Ed Sprague 296
Scott Stahoviak....... 296
Mike Stanley 297
Terry Steinbach....... 297
Dave Stevens 298
Kelly Stinnett 298
Kevin Stocker.......... 299
Todd Stottlemyre 299
Doug Strange.......... 300
Darryl Strawberry ... 300
Franklin Stubbs....... 301
B.J. Surhoff 301
Bill Swift 302

Greg Swindell 302
Jeff Tabaka.............. 303
Kevin Tapani 303
Tony Tarasco........... 304
Danny Tartabull....... 304
Ed Taubensee 305
Julian Tavarez 305
Mickey Tettleton.... 306
Bob Tewksbury 306
Frank Thomas 307
Jim Thome.............. 307
Milt Thompson 308
Robby Thompson ... 308
Ryan Thompson 309
Mike Timlin 309
Ozzie Timmons 310
Lee Tinsley 310
Salomon Torres 311
Steve Trachsel 311
Alan Trammell....... 312
Mike Trombley 312
Tom Urbani 313
Ismael Valdes 313
John Valentin 314
Jose Valentin 314
Fernando
Valenzuela.............. 315
Dave Valle 315
John Vander Wal..... 316
William
VanLandingham.......316
Todd Van Poppel.... 317
Andy Van Slyke 317
Greg Vaughn 318
Mo Vaughn 318
Randy Velarde......... 319
Robin Ventura......... 319
Quilvio Veras.......... 320
Dave Veres 320
Randy Veres 321
Ron Villone 321
Fernando Vina........ 322
Jose Vizcaino 322
Omar Vizquel 323
Paul Wagner 323
Tim Wakefield 324

Matt Walbeck........... 324
Larry Walker 325
Tim Wallach............. 325
Jerome Walton 326
Duane Ward 326
Turner Ward 327
Allen Watson........... 327
David Weathers....... 328
Lenny Webster........ 328
Bill Wegman 329
Walt Weiss 329
David Wells 330
David West 330
John Wetteland....... 331
Lou Whitaker 331
Devon White 332
Rick White 332
Rondell White 333
Mark Whiten 333
Matt Whiteside....... 334
Darrell Whitmore 334
Bob Wickman 335
Rick Wilkins 335
Bernie Williams 336
Brian Williams 336
Eddie Williams 337
Gerald Williams 337
Matt Williams......... 338
Dan Wilson 338
Trevor Wilson 339
Dave Winfield......... 339
Bobby Witt 340
Mark Wohlers 340
Brad Woodall 341
Todd Worrell 341
Anthony Young 342
Eric Young 342
Kevin Young 343
Todd Zeile 343

Rookie Prospects ... 344
Jeff Abbott 344
Bob Abreu 344
Willie Adams........... 345
George Arias 345
Kym Ashworth 346

8

CONTENTS

James Baldwin 346
Michael Barrett 347
Tony Batista 347
Howard Battle 348
Trey Beamon 348
David Bell 349
Mike Bell 349
Alan Benes 350
Yamil Benitez 350
Jaime Bluma 351
Hiram Bocachica 351
Jim Bonnici 352
Aaron Boone 352
Steve Bourgeois 353
Mark Brandenburg .. 353
Jamie Brewington ... 354
Jim Brower 354
Kevin Brown 355
John Burke 355
Homer Bush 356
Jay Canizaro 356
Raul Casanova 357
Luis Castillo 357
Ramon Castro 358
Roger Cedeno 358
Bobby Chouinard 359
McKay
Christensen 359
Tony Clark 360
Bartolo Colon 360
Rocky Coppinger 361
Steve Cox 361
Jacob Cruz 362
Jose Cruz Jr. 362
Wil Cunnane 363
Jeff D'Amico 363
Johnny Damon 364
Ben Davis 364
Jeff Davis 365
Tommy Davis 365
Edwin Diaz 366
David Doster 366
Matt Drews 367
Mike Drumright 367
Jermaine Dye 368
Scott Elarton 368
Darin Erstad 369
Ramon Fermin 369
Joe Fontenot 370
Tom Fordham 370
Tim Forkner 371
Brad Fullmer 371
Karim Garcia 372
Omar Garcia 372
Nomar
Garciaparra 373
Jason Giambi 373
Steve Gibralter 374
Derrick Gibson 374
Ed Giovanola 375
Wayne Gomes 375
Todd Greene 376
Ben Grieve 376
Vladimir Guerrero ... 377
Wilton Guerrero 377
Jose Guillen 378
Mike Gulan 378
Roy Halladay 379
Ryan Hancock 379
LaTroy Hawkins 380
Jimmy Haynes 380
Rodney
Henderson 381
Chad Hermansen 381
Dustin
Hermanson 382
Richard Hidalgo 382
Aaron Holbert 383
Damon Hollins 383
John Hope 384
Mike Hubbard 384
Scott Hunter 385
Edwin Hurtado 385
Jesse Ibarra 386
Jason
Isringhausen 386
Damian Jackson 387
Ryan Jackson 387
Marty Janzen 388
Ryan Jaroncyk 388
Corey Jenkins 389
Geoff Jenkins 389
Robin Jennings 390
Derek Jeter 390
Jonathan
Johnson 391
Andruw Jones 391
Jaime Jones 392
Jason Kendall 392
Brooks
Kieschnick 393
Paul Konerko 393
Marc Kroon 394
Todd Landry 394
Chris Latham 395
Juan LeBron 395
Derrek Lee 396
Jeff Liefer 396
Carlton Loewer 397
Mark Loretta 397
Andrew Lorraine 398
Fausto Macey 398
Dwight Maness 399
Felix Martinez 399
David McCarty 400
Quinton
McCracken 400
Jason McDonald 401
Ryan McGuire 401
Tony McKnight 402
Bill McMillon 402
Pepe McNeal 403
Rafael Medina 403
David Miller 404
Travis Miller 404
Ralph Milliard 405
Doug Million 405
Shea Morenz 406
Matt Morris 406
Damian Moss 407
Chad Mottola 407
Tony Mounce 408
Heath Murray 408
Matt Murray 409
Clemente Nunez 409
Sergio Nunez 410
Ryan Nye 410
Alex Ochoa 411

9

CONTENTS

Rey Ordonez 411
Rafael Orellano 412
Jay Payton 412
Neifi Perez 413
Charles Peterson 413
Jose Pett 414
Jorge Posada 414
Dante Powell 415
Jay Powell 415
Arquimedez Pozo 416
Ariel Prieto 416
Steve Rain 417
Gary Rath 417
Mark Redman 418
Brandon Reed 418
Pokey Reese 419
Bryan Rekar 419
Desi Relaford 420
Edgar Renteria 420
Ray Ricken 421
Adam Riggs 421
Marquis Riley 422
Armando Rios 422
Mariano Rivera 423
Ruben Rivera 423
Alex Rodriguez 424
Felix Rodriguez 424
Victor Rodriguez 425
Scott Rolen 425
Joe Rosselli 426
Glendon Rusch 426
Jason Ryan 427
Brian Sackinsky 427
Donnie Sadler 428
Julio Santana 428
Jason Schmidt 429
Dan Serafini 429
Richie Sexson 430
Alvie Shepherd 430
Bill Simas 431
Mike Sirotka 431
Steve Soderstrom ... 432
Clint Sodowsky 432
Scott Spiezio 433
Brian Stephenson ... 433
Shannon Stewart 434

Scott Sullivan 434
Jeff Suppan 435
Mike Sweeney 435
Andy Taulbee 436
Reggie Taylor 436
Amaury Telemaco ... 437
Jason Thompson 437
Michael Tucker 438
Ugie Urbina 438
Pedro Valdes 439
Jason Varitek 439
Andrew Vessel 440
Joe Vitiello 440
Terrell Wade 441
Billy Wagner 441
Bret Wagner 442
Matt Wagner 442
Todd Walker 443
Daryle Ward 443
Jeff Ware 444
John Wasdin 444
Pat Watkins 445
Chris Widger 445
Keith Williams 446
Shad Williams 446
Antone Williamson .. 447
Enrique Wilson 447
Paul Wilson 448
Jay Witasick 448
Bob Wolcott 449
Kerry Wood 449
Jamey Wright 450
Jaret Wright 450
David Yocum 451
Andy Yount 451

Team Overviews 452
Baltimore Orioles 453
Boston Red Sox 454
Detroit Tigers 455
New York Yankees .. 456
Toronto Blue Jays ... 457
Chicago White Sox . 458
Cleveland Indians 459
Kansas City Royals . 460

Milwaukee
Brewers 461
Minnesota Twins 462
California Angels 463
Oakland Athletics 464
Seattle Mariners 465
Texas Rangers 466
Atlanta Braves 467
Florida Marlins 468
Montreal Expos 469
New York Mets 470
Philadelphia
Phillies 471
Chicago Cubs 472
Cincinnati Reds 473
Houston Astros 474
Pittsburgh Pirates ... 475
St. Louis Cardinals .. 476
Colorado Rockies 477
Los Angeles
Dodgers 478
San Diego Padres ... 479
San Francisco
Giants 480

Hall of Fame 481

**Awards
and Highlights** 511

**Yearly Team and
Individual Leaders** .. 526

1995 Awards 672

CURRENT PLAYERS

Current Players and Rookie Prospects

In this section you'll find profiles of 800 players—first 600 current players and then 200 rookie prospects. The current players and rookie prospects are in alphabetical order.

Full major-league statistics are included with the current players. If a player played with two teams in both the American League and the National League in one season, both lines are presented in the "Major League Registers." If the player played with two teams in one league during a season, the statistics were combined to give you accurate information on how each player performed against one league in one season. At the bottom of most of the Major League Registers you'll find a "3 AVE" line. Players who qualified had their last three seasons' statistics averaged for each of the 10 categories. For batters to qualify for this line, they had to accumulate 150 at bats in each season. For starters to qualify, they had to pitch at least 60 innings each season. For relievers to qualify, they had to pitch at least 30 innings each season. If the player did not qualify for all three seasons but for only two years out of the last three, you'll find a "2 AVE" line. These lines give you a straightforward way to help you better predict how these players will do this summer. When calculating the averages, the totals for the 1994 season were increased by approximately 1.41, or 162 divided by 115. The totals for the 1995 season were increased by 1.125, or 162 divided by 144. This is to provide a more accurate picture of how a player will do over a full 162-game schedule.

The rookie prospects each have a "Professional Register." Included are statistics from each year that the player has been in organized baseball, from the Rookie leagues (**R**), Class-A (**A**), Double-A (**AA**), and Triple-A (**AAA**). If the player has played in the major leagues, each league's performance is also shown (**AL** and **NL**). If during one season a player played with more than one team on one minor league level, or if a player played with more than one AL or NL team, the statistics were combined.

The abbreviations for batters are: **BA** = batting average; **G** = games played; **AB** = at bats; **R** = runs scored; **H** = hits; **2B** = doubles; **3B** = triples; **HR** = home runs; **RBI** = runs batted in; **SB** = stolen bases. The abbreviations for pitchers are: **W** = wins; **L** = losses; **ERA** = earned run average; **G** = games; **CG** = complete games; **S** = saves; **IP** = innings pitched; **H** = hits; **ER** = earned runs; **BB** = bases on balls; **SO** = strikeouts. Note that for innings pitched, a .1 = ⅓ inning pitched, and .2 = ⅔ inning pitched.

The "Player Summary" box that accompanies each profile is an at-a-glance look at each player. The "Fantasy Value" line suggests a draft price for a fantasy baseball games. The price range is based on $260 budget for a 23-player roster. The "Card Value" line is a general estimate for determining the worth of a Mint 1996 regular-issue (base set) baseball card of that player. This estimate is based mostly on the future value gain of that player's card. Any error, variation, or specialty cards are not taken into account.

CURRENT PLAYERS

JIM ABBOTT

Position: Pitcher
Team: California Angels
Born: Sept. 19, 1967 Flint, MI
Height: 6'3" **Weight:** 200 lbs.
Bats: left **Throws:** left
Acquired: Traded by White Sox with Tim Fortugno for McKay Christensen, Andrew Lorraine, Bill Simas, and John Snyder, 7/95

Player Summary	
Fantasy Value	$10 to $12
Card Value	8¢ to 15¢
Will	show good control
Can't	avoid gopher balls
Expect	double-digit wins
Don't Expect	lots of Ks

After two disappointing years with the Yankees, Abbott regained the form that had made him one of the American League's top starters. He had made eight straight quality starts for the White Sox before the All-Star break, including a June 22 complete game that was his first in nearly a year. A victim of poor run support early in 1995, he had only managed a half-dozen wins before his trade to the Angels. The former University of Michigan star and Olympian never pitched in the minors. He wins by blending a fastball, a curveball, a change, and a forkball—often coaxing ground outs. His cut fastball rides in on right-handed hitters, giving him an advantage over other left-handed pitchers. Although he's not a strikeout pitcher, he rarely beats himself with walks, averaging about three per nine innings last year. He fields his position well and is adept at holding runners on base.

Major League Pitching Register

	W	L	ERA	G	CG	IP	H	ER	BB	SO
89 AL	12	12	3.92	29	4	181.1	190	79	74	115
90 AL	10	14	4.51	33	4	211.2	246	106	72	105
91 AL	18	11	2.89	34	5	243.0	222	78	73	158
92 AL	7	15	2.77	29	7	211.0	208	65	68	130
93 AL	11	14	4.37	32	4	214.0	221	104	73	95
94 AL	9	8	4.55	24	2	160.1	167	81	64	90
95 AL	11	8	3.70	30	4	197.0	209	81	64	86
Life	78	82	3.77	211	30	1418.1	1463	594	488	779
3 AVE	12	11	4.21	33	4	220.2	230	103	78	106

KURT ABBOTT

Position: Shortstop
Team: Florida Marlins
Born: June 2, 1969 Zanesville, OH
Height: 6' **Weight:** 170 lbs.
Bats: right **Throws:** right
Acquired: Traded by Athletics for Kerwin Moore, 12/93

Player Summary	
Fantasy Value	$7 to $9
Card Value	4¢ to 6¢
Will	show strong arm
Can't	handle sliders
Expect	home run binges
Don't Expect	terrific range

A streak hitter with surprising power for a shortstop, Abbott went on a home run tear in early July, victimizing All-Star starter Hideo Nomo, among others. Abbott would be far more dangerous, however, if he learned to be selective at the plate. Because he struck out about three times more often than he walked throughout much of the year, he did not compile a very good on-base percentage. He's also susceptible to low-and-outside sliders. He could add to his game by using his speed on the bases but running only rarely—a surprise for a player who topped a dozen steals three times in the minors. That quickness doesn't help much in the field either. He isn't comparable to Walt Weiss, the man Abbott succeeded at shortstop for Florida in 1994. Although he has good hands and a strong throwing arm, Abbott has only average range. He saw service as an outfielder and second baseman with Oakland in 1993 and could eventually evolve into a jack-of-all-trades. His first priority, however, will be showing more patience at the plate.

Major League Batting Register

	BA	G	AB	R	H	2B	3B	HR	RBI	SB
93 AL	.246	20	61	11	15	1	0	3	9	2
94 NL	.249	101	345	41	86	17	3	9	33	3
95 NL	.255	120	420	60	107	18	7	17	60	4
Life	.252	241	826	112	208	36	10	29	102	9
2 AVE	.252	139	479	63	121	22	6	16	57	4

CURRENT PLAYERS

KYLE ABBOTT

Position: Pitcher
Team: Philadelphia Phillies
Born: Feb. 18, 1968 Newburyport, MA
Height: 6'4" **Weight:** 215 lbs.
Bats: left **Throws:** left
Acquired: Signed as a free agent, 12/94

Player Summary
Fantasy Value	$0
Card Value	4¢ to 6¢
Will	depend upon fastball
Can't	always throw strikes
Expect	best job vs. lefties
Don't Expect	return to rotation

Before he went on the shelf with a sore left shoulder in July 1995, Abbott played an important role in the Philadelphia bullpen. Used primarily against left-handed hitters, he averaged six and one-half strikeouts per nine innings while yielding one hit per inning. The converted starter often struggled with his control, however, and encountered some problems with the long ball. But he proved adept at stranding inherited runners, making him likely to continue in his present bullpen deployment. The fastball pitcher from Long Beach State has already had a roller-coaster career. After seven years as a pro, it's apparent that he's neither the man whose 14 wins and 180 innings pitched led the 1991 Triple-A Pacific Coast League nor the man who fashioned a 1-14 record in his NL bow a year later. Abbott may never be a star, but he's already done better than father Larry, who never made it out of the minor leagues (1964 to '70). If he stays healthy and recaptures the control he displayed in the minors, Kyle should be able to assume a heavier workload.

Major League Pitching Register
	W	L	ERA	G	S	IP	H	ER	BB	SO
91 AL	1	2	4.58	5	0	19.2	22	10	13	12
92 NL	1	14	5.13	31	0	133.1	147	76	45	88
95 NL	2	0	3.81	18	0	28.1	28	12	16	21
Life	4	16	4.86	54	0	181.1	197	98	74	121

JUAN ACEVEDO

Position: Pitcher
Team: New York Mets
Born: May 5, 1970 Juarez, Mexico
Height: 6'2" **Weight:** 195 lbs.
Bats: right **Throws:** right
Acquired: Traded by Rockies with Arnold Gooch for Bret Saberhagen and a player to be named later, 7/95

Player Summary
Fantasy Value	$1
Card Value	5¢ to 8¢
Will	win as he learns
Can't	get all lefties
Expect	lively fastball
Don't Expect	erratic control

Acevedo led the Double-A Eastern League with 17 wins and a 2.37 earned run average in 1994, and league managers named him the No. 4 prospect in the league. In 1995, he jumped directly into the rotation of the Colorado Rockies. The thin air, coupled with his lack of experience, soon caused problems, however. But that didn't prevent the Mets from demanding he be part of the Bret Saberhagen trade on July 31. When he's right, Acevedo can be dominating. While pitching for Mexico in the 1994 Caribbean World Series, he blanked the talented team of major-league All-Stars playing for Puerto Rico. With the Rockies, however, he struggled with lefties, had trouble with his off-speed pitches, and couldn't throw strikes consistently. His best pitch is a fastball that has above-average velocity and exceptional movement. Acevedo needs to mix in more off-speed pitches, however, and pitch off the plate when ahead in the count. He's already shown a willingness to pitch inside. He turned pro when Colorado drafted him off the Parkland College (Illinois) campus in the 14th round of the 1992 draft.

Major League Pitching Register
	W	L	ERA	G	CG	IP	H	ER	BB	SO
95 NL	4	6	6.44	17	0	65.2	82	47	20	40
Life	4	6	6.44	17	0	65.2	82	47	20	40

CURRENT PLAYERS

MARK ACRE

Position: Pitcher
Team: Oakland Athletics
Born: Sept. 16, 1968 Concord, CA
Height: 6'8" **Weight:** 235 lbs.
Bats: right **Throws:** right
Acquired: Signed as a free agent, 8/91

Player Summary	
Fantasy Value	$2 to $4
Card Value	4¢ to 6¢
Will	pile up strikeouts
Can't	always find plate
Expect	possible closer role
Don't Expect	trouble with glove

Groomed for years as a possible successor to Oakland closer Dennis Eckersley, Acre has been hoisted by his own petard: an inability to throw the ball for strikes. Although he averaged more than eight strikeouts and less than eight hits per nine innings for much of 1995, he also yielded more than four walks over the same span. That is not acceptable for any relief pitcher, not to mention a closer. The towering New Mexico State product also has problems keeping the ball in the park. An unrefined power pitcher, Acre won't be a big-league success unless he develops off-speed pitches to complement his plus fastball. He also needs to show more consistency against right-handed hitters, who were far more successful against him last year than during his 1994 rookie campaign. As a result, too many of the runners he inherited crossed the plate. He holds runners well and shows surprising agility in the field for a man of his size. His future will be determined by his ability to improve his control and develop his repertoire.

Major League Pitching Register

	W	L	ERA	G	S	IP	H	ER	BB	SO
94 AL	5	1	3.41	34	0	34.1	24	13	23	21
95 AL	1	2	5.71	43	0	52.0	52	33	28	47
Life	6	3	4.80	77	0	86.1	76	46	51	68
2 AVE	4	2	4.67	48	0	53.1	46	28	32	41

RICK AGUILERA

Position: Pitcher
Team: Minnesota Twins
Born: Dec. 31, 1961 San Gabriel, CA
Height: 6'5" **Weight:** 205 lbs.
Bats: right **Throws:** right
Acquired: Signed as a free agent, 12/95

Player Summary	
Fantasy Value	$25 to $30
Card Value	5¢ to 8¢
Will	slam door
Can't	keep runners close
Expect	varied arsenal
Don't Expect	fielding woes

For the last six seasons, Aguilera has been one of the top closers in the major leagues. At the time of his 1995 trade to Boston, he was the only pitcher on the Minnesota staff who had allowed less hits than innings pitched. He also averaged about one strikeout per inning. He has good control of four pitches: a fastball, a slider, a curve, and a forkball, which ranks as his best pitch. Scouts say his stuff is as good today as it was when he had back-to-back 40-save seasons in 1991 and 1992. The Brigham Young product rarely blows a save opportunity. Minnesota fans thanked him with a standing ovation when he made his first Red Sox appearance July 7. A month later, Aguilera notched his 200th career save. Drafted as a third baseman, he retains infielder's instincts on the mound.

Major League Pitching Register

	W	L	ERA	G	S	IP	H	ER	BB	SO
85 NL	10	7	3.24	21	0	122.1	118	44	37	74
86 NL	10	7	3.88	28	0	141.2	145	61	36	104
87 NL	11	3	3.60	18	0	115.0	124	46	33	77
88 NL	0	4	6.93	11	0	24.2	29	19	10	16
89 NL	6	6	2.34	36	7	69.1	59	18	21	80
89 AL	3	5	3.21	11	0	75.2	71	27	17	57
90 AL	5	3	2.76	56	32	65.1	55	20	19	61
91 AL	4	5	2.35	63	42	69.0	44	18	30	61
92 AL	2	6	2.83	64	41	66.2	60	21	17	52
93 AL	4	3	3.11	65	34	72.1	60	25	14	59
94 AL	1	4	3.63	44	23	44.2	57	18	10	46
95 AL	3	3	2.60	52	32	55.1	46	16	13	52
Life	59	56	3.25	469	211	922.0	868	333	257	739
3 AVE	3	4	3.11	62	34	65.2	64	23	14	61

CURRENT PLAYERS

MIKE ALDRETE

Position: First base; outfield
Team: California Angels
Born: Jan. 29, 1961 Carmel, CA
Height: 5'11" **Weight:** 185 lbs.
Bats: left **Throws:** left
Acquired: Traded by Athletics for Demond Smith, 8/95

Player Summary
Fantasy Value $0
Card Value . . . . 4¢ to 6¢
Will . . . . hammer low fastballs
Can't . . . . generate much power
Expect . . . . trouble with lefties
Don't Expect . . . . daily duty

A valuable man to have on a ballclub, Aldrete serves as a backup first baseman, outfield reserve, and pinch hitter against right-handed pitching. He was especially valuable to Oakland last year when All-Star Mark McGwire was sidelined for short stretches by various injuries. A low fastball hitter who makes decent contact, Aldrete has trouble with breaking balls and high heat. He is also not much of a home run threat. He has hit as many as 15 homers only once in a pro career that began in 1983. Though he once stole 16 bases in a minor-league season, he is not much of a threat on the bases. He's a capable first baseman, however, though not nearly as polished as McGwire. Aldrete's work in the outfield is adequate at best, though he did play all three positions in 1995. He holds a bachelor's degree in communications from Stanford.

Major League Batting Register

	BA	G	AB	R	H	2B	3B	HR	RBI	SB
86 NL	.250	84	216	27	54	18	3	2	25	1
87 NL	.325	126	357	50	116	18	2	9	51	6
88 NL	.267	139	389	44	104	15	0	3	50	6
89 NL	.221	76	136	12	30	8	1	1	12	1
90 NL	.242	96	161	22	39	7	1	1	18	1
91 NL	.000	12	15	2	0	0	0	0	1	0
91 AL	.262	85	183	22	48	6	1	1	19	1
93 AL	.267	95	255	40	68	13	1	10	33	1
94 AL	.242	76	178	23	43	5	0	4	18	2
95 AL	.268	78	149	19	40	8	0	4	24	0
Life	.266	867	2039	261	542	98	9	35	251	19
2 AVE	.254	101	253	36	64	10	1	8	29	2

MANNY ALEXANDER

Position: Second base; infield
Team: Baltimore Orioles
Born: March 20, 1971 San Pedro de Macoris, Dominican Republic
Height: 5'10" **Weight:** 165 lbs.
Bats: right **Throws:** right
Acquired: Signed as an undrafted free agent, 2/88

Player Summary
Fantasy Value . . . . $3 to $5
Card Value . . . . 5¢ to 8¢
Will . . . . play great defense
Can't . . . . hit long ball
Expect . . . . best bat vs. lefties
Don't Expect . . . . frequent Ks

Less than six weeks after surprising the Baltimore coaching staff with his sudden strength during 1995 spring training, Alexander won the regular second-base job from trade import Bret Barberie. Once called the Orioles' shortstop-of-the-future, Alexander made the most of the opportunity. He is a contact hitter who last year collected almost as many walks as strikeouts throughout much of the season. He fares much better against left-handed pitching than against righties—and he has a future as a possible platoon infielder. He fattens his average with infield hits, and his slugging percentage was above .350 through much of the season. He is a definite threat to steal; he twice topped 40 steals in the minors. His quickness also helps him in the field, where he has a shortstop's range, reflexes, and throwing skills. He had led several minor leagues in putouts, assists, and fielding percentage as a shortstop, leading *Baseball America* to call him one of the best defensive infielders in the minors.

Major League Batting Register

	BA	G	AB	R	H	2B	3B	HR	RBI	SB
92 AL	.200	4	5	1	1	0	0	0	0	0
93 AL	.000	3	1	0	0	0	0	0	0	0
95 AL	.236	94	242	35	57	9	1	3	23	11
Life	.235	101	247	37	58	9	1	3	23	11

CURRENT PLAYERS

EDGARDO ALFONZO

Position: Second base; third base
Team: New York Mets
Born: Aug. 11, 1973 Station Teresa, Venezuela
Height: 5'11" **Weight:** 185 lbs.
Bats: right **Throws:** right
Acquired: Signed as a free agent, 2/91

Player Summary	
Fantasy Value	$3 to $5
Card Value	8¢ to 12¢
Will	make contact
Can't	show big power
Expect	hits vs. lefties
Don't Expect	patience

The youngest of three Alfonzo brothers in professional baseball, Edgardo pulled a double surprise: He not only made the Opening Day Mets' roster but found a spot in the lineup as the everyday third baseman. Signed as a shortstop, he had led his minor league in putouts, assists, double plays, and total chances. But he shifted to third two years later after the Mets signed Cuban defector Rey Ordonez. Alfonzo is a minor-league batting champ who twice reached double figures in home runs, and he held his own during his first look at National League pitchers. He made good contact, but he showed such impatience at the plate that he averaged about three strikeouts for every walk. Through much of the season, he hit about .300 against left-handed pitching. Alfonzo kept his errors to a minimum and showed good hands, quick reactions, and a strong throwing arm. He missed some games toward the end of the season last year because of a herniated disk in his back. Because of his speed and range, he might have a future at second base. His bat and glove are good enough for the hot corner as well.

Major League Batting Register

	BA	G	AB	R	H	2B	3B	HR	RBI	SB
95 NL	.278	101	335	26	93	13	5	4	41	1
Life	.278	101	335	26	93	13	5	4	41	1

LUIS ALICEA

Position: Second base
Team: Boston Red Sox
Born: July 29, 1965 Santurce, PR
Height: 5'10" **Weight:** 150 lbs.
Bats: both **Throws:** right
Acquired: Traded by Cardinals for Jeff McNeely and Nate Minchey, 12/94

Player Summary	
Fantasy Value	$6 to $8
Card Value	4¢ to 6¢
Will	provide defense
Can't	utilize speed
Expect	pop vs. lefties
Don't Expect	long slumps

St. Louis fans were surprised when the Cards shipped Alicea to Boston after the 1994 season. The former Florida State All-American is a dependable second baseman who made good contact and showed surprising pop from both sides of the plate. Alicea walks almost as much as he strikes out, steals some bases, and delivers occasional long balls. On July 28, he notched the first multihomer game of his career, marking the first time in 22 seasons that a Boston player homered from both sides of the plate in the same game (Reggie Smith did it last). A fastball hitter who's a better righty batter, Alicea is willing to wait for his pitch. He is also willing to take a few pitches with a speedy runner on base ahead of him. Alicea turns the double play, shows excellent range, and provides fine overall defense. His speed helps him in the field but he's not much of a threat to steal; he was thrown out stealing almost as many times as he was successful during much of last season.

Major League Batting Register

	BA	G	AB	R	H	2B	3B	HR	RBI	SB
88 NL	.212	93	297	20	63	10	4	1	24	1
91 NL	.191	56	68	5	13	3	0	0	0	0
92 NL	.245	85	265	26	65	9	11	2	32	2
93 NL	.279	115	362	50	101	19	3	3	46	11
94 NL	.278	88	205	32	57	12	5	5	29	4
95 AL	.270	132	419	64	113	20	3	6	44	13
Life	.255	569	1616	197	412	73	26	17	175	31
3 AVE	.275	129	374	56	103	19	4	6	45	10

CURRENT PLAYERS

ROBERTO ALOMAR

Position: Second base
Team: Toronto Blue Jays
Born: Feb. 5, 1968 Ponce, PR
Height: 6' **Weight:** 175 lbs.
Bats: both **Throws:** right
Acquired: Traded by Padres with Joe Carter for Fred McGriff and Tony Fernandez, 12/90

Player Summary	
Fantasy Value	$30 to $35
Card Value	20¢ to 80¢
Will	mix speed, power
Can't	handle all southpaws
Expect	Gold Glove level
Don't Expect	many errors

Even though Carlos Baerga was the starting second baseman for the 1995 AL All-Stars, Alomar is considered the game's top player at his position. Managers polled by *Baseball America* named him the league's top defensive second baseman, second-best bunter, third-best baserunner, and third-most exciting player. More than 10 teams tried to pry Alomar from the Blue Jays before the July 31 trading deadline. In addition to providing power and speed, he set an AL record with 90 consecutive errorless games before a botched July 4 grounder left him at 104—19 short of Ryne Sandberg's major-league mark. A much better left-handed hitter, Alomar reached double digits in homers for the second time in his major-league career in 1995. Time has not dulled his baserunning skills: He is rarely caught when he tries to steal. Alomar is a multiple Gold Glove winner, and he was named the MVP of the 1992 ALCS.

Major League Batting Register

	BA	G	AB	R	H	2B	3B	HR	RBI	SB
88 NL	.266	143	545	84	145	24	6	9	41	24
89 NL	.295	158	623	82	184	27	1	7	56	42
90 NL	.287	147	586	80	168	27	5	6	60	24
91 AL	.295	161	637	88	188	41	11	9	69	53
92 AL	.310	152	571	105	177	27	8	8	76	49
93 AL	.326	153	589	109	192	35	6	17	93	55
94 AL	.306	107	392	78	120	25	4	8	38	19
95 AL	.300	130	517	71	155	24	7	13	66	30
Life	.298	1151	4460	697	1329	230	48	77	499	296
3 AVE	.311	150	574	100	178	32	7	14	74	39

SANDY ALOMAR

Position: Catcher
Team: Cleveland Indians
Born: June 18, 1966 Salinas, PR
Height: 6'5" **Weight:** 200 lbs.
Bats: right **Throws:** right
Acquired: Traded by Padres with Chris James and Carlos Baerga for Joe Carter, 12/89

Player Summary	
Fantasy Value	$11 to $14
Card Value	5¢ to 8¢
Will	supply top defense
Can't	keep off DL
Expect	solid stick
Don't Expect	a workhorse

Alomar's 1995 season was a story of good news and bad news. The good news was a batting average at about the .300 level for the season. The bad news was that he posted that average during relatively few at bats. Last year, for the sixth time in as many seasons, Alomar spent long stretches on the disabled list. In fact, he was out until June 29 following surgery to repair torn knee cartilage. His career began with a bang when he was named AL Rookie of the Year in 1990. He has never played 100 games in any season since his freshman year, however. A line-drive hitter who can pull to left with power, he hits well in the clutch. When he played, he batted ninth in the power-packed Cleveland lineup last year. He also shines on defense, where he's a good game-caller, an improving handler of pitchers, and the owner of a strong throwing arm. Alomar is also adept at preventing wild pitches and blocking the plate.

Major League Batting Register

	BA	G	AB	R	H	2B	3B	HR	RBI	SB
88 NL	.000	1	0	0	0	0	0	0	0	0
89 NL	.211	7	19	1	4	1	0	1	6	0
90 AL	.290	132	445	60	129	26	2	9	66	4
91 AL	.217	51	184	10	40	9	0	0	7	0
92 AL	.251	89	299	22	75	16	0	2	26	3
93 AL	.270	64	215	24	58	7	1	6	32	3
94 AL	.288	80	292	44	84	15	1	14	43	8
95 AL	.300	66	203	32	61	6	0	10	35	3
Life	.272	490	1658	193	451	80	4	42	215	21
3 AVE	.287	84	285	41	82	12	1	12	44	6

CURRENT PLAYERS

MOISES ALOU

Position: Outfield
Team: Montreal Expos
Born: July 3, 1966 Atlanta, GA
Height: 6'3" **Weight:** 180 lbs.
Bats: right **Throws:** right
Acquired: Traded by Pirates with Scott Ruskin and Willie Greene for Zane Smith, 8/90

Player Summary	
Fantasy Value	$25 to $30
Card Value	8¢ to 20¢
Will	murder left-handers
Can't	escape streak label
Expect	solid fielding
Don't Expect	old speed

Moises Alou is the son of Felipe Alou, nephew of Matty and Jesus Alou, and cousin of Mel Rojas. Rarely has a single player had such strong baseball bloodlines. That legacy emerged in 1994, when Moises became a solid No. 3 hitter and an NL All-Star who finished third in the MVP voting. A line-drive hitter who is equally adept at bunting or driving high fastballs, he feasts on left-handed pitchers. He was also at his best with runners in scoring position and in clutch situations last season. Normally a patient hitter who peppers hits to all fields, he seemed to be pressing last year to compensate for the departures of Larry Walker and Marquis Grissom. Alou's production tailed off as a result. His baserunning was also down—the residue of a broken leg suffered late in the '93 campaign. He can still surprise the opposition with a bunt, however. He throws better than most left fielders, while also helping in right field when necessary. Not yet 30, Alou should be at the peak of his career.

Major League Batting Register

	BA	G	AB	R	H	2B	3B	HR	RBI	SB
90 NL	.200	16	20	4	4	0	1	0	0	0
92 NL	.282	115	341	53	96	28	2	9	56	16
93 NL	.286	136	482	70	138	29	6	18	85	17
94 NL	.339	107	422	81	143	31	5	22	78	7
95 NL	.273	93	344	48	94	22	0	14	58	4
Life	.295	467	1609	256	475	110	14	63	277	44
3 AVE	.304	130	488	79	148	32	4	22	87	10

WILSON ALVAREZ

Position: Pitcher
Team: Chicago White Sox
Born: March 24, 1970 Maracaibo, Venezuela
Height: 6'1" **Weight:** 175 lbs.
Bats: left **Throws:** left
Acquired: Traded by Rangers with Scott Fletcher and Sammy Sosa for Harold Baines and Fred Manrique, 7/89

Player Summary	
Fantasy Value	$9 to $16
Card Value	8¢ to 15¢
Will	look for '93 form
Can't	harness control
Expect	lefties to struggle
Don't Expect	runners to go

Alvarez learned the meaning of excess baggage the hard way. Too heavy when he reported to the abbreviated spring training of 1995, he wasn't able to shed the extra poundage before the season started. His abysmal first half contributed to the sudden ChiSox fall from grace. The most telling statistic was the .300-plus batting average posted against Alvarez by left-handed hitters over much of the season. Normally, the hard-throwing lefty has little trouble against southpaws. Another culprit was poor control. During much of the year, he averaged about five walks per nine innings—a pace that gave him a strikeout-to-walk ratio close to 1-to-1. These problems led to him completing fewer of his starts. When he's healthy, Alvarez blends a lively fastball with a curve that serves as his out pitch. He also throws a changeup and a slider. He's not much of a fielder but has learned to control the running game. In his second big-league start, he no-hit the Orioles.

Major League Pitching Register

	W	L	ERA	G	CG	IP	H	ER	BB	SO
89 AL	0	1	0.00	1	0	0.0	3	3	2	0
91 AL	3	2	3.51	10	2	56.1	47	22	29	32
92 AL	5	3	5.20	34	0	100.1	103	58	65	66
93 AL	15	8	2.95	31	1	207.2	168	68	122	155
94 AL	12	8	3.45	24	2	161.2	147	62	62	108
95 AL	8	11	4.32	29	8	175.0	171	84	93	118
Life	43	33	3.81	129	8	701.0	639	297	373	479
3 AVE	14	11	3.56	32	2	210.2	189	83	105	147

CURRENT PLAYERS

RICH AMARAL

Position: Outfield
Team: Seattle Mariners
Born: April 1, 1962 Visalia, CA
Height: 6' **Weight:** 175 lbs.
Bats: right **Throws:** right
Acquired: Signed as a free agent, 11/90

Player Summary	
Fantasy Value	$3 to $5
Card Value	4¢ to 6¢
Will	be a backup
Can't	hit long ball
Expect	use of speed
Don't Expect	infield play

Had he won Rookie of the Year honors in 1993 (he finished fifth), Amaral, then 31, would have been the oldest player ever to win the award. Instead, he had to settle for the knowledge that perseverance pays off. The former UCLA All-American spent nine years in the minors before reaching the big leagues. Signed as a second baseman, he spent most of his minor-league tenure as a speedy jack-of-all-trades. He reached Seattle that way too before beating out Bret Boone, then a rookie, for the regular second-base job. Found wanting defensively, Amaral shifted to the outfield, eventually supplanting Darren Bragg in left field. A singles hitter who steals bases, Amaral is most productive against lefties. He bunts, executes the hit-and-run, and goes the opposite way if necessary—all without fanning too often. His on-base percentage would be higher, however, if he walked more often. Because he runs well, Amaral is an acceptable outfielder. But his weak throwing arm precludes prolonged service anywhere but left field.

Major League Batting Register

	BA	G	AB	R	H	2B	3B	HR	RBI	SB
91 AL	.063	14	16	2	1	0	0	0	0	0
92 AL	.240	35	100	9	24	3	0	1	7	4
93 AL	.290	110	373	53	108	24	1	1	44	19
94 AL	.263	77	228	37	60	10	2	4	18	5
95 AL	.282	90	238	45	67	14	2	2	19	21
Life	.272	326	955	146	260	51	5	8	88	49
3 AVE	.278	107	321	52	89	18	2	3	30	17

BRADY ANDERSON

Position: Outfield
Team: Baltimore Orioles
Born: Jan. 18, 1964 Silver Spring, MD
Height: 6'1" **Weight:** 195 lbs.
Bats: left **Throws:** left
Acquired: Traded by Red Sox with Curt Schilling for Mike Boddicker, 7/88

Player Summary	
Fantasy Value	$16 to $19
Card Value	6¢ to 12¢
Will	reach base
Can't	reduce K rate
Expect	success stealing
Don't Expect	top bat vs. lefties

A leadoff man with speed and power, Anderson carved a niche in the American League record book last year. He stole 36 consecutive bases before Minnesota's Matt Walbeck nailed him July 3. For much of the season, over 33 percent of Anderson's hits went for extra bases. Although he doesn't produce the high batting average usually associated with top-of-the-lineup types, he draws so many walks that his on-base percentage is usually 100 points higher than his batting average. He struggles against left-handed pitchers and fans too often for a player not regarded as a home run hitter. In 1994, he had a .969 success ratio as a basestealer—a single-season record for a player with at least 30 steals. His defense is also exceptional. He has spent most of the last few years in left field, but he also saw time in center when rookie Curtis Goodwin began to fade.

Major League Batting Register

	BA	G	AB	R	H	2B	3B	HR	RBI	SB
88 AL	.212	94	325	31	69	13	4	1	21	10
89 AL	.207	94	266	44	55	12	2	4	16	16
90 AL	.231	89	234	24	54	5	2	3	24	15
91 AL	.230	113	256	40	59	12	3	2	27	12
92 AL	.271	159	623	100	169	28	10	21	80	53
93 AL	.262	142	560	87	147	36	8	13	66	24
94 AL	.263	111	453	78	119	25	5	12	48	31
95 AL	.262	143	554	108	145	33	10	16	64	26
Life	.250	945	3271	512	817	164	44	72	346	187
3 AVE	.262	153	607	106	159	36	9	16	69	32

CURRENT PLAYERS

BRIAN ANDERSON

Position: Pitcher
Team: California Angels
Born: April 26, 1972 Geneva, OH
Height: 6'1" **Weight:** 190 lbs.
Bats: both **Throws:** left
Acquired: First-round pick in 6/93 free-agent draft

Player Summary	
Fantasy Value	$3 to $5
Card Value	6¢ to 10¢
Will	show control
Can't	avoid gophers
Expect	excellent defense
Don't Expect	high whiff totals

The youngster in a veteran rotation last year, Anderson performed like an established big leaguer. The Wright State University product showed good control of his rising fastball, slider, and breaking ball. He averaged less than three walks per nine innings for much of the season, while yielding less hits than innings pitched and dominating right-handed hitters. A victim of his own control, he had some problems with gopher balls—especially against lefties. Batters usually put the ball into play against him, but often hit it on the ground. That's good, since he helps himself with his defense. He has quick reactions and a delivery that leaves him in good fielding position. His pickoff move needs work, however. Umpires called him for two balks in his first nine starts. Anderson is still learning. Though he's made remarkable strides for a pitcher who worked only six games in the minors, there's no substitute for big-league experience. He was the third pick in the nation in the 1993 free-agent draft.

Major League Pitching Register

	W	L	ERA	G	CG	IP	H	ER	BB	SO
93 AL	0	0	3.97	4	0	11.1	11	5	2	4
94 AL	7	5	5.22	18	0	101.2	120	59	27	47
95 AL	6	8	5.87	18	1	99.2	110	65	30	45
Life	13	13	5.46	40	1	212.2	241	129	59	96
2 AVE	8	8	5.51	23	1	127.3	146	78	36	58

GARRET ANDERSON

Position: Outfield
Team: California Angels
Born: June 30, 1972 Los Angeles, CA
Height: 6'3" **Weight:** 190 lbs.
Bats: left **Throws:** left
Acquired: Fourth-round pick in 6/90 free-agent draft

Player Summary	
Fantasy Value	$9 to $11
Card Value	20¢ to 40¢
Will	swing big stick
Can't	cut K rate
Expect	future batting title
Don't Expect	Gold Gloves

Although he didn't join the lineup until the eighth week last year, Anderson wasted little time becoming a contender in the Rookie of the Year race. He was AL Player of the Month for July, when his league-high .410 average was accompanied by seven homers, 22 runs scored, and 31 RBI in 25 games. That placed him first in average, second in RBI, and third in homers among all AL freshmen. After Tony Phillips moved from left field to third base to make room for him in the lineup, Anderson showed the wisdom of that switch with a home run in his first start. A confident hitter with a line-drive stroke, he has drawn comparisons to Chili Davis, Ken Griffey Jr., and seven-time batting king Rod Carew, California hitting coach. The source of the Carew comparison was Carew himself. Anderson has more power than Carew but lacks his patience at the plate. Anderson fanned about three times more than he walked last year. In 1994, he had a 27-game hitting streak in Triple-A, and he batted .321 with 12 homers and 102 RBI. He won't win a Gold Glove or basestealing title. But with that bat, who cares?

Major League Batting Register

	BA	G	AB	R	H	2B	3B	HR	RBI	SB
94 AL	.385	5	13	0	5	0	0	0	1	0
95 AL	.321	106	374	50	120	19	1	16	69	6
Life	.323	111	387	50	125	19	1	16	70	6

CURRENT PLAYERS

SHANE ANDREWS

Position: Third base; first base
Team: Montreal Expos
Born: Aug. 28, 1968 Dallas, TX
Height: 6'1" **Weight:** 215 lbs.
Bats: right **Throws:** right
Acquired: First-round pick in 6/90 free-agent draft

Player Summary	
Fantasy Value	$2 to $4
Card Value	5¢ to 8¢
Will	show some power
Can't	stop strikeouts
Expect	better fielding
Don't Expect	OK batting

In his first major-league season, Andrews split his time between the infield corners and showed flashes of power. The 10th draft pick in the nation in 1990, he has always impressed the Montreal organization with his long-ball potential. He sabotaged his own progress by demonstrating a tendency to fan far too frequently. During much of the season, while more than 40 percent of his hits went for extra bases, he fanned about three times per walk and couldn't boost his batting average above the Mendoza Line. Until he becomes more productive against lefties and learns to be selective at the plate, he is not likely to play every day. In the minors, Andrews led various leagues in home runs, walks, and strikeouts. In 1994 at Triple-A, he batted .254 with 16 homers and 85 RBI in 460 at bats. He batted .260 with 18 homers and 70 RBI in 442 at bats in Double-A in 1993. Last year, defensively, he demonstrated dramatic improvement in playing the hot corner, especially on throws. He has an adequate glove, but Andrews's challenge will be to improve his offense to the point where nobody worries about his glove.

Major League Batting Register

	BA	G	AB	R	H	2B	3B	HR	RBI	SB
95 NL	.214	84	220	27	47	10	1	8	31	1
Life	.214	84	220	27	47	10	1	8	31	1

ERIC ANTHONY

Position: Outfield; first base
Team: Cincinnati Reds
Born: Nov. 8, 1967 San Diego, CA
Height: 6'2' **Weight:** 195 lbs.
Bats: left **Throws:** left
Acquired: Signed as a free agent, 4/95

Player Summary	
Fantasy Value	$3 to $5
Card Value	4¢ to 6¢
Will	show good power
Can't	cut whiff total
Expect	hits vs. righties
Don't Expect	Gold Glove play

After watching his power production decline for three straight seasons, Anthony began a revival last year before going on the shelf with a strained patella tendon under his right knee July 14. Late in June, Anthony hit a 465-footer that was the longest in the majors at that point in the season. A streak hitter who generates enormous power with his leg-kicking stance, Anthony lacks discipline at the plate. Southpaws give him fits, and he struck out at an alarming rate: about three times per walk for much of the season last year. He did keep his slugging percentage above the .500 mark during much of the season, however. A first baseman in the minors, he had been an outfielder since reaching the majors with the Astros in 1989. But the Reds gave him a start at first on June 22. He is still more comfortable in the outfield, where he throws well enough to get by in right field. With his arm, however, he is probably better stationed in left field.

Major League Batting Register

	BA	G	AB	R	H	2B	3B	HR	RBI	SB
89 NL	.180	25	61	7	11	2	0	4	7	0
90 NL	.192	84	239	26	46	8	0	10	29	5
91 NL	.153	39	118	11	18	6	0	1	7	1
92 NL	.239	137	440	45	105	15	1	19	80	5
93 NL	.249	145	486	70	121	19	4	15	66	3
94 AL	.237	79	262	31	62	14	1	10	30	6
95 NL	.269	47	134	19	36	6	0	5	23	2
Life	.229	556	1740	209	399	70	6	64	242	22
2 AVE	.244	128	428	57	104	19	3	15	54	6

CURRENT PLAYERS

KEVIN APPIER

Position: Pitcher
Team: Kansas City Royals
Born: Dec. 6, 1967 Lancaster, CA
Height: 6'2" **Weight:** 190 lbs.
Bats: right **Throws:** right
Acquired: First-round pick in 6/87 free-agent draft

Player Summary	
Fantasy Value	$17 to $20
Card Value	7¢ to 15¢
Will	throw hard
Can't	flash top glove
Expect	more wins
Don't Expect	control trouble

Appier had two different seasons last year. The AL Pitcher of the Month in June (5-1, 2.40 ERA, 42 strikeouts, and 43 hits allowed in 45 innings), he had 11 wins by July 4. He was finally named to the All-Star Team after being overlooked for years. Then the roof fell in. In his seventh attempt at his 12th win July 25, he yielded seven runs in an 8-1 loss to the Yankees. Two days later, Appier was disabled with tendinitis of the right shoulder. The culprit could have been the four-man rotation of rookie manager Bob Boone. The hard-throwing Appier made eight starts with three days of rest. His repertoire includes a fastball, a slider, and a forkball—all delivered with an overhand delivery that's tough on the shoulder. When healthy, he blows right-handed hitters away and keeps the ball in the park. He's not adept at holding runners or fielding; an awkward follow-through leaves him on the first-base side of the mound.

Major League Pitching Register

	W	L	ERA	G	CG	IP	H	ER	BB	SO
89 AL	1	4	9.14	6	0	21.2	34	22	12	10
90 AL	12	8	2.76	32	3	185.2	179	57	54	127
91 AL	13	10	3.42	34	6	207.2	205	79	61	158
92 AL	15	8	2.46	30	3	208.1	167	57	68	150
93 AL	18	8	2.56	34	5	238.2	183	68	81	186
94 AL	7	6	3.83	23	1	155.0	137	66	63	145
95 AL	15	10	3.89	31	4	201.1	163	87	80	185
Life	81	54	3.22	190	22	1218.1	1068	436	419	961
3 AVE	15	9	3.41	34	4	227.1	186	86	87	199

ALEX ARIAS

Position: Infield
Team: Florida Marlins
Born: Nov. 20, 1967 New York, NY
Height: 6'3" **Weight:** 185 lbs.
Bats: right **Throws:** right
Acquired: Traded by Cubs with Gary Scott for Greg Hibbard, 11/92

Player Summary	
Fantasy Value	$0
Card Value	4¢ to 6¢
Will	fill reserve role
Can't	provide power
Expect	good pinch hitting
Don't Expect	speed

A versatile singles hitter who makes good contact, Arias is handy to have on the bench. Signed as a shortstop out of New York's George Washington High School, he's also comfortable at second and third. Although he lacks both power and speed, he has become a potent pinch hitter because of his selective batting eye. He walks more often than he strikes out, giving him an on-base percentage about 100 points higher than his batting average. An accomplished fielder, Arias led several leagues in chances, putouts, assists, double plays, and fielding percentage. He also led in triples once, but that must have been a fluke because he had more three-baggers in that year (11) than in the rest of his professional career combined. He's equally unlikely to duplicate the .293 average he produced for the Cubs during a 32-game trial at the end of the 1992 campaign. Acceptable on defense everywhere, he will probably not be a standout anywhere. But Arias is a useful big-league backup.

Major League Batting Register

	BA	G	AB	R	H	2B	3B	HR	RBI	SB
92 NL	.293	32	99	14	29	6	0	0	7	0
93 NL	.269	96	249	27	67	5	1	2	20	1
94 NL	.239	59	113	4	27	5	0	0	15	0
95 NL	.269	94	216	22	58	9	2	3	26	1
Life	.267	281	677	67	181	25	3	5	68	2
2 AVE	.269	101	246	26	66	8	2	3	25	1

CURRENT PLAYERS

RENE AROCHA

Position: Pitcher
Team: St. Louis Cardinals
Born: Feb. 24, 1966 Havana, Cuba
Height: 6' **Weight:** 180 lbs.
Bats: right **Throws:** right
Acquired: Signed as a free agent, 11/91

Player Summary	
Fantasy Value	$1 to $3
Card Value	4¢ to 6¢
Will	throw hard
Can't	prevent gophers
Expect	diverse arsenal
Don't Expect	control trouble

Before a strained right elbow sent him to the disabled list on Aug. 2, Arocha had been the workhorse of the St. Louis bullpen. A control pitcher who throws a fastball, forkball, and five other deliveries, Arocha throws harder as a reliever than he did as a starter. The reason is obvious: confined to an inning or two per stint, he no longer has to pace himself. Overwork and the aching elbow made him less effective last year than he was in 1994. Before the player strike sliced the last seven weeks off that season, he had posted the league's fifth-best bullpen ERA (2.36) and held hitters to a .228 batting average as a reliever. He finished with a 3-1 ratio of strikeouts to walks. Like many control pitchers, he has occasional problems with the gopher ball. Arocha helps himself with his bunting and fielding but isn't much of a hitter. He is adept at keeping runners close, however. A member of the Cuban national team for many years, Arocha spent only one year in the minors before reaching St. Louis. He will probably remain in the bullpen.

Major League Pitching Register

	W	L	ERA	G	S	IP	H	ER	BB	SO
93 NL	11	8	3.78	32	0	188.0	197	79	31	96
94 NL	4	4	4.01	45	11	33.0	94	37	21	62
95 NL	3	5	3.99	41	0	49.2	55	22	18	25
Life	18	17	3.87	118	11	320.2	346	138	70	183
3 AVE	7	6	3.89	47	5	120.1	130	52	27	70

ANDY ASHBY

Position: Pitcher
Team: San Diego Padres
Born: July 11, 1967 Kansas City, MO
Height: 6'5" **Weight:** 180 lbs.
Bats: right **Throws:** right
Acquired: Traded by Rockies with Doug Bochtler and Brad Ausmus for Greg Harris and Bruce Hurst, 7/93

Player Summary	
Fantasy Value	$15 to $18
Card Value	5¢ to 10¢
Will	get a dozen wins
Can't	win without support
Expect	ground outs
Don't Expect	gopher problems

The July 31 trade of Andy Benes made Ashby San Diego's No. 1 starter. That seemed like a tall order for a man whose career record prior to 1995 had been 11-29 with a 5.26 ERA. But Ashby has been improving with experience. During a 2-0 shutout at Pittsburgh June 19, he fanned a career-high 10 and got 13 ground outs while walking only two. It was his first shutout in 72 career starts. A sinkerballer who also throws a cut fastball, a slider, a changeup, and a curve, Ashby keeps hitters off-balance. During most of the 1995 season, he yielded less hits than innings pitched, kept the ball in the park, and averaged about three walks and seven strikeouts per game. He pitched well in clutch situations and was especially effective against right-handed batters. A good bunter who can also poke occasional singles, Ashby fields his position well. He's even corrected his biggest previous weakness: an inability to hold runners.

Major League Pitching Register

	W	L	ERA	G	CG	IP	H	ER	BB	SO
91 NL	1	5	6.00	8	0	42.0	41	28	19	26
92 NL	1	3	7.54	10	0	37.0	42	31	21	24
93 NL	3	10	6.80	32	0	123.0	168	93	56	77
94 NL	6	11	3.40	24	4	164.1	145	62	43	121
95 NL	12	10	2.94	31	2	192.2	180	63	62	150
Life	23	39	4.46	105	6	559.0	576	277	201	398
3 AVE	8	12	3.96	34	3	190.1	192	84	62	139

CURRENT PLAYERS

BILLY ASHLEY

Position: Outfield
Team: Los Angeles Dodgers
Born: July 11, 1970 Taylor, MI
Height: 6'7" **Weight:** 227 lbs.
Bats: right **Throws:** right
Acquired: Third-round pick in 6/88 free-agent draft

Player Summary
Fantasy Value	$2 to $4
Card Value	8¢ to 15¢
Will	hammer ball
Can't	show speed
Expect	Dave Kingman
Don't Expect	strong defense

Maybe the thin air of Albuquerque distorted the statistics. But the Dodgers, drooling at his power potential, handed Ashley their left-field job long before the '95 season started. It didn't last. After hitting .345 with 37 homers and 105 RBI in 388 Triple-A at bats, the 1994 *USA Today* Minor League Player of the Year was overmatched in the majors. During much of the season, he fanned about three times more than he walked, struggled against right-handers, and was guilty of such dreadful defense that he conjured up images of Dave Kingman. Bigger and stronger than ex-Dodger Darryl Strawberry, Ashley has frightening power. But his huge swing held him back, forcing the team to try changing his swing to a short, compact stroke. By July, with that project failed, he took his bat to the bench. At age 25, Ashley figures to find a big-league niche somewhere. It could be as a DH, first baseman, or even as an outfielder if his defense improves. At the moment, he's strictly a one-dimensional player; and it didn't work very well last summer.

Major League Batting Register
	BA	G	AB	R	H	2B	3B	HR	RBI	SB
92 NL	.221	29	95	6	21	5	0	2	6	0
93 NL	.243	14	37	0	9	0	0	0	6	0
94 NL	.333	2	6	0	2	1	0	0	0	0
95 NL	.237	81	215	17	51	5	0	8	27	0
Life	.235	126	353	23	83	11	0	10	33	0

PAUL ASSENMACHER

Position: Pitcher
Team: Cleveland Indians
Born: Dec. 10, 1960 Detroit, MI
Height: 6'3" **Weight:** 200 lbs.
Bats: left **Throws:** left
Acquired: Signed as a free agent, 4/95

Player Summary
Fantasy Value	$2 to $4
Card Value	4¢ to 6¢
Will	dominate left-handers
Can't	freeze basestealers
Expect	reliance on curve
Don't Expect	closer work

Although he's bounced around both leagues, Assenmacher has never forgotten to apply his college degree in business administration. He just goes about his business—holding leads for closers 40 or more times each season. A curveball specialist who also throws a changeup and an occasional fastball, he averaged less than six hits and three walks per nine innings for much of the season last year. He kept the ball in the park and stranded most of the runners he inherited. He was especially tough on lefties, though AL hitters as a whole managed a batting average under the .200 level against him for much of the season. He doesn't get opportunities to notch many saves. Yet, he still looks like the same guy who made 70 appearances for the Cubs three years in a row (1990 to '92). He helps himself with his fielding but doesn't keep runners from stealing.

Major League Pitching Register
	W	L	ERA	G	S	IP	H	ER	BB	SO
86 NL	7	3	2.50	61	7	68.1	61	19	26	56
87 NL	1	1	5.10	52	2	54.2	58	31	24	39
88 NL	8	7	3.06	64	5	79.1	72	27	32	71
89 NL	3	4	3.99	63	0	76.2	74	34	28	79
90 NL	7	2	2.80	74	10	103.0	90	32	36	95
91 NL	7	8	3.24	75	15	102.2	85	37	31	117
92 NL	4	4	4.10	70	8	68.0	72	31	26	67
93 NL	2	1	3.49	46	0	38.2	44	15	13	34
93 AL	2	2	3.12	26	0	17.1	10	6	9	11
94 AL	1	2	3.55	44	1	33.0	26	13	13	29
95 AL	6	2	2.82	47	0	38.1	32	12	12	40
Life	48	36	3.40	622	48	680.0	624	257	250	638
3 AVE	4	3	3.26	62	0	48.1	42	18	18	44

CURRENT PLAYERS

PEDRO ASTACIO

Position: Pitcher
Team: Los Angeles Dodgers
Born: Nov. 28, 1969 Hato Mayor, Dominican Republic
Height: 6'2" **Weight:** 195 lbs.
Bats: right **Throws:** right
Acquired: Signed as a free agent, 11/87

Player Summary
Fantasy Value . . . . $4 to $6
Card Value . . . . 4¢ to 6¢
Will . . . . seek old velocity
Can't . . . . keep ball in park
Expect . . . . control of sinker
Don't Expect . . . . return as starter

Once regarded as a bright young pitching prospect, Astacio has watched his ERA rise for four years in a row. After winning one of 20 starts over a two-year span, he was replaced in the rotation by Ismael Valdes. Astacio wasn't much better in the bullpen. Despite excellent control and a 3-1 ratio of strikeouts to walks for much of the year, he was often victimized by wild pitches and home runs. When he's right, he is a sinkerballer who gets a lot of ground outs. He also throws a sweeping curve and a changeup. He averaged about two and one-half walks and about six and one-half strikeouts per nine innings for much of the season. Some scouts, however, said his velocity declined last year. His running speed hasn't; he can leg out a bunt. Astacio is also a quick, agile fielder who pays close attention to enemy baserunners, though his pickoff move looks awkward. Like Carlos Perez, Astacio is an animated presence on the mound. But his ebullient personality would be appreciated more if he pitched like Perez.

Major League Pitching Register

	W	L	ERA	G	CG	IP	H	ER	BB	SO
92 NL	5	5	1.98	11	4	82.0	80	18	20	43
93 NL	14	9	3.57	31	3	186.1	165	74	68	122
94 NL	6	8	4.29	23	3	149.0	142	71	47	108
95 NL	7	8	4.24	48	1	104.0	103	49	29	80
Life	32	30	3.66	113	11	521.1	490	212	164	353
3 AVE	10	10	4.02	39	3	171.0	160	76	56	121

BRAD AUSMUS

Position: Catcher
Team: San Diego Padres
Born: April 14, 1969 New Haven, CT
Height: 5'11" **Weight:** 190 lbs.
Bats: right **Throws:** right
Acquired: Traded by Rockies with Doug Bochtler and Andy Ashby for Bruce Hurst and Greg Harris, 7/93

Player Summary
Fantasy Value . . . . $7 to $9
Card Value . . . . 5¢ to 10¢
Will . . . . nail base thieves
Can't . . . . hit long ball
Expect . . . . unexpected speed
Don't Expect . . . . poor batting mark

Catchers who can hit and throw are hard to find. Catchers who can run, hit, and throw are worth their weight in gold. Ausmus belongs in that category. He is a young receiver who has tackled the difficult job of replacing former Gold Glove receiver Benito Santiago. During his short time in the majors, Ausmus has shown even greater potential. While he can't match Santiago's power, Ausmus is a productive hitter, especially against right-handers. He'd be even better if he reduced the 2-1 ratio of strikeouts to walks that he accrued during much of last year and started smacking more line drives. His speed helps him avoid double plays and gives him a chance to steal his way into scoring position. When he tries, he usually succeeds. He's also good at stopping opponents from doing the same thing. He nailed nearly 40 percent of runners who tried to steal against him during much of 1995. An Ivy Leaguer (Dartmouth), Ausmus handles pitchers well, releases the ball quickly, and commands the confidence of his ballclub.

Major League Batting Register

	BA	G	AB	R	H	2B	3B	HR	RBI	SB
93 NL	.256	49	160	18	41	8	1	5	12	2
94 NL	.251	101	327	45	82	12	1	7	24	5
95 NL	.293	103	328	44	96	16	4	5	34	16
Life	.269	253	815	107	219	36	6	17	70	23
3 AVE	.267	102	330	44	88	14	2	7	28	9

CURRENT PLAYERS

STEVE AVERY

Position: Pitcher
Team: Atlanta Braves
Born: April 14, 1970 Trenton, MI
Height: 6'4" **Weight:** 180 lbs.
Bats: left **Throws:** left
Acquired: First-round pick in 6/88 free-agent draft

Player Summary	
Fantasy Value	$13 to $16
Card Value	10¢ to 20¢
Will	make comeback bid
Can't	stop running game
Expect	a batter
Don't Expect	control woes

After posting two 18-win seasons, winning a playoff MVP Award, and making the All-Star team, Avery was regarded as one of baseball's rising stars. But that was before his magic disappeared in 1994—the same year his premature son had a lengthy hospital stay. Changing his routine between starts so he could commute home, Avery developed problems with his delivery. Except for brief bursts of brilliance, those troubles persisted in 1995. As a result, he dropped four of his first 11 decisions—a significant plunge. A fastball-curveball pitcher who sometimes relies too heavily on his changeup, Avery often gets hit hard when he falls behind in the count. During the three years he won in double-digits, he showed good control. When he's right, he keeps the ball down and coaxes a lot of ground balls from opposing hitters. Avery helps himself with his batting, bunting, and fielding. He even hit his first two homers in 1995. He's also improved his pickoff move.

Major League Pitching Register

	W	L	ERA	G	CG	IP	H	ER	BB	SO
90 NL	3	11	5.64	21	1	99.0	121	62	45	75
91 NL	18	8	3.38	35	3	210.1	189	79	65	137
92 NL	11	11	3.20	35	2	233.2	216	83	71	129
93 NL	18	6	2.94	35	3	223.1	216	73	43	125
94 NL	8	3	4.04	24	1	151.2	127	68	55	122
95 NL	7	13	4.67	29	3	173.1	165	90	52	141
Life	65	52	3.75	179	13	1091.1	1034	455	331	729
3 AVE	12	8	3.85	34	3	210.2	194	90	60	152

BOBBY AYALA

Position: Pitcher
Team: Seattle Mariners
Born: July 8, 1968 Ventura, CA
Height: 6'3" **Weight:** 200 lbs.
Bats: right **Throws:** right
Acquired: Traded by Reds with Dan Wilson for Erik Hanson and Bret Boone, 11/93

Player Summary	
Fantasy Value	$16 to $19
Card Value	5¢ to 10¢
Will	close games
Can't	always nix gophers
Expect	success vs. righties
Don't Expect	pinpoint control

There are not many players who would dare to wear No. 13. Ayala is an exception. Despite so-called unlucky digits, the hard-throwing right-hander has found success in two seasons as Seattle's closer. He averaged about one strikeout and one hit per inning. He shows good control of three pitches: a fastball, a forkball, and a slider. The heater—his best pitch—has been timed at 95 mph. To reach a higher level, Ayala needs to improve his work against left-handed hitters; he's far more effective against righties. Although he had some problems with the long ball last summer, he succeeded because he fanned about two and one-half times as many men as he walked. He's best used to start an inning, since he sometimes has trouble with inherited runners. He's also prone to occasional spells of wildness. Ayala still needs work on his defense and pickoff move; his high leg kick and slow delivery don't help. He spent two years as a full-time starter in the minor leagues, but Ayala has shown himself to be a fine closer.

Major League Pitching Register

	W	L	ERA	G	S	IP	H	ER	BB	SO
92 NL	2	1	4.34	5	0	29.0	33	14	13	23
93 NL	7	10	5.60	43	3	98.0	106	61	45	65
94 AL	4	3	2.86	46	18	56.2	42	18	26	76
95 AL	6	5	4.44	63	19	71.0	73	35	30	77
Life	19	19	4.52	157	40	254.2	254	128	114	241
3 AVE	6	7	4.39	60	17	86.1	82	42	38	86

CURRENT PLAYERS

CARLOS BAERGA

Position: Second base
Team: Cleveland Indians
Born: Nov. 4, 1968 San Juan, PR
Height: 5'11" **Weight:** 165 lbs.
Bats: both **Throws:** right
Acquired: Traded by Padres with Sandy Alomar and Chris James for Joe Carter, 12/89

Player Summary	
Fantasy Value	$30 to $35
Card Value	20¢ to 60¢
Will	post MVP stats
Can't	reach on walks
Expect	multihit games
Don't Expect	Gold Glove play

There's really no good way to work Baerga. A dangerous hitter for both power and average, he makes exceptional contact: He didn't strike out in his first 88 at bats of 1995 before Erik Hanson got him twice in succession. Baerga seems to get better with a two-strike count. Equally destructive from both sides of the plate, he led the majors in multihit games throughout much of the season. He also was a league leader in hits and batting. Pitchers try to confuse him with a variety of high inside heat and low-and-away breaking balls but few succeed. Baerga gave AL hurlers a gift in '94 when he showed up 20 pounds overweight and started slowly. He didn't repeat the mistake last year. The resulting offensive explosion earned him his first starting All-Star assignment. In the field, he has quick reactions, good range, and a solid throwing arm. He is the only AL second baseman ever to hit .300 with 20 homers, 100 RBI, and 200 hits in a season; he's done it twice.

Major League Batting Register

	BA	G	AB	R	H	2B	3B	HR	RBI	SB
90 AL	.260	108	312	46	81	17	2	7	47	0
91 AL	.288	158	593	80	171	28	2	11	69	3
92 AL	.312	161	657	92	205	32	1	20	105	10
93 AL	.321	154	624	105	200	28	6	21	114	15
94 AL	.314	103	442	81	139	32	2	19	80	8
95 AL	.314	135	557	87	175	28	2	15	90	11
Life	.305	819	3185	491	971	165	15	93	505	47
3 AVE	.316	150	624	106	198	35	4	22	109	13

JEFF BAGWELL

Position: First base
Team: Houston Astros
Born: May 27, 1968 Boston, MA
Height: 6' **Weight:** 195 lbs.
Bats: right **Throws:** right
Acquired: Traded by Red Sox for Larry Andersen, 8/90

Player Summary	
Fantasy Value	$35 to $40
Card Value	80¢ to $2
Will	show big power
Can't	fret about Ks
Expect	top on-base mark
Don't Expect	defensive woes

A Triple Crown contender and unanimous MVP in 1994, Bagwell went begging for hits in April and May last year. He later found his stroke, raising his average 100 points in a two-month span that started just after Memorial Day. Then—for the second straight season—the University of Hartford product broke the fourth metacarpal bone of his left hand when hit by a pitch. The accident happened July 30 after he had hit .331 with 31 RBI for the month. The Astros were anticipating a strong stretch-drive performance from their No. 3 hitter. When healthy, he murders southpaws and hits home runs with distance and regularity. In 1994, he led the league in runs, total bases, RBI, and home run frequency, as well as in batting, slugging, and on-base average against lefties. His best-in-the-majors slugging percentage was a Ruthian .750. Once an easy strikeout victim, Bagwell now changes stances to meet the occasion. He's a good fielder too: a Gold Glove complemented his 1994 MVP Award.

Major League Batting Register

	BA	G	AB	R	H	2B	3B	HR	RBI	SB
91 NL	.294	156	554	79	163	26	4	15	82	7
92 NL	.273	162	586	87	160	34	6	18	96	10
93 NL	.320	142	535	76	171	37	4	20	88	13
94 NL	.368	110	400	104	147	32	2	39	116	15
95 NL	.290	114	448	88	130	29	0	21	87	12
Life	.306	684	2523	434	771	158	16	113	469	57
3 AVE	.327	142	534	107	175	38	2	33	116	16

CURRENT PLAYERS

HAROLD BAINES

Position: Designated hitter
Team: Chicago White Sox
Born: March 15, 1959 Easton, MD
Height: 6'2" **Weight:** 195 lbs.
Bats: left **Throws:** left
Acquired: Signed as a free agent, 12/95

Player Summary
Fantasy Value	$8 to $10
Card Value	6¢ to 12¢
Will	get on base
Can't	cure knee problems
Expect	contact, power
Don't Expect	outfield play

Baines talks softly but carries a big stick. On Aug. 2, he delivered the only hit against Toronto rookie Paul Menhart, but it was a second-inning homer in a 1-0 win. A rare power-hitter who makes good contact, Baines walks more often than he strikes out. While that gives him a high on-base percentage, it's not necessarily great stats. He doesn't run well because of chronic knee problems, but no ballclub would want to risk losing his booming bat. A pull hitter whose left-handed swing was perfect for Oriole Park at Camden Yards, he is dangerous against both righties and lefties. The White Sox re-signed Baines for '96.

Major League Batting Register

	BA	G	AB	R	H	2B	3B	HR	RBI	SB
80 AL	.255	141	491	55	125	23	6	13	49	2
81 AL	.286	82	280	42	80	11	7	10	41	6
82 AL	.271	161	608	89	165	29	8	25	105	10
83 AL	.280	156	596	76	167	33	2	20	99	7
84 AL	.304	147	569	72	173	28	10	29	94	1
85 AL	.309	160	640	86	198	29	3	22	113	1
86 AL	.296	145	570	72	169	29	2	21	88	2
87 AL	.293	132	505	59	148	26	4	20	93	0
88 AL	.277	158	599	55	166	39	1	13	81	0
89 AL	.309	146	505	73	156	29	1	16	72	0
90 AL	.284	135	415	52	118	15	1	16	65	0
91 AL	.295	141	488	76	144	25	1	20	90	0
92 AL	.253	140	478	58	121	18	0	16	76	1
93 AL	.313	118	416	64	130	22	0	20	78	0
94 AL	.294	94	326	44	96	12	1	16	54	0
95 AL	.299	127	385	60	115	19	1	24	63	0
Life	.289	2183	7871	1033	2271	387	48	301	1261	30
3 AVE	.302	131	436	64	132	20	1	23	75	0

BRET BARBERIE

Position: Second base; third base
Team: Baltimore Orioles
Born: Aug. 16, 1967 Long Beach, CA
Height: 5'11" **Weight:** 185 lbs.
Bats: both **Throws:** right
Acquired: Traded by Marlins for Jay Powell, 12/94

Player Summary
Fantasy Value	$3 to $5
Card Value	4¢ to 6¢
Will	hit righties hard
Can't	find old patience
Expect	a little pop
Don't Expect	regular spot

Barberie has always been a decent hitter, but he hasn't always been the same type of hitter. In his first three pro seasons, he was a contact man, walking much more often than fanning and posting high on-base percentages. Though he still draws some walks, he's gone in the other direction: hacking more and enjoying it less. Barberie last year fanned about twice for every base on ball. Using all fields, he collected a few doubles but was not much of a threat to hit a home run or steal a base. The switch-hitting infielder struggled so much last summer—especially against southpaws—that he lost his regular second-base job to Manny Alexander in May. At 28, Barberie's future could lie as an all-purpose infielder. The former Olympian and USC standout has played all four infield spots in the majors. Mostly a second baseman, he doesn't turn the double play all that well or show great range at the position. He led NL second basemen in errors in 1994 and had the third-lowest fielding percentage.

Major League Batting Register

	BA	G	AB	R	H	2B	3B	HR	RBI	SB
91 NL	.353	57	136	16	48	12	2	2	18	0
92 NL	.232	111	285	26	66	11	0	1	24	9
93 NL	.277	99	375	45	104	16	2	5	33	2
94 NL	.301	107	372	40	112	20	2	5	31	2
95 AL	.241	90	237	32	57	14	0	2	25	3
Life	.275	464	1405	159	387	73	6	15	131	16
3 AVE	.280	117	389	46	109	20	2	5	35	3

CURRENT PLAYERS

KEVIN BASS

Position: Outfield
Team: Baltimore Orioles
Born: May 12, 1959 Redwood City, CA
Height: 6′ **Weight:** 180 lbs.
Bats: both **Throws:** right
Acquired: Signed as a free agent, 4/95

Player Summary
Fantasy Value.................$1 to $3
Card Value....................4¢ to 6¢
Will......................get timely hits
Can't...................recapture speed
Expect....................hits vs. lefties
Don't Expect............to test his arm

Expecting to contend for the AL East title, Baltimore viewed Bass as a fourth outfielder who could play both corners, spell DH Harold Baines, and pinch-hit from either side of the plate. Bass gave them an even better bargain. The long-time Houston standout spent much of the year as the regular right fielder, filling in for the O's acquired Bobby Bonilla. The switch-hitting Bass is a better right-handed hitter, but he still delivered big hits as a lefty. His .386 batting average with runners in scoring position led the NL in 1994. He thrives in clutch situations and loves 3-2 counts. He still shows flashes of power and speed. Though he's lost some speed in the field, Bass compensates with great positioning and a powerful arm.

Major League Batting Register

	BA	G	AB	R	H	2B	3B	HR	RBI	SB
82 AL	.000	18	9	4	0	0	0	0	0	0
82 NL	.042	12	24	2	1	0	0	0	1	0
83 NL	.236	88	195	25	46	7	3	2	18	2
84 NL	.260	121	331	33	86	17	5	2	29	5
85 NL	.269	150	539	72	145	27	5	16	68	19
86 NL	.311	157	591	83	184	33	5	20	79	22
87 NL	.284	157	592	83	168	31	5	19	85	21
88 NL	.255	157	541	57	138	27	2	14	72	31
89 NL	.300	87	313	42	94	19	4	5	44	11
90 NL	.252	61	214	25	54	9	1	7	32	2
91 NL	.233	124	361	43	84	10	4	10	40	7
92 NL	.269	135	402	40	108	23	5	9	39	14
93 NL	.284	111	229	31	65	18	0	3	37	7
94 NL	.310	82	203	37	63	15	1	6	35	2
95 AL	.244	111	295	32	72	12	0	5	32	8
Life	.270	1571	4839	609	1308	248	40	118	611	151
3 AVE	.277	117	282	40	78	18	0	6	41	6

JASON BATES

Position: Second base; infield
Team: Colorado Rockies
Born: Jan. 5, 1971 Downey, CA
Height: 5′11″ **Weight:** 170 lbs.
Bats: both **Throws:** right
Acquired: Seventh-round pick in 6/92 free-agent draft

Player Summary
Fantasy Value.................$6 to $8
Card Value....................4¢ to 6¢
Will......................thrive in clutch
Can't...................hit left-handers
Expect....................patience at bat
Don't Expect...................big power

With smooth-fielding Walt Weiss ahead of him as the Colorado shortstop, Bates became a three-way infield backup last year. He began as the everyday second baseman but yielded in midseason to the hot bat of holdover Eric Young. A switch-hitter who hammers right-handed pitching, Bates got extra bases on about one-third of his hits in 1995. He shows unusual patience for a young player, padding his on-base percentage by drawing a healthy share of walks. He actually walked more often than he fanned in two of his three minor-league seasons. A scrappy player with a strong clutch bat, Bates was a surprise team leader in batting with runners in scoring position during much of the season. He has more power than many middle infielders; he reached double-digits in homers two years in a row at Triple-A Colorado Springs in 1992 and '93. Bates also has some speed: He swiped 18 bases as a first-year pro in 1992. That speed gives him good range in the field. He led one minor-league in double plays and another in fielding percentage—both as a shortstop. If he learns to hold his own against lefties, he'll see more playing time.

Major League Batting Register

	BA	G	AB	R	H	2B	3B	HR	RBI	SB
95 NL	.267	116	322	42	86	17	4	8	46	3
Life	.267	116	322	42	86	17	4	8	46	3

CURRENT PLAYERS

DANNY BAUTISTA

Position: Outfield
Team: Detroit Tigers
Born: May 24, 1972 Santo Domingo, Dominican Republic
Height: 5'11" **Weight:** 170 lbs.
Bats: right **Throws:** right
Acquired: Signed as a free agent, 6/89

Player Summary	
Fantasy Value	$4 to $6
Card Value	5¢ to 8¢
Will	show good speed
Can't	wait for walks
Expect	strong defense
Don't Expect	many home runs

Although he's supposed to be an outfielder, Danny Bautista hit more like pitcher Jose Bautista last summer. Even before he hit an 0-for-36 skid in August, Danny had trouble staying above the Mendoza Line. A fleet line-drive hitter who lacks patience at the plate, Bautista would be additionally valuable if he worked his way on base with walks more. He also needs to show improvement in his performance against left-handed pitchers. He doesn't have much power but does offer enough speed and defense to play any of the three outfield positions. He spent most of 1995 in right field. His speed (46 steals over a two-year span in the minors) gives him great range. He also has a compact batting stroke that should result in double-digit homers—something he never accomplished in the minors. His basic problem is that he doesn't make enough contact. While other young hitters are bothered by breaking balls, Bautista has trouble with heat. Rest assured that the word is out to the pitchers' union. Since the Tigers were not challenging for a playoff spot last summer, the team could be patient with Bautista.

Major League Batting Register
	BA	G	AB	R	H	2B	3B	HR	RBI	SB
93 AL	.311	17	61	6	19	3	0	1	9	3
94 AL	.232	31	99	12	23	4	1	4	15	1
95 AL	.203	89	271	28	55	9	0	7	27	4
Life	.225	137	431	46	97	16	1	12	51	8

JOSE BAUTISTA

Position: Pitcher
Team: San Francisco Giants
Born: July 25, 1964 Bani, Dominican Republic
Height: 6'2" **Weight:** 205 lbs.
Bats: right **Throws:** right
Acquired: Signed as a free agent, 4/95

Player Summary	
Fantasy Value	$1 to $3
Card Value	4¢ to 6¢
Will	seek comeback
Can't	keep ball in park
Expect	starter's arsenal
Don't Expect	high whiff totals

A rubber-armed relief pitcher who throws his forkball at two different speeds, Bautista had been expected to bolster the San Francisco bullpen last summer. Instead, he wound up fighting "The Curse of the Long Ball." He hardly looked like the pitcher who had made 58 relief outings—most of them first rate—in each of the two previous seasons for the Cubs. The former Oriole starter still has a starter's repertoire: a fastball, a curve, and a slider, in addition to the forkball. Though he's not a strikeout pitcher, he did manage a strikeout-to-walk ratio of nearly 3-to-1 in 1994. But his effectiveness went south while he went west. When he catches too much of the plate, hitters frequently catch too much of the ball. More than half of those went for extra bases. With so many baserunners, Bautista had trouble holding runners on last year. He does field well, however, and can swing the bat. Bautista is sometimes used as a pinch runner.

Major League Pitching Register
	W	L	ERA	G	S	IP	H	ER	BB	SO
88 AL	6	15	4.30	33	0	171.2	171	82	45	76
89 AL	3	4	5.31	15	0	78.0	84	46	15	30
90 AL	1	0	4.05	22	0	26.2	28	12	7	15
91 AL	0	1	16.88	5	0	5.1	13	10	5	3
93 NL	10	3	2.82	58	2	111.2	105	35	27	63
94 NL	4	5	3.89	58	1	69.1	75	30	17	45
95 NL	3	8	6.44	52	0	100.2	120	72	26	45
Life	27	36	4.59	243	3	563.1	596	287	142	277
3 AVE	6	6	4.42	66	1	107.2	115	53	27	59

CURRENT PLAYERS

ROD BECK

Position: Pitcher
Team: San Francisco Giants
Born: Aug. 3, 1968 Burbank, CA
Height: 6'1" **Weight:** 215 lbs.
Bats: right **Throws:** right
Acquired: Traded by Athletics for Charlie Corbell, 3/88

Player Summary	
Fantasy Value	$35 to $40
Card Value	5¢ to 10¢
Will	make comeback bid
Can't	prevent homers
Expect	improved control
Don't Expect	return to '93

Beck's enormous workload of recent years may have caught up with him last summer. After converting a record 41 straight save opportunities (including all 28 in 1994), he struggled with his control and his ability to keep the ball in the park. On July 9, he yielded a single, a walk, and a Fred McGriff homer to a 2-0 lead into a 3-2 defeat. Beck had eight blown saves over the first four months—the worst slump of his career. When he's on, the hard-throwing right-hander with a glowering stare and a Fu Manchu mustache unleashes his arsenal of low-90s fastballs, forkballs, and sliders. He had a 3-1 ratio of whiffs to walks in '94, but only had about a 2-1 ratio for much of the season last year. Left-handers pounded the two-time All-Star. His velocity has faded sharply since he had better than one strikeout per inning in 1993, his best year. Weight problems also have contributed to his demise. He does help himself with his fielding and ability to hold runners on.

Major League Pitching Register

	W	L	ERA	G	S	IP	H	ER	BB	SO
91 NL	1	1	3.78	31	1	52.1	53	22	13	38
92 NL	3	3	1.76	65	17	92.0	62	18	15	87
93 NL	3	1	2.16	76	48	79.1	57	19	13	86
94 NL	2	4	2.77	48	28	48.2	49	15	13	39
95 NL	5	6	4.45	60	33	58.2	60	29	21	42
Life	14	15	2.80	280	127	331.0	281	103	75	292
3 AVE	4	4	3.06	70	42	71.2	65	24	18	63

RICH BECKER

Position: Outfield
Team: Minnesota Twins
Born: Feb. 1, 1972 Aurora, IL
Height: 5'10" **Weight:** 180 lbs.
Bats: both **Throws:** left
Acquired: Third-round pick in 6/90 free-agent draft

Player Summary	
Fantasy Value	$6 to $8
Card Value	5¢ to 8¢
Will	use speed
Can't	handle left-handers
Expect	excellent defense
Don't Expect	Dykstra imitation

For years, scouts have been comparing Becker to Lenny Dykstra. Although he provided Dykstra-style speed, defense, power, and patience during his minor-league tenure, Becker wasn't able to quickly make the adjustment to big-league pitching. Like Dykstra, however, Becker spent extended time on the disabled list (knee problems). Given a full shot in center field last season, he ran into problems. As a switch-hitter who was buried by southpaws, he failed to make Dykstra-type contact, fanning about three times per walk. The weak on-base percentage that resulted gave him little chance to show his speed on the bases. Since Becker led two minor leagues in walks and another in doubles (many of them singles he stretched), it seems likely that he'll add patience to his game. While working his way up, he led various leagues in on-base percentage, total bases, runs scored, chances, and putouts. Already one of the game's best defensive center fielders, Becker has excellent range and an arm that is both accurate and powerful. But will he hit?

Major League Batting Register

	BA	G	AB	R	H	2B	3B	HR	RBI	SB
93 AL	.286	3	7	3	2	2	0	0	0	1
94 AL	.265	28	98	12	26	3	0	1	8	6
95 AL	.237	106	392	45	93	15	1	2	33	8
Life	.243	137	497	60	121	20	1	3	41	15

CURRENT PLAYERS

TIM BELCHER

Position: Pitcher
Team: Seattle Mariners
Born: Oct. 19, 1961 Mount Gilead, OH
Height: 6'3" **Weight:** 210 lbs.
Bats: right **Throws:** right
Acquired: Traded by Reds for Roger Salkeld, 5/95

Player Summary	
Fantasy Value	$1 to $3
Card Value	4¢ to 8¢
Will	win with defense
Can't	always throw strikes
Expect	baserunners
Don't Expect	high K total

Belcher has been a big winner and a big loser. He was a 15-game winner twice, and he lost 14 games in one year and 15 in another. He's far from the pitcher who led the National League with eight shutouts and 10 complete games in 1989, but he's not as bad as the 7-15 record and career-worst 5.89 ERA that he recorded five years later. He is simply a journeyman right-hander who wins when he keeps his fastball, forkball, and slider low in the strike zone. Since he's not a strikeout pitcher, he relies on help from his defense. He sometimes sabotages his own efforts with erratic control and an inability to keep the ball in the park. Much more effective against right-handed hitters, Belcher carries a good glove and holds baserunners close. He was a College All-American from Mt. Vernon Nazarene in Ohio.

Major League Pitching Register

	W	L	ERA	G	CG	IP	H	ER	BB	SO
87 NL	4	2	2.38	6	0	34.0	30	9	7	23
88 NL	12	6	2.91	36	4	179.2	143	58	51	152
89 NL	15	12	2.82	39	10	230.0	182	72	80	200
90 NL	9	9	4.00	24	5	153.0	136	68	48	102
91 NL	10	9	2.62	33	2	209.1	189	61	75	156
92 NL	15	14	3.91	35	2	227.2	201	99	80	149
93 NL	9	6	4.47	22	4	137.0	134	68	47	101
93 AL	3	5	4.40	12	1	71.2	64	35	27	34
94 AL	7	15	5.89	25	3	162.0	192	106	78	76
95 AL	10	12	4.52	28	1	179.1	188	90	88	96
Life	94	90	3.78	260	32	1583.2	1459	666	581	1089
3 AVE	11	15	4.98	34	3	213.1	227	118	94	117

STAN BELINDA

Position: Pitcher
Team: Boston Red Sox
Born: Aug. 6, 1966 Huntington, PA
Height: 6'3" **Weight:** 200 lbs.
Bats: right **Throws:** right
Acquired: Signed as a free agent, 4/95

Player Summary	
Fantasy Value	$5 to $7
Card Value	4¢ to 6¢
Will	set up
Can't	keep control steady
Expect	velocity
Don't Expect	gopher woes

Before the Red Sox obtained Rick Aguilera last July, Belinda was their primary late-inning closer. He later moved to the familiar set-up role he performed for Jeff Montgomery in two seasons with the Royals. Belinda is a fastball-forkball pitcher whose control sometimes wavers. In three full seasons as Pittsburgh's closer, Belinda never had more than 19 saves. But he topped 50 appearances three years in a row and reached that level again last year. Because he's a sidearmer, he is much more effective against right-handed hitters. For much of the season last year, he kept the ball in the park, averaged about two strikeouts per walk, and yielded about six hits and three and one-half walks per nine innings. Belinda stranded about 70 percent of the runners he inherited through much of the year—a figure that needs improvement. He is a fine fielder, but his high leg kick is an open invitation to basestealers.

Major League Pitching Register

	W	L	ERA	G	S	IP	H	ER	BB	SO
89 NL	0	1	6.10	8	0	10.1	13	7	2	10
90 NL	3	4	3.55	55	8	58.1	48	23	29	55
91 NL	7	5	3.45	60	16	78.1	50	30	35	71
92 NL	6	4	3.15	59	18	71.1	58	25	29	57
93 NL	3	1	3.61	40	19	42.1	35	17	11	30
93 AL	1	1	4.28	23	0	27.1	30	13	6	25
94 AL	2	2	5.14	37	1	49.0	47	28	24	37
95 AL	8	1	3.10	63	10	69.2	51	24	28	57
Life	30	19	3.70	345	72	406.2	332	167	164	342
3 AVE	5	2	4.00	62	11	72.1	63	32	27	57

CURRENT PLAYERS

DEREK BELL

Position: Outfield
Team: Houston Astros
Born: Dec. 11, 1968 Tampa, FL
Height: 6'2" **Weight:** 200 lbs.
Bats: right **Throws:** right
Acquired: Traded by Padres with Phil Plantier, Pedro Martinez, Doug Brocail, Craig Shipley, and Ricky Gutierrez for Ken Caminiti, Steve Finley, Andujar Cedeno, Robert Petagine, Brian Williams, and a player to be named later, 12/94

Player Summary
Fantasy Value	$30 to $35
Card Value	8¢ to 15¢
Will	knock in runs
Can't	get press
Expect	solid defense
Don't Expect	selective at bats

On the day the 1995 All-Star Team was announced, Bell was the NL's top hitter (.353), tied for first in RBI, and among the Top 10 in hits, stolen bases, and assists. Yet he was 22nd in the outfield voting. Overlooked as well in his two previous good years, the frustrated Bell banged out a single, double, and home run the next day. According to Merv Rettenmund, his former hitting coach at San Diego, Bell will eventually lead the league in homers. Because he hits the ball harder more consistently than anybody else, the coach says, all Bell has to do is learn to lift the ball more. More patience at the plate would help too. He struck out more than twice per walk. He hammers left-handed pitching and hits to all fields. In addition to his bat, he provides speed, defense, a strong arm, and a good attitude.

Major League Batting Register
	BA	G	AB	R	H	2B	3B	HR	RBI	SB
91 AL	.143	18	28	5	4	0	0	0	1	3
92 AL	.242	61	161	23	39	6	3	2	15	7
93 NL	.262	150	542	73	142	19	1	21	72	26
94 NL	.311	108	434	54	135	20	0	14	54	24
95 NL	.334	112	452	63	151	21	2	8	86	27
Life	.291	449	1617	218	471	66	6	45	228	87
3 AVE	.302	143	554	73	167	24	1	17	82	30

JAY BELL

Position: Shortstop
Team: Pittsburgh Pirates
Born: Dec. 11, 1965 Eglin Air Force Base, FL
Height: 6'1" **Weight:** 180 lbs.
Bats: right **Throws:** right
Acquired: Traded by Indians for Felix Fermin, 3/89

Player Summary
Fantasy Value	$8 to $10
Card Value	5¢ to 8¢
Will	hit-and-run
Can't	trim K ratio
Expect	occasional homers
Don't Expect	quick start

One of baseball's most durable performers, Bell participated in 828 of Pittsburgh's first 853 games in the 1990s—an accomplishment topped only by Cal Ripken among active shortstops. Warming with the weather, Bell homered twice against Houston on Aug. 6. He finished with double-digits in homers for the second time in his career. Power is hardly his primary contribution, however. Batting second in the lineup, he has become an accomplished hit-and-run artist, as well as a skilled bunter who once posted 39 sacrifices in a single season. A *Baseball America* poll of managers last year named him the NL's second-best bunter and defensive shortstop, and third-best hit-and-run man. A better batter against southpaws, Bell fans far too frequently for a guy who usually hits singles. He averaged about two whiffs per walk last year.

Major League Batting Register
	BA	G	AB	R	H	2B	3B	HR	RBI	SB
86 AL	.357	5	14	3	5	2	0	1	4	0
87 AL	.216	38	125	14	27	9	1	2	13	2
88 AL	.218	73	211	23	46	5	1	2	21	4
89 NL	.258	78	271	33	70	13	3	2	27	5
90 NL	.254	159	583	93	148	28	7	7	52	10
91 NL	.270	157	608	96	164	32	8	16	67	10
92 NL	.264	159	632	87	167	36	6	9	55	7
93 NL	.310	154	604	102	187	32	9	9	51	16
94 NL	.276	110	424	68	117	35	4	9	45	2
95 NL	.262	138	530	79	139	28	4	13	55	2
Life	.267	1071	4002	598	1070	220	43	70	390	58
3 AVE	.283	155	599	96	169	38	6	12	59	7

CURRENT PLAYERS

ALBERT BELLE

Position: Outfield
Team: Cleveland Indians
Born: Aug. 25, 1966 Shreveport, LA
Height: 6'2" **Weight:** 200 lbs.
Bats: right **Throws:** right
Acquired: Second-round pick in 6/87 free-agent draft

Player Summary
Fantasy Value .... $40 to $45
Card Value .... 75¢ to $1
Will .... hammer mistakes
Can't .... run for 30-30
Expect .... patience, power
Don't Expect .... bad glove

Belle is the cleanup hitter and anchor man of the powerful attack that made the Indians postseason participants last year for the first time since 1954. Once a victim of his own temperament, he has become a team leader both on and off the field. He had his fourth straight 30-homer year in 1995. A selective hitter who's willing to walk, he bid for a Triple Crown in 1994—his first .300 average was just two points behind batting champion Paul O'Neill. A deadly clutch hitter, Belle had been known as a streak hitter before his 1994 performance showed he had mastered the art of consistency. A student of hitting, the former Louisiana State standout is regarded as the best "mistake" hitter in the game. All hanging breaking balls are fair game. Belle has decent speed but doesn't steal much. His speed does help in the outfield, however, where he's worked hard to overcome a reputation as a below-average left fielder.

Major League Batting Register

	BA	G	AB	R	H	2B	3B	HR	RBI	SB
89 AL	.225	62	218	22	49	8	4	7	37	2
90 AL	.174	9	23	1	4	0	0	1	3	0
91 AL	.282	123	461	60	130	31	2	28	95	3
92 AL	.260	153	585	81	152	23	1	34	112	8
93 AL	.290	159	594	93	172	36	3	38	129	23
94 AL	.357	106	412	90	147	35	2	36	101	9
95 AL	.317	143	546	121	173	52	1	50	126	5
Life	.291	755	2839	468	827	185	13	194	603	50
3 AVE	.321	156	596	119	191	48	2	48	138	14

RAFAEL BELLIARD

Position: Shortstop; second base
Team: Atlanta Braves
Born: Oct. 24, 1961 Pueblo Nuevo, Mao, Dominican Republic
Height: 5'6" **Weight:** 150 lbs.
Bats: right **Throws:** right
Acquired: Signed as a free agent, 12/90

Player Summary
Fantasy Value $0
Card Value .... 4¢ to 6¢
Will .... fill sub role
Can't .... wait for walk
Expect .... great defense
Don't Expect .... a long ball

Sometimes good things come in small packages, and Belliard is a perfect example. A little guy with a great glove, he maintains a smiling disposition while waiting on the bench for a regular middle infielder to be sidelined by illness or injury. Once he gets into a game, he shows off quick reactions, excellent range, and a throwing arm often more powerful than those of the regulars he replaces. He was often used as a late-inning defensive replacement because of the value of his leather. A Punch-and-Judy hitter and terrific bunter, Belliard has earned the nickname "Hack-Man" for his tendency to swing at almost anything. He's hit only one home run in 14 seasons—one of the worst power outputs in baseball history—and walks infrequently as well.

Major League Batting Register

	BA	G	AB	R	H	2B	3B	HR	RBI	SB
82 NL	.500	9	2	3	1	0	0	0	0	1
83 NL	.000	4	1	1	0	0	0	0	0	0
84 NL	.227	20	22	3	5	0	0	0	0	4
85 NL	.200	17	20	1	4	0	0	0	1	0
86 NL	.233	117	309	33	72	5	2	0	31	12
87 NL	.207	81	203	26	42	4	3	1	15	5
88 NL	.213	122	286	28	61	0	4	0	11	7
89 NL	.214	67	154	10	33	4	0	0	8	5
90 NL	.204	47	54	10	11	3	0	0	6	1
91 NL	.249	149	353	36	88	9	2	0	27	3
92 NL	.211	144	285	20	60	6	1	0	14	0
93 NL	.228	91	79	6	18	5	0	0	6	0
94 NL	.242	46	120	9	29	7	1	0	9	0
95 NL	.222	75	180	12	40	2	1	0	7	2
Life	.224	989	2068	198	464	45	14	1	135	40

CURRENT PLAYERS

ANDY BENES

Position: Pitcher
Team: Seattle Mariners
Born: Aug. 20, 1967 Evansville, IN
Height: 6'6" **Weight:** 235 lbs.
Bats: right **Throws:** right
Acquired: Traded by Padres with Greg Keagle for Ron Villone and Marc Newfield, 7/95

Player Summary	
Fantasy Value	$12 to $15
Card Value	6¢ to 10¢
Will	register Ks
Can't	stop extra-base hits
Expect	15-plus wins
Don't Expect	more hits than frames

Before he fell victim to poor support in 1994, Benes was a double-digit winner in San Diego for four straight seasons. He made the NL All-Star Team in one of those seasons. So it was not surprising that Seattle, seeking a wild-card berth, traded for him on July 31. The Mariners hoped that he was over the streak that left him winless for 17 straight starts before his June 16 victory at Pittsburgh. A power pitcher who throws a fastball, a slider, and a straight change, Benes averaged about one strikeout per inning for the Pads and the M's last year. He also notched nearly a 3-1 ratio of whiffs to walks for San Diego, although he had some control trouble in Seattle. A former Olympian out of Evansville University, he helps himself with strong defense. Despite a windup that features a high leg kick, Benes has become adept at picking runners off. He also helps himself with his fielding. He was the nation's first pick in the 1988 draft.

Major League Pitching Register

	W	L	ERA	G	CG	IP	H	ER	BB	SO
89 NL	6	3	3.51	10	0	66.2	51	26	31	66
90 NL	10	11	3.60	32	2	192.1	177	77	69	140
91 NL	15	11	3.03	33	4	223.0	194	75	59	167
92 NL	13	14	3.35	34	2	231.1	230	86	61	169
93 NL	15	15	3.78	34	4	230.2	200	97	86	179
94 NL	6	14	3.86	25	2	172.1	155	74	51	189
95 NL	4	7	4.17	19	1	118.2	121	55	45	126
95 AL	7	2	5.86	12	0	63.0	72	41	33	45
Life	76	77	3.68	199	15	1298.0	1200	531	435	1081
3 AVE	12	15	4.11	35	3	225.2	212	103	82	213

ARMANDO BENITEZ

Position: Pitcher
Team: Baltimore Orioles
Born: Nov. 3, 1972 Ramon Santana, Dominican Republic
Height: 6'4" **Weight:** 180 lbs.
Bats: right **Throws:** right
Acquired: Signed as a free agent, 4/90

Player Summary	
Fantasy Value	$4 to $6
Card Value	10¢ to 15¢
Will	blaze ball
Can't	stop runners
Expect	huge K totals
Don't Expect	perfect control

Drooling at the thought that he might be a reincarnation of the young Lee Smith, the Orioles opened the 1995 season with Benitez as their closer-in-waiting. Control problems intervened, however, and the flame-throwing right-hander made several trips back to the minors, where he lacked previous Triple-A experience. Used almost exclusively in relief since turning pro in 1990, Benitez made his first big splash by striking out 112 batters in 67 innings while pitching for two Baltimore farms in 1993. That average of 15.04 strikeouts per nine innings led all of professional baseball. A year later, his ratio in Double-A ball was 13.31. He fanned the first big-league batter he faced, Albert Belle, on July 28, 1994. But the sharp control Benitez exhibited during that 10-inning prestrike audition did not return with him in 1995. He also needs to refine his slider, which complements his mid-90s fastball. As an alternative, he might want to learn another pitch, such as a forkball or a changeup. Without better control, however, he'll never be more than a middle reliever.

Major League Pitching Register

	W	L	ERA	G	S	IP	H	ER	BB	SO
94 AL	0	0	0.90	3	0	10.0	8	1	4	14
95 AL	1	5	5.66	44	2	47.2	37	30	37	56
Life	1	5	4.84	47	2	57.2	45	31	41	70

CURRENT PLAYERS

MIKE BENJAMIN

Position: Infield
Team: Philadelphia Phillies
Born: Nov. 22, 1965 Euclid, OH
Height: 6' **Weight:** 169 lbs.
Bats: right **Throws:** right
Acquired: Traded by Giants for Jeff Juden and Tommy Eason, 10/95

Player Summary
Fantasy Value	$1
Card Value	4¢ to 6¢
Will	play three spots
Can't	show patience
Expect	some speed
Don't Expect	consistent stick

After carrying a six-year batting average of .186 into the 1995 campaign, Benjamin was not likely to set the world on fire with his bat. But long hours in the batting cage with Giants hitting coach Bobby Bonds produced amazing results during a June series at Wrigley Field. Playing third in the absence of injured slugger Matt Williams, Benjamin went 6-for-7 on June 14, giving him a record 14 hits in three games. In 18 at bats, he had produced just two fewer hits than his season's total for 1994. He had also broken the three-game mark of 13 hits shared by Tim Salmon, Walt Dropo, and Joe Cronin. Not surprisingly, Benjamin's hits included 12 singles, a double, and a home run. He's basically an undisciplined singles hitter who doesn't make good contact or draw many walks. That hurts, since he has enough speed to steal some bases when he reaches. His value is directly linked to his ability to play three infield positions well. Benjamin signed as a shortstop out of Arizona State.

Major League Batting Register
	BA	G	AB	R	H	2B	3B	HR	RBI	SB
89 NL	.167	14	6	6	1	0	0	0	0	0
90 NL	.214	22	56	7	12	3	1	2	3	1
91 NL	.123	54	106	12	13	3	0	2	8	3
92 NL	.173	40	75	4	13	2	1	1	3	1
93 NL	.199	63	146	22	29	7	0	4	16	3
94 NL	.258	38	62	9	16	5	1	1	9	5
95 NL	.220	68	186	19	41	6	0	3	12	11
Life	.196	299	637	79	125	26	3	13	51	21

JASON BERE

Position: Pitcher
Team: Chicago White Sox
Born: May 26, 1971 Cambridge, MA
Height: 6'3" **Weight:** 185 lbs.
Bats: right **Throws:** right
Acquired: 36th-round pick in 6/90 free-agent draft

Player Summary
Fantasy Value	$6 to $8
Card Value	8¢ to 15¢
Will	win with control
Can't	prevent gophers
Expect	strikeouts
Don't Expect	more hits than frames

After posting a 24-7 record in less than two full years with the White Sox, Bere's 1995 collapse turned out to be a mystery. He did show some flashes of brilliance, including a 14-strikeout game on June 28 that left him two shy of Jack Harshman's 1954 club record. But Bere had such severe control problems that his excellent hits-to-innings ratio hardly mattered. Through much of the season, the hard-throwing New Englander was yielding almost seven walks per nine innings. Even when he threw strikes, his spotty control made his pitches too fat—resulting in long hits by opponents. He throws a fastball, an occasional curve, and the "fosh" changeup first popularized by former big-league pitcher Mike Boddicker. In addition to improving his control, Bere could help himself by improving his defensive skills—especially his inability to hold baserunners. Based upon his '95 showing, it's hard to tell that he was a 1994 All-Star. Bere now faces a long comeback trail before he can regain his stature as an up-and-coming star.

Major League Pitching Register
	W	L	ERA	G	CG	IP	H	ER	BB	SO
93 AL	12	5	3.47	24	1	142.2	109	55	81	129
94 AL	12	2	3.81	24	0	141.2	119	60	80	127
95 AL	8	15	7.19	27	1	137.2	151	110	106	110
Life	32	22	4.80	75	2	422.0	379	225	267	366
3 AVE	13	8	4.77	29	1	165.2	149	88	104	144

CURRENT PLAYERS

SEAN BERGMAN

Position: Pitcher
Team: Detroit Tigers
Born: April 11, 1970 Joliet, IL
Height: 6'4" **Weight:** 205 lbs.
Bats: right **Throws:** right
Acquired: Fourth-round pick in 6/91 free-agent draft

Player Summary	
Fantasy Value	$3 to $5
Card Value	8¢ to 12¢
Will	bank on changeup
Can't	shed blister hex
Expect	improving record
Don't Expect	rotation removal

The blisters that bothered Bergman during the first half of the 1995 season weren't in evidence Aug. 2. That was the night he registered his first big-league shutout with a 5-0 victory over the first-place Red Sox. Bergman's four-hitter included seven strikeouts and just one walk. The Southern Illinois University product blends an 87 mph moving fastball with an improving breaking ball and a changeup that rates as his No. 1 pitch. He tries to get ahead in the count early to set up the change. During his best minor-league season, at Triple-A Toledo in 1994, Bergman maintained a strikeout-to-walk ratio of about 3-to-1. That year, he went 11-8 with a 3.72 ERA for the Mud Hens. He was 8-9 with a 4.38 ERA in 1993 at Toledo. An intense competitor, he had two brief cups of coffee before breaking into the rebuilding Tiger rotation on a regular basis in 1995. Except for three relief outings for the '93 Tigers, Bergman has been used exclusively as a starter since beginning his pro ball career in 1988. He's long been regarded as one of the top pitching prospects in the Detroit organization.

Major League Pitching Register

	W	L	ERA	G	CG	IP	H	ER	BB	SO
93 AL	1	4	5.67	9	1	39.2	47	25	23	19
94 AL	2	1	5.60	3	0	17.2	22	11	7	12
95 AL	7	10	5.12	28	1	135.1	169	77	67	86
Life	10	15	5.28	40	2	192.2	238	113	97	117

GERONIMO BERROA

Position: Outfield
Team: Oakland Athletics
Born: March 18, 1965 Santo Domingo, Dominican Republic
Height: 6' **Weight:** 195 lbs.
Bats: right **Throws:** right
Acquired: Signed as a free agent, 1/94

Player Summary	
Fantasy Value	$14 to $17
Card Value	5¢ to 8¢
Will	hit with power
Can't	supply glove
Expect	good two-strike bat
Don't Expect	impatience

When he was hitting well early in the 1995 season, Berroa said he was using bats given to him by Kirby Puckett. They were the same weight and model as his own bats, but Berroa said the gift bats contained more hits because they had Puckett's name on them. In 1994 and early 1995, Puckett and Berroa had similar offensive numbers. The magic didn't last for Berroa, however. One of his problems last year was a sudden weakness against left-handed pitching. He had hit .341 against southpaws in 1994. Given more playing time as a result, he reached career power peaks last summer. He's become a much more selective hitter in recent seasons, allowing him to increase his long-ball production. A good two-strike hitter, Berroa has good power to left-center. He's worked hard to improve his once-dreadful defense, but is still prone to misjudging fly balls and making inaccurate throws. He's still best as a DH, however. Berroa has decent speed and will steal a base occasionally.

Major League Batting Register

	BA	G	AB	R	H	2B	3B	HR	RBI	SB
89 NL	.265	81	136	7	36	4	0	2	9	0
90 NL	.000	7	4	0	0	0	0	0	0	0
92 NL	.267	13	15	2	4	1	0	0	0	0
93 NL	.118	14	34	3	4	1	0	0	0	0
94 AL	.306	96	340	55	104	18	2	13	65	7
95 AL	.278	141	546	87	152	22	3	22	88	7
Life	.279	352	1075	154	300	46	5	37	162	14
2 AVE	.290	147	547	88	159	25	3	22	95	9

CURRENT PLAYERS

SEAN BERRY

Position: Third base; outfield
Team: Houston Astros
Born: April 22, 1966 Santa Monica, CA
Height: 5'11" **Weight:** 210 lbs.
Bats: right **Throws:** right
Acquired: Traded by Expos for Dave Veras and Raul Chavez, 12/95

Player Summary	
Fantasy Value	$8 to $10
Card Value	5¢ to 8¢
Will	try to add power
Can't	hit some righties
Expect	adequate fielding
Don't Expect	clutch production

After the Expos acquired Dave Silvestri from the Yankees last summer, manager Felipe Alou asked Berry—a college center fielder at UCLA—to begin taking fly balls in left field. The idea was to move Moises Alou from left to right, replacing Tony Tarasco, and play Berry in left against left-handed pitchers. While Berry had given Montreal good defense at third base, he had never delivered the power expected from the position. That's why the team promoted Shane Andrews and acquired Silvestri, a fellow 1995 rookie with a reputation as a minor-league slugger. If Berry's hitting could match his fielding, he'd be a star. But he shows such impatience at the plate that in 1995 he averaged about two strikeouts for every walk. He's not known for his clutch hitting and too often gets jammed at the plate. He has some speed, but not much success as a basestealer last summer. In '94, however, he was perfect in 14 attempts. As an infielder, Berry's arm is his best asset.

Major League Batting Register

	BA	G	AB	R	H	2B	3B	HR	RBI	SB
90 AL	.217	8	23	2	5	1	1	0	4	0
91 AL	.133	31	60	5	8	3	0	0	1	0
92 NL	.333	24	57	5	19	1	0	1	4	2
93 NL	.261	122	299	50	78	15	2	14	49	12
94 NL	.278	103	320	43	89	19	2	11	41	14
95 NL	.318	103	314	38	100	22	1	14	55	3
Life	.279	391	1073	143	299	61	6	40	154	31
3 AVE	.286	128	368	51	105	22	2	15	56	12

DAMON BERRYHILL

Position: Catcher
Team: Cincinnati Reds
Born: Dec. 3, 1963 Laguna, CA
Height: 6' **Weight:** 210 lbs.
Bats: both **Throws:** right
Acquired: Signed as a free agent, 11/94

Player Summary	
Fantasy Value	$0
Card Value	4¢ to 6¢
Will	add leadership
Can't	nail runners
Expect	well-called games
Don't Expect	solid batting mark

Although his reputation has superseded his statistics in recent seasons, Berryhill survives because he's a veteran catcher who switch-hits and has World Series experience. He's bounced around a bit—mainly because his major contribution is neither offense nor defense but leadership. He caught every postseason game pitched by the talented Atlanta staff in the 1992 and 1993 postseasons. He even contributed two key homers—one of them a game-winner. Berryhill bangs a few extra-base hits a year and excels at ripping pitchers' mistakes. His batting eye seems sharper when he gets more playing time. Patience is not one of his virtues, though he did draw a critical walk during the three-run, ninth-inning uprising that won the 1992 NL playoffs for the Braves. He doesn't nail many runners, but calls a good game, prevents wild pitches, and blocks the plate.

Major League Batting Register

	BA	G	AB	R	H	2B	3B	HR	RBI	SB
87 NL	.179	12	28	2	5	1	0	0	1	0
88 NL	.259	95	309	19	80	19	1	7	38	1
89 NL	.257	91	334	37	86	13	0	5	41	1
90 NL	.189	17	53	6	10	4	0	1	9	0
91 NL	.188	63	160	13	30	7	0	5	14	1
92 NL	.228	101	307	21	70	16	1	10	43	0
93 NL	.245	115	335	24	82	18	2	8	43	0
94 AL	.263	82	255	30	67	17	2	6	34	0
95 NL	.183	34	82	6	15	3	0	2	11	0
Life	.239	610	1863	158	445	98	6	44	234	3
2 AVE	.254	115	347	33	88	21	2	8	45	0

ANDRES BERUMEN

Position: Pitcher
Team: San Diego Padres
Born: April 5, 1971 Tijuana, Mexico
Height: 6'2" **Weight:** 205 lbs.
Bats: right **Throws:** right
Acquired: Traded by Marlins with Trevor Hoffman and Jose Martinez for Gary Sheffield and Rich Rodriguez, 6/93

Player Summary	
Fantasy Value	$1 to $3
Card Value	12¢ to 20¢
Will	work out of bullpen
Can't	cut walk ratio
Expect	more Ks than frames
Don't Expect	gopher troubles

When Berumen was included in the Gary Sheffield trade of June 1993, noted baseball columnist Peter Gammons predicted that the Padres' acquisition of Berumen would turn out to be a steal for San Diego. Used as both a starter and reliever in a minor-league career that began in 1989, Berumen made his big-league bow out of the bullpen on April 27, 1995. Throwing a mid-90s fastball with a smooth delivery, he held hitters around the Mendoza Line for a good portion of the season, until he ran into some tendinitis woes and was less effective. He also managed to keep the ball in the park. On the other hand, his control was so erratic that the Padres briefly sent him back to the minors to sharpen his breaking ball. For much of the year, he had more wild pitches and a higher walk ratio (about seven per nine innings) than any other Padre reliever. But he also had an excellent ratio of hits to innings. *Baseball America* rated him one of San Diego's Top 10 prospects in 1994. Berumen was originally selected by the Marlins from Kansas City in the second round of the 1992 expansion draft.

Major League Pitching Register

	W	L	ERA	G	S	IP	H	ER	BB	SO
95 NL	2	3	5.68	37	1	44.1	37	28	36	42
Life	2	3	5.68	37	1	44.1	37	28	36	42

DANTE BICHETTE

Position: Outfield
Team: Colorado Rockies
Born: Nov. 18, 1963 West Palm Beach, FL
Height: 6'3" **Weight:** 212 lbs.
Bats: right **Throws:** right
Acquired: Traded by Brewers for Kevin Reimer, 11/92

Player Summary	
Fantasy Value	$30 to $35
Card Value	30¢ to 50¢
Will	thrive at home
Can't	maintain pace
Expect	run production
Don't Expect	weak throws

Is Bichette the same guy who was once platooned with Darryl Hamilton? No manager would dare do that today, now that Bichette has shown he can hit .300 with power against both righties and lefties. Playing half his schedule in the alpine air of Denver's Coors Field, he seemingly has become one of the game's top sluggers. Before playing in the All-Star Game for the second year in a row, he had a 23-game hitting streak, the NL's longest. His .358 batting average led the NL on June 20. He set club records with 11 homers and 34 RBI in July. Bichette hit his first 17 home runs at home but hit the next three on the road. He fanned about four times more than he walked last year, but he managed to improve the results when he made contact. Instead of pulling everything, he went with the pitch and used all fields. Bichette owns an exceptional throwing arm, but shifted from right to left when an even better gun—Larry Walker—joined the team.

Major League Batting Register

	BA	G	AB	R	H	2B	3B	HR	RBI	SB
88 AL	.261	21	46	1	12	2	0	0	8	0
89 AL	.210	48	138	13	29	7	0	3	15	3
90 AL	.255	109	349	40	89	15	1	15	53	5
91 AL	.238	134	445	53	106	18	3	15	59	14
92 AL	.287	112	387	37	111	27	2	5	41	18
93 NL	.310	141	538	93	167	43	5	21	89	14
94 NL	.304	116	484	74	147	33	2	27	95	21
95 NL	.340	139	579	102	197	38	2	40	128	13
Life	.289	820	2966	413	858	183	15	126	488	88
3 AVE	.318	154	624	104	199	44	3	35	122	19

CURRENT PLAYERS

MIKE BIELECKI

Position: Pitcher
Team: California Angels
Born: July 31, 1959 Baltimore, MD
Height: 6'3" **Weight:** 195 lbs.
Bats: right **Throws:** right
Acquired: Signed as a free agent, 4/95

Player Summary
Fantasy Value $0
Card Value . . . . 4¢ to 6¢
Will . . . . mix four pitches
Can't . . . . complete his starts
Expect. . . . . spot starts
Don't Expect . . . . return to 1989

Although his career record reads like a railroad timetable, Bielecki enjoyed a surprising revival in California last summer. Deployed as both a starter and reliever, he showed flashes of brilliance before going on the shelf with an inflamed right shoulder in July. His best game came on July 2, when he yielded two hits in eight innings at Oakland. It was the first time he had pitched past the seventh inning in nine starts. Hardly a model of stamina, Bielecki had completed only seven of 162 big-league starts before joining the Angels. However, he does offer a diversified repertoire: a fastball, a forkball, a curveball, and a changeup, usually with good control. He kept the ball in the park for much of last season and allowed less hits than innings pitched. In 1989, his best season, Bielecki helped pitch the Cubs into the NLCS with an 18-7 performance.

Major League Pitching Register

	W	L	ERA	G	S	IP	H	ER	BB	SO
84 NL	0	0	0.00	4	0	4.1	4	0	0	1
85 NL	2	3	4.53	12	0	45.2	45	23	31	22
86 NL	6	11	4.66	31	0	148.2	149	77	83	83
87 NL	2	3	4.73	8	0	45.2	43	24	12	25
88 NL	2	2	3.35	19	0	48.1	55	18	16	33
89 NL	18	7	3.14	33	0	212.1	187	74	81	147
90 NL	8	11	4.93	36	1	168.0	188	92	70	103
91 NL	13	11	4.46	41	0	173.2	171	86	56	75
92 NL	2	4	2.57	19	0	80.2	77	23	27	62
93 AL	4	5	5.90	13	0	68.2	90	45	23	38
94 NL	2	0	4.00	19	0	27.0	28	12	12	18
95 AL	4	6	5.97	22	0	75.1	80	50	31	45
Life	63	63	4.29	257	1	1098.1	1117	524	442	652
2 AVE	4	6	5.94	19	0	76.2	90	51	29	44

CRIAG BIGGIO

Position: Second base
Team: Houston Astros
Born: Dec. 14, 1965 Smithtown, NY
Height: 5'11" **Weight:** 180 lbs.
Bats: right **Throws:** right
Acquired: First-round pick in 6/87 free-agent draft

Player Summary
Fantasy Value . . . . $30 to $35
Card Value . . . . 20¢ to 40¢
Will . . . . mix speed, power
Can't . . . . return to catcher
Expect . . . . top on-base mark
Don't Expect . . . . defensive lapses

Biggio turned the power back on in 1995. The former Seton Hall All-American—a converted catcher—won his first Gold Glove as a second baseman in 1994, when he led the NL with 44 doubles and 39 stolen bases. A contact hitter who shows patience at the plate, Biggio walked almost as often as he struck out during much of the 1995 season. He also had one of the best on-base percentages in the National League, keeping it about the .400 mark for much of the season. He is comfortable in any of the top three lineup positions, but hit second most often after the promotion of Brian Hunter last June. That spot is ideal for Biggio, who's one of the game's top hit-and-run men. He can also bunt, reach the gaps, and hit to the opposite field. He runs well and is rarely erased when he tries to steal. In four years as a second baseman, he's become one of the game's best all-around performers at his position. Biggio has been an All-Star four times.

Major League Batting Register

	BA	G	AB	R	H	2B	3B	HR	RBI	SB
88 NL	.211	50	123	14	26	6	1	3	5	6
89 NL	.257	134	443	64	114	21	2	13	60	21
90 NL	.276	150	555	53	153	24	2	4	42	25
91 NL	.295	149	546	79	161	23	4	4	46	19
92 NL	.277	162	613	96	170	32	3	6	39	38
93 NL	.287	155	610	98	175	41	5	21	64	15
94 NL	.318	114	437	88	139	44	5	6	56	39
95 NL	.302	141	553	123	167	30	2	22	77	33
Life	.285	1055	3880	615	1105	221	24	79	389	196
3 AVE	.302	158	616	120	186	46	5	18	77	36

CURRENT PLAYERS

WILLIE BLAIR

Position: Pitcher
Team: San Diego Padres
Born: Dec. 18, 1965 Paintsville, KY
Height: 6'1" **Weight:** 185 lbs.
Bats: right **Throws:** right
Acquired: Signed as a free agent, 4/95

Player Summary
Fantasy Value	$4 to $6
Card Value	4¢ to 6¢
Will	show velocity
Can't	always throw strikes
Expect	a look as a starter
Don't Expect	bat to help

Although he had losing records in each of his first five big-league seasons, Blair had shown enough potential to find a job with San Diego. In fact, he was handed the rotation vacancy created by the July 31 Andy Benes trade last year. Blair's first start in more than a year was a huge success: three singles and no runs in six innings against San Francisco on Aug. 3. A hard thrower who averaged about six and one-half strikeouts per nine innings for much of the '95 season, Blair has been held back only by erratic control. But he made dramatic strides in that department last season. In addition to his heater, he throws a cut fastball and a curve. But he'd be more effective as a starter if he added another pitch. He helps himself with his fielding and his ability to hold runners, but isn't much of a hitter. The Morehead State product has some ability as a pitcher, however. The Colorado Rockies made him a first-round pick in the expansion draft in 1992.

Major League Pitching Register
	W	L	ERA	G	S	IP	H	ER	BB	SO
90 AL	3	5	4.06	27	0	68.2	66	31	28	43
91 AL	2	3	6.75	11	0	36.0	58	27	10	13
92 NL	5	7	4.00	29	0	78.2	74	35	25	48
93 NL	6	10	4.75	46	0	146.0	184	77	42	84
94 NL	0	5	5.79	47	3	77.2	98	50	39	68
95 NL	7	5	4.34	40	0	114.0	112	55	45	83
Life	23	35	4.75	200	3	521.0	592	275	189	339
3 AVE	5	8	4.91	52	1	128.1	149	70	49	91

JEFF BLAUSER

Position: Shortstop
Team: Atlanta Braves
Born: Nov. 8, 1965 Los Gatos, CA
Height: 6'1" **Weight:** 180 lbs.
Bats: right **Throws:** right
Acquired: First-round pick in secondary phase of 6/84 free-agent draft

Player Summary
Fantasy Value	$7 to $9
Card Value	5¢ to 8¢
Will	provide some pop
Can't	stop striking out
Expect	steady glovework
Don't Expect	'93 bat

Once known as a shortstop who could hit but not field, Blauser has gone the other way over the past two seasons. In 1993, when he made the All-Star Team, he became the first Braves shortstop to top .300 since Alvin Dark in 1948. Blauser also hit a career-best 17 homers (two of them in the NL playoffs). In '94, however, his power seemed to evaporate and he started striking out with alarming frequency. Although he hit more long balls last year, his average fell for the second straight season. He fanned about twice for every walk, took too many good pitches, and tarnished his prized reputation as a good hit-and-run man. Perhaps 1993 was a fluke career year. It's a mystery why Bobby Cox left Blauser in the No. 2 hole all year, but it is no mystery why he left him alone at short. Blauser has become a defensive standout with quick reactions, good hands, and an arm that's improved over the years.

Major League Batting Register
	BA	G	AB	R	H	2B	3B	HR	RBI	SB
87 NL	.242	51	165	11	40	6	3	2	15	7
88 NL	.239	18	67	7	16	3	1	2	7	0
89 NL	.270	142	456	63	123	24	2	12	46	5
90 NL	.269	115	386	46	104	24	3	8	39	3
91 NL	.259	129	352	49	91	14	3	11	54	5
92 NL	.262	123	343	61	90	19	3	14	46	5
93 NL	.305	161	597	110	182	29	2	15	73	16
94 NL	.258	96	380	56	98	21	4	6	45	1
95 NL	.211	115	431	60	91	16	2	12	31	8
Life	.263	950	3177	463	835	156	23	82	356	50
3 AVE	.261	142	539	85	141	26	3	12	57	9

CURRENT PLAYERS

MIKE BLOWERS

Position: Third base
Team: Los Angeles Dodgers
Born: April 24, 1965 Wurzburg, West Germany
Height: 6'2" **Weight:** 210 lbs.
Bats: right **Throws:** right
Acquired: Traded by Mariners for Miguel Cairo and Willie Otanez, 11/95

Player Summary	
Fantasy Value	$9 to $11
Card Value	5¢ to 8¢
Will	burn lefties
Can't	display speed
Expect	run production
Don't Expect	high on-base mark

When he's hot, he's hot. Blowers knocked in eight runs against Boston on May 24 and added a pair of five-RBI games earlier in the season. Run production has never been his problem. The rap against Blowers included impatience at the plate, and an inability to swing a strong stick against right-handed pitchers. The former University of Washington standout fanned about twice as often as he walked last season. He also hit for a much higher average against lefties. His eyes light up when he sees runners in scoring position. To get his bat into the lineup when a lefty pitcher appeared, the Mariners tried him at first base, DH, and the outfield corners. He's a decent fielder with a solid throwing arm, but he lacks speed and quickness. Most of his errors come on boots. Although he led two minor leagues in fielding percentage, Blowers made four errors in a game while with the Yankees in 1990.

Major League Batting Register

	BA	G	AB	R	H	2B	3B	HR	RBI	SB
89 AL	.263	13	38	2	10	0	0	0	3	0
90 AL	.188	48	144	16	27	4	0	5	21	1
91 AL	.200	15	35	3	7	0	0	1	1	0
92 AL	.192	31	73	7	14	3	0	1	2	0
93 AL	.280	127	379	55	106	23	3	15	57	1
94 AL	.289	85	270	37	78	13	0	9	49	2
95 AL	.257	134	439	59	113	24	1	23	96	2
Life	.258	453	1378	179	355	67	4	54	229	6
3 AVE	.274	132	418	58	114	23	1	18	78	2

JOE BOEVER

Position: Pitcher
Team: Detroit Tigers
Born: Oct. 4, 1960 St. Louis, MO
Height: 6'1" **Weight:** 200 lbs.
Bats: right **Throws:** right
Acquired: Signed as a free agent, 8/93

Player Summary	
Fantasy Value	$2 to $4
Card Value	4¢ to 6¢
Will	use palmballs
Can't	always locate plate
Expect	middle relief
Don't Expect	stranded runners

A rubber-armed right-hander who can work often, Boever has spent the last several seasons as a middle reliever. His stints sometimes last two or three innings. When he has control, he keeps batters off-balance by blending the palmball—his best pitch—with a fastball and a slider. The UNLV product makes the trick pitch move right or left, which should make him equally effective against righties or lefties. Over the last two years, however, right-handers have eaten him alive. As a result, about half the runners Boever inherited for much of last year were able to score. Although he relies on his deceptive motion to distract batters, it's also slow enough to delight baserunners. He yields far too many steals for a reliever assigned to keep games closer. The fact that he's a weak fielder doesn't help. He once led four minor leagues in saves.

Major League Pitching Register

	W	L	ERA	G	S	IP	H	ER	BB	SO
85 NL	0	0	4.41	13	0	16.1	17	8	4	20
86 NL	0	1	1.66	11	0	21.2	19	4	11	8
87 NL	1	0	7.36	14	0	18.1	29	15	12	18
88 NL	0	2	1.77	16	1	20.1	12	4	1	7
89 NL	4	11	3.94	66	21	82.1	78	36	34	68
90 NL	3	6	3.36	67	14	88.1	77	33	51	75
91 NL	3	5	3.84	68	0	98.1	90	42	54	89
92 NL	3	6	2.51	81	2	111.1	103	31	45	67
93 AL	6	3	3.61	61	3	102.1	101	41	44	63
94 AL	9	2	3.98	46	3	81.1	80	36	37	49
95 AL	5	7	6.39	60	3	98.2	128	70	44	71
Life	34	43	3.90	503	47	739.1	734	320	337	535
3 AVE	8	5	4.68	64	4	109.2	119	57	49	71

CURRENT PLAYERS

TIM BOGAR

Position: Infield
Team: New York Mets
Born: Oct. 28, 1966 Indianapolis, IN
Height: 6'2" **Weight:** 198 lbs.
Bats: right **Throws:** right
Acquired: Eighth-round pick in 6/87 free-agent draft

Player Summary
Fantasy Value	$0
Card Value	4¢ to 6¢
Will	play any position
Can't	produce power
Expect	hits vs. lefties
Don't Expect	patience

A valuable utility player who makes good contact, Bogar in 1995 did some of his best hitting with runners in scoring position. He was especially productive against left-handed pitching. Signed as a shortstop out of Eastern Illinois University, Bogar has played everything but the bass fiddle since turning pro. He even pulled a "Cesar Tovar"—appearing at all nine positions in a Triple-A game. Basically a singles hitter who sprays hits to all fields, Bogar will surprise once in awhile with a home run or an extra-base hit up the alley. Since he gets so few chances to bat, he doesn't like waiting for walks. But he almost always puts the ball in play. Bogar is most comfortable at second base or shortstop, but does not embarrass himself at the infield corners or the outfield; nor does he complain about sitting on the bench. He'd see more action if he had more speed; however, because Bogar doesn't run all that well, he rarely gets the call as a pinch runner. He began his pro career in 1987 at Little Falls of the New York-Penn League.

Major League Batting Register
	BA	G	AB	R	H	2B	3B	HR	RBI	SB
93 NL	.244	78	205	19	50	13	0	3	25	0
94 NL	.154	50	52	5	8	0	0	2	5	1
95 NL	.290	78	145	17	42	7	0	1	21	1
Life	.249	206	402	41	100	20	0	6	51	2

WADE BOGGS

Position: Third base
Team: New York Yankees
Born: June 15, 1958 Omaha, NE
Height: 6'2" **Weight:** 197 lbs.
Bats: left **Throws:** right
Acquired: Signed as a free agent, 12/92

Player Summary
Fantasy Value	$7 to $9
Card Value	15¢ to 25¢
Will	remain an All-Star
Can't	use speed
Expect	extreme patience
Don't Expect	great power

Boggs remains one of baseball's best hitters. He's won five batting crowns and made the All-Star team in each of the last 11 years, including nine straight as the starting third baseman. If he maintains his present pace, and injuries or labor strife don't interfere, Boggs could reach the 3,000-hit milestone in 1998. Although he doesn't have speed to pad his average with bunts or infield hits, the former Boston star boosts his on-base percentage by refusing to swing at bad pitches. Even 0-2 counts don't bother him. In the field, he compensates for his lack of quickness by knowing how to play the hitters. He has nifty reactions, good hands, and an accurate arm—a combination that helped him win his first Gold Glove in 1994. Boggs may eventually move to first base.

Major League Batting Register
	BA	G	AB	R	H	2B	3B	HR	RBI	SB
82 AL	.349	104	338	51	118	14	1	5	44	1
83 AL	.361	153	582	100	210	44	7	5	74	3
84 AL	.325	158	625	109	203	31	4	6	55	3
85 AL	.368	161	653	107	240	42	3	8	78	2
86 AL	.357	149	580	107	207	47	2	8	71	0
87 AL	.363	147	551	108	200	40	6	24	89	1
88 AL	.366	155	584	128	214	45	6	5	58	2
89 AL	.330	156	621	113	205	51	7	3	54	2
90 AL	.302	155	619	89	187	44	5	6	63	0
91 AL	.332	144	546	93	181	42	2	8	51	1
92 AL	.259	143	514	62	133	22	4	7	50	1
93 AL	.302	143	560	83	169	26	1	2	59	0
94 AL	.342	97	366	61	125	19	1	11	55	2
95 AL	.324	126	460	76	149	22	4	5	63	1
Life	.334	1991	7599	1287	2541	489	53	103	864	19
3 AVE	.322	140	531	85	171	26	2	8	69	1

CURRENT PLAYERS

BRIAN BOHANON

Position: Pitcher
Team: Detroit Tigers
Born: Aug. 1, 1968 Denton, TX
Height: 6'2" **Weight:** 220 lbs.
Bats: left **Throws:** left
Acquired: Signed as a free agent, 4/95

Player Summary	
Fantasy Value	$0
Card Value	4¢ to 6¢
Will	see action
Can't	stop runners
Expect	duty vs. lefties
Don't Expect	a closer role

Bohanon saw a lot of action last year, his first pitching for the Tigers. The lefty appeared in 52 games, and he notched 100-plus innings. His earned run average was subpar, but he was effective in stretches. There were times that he was the only left-hander in the Detroit bullpen, so then-manager Sparky Anderson had to utilize Bohanon early and often. Originally a first-round draft pick by the Rangers in 1987, Bohanon shuttled back and forth between Triple-A Oklahoma City and Arlington for several years. He was an effective starter at times in the minor leagues, but he never really to seem to find his niche in Texas. He is not a strikeout pitcher, having almost five and one-half strikeouts per nine innings last year. Bohanon, however, allowed too many bases on balls to be effective and didn't stop left-handed batters well enough—they batted .250 against him. He also allowed too many inherited runners to score. About half of the baserunners he inherited reached pay dirt.

Major League Pitching Register

	W	L	ERA	G	S	IP	H	ER	BB	SO
90 AL	0	3	6.62	11	0	34.0	40	25	18	15
91 AL	4	3	4.84	11	0	61.1	66	33	23	34
92 AL	1	1	6.31	18	0	45.2	57	32	25	29
93 AL	4	4	4.76	36	0	92.2	107	49	46	45
94 AL	2	2	7.23	11	0	37.1	51	30	8	26
95 AL	1	1	5.54	52	1	105.2	121	65	41	63
Life	12	14	5.59	139	1	376.2	442	234	161	212
2 AVE	3	3	5.20	47	1	105.2	122	61	46	58

BARRY BONDS

Position: Outfield
Team: San Francisco Giants
Born: July 24, 1964 Riverside, CA
Height: 6'1" **Weight:** 185 lbs.
Bats: left **Throws:** left
Acquired: Signed as a free agent, 12/92

Player Summary	
Fantasy Value	$45 to $50
Card Value	50¢ to $1
Will	bid for MVP
Can't	make great throws
Expect	high on-base mark
Don't Expect	low power

When a broken foot knocked Matt Williams out of the lineup for half a season, Bonds was the lone power hitter left in San Francisco. Though frustrated when opponents pitched around him, the three-time MVP proved up to the task. An extremely patient power hitter who garnered more walks than strikeouts last year, Bonds led the NL in on-base percentage for much of the season, keeping the mark above the .400 level. He also ranked among the league leaders in home runs and RBI. The NL's top vote-getter for the All-Star Game, Bonds was elected to start for the fourth straight season. When he stole second against Colorado on June 28, it gave Barry and father Bobby 783 career steals—one more than previous leaders Maury and Bump Wills. Bonds has exceptional range in the outfield; his only weakness—an arm that is less than powerful—doesn't concern Gold Glove voters.

Major League Batting Register

	BA	G	AB	R	H	2B	3B	HR	RBI	SB
86 NL	.223	113	413	72	92	26	3	16	48	36
87 NL	.261	150	551	99	144	34	9	25	59	32
88 NL	.283	144	538	97	152	30	5	24	58	17
89 NL	.248	159	580	96	144	34	6	19	58	32
90 NL	.301	151	519	104	156	32	3	33	114	52
91 NL	.292	153	510	95	149	28	5	25	116	43
92 NL	.311	140	473	109	147	36	5	34	103	39
93 NL	.336	159	539	129	181	38	4	46	123	29
94 NL	.312	112	391	89	122	18	1	37	81	29
95 NL	.294	144	506	109	149	30	7	33	104	31
Life	.286	1425	5020	999	1436	306	48	292	864	340
3 AVE	.314	160	553	126	173	32	4	45	118	35

CURRENT PLAYERS

RICKY BONES

Position: Pitcher
Team: Milwaukee Brewers
Born: April 7, 1969 Salinas, PR
Height: 6′ **Weight:** 190 lbs.
Bats: right **Throws:** right
Acquired: Traded by Padres with Jose Valentin and Matt Mieske for Gary Sheffield, 3/91

Player Summary
Fantasy Value	$7 to $9
Card Value	4¢ to 6¢
Will	keep ball down
Can't	avoid gophers
Expect	rotation spot
Don't Expect	many Ks

Because he's not a strikeout pitcher, Bones has to rely on location, deception, and defense to win games. When he keeps the ball down, he's usually successful. In fact, he made the 1994 American League All-Star team. The only veteran in the Milwaukee rotation last season, Bones was hoping to finish with double-digits in victories for the third year in a row. He mixes a rising fastball with a sinking forkball and a big curveball that is only effective when low in the strike zone. His hanging curves tend to disappear over distant fences. He yielded about one hit per inning and around three walks per game in 1995. He helps himself with his fielding, and holds runners much better than he once did. When he's on, he gets more than his share of ground outs. Since there always seem to be runners on base when he pitches, many of those grounders turn into double plays. Bones is the kind of pitcher managers appreciate because he works many innings and always takes his turn.

Major League Pitching Register
	W	L	ERA	G	CG	IP	H	ER	BB	SO
91 NL	4	6	4.83	11	0	54.0	57	29	18	31
92 AL	9	10	4.57	31	0	163.1	169	83	48	65
93 AL	11	11	4.86	32	3	203.2	222	110	63	63
94 AL	10	9	3.43	24	4	170.2	166	65	45	57
95 AL	10	12	4.63	32	3	200.1	218	103	83	77
Life	44	48	4.43	130	10	792.0	832	390	257	293
3 AVE	12	12	4.27	34	4	222.2	234	106	73	77

BOBBY BONILLA

Position: Outfield; third base
Team: Baltimore Orioles
Born: Feb. 23, 1963 New York, NY
Height: 6′3″ **Weight:** 230 lbs.
Bats: both **Throws:** right
Acquired: Traded by Mets with Jimmy Williams for Damon Buford and Alex Ochoa, 7/95

Player Summary
Fantasy Value	$30 to $35
Card Value	8¢ to 15¢
Will	rip fastballs
Can't	reduce K rate
Expect	power
Don't Expect	strong defense

After compiling a .278 average in nine previous seasons, Bonilla was headed for his third .300 season when he was traded across league lines. A fastball hitter with power from both sides of the plate, he is more productive as a left-handed batter. He had three and one-half solid seasons with the Mets, though he never showed the consistent stroke that he had in Pittsburgh just before jumping at New York's megabucks offer. For the Mets and the Orioles in 1995, he was able to cut his strikeout-to-walk ratio. Usually a patient hitter who draws many bases on balls, Bonilla still showed a tendency to whiff. His rocky relationship with the New York media caused consternation. Power keeps Bonilla in the lineup since his defense is mediocre at best. He doesn't run well but has a decent arm.

Major League Batting Register
	BA	G	AB	R	H	2B	3B	HR	RBI	SB
86 AL	.269	75	234	27	63	10	2	2	26	4
86 NL	.240	63	192	28	46	6	2	1	17	4
87 NL	.300	141	466	58	140	33	3	15	77	3
88 NL	.274	159	584	87	160	32	7	24	100	3
89 NL	.281	163	616	96	173	37	10	24	86	8
90 NL	.280	160	625	112	175	39	7	32	120	4
91 NL	.302	157	577	102	174	44	6	18	100	2
92 NL	.249	128	438	62	109	23	0	19	70	4
93 NL	.265	139	502	81	133	21	3	34	87	3
94 NL	.290	108	403	60	117	24	1	20	67	1
95 NL	.325	80	317	49	103	25	4	18	53	0
95 AL	.333	61	237	47	79	12	4	10	46	0
Life	.284	1434	5191	809	1472	306	49	217	849	36
3 AVE	.297	150	564	91	168	32	4	31	98	1

CURRENT PLAYERS

BRET BOONE

Position: Second base
Team: Cincinnati Reds
Born: April 6, 1969 El Cajon, CA
Height: 5'10" **Weight:** 180 lbs.
Bats: right **Throws:** right
Acquired: Traded by Mariners with Erik Hanson for Bobby Ayala and Dan Wilson, 11/93

Player Summary	
Fantasy Value	$13 to $16
Card Value	8¢ to 15¢
Will	generate power
Can't	shake glove rap
Expect	clutch work
Don't Expect	errors

Boone has erased the good-hit, no-field tag that accompanied him through the Seattle organization. In fact, his error last July 15 ended a string of 400 chances and 79 games without a boot. The former USC standout has mastered the art of positioning himself on Astroturf, even standing in short right field on occasion. Boone's range has also proven better than originally advertised. No matter how well he fields, however, he will be regarded as an offense-oriented player. On July 23, his second home run of the game—a three-run shot off Randy Myers in the 10th—beat the Cubs 7-5. Boone mustered enough power last year to garner a career high in homers. His father, Bob, now Kansas City manager, was instrumental in reducing Bret's once long swing. His new compact swing helped make him a better contact hitter without sacrificing power. Most of his power is to left field, and he can poke singles the other way. The first third-generation player in baseball history, Bret is the grandson of Ray Boone.

Major League Batting Register

	BA	G	AB	R	H	2B	3B	HR	RBI	SB
92 AL	.194	33	129	15	25	4	0	4	15	1
93 AL	.251	76	271	31	68	12	2	12	38	2
94 NL	.320	108	381	59	122	25	2	12	68	3
95 NL	.267	138	513	63	137	34	2	15	68	5
Life	.272	355	1294	168	352	75	6	43	189	11
3 AVE	.284	128	462	62	131	28	2	15	70	4

PEDRO BORBON

Position: Pitcher
Team: Atlanta Braves
Born: Nov. 15, 1967 Mao, Dominican Republic
Height: 6'1" **Weight:** 205 lbs.
Bats: left **Throws:** left
Acquired: Signed as a free agent, 8/89

Player Summary	
Fantasy Value	$1 to $3
Card Value	5¢ to 8¢
Will	stifle lefties
Can't	always throw strikes
Expect	stranded runners
Don't Expect	huge Ks

The July 31 trade of Mike Stanton left Borbon as the lone left-hander in the Atlanta bullpen. But manager Bobby Cox didn't hesitate to place full confidence in the rookie. Before yielding a hit on June 14, he had pitched 8⅓ hitless innings in more than 12 appearances. At that point in the season, the opponents' batting average against him was about .100. The son of a former right-handed reliever, Borbon is especially effective against left-handed hitters. He averaged nearly one strikeout per inning and about eight hits per game throughout much of the season. His control is usually good, though he needs work to keep sharp. Borbon's repertoire includes a fastball, a curveball, and a changeup. He stranded most of the runners he inherited and kept the ball in the park. He's a competent fielder but needs work on his pickoff move. He isn't well-acquainted with the batter's box. He began his pro ball career in 1988 with the White Sox organization, was out of pro ball in 1989, and restarted his career with the Atlanta system in 1990.

Major League Pitching Register

	W	L	ERA	G	S	IP	H	ER	BB	SO
92 NL	0	1	6.75	2	0	1.1	2	1	1	1
93 NL	0	0	21.60	3	0	1.2	3	4	3	2
95 NL	2	2	3.09	41	2	32.0	29	11	17	33
Life	2	3	4.11	46	2	35.0	34	16	21	36

CURRENT PLAYERS

PAT BORDERS

Position: Catcher
Team: Houston Astros
Born: May 14, 1963 Columbus, OH
Height: 6'2" **Weight:** 205 lbs.
Bats: right **Throws:** right
Acquired: Traded by Royals for Rick Huisman, 8/95

Player Summary
Fantasy Value	$1 to $3
Card Value	4¢ to 6¢
Will	make contact
Can't	display speed
Expect	streaks
Don't Expect	poor fielding

After six seasons as Toronto's regular receiver, Borders moved to Kansas City as the right-handed platoon partner of Brent Mayne. It was a good move for Borders, who hammered left-handed pitching and got extra bases on more than one-third of his hits. He then moved to Houston to back up Tony Eusebio. A streak hitter who craves first-pitch fastballs, Borders has twice topped one dozen homers in a season. In one of those years, 1992, he got so hot during the World Series that he won MVP honors with a 9-for-20 performance (.450) that included a home run and three RBI. Though he lacks patience at the plate, he generally makes contact—especially on mistake pitches. He's a good receiver who calls a good game, handles his staff well, prevents wild pitches, and blocks the plate. While he was with KC, he had nailed about 40 percent of the runners who tried to steal against him.

Major League Batting Register
	BA	G	AB	R	H	2B	3B	HR	RBI	SB
88 AL	.273	56	154	15	42	6	3	5	21	0
89 AL	.257	94	241	22	62	11	1	3	29	2
90 AL	.286	125	346	36	99	24	2	15	49	0
91 AL	.244	105	291	22	71	17	0	5	36	0
92 AL	.242	138	480	47	116	26	2	13	53	1
93 AL	.254	138	488	38	124	30	0	9	55	2
94 AL	.247	85	295	24	73	13	1	3	26	1
95 AL	.231	52	143	14	33	8	1	4	13	0
95 NL	.114	11	35	1	4	0	0	0	0	0
Life	.252	804	2473	219	624	135	10	57	282	6
3 AVE	.243	110	368	30	89	19	1	6	35	1

MIKE BORDICK

Position: Shortstop
Team: Oakland Athletics
Born: July 21, 1965 Marquette, MI
Height: 5'11" **Weight:** 175 lbs.
Bats: right **Throws:** right
Acquired: Signed as a free agent, 7/86

Player Summary
Fantasy Value	$5 to $7
Card Value	4¢ to 6¢
Will	make contact
Can't	hit long ball
Expect	top defense
Don't Expect	media glare

While other players crave the media spotlight, Bordick just goes about his business in a quiet, efficient way. One of baseball's steadiest defensive shortstops, he is no automatic out at the plate. Bordick is a contact hitter who uses all fields, and is a tough man to strike out. In 1993—the last season uninterrupted by labor pains—he actually walked more often than he struck out. Bordick is more likely to steal a base than hit a home run, but doesn't do much of either. His claim to fame is his glove. He led two minor leagues in fielding percentage, and was doing the same in the AL at last year's All-Star break. To make sure his positioning is perfect, he studies the tendencies of rival hitters as well as his own pitchers. He has quick reactions, sure hands, good range, and a strong arm. His throws are accurate even from deep in the hole. Bordick can also turn the double play from either side of the bag; he played second when Walt Weiss was with Oakland prior to 1993.

Major League Batting Register
	BA	G	AB	R	H	2B	3B	HR	RBI	SB
90 AL	.071	25	14	0	1	0	0	0	0	0
91 AL	.238	90	235	21	56	5	1	0	21	3
92 AL	.300	154	504	62	151	19	4	3	48	12
93 AL	.249	159	546	60	136	21	2	3	48	10
94 AL	.253	114	391	38	99	18	4	2	37	7
95 AL	.264	126	428	46	113	13	0	8	44	11
Life	.263	668	2118	227	556	76	11	16	198	43
3 AVE	.255	154	526	55	134	20	3	5	50	11

CURRENT PLAYERS

TOBY BORLAND

Position: Pitcher
Team: Philadelphia Phillies
Born: May 29, 1969 Quitman, LA
Height: 6'6" **Weight:** 190 lbs.
Bats: right **Throws:** right
Acquired: 27th-round selection in 6/87 free-agent draft

Player Summary	
Fantasy Value	$3 to $5
Card Value	12¢ to 20¢
Will	retain relief role
Can't	freeze lefty bats
Expect	ground outs
Don't Expect	gopher woes

After spending parts of the previous three seasons at the Triple-A level, Borland became a valuable member of the Philadelphia bullpen in 1995. Deployed primarily as a set-up man and middle reliever, he improved his performance in direct proportion to the work he received. Borland finished July by stringing together 14⅔ innings without allowing an earned run. A sinker-slider pitcher who also throws a forkball, Borland is most effective when he keeps the ball down in the strike zone. He gets most of his outs by strikeout or ground ball. A quick worker, he yielded one hit per inning and about six whiffs per nine innings; however, he has periodic bouts of wildness. Through much of last year, he had problems with inherited runners. Thus far in his young career, he has been much more effective against right-handed batters. If he shows better results against southpaws, his big-league workload could approach the level of his 1993 duty log in the minors (70 appearances). Borland helps himself with his fielding.

Major League Pitching Register

	W	L	ERA	G	S	IP	H	ER	BB	SO
94 NL	1	0	2.36	24	1	34.1	31	9	14	26
95 NL	1	3	3.77	50	6	74.0	81	31	37	59
Life	2	3	3.32	74	7	108.1	112	40	51	85
2 AVE	1	2	3.25	45	4	66.1	67	24	31	52

CHRIS BOSIO

Position: Pitcher
Team: Seattle Mariners
Born: April 3, 1963 Carmichael, CA
Height: 6'3" **Weight:** 225 lbs.
Bats: right **Throws:** right
Acquired: Signed as a free agent, 12/92

Player Summary	
Fantasy Value	$6 to $8
Card Value	4¢ to 6¢
Will	try to stay healthy
Can't	win without control
Expect	variety of pitches
Don't Expect	lots of Ks

If Bosio could find consistency, he'd be a star. He won his first five decisions of 1995 and worked at least five innings in each of his first eight starts, yielding no more than three runs in any appearance through June 12. Then the slump came. He went winless for a month before beating Cleveland on July 29. The victim of six knee operations, Bosio is solid starter when healthy. He pitched a no-hitter against Boston in his first month with Seattle. He doesn't seem like the no-hit type, since he's not overpowering, but Bosio succeeds by keeping batters guessing. His fastball isn't much, but it looks better when blended with his forkball, slider, and curve—all of which he uses as changeups. He is a master of changing location and velocity, but struggles when he doesn't have control. He's also had some problems with temper tantrums. Bosio helps his own cause with first-rate fielding and a good pickoff move.

Major League Pitching Register

	W	L	ERA	G	CG	IP	H	ER	BB	SO
86 AL	0	4	7.01	10	0	34.2	41	27	13	29
87 AL	11	8	5.24	46	2	170.0	187	99	50	150
88 AL	7	15	3.36	38	9	182.0	190	68	38	84
89 AL	15	10	2.95	33	8	234.2	225	77	48	173
90 AL	4	9	4.00	20	4	132.2	131	59	38	76
91 AL	14	10	3.25	32	5	204.2	187	74	58	117
92 AL	16	6	3.62	33	4	231.1	223	93	44	120
93 AL	9	9	3.45	29	3	164.1	138	63	59	119
94 AL	4	10	4.32	19	4	125.0	137	60	40	67
95 AL	10	8	4.92	31	0	170.0	211	93	69	85
Life	90	89	3.89	291	39	1649.1	1670	713	457	1020
3 AVE	9	11	4.27	30	3	177.0	189	84	64	103

CURRENT PLAYERS

SHAWN BOSKIE

Position: Pitcher
Team: California Angels
Born: March 28, 1967 Hawthorne, NV
Height: 6'3" **Weight:** 205 lbs.
Bats: right **Throws:** right
Acquired: Signed as a free agent, 4/95

Player Summary	
Fantasy Value	$2 to $4
Card Value	4¢ to 6¢
Will	bid for rotation
Can't	keep off DL
Expect	five pitches
Don't Expect	great fastball

When Boskie won his first five decisions for the Angels last year, he seemed a good bet to finish with double-digits in victories for the first time in his six-year career. But a sprained right elbow sent him to the disabled list in July. His 5-0 start was the first by an Angel since Terry Clark in 1988. But Boskie's injury should not have been a surprise, because he has been on the DL four times in his short career. Because he has good control of five pitches, Boskie should be able to win more consistently. He throws sinking and cut fastballs plus a forkball, a curve, and a changeup. He often does his best pitching with runners in scoring position. He yielded about one hit per inning and less than three walks per game last year before the injury. Boskie is reasonably efficient against left-handed batters. The one-time infielder retains his old defensive skills, helping himself enormously on the mound. He's also good at holding runners.

Major League Pitching Register

	W	L	ERA	G	CG	IP	H	ER	BB	SO
90 NL	5	6	3.69	15	1	97.2	99	40	31	49
91 NL	4	9	5.23	28	0	129.0	150	75	52	62
92 NL	5	11	5.01	23	0	91.2	96	51	36	39
93 NL	5	3	3.43	39	0	65.2	63	25	21	39
94 NL	4	6	5.01	20	1	88.0	88	49	29	61
94 AL	0	1	6.75	2	0	2.2	4	2	1	0
95 AL	7	7	5.64	20	1	111.2	127	70	25	51
Life	30	43	4.79	147	3	586.1	627	312	195	301
3 AVE	6	7	4.95	31	1	106.1	112	59	30	61

RICKY BOTTALICO

Position: Pitcher
Team: Philadelphia Phillies
Born: Aug. 26, 1969 New Britain, CT
Height: 6'1" **Weight:** 209 lbs.
Bats: left **Throws:** right
Acquired: Signed as a nondrafted free agent, 7/91

Player Summary	
Fantasy Value	$7 to $9
Card Value	12¢ to 15¢
Will	blow righties away
Can't	always find plate
Expect	future as closer
Don't Expect	many gophers

During his days at Central Connecticut State, Bottalico did more catching than pitching. He was on the mound mostly in various summer leagues, though he pitched a one-hitter against Northeastern. That game boosted his confidence and led to his full-time conversion. Strictly a pitcher in the minors, he switched to the bullpen as a second-year pro and never looked back. After saving 49 games over his first two seasons, he broke into the big leagues as a set-up man. The velocity was always there, but he needed a quality off-speed pitch. He tried a slurve and a slider before Phillies pitching coach Johnny Podres convinced Bottalico to throw a big curve. The results were spectacular: Before Charlie O'Brien's Aug. 1 single, Bottalico had retired 24 consecutive batters. Through much of the season, right-handed batters were not able to compile a .200 batting average against him. But he occasionally struggled with his control. When that happened, the ball went a long way. With more experience, Bottalico should realize his potential as a closer.

Major League Pitching Register

	W	L	ERA	G	S	IP	H	ER	BB	SO
94 NL	0	0	0.00	3	0	3.0	3	0	1	3
95 NL	5	3	2.46	62	1	87.2	50	24	42	87
Life	5	3	2.38	65	1	90.2	53	24	43	90

CURRENT PLAYERS

RYAN BOWEN

Position: Pitcher
Team: Florida Marlins
Born: Feb. 10, 1968 Hanford, CA
Height: 6' **Weight:** 185 lbs.
Bats: right **Throws:** right
Acquired: Third-round pick from Astros in 11/92 expansion draft

Player Summary	
Fantasy Value	$0
Card Value	4¢ to 6¢
Will	show velocity
Can't	control pitches
Expect	do or die
Don't Expect	injury-free year

Bowen has reached a career crossroads. Suddenly more of a suspect than a prospect, he's had more injuries than victories over the past two years. When he does pitch, his control is so erratic that his performance is unpredictable. Idled last year after surgery to repair a ruptured knee tendon, Bowen has also had shoulder problems and a strained side muscle since winning eight games during Florida's fledgling season in 1993. One of those wins was his only big-league shutout. He has proven over the years that he can hit and run, but the jury is out as to whether he can pitch. He hasn't progressed much further than his third minor-league season, when he walked 116 batters in 139⅔ innings. But scouts drool over his live arm and outstanding stuff. Bowen's mid-90s fastball has velocity and movement and is practically unhittable when it follows his slider or curve. But batters with patience could work their way on base with walks. Bowen also had problems with fielding—thanks in part to his awkward follow-through.

Major League Pitching Register

	W	L	ERA	G	CG	IP	H	ER	BB	SO
91 NL	6	4	5.15	14	0	71.2	73	41	36	49
92 NL	0	7	10.96	11	0	33.2	48	41	30	22
93 NL	8	12	4.42	27	2	156.2	156	77	87	98
94 NL	1	5	4.94	8	1	47.1	50	26	19	32
95 NL	2	0	3.78	4	0	16.2	23	7	12	15
Life	17	28	5.30	64	3	326.0	350	192	184	216

DARREN BRAGG

Position: Outfield
Team: Seattle Mariners
Born: Sept. 7, 1969 Waterbury, CT
Height: 5'9" **Weight:** 180 lbs.
Bats: left **Throws:** right
Acquired: 22nd-round pick in 6/91 free-agent draft

Player Summary	
Fantasy Value	$2 to $4
Card Value	6¢ to 10¢
Will	reach base
Can't	swing steady bat
Expect	occasional power
Don't Expect	return to minors

A little leadoff type with surprising pop, Bragg had hoped to fill Seattle's 1995 vacancy in left field. He stumbled along the way, but did manage to hit a July 4 homer off Tiger Stadium's second-deck facade in right field. Once he gets off the minor-league shuttle, he has the ability to become a productive player. Blessed with a discriminating batting eye, he netted 105 walks—tops in the Class-A Carolina League—in his second season as a pro. Once on base, he's always a threat to run: his three 20-steal seasons in the minors included a 44-steal effort. The former Georgia Tech standout simply has to show some consistency with his bat. Bragg belted 17 homers to accompany a .350 average at Triple-A Calgary in 1994, but he had difficulty making the adjustment to big-league pitching. He's always worked hard to improve his game, however, and should be able to do whatever is necessary to stick with the varsity. The owner of a strong arm, Bragg led Triple-A Pacific Coast League outfielders in chances and double plays two years ago. He throws so well that he was once used as a mop-up pitcher.

Major League Batting Register

	BA	G	AB	R	H	2B	3B	HR	RBI	SB
94 AL	.158	8	19	4	3	1	0	0	2	0
95 AL	.234	52	145	20	34	5	1	3	12	9
Life	.226	60	164	24	37	6	1	3	14	9

CURRENT PLAYERS

JEFF BRANSON

Position: Infield
Team: Cincinnati Reds
Born: Jan. 26, 1967 Waynesboro, MS
Height: 6′ **Weight:** 180 lbs.
Bats: left **Throws:** right
Acquired: Second-round pick in 6/88 free-agent draft

Player Summary	
Fantasy Value	$2 to $4
Card Value	4¢ to 6¢
Will	hit in clutch
Can't	handle lefties
Expect	surprise power
Don't Expect	patience at bat

When Willie Greene failed to claim the Cincinnati third-base job last spring, the Reds replaced him with the left-right platoon of Branson and Mark Lewis. Branson had no trouble with the assignment: During his previous three years in the majors, he'd already played every infield position. He has always had a productive bat, though he struck out almost twice as much as he walked last year. A good clutch performer, he thrives with runners in scoring position and delivers surprising power. About one-third of his hits yielded extra bases last year. An aggressive hitter known to lunge for pitches outside the strike zone, he hits to all fields. But most of his power is to left field—especially against right-handed pitchers. In the field, he's best at second base, but he is almost as comfortable at third. He's not as fast in the wake of 1992 knee surgery, but he's no liability either. Though signed as a shortstop, the former Olympian no longer has the range to play there for extended periods.

Major League Batting Register

	BA	G	AB	R	H	2B	3B	HR	RBI	SB
92 NL	.296	72	115	12	34	7	1	0	15	0
93 NL	.241	125	381	40	92	15	1	3	22	4
94 NL	.284	58	109	18	31	4	1	6	16	0
95 NL	.260	122	331	43	86	18	2	12	45	2
Life	.260	377	936	113	243	44	5	21	98	6
2 AVE	.251	131	377	44	94	18	2	8	36	3

JEFF BRANTLEY

Position: Pitcher
Team: Cincinnati Reds
Born: Sept. 5, 1963 Florence, AL
Height: 5′11″ **Weight:** 180 lbs.
Bats: right **Throws:** right
Acquired: Signed as a free agent, 1/94

Player Summary	
Fantasy Value	$17 to $20
Card Value	5¢ to 8¢
Will	throw heat
Can't	prevent long ball
Expect	few hits
Don't Expect	runners to go

One of the most durable and successful closers in the majors, Brantley has worked at least 50 times for seven straight seasons. He keeps batters guessing whether he will throw his rising fastball, forkball, slider, or curve. For much of the season last year, he averaged one strikeout per inning and about three walks per game. Because he's always around the plate, he gives up an alarming share of gopher balls—his most glaring weakness. But his 3-1 ratio of strikeouts to walks means those homers often come with the bases empty. An intense competitor who throws hard, Brantley is especially brutal on first batters and right-handed hitters. But opponents on both sides of the plate batted only about .200 against him throughout much of the season. He fields his position well and keeps close watch on the running game. Even though he's a right-handed pitcher, few runners challenge him. He was an NL All-Star with the Giants in 1990.

Major League Pitching Register

	W	L	ERA	G	S	IP	H	ER	BB	SO
88 NL	0	1	5.66	9	1	20.2	22	13	6	11
89 NL	7	1	4.07	59	0	97.1	101	44	37	69
90 NL	5	3	1.56	55	19	86.2	77	15	33	61
91 NL	5	2	2.45	67	15	95.1	78	26	52	81
92 NL	7	7	2.95	56	7	91.2	67	30	45	86
93 NL	5	6	4.28	53	0	113.2	112	54	46	76
94 NL	6	6	2.48	50	15	65.1	46	18	28	63
95 NL	3	2	2.82	56	28	70.1	53	22	20	62
Life	38	28	3.12	405	85	641.0	556	222	267	509
3 AVE	6	6	3.29	62	18	94.2	79	35	36	78

CURRENT PLAYERS

DOUG BROCAIL

Position: Pitcher
Team: Houston Astros
Born: May 16, 1967 Clearfield, PA
Height: 6'5" **Weight:** 230 lbs.
Bats: left **Throws:** right
Acquired: Traded by Padres with Phil Plantier, Derek Bell, Pedro Martinez, Craig Shipley, and Ricky Gutierrez for Ken Caminiti, Steve Finley, Andujar Cedeno, Roberto Petagine, Brian Williams, and a player to be named later, 12/94

Player Summary	
Fantasy Value	$1 to $3
Card Value	5¢ to 8¢
Will	bear down
Can't	keep rotation berth
Expect	bunting skills
Don't Expect	economy-sized ERA

Although he's completed 10 years in pro ball, Brocail has yet to find his niche. Tried as both a starter and reliever, he has had mixed results. He began last year in the Houston bullpen but saw some starting service during the second half. A sinkerballer with fine control, he also throws a curveball, a slider, and a changeup. Because he yielded more hits than innings pitched for much of the 1995 season, his salvation was an ability to pitch well with runners in scoring position. He helps his own cause with his hitting and fielding. One of baseball's best bunters, he can always be counted on to move runners along. He's improved his once-awful ability to keep baserunners from stealing. A product of Lamar (Colorado) Community College, he was a first-round draft choice by San Diego in the 1986 draft. It's high time for Brocail to justify his status as a former first-rounder.

Major League Pitching Register

	W	L	ERA	G	S	IP	H	ER	BB	SO
92 NL	0	0	6.43	3	0	14.0	17	10	5	15
93 NL	4	13	4.56	24	0	128.1	143	65	42	70
94 NL	0	0	5.82	12	0	17.0	21	11	5	11
95 NL	6	4	4.19	36	1	77.1	87	36	22	39
Life	10	17	4.64	75	1	236.2	268	122	74	135
2 AVE	5	9	4.41	32	1	107.1	120	53	33	57

RICO BROGNA

Position: First base
Team: New York Mets
Born: April 18, 1970 Turner Falls, MA
Height: 6'2" **Weight:** 200 lbs.
Bats: left **Throws:** left
Acquired: Traded by Tigers for Alan Zinter, 4/94

Player Summary	
Fantasy Value	$15 to $18
Card Value	6¢ to 10¢
Will	kill righties
Can't	slash K rate
Expect	solid defense
Don't Expect	curve knocks

One year after he was a surprise star for a six-week stretch, Brogna reverted to mere mortal levels during the 1995 season. He still managed to hit about .300 against right-handed pitchers but struggled against most southpaws for much of the season. A young slugger who feasts on fastballs, he needs to learn patience at the plate. He had a strikeout-to-walk ratio of about 3-to-1 during much of the season. If he can master the art of hitting the curveball, that would help greatly. The top draft pick of the Tigers in 1988, he couldn't budge Cecil Fielder. Brogna began showing his potential only after the Mets moved him up from Triple-A Norfolk six weeks before the 1994 strike. During that time, he unveiled a 15-game hitting streak. Then last year, the Mets traded David Segui and handed the first-sack job to Brogna. He provides solid defense at first base. Though he doesn't run well, he knows how to stretch, scoop bad throws, and execute the tough 3-6-3 double play. Brogna once led the Double-A Eastern League in chances, putouts, assists, and double plays.

Major League Batting Register

	BA	G	AB	R	H	2B	3B	HR	RBI	SB
92 AL	.192	9	26	3	5	1	0	1	3	0
94 NL	.351	39	131	16	46	11	2	7	20	1
95 NL	.289	134	495	72	143	27	2	22	76	0
Life	.298	182	652	91	194	39	4	30	99	1

SCOTT BROSIUS

Position: Infield; outfield
Team: Oakland Athletics
Born: Aug. 15, 1966 Hillsboro, OR
Height: 6'1" **Weight:** 185 lbs.
Bats: right **Throws:** right
Acquired: 20th-round pick in 6/87 free-agent draft

Player Summary
Fantasy Value.................$6 to $8
Card Value ....4¢ to 6¢
Will ....fill many holes
Can't....................stop strikeouts
Expect ....extra-base hits
Don't Expect ....patience at bat

Talk about versatility: Brosius played everywhere but catcher and pitcher for Oakland last season. Most of his work came at third base, where the former middle infielder showed good range and fine hands. Most of his errors came on botched throws. Although about one-third of his hits netted extra bases last year, he does not hit with the ideal power associated with the hot corner. He did, however, bang two solo homers and one RBI single in a 5-2 win over Minnesota on June 20. If he practiced more patience at the plate, he'd become a more effective offensive weapon. Last year he fanned nearly twice for every walk. A pull hitter who loves a fastball diet, Brosius also needs to reduce the size of his swing and improve his production against left-handed pitchers. He's a good clutch hitter, however, and is also adept at moving runners up with a well-placed bunt. With the possible exceptions of Tony Phillips and Randy Velarde, few big-leaguers can match Brosius as jacks-of-all-trades.

Major League Batting Register

	BA	G	AB	R	H	2B	3B	HR	RBI	SB
91 AL	.235	36	68	9	16	5	0	2	4	3
92 AL	.218	38	87	13	19	2	0	4	13	3
93 AL	.249	70	213	26	53	10	1	6	25	6
94 AL	.238	96	324	31	77	14	1	14	49	2
95 AL	.263	123	388	69	102	19	2	17	46	4
Life	.247	363	1080	148	267	50	4	43	137	18
3 AVE	.250	115	369	49	92	17	2	15	49	4

KEVIN BROWN

Position: Pitcher
Team: Florida Marlins
Born: March 14, 1965 McIntyre, GA
Height: 6'4" **Weight:** 188 lbs.
Bats: right **Throws:** right
Acquired: Signed as a free agent, 12/95

Player Summary
Fantasy Value...............$12 to $15
Card Value ....5¢ to 8¢
Will ....coax grounders
Can't................win without support
Expect......................top control
Don't Expect.........smooth first frame

Since winning 21 games and starting the All-Star Game in 1992, Brown has watched his career do what his favorite pitch won't: sink. Last year, part of his problem was a dislocated first joint in his right index finger. In fairness to Brown, he didn't pitch all that poorly last year. His ERA for much of the season was analogous to his career ERA. A control artist, he throws a fastball, a slider, a curve, and a changeup in addition to his patented sinker. For much of the year, he averaged about two walks per game, yielded less hits than innings, kept the ball in the park, and maintained a fine strikeout-to-walk ratio. But he received about four runs of support per game last summer. The former Georgia Tech All-American helps his own cause with fine fielding and a polished pickoff move. If he can steer clear of injury and avoid first-inning troubles, he should return to peak form.

Major League Pitching Register

	W	L	ERA	G	CG	IP	H	ER	BB	SO
86 AL	1	0	3.60	1	0	5.0	6	2	0	4
88 AL	1	1	4.24	4	1	23.1	33	11	8	12
89 AL	12	9	3.35	28	7	191.0	167	71	70	104
90 AL	12	10	3.60	26	6	180.0	175	72	60	88
91 AL	9	12	4.40	33	0	210.2	233	103	90	96
92 AL	21	11	3.32	35	11	265.2	262	98	76	173
93 AL	15	12	3.59	34	12	233.0	228	93	74	142
94 AL	7	9	4.82	26	3	170.0	218	91	50	123
95 AL	10	9	3.60	26	3	172.1	155	69	48	117
Life	88	73	3.78	213	43	1451.0	1477	610	476	859
3 AVE	12	12	4.04	33	7	222.0	236	100	66	149

CURRENT PLAYERS

JERRY BROWNE

Position: Outfield; second base; third base
Team: Florida Marlins
Born: Feb. 13, 1966 Christiansted, St. Croix, Virgin Islands
Height: 5'10" **Weight:** 170 lbs.
Bats: both **Throws:** right
Acquired: Signed as a free agent, 1/94

Player Summary
Fantasy Value	$0
Card Value	4¢ to 6¢
Will	man five positions
Can't	show former speed
Expect	patience
Don't Expect	run production

Though he still answers to the nickname "Governor," baseball's Jerry Browne has had more notice recently than his California namesake. A switch-hitting contact hitter with extreme patience at the plate, Browne often compiles an on-base percentage 100 points higher than his batting average. Because he rarely swings at the first pitch, he gets a good look at opposing pitchers. He had more walks than strikeouts, made contact on more than half of his swings, and hit well with runners in scoring position for much of last year. Though he struggled against lefties, he previously had equal success from both sides of the plate. Displaced in Florida as leadoff man, Browne became a competent No. 2 batter. He's also competent in the field, where he plays five positions. Signed as a second baseman, he led several minor leagues in chances, putouts, assists, and fielding.

Major League Batting Register
	BA	G	AB	R	H	2B	3B	HR	RBI	SB
86 AL	.417	12	24	6	10	2	0	0	3	0
87 AL	.271	132	454	63	123	16	6	1	38	27
88 AL	.229	73	214	26	49	9	2	1	17	7
89 AL	.299	153	598	83	179	31	4	5	45	14
90 AL	.267	140	513	92	137	26	5	6	50	12
91 AL	.228	107	290	28	66	5	2	1	29	2
92 AL	.287	111	324	43	93	12	2	3	40	3
93 AL	.250	76	260	27	65	13	0	2	19	4
94 NL	.295	101	329	42	97	17	4	3	30	3
95 NL	.255	77	184	21	47	4	0	1	17	1
Life	.271	982	3190	431	866	135	25	23	288	73
3 AVE	.274	102	310	37	85	14	2	2	27	3

TOM BROWNING

Position: Pitcher
Team: Kansas City Royals
Born: April 28, 1960 Casper, WY
Height: 6'1" **Weight:** 190 lbs.
Bats: left **Throws:** left
Acquired: Signed as a free agent, 4/95

Player Summary
Fantasy Value	$0
Card Value	4¢ to 6¢
Will	seek big comeback
Can't	escape injury hex
Expect	excellent control
Don't Expect	defensive trouble

After spending 11 seasons with the Reds, Browning was looking forward to his first encounter with AL hitters. But a sore shoulder intervened, keeping him on the Kansas City DL most of last summer. At his age, he'll have to prove healthy again if he wants to hang onto a varsity job. When he's right, Browning can be a big winner. He won 20 as a rookie in 1985 and later topped one dozen wins in five other seasons. A control pitcher with a fastball, a curve, and a changeup, Browning is known for his ability to change speeds and throw each pitch exactly where he wants it. Though not a hard thrower, he has averaged three strikeouts per walk. He even threw a 1988 perfect game against Los Angeles. Browning helps himself with his fielding and pickoff move but has problems with the gopher ball. He also has a hard time staying off the disabled list.

Major League Pitching Register
	W	L	ERA	G	CG	IP	H	ER	BB	SO
84 NL	1	0	1.54	3	0	23.1	27	4	5	14
85 NL	20	9	3.55	38	6	261.1	242	103	73	155
86 NL	14	13	3.81	39	4	243.1	225	103	70	147
87 NL	10	13	5.02	32	2	183.0	201	102	61	117
88 NL	18	5	3.41	36	5	250.2	205	95	64	124
89 NL	15	12	3.39	37	9	249.2	241	94	64	118
90 NL	15	9	3.80	35	2	227.2	235	96	52	99
91 NL	14	14	4.18	36	1	230.1	241	107	56	115
92 NL	6	5	5.07	16	0	87.0	108	49	28	33
93 NL	7	7	4.74	21	0	114.0	159	60	20	53
94 NL	3	1	4.20	7	2	40.2	34	19	13	22
95 AL	0	2	8.10	2	0	10.0	13	9	5	3
Life	123	90	3.94	302	31	1921.0	1931	841	511	1000

CURRENT PLAYERS

JACOB BRUMFIELD

Position: Outfield
Team: Pittsburgh Pirates
Born: May 27, 1965 Bogalusa, LA
Height: 6′ **Weight:** 180 lbs.
Bats: right **Throws:** right
Acquired: Traded by Reds for Danny Clyburn, 10/94

Player Summary	
Fantasy Value	$8 to $10
Card Value	5¢ to 8¢
Will	devour left-handers
Can't	produce power
Expect	fine fielding
Don't Expect	full-time play

Before the Pirates gave him a chance to play every day, Brumfield had seemed destined to spend his entire career as a supporting player. His own versatility works against him, since he's a potent pinch hitter and pinch runner as well as a capable defensive performer at all three outfield spots. He murders left-handers, hitting about 60 points higher against them than he did against righties for much of the season last year. He also tends to get anxious at the plate, sometimes lunging at pitches outside the strike zone. For a leadoff-type hitter, he fanned a little too much. He has a little pop, but is far more likely to hit a double than a home run. While he is no Andy Van Slyke in center field, Brumfield holds his own with good speed and a strong arm. He spent most of 1995 sharing center with Al Martin and Midre Cummings. Originally signed by the Cubs, Brumfield spent time in the Kansas City system before reaching the majors with the 1992 Reds. He can play second or third in a pinch.

Major League Batting Register

	BA	G	AB	R	H	2B	3B	HR	RBI	SB
92 NL	.133	24	30	6	4	0	0	0	2	6
93 NL	.268	103	272	40	73	17	3	6	23	20
94 NL	.311	68	122	36	38	10	2	4	11	6
95 NL	.271	116	402	64	109	23	2	4	26	22
Life	.271	311	826	146	224	50	7	14	62	54
2 AVE	.270	117	362	56	98	21	3	5	26	22

DAMON BUFORD

Position: Outfield
Team: New York Mets
Born: June 12, 1970 Baltimore, MD
Height: 5′10 **Weight:** 170 lbs.
Bats: right **Throws:** right
Acquired: Traded by Orioles with Alex Ochoa for Bobby Bonilla and Jimmy Williams, 7/95

Player Summary	
Fantasy Value	$3 to $5
Card Value	6¢ to 10¢
Will	display great speed
Can't	always make contact
Expect	a leadoff type
Don't Expect	big power

The Buford name is familiar to Mets fans: father Don's leadoff homer against Tom Seaver in the 1969 World Series opener led to Baltimore's only win. While Damon doesn't have his dad's power, he could turn out to be a similar player. Blessed with great speed, he twice topped 40 steals in the minors. He has a line-drive bat that sprays hits to all fields. Although he hit 16 homers in 111 Triple-A games in 1994, Buford had never reached double-digits in power production previously. He'd be a fine leadoff man if he showed more patience at the plate and concentrated on making contact. Even ground balls would help, since he could fatten his average with infield hits. The former USC standout, who tried switch-hitting as a collegian, reverted to his natural right-handed style. He hopes to follow in the footsteps of Rickey Henderson, another right-handed leadoff hitter. Buford's speed helps in the outfield, where he led two leagues in assists and chances. Because his arm isn't great, his best position is left field.

Major League Batting Register

	BA	G	AB	R	H	2B	3B	HR	RBI	SB
93 AL	.228	53	79	18	18	5	0	2	9	2
94 AL	.500	4	2	2	1	0	0	0	0	0
95 AL	.063	24	32	6	2	0	0	0	2	3
95 NL	.235	44	136	24	32	5	0	4	12	7
Life	.213	125	249	50	53	10	0	6	23	12

CURRENT PLAYERS

JAY BUHNER

Position: Outfield
Team: Seattle Mariners
Born: Aug. 13, 1964 Louisville, KY
Height: 6'3" **Weight:** 205 lbs.
Bats: right **Throws:** right
Acquired: Traded by Yankees with Rick Balabon and Troy Evers for Ken Phelps, 7/88

Player Summary	
Fantasy Value	$25 to $30
Card Value	8¢ to 15¢
Will	generate power
Can't	cut strikeouts
Expect	improvement vs. lefties
Don't Expect	runners to test him

Whenever anyone mentions Seattle's outfield, the first name that comes to mind is Ken Griffey Jr. But AL managers know that Buhner should not be overlooked. He's hit more than 20 home runs five years in a row and doesn't hesitate to employ a powerful throwing arm that few runners challenge. Usually a devastating hitter against left-handed pitching, he struggled last season. He also had hamstring problems that cost him playing time. As a result, he reverted to some bad habits at the plate—mainly a propensity to strike out about twice as often as he walked. In 1994, he walked more often than he struck out for the first time in his career. That helped him post a .439 on-base percentage against lefties, ranking him in the league's top 10. If Buhner finds that patience, he could become an All-Star for the first time. However, he won't make it for his speed, because he doesn't run well.

Major League Batting Register

	BA	G	AB	R	H	2B	3B	HR	RBI	SB
87 AL	.227	7	22	0	5	2	0	0	1	0
88 AL	.215	85	261	36	56	13	1	13	38	1
89 AL	.275	58	204	27	56	15	1	9	33	1
90 AL	.276	51	163	16	45	12	0	7	33	2
91 AL	.244	137	406	64	99	14	4	27	77	0
92 AL	.243	152	543	69	132	16	3	25	79	0
93 AL	.272	158	563	91	153	28	3	27	98	2
94 AL	.279	101	358	74	100	23	4	21	68	0
95 AL	.262	126	470	86	123	23	0	40	121	0
Life	.257	875	2990	463	769	146	16	169	548	6
3 AVE	.271	147	532	97	144	29	3	34	110	1

SCOTT BULLETT

Position: Outfield
Team: Chicago Cubs
Born: Dec. 25, 1968 Martinsburg, WV
Height: 6'2" **Weight:** 190 lbs.
Bats: left **Throws:** left
Acquired: Traded by Pirates for Travis Willis, 3/94

Player Summary	
Fantasy Value	$3 to $5
Card Value	4¢ to 6¢
Will	use speed better
Can't	show patience
Expect	strong fielding
Don't Expect	big power

Before the midseason arrival of Luis Gonzalez from the Astros, Bullett was splitting time in left field with fellow freshman Ozzie Timmons, a right-handed hitter. Together, they combined for only five homers and five stolen bases over the first four months—hardly enough production to please the Cubs. A speeding Bullett from the minors, where he topped two-dozen steals for five seasons in a row from 1990 to '94, Scott will have to reach more to run more. That means showing much more patience at the plate: His on-base average was under the .300 mark for much of the season. Sometimes he seems more like he's in the Twilight Zone than the strike zone. He fanned far too often for a Punch-and-Judy hitter last year, rarely connected for extra-base hits, and didn't hit a respectable average against right-handed pitchers. In 1994, his one-year power splurge (13 Triple-A homers) was accompanied by a ridiculous strikeout-to-walk ratio of more than 5-to-1. Despite a fine defensive game that includes great range and a strong arm, Bullett won't win a regular job unless he returns to the running game big-time.

Major League Batting Register

	BA	G	AB	R	H	2B	3B	HR	RBI	SB
91 NL	.000	11	4	2	0	0	0	0	0	1
93 NL	.200	23	55	2	11	0	2	0	4	3
95 NL	.273	104	150	19	41	5	7	3	22	8
Life	.249	138	209	23	52	5	9	3	26	12

CURRENT PLAYERS

JIM BULLINGER

Position: Pitcher
Team: Chicago Cubs
Born: Aug. 21, 1965 New Orleans, LA
Height: 6'2" **Weight:** 185 lbs.
Bats: right **Throws:** right
Acquired: Ninth-round pick in 6/86 free-agent draft

Player Summary	
Fantasy Value	$5 to $7
Card Value	4¢ to 6¢
Will	thwart righty hitters
Can't	stop runners
Expect	ground-ball outs
Don't Expect	weak hitting

After missing time with elbow tendinitis in June, Bullinger had become the Cubs' biggest winner by August. He three-hit the Phils on July 30, winning 8-0, for his first shutout. He then extended his scoreless-innings streak to 19 with a 1-0 win against St. Louis on Aug. 5. He blends a sinking fastball with a slow curve—getting ground outs when he has his control. Though he averaged less than six strikeouts per nine innings for much of the 1995 season, Bullinger also yielded less hits than innings and about three walks per game. Because of his tantalizing curve, he's extremely effective against right-handed batters. The one-time shortstop is one of baseball's better-hitting pitchers. His home run in his first big-league at bat was no fluke. If anyone is a fifth infielder on the mound, he qualifies. He almost never makes an error. His weak spot is an inability to hold baserunners. The New Orleans University product uses his relief pitching background (20 Triple-A saves in '93) to leave runners dangling.

Major League Pitching Register

	W	L	ERA	G	CG	IP	H	ER	BB	SO
92 NL	2	8	4.66	39	1	85.0	72	44	54	36
93 NL	1	0	4.32	15	0	16.2	18	8	9	10
94 NL	6	2	3.60	33	1	100.0	87	40	34	72
95 NL	12	8	4.14	24	1	150.0	152	69	65	93
Life	21	18	4.12	111	3	351.2	329	161	162	211
2 AVE	11	6	3.89	37	1	155.0	147	67	61	103

DAVE BURBA

Position: Pitcher
Team: Cincinnati Reds
Born: July 7, 1966 Dayton, OH
Height: 6'4" **Weight:** 240 lbs.
Bats: right **Throws:** right
Acquired: Traded by Giants with Mark Portugal and Darren Lewis for Deion Sanders, Scott Service, John Roper, Dave McCarty, and Ricky Pickett, 7/95

Player Summary	
Fantasy Value	$5 to $7
Card Value	4¢ to 6¢
Will	quiet righty hitters
Can't	avoid long balls
Expect	more Ks than frames
Don't Expect	steady control

The Cincinnati Reds would not have made the Deion Sanders trade without getting Burba in return. A rubber-armed righty who has worked at least 50 times in each of the last three seasons, Burba is best used out of the bullpen—as a set-up man or even as a long reliever who can eat up innings. He can also start in a pinch. Burba's first three relief outings with the Reds were so good (no runs, three hits, and five strikeouts in 7⅓ innings) that Cincinnati put him into its injury-riddled rotation. He is a fastball-slider pitcher who also throws the forkball. He is especially tough on right-handed hitters. He averaged about one strikeout per inning and less than eight hits per nine innings for much of the year, but there were times that he struggled with his control. The Ohio State product also had periodic problems with the long ball. He's not much of a fielder or hitter but does a good job of controlling the running game.

Major League Pitching Register

	W	L	ERA	G	S	IP	H	ER	BB	SO
90 AL	0	0	4.50	6	0	8.0	8	4	2	4
91 AL	2	2	3.68	22	1	36.2	34	15	14	16
92 NL	2	7	4.97	23	0	70.2	80	39	31	47
93 NL	10	3	4.25	54	0	95.1	95	45	37	68
94 NL	3	6	4.38	57	0	74.0	59	36	45	84
95 NL	10	4	3.97	52	0	106.2	90	47	51	96
Life	27	22	4.28	214	1	391.1	366	186	180	335
3 AVE	8	5	4.18	64	0	106.1	93	50	53	105

CURRENT PLAYERS

JOHN BURKETT

Position: Pitcher
Team: Florida Marlins
Born: Nov. 28, 1964 New Brighton, PA
Height: 6'3" **Weight:** 205 lbs.
Bats: right **Throws:** right
Acquired: Signed as free agent, 4/95

Player Summary	
Fantasy Value	$7 to $9
Card Value	5¢ to 8¢
Will	offer wide repertoire
Can't	help with bat
Expect	decent control
Don't Expect	20 wins

During his tenure in the majors, Burkett has become one of the game's most dependable starters. In five of the last six years, his win total has finished in double-digits—including a 22-win season in 1993 that nearly pitched the Giants to a divisional title. A control pitcher who yielded about one hit per inning last year for Florida, he bamboozles batters with a diversified arsenal of pitches. The 1993 All-Star's sinking fastball looks a lot better as part of a package that also includes a slider, a curveball, a forkball, and a changeup. His two-year string of problems with right-handed hitters, however, remains a mystery. For much of the season last year, Burkett averaged about six strikeouts per game and induced ground balls when his pitches were working. He doesn't help himself with his hitting or fielding. Burkett does have some success in freezing potential basestealers, and is usually among the league leaders in throws to first base.

Major League Pitching Register

	W	L	ERA	G	CG	IP	H	ER	BB	SO
87 NL	0	0	4.50	3	0	6.0	7	3	3	5
90 NL	14	7	3.79	33	2	204.0	201	86	61	118
91 NL	12	11	4.18	36	3	206.2	223	96	60	131
92 NL	13	9	3.84	32	3	189.2	194	81	45	107
93 NL	22	7	3.65	34	2	231.2	224	94	40	145
94 NL	6	8	3.62	25	0	159.1	176	64	36	85
95 NL	14	14	4.30	30	4	188.1	208	90	57	126
Life	81	56	3.90	193	14	1185.2	1233	514	302	717
3 AVE	15	11	3.85	34	2	222.2	235	95	52	135

ELLIS BURKS

Position: Outfield
Team: Colorado Rockies
Born: Sept. 11, 1964 Vicksburg, MS
Height: 6'2" **Weight:** 202 lbs.
Bats: right **Throws:** right
Acquired: Signed as a free agent, 11/93

Player Summary	
Fantasy Value	$6 to $8
Card Value	4¢ to 6¢
Will	add some power
Can't	avoid injuries
Expect	strong defense
Don't Expect	stolen bases

No longer the 20-20 player he was as a rookie with the 1987 Red Sox, Burks is still productive when healthy. He was NL Player of the Month after hitting .413 with nine homers in April 1994. He then spent the remainder of the season nursing a torn ligament in his left wrist, however. By the time he returned, the Rockies had reduced him to a platoon role with Mike Kingery. That didn't sit well with Burks, a one-time Gold Glove center fielder who had made the AL All-Star team in 1990. A fastball hitter with a short, compact stroke, he is blessed with a keen batting eye that allows him to draw his share of walks. For much of the season, his on-base percentage was about 100 points higher than his batting average. His outfield range has declined, but he still throws well. He played all three outfield spots last year. He also did his best to avoid the DL; Burks had knee, shoulder, and back ailments before hurting his wrist.

Major League Batting Register

	BA	G	AB	R	H	2B	3B	HR	RBI	SB
87 AL	.272	133	558	94	152	30	2	20	59	27
88 AL	.294	144	540	93	159	37	5	18	92	25
89 AL	.303	97	399	73	121	19	6	12	61	21
90 AL	.296	152	588	89	174	33	8	21	89	9
91 AL	.251	130	474	56	119	33	3	14	56	6
92 AL	.255	66	235	35	60	8	3	8	30	5
93 NL	.275	146	499	75	137	24	4	17	74	6
94 NL	.322	42	149	33	48	8	3	13	24	3
95 NL	.266	103	278	41	74	10	6	14	49	7
Life	.281	1013	3720	589	1044	202	40	137	534	109
2 AVE	.271	131	406	61	110	18	5	16	65	7

CURRENT PLAYERS

MIKE BUTCHER

Position: Pitcher
Team: California Angels
Born: May 10, 1965 Davenport, IA
Height: 6'1" **Weight:** 200 lbs.
Bats: right **Throws:** right
Acquired: Signed as a free agent, 7/88

Player Summary	
Fantasy Value	$1
Card Value	4¢ to 6¢
Will	work middle relief
Can't	muster velocity
Expect	unreliable control
Don't Expect	closer deployment

A sinkerballing reliever who is usually rough on right-handers, Butcher was a key player in the California bullpen last summer. He won six of seven decisions, yielded about one hit per innings pitched, and, for the most part, stopped the running game. He did have problems with periodic control lapses, however, and also struggled to strand inherited runners. Not a strikeout artist, he is best deployed as a middle reliever or set-up man. He doesn't work more than one inning or two per appearance. His control wavers and hitters catch up to his deliveries once they see him a second time. In addition, heavy workloads would contradict his history of elbow problems. That's why Butcher has never made a start in the major leagues—even though he launched his career as a starter in the Kansas City system in 1986. A product of Northeastern Oklahoma A&M, he helps his own cause with good defensive skills. He'll probably never be a big-time star, but Butcher has proven himself a valuable journeyman middle reliever.

Major League Pitching Register

	W	L	ERA	G	S	IP	H	ER	BB	SO
92 AL	2	2	3.25	19	0	27.2	29	10	13	24
93 AL	1	0	2.86	23	8	28.1	21	9	15	24
94 AL	2	1	6.67	33	1	29.2	31	22	23	19
95 AL	6	1	4.73	40	0	51.1	49	27	31	29
Life	11	4	4.47	115	9	137.0	130	68	82	96

BRETT BUTLER

Position: Outfield
Team: Los Angeles Dodgers
Born: June 15, 1957 Los Angeles, CA
Height: 5'10" **Weight:** 160 lbs.
Bats: left **Throws:** left
Acquired: Traded by Mets for Scott Hunter and Dwight Maness, 8/95

Player Summary	
Fantasy Value	$12 to $15
Card Value	6¢ to 10¢
Will	set the table
Can't	hit ball over fence
Expect	bunts, infield hits
Don't Expect	low on-base mark

Even though he turned 38 last June, Butler played like a younger man. He again had a batting average about .300—thanks in part to his usual collection of bunts and infield hits. Managers polled by *Baseball America* named him the NL's No. 1 bunter. He can still swing the bat. He had two triples in a game at St. Louis on July 19, while in the process of stroking 15 hits in four games—one shy of Milt Stock's 1925 record. Butler shows patience at the plate, works deep into the count, fouls off deliveries he doesn't like, and uses all fields. Primarily a singles hitter, he usually walks as often as he strikes out. That gives him a good on-base percentage, plus a chance to run. In center field, Butler still gets great jumps and catches everything he reaches.

Major League Batting Register

	BA	G	AB	R	H	2B	3B	HR	RBI	SB
81 NL	.254	40	126	17	32	2	3	0	4	9
82 NL	.217	89	240	35	52	2	0	0	7	21
83 NL	.281	151	549	84	154	21	13	5	37	39
84 AL	.269	159	602	108	162	25	9	3	49	52
85 AL	.311	152	591	106	184	28	14	5	50	47
86 AL	.278	161	587	92	163	17	14	4	51	32
87 AL	.295	137	522	91	154	25	8	9	41	33
88 NL	.287	157	568	109	163	27	9	6	43	43
89 NL	.283	154	594	100	168	22	4	4	36	31
90 NL	.309	160	622	108	192	20	9	3	44	51
91 NL	.296	161	615	112	182	13	5	2	38	38
92 NL	.309	157	553	86	171	14	11	3	39	41
93 NL	.298	156	607	80	181	21	10	1	42	39
94 NL	.314	111	417	79	131	13	9	8	33	27
95 NL	.300	129	513	78	154	18	9	1	38	32
Life	.291	2074	7706	1285	2243	268	127	54	552	535
3 AVE	.304	152	591	93	180	20	11	4	44	38

CURRENT PLAYERS

EDGAR CACERES

Position: Second base; infield
Team: Kansas City Royals
Born: June 6, 1964 Lara, Venezuela
Height: 6'1" **Weight:** 170 lbs.
Bats: both **Throws:** right
Acquired: Signed as a minor-league free agent, 11/93

Player Summary	
Fantasy Value	$0
Card Value	15¢ to 20¢
Will	make contact
Can't	supply power
Expect	best work vs. righties
Don't Expect	fielding problems

In his first big-league at bat last June 8, Caceres hit a booming triple against Matt Whiteside of the Rangers. That was unexpected, since Caceres is basically a singles hitter not known for his power. As a switch-hitter, who for much of the 1995 season compiled a better batting average against right-handed pitchers, he made his mark as a rookie by playing all four infield positions. He spent most of his time at second base, filling the void for the suspended Jose Lind. But Caceres also made more than a half-dozen appearances at shortstop. He led two minor leagues in fielding percentage, once as a second baseman and once as a third baseman. A contact hitter who walks almost as often as he fans, he fanned once in every 11.85 plate appearances while hitting .317 at Triple-A New Orleans in 1993. He's twice topped two-dozen steals in a minor-league season. He was originally signed as a nondrafted free agent by the Dodgers, and then played in the organizations of the White Sox and Brewers before joining the Royals. A versatile athlete, Caceres was a four-sport star in high school: baseball, basketball, soccer, and volleyball. He launched his pro career in 1983.

Major League Batting Register

	BA	G	AB	R	H	2B	3B	HR	RBI	SB
95 AL	.239	55	117	13	28	6	2	1	17	2
Life	.239	55	117	13	28	6	2	1	17	2

KEN CAMINITI

Position: Third base
Team: San Diego Padres
Born: April 21, 1963 Hanford, CA
Height: 6' **Weight:** 200 lbs.
Bats: both **Throws:** right
Acquired: Traded by Astros with Steve Finley, Andujar Cedeno, Robert Petagine, Brian Williams, and a player to be named later for Phil Plantier, Derek Bell, Pedro Martinez, Doug Brocail, Craig Shipley, and Ricky Gutierrez, 12/94

Player Summary	
Fantasy Value	$18 to $21
Card Value	8¢ to 15¢
Will	feature fine arm
Can't	hit all righties
Expect	future Gold Glove
Don't Expect	any speed

NL managers polled by *Baseball America* last summer named Caminiti the second-best defensive third baseman (behind Matt Williams) and the owner of the second-best infield arm (behind Shawon Dunston). Caminiti could have finished first in either poll. He has instantaneous reactions and soft hands to accompany his cannon. He made more than his usual share of errors, but also contributed eye-popping plays not seen in San Diego since Graig Nettles. Caminiti is a natural right-handed hitter who hits for a higher average against lefties. He was hampered by lower back problems last year. He strikes out frequently but draws enough walks to build a solid on-base percentage. The former San Jose State All-American is not much of a threat to steal.

Major League Batting Register

	BA	G	AB	R	H	2B	3B	HR	RBI	SB
87 NL	.246	63	203	10	50	7	1	3	23	0
88 NL	.181	30	83	5	15	2	0	1	7	0
89 NL	.255	161	585	71	149	31	3	10	72	4
90 NL	.242	153	541	52	131	20	2	4	51	9
91 NL	.253	152	574	65	145	30	3	13	80	4
92 NL	.294	135	506	68	149	31	2	13	62	10
93 NL	.262	143	543	75	142	31	0	13	75	8
94 NL	.283	111	406	63	115	28	2	18	75	4
95 NL	.302	143	526	74	159	33	0	26	94	12
Life	.266	1091	3967	483	1055	213	13	101	539	51
3 AVE	.283	153	569	82	161	36	1	23	95	9

CURRENT PLAYERS

TOM CANDIOTTI

Position: Pitcher
Team: Los Angeles Dodgers
Born: Aug. 31, 1957 Walnut Creek, CA
Height: 6'2" **Weight:** 205 lbs.
Bats: right **Throws:** right
Acquired: Signed as free agent, 12/91

Player Summary	
Fantasy Value	$7 to $9
Card Value	5¢ to 8¢
Will	bank on knuckleball
Can't	avoid wild pitches
Expect	first-frame blues
Don't Expect	control lapses

Before the 1996 season ends, Candiotti will celebrate his 39th birthday. At an age when others have retired, he survives by throwing the knuckleball—an effortless pitch that pains both batters and catchers. Actually, he throws two knucklers: the usual slow-motion butterfly plus a harder version with last-second movement. Mixed with a curve and a cut fastball, that arsenal is often deadly—though he is an example of a pitcher with first-inning woes. When he lasts late into the game, he's practically unhittable. Poor run support hampered him last year. He yielded less than three walks per game much of last year; an accomplishment for someone who doesn't know where his pitches are going. Not surprisingly, he is usually among the league leaders in wild pitches. He helps himself with his bunting, batting, defense, and pickoff move.

Major League Pitching Register

	W	L	ERA	G	CG	IP	H	ER	BB	SO
83 AL	4	4	3.23	10	2	55.2	62	20	16	21
84 AL	2	2	5.29	8	0	32.1	38	19	10	23
86 AL	16	12	3.57	36	17	252.1	234	100	106	167
87 AL	7	18	4.78	32	7	201.2	193	107	93	111
88 AL	14	8	3.28	31	11	216.2	225	79	53	137
89 AL	13	10	3.10	31	4	206.0	188	71	55	124
90 AL	15	11	3.65	31	3	202.0	207	82	55	128
91 AL	13	13	2.65	34	6	238.0	202	70	73	167
92 NL	11	15	3.00	32	6	203.2	177	68	63	152
93 NL	8	10	3.12	33	2	213.2	192	74	71	155
94 NL	7	7	4.12	23	5	153.0	149	70	54	102
95 NL	7	14	3.50	30	1	190.1	187	74	58	141
Life	117	124	3.47	331	64	2165.1	2054	834	707	1428
3 AVE	9	12	3.58	33	3	214.1	204	85	71	152

JOHN CANGELOSI

Position: Outfield
Team: Houston Astros
Born: March 10, 1963 Brooklyn, NY
Height: 5'8" **Weight:** 160 lbs.
Bats: both **Throws:** right
Acquired: Signed as a free agent, 2/95

Player Summary	
Fantasy Value	$1 to $3
Card Value	4¢ to 6¢
Will	play well in a pinch
Can't	hit long balls
Expect	high on-base mark
Don't Expect	87-steals production

Cangelosi proved again last summer that he's the perfect spare part. A switch-hitter known for his speed and defense, he filled in for injured center fielder Brian Hunter, served as the right-handed half of a left-field platoon, and saw considerable service as a pinch hitter and pinch runner. During July, Cangelosi had six hits in six appearances, two shy of the Houston club record. A contact hitter with patience—not to mention a small strike zone—he can compile a lofty on-base percentage by walking more often than he fans. Looking at his 1995 numbers, it's hard to believe he was a career .236 hitter over eight previous seasons. A product of Miami-Dade (North) Community College, he is no longer the burner who once stole 87 bases in a minor-league season. But he still runs well enough to succeed about 80 percent of the time he tries. He is still good enough to serve as a productive fourth outfielder.

Major League Batting Register

	BA	G	AB	R	H	2B	3B	HR	RBI	SB
85 AL	.000	5	2	2	0	0	0	0	0	0
86 AL	.235	137	438	65	103	16	3	2	32	50
87 NL	.275	104	182	44	50	8	3	4	18	21
88 NL	.254	75	118	18	30	4	1	0	8	9
89 NL	.219	112	160	18	35	4	2	0	9	11
90 NL	.197	58	76	13	15	2	0	0	1	7
92 AL	.188	73	85	12	16	2	0	1	6	6
94 NL	.252	62	111	14	28	4	0	0	4	5
95 NL	.318	90	201	46	64	5	2	2	18	21
Life	.248	716	1373	232	341	45	11	9	96	130

CURRENT PLAYERS

JOSE CANSECO

Position: Designated hitter
Team: Boston Red Sox
Born: July 2, 1964 Havana, Cuba
Height: 6'3" **Weight:** 230 lbs.
Bats: right **Throws:** right
Acquired: Traded by Rangers for Otis Nixon and Luis Ortiz, 12/94

Player Summary
Fantasy Value	$25 to $30
Card Value	20¢ to 50¢
Will	maul the wall
Can't	stay healthy
Expect	power binges
Don't Expect	40-40 season

During seven seasons with Oakland, Canseco wondered aloud how well he might do if he played half his schedule in Fenway Park, home of the famed left-field Green Monster. He got his wish last summer, after two-plus seasons in Texas. He lost some first-half playing time with a torn muscle in his rib cage. By August, he had only 11 homers and four stolen bases—puny numbers for the only man in baseball history to go 40-40 (in 1988). He then got hot. While he still has the keen eye that lets him reach often on free passes, Canseco has never curbed his penchant for striking out—usually twice for every walk. His swing has recovered from the torn elbow ligament that idled him much of 1993. Injuries have taken a toll, however. Because he can't throw, Canseco is confined to DH duty. He loves left-handers and still has huge power.

Major League Batting Register
	BA	G	AB	R	H	2B	3B	HR	RBI	SB
85 AL	.302	29	96	16	29	3	0	5	13	1
86 AL	.240	157	600	85	144	29	1	33	117	15
87 AL	.257	159	630	81	162	35	3	31	113	15
88 AL	.307	158	610	120	187	34	0	42	124	40
89 AL	.269	65	227	40	61	9	1	17	57	6
90 AL	.274	131	481	83	132	14	2	37	101	19
91 AL	.266	154	572	115	152	32	1	44	122	26
92 AL	.244	119	439	74	107	15	0	26	87	6
93 AL	.255	60	231	30	59	14	1	10	46	6
94 AL	.282	111	429	88	121	19	2	31	90	15
95 AL	.306	102	396	64	121	25	1	24	81	4
Life	.271	1245	4711	796	1275	229	12	300	951	153
3 AVE	.285	110	427	75	122	23	2	27	88	11

RAMON CARABALLO

Position: Second base
Team: St. Louis Cardinals
Born: May 23, 1969 Rio San Juan, Dominican Republic
Height: 5'7" **Weight:** 150 lbs.
Bats: both **Throws:** right
Acquired: Traded by Braves for Aldo Pecorilli, 11/94

Player Summary
Fantasy Value	$0
Card Value	10¢ to 15¢
Will	show great speed
Can't	hit right-handers
Expect	improved defense
Don't Expect	patient approach

After recovering from tendinitis of the right knee, Caraballo found his stroke at Triple-A Louisville early in 1995. When the Cardinals needed a second baseman to replace the injured Geronimo Pena, Caraballo got the call. A little guy with big-time speed, he topped 40 steals twice during his minor-league career. Reaching base more often would help, however: He struggled to clear the Mendoza Line against right-handed pitchers last year. But he did deliver some big hits, including his first big-league homer, instrumental in a 6-4 win over the Cubs on June 29. Caraballo would be more productive if he showed patience at the plate. He fanned about four times more often than he walked last year. A good bunter, he is fast enough to fatten his average with infield hits or take extra bases. He had 37 extra-base hits at Triple-A Richmond in 1993. Because his quickness translates into great range, he should be able to overcome the defensive problems he encountered in St. Louis last year. In 1992, Caraballo led Triple-A International League second baseman in fielding.

Major League Batting Register
	BA	G	AB	R	H	2B	3B	HR	RBI	SB
93 NL	.000	6	0	0	0	0	0	0	0	0
95 NL	.202	34	99	10	20	4	1	2	3	3
Life	.202	40	99	10	20	4	1	2	3	3

CURRENT PLAYERS

CHUCK CARR

Position: Outfield
Team: Milwaukee Brewers
Born: Aug. 10, 1968 San Bernardino, CA
Height: 5'10" **Weight:** 165 lbs.
Bats: both **Throws:** right
Acquired: Traded by Marlins with Tyrone Narcisse for Juan Gonzalez, 12/95

Player Summary
Fantasy Value	$5 to $7
Card Value	5¢ to 8¢
Will	use great speed
Can't	swing better bat
Expect	strong fielding
Don't Expect	extra-base hits

Carr's speed compensates for his lack of power, limited hitting success, and unnecessary bravado. There's no question that Carr can fly. He led the NL with 58 steals in 1993. He took too many chances, however, and finished with a success ratio of 72 percent—unacceptable for someone who could challenge Deion Sanders to a footrace. If Carr could hit, he'd probably steal 100 times. But he has watched his average decline steadily from a peak of .353 on May 20, 1994. He showed considerably more patience in '95 than he had previously. His on-base percentage was about 100 points higher than his batting average through much of the season. When he's not bunting for a hit, he beats the ball into the ground and runs. He also runs well in the outfield, where his great range and ability to make dives erase some mistakes in judgement. He needs to remember, though, that hot dogs who can't hit end up smothered in mustard.

Major League Batting Register

	BA	G	AB	R	H	2B	3B	HR	RBI	SB
90 NL	.000	4	2	0	0	0	0	0	0	1
91 NL	.182	12	11	1	2	0	0	0	1	1
92 NL	.219	22	64	8	14	3	0	0	3	10
93 NL	.267	142	551	75	147	19	2	4	41	58
94 NL	.263	106	433	61	114	19	2	2	30	32
95 NL	.227	105	308	54	70	20	0	2	20	25
Life	.253	391	1369	199	347	61	4	8	95	127
3 AVE	.256	136	502	74	129	23	2	3	35	44

HECTOR CARRASCO

Position: Pitcher
Team: Cincinnati Reds
Born: Oct. 22, 1969 San Pedro de Macoris, Dominican Republic
Height: 6'2" **Weight:** 175 lbs.
Bats: right **Throws:** right
Acquired: Traded by Marlins with Gary Scott for Chris Hammond, 9/93

Player Summary
Fantasy Value	$2 to $4
Card Value	5¢ to 8¢
Will	star in future
Can't	maintain top control
Expect	velocity and movement
Don't Expect	gopher woes

After jumping from Class-A to the majors in 1994, Carrasco broke in with a bang. He held hitters to a .210 average and was even more effective with runners in scoring position (.192). The Marlins, who had given up on Carrasco after trying him as a starter in 1993, never dreamed he'd reach those levels. But the Reds took his ordinary arsenal of a fastball, a forkball, and a slider and made some fundamental changes. Teammate Jose Rijo, owner of one of the game's best sliders, spent long hours with his fellow Dominican providing private coaching lessons on the slider, forkball, and the art of pitching in general. Pitching coach Don Gullett, a former Cincinnati standout, changed the grip on Carrasco's fastball—a pitch that moves in on righties but away from lefties. The result was a pitcher who throws nearly 100 mph, yields less hits than innings, and almost never throws a home run ball. Carrasco's control is still erratic; he allowed about four walks per nine innings last year. He definitely has the potential to be a standout closer in the future, however.

Major League Pitching Register

	W	L	ERA	G	S	IP	H	ER	BB	SO
94 NL	5	6	2.24	45	6	56.1	42	14	30	41
95 NL	2	7	4.12	64	5	87.1	86	40	46	64
Life	7	13	3.38	109	11	143.2	128	54	76	105
2 AVE	5	8	3.28	68	7	88.1	78	32	47	65

CURRENT PLAYERS

MARK CARREON

Position: First base; outfield
Team: San Francisco Giants
Born: July 9, 1963 Chicago, IL
Height: 6' **Weight:** 195 lbs.
Bats: right **Throws:** left
Acquired: Signed as a free agent, 1/93

Player Summary
Fantasy Value	$5 to $7
Card Value	4¢ to 6¢
Will	maul left-handers
Can't	show much speed
Expect	strong pinch-bat
Don't Expect	powerful defense

The departure of All-Star Will Clark left a huge void at first base in San Francisco. When Todd Benzinger and J.R. Phillips failed to fill it in 1995, manager Dusty Baker turned to Carreon. Previously a backup outfielder and power-hitting pinch hitter (with about a .280 lifetime average in that role), he carried out his mission well. Batting behind Barry Bonds while injured slugger Matt Williams recuperated from a broken foot, Carreon provided a solid right-handed bat. He hit about 100 points higher against left-handers while providing power. Although he doesn't run well, he netted extra bases on about one-third of his hits. He would be a more valuable hitter if he showed better selectivity, but years as a pinch hitter taught him to come out hacking. No gazelle on the bases or in the field, Carreon has limited experience at first base. He is the son of former big-league catcher Camilo Carreon.

Major League Batting Register
	BA	G	AB	R	H	2B	3B	HR	RBI	SB
87 NL	.250	9	12	0	3	0	0	0	1	0
88 NL	.556	7	9	5	5	2	0	1	1	0
89 NL	.308	68	133	20	41	6	0	6	16	2
90 NL	.250	82	188	30	47	12	0	10	26	1
91 NL	.260	106	254	18	66	6	0	4	21	2
92 AL	.232	101	336	34	78	11	1	10	41	3
93 NL	.327	78	150	22	49	9	1	7	33	1
94 NL	.270	51	100	8	27	4	0	3	20	0
95 NL	.301	117	396	53	119	24	0	17	65	0
Life	.276	619	1578	190	435	74	2	58	224	9
2 AVE	.307	105	298	41	91	18	1	13	53	1

JOE CARTER

Position: Outfield
Team: Toronto Blue Jays
Born: March 7, 1960 Oklahoma City, OK
Height: 6'3" **Weight:** 215 lbs.
Bats: right **Throws:** right
Acquired: Traded by Padres with Roberto Alomar for Fred McGriff and Tony Fernandez, 12/90

Player Summary
Fantasy Value	$25 to $30
Card Value	15¢ to 40¢
Will	show power
Can't	notch walks
Expect	hits vs. lefties
Don't Expect	30-30 form

When Toronto placed its high-priced stars on the trading block last July, rival teams almost created a stampede in their haste to land Carter. One of the most consistent and prolific run-producers in the game, he had five 30-homer campaigns and eight 100-RBI years prior to 1995. He'd also been an All-Star four times. Even before his ninth-inning homer off Mitch Williams won the 1993 World Series, Carter had found the confines of the SkyDome conducive to his right-handed power stroke. The former Wichita State All-American unloads a powerful, uppercut swing at anything near home plate. Patience has never been one of his virtues: Carter rarely waits for walks. He makes surprising contact for a slugger. He also has surprising speed.

Major League Batting Register
	BA	G	AB	R	H	2B	3B	HR	RBI	SB
83 NL	.176	23	51	6	9	1	1	0	1	1
84 AL	.275	66	244	32	67	6	1	13	41	2
85 AL	.262	143	489	64	128	27	0	15	59	24
86 AL	.302	162	663	108	200	36	9	29	121	29
87 AL	.264	149	588	83	155	27	2	32	106	31
88 AL	.271	157	621	85	168	36	6	27	98	27
89 AL	.243	162	651	84	158	32	4	35	105	13
90 NL	.232	162	634	79	147	27	1	24	115	22
91 AL	.273	162	638	89	174	42	3	33	108	20
92 AL	.264	158	622	97	164	30	7	34	119	12
93 AL	.254	155	603	92	153	33	5	33	121	8
94 AL	.271	111	435	70	118	25	2	27	103	11
95 AL	.253	139	558	70	141	23	0	25	76	12
Life	.262	1749	6797	959	1782	345	41	327	1173	212
3 AVE	.259	156	615	90	159	31	3	33	117	12

CURRENT PLAYERS

VINNY CASTILLA

Position: Third base
Team: Colorado Rockies
Born: July 4, 1967 Oaxaca, Mexico
Height: 6'1" **Weight:** 175 lbs.
Bats: right **Throws:** right
Acquired: Second-round pick from Braves in 11/92 expansion draft

Player Summary	
Fantasy Value	$18 to $21
Card Value	10¢ to 20¢
Will	smash southpaws
Can't	notch many walks
Expect	clutch hitting
Don't Expect	any speed

All Castilla needed was a chance. In his first season as a full-time third baseman, the converted shortstop became an All-Star starter, replacing the injured Matt Williams. Castilla also became one of the NL's top sluggers, hitting as many home runs by the All-Star break as he had in four previous seasons. He likes to deliver in pairs: He had a half-dozen two-homer games over the first four months. He also accumulated a batting average over the .350 mark both at Coors Field, his high-altitude home park, and against left-handed pitching during most of the 1995 season. About 40 percent of his hits netted extra bases. A fastball hitter who can go the opposite way, Castilla cuts at anything near the plate. He fanned about three times more than he walked. He also didn't get many bunt hits or infield hits; speed is simply not his forte. At third, Castilla shows quick reactions, good hands, and a strong arm. His days as a utility infielder are history. He launched his pro career in 1987.

Major League Batting Register

	BA	G	AB	R	H	2B	3B	HR	RBI	SB
91 NL	.200	12	5	1	1	0	0	0	0	0
92 NL	.250	9	16	1	4	1	0	0	1	0
93 NL	.255	105	337	36	86	9	7	9	30	2
94 NL	.331	52	130	16	43	11	1	3	18	2
95 NL	.309	139	527	82	163	34	2	32	90	2
Life	.293	317	1015	136	297	55	10	44	139	6
2 AVE	.290	131	465	64	135	24	5	23	66	2

FRANK CASTILLO

Position: Pitcher
Team: Chicago Cubs
Born: April 1, 1969 El Paso, TX
Height: 6'1" **Weight:** 180 lbs.
Bats: right **Throws:** right
Acquired: Sixth-round pick in 6/87 free-agent draft

Player Summary	
Fantasy Value	$7 to $9
Card Value	4¢ to 6¢
Will	continue to develop
Can't	win without support
Expect	few walks
Don't Expect	weak hitting

After slipping back to the minors in 1994, Castillo was a long-shot to resurrect his career—let alone return to the Cubs rotation. But he silenced the skeptics by suddenly realizing the potential he had flashed only briefly in four previous seasons. He had a perfect game going June 15 before yielding a one-out, seventh-inning single to Mike Benjamin. By the end of the year, Castillo had emerged as perhaps the most effective of the five Chicago starters. A sinker-slider pitcher who also throws a curve and a change, Castillo is a control artist who for much of the season yielded less hits than innings and had a strikeout-to-walk ratio of nearly 3-to-1. He helps his own cause with his hitting, fielding, and pickoff move. That self-help is often necessary, since Castillo often got paltry support. Getting an average of less than four runs per game through much of the season prevented him from posting a better record. Castillo pitched a no-hitter in the minors.

Major League Pitching Register

	W	L	ERA	G	CG	IP	H	ER	BB	SO
91 NL	6	7	4.35	18	4	111.2	107	54	33	73
92 NL	10	11	3.46	33	0	205.1	179	79	63	135
93 NL	5	8	4.84	29	2	141.1	162	76	39	84
94 NL	2	1	4.30	4	0	23.0	25	11	5	19
95 NL	11	10	3.21	29	2	188.0	179	67	52	135
Life	34	37	3.86	113	9	669.1	652	287	192	446
2 AVE	9	10	3.86	31	2	176.1	182	76	49	118

CURRENT PLAYERS

TONY CASTILLO

Position: Pitcher
Team: Toronto Blue Jays
Born: March 1, 1963 Lara, Venezuela
Height: 5'10" **Weight:** 188 lbs.
Bats: left **Throws:** left
Acquired: Signed as a minor-league free agent, 1/93

Player Summary	
Fantasy Value	$7 to $9
Card Value	4¢ to 6¢
Will	show control
Can't	throw hard
Expect	frequent outings
Don't Expect	fielding problems

It pays to be in the right place at the right time. When simultaneous injuries idled Duane Ward, Darren Hall, Danny Cox, Mike Timlin, and Woody Williams last summer, Castillo became Toronto's interim closer. Although he had only three saves in six previous seasons, Castillo pretty much proved up to the task. He converted seven of his first nine chances, kept runners off base with good control, and kept the ball in the park. A rubber-armed righty, capable of working 50 times a season, Castillo mixes a fastball, slider, and a curve with generally good results. For much of the 1995 season he yielded less hits than innings, had some success in stopping the running game, and fared well against both righties and lefties. He's also a first-rate fielder. If his 1995 performance is a true test of his skills, he might have broken out of the strict role that he was a reliever to be used primarily against left-handers.

Major League Pitching Register

	W	L	ERA	G	S	IP	H	ER	BB	SO
88 AL	1	0	3.00	14	0	15.0	10	5	2	14
89 AL	1	1	6.11	17	1	17.2	23	12	10	10
89 NL	0	1	4.82	12	0	9.1	8	5	4	5
90 NL	5	1	4.23	52	1	76.2	93	36	20	64
91 NL	2	1	3.34	17	0	32.1	40	12	11	18
93 AL	3	2	3.38	51	0	50.2	44	19	22	28
94 AL	5	2	2.51	41	1	68.0	66	19	28	43
95 AL	1	5	3.22	55	13	72.2	64	26	24	38
Life	18	13	3.52	259	16	342.1	348	134	121	220
3 AVE	4	3	2.96	57	5	76.1	70	25	29	44

ANDUJAR CEDENO

Position: Shortstop
Team: San Diego Padres
Born: Aug. 21, 1969 La Romana, Dominican Republic
Height: 6'1" **Weight:** 168 lbs.
Bats: right **Throws:** right
Acquired: Traded by Astros with Ken Caminiti, Steve Finley, Roberto Petagine, Brian Williams, and a player to be named later for Phil Plantier, Derek Bell, Pedro Martinez, Doug Brocail, Craig Shipley, and Ricky Gutierrez, 12/94

Player Summary	
Fantasy Value	$5 to $7
Card Value	5¢ to 8¢
Will	hit left-handers
Can't	cut whiff ratio
Expect	fielding slumps
Don't Expect	contact hitting

Of all the players the Padres acquired in their huge trade with the Astros, Cedeno was the biggest disappointment. Viewed as a power-hitting shortstop with untapped potential, he spent most of the season trying to reach the Mendoza Line against right-handers. Though about one-third of his hits were for extra bases last year, he missed more often than he connected. When he saw a fastball—even if far from the strike zone—Cedeno went for it. A first-pitch swinger, he's made a conscious effort to convert to a compact stroke and to be more selective. If 1995 is an accurate barometer, however, those efforts have not paid off. His defense doesn't compensate for his erratic performance at the plate. He makes too many errors and often goes through fielding slumps where he makes them in bunches.

Major League Batting Register

	BA	G	AB	R	H	2B	3B	HR	RBI	SB
90 NL	.000	7	8	0	0	0	0	0	0	0
91 NL	.243	67	251	27	61	13	2	9	36	4
92 NL	.173	71	220	15	38	13	2	2	13	2
93 NL	.283	149	505	69	143	24	4	11	56	9
94 NL	.263	98	342	38	90	26	0	9	49	1
95 NL	.210	120	390	42	82	16	2	6	31	5
Life	.241	512	1716	191	414	92	10	37	185	21
3 AVE	.254	141	475	57	121	26	2	10	53	5

CURRENT PLAYERS

DOMINGO CEDENO

Position: Infield
Team: Toronto Blue Jays
Born: Nov. 4, 1968 La Romana, Dominican Republic
Height: 6'1" **Weight:** 170 lbs.
Bats: both **Throws:** right
Acquired: Signed as a free agent, 8/87

Player Summary	
Fantasy Value	$0
Card Value	5¢ to 8¢
Will	supply defense
Can't	learn strike zone
Expect	a good bunter
Don't Expect	much power

When heralded rookie Alex Gonzalez struggled against right-handers last season, Cedeno saw more action than the Blue Jays had anticipated. Though signed as a shortstop, Cedeno had come to spring training camp as a utility infielder capable of playing three positions. He has some speed and power, plus the ability to bunt, and he's equally effective from both sides of the plate. He showed little concept of the strike zone for much of the 1995 season, however, fanning three times for every walk. When he did connect, he contributed an element of surprise. His three-run homer at Baltimore on Aug. 1 capped a six-run, ninth-inning rally in a 12-10 Toronto victory. Cedeno had a career-best four RBI that night. A good fielder with a strong, accurate arm and good range, he is most comfortable at either shortstop or second base. His speed helps: During his minor-league career, Cedeno reached double-digits in steals three times and in triples twice. He also led one of his leagues in chances, putouts, assists, and double plays.

Major League Batting Register

	BA	G	AB	R	H	2B	3B	HR	RBI	SB
93 AL	.174	15	46	5	8	0	0	0	7	1
94 AL	.196	47	97	14	19	2	3	0	10	1
95 AL	.236	51	161	18	38	6	1	4	14	0
Life	.214	113	304	37	65	8	4	4	31	2

NORM CHARLTON

Position: Pitcher
Team: Seattle Mariners
Born: Jan. 6, 1963 Fort Polk, LA
Height: 6'3" **Weight:** 200 lbs.
Bats: both **Throws:** left
Acquired: Signed as a free agent, 6/95

Player Summary	
Fantasy Value	$10 to $13
Card Value	4¢ to 6¢
Will	silence southpaws
Can't	stop baserunners
Expect	whiff per inning
Don't Expect	pinpoint control

After missing the entire 1994 season while recovering from torn ligaments in his left elbow, Charlton made an impressive comeback last summer. An early-season disappointment in Philadelphia, he appeared more comfortable after returning to Seattle. There he resumed the short set-up role he held with the team two years earlier. For much of his time with the Mariners, he averaged about one strikeout per inning while holding hitters to a microscopic batting average under the .200 mark. He allowed an average of about five hits per nine AL innings last year. A fastball-forkball pitcher who also throws a slider, Charlton fields his position well but has trouble preventing runners from stealing. He's already recorded a minor miracle by resurrecting his career in the wake of "Tommy John surgery," and Charlton could become a closer again if he steers clear of injury.

Major League Pitching Register

	W	L	ERA	G	S	IP	H	ER	BB	SO
88 NL	4	5	3.96	10	0	61.1	60	27	20	39
89 NL	8	3	2.93	69	0	95.1	67	31	40	98
90 NL	12	9	2.74	56	2	154.1	131	47	70	117
91 NL	3	5	2.91	39	1	108.1	92	35	34	77
92 NL	4	2	2.99	64	26	81.1	79	27	26	90
93 AL	1	3	2.34	34	18	34.2	22	9	17	48
95 NL	2	5	7.36	25	0	22.0	23	18	15	12
95 AL	2	1	1.51	30	14	47.2	23	8	16	58
Life	36	33	3.00	327	61	605.0	497	202	238	539
2 AVE	3	5	3.05	48	17	56.2	37	19	26	63

JASON CHRISTIANSEN

Position: Pitcher
Team: Pittsburgh Pirates
Born: Sept. 21, 1969 Omaha, NE
Height: 6'5" **Weight:** 230 lbs.
Bats: right **Throws:** left
Acquired: Signed as a free agent, 7/91

Player Summary
Fantasy Value	$0
Card Value	12¢ to 15¢
Will	bank on big curve
Can't	leave runners on
Expect	lefties to cringe
Don't Expect	too many gophers

Left-handed hitters don't like to see Christiansen enter the game. A reliever used in both middle and set-up roles as a rookie last summer, he throws three pitches for strikes. The one lefties dread is a sweeping curve that is most effective down in the zone. When the curve isn't working, Christiansen gets hit. For much of the of the '95 campaign, however, that rarely happened. Lefties staggered with a batting average under the Mendoza Line against the towering southpaw for much of the season. Christiansen put up good numbers during four years in the minors, and he averaged more than one strikeout per inning. He nearly maintained that average last summer, when he also yielded about seven hits per nine innings. He kept the ball in the park and held baserunners well. He did have some problems with inherited runners, however, and also endured several bouts of control trouble, giving up about six walks a game. But he had one of the best ERAs in the Pirate bullpen well into the second half of the season. Signed out of a tryout camp, Christiansen appears to have a pretty bright future.

Major League Pitching Register
	W	L	ERA	G	S	IP	H	ER	BB	SO
95 NL	1	3	4.15	63	0	56.1	49	26	34	53
Life	1	3	4.15	63	0	56.1	49	26	34	53

ARCHI CIANFROCCO

Position: Infield; outfield
Team: San Diego Padres
Born: Oct. 6, 1966 Rome, NY
Height: 6'5" **Weight:** 215 lbs.
Bats: right **Throws:** right
Acquired: Traded by Expos for Tim Scott, 6/93

Player Summary
Fantasy Value	$1
Card Value	4¢ to 6¢
Will	back several spots
Can't	connect frequently
Expect	some power
Don't Expect	patience at bat

Because he plays several positions and provides power potential off the bench, Cianfrocco keeps surfacing in the major leagues. He hasn't had a full season yet, however, and probably won't unless he learns the dimensions of the strike zone. All too often, he seems determined to perform his Dave Kingman imitation, with all-or-nothing riding on every swing. A first-pitch, fastball hitter teased by breaking stuff out of the zone, Cianfrocco averaged about two strikeouts per walk for much of the season. When he did connect, one-third of his hits produced extra bases. He had two six-RBI games in his first 13 contests with the Padres after his July 14 promotion last year. The Purdue product runs well for a big man, but frequently doesn't steal. He moves and throws well enough to fill in at shortstop, but he is most comfortable at the infield or outfield corners. Though he has an inaccurate throwing arm, Cianfrocco once led Eastern League first basemen in assists and double plays. As a third baseman, he led one league in fielding percentage and another in errors.

Major League Batting Register
	BA	G	AB	R	H	2B	3B	HR	RBI	SB
92 NL	.241	86	232	25	56	5	2	6	30	3
93 NL	.243	96	296	30	72	11	2	12	48	2
94 NL	.219	59	146	9	32	8	0	4	13	2
95 NL	.263	51	118	22	31	7	0	5	31	0
Life	.241	292	792	86	191	31	4	27	122	7

JEFF CIRILLO

Position: Third base; second base
Team: Milwaukee Brewers
Born: Sept. 23, 1969 Pasadena, CA
Height: 6'2" **Weight:** 190 lbs.
Bats: right **Throws:** right
Acquired: 11th-round pick in 6/91 free-agent draft

Player Summary
Fantasy Value	$8 to $10
Card Value	6¢ to 10¢
Will	club left-handers
Can't	show much range
Expect	line drives
Don't Expect	third-base power

In his first full big-league season, Cirillo was so successful that he pushed veteran Kevin Seitzer into a swing-shift role involving both infield corners. Like Seitzer, Cirillo is a line-drive contact hitter with good patience but moderate power. He hits left-handed pitchers hard, steals a few bases, and fills in at the other three infield positions. The former Southern Cal communications major doesn't have the ideal power of a third baseman. In fact, he never hit more than 10 home runs in any of his four minor-league campaigns. But Cirillo compensated with a .300 stroke that helped him compile a high on-base percentage. He walked almost as much as he struck out for much of the 1995 campaign. He should improve that ratio as he gains experience. Despite limited range, he's a decent defensive third baseman with a solid arm. During his first minor-league season, he led his league in putouts, assists, and chances. Two years later, he posted a .417 on-base percentage. Continued production at that level will not only keep Cirillo in the majors but also in the starting lineup.

Major League Batting Register
	BA	G	AB	R	H	2B	3B	HR	RBI	SB
94 AL	.238	39	126	17	30	9	0	3	12	0
95 AL	.277	125	328	57	91	19	4	9	39	7
Life	.267	164	454	74	121	28	4	12	51	7

DAVE CLARK

Position: Outfield
Team: Pittsburgh Pirates
Born: Sept. 3, 1962 Tupelo, MS
Height: 6'2" **Weight:** 209 lbs.
Bats: left **Throws:** right
Acquired: Signed as a free agent, 1/92

Player Summary
Fantasy Value	$3 to $5
Card Value	4¢ to 6¢
Will	produce some pop
Can't	steal too often
Expect	OK on-base mark
Don't Expect	a Gold Glove

One of Pittsburgh manager Jim Leyland's platoon outfielders for several years, Clark last year shattered the myth that he can't hit left-handed pitching, with a mark over .400 for much of the season. A fastball hitter who makes surprising contact for a slugger, he doesn't surprise anyone with his strength. The product of Jackson State University is a former Olympic boxing hopeful. He hits with power to all fields. A fine clutch hitter, he is murder with the count in his favor. And he showed enough patience at the plate to post a respectable on-base percentage. He is capable of handling either corner. He hustles after everything hit in his direction, but is sometimes guilty of overzealousness. In a serious July 25 collision in right center with Jacob Brumfield, Clark suffered a broken collarbone, lost a tooth, and had cuts and abrasions.

Major League Batting Register
	BA	G	AB	R	H	2B	3B	HR	RBI	SB
86 AL	.276	18	58	10	16	1	0	3	9	1
87 AL	.207	29	87	11	18	5	0	3	12	1
88 AL	.263	63	156	11	41	4	1	3	18	0
89 AL	.237	102	253	21	60	12	0	8	29	0
90 NL	.275	84	171	22	47	4	2	5	20	7
91 AL	.200	11	10	1	2	0	0	0	1	0
92 NL	.212	23	33	3	7	0	0	2	7	0
93 NL	.271	110	277	43	75	11	2	11	46	1
94 NL	.296	86	223	37	66	11	1	10	46	2
95 NL	.281	77	196	30	55	6	0	4	24	3
Life	.264	603	1464	189	387	54	6	49	212	15
3 AVE	.283	106	271	43	77	11	1	10	46	2

CURRENT PLAYERS

JERALD CLARK

Position: Outfield; first base
Team: Minnesota Twins
Born: Aug. 10, 1963 Crockett, TX
Height: 6'4" **Weight:** 190 lbs.
Bats: right **Throws:** right
Acquired: Signed as a free agent, 3/95

Player Summary
Fantasy Value	$1
Card Value	4¢ to 6¢
Will	produce some power
Can't	reduce strikeouts
Expect	clutch hits
Don't Expect	sterling defense

Like the Padres and Rockies before them, the Twins were hoping for some offense when they plucked Clark out of Japan after a one-year exile. He continued to do what he's done in the past: supply occasional power, poke a few pinch hits, and add experience to a baby-faced ballclub. He also participated in the all-comers derby to replace retired first baseman Kent Hrbek. Clark missed much of the second half of 1995 with a severely sprained knee. Although he uses all fields and usually thrives in clutch situations, Clark deflates his value by not paying any attention to the strike zone. He has fanned three times more often than he walked during much of his major-league career, and he has often looked bad in the process. He has been effective against righties and lefties, but breaking balls give him fits. Clark moves well for a big man and could swipe a dozen bases if he tried. His defense isn't much, however.

Major League Batting Register
	BA	G	AB	R	H	2B	3B	HR	RBI	SB
88 NL	.200	6	15	0	3	1	0	0	3	0
89 NL	.195	17	41	5	8	2	0	1	7	0
90 NL	.267	53	101	12	27	4	1	5	11	0
91 NL	.228	118	369	26	84	16	0	10	47	2
92 NL	.242	146	496	45	120	22	6	12	58	3
93 NL	.282	140	478	65	135	26	6	13	67	9
95 AL	.339	36	109	17	37	8	3	3	15	3
Life	.257	516	1609	170	414	79	16	44	208	17

MARK CLARK

Position: Pitcher
Team: Cleveland Indians
Born: May 12, 1968 Bath, IL
Height: 6'5" **Weight:** 225 lbs.
Bats: right **Throws:** right
Acquired: Traded by Cardinals with Juan Andujar for Mark Whiten, 3/93

Player Summary
Fantasy Value	$5 to $7
Card Value	4¢ to 6¢
Will	seek old control
Can't	rack up Ks
Expect	ground outs
Don't Expect	economy-sized ERA

One year after posting the best record of his career, Clark did a complete about-face. He struggled so much that he even endured an unexpected brief exile to Triple-A, where he was sent to find his missing stuff. More effective after his recall, Clark was involved in a combined six-hit shutout of Oakland on July 23. But he moved to the bullpen four days later when Ken Hill came to Cleveland. A sinker-slider pitcher who also throws a forkball and a changeup, Clark is only effective when he locates those pitches effectively in and around the strike zone. Because he doesn't record many strikeouts, he tries to get batters out on ground balls. With his control slightly askew last summer, he was hit hard by both righties and lefties. He also yielded too many home runs. Sporadic use may have hurt him last summer, so Clark needs regular work to keep sharp. He's improved his defense, and he keeps his teammates on their toes with a fast-paced performance, but he still needs help with his pickoff move.

Major League Pitching Register
	W	L	ERA	G	CG	IP	H	ER	BB	SO
91 NL	1	1	4.03	7	0	22.1	17	10	11	13
92 NL	3	10	4.45	20	1	113.1	117	56	36	44
93 AL	7	5	4.28	26	1	109.1	119	52	25	57
94 AL	11	3	3.82	20	4	127.1	133	54	40	60
95 AL	9	7	5.27	22	2	124.2	143	73	42	68
Life	31	26	4.44	95	8	497.0	529	245	154	242
3 AVE	11	6	4.41	26	3	142.2	156	70	43	73

CURRENT PLAYERS

PHIL CLARK

Position: Outfield; first base
Team: San Diego Padres
Born: May 6, 1968 Crockett, TX
Height: 6' **Weight:** 205 lbs.
Bats: right **Throws:** right
Acquired: Claimed from Tigers on waivers, 4/93

Player Summary	
Fantasy Value	$1
Card Value	4¢ to 6¢
Will	back several spots
Can't	show much patience
Expect	surprising contact
Don't Expect	much catching duty

Because of his versatility, Clark has never had a chance to play regularly in the big leagues. In fact, it was a surprise when he squeezed into more than 100 games in 1993. But that just happened to be his most productive season with the bat. Signed as a catcher, Clark plays the outfield corners mostly, though he had some work at first base. He brings power off the bench when he pinch-hits. An aggressive hitter, he fanned almost three times more than he walked through much of 1995. Before knee surgery, Clark could even run; he once swiped 25 bases in the minors. He doesn't run much anymore and is not particularly gifted with a glove, though he does have a strong arm. He led two leagues in errors by a catcher, but also shared a league lead in double plays by a catcher. Clark's best positions on the field are first base or left field, but his best overall position is batter. He would make a fine DH. Although both played for the Padres, neither Phil nor brother Jerald were ever teammates in the majors.

TERRY CLARK

Position: Pitcher
Team: Baltimore Orioles
Born: Oct. 10, 1960 Los Angeles, CA
Height: 6'2" **Weight:** 196 lbs.
Bats: right **Throws:** right
Acquired: Signed as a free agent, 4/95

Player Summary	
Fantasy Value	$1
Card Value	4¢ to 6¢
Will	strand runners
Can't	record many Ks
Expect	heavy workload
Don't Expect	success vs. lefties

As a rookie with the Angels in 1988, Clark won his first five decisions. His bubble soon burst, however, and he spent the next five years in the minors before resurfacing in the Baltimore bullpen last summer. Strictly a reliever for almost nine years, Clark reached the majors for the first time only after becoming a starter. He returned to relief in '93 and reached career peaks in games (61) and saves (26) a year later, for Triple-A Richmond. Impressive during the strike-abbreviated spring training of 1995, Clark made Atlanta's 28-man Opening Day roster, but got little chance to show what he could do. When he didn't survive the May 15 cutdown date, Baltimore came calling. He rewarded the Orioles much of the season by dominating right-handed batters, stranding nearly 90 percent of the runners he inherited, and being extremely frugal with the home run ball. Not a power pitcher, Clark rarely beat himself. Clark has topped 50 appearances five times in a pro career that began in 1979.

Major League Batting Register

	BA	G	AB	R	H	2B	3B	HR	RBI	SB
92 AL	.407	23	54	3	22	4	0	1	5	1
93 NL	.313	102	240	33	75	17	0	9	33	2
94 NL	.215	61	149	14	32	6	0	5	20	1
95 NL	.216	75	97	12	21	3	0	2	7	0
Life	.278	261	540	62	150	30	0	17	65	4

Major League Pitching Register

	W	L	ERA	G	S	IP	H	ER	BB	SO
88 AL	6	6	5.07	15	0	94.0	120	53	31	39
89 AL	0	2	4.91	4	0	11.0	13	6	3	7
90 NL	0	0	13.50	1	0	4.0	9	6	3	2
95 NL	0	0	4.91	3	0	3.2	3	2	5	2
95 AL	2	5	3.46	38	1	39.0	40	15	15	18
Life	8	13	4.87	61	1	151.2	185	82	57	68

CURRENT PLAYERS

WILL CLARK

Position: First base
Team: Texas Rangers
Born: March 13, 1964 New Orleans, LA
Height: 6'1" **Weight:** 190 lbs.
Bats: left **Throws:** left
Acquired: Signed as a free agent, 11/93

Player Summary
Fantasy Value	$18 to $21
Card Value	15¢ to 25¢
Will	use all fields
Can't	avoid injury
Expect	good contact
Don't Expect	20 home runs

Injuries contributed to Clark's power shortfall last summer. The six-time All-Star suffered a sore elbow in June and a strained right groin muscle in July. Postseason surgery was needed to return the elbow to full strength. Clark, a durable star who once played the complete 162-game schedule, decided to play with the pain. Still a .300 hitter who makes good contact and hits to all fields, he compiles a high on-base percentage by walking more often than he fans. He is a feared clutch hitter. He shows more power and produces a higher average against right-handed pitchers. A former All-American at Mississippi State, Clark played on the 1984 U.S. Olympic team, won the Golden Spikes Award in '85, and was playing for the Giants a year later. He won a Gold Glove in 1991. Clark homered in his first minor-league at bat and first major-league at bat. Both came on the first swing.

Major League Batting Register
	BA	G	AB	R	H	2B	3B	HR	RBI	SB
86 NL	.287	111	408	66	117	27	2	11	41	4
87 NL	.308	150	529	89	163	29	5	35	91	5
88 NL	.282	162	575	102	162	31	6	29	109	9
89 NL	.333	159	588	104	196	38	9	23	111	8
90 NL	.295	154	600	91	177	25	5	19	95	8
91 NL	.301	148	565	84	170	32	7	29	116	4
92 NL	.300	144	513	69	154	40	1	16	73	12
93 NL	.283	132	491	82	139	27	2	14	73	2
94 AL	.329	110	389	73	128	24	2	13	80	5
95 AL	.302	123	454	85	137	27	3	16	92	0
Life	.302	1,393	5112	845	1543	300	42	205	881	57
3 AVE	.305	142	517	93	158	30	3	17	96	3

ROYCE CLAYTON

Position: Shortstop
Team: San Francisco Giants
Born: Jan. 2, 1970 Burbank, CA
Height: 6' **Weight:** 175 lbs.
Bats: right **Throws:** right
Acquired: First-round pick in 6/88 free-agent draft

Player Summary
Fantasy Value	$9 to $11
Card Value	6¢ to 10¢
Will	show good glove
Can't	cut whiff total
Expect	All-Star future
Don't Expect	home run crown

If Barry Larkin weren't in the National League, Clayton would be considered the heir apparent to Ozzie Smith as the NL's top shortstop. A burner whose speed gives him great range in the field, Clayton is especially adept at turning the double play. He has quick reactions, good hands, and a strong, accurate arm. His statistics suggest he makes many errors but that's because he reaches balls most others don't. Clayton also has more clout than many middle infielders. He had more than 30 extra-base hits last year. His weak point is impatience at the plate. He fanned about three times for every walk, denying himself a probable run at the league lead in stolen bases. Clayton topped 20 in each of the last two seasons and twice topped 30 in the minors. If he were on more, he'd steal more bases and score more runs, since his steals succeeded about 70 percent of the time last year. A fine bunter, Clayton should bunt for hits more often. Better contact would also give him value as a hit-and-run man.

Major League Batting Register
	BA	G	AB	R	H	2B	3B	HR	RBI	SB
91 NL	.115	9	26	0	3	1	0	0	2	0
92 NL	.224	98	321	31	72	7	4	4	24	8
93 NL	.282	153	549	54	155	21	5	6	70	11
94 NL	.236	108	385	38	91	14	6	3	30	23
95 NL	.244	138	509	56	124	29	3	5	58	24
Life	.249	506	1790	179	445	72	18	18	184	66
3 AVE	.254	153	555	57	141	24	6	5	59	23

CURRENT PLAYERS

ROGER CLEMENS

Position: Pitcher
Team: Boston Red Sox
Born: Aug. 4, 1962 Dayton, OH
Height: 6'4" **Weight:** 220 lbs.
Bats: right **Throws:** right
Acquired: First-round pick in 6/83 free-agent draft

Player Summary	
Fantasy Value	$14 to $17
Card Value	20¢ to 35¢
Will	seek comeback
Can't	avoid injuries
Expect	lower velocity
Don't Expect	fourth Cy Young

Clemens used to have the command and velocity that helped him capture three Cy Young Awards. Forced to use his breaking ball more often last summer, he complemented his fastball, forkball, and changeup with a circle change instead of a curveball. He also went through some on-the-job training in learning to mix pitches properly. Proof that his fastball had lost its hop came July 13, when the Rangers became the first team to rip him for four homers in one game. Idled for two months by a strained muscle in his right shoulder, he later suffered elbow swelling between appearances. The five-time All-Star, who led the league in ERA four times and strikeouts twice, did show signs of his old form.

Major League Pitching Register

	W	L	ERA	G	CG	IP	H	ER	BB	SO
84 AL	9	4	4.32	21	5	133.1	146	64	29	126
85 AL	7	5	3.29	15	3	98.1	83	36	37	74
86 AL	24	4	2.48	33	10	254.0	179	70	67	238
87 AL	20	9	2.97	36	18	281.2	248	93	83	256
88 AL	18	12	2.93	35	14	264.0	217	86	62	291
89 AL	17	11	3.13	35	8	253.1	215	88	93	230
90 AL	21	6	1.93	31	7	228.1	193	49	54	209
91 AL	18	10	2.62	35	13	271.1	219	79	65	241
92 AL	18	11	2.41	32	11	246.2	203	66	62	208
93 AL	11	14	4.46	29	2	191.2	175	95	67	160
94 AL	9	7	2.85	24	3	170.2	124	54	71	168
95 AL	10	5	4.18	23	0	140.0	141	65	60	132
Life	182	98	3.00	349	94	2533.1	2143	845	750	2333
3 AVE	12	10	3.73	30	2	196.2	169	81	78	182

BRAD CLONTZ

Position: Pitcher
Team: Atlanta Braves
Born: April 25, 1971 Stuart, VA
Height: 6'1" **Weight:** 180 lbs.
Bats: right **Throws:** right
Acquired: 10th-round pick in 6/92 free-agent draft

Player Summary	
Fantasy Value	$2 to $4
Card Value	6¢ to 10¢
Will	baffle batters
Can't	get all lefties
Expect	decent control
Don't Expect	many homers

Clontz could have been disappointed when teammate Greg Maddux was named NL Pitcher of the Month for July. A strong case could have been made for the sidearming rookie reliever. All Clontz did during the month was post a 6-0 record and 0.00 ERA over nine appearances. After a rocky start caused by nibbling and nit-picking, he resumed the fearless form he had shown as closer for Triple-A Richmond in 1994. Converting 41 of 44 opportunities (three of them in the playoffs) that year, he challenged the hitters, throwing his sinker-slider arsenal with the most pronounced submarine style since Dan Quisenberry's days in Kansas City. At his peak on July 15, Clontz fanned three of the five San Diego hitters he faced. Extremely tough on right-handed hitters, he was no pushover for lefties either. Hitting a 90-mph sinker thrown from down under is no picnic. A good control pitcher, he averaged about eight hits and seven strikeouts per nine innings for much of the season. The Virginia Tech product disposed of inherited runners, kept the ball in the park, and maintained close watch over the running game.

Major League Pitching Register

	W	L	ERA	G	S	IP	H	ER	BB	SO
95 NL	8	1	3.65	59	4	69.0	71	28	22	55
Life	8	1	3.65	59	4	69.0	71	28	22	55

CURRENT PLAYERS

GREG COLBRUNN

Position: First base
Team: Florida Marlins
Born: July 26, 1969 Fontana, CA
Height: 6′ **Weight:** 190 lbs.
Bats: right **Throws:** right
Acquired: Claimed from Expos on waivers, 10/93

Player Summary	
Fantasy Value	$13 to $16
Card Value	5¢ to 8¢
Will	produce power
Can't	wait for his pitch
Expect	fine clutch job
Don't Expect	defensive awards

The power long expected of Colbrunn finally started to surface last summer. He got red-hot in July, when he hit seven home runs from the All-Star break to the end of the month. If he made better contact, he would become even more productive. But he fanned about three times per walk for much of the 1995 season, leaving him with a low on-base percentage. Usually more productive against left-handed pitchers, Colbrunn had the reverse situation last year. He thrives on a fastball diet and hits to all fields. One-third of all his hits netted extra bases, and he did some of his best hitting in clutch situations. A converted catcher, Colbrunn has been hampered by knee and elbow problems during his short career. Colbrunn's knee problems were so severe that his success as a basestealer last summer (seven of his first eight) was a complete surprise. His range, arm, and footwork at first are below-average. But there's no other place to hide him in the National League.

Major League Batting Register

	BA	G	AB	R	H	2B	3B	HR	RBI	SB
92 NL	.268	52	168	12	45	8	0	2	18	3
93 NL	.255	70	153	15	39	9	0	4	23	4
94 NL	.303	47	155	17	47	10	0	6	31	1
95 NL	.277	138	528	70	146	22	1	23	89	11
Life	.276	307	1004	114	277	49	1	35	161	19
3 AVE	.279	97	322	39	90	16	0	13	56	6

ALEX COLE

Position: Outfield
Team: Minnesota Twins
Born: Aug. 17, 1965 Fayetteville, NC
Height: 6′2″ **Weight:** 175 lbs.
Bats: left **Throws:** left
Acquired: Signed as a free agent, 2/94

Player Summary	
Fantasy Value	$5 to $7
Card Value	4¢ to 6¢
Will	let it fly
Can't	hit homers
Expect	some bunts
Don't Expect	good glove

A fleet leadoff type with little power, Cole seemed en route to his best season in 1995 when he broke his leg and dislocated his right ankle at the end of May. He draws enough walks to fatten his on-base percentage, and also drops bunts that he beats out for hits. A better hitter against right-handers, he slaps hits to all fields, and he likes one breaking balls. He could contend for league leadership in steals if he received enough playing time. After leading three minor leagues in swipes, he once stole 40 bases in 63 games for the Indians. But Cole's speed doesn't help him in the outfield. His overall defense is below average. Cole had more errors and a lower fielding percentage than any other center fielder in 1994. He's best used as a three-position backup, pinch hitter, pinch runner, and DH. Cole launched his pro career in the St. Louis system in 1985 but spent nearly six years in the minors before Cleveland gave him his first big-league chance.

Major League Batting Register

	BA	G	AB	R	H	2B	3B	HR	RBI	SB
90 AL	.300	63	227	43	68	5	4	0	13	40
91 AL	.295	122	387	58	114	17	3	0	21	27
92 AL	.206	41	97	11	20	1	0	0	5	9
92 NL	.278	64	205	33	57	3	7	0	10	7
93 NL	.256	126	348	50	89	9	4	0	24	30
94 AL	.296	105	345	68	102	15	5	4	23	29
95 AL	.342	28	79	10	27	3	2	1	14	1
Life	.283	549	1688	273	477	53	25	5	110	143
2 AVE	.279	137	417	73	116	15	6	3	28	35

VINCE COLEMAN

Position: Outfield
Team: Seattle Mariners
Born: Sept. 22, 1961 Jacksonville, FL
Height: 6' **Weight:** 170 lbs.
Bats: both **Throws:** right
Acquired: Traded by Royals for Jim Converse, 8/95

Player Summary
Fantasy Value	$14 to $17
Card Value	4¢ to 6¢
Will	zip around bases
Can't	clear wall often
Expect	bunting for hits
Don't Expect	dazzling defense

Coleman thinks he can still beat Kenny Lofton in the 50-yard dash. Although Coleman is no longer the blur who topped 100 steals in three seasons, he can still fly. He still holds the major-league record for most consecutive steals without getting caught (50). Catchers do nail him a bit more often these days, however. He has bounced around a bit in recent seasons but swung the bat better last year than he had since 1990. Managers in a *Baseball America* poll last year named him the AL's third fastest runner (behind Lofton and Tom Goodwin). Coleman would be much more effective if he reached base more often but that has been a problem. He fanned about twice as much as he walked for much of 1995—a ratio that made him an unsatisfactory leadoff man. Coleman's bunts for hits sweeten his average with infield singles. His speed doesn't compensate for his erratic defense.

Major League Batting Register

	BA	G	AB	R	H	2B	3B	HR	RBI	SB
85 NL	.267	151	636	107	170	20	10	1	40	110
86 NL	.232	154	600	94	139	13	8	0	29	107
87 NL	.289	151	623	121	180	14	10	3	43	109
88 NL	.260	153	616	77	160	20	10	3	38	81
89 NL	.254	145	563	94	143	21	9	2	28	65
90 NL	.292	124	497	73	145	18	9	6	39	77
91 NL	.255	72	278	45	71	7	5	1	17	37
92 NL	.275	71	229	37	63	11	1	2	21	24
93 NL	.279	92	373	64	104	14	8	2	25	38
94 AL	.240	104	438	61	105	14	12	2	33	50
95 AL	.288	115	455	66	131	23	6	5	29	42
Life	.266	1332	5308	839	1411	175	88	27	342	740
3 AVE	.266	123	501	75	133	20	11	3	35	52

DARNELL COLES

Position: First base; third base; outfield
Team: St. Louis Cardinals
Born: June 2, 1962 San Bernardino, CA
Height: 6'1" **Weight:** 185 lbs.
Bats: right **Throws:** right
Acquired: Signed as a free agent, 4/95

Player Summary
Fantasy Value	$0
Card Value	4¢ to 6¢
Will	show some power
Can't	hit for average
Expect	decent contact
Don't Expect	any regular job

Because he plays so many positions and contributes occasional power as a pinch hitter, Coles continues to hang around the big leagues. After flirting with the Mendoza Line for two seasons, however, his grip is beginning to feel a bit tenuous. Though he has a good arm, Coles is more of a liability than a solution at either the infield or outfield corners, his four "best" positions. He once made 73 errors in 136 games as a minor-league shortstop. Talk about bad hands! When Coles connects—infrequently these days—he has pop; approximately one-third of his hits produce extra bases. He's even hit three home runs in a game twice—amazing for someone with such limited playing time.

Major League Batting Register

	BA	G	AB	R	H	2B	3B	HR	RBI	SB
83 AL	.283	27	92	9	26	7	0	1	6	0
84 AL	.161	48	143	15	23	3	1	0	6	2
85 AL	.237	27	59	8	14	4	0	1	5	0
86 AL	.273	142	521	67	142	30	2	20	86	6
87 AL	.181	53	149	14	27	5	1	4	15	0
87 NL	.227	40	119	20	27	8	0	6	24	1
88 NL	.232	68	211	20	49	13	1	5	36	1
88 AL	.292	55	195	32	57	10	1	10	34	3
89 AL	.252	146	535	54	135	21	3	10	59	5
90 AL	.209	89	215	22	45	7	1	3	20	0
91 NL	.214	11	14	1	3	0	0	0	0	0
92 NL	.312	55	141	16	44	11	2	3	18	1
93 AL	.253	64	194	26	49	9	1	4	26	1
94 AL	.210	48	143	15	30	6	1	4	15	0
95 NL	.225	63	138	13	31	7	0	3	16	0
Life	.245	936	2869	332	702	141	14	74	366	20

CURRENT PLAYERS

DAVID CONE

Position: Pitcher
Team: New York Yankees
Born: Jan. 2, 1963 Kansas City, MO
Height: 6'1" **Weight:** 190 lbs.
Bats: left **Throws:** right
Acquired: Traded by Blue Jays for Marty Janzen, Jason Jarvis, and Mike Gordon, 7/95

Player Summary	
Fantasy Value	$20 to $25
Card Value	10¢ to 20¢
Will	seek Cy Young
Can't	prevent home runs
Expect	lots of Ks
Don't Expect	control lapses

Cone continues to rank as one of the most durable and productive starting pitchers in baseball. The 1994 AL Cy Young Award winner has made the All-Star team three times and led his league in Ks twice. According to managers polled by *Baseball America* last year, only Randy Johnson has a better slider. Cone throws a fastball with velocity and movement, a forkball, and a curve that he uses as a changeup. He averaged about three walks, seven strikeouts, and eight hits per nine innings for much of the season. Before Toronto dumped his salary, Cone came within two outs of a no-hitter against Texas on June 17. He is usually among league leaders in innings, strikeouts, and complete games. He dominates right-handed batters, but has problems with stopping runners.

Major League Pitching Register

	W	L	ERA	G	CG	IP	H	ER	BB	SO
86 AL	0	0	5.56	11	0	22.2	29	14	13	21
87 NL	5	6	3.71	21	1	99.1	87	41	44	68
88 NL	20	3	2.22	35	8	231.1	178	57	80	213
89 NL	14	8	3.52	34	7	219.2	183	86	74	190
90 NL	14	10	3.23	31	6	211.2	177	76	65	233
91 NL	14	14	3.29	34	5	232.2	204	85	73	241
92 NL	13	7	2.88	27	7	196.2	162	63	82	214
92 AL	4	3	2.55	8	0	53.0	39	15	29	47
93 A	11	14	3.33	34	6	254.0	205	94	114	191
94 AL	16	5	2.94	23	4	171.2	130	56	54	132
95 AL	18	8	3.57	30	6	229.1	195	91	88	191
Life	129	78	3.17	288	50	1922.0	1589	678	716	1741
3 AVE	18	10	3.29	33	6	251.1	203	92	96	197

JEFF CONINE

Position: Outfield; first base
Team: Florida Marlins
Born: June 27, 1966 Tacoma, WA
Height: 6'1" **Weight:** 220 lbs.
Bats: right **Throws:** right
Acquired: First-round pick from Royals in 11/92 expansion draft

Player Summary	
Fantasy Value	$25 to $30
Card Value	6¢ to 10¢
Will	produce power
Can't	steal much anymore
Expect	high on-base mark
Don't Expect	tremendous defense

During his days at UCLA, Conine was a pitcher. He has since proven that he can swing the bat. In fact, his one swing in the 1995 All-Star Game resulted in a game-winning homer and All-Star MVP honors. An all-fields hitter with power and patience, he has improved in each of his three seasons with the Marlins. He walks often enough to compile a high on-base average, murders left-handed pitching, and gets extra bases on more than one-third of his hits. Although he topped 20 steals in each of his first three pro seasons, Conine doesn't run much anymore. But he's a world-class racquetball player who moves well enough to play left field. He has fine instincts and good hands, plus an accurate though not powerful throwing arm. Usually a durable performer, Conine spent two 10-day stints on the sidelines last year with a sore hamstring and strained shoulder. The day he returned from the shoulder ailment, he hit a three-run, game-winning homer against Mets' rookie Bill Pulsipher.

Major League Batting Register

	BA	G	AB	R	H	2B	3B	HR	RBI	SB
90 AL	.250	9	20	3	5	2	0	0	2	0
92 AL	.253	28	91	10	23	5	2	0	9	0
93 NL	.292	162	595	75	174	24	3	12	79	2
94 NL	.319	115	451	60	144	27	6	18	82	1
95 NL	.302	133	483	72	146	26	2	25	105	2
Life	.300	447	1640	220	492	84	13	55	277	5
3 AVE	.305	158	591	80	180	30	5	22	104	2

CURRENT PLAYERS

STEVE COOKE

Position: Pitcher
Team: Pittsburgh Pirates
Born: Jan. 14, 1970 Kanai, HI
Height: 6'6" **Weight:** 220 lbs.
Bats: right **Throws:** left
Acquired: 35th-round pick in 6/89 free-agent draft

Player Summary
Fantasy Value $0
Card Value .... 6¢ to 10¢
Will .... seek starting job
Can't .... live off memories
Expect .... plague of gophers
Don't Expect .... pinpoint control

Cooke is still trying to recapture the rookie form he showed with the 1993 Pirates. That year he made 32 starts, splitting 20 decisions for a bad ballclub, while topping 200 innings and maintaining a strikeout-to-walk ratio of better than 2-to-1. The Hawaiian lefty slipped badly in '94, however, when he was often victimized by the long ball, and spent much of last year on the shelf with left shoulder problems. Although he throws a sinking fastball, Cooke coaxes most batters to hit the ball in the air rather than on the ground. When the sinker doesn't sink, the results often stink. His other pitches—a changeup, a fast curve, and a slow curve—aren't exceptional. Cooke helps his own cause with his bunting and hitting skills; he even shows occasional alley power. His pickoff move still needs work, but he's adequate in the field otherwise. Even if he proves healthy, the Southern Idaho product will need to show improvement in many areas to reclaim his rotation spot.

Major League Pitching Register

	W	L	ERA	G	CG	IP	H	ER	BB	SO
92 NL	2	0	3.52	11	0	23.0	22	9	4	10
93 NL	10	10	3.89	32	3	210.2	207	91	59	132
94 NL	4	11	5.02	25	2	134.1	157	75	46	74
Life	16	21	4.28	68	5	368.0	386	175	109	216

SCOTT COOPER

Position: Third base
Team: St. Louis Cardinals
Born: Oct. 13, 1967 St. Louis, MO
Height: 6'3" **Weight:** 205 lbs.
Bats: left **Throws:** right
Acquired: Traded by Red Sox with Cory Bailey and a player to be named later for Mark Whiten and Rheal Cormier, 4/95

Player Summary
Fantasy Value .... $5 to $7
Card Value .... 5¢ to 8¢
Will .... try for comeback
Can't .... hit lefties
Expect .... good eye
Don't Expect .... homer barrage

After making the AL All-Star Team two years in a row, Cooper caught the hitting malaise that swallowed St. Louis last summer. A .164 July plunged his average from .308 on May 20 to about .230 by August. He proved so unsatisfactory against left-handers that he wound up sharing time at third with the right-handed hitting Darnell Coles. The numbers were embarrassing for Cooper, a St. Louis native. His only salvation was an ability to get walks, swelling his on-base percentage about 100 points above his batting average. He fanned too frequently for a man who hits mostly singles. His power is seemingly vanishing; perhaps he hasn't fully healed from the arthroscopic shoulder surgery he underwent during the winter of 1994-95. Cooper has led various minor leagues in chances, putouts, and assists. The owner of a strong but inaccurate throwing arm, he has mediocre range.

Major League Batting Register

	BA	G	AB	R	H	2B	3B	HR	RBI	SB
90 AL	.000	2	1	0	0	0	0	0	0	0
91 AL	.457	14	35	6	16	4	2	0	7	0
92 AL	.276	123	337	34	93	21	0	5	33	1
93 AL	.279	156	526	67	147	29	3	9	63	5
94 AL	.282	104	369	49	104	16	4	13	53	0
95 NL	.230	118	374	29	86	18	2	3	40	0
Life	.272	517	1642	185	446	88	11	30	196	6
3 AVE	.266	145	489	56	130	24	4	10	61	2

CURRENT PLAYERS

JOEY CORA

Position: Second base
Team: Seattle Mariners
Born: May 14, 1965 Caguas, PR
Height: 5'8" **Weight:** 155 lbs.
Bats: both **Throws:** right
Acquired: Signed as a free agent, 4/95

Player Summary
Fantasy Value	$6 to $8
Card Value	4¢ to 6¢
Will	make good contact
Can't	hit long ball
Expect	sacrifices
Don't Expect	sterling fielding

Big things sometimes come in small packages. Though not a power hitter, Cora is a solid contact hitter best-suited to hitting at the top of the order. He hits mostly singles, sweetening his average with bunts and infield rollers. He is also a capable basestealer, though he's never duplicated in the majors the 40-steal season that led the Pacific Coast League in 1989. The switch-hitting infielder slams left-handed pitching but is no easy out against right-handers. He walks about as much as he fans, though he really doesn't do much of either. Cora's value would jump if he bunted more often. In 1993, he led the American League with 19 sacrifice bunts and 48 bunts in play. He is a spray hitter who uses all fields. The Vanderbilt product has quick reactions, good hands, an adequate throwing arm, and moves well to his right. But he makes more boots than the typical second baseman and is not a strong fielder.

Major League Batting Register
	BA	G	AB	R	H	2B	3B	HR	RBI	SB
87 NL	.237	77	241	23	57	7	2	0	13	15
89 NL	.316	12	19	5	6	1	0	0	1	1
90 NL	.270	51	100	12	27	3	0	0	2	8
91 AL	.241	100	228	37	55	2	3	0	18	11
92 AL	.246	68	122	27	30	7	1	0	9	10
93 AL	.268	153	579	95	155	15	13	2	51	20
94 AL	.276	90	312	55	86	13	4	2	30	8
95 AL	.297	120	427	64	127	19	2	3	39	18
Life	.268	671	2028	318	543	67	25	7	163	91
3 AVE	.280	138	500	81	140	18	7	3	46	17

WIL CORDERO

Position: Shortstop
Team: Montreal Expos
Born: Oct. 3, 1971 Mayaguez, PR
Height: 6'2" **Weight:** 185 lbs.
Bats: right **Throws:** right
Acquired: Signed as a free agent, 5/88

Player Summary
Fantasy Value	$10 to $13
Card Value	8¢ to 15¢
Will	star with bat
Can't	target throws
Expect	two-base hits
Don't Expect	great defense

Like Jose Offerman, Cordero is a better hitter than his team expected but less of a fielder than advertised. For much of the 1995 season, he batted around .300 against both righties and lefties, drove the ball to all fields, and netted extra bases on about a third of his hits. He has topped 30 doubles three years in a row and has the power to clear the fences on occasion. Cordero loves inside fastballs and first-pitch mistakes, but he's become increasingly more selective in recent seasons. He still fanned about twice for every walk, but showed enough patience to fashion an on-base mark about 50 points higher than his batting average. A double-digit basestealer, Cordero is not thrown out often. In the field, his reactions, range, and hands are fine, but his strong arm is not always accurate. He has a penchant for making spectacular plays but booting the easy ones. Cordero has seen some big-league service at second, third, and the outfield—positions that may be in his future.

Major League Batting Register
	BA	G	AB	R	H	2B	3B	HR	RBI	SB
92 NL	.302	45	126	17	38	4	1	2	8	0
93 NL	.248	138	475	56	118	32	2	10	58	12
94 NL	.294	110	415	65	122	30	3	15	63	16
95 NL	.286	131	514	64	147	35	2	10	49	9
Life	.278	424	1530	202	425	101	8	37	178	37
3 AVE	.278	147	546	73	152	38	3	14	67	15

CURRENT PLAYERS

MARTY CORDOVA

Position: Outfield
Team: Minnesota Twins
Born: July 10, 1969 Las Vegas, NV
Height: 6'2" **Weight:** 200 lbs.
Bats: right **Throws:** right
Acquired: 10th-round selection in 6/89 free-agent draft

Player Summary	
Fantasy Value	$16 to $19
Card Value	15¢ to 25¢
Will	hit the long ball
Can't	show good glove
Expect	some speed
Don't Expect	weak arm

If not for serious wrist and shoulder injuries in the minors, Cordova might have reached the majors before 1995. But the timing of the former UNLV standout couldn't have been better, because he arrived just as the Twins were frantically searching for a successor to veteran outfielder Shane Mack. Ready, willing, and able, Cordova became the Minnesota left fielder, adding power, speed, and defense to the lineup. He did so well that by the end of the season he was named the AL Rookie of the Year. Though he fanned about twice as much as he walked for much of the 1995 season, he compensated by collecting extra bases on about half of his hits. He teamed with Kirby Puckett and Pedro Munoz last summer to supply almost all of the club's home run power. Cordova has led various minor leagues in total bases, slugging, strikeouts, home runs, RBI, and fielding percentage. He reached double-digits in steals four straight years. He also reached double-digits in outfield assists last year. Despite his speed and strong throwing arm, Cordova is not considered a good outfielder. He might eventually move to first.

Major League Batting Register

	BA	G	AB	R	H	2B	3B	HR	RBI	SB
95 AL	.277	137	512	81	142	27	4	24	84	20
Life	.277	137	512	81	142	27	4	24	84	20

RHEAL CORMIER

Position: Pitcher
Team: Boston Red Sox
Born: April 23, 1967 Moncton, New Brunswick, Canada
Height: 5'10" **Weight:** 185 lbs.
Bats: left **Throws:** left
Acquired: Traded by Cardinals with Mark Whiten for Scott Cooper, Cory Bailey, and a player to be named later, 4/95

Player Summary	
Fantasy Value	$2 to $4
Card Value	4¢ to 6¢
Will	join rotation
Can't	avoid gophers
Expect	great control
Don't Expect	more injuries

Control is Cormier's biggest asset. For much of the 1995 season, he averaged about two walks per game, allowing him to maintain a strikeout-to-walk ratio of better than 2-to-1. A member of the 1988 Canadian Olympic team, Cormier was a career starter before Boston placed him in the bullpen last spring. Although the results were encouraging, the Red Sox spotted him in the rotation in August. He rewarded them by winning his first two starts in the heat of the AL East title chase. His best pitch is a sharp-breaking slider, which he blends with a good changeup, a roundhouse curve, and a sinking fastball that doesn't always sink. When he gets his pitches up, Cormier is susceptible to the long ball. On the plus side, he dominated left-handed hitters, fielded his position well, and didn't hesitate to show off his fine pick-off move. As a reliever, he handled inherited runners well, stranding about 75 percent of them during much of the year.

Major League Pitching Register

	W	L	ERA	G	CG	IP	H	ER	BB	SO
91 NL	4	5	4.12	11	2	67.2	74	31	8	38
92 NL	10	10	3.68	31	3	186.0	194	76	33	117
93 NL	7	6	4.33	38	1	145.1	163	70	27	75
94 NL	3	2	5.45	7	0	39.2	40	24	7	26
95 AL	7	5	4.07	48	0	115.0	131	52	31	69
Life	31	28	4.11	135	6	553.2	602	253	106	325
2 AVE	7	6	4.21	46	1	137.1	155	64	31	76

CURRENT PLAYERS

TRIPP CROMER

Position: Shortstop; second base
Team: St. Louis Cardinals
Born: Nov. 21, 1967 Lake City, SC
Height: 6'2" **Weight:** 165 lbs.
Bats: right **Throws:** right
Acquired: Third-round pick in 6/89 free-agent draft

Player Summary	
Fantasy Value	$1 to $3
Card Value	6¢ to 10¢
Will	show a little pop
Can't	learn strike zone
Expect	long cold spells
Don't Expect	Ozzie Smith

With Ozzie Smith idled by arthroscopic surgery on his throwing shoulder, Cromer got his first prolonged exposure to big-league pitching. Although he showed flashes of power, he also endured long stretches of futility, including a .177 batting average in July. His chief problem was impatience. He fanned five times more than he walked for much of the season. He doesn't have much speed either, so he can't bunt or count on infield hits to fatten his batting average. Although he had some defensive problems last year, Cromer had led two minor leagues in fielding percentage. He has quick reactions, good hands, and an ability to turn the double play. He'll never replace the acrobatic Wizard of Oz, but who could? If Cromer can raise his average against left-handed pitchers and learn the strike zone, he's likely to last a long time in the majors. Without those improvements, however, he probably will never amount to more than a utility infielder. Though signed as a shortstop, he spent some time last year at second base. Cromer is a product of South Carolina University.

Major League Batting Register

	BA	G	AB	R	H	2B	3B	HR	RBI	SB
93 NL	.087	10	23	1	2	0	0	0	0	0
94 NL	.000	2	0	1	0	0	0	0	0	0
95 NL	.226	105	345	36	78	19	0	5	18	0
Life	.217	117	368	38	80	19	0	5	18	0

JOHN CUMMINGS

Position: Pitcher
Team: Los Angeles Dodgers
Born: May 10, 1969 Torrance, CA
Height: 6'3" **Weight:** 200 lbs.
Bats: left **Throws:** left
Acquired: Signed as a free agent, 4/95

Player Summary	
Fantasy Value	$1
Card Value	4¢ to 6¢
Will	retain relief role
Can't	show much velocity
Expect	stranded runners
Don't Expect	control lapses

Before Mark Guthrie arrived in the Kevin Tapani trade, Cummings was the lone left-hander on the Dodger pitching staff. Used exclusively in relief for the first time in a pro career that began in 1990, he made the most of this opportunity. Though used only sporadically, he held opposing hitters under the Mendoza Line for much of the season, kept the ball in the park, and prospered against teams whose lineups lean to the left. He blends a big-breaking curveball with a high-80s fastball, a changeup, and a slider. Although he once won a strikeout crown in the minors, Cummings has become a finesse pitcher who changes speeds and relies on proper pitch location. An over-the-top control artist who uses the upper half of the strike zone, he stranded 10 of the first 11 runners he inherited last year before falling off. Part of the reason was an ability to keep runners close. He is also a good fielder. The USC product seems to have found his niche as a quality set-up pitcher; expect to see him used more often this summer.

Major League Pitching Register

	W	L	ERA	G	S	IP	H	ER	BB	SO
93 AL	0	6	6.02	10	0	46.1	59	31	16	19
94 AL	2	4	5.63	17	0	64.0	66	40	37	33
95 AL	0	0	11.81	4	0	5.1	8	7	7	4
95 NL	3	1	3.00	35	0	39.0	38	13	10	21
Life	5	11	5.30	66	0	154.2	171	91	70	77
2 AVE	3	3	5.07	34	0	70.1	72	39	36	37

CURRENT PLAYERS

CHAD CURTIS

Position: Outfield
Team: Detroit Tigers
Born: Nov. 6, 1968 Marion, IN
Height: 5'10" **Weight:** 175 lbs.
Bats: right **Throws:** right
Acquired: Traded by Angels for Tony Phillips, 4/95

Player Summary
Fantasy Value	$19 to $22
Card Value	5¢ to 8¢
Will	score runs often
Can't	hit all righties
Expect	surprising power
Don't Expect	deadbeat defense

Seldom has a trade helped both parties so much. Tony Phillips gave the Angels veteran spark, while Curtis gave the Tigers youth, speed, and great defense in center field. He also produced the most power of his four-year career following a winter of workouts. The first Tiger to top 20 steals since Milt Cuyler in 1991, Curtis is among the handful of leadoff men whose bats are strong enough to bat third if needed. He pounds left-handed pitching, walks often enough to maintain a high on-base percentage, and nets extra bases on about one-third of his hits. He also fattens his average with bunts and infield hits. The sharp improvement in his offensive game moved Curtis toward the top of the AL in runs scored. An aggressive runner who is nailed too frequently on the bases, he has the range to make spectacular plays in the outfield. His positioning is sometimes questionable. He has quick reactions and quicker feet to overcome some problems, however. Curtis led the American League with 16 assists in 1992.

Major League Batting Register

	BA	G	AB	R	H	2B	3B	HR	RBI	SB
92 AL	.259	139	441	59	114	16	2	10	46	43
93 AL	.285	152	583	94	166	25	3	6	59	48
94 AL	.256	114	453	67	116	23	4	11	50	25
95 AL	.268	144	586	96	157	29	3	21	67	27
Life	.268	549	2063	316	553	93	12	48	222	143
3 AVE	.269	158	627	99	169	30	4	15	68	38

MILT CUYLER

Position: Outfield
Team: Detroit Tigers
Born: Oct. 7, 1968 Macon, GA
Height: 5'10" **Weight:** 175 lbs.
Bats: both **Throws:** right
Acquired: Second-round pick in 6/86 free-agent draft

Player Summary
Fantasy Value	$1
Card Value	4¢ to 6¢
Will	boost defense
Can't	show patience
Expect	dynamic speed
Don't Expect	the long ball

During his days in the minor leagues, Cuyler was perfectly willing to wait for walks, then use his blinding speed to advance around the bases. Since reaching the majors, however, his patience has evaporated. Last year, he compiled about a 2-1 strikeout-to-walk ratio. Since he rarely makes contact from either side, he needs walks and bunts to boost his on-base percentage to acceptable levels. After all, he can't steal first base. When his patience prevailed in the minors, Cuyler produced a pair of 50-steal seasons. One of them included a league-high 100 runs scored. To make maximum mileage out of his speed, he also has to avoid the knee problems that have plagued him in the past. In the outfield, he has good reactions, terrific range, and the ability to outrace anything in his vicinity. Because he doesn't have a strong arm, left field is his best position. The former center fielder spent time there last summer after the Tigers acquired Chad Curtis.

Major League Batting Register

	BA	G	AB	R	H	2B	3B	HR	RBI	SB
90 AL	.255	19	51	8	13	3	1	0	8	1
91 AL	.257	154	475	77	122	15	7	3	33	41
92 AL	.241	89	291	39	70	11	1	3	28	8
93 AL	.213	82	249	46	53	11	7	0	19	13
94 AL	.241	48	116	20	28	3	1	1	11	5
95 AL	.205	41	88	15	18	1	4	0	5	2
Life	.239	433	1270	205	304	44	21	7	104	70

CURRENT PLAYERS

RON DARLING

Position: Pitcher
Team: Oakland Athletics
Born: Aug. 19, 1960 Honolulu, HI
Height: 6'3" **Weight:** 195 lbs.
Bats: right **Throws:** right
Acquired: Traded by Expos for Matt Grott and Russell Cormier, 7/91

Player Summary
Fantasy Value	$0
Card Value	4¢ to 6¢
Will	seek to keep job
Can't	keep ball in park
Expect	many ground balls
Don't Expect	pinpoint control

No longer the darling of the starting rotation, this veteran is just a shadow of the man who reached double-digit victories eight times. Darling is a power pitcher unable to make a smooth transition to a finesse style. He still banks heavily on his familiar fastball-forkball combination, but he can't come up with the velocity or location he once used. He also throws a cut fastball, a changeup, and a curveball. When he's on, he gets ground-ball outs. Too often, however, his pitches have been too far out of the strike zone—or too much in the middle. When that happens, hitters tee off, sending the ball over distant fences. Darling yielded almost 11 hits per nine innings and had trouble with gopher balls. Left-handed hitters owned him.

Major League Pitching Register
	W	L	ERA	G	CG	IP	H	ER	BB	SO
83 NL	1	3	2.80	5	1	35.1	31	11	17	23
84 NL	12	9	3.81	33	2	205.2	179	87	104	136
85 NL	16	6	2.90	36	4	248.0	214	80	114	167
86 NL	15	6	2.81	34	4	237.0	203	74	81	184
87 NL	12	8	4.29	32	2	207.2	183	99	96	167
88 NL	17	9	3.25	34	7	240.2	218	87	60	161
89 NL	14	14	3.52	33	4	217.1	214	85	70	153
90 NL	7	9	4.50	33	1	126.0	135	63	44	99
91 NL	5	8	4.37	20	0	119.1	121	58	33	69
91 AL	3	7	4.08	12	0	75.0	64	34	38	60
92 AL	15	10	3.66	33	4	206.1	198	84	72	99
93 AL	5	9	5.16	31	3	178.0	198	102	72	95
94 AL	10	11	4.50	25	4	160.0	162	80	59	108
95 AL	4	7	6.23	21	1	104.0	124	72	46	69
Life	136	116	3.87	382	37	2360.1	2244	1016	906	1590
3 AVE	8	11	5.11	30	3	173.0	189	99	69	108

DANNY DARWIN

Position: Pitcher
Team: Texas Rangers
Born: Oct. 25, 1955 Bonham, TX
Height: 6'3" **Weight:** 195 lbs.
Bats: right **Throws:** right
Acquired: Signed as a free agent, 8/95

Player Summary
Fantasy Value	$0
Card Value	4¢ to 6¢
Will	seek another year
Can't	prevent gophers
Expect	sinkers
Don't Expect	low ERA

Just when he thought his career was over, Darwin resurfaced with the Rangers during the dog days of August. Desperate for a warm body to stick into an injury-riddled rotation, Texas took a flyer on the former ERA king. While splitting his first four decisions, Darwin showed flashes of his old form. But that didn't last. A finesse pitcher with good control, he has difficulty with left-handed batters. When his sinker doesn't sink, it often disappears over the fence. Darwin probably should place more stock in his slider, curveball, and forkball. Recent injuries (back, rib cage) and age have taken a toll.

Major League Pitching Register
	W	L	ERA	G	CG	IP	H	ER	BB	SO
78 AL	1	0	4.15	3	0	8.2	11	4	1	8
79 AL	4	4	4.04	20	1	78.0	50	35	30	58
80 AL	13	4	2.63	53	0	109.2	98	32	50	104
81 AL	9	9	3.64	22	6	146.0	115	59	57	98
82 AL	10	8	3.44	56	0	89.0	95	34	37	61
83 AL	8	13	3.49	28	9	183.0	175	71	62	92
84 AL	8	12	3.94	35	5	223.2	249	98	54	123
85 AL	8	18	3.80	39	11	217.2	212	92	65	125
86 AL	6	8	3.52	27	5	130.1	120	51	35	80
86 NL	5	2	2.32	12	1	54.1	50	14	9	40
87 NL	9	10	3.59	33	3	195.2	184	78	69	134
88 NL	8	13	3.84	44	3	192.0	189	82	48	129
89 NL	11	4	2.36	68	0	122.0	92	32	33	104
90 NL	11	4	2.21	48	3	162.2	136	40	31	109
91 AL	3	6	5.16	12	0	68.0	71	39	15	42
92 AL	9	9	3.96	51	2	161.1	159	71	53	124
93 AL	15	11	3.26	34	2	229.1	196	83	49	130
94 AL	7	5	6.30	13	0	75.2	101	53	24	54
95 AL	3	10	7.45	20	1	99.0	131	82	31	58
Life	148	150	3.71	618	52	2546.0	2434	1050	753	1673
3 AVE	9	10	5.03	25	1	149.1	162	83	39	90

CURRENT PLAYERS

DARREN DAULTON

Position: Catcher
Team: Philadelphia Phillies
Born: Jan. 3, 1962 Arkansas City, KS
Height: 6'2" **Weight:** 190 lbs.
Bats: left **Throws:** right
Acquired: 25th-round pick in 6/80 free-agent draft

Player Summary
Fantasy Value	$12 to $15
Card Value	8¢ to 15¢
Will	join NL All-Stars
Can't	run much anymore
Expect	more power
Don't Expect	poor on-base mark

Though Daulton didn't supply his usual power last summer, he didn't compromise his reputation as one of baseball's most patient hitters. He walked as much as he fanned, allowing him to compile an on-base percentage 100 points higher than his batting average. Batting from an open stance, he hits to all fields against right-handers but tries to pull lefties or take them up the middle. The three-time All-Star is usually more successful against righties. In 1992, Daulton led the NL in RBI. But he's also had eight knee operations that, as a result, have limited his mobility. No matter, Daulton's overall defense is so good that talk of moving him to first base was shelved. A skilled handler of pitchers, Daulton is particularly adept at preventing wild pitches and blocking the plate. His throwing arm is strong.

Major League Batting Register
	BA	G	AB	R	H	2B	3B	HR	RBI	SB
83 NL	.333	2	3	1	1	0	0	0	0	0
85 NL	.204	36	103	14	21	3	1	4	11	3
86 NL	.225	49	138	18	31	4	0	8	21	2
87 NL	.194	53	129	10	25	6	0	3	13	0
88 NL	.208	58	144	13	30	6	0	1	12	2
89 NL	.201	131	368	29	74	12	2	8	44	2
90 NL	.268	143	459	62	123	30	1	12	57	7
91 NL	.196	89	285	36	56	12	0	12	42	5
92 NL	.270	145	485	80	131	32	5	27	109	11
93 NL	.257	147	510	90	131	35	4	24	105	5
94 NL	.300	69	257	43	77	17	1	15	56	4
95 NL	.249	98	342	44	85	19	3	9	55	3
Life	.244	1020	3223	440	785	176	17	123	525	44
3 AVE	.267	118	419	67	112	27	3	18	82	5

CHILI DAVIS

Position: Designated hitter
Team: California Angels
Born: Jan. 17, 1960 Kingston, Jamaica
Height: 6'3" **Weight:** 210 lbs.
Bats: both **Throws:** right
Acquired: Signed as a free agent, 12/92

Player Summary
Fantasy Value	$12 to $15
Card Value	8¢ to 15¢
Will	swing big bat
Can't	play the field
Expect	power
Don't Expect	basestealing

Contrary to popular opinion, it is possible to teach an old dog new tricks. Davis showed last summer, his 15th in the majors, that he could put into practice what California batting coach Rod Carew had been preaching: show patience and make contact. Walking more often than he fanned for the first time as a pro, Davis also produced the best batting and on-base averages of his career. Davis has come a long way from the days when he routinely fanned 100 times. Equally effective against righties and lefties, he's a low-fastball hitter who loves late-inning pressure situations. Although Davis once stole 40 bases in the minors, advancing age and aching knees have taken away his running game. He rarely bunts, works the hit-and-run, or returns to his original position as an outfielder.

Major League Batting Register
	BA	G	AB	R	H	2B	3B	HR	RBI	SB
81 NL	.133	8	15	1	2	0	0	0	0	2
82 NL	.261	154	641	86	167	27	6	19	76	24
83 NL	.233	137	486	54	113	21	2	11	59	10
84 NL	.315	137	499	87	157	21	6	21	81	12
85 NL	.270	136	481	53	130	25	2	13	56	15
86 NL	.278	153	526	71	146	28	3	13	70	16
87 NL	.250	149	500	80	125	22	1	24	76	16
88 AL	.268	158	600	81	161	29	3	21	93	9
89 AL	.271	154	560	81	152	24	1	22	90	3
90 AL	.265	113	412	58	109	17	1	12	58	1
91 AL	.277	153	534	84	148	34	1	29	93	5
92 AL	.288	138	444	63	128	27	2	12	66	4
93 AL	.243	153	573	74	139	32	0	27	112	4
94 AL	.311	108	392	72	122	18	1	26	84	3
95 AL	.318	119	424	81	135	23	0	20	86	3
Life	.273	1970	7087	1026	1934	348	29	270	1100	127
3 AVE	.289	146	534	89	154	28	0	29	109	4

83

CURRENT PLAYERS

RUSS DAVIS

Position: Third base; first base
Team: Seattle Mariners
Born: Sept. 13, 1969 Birmingham, AL
Height: 6' **Weight:** 170 lbs.
Bats: right **Throws:** right
Acquired: Traded by Yankees with Sterling Hitchcock for Jim Mecir, Jeff Nelson, and Tino Martinez, 12/950

Player Summary
Fantasy Value . . . . $6 to $8
Card Value . . . . 8¢ to 12¢
Will . . . . produce power
Can't . . . . hit righties hard
Expect . . . . good glove
Don't Expect . . . . patience at bat

Davis must feel like a yo-yo. For the past two seasons, he's been up and down more often than an elevator in the Empire State Building. A minor-league slugger with impressive credentials, he couldn't crack a Yankee lineup that had veteran stars Wade Boggs at third base and Don Mattingly at first. Signed as a third baseman out of Shelton State Junior College in his native Alabama, Davis also played some second during three of his minor-league seasons. He's best defensively at third, however. He has led various leagues in chances, putouts, assists, and fielding percentage. Best known for his power potential, Davis slammed 73 homers in the three minor-league years immediately preceding the 1995 campaign. He pounds left-handed pitching, but he needs to develop more discipline. Last year for the Yanks, Davis averaged about two strikeouts per walk. He was the Eastern League MVP in 1992, when he led the Double-A circuit in total bases and slugging percentage. He was twice runner-up for the International League's home run crown.

Major League Batting Register

	BA	G	AB	R	H	2B	3B	HR	RBI	SB
94 AL	.143	4	14	0	2	0	0	0	1	0
95 AL	.276	40	98	14	27	5	2	2	12	0
Life	.259	44	112	14	29	5	2	2	13	0

ANDRE DAWSON

Position: Outfield
Team: Florida Marlins
Born: July 10, 1954 Miami, FL
Height: 6'3" **Weight:** 195 lbs.
Bats: right **Throws:** right
Acquired: Signed as a free agent, 4/95

Player Summary
Fantasy Value . . . . $5 to $7
Card Value . . . . 10¢ to 20¢
Will . . . . still scare hurlers
Can't . . . . run like the old days
Expect . . . . a leader
Don't Expect . . . . knees

Dawson improved his on-base average by about 30 points in 1995 compared to 1994, and he proved a valuable veteran addition to the Marlins. He does play in pain. He needs to spend hours before every game stretching and after every game icing. But his example provides fine leadership for his teammates and foes alike. A certain Hall of Famer, Dawson was a great fielder as well as a fine hitter, but he has lost too much range to be much of an effective fielder anymore. Don't be surprised to see him in a front-office job or managing in a few years. Dawson is one of the most highly respected players in the game.

Major League Batting Register

	BA	G	AB	R	H	2B	3B	HR	RBI	SB
76 NL	.235	24	85	9	20	4	1	0	7	1
77 NL	.282	139	525	64	148	26	9	19	65	21
78 NL	.253	157	609	84	154	24	8	25	72	28
79 NL	.275	155	639	90	176	24	12	25	92	35
80 NL	.308	151	577	96	178	41	7	17	87	34
81 NL	.302	103	394	71	119	21	3	24	64	26
82 NL	.301	148	608	107	183	37	7	23	83	39
83 NL	.299	159	633	104	189	36	10	32	113	25
84 NL	.248	138	533	73	132	23	6	17	86	13
85 NL	.255	139	529	65	135	27	2	23	91	13
86 NL	.284	130	496	65	141	32	2	20	78	18
87 NL	.287	153	621	90	178	24	2	49	137	11
88 NL	.303	157	591	78	179	31	8	24	79	12
89 NL	.252	118	416	62	105	18	6	21	77	8
90 NL	.310	147	529	72	164	28	5	27	100	16
91 NL	.272	149	563	69	153	21	4	31	104	4
92 NL	.277	143	542	60	150	27	2	22	90	6
93 AL	.273	121	461	44	126	29	1	13	67	2
94 AL	.240	75	292	34	70	18	0	16	48	2
95 NL	.257	79	226	30	58	10	3	8	37	0
Life	.279	2585	9869	1367	2758	501	98	436	1577	314
3 AVE	.257	105	376	42	97	22	1	15	59	2

CURRENT PLAYERS

STEVE DECKER

Position: Catcher
Team: Florida Marlins
Born: Oct. 25, 1965 Rock Island, IL
Height: 6'3" **Weight:** 205 lbs.
Bats: right **Throws:** right
Acquired: Second-round pick from Giants in 11/92 expansion draft

Player Summary	
Fantasy Value	$0
Card Value	4¢ to 6¢
Will	produce some power
Can't	avoid disabled list
Expect	strong throwing arm
Don't Expect	much speed

Injuries have delayed Decker's chance to capitalize on the power potential he displayed in the minors. He had back surgery in 1993 and a broken right arm in 1994. He even sprained his foot once while trying to duck an autograph seeker. Decker did manage to make a major impression, however, when he hit .390 for Triple-A Edmonton in '94. It was the highest average for a PCL player with at least 200 at bats since Dan Gladden's .397 in 1984. Signed by the Giants after leading Lewis & Clark State College to the NAIA World Series, Decker hit his first big-league homer in his second game. Before his 1990 promotion, he had thrown out 42 percent of the runners who attempted to steal against him in the Double-A Texas League. He is a patient hitter who's willing to wait out a walk. For much of last season, his on-base percentage was about 80 points higher than his batting average. Decker is more productive against left-handed pitchers. He was a fine fill-in when Charles Johnson was idled with a broken hand in August.

Major League Batting Register

	BA	G	AB	R	H	2B	3B	HR	RBI	SB
90 NL	.296	15	54	5	16	2	0	3	8	0
91 NL	.206	79	233	11	48	7	1	5	24	0
92 NL	.163	15	43	3	7	1	0	0	1	0
93 NL	.000	8	15	0	0	0	0	0	1	0
95 NL	.226	51	133	12	30	2	1	3	13	1
Life	.211	168	478	31	101	12	2	11	47	1

JOSE DeLEON

Position: Pitcher
Team: Montreal Expos
Born: Dec. 20, 1960 Rancho Viejo, Dominican Republic
Height: 6'3" **Weight:** 215 lbs.
Bats: right **Throws:** right
Acquired: Traded by White Sox for Jeff Shaw, 8/95

Player Summary	
Fantasy Value	$1 to $3
Card Value	4¢ to 6¢
Will	be tough to hit
Can't	always find plate
Expect	four good pitches
Don't Expect	a starter job

During his days as a starter, DeLeon topped 200 innings three times and 200 strikeouts twice. Although scouts raved at his stuff, he managed to lose with alarming frequency. Strictly a middle reliever these days, DeLeon no longer has to maintain the velocity on his fastball for six or seven innings. He still throws in the low 90s, but blends the heater with a slider, a forkball, and a changeup. All four are quality pitches. He doesn't have the luxury of location, however. Lefty hitters give him a hard time, and the long ball is a constant threat. He stranded a good percent of inherited runners and kept basestealers in check.

Major League Pitching Register

	W	L	ERA	G	S	IP	H	ER	BB	SO
83 NL	7	3	2.83	15	0	108.0	75	34	47	118
84 NL	7	13	3.74	30	0	192.1	147	80	92	153
85 NL	2	19	4.70	31	3	162.2	138	85	89	149
86 NL	3	8.27	9	1	16.1	17	15	17	11
86 AL	4	5	2.96	13	0	79.0	49	26	42	68
87 AL	11	12	4.02	33	0	206.0	177	92	97	153
88 NL	13	10	3.67	34	0	225.1	198	92	86	208
89 NL	16	12	3.05	36	0	244.2	173	83	80	201
90 NL	7	19	4.43	32	0	182.2	168	90	86	164
91 NL	5	9	2.71	28	0	162.2	144	49	61	118
92 NL	2	9	4.37	32	0	117.1	111	57	48	79
93 NL	3	0	3.26	24	0	47.0	39	17	27	34
93 AL	0	1	1.74	11	0	10.1	5	2	3	6
94 AL	3	2	3.36	42	2	67.0	48	25	31	67
95 AL	5	3	5.19	38	0	67.2	60	39	28	53
95 NL	0	1	7.56	7	0	8.1	7	7	7	12
Life	86	119	3.76	415	6	1897.1	1556	793	841	1594
3 AVE	4	2	4.02	48	1	79.1	62	35	38	69

CURRENT PLAYERS

CARLOS DELGADO

Position: First base; outfield
Team: Toronto Blue Jays
Born: June 25, 1972 Aguadilla, PR
Height: 6'3" **Weight:** 220 lbs.
Bats: left **Throws:** right
Acquired: Signed as a free agent, 10/88

Player Summary
Fantasy Value	$6 to $8
Card Value	10¢ to 20¢
Will	hit a ton
Can't	steal much
Expect	hot streaks
Don't Expect	strong arm

There's no question about it: Delgado's best position is batter. He spent his first five years in the minors as a catcher, opened the 1994 season as Toronto's left fielder, then spent last year learning to play first base at the Triple-A level. The lumbering left-handed hitter, a slightly smaller version of Cecil Fielder, is a perfect DH. In two seasons, he won consecutive minor-league MVP awards and totaled 55 homers and 202 RBI. He then connected in five of the first seven AL games he started. Though guilty of frequent strikeouts, Delgado also has unusual patience for a young slugger. During his second MVP campaign, he had more walks than strikeouts and as many bases on balls as RBI (102). A wrist hitter who's likely to give righties fits, Delgado has already hit the glass of the SkyDome's Windows restaurant. As a catcher, he led various minor leagues in chances, putouts, assists, and double plays, but he also led loops in passed balls and errors. His arm isn't the greatest, either. But this guy can really hit.

Major League Batting Register
	BA	G	AB	R	H	2B	3B	HR	RBI	SB
93 AL	.000	2	1	0	0	0	0	0	0	0
94 AL	.215	43	130	17	28	2	0	9	24	1
95 AL	.165	37	91	7	15	3	0	3	11	0
Life	.194	82	222	24	43	5	0	12	35	1

RICH DeLUCIA

Position: Pitcher
Team: St. Louis Cardinals
Born: Oct. 7, 1964 Reading, PA
Height: 6' **Weight:** 185 lbs.
Bats: right **Throws:** right
Acquired: Rule 5 draft pick from Orioles, 12/94

Player Summary
Fantasy Value	$2 to $4
Card Value	4¢ to 6¢
Will	remain in relief
Can't	always find plate
Expect	good K ratio
Don't Expect	rotation return

Before Seattle turned him into a reliever three years ago, DeLucia was used almost exclusively as a starter since turning pro in 1986. With St. Louis, he held hitters to a batting average befitting Mario Mendoza, but DeLucia occasionally succumbed to a lack of control. He averaged about four walks per nine innings, sabotaging ratios of more than seven strikeouts and less than seven hits over that same span. Most of the hits he gave up were singles—even though DeLucia yielded more fly balls than grounders. Capable of working often and delivering several innings at a time, he is a dependable middle reliever. He helps his own cause with excellent defense and a fine pickoff move. DeLucia is especially difficult for right-handed hitters. He had a career high in appearances last summer, when he was one of the busiest pitchers in the St. Louis bullpen. During his first pro year, the hard-throwing University of Tennessee product led the Northwest League in earned run average.

Major League Pitching Register
	W	L	ERA	G	S	IP	H	ER	BB	SO
90 AL	1	2	2.00	5	0	36.0	30	8	9	20
91 AL	12	13	5.09	32	0	182.0	176	103	78	98
92 AL	3	6	5.49	30	1	83.2	100	51	35	66
93 AL	3	6	4.64	30	0	42.2	46	22	23	48
94 NL	0	0	4.22	8	0	10.2	9	5	5	15
95 NL	8	7	3.39	56	0	82.1	63	31	36	76
Life	27	34	4.53	161	1	437.1	424	220	186	323
2 AVE	6	7	3.78	47	0	67.2	58	28	32	67

CURRENT PLAYERS

DELINO DeSHIELDS

Position: Second base
Team: Los Angeles Dodgers
Born: Jan. 15, 1969 Seaford, DE
Height: 6'1" **Weight:** 170 lbs.
Bats: left **Throws:** right
Acquired: Traded by Expos for Pedro Martinez, 11/93

Player Summary	
Fantasy Value	$12 to $15
Card Value	6¢ to 10¢
Will	hit comeback trail
Can't	reach fences
Expect	great speed
Don't Expect	Gold Gloves

Four times in his six-year career, DeShields has stolen at least 40 bases. It didn't happen last season, when the Villanova product was plagued by chronic pain near his left hip and thigh. Determined not to do further damage, he decided to return to full health before he returned to the lineup. The Dodgers disapproved, thinking he was placing himself ahead of the team. He is a patient hitter who knows a walk will give him a chance to run. DeShields led the league in most pitches seen per plate appearance in 1994. He's cut his once-alarming strikeout rate (151 to lead the NL in 1991), helping him put more balls into play. Not much of a power threat, DeShields sprays hits to all fields, though he usually takes lefties the opposite way. His on-base percentage was about 100 points higher than his batting average last year. He's a good percentage basestealer and a decent defensive player whose best asset is his incredible range. DeShields got four hits in his first major-league game.

Major League Batting Register

	BA	G	AB	R	H	2B	3B	HR	RBI	SB
90 NL	.289	129	499	69	144	28	6	4	45	42
91 NL	.238	151	563	83	134	15	4	10	51	56
92 NL	.292	135	530	82	155	19	8	7	56	46
93 NL	.295	123	481	75	142	17	7	2	29	43
94 NL	.250	89	320	51	80	11	3	2	33	27
95 NL	.256	127	425	66	109	18	3	8	37	39
Life	.271	754	2818	426	764	108	31	33	251	253
3 AVE	.268	130	470	74	126	18	5	5	39	42

MIKE DEVEREAUX

Position: Outfield
Team: Atlanta Braves
Born: April 10, 1963 Casper, WY
Height: 6' **Weight:** 191 lbs.
Bats: right **Throws:** right
Acquired: Traded by White Sox for Andre King, 8/95

Player Summary	
Fantasy Value	$2 to $4
Card Value	5¢ to 8¢
Will	swing strong stick
Can't	make strong throws
Expect	acrobatic defense
Don't Expect	100 RBI

Reports of Devereaux's demise were greatly exaggerated. One year after his batting average dwindled to a career low, he did a complete turnaround. Usually much better against southpaws, he batted equally well against lefties and righties for the White Sox last summer. He also made a significant reduction in a strikeout-to-walk ratio that had exceeded 3-to-1 in 1994. Showing more patience at the plate helped: Devereaux posted a healthy on-base percentage, reached more often, and stole more bases than he had in the previous two years combined. Devereaux didn't display the authority of his 24-homer, 107-RBI year in 1992, but he did get extra bases on about one-third of his hits. Known as a top center fielder in Baltimore, Devereaux was a right fielder for the White Sox and a fill-in for the Braves. The Arizona State product doesn't have a cannon but has great range.

Major League Batting Register

	BA	G	AB	R	H	2B	3B	HR	RBI	SB
87 NL	.222	19	54	7	12	3	0	0	4	3
88 NL	.116	30	43	4	5	1	0	0	2	0
89 AL	.266	122	391	55	104	14	3	8	46	22
90 AL	.240	108	367	48	88	18	1	12	49	13
91 AL	.260	149	608	82	158	27	10	19	59	16
92 AL	.276	156	653	76	180	29	11	24	107	10
93 AL	.250	131	527	72	132	31	3	14	75	3
94 AL	.203	85	301	35	61	8	2	9	33	1
95 AL	.306	92	333	48	102	21	1	10	55	6
95 NL	.255	29	55	7	14	3	0	1	8	2
Life	.257	921	3332	434	856	155	31	97	438	76
3 AVE	.251	129	463	61	116	23	2	13	64	4

CURRENT PLAYERS

ALEX DIAZ

Position: Outfield; infield
Team: Seattle Mariners
Born: Oct. 5, 1968 Brooklyn, NY
Height: 5'11" **Weight:** 180 lbs.
Bats: both **Throws:** right
Acquired: Claimed from Brewers on waivers, 10/94

Player Summary	
Fantasy Value	$1 to $3
Card Value	4¢ to 6¢
Will	serve as reserve
Can't	reach the fences
Expect	contact hitting
Don't Expect	good on-base mark

When Ken Griffey Jr. missed long stretches of 1995 with a fractured wrist, Diaz got most of the playing time in center field. The switch-hitting utility player acquitted himself well. A contact hitter who neither whiffs nor walks frequently, Diaz is a slap-and-run guy whose game revolves around his speed. Power is not his calling card. He twice topped 40 steals in the minors, and he showed last summer that he has not forgotten his roots. His stolen-base success rate didn't thrill anyone, however. Originally signed as a shortstop by the Mets, Diaz has played three infield and all outfield positions during his brief big-league career. Because his speed gives him great range, he is best in the outfield, where he also has a strong throwing arm. He is also useful as a pinch hitter and pinch runner. He was more productive against left-handed pitchers last season. Diaz has led various minor leagues in triples, stolen bases, and errors by a shortstop (an unbelievable 72 in 123 games).

Major League Batting Register

	BA	G	AB	R	H	2B	3B	HR	RBI	SB
92 AL	.111	22	9	5	1	0	0	0	1	3
93 AL	.319	32	69	9	22	2	0	0	1	5
94 AL	.251	79	187	17	47	5	7	1	17	5
95 AL	.248	103	270	44	67	14	0	3	27	18
Life	.256	236	535	75	137	21	7	4	46	31
2 AVE	.250	114	284	37	71	11	5	2	27	14

MARIO DIAZ

Position: Infield
Team: Florida Marlins
Born: Jan. 10, 1962 Humacao, PR
Height: 5'10" **Weight:** 160 lbs.
Bats: right **Throws:** right
Acquired: Signed as a free agent, 5/94

Player Summary	
Fantasy Value	$0
Card Value	4¢ to 6¢
Will	play anywhere
Can't	wait for walks
Expect	decent defense
Don't Expect	any power show

If Webster produced an illustrated dictionary, the face of Mario Diaz would be opposite the word "utility infielder." In a pro career that started in 1979, he's done everything but pitch and catch. He even spent the obligatory overtime in the minors—nearly nine years before catching his first breath of big-league air. A .259 career hitter before 1995, Diaz used to show more patience at the plate. But his at bats have become so few and far between that he's afraid to waste one. It's virtually impossible to walk Diaz, but he almost always puts the ball in play. Bunts and infield rollers fatten his average, though Diaz is not a speed merchant by any stretch of the imagination. He's never reached double-digit steals as a pro. Usually a terror against left-handers, Diaz disappointed in that department last season. He is a good opposite-field hitter. Diaz is competent though not spectacular in the field. He does not have a powerful throwing arm.

Major League Batting Register

	BA	G	AB	R	H	2B	3B	HR	RBI	SB
87 AL	.304	11	23	4	7	0	1	0	3	0
88 AL	.306	28	72	6	22	5	0	0	9	0
89 AL	.135	52	74	9	10	0	0	1	7	0
90 NL	.136	16	22	0	3	1	0	0	1	0
91 AL	.264	96	182	24	48	7	0	1	22	0
92 AL	.226	19	31	2	7	1	0	0	1	0
93 AL	.273	71	205	24	56	10	1	2	24	1
94 AL	.323	32	77	10	25	4	2	0	11	0
95 NL	.230	49	87	5	20	3	0	1	6	0
Life	.256	374	773	84	198	31	4	5	84	1

CURRENT PLAYERS

ROB DIBBLE

Position: Pitcher
Team: Milwaukee Brewers
Born: Jan. 24, 1964 Bridgeport, CT
Height: 6'4" **Weight:** 235 lbs.
Bats: left **Throws:** right
Acquired: Signed as a free agent, 7/95

Player Summary	
Fantasy Value	$0
Card Value	4¢ to 6¢
Will	seek old heat
Can't	find the plate
Expect	many strikeouts
Don't Expect	many hits

Wildness, shoulder problems, and an explosive temperament have reduced Dibble from All-Star closer to mop-up man. Released by the White Sox—a team that really needed relief help—Dibble hooked on with the Brewers. Milwaukee insisted that he polish his mechanics at their Triple-A club. It was quite a comedown for a man who once set a major-league record with a nine-inning average of 13.55 strikeouts (with the 1991 Reds). A fastball-slider pitcher who's extremely tough to hit, Dibble is his own worst enemy. More often than not, he has serious control problems, involving wild pitches as well as walks. Baserunners love his deliberate, high-kicking windup. He also has a follow-through that places him in poor position to anything—even bunts. He doesn't have the velocity that allowed him to rack up 100 strikeouts a year over four seasons. Now that he's two years removed from his 1994 shoulder surgery, Dibble may demonstrate some old skills.

Major League Pitching Register

	W	L	ERA	G	S	IP	H	ER	BB	SO
88 NL	1	1	1.82	37	0	59.1	43	12	21	59
89 NL	10	5	2.09	74	2	99.0	62	23	39	141
90 NL	8	3	1.74	68	11	98.0	62	19	34	136
91 NL	3	5	3.17	67	31	82.1	67	29	25	124
92 NL	3	5	3.07	63	25	70.1	48	24	31	110
93 NL	1	4	6.48	45	19	41.2	34	30	42	49
95 NL	1	2	7.18	31	1	26.1	16	21	46	26
Life	27	25	2.98	385	89	477.0	332	158	238	645

JERRY DiPOTO

Position: Pitcher
Team: New York Mets
Born: May 24, 1968 Jersey City, NJ
Height: 6'2" **Weight:** 200 lbs.
Bats: right **Throws:** right
Acquired: Traded by Indians with Paul Byrd, Dave Mlicki, and Jesus Azuaje for Jeromy Burnitz and Joe Roa, 11/94

Player Summary	
Fantasy Value	$1 to $3
Card Value	4¢ to 6¢
Will	get many calls
Can't	work as closer
Expect	grounders
Don't Expect	gopher trouble

A sinker-slider pitcher who answers frequent relief calls, DiPoto showed last summer that he had rebounded nicely from removal of a cancerous thyroid gland. In his first season with the Mets, he became the busiest member of the New York bullpen. For much of the season, he yielded less hits than innings, displayed decent but not razor-sharp control, and was especially adept at preventing the long ball. As a rookie in 1993, he did not allow a homer in 56⅓ innings. A starter during his minor-league days, DiPoto is durable when healthy. He made a combined 80 appearances between the Indians and Triple-A Charlotte in 1993. He averaged about five strikeouts per nine innings, and he stranded around 75 percent of the runners he inherited. He'd be more effective if his control were more reliable. He allowed about three and one-half walks per nine innings. DiPoto began his career at Watertown of the New York-Penn League in 1989. He reached the majors in '93, saving 11 games in 46 appearances.

Major League Pitching Register

	W	L	ERA	G	S	IP	H	ER	BB	SO
93 AL	4	4	2.40	46	11	56.1	57	15	30	41
94 AL	0	0	8.04	7	0	15.2	26	14	10	9
95 NL	4	6	3.78	58	2	78.2	77	33	29	49
Life	8	10	3.70	111	13	150.2	160	62	69	99
2 AVE	4	5	3.24	56	7	72.2	72	26	31	48

CURRENT PLAYERS

GARY DiSARCINA

Position: Shortstop
Team: California Angels
Born: Nov. 19, 1967 Malden, MA
Height: 6'1" **Weight:** 178 lbs.
Bats: right **Throws:** right
Acquired: Sixth-round pick in 6/88 free-agent draft

Player Summary	
Fantasy Value	$5 to $7
Card Value	5¢ to 8¢
Will	bang clutch hits
Can't	hit homers often
Expect	contact
Don't Expect	trouble in field

Score another one for Rod Carew. Before the lessons of the California hitting coach took root, DiSarcina had compiled a .242 batting average and hit nine home runs over three full seasons. But that was before Carew taught DiSarcina the importance of getting his hands through the hitting zone and not taking such a big stride. With quicker hands and added off-season muscle, DiSarcina reached new peaks in doubles, homers, extra-base hits, and batting average by midseason. He even made the All-Star team for the first time. A contact hitter with patience, he hits the ball where it is pitched. In 1995, he played through back problems but was disabled for the year on Aug. 3 after tearing a ligament in his left thumb. The Angels panicked, since the University of Massachusetts product had made only five errors all season. His exceptional range and strong, accurate arm have made DiSarcina one of baseball's premier defensive shortstops.

Major League Batting Register

	BA	G	AB	R	H	2B	3B	HR	RBI	SB
89 AL	.000	2	0	0	0	0	0	0	0	0
90 AL	.140	18	57	8	8	1	1	0	0	1
91 AL	.211	18	57	5	12	2	0	0	3	0
92 AL	.247	157	518	48	128	19	0	3	42	9
93 AL	.238	126	416	44	99	20	1	3	45	5
94 AL	.260	112	389	53	101	14	2	3	33	3
95 AL	.307	99	362	61	111	28	6	5	41	7
Life	.255	532	1799	219	459	84	10	14	164	25
3 AVE	.267	132	457	62	122	24	4	4	46	6

GLENN DISHMAN

Position: Pitcher
Team: San Diego Padres
Born: Nov. 5, 1970 Baltimore, MD
Height: 6'1" **Weight:** 195 lbs.
Bats: right **Throws:** left
Acquired: Signed as a nondrafted free agent, 6/93

Player Summary	
Fantasy Value	$3 to $5
Card Value	10¢ to 15¢
Will	quiet lefty bats
Can't	avoid gopher ball
Expect	terrific control
Don't Expect	return to minors

After topping the 1994 Double-A Texas League in strikeouts (with 165, 35 more than the runner-up), Dishman won six of nine Triple-A decisions last year while recording the best earned run average in the hitter-friendly Pacific Coast League. That prompted his promotion to the Padres, where he made his big-league debut on June 22 with a 3-2 loss to the Rockies. In each of his first three starts, he yielded three runs, including a solo home run in the third inning. Since Dishman wears No. 33, the numerologists had a field day. A control artist out of Texas Christian University, he relies on an outstanding changeup to set up his fastball. Extremely effective against left-handed hitters, he yielded about as many hits as innings for much of 1995. He showed that he can control the running game and has only occasional problems with the long ball. He split his first eight big-league decisions while joining Andy Ashby and Joey Hamilton as the workhorses of the San Diego staff. In both of his minor-league seasons, Dishman had about a 4-1 ratio of strikeouts to walks. He pitched a no-hitter in 1993.

Major League Pitching Register

	W	L	ERA	G	CG	IP	H	ER	BB	SO
95 NL	4	8	5.01	19	0	97.0	104	54	34	43
Life	4	8	5.01	19	0	97.0	104	54	34	43

CURRENT PLAYERS

JOHN DOHERTY

Position: Pitcher
Team: Detroit Tigers
Born: June 11, 1967 Bronx, NY
Height: 6'4" **Weight:** 190 lbs.
Bats: right **Throws:** right
Acquired: 19th-round pick in 6/89 free-agent draft

Player Summary	
Fantasy Value	$1 to $3
Card Value	4¢ to 6¢
Will	hope sinker sinks
Can't	stop all lefties
Expect	reliable control
Don't Expect	big whiffs

Doherty is still searching for his niche in the big leagues. He began his pro career as a closer, became a full-time starter four years later, then returned to a relief role in 1995. His reviews were mixed. A sinkerballer who needs grounders to survive, Doherty pitched so well during the first half of the season that teammates were upset when he was omitted from the All-Star roster. But the second half was such a debacle that his future remains uncertain. He has good control, allowing about three walks per nine innings, and he keeps the ball in the park. Playing half his games in hitter-friendly Tiger Stadium didn't help, but he also courted disaster when his sinker didn't sink. His other pitches—a curve, a slider, and a change—aren't as good. Doherty stranded about 50 percent of the runners he inherited last year, and he has difficulty with left-handed hitters. After two bad years in a row, the graduate of Concordia College in New York hopes to regain the winning form he showed in 1992 and 1993.

Major League Pitching Register

	W	L	ERA	G	S	IP	H	ER	BB	SO
92 AL	7	4	3.88	47	3	116.0	131	50	25	37
93 AL	14	11	4.44	32	0	184.2	205	91	48	63
94 AL	6	7	6.48	18	0	101.1	139	73	26	28
95 AL	5	9	5.10	48	6	113.0	130	64	37	46
Life	32	31	4.86	145	9	515.0	605	278	136	174
3 AVE	9	10	5.26	37	2	151.1	182	89	42	51

JIM DOUGHERTY

Position: Pitcher
Team: Houston Astros
Born: March 8, 1968 Brentwood, NY
Height: 6' **Weight:** 210 lbs.
Bats: right **Throws:** right
Acquired: 26th-round pick in 6/90 free-agent draft

Player Summary	
Fantasy Value	$1 to $3
Card Value	6¢ to 8¢
Will	stay in middle
Can't	close games
Expect	lefties to hit him
Don't Expect	many Ks

Dougherty was an important part of the Astro bullpen last year. When he appeared in 56 games as a rookie, it was the fifth straight year that he topped 50 games in his five years as a professional ballplayer. A sidearmer who uses finesse and a changeup, he is able to stop right-handed batters from beating him. He held righties to a .225 batting average last year. On the flip side, however, is his problems with lefties. Dougherty allowed left-handed hitters to knock him at a .425 clip. That led to him allowing more hits than innings. A closer in the minor leagues, Dougherty will not be anything more than a middle reliever until he learns to get a higher percentage of lefties out. He led the minors in total saves from 1991 to 1994. Dougherty led the Triple-A Pacific Coast League with 21 saves, going 5-4 with a 4.12 ERA. He also led the Double-A Texas League with 36 saves in 1993. A North Carolina product, Dougherty needs to cut down the number of free passes he allows, since he is not going to be a strikeout pitcher.

Major League Pitching Register

	W	L	ERA	G	S	IP	H	ER	BB	SO
95 NL	8	4	4.92	56	0	67.2	76	37	25	49
Life	8	4	4.92	56	0	67.2	76	37	25	49

CURRENT PLAYERS

DOUG DRABEK

Position: Pitcher
Team: Houston Astros
Born: July 25, 1962 Victoria, TX
Height: 6'1" **Weight:** 185 lbs.
Bats: right **Throws:** right
Acquired: Signed as a free agent, 12/92

Player Summary	
Fantasy Value	$13 to $16
Card Value	5¢ to 8¢
Will	thrive under pressure
Can't	muster old speed
Expect	some brilliance
Don't Expect	another Cy Young

Although he's one of the most durable starters in the majors, Drabek has never repeated the consistent excellence of his 1990 Cy Young Award season. Last year, he was either very good or very bad. His three-hitter blanked the Dodgers, 4-0, on his 33rd birthday, giving him his first shutout in more than a year. Five days later, he won his third straight start with a 7-1 win at San Diego. Drabek has good control of four pitches: a fastball, a slider, a changeup, and a curve. His location compensates for lack of velocity so well that he fanned about eight batters per nine innings through much of the year. He yielded about one hit per inning and kept the ball from leaving the park. He is equally effective against lefties and righties. One of baseball's better-hitting pitchers, he helps himself with the glove as well as the bat. He has both speed and savvy on the bases.

Major League Pitching Register

	W	L	ERA	G	CG	IP	H	ER	BB	SO
86 AL	7	8	4.10	27	0	131.2	126	60	50	76
87 NL	11	12	3.88	29	1	176.1	165	76	46	120
88 NL	15	7	3.08	33	3	219.1	194	75	50	127
89 NL	14	12	2.80	35	8	244.1	215	76	69	123
90 NL	22	6	2.76	33	9	231.1	190	71	56	131
91 NL	15	14	3.07	35	5	234.2	245	80	62	142
92 NL	15	11	2.77	34	10	256.2	218	79	54	177
93 NL	9	18	3.79	34	7	237.2	242	100	60	157
94 NL	12	6	2.84	23	6	164.2	132	52	45	121
95 NL	10	9	4.77	31	2	185.0	205	98	54	143
Life	130	103	3.32	314	51	2081.2	1932	767	546	1317
3 AVE	12	12	3.76	34	6	225.2	220	95	61	163

DARREN DREIFORT

Position: Pitcher
Team: Los Angeles Dodgers
Born: May 18, 1972 Wichita, KS
Height: 6'2" **Weight:** 205 lbs.
Bats: right **Throws:** right
Acquired: First-round pick in 6/93 free-agent draft

Player Summary	
Fantasy Value	$1 to $3
Card Value	8¢ to 12¢
Will	seek medical miracle
Can't	always throw strikes
Expect	good hitting ability
Don't Expect	immediate stardom

Dreifort won the Golden Spikes Award, given annually to the nation's best amateur. He also made the U.S. Olympic team, and he was a three-time All-American at Wichita State. Lately, however, Dreifort has spent more time mending his injuries than trying to add to his trophies. The star-crossed right-hander, drafted less than three years ago, has already encountered arm, shoulder, and elbow problems. He missed all of 1995 after March 14 surgery to replace a torn ligament in his right elbow. Should he return to full health, Dreifort may switch from short relief, where he had an unsuccessful 1994 trial, to the starting rotation. Strictly a starter in college, he had a 26-5 record, .318 batting average, and 25 homers in 314 at bats (he doubled as the team's designated hitter). His arsenal includes a rising fastball, a low-90s sinker with good movement, a late-breaking slider, and a slow curve. Dreifort decimates right-handed hitters, but needs to improve against lefties and show better overall control. He helps himself with strong defense as well as his bat. He hit an RBI pinch single in his first NL at bat.

Major League Pitching Register

	W	L	ERA	G	S	IP	H	ER	BB	SO
94 NL	0	5	6.21	27	6	29.0	45	20	15	22
Life	0	5	6.21	27	6	29.0	45	20	15	22

CURRENT PLAYERS

MARIANO DUNCAN

Position: Infield
Team: New York Yankees
Born: March 13, 1963 San Pedro de Macoris, Dominican Republic
Height: 6′ **Weight:** 185 lbs.
Bats: right **Throws:** right
Acquired: Signed as a free agent, 12/95

Player Summary	
Fantasy Value	$2 to $4
Card Value	4¢ to 6¢
Will	fill many holes
Can't	wait for walks
Expect	good clutch bat
Don't Expect	strong fielding

Mariano Duncan walks less often than Bill Clinton and Newt Gingrich agree on an issue. Duncan simply doesn't accept free passes, preferring instead to swing at anything remotely resembling pitches he can reach. Although he's a pretty solid hitter—especially against lefties—he could bring home a batting average that's better than his on-base percentage. Now there's a rare feat. Primarily a singles hitter who pads his average with infield hits, Duncan goes with the pitch, trying to hit it hard to any field. In 1990, he reached double figures in doubles, triples, and homers—the only time he finished over .300. These days, he's too aggressive, often lunging at unhittable pitches. Originally a shortstop, he has made himself a jack-of-all-trades, capable of playing all four infield spots as well as left field. He's not great at any.

SHAWON DUNSTON

Position: Shortstop
Team: Chicago Cubs
Born: March 21, 1963 Brooklyn, NY
Height: 6′1″ **Weight:** 175 lbs.
Bats: right **Throws:** right
Acquired: First-round pick in 6/82 free-agent draft

Player Summary	
Fantasy Value	$9 to $11
Card Value	5¢ to 8¢
Will	provide some power
Can't	reduce whiff rate
Expect	great infield arm
Don't Expect	another .300 year

A few years ago, they thought he was through. Dunston's back problems were so severe that he got into only 25 games in the 1992 and 1993 seasons combined. He made a pretty good comeback in '94—but nothing like last season's. A career .261 hitter before 1995, he suddenly spent most of the summer above .330. Batting coach Billy Williams said Dunston was opening up his stance more and not jumping at pitches he couldn't hit. His performance was even more surprising in view of his 8-1 ratio of strikeouts to walks—by far the worst of his career. He pounded left-handers and netted extra bases on about one-third of his hits. Once a burner, Dunston doesn't run much anymore because of his back problems. The two-time All-Star still has the NL's best infield arm. He has good instincts, great range, and the ability to turn two.

Major League Batting Register

	BA	G	AB	R	H	2B	3B	HR	RBI	SB
85 NL	.244	142	562	74	137	24	6	6	39	38
86 NL	.229	109	407	47	93	7	0	8	30	48
87 NL	.215	76	261	31	56	8	1	6	18	11
89 NL	.248	94	258	32	64	15	2	3	21	9
90 NL	.306	125	435	67	133	22	11	10	55	13
91 NL	.258	100	333	46	86	7	4	12	40	5
92 NL	.267	142	574	71	153	40	3	8	50	23
93 NL	.282	124	496	68	140	26	4	11	73	6
94 NL	.268	88	347	49	93	22	1	8	48	10
95 NL	.287	81	265	36	76	14	2	6	36	1
Life	.262	1081	3938	521	1031	185	34	78	410	164
3 AVE	.278	113	428	59	119	24	3	10	60	7

Major League Batting Register

	BA	G	AB	R	H	2B	3B	HR	RBI	SB
85 NL	.260	74	250	40	65	12	4	4	18	11
86 NL	.250	150	581	66	145	37	3	17	68	13
87 NL	.246	95	346	40	85	18	3	5	22	12
88 NL	.249	155	575	69	143	23	6	9	56	30
89 NL	.278	138	471	52	131	20	6	9	60	19
90 NL	.262	146	545	73	143	22	8	17	66	25
91 NL	.260	142	492	59	128	22	7	12	50	21
92 NL	.315	18	73	8	23	3	1	0	2	2
93 NL	.400	7	10	3	4	2	0	0	2	0
94 NL	.278	88	331	38	92	19	0	11	35	3
95 NL	.296	127	477	58	141	30	6	14	69	10
Life	.265	1140	4151	506	1100	208	44	98	448	146
2 AVE	.287	133	501	59	144	30	3	16	63	8

CURRENT PLAYERS

RAY DURHAM

Position: Second base
Team: Chicago White Sox
Born: Nov. 30, 1971 Charlotte, NC
Height: 5'8" **Weight:** 170 lbs.
Bats: both **Throws:** right
Acquired: Fifth-round pick in 6/90 free-agent draft

Player Summary	
Fantasy Value	$10 to $13
Card Value	10¢ to 20¢
Will	improve over time
Can't	stop striking out
Expect	pretty good power
Don't Expect	return to leadoff

When he learns patience at the plate, Durham should develop into a first-rate leadoff man. He has the speed, the baserunning skills, and surprising power for a little guy. He reached the White Sox last summer after finishing the 1994 campaign batting .296 with 33 doubles, 12 triples, 16 homers, 34 stolen bases, and 89 runs scored at Triple-A Nashville. He was named the No. 4 prospect in the American Association that year. Thanks to his outstanding range, Durham also led American Association second basemen in chances, putouts, assists, double plays, and fielding percentage. In his last two minor-league seasons, he ranked first in his league in three-base hits. He showed flashes of that potential in Chicago but struggled so much against right-handers that he wound up sharing playing time with Norberto Martin. Durham also lost the leadoff job he held early in the season; a 3-1 ratio of strikeouts to walks made it risky business to bat him first. When he reaches more often and learns the pitchers better, Durham could exceed the 30-steal form he displayed during his last two minor-league campaigns. At 24, his future is bright.

Major League Batting Register

	BA	G	AB	R	H	2B	3B	HR	RBI	SB
95 AL	.257	125	471	68	121	27	6	7	51	18
Life	.257	125	471	68	121	27	6	7	51	18

MIKE DYER

Position: Pitcher
Team: Pittsburgh Pirates
Born: Sept. 8, 1966 Upland, CA
Height: 6'3" **Weight:** 200 lbs.
Bats: right **Throws:** right
Acquired: Signed as a free agent, 1/94

Player Summary	
Fantasy Value	$0
Card Value	10¢ to 15¢
Will	work middle relief
Can't	silence lefty bats
Expect	sinkers, grounders
Don't Expect	sensational control

A rare veteran on a young pitching staff last summer, Dyer held his own as a middle reliever and set-up man. The former Minnesota starter, who's much more effective against right-handed hitters, stranded most of the runners he inherited during much of the 1995 season, while topping three-dozen appearances for the first time in his brief big-league career. Although Dyer showed decent control last year (about three and one-half walks per nine innings), he threw too many wild pitches for a reliever and also encountered more than his share of gopher balls. Allowing more hits than innings pitched didn't help. A sinkerballer who gets lots of grounders when he's on, Dyer also throws a changeup and a slider. He showed last summer that he's completely healed from the shoulder problems that caused him to miss the entire 1991 campaign. Previously poor at controlling the running game, Dyer did better in that department last summer. A product of California's Citrus College, he broke into pro ball in the Minnesota system in 1986.

Major League Pitching Register

	W	L	ERA	G	S	IP	H	ER	BB	SO
89 AL	4	7	4.82	16	0	71.0	74	38	37	37
94 NL	1	1	5.87	14	4	15.1	15	10	12	13
95 NL	4	5	4.34	55	0	74.2	81	36	30	53
Life	9	13	4.70	85	4	161.0	170	84	79	103

CURRENT PLAYERS

LENNY DYKSTRA

Position: Outfield
Team: Philadelphia Phillies
Born: Feb. 10, 1963 Santa Ana, CA
Height: 5'10" **Weight:** 190 lbs.
Bats: left **Throws:** left
Acquired: Traded by Mets with Roger McDowell for Juan Samuel, 6/89

Player Summary	
Fantasy Value	$11 to $14
Card Value	8¢ to 12¢
Will	reach base often
Can't	show strong arm
Expect	patience
Don't Expect	injury-free year

A healthy Dykstra is the prototypical leadoff man. Patience personified, he'll work deep into the count, wait for a walk, bunt for a hit, beat out a roller, slap a liner to any field, or even hit the ball out. The only problem is his penchant for landing on the disabled list with alarming regularity. In 1993, he led the NL in at bats, runs, hits, walks, and putouts. He had previously topped the NL in on-base percentage. Suffering from thickening of the spinal cord, he tried medication, then rest (he missed most of June with back pain). Then knee surgery sent him back to the DL, ending his season, in late July. In recent years, he's had a car wreck, a broken collarbone, and appendicitis, plus other problems. Dykstra could pick up where he left off. The three-time All-Star has enough speed to steal some bases and supply strong, sometimes spectacular defense in center.

Major League Batting Register

	BA	G	AB	R	H	2B	3B	HR	RBI	SB
85 NL	.254	83	236	40	60	9	3	1	19	15
86 NL	.295	147	431	77	127	27	7	8	45	31
87 NL	.285	132	431	86	123	37	3	10	43	27
88 NL	.270	126	429	57	116	19	3	8	33	30
89 NL	.237	146	511	66	121	32	4	7	32	30
90 NL	.325	149	590	106	192	35	3	9	60	33
91 NL	.297	63	246	48	73	13	5	3	12	24
92 NL	.301	85	345	53	104	18	0	6	39	30
93 NL	.305	161	637	143	194	44	6	19	66	37
94 NL	.273	84	315	68	86	26	5	5	24	15
95 NL	.264	62	254	37	67	15	1	2	18	10
Life	.285	1238	4425	781	1263	275	40	78	391	282
3 AVE	.286	116	455	93	130	33	5	9	40	23

DAMION EASLEY

Position: Second base; shortstop
Team: California Angels
Born: Nov. 11, 1969 Oakland, CA
Height: 5'11" **Weight:** 155 lbs.
Bats: right **Throws:** right
Acquired: 30th-round pick in 6/88 free-agent draft

Player Summary	
Fantasy Value	$1 to $3
Card Value	4¢ to 6¢
Will	seek bat revival
Can't	hit right-handers
Expect	display of speed
Don't Expect	great power

For the second year in a row, Easley was a disappointment with a bat in his hands. There were contributing factors, however, including a first-half wrist injury and a serious bout with migraine headaches during the second half. Complicating his inability to recapture his .300 stroke of 1993 was a forced position shift in August. When incumbent shortstop Gary DiSarcina tore a ligament in his left thumb, Easley shifted from second base—his best spot—to short. It was not exactly a smooth transfer. A singles hitter who uses all fields, Easley struggles against right-handed pitching. His best bet would be to hit the ball down and run but he often does the opposite, producing lazy fly balls. However, he can bunt. Because the Long Beach City College product has played three infield positions in his career, he's earning an unwanted reputation as a utility player. But Easley must show more consistency with the bat and demonstrate an ability to turn the double play before he can nail down a single spot.

Major League Batting Register

	BA	G	AB	R	H	2B	3B	HR	RBI	SB
92 AL	.258	47	151	14	39	5	0	1	12	9
93 AL	.313	73	230	33	72	13	2	2	22	6
94 AL	.215	88	316	41	68	16	1	6	30	4
95 AL	.216	114	357	35	77	14	2	4	35	5
Life	.243	322	1054	123	256	48	5	13	99	24
3 AVE	.236	108	359	43	85	17	2	5	35	6

DENNIS ECKERSLEY

Position: Pitcher
Team: Oakland Athletics
Born: Oct. 3, 1954 Oakland, CA
Height: 6'2" **Weight:** 195 lbs.
Bats: right **Throws:** right
Acquired: Traded by Cubs with Dan Rohn for Dave Wilder, Brian Guinn, and Mark Leonette, 4/87

Player Summary	
Fantasy Value	$20 to $25
Card Value	6¢ to 10¢
Will	try another year
Can't	tame all lefties
Expect	pinpoint control
Don't Expect	another Cy Young

The great control is still there, but this Cooperstown-bound closer is definitely showing signs of slipping. Eckersley's velocity has declined, and he's only a shadow of the man who once converted 36 straight save opportunities in the same season—a record broken by Jose Mesa in 1995. Eckersley is the only man ever to have a season with more saves than hits and walks combined. Still a sinkerballer, the '92 AL MVP and Cy Young Award winner also throws a slider, a forkball, and a changeup.

Major League Pitching Register

	W	L	ERA	G	S	IP	H	ER	BB	SO
75 AL	13	7	2.60	34	0	186.2	147	54	90	152
76 AL	13	12	3.43	36	1	199.1	155	76	78	200
77 AL	14	13	3.53	33	0	247.1	214	97	54	191
78 AL	20	8	2.99	35	0	268.1	258	89	71	162
79 AL	17	10	2.99	33	0	246.2	234	82	59	150
80 AL	12	14	4.28	30	0	197.2	188	94	44	121
81 AL	9	8	4.27	23	0	154.0	160	73	35	79
82 AL	13	13	3.73	33	0	224.1	228	93	43	127
83 AL	9	13	5.61	28	0	176.1	223	110	39	77
84 AL	4	4	5.01	9	0	64.2	71	36	13	33
84 NL	10	8	3.03	24	0	160.1	152	54	36	81
85 NL	11	7	3.08	25	0	169.1	145	58	19	117
86 NL	6	11	4.57	33	0	201.0	226	102	43	137
87 AL	6	8	3.03	54	16	115.2	99	39	17	113
88 AL	4	2	2.35	60	45	72.2	52	19	11	70
89 AL	4	0	1.56	51	33	57.2	32	10	3	55
90 AL	4	2	0.61	63	48	73.1	41	5	4	73
91 AL	5	4	2.96	67	43	76.0	60	25	9	87
92 AL	7	1	1.91	69	51	80.0	62	17	11	93
93 AL	2	4	4.16	64	36	67.0	67	31	13	80
94 AL	5	4	4.26	45	19	44.1	49	21	13	47
95 AL	4	6	4.83	52	29	50.1	53	27	11	40
Life	192	159	3.48	901	323	3133.0	2916	1212	716	2285
3 AVE	5	5	4.40	62	32	62.1	65	30	15	64

JIM EDMONDS

Position: Outfield
Team: California Angels
Born: June 27, 1970 Fullerton, CA
Height: 6'1" **Weight:** 190 lbs.
Bats: left **Throws:** left
Acquired: Seventh-round pick in 6/88 free-agent draft

Player Summary	
Fantasy Value	$20 to $25
Card Value	8¢ to 15¢
Will	generate fine power
Can't	reduce K ratio
Expect	good at bats
Don't Expect	great speed

Another protégé of California hitting coach Rod Carew, Edmonds blossomed into an All-Star in his second full season. Spending long hours in the weight room and the batting cage helped Edmonds, but Carew's counsel made the deepest impression. The Hall of Famer told Edmonds to have one good at bat at a time and that the homers would come naturally, since he considered Edmonds the strongest man on the ballclub. Although he fanned more frequently than any other Angel (about three times more than he walks), Edmonds soon proved Carew right. He uncorked a 23-game hitting streak, made the All-Star team for the first time, and set a club record by scoring in 12 consecutive games. After hitting five homers in his first 112 AL games, Edmonds exploded. On Aug. 9, he homered in his third straight game for the second time. Edmonds is equally potent against both right-handers and left-handers. He doesn't steal much. Edmonds is a fine center fielder, sandwiched between Tim Salmon and Garret Anderson in an outstanding young outfield.

Major League Batting Register

	BA	G	AB	R	H	2B	3B	HR	RBI	SB
93 AL	.246	18	61	5	15	4	1	0	4	0
94 AL	.273	94	289	35	79	13	1	5	37	4
95 AL	.290	141	558	120	162	30	4	33	107	1
Life	.282	253	908	160	256	47	6	38	148	5
2 AVE	.284	146	517	92	147	26	3	22	86	3

CURRENT PLAYERS

JIM EISENREICH

Position: Outfield
Team: Philadelphia Phillies
Born: April 18, 1959 St. Cloud, MN
Height: 5'11" **Weight:** 195 lbs.
Bats: left **Throws:** left
Acquired: Signed as a free agent, 1/93

Player Summary	
Fantasy Value	$7 to $9
Card Value	4¢ to 6¢
Will	try all fields
Can't	hit left-handers
Expect	more platooning
Don't Expect	numerous homers

Platooning has been kind to Eisenreich. He hits well against right-handers but struggles against southpaws. He supplies such good defense that he often gets into games that he doesn't start as a late-inning replacement. A contact hitter whose extra-base hits are usually doubles, Eisenreich walks about as often as he fans. He does his best hitting with runners in scoring position. A product of St. Cloud State in Minnesota, he hit a rare home run in the 1993 World Series but usually slaps line drives to all fields. When he's hot, he's hot. Eisenreich batted .398 over the 40-game stretch that ended June 26 and made a serious bid to make the All-Star team for the first time. He is still pretty speedy, which translates to good range in the outfield, where he's capable at all three spots but spends most of his time in right. He has good reactions and a decent arm.

Major League Batting Register

	BA	G	AB	R	H	2B	3B	HR	RBI	SB
82 AL	.303	34	99	10	30	6	0	2	9	0
83 AL	.286	2	7	1	2	1	0	0	0	0
84 AL	.219	12	32	1	7	1	0	0	3	2
87 AL	.238	44	105	10	25	8	2	4	21	1
88 AL	.218	82	202	26	44	8	1	1	19	9
89 AL	.293	134	475	64	139	33	7	9	59	27
90 AL	.280	142	496	61	139	29	7	5	51	12
91 AL	.301	135	375	47	113	22	3	2	47	5
92 AL	.269	113	353	31	95	13	3	2	28	11
93 NL	.318	153	362	51	115	17	4	7	54	5
94 NL	.300	104	290	42	87	15	4	4	43	6
95 NL	.316	129	377	46	119	22	2	10	55	10
Life	.288	1084	3173	390	915	175	33	46	389	88
3 AVE	.311	148	398	54	124	21	4	8	59	8

CAL ELDRED

Position: Pitcher
Team: Milwaukee Brewers
Born: Nov. 24, 1967 Cedar Rapids, IA
Height: 6'4" **Weight:** 215 lbs.
Bats: right **Throws:** right
Acquired: First-round pick in 6/89 free-agent draft

Player Summary	
Fantasy Value	$7 to $9
Card Value	5¢ to 8¢
Will	return to old job
Can't	always find plate
Expect	double-digit wins
Don't Expect	big workloads

Too much work can be detrimental to a young pitcher. The Brewers learned that lesson last year when projected staff ace Cal Eldred was sidelined with elbow problems. He had worked an AL-high 437 innings in 1993 and 1994. At age 25 in '93, he threw 130 pitches in 11 of his starts and 140 in five others. Eldred may have to modify his over-the-top delivery and emphasis on the curve. When he went 11-2 with a 1.79 ERA as a rookie in 1992, he had a 3-1 ratio of strikeouts to walks, yielded fewer hits than innings, and kept the ball in the park. He's had problems with his control since then, however. Eldred throws a moving fastball, a curve that breaks down, and a changeup. To keep batters guessing, he also throws his curve at different speeds. He helps his own cause with excellent defense but needs work at holding runners. The University of Iowa product was the 17th player picked in the 1989 amateur draft. He was named by *The Sporting News* as the AL Rookie Pitcher of the Year for 1992.

Major League Pitching Register

	W	L	ERA	G	CG	IP	H	ER	BB	SO
91 AL	2	0	4.50	3	0	16.0	20	8	6	10
92 AL	11	2	1.79	14	2	100.1	76	20	23	62
93 AL	16	16	4.01	36	8	258.0	232	115	91	180
94 AL	11	11	4.68	25	6	179.0	158	93	84	98
95 AL	1	1	3.42	4	0	23.2	24	9	10	18
Life	41	30	3.82	82	16	577.0	510	245	214	363
2 AVE	16	16	4.34	36	8	255.0	227	123	105	159

CURRENT PLAYERS

JOHN ERICKS

Position: Pitcher
Team: Pittsburgh Pirates
Born: Sept. 16, 1967 Oak Lawn, IL
Height: 6'7" **Weight:** 255 lbs.
Bats: right **Throws:** right
Acquired: Signed as a minor-league free agent, 2/93

Player Summary
Fantasy Value	$1
Card Value	10¢ to 15¢
Will	bury righty batters
Can't	win without support
Expect	few homers
Don't Expect	the sophomore jinx

Ericks showed last summer that he had fully recovered from the shoulder surgery that sidelined him for the entire 1993 campaign. Joining the Pirates on June 24, the towering right-hander got his first win 10 days later, when he worked seven scoreless innings against Philadelphia. Ericks notched the first complete game of his six-year pro career when he beat the Mets 3-2 on July 8. He fanned seven, walked one, and yielded five hits. He added his first big-league hit for good measure. The Pirates knew Ericks had promise after he fanned 135 hitters in 109 Double-A innings in 1994. When he hits his spots, he can be intimidating. He blends breaking balls with fastballs that he works up-the-ladder on opposing hitters. The heater has been clocked at 95 mph. For much of the 1995 season, he yielded less hits than innings, kept the ball in the park, maintained around a 2-1 ratio of whiffs to walks, and averaged about three walks per game. The University of Illinois product is extremely potent against right-handed hitters. He was originally chosen by the St. Louis Cardinals in the first round of the 1988 amateur draft.

Major League Pitching Register
	W	L	ERA	G	CG	IP	H	ER	BB	SO
95 NL	3	9	4.58	19	1	106.0	108	54	50	80
Life	3	9	4.58	19	1	106.0	108	54	50	80

SCOTT ERICKSON

Position: Pitcher
Team: Baltimore Orioles
Born: Feb. 2, 1968 Long Beach, CA
Height: 6'4" **Weight:** 220 lbs.
Bats: right **Throws:** right
Acquired: Traded by Twins for Scott Klingenbeck and Kimera Bartee, 7/95

Player Summary
Fantasy Value	$7 to $9
Card Value	5¢ to 8¢
Will	bank on sinker
Can't	silence lefties
Expect	many grounders
Don't Expect	20 wins

In his first full season, Erickson won 20 games. Three years later, he pitched a no-hitter. In between, he earned an unwanted reputation as a complainer who couldn't or wouldn't pitch on turf. Tired of dealing with a pitcher they thought had a million-dollar arm and 10-cent head, the Twins sent Erickson's salary east to Baltimore last July. Since Oriole Park at Camden Yards has a natural carpet, his sinker could be more effective there. Erickson, who also throws a slider and a changeup, was never a high-strikeout pitcher—even in his 200-inning seasons. He relies on getting grounders his fielders can handle. The former University of Arizona All-American has good control but struggles against left-handed hitters and throws more than his share of home run balls. Almost unhittable during the first half of his 20-win season in 1991, Erickson hasn't been the same pitcher since forearm and elbow problems sent him to the disabled list that summer.

Major League Pitching Register
	W	L	ERA	G	CG	IP	H	ER	BB	SO
90 AL	8	4	2.87	19	1	113.0	108	36	51	53
91 AL	20	8	3.18	32	5	204.0	189	72	71	108
92 AL	13	12	3.40	32	5	212.0	197	80	83	101
93 AL	8	19	5.19	34	1	218.2	266	126	71	116
94 AL	8	11	5.44	23	2	144.0	173	87	59	104
95 AL	13	10	4.81	32	7	196.1	213	105	67	106
Life	70	64	4.19	172	21	1088.0	1146	506	402	588
3 AVE	11	15	5.14	34	4	213.2	250	122	76	127

CURRENT PLAYERS

VAUGHN ESHELMAN

Position: Pitcher
Team: Boston Red Sox
Born: May 22, 1969 Philadelphia, PA
Height: 6'3" **Weight:** 205 lbs.
Bats: left **Throws:** left
Acquired: Rule 5 draft pick from Orioles, 12/94

Player Summary
Fantasy Value	$1
Card Value	8¢ to 12¢
Will	coax ground-ball outs
Can't	always locate plate
Expect	more starts
Don't Expect	injury-free year

A finesse pitcher who can blow the ball by hitters in critical situations, Eshelman broke into the big leagues with a bang last spring. Filling in for injured veteran Zane Smith, Eshelman won his first three decisions, one of them against the arch-rival Yankees in his May 1 debut. In that game, he fanned eight batters while working six scoreless innings. He is a ground-ball pitcher who keeps the ball in the park. Eshelman's fine start was short-circuited by a shoulder strain that landed him on the disabled list. He later returned to the Red Sox rotation. A survivor of "Tommy John surgery" on his pitching elbow, Eshelman missed that entire year. He takes a unique mental approach into every game. He's an advocate of Taoism, a Chinese philosophy that urges people to control only those things within their grasp. Eshelman says the philosophy gives him happiness and contentment. Eshelman was 11-9 at Double-A Bowie in 1994, with a 4.00 ERA, 133 strikeouts, and 60 bases on balls in 166 ⅓ innings. He had two big years at the University of Houston before turning pro.

Major League Pitching Register
	W	L	ERA	G	CG	IP	H	ER	BB	SO
95 AL	6	3	4.85	23	0	81.2	86	44	36	41
Life	6	3	4.85	23	0	81.2	86	44	36	41

ALVARO ESPINOZA

Position: Shortstop; third base
Team: Cleveland Indians
Born: Feb. 19, 1962 Valencia, Venezuela
Height: 6' **Weight:** 190 lbs.
Bats: right **Throws:** right
Acquired: Signed as free agent, 4/92

Player Summary
Fantasy Value	$0
Card Value	4¢ to 6¢
Will	back up infield
Can't	learn strike zone
Expect	strong glove
Don't Expect	any power

For the past two years, Espinoza has played every infield position for the Indians. He's also seen some service as a DH and pinch hitter. A singles hitter with no power or patience, Espinoza stays in the majors strictly because of his versatility, willingness to wait his turn on the bench, and ability to supply strong defense at several positions. He's best at shortstop, his original position, where he shows quick reactions, surprising range for a man without much speed, and a powerful throwing arm. He's no Omar Vizquel, but Espinoza is hardly a bad short-term replacement. A hitter he's not. He would swing at a beach ball if it fell out of the stands. A pure hacker, the guy's a sucker for good breaking balls. Espinoza is a professional bench-warmer, an understudy with no chance to become a star. But baseball needs players like him.

Major League Batting Register
	BA	G	AB	R	H	2B	3B	HR	RBI	SB
84 AL	.000	1	0	0	0	0	0	0	0	0
85 AL	.263	32	57	5	15	2	0	0	9	0
86 AL	.214	37	42	4	9	1	0	0	1	0
88 AL	.000	3	3	0	0	0	0	0	0	0
89 AL	.282	146	503	51	142	23	1	0	41	3
90 AL	.224	150	438	31	98	12	2	2	20	1
91 AL	.256	148	480	51	123	23	2	5	33	4
93 AL	.278	129	263	34	73	15	0	4	27	2
94 AL	.238	90	231	27	55	13	0	1	19	1
95 AL	.252	66	143	15	36	4	0	2	17	0
Life	.255	802	2160	218	551	93	5	14	167	11
2 AVE	.256	128	294	36	75	17	0	3	27	2

99

CURRENT PLAYERS

TONY EUSEBIO

Position: Catcher
Team: Houston Astros
Born: April 27, 1967 San Jose de Los Llamos, Dominican Republic
Height: 6'2" **Weight:** 180 lbs.
Bats: right **Throws:** right
Acquired: Signed as a free agent, 5/85

Player Summary	
Fantasy Value	$3 to $5
Card Value	5¢ to 8¢
Will	swing solid stick
Can't	supply much power
Expect	good throwing arm
Don't Expect	poor on-base mark

The hitting ability was always there. But Eusebio also needed an opportunity. That came on July 9, when Houston trade acquisition Rick Wilkins underwent surgery to repair a cervical disc in his neck. An opposite-field contact hitter with occasional gap power, Eusebio kept his job with a booming bat. For much of the season, he had a batting average over the .300 mark and an on-base percentage over .375—thanks to his willingness to wait for walks. He's usually more effective against left-handers but didn't discriminate in 1995. He did, however, learn to handle a pitching staff. Although he could always throw, Eusebio needed exposure to the big-league arts of game-calling and catcher-pitcher relations. He's good at preventing wild pitches, blocking the plate, and serving as his club's quarterback on the field. Eusebio nailed about 30 percent of the runners who try to steal against him. He led several minor leagues in fielding percentage and double plays by a catcher.

CARL EVERETT

Position: Outfield
Team: New York Mets
Born: June 3, 1971 Tampa, FL
Height: 6' **Weight:** 190 lbs.
Bats: both **Throws:** right
Acquired: Traded by Marlins for Quilvio Veras, 11/94

Player Summary	
Fantasy Value	$7 to $9
Card Value	6¢ to 10¢
Will	become future star
Can't	cut K ratio
Expect	strong arm
Don't Expect	return to minors

During his second stint with the Mets last summer, Everett showed the plate discipline he had lacked earlier. He was able to compile an on-base average over the .330 mark for the majority of the season. Everett had opened the season by fanning 18 times in his first 57 at bats—forcing his return to Triple-A. After hitting .300 in 67 games in the minors, he was back as New York's No. 3 hitter and right fielder. Shortly after his return, he reached base nine consecutive times, five short of Pedro Guerrero's NL record. A former first-round draft choice of the Yankees, Everett is a five-tools player. He still fans far more often than he walks but not quite so often as he once did. When he learns to be more selective, he will draw more walks, steal more bases, and see better pitches to hit. He also needs to improve his performance against southpaws. His speed helps him in the outfield, where he has fine range and a strong arm. Everett was signed out of the same high school program that sent Gary Sheffield and Dwight Gooden to the majors.

Major League Batting Register

	BA	G	AB	R	H	2B	3B	HR	RBI	SB
91 NL	.105	10	19	4	2	1	0	0	0	0
94 NL	.296	55	159	18	47	9	1	5	30	0
95 NL	.299	113	368	46	110	21	1	6	58	0
Life	.291	178	546	68	159	31	2	11	88	0
2 AVE	.298	102	319	39	95	18	1	7	54	0

Major League Batting Register

	BA	G	AB	R	H	2B	3B	HR	RBI	SB
93 NL	.105	11	19	0	2	0	0	0	0	1
94 NL	.216	16	51	7	11	1	0	2	6	4
95 NL	.260	79	289	48	75	13	1	12	54	2
Life	.245	106	359	55	88	14	1	14	60	7

CURRENT PLAYERS

JORGE FABREGAS

Position: Catcher
Team: California Angels
Born: March 13, 1970 Miami, FL
Height: 6'3" **Weight:** 205 lbs.
Bats: left **Throws:** right
Acquired: Supplemental second-round pick in 6/91 free-agent draft

Player Summary
Fantasy Value	$1 to $2
Card Value	6¢ to 8¢
Will	show fine arm
Can't	flash top leather
Expect	improvement
Don't Expect	power

Fabregas is a left-handed hitting catcher, which makes him a relative rarity to begin with. He does not have a great glove. He was a third baseman and a designated hitter at the University of Miami, where he was a backup to Marlins catcher Charles Johnson. Fabregas led the Class-A California League with 17 errors, and he had six errors last year. But he is improving with the leather every season. His arm is more than adequate. He threw out almost 40 percent of the runners trying to steal against him last year. It is the lumber that Fabregas has to worry about. When the Angels drafted him in 1991, they thought they would be getting a fine hitter who would have to grow into the catcher role. After all, he was a second-team All-American who was on Miami's top ten list in many batting categories, including average, RBI, and slugging percentage. Fabregas has not yet made the adjustment to pro pitching. He batted about .180 against lefties last year, and at this point, he looks like a platoon player. If Fabregas makes the adjustment with his bat, he may have the talent to land a starting job in the big leagues.

Major League Batting Register
	BA	G	AB	R	H	2B	3B	HR	RBI	SB
94 AL	.283	43	127	12	36	3	0	0	16	2
95 AL	.247	73	227	24	56	10	0	1	22	0
Life	.260	116	354	36	92	13	0	1	38	2

RIKKERT FANEYTE

Position: Outfield
Team: Texas Rangers
Born: May 31, 1969 Amsterdam, Netherlands
Height: 6'1" **Weight:** 170 lbs.
Bats: right **Throws:** right
Acquired: Traded by Giants for a player to be named later, 12/95

Player Summary
Fantasy Value	$0
Card Value	10¢ to 15¢
Will	play sound defense
Can't	find former stroke
Expect	a few swipes
Don't Expect	poor on-base mark

The third Dutch player in major-league history has yet to show he can handle a bat. Though he twice topped .300 at Triple-A Phoenix, Faneyte had been overpowered in limited playing time with the Giants. The one saving grace of his offense is a good batting eye, which he uses to pile up more than his share of walks. As a result, his on-base percentage stood about 100 points higher than his batting average during most of the 1995 season. A former member of the Dutch national team, Faneyte honed his skills at Miami-Dade Community College South before turning pro. He showed some power, speed, and skill in the minors, where he stole at least 15 bases four times and led one league in fielding percentage. He is a fine defensive center fielder with quick reactions, good instincts, and excellent range. He also has a better throwing arm than Deion Sanders, who displaced Darren Lewis in center last summer. Faneyte played all three outfield spots for the Giants, although center is certainly his best position.

Major League Batting Register
	BA	G	AB	R	H	2B	3B	HR	RBI	SB
93 NL	.133	7	15	2	2	0	0	0	0	0
94 NL	.115	19	26	1	3	3	0	0	4	0
95 NL	.198	46	86	7	17	4	1	0	4	1
Life	.173	72	127	10	22	7	1	0	8	1

CURRENT PLAYERS

JEFF FASSERO

Position: Pitcher
Team: Montreal Expos
Born: Jan. 5, 1963 Springfield, IL
Height: 6'1" **Weight:** 195 lbs.
Bats: left **Throws:** left
Acquired: Signed as a minor-league free agent, 1/91

Player Summary	
Fantasy Value	$8 to $10
Card Value	6¢ to 10¢
Will	get grounders
Can't	stop running game
Expect	solid work
Don't Expect	control problems

Fassero has come full circle. He went from starter to workhorse reliever to starter again. Returned to the rotation midway through the 1993 campaign, he has definitely found his niche. The keys to his success were destroying left-handed hitters and avoiding gopher balls. Through much of the season, he averaged about three walks and eight strikeouts per nine innings. Fassero yielded less hits than innings in his first four seasons, though he struggled last summer. He got most of his outs on grounders, thanks to a repertoire that includes a heavy sinker, a hard slider, an occasional changeup, and a forkball that he throws on any count. The University of Mississippi product still attracted considerable interest from other clubs in the trade market, however. He fields his position well and helps himself by bunting runners along. He's still stymied over how to stop the running game. Even though he faces first base when he sets, he fares poorly in freezing potential basestealers.

Major League Pitching Register

	W	L	ERA	G	CG	IP	H	ER	BB	SO
91 NL	2	5	2.44	51	0	55.1	39	15	17	42
92 NL	8	7	2.84	70	0	85.2	81	27	34	63
93 NL	12	5	2.29	56	1	149.2	119	38	54	140
94 NL	8	6	2.99	21	1	138.2	119	46	40	119
95 NL	13	14	4.33	30	1	189.0	207	91	74	164
Life	43	37	3.16	228	36	618.1	565	217	219	528
3 AVE	13	10	3.31	40	1	185.2	173	68	65	164

FELIX FERMIN

Position: Shortstop; second base
Team: Seattle Mariners
Born: Oct. 9, 1963 Mao Valverde, Dominican Republic
Height: 5'11" **Weight:** 170 lbs.
Bats: right **Throws:** right
Acquired: Traded by Indians with Reggie Jefferson and cash for Omar Vizquel, 12/93

Player Summary	
Fantasy Value	$0
Card Value	4¢ to 6¢
Will	carry good glove
Can't	reach the fences
Expect	contact hitting
Don't Expect	patience at plate

Fresh off a .300 season in 1994—his first in a pro career that began in 1983—Fermin suddenly forgot how to hit last summer. He struggled to surface above the Mendoza Line, lost his job to Luis Sojo, and kept looking over his shoulder for the imminent recall of phenom Alex Rodriguez. The only thing Fermin did right was make terrific contact: five strikeouts in his first 150 at bats. He walked about as frequently, however, leaving him with one of the league's lowest on-base percentages. Usually a good hit-and-run man, Fermin is even better at bunting. Since he is unlikely to homer, he'd be wise to try bunting for base hits as often as possible. Fermin's forte remains his fine defense—especially at shortstop. He has quick reactions, good hands, and a strong arm. He turns the double play well from both sides of second base. Fermin led three minor leagues in fielding percentage.

Major League Batting Register

	BA	G	AB	R	H	2B	3B	HR	RBI	SB
87 NL	.250	23	68	6	17	0	0	0	4	0
88 NL	.276	43	87	9	24	0	2	0	2	3
89 AL	.238	156	484	50	115	9	1	0	21	6
90 AL	.256	148	414	47	106	13	2	1	40	3
91 AL	.262	129	424	30	111	13	2	0	31	5
92 AL	.270	79	215	27	58	7	2	0	13	0
93 AL	.262	140	480	48	126	16	2	2	45	4
94 AL	.317	101	379	52	120	21	0	1	35	4
95 AL	.195	73	200	21	39	6	0	0	15	2
Life	.260	892	2751	290	716	85	11	4	206	27
3 AVE	.274	121	413	48	113	17	1	1	37	4

CURRENT PLAYERS

ALEX FERNANDEZ

Position: Pitcher
Team: Chicago White Sox
Born: Aug. 13, 1969 Miami Beach, FL
Height: 6'1" **Weight:** 205 lbs.
Bats: right **Throws:** right
Acquired: First-round pick in 6/90 free-agent draft

Player Summary	
Fantasy Value	$18 to $21
Card Value	6¢ to 10¢
Will	remain staff ace
Can't	retire all lefties
Expect	better whiff ratio
Don't Expect	great control

When Fernandez went 18-9 in 1993, the White Sox believed he was about to realize his promise. But his performance deteriorated so sharply over the next two seasons that all predictions have been placed on the back burner. After a bad first half in 1995, he needed a three-game winning streak to reach .500 on Aug. 21. That is not what the ChiSox had in mind for him. Bouts of control trouble, careless mistakes, and left-handed batters posed problems for Fernandez. He should have better command of his four pitches: a fastball, a slider, a curveball, and a changeup. When he's on top of his game, Fernandez coaxes a lot of ground outs. A power pitcher, he had about a 2-1 ratio of strikeouts to walks in '95. Three of his 11 victories in 1994 were shutouts. He helps himself with fine defense, including a pickoff move that prevents basestealers from running wild when he's on the mound. The Miami-Dade South Community College product is a former Golden Spikes Award winner.

Major League Pitching Register

	W	L	ERA	G	CG	IP	H	ER	BB	SO
90 AL	5	5	3.80	13	3	87.2	89	37	34	61
91 AL	9	13	4.51	34	2	191.2	186	96	88	145
92 AL	8	11	4.27	29	4	187.2	199	89	50	95
93 AL	18	9	3.13	34	3	247.1	221	86	67	169
94 AL	11	7	3.86	24	4	170.1	163	73	50	122
95 AL	12	8	3.80	30	5	203.2	200	86	65	159
Life	63	53	3.86	164	21	1088.1	1058	467	354	751
3 AVE	16	9	3.59	34	5	238.2	225	95	70	173

SID FERNANDEZ

Position: Pitcher
Team: Philadelphia Phillies
Born: Oct. 12, 1962 Honolulu, HI
Height: 6'1" **Weight:** 230 lbs.
Bats: left **Throws:** left
Acquired: Signed as a free agent, 7/95

Player Summary	
Fantasy Value	$5 to $7
Card Value	5¢ to 8¢
Will	yield few safeties
Can't	keep ball in park
Expect	lefties to wither
Don't Expect	low K rate

Always tough to hit, Fernandez won 16 games once and 14 games twice—even though he often received poor run support. In his first seven starts with the Phils last summer, opposing batters hit .187 (.130 by lefties). The two-time All-Star throws a short-arm fastball that rises, a slow curve, and a tantalizing changeup. After an unimpressive debut with the Phils, Fernandez fanned 17 and walked three in his next 13 innings. He had about a 4-1 ratio of strikeouts to walks for the Phils through much of the season. Because he's a fly-ball pitcher, he is prone to occasional gophers. However, he was helped immensely by Philly pitching coach Johnny Podres last year. He had a collarbone problem, one of many injuries that have plagued him in recent years, and he has trouble holding runners.

Major League Pitching Register

	W	L	ERA	G	CG	IP	H	ER	BB	SO
83 NL	0	1	6.00	2	0	6.0	7	4	7	9
84 NL	6	6	3.50	15	0	90.0	74	35	34	62
85 NL	9	9	2.80	26	3	170.1	108	53	80	180
86 NL	16	6	3.52	32	2	204.1	161	80	91	200
87 NL	12	8	3.81	28	3	156.0	130	66	67	134
88 NL	12	10	3.03	31	1	187.0	127	63	70	189
89 NL	14	5	2.83	35	6	219.1	157	69	75	198
90 NL	9	14	3.46	30	2	179.1	130	69	67	181
91 NL	1	3	2.86	8	0	44.0	36	14	9	31
92 NL	14	11	2.73	32	5	214.2	162	65	67	193
93 NL	5	6	2.93	18	1	119.2	82	39	36	81
94 NL	6	6	5.15	19	2	115.1	109	66	46	95
95 NL	0	4	7.39	8	0	28.0	36	23	17	31
95 NL	6	1	3.34	11	0	64.2	48	24	21	79
Life	110	90	3.35	295	25	1798.2	1367	670	687	1663
3 AVE	7	7	4.31	22	1	128.2	110	62	48	113

TONY FERNANDEZ

Position: Shortstop
Team: New York Yankees
Born: June 30, 1962 San Pedro de Macoris, Dominican Republic
Height: 6'2" **Weight:** 175 lbs.
Bats: both **Throws:** right
Acquired: Signed as a free agent, 12/94

Player Summary	
Fantasy Value	$3 to $5
Card Value	5¢ to 8¢
Will	make good contact
Can't	hit all righties
Expect	defensive skills
Don't Expect	home run barrage

When the Yankees decided to give Derek Jeter more development time in the minors, they brought Fernandez back to New York with a two-year, $3 million contract. A switch-hitter who makes good contact, Fernandez also shows enough patience to produce a fine on-base percentage. He's had several seasons in which he's walked more often than he's struck out. A switch-hitter who's better left-handed, he can sacrifice, bunt for a base hit, or work the hit-and-run. He's never been a power hitter or RBI man. The four-time All-Star was thrown out about half the time he tried (which wasn't much) in 1995. Fernandez remains a fine fielder, but no longer at his previous Gold Glove level. He reacts quickly, turns two, and throws well.

Major League Batting Register

	BA	G	AB	R	H	2B	3B	HR	RBI	SB
83 AL	.265	15	34	5	9	1	1	0	2	0
84 AL	.270	88	233	29	63	5	3	3	19	5
85 AL	.289	161	564	71	163	31	10	2	51	13
86 AL	.310	163	687	91	213	33	9	10	65	25
87 AL	.322	146	578	90	186	29	8	5	67	32
88 AL	.287	154	648	76	186	41	4	5	70	15
89 AL	.257	140	573	64	147	25	9	11	64	22
90 AL	.276	161	635	84	175	27	17	4	66	26
91 NL	.272	145	558	81	152	27	5	4	38	23
92 NL	.275	155	622	84	171	32	4	4	37	20
93 NL	.225	48	173	20	39	5	2	1	14	6
93 AL	.306	94	353	45	108	18	9	4	50	15
94 NL	.279	104	366	50	102	18	6	8	50	12
95 AL	.245	108	384	57	94	20	2	5	45	6
Life	.282	1682	6408	847	1808	312	89	66	638	220
3 AVE	.269	137	491	67	132	24	7	7	62	15

MIKE FETTERS

Position: Pitcher
Team: Milwaukee Brewers
Born: Dec. 19, 1964 Van Nuys, CA
Height: 6'4" **Weight:** 212 lbs.
Bats: right **Throws:** right
Acquired: Traded by Angels with Glenn Carter for Chuck Crim, 12/91

Player Summary	
Fantasy Value	$13 to $16
Card Value	4¢ to 6¢
Will	keep ball in park
Can't	avoid baserunners
Expect	lots of grounders
Don't Expect	trouble in clutch

He averages one strikeout per inning. He rarely blows a save opportunity. And he never—repeat never—lets a batter hit the ball over the fence. So why can't Fetters get the recognition he deserves? Pitching in Milwaukee, with its modicum of national publicity, could be the problem. The Pepperdine product aims for the corners of the plate with his sinking fastball, forkball, slider, curve, and changeup. Fetters walks more than most other closers and also yields more hits, though most are singles. He's an expert at getting batters to hit the ball on the ground, helping him get double plays at critical moments. Converted to relief during his fifth pro season, he blossomed into a bullpen star after changing his delivery to a more over-the-top style with Milwaukee in 1992. Two years later, he moved from middle relief to closing. Fetters is a fine fielder with a good pickoff move. He shows no signs of the elbow woes that plagued him in 1993.

Major League Pitching Register

	W	L	ERA	G	S	IP	H	ER	BB	SO
89 AL	0	0	8.10	1	0	3.1	5	3	1	4
90 AL	1	1	4.12	26	1	67.2	77	31	20	35
91 AL	2	5	4.84	19	0	44.2	53	24	28	24
92 AL	5	1	1.87	50	2	62.2	38	13	24	43
93 AL	3	3	3.34	45	0	59.1	59	22	22	23
94 AL	1	4	2.54	42	17	46.0	41	13	27	31
95 AL	0	3	3.38	40	22	34.2	40	13	20	33
Life	12	17	3.36	223	42	318.1	313	119	142	193
3 AVE	1	4	3.03	50	16	54.1	54	18	28	35

CURRENT PLAYERS

CECIL FIELDER

Position: First base
Team: Detroit Tigers
Born: Sept. 21, 1963 Los Angeles, CA
Height: 6'3" **Weight:** 250 lbs.
Bats: right **Throws:** right
Acquired: Signed as a free agent, 1/90

Player Summary	
Fantasy Value	$18 to $22
Card Value	8¢ to 12¢
Will	clear walls often
Can't	provide any speed
Expect	enormous strength
Don't Expect	high batting mark

Although he's still a dangerous slugger, Fielder has seen his run production slip over the last three seasons. A three-time RBI king who twice topped the AL in homers, he is prone to long slumps. He went more than a month without a home run in midseason last year. Fielder still managed to become the first Tiger to top 25 homers in each of his first six seasons. Frequent strikeouts accompany the Fielder power explosion; he fans more than 100 times per season, with three years above the 150-K mark. He is a pull hitter who likes low-and-away fastballs, pitches that allow him to extend his powerful arms. He hits with power to all fields but is slower than a tortoise. He also doesn't have the defensive range of the average first baseman, but he does have good instincts, quick reactions, soft hands, and an accurate arm. Fielder has led his position in double plays and assists.

Major League Batting Register

	BA	G	AB	R	H	2B	3B	HR	RBI	SB
85 AL	.311	30	74	6	23	4	0	4	16	0
86 AL	.157	34	83	7	13	2	0	4	13	0
87 AL	.269	82	175	30	47	7	1	14	32	0
88 AL	.230	74	174	24	40	6	1	9	23	0
90 AL	.277	159	573	104	159	25	1	51	132	0
91 AL	.261	162	624	102	163	25	0	44	133	0
92 AL	.244	155	594	80	145	22	0	35	124	0
93 AL	.267	154	573	80	153	23	0	30	117	0
94 AL	.259	109	425	67	110	16	2	28	90	0
95 AL	.243	136	494	70	120	18	1	31	82	0
Life	.257	1095	3789	570	973	148	6	250	762	0
3 AVE	.256	154	576	84	148	22	1	35	112	0

CHUCK FINLEY

Position: Pitcher
Team: California Angels
Born: Nov. 26, 1962 Monroe, LA
Height: 6'6" **Weight:** 212 lbs.
Bats: left **Throws:** left
Acquired: First-round pick in 6/85 free-agent draft

Player Summary	
Fantasy Value	$12 to $15
Card Value	5¢ to 8¢
Will	remain a winner
Can't	count on control
Expect	good clutch work
Don't Expect	righties to rally

Finley has been one of baseball's best left-handers since 1989. He's led the American League in innings, complete games, and starts. He has made the All-Star team three times, including 1995. Not known as a hard thrower, he relies on finesse, deception, and location. By cutting his fastball, he makes the pitch run away from right-handed hitters. As a result, he's usually more effective against righties than he is against lefties. The Northeast Louisiana product also throws a forkball and a slurve. However, he does encounter occasional control trouble (with wild pitches as well as walks). Finley averaged about eight and one-half hits and four walks over nine innings for much of the season last year. He is not much of a pickoff artist or fielder. The wily veteran often coaxes ground outs from opposing hitters and keeps the ball in the park.

Major League Pitching Register

	W	L	ERA	G	CG	IP	H	ER	BB	SO
86 AL	3	1	3.30	25	0	46.1	40	17	23	37
87 AL	2	7	4.67	35	0	90.2	102	47	43	63
88 AL	9	15	4.17	31	2	194.1	191	90	82	111
89 AL	16	9	2.57	29	9	199.2	171	57	82	156
90 AL	18	9	2.40	32	7	236.0	210	63	81	177
91 AL	18	9	3.80	34	4	227.1	205	96	101	171
92 AL	7	12	3.96	31	4	204.1	212	90	98	124
93 AL	16	14	3.15	35	13	251.1	243	88	82	187
94 AL	10	10	4.32	25	7	183.1	178	88	71	148
95 AL	15	12	4.21	32	2	203.0	192	95	93	195
Life	114	98	3.58	309	48	1836.1	1744	731	756	1369
3 AVE	16	14	3.89	35	8	246.1	237	106	96	205

CURRENT PLAYERS

STEVE FINLEY

Position: Outfield
Team: San Diego Padres
Born: March 12, 1965 Union City, TN
Height: 6'2" **Weight:** 175 lbs.
Bats: left **Throws:** left
Acquired: Traded by Astros with Ken Caminiti, Andujar Cedeno, Roberto Petagine, Brian Williams and a player to be named later for Phil Plantier, Derek Bell, Pedro Martinez, Doug Brocail, Craig Shipley, and Ricky Gutierrez, 12/94

Player Summary
Fantasy Value	$14 to $17
Card Value	5¢ to 8¢
Will	terrorize rivals
Can't	get proper press
Expect	high on-base mark
Don't Expect	a dozen homers

With Bip Roberts sidelined for long stretches last summer, San Diego shifted Finley from second to first in the lineup. Although he prefers the No. 2 spot, he was even more productive as a leadoff man. In his first 47 games at the top, he batted .390 with 22 steals and 49 runs scored. A contact hitter with considerable patience, Finley walks about as often as he fans. Equally effective against righties or lefties, he's also an accomplished bunter (Finley had 21 bunts in play during the 1994 campaign). The Southern Illinois product often ranks among the league leaders in runs, hits, triples, stolen bases, and on-base percentage. Finley has topped 30 steals three times. Because of his speed and aggressiveness, he's a high-percentage base-stealer. He's also a wide-ranging center fielder with a strong throwing arm.

Major League Batting Register
	BA	G	AB	R	H	2B	3B	HR	RBI	SB
89 AL	.249	81	217	35	54	5	2	2	25	17
90 AL	.256	142	464	46	119	16	4	3	37	22
91 NL	.285	159	596	84	170	28	10	8	54	34
92 NL	.292	162	607	84	177	29	13	5	55	44
93 NL	.266	142	545	69	145	15	13	8	44	19
94 NL	.276	94	373	64	103	16	5	11	33	13
95 NL	.297	139	562	104	167	23	8	10	44	36
Life	.278	919	3364	486	935	132	55	47	292	185
3 AVE	.281	144	568	92	159	21	10	12	47	26

JOHN FLAHERTY

Position: Catcher
Team: Detroit Tigers
Born: Oct. 21, 1967 New York, NY
Height: 6'1" **Weight:** 202 lbs.
Bats: right **Throws:** right
Acquired: Traded by Red Sox for Rich Rowland, 4/94

Player Summary
Fantasy Value	$3 to $5
Card Value	5¢ to 8¢
Will	show some power
Can't	hit left-handers
Expect	strong fielding
Don't Expect	few Ks

Private lessons with Tiger hitting coach Larry Herndon worked wonders for Flaherty last season. After flunking two trials with the Red Sox, the young receiver suddenly showed he could handle a bat. Stronger after a winter of workouts, he started driving the ball instead of lofting it. He hammered two home runs in a 5-2 win over Milwaukee on June 24, and reached double-digits before Labor Day. Flaherty had never hit more than seven homers in a professional career that began in 1988. Though about one-third of his hits netted extra bases last year, he would be even more productive if he mastered the strike zone; he fanned about three times per walk. His futility against left-handers is another problem area that needs improvement. He doesn't steal much—few catchers do—but supplies so much defense that Detroit management can't complain. Sparky Anderson, his manager last year, called Flaherty the best defensive catcher in the AL. He was drafted by the Red Sox in 1988 in the 25th round out of George Washington University.

Major League Batting Register
	BA	G	AB	R	H	2B	3B	HR	RBI	SB
92 AL	.197	35	66	3	13	2	0	0	2	0
93 AL	.120	13	25	3	3	2	0	0	2	0
94 AL	.150	34	40	2	6	1	0	0	4	0
95 AL	.243	112	354	39	86	22	1	11	40	0
Life	.223	194	485	47	108	27	1	11	48	0

CURRENT PLAYERS

DAVE FLEMING

Position: Pitcher
Team: Kansas City Royals
Born: Nov. 7, 1969 Queens, NY
Height: 6'3" **Weight:** 200 lbs.
Bats: left **Throws:** left
Acquired: Traded by Mariners for Bob Milacki, 7/95

Player Summary	
Fantasy Value	$0
Card Value	4¢ to 6¢
Will	need big comeback
Can't	rack up strikeouts
Expect	wins with control
Don't Expect	gopher-ball trouble

Seldom has a player fallen so far so fast. Fleming's performance has declined dramatically since his 17-10 rookie year with the 1992 Mariners. Control trouble and injuries haven't helped, but Seattle gave up the ghost after the pitcher's ERA fell off the map. He even returned to the minors last year after his trade to the Royals. But left-handers with recent success don't stay hidden long. Recalled in late August, Fleming tried to recapture the form that brought him to the big leagues in the first place. He is a sinkerballer who doesn't throw hard. To succeed, he needs to change speeds and place his pitches in precise locations. The University of Georgia product, who also throws a curveball and a changeup, keeps the ball in the park but allows more hits than innings pitched. Fortunately, he's adept at fielding his position and holding runners on base. During his rookie year, everything worked for Fleming. If he returns to that level, he could regain his place as a solid starter.

Major League Pitching Register

	W	L	ERA	G	CG	IP	H	ER	BB	SO
91 AL	1	0	6.62	9	0	17.2	19	13	3	11
92 AL	17	10	3.39	33	7	228.1	225	86	60	112
93 AL	12	5	4.36	26	1	167.1	189	81	67	75
94 AL	7	11	6.46	23	0	117.0	152	84	65	65
95 AL	1	6	5.96	25	1	80.0	84	53	53	40
Life	38	32	4.67	116	9	610.1	669	317	248	303
3 AVE	8	9	5.52	29	1	141.0	166	86	73	71

DARRIN FLETCHER

Position: Catcher
Team: Montreal Expos
Born: Oct. 3, 1966 Elmhurst, IL
Height: 6'1" **Weight:** 198 lbs.
Bats: left **Throws:** right
Acquired: Traded by Phillies with cash for Barry Jones, 12/91

Player Summary	
Fantasy Value	$4 to $6
Card Value	4¢ to 6¢
Will	ravage righties
Can't	bring speed
Expect	exceptional contact
Don't Expect	defensive problems

Buried north of the border for the last three years, Fletcher does not receive the recognition he deserves. But he's quietly become one of baseball's best all-around backstops. A 1994 All-Star, he enjoyed his finest season last year. Platooning with righty-hitting Tim Laker, Fletcher finished about 50 points above his previous career average and dramatically increased his success in throwing out would-be basestealers. He is a terrific contact hitter who thrives in clutch situations. Fletcher walked more than he fanned last year, yielding a high on-base percentage to complement his batting average. He ripped right-handers and delivered extra bases on nearly one-third of his hits. Fletcher nailed about 35 percent of opposing runners last year, a big improvement on his league-low 16 percent in 1994. The University of Illinois product handles his pitchers well, calls good games, and is skilled at preventing wild pitches and blocking the plate.

Major League Batting Register

	BA	G	AB	R	H	2B	3B	HR	RBI	SB
89 NL	.500	5	8	1	4	0	0	1	2	0
90 NL	.130	21	23	3	3	1	0	0	1	0
91 NL	.228	46	136	5	31	8	0	1	12	0
92 NL	.243	83	222	13	54	10	2	2	26	0
93 NL	.255	133	396	33	101	20	1	9	60	0
94 NL	.260	94	285	28	74	18	1	10	57	0
95 NL	.286	110	350	42	100	21	1	11	45	0
Life	.258	482	1420	125	367	78	5	34	203	0
3 AVE	.267	130	397	40	106	23	1	12	64	0

CURRENT PLAYERS

SCOTT FLETCHER

Position: Second base; shortstop
Team: Detroit Tigers
Born: July 30, 1958 Fort Walton Beach, FL
Height: 5'11" **Weight:** 173 lbs.
Bats: right **Throws:** right
Acquired: Signed as a free agent, 4/95

Player Summary	
Fantasy Value	$0
Card Value	4¢ to 6¢
Will	hit to all fields
Can't	produce power
Expect	patience at plate
Don't Expect	clutch hits

Fletcher hangs onto his big-league berth because of experience, defensive ability, and versatility. He played all three bases for Detroit last year while contributing an on-base percentage 100 points higher than his batting average. A contact hitter without much power, he does have patience. He walks about as much as he fans, even when rusty from long spells on the bench. He's also adept at bunting or working a hit-and-run play. Fletcher sprays singles to all fields, but also hits a lot of ground balls that become double plays with men on base. The former Georgia Southern shortstop counters by turning the double play on opponents from second base. Some of his range is gone, but he still has good instincts, soft hands, and a decent throwing arm. He rarely makes an error.

Major League Batting Register

	BA	G	AB	R	H	2B	3B	HR	RBI	SB
81 NL	.217	19	46	6	10	4	0	0	1	0
82 NL	.167	11	24	4	4	0	0	0	1	1
83 AL	.237	114	262	42	62	16	5	3	31	5
84 AL	.250	149	456	46	114	13	3	3	35	10
85 AL	.256	119	301	38	77	8	1	2	31	5
86 AL	.300	147	530	82	159	34	5	3	50	12
87 AL	.287	156	588	82	169	28	4	5	63	13
88 AL	.276	140	515	59	142	19	4	0	47	8
89 AL	.253	142	546	77	138	25	2	1	43	2
90 AL	.242	151	509	54	123	18	3	4	56	1
91 AL	.206	90	248	14	51	10	1	1	28	0
92 AL	.275	123	386	53	106	18	3	3	51	17
93 AL	.285	121	480	81	137	31	5	5	45	16
94 AL	.227	63	185	31	42	9	1	3	11	8
95 AL	.231	67	182	19	42	10	1	1	17	1
Life	.262	1612	5258	688	1376	243	38	34	510	99
3 AVE	.257	95	315	49	81	18	3	3	27	9

KEVIN FLORA

Position: Outfield; second base
Team: Philadelphia Phillies
Born: June 10, 1969 Fontana, CA
Height: 6' **Weight:** 185 lbs.
Bats: right **Throws:** right
Acquired: Traded by Angels with Russ Springer for Dave Gallagher, 8/95

Player Summary	
Fantasy Value	$1 to $3
Card Value	4¢ to 8¢
Will	maximize speed
Can't	avoid injuries
Expect	outfield berth
Don't Expect	patience at bat

Although injuries and personal tragedy delayed his ascent to the majors, Flora got a new start last summer when the Phillies needed a fleet leadoff man to replace sidelined veteran Lenny Dykstra. One of 15 Angels protected in the 1992 expansion draft, Flora has always had good tools. He had 15 triples, 12 homers, and 40 steals in 124 games as a Double-A Texas League second baseman in 1992. He suffered a major setback a year later due to personal reasons. Recurring knee problems, an ankle injury, and other ailments chopped time off several seasons. Last year, Flora had to overcome a hamstring problem before showcasing his skills at Triple-A Vancouver. He was hitting .298 with 14 RBI in 38 games at the time of his trade. Originally signed as a shortstop, he faces a bright future as an outfielder because of his exceptional range. Flora has shown that he can hold his own as an infielder, too. He's a high-percentage basestealer who would be even more effective if he showed more selectivity at the plate. Flora knocked in five runs with his first eight hits for the Phillies.

Major League Batting Register

	BA	G	AB	R	H	2B	3B	HR	RBI	SB
91 AL	.125	3	8	1	1	0	0	0	0	1
95 AL	.000	2	1	1	0	0	0	0	0	0
95 NL	.213	24	75	12	16	3	0	2	7	1
Life	.202	29	84	14	17	3	0	2	7	2

CURRENT PLAYERS

CLIFF FLOYD

Position: First base; outfield
Team: Montreal Expos
Born: Dec. 5, 1972 Chicago, IL
Height: 6'4" **Weight:** 220 lbs.
Bats: left **Throws:** right
Acquired: First-round pick in 6/91 free-agent draft

Player Summary	
Fantasy Value	$7 to $9
Card Value	12¢ to 20¢
Will	improve his power
Can't	reduce strikeouts
Expect	more use of speed
Don't Expect	lingering injury

The pennant hopes of the 1995 Expos evaporated last May when Floyd needed surgery to repair an injured left wrist. Although he didn't display the power the team expected during his rookie year in 1994, he is still counted on to fulfill his potential as a Willie McCovey type with speed. A big first baseman who can really move, Floyd may have a future in the outfield. He played both spots while winning Minor League Player of the Year honors from *The Sporting News* in 1993. His three-club totals that season included 29 homers, 121 RBI, and 33 steals. Floyd has already shown he can hit big-league left-handers, deliver with runners in scoring position, and come through in late-inning pressure situations. His biggest problem is impatience at the plate. He fanned about three times more than he walked last year. A two-time RBI champion in the minors, Floyd once finished a season with double-digits in doubles, triples, and home runs. He was Eastern League MVP in 1993, the same year *Baseball America* named him the league's top prospect.

Major League Batting Register

	BA	G	AB	R	H	2B	3B	HR	RBI	SB
93 NL	.226	10	31	3	7	0	0	1	2	0
94 NL	.281	100	334	43	94	19	4	4	41	10
95 NL	.130	29	69	6	9	1	0	1	8	3
Life	.253	139	434	52	110	20	4	6	51	13

CHAD FONVILLE

Position: Second base; shortstop
Team: Los Angeles Dodgers
Born: March 5, 1971 Jacksonville, NC
Height: 5'6" **Weight:** 155 lbs.
Bats: both **Throws:** right
Acquired: Claimed on waivers from Expos, 6/95

Player Summary	
Fantasy Value	$6 to $8
Card Value	12¢ to 20¢
Will	show great speed
Can't	clear the fences
Expect	Bip Roberts type
Don't Expect	sterling defense

A little guy who tries to make the most of limited skills, Fonville jumped from Class-A to the majors after Montreal snatched him from San Francisco in the Rule 5 draft. Why the Expos let him escape so quickly remains one of baseball's many mysteries. A switch-hitting singles hitter out of Louisburg (North Carolina) Junior College, Fonville has already drawn comparisons to Bip Roberts. Both have the capacity to play several positions and drive rivals daffy with their speed. A better right-handed hitter, Fonville holds his own as a lefty. He's much more likely to steal a base than deliver an extra-base hit, but he does have the ability to drive the ball. He once finished a minor-league season with 16 doubles and 10 triples. That same summer, he had 52 stolen bases. He made a fine fill-in for Delino DeShields after injuries sidelined the second baseman last summer. Although he covers lots of ground, Fonville needs to refine his fielding. He made far too many errors. If he ever wants to play every day, he'll also have to return to his old selective ways at the plate.

Major League Batting Register

	BA	G	AB	R	H	2B	3B	HR	RBI	SB
95 NL	.278	102	320	43	89	6	1	0	16	20
Life	.278	102	320	43	89	6	1	0	16	20

CURRENT PLAYERS

TONY FOSSAS

Position: Pitcher
Team: St. Louis Cardinals
Born: Sept. 23, 1957 Havana, Cuba
Height: 6' **Weight:** 187 lbs.
Bats: left **Throws:** left
Acquired: Signed as a free agent, 4/95

Player Summary
Fantasy Value	$1
Card Value	4¢ to 6¢
Will	retire lefties
Can't	field position
Expect	frequent games
Don't Expect	gopher trouble

At an age when most of his contemporaries are contemplating retirement, Fossas keeps right on rolling. His life seems divided into thirds: one-third of an inning here, two-thirds there. A true baseball specialist, his job is to come in and retire one or two left-handed hitters. In the years that he topped 60 appearances, he finished with far more games than innings pitched. The guy doesn't stay long, but he's good at what he does. A fastball-slider pitcher with a sidearm delivery, Fossas is a formidable presence when lefties come to bat. For much of 1995, he held them beneath a composite .250 batting average, yielding about seven hits and three walks per game while averaging one strikeout per inning. Fossas seems to be improving with age. He also avoided the gopher-ball problems that have plagued him in the past. His pickoff move is so sound that baserunners seldom mount a challenge.

Major League Pitching Register
	W	L	ERA	G	S	IP	H	ER	BB	SO
88 AL	0	0	4.76	5	0	5.2	11	3	2	4
89 AL	2	2	3.54	51	1	61.0	57	24	22	42
90 AL	2	3	6.44	32	0	29.1	44	21	10	24
91 AL	3	2	3.47	64	1	57.0	49	22	28	29
92 AL	1	2	2.43	60	2	29.2	31	8	14	19
93 AL	1	1	5.17	71	0	40.0	38	23	15	39
94 AL	2	0	4.76	44	1	34.0	35	18	15	31
95 NL	3	0	1.47	58	0	36.2	28	6	10	40
Life	14	10	3.84	385	5	293.1	293	125	116	224
3 AVE	2	0	3.84	56	0	43.1	40	18	16	43

KEVIN FOSTER

Position: Pitcher
Team: Chicago Cubs
Born: Jan. 13, 1969 Evanston, IL
Height: 6'1" **Weight:** 170 lbs.
Bats: right **Throws:** right
Acquired: Traded by Phillies for Shawn Boskie, 4/94

Player Summary
Fantasy Value	$7 to $9
Card Value	5¢ to 8¢
Will	rack up strikeouts
Can't	avoid gopher balls
Expect	great pickoff move
Don't Expect	defensive woes

It shouldn't be surprising that Foster is still learning how to pitch. Signed as a third baseman out of Kishwaukee College in Illinois, he spent two years as an infielder before switching to the mound in 1990. An aggressive worker, his tendency to pitch up in the strike zone hurt him in Wrigley Field. Foster has flashes of brilliance. He pitched eight shutout innings and tied his career high with nine strikeouts in a 3-0 win at New York on July 4. But he also threw more home run balls than any other NL pitcher. For much of the 1995 season, he yielded less hits than innings, fanned about eight hitters per game, and displayed decent control (three and one-half walks). He also does an excellent job of monitoring the running game and fielding his position, where he's literally a fifth infielder. He's not much of a hitter, however. A skinny pitcher who throws hard, Foster features a rising fastball, a curveball, and a changeup. His outs come on strikeouts or fly balls—a dangerous game plan for a pitcher working half his schedule in the Windy City.

Major League Pitching Register
	W	L	ERA	G	CG	IP	H	ER	BB	SO
93 NL	0	1	14.85	2	0	6.2	13	11	7	6
94 NL	3	4	2.89	13	0	81.0	70	26	35	75
95 NL	12	11	4.51	30	0	167.2	149	84	65	146
Life	15	16	4.27	45	0	255.1	232	121	107	227
2 AVE	9	9	3.90	26	0	151.1	133	66	61	135

CURRENT PLAYERS

JOHN FRANCO

Position: Pitcher
Team: New York Mets
Born: Sept. 17, 1960 Brooklyn, NY
Height: 5'10" **Weight:** 185 lbs.
Bats: left **Throws:** left
Acquired: Traded by Reds with Don Brown for Kip Gross and Randy Myers, 12/89

Player Summary	
Fantasy Value	$20 to $25
Card Value	5¢ to 8¢
Will	bank on slow change
Can't	make 60 appearances
Expect	righties to struggle
Don't Expect	gopher woes

It looks like a screwball. It moves like a screwball. But it's actually a slow changeup that gives this little lefty a potent weapon against right-handed hitters. Franco is more effective against righties than lefties, though he yields less hits than innings against all comers. A control artist who struck out about two and one-half batters for every walk, he is effective at getting batters to hit ground balls. Blending fastballs and sliders with the change, he tries to jam hitters inside. A five-time All-Star, Franco is still a valuable closer who strands most runners, rarely throws a gopher ball, and converts most of his save opportunities. Few runners challenge the St. John's product, who has a fine pickoff move. Franco is also a first-rate fielder. His main worry is a return of recurring elbow problems that plagued him as recently as 1993.

Major League Pitching Register

	W	L	ERA	G	S	IP	H	ER	BB	SO
84 NL	6	2	2.61	54	4	79.1	74	23	36	55
85 NL	12	3	2.18	67	12	99.0	83	24	40	61
86 NL	6	6	2.94	74	29	101.0	90	33	44	84
87 NL	8	5	2.52	68	32	82.0	76	23	27	61
88 NL	6	6	1.57	70	39	86.0	60	15	27	46
89 NL	4	8	3.12	60	32	80.2	77	28	36	60
90 NL	5	3	2.53	55	33	67.2	66	19	21	56
91 NL	5	9	2.93	52	30	55.1	61	18	18	45
92 NL	6	2	1.64	31	15	33.0	24	6	11	20
93 NL	4	3	5.20	35	10	36.1	46	21	19	29
94 NL	1	4	2.70	47	30	50.0	47	15	19	42
95 NL	5	3	2.44	48	29	51.2	48	14	17	41
Life	68	54	2.62	661	295	822.0	752	239	315	600
3 AVE	4	4	3.16	52	28	55.1	55	19	22	45

JULIO FRANCO

Position: First base
Team: Cleveland Indians
Born: Aug. 23, 1961 San Pedro de Macoris, Dominican Republic
Height: 6'1" **Weight:** 185 lbs.
Bats: right **Throws:** right
Acquired: Signed as a free agent, 12/95

Player Summary	
Fantasy Value	$10 to $15
Card Value	6¢ to 10¢
Will	hit to all fields
Can't	show OK glove
Expect	great clutch work
Don't Expect	'94's RBI

Franco signed a contract to play with Lotte in the Japanese Pacific League for the 1995 season while the strike was still going on, not knowing if there was going to be major-league baseball in the States. He batted .306 with 58 RBI, and then he signed a contract to play in Cleveland in '96. In 1994, he was installed as the White Sox DH and cleanup man, batting behind Frank Thomas. Franco collected 48 RBI on his first 47 hits, finishing with 98 in 113 games. He also managed to reach a career peak with 20 homers. A line-drive hitter with a batting crown (in 1991), Franco hits with authority to all fields. He murders left-handed pitchers. Slowed by chronic knee problems, the three-time All-Star still steals occasionally and is rarely caught trying. Franco was the 1990 All-Star Game MVP.

Major League Batting Register

	BA	G	AB	R	H	2B	3B	HR	RBI	SB
82 NL	.276	16	29	3	8	1	0	0	3	0
83 AL	.273	149	560	68	153	24	8	8	80	32
84 AL	.286	160	658	82	188	22	5	3	79	19
85 AL	.288	160	636	97	183	33	4	6	90	13
86 AL	.306	149	599	80	183	30	5	10	74	10
87 AL	.319	128	495	86	158	24	3	8	52	32
88 AL	.303	152	613	88	186	23	6	10	54	25
89 AL	.316	150	548	80	173	31	5	13	92	21
90 AL	.296	157	582	96	172	27	1	11	69	31
91 AL	.341	146	589	108	201	27	3	15	78	36
92 AL	.234	35	107	19	25	7	0	2	8	1
93 AL	.289	144	532	85	154	31	3	14	84	9
94 AL	.319	112	433	72	138	19	2	20	98	8
Life	.301	1658	6381	964	1922	299	45	120	861	237

CURRENT PLAYERS

LOU FRAZIER

Position: Outfield
Team: Texas Rangers
Born: Jan. 26, 1965 St. Louis, MO
Height: 6'2" **Weight:** 180 lbs.
Bats: both **Throws:** right
Acquired: Traded by Expos for Hector Fajardo, 7/95

Player Summary	
Fantasy Value	$2 to $4
Card Value	4¢ to 6¢
Will	run like the wind
Can't	reach the fences
Expect	great batting eye
Don't Expect	a regular spot

Once he got into the lineup, it was hard to get him out. Acquired to provide speed and defense off the bench in the late innings, Frazier hardly had time to gather splinters in Texas. He got 10 hits in his first 35 Texas at bats (.286), scoring eight runs and stealing six bases in as many tries over that same period. He even had a four-RBI game Aug. 9. A spray hitter with little power, he's better batting left-handed. Originally signed as a shortstop by the Astros out of Scottsdale Community College, Frazier has played everywhere but pitcher and catcher during his pro career. He twice led minor leagues in stolen bases—once by swiping 87 in a 130-game season. Blessed with a tremendous batting eye, he twice had 90-walk seasons in the minors. He's been less patient in the majors, however, as he's tried to bat his way off the bench. Frazier would be much more valuable if he waited for walks, then turned on his speed. That speed gives him great range in the outfield, where he's most often used in left field. He has also filled in at second base.

Major League Batting Register

	BA	G	AB	R	H	2B	3B	HR	RBI	SB
93 NL	.286	112	189	27	54	7	1	1	16	17
94 NL	.271	76	140	25	38	3	1	0	14	20
95 NL	.190	35	63	6	12	2	0	0	3	4
95 AL	.212	49	99	19	21	2	0	0	8	9
Life	.255	272	491	77	125	14	2	1	41	50
2 AVE	.245	103	186	28	46	6	1	1	14	16

MARVIN FREEMAN

Position: Pitcher
Team: Colorado Rockies
Born: April 10, 1963 Chicago, IL
Height: 6'7" **Weight:** 222 lbs.
Bats: right **Throws:** right
Acquired: Signed as a free agent, 10/93

Player Summary	
Fantasy Value	$1 to $3
Card Value	4¢ to 6¢
Will	hit comeback trail
Can't	always find plate
Expect	grounders
Don't Expect	hits from righties

One year after becoming Colorado's top starter, Freeman fell victim to control problems and injuries. He finished a rough first half by throwing seven scoreless innings at the Expos on July 9. In that game, he changed his mechanics, pausing at the top of his delivery to give his arm a chance to catch up with the rest of his body. Unable to maintain any consistency, however, Freeman was relegated to relief less than a month later. Then he went on the DL with a strained oblique muscle. When he has his control and his health, he has the ability to win in the majors. He uses a sinker, a slider, and a forkball to force batters to hit the ball on the ground. During his breakthrough season in 1994, Freeman yielded less than two walks per game. He's especially effective against right-handed hitters. The Jackson State product doesn't help himself with his fielding or pickoff move. He once pitched a Triple-A no-hitter.

Major League Pitching Register

	W	L	ERA	G	CG	IP	H	ER	BB	SO
86 NL	2	0	2.25	7	0	16.0	6	4	10	8
88 NL	2	3	6.10	11	0	51.2	55	35	43	37
89 NL	0	0	6.00	1	0	3.0	2	2	5	0
90 NL	1	2	4.31	25	0	48.0	41	23	17	38
91 NL	1	0	3.00	34	0	48.0	37	16	13	34
92 NL	7	5	3.22	58	0	64.1	61	23	29	41
93 NL	2	0	6.08	21	0	23.2	24	16	10	25
94 NL	10	2	2.80	19	0	112.2	113	35	23	67
95 NL	3	7	5.89	22	0	94.2	122	62	41	61
Life	28	19	4.21	194	0	462.0	461	216	191	311
2 AVE	9	5	4.04	26	0	132.3	148	60	39	82

CURRENT PLAYERS

JEFF FRYE

Position: Second base
Team: Texas Rangers
Born: Aug. 31, 1966 Oakland, CA
Height: 5'9" **Weight:** 165 lbs.
Bats: right **Throws:** right
Acquired: 30th-round pick in 6/88 free-agent draft

Player Summary
Fantasy Value	$4 to $6
Card Value	4¢ to 6¢
Will	reach base often
Can't	escape injuries
Expect	contact hitting
Don't Expect	extra-base hits

Injuries have interfered with Frye's progress during each of the last three seasons. He missed all of 1993 after tearing an anterior cruciate ligament in his right knee. He then broke his wrist when hit by a pitch during winter ball just before 1994 spring training. A sore right hamstring disabled him twice during the first half of 1995. Frye still finished with the most at bats of his brief big-league career, however. A singles hitter and good bunter who makes contact, he is a master of bat control. He had more walks than strikeouts in six of his eight pro seasons. He also batted .300 in three seasons in the minors, including a .313 effort in 1989 that led the Class-A South Atlantic League. A good two-strike hitter, he hits well with runners in scoring position, produces in late-inning pressure situations, and rarely grounds into double plays. He's lost some speed since the knee injury but still covers lots of ground at second. His defense is sound, and he turns the double play with little difficulty. Frye was a first-team NAIA All-American at Southeastern Oklahoma State in 1988.

Major League Batting Register
	BA	G	AB	R	H	2B	3B	HR	RBI	SB
92 AL	.256	67	199	24	51	9	1	1	12	1
94 AL	.327	57	205	37	67	20	3	0	18	6
95 AL	.278	90	313	38	87	15	2	4	29	3
Life	.286	214	717	99	205	44	6	5	59	10
2 AVE	.300	91	320	47	96	23	3	2	29	6

TRAVIS FRYMAN

Position: Third base
Team: Detroit Tigers
Born: March 25, 1969 Lexington, KY
Height: 6'2" **Weight:** 190 lbs.
Bats: right **Throws:** right
Acquired: Third-round pick in 6/87 free-agent draft

Player Summary
Fantasy Value	$17 to $20
Card Value	12¢ to 20¢
Will	supply pop
Can't	stop strikeouts
Expect	powerful throws
Don't Expect	return to short

Entering his seventh season in the majors, Fryman is still struggling to master the strike zone. Before 1995, he averaged about three strikeouts per walk and even had the dubious distinction of leading the majors in Ks (128 in 114 games in 1994). Showing more patience last summer, his walks were up and strikeouts down—but his power also suffered. His best game came Aug. 2, when he homered twice in a 5-0 win over Boston. A three-time All-Star who had as many 90-RBI years, he should be much more successful against southpaws. But they gave him fits almost all of last year. Fryman's patience helped him finish with a healthy on-base percentage. He steals a handful of bases each year but is only an average runner. He is better in the field, where his powerful arm is his biggest asset. Managers told *Baseball America* last summer that he owns the league's second-best infield arm (behind Mike Blowers). A converted shortstop, Fryman has good reactions and good hands at the hot corner.

Major League Batting Register
	BA	G	AB	R	H	2B	3B	HR	RBI	SB
90 AL	.297	66	232	32	69	11	1	9	27	3
91 AL	.259	149	557	65	144	36	3	21	91	12
92 AL	.266	161	659	87	175	31	4	20	96	8
93 AL	.300	151	607	98	182	37	5	22	97	9
94 AL	.263	114	464	66	122	34	5	18	85	2
95 AL	.275	144	567	79	156	21	5	15	81	4
Life	.275	785	3086	427	848	170	23	105	477	38
3 AVE	.279	158	633	93	176	36	6	21	103	5

CURRENT PLAYERS

GARY GAETTI

Position: Third base; first base
Team: Kansas City Royals
Born: Aug. 19, 1958 Centralia, IL
Height: 6′ **Weight:** 200 lbs.
Bats: right **Throws:** right
Acquired: Signed as a free agent, 6/93

Player Summary	
Fantasy Value	$9 to $11
Card Value	5¢ to 8¢
Will	defy Father Time
Can't	display any speed
Expect	good power
Don't Expect	throwing errors

Fading veterans rarely return to the Fountain of Youth. But Gaetti was a notable exception last summer. After failing to hit 20 homers for six seasons, he suddenly cleared 30—finishing with his finest all-around season since 1987. The rebuilding Royals had retained Gaetti only to add experience. Not even sure he could play every day, they had been prepared to make rookie Joe Randa their regular third baseman. But Gaetti would have none of that. The two-time All-Star led the team in homers and RBI despite a mysterious inability to hit left-handers. He doesn't have much speed but retains quick reactions at third, where he won Gold Gloves from 1986 to 1989. The owner of a strong arm, Gaetti is a fine fielder, adept at charging rollers or snaring liners headed for the corner.

Major League Batting Register

	BA	G	AB	R	H	2B	3B	HR	RBI	SB
81 AL	.192	9	26	4	5	0	0	2	3	0
82 AL	.230	145	508	59	117	25	4	25	84	0
83 AL	.245	157	584	81	143	30	3	21	78	7
84 AL	.262	162	588	55	154	29	4	5	65	11
85 AL	.246	160	560	71	138	31	0	20	63	13
86 AL	.287	157	596	91	171	34	1	34	108	14
87 AL	.257	154	584	95	150	36	2	31	109	10
88 AL	.301	133	468	66	141	29	2	28	88	7
89 AL	.251	130	498	63	125	11	4	19	75	6
90 AL	.229	154	577	61	132	27	5	16	85	6
91 AL	.246	152	586	58	144	22	1	18	66	5
92 AL	.226	130	456	41	103	13	2	12	48	3
93 AL	.245	102	331	40	81	20	1	14	50	1
94 AL	.287	90	327	53	94	15	3	12	57	0
95 AL	.261	137	514	76	134	27	0	35	96	3
Life	.254	1972	7203	914	1832	349	32	292	1075	86
3 AVE	.266	128	457	67	121	24	2	23	79	1

GREG GAGNE

Position: Shortstop
Team: Los Angeles Dodgers
Born: Nov. 12, 1961 Fall River, MA
Height: 5′11″ **Weight:** 172 lbs.
Bats: right **Throws:** right
Acquired: Signed as a free agent, 11/95

Player Summary	
Fantasy Value	$4 to $6
Card Value	4¢ to 6¢
Will	supply strong defense
Can't	hit for high average
Expect	swing on first pitch
Don't Expect	less than 20 doubles

Even if Gagne didn't hit as well as he does, many clubs would gladly make him their shortstop. Although he lacks the flash of an Omar Vizquel, Gagne remains one of baseball's best defensive shortstops. He has quick reactions, soft hands, and a strong, accurate arm. He scoops anything hit in his direction, even adding acrobatics when necessary. Although he's never won a Gold Glove, Gagne has led the AL in putouts and fielding percentage. He's no slouch at the plate, either. A first-pitch, fastball hitter, he sprays singles to all fields but also has enough gap power to hit 20 doubles a year—something he'd done 10 years in a row. He's also finished with double-digits in homers four times, and has even hit four homers in 24 postseason games. Gagne shares the major-league record for most inside-the-park homers in one game (two).

Major League Batting Register

	BA	G	AB	R	H	2B	3B	HR	RBI	SB
83 AL	.111	10	27	2	3	1	0	0	3	0
84 AL	.000	2	1	0	0	0	0	0	0	0
85 AL	.225	114	293	37	66	15	3	2	23	10
86 AL	.250	156	472	63	118	22	6	12	54	12
87 AL	.265	137	437	68	116	28	7	10	40	6
88 AL	.236	149	461	70	109	20	6	14	48	15
89 AL	.272	149	460	69	125	29	7	9	48	11
90 AL	.235	138	388	38	91	22	3	7	38	8
91 AL	.265	139	408	52	108	23	3	8	42	11
92 AL	.246	146	439	53	108	23	0	7	39	6
93 AL	.280	159	540	66	151	32	3	10	57	10
94 AL	.259	107	375	39	97	23	3	7	51	10
95 AL	.256	120	430	58	110	25	4	6	49	3
Life	.254	1526	4731	615	1202	263	45	92	492	102
3 AVE	.265	148	517	62	137	31	4	9	61	9

CURRENT PLAYERS

ANDRES GALARRAGA

Position: First base
Team: Colorado Rockies
Born: June 18, 1961 Caracas, Venezuela
Height: 6'3" **Weight:** 235 lbs.
Bats: right **Throws:** right
Acquired: Signed as a free agent, 11/92

Player Summary
Fantasy Value	$25 to $30
Card Value	10¢ to 15¢
Will	supply power
Can't	stop striking out
Expect	excellent defense
Don't Expect	high on-base mark

When he posted a league-best .370 average in 1993, Galarraga fanned about three times per walk. Last year, with the ratio approaching 5-to-1 for much of the season, he struggled to reach .300. But the power hasn't disappeared. Using an open stance suggested by Colorado manager Don Baylor, Galarraga became the fourth player to hit three home runs in three innings—each farther than the one before. Angered at being left off the All-Star squad for the second straight year, Galarraga went 7-for-9 with three homers and 10 RBI in the first two games after the announcement. He punishes lefties, holds his own against righties, and hits with power to all fields. He has surprising speed and will steal a few bases. Galarraga earned his "Big Cat" nickname with his graceful fielding. The former Gold Glove winner has good instincts, quick reactions, and soft hands.

Major League Batting Register

	BA	G	AB	R	H	2B	3B	HR	RBI	SB
85 NL	.187	24	75	9	14	1	0	2	4	1
86 NL	.271	105	321	39	87	13	0	10	42	6
87 NL	.305	147	551	72	168	40	3	13	90	7
88 NL	.302	157	609	99	184	42	8	29	92	13
89 NL	.257	152	572	76	147	30	1	23	85	12
90 NL	.256	155	579	65	148	29	0	20	87	10
91 NL	.219	107	375	34	82	13	2	9	33	5
92 NL	.243	95	325	38	79	14	2	10	39	5
93 NL	.370	120	470	71	174	35	4	22	98	2
94 NL	.319	103	417	77	133	21	0	31	85	8
95 NL	.280	143	554	89	155	29	3	31	106	12
Life	.283	1308	4848	669	1371	267	23	200	761	81
3 AVE	.319	142	560	93	179	32	2	34	112	9

DAVE GALLAGHER

Position: Outfield
Team: California Angels
Born: Sept. 20, 1960 Trenton, NJ
Height: 6' **Weight:** 180 lbs.
Bats: right **Throws:** right
Acquired: Traded by Phillies for Kevin Flora and Russ Springer, 8/95

Player Summary
Fantasy Value	$0
Card Value	4¢ to 6¢
Will	back up four spots
Can't	show much power
Expect	strong fielding
Don't Expect	a hint of speed

Though Gallagher rarely hits a home run or steals a base, he's a valuable player because of his versatility, defensive skills, and attitude. A contact hitter who walks about as often as he strikes out, he goes with the pitch and uses the whole field. Often used as a pinch hitter, especially against left-handed pitching, Gallagher is strictly a singles hitter these days, though he once delivered a career-best 22 doubles for the 1989 White Sox. He played 161 games for that team, mainly because he provided such sound outfield defense. Despite sub-standard range (especially in center), he has quick reactions, soft hands, and a strong throwing arm. He makes an error as often as he hits a home run (almost never). Gallagher had a good year for Philadelphia last year before the Angels added him as late-summer title insurance. He's a terrific positive influence in the clubhouse.

Major League Batting Register

	BA	G	AB	R	H	2B	3B	HR	RBI	SB
87 AL	.111	15	36	2	4	1	1	0	1	2
88 AL	.303	101	347	59	105	15	3	5	31	5
89 AL	.266	161	601	74	160	22	2	1	46	5
90 AL	.254	68	126	12	32	4	1	0	7	1
91 AL	.293	90	270	32	79	17	0	1	30	2
92 NL	.240	98	175	20	42	11	1	1	21	4
93 NL	.274	99	201	34	55	12	2	6	28	1
94 NL	.224	89	152	27	34	5	0	2	14	0
95 NL	.318	62	157	12	50	12	0	1	12	0
95 AL	.188	11	16	1	3	1	0	0	0	0
Life	.271	794	2081	273	564	100	10	17	190	20
3 AVE	.267	102	203	29	54	11	1	3	20	0

CURRENT PLAYERS

MIKE GALLEGO

Position: Shortstop; second base; third base
Team: Oakland Athletics
Born: Oct. 31, 1960 Whittier, CA
Height: 5'8" **Weight:** 160 lbs.
Bats: right **Throws:** right
Acquired: Signed as a minor-league free agent, 4/95

Player Summary
Fantasy Value	$1 to $3
Card Value	4¢ to 6¢
Will	make contact
Can't	steal bases often
Expect	fine on-base mark
Don't Expect	big power barrage

Although Gallego returned to his Oakland roots last season, he couldn't reclaim his old job at second base. Receiving limited at bats early because of torn tissue and a strain of his left arch, he found Brent Gates and Mike Bordick entrenched at second and short, respectively. Gallego wound up playing every infield spot but first, and served as an occasional pinch hitter. A capable bat-handler, he once tied for the AL lead in sacrifice bunts (17 in 1990). He is a contact hitter with plenty of patience, and he usually posts an on-base percentage far above his batting average. Most of his extra-base hits are doubles. Always trying to move runners up, Gallego sprays hits to all fields and occasionally bunts for a hit. He steals only a few bases per year, however. Signed as a second baseman, he has also played short, third, and the outfield.

Major League Batting Register

	BA	G	AB	R	H	2B	3B	HR	RBI	SB
85 AL	.208	76	77	13	16	5	1	1	9	1
86 AL	.270	20	37	2	10	2	0	0	4	0
87 AL	.250	72	124	18	31	6	0	2	14	0
88 AL	.209	129	277	38	58	8	0	2	20	2
89 AL	.252	133	357	45	90	14	2	3	30	7
90 AL	.206	140	389	36	80	13	2	3	34	5
91 AL	.247	159	482	67	119	15	4	12	49	6
92 AL	.254	53	173	24	44	7	1	3	14	0
93 AL	.283	119	403	63	114	20	1	10	54	3
94 AL	.239	89	306	39	73	17	1	6	41	0
95 AL	.233	43	120	11	28	0	0	0	8	0
Life	.242	1033	2745	356	663	107	12	42	277	24
2 AVE	.260	122	417	59	108	22	1	9	56	2

RON GANT

Position: Outfield
Team: Cincinnati Reds
Born: March 2, 1965 Victoria, TX
Height: 6' **Weight:** 172 lbs.
Bats: right **Throws:** right
Acquired: Signed as a free agent, 6/94

Player Summary
Fantasy Value	$25 to $30
Card Value	15¢ to 25¢
Will	try 30-30 again
Can't	throw ball well
Expect	frequent homers
Don't Expect	strong fielding

There's no longer any doubt about Gant's recovery. Out for the entire 1994 season with a multiple compound fracture of his right leg (the result of a dirt-bike accident), he returned after the Reds gave him an incentive-laden contract. The owner of baseball's biggest biceps should have asked for more. He resumed his rampage against NL pitchers, ranking among the league leaders in home runs, RBI, slugging, and on-base percentage. The two-time 30-30 man also showed he could still be a high-percentage basestealer. Gant had four extra-inning, game-winning homers—a single-season record—by July 1. A dead pull hitter who feasts on fastballs, Gant fans frequently but will also wait for his pitch. His frequent walks yielded an on-base mark 100 points higher than his batting average. Once an iron-gloved infielder, Gant gets by in left field despite bad hands and a substandard arm. He is a two-time All-Star.

Major League Batting Register

	BA	G	AB	R	H	2B	3B	HR	RBI	SB
87 NL	.265	21	83	9	22	4	0	2	9	4
88 NL	.259	146	563	85	146	28	8	19	60	19
89 NL	.177	75	260	26	46	8	3	9	25	9
90 NL	.303	152	575	107	174	34	3	32	84	33
91 NL	.251	154	561	101	141	35	3	32	105	34
92 NL	.259	153	544	74	141	22	6	17	80	32
93 NL	.274	157	606	113	166	27	4	36	117	26
95 NL	.276	119	410	79	113	19	4	29	88	23
Life	.263	977	3602	594	949	177	31	176	568	180
2 AVE	.275	145	534	101	147	24	4	34	108	26

CURRENT PLAYERS

CARLOS GARCIA

Position: Second base
Team: Pittsburgh Pirates
Born: Oct. 15, 1967 Tachira, Venezuela
Height: 6'1" **Weight:** 185 lbs.
Bats: right **Throws:** right
Acquired: Signed as a free agent, 1/87

Player Summary	
Fantasy Value	$7 to $9
Card Value	5¢ to 8¢
Will	swing potent bat
Can't	stage power show
Expect	speed to be used
Don't Expect	high on-base mark

Garcia wears No. 13 as a tribute to his idol, former Cincinnati shortstop Dave Concepcion. But he started playing like Concepcion only recently. Garcia had six RBI in an 11-7 win over Los Angeles on June 15, and completed a 21-game hitting streak 13 days later. Garcia hit .365 during the streak, helping him maintain a .300-plus average as the season entered its last month. Though he strikes out twice as much as he walks, he is a productive hitter when he connects. An aggressive wrist hitter with good bat speed, Garcia nets extra bases on more than a quarter of his hits, though few are home runs. He also puts many bunts into play. He would have stolen more often last year if a strained left hamstring had not interfered. He was disabled with the injury on Aug. 1. Signed as a shortstop, Garcia spent his first five minor-league seasons there before switching to second at the big-league level. He has good reactions, soft hands, and a strong arm. Garcia was an All-Star reserve in 1994.

MIKE GARDINER

Position: Pitcher
Team: Detroit Tigers
Born: Oct. 19, 1965 Sarnia, Ontario
Height: 6' **Weight:** 200 lbs.
Bats: both **Throws:** right
Acquired: Signed as a free agent, 8/93

Player Summary	
Fantasy Value	$0
Card Value	4¢ to 6¢
Will	try for comeback
Can't	stop gopher balls
Expect	more relief work
Don't Expect	many strikeouts

Had he stayed healthy last year, Gardiner could have proved much-needed relief to Detroit's youthful starting rotation. Instead, he missed virtually the entire season with severe allergies and a sinus infection. At age 30, the 1984 Canadian Olympian could make a strong comeback. When he has control of his fastball, forkball, slider, and curve, he dominates right-handed hitters and strands most of the runners he inherits. A converted starter, Gardiner has the stamina to work several innings per outing. Though not a strikeout pitcher, he coaxes lots of grounders when his location is working. When it isn't, he's prone to throwing occasional gopher balls. Gardiner has no problems holding runners or fielding his position. He was an 18th-round draft choice by Seattle out of Indiana State. He pitched in the majors for Seattle, Boston, and Montreal in addition to Detroit.

Major League Batting Register

	BA	G	AB	R	H	2B	3B	HR	RBI	SB
90 NL	.500	4	4	1	2	0	0	0	0	0
91 NL	.250	12	24	2	6	0	2	0	1	0
92 NL	.205	22	39	4	8	1	0	0	4	0
93 NL	.269	141	546	77	147	25	5	12	47	18
94 NL	.277	98	412	49	114	15	2	6	28	18
95 NL	.294	104	367	41	108	24	2	6	50	8
Life	.277	381	1392	174	385	65	11	24	130	44
3 AVE	.279	132	513	64	143	24	3	9	48	17

Major League Pitching Register

	W	L	ERA	G	S	IP	H	ER	BB	SO
90 AL	0	2	10.66	5	0	12.2	22	15	5	6
91 AL	9	10	4.85	22	0	130.0	140	70	47	91
92 AL	4	10	4.75	28	0	130.2	126	69	58	79
93 NL	2	3	5.21	24	0	38.0	40	22	19	21
93 AL	0	0	3.97	10	0	11.1	12	5	7	4
94 AL	2	2	4.14	38	5	58.2	53	27	23	31
95 AL	0	0	14.59	9	0	12.1	27	20	2	7
Life	17	27	5.21	136	5	393.2	420	228	161	239
2 AVE	2	3	4.43	44	4	65.2	63	33	29	34

CURRENT PLAYERS

MARK GARDNER

Position: Pitcher
Team: Florida Marlins
Born: March 1, 1962 Los Angeles, CA
Height: 6'1" **Weight:** 190 lbs.
Bats: right **Throws:** right
Acquired: Signed as a free agent, 1/94

Player Summary
Fantasy Value	$1
Card Value	4¢ to 6¢
Will	seek regular slot
Can't	prevent long ball
Expect	good pickoff move
Don't Expect	another no-hitter

Gardner has a way of confusing his managers. He has moments of brilliance as both a starter and reliever, but never shows enough consistency to nail down either job. As a reliever last year, he stranded the first 16 runners he inherited. As an emergency starter, he threw a 6-0 shutout against St. Louis on July 9, fanning eight and walking none. Gardner even made the record books with a nine-inning no-hitter against Los Angeles on July 26, 1991. He lost, 1-0, after yielding two hits in the 10th. He yielded about one hit per inning for much of the 1995 season while averaging around seven and one-half whiffs per game. He gets most of those Ks on a big-breaking curve, which he blends with a fastball and a changeup. When his control is off, Gardner's pitches quickly become gophers. He's much more effective against right-handed hitters. He helps himself with an outstanding pickoff move, but neither his fielding nor his hitting deserve much comment.

Major League Pitching Register

	W	L	ERA	G	CG	IP	H	ER	BB	SO
89 NL	0	3	5.13	7	0	26.1	26	15	11	21
90 NL	7	9	3.42	27	3	152.2	129	58	61	135
91 NL	9	11	3.85	27	0	168.1	139	72	75	107
92 NL	12	10	4.36	33	0	179.2	179	87	60	132
93 AL	4	6	6.19	17	0	91.2	92	63	36	54
94 NL	4	4	4.87	20	0	92.1	97	50	30	57
95 NL	5	5	4.49	39	1	102.1	109	51	43	87
Life	41	48	4.38	170	4	813.1	771	396	316	593
3 AVE	5	6	5.10	30	0	112.2	117	64	42	77

BRENT GATES

Position: Second base
Team: Oakland Athletics
Born: March 14, 1970 Grand Rapids, MI
Height: 6'1" **Weight:** 180 lbs.
Bats: both **Throws:** right
Acquired: First-round pick in 6/91 free-agent draft

Player Summary
Fantasy Value	$7 to $9
Card Value	5¢ to 8¢
Will	enjoy hot stretches
Can't	clear fences often
Expect	hits vs. lefties
Don't Expect	many steals

When Gates launched a long hitting streak last August, the A's weren't surprised; the one-time University of Minnesota shortstop had a 35-game hitting streak in the minors. His big-league tear showed that he had healed completely from the wrist and knee injuries that hampered his progress in 1994. A switch-hitter who's more productive against lefties, Gates fans too frequently for a nonslugger, but he compensates by showing enough patience to produce an on-base percentage about 50 points higher than his batting average. A good clutch hitter, he slaps hard grounders to all fields. He has some alley power but isn't a threat to reach double digits in home runs or stolen bases. While Gates may never become a Gold Glove candidate at second, he once led a minor league in chances, putouts, assists, and double plays. He has quick reactions, soft hands, and a strong throwing arm, plus range that is more than acceptable. As a collegian, Gates broke many of the college records set by Terry Steinbach, later his teammate with Oakland.

Major League Batting Register

	BA	G	AB	R	H	2B	3B	HR	RBI	SB
93 AL	.290	139	535	64	155	29	2	7	69	7
94 AL	.283	64	233	29	66	11	1	2	24	3
95 AL	.254	136	524	60	133	24	4	5	56	3
Life	.274	339	1292	153	354	64	7	14	149	13
3 AVE	.274	127	484	57	133	24	3	5	55	5

BENJI GIL

Position: Shortstop
Team: Texas Rangers
Born: Oct. 6, 1972 Tijuana, Mexico
Height: 6'2" **Weight:** 182 lbs.
Bats: right **Throws:** right
Acquired: First-round pick in 6/91 free-agent draft

Player Summary	
Fantasy Value	$3 to $5
Card Value	6¢ to 10¢
Will	play great defense
Can't	reduce whiff ratio
Expect	gradual improvement
Don't Expect	solid on-base mark

The potential is obvious. But even if Gil never brings his minor-league power and speed production to the majors, his exceptional defense should keep him in the big leagues. A bust in two 1993 AL trials, Gil surfaced again last spring after two strong years in the upper minors. He supplied strong defense at short but had a 1-for-32 skid in August that gave him the dubious distinction of leading both leagues in strikeouts. Until he reduces his ratio of strikeouts to walks—which was about 5-to-1 last year—and swings a respectable stick against left-handed pitchers, Gil will only be considered half a shortstop. But what a half! He netted extra bases on about one-third of his hits and fielded his position like a human vacuum cleaner. He has instant reactions, exceptional range, good hands, and a powerful throwing arm. In 1994, he led the Triple-A American Association in chances, putouts, assists, and double plays. He got his first big-league hit against Boston ace Roger Clemens. At 23, Gil has a bright future.

Major League Batting Register

	BA	G	AB	R	H	2B	3B	HR	RBI	SB
93 AL	.123	22	57	3	7	0	0	0	2	1
95 AL	.219	130	415	36	91	20	3	9	46	2
Life	.208	152	472	39	98	20	3	9	48	3

BERNARD GILKEY

Position: Outfield
Team: St. Louis Cardinals
Born: Sept. 24, 1966 St. Louis, MO
Height: 6' **Weight:** 170 lbs.
Bats: right **Throws:** right
Acquired: Signed as a free agent, 8/84

Player Summary	
Fantasy Value	$14 to $17
Card Value	5¢ to 8¢
Will	show some sock
Can't	find old speed
Expect	good clutch bat
Don't Expect	stellar defense

Gilkey gives his club speed plus power at the top of the lineup, but he does not supply enough of either to suggest Rickey Henderson or Kenny Lofton. Though he once swiped 107 bases over a two-year span in the minors, Gilkey hasn't shown the same speed in the National League. Nor has he shown the same patience which once allowed him to build up huge on-base percentages. He had more walks than strikeouts in five straight minor-league campaigns but has never done it in the majors. He does make decent contact, however, and draws enough passes to post an on-base average about 50 points above his batting average. He loves left-handers and thrives in clutch situations. He also got extra bases on about one-third of his hits last year. He usually succeeds when he tries to steal. Although he's not considered a great defender, Gilkey outruns his own mistakes, snares balls headed for the alley, and throws well for a left fielder. He led the NL with 19 assists in 1993.

Major League Batting Register

	BA	G	AB	R	H	2B	3B	HR	RBI	SB
90 NL	.297	18	64	11	19	5	2	1	3	6
91 NL	.216	81	268	28	58	7	2	5	20	14
92 NL	.302	131	384	56	116	19	4	7	43	18
93 NL	.305	137	557	99	170	40	5	16	70	15
94 NL	.253	105	380	52	96	22	1	6	45	15
95 NL	.298	121	480	73	143	33	4	17	69	12
Life	.282	593	2133	319	602	126	18	52	250	80
3 AVE	.286	140	544	85	155	36	4	15	70	17

CURRENT PLAYERS

JOE GIRARDI

Position: Catcher
Team: New York Yankees
Born: Oct. 14, 1964 Peoria, IL
Height: 6' **Weight:** 195 lbs.
Bats: right **Throws:** right
Acquired: Traded by Rockies for Mike DeJean and a player to be named later, 11/95

Player Summary	
Fantasy Value	$5 to $7
Card Value	4¢ to 6¢
Will	move runners along
Can't	show more patience
Expect	good game-calling
Don't Expect	any speed

If Girardi could build a catcher from scratch, he might use himself as a model. Using his Northwestern degree in industrial engineering, he'd create a sturdy, strong-armed receiver able to prevent wild pitches, block the plate, call a good game, and hold up his end on offense. The Girardi model might fan frequently but would make contact often enough to hit second in the lineup. That is an unlikely place for a hitter without speed, but a good spot for a hit-and-run man whose bunts and opposite-field grounders move runners up. He is a sound singles hitter who loves late-inning pressure spots. A thinking man's catcher, Girardi is highly regarded for his game-calling skills. His success rate at nailing basestealers has declined over the last three years, however. He also had trouble hitting left-handed pitchers last summer. But he also avoided his usual bout with chronic back problems. As a result, he assumed his heaviest workload since 1990.

Major League Batting Register

	BA	G	AB	R	H	2B	3B	HR	RBI	SB
89 NL	.248	59	157	15	39	10	0	1	14	2
90 NL	.270	133	419	36	113	24	2	1	38	8
91 NL	.191	21	47	3	9	2	0	0	6	0
92 NL	.270	91	270	19	73	3	1	1	12	0
93 NL	.290	86	310	35	90	14	5	3	31	6
94 NL	.276	93	330	47	91	9	4	4	34	3
95 NL	.262	125	462	63	121	17	2	8	55	3
Life	.269	608	1995	218	536	79	14	18	190	22
3 AVE	.274	119	432	57	118	15	4	6	47	5

BRIAN GIVENS

Position: Pitcher
Team: Milwaukee Brewers
Born: Nov. 6, 1965 Lompac, CA
Height: 6'6" **Weight:** 220 lbs.
Bats: right **Throws:** left
Acquired: Signed as a minor-league free agent, 10/94

Player Summary	
Fantasy Value	$0
Card Value	6¢ to 10¢
Will	bank on curveball
Can't	always find plate
Expect	berth in rotation
Don't Expect	new elbow trouble

Givens is living proof that patience pays off. He not only spent 12 years in the minors, but also endured five elbow operations, including "Tommy John surgery" in 1991. His odyssey spanned a dozen teams in five different organizations, but he never got a chance in the big leagues before 1995. He made it only after serving as a replacement during the protracted player strike that sliced three weeks off the front of the season. A former fireballer who now blends a huge curve with a sharp cut fastball, Givens got his first win July 16 when he yielded three hits in eight innings against the White Sox. He made another impressive showing Aug. 21 against Kansas City, yielding five hits in eight innings. He yielded about one hit per inning, kept the ball in the park, and held lefties around the Mendoza Line. He did suffer bouts of control trouble, however. Primarily a starter in the minors, he never won more than eight games in one season. He was originally the property of the Mets. Givens went 4-7 with a 3.68 ERA in 36 games (13 starts) for Birmingham in 1994. He averaged more than one strikeout per inning in two minor-league seasons.

Major League Pitching Register

	W	L	ERA	G	S	IP	H	ER	BB	SO
95 AL	5	7	4.95	19	0	107.1	116	59	54	73
Life	5	7	4.95	19	0	107.1	116	59	54	73

CURRENT PLAYERS

TOM GLAVINE

Position: Pitcher
Team: Atlanta Braves
Born: March 25, 1966 Concord, MA
Height: 6' **Weight:** 175 lbs.
Bats: left **Throws:** left
Acquired: Second-round pick in 6/84 free-agent draft

Player Summary	
Fantasy Value	$20 to $25
Card Value	12¢ to 20¢
Will	win most starts
Can't	capture K crown
Expect	fine hitting
Don't Expect	gopher woes

If he weren't on the same staff as Greg Maddux, Glavine would be a No. 1 starter. A 20-game winner for three straight years (1991 to '93), he has been the game's most successful southpaw over the last five seasons. Managers told *Baseball America* last year that Glavine owns the league's best changeup, even ahead of Maddux. Glavine blends the pitch with a fastball, a slider, and a curve—throwing all four for strikes. Though he's not a strikeout artist, Glavine maintained a 2-1 ratio of whiffs to walks for much of the 1995 season. He is extremely stingy with the home run ball. Glavine, a three-time All-Star, paints the outside corners with his changeup, then shocks hitters by coming inside with his fastball. The NL's 1991 Cy Young Award winner helps himself off the mound. Sometimes used as a pinch hitter or pinch runner, Glavine is also a fine fielder whose failure to win a Gold Glove is a mystery.

Major League Pitching Register

	W	L	ERA	G	CG	IP	H	ER	BB	SO
87 NL	2	4	5.54	9	0	50.1	55	31	33	20
88 NL	7	17	4.56	34	1	195.1	201	99	63	84
89 NL	14	8	3.68	29	6	186.0	172	76	40	90
90 NL	10	12	4.28	33	1	214.1	232	102	78	129
91 NL	20	11	2.55	34	9	246.2	201	70	69	192
92 NL	20	8	2.76	33	7	225.0	197	69	70	129
93 NL	22	6	3.20	36	4	239.1	236	85	90	120
94 NL	13	9	3.97	25	2	165.1	173	73	70	140
95 NL	16	7	3.08	29	3	198.2	182	68	66	127
Life	124	82	3.52	262	33	1721.0	1649	673	579	1031
3 AVE	19	9	3.42	35	3	231.2	228	88	88	153

CHRIS GOMEZ

Position: Shortstop; second base
Team: Detroit Tigers
Born: June 16, 1971 Los Angeles, CA
Height: 6'1" **Weight:** 183 lbs.
Bats: right **Throws:** right
Acquired: Third-round pick in 6/92 free-agent draft

Player Summary	
Fantasy Value	$5 to $7
Card Value	6¢ to 10¢
Will	improve over time
Can't	cut strikeout rate
Expect	some show of power
Don't Expect	defensive problems

A middle infielder with surprising pop, Gomez is still learning on the job. He got extra bases on more than one-third of his hits during much of the 1995 season but didn't make enough contact—especially against right-handed pitchers. When he does hit, however, he can be an offensive force. His 4-for-5 day at Boston on July 1 spurred an 11-2 victory. A power hitter with an aluminum bat at Long Beach State, Gomez started slowly after converting to wood as a pro. But winter weight training, plus a shortened swing, helped eliminate his reputation as a Punch-and-Judy hitter. His manager last season, Sparky Anderson, suggests that Gomez is another Dave Concepcion—a flashy fielder whose hitting improved as he gained experience. There's no doubt about Gomez's defense. Though signed as a shortstop, he's equally skilled at second base. He turns the double play from either spot, shows good range, and throws with enough power and accuracy to go deep in the shortstop hole. Gomez should continue to accumulate at bats this season.

Major League Batting Register

	BA	G	AB	R	H	2B	3B	HR	RBI	SB
93 AL	.250	46	128	11	32	7	1	0	11	2
94 AL	.257	84	296	32	76	19	0	8	53	5
95 AL	.223	123	431	49	96	20	2	11	50	4
Life	.239	253	855	92	204	46	3	19	114	11
2 AVE	.238	128	451	50	108	25	1	12	65	6

CURRENT PLAYERS

LEO GOMEZ

Position: Third base
Team: Baltimore Orioles
Born: March 2, 1967 Canovanas, PR
Height: 6′ **Weight:** 202 lbs.
Bats: right **Throws:** right
Acquired: Signed as a free agent, 12/85

Player Summary
Fantasy Value	$3 to $5
Card Value	4¢ to 6¢
Will	show good power
Can't	steal any bases
Expect	patience at bat
Don't Expect	trouble vs. lefties

After four years as Baltimore's more-or-less regular third baseman, Gomez not only battled a foot injury last summer but lost his job to the right-left platoon of Jeff Manto and Jeff Huson. When healthy, Gomez is a power hitter with patience. He walks almost as often as he fans, yielding an on-base percentage much higher than his batting average. That helps, since he has a well-deserved reputation as a low-average, high-power player. He got extra bases on nearly half his hits in 1994. Gomez loves left-handed pitching and runners in scoring position. Although he doesn't have the speed to steal a base, he moves well enough to supply decent defense. His .975 fielding percentage in 1994 ranked second among AL third basemen. He has quick reactions, good hands, and a strong, accurate throwing arm. He led one minor league in assists and another in double plays. Gomez has played all four infield positions during a professional career that began in 1986.

Major League Batting Register
	BA	G	AB	R	H	2B	3B	HR	RBI	SB
90 AL	.231	12	39	3	9	0	0	0	1	0
91 AL	.233	118	391	40	91	17	2	16	45	1
92 AL	.265	137	468	62	124	24	0	17	64	2
93 AL	.197	71	244	30	48	7	0	10	25	0
94 AL	.274	84	285	46	78	20	0	15	56	0
95 AL	.236	53	127	16	30	5	0	4	12	0
Life	.245	475	1554	197	380	73	2	62	203	3
2 AVE	.245	95	323	47	79	18	0	16	52	0

ALEX GONZALEZ

Position: Shortstop
Team: Toronto Blue Jays
Born: April 8, 1973 Miami, FL
Height: 6′ **Weight:** 182 lbs.
Bats: right **Throws:** right
Acquired: 14th-round pick in 6/91 free-agent draft

Player Summary
Fantasy Value	$8 to $10
Card Value	6¢ to 10¢
Will	swing solid bat
Can't	stop strikeouts
Expect	All-Star future
Don't Expect	fielding lapses

At the tender age of 23, Gonzalez has already drawn comparisons with Cal Ripken and Barry Larkin, baseball's two All-Star shortstops. The reasons are obvious: power, speed, and dazzling defensive skills. Scouts insist Gonzalez will hit for average and power (61 steals and 28 homers in his last two minor-league years). During the 1995 season, he netted extra bases on one-third of his hits. A .300 hitter against lefties, he needs to boost his production against right-handers and become a more selective hitter. Until he trims his ratio of strikeouts to walks, Gonzalez won't be able to make maximum use of his speed. Not on the bases, anyway. In the field, he ranges far and wide to demonstrate his acrobatic agility and shotgun arm. Before reaching the majors, he led his minor league in chances, putouts, and assists three years in a row. He's also finished first in double plays and fielding percentage. The son of an electrical engineering professor at the University of Miami, Gonzalez turned down a full scholarship offer to turn pro.

Major League Batting Register
	BA	G	AB	R	H	2B	3B	HR	RBI	SB
94 AL	.151	15	53	7	8	3	1	0	1	3
95 AL	.243	111	367	51	89	19	4	10	42	4
Life	.231	126	420	58	97	22	5	10	43	7

CURRENT PLAYERS

JUAN GONZALEZ

Position: Designated hitter
Team: Texas Rangers
Born: Oct. 16, 1969 Vega Baja, PR
Height: 6'3" **Weight:** 215 lbs.
Bats: right **Throws:** right
Acquired: Signed as a free agent, 5/86

Player Summary
Fantasy Value	$25 to $30
Card Value	30¢ to 60¢
Will	produce great power
Can't	utilize speed
Expect	extra-base hits
Don't Expect	many walks

Gonzalez takes the hitter part of the DH equation seriously; he doesn't stand at the plate with the bat on his shoulder. He fanned almost four times more than he walked in 1995, figuring four bases with one swing beats one base with four balls. He pounds left-handed pitching, nets extra bases on nearly half his hits, and averages about one home run per one dozen at bats. Yet his on-base percentage was only a few points better than his batting average. Once a wild hacker, Gonzalez has learned to make better contact. On Aug. 21, he had a grand-slam homer and single in the same inning against Minnesota. When healthy, Gonzalez is a force. He won consecutive AL home run crowns in 1992 and 1993, and his .632 slugging percentage in 1993 led the American League. But he spent almost two months on the DL with neck, back, and shoulder problems. Convinced that weightlifting was a factor, Gonzalez stopped the practice in May. He missed 55 of the first 98 Texas games last year.

Major League Batting Register

	BA	G	AB	R	H	2B	3B	HR	RBI	SB
89 AL	.150	24	60	6	9	3	0	1	7	0
90 AL	.289	25	90	11	26	7	1	4	12	0
91 AL	.264	142	545	78	144	34	1	27	102	4
92 AL	.260	155	584	77	152	24	2	43	109	0
93 AL	.310	140	536	105	166	33	1	46	118	4
94 AL	.275	107	422	57	116	18	4	19	85	6
95 AL	.295	90	352	57	104	20	2	27	82	0
Life	.277	683	2589	391	717	139	11	167	515	14
3 AVE	.292	131	509	83	149	27	3	34	110	4

LUIS GONZALEZ

Position: Outfield
Team: Chicago Cubs
Born: Sept. 3, 1967 Tampa, FL
Height: 6'2" **Weight:** 180 lbs.
Bats: left **Throws:** right
Acquired: Traded by Astros with Scott Servais for Rick Wilkins, 6/95

Player Summary
Fantasy Value	$9 to $11
Card Value	6¢ to 10¢
Will	use all fields
Can't	hit 20 homers
Expect	two-base hits
Don't Expect	a powerful arm

Before his trade to the Cubs, Gonzalez was a .351 career hitter against Chicago—mainly because he sees the ball well at Wrigley Field. Escaping the cavernous Astrodome should have been a blessing for him, but he started slowly in his new uniform. He finally perked up after taking extended batting practice from left-handed pitching assistant Les Strode and reducing the leg-kick in his batting stance. The result was a .403 spurt over an 18-game stretch in late August. An aggressive hitter who sends line drives to all fields, Gonzalez shows enough patience to post an on-base percentage about 75 points higher than his batting average. He usually smacks more than 20 doubles per season but has never hit that many homers in the big leagues. He did not try to steal many bases last season. He did, however, continue to improve in left field. Signed as a third baseman out of South Alabama, Gonzalez has quick reactions, good range, and soft hands, although his throwing arm is average.

Major League Batting Register

	BA	G	AB	R	H	2B	3B	HR	RBI	SB
90 NL	.190	12	21	1	4	2	0	0	0	0
91 NL	.254	137	473	51	120	28	9	13	69	10
92 NL	.243	122	387	40	94	19	3	10	55	7
93 NL	.300	154	540	82	162	34	3	15	72	20
94 NL	.273	112	392	57	107	29	4	8	67	15
95 NL	.276	133	471	69	130	29	8	13	69	6
Life	.270	670	2284	300	617	141	27	59	332	58
3 AVE	.283	154	541	80	153	36	6	14	81	16

CURRENT PLAYERS

DWIGHT GOODEN

Position: Pitcher
Team: New York Yankees
Born: Nov. 16, 1964 Tampa, FL
Height: 6'3" **Weight:** 210 lbs.
Bats: right **Throws:** right
Acquired: Signed as a free agent, 10/95

Player Summary
Fantasy Value................ $3 to $5
Card Value .... 6¢ to 10¢
Will............... have major problems
Can't........................ forget past
Expect .... another shot
Don't Expect 1985

Suspended for the 1995 season for violating his drug aftercare program, Gooden looks to restart his career. He is not the same pitcher who dominated hitters in 1985. The question that remains, however, is whether he is the same pitcher who turned in back-to-back respectable seasons for bad Mets ballclubs in 1992 and '93. He learned how to pitch without great stuff in those two years. Before he was suspended in 1994, he had strained a ligament in his big toe. He had shoulder problems previously. The year layoff might help Gooden physically. Mentally, he is a major question mark. It is hard to believe that he can comeback from a year and one-half layoff and be an effective starter right away. If he can't muster some kind of velocity, at least enough to make his previously fine curveball effective, he might have to spend the beginning part of 1996 in the bullpen.

Major League Pitching Register

	W	L	ERA	G	CG	IP	H	ER	BB	SO
84 NL	17	9	2.60	31	7	218.0	161	63	73	276
85 NL	24	4	1.53	35	16	276.2	198	47	69	268
86 NL	17	6	2.84	33	12	250.0	197	79	80	200
87 NL	15	7	3.21	25	7	179.2	162	64	53	148
88 NL	18	9	3.19	34	10	248.1	242	88	57	175
89 NL	9	4	2.89	19	0	118.1	93	38	47	101
90 NL	19	7	3.83	34	2	232.2	229	99	70	223
91 NL	13	7	3.60	27	3	190.0	185	76	56	150
92 NL	10	13	3.67	31	3	206.0	197	84	70	145
93 NL	12	15	3.45	29	7	208.2	188	80	61	149
94 NL	3	4	6.31	7	0	41.1	46	29	15	40
Life	157	85	3.10	305	67	2169.2	1898	747	651	1875

CURTIS GOODWIN

Position: Outfield
Team: Baltimore Orioles
Born: Sept. 30, 1972 Oakland, CA
Height: 5'11" **Weight:** 180 lbs.
Bats: left **Throws:** left
Acquired: 12th-round pick in 6/91 free-agent draft

Player Summary
Fantasy Value................ $9 to $11
Card Value .... 6¢ to 10¢
Will.................... use great speed
Can't.................... cut whiff ratio
Expect .... steals, defense
Don't Expect .... home run power

A single to Goodwin is like a double or triple to anyone else. World-class speed makes the difference. Once he reaches, he is off to the races. He was nailed only four times in his first 25 big-league steal attempts. Promoted from Triple-A on June 2, Goodwin went 22-for-57 in his first 15 games and had 16 multihit games during his first month in the majors. He even hit the sixth homer of his professional career July 1 at Toronto. A better hitter against right-handed pitching, Goodwin cooled after his hot start. But his slumps should be short: Speed merchants can always bunt for a hit or beat out an infield roller. He could also improve his game by walking more often. The more than 3-1 ratio of strikeouts to walks that he notched last year is more appropriate for a power hitter because it depresses his potential on-base percentage. Although he is still a raw talent, he has been compared to Kenny Lofton; but Goodwin is actually more like Vince Coleman because of his all-speed, no-power package. Goodwin had 25 straight steals in Triple-A last year before being caught in a rundown. His speed translates into tremendous range in center field.

Major League Batting Register

	BA	G	AB	R	H	2B	3B	HR	RBI	SB
95 AL	.263	87	289	40	76	11	3	1	24	22
Life	.263	87	289	40	76	11	3	1	24	22

CURRENT PLAYERS

TOM GOODWIN

Position: Outfield
Team: Kansas City Royals
Born: July 27, 1968 Fresno, CA
Height: 6'1" **Weight:** 170 lbs.
Bats: left **Throws:** right
Acquired: Claimed from Dodgers on waivers, 1/94

Player Summary	
Fantasy Value	$8 to $10
Card Value	5¢ to 8¢
Will	run like the wind
Can't	provide any power
Expect	top rank in steals
Don't Expect	trouble with glove

Ex-teammate Vince Coleman, who's done it three times, says Goodwin is the only man in the majors who could steal 100 bases in a season. The Kansas City Player of the Month for June (.315, 13 swipes), Goodwin reached base 12 times in 13 tries (nine singles, two walks, one hit-by-pitch). He stole two bases June 28 to take over the league lead. He also fattened his average by collecting 27 infield hits among his first 86 big-league safeties. The kid can fly. He had three 50-steal seasons in the minors before becoming a regular for the first time with the 1995 Royals. Last year, he finished in a tie for second in the AL in swipes. A spray hitter, he was equally effective against righties and lefties last year. After the August promotion of Johnny Damon, Goodwin dropped from first to second in the lineup and shifted from center field to left. The former Fresno State All-American and U.S. Olympian has outstanding range. He once led the Double-A Texas League in fielding percentage. No one noticed, since Goodwin also stole 120 bases in his first 165 pro games.

Major League Batting Register

	BA	G	AB	R	H	2B	3B	HR	RBI	SB
91 NL	.143	16	7	3	1	0	0	0	0	1
92 NL	.233	57	73	15	17	1	1	0	3	7
93 NL	.294	30	17	6	5	1	0	0	1	1
94 AL	.000	2	2	0	0	0	0	0	0	0
95 AL	.287	133	480	72	138	16	3	4	28	50
Life	.278	238	579	96	161	18	4	4	32	59

TOM GORDON

Position: Pitcher
Team: Kansas City Royals
Born: Nov. 18, 1967 Sebring, FL
Height: 5'9" **Weight:** 160 lbs.
Bats: right **Throws:** right
Acquired: Sixth-round pick in 6/86 free-agent draft

Player Summary	
Fantasy Value	$5 to $7
Card Value	5¢ to 8¢
Will	bank on curve
Can't	always find plate
Expect	lots of grounders
Don't Expect	mastery

Gordon's teams have always considered him "The Man with the Golden Arm." A starter in the minors, he spent four of his first five big-league summers working mostly in relief—once finishing with more strikeouts than innings pitched. Strictly a starter in each of the last two years, he was often a victim of poor run support; not to mention his own control troubles. A curveball specialist who also throws a rising fastball and a changeup, Gordon gets numerous ground outs because of his over-the-top delivery. Especially effective against right-handed batters, he keeps the ball in the park and makes a concerted effort to keep baserunners close. He's also a good fielder. He yielded about one hit per inning last season. Warming with the weather last summer, he had a 2.70 ERA and a 2-1 ratio of strikeouts to walks during an eight-start streak that ended July 22. With better support, plus better control, Gordon can still become a top pitcher.

Major League Pitching Register

	W	L	ERA	G	CG	IP	H	ER	BB	SO
88 AL	0	2	5.17	5	0	15.2	16	9	7	18
89 AL	17	9	3.64	49	1	163.0	122	66	86	153
90 AL	12	11	3.73	32	6	195.1	192	81	99	175
91 AL	9	14	3.87	45	1	158.0	129	68	87	167
92 AL	6	10	4.59	40	0	117.2	116	60	55	98
93 AL	12	6	3.58	48	2	155.2	125	62	77	143
94 AL	11	7	4.35	24	0	155.1	136	75	87	126
95 AL	12	12	4.43	31	2	189.0	204	93	89	119
Life	79	71	4.02	274	12	1149.2	1040	514	587	999
3 AVE	14	10	4.17	39	1	195.1	182	91	100	151

CURRENT PLAYERS

JIM GOTT

Position: Pitcher
Team: Pittsburgh Pirates
Born: Aug. 3, 1959 Hollywood, CA
Height: 6'4" **Weight:** 220 lbs.
Bats: right **Throws:** right
Acquired: Signed as a free agent, 4/95

Player Summary
Fantasy Value $0
Card Value .... 4¢ to 6¢
Will............... seek medical miracle
Can't .... always throw strikes
Expect .... small workload
Don't Expect............... many saves

Gott personifies Pittsburgh's reluctance to invest in free agents. Signed to lend veteran stability to a young bullpen, he spent three stints on the disabled list before elbow and shoulder problems shut him down. Gott now needs to recover from the same shoulder-capsule repair procedure pioneered on Orel Hershiser in 1991. An injury to Gott is no surprise; since 1986, he's been on the DL for rotator-cuff, elbow, and shoulder problems, as well as appendicitis and other ailments. When healthy, he is reliable and effective. His curve breaks straight down, making it act like a forkball and driving left-handed hitters to distraction. Gott's fastball and slider are merely diversions. Despite some control trouble, he succeeds by keeping the ball down and in the park and keeping baserunners close.

Major League Pitching Register

	W	L	ERA	G	S	IP	H	ER	BB	SO
82 AL	5	10	4.43	30	0	136.0	134	67	66	82
83 AL	9	14	4.74	34	0	176.2	195	93	68	121
84 AL	7	6	4.02	35	2	109.2	93	49	49	73
85 NL	7	10	3.88	26	0	148.1	144	64	51	78
86 NL	0	0	7.62	9	1	13.0	16	11	13	9
87 NL	1	2	3.41	55	13	87.0	81	33	40	90
88 NL	6	6	3.49	67	34	77.1	68	30	22	76
89 NL	0	0	0.00	1	0	0.2	1	0	1	1
90 NL	3	5	2.90	50	3	62.0	59	20	34	44
91 NL	4	3	2.96	55	2	76.0	63	25	32	73
92 NL	3	3	2.45	68	6	88.0	72	24	41	75
93 NL	4	8	2.32	62	25	77.2	71	20	17	67
94 NL	5	3	5.94	37	2	36.1	46	24	20	29
95 NL	2	4	6.03	25	3	31.1	38	21	12	19
Life	56	74	3.87	554	91	1120.0	1081	481	466	837
3 AVE	4	6	4.25	47	10	54.2	60	26	20	43

MARK GRACE

Position: First base
Team: Chicago Cubs
Born: June 28, 1964 Winston-Salem, NC
Height: 6'2" **Weight:** 190 lbs.
Bats: left **Throws:** left
Acquired: 24th-round pick in 6/85 free-agent draft

Player Summary
Fantasy Value............... $15 to $18
Card Value .... 10¢ to 20¢
Will .... bang two-base hits
Can't .... steal bases often
Expect .... Gold Glove defense
Don't Expect......... more Ks than walks

He's not fast. He doesn't have a lot of power. He struggles against left-handed pitchers. But Grace keeps reinforcing his reputation as one of baseball's best first basemen. A contact hitter who walks much more often than he strikes out, he's always among the league leaders in on-base percentage. He's also among the leaders in extra-base hits, thanks to a high number of doubles. The first National Leaguer with 50 doubles since Pete Rose had 51 in 1978, Grace broke Charlie Grimm's 1932 team record for two-base hits by a left-handed hitter. The two-time All-Star goes with the pitch, sending the ball to all fields with good power to the alleys. He does his best hitting in clutch situations and with runners in scoring position. Grace rarely steals a base but is adept at stealing bases away from the opposition. The Gold Glover has great reactions at first base, where he's led his league in chances, putouts, assists, and double plays.

Major League Batting Register

	BA	G	AB	R	H	2B	3B	HR	RBI	SB
88 NL	.296	134	486	65	144	23	4	7	57	3
89 NL	.314	142	510	74	160	28	3	13	79	14
90 NL	.309	157	589	72	182	32	1	9	82	15
91 NL	.273	160	619	87	169	28	5	8	58	3
92 NL	.307	158	603	72	185	37	5	9	79	6
93 NL	.325	155	594	86	193	39	4	14	98	8
94 NL	.298	106	403	55	120	23	3	6	44	0
95 NL	.326	143	552	97	180	51	3	16	92	6
Life	.306	1155	4356	608	1333	261	28	82	589	55
3 AVE	.317	155	594	91	188	43	4	13	88	5

CURRENT PLAYERS

JOE GRAHE

Position: Pitcher
Team: Colorado Rockies
Born: June 14, 1967 West Palm Beach, FL
Height: 6' **Weight:** 200 lbs.
Bats: right **Throws:** right
Acquired: Signed as a free agent, 12/94

Player Summary	
Fantasy Value	$0
Card Value	4¢ to 6¢
Will	try to get well
Can't	stop lefty bats
Expect	control lapses
Don't Expect	great velocity

The jury is still out on Joe Grahe. Should he start or relieve? A starter in the minors, Grahe gave the Angels three good years in relief before rotator cuff problems hampered his performance late in the 1993 campaign. The former University of Miami strikeout artist returned to the rotation with the Rockies last year before shoulder problems sent him to the sidelines again. In his 11-3 win over San Diego June 25, Grahe gave up one run on three walks and four hits, but failed to fan anyone during his five-inning stint. Although he did a remarkable job of keeping the ball in the park at Coors Field, he averaged only one strikeout per walk. He gets hammered when his control wavers. Lefty hitters also give him grief. Grahe throws a fastball, a curve, a slider, and a changeup. But he can't maintain great velocity. He helps himself, however, by keeping runners close and fielding his position well. Before he can reclaim a rotation spot, he'll have to prove 100 percent healthy.

Major League Pitching Register

	W	L	ERA	G	S	IP	H	ER	BB	SO
90 AL	3	4	4.98	8	0	43.1	51	24	23	25
91 AL	3	7	4.81	18	0	73.0	84	39	33	40
92 AL	5	6	3.52	46	21	94.2	85	37	39	39
93 AL	4	1	2.86	45	11	56.2	54	18	25	31
94 AL	2	5	6.65	40	13	43.1	68	32	18	26
95 NL	4	3	5.08	17	0	56.2	69	32	27	27
Life	21	26	4.46	174	45	367.2	411	182	165	188
2 AVE	3	4	4.82	51	15	58.2	75	32	25	34

CRAIG GREBECK

Position: Infield
Team: Chicago White Sox
Born: Dec. 29, 1964 Johnstown, PA
Height: 5'8" **Weight:** 160 lbs.
Bats: right **Throws:** right
Acquired: Signed as a free agent, 8/86

Player Summary	
Fantasy Value	$0
Card Value	4¢ to 6¢
Will	back up three spots
Can't	hit many homers
Expect	patient at bats
Don't Expect	speed

One of baseball's best utility players, Grebeck has spent the last six years as a caddie to White Sox shortstop Ozzie Guillen, often spelling him against difficult left-handed pitchers. Grebeck showed last summer that he had completely recovered from the ankle injury that shortened his season in 1994. A contact hitter with patience, he walks about as much as he fans. As a result, his on-base average was 100 points higher than his batting average in 1995. Grebeck will surprise the opposition with an occasional tater, but he is mostly a singles hitter who sprays the ball to all fields. He loves fastballs and late-inning pressure situations, making him an effective pinch hitter. And he hits right-handed pitching even better than he hits lefties. Best at shortstop, his original position, Grebeck also provides more than adequate defense at third and second. The former Cal State standout is an avid golfer who once played in the World Series of Beach Volleyball.

Major League Batting Register

	BA	G	AB	R	H	2B	3B	HR	RBI	SB
90 AL	.168	59	119	7	20	3	1	1	9	0
91 AL	.281	107	224	37	63	16	3	6	31	1
92 AL	.268	88	287	24	77	21	2	3	35	0
93 AL	.226	72	190	25	43	5	0	1	12	1
94 AL	.309	35	97	17	30	5	0	0	5	0
95 AL	.260	53	154	19	40	12	0	1	18	0
Life	.255	414	1071	129	273	62	6	12	110	2
2 AVE	.242	66	182	23	44	9	0	1	16	1

CURRENT PLAYERS

SHAWN GREEN

Position: Outfield
Team: Toronto Blue Jays
Born: Nov. 10, 1972 Des Plaines, IL
Height: 6'4" **Weight:** 190 lbs.
Bats: left **Throws:** left
Acquired: First-round pick in 6/91 free-agent draft

Player Summary	
Fantasy Value	$10 to $13
Card Value	10¢ to 15¢
Will	improve quickly
Can't	hit left-handers
Expect	power to develop
Don't Expect	fielding woes

Even before he stepped into the Toronto lineup last year, Green had been billed as the second coming of John Olerud: a quiet, articulate collegian with a classic left-handed swing. In 1994, Green had shown some speed and power at Triple-A Syracuse, where he led the International League with a .344 batting average and .996 fielding percentage. Managers later named him the league's No. 1 prospect in a *Baseball America* poll. Solving big-league pitching wasn't so simple, however. Struggling against southpaws, he found himself in a right-field platoon with Candy Maldonado. To win the job outright, Green will have to reduce a strikeout-to-walk ratio of about 3-to-1 and jump-start his running game. More power would also help. A good outfielder with a powerful arm, Green is a five-tools player with star potential, according to several minor-league managers. He can bunt, beat out an infield hit, or rip liners to all fields. He is a hard-working, coachable player. Green was a straight-A high school student before enrolling in Stanford, where he's working on a psychology degree.

Major League Batting Register

	BA	G	AB	R	H	2B	3B	HR	RBI	SB
93 AL	.000	3	6	0	0	0	0	0	0	0
94 AL	.091	14	33	1	3	1	0	0	1	1
95 AL	.288	121	379	52	109	31	4	15	54	1
Life	.268	138	418	53	112	32	4	15	55	2

TYLER GREEN

Position: Pitcher
Team: Philadelphia Phillies
Born: Feb. 18, 1970 Springfield, OH
Height: 6'5" **Weight:** 204 lbs.
Bats: right **Throws:** right
Acquired: First-round pick in 6/91 free-agent draft

Player Summary	
Fantasy Value	$1 to $3
Card Value	8¢ to 12¢
Will	seek All-Star form
Can't	silence lefty bats
Expect	self-help at plate
Don't Expect	patient management

It was a year of mastery and mystery for Green. Pressed into starting service after injuries felled several veterans, he pitched well enough to make the NL All-Star Team as a rookie. On July 1, he led the NL in complete games, tied for first in shutouts, and was second in wins, fifth in innings, and sixth in ERA. When his knuckle-curve wasn't working, a searing fastball sufficed. He fixed the alleged delivery glitches that produced a 7-16 Triple-A mark in 1994. After the All-Star Game, however, Greene's glitter faded fast. In his first eight second-half starts, he went 0-4 with an 8.68 ERA. He hit a three-run homer in one game but was knocked out in the second inning. Perhaps past shoulder or elbow problems were interfering. Not a strikeout pitcher, Green needs good location to survive. He didn't always have it last year, when he yielded about one hit per inning and four walks per nine. He also had problems with the long ball—especially against lefties. Green fields his position well and has a good pickoff move. He was the 10th overall selection in the 1991 amateur draft after a 21-8 career record at Wichita State.

Major League Pitching Register

	W	L	ERA	G	CG	IP	H	ER	BB	SO
93 NL	0	0	7.36	3	0	7.1	16	6	5	7
95 NL	8	9	5.31	26	4	140.2	157	83	66	85
Life	8	9	5.41	29	4	148.0	173	89	71	92

CURRENT PLAYERS

TOMMY GREENE

Position: Pitcher
Team: Philadelphia Phillies
Born: April 6, 1967 Lumberton, NC
Height: 6'5" **Weight:** 225 lbs.
Bats: right **Throws:** right
Acquired: Traded by Braves with Dale Murphy for Jeff Parrett, Jim Vatcher, and Victor Rosario, 8/90

Player Summary
Fantasy Value	$1
Card Value	5¢ to 8¢
Will	start when healthy
Can't	heal weak shoulder
Expect	good work at plate
Don't Expect	another no-hitter

When his shoulder isn't killing him, Greene proved that he can be a 200-inning starter who wins often and yields less hits than innings. But he's spent more time on the disabled list than on the active roster over the last four years. Perpetual shoulder aches, including a small tear in the rotator cuff, have kept Greene out of action. When he did work, he was only a shadow of his former self. A fastball-slider pitcher who also throws a curve and a changeup, he can be overpowering when he has proper location. Two years after a 1991 no-hitter against Montreal, he opened the season with eight straight wins. He hasn't done much since, however, despite lots of rehab time in the minors. Although Greene has problems holding runners close, he compensates with a solid glove and surprising bat. He has some home run power, and he has appeared as a pinch hitter and pinch runner. Greene pitched in the World Series for the 1993 Phillies.

Major League Pitching Register
	W	L	ERA	G	CG	IP	H	ER	BB	SO
89 NL	1	2	4.10	4	1	26.1	22	12	6	17
90 NL	3	3	5.08	15	0	51.1	50	29	26	21
91 NL	13	7	3.38	36	3	207.2	177	78	66	154
92 NL	3	3	5.32	13	0	64.1	75	38	34	39
93 NL	16	4	3.42	31	7	200.0	175	76	62	167
94 NL	2	0	4.54	7	0	35.2	37	18	22	28
95 NL	0	5	8.29	11	0	33.2	45	31	20	24
Life	38	24	4.10	117	11	619.0	581	282	236	450

WILLIE GREENE

Position: Third base
Team: Cincinnati Reds
Born: Sept. 23, 1971 Milledgeville, GA
Height: 5'11" **Weight:** 184 lbs.
Bats: left **Throws:** right
Acquired: Traded by Expos with Dave Martinez and Scott Ruskin for John Wetteland and Bill Risley, 12/91

Player Summary
Fantasy Value	$2
Card Value	6¢ to 8¢
Will	try to gain job
Can't	worry about '95
Expect	every chance
Don't Expect	instant stardom

Greene probably has just about had it. He was bounced from the Cincinnati lineup and back to Triple-A Indianapolis after a few games at the beginning of the 1995 season by then-Reds manager Davey Johnson. Of course, Greene didn't really hit all that well in his early-season trial, but he never was given the opportunity to get out of his slump. The Reds went with a platoon of Mark Lewis and Jeff Branson at third base for much of the year. Greene went back to Indianapolis and performed well, again. He is ready to prove Johnson and those who are saying that he is just a Triple-A player wrong. He has hit 20 homers in the minors, but he doesn't show much patience at the plate. Greene has always had healthy walk totals but still fans too frequently. He doesn't steal much but has more speed than most other third basemen. A converted shortstop, he has led several minor leagues in putouts, double plays, and fielding percentage, as well as errors. He was once a first-round draft selection of the Pirates.

Major League Batting Register
	BA	G	AB	R	H	2B	3B	HR	RBI	SB
92 NL	.269	29	93	10	25	5	2	2	13	0
93 NL	.160	15	50	7	8	1	1	2	5	0
94 NL	.216	16	37	5	8	2	0	0	3	0
95 NL	.105	8	19	1	2	0	0	0	0	0
Life	.216	68	199	23	43	8	3	4	21	0

CURRENT PLAYERS

MIKE GREENWELL

Position: Outfield
Team: Boston Red Sox
Born: July 18, 1963 Louisville, KY
Height: 6' **Weight:** 200 lbs.
Bats: left **Throws:** right
Acquired: Third-round pick in 6/82 free-agent draft

Player Summary	
Fantasy Value	$11 to $14
Card Value	5¢ to 8¢
Will	make good contact
Can't	display much speed
Expect	hits to all fields
Don't Expect	home run explosion

After years of watching Ted Williams, Carl Yastrzemski, and Jim Rice, it's still strange to see a Red Sox left fielder who doesn't crush numerous homers. But that's not Greenwell's game. Greenwell has compiled a .300 lifetime average and mastered the difficult art of playing Fenway Park's Green Monster. A fastball hitter who smacks line drives to all fields, he hits well over .300 against righties and holds his own against southpaws. During much of the 1995 season, he made good contact and had an on-base percentage about 50 points above his batting average. Though he's not the slowest man in the league, Greenwell is not much of a basestealer. He bangs into more than his share of double plays. He moves well enough in left field, however, and he knows how to play the hitters. He gets the ball back to the infield in a hurry; a quick release compensates for an average arm.

Major League Batting Register

	BA	G	AB	R	H	2B	3B	HR	RBI	SB
85 AL	.323	17	31	7	10	1	0	4	8	1
86 AL	.314	31	35	4	11	2	0	0	4	0
87 AL	.328	125	412	71	135	31	6	19	89	5
88 AL	.325	158	590	86	192	39	8	22	119	16
89 AL	.308	145	578	87	178	36	0	14	95	13
90 AL	.297	159	610	71	181	30	6	14	73	8
91 AL	.300	147	544	76	163	26	6	9	83	15
92 AL	.233	49	180	16	42	2	0	2	18	2
93 AL	.315	146	540	77	170	38	6	13	72	5
94 AL	.269	95	327	60	88	25	1	11	45	2
95 AL	.297	120	481	67	143	25	4	15	76	9
Life	.303	1192	4328	622	1313	255	37	123	682	76
3 AVE	.295	134	514	79	152	34	4	15	74	6

RUSTY GREER

Position: Outfield; first base
Team: Texas Rangers
Born: Jan. 21, 1969 Fort Rucker, AL
Height: 6' **Weight:** 190 lbs.
Bats: left **Throws:** left
Acquired: 10th-round pick in 6/90 free-agent draft

Player Summary	
Fantasy Value	$8 to $10
Card Value	4¢ to 6¢
Will	show patience
Can't	cut strikeout rate
Expect	good defense
Don't Expect	frequent home runs

No matter what he does for the rest of his career, Greer will always be remembered by Rangers fans for the diving, ninth-inning catch that preserved the 1994 perfect game of Texas teammate Kenny Rogers. Greer finished that season with a .314 average in 80 games but fell to more realistic levels last summer. A line-drive hitter with surprising patience, he has saved some of his best work for clutch situations—especially when runners are in scoring position. Though better against right-handers, he hits lefties well enough to stay in the lineup when southpaws work. Greer tries to pull left-handers while hitting to all fields against righties. He strikes out more than a non-slugger should, however, but compensates by drawing lots of walks. His on-base percentage hovered one hundred points above his batting average most of last year. Greer has some speed but shows it mostly in his outfield play. He plays all three positions, plus first base, but spent most of last year in right—a surprise because of his mediocre arm. Greer attended the University of Montevallo in his native Alabama.

Major League Batting Register

	BA	G	AB	R	H	2B	3B	HR	RBI	SB
94 AL	.314	80	277	36	87	16	1	10	46	0
95 AL	.271	131	417	58	113	21	2	13	61	3
Life	.288	211	694	94	200	37	3	23	107	3
2 AVE	.291	130	430	58	125	23	2	14	67	2

CURRENT PLAYERS

KEN GRIFFEY JR.

Position: Outfield
Team: Seattle Mariners
Born: Nov. 21, 1969 Donora, PA
Height: 6'3" **Weight:** 195 lbs.
Bats: left **Throws:** left
Acquired: First-round pick in 6/87 free-agent draft

Player Summary	
Fantasy Value	$40 to $45
Card Value	$2 to $3
Will	show great power
Can't	join 30-30 group
Expect	future MVP award
Don't Expect	trouble in field

Griffey can do it all: hit for average, hit for power, run, throw, and field. His only problem is he knows no limits. While chasing a fly ball last May 26, he crashed into the outfield wall and fractured his left wrist. That injury cost Griffey 11 weeks and 73 games in a season already shortened three weeks at the start by the player strike. When healthy, Griffey is one of the game's top talents. He's led the AL in home runs, total bases, and outfielder double plays. He's also won five Gold Gloves, started five All-Star Games, and earned All-Star MVP honors. It's just a matter of time before he's the regular-season MVP as well. A wrist hitter with a smooth stroke, Griffey hits the ball hard to all fields, though most of his power is to right-center. A *Baseball America* poll of AL managers last spring named Griffey the most exciting player, second-best defensive outfielder (to Kenny Lofton), and third-best hitter (after Edgar Martinez and Frank Thomas). Griffey also has a fine arm.

Major League Batting Register

	BA	G	AB	R	H	2B	3B	HR	RBI	SB
89 AL	.264	127	455	61	120	23	0	16	61	16
90 AL	.300	155	597	91	179	28	7	22	80	16
91 AL	.327	154	548	76	179	42	1	22	100	18
92 AL	.308	142	565	83	174	39	4	27	103	10
93 AL	.309	156	582	113	180	38	3	45	109	17
94 AL	.323	111	433	94	140	24	4	40	90	11
95 AL	.258	72	260	52	67	7	0	17	42	4
Life	.302	917	3440	570	1039	201	19	189	585	92
3 AVE	.305	131	495	101	151	27	3	40	94	12

MARQUIS GRISSOM

Position: Outfield
Team: Atlanta Braves
Born: April 17, 1967 Atlanta, GA
Height: 5'11" **Weight:** 190 lbs.
Bats: right **Throws:** right
Acquired: Traded by Expos for Roberto Kelly, Tony Tarasco, Esteban Yan, and cash, 4/95

Player Summary	
Fantasy Value	$25 to $30
Card Value	10¢ to 15¢
Will	deliver some power
Can't	wait for his pitch
Expect	Gold Glove defense
Don't Expect	solid on-base mark

Atlanta learned last season that ex-Brave Otis Nixon is a better leadoff man than Grissom. Grissom has slowed considerably since swiping 154 bases in two seasons (1991 and 1992). He no longer tries to smack the ball on the ground and run or bunt for a base hit. Instead, he tries to hit every pitch out of the park—a bad habit that developed during his 19-homer season for the Expos in 1993. Batting third most of that year, he could afford to take big swings. As a leadoff man, Grissom needs to show much more patience and cut down on his strikeout total, which is too high for a man not considered a power hitter. Even when he's ahead in the count, Grissom often lunges for pitches outside the strike zone. He began to run more late last summer after a heel injury healed. He hasn't sacrificed any speed in center, where he's still the NL's best. The Gold Glove winner shows uncanny instincts, an ability to run back on the ball, and a strong arm.

Major League Batting Register

	BA	G	AB	R	H	2B	3B	HR	RBI	SB
89 NL	.257	26	74	16	19	2	0	1	2	1
90 NL	.257	98	288	42	74	14	2	3	29	22
91 NL	.267	148	558	73	149	23	9	6	39	76
92 NL	.276	159	653	99	180	39	6	14	66	78
93 NL	.298	157	630	104	188	27	2	19	95	53
94 NL	.288	110	475	96	137	25	4	11	45	36
95 NL	.258	139	551	80	142	23	3	12	42	29
Life	.275	837	3229	510	889	153	26	66	318	295
3 AVE	.282	156	640	110	180	29	4	16	69	45

CURRENT PLAYERS

KEVIN GROSS

Position: Pitcher
Team: Texas Rangers
Born: June 8, 1961 Downey, CA
Height: 6'5" **Weight:** 215 lbs.
Bats: right **Throws:** right
Acquired: Signed as a free agent, 12/94

Player Summary
Fantasy Value	$2 to $4
Card Value	4¢ to 6¢
Will	retain rotation berth
Can't	win without control
Expect	frequent grounders
Don't Expect	200 innings

Gross was abominable early last season. A sinkerballer who depends upon location, he gets clobbered when he pitches up in the strike zone. That's what happened early in '95. He changes speeds on all his pitches, and throws a curveball and a changeup in addition to the sinking fastball. He usually averages about three strikeouts per walk. But his second-half showing proved that the wily veteran still has something left. The author of a 1992 no-hitter, Gross has his moments of brilliance. He helps himself by fielding his position well and keeping a close eye on the running game. He has a good move for a right-hander, though his slow, high-kicking motion gives runners a head start. While Gross may no longer be a workhorse, he's still a dependable starter when his location is good.

Major League Pitching Register
	W	L	ERA	G	CG	IP	H	ER	BB	SO
83 NL	4	6	3.56	17	1	96.0	100	38	35	66
84 NL	8	5	4.12	44	1	129.0	140	59	44	84
85 NL	15	13	3.41	38	6	205.2	194	78	81	151
86 NL	12	12	4.02	37	7	241.2	240	108	94	154
87 NL	9	16	4.35	34	3	200.2	205	97	87	140
88 NL	12	14	3.69	33	5	231.2	209	95	89	162
89 NL	11	12	4.38	31	4	201.1	188	98	88	158
90 NL	9	12	4.57	31	2	163.1	171	83	65	111
91 NL	10	11	3.58	46	0	115.2	123	46	50	95
92 NL	8	13	3.17	34	4	204.2	182	72	77	158
93 NL	13	13	4.14	33	3	202.1	224	93	74	150
94 NL	9	7	3.60	25	1	157.1	162	63	43	124
95 AL	9	15	5.54	31	4	183.2	200	113	89	106
Life	129	149	4.02	434	41	2333.0	2338	1043	916	1629
3 AVE	12	13	4.41	34	2	210.2	226	103	78	148

MARK GRUDZIELANEK

Position: Infield
Team: Montreal Expos
Born: June 30, 1970 Milwaukee, WI
Height: 6'1" **Weight:** 185 lbs.
Bats: right **Throws:** right
Acquired: 11th-round pick in 6/91 free-agent draft

Player Summary
Fantasy Value	$3 to $5
Card Value	8¢ to 10¢
Will	play strong defense
Can't	clear fences often
Expect	many steal attempts
Don't Expect	much power

When the Expos decided Wil Cordero did not throw well enough to play shortstop every day, they handed his job to Grudzielanek. That didn't happen until August, after Grudzielanek had spent two months in the minors sharpening his offensive skills. He had hit just .248 with a single home run during a 47-game trial earlier in the season. A world-beater against lefties and on his home turf at Olympic Stadium during the 1995 season, he fared poorly against righties and on the road. Used mostly at third during his earlier stay, Grudzielanek is more at home as a shortstop. His .958 fielding percentage led Double-A Eastern League shortstops in 1994, the same year he won the MVP Award with a league-best 37 doubles plus 11 homers, a .322 batting average, and a career-high 32 steals. Grudzielanek also showed some patience at the plate for the first time in his four-year pro career. He's obviously over the heel injuries that have plagued him in the past. If he delivers the speed and defense his minor-league numbers suggest, Grudzielanek could become a valuable player.

Major League Batting Register
	BA	G	AB	R	H	2B	3B	HR	RBI	SB
95 NL	.245	78	269	27	66	12	2	1	20	8
Life	.245	78	269	27	66	12	2	1	20	8

CURRENT PLAYERS

EDDIE GUARDADO

Position: Pitcher
Team: Minnesota Twins
Born: Oct. 2, 1970 Stockton, CA
Height: 6' **Weight:** 193 lbs.
Bats: right **Throws:** left
Acquired: 21st-round pick in 6/90 free-agent draft

Player Summary	
Fantasy Value	$0
Card Value	4¢ to 6¢
Will	seek old control
Can't	stop gopher balls
Expect	more relief work
Don't Expect	hits by lefties

During his days in the minors, Guardado developed a reputation as a control artist. He had strikeout-to-walk ratios of better than 3-to-1 for four different ballclubs in a pro career that began in 1991. He has yet to show that same sharpness in the majors, however. In his year-plus with the Twins, the southpaw excelled in only one area: retiring left-handed hitters. While he pitches like Popeye against lefties—holding them under the Mendoza Line—he's more like Olive Oyl against righties. They salivate when they see him coming. Guardado also had trouble keeping the ball in the park, stranding inherited runners, and maintaining control of his fastball, changeup, and breaking balls during the season. If he weren't so good at controlling the running game, his hefty ERA would be even worse. Exclusively a starter in the minors, Guardado spent most of last year in the bullpen after getting blown out of his rotation spot. Drafted out of San Joaquin Delta College in California, Guardado pitched a no-hitter as a first-year pro in 1991.

Major League Pitching Register

	W	L	ERA	G	S	IP	H	ER	BB	SO
93 AL	3	8	6.18	19	0	94.2	123	65	36	46
94 AL	0	2	8.47	4	0	17.0	26	16	4	8
95 AL	4	9	5.12	51	2	91.1	99	52	45	71
Life	7	19	5.90	74	2	203.0	248	133	85	125
2 AVE	4	9	5.63	38	1	98.2	117	62	43	63

MARK GUBICZA

Position: Pitcher
Team: Kansas City Royals
Born: Aug. 14, 1962 Philadelphia, PA
Height: 6'5" **Weight:** 220 lbs.
Bats: right **Throws:** right
Acquired: Second-round pick in 6/81 free-agent draft

Player Summary	
Fantasy Value	$7 to $9
Card Value	4¢ to 6¢
Will	win with support
Can't	get frequent Ks
Expect	outs on grounders
Don't Expect	control problems

For six straight seasons, Gubicza was a double-digit winner for the Royals. But that was before shoulder problems reduced his velocity, forcing him to rely on proper location of his sinker, slider, curve, and changeup. A control artist, he got an unexpected boost last year when the Royals rookie manager, former catcher Bob Boone, built Gubicza's confidence by telling him to challenge the hitters. He responded with the first one-hitter of his 10-year career, 7-0 against Oakland June 15. By season's end, the two-time All-Star had put together his best season since 1989. He dominated right-handed batters, kept the ball in the park, and had some success with the running game. Not a power pitcher, Gubicza gets most of his outs on grounders. He helps himself with fine defensive skills.

Major League Pitching Register

	W	L	ERA	G	CG	IP	H	ER	BB	SO
84 AL	10	14	4.05	29	4	189.0	172	85	75	111
85 AL	14	10	4.06	29	0	177.1	160	80	77	99
86 AL	12	6	3.64	35	3	180.2	155	73	84	118
87 AL	13	18	3.98	35	10	241.2	231	107	120	166
88 AL	20	8	2.70	35	8	269.2	237	81	83	183
89 AL	15	11	3.04	36	8	255.0	252	86	63	173
90 AL	4	7	4.50	16	2	94.0	101	47	38	71
91 AL	9	12	5.68	26	0	133.0	168	84	42	89
92 AL	7	6	3.72	18	2	111.1	110	46	36	81
93 AL	5	8	4.66	49	0	104.1	128	54	43	80
94 AL	7	9	4.50	22	0	130.0	158	65	26	59
95 AL	12	14	3.75	33	3	213.1	222	89	62	81
Life	128	123	3.85	363	40	2099.1	2094	897	749	1311
3 AVE	9	12	4.19	39	1	176.1	200	82	50	85

CURRENT PLAYERS

OZZIE GUILLEN

Position: Shortstop
Team: Chicago White Sox
Born: Jan. 20, 1964 Ocumare del Tuy, Venezuela
Height: 5'11" **Weight:** 150 lbs.
Bats: left **Throws:** right
Acquired: Traded by Padres with Tim Lollar, Bill Long, and Luis Salazar for LaMarr Hoyt, Todd Simmons, and Kevin Kristan, 12/84

Player Summary	
Fantasy Value	$4 to $6
Card Value	4¢ to 6¢
Will	make good contact
Can't	hit ball over wall
Expect	sterling fielding
Don't Expect	solid on-base mark

There's little doubt that Guillen's glove keeps him in the lineup. He has little power and struggles so much against southpaws that he was often lifted last year. He is a first-ball, fastball hitter who makes good contact. But continual strikeouts squander his chance to bunt his way on, beat out an infield roller, or spray an opposite-field single. His on-base percentage is unpleasant. The one-time speed merchant no longer steals much, thanks to a 1992 knee surgery, but he still supplies acrobatics at shortstop. His instincts, reactions, and positioning are outstanding. He still has good range. The three-time All-Star is one of the best at turning the double play. Guillen was AL Rookie of the Year in 1985 and a Gold Glove winner in 1990.

Major League Batting Register

	BA	G	AB	R	H	2B	3B	HR	RBI	SB
85 AL	.273	150	491	71	134	21	9	1	33	7
86 AL	.250	159	547	58	137	19	4	2	47	8
87 AL	.279	149	560	64	156	22	7	2	51	25
88 AL	.261	156	566	58	148	16	7	0	39	25
89 AL	.253	155	597	63	151	20	8	1	54	36
90 AL	.279	160	516	61	144	21	4	1	58	13
91 AL	.273	154	524	52	143	20	3	3	49	21
92 AL	.200	12	40	5	8	4	0	0	7	1
93 AL	.280	134	457	44	128	23	4	4	50	5
94 AL	.288	100	365	46	105	9	5	1	39	5
95 AL	.248	122	415	50	103	20	3	1	41	6
Life	.267	1451	5078	572	1357	195	54	16	468	152
3 AVE	.272	137	479	55	131	19	5	2	50	6

MARK GUTHRIE

Position: Pitcher
Team: Los Angeles Dodgers
Born: Sept. 22, 1965 Buffalo, NY
Height: 6'4" **Weight:** 202 lbs.
Bats: both **Throws:** left
Acquired: Traded by Twins with Kevin Tapani for Jose Parra, Chris Latham, Greg Hansell, and Ron Coomer, 7/95

Player Summary	
Fantasy Value	$1
Card Value	4¢ to 6¢
Will	provide relief
Can't	fret about shoulder
Expect	reliable control
Don't Expect	return to rotation

Primarily a starter for his first five years as a pro, Guthrie became a dependable middle reliever after Minnesota moved him to the bullpen on a full-time basis in 1992. A control artist who in 1995 notched about a 3-1 ratio of strikeouts to walks, Guthrie massacred left-handed hitters but was also effective against righties. His repertoire includes a fastball, a forkball, and a curveball. Because of his efficiency against first batters, Guthrie strands most of the runners he inherits. He is also adept at keeping the ball in the park. The Louisiana State product, healed completely from a shoulder blood clot that cost him much of the 1993 campaign, is capable of working more than 50 times a year. Often used to dispose of one or two lefty hitters at a time, his stints are usually brief. The lanky lefty helps himself with one of baseball's better pickoff moves, as well as good defensive skills.

Major League Pitching Register

	W	L	ERA	G	S	IP	H	ER	BB	SO
89 AL	2	4	4.55	13	0	57.1	66	29	21	38
90 AL	7	9	3.79	24	0	144.2	154	61	39	101
91 AL	7	5	4.32	41	2	98.0	116	47	41	72
92 AL	2	3	2.88	54	5	75.0	59	24	23	76
93 AL	2	1	4.71	22	0	21.0	20	11	16	15
94 AL	4	2	6.14	50	1	51.1	65	35	18	38
95 AL	5	3	3.46	36	0	42.1	47	21	16	48
95 NL	0	2	3.66	24	0	19.2	19	8	9	19
Life	29	29	4.17	264	8	509.1	546	236	183	407
2 AVE	6	4	5.19	69	1	70.2	83	41	27	64

CURRENT PLAYERS

RICKY GUTIERREZ

Position: Shortstop
Team: Houston Astros
Born: May 23, 1970 Miami, FL
Height: 6'1" **Weight:** 175 lbs.
Bats: right **Throws:** right
Acquired: Traded by Padres with Derek Bell, Doug Brocail, Pedro Martinez, Phil Plantier, and Craig Shipley for Ken Caminiti, Steve Finley, Andujar Cedeno, Roberto Petagine, Brian Williams, and a player to be named later, 12/94

Player Summary	
Fantasy Value	$1
Card Value	4¢ to 6¢
Will	hit southpaws
Can't	provide power
Expect	range at short
Don't Expect	patient at bats

With expansion just around the corner, Gutierrez may get another chance at a regular job in the big leagues. But he's not likely to get an extended trial from any established club. Though he filled in for injured rookie Orlando Miller in Houston last August, Gutierrez proved to be an erratic performer—at bat and in the field. He fans far too frequently for a singles hitter, never walks, and is an automatic out against right-handed pitching. Gutierrez has forgotten how to be selective at the plate. When he waited for walks in 1994, his batting and on-base averages were in the range of respectability. Reaching more often would help, since he can run. He doesn't steal much, however. In the field, his range is his best asset. He doesn't have good hands and makes too many boots on routine plays. Gutierrez has a strong but unreliable throwing arm. A potential utility infielder, he's seen some action at second and third.

Major League Batting Register

	BA	G	AB	R	H	2B	3B	HR	RBI	SB
93 NL	.251	133	438	76	110	10	5	5	26	4
94 NL	.240	90	275	27	66	11	2	1	28	2
95 NL	.276	52	156	22	43	6	0	0	12	5
Life	.252	275	869	125	219	27	7	6	66	11
3 AVE	.251	106	334	46	84	11	3	2	26	4

JOSE GUZMAN

Position: Pitcher
Team: Chicago Cubs
Born: April 9, 1963 Santa Isabel, PR
Height: 6'3" **Weight:** 198 lbs.
Bats: right **Throws:** right
Acquired: Signed as a free agent, 12/92

Player Summary	
Fantasy Value	$0
Card Value	4¢ to 6¢
Will	need major miracle
Can't	shake shoulder woes
Expect	struggle for job
Don't Expect	strong fielding

Severe shoulder problems have kept Guzman sidelined for four of the last seven seasons. He had arthroscopic surgery on June 1, 1994, but still missed most of that year and virtually all of 1995. In fact, he's given the Cubs only 14 wins in the first three seasons of a four-year, $14 million contract. At a million dollars a win, it's no wonder Cubs management is screaming bloody murder. Even a 20-win season wouldn't justify the missed time, medical bills, and millions poured down the tubes. Besides, it ain't gonna happen. Even when he's healthy, Guzman gives up too many walks and too many homers. With a five-pitch repertoire, he should do better. He throws a sinker, a slider, a forkball, a curve, and a changeup. Not a strong fielder, his high-kicking delivery encourages runners to steal. Unless he's fully recovered, Guzman will have lots of runners to worry about.

Major League Pitching Register

	W	L	ERA	G	CG	IP	H	ER	BB	SO
85 AL	3	2	2.76	5	0	32.2	27	10	14	24
86 AL	9	15	4.54	29	2	172.1	199	87	60	87
87 AL	14	14	4.67	37	6	208.1	196	108	82	143
88 AL	11	13	3.70	30	6	206.2	180	85	82	157
91 AL	13	7	3.08	25	5	169.2	152	58	84	125
92 AL	16	11	3.66	33	5	224.0	229	91	73	179
93 NL	12	10	4.34	30	2	191.0	188	92	74	163
94 NL	2	2	9.15	4	0	19.2	22	20	13	11
Life	80	74	4.05	193	26	1224.1	1193	551	482	889

CURRENT PLAYERS

JUAN GUZMAN

Position: Pitcher
Team: Toronto Blue Jays
Born: Oct. 28, 1966 Santo Domingo, Dominican Republic
Height: 5'11" **Weight:** 190 lbs.
Bats: right **Throws:** right
Acquired: Traded by Dodgers for Mike Sharperson, 9/87

Player Summary	
Fantasy Value	$4 to $6
Card Value	5¢ to 8¢
Will	seek comeback
Can't	throw strikes
Expect	good velocity
Don't Expect	great defense

Erratic control and shoulder problems hit Guzman so hard last season that he lost his spot in the Toronto rotation, spent time on the disabled list, and watched his ERA rise. His best game came July 14, when he held Seattle to one earned run in eight innings. He had not thrown so hard in quite some time. Guzman could not continue his good work, however. A fastball-slider pitcher who also throws a forkball and a changeup, he has always had trouble finding the plate. Before leading the American League in wild pitches twice, he did the same thing three times in the minors. When healthy, Guzman worries most about walks and gopher balls. He takes the bats out of right-handers' hands and generates enough velocity on his heater to blaze his way out of trouble. But he's not a good fielder or pickoff artist. Guzman is also prone to lapses of concentration, especially when working behind in the count. This is make-or-break time.

Major League Pitching Register

	W	L	ERA	G	CG	IP	H	ER	BB	SO
91 AL	10	3	2.99	23	1	138.2	98	46	66	123
92 AL	16	5	2.64	28	2	180.2	135	53	72	165
93 AL	14	3	3.99	33	2	221.0	211	98	110	194
94 AL	12	11	5.68	25	2	147.1	165	93	76	124
95 AL	4	14	6.32	24	3	135.1	151	95	73	94
Life	56	36	4.21	133	9	823.0	760	385	397	700
3 AVE	12	11	5.20	32	3	193.1	204	112	100	158

CHRIS GWYNN

Position: Outfield
Team: Los Angeles Dodgers
Born: Oct. 13, 1964 Los Angeles, CA
Height: 6' **Weight:** 210 lbs.
Bats: left **Throws:** left
Acquired: Signed as a free agent, 4/94

Player Summary	
Fantasy Value	$0
Card Value	4¢ to 6¢
Will	pinch-hit often
Can't	generate power
Expect	contact hitting
Don't Expect	patient at bats

During their college careers at San Diego State, Chris Gwynn gave more hint of future promise than brother Tony. Chris, not Tony, was the All-American who went on to play for the U.S. Olympic team. As professionals, however, Chris quickly acquired a part-timer tag; perhaps because he never showed the same speed or defensive skills as his older brother. He has never played in more than 112 games in a pro career that began in 1985. Another factor keeping Chris on the bench is his pinch-hitting ability. A contact hitter who sends line-drives to all fields, he's especially potent against right-handed pitchers. Gwynn doesn't walk, steal, or deliver extra-base hits. He moved into second place, behind Manny Mota, on the Dodgers' career pinch-hitting list last year before he was disabled in August with pain in his right knee. Though Chris plays best in left, he runs and throws well enough to play all three outfield spots.

Major League Batting Register

	BA	G	AB	R	H	2B	3B	HR	RBI	SB
87 NL	.219	17	32	2	7	1	0	0	2	0
88 NL	.182	12	11	1	2	0	0	0	0	0
89 NL	.235	32	68	8	16	4	1	0	7	1
90 NL	.284	101	141	19	40	2	1	5	22	0
91 NL	.252	94	139	18	35	5	1	5	22	1
92 NL	.286	34	84	10	24	3	2	1	7	0
93 NL	.300	103	287	36	86	14	4	1	25	0
94 NL	.268	58	71	9	19	0	0	3	13	0
95 NL	.214	67	84	8	18	3	2	1	10	0
Life	.269	518	917	111	247	32	11	16	108	2

CURRENT PLAYERS

TONY GWYNN

Position: Outfield
Team: San Diego Padres
Born: May 9, 1960 Los Angeles, CA
Height: 5'11" **Weight:** 205 lbs.
Bats: left **Throws:** left
Acquired: Third-round pick in 6/81 free-agent draft

Player Summary
Fantasy Value	$20 to $25
Card Value	25¢ to 50¢
Will	chase batting crown
Can't	clear fences often
Expect	All-Star selection
Don't Expect	old speed

Pitchers still can't handle Gwynn. The supreme contact hitter, he won his sixth batting crown and second in a row last year. Gwynn murders right-handed pitching, hits well over .300 against lefties, and rarely fans. The 11-time All-Star, who has also led the NL in hits, is so confident at the plate that he doesn't display his old patience. As a result, his on-base average hovers only about 40 points above his batting average. Still, he's on base often. He had his first career grand slam on Aug. 22. His .394 average in 1994 was baseball's best since Ted Williams hit .406 in 1941. Gwynn is now three seasons short of Stan Musial's NL-best 16 straight .300 years. Gwynn is a five-time Gold Glove outfielder.

Major League Batting Register

	BA	G	AB	R	H	2B	3B	HR	RBI	SB
82 NL	.289	54	190	33	55	12	2	1	17	8
83 NL	.309	86	304	34	94	12	2	1	37	7
84 NL	.351	158	606	88	213	21	10	5	71	33
85 NL	.317	154	622	90	197	29	5	6	46	14
86 NL	.329	160	642	107	211	33	7	14	59	37
87 NL	.370	157	589	119	218	36	13	7	54	56
88 NL	.313	133	521	64	163	22	5	7	70	26
89 NL	.336	158	604	82	203	27	7	4	62	40
90 NL	.309	141	573	79	177	29	10	4	72	17
91 NL	.317	134	530	69	168	27	11	4	62	8
92 NL	.317	128	520	77	165	27	3	6	41	3
93 NL	.358	122	489	70	175	41	3	7	59	14
94 NL	.394	110	419	79	165	35	1	12	64	5
95 NL	.368	135	535	82	197	33	1	9	90	17
Life	.336	1830	7144	1073	2401	384	80	87	804	285
3 AVE	.374	143	560	91	210	42	2	11	83	13

JOHN HABYAN

Position: Pitcher
Team: California Angels
Born: Jan. 29, 1964 Bayshore, NY
Height: 6'2" **Weight:** 195 lbs.
Bats: right **Throws:** right
Acquired: Traded by Cardinals for Mark Sweeney, 7/95

Player Summary
Fantasy Value	$2 to $4
Card Value	4¢ to 6¢
Will	answer bell often
Can't	retire all lefties
Expect	stranded runners
Don't Expect	gopher troubles

A sinker-slider pitcher who gets lots of ground balls, Habyan has been a bullpen workhorse since making a full-time shift to relief with the 1991 Yankees. Used mostly as a middle man, he stranded a high percentage of inherited runners and did some of his best pitching with runners in scoring position in 1995. More effective against right-handed hitters, Habyan succeeds by keeping runners off base. He seldom suffered bouts of control trouble and kept the ball in the park. He averaged almost one strikeout per inning. Habyan, who also throws a curveball, helps himself with outstanding defense but has trouble holding runners close. In 1985, he pitched a Triple-A no-hitter. Habyan pitched for the Orioles, Yankees, Royals, and Cardinals before the Angels picked him up as pennant-race insurance late last season.

Major League Pitching Register

	W	L	ERA	G	S	IP	H	ER	BB	SO
85 AL	1	0	0.00	2	0	2.2	3	0	0	2
86 AL	1	3	4.44	6	0	26.1	24	13	18	14
87 AL	6	7	4.80	27	1	116.1	110	62	40	64
88 AL	1	0	4.30	7	0	14.2	22	7	4	4
90 AL	0	0	2.08	6	0	8.2	10	2	2	4
91 AL	4	2	2.30	66	2	90.0	73	23	20	70
92 AL	5	6	3.84	56	7	72.2	84	31	21	44
93 AL	2	1	4.15	48	1	56.1	59	26	20	39
94 NL	1	0	3.23	52	1	47.1	50	17	20	46
95 NL	2	2	2.88	31	0	40.2	32	13	15	35
95 AL	1	2	4.13	28	0	32.2	36	15	12	25
Life	25	23	3.70	329	12	508.1	503	209	172	347
3 AVE	3	2	3.57	63	1	68.2	69	27	26	57

CURRENT PLAYERS

CHIP HALE

Position: Second base
Team: Minnesota Twins
Born: Dec. 2, 1964 Santa Clara, CA
Height: 5'11" **Weight:** 191 lbs.
Bats: left **Throws:** right
Acquired: 17th-round pick in 6/87 free-agent draft

Player Summary	
Fantasy Value	$0
Card Value	4¢ to 6¢
Will	deliver in pinch
Can't	clear the fences
Expect	contact hitting
Don't Expect	patient at bats

Few hitters handle the pressure of coming off the bench cold and swinging a hot bat. Hale is a notable exception. He went 11-for-31 as a pinch hitter in 1994, and went 4-for-8 with six RBI immediately after his June 8 promotion from Triple-A last year. A singles hitter who makes contact, Hale and home runs are usually not invited to the same party. But there are exceptions. His one-out homer in the top of the 10th last Aug. 20 tilted an 8-7 verdict to the Twins. An aggressive hitter known for his potency against right-handers, Hale actually had a higher average against lefties over the last two seasons. He rarely walks, steals, or collects extra-base hits. He once collected eight consecutive hits, mostly as a pinch hitter, over a two-week span. Signed as a second baseman, the University of Arizona alumnus has played everywhere but catcher during a pro career that began in 1987. Hale led several minor leagues in chances, putouts, assists, double plays, and fielding percentage at second base.

Major League Batting Register

	BA	G	AB	R	H	2B	3B	HR	RBI	SB
89 AL	.209	28	67	6	14	3	0	0	4	0
90 AL	.000	1	2	0	0	0	0	0	2	0
93 AL	.333	69	186	25	62	6	1	3	27	2
94 AL	.263	67	118	13	31	9	0	1	11	0
95 AL	.262	69	103	10	27	4	0	2	18	0
Life	.282	234	476	54	134	22	1	6	62	2

DARREN HALL

Position: Pitcher
Team: Los Angeles Dodgers
Born: July 14, 1964 Marysville, OH
Height: 6'3" **Weight:** 205 lbs.
Bats: right **Throws:** right
Acquired: Signed as a free agent, 11/95

Player Summary	
Fantasy Value	$2 to $4
Card Value	5¢ to 8¢
Will	close if sound
Can't	quiet righties
Expect	frequent calls
Don't Expect	gopher trouble

One year after his impressive debut as a replacement closer for the injured Duane Ward, Hall ran into physical problems of his own. When a strained right elbow kept him sidelined for long stretches, journeyman southpaw Tony Castillo took over as Toronto's closer. Hall was left to contemplate his future. He hopes it will be in the Dodger bullpen, since he spent more than eight years in the minors before he finally reached the majors. For that to happen, Hall has to regain his 1994 form—or at least most of it. By converting 17 of 20 opportunities that summer, he led the American League with an 85 percent success ratio. A power pitcher who had more strikeouts than innings pitched in two minor-league stops, Hall blends a sinking fastball with a curveball and a slider. In 1994, he yielded only three home runs. He also stranded all 12 runners he inherited—a key statistic in the event he moves from closer to set-up duty. He's a decent but not spectacular fielder with an adequate pickoff move. When healthy, Hall can answer the call often.

Major League Pitching Register

	W	L	ERA	G	S	IP	H	ER	BB	SO
94 AL	2	3	3.41	30	17	31.2	26	12	14	28
95 AL	0	2	4.41	17	3	16.1	21	8	9	11
Life	2	5	3.75	47	20	48.0	47	20	23	39

CURRENT PLAYERS

BOB HAMELIN

Position: Designated hitter
Team: Kansas City Royals
Born: Nov. 29, 1967 Elizabeth, NJ
Height: 6′ **Weight:** 235 lbs.
Bats: left **Throws:** left
Acquired: Second-round pick in 6/88 free-agent draft

Player Summary
Fantasy Value................$8 to $10
Card Value....................5¢ to 8¢
Will.........................provide power
Can't...................even think of speed
Expect............make-or-break season
Don't Expect.............much defense

Is Bob Hamelin the second coming of Joe Charbonneau? Hamelin, the 1994 AL Rookie of the Year, suffered the supreme sophomore jinx, spending most of last summer in the minors after reporting to spring training 25 pounds overweight. His mobility—never the best—suffered, and his bat speed declined in direct proportion. Although he homered in consecutive games for the Royals on July 13 and 14, Hamelin lasted only a month during his second tour with the varsity. Without a complete turnaround, he could become a second Charbonneau, a Cleveland Rookie of the Year in 1980 who was out of the game a short time later. Hamelin has had a career-long bout with back problems, but he is a prolific power producer when healthy. About one-half of his hits netted extra bases in 1994. Better against right-handers, he's deadly when he gets ahead in the count. Hamelin shows surprising patience for a slugger. Because the former UCLA first baseman can't match Wally Joyner's glove, Hamelin spent his first years in the majors as a designated hitter.

Major League Batting Register

	BA	G	AB	R	H	2B	3B	HR	RBI	SB
93 AL	.224	16	49	2	11	3	0	2	5	0
94 AL	.282	101	312	64	88	25	1	24	65	4
95 AL	.168	72	208	20	35	7	1	7	25	0
Life	.236	189	569	86	134	35	2	33	95	4
2 AVE	.243	112	337	56	82	22	1	21	60	3

DARRYL HAMILTON

Position: Outfield
Team: Milwaukee Brewers
Born: Dec. 3, 1964 Baton Rouge, LA
Height: 6′1″ **Weight:** 180 lbs.
Bats: left **Throws:** right
Acquired: 11th-round pick in 6/86 free-agent draft

Player Summary
Fantasy Value..................$5 to $7
Card Value.....................4¢ to 6¢
Will.........................reach base often
Can't...................show great power
Expect.....................display of speed
Don't Expect...............fielding woes

Hamilton makes up for his lack of power with his excellent knowledge of the strike zone. He works deep into the count, makes contact when he swings, and shows enough patience to tally more walks than strikeouts. As a result, his on-base percentage hovered about 75 points above his batting average for much of the 1995 season. Hamilton fattens his average with bunts and infield hits. A better hitter with two strikes, he's also formidable in clutch situations. He is completely healed from the elbow operation that shortened his 1994 campaign. He's also had past shoulder problems. Hamilton, who once reacted to lefties like Superman reacts to kryptonite, now hits for a respectable average against southpaws. His success ratio as a base-stealer is even more impressive; he's rarely thrown out. If healthy, Hamilton could swipe 40 again. His speed helps in the outfield, where he has more than enough range to play center every day. He also throws well.

Major League Batting Register

	BA	G	AB	R	H	2B	3B	HR	RBI	SB
88 AL	.184	44	103	14	19	4	0	1	11	7
90 AL	.295	89	156	27	46	5	0	1	18	10
91 AL	.311	122	405	64	126	15	6	1	57	16
92 AL	.298	128	470	67	140	19	7	5	62	41
93 AL	.310	135	520	74	161	21	1	9	48	21
94 AL	.262	36	141	23	37	10	1	1	13	3
95 AL	.271	112	398	54	108	20	6	5	44	11
Life	.290	666	2193	323	637	94	21	23	253	109
2 AVE	.292	131	484	67	141	22	4	7	49	17

CURRENT PLAYERS

JOEY HAMILTON

Position: Pitcher
Team: San Diego Padres
Born: Sept. 9, 1970 Statesboro, GA
Height: 6'4" **Weight:** 220 lbs.
Bats: right **Throws:** right
Acquired: First-round pick in 6/91 free-agent draft

Player Summary	
Fantasy Value	$14 to $17
Card Value	5¢ to 8¢
Will	work fast games
Can't	win whiff title
Expect	reliable control
Don't Expect	runners to steal

Hamilton likes to make quick work of the opposition. He finished a 2-0 four-hitter against Colorado June 24 in one hour and 55 minutes, the fastest game in the majors at that point of the season. It was the second whitewash in three starts for the young control artist, who maintained a strikeout-to-walk ratio of about 2-to-1 in 1995. Although last year was his first full season, Hamilton possesses poise far beyond his youth and limited experience. He blends a sinker and a slider with a cut fastball, a curveball, and a changeup—throwing all five pitches for strikes. Last year he allowed an average of about two walks per nine innings. Most of his outs come on ground balls. Hamilton keeps the ball in the park, controls the running game exceptionally well, and helps himself with his fielding. His once-laughable hitting is even coming around. After going 0-for-57 to start his career, he finally got a hit on June 9. The second-team All-American at Georgia Southern has had problems with a bulging waistline and tender shoulder. If he stays fit, Hamilton could become a star.

Major League Pitching Register

	W	L	ERA	G	CG	IP	H	ER	BB	SO
94 NL	9	6	2.98	16	1	108.2	98	36	29	61
95 NL	6	9	3.08	31	2	204.1	189	70	56	123
Life	15	15	3.05	47	3	313.0	287	106	85	184
2 AVE	10	9	3.04	29	2	191.2	175	65	52	112

CHRIS HAMMOND

Position: Pitcher
Team: Florida Marlins
Born: Jan. 21, 1966 Atlanta, GA
Height: 6' **Weight:** 190 lbs.
Bats: left **Throws:** left
Acquired: Traded by Reds for Gary Scott and Hector Carrasco, 3/92

Player Summary	
Fantasy Value	$4 to $6
Card Value	5¢ to 10¢
Will	keep ERA down
Can't	field position
Expect	surprising bat
Don't Expect	rival steals

Injuries have wreaked havoc with Hammond's career over the last two seasons. After battling a bad back in 1994, he tried a stretching regimen to combat the chronic pain last year. Then he was disabled in August with shoulder tendinitis. When healthy, Hammond shows flashes of the form that enabled him to have two spectacular seasons in the high minors (16-5 and 15-1). He reeled off 24 consecutive scoreless innings, a Florida club record, in 1994. He had a pair of shutouts before Labor Day last year. One of them was a 4-0 three-hitter at Los Angeles July 13 that lowered his ERA to 2.28, third in the NL at the time. Hammond has outstanding control of a fastball, a slider, a curve, and a slow change. For much of the 1995 season, he averaged about two walks per game, yielded less hits than innings, and had about two and one-half strikeouts for every walk. He helps himself with a potent bat (he hit a grand slam May 29) and a perfected pickoff move. Hammond's weak spot is his fielding.

Major League Pitching Register

	W	L	ERA	G	CG	IP	H	ER	BB	SO
90 NL	0	2	6.35	3	0	11.1	13	8	12	4
91 NL	7	7	4.06	20	0	99.2	92	45	48	50
92 NL	7	10	4.21	28	0	147.1	149	69	55	79
93 NL	11	12	4.66	32	1	191.0	207	99	66	108
94 NL	4	4	3.07	13	1	73.1	79	25	23	40
95 NL	9	6	3.80	25	3	161.0	157	68	47	126
Life	38	41	4.13	121	5	683.2	697	314	251	407
3 AVE	9	8	3.99	26	2	158.0	165	70	50	102

CURRENT PLAYERS

JEFFREY HAMMONDS

Position: Outfield
Team: Baltimore Orioles
Born: March 5, 1971 Plainfield, NJ
Height: 6' **Weight:** 195 lbs.
Bats: right **Throws:** right
Acquired: First-round pick in 6/92 free-agent draft

Player Summary	
Fantasy Value	$9 to $11
Card Value	8¢ to 12¢
Will	show speed
Can't	escape injuries
Expect	run production
Don't Expect	patient at bats

Hammonds has been hampered by his own personal injury wave over the past several seasons. He started the 1995 campaign at Double-A Bowie while rehabbing from off-season knee surgery, then he later spent long stretches on the DL with neck and shoulder problems. He has also had a wrist injury, concussion, herniated disc in his neck, and a strained right knee. The healthy Hammonds has a world of potential. The former Stanford standout was a two-time All-American who started in center field for the 1992 U.S. Olympic team. He could evolve into a 30-30 man, according to several scouts. A pull hitter against lefties, he hits to all fields against right-handers. He'll be more productive when he masters the strike zone—he fans about twice per walk. If he reaches more, he'll run more, though Hammonds may never reach the 50-steal level once predicted for him. His speed helps in the outfield, however, where his range compensates for a mediocre arm. The first player from the 1992 draft to reach the majors, Hammonds hopes to play a full season for the first time.

Major League Batting Register

	BA	G	AB	R	H	2B	3B	HR	RBI	SB
93 AL	.305	33	105	10	32	8	0	3	19	4
94 AL	.296	68	250	45	74	18	2	8	31	5
95 AL	.242	57	178	18	43	9	1	4	23	4
Life	.280	158	533	73	149	35	3	15	73	13
2 AVE	.276	80	276	42	76	18	2	8	35	6

MIKE HAMPTON

Position: Pitcher
Team: Houston Astros
Born: Sept. 9, 1972 Brooksville, FL
Height: 5'10" **Weight:** 180 lbs.
Bats: right **Throws:** left
Acquired: Traded by Mariners with Mike Felder for Eric Anthony, 12/93

Player Summary	
Fantasy Value	$10 to $13
Card Value	6¢ to 10¢
Will	coax ground balls
Can't	hold runners on
Expect	spot in rotation
Don't Expect	return to relief

After he saw Hampton pitch last summer, St. Louis manager Mike Jorgensen wondered aloud why the Houston lefty was only a fifth starter. A control artist who blends a cut fastball with a changeup and a slurve, Hampton moved into the Astro rotation last spring after spending all of 1994 in the bullpen. He didn't complete any of his first 17 starts, but did throw eight scoreless innings in a 9-0 win over the Cardinals June 28. While the changeup keeps batters off-stride, the slurve is actually his best pitch. Through much of the 1995 season, he yielded about eight and one-half hits, seven strikeouts, and three walks per nine innings. He's especially stingy with the home run ball. When his location is on, Hampton keeps his infielders occupied handling ground balls. His weaknesses are retiring left-handed hitters and holding runners close. He improved against lefties last year but should do even better. Hampton has no problems as a fielder but doesn't show much in the batter's box. No one is complaining, however.

Major League Pitching Register

	W	L	ERA	G	S	IP	H	ER	BB	SO
93 AL	1	3	9.53	13	1	17.0	28	18	17	8
94 NL	2	1	3.70	44	0	41.1	46	17	16	24
95 NL	9	8	3.35	24	0	150.2	141	56	49	115
Life	12	12	3.92	81	0	209.0	215	91	82	147
2 AVE	6	5	3.44	44	0	113.2	112	43	39	82

CURRENT PLAYERS

CHRIS HANEY

Position: Pitcher
Team: Kansas City Royals
Born: Nov. 16, 1968 Baltimore, MD
Height: 6'3" **Weight:** 195 lbs.
Bats: left **Throws:** left
Acquired: Traded by Expos with Bill Sampen for Sean Berry and Archie Corbin, 8/92

Player Summary	
Fantasy Value	$7 to $9
Card Value	4¢ to 6¢
Will	rely on location
Can't	avoid home runs
Expect	complete recovery
Don't Expect	perfect control

Haney was among the American League's ERA leaders on July 17 when he was sidelined by a herniated disc in his back. At the time, he was pitching the best ball of his big-league career and seemed poised for a breakthrough season. A finesse pitcher who's much more effective against left-handed hitters, Haney blends a fastball, a slider, and a curve in a repertoire that begs for a changeup. Because he doesn't register many strikeouts, he needs precise location of his pitches to succeed. He doesn't always have it. Nor is he always able to keep the ball in the park. Haney yielded about one hit per inning plus three and one-half walks and strikeouts per game. He helps himself by holding runners well, but is no better than adequate as a fielder. The son of former big-league backstop Larry Haney, Chris began his career in the Montreal farm system in 1990 after he was drafted off the University of North Carolina's Charlotte campus in the second round.

Major League Pitching Register

	W	L	ERA	G	CG	IP	H	ER	BB	SO
91 NL	3	7	4.04	16	0	84.2	94	38	43	51
92 NL	2	3	5.45	9	1	38.0	40	23	10	27
92 AL	2	3	3.86	7	1	42.0	35	18	16	27
93 AL	9	9	6.02	23	1	124.0	141	83	53	65
94 AL	2	2	7.31	6	0	28.1	36	23	11	18
95 AL	3	4	3.65	16	1	81.1	78	33	33	31
Life	21	28	4.93	77	4	398.1	424	218	166	219
2 AVE	6	7	5.02	21	1	108.1	114	60	45	50

DAVE HANSEN

Position: Third base
Team: Los Angeles Dodgers
Born: Nov. 24, 1968 Long Beach, CA
Height: 6' **Weight:** 180 lbs.
Bats: left **Throws:** right
Acquired: Second-round pick in 6/86 free-agent draft

Player Summary	
Fantasy Value	$1
Card Value	4¢ to 6¢
Will	hit right-handers
Can't	clear the fences
Expect	many pinch hits
Don't Expect	prolonged action

Don't expect Hansen to steal a base or hit a home run. Do expect him to produce a lot of pinch hits. Hansen had 18 pinch hits, a single-season Dodger record, in 1993. He saw more action last year when regular third baseman Tim Wallach was sidelined by injury. A contact hitter who walks more often than he fans, Hansen hits right-handers well but struggles against southpaws. After Wallach went down, rookie Garey Ingram and Hansen formed a good left-right platoon. Hansen has a good idea of the strike zone, and walked often enough last year to inflate his on-base percentage by 70 points over his batting average. He's also a capable third baseman with good instincts, quick reactions, soft hands, and a reliable throwing arm. He led various minor leagues in chances, putouts, assists, double plays, and fielding percentage. Recurring back problems have hampered Hansen's ability to answer the bell every day. But his lack of power and prowess in the pinch may have hurt him even more.

Major League Batting Register

	BA	G	AB	R	H	2B	3B	HR	RBI	SB
90 NL	.143	5	7	0	1	0	0	0	1	0
91 NL	.268	53	56	3	15	4	0	1	5	1
92 NL	.214	132	341	30	73	11	0	6	22	0
93 NL	.362	84	105	13	38	3	0	4	30	0
94 NL	.341	40	44	3	15	3	0	0	5	0
95 NL	.287	100	181	19	52	10	0	1	14	0
Life	.264	414	734	68	194	31	0	12	77	1

CURRENT PLAYERS

ERIK HANSON

Position: Pitcher
Team: Boston Red Sox
Born: May 18, 1965 Kinnelon, NJ
Height: 6'6" **Weight:** 210 lbs.
Bats: right **Throws:** right
Acquired: Signed as a free agent, 4/95

Player Summary	
Fantasy Value	$8 to $10
Card Value	6¢ to 10¢
Will	win starts often
Can't	find former heat
Expect	several Ks
Don't Expect	gopher problems

How much better might Hanson have been last summer? After making the All-Star team for the first time, he developed a sore elbow that prevented him from throwing his best pitch, an overhand curveball. That reduced his repertoire to a fastball, a changeup, and a hybrid that is part slider and part cut-fastball. A former power pitcher who once fanned 211 AL hitters, Hanson now relies on location, finesse, and a deceptive motion to fool rival hitters. The formula apparently works. Hanson yielded less hits than innings, kept the ball in the park, and notched a strikeout-to-walk ratio of better than 2-to-1. He had about three walks and seven whiffs per game. He's more effective against lefties than righties. Hanson helps himself by fielding his position well and keeping close watch on the running game. The Wake Forest product was a second-round draft choice by Seattle in 1986.

Major League Pitching Register

	W	L	ERA	G	CG	IP	H	ER	BB	SO
88 AL	2	3	3.24	6	0	41.2	35	15	12	36
89 AL	9	5	3.18	17	1	113.1	103	40	32	75
90 AL	18	9	3.24	33	5	236.0	205	85	68	211
91 AL	8	8	3.81	27	2	174.2	182	74	56	143
92 AL	8	17	4.82	31	6	186.2	209	100	57	112
93 AL	11	12	3.47	31	7	215.0	215	83	60	163
94 AL	5	5	4.11	22	0	122.2	137	56	23	101
95 AL	15	5	4.24	29	1	186.2	187	88	59	139
Life	76	64	3.81	196	22	1276.2	1273	541	367	980
3 AVE	12	8	3.93	32	3	199.2	206	87	53	154

MIKE HARKEY

Position: Pitcher
Team: California Angels
Born: Oct. 25, 1966 San Diego, CA
Height: 6'5" **Weight:** 235 lbs.
Bats: right **Throws:** right
Acquired: Claimed from Athletics on waivers, 7/95

Player Summary	
Fantasy Value	$0
Card Value	4¢ to 6¢
Will	seek starting job
Can't	quiet lefty bats
Expect	gopher problems
Don't Expect	injury-free year

Harkey pitches best when he doesn't worry about his past shoulder problems and control woes and just rears back and fires the ball. He did just that last summer. Filling in for Shawn Boskie, Harkey won his first three Angel decisions. In a 9-2 complete-game win over Texas, Harkey kept the pitch count down, challenged the hitters, and looked like the pitcher who went 12-6 for the Cubs as a 1990 rookie. Though Harkey seems to be getting over his previous control problems, he still catches too much of the plate with his fastball, curve, and slider. Good hitters can hit good fastballs if they're not in the right location. That's why he yielded more hits than innings and throws too many home run balls. Lefties light him up and righties don't roll over against him. Harkey hurts his own cause with poor defense and an inability to hold runners close. A former first-round draft choice out of Cal State Fullerton, Harkey has had more than his share of injuries.

Major League Pitching Register

	W	L	ERA	G	CG	IP	H	ER	BB	SO
88 NL	0	3	2.60	5	0	34.2	33	10	15	18
90 NL	12	6	3.26	27	2	173.2	153	63	59	94
91 NL	0	2	5.30	4	0	18.2	21	11	6	15
92 NL	4	0	1.89	7	0	38.0	34	8	15	21
93 NL	10	10	5.26	28	1	157.1	187	92	43	67
94 NL	1	6	5.79	24	0	91.2	125	59	35	39
95 AL	8	9	5.44	26	1	127.1	155	77	47	56
Life	35	36	4.49	121	4	641.1	708	320	220	310
3 AVE	7	10	5.48	30	1	143.2	179	87	48	62

CURRENT PLAYERS

PETE HARNISCH

Position: Pitcher
Team: New York Mets
Born: Sept. 23, 1966 Commack, NY
Height: 6' **Weight:** 207 lbs.
Bats: right **Throws:** right
Acquired: Traded by Astros for Andy Beckerman, 11/94

Player Summary	
Fantasy Value	$7 to $9
Card Value	5¢ to 8¢
Will	try to prove sound
Can't	win without slider
Expect	200 innings if OK
Don't Expect	control lapses

When Harnisch had his two big years for Houston, he capitalized on his ability to finish off hitters. He mixed his fastball and slider with a cut fastball, a slow curve, and a changeup. He couldn't do that last summer, when the slider gave him fits. Unable to show his usual good control, he was hit hard; he was among the NL leaders in extra-base hits allowed per nine innings. As a result, he dropped eight of his 10 decisions. The Fordham product got untracked July 16, when he had a seven-hit, eight-K game in eight innings against Colorado. Three weeks later, however, Harnisch was disabled with a shoulder injury that required surgery. He had torn a shoulder tendon in 1994, tried pitching through the pain, but spent a month on the DL anyway. When healthy, he is a tough competitor who dominates righties. He topped the NL with four shutouts in 1993. Harnisch can bunt, hit, and field, but doesn't hold runners well.

Major League Pitching Register

	W	L	ERA	G	CG	IP	H	ER	BB	SO
88 AL	0	2	5.54	2	0	13.0	13	8	9	10
89 AL	5	9	4.62	18	2	103.1	97	53	64	70
90 AL	11	11	4.34	31	3	188.2	189	91	86	122
91 NL	12	9	2.70	33	4	216.2	169	65	83	172
92 NL	9	10	3.70	34	0	206.2	182	85	64	164
93 NL	16	9	2.98	33	5	217.2	171	72	79	185
94 NL	8	5	5.40	17	1	95.0	100	57	39	62
95 NL	2	8	3.68	18	0	110.0	111	45	24	82
Life	63	63	3.72	186	15	1151.0	1032	476	448	867
3 AVE	10	8	3.84	26	2	158.1	146	68	54	122

GENE HARRIS

Position: Pitcher
Team: Baltimore Orioles
Born: Dec. 5, 1964 Sebring, FL
Height: 5'11" **Weight:** 195 lbs.
Bats: right **Throws:** right
Acquired: Traded by Phillies for Andy Van Slyke, 6/95

Player Summary	
Fantasy Value	$1 to $3
Card Value	4¢ to 6¢
Will	throw late heat
Can't	locate the plate
Expect	steals by rivals
Don't Expect	frequent gophers

For a guy with such great stuff, Harris bounces around a lot. Signed by Montreal, he's pitched in the majors for the Expos, Mariners, Padres, Tigers, Phillies, and Orioles—all within the last six years. One problem is his elbow, so sore lately that he hasn't pitched much in two seasons. His biggest problem, however, is control—or lack of it. Even during his 23-save season in 1993, Harris walked almost as many as he struck out. Since erratic control nullifies the advantage of yielding less hits than innings, he has an obvious problem. A sinker-slider pitcher who also throws a change, he gets his outs on strikeouts or grounders. When he was sound, Harris notched six strikeouts and five and one-half walks per nine innings. He keeps the ball in the park and fields his position but can't hold runners. He'll have to prove healthy before he gets another chance.

Major League Pitching Register

	W	L	ERA	G	S	IP	H	ER	BB	SO
89 NL	1	1	4.95	11	0	20.0	16	11	10	11
89 AL	1	4	6.48	10	1	33.1	47	24	15	14
90 AL	1	2	4.74	25	0	38.0	31	20	30	43
91 AL	0	0	4.05	8	1	13.1	15	6	10	6
92 AL	0	0	7.00	9	0	9.0	8	7	6	6
92 NL	0	2	2.95	14	0	21.1	15	7	9	19
93 NL	6	6	3.03	59	23	59.1	57	20	37	39
94 NL	1	1	8.03	13	0	12.1	21	11	8	9
94 AL	0	0	7.15	11	1	11.1	13	9	4	10
95 NL	2	2	4.26	21	0	19.0	19	9	8	9
95 AL	0	0	4.50	3	0	4.0	4	2	1	4
Life	12	18	4.71	183	26	241.0	246	126	138	170

CURRENT PLAYERS

LENNY HARRIS

Position: Infield
Team: Cincinnati Reds
Born: Oct. 28, 1964 Miami, FL
Height: 5'10" **Weight:** 195 lbs.
Bats: left **Throws:** right
Acquired: Signed as a free agent, 11/93

Player Summary
Fantasy Value	$1
Card Value	4¢ to 6¢
Will	fill any vacancy
Can't	help on defense
Expect	many pinch hits
Don't Expect	long-ball power

A true baseball handyman, Harris is good at playing several different positions but isn't good enough to play any of them for a prolonged period of time. Signed as a third baseman, he has played all four infield positions, plus the outfield corners, in the majors. He's made his biggest mark, however, as a productive pinch hitter against right-handed pitching. He is an aggressive contact hitter who rips liners to all fields. However, Harris rarely walks, fans, or connects for a home run. Even though his hits are usually singles, he is an effective weapon on the bench. He'll beat out bunts and infield hits, steal a few bases, and succeed at a high percentage of his steal attempts. Because of his bad hands and inability to turn the double play at second, Harris spent most of last year backing the infield corners. Prone to mental errors and booting routine plays, he is far better with a bat in his hands than he is with a glove.

BRYAN HARVEY

Position: Pitcher
Team: Florida Marlins
Born: June 2, 1963 Chattanooga, TN
Height: 6'2" **Weight:** 215 lbs.
Bats: right **Throws:** right
Acquired: First-round pick from Angels in 11/92 expansion draft

Player Summary
Fantasy Value	$4 to $6
Card Value	5¢ to 8¢
Will	try new comeback
Can't	prevent injuries
Expect	strikeouts
Don't Expect	frequent gophers

Harvey worked at least 50 games five times, reached the 45-save level twice, had two other 25-save campaigns, and made the All-Star team twice. But he's also spent long stretches on the sidelines while recuperating from surgery, usually involving his fragile right elbow. Out most of the last two seasons, Harvey will try to prove this spring that he's healed from the torn elbow ligament that idled him early last year. When healthy, he has been considered baseball's best closer. His icy stare alone has been known to intimidate batters. He is a fastball-forkball pitcher with exceptional control. In the past, Harvey yielded few hits, fewer homers, and more strikeouts than innings pitched. Harvey did not blow many save opportunities. In 1993, his one-win, 45-save season for the Marlins gave him a hand in a record 71.9 percent of his team's victories. He was signed out of the University of North Carolina-Charlotte.

Major League Batting Register
	BA	G	AB	R	H	2B	3B	HR	RBI	SB
88 NL	.372	16	43	7	16	1	0	0	8	4
89 NL	.236	115	335	36	79	10	1	3	26	14
90 NL	.304	137	431	61	131	16	4	2	29	15
91 NL	.287	145	429	59	123	16	1	3	38	12
92 NL	.271	135	347	28	94	11	0	0	30	19
93 NL	.237	107	160	20	38	6	1	2	11	3
94 NL	.310	66	100	13	31	3	1	0	14	7
95 NL	.208	101	197	32	41	8	3	2	16	10
Life	.271	822	2042	256	553	71	11	12	172	84
2 AVE	.220	110	191	28	42	8	2	2	15	7

Major League Pitching Register
	W	L	ERA	G	S	IP	H	ER	BB	SO
87 AL	0	0	0.00	3	0	5.0	6	0	2	3
88 AL	7	5	2.13	50	17	76.0	59	18	20	67
89 AL	3	3	3.44	51	25	55.0	36	21	41	78
90 AL	4	4	3.22	54	25	64.1	45	23	35	82
91 AL	2	4	1.60	67	46	78.2	51	14	17	101
92 AL	0	4	2.83	25	13	28.2	22	9	11	34
93 NL	1	5	1.70	59	45	69.0	45	13	13	73
94 NL	0	0	5.23	12	6	10.1	12	6	4	10
95 NL	0	0	0.00	1	0	0.0	2	3	1	0
Life	17	25	2.49	322	177	387.0	278	107	144	448

CURRENT PLAYERS

CHARLIE HAYES

Position: Third base
Team: Philadelphia Phillies
Born: May 29, 1965 Hattiesburg, MS
Height: 6' **Weight:** 205 lbs.
Bats: right **Throws:** right
Acquired: Signed as a free agent, 4/95

Player Summary	
Fantasy Value	$7 to $9
Card Value	5¢ to 8¢
Will	hit lefties hard
Can't	avoid double plays
Expect	some power
Don't Expect	impatient at bats

In his second tour with the Phillies, Hayes proved to be far more patient at the plate. Although he still fanned more frequently than anyone else on the team, he also drew enough walks to boost his on-base percentage about 70 points higher than his batting average. A fastball hitter who hits "mistakes" of any variety, Hayes hits to all fields against right-handed pitchers but tries to pull lefties. His .305 average and 72 extra-base hits of 1993 were aided by the altitude of Colorado. He is good for 10 to 20 homers in any climate, however. He hammers left-handed pitching. On the minus side, he bangs into numerous double plays. Hayes steals a handful of bases a year, but moves well enough to provide solid defense at third. He has quick reactions, good range, soft hands, and a strong arm, though his errors usually come on bad throws. He's led his league in chances, assists, and double plays by a third baseman.

Major League Batting Register

	BA	G	AB	R	H	2B	3B	HR	RBI	SB
88 NL	.091	7	11	0	1	0	0	0	0	0
89 NL	.257	87	304	26	78	15	1	8	43	3
90 NL	.258	152	561	56	145	20	0	10	57	4
91 NL	.230	142	460	34	106	23	1	12	53	3
92 AL	.257	142	509	52	131	19	2	18	66	3
93 NL	.305	157	573	89	175	45	2	25	98	11
94 NL	.288	113	423	46	122	23	4	10	50	3
95 NL	.276	141	529	58	146	30	3	11	85	5
Life	.268	941	3370	361	904	175	13	94	452	32
3 AVE	.290	158	588	73	170	37	4	17	88	7

SCOTT HEMOND

Position: Catcher; infield
Team: St. Louis Cardinals
Born: Nov. 18, 1965 Taunton, MA
Height: 6' **Weight:** 215 lbs.
Bats: right **Throws:** right
Acquired: Signed as a free agent, 4/95

Player Summary	
Fantasy Value	$1 to $3
Card Value	4¢ to 6¢
Will	play anywhere
Can't	cut strikeouts
Expect	strong defense
Don't Expect	power explosion

With the possible exception of Craig Biggio, who made the All-Star team as both a catcher and second baseman, few big-league backstops are as versatile as Hemond. The former South Florida All-American has done everything but pitch in the major leagues. Though he's an impatient hitter who in 1995 fanned more than twice per walk, Hemond shows some power when he makes contact. Unfortunately for his team, that's not very often. He's more likely to steal a base than he is to blast an extra-base hit. He's never swiped more than 14 in the majors but once pilfered 45 as a regular in the minors. He is also adept at stopping others from stealing; he has nailed more than 40 percent of those who try to run on him in the past. A solid defensive catcher, Hemond calls a good game, prevents wild pitches, and blocks the plate well. He's quite competent at third base too; he once led the Double-A Southern League in assists and chances.

Major League Batting Register

	BA	G	AB	R	H	2B	3B	HR	RBI	SB
89 AL	.000	4	0	2	0	0	0	0	0	0
90 AL	.154	7	13	0	2	0	0	0	1	0
91 AL	.217	23	23	4	5	0	0	0	0	1
92 AL	.225	25	40	8	9	1	0	0	1	1
93 AL	.256	91	215	31	55	16	0	6	26	14
94 AL	.222	91	198	23	44	11	0	3	20	7
95 NL	.144	57	118	11	17	1	0	3	9	0
Life	.217	298	607	79	132	30	0	12	58	23
2 AVE	.237	110	247	32	58	16	0	5	27	12

CURRENT PLAYERS

RICKEY HENDERSON

Position: Outfield
Team: Oakland Athletics
Born: Dec. 25, 1958 Chicago, IL
Height: 5'10" **Weight:** 190 lbs.
Bats: right **Throws:** left
Acquired: Signed as a free agent, 12/93

Player Summary	
Fantasy Value	$16 to $19
Card Value	8¢ to 12¢
Will	reach base often
Can't	show former power
Expect	gradual slowdown
Don't Expect	another MVP year

After winning 11 stolen-base titles, Henderson seems to be slowing down. Though he's still a high-percentage basestealer, the frequency has definitely declined. However, he still has a quick bat. Henderson's on-base percentage still ranks near the top of the list, and he retains his reputation as one of baseball's best leadoff men. Batting from a deep crouch that minimizes his strike zone, he loves high fastballs. He's hit more leadoff homers than anyone in history. Though he once won a Gold Glove, Henderson is not a great outfielder. His throwing is weak and his speed compensates for mistakes in judgement. He was the regular-season MVP in 1990 and the Championship Series MVP in 1989.

Major League Batting Register

	BA	G	AB	R	H	2B	3B	HR	RBI	SB
79 AL	.274	89	351	49	96	13	3	1	26	33
80 AL	.303	158	591	111	179	22	4	9	53	100
81 AL	.319	108	423	89	135	18	7	6	35	56
82 AL	.267	149	536	119	143	24	4	10	51	130
83 AL	.292	145	513	105	150	25	7	9	48	108
84 AL	.293	142	502	113	147	27	4	16	58	66
85 AL	.314	143	547	146	172	28	5	24	72	80
86 AL	.263	153	608	130	160	31	5	28	74	87
87 AL	.291	95	358	78	104	17	3	17	37	41
88 AL	.305	140	554	118	169	30	2	6	50	93
89 AL	.274	150	541	113	148	26	3	12	57	77
90 AL	.325	136	489	119	159	33	3	28	61	65
91 AL	.268	134	470	105	126	17	1	18	57	58
92 AL	.283	117	396	77	112	18	3	15	46	48
93 AL	.289	134	481	114	139	22	2	21	59	53
94 AL	.260	87	296	66	77	13	0	6	20	22
95 AL	.300	112	407	67	122	31	1	9	54	32
Life	.290	2192	8063	1719	2338	395	57	235	858	1149
3 AVE	.284	128	452	94	128	25	1	13	49	40

TOM HENKE

Position: Pitcher
Team: St. Louis Cardinals
Born: Dec. 21, 1957 Kansas City, MO
Height: 6'5" **Weight:** 225 lbs.
Bats: right **Throws:** right
Acquired: Signed as a free agent, 12/94

Player Summary	
Fantasy Value	$19 to $22
Card Value	5¢ to 8¢
Will	throw late heat
Can't	hold runners on
Expect	frequent calls
Don't Expect	control trouble

With his 1994 back problems behind him, Henke hoisted himself back into the relief pitching elite last summer. Pitching in the NL for the first time in his career, he converted his first 23 save opportunities, three short of his career best, before finally blowing one. He blew only two all season. Henke did it by fanning nearly eight hitters, walking about three batters, and yielding about seven hits over nine innings for much of the season. His combination of a sinker, a slider, and a forkball results in ground balls and strikeouts. He holds hitters to a low average, gives up few homers, and strands a high percentage of inherited runners. He hurts his own cause with erratic fielding and an inability to keep runners close. An All-Star in both leagues, Henke in 1995 recorded his 300th career save.

Major League Pitching Register

	W	L	ERA	G	S	IP	H	ER	BB	SO
82 AL	1	0	1.15	8	0	15.2	14	2	8	9
83 AL	1	0	3.38	8	1	16.0	16	6	4	17
84 AL	1	1	6.35	25	2	28.1	36	20	20	25
85 AL	3	3	2.03	28	13	40.0	29	9	8	42
86 AL	9	5	3.35	63	27	91.1	63	34	32	118
87 AL	0	6	2.49	72	34	94.0	62	26	25	128
88 AL	4	4	2.91	52	25	68.0	60	22	24	66
89 AL	8	3	1.92	64	20	89.0	66	19	25	116
90 AL	2	4	2.17	61	32	74.2	58	18	19	75
91 AL	0	2	2.32	49	32	50.1	33	13	11	53
92 AL	3	2	2.26	57	34	55.2	40	14	22	46
93 AL	5	5	2.91	66	40	74.1	55	24	27	79
94 AL	3	6	3.79	37	15	38.0	33	16	12	39
95 NL	1	1	1.82	52	36	54.1	42	11	18	48
Life	41	42	2.67	642	311	789.2	607	234	255	861
3 AVE	3	5	2.81	59	34	63.1	50	20	21	63

CURRENT PLAYERS

MIKE HENNEMAN

Position: Pitcher
Team: Houston Astros
Born: Dec. 11, 1961 St. Charles, MO
Height: 6'4" **Weight:** 205 lbs.
Bats: right **Throws:** right
Acquired: Traded by Tigers for Phil Nevin, 7/95

Player Summary
Fantasy Value	$4 to $6
Card Value	5¢ to 8¢
Will	stifle rallies
Can't	stop southpaws
Expect	heavy workload
Don't Expect	rivals to steal

Henneman carried a hefty bullpen workload in Detroit for seven years before collapsing under the strain in 1994. But he rebounded so well last year that the Astros acquired him as insurance for the wild-card race. From 1987 to 1993, the Oklahoma State product pitched at least 55 times, often working multi-inning stints. He even made the All-Star team once. A sinker-slider pitcher who also throws a forkball—all from a three-quarters motion—Henneman has always been more effective against right-handed hitters. He usually yields less hits than innings and keeps the ball in the park. Henneman also customarily strands a high percentage of the runners he inherits. Because of his quick delivery and quick move, he allows few baserunners to take liberties. He's not nearly as spectacular with the glove, though he's no slouch either.

Major League Pitching Register

	W	L	ERA	G	S	IP	H	ER	BB	SO
87 AL	11	3	2.98	55	7	96.2	86	32	30	75
88 AL	9	6	1.87	65	22	91.1	72	19	24	58
89 AL	11	4	3.70	60	8	90.0	84	37	51	69
90 AL	8	6	3.05	69	22	94.1	90	32	33	50
91 AL	10	2	2.88	60	21	84.1	81	27	34	61
92 AL	2	6	3.96	60	24	77.1	75	34	20	58
93 AL	5	3	2.64	63	24	71.2	69	21	32	58
94 AL	1	3	5.19	30	8	34.2	43	20	17	27
95 AL	0	1	1.53	29	18	29.1	24	5	9	24
95 NL	0	1	3.00	21	8	21.0	21	7	4	19
Life	57	35	3.05	512	162	690.2	645	234	254	499
3 AVE	2	3	3.18	54	22	58.2	60	21	24	48

BUTCH HENRY

Position: Pitcher
Team: Boston Red Sox
Born: Oct. 7, 1968 El Paso, TX
Height: 6'1" **Weight:** 195 lbs.
Bats: left **Throws:** left
Acquired: Claimed from Expos on waivers, 10/95

Player Summary
Fantasy Value	$1
Card Value	5¢ to 8¢
Will	win when healthy
Can't	hold runners on
Expect	pinpoint control
Don't Expect	gopher problems

Though overshadowed by Carlos Perez, Pedro Martinez, and Jeff Fassero in Montreal last year, Henry was the most effective member of the rotation before he was sidelined by injury. That happened Aug. 15, when he tore a ligament in his pitching elbow. The subsequent surgery could keep him sidelined for a chunk of the 1996 season. When healthy, Henry is a sinker-slider pitcher who also throws a curve. Last year, he emphasized location over velocity, maintained a 2-1 ratio of strikeouts to walks, and kept the ball in the park. Working from the stretch, even with the bases empty, Henry has no trouble painting both corners of the plate—thanks to a subtle change in his delivery made two years ago. A lower arm angle made a vast difference in his control, which now ranks among the best in both leagues. Since he also yielded about one hit per inning in 1995, Henry was highly effective. He'll never win a Gold Glove Award or be mentioned as a standout pickoff artist, but Henry does help himself with the bat on occasion.

Major League Pitching Register

	W	L	ERA	G	CG	IP	H	ER	BB	SO
92 NL	6	9	4.02	28	2	165.2	185	74	41	96
93 NL	3	9	6.12	30	1	103.0	135	70	28	47
94 NL	8	3	2.43	24	0	107.1	97	29	20	70
95 NL	7	9	2.84	21	1	126.2	133	40	28	60
Life	24	30	3.81	103	4	502.2	550	213	117	273
3 AVE	7	8	3.54	29	1	131.2	140	52	29	71

CURRENT PLAYERS

DOUG HENRY

Position: Pitcher
Team: New York Mets
Born: Dec. 10, 1963 Sacramento, CA
Height: 6'4" **Weight:** 185 lbs.
Bats: right **Throws:** right
Acquired: Traded by Brewers for Javier Gonzalez and Fernando Vina, 11/94

Player Summary	
Fantasy Value	$2 to $4
Card Value	4¢ to 6¢
Will	keep average down
Can't	avoid gopher balls
Expect	middle relief job
Don't Expect	many walks

For the better part of two seasons, Henry was Milwaukee's No. 1 closer. But that was before shoulder tendinitis and serious control trouble short-circuited his career. Henry even returned to the minors for a spell before the Brewers shipped him across league lines to the Mets. He got his first big-league saves since 1993, but he was much more effective as a set-up man. He throws a sinker, a slider, a forkball, and a changeup for strikes. If not for an alarming tendency to yield gopher balls, Henry would be much more effective. For much of the 1995 season, he held hitters right around the Mendoza Line, yielding about seven hits and three walks per nine innings while averaging one strikeout per inning. Henry has trouble with first pitches and first batters, however, making him a liability when inserted with runners on base. Henry's inability to hold runners close also hampers his effectiveness in such situations. He's passable but not spectacular in the field.

Major League Pitching Register

	W	L	ERA	G	S	IP	H	ER	BB	SO
91 AL	2	1	1.00	32	15	36.0	16	4	14	28
92 AL	1	4	4.02	68	29	65.0	64	29	24	52
93 AL	4	4	5.56	54	17	55.0	67	34	25	38
94 AL	2	3	4.60	25	0	31.1	32	16	23	20
95 NL	3	6	2.96	51	4	67.0	48	22	25	62
Life	12	18	3.72	230	65	254.1	227	105	111	200
3 AVE	3	5	4.19	49	7	58.0	55	27	29	45

PAT HENTGEN

Position: Pitcher
Team: Toronto Blue Jays
Born: Nov. 13, 1968 Detroit, MI
Height: 6'2" **Weight:** 200 lbs.
Bats: right **Throws:** right
Acquired: Fifth-round pick in 6/86 free-agent draft

Player Summary	
Fantasy Value	$14 to $17
Card Value	5¢ to 8¢
Will	win with control
Can't	stop gopher balls
Expect	double-digit wins
Don't Expect	high whiff totals

For the first six years of his career, Hentgen was a starter. Then he was a reliever. Then he was a starter again. He's cleared those revolving doors, but he hasn't shown the ability to win consistently in the majors. Given good run support in 1993, Hentgen went 19-9 in his first season in a big-league rotation. His win column has dropped dramatically in the two years since, however. A bad first half last year included a winless June and a nine-walk game, a Toronto club record, in July. But Hentgen improved his velocity and sharpened his curve during the season's second half. The two-time All-Star also throws a cut fastball and a changeup. However, he is not a strikeout pitcher. He needs proper location to convert his pitches into ground outs. Most of last year, he had trouble finding the plate. Once an easy mark for baserunners, Hentgen has become much more successful over the last two years. He's otherwise adequate in the field. He is more effective against right-handed hitters.

Major League Pitching Register

	W	L	ERA	G	CG	IP	H	ER	BB	SO
91 AL	0	0	2.45	3	0	7.1	5	2	3	3
92 AL	5	2	5.36	28	0	50.1	49	30	32	39
93 AL	19	9	3.87	34	3	216.1	215	93	74	122
94 AL	13	8	3.40	24	6	174.2	158	66	59	147
95 AL	10	14	5.11	30	2	200.2	236	114	90	135
Life	47	33	4.23	119	11	649.1	663	305	258	446
3 AVE	16	12	4.11	34	5	229.2	234	105	86	160

CURRENT PLAYERS

GIL HEREDIA

Position: Pitcher
Team: Montreal Expos
Born: Oct. 26, 1965 Nogales, AZ
Height: 6'1" **Weight:** 205 lbs.
Bats: right **Throws:** right
Acquired: Claimed from Giants on waivers, 8/92

Player Summary
Fantasy Value.................$1 to $3
Card Value....................4¢ to 6¢
Will .... work best from pen
Can't............... stop swingman role
Expect .... numerous grounders
Don't Expect .... gopher woes

Heredia has been trying to establish a niche in the majors for the past five seasons. Most effective when used mostly in relief in 1994, he's also had his moments as a starter. Heredia began 1995 in the Montreal rotation, moved to the pen in July, then enjoyed his best game of the season as an emergency starter Aug. 8. In that game, he held Houston to three hits in five innings of a 6-0 win. He fanned six and walked none. When his sinker, slider, forkball, and curve are working, Heredia gets lots of ground balls. Though he's not a power pitcher, he maintains a fine ratio of strikeouts to walks because of exceptional control. The University of Arizona product yields more hits than innings, but usually keeps those hits in the ballpark. Equally effective against righties and lefties, Heredia has no qualms about pitching inside. He can hit, field, and hold runners, but would be best-served by some definite decision ending his swingman status. He once pitched 15 complete games in the Mexican League.

Major League Pitching Register

	W	L	ERA	G	S	IP	H	ER	BB	SO
91 NL	0	2	3.82	7	0	33.0	27	14	7	13
92 NL	2	3	4.23	20	0	44.2	44	21	20	22
93 NL	4	2	3.92	20	2	57.1	66	25	14	40
94 NL	6	3	3.46	39	0	75.1	85	29	13	62
95 NL	5	6	4.31	40	1	119.0	137	57	21	74
Life	17	16	3.99	126	3	329.1	359	146	75	211
3 AVE	6	4	3.93	40	1	99.1	113	43	19	70

CARLOS HERNANDEZ

Position: Catcher
Team: Los Angeles Dodgers
Born: May 24, 1967 Bolivar, Venezuela
Height: 5'11" **Weight:** 185 lbs.
Bats: right **Throws:** right
Acquired: Signed as free agent, 10/84

Player Summary
Fantasy Value $0
Card Value .... 4¢ to 6¢
Will .... show good arm
Can't................... provide power
Expect .... understudy job
Don't Expect .... patient at bats

Somebody has to do it, but it's tough to play behind Mike Piazza. Though Hernandez showed great hitting potential himself in the minors, he has been the caddie for the All-Star slugger for the past two seasons. Though his hitting suffers from prolonged time on the bench, Hernandez never misses a beat on defense. He nailed 50 percent of the runners who challenged him last year, and handled his pitchers well. He is an expert at such backstopping chores as preventing wild pitches and blocking the plate. Hernandez led several minor leagues in chances, putouts, assists, and double plays. Given playing time, he also had five .300 seasons—including a .345 year at Triple-A Albuquerque. Never patient, Hernandez has gotten even more aggressive sitting on the bench. Don't count on him to draw a walk or hit the ball over the fence. Against left-handers who throw hard, however, Hernandez can be a potent force. Signed as a third baseman, Hernandez converted to catching in his second season as a pro.

Major League Batting Register

	BA	G	AB	R	H	2B	3B	HR	RBI	SB
90 NL	.200	10	20	2	4	1	0	0	1	0
91 NL	.214	15	14	1	3	1	0	0	1	1
92 NL	.260	69	173	11	45	4	0	3	17	0
93 NL	.253	50	99	6	25	5	0	2	7	0
94 NL	.219	32	64	6	14	2	0	2	6	0
95 NL	.149	45	94	3	14	1	0	2	8	0
Life	.226	221	464	29	105	14	0	9	40	1

CURRENT PLAYERS

JEREMY HERNANDEZ

Position: Pitcher
Team: Florida Marlins
Born: July 7, 1966 Burbank, CA
Height: 6'6" **Weight:** 195 lbs.
Bats: right **Throws:** right
Acquired: Traded by Indians for Matt Turner, 4/94

Player Summary	
Fantasy Value	$1
Card Value	4¢ to 6¢
Will	fill set-up role
Can't	always find plate
Expect	stranded runners
Don't Expect	homer woes

Hernandez pitched fewer than six innings for the Marlins last year before suffering a recurrence of the neck problems that plagued him in 1994. After getting off to a good start in the Florida bullpen that spring, he had surgery to repair two herniated discs. When healthy, Hernandez is a power pitcher who has tallied a 2-1 ratio of strikeouts to walks with his three-pitch arsenal: fastball, forkball, and slurve. The former Cal State Northridge standout, who uses a three-quarters delivery, gets lots of ground balls when his location is good. When it isn't, hitters tag him for home runs. Hernandez has had some control problems during his career. He strands the bulk of the runners he inherits, however, and holds runners close. A competent set-up man who's also had some success as a closer, Hernandez can work multiple-inning stints. He helps himself with his defense. Hernandez broke in as a starter in the St. Louis system in 1987. He was converted to relief four years later.

Major League Pitching Register

	W	L	ERA	G	S	IP	H	ER	BB	SO
91 NL	0	0	0.00	9	2	14.1	8	0	5	9
92 NL	1	4	4.17	26	1	36.2	39	17	11	25
93 NL	0	2	4.72	21	0	34.1	41	18	7	26
93 AL	6	5	3.14	49	8	77.1	75	27	27	44
94 NL	3	3	2.70	21	9	23.1	16	7	14	13
95 NL	0	0	11.57	7	0	7.0	12	9	3	5
Life	10	14	3.64	133	20	193.0	191	78	67	122

JOSE HERNANDEZ

Position: Infield
Team: Chicago Cubs
Born: July 14, 1969 Vega Alta, PR
Height: 6'1" **Weight:** 180 lbs.
Bats: right **Throws:** right
Acquired: Traded by Indians for Heathcliff Slocumb, 6/93

Player Summary	
Fantasy Value	$2 to $4
Card Value	5¢ to 8¢
Will	back three spots
Can't	hit right-handers
Expect	extra-base hits
Don't Expect	erratic defense

Baseball is full of surprises. The sudden power of Hernandez last summer was one of them. In eight previous seasons as a pro, he had never reached double-digits in home runs. That changed last summer, even though the versatile Hernandez played only sparingly. Signed as a shortstop out of Puerto Rico's American University, he spent 1995 as a three-position infielder, with most of his time as Shawon Dunston's understudy at shortstop. Though Hernandez fanned an unacceptable five times more often than he walked, nearly half his hits went for extra bases. Showing more power than speed was surprising for him. He once had a minor-league season with 11 steals and one homer. He doesn't try to steal much, though he has some athletic ability. A competent gloveman with a strong arm, Hernandez has quick reactions and good range, though he made an uncharacteristic nine errors last year. Originally signed as a nondrafted free agent by Texas, he began his career in 1987. He has played for the Rangers, Indians, and Cubs.

Major League Batting Register

	BA	G	AB	R	H	2B	3B	HR	RBI	SB
91 AL	.184	45	98	8	18	2	1	0	4	0
92 AL	.000	3	4	0	0	0	0	0	0	0
94 NL	.242	56	132	18	32	2	3	1	9	2
95 NL	.245	93	245	37	60	11	4	13	40	1
Life	.230	197	479	63	110	15	8	14	53	3

CURRENT PLAYERS

ROBERTO HERNANDEZ

Position: Pitcher
Team: Chicago White Sox
Born: Nov. 11, 1964 Santurce, PR
Height: 6'4" **Weight:** 220 lbs.
Bats: right **Throws:** right
Acquired: Traded by Angels with Mark Doran for Mark Davis, 8/89

Player Summary	
Fantasy Value	$30 to $35
Card Value	5¢ to 8¢
Will	get strikeouts
Can't	harness control
Expect	30 saves
Don't Expect	stolen bases

Most pitchers would be proud to own a strikeout-to-walk ratio of 3-to-1. But not Hernandez, who knows his 1995 ratio should have been much better. While the flame-thrower averaged more than a dozen strikeouts per nine innings, he also walked more than four batters over that same span. He also threw an alarming number of long balls. The results included an inflated ERA, double-digits in blown saves, and a substandard performance in trying to strand inherited runners. Kept as the closer because the White Sox had nobody else, Hernandez didn't come close to his 1992 or 1993 numbers in the same role. His arsenal of a sinker, a slider, and a forkball is formidable when combined with control. When the pitches are fat or flat, they tend to go a long way in the opposite direction. Hernandez does help himself by fielding his position and freezing the running game (a quick delivery and steady stream of hard stuff help). A starter in the minors, Hernandez became a full-time reliever in 1992.

Major League Pitching Register

	W	L	ERA	G	S	IP	H	ER	BB	SO
91 AL	1	0	7.80	9	0	15.0	18	13	7	6
92 AL	7	3	1.65	43	12	71.0	45	13	20	68
93 AL	3	4	2.29	70	38	78.2	66	20	20	71
94 AL	4	4	4.91	45	14	47.2	44	26	19	50
95 AL	3	7	3.92	60	32	59.2	63	26	28	84
Life	18	18	3.24	227	96	272.0	236	98	94	279
3 AVE	4	6	3.63	67	31	70.2	66	29	26	79

XAVIER HERNANDEZ

Position: Pitcher
Team: Cincinnati Reds
Born: Aug. 16, 1965 Port Arthur, TX
Height: 6'2" **Weight:** 185 lbs.
Bats: left **Throws:** right
Acquired: Signed as a free agent, 12/94

Player Summary	
Fantasy Value	$1 to $3
Card Value	4¢ to 6¢
Will	keep set-up role
Can't	avoid long hits
Expect	some strikeouts
Don't Expect	righties to hit him

For most of his big-league career, Hernandez has been capable of working often, but incapable of nailing down games in the ninth inning. A sinker-slider pitcher who also throws a forkball, Hernandez throws the ball over the plate and dominates right-handed hitters. Lefties, however, are another story. Though he gets lots of strikeouts, he yields too many extra-base hits and makes too many wild pitches—the result of forkballs in the dirt. He also has problems preventing inherited runners from scoring. Hernandez had an inflated ERA, two blown saves, and a 50-50 record with inherited runners. He was a far cry from the pitcher who posted a 2.11 ERA in 77 appearances for the 1992 Astros and maintained a 4-1 ratio of whiffs to walks in '93. Perhaps the strain of working 149 games those two years is getting to him. A bust as a closer for the '94 Yankees, Hernandez is happier working in set-up gigs. He helps himself with his glove but had trouble holding runners last summer.

Major League Pitching Register

	W	L	ERA	G	S	IP	H	ER	BB	SO
89 AL	1	0	4.76	7	0	22.2	25	12	8	7
90 NL	2	1	4.62	34	0	62.1	60	32	24	24
91 NL	2	7	4.71	32	3	63.0	66	33	32	55
92 NL	9	1	2.11	77	7	111.0	81	26	42	96
93 NL	4	5	2.61	72	9	96.2	75	28	28	101
94 AL	4	4	5.85	31	6	40.0	48	26	21	37
95 NL	7	2	4.60	59	3	90.0	95	46	31	84
Life	29	20	3.76	312	28	485.2	450	203	186	404
3 AVE	6	4	4.12	61	7	85.1	83	39	31	83

CURRENT PLAYERS

OREL HERSHISER

Position: Pitcher
Team: Cleveland Indians
Born: Sept. 16, 1958 Buffalo, NY
Height: 6'3" **Weight:** 192 lbs.
Bats: right **Throws:** right
Acquired: Signed as a free agent, 4/95

Player Summary
Fantasy Value	$11 to $14
Card Value	6¢ to 10¢
Will	hope sinker sinks
Can't	record strikeouts
Expect	experience to help
Don't Expect	route-going efforts

He still doesn't throw hard, register many strikeouts, or finish what he starts. But Hershiser knows how to pitch. In his first AL campaign, he topped a dozen wins for the sixth time—the first time since 1989. Though he missed time with a sprained back in midseason, he went 7-2 over the first 10 starts after his return. In one of those games, a 7-3 win at Toronto Aug. 21, he fanned eight and walked none. Although 1990 shoulder surgery has robbed him of his former Cy Young Award form, Hershiser hasn't changed his pitching pattern much. He still throws a sinker, a slider, a curveball, and a pair of changeups. He succeeds by changing speeds and location. The Bowling Green State product dominates right-handed batters and helps himself with strong defense and a good pickoff move. He's also a good hitter and bunter.

Major League Pitching Register
	W	L	ERA	G	CG	IP	H	ER	BB	SO
83 NL	0	0	3.38	8	0	8.0	7	3	6	5
84 NL	11	8	2.66	45	8	189.2	160	56	50	150
85 NL	19	3	2.03	36	9	239.2	179	54	68	157
86 NL	14	14	3.85	35	8	231.1	213	99	86	153
87 NL	16	16	3.06	37	10	264.2	247	90	74	190
88 NL	23	8	2.26	35	15	267.0	208	67	73	178
89 NL	15	15	2.31	35	8	256.2	226	66	77	178
90 NL	1	1	4.26	4	0	25.1	26	12	4	16
91 NL	7	2	3.46	21	0	112.0	112	43	32	73
92 NL	10	15	3.67	33	1	210.2	209	86	69	130
93 NL	12	14	3.59	33	5	215.2	201	86	72	141
94 NL	6	6	3.79	21	1	135.1	146	57	42	72
95 AL	16	6	3.87	26	1	167.1	151	72	51	111
Life	150	108	3.06	369	66	2323.1	2085	791	704	1554
3 AVE	13	10	3.74	31	2	198.2	192	82	63	122

GREG HIBBARD

Position: Pitcher
Team: Seattle Mariners
Born: Sept. 13, 1964 New Orleans, LA
Height: 6' **Weight:** 190 lbs.
Bats: left **Throws:** left
Acquired: Signed as a free agent, 1/94

Player Summary
Fantasy Value	$0
Card Value	5¢ to 8¢
Will	try to prove sound
Can't	field well
Expect	ground outs
Don't Expect	many whiffs

Hibbard missed the entire 1995 season while recuperating from a partially torn rotator cuff in his pitching shoulder. The injury, which also sidelined him for a sizeable chunk of the '94 campaign, was detrimental to Seattle. The Mariners got only a 1-5 record from Hibbard in the first two years of their investment. When healthy, the University of Alabama product mixes his sinkerball with a slider, a curve, and a changeup. Not a power pitcher, he's never had triple-digit strikeouts in a career that started in 1986. Getting ground balls is another matter, however. Hibbard does that very well, especially against left-handed hitters. He also keeps the ball in the park, thrives in clutch situations, and holds runners so close that they rarely try to steal against him. Beyond his physical problems, Hibbard has a real problem with his fielding. He's sometimes guilty of inadvertently hurting his own cause.

Major League Pitching Register
	W	L	ERA	G	CG	IP	H	ER	BB	SO
89 AL	6	7	3.21	23	2	137.1	142	49	41	55
90 AL	14	9	3.16	33	3	211.0	202	74	55	92
91 AL	11	11	4.31	32	5	194.0	196	93	57	71
92 AL	10	7	4.40	31	0	176.0	187	86	57	69
93 NL	15	11	3.96	31	1	191.0	209	84	47	82
94 AL	1	5	6.69	15	0	80.2	115	60	31	39
Life	57	50	4.05	165	11	990.0	1051	446	288	408

CURRENT PLAYERS

BRYAN HICKERSON

Position: Pitcher
Team: Colorado Rockies
Born: Oct. 13, 1963 Bemidji, MN
Height: 6'2" **Weight:** 195 lbs.
Bats: left **Throws:** left
Acquired: Traded by Cubs for future considerations, 7/95

Player Summary	
Fantasy Value	$0
Card Value	4¢ to 6¢
Will	remain in relief
Can't	sit lefties down
Expect	wavering control
Don't Expect	huge strikeouts

In four short years, Hickerson's steadily rising ERA has jumped from respectable to reprehensible. Once a valuable middle reliever who yielded less hits than innings and fanned about three times more men than he walked, Hickerson has fallen on hard times. He yielded far too many walks, hits, and homers last year—even before he landed at Coors Field. The University of Minnesota graduate has bounced from the Giants to the Cubs to the Rockies in recent seasons because of his inability to pitch with any consistency. Even last year's full-time return to relief, where Hickerson enjoyed his greatest success, didn't help. His rising fastball, forkball, and slider weren't sharp. Lefties hit him hard for the second year in a row, and he battled to retire just over half of the runners he inherited. An adequate fielder, Hickerson helps himself with a good pickoff move and surprising success at the plate. Unless his pitching improves, however, his job could be in jeopardy.

Major League Pitching Register

	W	L	ERA	G	S	IP	H	ER	BB	SO
91 NL	2	2	3.60	17	0	50.0	53	20	17	43
92 NL	5	3	3.09	61	0	87.1	74	30	21	68
93 NL	7	5	4.26	47	0	120.1	137	57	39	69
94 NL	4	8	5.40	28	1	98.1	118	59	38	59
95 NL	3	3	8.57	56	1	48.1	69	46	28	40
Life	21	21	4.72	209	2	404.1	451	212	143	279
3 AVE	5	7	5.51	50	1	104.2	127	64	41	66

BOB HIGGINSON

Position: Outfield
Team: Detroit Tigers
Born: Aug. 18, 1970 Philadelphia, PA
Height: 5'11" **Weight:** 180 lbs.
Bats: left **Throws:** right
Acquired: 12th-round pick in 6/92 free-agent draft

Player Summary	
Fantasy Value	$5 to $7
Card Value	12¢ to 20¢
Will	boost his power
Can't	hit left-handers
Expect	increased speed
Don't Expect	low on-base mark

Though he was platooned for a good pa of his rookie year in 1995, Higginson ha enough time to make a positive first im pression. He showed a selective battin eye, considerable power, and a tremendou throwing arm. Blessed with good bat spee and gap power, the Temple product pro duced his best game Aug. 16, when he h two singles and a three-run homer, stole base, and had two assists from right field i a 7-4 loss to Toronto. Higginson walked s often that he posted an on-base percent age about 100 points higher than his bat ting average. He hit poorly in limited actio against lefties and didn't make much of dent against righties either. He'll have to im prove in that category. If he does, his powe and speed should increase in direct pro portion—maybe beyond the 16-steal, 23 homer performance he staged in his las Triple-A campaign. One of the mystifyin aspects of his rookie year was his wea stick at home; Tiger Stadium is widely re garded as one of the best hitters' parks i the majors. Then again, Higginson did no have the advantage of batting against th Tiger pitching staff.

Major League Batting Register

	BA	G	AB	R	H	2B	3B	HR	RBI	SB
95 AL	.224	131	410	61	92	17	5	14	43	6
Life	.224	131	410	61	92	17	5	14	43	6

CURRENT PLAYERS

GLENALLEN HILL

Position: Outfield
Team: San Francisco Giants
Born: March 22, 1965 Santa Cruz, CA
Height: 6'2" **Weight:** 205 lbs.
Bats: right **Throws:** right
Acquired: Signed as a free agent, 4/95

Player Summary	
Fantasy Value	$17 to $20
Card Value	5¢ to 8¢
Will	show great power
Can't	avoid strikeouts
Expect	more 20-20 years
Don't Expect	strong throws

Given the most at bats of his career last summer, Hill finally realized the 20-20 potential that had long been predicted for him. Private tutoring from San Francisco batting coach Bobby Bonds helped. Hill, who tallied extra bases on about 40 percent of his hits last year, had hit only 25 homers in the two previous seasons combined before joining the Giants. His big season helped fill the void created by the three-month absence of 1994 home run king Matt Williams. Big things had been expected from Hill even before he led the Triple-A International League in runs, hits, triples, homers, total bases, and slugging in 1989. A victim of his own anxiety, however, Hill hurt his chances by fanning too frequently. But he has made a big improvement over his 211 strikeouts in 131 games as a third-year pro. A high-percentage basestealer, Hill also uses his speed well in the outfield. Since his arm isn't accurate or strong, he's best in left field.

Major League Batting Register

	BA	G	AB	R	H	2B	3B	HR	RBI	SB
89 AL	.288	19	52	4	15	0	0	1	7	2
90 AL	.231	84	260	47	60	11	3	12	32	8
91 AL	.253	35	99	14	25	5	2	3	11	2
91 AL	.258	72	221	29	57	8	2	8	25	6
92 AL	.241	102	369	38	89	16	1	18	49	9
93 AL	.224	66	174	19	39	7	2	5	25	7
93 AL	.345	31	87	14	30	7	0	10	22	1
94 AL	.297	89	269	48	80	12	1	10	38	19
95 NL	.264	132	497	71	131	29	4	24	86	25
Life	.260	595	2028	290	526	95	15	91	295	79
3 AVE	.274	124	400	60	110	21	3	19	66	21

KEN HILL

Position: Pitcher
Team: Cleveland Indians
Born: Dec. 14, 1965 Lynn, MA
Height: 6'2" **Weight:** 175 lbs.
Bats: right **Throws:** right
Acquired: Traded by Cardinals for David Bell, Rick Heiserman, and Pepe McNeal, 7/95

Player Summary	
Fantasy Value	$9 to $11
Card Value	6¢ to 10¢
Will	seek former form
Can't	stop running game
Expect	few hits
Don't Expect	long-ball woes

When Hill came to Cleveland last year, the Indians immediately spotted several flaws in his delivery. He simply wasn't the same pitcher who had won 41 games over the previous three seasons. In fact, it was hard to believe he finished second to Greg Maddux in the 1994 NL Cy Young Award voting. Cleveland had been hoping that Hill would return to being the control pitcher who blends a sinker, a slider, and a forkball (his strikeout pitch) with an occasional rising fastball. Not afraid to pitch inside, he gets most of his outs on grounders. When he's right, Hill dominates right-handed batters and is stingy with the home run ball. He works off a three-quarters delivery that is deceiving to righty hitters. His skills are pretty good, and he helps himself with his defense. Hill has problems holding runners, however, and his slow delivery gives potential basestealers a head start.

Major League Pitching Register

	W	L	ERA	G	CG	IP	H	ER	BB	SO
88 NL	0	1	5.14	4	0	14.0	16	8	6	6
89 NL	7	15	3.80	33	2	196.2	186	83	99	112
90 NL	5	6	5.49	17	1	78.2	79	48	33	58
91 NL	11	10	3.57	30	0	181.1	147	72	67	121
92 NL	16	9	2.68	33	3	218.0	187	65	75	150
93 NL	9	7	3.23	28	2	183.2	163	66	74	90
94 NL	16	5	3.32	23	2	154.2	145	57	44	85
95 NL	6	7	5.06	18	0	110.1	125	62	45	50
95 AL	4	1	3.98	12	1	74.2	77	33	32	48
Life	74	61	3.67	198	11	1212.0	1125	494	475	720
3 AVE	14	8	3.74	31	2	205.3	198	84	74	107

CURRENT PLAYERS

STERLING HITCHCOCK

Position: Pitcher
Team: Seattle Mariners
Born: April 29, 1971 Fayetteville, NC
Height: 6'1" **Weight:** 192 lbs.
Bats: left **Throws:** left
Acquired: Traded by Yankees with Russ Davis for Jim Mecir, Jeff Nelson, and Tino Martinez, 12/95

Player Summary	
Fantasy Value	$8 to $10
Card Value	5¢ to 8¢
Will	try to deflate ERA
Can't	keep runners close
Expect	a diversified arsenal
Don't Expect	few gophers

Hitchcock had his first full shot as a big-league starter last season. The results were mixed. The highlight of an erratic first half was a four-hit shutout of the Orioles, but he struggled to keep his ERA below 5.00. Hitchcock eventually proved so erratic that Yankee manager Buck Showalter returned him to the bullpen to work out some of his problems. Though he yielded less hits than innings and showed good control for a young southpaw, Hitchcock has a horrible time controlling the running game. He also throws more than his share of homers. A sinker-slider pitcher who also has a four-seam fastball, a changeup, and a forkball, Hitchcock should be much more effective against left-handed hitters. He's no better than adequate in the field and his pickoff move is pathetic. That weakness helped inflate his ERA. To remain a big-leaguer, he'll need more consistency. Exclusively a starter in the minors, Hitchcock made his first relief outings at the big-league level in 1994.

Major League Pitching Register

	W	L	ERA	G	CG	IP	H	ER	BB	SO
92 AL	0	2	8.31	3	0	13.0	23	12	6	6
93 AL	1	2	4.65	6	0	31.0	32	16	14	26
94 AL	4	1	4.20	23	1	49.1	48	23	29	37
95 AL	11	10	4.70	27	4	168.1	155	88	68	121
Life	16	15	4.78	59	5	261.2	258	139	117	190
2 AVE	9	6	4.57	31	3	129.1	121	66	59	94

TREVOR HOFFMAN

Position: Pitcher
Team: San Diego Padres
Born: Oct. 13, 1967 Bellflower, CA
Height: 6'1" **Weight:** 200 lbs.
Bats: right **Throws:** right
Acquired: Traded by Marlins with Jose Martinez and Andres Beruman for Gary Sheffield and Rich Rodriguez, 6/93

Player Summary	
Fantasy Value	$25 to $30
Card Value	5¢ to 8¢
Will	save many games
Can't	find former form
Expect	last-inning heat
Don't Expect	control problems

What a difference a year can make. In 1994, Hoffman ranked second among NL relievers in fewest baserunners allowed per nine innings with nine and one-half. Last year his control was off just a tad for much of the season. Hoffman yielded more than twice the number of home runs he had allowed the year before. The result was seven blown saves before Labor Day. After holding hitters to a .173 average in 1994, Hoffman had trouble staging an encore. There's nothing wrong with his arsenal. He is able to bring a mid-90s fastball, a slider, and a curve that he often uses as a changeup. Had he stayed with the Marlins, he might have perfected the forkball Bryan Harvey was teaching him. Not that Hoffman needs any more weapons. He strands most runners he inherits and helps himself as a hitter and fielder (he's a converted infielder). After making a concerted effort to improve his pickoff move, Hoffman now holds runners well. His older brother Glenn was a Red Sox shortstop.

Major League Pitching Register

	W	L	ERA	G	S	IP	H	ER	BB	SO
93 NL	4	6	3.90	67	5	90.0	80	39	39	79
94 NL	4	4	2.57	47	20	56.0	39	16	20	68
95 NL	7	4	3.88	55	31	53.1	48	23	14	52
Life	15	14	3.52	169	56	199.1	167	78	73	199
3 AVE	6	5	3.44	65	23	76.1	63	29	28	78

CURRENT PLAYERS

CHRIS HOILES

Position: Catcher
Team: Baltimore Orioles
Born: March 20, 1965 Bowling Green, OH
Height: 6′ **Weight:** 213 lbs.
Bats: right **Throws:** right
Acquired: Traded by Tigers with Cesar Mejia and Robinson Garces for Fred Lynn, 9/88

Player Summary	
Fantasy Value	$13 to $16
Card Value	5¢ to 8¢
Will	show good power
Can't	steal any bases
Expect	slow first half
Don't Expect	shabby fielding

Although his batting average has sagged, Hoiles showed last summer that he's still one of baseball's best-hitting backstops. Despite his usual slow start, he netted extra bases on about half his hits and pounded left-handers. A patient hitter who's willing to wait for walks (especially against right-handers), Hoiles is no stranger to high on-base percentages. Last year, there was a difference of about 100 points between his on-base mark and his batting average. A pull hitter against lefties, he sometimes hits to the opposite field against right-handed pitchers. He doesn't run well, but Hoiles moves well behind the plate. He calls a good game, handles his pitchers well, prevents wild pitches, and knows how to block the plate. Hoiles nailed about one-third of the baserunners who tried to steal against him last year. The Eastern Michigan product has led AL receivers in chances, putouts, and fielding percentage.

Major League Batting Register

	BA	G	AB	R	H	2B	3B	HR	RBI	SB
89 AL	.111	6	9	0	1	1	0	0	1	0
90 AL	.190	23	63	7	12	3	0	1	6	0
91 AL	.243	107	341	36	83	15	0	11	31	0
92 AL	.274	96	310	49	85	10	1	20	40	0
93 AL	.310	126	419	80	130	28	0	29	82	1
94 AL	.247	99	332	45	82	10	0	19	53	2
95 AL	.250	114	352	53	88	15	1	19	58	1
Life	.263	571	1826	270	481	82	2	99	271	4
3 AVE	.269	131	428	68	115	20	0	26	74	2

TODD HOLLANDSWORTH

Position: Outfield
Team: Los Angeles Dodgers
Born: April 20, 1973 Dayton, OH
Height: 6'2″ **Weight:** 193 lbs.
Bats: left **Throws:** left
Acquired: Third-round pick in 6/91 free-agent draft

Player Summary	
Fantasy Value	$5 to $7
Card Value	12¢ to 15¢
Will	show some sock
Can't	avoid injuries
Expect	20-20 potential
Don't Expect	patient at bats

Though injuries (broken wrist, thumb) interfered with his rookie season in 1995, Hollandsworth hinted at a bright big-league future. He played so well in July that he drew comparisons to Kirk Gibson, the oft-injured former Dodger outfielder and clubhouse leader. Before Brett Butler returned, Hollandsworth played center field (for the first time in four years) and batted first (for the first time ever). A blue-chip prospect who has always been one of the youngest players in his league, Hollandsworth showed power, speed, and heart during his days on the active list last year. He has definite 20-20 potential. When managers named him the seventh-best prospect in the Triple-A Pacific Coast League in 1994, one of them told *Baseball America* that Hollandsworth will drive in runs, hit for power and average, and steal bases. He needs to practice more patience, however. Throughout his career, Hollandsworth has fanned more than twice for every walk. Defense isn't his forte either, though he has good range and a strong throwing arm. He had a .343 on-base percentage at Triple-A Albuquerque in 1994.

Major League Batting Register

	BA	G	AB	R	H	2B	3B	HR	RBI	SB
95 NL	.233	41	103	16	24	2	0	5	13	2
Life	.233	41	103	16	24	2	0	5	13	2

CURRENT PLAYERS

DAVE HOLLINS

Position: First base
Team: Boston Red Sox
Born: May 25, 1966 Buffalo, NY
Height: 6'1" **Weight:** 195 lbs.
Bats: both **Throws:** right
Acquired: Traded by Phillies for Mark Whiten, 7/95

Player Summary	
Fantasy Value	$3 to $5
Card Value	6¢ to 10¢
Will	provide some pop
Can't	reduce strikeouts
Expect	good batting eye
Don't Expect	powerful throwing

In baseball, heroes can become goats in the blink of an eye. It happened to Hollins, though a personal injury wave played a major role in the transformation. He totaled 45 homers, 186 RBI, and 161 walks for the Phillies in 1992 and 1993. But he broke his hand twice in '94, then missed time with complications from diabetes and a broken wrist last year. He lost his job to Gregg Jefferies and eventually lost his roster spot. When healthy, Hollins is an intense competitor with power, patience, and the ability to switch-hit. Though better right-handed, he has power from both sides of the plate. Because he has a big swing, Hollins fans frequently. But he also builds a high on-base percentage with his willingness to walk. The University of South Carolina product does his best hitting with runners in scoring position. Although batter is his best position, he can be hidden at first, where his erratic throwing arm is not too obvious.

Major League Batting Register

	BA	G	AB	R	H	2B	3B	HR	RBI	SB
90 NL	.184	72	114	14	21	0	0	5	15	0
91 NL	.298	56	151	18	45	10	2	6	21	1
92 NL	.270	156	586	104	158	28	4	27	93	9
93 NL	.273	143	543	104	148	30	4	18	93	2
94 NL	.222	44	162	28	36	7	1	4	26	1
95 NL	.229	65	205	46	47	12	2	7	25	1
95 AL	.154	5	13	2	2	0	0	0	1	0
Life	.258	541	1774	316	457	87	13	67	274	14
3 AVE	.250	95	339	66	85	18	3	11	53	2

DARREN HOLMES

Position: Pitcher
Team: Colorado Rockies
Born: April 25, 1966 Asheville, NC
Height: 6' **Weight:** 200 lbs.
Bats: right **Throws:** right
Acquired: First-round pick from Brewers in 11/92 expansion draft

Player Summary	
Fantasy Value	$3 to $5
Card Value	4¢ to 6¢
Will	answer bell often
Can't	always find plate
Expect	whiff per inning
Don't Expect	gopher problems

During his roller-coaster career as a big-league reliever, Holmes has solved some mysteries and created others. He's been good at times and bad at times, but he was mostly mediocre before last season. Free of the elbow problems that plagued him in 1994, Holmes regained his rank as the Rockies' No. 1 closer and pitched very effectively—considering that he played half his schedule in Coors Field, baseball's best hitters' park. Equipped with an extensive arsenal for a closer (a sinker, a slider, a curve, and a change), Holmes yielded less hits than innings, kept the ball in the park, and stranded about 70 percent of the runners he inherited. He had some problems with control, however, and maintains a 2-1 ratio of strikeouts to walks—even though he averaged nearly one strikeout per inning. Usually more effective against right-handers, Holmes had the opposite reaction last year. He helps himself by holding runners close and fielding his position.

Major League Pitching Register

	W	L	ERA	G	S	IP	H	ER	BB	SO
90 NL	0	1	5.19	14	0	17.1	15	10	11	19
91 AL	1	4	4.72	40	3	76.1	90	40	27	59
92 AL	4	4	2.55	41	6	42.1	35	12	11	31
93 NL	3	3	4.05	62	25	66.2	56	30	20	60
94 NL	0	3	6.35	29	3	28.1	35	20	24	33
95 NL	6	1	3.24	68	14	66.2	59	24	28	61
Life	14	16	4.11	254	51	297.2	290	136	121	263
2 AVE	5	2	3.62	69	20	70.2	61	29	26	64

CURRENT PLAYERS

RICK HONEYCUTT

Position: Pitcher
Team: New York Yankees
Born: June 29, 1954 Chattanooga, TN
Height: 6'1" **Weight:** 190 lbs.
Bats: left **Throws:** left
Acquired: Purchased from Athletics, 9/95

Player Summary
Fantasy Value	$0
Card Value	4¢ to 6¢
Will	keep set-up spot
Can't	produce velocity
Expect	superb control
Don't Expect	many strikeouts

Honeycutt is coming off his best season since switching from starting to set-up relief work in 1988. Merciless against left-handers, he is a control artist, getting most of his outs on ground balls. His sinker, slider, and cut fastball still baffle big-league hitters. He strands a high percentage of inherited runners, keeps the ball in the park, and answers frequent relief calls. A good fielder who holds runners well, Honeycutt has appeared at least 40 times in seven seasons. The University of Tennessee graduate was a starter when he turned pro in 1976. Honeycutt made the AL All-Star Team twice.

Major League Pitching Register
	W	L	ERA	G	S	IP	H	ER	BB	SO
77 AL	0	1	4.34	10	0	29.0	26	14	11	17
78 AL	5	11	4.89	26	0	134.1	150	73	49	50
79 AL	11	12	4.04	33	0	194.0	201	87	67	83
80 AL	10	17	3.94	30	0	203.1	221	89	60	79
81 AL	11	6	3.31	20	0	127.2	120	47	17	40
82 AL	5	17	5.27	30	0	164.0	201	96	54	64
83 AL	14	8	2.42	25	0	174.2	168	47	37	56
83 NL	2	3	5.77	9	0	39.0	46	25	13	18
84 NL	10	9	2.84	29	0	183.2	180	58	51	75
85 NL	8	12	3.42	31	1	142.0	141	54	49	67
86 NL	11	9	3.32	32	0	171.0	164	63	45	100
87 NL	2	12	4.59	27	0	115.2	133	59	45	92
87 AL	1	4	5.32	7	0	23.2	25	14	9	10
88 AL	3	2	3.50	55	7	79.2	74	31	25	47
89 AL	2	2	2.35	64	12	76.2	56	20	26	52
90 AL	2	2	2.70	63	7	63.1	46	19	22	38
91 AL	2	4	3.58	43	0	37.2	37	15	20	26
92 AL	1	4	3.69	54	3	39.0	41	16	10	32
93 AL	1	4	2.81	52	1	41.2	30	13	20	21
94 AL	1	2	7.20	42	1	25.0	37	20	9	18
95 AL	5	1	2.96	52	2	45.2	39	15	10	21
Life	107	142	3.73	734	34	2110.2	2136	875	649	1006
2 AVE	3	3	2.89	55	2	46.2	37	15	16	22

DWAYNE HOSEY

Position: Outfield
Team: Boston Red Sox
Born: March 11, 1967 Sharon, PA
Height: 5'10" **Weight:** 175 lbs.
Bats: both **Throws:** right
Acquired: Claimed from Royals on waivers, 8/95

Player Summary
Fantasy Value	$2 to $4
Card Value	8¢ to 12¢
Will	fine a role
Can't	regain youth
Expect	a fine bat
Don't Expect	huge speed

You *can* get there from here. Hosey's long crusade through the minors went through Kansas City and ended in Fenway Park as a part-time center fielder for the division-winning Red Sox. Drafted in the 13th round of the 1987 draft by the White Sox out of Pasadena City College, Hosey rambled through five organizations before ending up in Boston. He was the Triple-A American Association MVP in 1994. For Omaha that year, he batted .333 with 27 homers, 80 RBI, 95 runs scored, and 27 stolen bases. In 1995 at Omaha, he showed some power and speed, with double-digits in both steals and homers, while hitting for a respectable average. Kansas City found him expendable, however, when the team called up phenom outfielder Johnny Damon from Double-A. Hosey was what the doctor ordered in Boston. Down the stretch, he garnered a .408 on-base average and a .618 slugging percentage. While those numbers will be hard to match, make no mistake: Hosey can hit. He is also a capable fielder with a fine arm. He led league outfielders with five double plays in 1994. Hosey has had three 30-swipe seasons in the minors.

Major League Batting Register
	BA	G	AB	R	H	2B	3B	HR	RBI	SB
95 AL	.338	24	68	20	23	8	1	3	7	6
Life	.338	24	68	20	23	8	1	3	7	6

CURRENT PLAYERS

THOMAS HOWARD

Position: Outfield
Team: Cincinnati Reds
Born: Dec. 11, 1964 Middletown, OH
Height: 6'2" **Weight:** 200 lbs.
Bats: both **Throws:** right
Acquired: Traded by Indians for Randy Milligan, 8/93

Player Summary
Fantasy Value	$2 to $4
Card Value	5¢ to 8¢
Will	poke pinch hits
Can't	show much power
Expect	clutch hitting
Don't Expect	regular status

Because of his speed, power, and defensive skills at all three outfield positions, Howard is an extremely valuable spare part. In addition to pinch-running and pinch-hitting assignments, he's also able to step in for any injured regular. In the first 15 games after the Deion Sanders swap last summer, Howard hit .341 with two homers and six RBI. He also had a stretch of eight hits in 17 at bats as a pinch hitter. A far better hitter against right-handed pitching, he shows enough patience to push his on-base average about 50 points higher than his actual batting mark. He's also a high-percentage basestealer. Despite limited playing time in 1995, Thomas swiped the most bases of his big-league career. That speed helps him in the outfield, where he has the range for center and the arm for right. The former Ball State All-American played for the Padres and Indians before joining the Reds.

Major League Batting Register
	BA	G	AB	R	H	2B	3B	HR	RBI	SB
90 NL	.273	20	44	4	12	2	0	0	0	0
91 NL	.249	106	281	30	70	12	3	4	22	10
92 NL	.333	5	3	1	1	0	0	0	0	0
92 AL	.277	117	358	36	99	15	2	2	32	15
93 AL	.236	74	178	26	42	7	0	3	23	5
93 NL	.277	38	141	22	39	8	3	4	13	5
94 NL	.264	83	178	24	47	11	0	5	24	4
95 NL	.302	113	281	42	85	15	2	3	26	17
Life	.270	556	1464	185	395	70	10	21	140	56
3 AVE	.274	119	295	43	81	16	2	6	33	12

STEVE HOWE

Position: Pitcher
Team: New York Yankees
Born: March 10, 1958 Pontiac, MI
Height: 5'11" **Weight:** 196 lbs.
Bats: left **Throws:** left
Acquired: Signed as a free agent, 12/92

Player Summary
Fantasy Value	$0
Card Value	4¢ to 6¢
Will	smother southpaws
Can't	avoid bad streaks
Expect	make-or-break year
Don't Expect	left-handed homers

Howe has had alternating good and bad years since the Yankees rescued him from baseball's scrap heap in 1991. Last year was bad. The former Michigan All-American and NL Rookie of the Year encountered severe turbulence last year. He threw Dave Nilsson a home run ball that was only the second Howe has yielded to a left-handed hitter since 1983. When he's on, he busts batters in and out, working both corners. He helps himself with his fielding and pickoff move. His command suffers when he gets the ball up. Howe's arsenal includes a fastball, a slider, a curve, and a changeup—pitches he threw consistently for strikes in 1994 but not in 1995. He also stranded a higher percentage of inherited runners and threw fewer gophers in '94. Howe is still very effective against lefties, but righties relished his appearances.

Major League Pitching Register
	W	L	ERA	G	S	IP	H	ER	BB	SO
80 NL	7	9	2.66	59	17	84.2	83	25	22	39
81 NL	5	3	2.50	41	8	54.0	51	15	18	32
82 NL	7	5	2.08	66	13	99.1	87	23	17	49
83 NL	4	7	1.44	46	18	68.2	55	11	12	52
85 NL	1	1	4.91	19	3	22.0	30	12	5	11
85 AL	2	3	6.16	13	0	19.0	28	13	7	10
87 AL	3	3	4.31	24	1	31.1	33	15	8	19
91 AL	3	1	1.68	37	3	48.1	39	9	7	34
92 AL	3	0	2.45	20	6	22.0	9	6	3	12
93 AL	3	5	4.97	51	4	50.2	58	28	10	19
94 AL	3	0	1.80	40	15	40.0	28	8	7	18
95 AL	6	3	4.96	56	2	49.0	66	27	17	28
Life	47	40	2.93	472	90	589.0	567	192	133	323
3 AVE	5	3	3.87	57	9	54.1	57	23	13	25

CURRENT PLAYERS

JOHN HUDEK

Position: Pitcher
Team: Houston Astros
Born: Aug. 8, 1966 Tampa, FL
Height: 6'1" **Weight:** 200 lbs.
Bats: both **Throws:** right
Acquired: Claimed from Tigers on waivers, 7/93

Player Summary	
Fantasy Value	$17 to $20
Card Value	8¢ to 12¢
Will	seek big comeback
Can't	always find plate
Expect	fastball velocity
Don't Expect	fielding woes

In 1994, he became the first pitcher to make an All-Star team before earning his first major-league victory. Hudek got that win, plus another, in 1995. But then he submitted to surgery that removed a rib from under the collarbone, relieving a blocked vein in his right arm. Although the injury was considered career-threatening, the Astros hope a clean bill of health will help Hudek regain his fine form of '94. A flamethrower who mixes in a slider and changeup, he hits radar guns at 95 mph. His heater rises or sinks—giving hitters different looks. Though Hudek has had some control problems in the past, his average of about one strikeout per inning helps compensate. Hitters managed only a .174 batting average against the hard-throwing Hudek in 1994. When operating at full capacity, he strands inherited runners, helps himself with agile defensive play, and continues to improve a pickoff move that was once mediocre. A product of Florida Southern, he spent more than six years in the minors before reaching Houston as an understudy to Mitch Williams. Within two months, Hudek had the starring role.

Major League Pitching Register

	W	L	ERA	G	S	IP	H	ER	BB	SO
94 NL	0	2	2.97	42	16	39.1	24	13	18	39
95 NL	2	2	5.40	19	7	20.0	19	12	5	29
Life	2	4	3.79	61	23	59.1	43	25	23	68

REX HUDLER

Position: Infield; outfield
Team: California Angels
Born: Sept. 2, 1960 Tempe, AZ
Height: 6' **Weight:** 195 lbs.
Bats: right **Throws:** right
Acquired: Signed as a free agent, 4/94

Player Summary	
Fantasy Value	$2 to $4
Card Value	4¢ to 6¢
Will	plug any hole
Can't	show much pop
Expect	all-out style
Don't Expect	bases on balls

If hustle is the name of the game, then Hudler plays it well. At an age when most of his contemporaries are contemplating retirement, the veteran utility player does his Energizer Bunny imitation. He keeps going and going and going. A singles hitter who in 1995 struck out about five times more often than he walked, Hudler substitutes aggressiveness for power. He gives 110 percent effort in everything he does, plays anywhere he's asked, and provides a satisfactory—though not spectacular—performance against left-handed pitching. He doesn't steal often but still runs well enough to succeed whenever he tries. Hudler hustles after everything his way in the outfield but is best-suited to left field because of a weak throwing arm. His best position may be second base, where he was stationed much of last year. Originally signed as a shortstop by the Yankees, Hudler started his pro career in 1978.

Major League Batting Register

	BA	G	AB	R	H	2B	3B	HR	RBI	SB
84 AL	.143	9	7	2	1	1	0	0	0	0
85 AL	.157	20	51	4	8	0	1	0	1	0
86 AL	.000	14	1	1	0	0	0	0	0	1
88 NL	.273	77	216	38	59	14	2	4	14	29
89 NL	.245	92	155	21	38	7	0	6	13	15
90 NL	.282	93	220	31	62	11	2	7	22	18
91 NL	.227	101	207	21	47	10	2	1	15	12
92 NL	.245	61	98	17	24	4	0	3	5	2
94 AL	.298	56	124	17	37	8	0	8	20	2
95 NL	.265	84	223	30	59	16	0	6	27	12
Life	.257	607	1302	182	335	71	7	35	117	91

CURRENT PLAYERS

MIKE HUFF

Position: Outfield
Team: Toronto Blue Jays
Born: Aug. 11, 1963 Honolulu, HI
Height: 6'1" **Weight:** 190 lbs.
Bats: right **Throws:** right
Acquired: Traded by White Sox for Domingo Martinez, 3/94

Player Summary	
Fantasy Value	$1
Card Value	4¢ to 6¢
Will	serve as reserve
Can't	deliver long hits
Expect	excellent defense
Don't Expect	high whiff ratio

Although he's a fine defensive outfielder with a strong throwing arm, Huff has never had the chance to play regularly in the major leagues. Though he did hit .300 the only time he received more than 200 at bats, he never seemed to show the same authority at the plate that he had shown in the minors. A selective hitter who walks as often as he fans, Huff seldom hits anything more than a single. He's not much of a basestealer, so he's a station-to-station man on the bases. Huff does have some speed, however, and he fattens his average with bunts and infield hits. His speed also helps in the outfield, where he has the range for center and the arm for right. Because he knows the hitters, he gets great jumps, allowing him to snare balls headed for the gaps. A five-time .300 hitter in the minors, he led two leagues in double plays by an outfielder. Originally signed by the Dodgers, Huff launched his pro baseball career in 1985. He can play second base as well as the outfield.

Major League Batting Register

	BA	G	AB	R	H	2B	3B	HR	RBI	SB
89 NL	.200	12	25	4	5	1	0	1	2	0
91 AL	.251	102	243	42	61	10	2	3	25	14
92 AL	.209	60	115	13	24	5	0	0	8	1
93 AL	.182	43	44	4	8	2	0	0	6	1
94 AL	.304	80	207	31	63	15	3	3	25	2
95 AL	.232	61	138	14	32	9	1	1	9	1
Life	.250	358	772	108	193	42	6	9	75	19

TODD HUNDLEY

Position: Catcher
Team: New York Mets
Born: May 27, 1969 Martinsville, VA
Height: 5'11" **Weight:** 185 lbs.
Bats: both **Throws:** right
Acquired: Second-round pick in 6/87 free-agent draft

Player Summary	
Fantasy Value	$10 to $13
Card Value	6¢ to 10¢
Will	show selective eye
Can't	steal bases
Expect	more homers than dad
Don't Expect	pitchers to complain

After failing to realize his potential during his first three seasons, Hundley made major strides last summer. He became a more selective hitter, pounded left-handers, and showed great improvement in his handling of the pitching staff. Before breaking his left wrist in a July 22 home-plate collision with Eric Young, Hundley had hit .341 with nine homers and 24 RBI over a 28-game stretch. His overall performance indicated he was following the footsteps of his father, former All-Star receiver Randy Hundley. Todd's biggest improvement last year was his willingness to wait for walks. Refusing to chase bad pitches, his average climbed about 50 points and his on-base percentage jumped 100 points beyond that. A strong defensive catcher with a good arm, Hundley nailed about 30 percent of the runners who try to steal against him in 1995. Hundley's game-calling improved so much last summer that he earned the confidence of his club's young pitchers.

Major League Batting Register

	BA	G	AB	R	H	2B	3B	HR	RBI	SB
90 NL	.209	36	67	8	14	6	0	0	2	0
91 NL	.133	21	60	5	8	0	1	1	7	0
92 NL	.209	123	358	32	75	17	0	7	32	3
93 NL	.228	130	417	40	95	17	2	11	53	1
94 NL	.237	91	291	45	69	10	1	16	42	2
95 NL	.280	90	275	39	77	11	0	15	51	1
Life	.230	491	1468	169	338	61	4	50	187	7
3 AVE	.245	120	379	49	93	14	1	17	57	2

CURRENT PLAYERS

BRIAN HUNTER

Position: Outfield
Team: Houston Astros
Born: March 5, 1971 Portland, OR
Height: 6'4" **Weight:** 180 lbs.
Bats: right **Throws:** right
Acquired: Second-round pick in 6/89 free-agent draft

Player Summary	
Fantasy Value	$14 to $17
Card Value	10¢ to 15¢
Will	set the table well
Can't	reduce whiff rate
Expect	exceptional speed
Don't Expect	homer outburst

Even though he doesn't have a cape, Hunter can fly. Timed at 3.6 seconds from home to first base, he had 10 infield hits in the first five weeks after his recall from the minors June 13. Hunter had five consecutive minor-league seasons with at least 30 steals, including a career-best 49 on the Triple-A level in 1994. That same year, he also led the Pacific Coast League in runs (113), hits (191), and batting (.372). League managers polled by *Baseball America* named Hunter the loop's top prospect that year. A prototypical leadoff man, Hunter had been on a .374 tear over the 21-game span in 1995 just before a pitch broke his wrist in July. Though it was only 15 games, the layoff hurt, since Hunter fell into a prolonged slump after his return. He bats from an unorthodox stance, coupled with numerous hitches and lots of movement at the plate. He sprays singles all over the diamond, but does have some power. He is a wide-ranging center fielder who reaches balls others can't. Hunter was the reason the Astros traded Kenny Lofton in 1991.

Major League Batting Register

	BA	G	AB	R	H	2B	3B	HR	RBI	SB
94 NL	.250	6	24	2	6	1	0	0	0	2
95 NL	.302	78	321	52	97	14	5	2	28	24
Life	.299	84	345	54	103	15	5	2	28	26

BRIAN HUNTER

Position: First base; outfield
Team: Cincinnati Reds
Born: March 4, 1968 El Toro, CA
Height: 6' **Weight:** 195 lbs.
Bats: right **Throws:** left
Acquired: Traded by Pirates for Micah Franklin, 7/94

Player Summary	
Fantasy Value	$1
Card Value	4¢ to 6¢
Will	hit lefties hard
Can't	dump platoon tag
Expect	occasional power
Don't Expect	dazzling defense

If Hunter can hang on until expansion in 1998, he'll probably get another crack at a regular job. He has never lived up to the early promise he showed with the Braves. Years of platooning may have hurt, since he developed a reputation for hitting lefties but sitting against righties. Memories of his game-seven homer in the 1991 NLCS still bring a smile to Atlanta fans. A fastball hitter with quick wrists, Hunter would be a much more productive player if he learned the strike zone. Even while hitting a career-best 15 homers in 1994, he fanned nearly four times per walk. Hunter doesn't have the speed to leg out bunts, infield hits, or triples and almost never steals a base. He won't win awards for fielding either. Because he throws as poorly as he runs, Hunter's best position is designated hitter, but he can play first base. A broken hand hampered Hunter last year, but he wouldn't have played much anyway as the Reds used nine other first basemen.

Major League Batting Register

	BA	G	AB	R	H	2B	3B	HR	RBI	SB
91 NL	.251	97	271	32	68	16	1	12	50	0
92 NL	.239	102	238	34	57	13	2	14	41	1
93 NL	.138	37	80	4	11	3	1	0	8	0
94 NL	.234	85	256	34	60	16	1	15	57	0
95 NL	.215	40	79	9	17	6	0	1	9	2
Life	.231	361	924	113	213	54	5	42	165	3

CURRENT PLAYERS

JEFF HUSON

Position: Infield
Team: Baltimore Orioles
Born: Aug. 15, 1964 Scottsdale, AZ
Height: 6'3" **Weight:** 180 lbs.
Bats: left **Throws:** right
Acquired: Signed as a minor-league free agent, 12/94

Player Summary	
Fantasy Value	$0
Card Value	4¢ to 6¢
Will	serve as a "supersub"
Can't	clear the fences
Expect	patience at bat
Don't Expect	regular play

When Huson is healthy, he's a solid utility player who can play three infield positions as well as the outfield. Avoiding serious injury, however, has been a major handicap to his career. He had a torn tendon in his left knee in 1991, and a torn right rotator cuff and broken left big toe in '93. He spent all of 1994 in the minors before Baltimore rescued him. When Jeff Manto struggled against right-handed pitching, Huson provided a perfect platoon partner at third base. Though he doesn't have Manto's power, Huson offers more speed, better contact, and a higher on-base percentage. Walking about as much as he fanned during much of last year, he boasted an on-base percentage about 75 points above his batting average. He has sure instincts, good range, and sure hands at third base, though his best position is shortstop. Huson spent three seasons as the regular shortstop for the Rangers. He doesn't figure to return to daily duty but could see considerable playing time because of his versatility.

Major League Batting Register

	BA	G	AB	R	H	2B	3B	HR	RBI	SB
88 NL	.310	20	42	7	13	2	0	0	3	2
89 NL	.162	32	74	1	12	5	0	0	2	3
90 AL	.240	145	396	57	95	12	2	0	28	12
91 AL	.213	119	268	36	57	8	3	2	26	8
92 AL	.261	123	318	49	83	14	3	4	24	18
93 AL	.133	23	45	3	6	1	1	0	2	0
95 AL	.248	66	161	24	40	4	2	1	19	5
Life	.235	528	1304	177	306	46	11	7	104	48

DANNY JACKSON

Position: Pitcher
Team: St. Louis Cardinals
Born: Jan. 5, 1962 San Antonio, TX
Height: 6' **Weight:** 205 lbs.
Bats: right **Throws:** left
Acquired: Signed as a free agent, 12/94

Player Summary	
Fantasy Value	$5 to $7
Card Value	4¢ to 6¢
Will	seek new comeback
Can't	approach '88 form
Expect	12 wins if sound
Don't Expect	control struggles

Jackson must feel like a human pin cushion. He has had everything from recurring shoulder problems to torn ankle ligaments, strained groin, lower abdominal strain, and toe surgery. He also suffered from a reaction to medication for thyroid cancer—a condition that required surgery during the winter of 1994-95. Still, the Cardinals thought he was worth a three-year, $10.8 million pact. Perhaps they were thinking of 1988, when he matched Orel Hershiser's 23-8 record, or even 1994, when Jackson made the All-Star team for the second time. Last year, however, wasn't great, baseball wise, though he held up pretty well, considering everything. A sinker-slider pitcher who also throws a changeup, Jackson gets his outs on ground balls and strikeouts. He hurts his own cause with below-average fielding and an ineffective pickoff move.

Major League Pitching Register

	W	L	ERA	G	CG	IP	H	ER	BB	SO
83 AL	1	1	5.21	4	0	19.0	26	11	6	9
84 AL	2	6	4.26	15	1	76.0	84	36	35	40
85 AL	14	12	3.42	32	4	208.0	209	79	76	114
86 AL	11	12	3.20	32	4	185.2	177	66	79	115
87 AL	9	18	4.02	36	11	224.0	219	100	109	152
88 NL	23	8	2.73	35	15	260.2	206	79	71	161
89 NL	6	11	5.60	20	1	115.2	122	72	57	70
90 NL	6	6	3.61	22	0	117.1	119	47	40	76
91 NL	1	5	6.75	17	0	70.2	89	53	48	31
92 NL	8	13	3.84	34	0	201.1	211	86	77	97
93 NL	12	11	3.77	32	2	210.1	214	88	80	120
94 NL	14	6	3.26	25	4	179.1	183	65	46	129
95 NL	2	12	5.90	19	2	100.2	120	66	48	52
Life	109	121	3.88	323	44	1968.2	1979	848	772	1166
3 AVE	11	11	3.96	30	3	192.2	202	85	66	120

CURRENT PLAYERS

MIKE JACKSON

Position: Pitcher
Team: Cincinnati Reds
Born: Dec. 22, 1964 Houston, TX
Height: 6' **Weight:** 185 lbs.
Bats: right **Throws:** right
Acquired: Signed as a free agent, 4/95

Player Summary	
Fantasy Value	$4 to $6
Card Value	4¢ to 6¢
Will	yield few safeties
Can't	resume old workload
Expect	quality work
Don't Expect	shaky control

One of the game's premier set-up men, Jackson has always been extremely difficult to hit. In 1994, he held hitters to a .164 average and averaged 11 strikeouts per nine innings. He wasn't that impressive last year, his first with the Reds, but his numbers were still good. He topped 60 appearances six years in a row, then developed a case of elbow tendinitis—probably the result of throwing too many sliders. He's also had knee problems. Basically a two-pitch pitcher, Jackson seldom deviates from his fastball-slider arsenal, though he's been known to throw a forkball on occasion. After averaging two walks per nine innings in '94, Jackson couldn't keep the same control last season. But he stranded most of the runners he inherited and didn't throw too many home run balls. The former high school infielder has good defensive instincts and a superb pickoff move. Few runners challenge him.

Major League Pitching Register

	W	L	ERA	G	S	IP	H	ER	BB	SO
86 NL	0	0	3.38	9	0	13.1	12	5	4	3
87 NL	3	10	4.20	55	1	109.1	88	51	56	93
88 AL	6	5	2.63	62	4	99.1	74	29	43	76
89 AL	4	6	3.17	65	7	99.1	81	35	54	94
90 AL	5	7	4.54	63	3	77.1	64	39	44	69
91 AL	7	7	3.25	72	14	88.2	64	32	34	74
92 AL	6	6	3.73	67	2	82.0	76	34	33	80
93 NL	6	6	3.03	81	1	77.1	58	26	24	70
94 NL	3	2	1.49	36	4	42.1	23	7	11	51
95 NL	6	1	2.39	40	2	49.0	38	13	19	41
Life	46	50	3.30	550	38	738.0	578	271	322	651
3 AVE	6	3	2.37	59	3	64.1	44	17	20	63

JASON JACOME

Position: Pitcher
Team: Kansas City Royals
Born: Nov. 24, 1970 Tulsa, OK
Height: 6'1" **Weight:** 175 lbs.
Bats: left **Throws:** left
Acquired: Traded by Mets with Allen McDill for Gino Morones, John Carter, and Derek Wallace, 7/95

Player Summary	
Fantasy Value	$1 to $3
Card Value	5¢ to 8¢
Will	rely on control
Can't	avoid home runs
Expect	ground-ball outs
Don't Expect	many strikeouts

Even though they have lots of young arms ripening on their farms, the New York Mets might have been too quick to pull the plug on Jacome. After he turned in five poor 1995 starts, they dropped him to the minors, then peddled him to Kansas City in a trade that merited only an agate footnote in the daily transactions box. All of a sudden, Jacome returned to the form he had shown as a rookie in 1994. A control pitcher whose arsenal includes a sinker, a slider, a curve, and a change, Jacome got his first big-league win in more than a year on Aug. 10. He worked the first seven innings in a 5-0 decision over the Angels, yielding four hits and two walks while fanning three. Though he allowed more hits than innings for Kansas City in 1995, he kept other runners to a minimum, averaging about two walks per game and giving him a strikeout-to-walk ratio near 2-to-1. A sound fielder, he's also adept at keeping the running game in check. When he's right, he gets lots of grounders, though he did throw more than his usual share of home runs last summer.

Major League Pitching Register

	W	L	ERA	G	CG	IP	H	ER	BB	SO
94 NL	4	3	2.67	8	1	54.0	54	16	17	30
95 NL	0	4	10.29	5	0	21.0	33	24	15	11
95 AL	4	6	5.36	15	1	84.0	101	50	21	39
Life	8	13	5.09	28	2	159.0	188	90	53	80

CURRENT PLAYERS

JOHN JAHA

Position: First base
Team: Milwaukee Brewers
Born: May 27, 1966 Portland, OR
Height: 6'1" **Weight:** 195 lbs.
Bats: right **Throws:** right
Acquired: 14th-round pick in 6/84 free-agent draft

Player Summary	
Fantasy Value	$10 to $13
Card Value	5¢ to 8¢
Will	improve
Can't	steal bases often
Expect	outstanding power
Don't Expect	impatience at bat

Even though he lost time with groin problems in June, Jaha enjoyed his best season in the majors. He showed more patience, made more contact, and showed significant gains in his batting and on-base percentages. There's no question about his eye: He led two minor leagues in walks, twice topped 100 in a season. He also won a pair of minor-league home run crowns. Still a first-pitch, fastball hitter with power to all fields, Jaha reduced his 1995 ratio of strikeouts to walks. He also stopped trying to pull every pitch. Though he shared time at first with B.J. Surhoff and Kevin Seitzer, Jaha hit over .300 against both lefties and righties—a big improvement for a slugger whose performance once paled against right-handers. Free of his 1994 knee problems and hitch in his swing, he netted extra bases on about 40 percent of his hits. The two-time minor-league MVP also improved his defense, which ranked last in the AL two years ago. Signed as a third baseman, he shifted to first a year later.

Major League Batting Register

	BA	G	AB	R	H	2B	3B	HR	RBI	SB
92 AL	.226	47	133	17	30	3	1	2	10	10
93 AL	.264	153	515	78	136	21	0	19	70	13
94 AL	.241	84	291	45	70	14	0	12	39	3
95 AL	.313	88	316	59	99	20	2	20	65	2
Life	.267	372	1255	199	335	58	3	53	184	28
3 AVE	.270	123	427	69	115	21	1	19	66	6

CHRIS JAMES

Position: Outfield
Team: Boston Red Sox
Born: Oct. 4, 1962 Rusk, TX
Height: 6'1" **Weight:** 190 lbs.
Bats: right **Throws:** right
Acquired: Traded by Royals for Wes Chamberlain and cash, 8/95

Player Summary	
Fantasy Value	$1
Card Value	4¢ to 6¢
Will	hit left-handers
Can't	show strong arm
Expect	some pinch hits
Don't Expect	return to lineup

After missing most of last season's first half with a strained left shoulder, James changed teams when the Red Sox required another right-handed bat as pennant-race insurance. Though used mostly as a designated hitter, he also subbed in the outfield corners. He has topped 140 games only twice in a pro career that started in 1982. He hit .349 against left-handed pitching in 1994 and posted an on-base percentage 100 points higher than his batting average. Because of his power and ability to hit lefties, James is a good pinch hitter. He once had two pinch homers in an eight-game stretch for the Rangers. On the minus side, however, is his tendency to strike out. Once a 20-steal man in the minors, James no longer runs very well. That limits his range in the outfield, where elbow, shoulder, and hand injuries have weakened his once-powerful arm.

Major League Batting Register

	BA	G	AB	R	H	2B	3B	HR	RBI	SB
86 NL	.283	16	46	5	13	3	0	1	5	0
87 NL	.293	115	358	48	105	20	6	17	54	3
88 NL	.242	150	566	57	137	24	1	19	66	7
89 NL	.243	132	482	55	117	17	2	13	65	5
90 NL	.299	140	528	62	158	32	4	12	70	4
91 AL	.238	115	437	31	104	16	2	5	41	3
92 NL	.242	111	248	25	60	10	4	5	32	2
93 NL	.256	65	129	19	33	10	1	6	19	2
93 AL	.355	8	31	5	11	1	0	3	7	0
94 AL	.256	52	133	28	34	8	4	7	19	0
95 AL	.268	42	82	8	22	4	0	2	8	1
Life	.261	946	3040	343	794	145	24	90	386	27

CURRENT PLAYERS

DION JAMES

Position: Outfield
Team: New York Yankees
Born: Nov. 9, 1962 Philadelphia, PA
Height: 6'1" **Weight:** 185 lbs.
Bats: left **Throws:** left
Acquired: Signed as a free agent, 4/95

Player Summary	
Fantasy Value	$1
Card Value	4¢ to 6¢
Will	play varied roles
Can't	reach the fences
Expect	hits vs. righties
Don't Expect	great arm

After spending a season in Japan, James returned to the Yankees last year and picked up where he left off. An exceptional contact hitter who walks more than he fans, he swings a solid .300 bat against right-handed pitching. He is a swing man who helped the Yankees reach postseason play for the first time since 1981. He played both outfield corners and first base, pinch-hit, and served as a left-handed DH before the arrival of Darryl Strawberry. A singles hitter who punches the ball to all fields, James rarely walks, fans, hits a home run, steals a base, or makes an error in the outfield. He plays all three positions but is best in left because his arm hardly resembles a bazooka. James hit .409 for the Yankees as a pinch hitter in 1993. He batted .263 in Japan in 1994. Originally signed by the Brewers, he also played for the Braves and Indians before coming to the Bronx.

Major League Batting Register

	BA	G	AB	R	H	2B	3B	HR	RBI	SB
83 AL	.100	11	20	1	2	0	0	0	1	1
84 AL	.295	128	387	52	114	19	5	1	30	10
85 AL	.224	18	49	5	11	1	0	0	3	0
87 NL	.312	134	494	80	154	37	6	10	61	10
88 NL	.256	132	386	46	99	17	5	3	30	9
89 NL	.259	63	170	15	44	7	0	1	11	1
89 AL	.306	71	245	26	75	11	0	4	29	1
90 AL	.274	87	248	28	68	15	2	1	22	5
92 AL	.262	67	145	24	38	8	0	3	17	1
93 AL	.332	115	343	62	114	21	2	7	36	0
95 AL	.287	85	209	22	60	6	1	2	26	4
Life	.289	911	2696	361	779	142	21	32	266	42
2 AVE	.314	105	289	43	91	14	2	5	33	2

STAN JAVIER

Position: Outfield
Team: San Francisco Giants
Born: Sept. 1, 1965 San Pedro de Macoris, Dominican Republic
Height: 6' **Weight:** 185 lbs.
Bats: both **Throws:** right
Acquired: Signed as a free agent, 12/95

Player Summary	
Fantasy Value	$15 to $18
Card Value	4¢ to 6¢
Will	use great glove
Can't	count on power
Expect	40-steal speed
Don't Expect	return to bench

Before changing his stance a few years ago, Javier couldn't shake the good-field, no-hit tag that shadowed him. When his average rose in 1993, however, the fleet center fielder got the opportunity to start in 1994. A contact hitter with considerable patience, Javier will never be mistaken for a slugger. His game is speed and defense, though he's far from the automatic out he once was. Javier is actually dangerous against left-handed pitching, finishing above .300 against southpaws two years in a row. While he hits for a better average batting right-handed, he has more power left-handed. A good bunter, Javier also fattens his average with infield hits. His speed gives him great range in center, where he owns an accurate arm. Javier's dad, Julian, also played in the majors.

Major League Batting Register

	BA	G	AB	R	H	2B	3B	HR	RBI	SB
84 AL	.143	7	7	1	1	0	0	0	0	0
86 AL	.202	59	114	13	23	8	0	0	8	8
87 AL	.185	81	151	22	28	3	1	2	9	3
88 AL	.257	125	397	49	102	13	3	2	35	20
89 AL	.248	112	310	42	77	12	3	1	28	12
90 AL	.242	19	33	4	8	0	2	0	3	0
90 NL	.304	104	276	56	84	9	4	3	24	15
91 NL	.205	121	176	21	36	5	3	1	11	7
92 NL	.249	130	334	42	83	17	1	1	29	29
93 AL	.291	92	237	33	69	10	4	3	28	12
94 AL	.272	109	419	75	114	23	0	10	44	24
95 AL	.278	130	442	81	123	20	2	8	56	36
Life	.258	1089	2896	439	748	120	23	31	275	155
3 AVE	.278	131	441	77	123	22	2	9	51	29

CURRENT PLAYERS

GREGG JEFFERIES

Position: First base; outfield
Team: Philadelphia Phillies
Born: Aug. 1, 1967 Burlingame, CA
Height: 5'10" **Weight:** 180 lbs.
Bats: both **Throws:** right
Acquired: Signed as a free agent, 12/94

Player Summary	
Fantasy Value	$20 to $25
Card Value	8¢ to 12¢
Will	hit to all fields
Can't	shake selfish tag
Expect	some pop
Don't Expect	a Gold Glove

After two solid seasons in St. Louis, Jefferies had a controversial debut in the City of Brotherly Love. Assigned to the outfield—an unfamiliar position—he spent so much time thinking about his defense that his offense suffered. Only after he returned to first in July did Jefferies start to hit. On Aug. 25, he became the first Phillie to hit for the cycle in 32 years. Though he lost playing time with an inflamed left thumb, Jefferies still finished with his third straight .300 season. He's heard complaints that he was more concerned about his own success than the team's. A contact hitter who walks more than he fans, Jefferies hit better against lefties last year but hit better against righties in 1994. A top two-strike hitter, he uses all fields against right-handers but goes up-the-middle against southpaws. He can bunt, work the hit-and-run, and collect infield hits. Jefferies can also motor around the bases.

Major League Batting Register

	BA	G	AB	R	H	2B	3B	HR	RBI	SB
87 NL	.500	6	6	0	3	1	0	0	2	0
88 NL	.321	29	109	19	35	8	2	6	17	5
89 NL	.258	141	508	72	131	28	2	12	56	21
90 NL	.283	153	604	96	171	40	3	15	68	11
91 NL	.272	136	486	59	132	19	2	9	62	26
92 AL	.285	152	604	66	172	36	3	10	75	19
93 NL	.342	142	544	89	186	24	3	16	83	46
94 NL	.325	103	397	52	129	27	1	12	55	12
95 NL	.306	114	480	69	147	31	2	11	56	9
Life	.296	976	3738	522	1106	214	18	91	474	149
3 AVE	.324	138	548	80	178	32	2	15	74	24

REGGIE JEFFERSON

Position: First base
Team: Boston Red Sox
Born: Sept. 25, 1968 Tallahassee, FL
Height: 6'4" **Weight:** 210 lbs.
Bats: left **Throws:** left
Acquired: Signed as a free agent, 4/95

Player Summary	
Fantasy Value	$3 to $5
Card Value	4¢ to 6¢
Will	supply power
Can't	stay healthy
Expect	pivotal year
Don't Expect	good defense

It would be fun to find out how Jefferson would do if he could stay healthy. Once a highly regarded prospect in the Cincinnati system, he has had elbow, back, and hamstring problems—among other injuries—and played in more than 63 big-league games only once. Signed by Boston because of his strong career performance at Fenway Park, Jefferson again failed to stay sound long enough for a thorough trial. When he did play, he hit righties hard and delivered enough power to suggest a 25-homer, 100-RBI year if he maintained such production over the full schedule. Jefferson is an aggressive batter who stopped switch-hitting during the 1994 season. Speed is out of the question: He has stolen one base in his big-league career. Jefferson's best position is designated hitter. He has problems scooping throws and isn't adept at turning the 3-6-3 double play. His mobility around the bag is also negligible. The 1996 season could be a make-or-break year for Jefferson.

Major League Batting Register

	BA	G	AB	R	H	2B	3B	HR	RBI	SB
91 NL	.143	5	7	1	1	0	0	1	1	0
91 AL	.198	26	101	10	20	3	0	2	12	0
92 AL	.337	24	89	8	30	6	2	1	6	0
93 AL	.249	113	366	35	91	11	2	10	34	1
94 AL	.327	63	162	24	53	11	0	8	32	0
95 AL	.289	46	121	21	35	8	0	5	26	0
Life	.272	277	846	99	230	39	4	27	111	1
2 AVE	.279	101	297	34	83	13	1	11	40	1

CURRENT PLAYERS

CHARLES JOHNSON

Position: Catcher
Team: Florida Marlins
Born: July 20, 1971 Ft. Pierce, FL
Height: 6'2" **Weight:** 215 lbs.
Bats: right **Throws:** right
Acquired: First-round pick in 6/92 free-agent draft

Player Summary
Fantasy Value	$8 to $10
Card Value	10¢ to 15¢
Will	nail basestealers
Can't	hit righties hard
Expect	long-distance bat
Don't Expect	defensive trouble

Preceded by reports of his powerful bat and even stronger throwing arm, Johnson jumped from Double-A into Florida's catching job, filling the gap created by Benito Santiago's departure. Anxious to impress, Johnson struggled at the plate, hitting .147 in his first 43 games. He never missed a beat in the field, however, nailing 34 of the first 70 runners who tested him and snapping Barry Larkin's string of 15 consecutive steals. Warming with the weather, Johnson's bat started booming. At one point, 13 of 24 hits went for extra bases. By the time the smoke cleared, the University of Miami All-American had become a hometown hero. Thanks to a good batting eye, his on-base average was 100 points higher than his batting average. He hammered left-handed pitching and nailed 43 percent of would-be basestealers. The former Olympian blocks the plate like a tank, digs out balls in the dirt, and gets good marks for his game-calling. Disabled when a Bret Saberhagen pitch broke his hand in August, Johnson enters 1996 with a clean bill of health and a bright future.

Major League Batting Register
	BA	G	AB	R	H	2B	3B	HR	RBI	SB
94 NL	.455	4	11	5	5	1	0	1	4	0
95 NL	.251	97	315	40	79	15	1	11	39	0
Life	.258	101	326	45	84	16	1	12	43	0

HOWARD JOHNSON

Position: Outfield; third base
Team: Chicago Cubs
Born: Nov. 29, 1960 Clearwater, FL
Height: 5'10" **Weight:** 195 lbs.
Bats: both **Throws:** right
Acquired: Signed as a free agent, 4/95

Player Summary
Fantasy Value	$1
Card Value	4¢ to 6¢
Will	try to hang on
Can't	cut strikeouts
Expect	occasional pop
Don't Expect	major comeback

How far the mighty have fallen. After leading the NL with 38 homers and 117 RBI in 1991, Johnson went into a four-year funk that hit bottom last summer. He was relegated to part-time duty with the Cubs. Johnson's eighth career pinch homer, delivered in June, showed he still has flashes of his former power. But he fans far too frequently, especially against left-handers. A fastball hitter who tries to pull everything, Johnson tries to be selective. He walks enough to make his on-base percentage respectable when compared to his batting average. Chronic shoulder problems, plus knee and wrist injuries and a viral infection, have reduced the two-time All-Star to a shadow of his former self. He holds the NL career and single-season records for most home runs by a switch-hitter.

Major League Batting Register
	BA	G	AB	R	H	2B	3B	HR	RBI	SB
82 AL	.316	54	155	23	49	5	0	4	14	7
83 AL	.212	27	66	11	14	0	0	3	5	0
84 AL	.248	116	355	43	88	14	1	12	50	10
85 NL	.242	126	389	38	94	18	4	11	46	6
86 NL	.245	88	220	30	54	14	0	10	39	8
87 NL	.265	157	554	93	147	22	1	36	99	32
88 NL	.230	148	495	85	114	21	1	24	68	23
89 NL	.287	153	571	104	164	41	3	36	101	41
90 NL	.244	154	590	89	144	37	3	23	90	34
91 NL	.259	156	564	108	146	34	4	38	117	30
92 NL	.223	100	350	48	78	19	0	7	43	22
93 NL	.238	72	235	32	56	8	2	7	26	6
94 NL	.211	93	227	30	48	10	2	10	40	11
95 NL	.195	87	169	26	33	4	1	7	22	1
Life	.249	1531	4940	760	1229	247	22	228	760	231
3 AVE	.216	100	248	35	54	9	2	10	36	8

CURRENT PLAYERS

LANCE JOHNSON

Position: Outfield
Team: Chicago White Sox
Born: July 7, 1963 Cincinnati, OH
Height: 5'11" **Weight:** 159 lbs.
Bats: left **Throws:** left
Acquired: Traded by Cardinals with Ricky Horton for Jose DeLeon, 2/88

Player Summary	
Fantasy Value	$20 to $25
Card Value	5¢ to 8¢
Will	run like the wind
Can't	hit lefties hard
Expect	triples
Don't Expect	patience at bat

Don't tell Johnson a triple is baseball's toughest hit. He led the AL in three-baggers four straight years before 1995 and made a serious bid to extend that streak. During a 6-for-6 game at Minnesota Sept. 23, he became the first player since 1987 to hit three triples, tying league records for hits and triples in a nine-inning contest. His two-digit finish in doubles, triples, and homers was the first of his career. A speed merchant who bats first, Johnson could be more valuable if he showed patience at the plate. He makes good contact but doesn't reach often enough to post a high on-base percentage—negating his speed. Johnson is seldom caught in the act of stealing bases. The fleet center fielder has quick reactions, spectacular range, and soft hands. The South Alabama product has led the league in putouts and fielding percentage, and even managed 11 assists twice despite a mediocre throwing arm.

Major League Batting Register

	BA	G	AB	R	H	2B	3B	HR	RBI	SB
87 NL	.220	33	59	4	13	2	1	0	7	6
88 AL	.185	33	124	11	23	4	1	0	6	6
89 AL	.300	50	180	28	54	8	2	0	16	16
90 AL	.285	151	541	76	154	18	9	1	51	36
91 AL	.274	159	588	72	161	14	13	0	49	26
92 AL	.279	157	567	67	158	15	12	3	47	41
93 AL	.311	147	540	75	168	18	14	0	47	35
94 AL	.277	106	412	56	114	11	14	3	54	26
95 AL	.306	142	607	98	186	18	12	10	57	40
Life	.285	978	3618	487	1031	108	78	17	334	232
3 AVE	.298	152	601	88	179	18	16	5	62	39

MARK JOHNSON

Position: First base
Team: Pittsburgh Pirates
Born: Oct. 17, 1967 Worcester, MA
Height: 6'4" **Weight:** 230 lbs.
Bats: left **Throws:** left
Acquired: 20th-round pick in 6/90 free-agent draft

Player Summary	
Fantasy Value	$2 to $4
Card Value	15¢ to 20¢
Will	provide some power
Can't	handle left-handers
Expect	walks
Don't Expect	a top average

Just because he mimics Mel Ott's stance doesn't mean Johnson hits like the late Hall of Famer. Johnson did produce at the right time, however, hitting a 475-foot homer against Curt Schilling in a 1995 exhibition game. That shot helped Johnson earn a share of Pittsburgh's first-base job last spring. He got off to a good start, showing some of the power that had earned him Double-A Southern League MVP honors in 1994 (when he had 24 homers). But inexperience eventually caught up to Johnson. When his average plunged toward the Mendoza Line in August, he was optioned to Calgary for much-needed Triple-A experience. Johnson should be back. He showed promise last year, walking enough to push his on-base percentage more than 100 points beyond his batting average. Unless he improves against lefties, however, Johnson may never amount to more than a platoon player. He has the size and strength to be a productive hitter, and also moves well enough to steal a few bases and sub as an outfielder. Johnson is a former Dartmouth quarterback who has a psychology degree from the Ivy League school.

Major League Batting Register

	BA	G	AB	R	H	2B	3B	HR	RBI	SB
95 NL	.208	79	221	32	46	6	1	13	28	5
Life	.208	79	221	32	46	6	1	13	28	5

CURRENT PLAYERS

RANDY JOHNSON

Position: Pitcher
Team: Seattle Mariners
Born: Sept. 10, 1963 Walnut Creek, CA
Height: 6'10" **Weight:** 225 lbs.
Bats: right **Throws:** left
Acquired: Traded by Expos with Gene Harris and Brian Holman for Mark Langston and Mike Campbell, 5/89

Player Summary
Fantasy Value	$25 to $30
Card Value	30¢ to 60¢
Will	dominate league
Can't	hold runners on
Expect	strikeout crown
Don't Expect	gopher problems

Baseball's most overpowering pitcher, Johnson has won four consecutive K crowns, pitched a no-hitter, and compiled a better winning percentage than his team's over the last six years. Last season, he had more strikeouts per nine innings than any starter in history at 12.35, breaking Nolan Ryan's 1987 record of 11.48. A four-time All-Star who started the 1995 game for the AL, Johnson is virtually untouchable against left-handed batters. He's hardly a soft touch against righties, allowing less than seven hits per nine innings. With his fastball and slider both rated the league's best by AL managers, it hardly seems fair that Johnson also throws a curve. He is the tallest player in baseball history. He missed 10 days with shoulder tendinitis last year but still was the major factor in Seattle's strong finish. He showed that he was a money pitcher in the postseason.

Major League Pitching Register

	W	L	ERA	G	CG	IP	H	ER	BB	SO
88 NL	3	0	2.42	4	1	26.0	23	7	7	25
89 NL	0	4	6.67	7	0	29.2	29	22	26	26
89 AL	7	9	4.40	22	2	131.0	118	64	70	104
90 AL	14	11	3.65	33	5	219.2	174	89	120	194
91 AL	13	10	3.98	33	2	201.1	151	89	152	228
92 AL	12	14	3.77	31	6	210.1	154	88	144	241
93 AL	19	8	3.24	35	10	255.1	185	92	99	308
94 AL	13	6	3.19	23	9	172.0	132	61	72	204
95 AL	18	2	2.48	30	6	214.1	159	59	65	294
Life	99	64	3.52	218	41	1459.2	1125	571	755	1624
3 AVE	19	6	2.98	34	10	246.1	183	81	91	309

BOBBY JONES

Position: Pitcher
Team: New York Mets
Born: Feb. 10, 1970 Fresno, CA
Height: 6'4" **Weight:** 210 lbs.
Bats: right **Throws:** right
Acquired: Supplemental first-round pick in 6/91 free-agent draft

Player Summary
Fantasy Value	$8 to $10
Card Value	10¢ to 15¢
Will	use control
Can't	throw hard
Expect	sacrifices
Don't Expect	many walks

The 1995 trade of Bret Saberhagen made Jones the ace of the Mets in his second full season. Though he staggered in late summer, he also showed flashes of great promise. A control pitcher who yielded about one hit per inning last year, Jones moves the ball around and changes speeds. He blends a cut fastball with a sinker, a curveball, and a changeup—his best pitch. Though he averaged about six strikeouts per game, his better than 2-1 ratio of whiffs to walks is deceptive because he does not throw hard. To him, location is far more important than velocity. The former Fresno State standout gives up occasional gopher balls but has a bigger problem holding runners on base. He allowed more steals last summer than any other Mets' pitcher. A good defensive player, Jones also helps himself with exceptional skills as a bunter. For most of 1995, he led the majors—including position players—in sacrifices. Jones was College Pitcher of the Year in 1991 and the Double-A Eastern League Pitcher of the Year in 1992.

Major League Pitching Register

	W	L	ERA	G	CG	IP	H	ER	BB	SO
93 NL	2	4	3.65	9	0	61.2	61	25	22	35
94 NL	12	7	3.15	24	1	160.0	157	56	56	80
95 NL	10	10	4.19	30	3	195.2	209	91	53	127
Life	24	21	3.71	63	4	417.1	427	172	131	242
3 AVE	10	8	3.66	26	2	169.1	172	69	54	97

CURRENT PLAYERS

CHIPPER JONES

Position: Third base
Team: Atlanta Braves
Born: April 24, 1972 DeLand, FL
Height: 6'3" **Weight:** 195 lbs.
Bats: both **Throws:** right
Acquired: First-round pick in 6/90 free-agent draft

Player Summary	
Fantasy Value	$18 to $21
Card Value	40¢ to 70¢
Will	improve his average
Can't	recapture old speed
Expect	clutch power
Don't Expect	impatience at bat

The hype was considerable. Even before the 1995 Braves installed Jones as their third baseman and No. 3 hitter, many scouts were calling him the best infield prospect since Cal Ripken Jr. was a rookie. Jones did nothing to discourage them. Fully healed from the torn knee ligament that idled him in 1994, he showed homer power, run-scoring ability, and a knack of driving in runs. He also played such a strong third base that he made Atlanta fans forget predecessor Terry Pendleton. The switch-hitting Jones, a natural right-handed batter, won a game with his first big-league homer, at New York on May 9, and later hit two other ninth inning game-winners. He also stole some bases, though he didn't display the speed that allowed him to top 20 twice in the minors. Since he's a selective hitter, Jones should jump over .300 once he learns to make better contact. He led the Triple-A International League in runs, hits, and triples in 1993. His quick reflexes and powerful throwing arm make the converted shortstop a future Gold Glove candidate. A natural athlete, he can also play the outfield.

Major League Batting Register

	BA	G	AB	R	H	2B	3B	HR	RBI	SB
93 NL	.667	8	3	2	2	1	0	0	0	0
95 NL	.265	140	524	87	139	22	3	23	86	8
Life	.268	148	527	89	141	23	3	23	86	8

CHRIS JONES

Position: Outfield
Team: New York Mets
Born: Dec. 16, 1965 Utica, NY
Height: 6'2" **Weight:** 205 lbs.
Bats: right **Throws:** right
Acquired: Signed as a free agent, 12/94

Player Summary	
Fantasy Value	$1
Card Value	4¢ to 6¢
Will	hit in pinch
Can't	play defense
Expect	power to help
Don't Expect	regular duty

Though he spends much of his time on the bench, Jones is always ready when asked to play. His power served him well in his role as the Mets' primary pinch hitter last summer. Before Labor Day, he had three pinch homers and a pinch-hitting batting average of .381. Jones, who netted extra bases on about one-third of his hits last year, can't crack the everyday lineup because of weak defense and a tendency to strike out more than three times for every walk. But he thrives in the pressurized world of pinch hitting, concentrating more when he comes to bat in the late innings of close games. After spending parts of four previous seasons in the majors, he lasted the full year for the first time in 1995. While he made a positive impression for his work in the pinch, he didn't earn points for his defensive skills—or lack of them. Jones has some speed but doesn't steal many bases. The one-time Colorado center fielder is best in left because of his weak arm. Jones began his career in the Cincinnati system in 1984.

Major League Batting Register

	BA	G	AB	R	H	2B	3B	HR	RBI	SB
91 NL	.292	52	89	14	26	1	2	2	6	2
92 NL	.190	54	63	7	12	2	1	1	4	3
93 NL	.273	86	209	29	57	11	4	6	31	9
94 NL	.300	21	40	6	12	2	1	0	2	0
95 NL	.280	79	182	33	51	6	2	8	31	2
Life	.271	292	583	89	158	22	10	17	74	16
2 AVE	.276	87	207	33	57	9	3	8	33	6

CURRENT PLAYERS

DOUG JONES

Position: Pitcher
Team: Baltimore Orioles
Born: June 24, 1957 Covina, CA
Height: 6'2" **Weight:** 195 lbs.
Bats: right **Throws:** right
Acquired: Signed as a free agent, 4/95

Player Summary	
Fantasy Value	$10 to $13
Card Value	4¢ to 6¢
Will	exceed 20 saves
Can't	find consistency
Expect	improved control
Don't Expect	a big future

Though he led Baltimore's bullpen in saves last summer and converted all but a handful of opportunities, Jones was wildly inconsistent. He finished with a bloated ERA, maintaining the pattern of alternating good and bad years he began in 1990. His control was off, and right-handed batters—usually his easiest prey—feasted on the diet of changeups (thrown at three different speeds). He occasionally shows a not-too-swift fastball. Age could be catching up with him. Last year, he lost his ability to keep walks and home runs to a bare minimum. But his strikeout ratio rose—perhaps because he was back in the AL after a three-year absence. He is not a great fielder but remains deceptive enough that runners rarely test him. For someone who doesn't throw hard, Jones has a quick delivery and a good pickoff move. He's been an All-Star five times.

Major League Pitching Register

	W	L	ERA	G	S	IP	H	ER	BB	SO
82 AL	0	0	10.13	4	0	2.2	5	3	1	1
86 AL	1	0	2.50	11	1	18.0	18	5	6	12
87 AL	6	5	3.15	49	8	91.1	101	32	24	87
88 AL	3	4	2.27	51	37	83.1	69	21	16	72
89 AL	7	10	2.34	59	32	80.2	76	21	13	65
90 AL	5	5	2.56	66	43	84.1	66	24	22	55
91 AL	4	8	5.54	36	7	63.1	87	39	17	48
92 NL	11	8	1.85	80	36	111.2	96	23	17	93
93 NL	4	10	4.54	71	26	85.1	102	43	21	66
94 NL	2	4	2.17	47	27	54.0	55	13	6	38
95 AL	0	4	5.01	52	22	46.2	55	26	16	42
Life	43	58	3.12	526	239	721.1	730	250	159	579
3 AVE	2	7	3.81	65	30	71.1	80	30	16	56

TODD JONES

Position: Pitcher
Team: Houston Astros
Born: April 24, 1968 Marietta, GA
Height: 6'3" **Weight:** 200 lbs.
Bats: left **Throws:** right
Acquired: Supplemental first-round pick in 6/89 free-agent draft

Player Summary	
Fantasy Value	$9 to $11
Card Value	4¢ to 6¢
Will	throw late heat
Can't	find strike zone
Expect	righties to reel
Don't Expect	trouble fielding

Jones is the hard-throwing reliever who served as Houston's 1995 closer after John Hudek's injury but before Mike Henneman's arrival. Jones probably would have held the job longer if his control had not betrayed him. Though he averaged about one strikeout per inning last year, Jones cannot always find the plate with his fastball, slider, curveball, and changeup. The fastball rises—making him extremely effective against right-handed batters. But he was better against righties in '94, when used as a set-up man, than he was last year. He also has occasional problems keeping the ball in the park and stranding inherited runners. Signed as a starter out of Alabama's Jacksonville State College, Jones moved to the bullpen in 1992. He's capable of working often and handling multi-inning stints. Though he doesn't bat much, he is no automatic out when he comes to the plate. He also helps himself with agile fielding and a quick move to first. Jones was Houston's compensation pick for the Rangers' signing of free-agent Nolan Ryan.

Major League Pitching Register

	W	L	ERA	G	S	IP	H	ER	BB	SO
93 NL	1	2	3.13	27	2	37.1	28	13	15	25
94 NL	5	2	2.72	48	5	72.2	52	22	26	63
95 NL	6	5	3.07	68	15	99.2	89	34	52	96
Life	12	9	2.96	143	22	209.2	169	69	93	184
3 AVE	5	3	2.94	57	9	83.2	67	27	37	74

CURRENT PLAYERS

BRIAN JORDAN

Position: Outfield
Team: St. Louis Cardinals
Born: March 26, 1967 Baltimore, MD
Height: 6'1" **Weight:** 205 lbs.
Bats: right **Throws:** right
Acquired: First-round pick in 6/88 free-agent draft

Player Summary	
Fantasy Value	$20 to $25
Card Value	8¢ to 12¢
Will	hit ball hard
Can't	cut whiff rate
Expect	power, speed
Don't Expect	sloppy defense

Given the most playing time of his career, Jordan spent 1995 battling Ray Lankford for team leadership in home runs, RBI, and stolen bases. No player had led the Cardinals in both RBI and steals since Stan Musial in 1948. Jordan, who has also played pro football as a safety for the Atlanta Falcons, never played more than 67 games in any of his three previous seasons. Injuries idled him twice, but an overcrowded outfield also hampered his progress. The 1995 trade of Mark Whiten ended that logjam. Playing every day, Jordan has 30-30 potential. The strike-shortened season worked against him last year, but he still joined Lankford in the 20-20 ranks. To steal more, Jordan needs to reach more—a tough task for an overly aggressive hitter who fans too much. He flubbed a brief fling as leadoff man because his on-base percentage wasn't high enough. As an outfielder, though, he's a standout, with the range for center field and the arm for right. He gets good jumps and seldom makes an error.

Major League Batting Register

	BA	G	AB	R	H	2B	3B	HR	RBI	SB
92 NL	.207	55	193	17	40	9	4	5	22	7
93 NL	.309	67	223	33	69	10	6	10	44	6
94 NL	.258	53	178	14	46	8	2	5	15	4
95 NL	.296	131	490	83	145	20	4	22	81	24
Life	.277	306	1084	147	300	47	16	42	162	41
3 AVE	.290	96	342	49	99	15	4	14	52	13

WALLY JOYNER

Position: First base
Team: Kansas City Royals
Born: June 16, 1962 Atlanta, GA
Height: 6'2" **Weight:** 198 lbs.
Bats: left **Throws:** left
Acquired: Signed as a free agent, 12/91

Player Summary	
Fantasy Value	$10 to $13
Card Value	5¢ to 8¢
Will	knock runs home
Can't	hit all lefties
Expect	strong fielding
Don't Expect	frequent homers

Although first base is considered a power position, Joyner no longer fits that profile. A contact hitter with patience, he usually walks more than he fans, then sends line drives to all fields when he connects. He's twice as likely to hit a double than a home run, but he's still a solid clutch hitter who collects a healthy share of RBI. Gary Gaetti joined Joyner as veterans in a sea of rookies, and they formed a fine left-right punch for the Royals last year. Joyner doesn't pad his average with infield hits. As a runner, he is mediocre at best. He's a graceful fielder, however, and has led AL first basemen in chances, putouts, assists, double plays, and fielding percentage. If Don Mattingly weren't in the same league, Joyner might own multiple Gold Gloves. Joyner was an AL All-Star in 1986, three years after the Angels drafted him off the Brigham Young campus.

Major League Batting Register

	BA	G	AB	R	H	2B	3B	HR	RBI	SB
86 AL	.290	154	593	82	172	27	3	22	100	5
87 AL	.285	149	564	100	161	33	1	34	117	8
88 AL	.295	158	597	81	176	31	2	13	85	8
89 AL	.282	159	593	78	167	30	2	16	79	3
90 AL	.268	83	310	35	83	15	0	8	41	2
91 AL	.301	143	551	79	166	34	3	21	96	2
92 AL	.269	149	572	66	154	36	2	9	66	11
93 AL	.292	141	497	83	145	36	3	15	65	5
94 AL	.311	97	363	52	113	20	3	8	57	3
95 AL	.310	131	465	69	144	28	0	12	83	3
Life	.290	1364	5105	725	1481	290	19	158	789	50
3 AVE	.304	142	510	78	155	32	2	13	80	4

CURRENT PLAYERS

JEFF JUDEN

Position: Pitcher
Team: San Francisco Giants
Born: Jan. 19, 1971 Salem, MA
Height: 6'8" **Weight:** 265 lbs.
Bats: right **Throws:** right
Acquired: Traded by Phillies with Tommy Eason for Mike Benjamin, 10/95

Player Summary	
Fantasy Value	$0
Card Value	4¢ to 6¢
Will	rattle righties
Can't	throw strikes
Expect	rotation trial
Don't Expect	J.R. Richard

After the Astros made him a first-round draft choice in 1989, Juden had Houston convinced he was the second coming of J.R. Richard, the former All-Star and strikeout king. But Juden's inability to control his sizzling fastball has kept him in the minors for most of his seven-year professional career. He surfaced twice with Houston and twice with the Phillies. Each time, Juden was betrayed by his ongoing battle with control problems. Though he's extremely tough on right-handed hitters, he has trouble with lefties. Overall, he yielded less hits than innings but gives up more than his share of long balls. For much of the 1995 season, Juden fanned more than six per nine innings but also allowed nearly five walks per game. That ratio just won't cut it in the big leagues. He did show flashes of potential late last summer, however. He yielded three hits and one run in a seven-inning stint against the Mets Aug. 10. He's still young enough to conquer his control problems and strong enough to get by with his blazer.

Major League Pitching Register

	W	L	ERA	G	CG	IP	H	ER	BB	SO
91 NL	0	2	6.00	4	0	18.0	19	12	7	11
93 NL	0	1	5.40	2	0	5.0	4	3	4	7
94 NL	1	4	6.18	6	0	27.2	29	19	12	22
95 NL	2	4	4.02	13	1	62.2	53	28	31	47
Life	3	11	4.92	25	1	113.1	105	62	54	87

DAVID JUSTICE

Position: Outfield
Team: Atlanta Braves
Born: April 14, 1966 Cincinnati, OH
Height: 6'3" **Weight:** 200 lbs.
Bats: left **Throws:** left
Acquired: Fourth-round pick in 6/85 free-agent draft

Player Summary	
Fantasy Value	$19 to $22
Card Value	20¢ to 35¢
Will	provide big power
Can't	prevent injuries
Expect	hustling defense
Don't Expect	much basestealing

Will the real Justice please stand up? Is he the guy who had 40 homers and 120 RBI in 1993 or the one who hit .313 a year later? The composite could be somewhere in the middle—if he stays healthy. Last year, the two-time All-Star was disabled June 2 with torn ligaments in front of his right shoulder. Justice, who also missed time in 1991 and 1992, had to alter his trademark swing when he returned and his production dropped. Usually a dangerous clutch hitter with a good batting eye, he walks more often than he strikes out. He has power to all fields. However, he struggled against southpaws in 1995 and that was atypical. His fine on-base percentage was vintage Justice; he ranked second in the NL with a .427 on-base mark in 1994. Atlanta's unofficial team leader, he sets a fine example with his brand of all-out hustle. He races after anything hit toward right field, often diving to make a catch. Justice has a strong arm and ranks among NL leaders in assists.

Major League Batting Register

	BA	G	AB	R	H	2B	3B	HR	RBI	SB
89 NL	.235	16	51	7	12	3	0	1	3	2
90 NL	.282	127	439	76	124	23	2	28	78	11
91 NL	.275	109	396	67	109	25	1	21	87	8
92 NL	.256	144	484	78	124	19	5	21	72	2
93 NL	.270	157	585	90	158	15	4	40	120	3
94 NL	.313	104	352	61	110	16	2	19	59	2
95 NL	.253	120	411	73	104	17	2	24	78	4
Life	.273	777	2718	452	741	118	16	154	497	32
3 AVE	.279	146	514	86	143	19	3	31	97	3

CURRENT PLAYERS

SCOTT KAMIENIECKI

Position: Pitcher
Team: New York Yankees
Born: April 19, 1964 Mt. Clemens, MI
Height: 6′ **Weight:** 195 lbs.
Bats: right **Throws:** right
Acquired: 14th-round pick in 6/86 free-agent draft

Player Summary	
Fantasy Value	$5 to $7
Card Value	5¢ to 8¢
Will	fight for berth
Can't	find strike zone
Expect	ground-ball outs
Don't Expect	high whiff total

Though he lost two months with a strained elbow ligament, Kamieniecki remained in the Yankee rotation when physically able. He wasn't as effective as he had been in 1994, however, because he was betrayed by his control. The University of Michigan graduate (degree in physical education) finished the year with more walks than strikeouts—a flaw he will have to fix to guarantee his big-league future. When he's right, Kamieniecki combines a fastball, a curveball, a slider, and a changeup, hoping to coax ground balls from guessing batters. Using guile rather than heat, he tries to change speeds and locate his pitches in and around the strike zone. When he fails, he gets hit hard. Kamieniecki yields about one hit per inning—a decent ratio—but has occasional homer trouble. His career record suggests that he's a better pitcher with more rest between starts. He is a fine fielder who holds runners well for a right-handed pitcher. Kamieniecki was Jim Abbott's roommate in college.

Major League Pitching Register

	W	L	ERA	G	CG	IP	H	ER	BB	SO
91 AL	4	4	3.90	9	0	55.1	54	24	22	34
92 AL	6	14	4.36	28	4	188.0	193	91	74	88
93 AL	10	7	4.08	30	2	154.1	163	70	59	72
94 AL	8	6	3.76	22	1	117.1	115	49	59	71
95 AL	7	6	4.01	17	1	89.2	83	40	49	43
Life	35	37	4.08	106	8	604.2	608	274	263	308
3 AVE	10	7	3.94	27	2	140.2	139	61	66	73

RON KARKOVICE

Position: Catcher
Team: Chicago White Sox
Born: Aug. 8, 1963 Union, NJ
Height: 6′1″ **Weight:** 215 lbs.
Bats: right **Throws:** right
Acquired: First-round pick in 6/82 free-agent draft

Player Summary	
Fantasy Value	$4 to $6
Card Value	4¢ to 6¢
Will	show great arm
Can't	cut strikeouts
Expect	occasional pop
Don't Expect	decent average

Karkovice never mastered the hitting lessons of White Sox coach Walt Hriniak. Karkovice does draw enough walks to push his on-base percentage almost 100 points higher than his batting average. He is always a threat to duplicate his 20-homer campaign of 1993. A better hitter against left-handers, he was lifted for Mike LaValliere against tough southpaws last summer. Karkovice is really known for his strong defense, which AL managers rated the league's best in consecutive *Baseball America* polls. A good handler of pitchers, Karkovice calls a good game, prevents wild pitches, and blocks the plate like a hockey goalie. Then there's the arm, a rocket that always ranks among the league leaders in catching basestealers. During his 1993 career year, Karkovice nailed 50 percent, and 60 percent in the All-Star Game.

Major League Batting Register

	BA	G	AB	R	H	2B	3B	HR	RBI	SB
86 AL	.247	37	97	13	24	7	0	4	13	1
87 AL	.071	39	85	7	6	0	0	2	7	3
88 AL	.174	46	115	10	20	4	0	3	9	4
89 AL	.264	71	182	21	48	9	2	3	24	0
90 AL	.246	68	183	30	45	10	0	6	20	2
91 AL	.246	75	167	25	41	13	0	5	22	0
92 AL	.237	123	342	39	81	12	1	13	50	10
93 AL	.228	128	403	60	92	17	1	20	54	2
94 AL	.213	77	207	33	44	9	1	11	29	0
95 AL	.217	113	323	44	70	14	1	13	51	2
Life	.224	777	2104	282	471	95	6	80	279	24
3 AVE	.220	121	353	52	78	15	1	17	51	1

CURRENT PLAYERS

SCOTT KARL

Position: Pitcher
Team: Milwaukee Brewers
Born: Aug. 9, 1971 Fontana, CA
Height: 6'2" **Weight:** 195 lbs.
Bats: left **Throws:** left
Acquired: Sixth-round pick in 6/92 free-agent draft

Player Summary
Fantasy Value.................$2 to $4
Card Value ....10¢ to 15¢
Will .... get ground outs
Can't..................... avoid wildness
Expect .... starting berth
Don't Expect............. gopher trouble

A sinkerballing southpaw from the University of Hawaii, Karl got his first win in his second start, beating Oakland 5-2 on July 6. He is a smart pitcher who knows what's going on in the game, and he has poise beyond his years. Private sessions with New Orleans pitching coach Bill Campbell, a former big-leaguer, helped Karl rediscover his changeup—his best pitch. Not a power pitcher, Karl gets most of his outs on ground balls. He yielded more hits than innings last year but kept the ball in the park. His biggest problem is occasional bouts of wildness. Karl, who spent less than four years in the minors, had three separate stints in Milwaukee last season. He pitched well against left-handed hitters but had some trouble with righties. He was exclusively a starter in the minors, leading the Double-A Texas League with 180 innings pitched in 1993. He divided his time in the majors between the rotation and the bullpen. His future seems to lie as a starter, however. Karl knows how to field his position but still needs to perfect his pickoff move. Even though he faces first base, most of the runners who challenged him succeeded.

Major League Pitching Register

	W	L	ERA	G	CG	IP	H	ER	BB	SO
95 AL	6	7	4.14	25	1	124.0	141	57	50	59
Life	6	7	4.14	25	1	124.0	141	57	50	59

ERIC KARROS

Position: First base
Team: Los Angeles Dodgers
Born: Nov. 4, 1967 Hackensack, NJ
Height: 6'4" **Weight:** 205 lbs.
Bats: right **Throws:** right
Acquired: Sixth-round pick in 6/88 free-agent draft

Player Summary
Fantasy Value.............. $19 to $22
Card Value ....12¢ to 20¢
Will .... hit ball far
Can't .... stop whiffing
Expect .... run production
Don't Expect .... stolen bases

Suddenly, Karros started hitting again last summer. After watching his RBI total fall two straight years after his Rookie-of-the-Year season in 1992, he compensated by making better contact and not trying to pull every pitch. By reducing his rookie-level ratio of three strikeouts per walk, he boosted both his batting and his on-base averages. Karros finished with career highs in batting, homers, and RBI. A better hitter against lefties, the UCLA product was hitting .315 with a team-best 14 homers and 46 RBI when the NL All-Stars were announced—without his name included. A month later, he won consecutive games with late-inning homers, a two-run shot in the 12th against the Giants on Aug. 7, and a solo blast in the eighth against St. Louis the next night. He has made improvements in the field, however. Once a defensive liability, there's now talk of shifting him to third—a position he played in the minors. Karros led several minor leagues in chances, putouts, and assists.

Major League Batting Register

	BA	G	AB	R	H	2B	3B	HR	RBI	SB
91 NL	.071	14	14	0	1	0	0	0	1	0
92 NL	.257	149	545	63	140	30	1	20	88	2
93 NL	.247	158	619	74	153	27	2	23	80	0
94 NL	.266	111	406	51	108	21	1	14	46	2
95 NL	.298	143	551	83	164	29	3	32	105	4
Life	.265	575	2135	271	566	108	7	89	320	8
3 AVE	.270	158	604	80	163	30	2	26	88	2

CURRENT PLAYERS

STEVE KARSAY

Position: Pitcher
Team: Oakland Athletics
Born: March 24, 1972 College Point, NY
Height: 6'3" **Weight:** 205 lbs.
Bats: right **Throws:** right
Acquired: Traded by Blue Jays with Jose Herrera for Rickey Henderson, 7/93

Player Summary	
Fantasy Value	$1
Card Value	4¢ to 6¢
Will	try to heal fast
Can't	shake injury hex
Expect	trial as starter
Don't Expect	runners to steal

At the time of his trade to Oakland three years ago, Karsay was considered the top pitching prospect in the Toronto organization. He has yet to deliver on that promise, however. He won only four games for the Athletics before submitting to surgery to replace a damaged ligament in his pitching arm. The operation, performed on June 20, 1995, could keep him sidelined until 1997. Karsay previously had arthroscopic surgery on his right elbow. He did have a good reputation as a starter in the minors, however. He showed poise, confidence, and control. Karsay mixes a low-90s fastball, a late-breaking slider, and a changeup. He averaged more than one strikeout per inning in the Double-A Southern League in 1993. The former first-round draft choice figures to yield less hits than innings and keep the ball in the park. He fields his position well and keeps close watch on baserunners. He's worked hard to improve his slide-step pickoff move. Scouts believe Karsay will become a big winner if he overcomes his health problems. He's a coachable player who is willing to learn.

MIKE KELLY

Position: Outfield
Team: Atlanta Braves
Born: June 2, 1970 Los Angeles, CA
Height: 6'4" **Weight:** 195 lbs.
Bats: right **Throws:** right
Acquired: First-round pick in 6/91 free-agent draft

Player Summary	
Fantasy Value	$2 to $4
Card Value	8¢ to 12¢
Will	hit with power
Can't	cut strikeouts
Expect	fight to stick
Don't Expect	trip to minors

If he ever learns to stop striking out, Kelly could blossom into the star college coach Jim Brock envisioned at Arizona State. While there, Brock said Kelly was more advanced than Barry Bonds at the same stage of his career. Between college and the majors, however, Kelly's career stalled. He showed both speed and power in the minors, but struck out so often in Atlanta that Braves manager Bobby Cox abandoned the right-left platoon of Kelly and Ryan Klesko in left field. That was a blow for Kelly, a former All-American who had also won College Player of the Year honors and the Golden Spikes Award. The second overall pick in the 1991 amateur draft, he has already been a 20-20 player in the minors. Given enough playing time, he'd do at least that well in the majors, with 30-30 also within his grasp. But he must make contact first. Because of his speed, Kelly could fatten his average with bunts and infield hits. With men on base, however, he wants to swing away. He netted extra bases on more than one-third of his hits. A good outfielder who's best in center, Kelly has great range and a strong arm.

Major League Pitching Register

	W	L	ERA	G	CG	IP	H	ER	BB	SO
93 AL	3	3	4.04	8	0	49.0	49	22	16	33
94 AL	1	1	2.57	4	1	28.0	26	8	8	15
Life	4	4	3.51	12	1	77.0	75	30	24	48

Major League Batting Register

	BA	G	AB	R	H	2B	3B	HR	RBI	SB
94 NL	.273	30	77	14	21	10	1	2	9	0
95 NL	.190	97	137	26	26	6	1	3	17	7
Life	.220	127	214	40	47	16	2	5	26	7

CURRENT PLAYERS

PAT KELLY

Position: Second base
Team: New York Yankees
Born: Oct. 10, 1967 Philadelphia, PA
Height: 6' **Weight:** 180 lbs.
Bats: right **Throws:** right
Acquired: Ninth-round pick in 6/88 free-agent draft

Player Summary

Fantasy Value	$7 to $9
Card Value	4¢ to 6¢
Will	add solid defense
Can't	hit long ball
Expect	bunts and singles
Don't Expect	patience at plate

Though he's starting his sixth big-league season, Kelly is still trying to shake the good-field, no-hit tag that has followed him most of his career. Yankee manager Buck Showalter benched Kelly for Randy Velarde during the team's late-September drive for the wild-card playoff slot. Earlier in the year, Kelly lost playing time when he needed arthroscopic surgery to repair torn ligaments in his left wrist. A far better hitter against left-handed pitchers, he would win more playing time if he reached base more often. To do that, he needs to show more patience at the plate. A good bunter whose 14 sacrifices led the league in 1994, Kelly could also bunt for hits more often. A spray hitter who sends singles to all fields, he occasionally surprises with his power. But he is more likely to steal a base than he is to hit a home run. Kelly's forte is his fielding. He has quick reactions, fine range, and a decent throwing arm. The Yankees drafted him off the campus of Pennsylvania's West Chester College.

Major League Batting Register

	BA	G	AB	R	H	2B	3B	HR	RBI	SB
91 AL	.242	96	298	35	72	12	4	3	23	12
92 AL	.226	106	318	38	72	22	2	7	27	8
93 AL	.273	127	406	49	111	24	1	7	51	14
94 AL	.280	93	286	35	80	21	2	3	41	6
95 AL	.237	89	270	32	64	12	1	4	29	8
Life	.253	511	1578	189	399	91	10	24	171	48
3 AVE	.266	119	371	45	99	22	2	5	47	10

ROBERTO KELLY

Position: Outfield
Team: Los Angeles Dodgers
Born: Oct. 1, 1964 Panama City, Panama
Height: 6'4" **Weight:** 185 lbs.
Bats: right **Throws:** right
Acquired: Traded by Expos with Joey Eischen for Henry Rodriguez and Jeff Treadway, 5/95

Player Summary

Fantasy Value	$12 to $15
Card Value	5¢ to 7¢
Will	hit in clutch
Can't	cut strikeouts
Expect	strong defense
Don't Expect	homer barrage

Kelly has never mastered the strike zone. As a result, he has a low on-base percentage—especially for a man who can run as well as he does. A dreadful leadoff man because of his penchant for striking out, Kelly is more productive lower in the order. He's a good clutch hitter with some power, but he has become more of a singles hitter in recent seasons. He's better against left-handers. It's not likely Kelly can repeat his 20-20 season of 1991, though 20 steals should be easy pickings. Kelly hits well with runners in scoring position and in late-inning pressure situations. He's as aggressive on the bases as he is at the plate, though that's not always good. He shifted to left after the Dodgers reacquired Brett Butler last year. Kelly showed that he still has great range, good hands, and a solid arm. He has been an All-Star in both leagues.

Major League Batting Register

	BA	G	AB	R	H	2B	3B	HR	RBI	SB
87 AL	.269	23	52	12	14	3	0	1	7	9
88 AL	.247	38	77	9	19	4	1	1	7	5
89 AL	.302	137	441	65	133	18	3	9	48	35
90 AL	.285	162	641	85	183	32	4	15	61	42
91 AL	.267	126	486	68	130	22	2	20	69	32
92 AL	.272	152	580	81	158	31	2	10	66	28
93 NL	.319	78	320	44	102	17	3	9	35	21
94 NL	.293	110	434	73	127	23	3	9	45	19
95 NL	.278	136	504	58	140	23	2	7	57	19
Life	.285	962	3535	495	1006	173	20	81	395	210
3 AVE	.293	.129	499	71	146	25	3	10	54	23

CURRENT PLAYERS

JEFF KENT

Position: Second base
Team: New York Mets
Born: March 7, 1968 Bellflower, CA
Height: 6'1" **Weight:** 185 lbs.
Bats: right **Throws:** right
Acquired: Traded by Blue Jays with Ryan Thompson for David Cone, 8/92

Player Summary	
Fantasy Value	$13 to $16
Card Value	5¢ to 8¢
Will	hit the long ball
Can't	stop striking out
Expect	shift from second
Don't Expect	Gold Glove defense

Controversy has shadowed Kent during his short career in the majors. He's heard complaints about his attitude, his defensive shortcomings, his approximately 3-1 ratio of strikeouts to walks, and his frequent inability to hit in the clutch. But few middle infielders produce his kind of power. Disabled in July with strained ligaments in his right shoulder, Kent resumed his long-ball hitting after he returned. A fastball hitter who usually rips lefties, he loves to turn on inside pitches. He hits a lot of balls in the air. The USC product is no longer the basestealer he was during his first three pro seasons. He does run the bases well. He has quick reactions and good range at second base. He had defensive problems, particularly in turning the double play. Although he reduced his error total last season after leading the league two years in a row, he's still regarded as a defensive liability at the position. A move somewhere else might still be in the offing.

Major League Batting Register

	BA	G	AB	R	H	2B	3B	HR	RBI	SB
92 AL	.240	65	192	36	46	13	1	8	35	2
92 NL	.239	37	113	16	27	8	1	3	15	0
93 NL	.270	140	496	65	134	24	0	21	80	4
94 NL	.292	107	415	53	121	24	5	14	68	1
95 NL	.278	125	472	65	131	22	3	20	65	3
Life	.272	474	1688	235	459	91	10	66	263	10
3 AVE	.280	144	537	71	151	28	3	21	83	3

JIMMY KEY

Position: Pitcher
Team: New York Yankees
Born: April 22, 1961 Huntsville, AL
Height: 6'1" **Weight:** 190 lbs.
Bats: right **Throws:** left
Acquired: Signed as a free agent, 11/92

Player Summary	
Fantasy Value	$8 to $10
Card Value	8¢ to 12¢
Will	seek medical miracle
Can't	freeze running game
Expect	15 wins if sound
Don't Expect	frequent strikeouts

Key may not be able to fulfill the year remaining on his four-year contract. The 1994 Cy Young Award runner-up had career-threatening rotator cuff surgery last July after five starts. The arthroscopic shoulder surgery of October 1994 hadn't solved his problems. The Yankees missed him; he has had a better winning percentage in pinstripes than Whitey Ford. When healthy, Key is a control pitcher who mixes a fastball, a slider, a curve, and a changeup. He keeps the ball in the park and dominates left-handed hitters. But he does not throw hard enough to rank among the league leaders in strikeouts. Key helps himself with his fielding but has some trouble holding runners. Signed off the Clemson campus by the Blue Jays in 1982, the four-time All-Star was named AL Pitcher of the Year by *The Sporting News* in both 1987 and 1994.

Major League Pitching Register

	W	L	ERA	G	CG	IP	H	ER	BB	SO
84 AL	4	5	4.65	63	0	62.0	70	32	32	44
85 AL	14	6	3.00	35	3	212.2	188	71	50	85
86 AL	14	11	3.57	36	4	232.0	222	92	74	141
87 AL	17	8	2.76	36	8	261.0	210	80	66	161
88 AL	12	5	3.29	21	2	131.1	127	48	30	65
89 AL	13	14	3.88	33	5	216.0	226	93	27	118
90 AL	13	7	4.25	27	0	154.2	169	73	22	88
91 AL	16	12	3.05	33	2	209.1	207	71	44	125
92 AL	13	13	3.53	33	4	216.2	205	85	59	117
93 AL	18	6	3.00	34	4	236.2	219	79	43	173
94 AL	17	4	3.27	25	1	168.0	177	61	52	97
95 AL	1	2	5.64	5	0	30.1	40	19	6	14
Life	152	93	3.40	381	33	2130.2	2060	804	505	1228
2 AVE	21	6	3.14	35	3	236.1	234	82	58	155

CURRENT PLAYERS

DARRYL KILE

Position: Pitcher
Team: Houston Astros
Born: Dec. 2, 1968 Garden Grove, CA
Height: 6'5" **Weight:** 185 lbs.
Bats: right **Throws:** right
Acquired: 30th-round pick in 6/87 free-agent draft

Player Summary	
Fantasy Value	$5 to 7¢
Card Value	6¢ to 10¢
Will	seek out '93 form
Can't	locate home plate
Expect	last-chance trial
Don't Expect	homer woes

"Steve Blass" disease is alive and well in Darryl Kile. A 15-game winner who made the All-Star team and pitched a no-hitter in 1993, Kile hasn't been able to throw strikes for the last two seasons. Things got so bad last year, in fact, that the Astros had to return him to the minors for a refresher course on the strike zone. While Kile usually yields less hits than innings and fans nearly eight batters per game, his control is often his worst enemy. He averaged more than five walks per nine innings last year—often reminding observers of Blass, the former Pittsburgh World Series hero whose career ended after a sudden inability to locate the plate. A curveball specialist whose pet pitch has a big drop, Kile also throws a fastball and a changeup. When he has his control, he gets his outs on strikeouts and ground outs. But the walks, wild pitches, and related temper tantrums haven't helped him regain his 1993 form. Kile can bunt, hit, and field but needs work on his pickoff move.

Major League Pitching Register

	W	L	ERA	G	CG	IP	H	ER	BB	SO
91 NL	7	11	3.69	37	0	153.2	144	63	84	100
92 NL	5	10	3.95	22	2	125.1	124	55	63	90
93 NL	15	8	3.51	32	4	171.2	152	67	69	141
94 NL	9	6	4.57	24	0	147.2	153	75	82	105
95 NL	4	12	4.96	25	0	127.0	114	70	73	113
Life	40	47	4.09	140	6	725.1	687	330	371	549
3 AVE	11	10	4.33	31	1	174.2	165	84	89	139

JEFF KING

Position: Third base
Team: Pittsburgh Pirates
Born: Dec. 26, 1964 Marion IN
Height: 6'1" **Weight:** 180 lbs.
Bats: right **Throws:** right
Acquired: First-round pick in 6/86 free-agent draft

Player Summary	
Fantasy Value	$10 to $13
Card Value	5¢ to 8¢
Will	produce some power
Can't	steal bases often
Expect	patience, contact
Don't Expect	Gold Gloves

King finally came into his own as a slugger last summer. Before he clouted two homers in an inning at San Francisco Aug. 8, no Pirate had done that in 101 years. Less than one month earlier, his two-homer game sparked a 9-2 win over St. Louis. Though disabled with a wrist injury in June, King finished with a career high in home runs. He'd do even better if the men hitting behind him were more productive. Pitchers started pitching around King two years ago, when he knocked in a career-best 98 runs. He has enough patience to walk almost as much as he fans, and makes better contact than most long-ball hitters. As a result, his on-base percentage towers above his batting average. He can play any of the four infield positions. The former Arkansas All-American—the first player chosen in the 1986 amateur draft—has quick reactions, good hands, and an accurate throwing arm. Signed as a third baseman, he also spent considerable time at first last year.

Major League Batting Register

	BA	G	AB	R	H	2B	3B	HR	RBI	SB
89 NL	.195	75	215	31	42	13	3	5	19	4
90 NL	.245	127	371	46	91	17	1	14	53	3
91 NL	.239	33	109	16	26	1	1	4	18	3
92 NL	.231	130	480	56	111	21	2	14	65	4
93 NL	.295	158	611	82	180	35	3	9	98	8
94 NL	.263	94	339	36	89	23	0	5	42	3
95 NL	.265	122	445	61	118	27	2	18	87	7
Life	.256	739	2570	328	657	137	12	69	382	32
3 AVE	.276	143	530	67	146	33	2	12	85	7

CURRENT PLAYERS

MIKE KINGERY

Position: Outfield
Team: Colorado Rockies
Born: March 29, 1961 St. James, MN
Height: 6′ **Weight:** 185 lbs.
Bats: left **Throws:** left
Acquired: Signed as a free agent, 12/93

Player Summary	
Fantasy Value	$5 to $7
Card Value	4¢ to 6¢
Will	make good contact
Can't	clear walls often
Expect	backup assignment
Don't Expect	luck with lefties

Though he couldn't maintain the brilliance of his 1994 campaign, Kingery remained a valuable contributor to Colorado's surprise season last summer. Though he struggled against left-handed pitchers, he made such good contact (more walks than strikeouts) that his on-base percentage was 80 points higher than his batting average. He spent most of the season platooning with Ellis Burks. Kingery is primarily a singles hitter who uses all fields. His stats suggest a little power, but playing half the schedule in Denver would help anyone. Kingery used his speed to good advantage last year, reaching a career peak in stolen bases. He can play all three outfield positions, as well as first base, but seems most comfortable in center field. An excellent fourth outfielder, Kingery played for the Royals, Mariners, Giants, and Athletics before joining the Rockies. Kansas City signed him as a nondrafted free agent in 1979.

Major League Batting Register

	BA	G	AB	R	H	2B	3B	HR	RBI	SB
86 AL	.258	62	209	25	54	8	5	3	14	7
87 AL	.280	120	354	38	99	25	4	9	52	7
88 AL	.203	57	123	21	25	6	0	1	9	3
89 AL	.224	31	76	14	17	3	0	2	6	1
90 NL	.295	105	274	24	61	7	1	0	24	6
91 NL	.182	91	110	13	20	2	2	0	8	1
92 AL	.107	12	28	3	3	0	0	0	1	0
94 NL	.349	105	301	56	105	27	8	4	41	5
95 NL	.269	119	350	66	94	18	4	8	37	13
Life	.272	702	1758	260	478	96	24	27	192	43
2 AVE	.310	141	409	77	127	29	8	7	50	11

WAYNE KIRBY

Position: Outfield
Team: Cleveland Indians
Born: Jan. 22, 1964 Williamsburg, VA
Height: 5′11″ **Weight:** 185 lbs.
Bats: left **Throws:** right
Acquired: Signed as a free agent, 12/90

Player Summary	
Fantasy Value	$2 to $4
Card Value	4¢ to 6¢
Will	make contact
Can't	show patience
Expect	strong throws
Don't Expect	home run power

Given enough playing time, Kirby swings a solid bat. Neither happened in 1995, however, when he split his time as chief understudy for Kenny Lofton in center and Manny Ramirez in right. Though he makes enough contact to be a good hit-and-run man, Kirby marches to the plate with an overly aggressive approach. He fans about three times more than he walks, negating his value as a basestealer. His poor on-base percentage of 1995 was a combination of impatience at the plate and weak performance against right-handers—normally his country cousins. His average against righties dipped some 100 points from its 1994 level of .297. He had even more difficulties on the road, where he was far below the Mendoza Line. Kirby would like to return to his form of 1992, when he led the Triple-A Pacific Coast League in runs, hits, and triples while batting .345 and stealing 51 bases. His speed helps in the outfield, where he has great range and a powerful arm. Kirby's 19 assists tied Bernard Gilkey for baseball's best in 1993.

Major League Batting Register

	BA	G	AB	R	H	2B	3B	HR	RBI	SB
91 AL	.209	21	43	4	9	2	0	0	5	1
92 AL	.167	21	18	9	3	1	0	0	1	0
93 AL	.269	131	458	71	123	19	5	6	60	17
94 AL	.293	78	191	33	56	6	0	5	23	11
95 AL	.207	101	188	29	39	10	2	1	14	10
Life	.256	352	898	146	230	38	7	13	103	39
3 AVE	.262	118	313	50	82	13	2	5	36	15

CURRENT PLAYERS

RYAN KLESKO

Position: Outfield; first base
Team: Atlanta Braves
Born: June 12, 1971 Westminster, CA
Height: 6'3" **Weight:** 220 lbs.
Bats: left **Throws:** left
Acquired: Fifth-round pick in 6/89 free-agent draft

Player Summary
Fantasy Value	$18 to $21
Card Value	25¢ to 50¢
Will	punish righties
Can't	solve all southpaws
Expect	long homers
Don't Expect	Gold Gloves

Like David Justice, Klesko was benched against left-handed pitchers for most of his rookie season. When manager Bobby Cox continued the practice last year, however, Klesko complained loud and long—and announced he'd be a 30-homer, 100-RBI performer if he played every day. He finally got his chance after the All-Star Game. Though Klesko hits far better against righties, he's hardly an automatic out against southpaws. He shows surprising patience for a young player, walking often enough to post a .400 on-base percentage. But Klesko would rather swing the bat. He hit 11 homers in a 38-game midseason stretch after recovering from a slow start. He'll also leap and dive for balls hit to left field, an unfamiliar position he's still learning. A first baseman by trade, he couldn't budge Fred McGriff during his first two years in Atlanta. Klesko has made dramatic improvements in his defense but will never win a Gold Glove. He runs well for a big man and works hard to maintain top physical condition.

Major League Batting Register
	BA	G	AB	R	H	2B	3B	HR	RBI	SB
92 NL	.000	13	14	0	0	0	0	0	1	0
93 NL	.353	22	17	3	6	1	0	2	5	0
94 NL	.278	92	245	42	68	13	3	17	47	1
95 NL	.310	107	329	48	102	25	2	23	70	5
Life	.291	234	605	93	176	39	5	42	123	6
2 AVE	.294	125	358	57	105	23	3	25	72	4

CHUCK KNOBLAUCH

Position: Second base
Team: Minnesota Twins
Born: July 7, 1968 Houston, TX
Height: 5'9" **Weight:** 175 lbs.
Bats: right **Throws:** right
Acquired: First-round pick in 6/89 free-agent draft

Player Summary
Fantasy Value	$30 to $35
Card Value	12¢ to 20¢
Will	get on
Can't	reverse whiff rate
Expect	lofty on-base mark
Don't Expect	huge RBI

One of baseball's most effective but least-publicized leadoff men, Knoblauch added power to his résumé last summer. He hit more homers in 1995 but still produced the best batting average of his career. Blessed with a good eye, Knoblauch draws enough walks to boost his on-base percentage about 80 points beyond his average. But he's no longer the contact man who walks more often than he strikes out, as he did in his first three seasons. He now fans frequently for a first-place hitter but still reaches base so often (40 percent of the time) that no one's complaining. When he does make contact, he hits the ball extremely well. He's topped 30 steals three times but was nailed more often last year than the season before. In a 1995 *Baseball America* survey, AL managers named him the No. 2 hit-and-run man and defensive second baseman. He has quick reflexes, excellent range, and soft hands—plus a strong enough arm to play short, his original position. The Texas A&M product has made the All-Star team twice.

Major League Batting Register
	BA	G	AB	R	H	2B	3B	HR	RBI	SB
91 AL	.281	151	565	78	159	24	6	1	50	25
92 AL	.297	155	600	104	178	19	6	2	56	34
93 AL	.277	153	602	82	167	27	4	2	41	29
94 AL	.312	109	445	85	139	45	3	5	51	35
95 AL	.333	136	538	107	179	34	8	11	63	46
Life	.299	704	2750	456	822	149	27	21	261	169
3 AVE	.308	153	611	107	188	43	6	7	61	43

CURRENT PLAYERS

RANDY KNORR

Position: Catcher
Team: Toronto Blue Jays
Born: Nov. 12, 1968 San Gabriel, CA
Height: 6'2" **Weight:** 215 lbs.
Bats: right **Throws:** right
Acquired: 10th-round pick in 6/86 free-agent draft

Player Summary
Fantasy Value	$0
Card Value	4¢ to 6¢
Will	hit southpaws
Can't	wait for walks
Expect	occasional pop
Don't Expect	strong throws

Because of his solid defense, Knorr opened the 1995 season as Toronto's top catcher. But inconsistency at the plate, followed by a broken thumb, eventually cost him the job. Despite his limited playing time, Knorr collected extra bases on one-third of his hits and hit well over .300 against left-handers. That gave him an edge over Lance Parrish and Angel Martinez. Knorr would be more valuable, however, if he reduced his ratio of strikeouts to walks. He has never met a fastball he didn't like—even if it was out of the strike zone. He doesn't run at all but used to be good at stopping opponents from running. In recent seasons, however, his success rate against potential basestealers has dropped to the 20-percent range. That's equivalent to the Mendoza Line of catching. Knorr still calls a good game, handles his pitchers well, and performs such other duties as preventing wild pitches and blocking the plate. Several Toronto pitchers specifically requested that he catch their games.

Major League Batting Register
	BA	G	AB	R	H	2B	3B	HR	RBI	SB
91 AL	.000	3	1	0	0	0	0	0	0	0
92 AL	.263	8	19	1	5	0	0	1	2	0
93 AL	.248	39	101	11	25	3	2	4	20	0
94 AL	.242	40	124	20	30	2	0	7	19	0
95 AL	.212	45	132	18	28	8	0	3	16	0
Life	.233	135	377	50	88	13	2	15	57	0

TIM LAKER

Position: Catcher
Team: Montreal Expos
Born: Nov. 27, 1969 Encino, CA
Height: 6'3" **Weight:** 200 lbs.
Bats: right **Throws:** right
Acquired: Sixth-round pick in 6/88 free-agent draft

Player Summary
Fantasy Value	$4 to $6
Card Value	4¢ to 6¢
Will	throw hard
Can't	steal much
Expect	a few hits
Don't Expect	daily duty

Before the 1995 season opened, the Montreal Expos planned to use Laker in a right-left platoon with Darrin Fletcher. But Laker's failure to hit—especially against lefties—scuttled that plan. His futility at the plate was a disappointment. His .309 average had placed fifth in the Triple-A International League the year before. Laker had also shown some power (12 homers) and speed (11 steals) while winning the circuit's All-Star honors. He's been a bust in three tries with the Expos, however, though he's still considered a hot property because of his throwing arm. Laker has led several leagues in assists and chances, though he also led five times in errors—the result of an over-aggressive attitude toward base-stealers. A product of California's Oxnard College, Laker has some hitting production. One-third of his hits for the Expos last year netted extra bases. Though signed as a catcher, he has also played some first base and outfield during a pro career that began in 1988. He is considered to be an excellent defensive receiver.

Major League Batting Register
	BA	G	AB	R	H	2B	3B	HR	RBI	SB
92 NL	.217	28	46	8	10	3	0	0	4	1
93 NL	.198	43	86	3	17	2	1	0	7	2
95 NL	.234	64	141	17	33	8	1	3	20	0
Life	.220	135	273	28	60	13	2	3	31	3

CURRENT PLAYERS

MARK LANGSTON

Position: Pitcher
Team: California Angels
Born: Aug. 20, 1960 San Diego, CA
Height: 6'2" **Weight:** 190 lbs.
Bats: right **Throws:** left
Acquired: Signed as a free agent, 12/89

Player Summary	
Fantasy Value	$7 to $9
Card Value	6¢ to 10¢
Will	remain a winner
Can't	avoid gophers
Expect	good strikeout ratio
Don't Expect	a K crown

Showing he was fully recovered from the lingering effects of elbow surgery, Langston regained the form that has earned him at least a dozen wins in nine different seasons. He is no longer the same power pitcher he was before the bone chips were removed. He has fine control, but he has a penchant for throwing home run balls. The four-time All-Star tries to keep batters guessing by blending his fastball with a cutter, a slider, a curve, and a straight change. He generally succeeds but would do better if he didn't have so much trouble with left-handed hitters—usually easy pickings for him. The San Jose State product kills himself with a top pickoff move and Gold Glove-caliber defensive skills. Langston teamed with lefties Jim Abbott and Chuck Finley to give the Angels a Big Three last year.

Major League Pitching Register

	W	L	ERA	G	CG	IP	H	ER	BB	SO
84 AL	17	10	3.40	35	5	225.0	188	85	118	204
85 AL	7	14	5.47	24	2	126.2	122	77	91	72
86 AL	12	14	4.85	37	9	239.1	234	129	123	245
87 AL	19	13	3.84	35	14	272.0	242	116	114	262
88 AL	15	11	3.34	35	9	261.1	222	97	110	235
89 AL	4	5	3.56	10	2	73.1	60	29	19	60
89 NL	12	9	2.39	24	6	176.2	138	47	93	175
90 AL	10	17	4.40	33	5	223.0	215	109	104	195
91 AL	19	8	3.00	34	7	246.1	190	82	96	183
92 AL	13	14	3.66	32	9	229.0	206	93	74	174
93 AL	16	11	3.20	35	7	256.1	220	91	85	196
94 AL	7	8	4.68	18	2	119.1	121	62	54	109
95 AL	15	7	4.63	31	2	200.1	212	103	64	142
Life	166	141	3.81	383	79	2648.2	2370	1120	1145	2252
3 AVE	14	10	4.07	32	4	216.1	210	98	78	170

RAY LANKFORD

Position: Outfield
Team: St. Louis Cardinals
Born: June 5, 1967 Modesto, CA
Height: 5'11" **Weight:** 180 lbs.
Bats: left **Throws:** left
Acquired: Third-round pick in 6/87 free-agent draft

Player Summary	
Fantasy Value	$19 to $22
Card Value	8¢ to 12¢
Will	swing strong bat
Can't	quit striking out
Expect	good use of speed
Don't Expect	trouble in field

Lankford can hit anywhere in the lineup. He has speed and power, and enough patience to compile a fine on-base percentage. Deployed most of last year as the Cardinals' No. 3 hitter, he waged a battle with Brian Jordan for team leadership in home runs, RBI, and stolen bases. Eventually, both became 20-20 men—Lankford for the second time in his five-year career. Although he's struck out 100 times in all five seasons, Lankford compensates when he connects. He had 24 RBI in a 13-game stretch through July 23, for example. He may not be the same speed merchant who swiped 40 bases in successive seasons in 1991 and 1992, but he succeeds on most of his steal efforts. Lankford's speed also helps him in center field, where he has quick reactions, good instincts, and outstanding range—often running down potential extra-base hits headed for the gaps. He also has a solid throwing arm. Lankford was drafted by St. Louis off the Modesto Junior College campus in California.

Major League Batting Register

	BA	G	AB	R	H	2B	3B	HR	RBI	SB
90 NL	.286	39	126	12	36	10	1	3	12	8
91 NL	.251	151	566	83	142	23	15	9	69	44
92 NL	.293	153	598	87	175	40	6	20	86	42
93 NL	.238	127	407	64	97	17	3	7	45	14
94 NL	.267	109	416	89	111	25	5	19	57	11
95 NL	.277	132	483	81	134	35	2	25	82	24
Life	.268	711	2596	416	695	150	32	83	351	143
3 AVE	.263	143	512	93	135	31	4	21	73	19

CURRENT PLAYERS

MIKE LANSING

Position: Second base
Team: Montreal Expos
Born: April 3, 1968 Rawlins, WY
Height: 6′ **Weight:** 175 lbs.
Bats: right **Throws:** right
Acquired: Purchased from Miami (independent team), 9/91

Player Summary
Fantasy Value	$9 to $11
Card Value	4¢ to 6¢
Will	show some pop
Can't	cut strikeouts
Expect	solid defense
Don't Expect	homer barrage

If he were a better hitter, Lansing could contend for league leadership in stolen bases. But the patience he showed in two previous years declined in 1995. Lansing had a strikeout-to-walk ratio of more than 2-to-1. That may be OK for a pitcher but not for a second baseman who doesn't reach double-digits in homers. Effective against righties and lefties, he netted extra bases on more than one-third of his hits but fans too frequently to hit near the top of the lineup. That negates his basestealing potential, which is considerable. His speed also helps him fatten his average with bunts and infield hits. He'd be a good hit-and-run man if he made better contact. The Wichita State product, previously used as a three-position utility player, has settled in as an everyday second baseman. His speed gives him good range and helps him turn the double play. Lansing has quick reactions, soft hands, and a strong throwing arm. He made only a handful of errors last year. Lansing began his pro career with the independent Miami Miracle in 1990.

Major League Batting Register
	BA	G	AB	R	H	2B	3B	HR	RBI	SB
93 NL	.287	141	491	64	141	29	1	3	45	23
94 NL	.266	106	394	44	105	21	2	5	35	12
95 NL	.255	127	467	47	119	30	2	10	62	27
Life	.270	374	1352	155	365	80	5	18	142	62
3 AVE	.269	144	524	60	141	31	2	7	55	23

BARRY LARKIN

Position: Shortstop
Team: Cincinnati Reds
Born: April 28, 1964 Cincinnati, OH
Height: 6′ **Weight:** 185 lbs.
Bats: right **Throws:** right
Acquired: First-round pick in 6/85 free-agent draft

Player Summary
Fantasy Value	$30 to $35
Card Value	20¢ to 35¢
Will	swing potent bat
Can't	shrink spotlight
Expect	exceptional speed
Don't Expect	weak on-base mark

Shortstops are usually noted for their defense rather than offense. Larkin, however, is a notable exception. A real baseball catalyst, he contributes in every area: batting average, on-base percentage, power production, stolen bases, and fielding. A contact hitter who walks more often than he fans, Larkin always seems to be on base. And he doesn't settle for just one, finishing with a career high in steals last year. He rarely failed to complete an attempted steal. The 1995 NL MVP also started the All-Star Game for the third year in a row. He is a former Michigan All-American and U.S. Olympian. A fastball hitter who uses all fields, he can turn on the power. He ended Ozzie Smith's Gold Glove string in 1994 and has taken over as the NL's best defensive shortstop. Larkin has quick reactions, soft hands, a powerful throwing arm, and the best range of anyone in the league.

Major League Batting Register
	BA	G	AB	R	H	2B	3B	HR	RBI	SB
86 NL	.283	41	159	27	45	4	3	3	19	8
87 NL	.244	125	439	64	107	16	2	12	43	21
88 NL	.296	151	588	91	174	32	5	12	56	40
89 NL	.342	97	325	47	111	14	4	4	36	10
90 NL	.301	158	614	85	185	25	6	7	67	30
91 NL	.302	123	464	88	140	27	4	20	69	24
92 NL	.304	140	533	76	162	32	6	12	78	15
93 NL	.315	100	384	57	121	20	3	8	51	14
94 NL	.279	110	427	78	119	23	5	9	52	26
95 NL	.319	131	496	98	158	29	6	15	66	51
Life	.298	1176	4429	711	1322	222	44	102	537	239
3 AVE	.302	134	515	92	155	28	6	13	66	36

CURRENT PLAYERS

MIKE LaVALLIERE

Position: Catcher
Team: Chicago White Sox
Born: Aug. 18, 1960 Charlotte, NC
Height: 5'9" **Weight:** 210 lbs.
Bats: left **Throws:** right
Acquired: Signed as a free agent, 5/93

Player Summary
Fantasy Value	$0
Card Value	4¢ to 6¢
Will	help the defense
Can't	reach the fences
Expect	action vs. righties
Don't Expect	any speed

If not for his defense, LaValliere would not be in the big leagues. The one-time Gold Glove recipient nails about half the runners who try to steal against him, calls games well, snares potential wild pitches, and blocks the plate like a tank. His Kirby Puckett-like physique helps, but the comparisons end there. When it comes to hitting, LaValliere is lucky to see occasional action against left-handers. Never more than a singles hitter, his average dropped dramatically last summer. He hit right-handers better than platoon partner Ron Karkovice but could hardly brag about his performance. Once a good contact hitter who always had more walks than strikeouts, LaValliere went the other way last summer. When he does reach, he is a liability on the bases. He has no speed to speak of. It almost takes a triple for him to score from second base.

Major League Batting Register
	BA	G	AB	R	H	2B	3B	HR	RBI	SB
84 NL	.000	6	7	0	0	0	0	0	0	0
85 NL	.147	12	34	2	5	1	0	0	6	0
86 NL	.234	110	303	18	71	10	2	3	30	0
87 NL	.300	121	340	33	102	19	0	1	36	0
88 NL	.261	120	352	24	92	18	0	2	47	3
89 NL	.316	68	190	15	60	10	0	2	23	0
90 NL	.258	96	279	27	72	15	0	3	31	0
91 NL	.289	108	336	25	97	11	2	3	41	2
92 NL	.256	95	293	22	75	13	1	2	29	0
93 NL	.200	1	5	0	1	0	0	0	0	0
93 AL	.258	37	97	6	25	2	0	0	8	0
94 AL	.281	59	139	6	39	4	0	1	24	0
95 AL	.245	46	98	7	24	6	0	1	19	0
Life	.268	879	2473	185	663	109	5	18	294	5

PHIL LEFTWICH

Position: Pitcher
Team: California Angels
Born: May 19, 1969 Lynchburg, VA
Height: 6'5" **Weight:** 205 lbs.
Bats: right **Throws:** right
Acquired: Second-round pick in 6/90 free-agent draft

Player Summary
Fantasy Value	$0
Card Value	5¢ to 8¢
Will	seek starting berth
Can't	prevent homers
Expect	clean bill of health
Don't Expect	control trouble

Though injuries had Leftwich sidelined for most of the 1995 campaign, he returned in time to post a 2-0 record and 2.79 ERA in five Triple-A starts, then fan 10 in the opener of the Pacific Coast League playoffs. That he even pitched at all was encouraging to Leftwich, who spent the bulk of the year recovering from arthroscopic shoulder surgery. The shoulder had been bothering him the year before, but Leftwich attributed his poor record to more obvious ailments involving his foot and leg. As a rookie in 1993, he had made a fine first impression. A sinker-slider pitcher with a developing changeup, Leftwich gets outs by ground balls rather than strikeouts. Because he's usually around the plate, he has some problems keeping the ball in the park. But he doesn't put men on base with walks either. The former Radford star has the size, stamina, and strength to develop into a front-line starter if given a clean bill of health. But he faces considerable competition in his bid to regain a spot in the starting rotation.

Major League Pitching Register
	W	L	ERA	G	CG	IP	H	ER	BB	SO
93 AL	4	6	3.79	12	1	80.2	81	34	27	31
94 AL	5	10	5.68	20	1	114.0	127	72	42	67
Life	9	16	4.90	32	2	194.2	208	106	69	98

CURRENT PLAYERS

AL LEITER

Position: Pitcher
Team: Toronto Blue Jays
Born: Oct. 23, 1965 Toms River, NJ
Height: 6'3" **Weight:** 215 lbs.
Bats: left **Throws:** left
Acquired: Traded by Yankees for Jesse Barfield, 4/89

Player Summary
Fantasy Value	$6 to $8
Card Value	4¢ to 6¢
Will	become staff ace
Can't	find strike zone
Expect	ground balls
Don't Expect	more bad support

After Randy Johnson, Leiter was the American League's top southpaw power pitcher in 1995. He was also the most effective starter on the Toronto staff. Once regarded as the top prospect in the Yankee system, Leiter battled the injury bug for five years before starting to realize his potential. Between 1988 and 1993, he had two shoulder operations and a serious elbow injury. He still has occasional blister problems. The victim of poor run support last season, Leiter still managed to reach double-digits in wins for the first time in a pro career that started in 1984. He compensated for control problems by posting a nine-inning average of less than eight hits. He holds hitters to a respectable average, keeps the ball in the park, and stops half the basestealers who run. A sinker-slider pitcher who gets ground balls, Leiter also throws a curve and a changeup. He works from a three-quarters delivery.

Major League Pitching Register
	W	L	ERA	G	CG	IP	H	ER	BB	SO
87 AL	2	2	6.35	4	0	22.2	24	16	15	28
88 AL	4	4	3.92	14	0	57.1	49	25	33	60
89 AL	1	2	5.67	5	0	33.1	32	21	23	26
90 AL	0	0	0.00	4	0	6.1	1	0	2	5
91 AL	0	0	27.00	3	0	1.2	3	5	5	1
92 AL	0	0	9.00	1	0	1.1	1	1	2	0
93 AL	9	6	4.11	34	1	105.0	93	48	56	66
94 AL	6	7	5.08	20	1	111.2	125	63	65	100
95 AL	11	11	3.64	28	2	183.0	162	74	108	153
Life	33	32	4.36	113	4	522.0	490	253	309	439
3 AVE	10	9	4.23	31	2	156.1	150	73	90	126

MARK LEITER

Position: Pitcher
Team: San Francisco Giants
Born: April 13, 1963 Joliet, IL
Height: 6'3" **Weight:** 210 lbs.
Bats: right **Throws:** right
Acquired: Signed as a free agent, 4/95

Player Summary
Fantasy Value	$5 to $7
Card Value	5¢ to 8¢
Will	show good control
Can't	fan many hitters
Expect	outs on grounders
Don't Expect	runners to steal

Like his brother Al, Mark Leiter would have had a better win-loss record for 1995 had he received better run support. A full-time starter for the first time in his six-year career, Leiter became the surprise ace of the San Francisco staff in his first NL campaign. He completed more games than the rest of the rotation combined and threw his first big-league shutout. Leiter's best game, however, was a July 26 two-hitter against the Reds that featured eight strikeouts and no walks. A sinker-slider pitcher who also throws a curve and a forkball, he doesn't fan as many hitters as his brother but has much more control. Leiter does his best pitching with runners in scoring position. He also holds runners well, thanks to a quick delivery, but his defense is otherwise mediocre. Leiter's follow-through leaves him in poor fielding position. He showed no effects of his four shoulder operations last year but a recurrence is always a concern. Leiter began his career in the Baltimore system in 1983.

Major League Pitching Register
	W	L	ERA	G	S	IP	H	ER	BB	SO
90 AL	1	1	6.84	8	0	26.1	33	20	9	21
91 AL	9	7	4.21	38	1	134.2	125	63	50	103
92 AL	8	5	4.18	35	0	112.0	116	52	43	75
93 AL	6	6	4.72	27	0	106.2	111	56	44	70
94 AL	4	7	4.72	40	2	95.1	99	50	35	71
95 NL	10	12	3.82	30	7	195.2	185	83	55	129
Life	38	38	4.35	178	10	670.2	669	324	236	469
3 AVE	8	10	4.29	39	3	153.2	153	73	52	105

CURRENT PLAYERS

SCOTT LEIUS

Position: Third base
Team: Minnesota Twins
Born: Sept. 24, 1965 Yonkers, NY
Height: 6'3" **Weight:** 185 lbs.
Bats: right **Throws:** right
Acquired: 13th-round pick in 6/86 free-agent draft

Player Summary	
Fantasy Value	$2 to $4
Card Value	4¢ to 6¢
Will	play good defense
Can't	hit the long ball
Expect	patience
Don't Expect	high batting mark

While he hits for a low average, Leius contributes to the offense by showing patience at the plate and making good contact. He walks as much as he fans, boosting his on-base percentage 100 points above his batting average. He also collects two-dozen extra-base hits per year, though his 1995 home run total fell after its career-best level of the year before. Despite a game-winning homer in the 1991 World Series, Leius seldom succeeds in late-inning pressure situations or with runners in scoring position. Minnesota's middle infielders actually supplied more power last summer than the men at the corners, even though first and third are generally considered power positions. Leius still hits like the shortstop he once was. Leius has sharp reactions, good range, and superior hands, but his arm isn't as strong as it was before 1993 rotator-cuff surgery. Though he isn't a basestealer, the Concordia College product has good mobility around the bag.

Major League Batting Register

	BA	G	AB	R	H	2B	3B	HR	RBI	SB
90 AL	.240	14	25	4	6	1	0	1	4	0
91 AL	.286	109	199	35	57	7	2	5	20	5
92 AL	.249	129	409	50	102	18	2	2	35	6
93 AL	.167	10	18	4	3	0	0	0	2	0
94 AL	.246	97	350	57	86	16	1	14	49	2
95 AL	.247	117	372	51	92	16	5	4	45	2
Life	.252	476	1373	201	346	58	10	26	155	15
2 AVE	.246	134	456	69	112	20	4	12	60	3

MARK LEMKE

Position: Second base
Team: Atlanta Braves
Born: Aug. 13, 1965 Utica, NY
Height: 5'9" **Weight:** 167 lbs.
Bats: both **Throws:** right
Acquired: 27th-round pick in 6/83 free-agent draft

Player Summary	
Fantasy Value	$2 to $4
Card Value	5¢ to 8¢
Will	hit in clutch
Can't	count on speed
Expect	strong defense
Don't Expect	home run swing

After struggling with the bat for most of 1995, Lemke staged a late-season rush that coincided with his elevation from eighth to second in the Atlanta batting order, and his recovery from nagging hamstring problems. Though neither a slugger nor a speedster, he delivered numerous timely hits en route to career highs in triples and stolen bases. A contact hitter with patience, Lemke walks more than he fans. He is productive from both sides of the plate. Because of a hustling style and willingness to get dirty, he has long been a favorite of Atlanta manager Bobby Cox's. Lemke has also caught the attention of other managers, who named him the NL's top defensive second baseman in *Baseball America*. Lemke's error on May 11 was his first in 78 games. He's a top double-play man with quick reactions, good range, and an accurate arm. He's led the NL in chances, putouts, and fielding percentage.

Major League Batting Register

	BA	G	AB	R	H	2B	3B	HR	RBI	SB
88 NL	.224	16	58	8	13	4	0	0	2	0
89 NL	.182	14	55	4	10	2	1	2	10	0
90 NL	.226	102	239	22	54	13	0	0	21	0
91 NL	.234	136	269	36	63	11	2	2	23	1
92 NL	.227	155	427	38	97	7	4	6	26	0
93 NL	.252	151	493	52	124	19	2	7	49	1
94 NL	.294	104	350	40	103	15	0	3	31	0
95 NL	.253	116	399	42	101	16	5	5	38	2
Life	.247	794	2290	242	565	87	14	25	200	4
3 AVE	.267	143	478	52	128	19	3	6	45	1

CURRENT PLAYERS

CURTIS LESKANIC

Position: Pitcher
Team: Colorado Rockies
Born: April 2, 1968 Homestead, PA
Height: 6′ **Weight:** 180 lbs.
Bats: right **Throws:** right
Acquired: Third-round pick from Twins in 11/92 expansion draft

Player Summary	
Fantasy Value	$9 to $11
Card Value	5¢ to 8¢
Will	throw late heat
Can't	lay down a bunt
Expect	ground outs
Don't Expect	control trouble

Big-league managers covet hard-throwing relievers who can throw strikes. Leskanic certainly qualifies. The busiest member of the Colorado bullpen last summer, he fanned about 10 hitters per nine innings. The ratio of strikeouts to walks was a major improvement for Leskanic, a one-time minor-league strikeout king whose control problems kept him in the minors for five years. Overpowering against right-handed hitters, the young sinkerballer often worked multi-inning stints in his role as a set-up man. Considering he pitched half his games in the Coors Field bandbox, Leskanic also did a good job of keeping the ball in the park. A starter in the minors, he moved to full-time relief duty only last year. The move was a good one: Over an 11-game stretch through June 22, he had a win, three saves, and a 1.08 ERA. Because of his quick delivery, Leskanic holds runners well. He's not a bad hitter or fielder but hasn't mastered the art of bunting. Leskanic was drafted off the Louisiana State campus by the Cleveland Indians in 1989.

Major League Pitching Register

	W	L	ERA	G	S	IP	H	ER	BB	SO
93 NL	1	5	5.37	18	0	57.0	59	34	27	30
94 NL	1	1	5.64	8	0	22.1	27	14	10	17
95 NL	6	3	3.40	76	10	98.0	83	37	33	107
Life	8	9	4.31	102	10	177.1	169	85	70	154

DARREN LEWIS

Position: Outfield
Team: Chicago White Sox
Born: Aug. 28, 1967 Berkeley, CA
Height: 6′ **Weight:** 175 lbs.
Bats: right **Throws:** right
Acquired: Signed as a free agent, 12/95

Player Summary	
Fantasy Value	$9 to $11
Card Value	5¢ to 8¢
Will	rely on speed
Can't	hit ball over wall
Expect	Gold Glove defense
Don't Expect	great arm

If Lewis were a better hitter, he'd showcase his considerable speed and defensive skills. Instead, his lack of power and penchant for fanning landed him in a platoon with Thomas Howard last year. Though Lewis makes decent contact, he'd be more valuable if he waited for walks. Neither his average nor his on-base percentage justify keeping him in the lineup—let alone as the leadoff man. Lewis fattens his average with bunts and infield hits but likes to swing away. Nobody expects him to duplicate the .340 batting average he produced in Triple-A, but an on-base percentage in that neighborhood would help. He had an NL-best nine triples in 1994. A better base-stealing percentage would help too; Lewis fails too frequently for a man with his speed. He seldom fails in center field, however. He holds major-league records for chances and consecutive errorless games by an outfielder. He won a Gold Glove in 1994.

Major League Batting Register

	BA	G	AB	R	H	2B	3B	HR	RBI	SB
90 AL	.229	25	35	4	8	0	0	0	1	2
91 NL	.248	72	222	41	55	5	3	1	15	13
92 NL	.231	100	320	38	74	8	1	1	18	28
93 NL	.253	136	522	84	132	17	7	2	48	46
94 NL	.257	114	451	70	116	15	9	4	29	30
95 NL	.250	132	472	66	118	13	3	1	24	32
Life	.249	579	2022	303	503	58	23	9	135	151
3 AVE	.254	148	563	86	143	18	8	3	39	41

CURRENT PLAYERS

MARK LEWIS

Position: Infield
Team: Detroit Tigers
Born: Nov. 30, 1969 Hamilton, OH
Height: 6'1" **Weight:** 190 lbs.
Bats: right **Throws:** right
Acquired: Traded by Reds with C.J. Nitkowski and Dave Tuttle for David Wells, 11/95

Player Summary
Fantasy Value................. $2 to $4
Card Value.................... 4¢ to 6¢
Will...................... feast off lefties
Can't.................. swipe bases often
Expect...................... platoon work
Don't Expect.......... sensational glove

The continued failure of Willie Greene to stick with the Reds created an opportunity for Lewis last season. Instead of filling the utility role that had been projected for him, he contributed to a fine right-left platoon with Jeff Branson at third base. A singles hitter who murders left-handed pitching, Lewis posted a lofty on-base percentage by combining patience at the plate with his ability to make contact. Most of his extra-base hits are doubles, though Lewis once had a 17-homer campaign in Triple-A. He could be a late bloomer as a hitter. Some scouts believe that Lewis will still develop some power. Lewis doesn't steal bases or provide good range at shortstop, his original position. The former starting shortstop for Cleveland, he lost the job with erratic defense. He's much better at third, where the same range and long throws are not required. Lewis was the second player chosen in the 1988 draft.

Major League Batting Register

	BA	G	AB	R	H	2B	3B	HR	RBI	SB
91 AL	.264	84	314	29	83	15	1	0	30	2
92 AL	.264	122	413	44	109	21	0	5	30	4
93 AL	.250	14	52	6	13	2	0	1	5	3
94 AL	.205	20	73	6	15	5	0	1	8	1
95 NL	.339	81	171	25	58	13	1	3	30	0
Life	.272	321	1023	110	278	56	2	10	103	10

JIM LEYRITZ

Position: Catcher; first base
Team: New York Yankees
Born: Dec. 27, 1963 Lakewood, OH
Height: 6' **Weight:** 190 lbs.
Bats: right **Throws:** right
Acquired: Signed as a free agent, 8/85

Player Summary
Fantasy Value................. $5 to $7
Card Value.................... 4¢ to 6¢
Will................... provide good pop
Can't.................... shed utility tag
Expect................... solid clutch bat
Don't Expect.......... low on-base mark

For Leyritz, versatility is more of a curse than a blessing. His ability to catch, play first, or patrol the outfield corners makes management consider him good at several positions but great at none. That eats into the playing time of the power-hitting University of Kentucky product. In six years with the Yankees, he has never played in 100 games. But he's certainly swung the bat well. A solid clutch hitter with considerable patience, Leyritz walks often enough to push his on-base percentage 100 points higher than his batting average. When he connects, he hits with power to all fields. In 1993 and 1994, he had 31 homers and 111 RBI in 508 trips. Though Leyritz has little speed, he moves well enough to provide decent range at both infield and outfield corners. He's also a competent catcher, though he nails only 20 percent of the runners who challenge him. The last time Leyritz was a regular, he won a batting title, hitting .315 for Double-A Albany-Colonie in 1989.

Major League Batting Register

	BA	G	AB	R	H	2B	3B	HR	RBI	SB
90 AL	.257	92	303	28	78	13	1	5	25	2
91 AL	.182	32	77	8	14	3	0	0	4	0
92 AL	.257	63	144	17	37	6	0	7	26	0
93 AL	.309	95	259	43	80	14	0	14	53	0
94 AL	.265	75	249	47	66	12	0	17	58	0
95 AL	.269	77	264	37	71	12	0	7	37	1
Life	.267	434	1296	180	346	60	1	50	203	3
3 AVE	.279	96	302	50	84	15	0	15	59	0

CURRENT PLAYERS

JOSE LIMA

Position: Pitcher
Team: Detroit Tigers
Born: Sept. 30, 1972 Santiago, Dominican Republic
Height: 6'2" **Weight:** 170 lbs.
Bats: right **Throws:** right
Acquired: Signed as nondrafted free agent, 7/89

Player Summary

Fantasy Value	$1
Card Value	6¢ to 10¢
Will	take the ball
Can't	quiet lefty bats
Expect	dynamic changeup
Don't Expect	control woes

After off-season surgery to remove seven bone chips from his right elbow, Lima started last season at Class-A Lakeland, where the spring weather is warm. Promoted to Triple-A Toledo, where he pitched a 1994 no-hitter, he went 5-3 with a 3.01 ERA before Detroit added him to its rotation. Though he showed good control (two and one-half walks per nine innings), Lima was shell-shocked. He yielded too many hits and too many homers—especially to left-handed hitters, who combined to hit well over .300 against him. Lima's problem was a dramatic drop in velocity from 1992, when he led Detroit's minor-league system in strikeouts with 137 in 151 innings. When contrasted with his dazzling changeup, however, he has more than enough velocity to succeed in the majors. His Triple-A no-hitter came during a 24-inning scoreless streak that coincided with the players' strike. Similar success in Detroit would certainly cement Lima's foothold in the majors. An outgoing personality who's a champion at dominoes, he kept a "lucky" rock in his back pocket during the no-hitter.

Major League Pitching Register

	W	L	ERA	G	CG	IP	H	ER	BB	SO
94 AL	0	1	13.50	3	0	6.2	11	10	3	7
95 AL	3	9	6.11	15	0	73.2	85	50	18	37
Life	3	10	6.72	18	0	80.1	96	60	21	44

FELIPE LIRA

Position: Pitcher
Team: Detroit Tigers
Born: April 26, 1972 Miranda, Venezuela
Height: 6' **Weight:** 170 lbs.
Bats: right **Throws:** right
Acquired: Signed as a nondrafted free agent, 2/90

Player Summary

Fantasy Value	$1
Card Value	12¢ to 15¢
Will	keep ball down
Can't	be overpowering
Expect	trial as closer
Don't Expect	control trouble

A control artist who keeps the ball down, Lira found some success as a rookie with the Tigers last summer. Signed as a starter in 1990, he moved to the bullpen two years later for a one-year trial before returning to the rotation. Lira led the organization in strikeouts in 1993 and pitched a seven-inning no-hitter in 1994. That earned a promotion to Detroit, where he went 6-6 with a 4.15 ERA in 16 starts before Sparky Anderson returned Lira to the pen in late August. The manager praised Lira's ability to throw strikes, his makeup, and the movement of his above-average forkball. Anderson also predicted that Lira will have a long career. The wiry reliever yielded one hit per inning and averaged about five and one-half strikeouts per game last year. The rest of his outs usually came on ground balls. Lira's gopher-ball total should decrease as he gains experience and masters the difficult art of pitching half the schedule in a hitters' haven. A competent fielder, he has an exceptional pickoff move for a right-hander. He nailed more than half the men who challenged him.

Major League Pitching Register

	W	L	ERA	G	CG	IP	H	ER	BB	SO
95 AL	9	13	4.31	37	0	146.1	151	70	56	89
Life	9	13	4.31	37	0	146.1	151	70	56	89

CURRENT PLAYERS

NELSON LIRIANO

Position: Second base
Team: Pittsburgh Pirates
Born: June 3, 1964 Puerto Plata, Dominican Republic
Height: 5'10" **Weight:** 178 lbs.
Bats: both **Throws:** right
Acquired: Claimed from Rockies on waivers, 10/94

Player Summary
Fantasy Value	$1
Card Value	4¢ to 6¢
Will	deliver in clutch
Can't	clear walls often
Expect	hits vs. righties
Don't Expect	adequate fielding

Although he's been around the big leagues for eight years, Liriano has gotten into 100 games only once, as the regular second baseman for the 1989 Blue Jays. His versatility and pinch-hitting prowess may have worked against him, keeping him available for the late innings. An opposite-field spray hitter who's better left-handed, Liriano makes good contact. He walks almost as much as he fans but doesn't do either too often. Nor does he hit home runs or steal bases. Liriano's expertise lies in hitting with runners in scoring position. His average in the clutch is usually higher than his overall batting mark. He doesn't see much action on the field. He has bad hands and an erratic arm, negating the value of his range at second base. He is even more of a liability at shortstop and third base. On the bench or in the clubhouse, however, Liriano is a positive presence who lends experience to a young ballclub.

Major League Batting Register

	BA	G	AB	R	H	2B	3B	HR	RBI	SB
87 AL	.241	37	158	29	38	6	2	2	10	13
88 AL	.264	99	276	36	73	6	2	3	23	12
89 AL	.263	132	418	51	110	26	3	5	53	16
90 AL	.234	103	355	46	83	12	9	1	28	8
91 AL	.409	10	22	5	9	0	0	0	1	0
93 NL	.305	48	151	28	46	6	3	2	15	6
94 NL	.255	87	255	39	65	17	5	3	31	0
95 NL	.286	107	259	29	74	12	1	5	38	2
Life	.263	623	1894	263	498	85	25	21	199	57
3 AVE	.275	97	267	39	74	14	4	4	34	3

PAT LISTACH

Position: Infield; outfield
Team: Milwaukee Brewers
Born: Sept. 12, 1967 Natchitoches, LA
Height: 5'9" **Weight:** 170 lbs.
Bats: right **Throws:** right
Acquired: Fifth-round pick in 6/88 free-agent draft

Player Summary
Fantasy Value	$2 to $4
Card Value	5¢ to 8¢
Will	show some speed
Can't	reach base often
Expect	decent fielding
Don't Expect	extra-base hits

The more Listach plays, the more his 1992 Rookie of the Year Award reeks of highway robbery. Kenny Lofton, who also merited it, has blossomed into an MVP contender, while Listach has had a chronic case of the sophomore jinx. A .290 hitter with 54 steals as a shortstop in 1992, Listach has become a weak-hitting baseball nomad. Equally inept against both righties and lefties, he almost never collects an extra-base hit. An average of more than two strikeouts per walk hasn't helped. The Arizona State product spent most of his time last year at second, but also saw considerable service at shortstop and center field. He still has some speed but doesn't reach often enough to approach his 1992 stolen-base total. In fairness to Listach, his fast fall from stardom was probably accelerated by injuries. He's had knee surgery and back and hamstring problems. That doesn't stop Listach from playing good defense, however. He has great range and a strong arm, but all that moving around hasn't helped his psyche.

Major League Batting Register

	BA	G	AB	R	H	2B	3B	HR	RBI	SB
92 AL	.290	149	579	93	168	19	6	1	47	54
93 AL	.244	98	356	50	87	15	1	3	30	18
94 AL	.296	16	54	8	16	3	0	0	2	2
95 AL	.219	101	334	35	73	8	2	0	25	13
Life	.260	364	1323	186	344	45	9	4	104	87
2 AVE	.231	106	366	45	85	12	2	2	29	16

CURRENT PLAYERS

SCOTT LIVINGSTONE

Position: Third base; first base
Team: San Diego Padres
Born: July 15, 1965 Dallas, TX
Height: 6' **Weight:** 190 lbs.
Bats: left **Throws:** right
Acquired: Traded by Tigers for Gene Harris, 5/94

Player Summary	
Fantasy Value	$1
Card Value	4¢ to 6¢
Will	hit righties
Can't	reach on walk
Expect	solid average
Don't Expect	accurate arm

The line-drive stroke that earned Livingstone All-American honors at Texas A&M resurfaced last summer. Moving across the diamond from his original position at third base, he formed a perfect platoon partner for righty-hitting first baseman Eddie Williams. A singles hitter without much power or patience, Livingstone specializes in making contact and hitting to all fields. He doesn't walk or strike out very often, leaving him with an on-base percentage only about 40 points above his batting average. But he does hit. He delivered the first .300 season of his big-league career and his second as a pro. Livingstone, who also filled in at second and third, can pinch-hit when he's not in the lineup. He hits well in clutch situations, though he's still searching for his vanished collegiate power stroke. Because of his erratic arm and limited range, Livingstone is better at first than at third. But his best position could be DH, his assignment during his college days.

Major League Batting Register

	BA	G	AB	R	H	2B	3B	HR	RBI	SB
91 AL	.291	44	127	19	37	5	0	2	11	2
92 AL	.282	117	354	43	100	21	0	4	46	1
93 AL	.293	98	304	39	89	10	2	2	39	1
94 AL	.217	15	23	0	5	1	0	0	1	0
94 NL	.272	57	180	11	49	12	1	2	10	2
95 NL	.337	99	196	26	66	15	0	5	32	2
Life	.292	430	1184	138	346	64	3	15	139	8
3 AVE	.295	104	270	28	80	15	1	3	30	2

GRAEME LLOYD

Position: Pitcher
Team: Milwaukee Brewers
Born: April 9, 1967 Victoria, Australia
Height: 6'7" **Weight:** 215 lbs.
Bats: left **Throws:** left
Acquired: Traded by Phillies for John Trisler, 12/92

Player Summary	
Fantasy Value	$1 to $3
Card Value	4¢ to 6¢
Will	answer calls often
Can't	strike batters out
Expect	solid pickoff move
Don't Expect	lefties to hit

A tall Australian who stifles southpaw hitters, Lloyd has spent his three big-league summers working as a set-up man. He yields less hits than innings but has occasional problems preventing the long ball. Lloyd leans on a three-pitch arsenal that includes a sinking fastball, a curve, and a changeup. Not a power pitcher, he tries to get ground-ball outs. Though generally effective against first batters, he has first-pitch problems with many of the hitters he faces. A rubber-armed lefty who can work often, Lloyd missed his third straight year of 40-plus appearances because of a finger injury that disabled him in August. He helps his own cause with solid fielding and a quick pickoff move. Few runners challenge him. A closer during his minor-league tenure in the Toronto system, Lloyd reached double-digits in saves twice. He saved 38 games over a two-year span in 1991 and 1992, convincing the Phillies to make him a Rule 5 draft selection. One day later, however, Lloyd was dealt to the Brewers. He figures to remain in middle relief.

Major League Pitching Register

	W	L	ERA	G	S	IP	H	ER	BB	SO
93 AL	3	4	2.83	55	0	63.2	64	20	13	31
94 AL	2	3	5.17	43	3	47.0	49	27	15	31
95 AL	0	5	4.50	33	4	32.0	28	16	8	13
Life	5	12	3.97	131	7	142.2	141	63	36	75
3 AVE	2	5	4.13	51	3	55.1	55	25	14	30

CURRENT PLAYERS

ESTEBAN LOAIZA

Position: Pitcher
Team: Pittsburgh Pirates
Born: Dec. 31, 1971 Tijuana, Mexico
Height: 6'4" **Weight:** 190 lbs.
Bats: right **Throws:** right
Acquired: Signed as a nondrafted free agent, 3/91

Player Summary	
Fantasy Value	$2 to $4
Card Value	10¢ to 15¢
Will	find strike zone
Can't	hold baserunners
Expect	to learn for future
Don't Expect	control problems

A power pitcher with good control, Loaiza jumped directly from the Double-A level into the Pittsburgh rotation. Though still perfecting his slider, the svelte right-hander has the size and strength to become a standout starter. His fastball has been timed at 95 mph, and his changeup and curve keep hitters guessing. Inexperience and inconsistency hurt Loaiza last year, when he yielded too many hits and too many homers to prevent his ERA from ballooning to unacceptable levels. He fanned less than five hitters per nine innings—well below his minor-league average—and had more trouble with right-handed hitters than against lefties. His only complete game came on July 9, when he beat the Mets, 6-3. Loaiza previously pitched the first seven innings of a 1-0 win at Montreal on June 25. In that game, he walked one, fanned one, and kept the ball down, getting lots of ground outs. A one-time catcher who pitched in Tijuana summer leagues, Loaiza is learning on the job. Though hitters have trouble picking up his pitches, he hasn't mastered the art of getting by without his best stuff. He also needs more work on his pickoff move.

Major League Pitching Register

	W	L	ERA	G	CG	IP	H	ER	BB	SO
95 NL	8	9	5.16	32	1	172.2	205	99	55	85
Life	8	9	5.16	32	1	172.2	205	99	55	85

KEITH LOCKHART

Position: Second base; third base
Team: Kansas City Royals
Born: Nov. 10, 1964 Whittier, CA
Height: 5'10" **Weight:** 170 lbs.
Bats: left **Throws:** right
Acquired: Signed as a minor-league free agent, 11/94

Player Summary	
Fantasy Value	$2 to $4
Card Value	10¢ to 15¢
Will	show some power
Can't	hit left-handers
Expect	contact hitting
Don't Expect	shaky fielding

During a pro career that started in 1986, Lockhart has played all nine positions. He's best at second, his original spot, but also acquits himself well at third. A 20-20 man in the minors, he contributes surprising speed and power for a middle infielder of his size. Primarily a platoon player last year, he hit more than .300 against right-handed pitching but barely exceeded his weight against southpaws. His leadoff homer at Boston on July 17 helped the Royals to a 4-3 victory and climaxed a 21-game hot streak that featured a .414 batting average. Though he's a contact hitter who seldom walks or fans, Lockhart connects for extra bases on nearly one-third of his hits. He's also a high-percentage basestealer. He led Class-A Midwest League third basemen in double plays in 1987 and Triple-A American Association second basemen in chances, putouts, and assists two years later. His high average last season was no surprise: Lockhart had four .300 seasons in the minors before San Diego gave him his first look at big-league pitching in 1994. He started his career in the Cincinnati organization.

Major League Batting Register

	BA	G	AB	R	H	2B	3B	HR	RBI	SB
94 NL	.209	27	43	4	9	0	0	2	6	1
95 AL	.321	94	274	41	88	19	3	6	33	8
Life	.306	121	317	45	97	19	3	8	39	9

CURRENT PLAYERS

KENNY LOFTON

Position: Outfield
Team: Cleveland Indians
Born: May 31, 1967 East Chicago, IN
Height: 6' **Weight:** 180 lbs.
Bats: left **Throws:** left
Acquired: Traded by Astros with Dave Rohde for Willie Blair and Eddie Taubensee, 12/91

Player Summary	
Fantasy Value	$35 to $40
Card Value	60¢ to $1.00
Will	drive rivals crazy
Can't	handle all lefties
Expect	spectacular defense
Don't Expect	few steals

The stats tell all: In 1994, Lofton led the AL in hits, singles, and steals while finishing second in at bats, runs, leadoff on-base percentage, batting average against right-handers, and bunts in play. He was third in triples. Lofton's credentials include four stolen-base crowns and two All-Star appearances. Hamstring problems and the strike-shortened season lowered his numbers last year but hardly tarnished his star. On July 8, he had two triples, two RBI, two runs scored, and a steal of home in a 7-3 win over Seattle. His 3-for-5 performance on Aug. 1 included a bunt single, a double, and an outfield assist. A better hitter against righties, Lofton is no automatic out against southpaws. He hit .331 against lefties in '94, though that figure fell sharply last summer. He also fanned more than he walked for the second straight year. That damaged his on-base percentage. Nothing hurt the Gold Glover in center, however, where his exceptional range, leaps, and dives have become legend.

Major League Batting Register

	BA	G	AB	R	H	2B	3B	HR	RBI	SB
91 NL	.203	20	74	9	15	1	0	0	0	2
92 AL	.285	148	576	96	164	15	8	5	42	66
93 AL	.325	148	569	116	185	28	8	1	42	70
94 AL	.349	112	459	105	160	32	9	12	57	60
95 AL	.310	118	481	93	149	22	13	7	53	54
Life	.312	546	2159	419	673	98	38	25	194	252
3 AVE	.329	146	586	123	193	33	12	9	61	72

TONY LONGMIRE

Position: Outfield
Team: Philadelphia Phillies
Born: Aug. 12, 1968 Vallejo, CA
Height: 6'1" **Weight:** 202 lbs.
Bats: left **Throws:** right
Acquired: Traded by Pirates with Wes Chamberlain and Julio Peguero for Carmelo Martinez, 9/90

Player Summary	
Fantasy Value	$1 to $3
Card Value	5¢ to 8¢
Will	pinch-hit
Can't	avoid Ks
Expect	some drama
Don't Expect	strong arm

Before a sore left wrist sent him to the DL Aug. 8, Longmire built up a reputation as a solid sub and pinch hitter with a flair for the dramatic. On June 15, his three-run pinch homer with two outs in the ninth helped the Phillies beat Houston, 4-2. Another late pinch homer with two men on beat Pittsburgh, 6-4, and landed in a level of Veterans Stadium untouched since Fred McGriff reached the same seats during the 1993 NL Championship Series. Not usually a power-hitter, Longmire reached double-digits in homers only once in a pro career that began in the Pittsburgh system in 1986. He never met a fastball he didn't like. But he hasn't learned to swing only at the ones he can hit. Longmire fans too frequently—a career-long problem—and doesn't walk enough to post a solid on-base average. His fielding may preclude the possibility of regular duty. He doesn't throw well enough for right, provide the range needed for center, or have the soft hands necessary for decent defense in left. He'd be great as a designated hitter.

Major League Batting Register

	BA	G	AB	R	H	2B	3B	HR	RBI	SB
93 NL	.231	11	13	1	3	0	0	0	1	0
94 NL	.237	69	139	10	33	11	0	0	17	2
95 NL	.356	59	104	21	37	7	0	3	19	1
Life	.285	139	256	32	73	18	0	3	37	3

CURRENT PLAYERS

JAVIER LOPEZ

Position: Catcher
Team: Atlanta Braves
Born: Nov. 5, 1970 Ponce, PR
Height: 6'3" **Weight:** 185 lbs.
Bats: right **Throws:** right
Acquired: Signed as a free agent, 11/87

Player Summary
Fantasy Value	$10 to $13
Card Value	12¢ to 20¢
Will	deliver dramatic hits
Can't	notch walks
Expect	a solid average
Don't Expect	Gold Gloves

Lopez emerged as a star in his second big-league season. The first Atlanta catcher to hit .300 since Joe Torre in 1966, Lopez did his best hitting last year with runners in scoring position. While splitting time behind the plate with veteran Charlie O'Brien, Lopez hit well over .300 against right-handers at home and on the road. He also showed more patience at the plate, reducing his ratio of strikeouts to walks from its rookie-year level of 4-to-1. But Lopez still walks so rarely that his on-base percentage is only 30 points higher than his batting average. His performance against left-handed pitchers also should be better. Though he's still learning, he has made major strides in his defense. His game-calling has improved to the point where Atlanta pitchers no longer complain about throwing to him. Missed signs and mound meetings were once Lopez trademarks. He is the owner of a strong arm. His mechanics are better, but he sometimes fails to make the weight-shifts required to get his body in front of wild pitches.

Major League Batting Register
	BA	G	AB	R	H	2B	3B	HR	RBI	SB
92 NL	.375	9	16	3	6	2	0	0	2	0
93 NL	.375	8	16	1	6	1	1	1	2	0
94 NL	.245	80	277	27	68	9	0	13	35	0
95 NL	.315	100	333	37	105	11	4	14	51	0
Life	.288	197	642	68	185	23	5	28	90	0
2 AVE	.280	113	382	40	107	13	2	17	53	0

JOHN MABRY

Position: First base; outfield
Team: St. Louis Cardinals
Born: Oct. 17, 1970 Wilmington, DE
Height: 6'4" **Weight:** 195 lbs.
Bats: left **Throws:** right
Acquired: Sixth-round pick in 6/91 free-agent draft

Player Summary
Fantasy Value	$8 to $10
Card Value	8¢ to 12¢
Will	hit line drives
Can't	find a position
Expect	contact hitting
Don't Expect	signs of speed

The free-agent departure of Gregg Jefferies opened the door for Mabry in St. Louis last summer. He responded with a quick bat, especially on the artificial turf of Busch Stadium. A contact hitter with some power, he collected more than two-dozen extra-base hits in limited playing time. Though used mainly against right-handers, he'll probably earn more playing time against lefties as he gains experience. He went 5-for-11 in the Dodger series that ended June 21 and 9-for-13 during a Colorado weekend series that ended Aug. 27. He also had several four-hit games. Though there's little doubt about his bat, finding a position could be the key to Mabry's future. He spent most of his rookie year at first base, where his powerful throwing arm was wasted. Also used in the outfield corners, he's best in right, where a shotgun is handy. Mabry doesn't have the speed or range for center, however. With Wade Boggs the exception, few players hit first or second unless they're accomplished basestealers. Because of his ability to get on base, Mabry could soon join that select group.

Major League Batting Register
	BA	G	AB	R	H	2B	3B	HR	RBI	SB
94 NL	.304	6	23	2	7	3	0	0	3	0
95 NL	.307	129	388	35	119	21	1	5	41	0
Life	.307	135	411	37	126	24	1	5	44	0

CURRENT PLAYERS

MIKE MACFARLANE

Position: Catcher
Team: Boston Red Sox
Born: April 12, 1964 Stockton, CA
Height: 6'1" **Weight:** 200 lbs.
Bats: right **Throws:** right
Acquired: Signed as a free agent, 4/95

Player Summary
Fantasy Value	$8 to $10
Card Value	4¢ to 6¢
Will	hit lefties hard
Can't	run on bad knees
Expect	extra-base hits
Don't Expect	flawless defense

The marriage of Macfarlane's power and Fenway Park's Green Monster seemed like a good idea. But the Red Sox began to have doubts after he staggered through a first-half slump. Though his play improved over the last three months, he was sluggish against right-handers all season. Though he usually hits them better than lefties, he had trouble hitting his weight against right-handers in 1995. Manager Kevin Kennedy even resorted to lifting Macfarlane for Bill Haselman against tougher pitchers. Macfarlane draws enough bases on balls to push his on-base percentage about 100 points higher than his batting average. A fastball hitter who crowds the plate and likes to pull, he hits lefties hard. Macfarlane handles pitchers well and knows how to block the plate but has trouble snaring pitches in the dirt. His throwing is solid: He nailed 35 percent of the runners who tried to steal against him last summer.

Major League Batting Register

	BA	G	AB	R	H	2B	3B	HR	RBI	SB
87 AL	.211	8	19	0	4	1	0	0	3	0
88 AL	.265	70	211	25	56	15	0	4	26	0
89 AL	.223	69	157	13	35	6	0	2	19	0
90 AL	.255	124	400	37	102	24	4	6	58	1
91 AL	.277	84	267	34	74	18	2	13	41	1
92 AL	.234	129	402	51	94	28	3	17	48	1
93 AL	.273	117	388	55	106	27	0	20	67	2
94 AL	.255	92	314	53	80	17	3	14	47	1
95 AL	.225	115	364	45	82	18	1	15	51	2
Life	.251	808	2522	313	633	154	13	91	360	8
3 AVE	.251	125	413	60	104	24	2	19	64	2

GREG MADDUX

Position: Pitcher
Team: Atlanta Braves
Born: April 14, 1966 San Angelo, TX
Height: 6' **Weight:** 170 lbs.
Bats: right **Throws:** right
Acquired: Signed as a free agent, 12/92

Player Summary
Fantasy Value	$30 to $35
Card Value	80¢ to $1.50
Will	pursue Cy Young
Can't	hold runners close
Expect	Cooperstown future
Don't Expect	ball to leave park

Before Maddux did it in 1994 and 1995, no NL right-hander had posted ERAs of less than 1.80 two years in a row since 1915. And no pitcher had ever won four straight Cy Young Awards. Maddux will throw any of his five pitches (sinker, slider, cut fastball, curve, circle change) on any count. He rarely misses a turn, and he has led the league in ERA and complete games three years in a row, and wins and shutouts two straight years. The only thing he doesn't do brilliantly is hold runners close. The four-time All-Star just missed a no-hitter last year when Jeff Bagwell hit an eighth-inning homer (the only hit) on May 28. Maddux also had a streak of 51 straight innings without a walk. His Sept. 16 win at Cincinnati was his 17th straight on the road, a record. He has never yielded more than two homers in a game. A good hitter and bunter, Maddux is a Gold Glove fielder.

Major League Pitching Register

	W	L	ERA	G	CG	IP	H	ER	BB	SO
86 NL	2	4	5.52	6	1	31.0	44	19	11	20
87 NL	6	14	5.61	30	1	155.2	181	97	74	101
88 NL	18	8	3.18	34	9	249.0	230	88	81	140
89 NL	19	12	2.95	35	7	238.1	222	78	82	135
90 NL	15	15	3.46	35	8	237.0	242	91	71	144
91 NL	15	11	3.35	37	7	263.0	232	98	66	198
92 NL	20	11	2.18	35	9	268.0	201	65	70	199
93 NL	20	10	2.36	36	8	267.0	228	70	52	197
94 NL	16	6	1.56	25	10	202.0	150	35	31	156
95 NL	19	2	1.63	28	10	209.2	147	38	23	181
Life	150	93	2.88	301	70	2120.2	1877	679	561	1471
3 AVE	21	7	1.85	34	11	262.1	202	54	41	207

CURRENT PLAYERS

MIKE MADDUX

Position: Pitcher
Team: Boston Red Sox
Born: Aug. 27, 1961 Dayton, OH
Height: 6'2" **Weight:** 180 lbs.
Bats: left **Throws:** right
Acquired: Signed as a free agent, 4/95

Player Summary	
Fantasy Value	$2 to $4
Card Value	4¢ to 6¢
Will	vex righties
Can't	emulate Greg
Expect	bullpen duty
Don't Expect	poor control

The last name may be the same but the results are different. Greg Maddux's older brother Mike has had more of a struggle than his sibling. Primarily a middle reliever, Maddux had made only 37 starts in nine years before the Red Sox added three to that total last summer. Like his brother, Maddux has excellent control. But he doesn't have the same success against left-handed hitters or the same ability to work out of jams. He is a journeyman who pitched for four clubs before Boston. Mixing a fastball, a slider, a curve, and a changeup, he tries to get grounders by keeping the ball down. On the rare occasion when everything works, Maddux can be brilliant. His 1995 highlight was a five-inning stint of perfect pitching against the Yankees in late summer. He has trouble stranding inherited runners and controlling the running game.

Major League Pitching Register

	W	L	ERA	G	S	IP	H	ER	BB	SO
86 NL	3	7	5.42	16	0	78.0	88	47	34	44
87 NL	2	0	2.65	7	0	17.0	17	5	5	15
88 NL	4	3	3.76	25	0	88.2	91	37	34	59
89 NL	1	3	5.15	16	1	43.2	52	25	14	26
90 NL	0	1	6.53	11	0	20.2	24	15	4	11
91 NL	7	2	2.46	64	5	98.2	78	27	27	57
92 NL	2	2	2.37	50	5	79.2	71	21	24	60
93 NL	3	8	3.60	58	5	75.0	67	30	27	57
94 NL	2	1	5.11	27	2	44.0	45	25	13	32
95 NL	1	0	9.00	8	0	9.0	14	9	3	4
95 AL	4	1	3.61	36	1	89.2	86	36	15	65
Life	29	28	3.87	318	19	644.0	633	277	200	430
3 AVE	4	4	4.20	49	3	82.1	81	39	22	60

DAVE MAGADAN

Position: Third base; first base
Team: Houston Astros
Born: Sept. 30, 1962 Tampa, FL
Height: 6'3" **Weight:** 195 lbs.
Bats: left **Throws:** right
Acquired: Signed as a free agent, 4/95

Player Summary	
Fantasy Value	$2 to $4
Card Value	4¢ to 6¢
Will	wait for pitch
Can't	count on speed
Expect	walks
Don't Expect	run production

Because he has no power or speed, Magadan has been a backup for most of his career in the majors. Only four times has he played in 100 games and only twice more than 130. He's most valuable playing first or third against right-handed pitchers or pinch-hitting. Magadan is an expert at waiting for walks. A good contact man, he walks considerably more than he fans, pushing his on-base percentage—one of the league's best—more than 100 points above his batting average. Magadan won't steal when he reaches, but he always finds a way to get on. He spent most of last year in a platoon with Craig Shipley at Houston's hot corner. Magadan also spent some time at first. He's better at first because of his lack of a great arm. The former Alabama All-American and Golden Spikes Award winner is good at turning the 3-6-3 double play. He is a cousin of Seattle pilot Lou Piniella.

Major League Batting Register

	BA	G	AB	R	H	2B	3B	HR	RBI	SB
86 NL	.444	10	18	3	8	0	0	0	3	0
87 NL	.318	85	192	21	61	13	1	3	24	0
88 NL	.277	112	314	39	87	15	0	1	35	0
89 NL	.286	127	374	47	107	22	3	4	41	1
90 NL	.328	144	451	74	148	28	6	6	72	2
91 NL	.258	124	418	58	108	23	0	4	51	1
92 NL	.283	99	321	33	91	9	1	3	28	1
93 NL	.286	66	227	22	65	12	0	4	29	0
93 AL	.259	71	228	27	59	11	0	1	21	2
94 NL	.275	74	211	30	58	7	0	1	17	0
95 NL	.313	127	348	44	109	24	0	2	51	2
Life	.290	1039	3102	398	901	164	11	29	372	9
3 AVE	.287	128	381	47	109	20	0	3	44	1

CURRENT PLAYERS

PAT MAHOMES

Position: Pitcher
Team: Minnesota Twins
Born: Aug. 9, 1970 Bryan, TX
Height: 6'4" **Weight:** 210 lbs.
Bats: right **Throws:** right
Acquired: Sixth-round pick in 6/88 free-agent draft

Player Summary	
Fantasy Value	$1
Card Value	5¢ to 8¢
Will	overpower righties
Can't	stop the long ball
Expect	unreliable control
Don't Expect	return to rotation

After leading two minor leagues in earned run average and showing flashes of brilliance as a 1994 rookie, Mahomes didn't produce the results that Minnesota expected of him last year. After starting the year as the No. 3 starter, he stumbled so badly that he was moved to the bullpen in June. The move paid dividends, since Mahomes is a rubber-armed righty who can pitch every day, even though he throws hard from his first pitch through his last. He mixes a live fastball and a sharp-breaking curve with a so-so slider and a changeup. Though he had trouble with left-handed batters, Mahomes overpowered right-handers, yielded one hit per inning, and averaged nearly seven strikeouts per nine innings. To cement his big-league future, he'll have to improve erratic control, improve his low-yield pickoff move, and stop feeding hitters a steady gopher-ball diet. Mahomes fields his position well for a big man and moves well enough to make occasional appearances as a pinch runner.

Major League Pitching Register

	W	L	ERA	G	S	IP	H	ER	BB	SO
92 AL	3	4	5.04	14	0	69.2	73	39	37	44
93 AL	1	5	7.71	12	0	37.1	47	32	16	23
94 AL	9	5	4.72	21	0	120.0	121	63	62	53
95 AL	4	10	6.37	47	3	94.2	100	67	47	67
Life	17	24	5.62	94	3	321.2	341	201	162	187
2 AVE	9	9	5.36	41	2	137.1	141	82	70	75

CANDY MALDONADO

Position: Outfield
Team: Texas Rangers
Born: Sept. 5, 1960 Humacao, PR
Height: 6' **Weight:** 195 lbs.
Bats: right **Throws:** right
Acquired: Traded by Blue Jays for a player to be named later, 8/95

Player Summary	
Fantasy Value	$1
Card Value	4¢ to 6¢
Will	hit with power
Can't	show any speed
Expect	pinch-hit duty
Don't Expect	strong defense

Webster's definition of journeyman might mention Maldonado. In the last 10 years, he's played for seven different teams—some of them twice. He hasn't been a regular since 1992; teams keep him around to pinch-hit against left-handers, back both outfield corners, or serve as a DH. Exactly half of his first 50 hits last year went for extra bases. His bat has helped six teams reach the LCS. Though he fans as often as he gets a hit, Maldonado also draws enough walks to inflate his on-base percentage. He rarely runs when he reaches, however. Maldonado's lack of speed doesn't help in the outfield. His reactions, range, and hands all are below-average.

Major League Batting Register

	BA	G	AB	R	H	2B	3B	HR	RBI	SB
81 NL	.083	11	12	0	1	0	0	0	0	0
82 NL	.000	6	4	0	0	0	0	0	0	0
83 NL	.194	42	62	5	12	1	1	1	6	0
84 NL	.268	116	254	25	68	14	0	5	28	0
85 NL	.225	121	213	20	48	7	1	5	19	1
86 NL	.252	133	405	49	102	31	3	18	85	4
87 NL	.292	118	442	69	129	28	4	20	85	8
88 NL	.255	142	499	53	127	23	1	12	68	6
89 NL	.217	129	345	39	75	23	0	9	41	4
90 AL	.273	155	590	76	161	32	2	22	95	3
91 AL	.250	86	288	37	72	15	0	12	48	4
92 AL	.272	137	489	64	133	25	4	20	66	2
93 NL	.186	70	140	8	26	5	0	3	15	0
93 AL	.247	28	81	11	20	2	0	5	20	0
94 AL	.196	42	92	14	18	5	1	5	12	1
95 AL	.263	74	190	28	50	16	0	9	30	1
Life	.254	1410	4106	498	1042	227	17	146	618	34
2 AVE	.235	91	217	25	51	13	0	9	34	1

CURRENT PLAYERS

JEFF MANTO

Position: Third base
Team: Baltimore Orioles
Born: Aug. 23, 1964 Bristol, PA
Height: 6'3" **Weight:** 210 lbs.
Bats: right **Throws:** right
Acquired: Traded by Mets for future considerations, 5/94

Player Summary	
Fantasy Value	$1 to $3
Card Value	5¢ to 8¢
Will	slam southpaws
Can't	show any speed
Expect	home run swing
Don't Expect	sloppy defense

Manto has spent most of his 11-year career in the minors. That was before he took the advice of Charlie Manuel, now Cleveland hitting coach, and became a power hitter. When Manto led the 1994 Triple-A International League in on-base percentage, total bases, home runs, and RBI, the Orioles gave him a chance. After becoming the regular third baseman May 17, Manto hit .290 with 10 homers and 22 RBI in the first month. He even tied a record with home runs in four consecutive at bats in early June. Though he couldn't maintain the pace, Manto had made his mark before hamstring problems sent him to the sidelines. The Temple University product showed a strong bat against southpaw pitching, plus the ability to collect extra-base hits. However, he struggled so much against right-handers that he wound up sharing his position with Jeff Huson. Manto can play first and third. A two-time MVP in the minors, he led several leagues in chances, assists, double plays, and fielding percentage. Manto has played every position but pitcher.

Major League Batting Register

	BA	G	AB	R	H	2B	3B	HR	RBI	SB
90 AL	.224	30	76	12	17	5	1	2	14	0
91 AL	.211	47	128	15	27	7	0	2	13	2
93 NL	.056	8	18	0	1	0	0	0	0	0
95 AL	.256	89	254	31	65	9	0	17	38	0
Life	.231	174	476	58	110	21	1	21	65	2

KIRT MANWARING

Position: Catcher
Team: San Francisco Giants
Born: July 15, 1965 Elmira, NY
Height: 5'11" **Weight:** 203 lbs.
Bats: right **Throws:** right
Acquired: Second-round pick in 6/86 free-agent draft

Player Summary	
Fantasy Value	$2 to $4
Card Value	4¢ to 6¢
Will	throw well
Can't	show speed
Expect	good glove
Don't Expect	home runs

He has no speed, little power, and not much of a batting average. But his defense is so solid that Manwaring remains one of baseball's top-ranked receivers. The one-time Gold Glove winner is a terrific handler of pitchers. He calls a great game, shifts his weight to block balls, converts foul tips into strikeouts, and makes a formidable obstacle when he guards the plate by planting his squat frame in front of the plate. The owner of a fine throwing arm, his success rate dropped from 44 percent in 1992 to 28 percent last year because San Francisco's young pitchers failed to keep runners close. He is no better than average as a hitter. However, Manwaring does have his moments at the plate. He homered twice in a 13-8 loss to Houston on July 14, for example. Normally a singles hitter who uses all fields, he fans too much to post high batting or on-base averages. Manwaring is more likely to hit a home run than steal a base.

Major League Batting Register

	BA	G	AB	R	H	2B	3B	HR	RBI	SB
87 NL	.143	6	7	0	1	0	0	0	0	0
88 NL	.250	40	116	12	29	7	0	1	15	0
89 NL	.210	85	200	14	42	4	2	0	18	2
90 NL	.154	8	13	0	2	0	1	0	1	0
91 NL	.225	67	178	16	40	9	0	0	19	1
92 NL	.244	109	349	24	85	10	5	4	26	2
93 NL	.275	130	432	48	119	15	1	5	49	1
94 NL	.250	97	316	30	79	17	1	1	29	1
95 NL	.251	118	379	21	95	15	2	4	36	1
Life	.247	660	1990	165	492	77	12	15	193	8
3 AVE	.259	133	435	38	112	19	2	4	43	1

TOM MARSH

Position: Outfield
Team: Philadelphia Phillies
Born: Dec. 27, 1965 Toledo, OH
Height: 6'2" **Weight:** 190 lbs.
Bats: right **Throws:** right
Acquired: 16th-round pick in 6/88 free-agent draft

Player Summary	
Fantasy Value	$1
Card Value	4¢ to 6¢
Will	fill a role
Can't	run too well
Expect	a strong arm
Don't Expect	a starting job

Marsh was one of the many role players utilized by the Phillies last year. A long-term member of the organization, he has been an adequate player throughout his professional career. Marsh had a .422 slugging percentage in 1995. He is an impatient hitter, waiting for only four walks last year while striking out 25 times. If he would quit swinging on so many pitches out of the strike zone, he would see better pitches to drive. He played the majority of his games in left field last year, though he also saw some action in center and right. One of the best tools that Marsh brings to the table is his fine arm. He led the Triple-A International League with 14 assists in 1994, and he led the IL in double plays in 1993. He had two assists last year in limited duty with the Phillies. He is not a speed demon, but he has enough wheels to play center field for short stretches. He does not steal many bases. Marsh holds the single-season and career marks in home runs at the University of Toledo.

Major League Batting Register

	BA	G	AB	R	H	2B	3B	HR	RBI	SB
92 NL	.200	42	125	7	25	3	2	2	16	0
94 NL	.278	8	18	3	5	1	1	0	3	0
95 NL	.294	43	109	13	32	3	1	3	15	0
Life	.246	93	252	23	62	7	4	5	34	0

AL MARTIN

Position: Outfield
Team: Pittsburgh Pirates
Born: Nov. 24, 1967 West Covina, CA
Height: 6'2" **Weight:** 210 lbs.
Bats: left **Throws:** left
Acquired: Signed as a free agent, 11/91

Player Summary	
Fantasy Value	$14 to $17
Card Value	6¢ to 10¢
Will	rip righties
Can't	stop whiffing
Expect	20-20 future
Don't Expect	strong throws

Although he has enough speed and power to reach the 20-20 club, Martin has been limited in his playing time because of his problems with left-handed pitchers. Once compared to Barry Bonds—the man he replaced as Pittsburgh's left fielder—Martin has not come close. Unlike Bonds, Martin fans far too frequently (twice per walk) to maximize his talents. He doesn't draw enough walks to post a high on-base percentage. Nor does he produce Bonds-like power. Though he hits .300 against right-handed pitching and gets extra bases on nearly one-third of his hits, Martin is a still-developing player. His baserunning needs work, as he was erased more than one-third of the time in 1995, and his defense also needs improvement. He charges balls well, but Martin's throwing is seldom strong and only occasionally accurate. He's actually looked better in center when tried there in spots. The chance to show off his speed helped him relax. Originally inked by the Braves, Martin began his pro career in 1985.

Major League Batting Register

	BA	G	AB	R	H	2B	3B	HR	RBI	SB
92 NL	.167	12	12	1	2	0	1	0	2	0
93 NL	.281	143	480	85	135	26	8	18	64	16
94 NL	.286	82	276	48	79	12	4	9	33	15
95 NL	.282	124	439	70	124	25	3	13	41	20
Life	.282	361	1207	204	340	63	16	40	140	51
3 AVE	.283	133	454	77	129	24	6	15	52	20

CURRENT PLAYERS

NORBERTO MARTIN

Position: Second base; infield
Team: Chicago White Sox
Born: Dec. 10, 1966 Santo Domingo, Dominican Republic
Height: 5'10" **Weight:** 164 lbs.
Bats: right **Throws:** right
Acquired: Signed as a nondrafted free agent, 3/84

Player Summary	
Fantasy Value	$0
Card Value	4¢ to 6¢
Will	show arm
Can't	forget to walk
Expect	fine fielding
Don't Expect	a starting spot

Martin suffered through a decade of minor-league baseball before he made a significant impact on the White Sox back in 1994. A backup at second base, shortstop, and third base, Martin also saw some playing time at the outfield corners. He has quickness and a pretty fair arm, and he is widely known around the league as a glove man. However, he does fill in adequately in the outfield when called upon. He fought Craig Grebeck for playing time for much of the last two seasons. The reason Martin didn't see more playing time is that he is a hacker at bat. He took only three bases on balls last season. His on-base average was only 12 points higher than his batting average. He also had 25 strikeouts, for an 8-1 strikeout-to-walk ratio. Martin must improve if he wants to remain in the major leagues. In 1993, he led the Triple-A American Association in at bats and hits, and he notched a .309 batting average. That year, Martin had 26 walks and 59 strikeouts.

Major League Batting Register

	BA	G	AB	R	H	2B	3B	HR	RBI	SB
93 AL	.357	8	14	3	5	0	0	0	2	0
94 AL	.275	45	131	19	36	7	1	1	16	4
95 AL	.269	72	160	17	43	7	4	2	17	5
Life	.275	125	305	39	84	14	5	3	35	9

ANGEL MARTINEZ

Position: Catcher
Team: Toronto Blue Jays
Born: Oct. 3, 1972 Villa Mella, Dominican Republic
Height: 6'4" **Weight:** 200 lbs.
Bats: left **Throws:** right
Acquired: Signed as a nondrafted free agent, 1/90

Player Summary	
Fantasy Value	$1 to $3
Card Value	12¢ to 20¢
Will	play solid defense
Can't	hit lefty pitchers
Expect	impatient at bats
Don't Expect	long-distance hits

As a rookie last year, Martinez made a handsome addition to Toronto's catching corps. Deployed exclusively against right-handed pitchers, the lefty-hitting backstop shared his spot with Lance Parrish and Randy Knorr. Martinez even contributed occasional extra-base hits. Though he fans about six times more than he walks, he maintains a decent batting average against right-handers. He adds no speed, however, and is overmatched by the league's better pitchers. His hitting should improve as he gains experience. Martinez, who started the season on the Double-A level, handled Toronto pitchers so well that the team ERA showed a marked improvement when he was behind the plate. He also nailed a healthy 40 percent of the runners who tried to steal against him. A sound defensive receiver, he snags balls in the dirt, blocks the plate well, and calls good games. His arrival convinced the Blue Jays to shelve the catching future of Carlos Delgado—now a first baseman and outfielder. Martinez was in the Class-A Florida State League in 1994, where he was tabbed as the loop's No. 8 prospect by *Baseball America*.

Major League Batting Register

	BA	G	AB	R	H	2B	3B	HR	RBI	SB
95 AL	.241	62	191	12	46	12	0	2	25	0
Life	.241	62	191	12	46	12	0	2	25	0

CURRENT PLAYERS

DAVE MARTINEZ

Position: Outfield; first base
Team: Chicago White Sox
Born: Sept. 26, 1964 New York, NY
Height: 5'10" **Weight:** 170 lbs.
Bats: left **Throws:** left
Acquired: Signed as a free agent, 4/95

Player Summary
Fantasy Value	$3 to $5
Card Value	4¢ to 6¢
Will	supply solid defense
Can't	hit homers often
Expect	pinch-hitting chores
Don't Expect	at bats vs. lefties

Martinez is one of baseball's best role players. He plays all three outfield positions well, fills in at first base, and serves as a potent pinch hitter against right-handed pitching. Known mostly for his defensive skills, Martinez enjoyed a career year as a hitter in 1995. Playing roughly half the time, he hit .300 for the first time and contributed more than 20 extra-base hits—something he hadn't done since 1992. A low-ball, fastball hitter who hits to the opposite field, Martinez sometimes surprises with his power. But he's only reached double-digits in home runs once. His basestealing days are over; however, he still runs well enough to provide fine outfield defense. He has quick reactions, great range, and good hands, while his arm is accurate. He also acquits himself so well at first that the White Sox used him there after making Frank Thomas a DH in late summer.

Major League Batting Register
	BA	G	AB	R	H	2B	3B	HR	RBI	SB
86 NL	.139	53	108	13	15	1	1	1	7	4
87 NL	.292	142	459	70	134	18	8	8	36	16
88 NL	.255	138	447	51	114	13	6	6	46	23
89 NL	.274	126	361	41	99	16	7	3	27	23
90 NL	.279	118	391	60	109	13	5	11	39	13
91 NL	.295	124	396	47	117	18	5	7	42	16
92 NL	.254	135	393	47	100	20	5	3	31	12
93 NL	.241	91	241	28	58	12	1	5	27	6
94 NL	.247	97	235	23	58	9	3	4	27	3
95 AL	.307	119	303	49	93	16	4	5	37	8
Life	.269	1143	3334	429	897	136	45	53	319	124
3 AVE	.268	121	304	39	81	14	3	5	36	6

DENNIS MARTINEZ

Position: Pitcher
Team: Cleveland Indians
Born: May 14, 1955 Granada, Nicaragua
Height: 6'1" **Weight:** 180 lbs.
Bats: right **Throws:** right
Acquired: Signed as a free agent, 12/93

Player Summary
Fantasy Value	$10 to $13
Card Value	10¢ to 15¢
Will	throw strikes
Can't	fret about age
Expect	two-digit wins
Don't Expect	gopher trouble

When he won his first nine decisions last summer, Martinez had the best start by a Cleveland pitcher since 1961. The team hardly expected such success from Martinez, whose son pitches in the Indians system. Though he lost playing time with knee problems, Martinez silenced skeptics. He is a control pitcher who throws a fastball, a slurve, and a changeup. An agile athlete, he fields his position well and keeps a close eye on the running game. The four-time All-Star once pitched a perfect game for Montreal.

Major League Pitching Register
	W	L	ERA	G	CG	IP	H	ER	BB	SO
76 AL	1	2	2.60	4	1	27.2	23	8	8	18
77 AL	14	7	4.10	42	6	166.2	157	76	64	107
78 AL	16	11	3.52	40	15	276.1	257	108	93	142
79 AL	15	16	3.66	40	18	292.1	279	119	78	132
80 AL	6	4	3.97	25	2	99.2	103	44	44	42
81 AL	14	5	3.32	25	9	179.0	173	66	62	88
82 AL	16	12	4.21	40	10	252.0	262	118	87	111
83 AL	7	16	5.53	32	4	153.0	209	94	45	71
84 AL	6	9	5.02	34	2	141.2	145	79	37	77
85 AL	13	11	5.15	33	3	180.0	203	103	63	68
86 AL	0	0	6.75	4	0	6.2	11	5	2	2
86 NL	3	6	4.59	19	1	98.0	103	50	28	63
87 NL	11	4	3.30	22	2	144.2	133	53	40	84
88 NL	15	13	2.72	34	9	235.1	215	71	55	120
89 NL	16	7	3.18	34	5	232.0	227	82	49	142
90 NL	10	11	2.95	32	7	226.0	191	74	49	156
91 NL	14	11	2.39	31	9	222.0	187	59	62	123
92 NL	16	11	2.47	32	6	226.1	172	62	60	147
93 NL	15	9	3.85	35	2	224.2	211	96	64	138
94 AL	11	6	3.52	24	7	176.2	166	69	44	92
95 AL	12	5	3.08	28	3	187.0	174	64	46	99
Life	231	176	3.60	610	120	3747.2	3601	1500	1080	2022
3 AVE	15	8	3.49	33	5	227.2	214	88	59	126

204

CURRENT PLAYERS

EDGAR MARTINEZ

Position: Third base
Team: Seattle Mariners
Born: Jan. 2, 1963 New York, NY
Height: 5'11" **Weight:** 175 lbs.
Bats: right **Throws:** right
Acquired: Signed as a free agent, 12/82

Player Summary
Fantasy Value. . . . . $25 to $30
Card Value . . . . 15¢ to 30¢
Will . . . . keep batting crown
Can't. . . . . steal bases often
Expect . . . . homers, RBI
Don't Expect. . . . . more Ks than walks

Patience pays off. After struggling for two years with shoulder, wrist, ankle, and hamstring problems, Martinez resumed the form that enabled him to win the 1992 AL batting crown. This time, he was even better. Refusing to swing at anything but strikes, he drew more than 100 walks for the first time in his career. He finished with his second batting title while ranking among the league leaders in runs, hits, slugging, and doubles. Martinez reached base nearly 50 percent of the time—an astronomical figure. A line-drive hitter with great bat speed, he crushes left-handed pitching and pounds 0-2 pitches. He nets extra bases on more than 40 percent of his hits, an amazing ratio for a batting king. An advocate of working with weights, he could also preach the value of his unorthodox batting stance. A third baseman by trade, Martinez spent most of last year as a DH—a move designed to conserve his legs.

Major League Batting Register

	BA	G	AB	R	H	2B	3B	HR	RBI	SB
87 AL	.372	13	43	6	16	5	2	0	5	0
88 AL	.281	14	32	0	9	4	0	0	5	0
89 AL	.240	65	171	20	41	5	0	2	20	2
90 AL	.302	144	487	71	147	27	2	11	49	1
91 AL	.307	150	544	98	167	35	1	14	52	0
92 AL	.343	135	528	100	181	46	3	18	73	14
93 AL	.237	42	135	20	32	7	0	4	13	0
94 AL	.285	89	326	47	93	23	1	13	51	6
95 AL	.356	145	511	121	182	52	0	29	113	4
Life	.313	797	2777	483	868	204	9	91	381	27
2 AVE	.325	144	517	101	168	45	1	25	99	6

PEDRO MARTINEZ

Position: Pitcher
Team: Montreal Expos
Born: July 25, 1971 Manoguayabo, Dominican Republic
Height: 5'11" **Weight:** 170 lbs
Bats: right **Throws:** right
Acquired: Traded by Dodgers for Delino DeShields, 11/93

Player Summary
Fantasy Value. . . . . $14 to $17
Card Value . . . . 12¢ to 20¢
Will . . . . escape tough jams
Can't. . . . . shake controversy
Expect . . . . exceptional stuff
Don't Expect. . . . . runners to steal

Good things often come in small packages. A younger, smaller version of brother Ramon, Pedro Martinez may have even more potential. After pitching eight hitless innings against the Reds in 1994, he worked nine perfect innings against the Padres last year. During his four-hit shutout at St. Louis on July 4, the Cards were baffled by his circle change while looking for his 95 mph fastball. Martinez learned the changeup from Ramon while playing catch in the backyard, and Pedro also throws a curveball. Because he's always around the plate, Martinez gives up his share of home runs. Brawls have started when he has hit the next batter after giving up a gopher. He has an unwanted reputation as a headhunter because of his penchant for pitching inside. But the style must work: Martinez is expert at working out of jams, especially with runners in scoring position. He doesn't hit or field like Ramon but he's better at freezing the running game. Martinez should be a star for years to come.

Major League Pitching Register

	W	L	ERA	G	CG	IP	H	ER	BB	SO
92 NL	0	1	2.25	2	0	8.0	6	2	1	8
93 NL	10	5	2.61	65	0	107.0	76	31	57	119
94 NL	11	5	3.42	24	1	144.2	115	55	45	142
95 NL	14	10	3.51	30	2	194.2	158	76	66	174
Life	35	21	3.25	121	3	454.1	355	164	169	443
3 AVE	14	8	3.30	44	1	176.2	139	65	65	172

CURRENT PLAYERS

RAMON MARTINEZ

Position: Pitcher
Team: Los Angeles Dodgers
Born: March 22, 1968 Santo Domingo, Dominican Republic
Height: 6'4" **Weight:** 173 lbs.
Bats: left **Throws:** right
Acquired: Signed as a free agent, 9/84

Player Summary	
Fantasy Value	$12 to $15
Card Value	6¢ to 10¢
Will	win games often
Can't	whiff 200 again
Expect	good bat
Don't Expect	flawless control

Though he once threw harder, Martinez showed last summer that he had made the transition from power to experience. He enjoyed his biggest year since 1991. He threw a 7-0 no-hitter at the Marlins July 15, but a 3-2 walk to Tommy Gregg spoiled the perfect game. Junking his breaking ball after the third inning, Martinez fooled Florida hitters with location of down and away fastballs. The former 20-game winner mixes a fastball, a slurve, and a circle change. Martinez has occasional lapses of control; he led the 1993 NL in walks. He dominates right-handed hitters and keeps the ball in the park, however. And he helps his own cause more than most pitchers. He can hit, run, field, and hold runners. Basestealers think twice before challenging him. The 1984 Dominican Olympian is no longer the pitcher who once fanned 18 hitters in one game, but he's still a solid front-line starter.

Major League Pitching Register

	W	L	ERA	G	CG	IP	H	ER	BB	SO
88 NL	1	3	3.79	9	0	35.2	27	15	22	23
89 NL	6	4	3.19	15	2	98.2	79	35	41	89
90 NL	20	6	2.92	33	12	234.1	191	76	67	223
91 NL	17	13	3.27	33	6	220.1	190	80	69	150
92 NL	8	11	4.00	25	1	150.2	141	67	69	101
93 NL	10	12	3.44	32	4	211.2	202	81	104	127
94 NL	12	7	3.97	24	4	170.0	160	75	56	119
95 NL	17	7	3.66	30	4	206.1	176	84	81	138
Life	91	63	3.48	201	33	1327.2	1166	513	509	970
3 AVE	15	10	3.70	33	5	227.1	208	94	91	150

TINO MARTINEZ

Position: First base
Team: New York Yankees
Born: Dec. 7, 1967 Tampa, FL
Height: 6'2" **Weight:** 205 lbs.
Bats: left **Throws:** left
Acquired: Traded by Mariners with Jeff Nelson and Jim Mecir for Sterling Hitchcock and Russ Davis, 12/95

Player Summary	
Fantasy Value	$20 to $25
Card Value	10¢ to 15¢
Will	continue to improve
Can't	shed Mattingly shadow
Expect	power and defense
Don't Expect	low on-base mark

The Yankees are replacing Don Mattingly with Tino Martinez. It's hard to believe Martinez was ever platooned. A better hitter against lefties, he became Seattle's top run producer during the three months Ken Griffey Jr. was idled by injury last year. Martinez walked often enough to hike his on-base percentage. He hits to all fields against right-handed pitchers, but goes up the middle against lefties. He rarely swings at the first pitch. He came to 1995 spring training 12 pounds lighter. That helped him get off to such a good start that he made the All-Star squad. A fine first baseman, Martinez knows how to charge bunts, stretch for bad throws, and work the 3-6-3 double play. While earning All-American honors at the University of Tampa, he fanned only 34 times in 636 at bats. He later played for the U.S. team that won the gold medal in 1988. Martinez was Minor League Player of the Year two years later.

Major League Batting Register

	BA	G	AB	R	H	2B	3B	HR	RBI	SB
90 AL	.221	24	68	4	15	4	0	0	5	0
91 AL	.205	36	112	11	23	2	0	4	9	0
92 AL	.257	136	460	53	118	19	2	16	66	2
93 AL	.265	109	408	48	108	25	1	17	60	0
94 AL	.261	97	329	42	86	21	0	20	61	1
95 AL	.293	141	519	92	152	35	3	31	111	0
Life	.265	543	1896	250	502	106	6	88	312	3
3 AVE	.275	135	485	70	133	31	1	27	90	0

CURRENT PLAYERS

DON MATTINGLY

Position: First base
Team: New York Yankees
Born: April 20, 1961 Evansville, IN
Height: 6' **Weight:** 192 lbs.
Bats: left **Throws:** left
Acquired: 19th-round pick in 6/79 free-agent draft

Player Summary	
Fantasy Value	$6 to $8
Card Value	50¢ to $1.00
Will	make solid contact
Can't	recapture old swing
Expect	award-winning glove
Don't Expect	few injuries

Mattingly is uncertain of his future. He has won an MVP Award and a batting title. He won his first Gold Glove in 1985 and has dominated the voting since. But he is not the player who led the AL in doubles three times, hits twice, and RBI once. Chronic back problems have sapped his power; he hit only one homer in his first 226 at bats last year before connecting for three in 14 at bats during a 27-for-60 (.450) outburst right after the All-Star break. The long-time Yankee captain was victimized by a strained hamstring and eye infection last summer. He did pass Babe Ruth on the team's doubles list July 4. Mattingly walks as much as he fans. With his glove, he reacts instinctively, charges and throws well, and turns the tough 3-6-3.

Major League Batting Register

	BA	G	AB	R	H	2B	3B	HR	RBI	SB
82 AL	.167	7	12	0	2	0	0	0	1	0
83 AL	.283	91	279	34	79	15	4	4	32	0
84 AL	.343	153	603	91	207	44	2	23	110	1
85 AL	.324	159	652	107	211	48	3	35	145	2
86 AL	.352	162	677	117	238	53	2	31	113	0
87 AL	.327	141	569	93	186	38	2	30	115	1
88 AL	.311	144	599	94	186	37	0	18	88	1
89 AL	.303	158	631	79	191	37	2	23	113	3
90 AL	.256	102	394	40	101	16	0	5	42	1
91 AL	.288	152	587	64	169	35	0	9	68	2
92 AL	.287	157	640	89	184	40	0	14	86	3
93 AL	.291	134	530	78	154	27	2	17	86	0
94 AL	.304	97	372	62	113	20	1	6	51	0
95 AL	.288	128	458	59	132	32	2	7	49	0
Life	.307	1785	7003	1007	2153	442	20	222	1099	14
3 AVE	.294	138	523	77	154	30	2	11	71	0

DERRICK MAY

Position: Outfield
Team: Houston Astros
Born: July 14, 1968 Rochester, NY
Height: 6'4" **Weight:** 205 lbs.
Bats: left **Throws:** right
Acquired: Traded by Brewers for Tommy Nevers, 7/95

Player Summary	
Fantasy Value	$4 to $6
Card Value	5¢ to 8¢
Will	hit in clutch
Can't	go for fences
Expect	solid contact
Don't Expect	strong throws

When James Mouton struggled against right-handers last summer, the Astros found him a lefty platoon partner. The son of former big leaguer Dave May, Derrick had little trouble crossing league lines since he had spent most of his career with the Cubs. A line-drive hitter with power to the gaps, May makes good contact when he swings—especially on a 3-2 count (he hit a league-high .476 in 1994). But he's also patient enough to walk as much as he fans (which is not often). Though he hits to all fields against right-handers but pulls against lefties, he's had more success against southpaws two years in a row. May has reached double-digits in homers only once in a pro career that started in 1986. He's reached double-digits in steals four times—once in the majors. May also has some problems in the outfield. His arm is weak—the result of chronic shoulder problems—and his judgement is sometimes questionable.

Major League Batting Register

	BA	G	AB	R	H	2B	3B	HR	RBI	SB
90 NL	.246	17	61	8	15	3	0	1	11	1
91 NL	.227	15	22	4	5	2	0	1	3	0
92 NL	.274	124	351	33	96	11	0	8	45	5
93 NL	.295	128	465	62	137	25	2	10	77	10
94 NL	.284	100	345	43	98	19	2	8	51	3
95 AL	.248	32	113	15	28	3	1	1	9	0
95 NL	.301	78	206	29	62	15	1	8	41	5
Life	.282	494	1563	194	441	78	6	37	237	24
3 AVE	.287	131	437	57	125	24	2	10	68	7

CURRENT PLAYERS

BRENT MAYNE

Position: Catcher
Team: Kansas City Royals
Born: April 19, 1968 Loma Linda, CA
Height: 6'1" **Weight:** 190 lbs.
Bats: left **Throws:** right
Acquired: First-round pick in 6/89 free-agent draft

Player Summary	
Fantasy Value	$1 to $3
Card Value	4¢ to 6¢
Will	call good game
Can't	hit home runs
Expect	a few doubles
Don't Expect	nailed runners

Mayne has no power, no speed, and no luck against left-handed pitchers. But he's a regular catcher because of his stalwart defense. Once forming a fine left-right platoon with Mike Macfarlane, Mayne inherited the full-time job when Macfarlane went to Boston via free agency. Not matching Macfarlane's power, Mayne did provide a better glove. A good game-caller who knows how to handle pitchers, he snares potential wild pitches and blocks the plate against incoming runners. He has nailed only 27 percent of rival baserunners over the last two seasons, however. Mayne fans twice per walk, and can't hit his weight against left-handed pitchers. Given more playing time, he reached a career high in doubles last season. Despite his shortcomings, however, he has always been popular with management because of his aggressive, hustling style of play. If the Cal State Fullerton product ever lifts that average, he could become a standout.

Major League Batting Register

	BA	G	AB	R	H	2B	3B	HR	RBI	SB
90 AL	.231	5	13	2	3	0	0	0	1	0
91 AL	.251	85	231	22	58	8	0	3	31	2
92 AL	.225	82	213	16	48	10	0	0	18	0
93 AL	.254	71	205	22	52	9	1	2	22	3
94 AL	.257	46	144	19	37	5	1	2	20	1
95 AL	.251	110	307	23	77	18	1	1	27	0
Life	.247	399	1113	104	275	50	3	8	119	6
2 AVE	.252	97	275	24	69	15	1	2	26	2

KIRK McCASKILL

Position: Pitcher
Team: Chicago White Sox
Born: April 9, 1961 Kapuskasing, Ontario
Height: 6'1" **Weight:** 196 lbs.
Bats: right **Throws:** right
Acquired: Signed as a free agent, 12/91

Player Summary	
Fantasy Value	$2 to $4
Card Value	4¢ to 6¢
Will	fight for spot
Can't	rely on reputation
Expect	top pickoff move
Don't Expect	rotation return

McCaskill must be hanging on with experience instead of performance. Once a stalwart starter, he's had two dreadful years in the three seasons since his conversion to the bullpen. Last year was one of them. He yields too many hits and too many homers to keep his ERA at respectable levels. The only thing McCaskill did well in 1995 was strand inherited runners. He permitted the league to hit .300 against him, and blew three of his five save opportunities. A curveball specialist who also throws a fastball, a slider, and a changeup, McCaskill needs location to be effective. When he has it, ground balls result. The former All-American hockey player at the University of Vermont is an agile athlete who fields his position well. Next to Armando Reynoso, McCaskill may rank as the right-hander with the game's best pickoff move. Few runners test it.

Major League Pitching Register

	W	L	ERA	G	S	IP	H	ER	BB	SO
85 AL	12	12	4.70	30	0	189.2	189	99	64	102
86 AL	17	10	3.36	34	0	246.1	207	92	92	202
87 AL	4	6	5.67	14	0	74.2	84	47	34	56
88 AL	8	6	4.31	23	0	146.1	155	70	61	98
89 AL	15	10	2.93	32	0	212.0	202	69	59	107
90 AL	12	11	3.25	29	0	174.1	161	63	72	78
91 AL	10	19	4.26	30	0	177.2	193	84	66	71
92 AL	12	13	4.18	34	0	209.0	193	97	95	109
93 AL	4	8	5.23	30	2	113.2	144	66	36	65
94 AL	1	4	3.42	40	3	52.2	51	20	22	37
95 AL	6	4	4.89	55	2	81.0	97	44	33	50
Life	101	103	4.03	351	7	1677.1	1676	751	634	975
3 AVE	4	6	4.63	49	3	92.2	108	48	35	58

CURRENT PLAYERS

BEN McDONALD

Position: Pitcher
Team: Baltimore Orioles
Born: Nov. 24, 1967 Baton Rouge, LA
Height: 6'7" **Weight:** 212 lbs.
Bats: right **Throws:** right
Acquired: First-round pick in 6/89 free-agent draft

Player Summary	
Fantasy Value	$11 to $14
Card Value	8¢ to 12¢
Will	regain rotation role
Can't	realize his promise
Expect	clean bill of health
Don't Expect	relief work

At age 28, McDonald has yet to show the potential that made him an All-American, College Player of the Year, Golden Spikes Award winner, and U.S. Olympian. The towering right-hander, who spent much of last summer sidelined with shoulder tendinitis, has never won more than 14 games in a season. And his earned run averages have lived up to their name—average. Since he has good control and an extensive repertoire, the former Louisiana State star should have better results. McDonald's arsenal includes two curves plus a forkball, a changeup, and a hybrid pitch that's part slider and part cut-fastball. When he keeps the ball down, he gets ground-ball outs. When he doesn't, he gives up home runs. He has pitched two one-hitters, the latest in 1994. Though he's a good fielder—especially for a big man—his slow delivery gives potential basestealers a head-start. McDonald was the first player chosen in the 1989 amateur draft.

Major League Pitching Register

	W	L	ERA	G	CG	IP	H	ER	BB	SO
89 AL	1	0	8.59	6	0	7.1	8	7	4	3
90 AL	8	5	2.43	21	3	118.2	88	32	35	65
91 AL	6	8	4.84	21	1	126.1	126	68	43	85
92 AL	13	13	4.24	35	4	227.0	213	107	74	158
93 AL	13	14	3.39	34	7	220.1	185	83	86	171
94 AL	14	7	4.06	24	5	157.1	151	71	54	94
95 AL	3	6	4.16	14	1	80.0	67	37	38	62
Life	58	53	3.89	155	21	937.0	838	405	334	638
3 AVE	12	10	3.80	28	5	177.1	158	75	68	124

JACK McDOWELL

Position: Pitcher
Team: New York Yankees
Born: Jan. 16, 1966 Van Nuys, CA
Height: 6'5" **Weight:** 179 lbs.
Bats: right **Throws:** right
Acquired: Traded by White Sox for Keith Heberling and Lyle Mouton, 12/94

Player Summary	
Fantasy Value	$16 to $19
Card Value	12¢ to 20¢
Will	remain big winner
Can't	avoid gophers
Expect	solid second half
Don't Expect	long-lived slumps

Down the stretch, baseball has few better pitchers than McDowell. In 1995, his first year with the Yankees, he started slowly after inheriting the staff ace role vacated by the injured Jimmy Key. Later, McDowell was fined $5,000 for making an obscene gesture to fans. But his three-hit shutout of Baltimore on Aug. 7, started a stretch run that enabled him to win at least 15 games for the fourth time in the last five years. The former Stanford standout uses his forkball to set up his fastball and curve. When he's right, McDowell gets better as the game goes on. He gets his outs on grounders and strikeouts. McDowell is prone to gophers, however, and attempting to freeze the running game also gives him problems. Otherwise, he is known for strong finishes. He's led the AL in starts and complete games twice, and wins and shutouts once each. McDowell won the Cy Young Award in 1993, one of his three All-Star years.

Major League Pitching Register

	W	L	ERA	G	CG	IP	H	ER	BB	SO
87 AL	3	0	1.93	4	0	28.0	16	6	6	15
88 AL	5	10	3.97	26	1	158.2	147	70	68	84
90 AL	14	9	3.82	33	4	205.0	189	87	77	165
91 AL	17	10	3.41	35	15	253.2	212	96	82	191
92 AL	20	10	3.18	34	13	260.2	247	92	75	178
93 AL	22	10	3.37	34	10	256.2	261	96	69	158
94 AL	10	9	3.73	25	6	181.0	186	75	42	127
95 AL	15	10	3.93	30	8	217.2	211	95	78	157
Life	106	68	3.56	221	57	1561.1	1469	617	497	1075
3 AVE	18	11	3.67	34	9	252.1	253	103	72	171

CURRENT PLAYERS

ROGER McDOWELL

Position: Pitcher
Team: Texas Rangers
Born: Dec. 21, 1960 Cincinnati, OH
Height: 6'1" **Weight:** 185 lbs.
Bats: right **Throws:** right
Acquired: Signed as a free agent, 4/95

Player Summary	
Fantasy Value	$1
Card Value	4¢ to 6¢
Will	work many games
Can't	strike guys out
Expect	ground-ball outs
Don't Expect	gopher problems

After a rocky start with the Rangers last summer, McDowell settled down to become an effective set-up man. Because of his effectiveness against first batters, he strands most of the runners he inherits. He is a sinkerballer who needs work to stay sharp. Though his hard sinker looks like a screwball to right-handed hitters, McDowell was actually more effective against lefties last year. He also throws a slider. He doesn't get many strikeouts against anyone, since his pitches produce ground balls when he throws them to the right spots. He has been strictly a set-up guy for the last three years. McDowell keeps the ball in the park, helps himself with solid fielding, and keeps a close watch on enemy baserunners. He has an excellent pickoff move. McDowell launched his career in 1982 after the Mets signed him off the campus of Bowling Green State.

Major League Pitching Register

	W	L	ERA	G	S	IP	H	ER	BB	SO
85 NL	6	5	2.83	62	17	127.1	108	40	37	70
86 NL	14	9	3.02	75	22	128.0	107	43	42	65
87 NL	7	5	4.16	56	25	88.2	95	41	28	32
88 NL	5	5	2.63	62	16	89.0	80	26	31	46
89 NL	4	8	1.96	69	23	92.0	79	20	38	47
90 NL	6	8	3.86	72	22	86.1	92	37	35	39
91 NL	9	9	2.93	71	10	101.1	100	33	48	50
92 NL	6	10	4.09	65	14	83.2	103	38	42	50
93 NL	5	3	2.25	54	2	68.0	76	17	30	27
94 NL	0	3	5.23	32	0	41.1	50	24	22	29
95 AL	7	4	4.02	64	4	85.0	86	38	34	49
Life	69	69	3.24	682	155	990.2	976	357	387	504
3 AVE	4	4	3.80	57	2	74.0	81	31	33	41

CHUCK McELROY

Position: Pitcher
Team: Cincinnati Reds
Born: Oct. 1, 1967 Galveston, TX
Height: 6' **Weight:** 195 lbs.
Bats: left **Throws:** left
Acquired: Traded by Cubs for Larry Luebbers, Mike Anderson, and Darron Cox, 12/93

Player Summary	
Fantasy Value	$2 to $4
Card Value	4¢ to 6¢
Will	seek comeback
Can't	retire first batters
Expect	superb pickoff move
Don't Expect	top control

Before his struggles of 1995, McElroy had earned a reputation as a solid set-up man specializing in retiring left-handed hitters. The one-time Philadelphia signee yielded more hits than innings last year for the second time in his career. He has good command of his fastball, forkball, and slider. He often has problems with first batters, however—making it difficult for him to strand inherited runners. McElroy sometimes has control trouble as well. His ratio of strikeouts to walks last year was down from its 1994 level. McElroy disguises his pitches with his deceptive three-quarters delivery, but he didn't fool lefties last season. Their average against him climbed 50 points from the year before. McElroy might have been weakened from a bout with the chicken pox or rusty from lack of work. He can hit, field, and hold runners. A minor-league starter, McElroy has never opened a big-league game.

Major League Pitching Register

	W	L	ERA	G	S	IP	H	ER	BB	SO
89 NL	0	0	1.74	11	0	10.1	12	2	4	8
90 NL	0	1	7.71	16	0	14.0	24	12	10	16
91 NL	6	2	1.95	71	3	101.1	73	22	57	92
92 NL	4	7	3.55	72	6	83.2	73	33	51	83
93 NL	2	2	4.56	49	0	47.1	51	24	25	31
94 NL	1	2	2.34	52	5	57.2	52	15	15	38
95 NL	3	4	6.02	44	0	40.1	46	27	15	27
Life	16	18	3.43	315	14	354.2	331	135	177	295
3 AVE	2	3	3.91	57	2	57.2	59	25	21	38

WILLIE McGEE

Position: Outfield
Team: Boston Red Sox
Born: Nov. 2, 1958 San Francisco, CA
Height: 6'1" **Weight:** 185 lbs.
Bats: both **Throws:** right
Acquired: Signed as a free agent, 6/95

Player Summary	
Fantasy Value	$2 to $4
Card Value	5¢ to 8¢
Will	burn left-handers
Can't	coax many walks
Expect	good glove
Don't Expect	speed to return

McGee showed last summer that he had recovered from the torn Achilles tendon and dislocated ankle that plagued him in 1994. Though no longer a burner, he still swings a solid bat—especially against left-handers. He reached the Red Sox on July 5 and formed a fine right field platoon with lefty-hitting Troy O'Leary. McGee also spent some time in center and left. A two-time batting champ and three-time Gold Glove winner, McGee has never been known for his patience at bat. The result was an on-base average only about 20 points above his batting average. He gets his share of bunts and infield hits. In the outfield, he has good range and a solid arm. The former MVP hit for the cycle on June 23, 1984, while with St. Louis.

Major League Batting Register

	BA	G	AB	R	H	2B	3B	HR	RBI	SB
82 NL	.296	123	422	43	125	12	8	4	56	24
83 NL	.286	147	601	75	172	22	8	5	75	39
84 NL	.291	145	571	82	166	19	11	6	50	43
85 NL	.353	152	612	114	216	26	18	10	82	56
86 NL	.256	124	497	65	127	22	7	7	48	19
87 NL	.285	153	620	76	177	37	11	11	105	16
88 NL	.292	137	562	73	164	24	6	3	50	41
89 NL	.236	58	199	23	47	10	2	3	17	8
90 NL	.335	125	501	76	168	32	5	3	62	28
90 AL	.274	29	113	23	31	3	2	0	15	3
91 NL	.312	131	497	67	155	30	3	4	43	17
92 NL	.297	138	474	56	141	20	2	1	36	13
93 NL	.301	130	475	53	143	28	1	4	46	10
94 NL	.282	45	156	19	44	3	0	5	23	3
95 AL	.285	67	200	32	57	11	3	2	15	5
Life	.297	1704	6500	877	1933	299	87	68	723	325
3 AVE	.293	90	307	39	90	15	1	4	32	7

FRED McGRIFF

Position: First base
Team: Atlanta Braves
Born: Oct. 31, 1963 Tampa, FL
Height: 6'3" **Weight:** 215 lbs.
Bats: left **Throws:** left
Acquired: Traded by Padres for Melvin Nieves, Donnie Elliott, and Vince Moore, 7/93

Player Summary	
Fantasy Value	$25 to $30
Card Value	20¢ to 30¢
Will	drive the ball
Can't	count on speed
Expect	run production
Don't Expect	great throwing

Before falling victim to the strike-shortened season, McGriff had hit at least 30 home runs seven years in a row. After getting a pair on Opening Day, he struggled to pull every pitch while pitchers worked him outside. A late-summer decision to hit each ball where it was pitched produced a prompt rise in both power and batting average. Though the Atlanta cleanup man suffered when No. 5 hitter David Justice was idled by injury, McGriff did manage a 460-foot homer at Denver's Coors Field on June 17. A better hitter against righties, McGriff is far from an automatic out against lefties. Though he fans frequently, the three-time All-Star also has enough patience to wait for a healthy share of walks. McGriff makes an imposing target for infielders' throws, and is adequate around the bag. He's no Sid Bream on the 3-6-3 double play, however.

Major League Batting Register

	BA	G	AB	R	H	2B	3B	HR	RBI	SB
86 AL	.200	3	5	1	1	0	0	0	0	0
87 AL	.247	107	295	58	73	16	0	20	43	3
88 AL	.282	154	536	100	151	35	4	34	82	6
89 AL	.269	161	551	98	148	27	3	36	92	7
90 AL	.300	153	557	91	167	21	1	35	88	5
91 AL	.278	153	528	84	147	19	1	31	106	4
92 NL	.286	152	531	79	152	30	4	35	104	8
93 NL	.291	151	557	111	162	29	2	37	101	5
94 NL	.318	113	424	81	135	25	1	34	94	7
95 NL	.280	144	528	85	148	27	1	27	93	3
Life	.285	1291	4512	788	1284	229	17	289	803	48
3 AVE	.297	157	583	107	173	32	2	38	113	6

CURRENT PLAYERS

MARK McGWIRE

Position: First base
Team: Oakland Athletics
Born: Oct. 1, 1963 Pomona, CA
Height: 6'5" **Weight:** 225 lbs.
Bats: right **Throws:** right
Acquired: First-round pick in 6/84 free-agent draft

Player Summary
Fantasy Value	$20 to $25
Card Value	15¢ to 20¢
Will	hit frequent homers
Can't	steal many bases
Expect	high on-base mark
Don't Expect	injury-free year

McGwire was leading the American League with 22 homers and 55 RBI on July 1, but injuries intervened for the third year in a row. He missed five games after a David Cone beaning, 13 games with a badly bruised toe, then more time when his back flared up. In the two previous years, he missed 202 of 276 games with a heel injury that needed surgery twice. The seven-time All-Star still has one of the game's great power strokes. On June 10, he became the first Oakland batter to hit three homers in a game twice. Teammate Dennis Eckersley said McGwire's swing is more compact and powerful than it was when he hit a rookie-record 49 homers in 1987. The statistics agree; projected over a full season, McGwire would have topped 61 homers. A former Olympian, All-American, and College Player of the Year at USC, McGwire walks more than he fans. He won a Gold Glove at first base in 1990.

Major League Batting Register

	BA	G	AB	R	H	2B	3B	HR	RBI	SB
86 AL	.189	18	53	10	10	1	0	3	9	0
87 AL	.289	151	557	97	161	28	4	49	118	1
88 AL	.260	155	550	87	143	22	1	32	99	0
89 AL	.231	143	490	74	113	17	0	33	95	1
90 AL	.235	156	523	87	123	16	0	39	108	2
91 AL	.201	154	483	62	97	22	0	22	75	2
92 AL	.268	139	467	87	125	22	0	42	104	0
93 AL	.333	27	84	16	28	6	0	9	24	0
94 AL	.252	47	135	26	34	3	0	9	25	0
95 AL	.274	104	317	75	87	13	0	39	90	1
Life	.252	1094	3659	621	921	150	5	277	747	7

MARK McLEMORE

Position: Second base; outfield
Team: Texas Rangers
Born: Oct. 4, 1964 San Diego, CA
Height: 5'11" **Weight:** 195 lbs.
Bats: both **Throws:** right
Acquired: Signed as a free agent, 12/94

Player Summary
Fantasy Value	$6 to $8
Card Value	4¢ to 6¢
Will	show patience
Can't	clear fences
Expect	opposite-field hits
Don't Expect	average above .300

Because of his versatility, speed, and selective approach to hitting, McLemore is a valuable man to have on a ballclub. He is a switch-hitter who's usually more productive against right-handers. He shows considerable patience at the plate, walking almost as much as he fans. That boosted his on-base percentage about 80 points above his batting average. McLemore gets most of his hits to the opposite field. He doesn't have much power but compensates with speed. He steals more than 20 bases a season, moves runners along with sacrifice bunts, and fattens his average with infield hits. McLemore's judgement on the bases is questionable at times, since he's thrown out too frequently. He's a good defender, however, with quick reactions and good range at both second base and left field. He's also played right field, but doesn't make the strong throws required for prolonged duty there.

Major League Batting Register

	BA	G	AB	R	H	2B	3B	HR	RBI	SB
86 AL	.000	5	4	0	0	0	0	0	0	0
87 AL	.236	138	433	61	102	13	3	3	41	25
88 AL	.240	77	233	38	56	11	2	2	16	13
89 AL	.243	32	103	12	25	3	1	0	14	6
90 AL	.150	28	60	6	9	2	0	0	2	1
91 NL	.148	21	61	6	9	1	0	0	2	0
92 AL	.246	101	228	40	56	7	2	0	27	11
93 AL	.284	148	581	81	165	27	5	4	72	21
94 AL	.257	104	343	44	88	11	1	3	29	20
95 AL	.261	129	467	73	122	20	5	5	41	21
Life	.251	783	2513	361	632	95	19	17	244	118
3 AVE	.268	147	530	75	142	22	4	5	53	24

CURRENT PLAYERS

GREG McMICHAEL

Position: Pitcher
Team: Atlanta Braves
Born: Dec. 1, 1966 Knoxville, TN
Height: 6'3" **Weight:** 215 lbs.
Bats: right **Throws:** right
Acquired: Signed as a minor-league free agent, 4/91

Player Summary	
Fantasy Value	$4 to $6
Card Value	4¢ to 6¢
Will	answer bell often
Can't	avoid homers
Expect	various changeups
Don't Expect	pinpoint control

Though he averages almost one strikeout per inning, McMichael is not a power pitcher. His pet delivery is a changeup that he can break in several different directions. Mixed with his fastball and slider, and thrown to the right spot, the McMichael changeup can be as effective as a Mark Wohlers fastball. The NL batting average against McMichael in 1995 was right on the Mendoza Line. But too many of the hits he yielded disappeared over the outfield wall. After throwing only one home run in '94, McMichael allowed homers in successive games Sept. 23 and 24, increasing his season's total to eight. Despite such setbacks, however, the season was a success for the University of Tennessee product. Moved to a set-up role after two years of closing, McMichael made more than 60 appearances for the second time in three seasons. He stranded a high percentage of the runners he inherited. He had some control problems, but McMichael gets a lot of ground balls. His fielding abilities help, but his pickoff move needs work.

Major League Pitching Register

	W	L	ERA	G	S	IP	H	ER	BB	SO
93 NL	2	3	2.06	74	19	91.2	68	21	29	89
94 NL	4	6	3.84	51	21	58.2	66	25	19	47
95 NL	7	2	2.79	67	2	80.2	64	25	32	74
Life	13	11	2.77	192	42	231.0	198	71	80	210
3 AVE	5	5	2.86	74	17	88.2	78	28	31	79

BRIAN McRAE

Position: Outfield
Team: Chicago Cubs
Born: Aug. 27, 1967 Bradenton, FL
Height: 6' **Weight:** 180 lbs.
Bats: both **Throws:** right
Acquired: Traded by Royals for Derek Wallace and Geno Morones, 4/95

Player Summary	
Fantasy Value	$16 to $19
Card Value	6¢ to 10¢
Will	use good speed
Can't	cut whiff rate
Expect	bunts, doubles
Don't Expect	lousy fielding

In their impatience to unload a hefty salary, the Royals gave the Cubs a fine center fielder and leadoff man. It was a match made in heaven. McRae reached career highs in runs, doubles, and batting. He also gave the Cubs their best center-field player since Bobby Dernier won a Gold Glove in 1984. A better right-handed batter, the switch-hitting McRae is more likely to bunt than hit a home run. He also fattens his average with infield hits, stretches long singles, and rattles rival pitchers once he reaches. He has a good success ratio as a basestealer. Once a wild hacker, McRae has reduced his strikeout-to-walk deficit. His on-base percentage is acceptable. His gap power placed him among NL leaders in doubles last year. In the field, McRae cuts off extra-base hits and gets great jumps. Because of his acrobatic play and hustling style, McRae's mediocre arm is only a minor handicap. He's the son of former player and manager Hal McRae.

Major League Batting Register

	BA	G	AB	R	H	2B	3B	HR	RBI	SB
90 AL	.286	46	168	21	48	8	3	2	23	4
91 AL	.261	152	629	86	164	28	9	8	64	20
92 AL	.223	149	533	63	119	23	5	4	52	18
93 AL	.282	153	627	78	177	28	9	12	69	23
94 AL	.273	114	436	71	119	22	6	4	40	28
95 NL	.288	137	580	92	167	38	7	12	48	27
Life	.267	751	2973	411	794	147	39	42	296	120
3 AVE	.281	156	631	94	178	34	8	10	60	31

CURRENT PLAYERS

RUSTY MEACHAM

Position: Pitcher
Team: Kansas City Royals
Born: Jan. 27, 1968 Stuart, FL
Height: 6'2" **Weight:** 175 lbs.
Bats: right **Throws:** right
Acquired: Claimed from Tigers on waivers, 10/91

Player Summary	
Fantasy Value	$1
Card Value	4¢ to 6¢
Will	keep set-up job
Can't	avoid home runs
Expect	ground-ball outs
Don't Expect	control trouble

Meacham has not been the same pitcher since tearing a ligament in his right elbow during the 1993 campaign. He missed most of that season before working his way back to the majors via Omaha, Kansas City's Triple-A farm, in '94. Meacham spent all of last year searching for his 1992 form. That year, he worked a career-best 64 games while serving as a superb set-up man for closer Jeff Montgomery. A sinker-slider pitcher who also throws a curve and a forkball, Meacham is a fast-working sidearmer with good control. Even though he struggled last summer, he allowed less than three walks per game. Not a power pitcher, Meacham tries to coax ground outs by keeping the ball down. But he's had uncharacteristic gopher trouble over the past two seasons. In 1995, the league hit .300 against him—the main reason Meacham had so little success against runners he inherited. His motion confuses baserunners, who rarely try to steal against him. His defense is otherwise no better than average.

Major League Pitching Register

	W	L	ERA	G	S	IP	H	ER	BB	SO
91 AL	2	1	5.20	10	0	27.2	35	16	11	14
92 AL	10	4	2.74	64	2	101.2	88	31	21	64
93 AL	2	4	5.57	15	0	21.0	31	13	5	13
94 AL	3	3	3.73	36	4	50.2	51	21	12	36
95 AL	4	3	4.98	49	2	59.2	72	33	19	30
Life	21	13	3.94	174	8	260.2	277	114	68	157
2 AVE	4	4	4.33	53	4	68.3	76	33	19	42

PAT MEARES

Position: Shortstop
Team: Minnesota Twins
Born: Sept. 6, 1968 Salina, KS
Height: 6' **Weight:** 185 lbs.
Bats: right **Throws:** right
Acquired: 15th-round pick in 6/90 free-agent draft

Player Summary	
Fantasy Value	$5 to $7
Card Value	4¢ to 6¢
Will	play solid game
Can't	coax more walks
Expect	extra-base hits
Don't Expect	few Ks

A fine-fielding shortstop with some speed, Meares was strictly a singles hitter before 1995. In fact, his only two big-league homers had come in the same game. But he muscled up last year, and reached double-digits in home runs for the first time in a pro career that started in 1990. He also reached new highs in doubles and triples, helping him net extra bases on one-third of his hits. Meares should show some more patience at the plate. Though he makes decent contact, he fanned too frequently, leaving him with an on-base percentage only about 30 points higher than his batting average. He doesn't reach base often enough to hit at the top of the lineup, but the Twins tried him at that spot anyway. A pull hitter against lefties, Meares uses all fields (and hits for a higher average) against right-handers. Meares was once regarded as an erratic infielder. He now shows quick reactions, fine range, good hands, and a strong arm. He played center field for the 1989 Wichita State team that won the College World Series.

Major League Batting Register

	BA	G	AB	R	H	2B	3B	HR	RBI	SB
93 AL	.251	111	346	33	87	14	3	0	33	4
94 AL	.266	80	229	29	61	12	1	2	24	5
95 AL	.269	116	390	57	105	19	4	12	49	10
Life	.262	307	965	119	253	45	8	14	106	19
3 AVE	.263	118	369	46	97	17	3	5	41	7

CURRENT PLAYERS

ROBERTO MEJIA

Position: Second base
Team: Colorado Rockies
Born: April 14, 1972 Hato Mayor, Dominican Republic
Height: 5'11" **Weight:** 165 lbs.
Bats: right **Throws:** right
Acquired: Second-round pick from Dodgers in 11/92 expansion draft

Player Summary
Fantasy Value	$1
Card Value	4¢ to 6¢
Will	show some speed
Can't	stop strikeouts
Expect	extra-base hits
Don't Expect	strong fielding

In all three years of their existence, the Colorado Rockies have tried to make Mejia their regular second baseman. Although he attracts ridiculous numbers of All-Star votes, the hard-swinging keystone sacker just can't seem to hold the job. Because of his speed and power potential, Mejia was once regarded as a hot prospect by the Dodgers. He's still just 23, but that 0-for-3 record in big-league trials is starting to work against him. Both his bat and defense need work. A wild swinger, Mejia strikes out far too frequently—more than twice for every walk. When he does connect, about one-third of his hits result in extra bases. In the field, his erratic arm and inability to turn the double play nullify his great range. He's also spinning his wheels on the bases. He would steal frequently if he could read pitchers better. Injuries have interfered with Mejia's march to the majors, but his own handicaps have hurt him more. This could be a make-or-break year for him.

Major League Batting Register
	BA	G	AB	R	H	2B	3B	HR	RBI	SB
93 NL	.231	65	229	31	53	14	5	5	20	4
94 NL	.241	38	116	11	28	8	1	4	14	3
95 NL	.154	23	52	5	8	1	0	1	4	0
Life	.224	126	397	47	89	23	6	10	38	7

ORLANDO MERCED

Position: Outfield; first base
Team: Pittsburgh Pirates
Born: Nov. 2, 1966 San Juan, PR
Height: 5'11" **Weight:** 170 lbs.
Bats: left **Throws:** right
Acquired: Signed as a free agent, 2/85

Player Summary
Fantasy Value	$12 to $15
Card Value	6¢ to 10¢
Will	hit righties hard
Can't	go for Gold Glove
Expect	extra-base knocks
Don't Expect	weak clutch stick

Playing for a manager who loves to platoon has kept Merced on the bench more than he would like in recent seasons. A former switch-hitter who went all-lefty in 1993, Merced pounds right-handers but often sits against southpaws. That may not be a good game plan, since he hit for a better average (.281) against lefties in 1994 than he did against righties (.269). A good clutch hitter, he's not much of a home run man. He bangs into more than his share of double plays. Once a dead fastball hitter, he's improving his work against breaking stuff. He's not improving his on-base percentage, however. Merced still fans twice as much as he walks, depriving him of many chances to use his speed on the bases. When he runs, he usually makes it. He's best defensively at first base, where his mediocre arm doesn't come into play so often. He has no problems with his reactions, range, hands, or footwork at the bag. In 1991, Merced homered in his first Championship Series at bat.

Major League Batting Register
	BA	G	AB	R	H	2B	3B	HR	RBI	SB
90 NL	.208	25	24	3	5	1	0	0	0	0
91 NL	.275	120	411	83	113	17	2	10	50	8
92 NL	.247	134	405	50	100	28	5	6	60	5
93 NL	.313	137	447	68	140	26	4	8	70	3
94 NL	.272	108	386	48	105	21	3	9	51	4
95 NL	.300	132	487	75	146	29	4	15	83	7
Life	.282	656	2160	327	609	122	18	48	314	27
3 AVE	.294	146	513	73	151	29	4	13	78	6

215

CURRENT PLAYERS

KENT MERCKER

Position: Pitcher
Team: Atlanta Braves
Born: Feb. 1, 1968 Dublin, OH
Height: 6'2" **Weight:** 195 lbs.
Bats: left **Throws:** left
Acquired: First-round pick in 6/86 free-agent draft

Player Summary	
Fantasy Value	$5 to $7
Card Value	6¢ to 10¢
Will	pitch out of jams
Can't	finish his starts
Expect	good whiff totals
Don't Expect	lefties to hit

A man who rarely finishes what he starts, Mercker completed two of his first 46 big-league starts, one of them a no-hitter against the Dodgers. Though he's generally stingy with hits, he has bouts of wildness that create self-made jams. His stuff is so good, however, that he can often escape unscathed. A power pitcher who also throws a curve, a slider, and a changeup, Mercker gets into trouble when he places too much stock in the change. His forte is pure heat but catchers constantly remind him to throw it. He does his best work against lefties and with runners in scoring position. His ratio of strikeouts to walks is better in 1994 than last year. A minor-league starter who began his big-league career in the bullpen, Mercker is more effective with more rest. He sometimes tires suddenly. He's a good fielder and improving hitter but baserunners give him fits. He is a quality pitcher for six innings and a question-mark beyond.

Major League Pitching Register

	W	L	ERA	G	CG	IP	H	ER	BB	SO
89 NL	0	0	12.46	2	0	4.1	8	6	6	4
90 NL	4	7	3.17	36	0	48.1	43	17	24	39
91 NL	5	3	2.58	50	0	73.1	56	21	35	62
92 NL	3	2	3.42	53	0	68.1	51	26	35	49
93 NL	3	1	2.86	43	0	66.0	52	21	36	59
94 NL	9	4	3.45	20	2	112.1	90	43	45	111
95 NL	7	8	4.15	29	0	143.0	140	66	61	102
Life	31	25	3.49	233	2	515.2	440	200	242	426
3 AVE	8	5	3.64	35	1	128.0	112	52	56	110

MATT MERULLO

Position: Catcher
Team: Minnesota Twins
Born: Aug. 15, 1965 Ridgefield, CT
Height: 6'2" **Weight:** 200 lbs.
Bats: left **Throws:** right
Acquired: Signed as a free agent, 12/94

Player Summary	
Fantasy Value	$0
Card Value	4¢ to 6¢
Will	get hits
Can't	start
Expect	DH duty
Don't Expect	great glove

Merullo joins the ranks of the good-hitting catchers that have scraped out major-league careers despite having less-than-average gloves. A lefty-hitting backstopper, Merullo batted .438 against southpaws, but curiously hit only .252 against right-handers. He also had a fine .335 on-base average. He has been a good hitter for years, leading the Triple-A American Association with a .332 batting average in 1993. Unfortunately for Merullo, his glove is nowhere as good as his stick. He had three errors last year in only 339 innings as a catcher and led the Double-A Southern League in both errors and passed balls. He threw out only five potential basestealers in 1995, while 36 were successful. But the Twins have had a history of waiting for good-hitting catchers to come around with the glove: Brian Harper led Minnesota to a world championship in 1991. So there is hope for Merullo. He was on the U.S. National Team in 1985, after playing at North Carolina with Walt Weiss, B.J. Surhoff, and Scott Bankhead.

Major League Batting Register

	BA	G	AB	R	H	2B	3B	HR	RBI	SB
89 AL	.222	31	81	5	18	1	0	1	8	0
91 AL	.229	80	140	8	32	1	0	5	21	0
92 AL	.180	24	50	3	9	1	1	0	3	0
93 AL	.050	8	20	1	1	0	0	0	0	0
94 AL	.100	4	10	1	1	0	0	0	0	0
95 AL	.282	76	195	19	55	14	1	1	27	0
Life	.234	223	496	37	116	17	2	7	59	0

CURRENT PLAYERS

JOSE MESA

Position: Pitcher
Team: Cleveland Indians
Born: May 22, 1966 Azua, Dominican Republic
Height: 6'3" **Weight:** 222 lbs.
Bats: right **Throws:** right
Acquired: Traded by Orioles for Kyle Washington, 7/92

Player Summary
Fantasy Value................$30 to $35
Card Value ....8¢ to 12¢
Will........................own the ninth
Can't...............................field
Expect....................velocity, control
Don't Expect ....pace to last

Before last year, Mesa had four saves in 13 pro seasons. Then the Indians, unable to trade for Bryan Harvey, made Mesa their closer by default. He quickly became the talk of the league, converting dozens of opportunities, making the All-Star Team, and blowing all hitters away. A hard-throwing right-hander who can work often, he complained when Cleveland moved him from the rotation to middle relief in 1994. But he tended to lose concentration as a starter. Things have changed. Paying less attention to his slow curve and forkball as a reliever, Mesa worked to add velocity and command to his fastball. It picked up several miles per hour, reaching 95 to 98 mph. Keeping his slider, he added a two-seam sinker to get more grounders. His ERA could only be seen with a microscope. He couldn't test his pickoff move much because few reached against him. Mesa's fielding was his only apparent weakness.

Major League Pitching Register

	W	L	ERA	G	S	IP	H	ER	BB	SO
87 AL	1	3	6.03	6	0	31.1	38	21	15	17
90 AL	3	2	3.86	7	0	46.2	37	20	27	24
91 AL	6	11	5.97	23	0	123.2	151	82	62	64
92 AL	7	12	4.54	28	0	160.2	169	82	70	62
93 AL	10	12	4.92	34	0	208.2	232	114	62	118
94 AL	7	5	3.82	51	2	73.0	71	31	26	63
95 AL	3	0	1.13	62	46	64.0	49	8	17	58
Life	37	45	4.55	211	48	708.0	747	358	279	406
3 AVE	8	6	3.91	59	18	128.1	129	56	39	91

DAN MICELI

Position: Pitcher
Team: Pittsburgh Pirates
Born: Sept. 9, 1970 Newark, NJ
Height: 6' **Weight:** 207 lbs.
Bats: right **Throws:** right
Acquired: Traded by Royals with Jon Lieber for Stan Belinda, 7/93

Player Summary
Fantasy Value................$17 to $20
Card Value ....8¢ to 12¢
Will....................convert most saves
Can't..................avoid some gophers
Expect....................righties to suffer
Don't Expect ....low K rate

A reliever with more strikeouts than innings pitched in six minor-league seasons, Miceli became Pittsburgh's top closer last summer. Though he had pitched only 32 previous innings in the majors, he made the most of his opportunity. He averaged almost one whiff per inning and about eight hits and three and one-half walks per nine innings. He converted 16 of his first 20 save chances, and held right-handers to a microscopic batting mark. When he improves his work against lefties and sharpens his control, Miceli could move into the elite ranks of late-inning firemen. He gains confidence every time out. He mixes a low-90s fastball with a still-not-perfected slider. When he's on, however, Miceli's heat is enough to survive his usual one-inning stint. Inherited runners give him trouble, however, and he's prone to throwing the gopher ball. Miceli holds runners well for a right-hander and is more than competent in the field. He's likely to become a far better closer than the veteran for whom he was traded, Stan Belinda.

Major League Pitching Register

	W	L	ERA	G	S	IP	H	ER	BB	SO
93 NL	0	0	5.06	9	0	5.1	6	3	3	4
94 NL	2	1	5.93	28	2	27.1	28	18	11	27
95 NL	4	4	4.66	58	21	58.0	61	30	28	56
Life	6	5	5.06	95	23	90.2	95	51	42	87

CURRENT PLAYERS

MATT MIESKE

Position: Outfield
Team: Milwaukee Brewers
Born: Feb. 13, 1968 Midland, MI
Height: 6' **Weight:** 185 lbs.
Bats: right **Throws:** right
Acquired: Traded by Padres with Ricky Bones and Jose Valentin for Gary Sheffield and Geoff Kellogg, 3/92

Player Summary	
Fantasy Value	$6 to $8
Card Value	5¢ to 8¢
Will	show better power
Can't	handle right-handers
Expect	surprising contact
Don't Expect	low on-base mark

Productive against lefties but ineffective against right-handers, Mieske wound up in a 1995 right-field platoon—first with Turner Ward and later with Dave Nilsson. The move might have been temporary, since Mieske has yet to realize the enormous potential he displayed during his minor-league tenure. He led various circuits in batting, home runs, RBI, hits, runs, walks, on-base percentage, total bases, chances, putouts, and assists. He once stole 39 bases in 133 games. For a power-hitter, Mieske makes good contact and shows enough patience to compile an on-base percentage almost 100 points higher than his batting average. His power is reflected in the fact that one-third of his hits go for extra bases. Mieske pulls the ball against lefties but uses all fields when he faces righties. He's still learning to use his speed on the bases and in the outfield. Mieske has good range and an arm that makes the long, hard throws from right. The two-time minor-league MVP was also an Academic All-American at Western Michigan.

Major League Batting Register

	BA	G	AB	R	H	2B	3B	HR	RBI	SB
93 AL	.241	23	58	9	14	0	0	3	7	0
94 AL	.259	84	259	39	67	13	1	10	38	3
95 AL	.251	117	267	42	67	13	1	12	48	2
Life	.253	224	584	90	148	26	2	25	93	5
2 AVE	.255	125	333	51	85	16	1	14	54	3

ORLANDO MILLER

Position: Shortstop
Team: Houston Astros
Born: Jan. 13, 1969 Changuinola, Panama
Height: 6'1" **Weight:** 180 lbs.
Bats: right **Throws:** right
Acquired: Traded by Yankees for Dave Silvestri and Daven Bond, 3/90

Player Summary	
Fantasy Value	$4 to $6
Card Value	15¢ to 20¢
Will	earn future stardom
Can't	cut strikeout ratio
Expect	defense
Don't Expect	zero power

Before he reached the big leagues, Miller built a reputation as a strong-fielding shortstop with a potent bat and a matching temper. If not for that temper—plus the presence of Andujar Cedeno in a Houston uniform—Miller might have reached the majors after posting double figures in doubles, triples, and homers for Triple-A Tucson in 1993. But a 5-1 ratio of strikeouts to walks, plus a league-leading 33 errors, convinced the Astros another year in the high minors wouldn't hurt. After that year, they made room for him by trading Cedeno. Miller didn't disappoint. He had three hits and five RBI in an 11-0 game against St. Louis on June 26, and two homers in an Aug. 6 game at Pittsburgh. Miller has stolen in double-digits only once as a pro, but there's no doubt he can move. He has quick reactions, great range, and a gun for a throwing arm—attributes that made Miller the best defensive infielder in the Houston organization before he reached the majors. If the one-time Yankee farmhand cuts his strikeouts and keeps his cool, Miller will become a star.

Major League Batting Register

	BA	G	AB	R	H	2B	3B	HR	RBI	SB
94 NL	.325	16	40	3	13	0	1	2	9	1
95 NL	.262	92	324	36	85	20	1	5	36	3
Life	.269	108	364	39	98	20	2	7	45	4

CURRENT PLAYERS

MICHAEL MIMBS

Position: Pitcher
Team: Philadelphia Phillies
Born: Feb. 13, 1969 Macon, GA
Height: 6'2" **Weight:** 182 lbs.
Bats: left **Throws:** left
Acquired: Rule 5 draft pick from Expos, 12/94

Player Summary
Fantasy Value	$1 to $3
Card Value	10¢ to 15¢
Will	seek starting spot
Can't	pierce strike zone
Expect	lefties to struggle
Don't Expect	gopher troubles

Opportunity knocked for Mimbs last spring. Two years after pitching in the independent Northern League, he was a starter for a big-league contender. Stepping into the rotation slot created by Tommy Greene's shoulder problems, Mimbs rolled to a 6-2 record and 3.74 ERA in his first 11 starts. He went all the way twice—once with his first big-league shutout. He yielded less hits than innings and was extremely stingy with the home run ball. He's especially effective against left-handed batters and has a terrific pickoff move. All of those attributes, however, did not save his rotation job after the acquisition of Sid Fernandez, promotion of Jeff Juden, and return of Greene from the disabled list. The culprit was control, or lack of it. Mimbs walked nearly five men per nine innings and threw too many wild pitches in key situations in 1995. Since he's not a strikeout pitcher, his ratio of whiffs to walks needs improvement. Mimbs started his career in the Dodger organization with his twin brother, Mark. At 27, Michael will certainly get another long look.

Major League Pitching Register
	W	L	ERA	G	CG	IP	H	ER	BB	SO
95 NL	9	7	4.15	35	2	136.2	127	63	75	93
Life	9	7	4.15	35	2	136.2	127	63	75	93

ANGEL MIRANDA

Position: Pitcher
Team: Milwaukee Brewers
Born: Nov. 9, 1969 Arecibo, PR
Height: 6'1" **Weight:** 195 lbs.
Bats: left **Throws:** left
Acquired: Signed as a nondrafted free agent, 3/87

Player Summary
Fantasy Value	$1 to $3
Card Value	4¢ to 6¢
Will	rely on screwball
Can't	evade injury wave
Expect	lapses of control
Don't Expect	job security

A screwball specialist with fine potential, Miranda has been on a three-year treadmill because of injuries. After disabling shoulder problems in the spring of '93, he tore his anterior cruciate ligament in winter ball and needed surgical repair. He returned the following June but did not pitch with the confidence he had displayed the year before. Miranda needed more knee surgery in '95, going under the knife to repair loose left-knee cartilage in late June. Again, he was ineffective when he returned. He was a power pitcher in the minors, with more strikeouts than innings in each of his first five seasons. In his last two years in Milwaukee, on the other hand, he had more walks than strikeouts. He was also hit hard and long anytime he made any of his deliveries too fat. He tries to mask the screwball with a moving fastball. Though he still has problems in the field, Miranda has improved a once-awful pickoff move. Improving his pitching is a bigger priority, however. Miranda needs to keep off the DL and learn whether he can win in the majors.

Major League Pitching Register
	W	L	ERA	G	CG	IP	H	ER	BB	SO
93 AL	4	5	3.30	22	2	120.0	100	44	52	88
94 AL	2	5	5.28	8	1	46.0	39	27	27	24
95 AL	4	5	5.23	30	0	74.0	83	43	49	45
Life	10	15	4.28	60	3	240.0	222	114	128	157
2 AVE	4	5	4.09	28	1	102.0	97	46	54	69

CURRENT PLAYERS

DAVE MLICKI

Position: Pitcher
Team: New York Mets
Born: June 8, 1968 Cleveland, OH
Height: 6'4" **Weight:** 190 lbs.
Bats: right **Throws:** right
Acquired: Traded by Indians with Jerry DiPoto, Paul Byrd, and Jesus Azuaje for Jeromy Burnitz and Joe Roa, 11/94

Player Summary
Fantasy Value	$4 to $6
Card Value	4¢ to 6¢
Will	offer good curve
Can't	keep ball in park
Expect	good strikeout ratio
Don't Expect	double-digit wins

After spending five years in the minors, Mlicki opened the 1995 campaign in the Mets' starting rotation. A curveball specialist who tries to keep batters guessing by mixing in a heater, Mlicki relies on quality control. He yielded less hits than innings and less than three walks per game last year. He is frequently victimized by the long ball, however, because he's around the plate so much. He yielded 20 home runs in his first 91 innings. That problem eventually caused his demotion to the bullpen after the promotion of Jason Isringhausen from the minor leagues. Returning when Bret Saberhagen was injured, Mlicki fanned 10 hitters in seven innings to beat the Marlins, 5-2, on Aug. 7. He had been winless in seven previous starts. Mlicki is much more effective against right-handed hitters. He's competent in the field but not so good at holding runners. If he hangs around for two more seasons, he could prove to be a very fine starter for one of the new expansion teams. His immediate future seems to lie in spot starting and long relief.

Major League Pitching Register
	W	L	ERA	G	CG	IP	H	ER	BB	SO
92 AL	0	2	4.98	4	0	21.2	23	12	16	16
93 AL	0	0	3.38	3	0	13.1	11	5	6	7
95 NL	9	7	4.26	29	0	160.2	160	76	54	123
Life	9	9	4.28	36	0	195.2	194	93	76	146

PAUL MOLITOR

Position: Designated hitter
Team: Minnesota Twins
Born: Aug. 22, 1956 St. Paul, MN
Height: 6' **Weight:** 185 lbs.
Bats: right **Throws:** right
Acquired: Signed as a free agent, 12/95

Player Summary
Fantasy Value	$18 to $21
Card Value	20¢ to 30¢
Will	approach 3,000 hits
Can't	recapture old power
Expect	Hall of Fame
Don't Expect	deployment in field

Molitor got off to a slow start. Then the injuries started. Chronic shoulder problems, complicated by strained muscles on his right side, forced Molitor to cut down his swing—short-circuiting the power that had produced 64 extra-base hits in 1993. Although he got his 200th career homer and his 1,000th RBI, the seven-time All-Star was moved from third to second in the Toronto lineup. Molitor still makes good contact, walking more than he fans, but doesn't hit with his former authority. The former All-American shortstop from the University of Minnesota has been reduced to a full-time DH. Molitor was the 1993 World Series MVP.

Major League Batting Register
	BA	G	AB	R	H	2B	3B	HR	RBI	SB
78 AL	.273	125	521	73	142	26	4	6	45	30
79 AL	.322	140	584	88	188	27	16	9	62	33
80 AL	.304	111	450	81	137	29	2	9	37	34
81 AL	.267	64	251	45	67	11	0	2	19	10
82 AL	.302	160	666	136	201	26	8	19	71	41
83 AL	.270	152	608	95	164	28	6	15	47	41
84 AL	.217	13	46	3	10	1	0	0	6	1
85 AL	.297	140	576	93	171	28	3	10	48	21
86 AL	.281	105	437	62	123	24	6	9	55	20
87 AL	.353	118	465	114	164	41	5	16	75	45
88 AL	.312	154	609	115	190	34	6	13	60	41
89 AL	.315	155	615	84	194	35	4	11	56	27
90 AL	.285	103	418	64	119	27	6	12	45	18
91 AL	.325	158	665	133	216	32	13	17	75	19
92 AL	.320	158	609	89	195	36	7	12	89	31
93 AL	.332	160	636	121	211	37	5	22	111	22
94 AL	.341	115	454	86	155	30	4	14	75	20
95 AL	.270	130	525	63	142	31	2	15	60	12
Life	.305	2261	9135	1545	2789	503	97	211	1036	466
3 AVE	.316	156	622	104	196	38	4	20	95	21

CURRENT PLAYERS

RAUL MONDESI

Position: Outfield
Team: Los Angeles Dodgers
Born: March 12, 1971 San Cristobal, Dominican Republic
Height: 5'11" **Weight:** 202 lbs.
Bats: right **Throws:** right
Acquired: Signed as a free agent, 6/88

Player Summary	
Fantasy Value	$20 to $25
Card Value	30¢ to 60¢
Will	show five tools
Can't	wait for good pitch
Expect	All-Star stats
Don't Expect	catchers to get him

He throws like Roberto Clemente. He hits for power and average. He runs like the wind. The only thing Mondesi can't do is reduce a strikeout-to-walk ratio of about 3-to-1. The 1994 NL Rookie of the Year blossomed into an MVP contender last year. He hit a 463-foot homer in Denver May 5. He nailed Mark Portugal at first base on an apparent base hit. And Mondesi stole 18 consecutive bases before Charles Johnson, the league's best, ended the string July 16. A five-tools player, Mondesi hits with power to all fields, steals at will, and collects extra bases on more than one-third of his hits. Few runners challenge his powerful throwing arm, which helped him lead the majors with 16 assists in 1994. Mondesi may be getting even better: last year's home run total was his best in a pro career that began in 1990. He still needs to make better contact and boost his production against left-handed pitchers (so far, he's done more damage to righties). When he masters those arts, nothing should stop Mondesi from joining the 30-30 club.

Major League Batting Register

	BA	G	AB	R	H	2B	3B	HR	RBI	SB
93 NL	.291	42	86	13	25	3	1	4	10	4
94 NL	.306	112	434	63	133	27	8	16	56	11
95 NL	.285	139	536	91	153	23	6	26	88	27
Life	.295	293	1056	167	311	53	15	46	154	42
2 AVE	.296	157	607	96	180	32	9	26	89	23

JEFF MONTGOMERY

Position: Pitcher
Team: Kansas City Royals
Born: Jan. 7, 1962 Wellston, OH
Height: 5'11" **Weight:** 180 lbs.
Bats: right **Throws:** right
Acquired: Traded by Reds for Van Snider, 2/88

Player Summary	
Fantasy Value	$25 to $30
Card Value	6¢ to 10¢
Will	induce double plays
Can't	quiet lefty hitters
Expect	few homers
Don't Expect	middle relief

For the past six years, Montgomery has been one of baseball's best closers, making the All-Star squad twice. The holder of a Bachelor of Science degree in computer science from Marshall University, Montgomery has also made a science of relief pitching. He usually finishes with more appearances and innings pitched than his fellow closers, but his ERA rarely suffers. He makes life miserable for right-handed hitters and is especially effective with runners in scoring position. He helps himself by coaxing double-play balls in crucial situations. He adds good defense and a competent pickoff move. Montgomery mixes a fastball, a slider, a curve, and a changeup, but he often relies on pure heat under pressure. Montgomery managed to top 20 saves for the sixth straight season. Even with his K total down, he managed a fine strikeout-to-walk ratio, yielded only seven hits per nine innings, kept the ball in the park, and controlled the running game.

Major League Pitching Register

	W	L	ERA	G	S	IP	H	ER	BB	SO
87 NL	2	2	6.52	14	0	19.1	25	14	9	13
88 AL	7	2	3.45	45	1	62.2	54	24	30	47
89 AL	7	3	1.37	63	18	92.0	66	14	25	94
90 AL	6	5	2.39	73	24	94.1	81	25	34	94
91 AL	4	4	2.90	67	33	90.0	83	29	28	77
92 AL	1	6	2.18	65	39	82.2	61	20	27	69
93 AL	7	5	2.27	69	45	87.1	65	22	23	66
94 AL	2	3	4.03	42	27	44.2	48	20	15	50
95 AL	2	3	3.43	54	31	65.2	60	25	25	49
Life	38	33	2.72	492	218	638.2	543	193	216	559
3 AVE	4	4	3.14	63	39	74.2	67	26	24	64

CURRENT PLAYERS

MIKE MOORE

Position: Pitcher
Team: Detroit Tigers
Born: Nov. 26, 1959 Eakly, OK
Height: 6'4" **Weight:** 205 lbs.
Bats: right **Throws:** right
Acquired: Signed as a free agent, 12/92

Player Summary	
Fantasy Value	$0
Card Value	4¢ to 6¢
Will	seek comeback
Can't	nail basestealers
Expect	early retirement
Don't Expect	gophers to stop

Someone must like what they see in Mike Moore: his earned run average has gone up in each of the last four seasons, but he was still the Opening Day starter for the 1995 Tigers. He got the job by keeping himself in good shape during the eight-month player strike. But his physical form did not prevent the most dreadful slump of his career. Over a 13-start span that ended Aug. 2, he dropped nine of 10 decisions while yielding a 9.62 ERA. Because he lacks the fastball to set up his curve and forkball, Moore needs precise location to win. When he doesn't have it, he falls behind, and ends up making fat pitches to compensate. That happened a lot last year. He was among the league leaders in hits and home runs surrendered. His inability to halt the running game compounds the felony.

Major League Pitching Register

	W	L	ERA	G	CG	IP	H	ER	BB	SO
82 AL	7	14	5.36	28	1	144.1	159	86	79	73
83 AL	6	8	4.71	22	3	128.0	130	67	60	108
84 AL	7	17	4.97	34	6	212.0	236	117	85	158
85 AL	17	10	3.46	35	14	247.0	230	95	70	155
86 AL	11	13	4.30	38	11	266.0	279	127	94	146
87 AL	9	19	4.71	33	12	231.0	268	121	84	115
88 AL	9	15	3.78	37	9	228.2	196	96	63	182
89 AL	19	11	2.61	35	6	241.2	193	70	83	172
90 AL	13	15	4.65	33	3	199.1	204	103	84	73
91 AL	17	8	2.96	33	3	210.0	176	69	105	153
92 AL	17	12	4.12	36	2	223.0	229	102	103	117
93 AL	13	9	5.22	36	4	213.2	227	124	89	89
94 AL	11	10	5.42	25	4	154.1	152	93	89	62
95 AL	5	15	7.53	25	1	132.2	179	111	68	64
Life	161	176	4.39	450	79	2831.2	2858	1381	1156	1667
3 AVE	11	13	5.89	33	4	193.2	214	127	97	83

MICKEY MORANDINI

Position: Second base
Team: Philadelphia Phillies
Born: April 22, 1966 Kittanning, PA
Height: 5'11" **Weight:** 170 lbs.
Bats: left **Throws:** right
Acquired: Fifth-round pick in 6/88 free-agent draft

Player Summary	
Fantasy Value	$6 to $8
Card Value	6¢ to 10¢
Will	hit to all fields
Can't	handle all lefties
Expect	Gold Glove defense
Don't Expect	double-digit power

Before last summer, Morandini's reaction to left-handed pitching was like Popeye's reaction to an empty spinach can. But the former Olympian from the University of Indiana showed enough improvement in 1995 that he became an All-Star. He was able to bat .229 against southpaws last year. He also escaped the onus of the platoon system that had plagued him since his arrival in the majors. A contact hitter who shows some patience, Morandini sprays hits to all fields but also produces some power. He'll even pop the ball over the fence on occasion. A double-digit basestealer with a high success rate, Morandini saves most of his speed for the field. The converted shortstop is a sure-handed second baseman who once turned an unassisted triple-play. He makes even difficult double plays seem routine. Morandini has terrific reactions, great range, and a solid arm. He makes only a handful of errors each season. A Gold Glove could be in his future.

Major League Batting Register

	BA	G	AB	R	H	2B	3B	HR	RBI	SB
90 NL	.241	25	79	9	19	4	0	1	3	3
91 NL	.249	98	325	38	81	11	4	1	20	13
92 NL	.265	127	422	47	112	8	8	3	30	8
93 NL	.247	120	425	57	105	19	9	3	33	13
94 NL	.292	87	274	40	80	16	5	2	26	10
95 NL	.283	127	494	65	140	34	7	6	49	9
Life	.266	584	2019	256	537	92	33	16	161	56
3 AVE	.275	128	456	62	125	27	8	4	42	12

CURRENT PLAYERS

MIKE MORGAN

Position: Pitcher
Team: St. Louis Cardinals
Born: Oct. 8, 1959 Tulare, CA
Height: 6'2" **Weight:** 215 lbs.
Bats: right **Throws:** right
Acquired: Traded by Cubs with Paul Torres and Francisco Morales for Todd Zeile, 6/95

Player Summary	
Fantasy Value	$6 to $8
Card Value	4¢ to 6¢
Will	always throw strikes
Can't	avoid disabled list
Expect	ground outs
Don't Expect	15 wins

Infielders better pay attention when Morgan pitches. When he's right, batters produce a torrent of ground balls. That happened last July 3, when the veteran right-hander worked eight and one-third hitless innings against Montreal before Wil Cordero beat out an infield single. Morgan needs location to survive, since he doesn't get a lot of strikeouts. Morgan throws a two-seam fastball that sinks, plus a slider, a forkball, and a circle change that was inspired by the success of Greg Maddux. Morgan's fielding is fine, but his hitting and pickoff move aren't. His top priority is avoiding the disabled list. In recent seasons, he's had shoulder and elbow problems, back spasms, and migraine headaches.

Major League Pitching Register

	W	L	ERA	G	CG	IP	H	ER	BB	SO
78 AL	0	3	7.30	3	0	12.1	19	10	8	0
79 AL	2	10	5.94	13	2	77.1	102	51	50	17
82 AL	7	11	4.37	30	2	150.1	167	73	67	71
83 AL	0	3	5.16	16	0	45.1	48	26	21	22
85 AL	1	1	12.00	2	0	6.0	11	8	5	2
86 AL	11	17	4.53	37	9	216.1	243	109	86	116
87 AL	12	17	4.65	34	8	207.0	245	107	53	85
88 AL	1	6	5.43	22	2	71.1	70	43	23	29
89 NL	8	11	2.53	40	0	152.2	130	43	33	72
90 NL	11	15	3.75	33	6	211.0	216	88	60	106
91 NL	14	10	2.78	34	5	236.1	197	73	61	140
92 NL	16	8	2.55	34	6	240.0	203	68	79	123
93 NL	10	15	4.03	32	1	207.2	206	93	74	111
94 NL	2	10	6.69	15	1	80.2	111	60	35	57
95 NL	7	7	3.56	21	1	131.1	133	56	34	61
Life	102	144	3.98	366	44	2045.2	2101	904	689	1012
3 AVE	7	12	4.53	26	1	156.0	171	79	54	87

HAL MORRIS

Position: First base
Team: Cincinnati Reds
Born: April 9, 1965 Fort Rucker, AL
Height: 6'4" **Weight:** 210 lbs.
Bats: left **Throws:** left
Acquired: Traded by Yankees with Rodney Imes for Tim Leary and Van Snider, 12/89

Player Summary	
Fantasy Value	$11 to $14
Card Value	6¢ to 10¢
Will	return to .300
Can't	hit left-handers
Expect	decent defense
Don't Expect	many home runs

Although Morris took a batting average over .300 into the 1995 campaign, hamstring problems and a slow start left him short of his lifetime mark. His on-base percentage was about 50 points below the .385 mark he posted in 1994. Anxiety to produce big hits made Morris an impatient hitter. He struggled in his few swings against southpaws. Never regarded as a home run hitter, Morris muscles line drives into the gaps. He hits the ball hard to all fields but also raps into numerous double plays. He was one of the few slow runners with the Reds last summer. The former University of Michigan star is a solid defensive player who can scoop and stretch as well as any first baseman. His arm is more than adequate—the result of his experience as an outfielder. A past contender for the batting crown, Morris might make future bids if he avoids the DL and sees enough action to maintain his batting stroke.

Major League Batting Register

	BA	G	AB	R	H	2B	3B	HR	RBI	SB
88 AL	.100	15	20	1	2	0	0	0	0	0
89 AL	.278	15	18	2	5	0	0	0	4	0
90 NL	.340	107	309	50	105	22	3	7	36	9
91 NL	.318	136	478	72	152	33	1	14	59	10
92 NL	.271	115	395	41	107	21	3	6	53	6
93 NL	.317	101	379	48	120	18	0	7	49	2
94 NL	.335	112	436	60	146	30	4	10	78	6
95 NL	.279	101	359	53	100	25	2	11	51	1
Life	.308	702	2394	327	737	149	13	55	330	34
3 AVE	.314	124	466	64	146	29	3	11	72	4

CURRENT PLAYERS

JAMES MOUTON

Position: Outfield
Team: Houston Astros
Born: Dec. 29, 1968 Denver, CO
Height: 5'9" **Weight:** 175 lbs.
Bats: right **Throws:** right
Acquired: Seventh-round pick in 6/91 free-agent draft

Player Summary
Fantasy Value	$8 to $10
Card Value	8¢ to 12¢
Will	back three spots
Can't	find old offense
Expect	tremendous speed
Don't Expect	few strikeouts

If anyone knows the meaning of a swing shift in baseball, it's Mouton. The converted second baseman was handed Houston's right-field job as a 1994 rookie, but he never lived up to his reputation as a minor-league speed merchant with a potent bat. He returned in '95 as an all-purpose reserve, filling in at all three outfield spots. Though he still fanned about three times for every walk, Mouton made himself much more valuable by swinging a more potent bat (not trying to pull everything helped). For the second straight year, he strangled southpaws but struggled against righties. Almost a third of his hits netted extra bases, and he topped two-dozen steals. Mouton hits to all fields against lefties but tries to go up the middle against right-handers. That formula worked in the minors, where he led different leagues in runs, hits, doubles, triples, total bases, and steals. Converted because of his bad hands at second (84 boots over a two-year span), Mouton is much better in the outfield, where he makes maximum mileage out of his great range. His arm isn't much.

Major League Batting Register
	BA	G	AB	R	H	2B	3B	HR	RBI	SB
94 NL	.245	99	310	43	76	11	0	2	16	24
95 NL	.262	104	298	42	78	18	2	4	27	25
Life	.253	203	608	85	154	29	2	6	43	49
2 AVE	.252	128	386	54	97	18	1	4	26	31

LYLE MOUTON

Position: Outfield
Team: Chicago White Sox
Born: May 14, 1969 Layfayette, LA
Height: 6'4" **Weight:** 240 lbs.
Bats: right **Throws:** right
Acquired: Traded by Yankees with Keith Heberling for Jack McDowell, 2/95

Player Summary
Fantasy Value	$2 to $4
Card Value	8¢ to 12¢
Will	show power
Can't	rely on speed
Expect	a long look
Don't Expect	a Gold Glove

Considered a throw-in player to a lopsided trade, Mouton hit .300 in the bigs, giving the White Sox fans something to cheer about in an otherwise tough year. The White Sox decided to part with former Cy Young winner Jack McDowell in a cost-cutting move, and they received a surprise in return. In 1994, Mouton hit .307 with 12 homers and 42 RBI at Double-A Albany, and he notched a .314 batting average with four homers and 32 RBI at Triple-A Columbus. Last year, he proved that those numbers were no fluke. He tallied a .475 slugging percentage, and was patient enough to wait for 19 walks, upping his on-base average to .373. He continues to work on cutting his strikeout rate. Mouton had one strikeout less than every four at bats last year. The Louisiana State product has adequate speed for the field. He also has a good arm, and he can play right field. Mouton stole 18 bases during one season in the minors, though he didn't run very much last year for the White Sox. Mouton was a member of the 1991 national championship baseball team at LSU.

Major League Batting Register
	BA	G	AB	R	H	2B	3B	HR	RBI	SB
95 AL	.302	58	179	23	54	16	0	5	27	1
Life	.302	58	179	23	54	16	0	5	27	1

CURRENT PLAYERS

JAMIE MOYER

Position: Pitcher
Team: Baltimore Orioles
Born: Nov. 18, 1962 Sellersville, PA
Height: 6′ **Weight:** 170 lbs.
Bats: left **Throws:** left
Acquired: Signed as a minor-league free agent, 12/92

Player Summary	
Fantasy Value	$4 to $6
Card Value	4¢ to 6¢
Will	win with finesse
Can't	keep ball in park
Expect	top control
Don't Expect	high whiff totals

A left-hander with finesse, Moyer manages to win without many strikeouts or ground balls. He relies on good control of a fastball, a slider, a curve, and a changeup that ranks as his best pitch. He maintains a good tempo and changes speeds well. In his best game last year, Moyer beat Milwaukee 2-0 on June 26, allowing two hits in seven innings. That started a string of victories that lasted nearly six weeks. Moyer fields his position well. He has some problems keeping the ball in the park and preventing baserunners from stealing, however. The home run has plagued Moyer throughout his career. He once led the American Association in home runs allowed, and he gave up 23 in 23 AL starts in 1994. Moyer is more effective against righties than lefties—the reverse of what's expected. He remains a good fourth starter, however. Moyer once pitched three straight no-hitters in high school.

Major League Pitching Register

	W	L	ERA	G	CG	IP	H	ER	BB	SO
86 NL	7	4	5.05	16	1	87.1	107	49	42	45
87 NL	12	15	5.10	35	1	201.0	210	114	97	147
88 NL	9	15	3.48	34	3	202.0	212	78	55	121
89 AL	4	9	4.86	15	1	76.0	84	41	33	44
90 AL	2	6	4.66	33	1	102.1	115	53	39	58
91 NL	0	5	5.74	8	0	31.1	38	20	16	20
93 AL	12	9	3.43	25	3	152.0	154	58	38	90
94 AL	5	7	4.77	23	0	149.0	158	79	38	87
95 AL	8	6	5.21	27	0	115.2	117	67	30	65
Life	59	76	4.51	216	10	1116.2	1195	559	388	677
3 AVE	9	9	4.48	29	1	164.1	169	82	42	95

TERRY MULHOLLAND

Position: Pitcher
Team: San Francisco Giants
Born: March 9, 1963 Uniontown, PA
Height: 6′3″ **Weight:** 200 lbs.
Bats: right **Throws:** left
Acquired: Signed as a free agent, 4/95

Player Summary	
Fantasy Value	$4 to $6
Card Value	4¢ to 6¢
Will	show superb control
Can't	prevent gopher balls
Expect	final comeback bid
Don't Expect	basestealers to try

Mulholland pitched a no-hitter in 1990, won 16 games a year later, worked a league-high 12 complete games in 1992, and started the All-Star Game for the NL in '93. Then came a 1994 trade to the Yankees and complete disaster. Back in the NL in '95, Mulholland was San Francisco's Opening Day starter. But he was even worse with the Giants than he had been with the Yankees. He still has good control and the game's best pickoff move. Mulholland's deliveries have somehow become a feast for right-handed hitters, however. The former Philadelphia standout throws a sinker, a slider, and a changeup. But he gets hurt when the sinker doesn't sink. He gets numerous ground balls when his pitches are working. A martial arts enthusiast and an aggressive competitor, Mulholland failed in his efforts to nibble at the corners. He lost the edge on his control and tended to lose concentration too.

Major League Pitching Register

	W	L	ERA	G	CG	IP	H	ER	BB	SO
86 NL	1	7	4.94	15	0	54.2	51	30	35	27
88 NL	2	1	3.72	9	2	46.0	50	19	7	18
89 AL	4	7	4.92	25	2	115.1	137	63	36	66
90 NL	9	10	3.34	33	6	180.2	172	67	42	75
91 NL	16	13	3.61	34	8	232.0	231	93	49	142
92 NL	13	11	3.81	32	12	229.0	227	97	46	125
93 NL	12	9	3.25	29	7	191.0	177	69	40	116
94 AL	6	7	6.49	24	2	120.2	150	87	37	72
95 NL	5	13	5.80	29	2	149.0	190	96	38	65
Life	68	78	4.24	230	41	1318.1	1385	621	330	706
3 AVE	9	11	5.10	32	4	176.1	201	100	45	97

CURRENT PLAYERS

BOBBY MUNOZ

Position: Pitcher
Team: Philadelphia Phillies
Born: March 3, 1968 Rio Piedras, PR
Height: 6'7" **Weight:** 237 lbs.
Bats: right **Throws:** right
Acquired: Traded by Yankees with Kevin Jordan and Ryan Karp for Terry Mulholland and Jeff Patterson, 2/94

Player Summary
Fantasy Value	$4 to $6
Card Value	4¢ to 6¢
Will	rejoin the rotation
Can't	freeze baserunners
Expect	self-help with bat
Don't Expect	frequent strikeouts

When baseball's labor pains ended for everybody else, they lasted for Munoz. Too heavy when he reported after the eight-month layoff, he injured his elbow and missed half the season. He made only three starts for the Phils before returning to the DL with more elbow miseries Aug. 8. The loss of Munoz was a severe blow, since he was Philadelphia's most consistent starter in 1994. A hard-throwing starter in the minors, he made it to the majors as a member of the 1993 Yankee bullpen. But irregular work interfered with his control. Traded across league lines, he was magnificent as a replacement for the injured Curt Schilling in 1994. During a two-hitter at Florida, Munoz didn't walk a man and retired the last 23 hitters. He throws a fastball, a slider, and a changeup. He fares well against left-handed hitters—mainly because his fastball tails away from them. His fielding and pickoff moves need work. If he stays healthy and keeps his control, Munoz could be a sound starter.

Major League Pitching Register
	W	L	ERA	G	CG	IP	H	ER	BB	SO
93 AL	3	3	5.32	38	0	45.2	48	27	26	33
94 NL	7	5	2.67	21	1	104.1	101	31	35	59
95 NL	0	2	5.74	3	0	15.2	15	10	9	6
Life	10	10	3.69	62	1	165.2	164	68	70	98
2 AVE	6	5	3.30	34	1	96.2	95	35	38	58

MIKE MUNOZ

Position: Pitcher
Team: Colorado Rockies
Born: July 12, 1965 Baldwin Park, CA
Height: 6'2" **Weight:** 200 lbs.
Bats: left **Throws:** left
Acquired: Signed as a minor-league free agent, 5/93

Player Summary
Fantasy Value	$0
Card Value	5¢ to 8¢
Will	coax ground outs
Can't	find home plate
Expect	improved control
Don't Expect	lesser workload

If Munoz ever masters the art of throwing strikes, he could become one of baseball's best left-handed relievers. He strands a healthy percentage of the runners he inherits. A sinkerballer who gets lots of ground outs when he's on, Munoz changes gears against right-handed hitters. His pitch of choice then becomes a screwball that is usually highly effective. He was more effective in 1994, when he held hitters to a .223 average and was even tougher with runners on base (.186). A workhorse who holds first batters below the Mendoza Line, Munoz's struggles last year were all attributed to erratic control. He helps himself with his fielding but doesn't hold runners well for a left-hander. That won't prevent him from getting frequent calls, however. His main worries are regaining his control and surviving the strain of his workload. A product of Cal Poly Pomona, Munoz broke into pro ball in the Dodger system in 1986.

Major League Pitching Register
	W	L	ERA	G	S	IP	H	ER	BB	SO
89 NL	0	0	16.88	3	0	2.2	5	5	2	3
90 NL	0	1	3.18	8	0	5.2	6	2	3	2
91 AL	0	0	9.64	6	0	9.1	14	10	5	3
92 AL	1	2	3.00	65	2	48.0	44	16	25	23
93 AL	0	1	6.00	8	0	3.0	4	2	6	1
93 NL	2	1	4.50	21	0	18.0	21	9	9	16
94 NL	4	2	3.74	57	1	45.2	37	19	31	32
95 NL	2	4	7.42	64	2	43.2	54	36	27	37
Life	9	11	5.06	232	5	176.0	185	99	108	117
2 AVE	4	4	5.34	76	2	56.3	56	34	37	43

CURRENT PLAYERS

PEDRO MUNOZ

Position: Outfield
Team: Minnesota Twins
Born: Sept. 19, 1968 Ponce, PR
Height: 5'11" **Weight:** 170 lbs.
Bats: right **Throws:** right
Acquired: Traded by Blue Jays with Nelson Liriano for John Candelaria, 7/90

Player Summary
Fantasy Value................$9 to $11
Card Value.....................5¢ to 8¢
Will.............................show power
Can't.......................cut whiff ratio
Expect..............best bat vs. lefties
Don't Expect ....a hint of speed

A beacon in the fog that engulfed the Twins last year, Munoz showed more muscle than he had in any previous season. During one stretch in July, he blasted five of the Twins' seven home runs. An impatient hitter who fanned about four times more than he walked last year, Munoz has power to all fields when he connects. As a result, the former pull hitter has watched his average climb three years in a row. He is especially productive against left-handed pitching. He also thrives in the Metrodome, a haven for hitters. He's deadly with the count in his favor, especially on a 3-1 pitch. Munoz spent most of last year as a DH, though he also saw some service in right field. He's not much of a fielder, however, and his weak arm is better-suited to left field or first base. One of many who tried to fill the Kent Hrbek void, Munoz played his first-ever games at first last summer. He was a double-digit basestealer in the minors, but he doesn't run much anymore in the wake of knee surgery.

Major League Batting Register

	BA	G	AB	R	H	2B	3B	HR	RBI	SB
90 AL	.271	22	85	13	23	4	1	0	5	3
91 AL	.283	51	138	15	39	7	1	7	26	3
92 AL	.270	127	418	44	113	16	3	12	71	4
93 AL	.233	104	326	34	76	11	1	13	38	1
94 AL	.295	75	244	35	72	15	2	11	36	0
95 AL	.301	104	376	45	113	17	0	18	58	0
Life	.275	483	1587	186	436	70	8	61	234	11
3 AVE	.279	109	364	45	102	17	1	16	51	0

EDDIE MURRAY

Position: Designated hitter; first base
Team: Cleveland Indians
Born: Feb. 24, 1956 Los Angeles, CA
Height: 6'2" **Weight:** 224 lbs.
Bats: both **Throws:** right
Acquired: Signed as a free agent, 12/93

Player Summary
Fantasy Value................$9 to $11
Card Value ....20¢ to 30¢
Will ....knock runners in
Can't................show much speed
Expect ....patience at bat
Don't Expect ....much glove time

Murray still has the bat speed of a much younger man. He's on target to join Hank Aaron and Willie Mays as the only men with 500 homers and 3,000 hits. Murray stroked the milestone single June 30 against Mike Trombley at Minnesota. It made Murray the second switch-hitter to reach 3,000 (with Pete Rose). A consistent performer, Murray is one of three hitters to reach 3,000 hits without a 200-hit season. A good batting eye helps; the eight-time All-Star makes good contact for a slugger and draws enough walks to compile a healthy on-base average. The three-time Gold Glove winner will take an occasional turn at first base.

Major League Batting Register

	BA	G	AB	R	H	2B	3B	HR	RBI	SB
77 AL	.283	160	611	81	173	29	2	27	88	0
78 AL	.285	161	610	85	174	32	3	27	95	6
79 AL	.295	159	606	90	179	30	2	25	99	10
80 AL	.300	158	621	100	186	36	2	32	116	7
81 AL	.294	99	378	57	111	21	2	22	78	2
82 AL	.316	151	550	87	174	30	1	32	110	7
83 AL	.306	156	582	115	178	30	3	33	111	5
84 AL	.306	162	588	97	180	26	3	29	110	10
85 AL	.297	156	583	111	173	37	1	31	124	5
86 AL	.305	137	495	61	151	25	1	17	84	3
87 AL	.277	160	618	89	171	28	3	30	91	1
88 AL	.284	161	603	75	171	27	2	28	84	5
89 NL	.247	160	594	66	147	29	1	20	88	7
90 NL	.330	155	558	96	184	22	3	26	95	8
91 NL	.260	153	576	69	150	23	1	19	96	10
92 NL	.261	156	551	64	144	37	2	16	93	4
93 NL	.285	154	610	77	174	28	1	27	100	2
94 NL	.254	108	433	57	110	21	1	17	76	8
95 AL	.323	113	436	68	141	21	0	21	82	5
Life	.290	2819	10603	1545	3071	532	34	479	1820	105
3 AVE	.285	144	570	78	163	27	1	25	100	6

MIKE MUSSINA

Position: Pitcher
Team: Baltimore Orioles
Born: Dec. 8, 1968 Williamsport, PA
Height: 6' **Weight:** 182 lbs.
Bats: right **Throws:** right
Acquired: First-round pick in 6/90 free-agent draft

Player Summary	
Fantasy Value	$20 to $25
Card Value	40¢ to 80¢
Will	win most starts
Can't	prevent gophers
Expect	amazing control
Don't Expect	strikeout crown

A high-percentage winner, Mussina just missed winning a Cy Young Award in his third full season in 1994. Rewarded with a two-year, $6.925 million contract, he struggled early in '95 before resuming his winning ways. His 4-3 win over the White Sox July 28 made Mussina the first 12-game winner in the majors. A control artist who yields less hits than innings, Mussina mixes five pitches: a fastball, a sinker, a slider, a knuckle-curve, and a changeup generally regarded as the American League's best. Though not a strikeout pitcher, Mussina wins because he's so stingy with bases on balls. He constantly coaxes ground outs from opposing hitters. The former Stanford standout, who holds an economics degree, does his best pitching in clutch situations. He has one of the league's best pickoff moves—rare for a right-hander—and is also a first-rate fielder. Mussina's .700 winning percentage leads all active pitchers with at least 50 wins. Mussina has made the All-Star team four times.

Major League Pitching Register

	W	L	ERA	G	CG	IP	H	ER	BB	SO
91 AL	4	5	2.87	12	2	87.2	77	28	21	52
92 AL	18	5	2.54	32	8	241.0	212	68	48	130
93 AL	14	6	4.46	25	3	167.2	163	83	44	117
94 AL	16	5	3.06	24	3	176.1	163	60	42	99
95 AL	19	9	3.29	32	7	221.2	187	81	50	158
Life	71	30	3.22	125	23	894.1	802	320	205	556
3 AVE	19	8	3.50	32	5	221.2	201	86	53	145

GREG MYERS

Position: Catcher
Team: Minnesota Twins
Born: April 14, 1966 Riverside, CA
Height: 6'2" **Weight:** 206 lbs.
Bats: left **Throws:** right
Acquired: Signed as a free agent, 12/95

Player Summary	
Fantasy Value	$2 to $4
Card Value	4¢ to 6¢
Will	maintain platoon
Can't	handle staff well
Expect	little power
Don't Expect	patience

Although he once pounded 20 minor-league homers, Myers has never approached that level during his eight-year tenure in the majors. He strikes out too much, doesn't walk enough, and is absolutely no threat to steal a base. Plagued by periodic shoulder and knee problems, Myers hangs on primarily because lefty-hitting catchers are hard to find. He's not even a defensive whiz, although he surprised observers by nailing 46 percent of the runners who tried to steal against him in 1994. Myers, whose arm used to be better, was far less successful last summer. Not regarded as much of a game-caller or handler of pitchers, Myers does have good hands and basic receiving skills. That includes plate-blocking and prevention of wild pitches. Platooned throughout his career, Myers has never appeared in more than 108 games in a season. Though he's been around for awhile, he's only 30.

Major League Batting Register

	BA	G	AB	R	H	2B	3B	HR	RBI	SB
87 AL	.111	7	9	1	1	0	0	0	0	0
89 AL	.114	17	44	0	5	2	0	0	1	0
90 AL	.236	87	250	33	59	7	1	5	22	0
91 AL	.262	107	309	25	81	22	0	8	36	0
92 AL	.231	30	78	4	18	7	0	1	13	0
93 AL	.255	108	290	27	74	10	0	7	40	3
94 AL	.246	45	126	10	31	6	0	2	8	0
95 AL	.260	85	273	35	71	12	2	9	38	0
Life	.247	486	1379	135	340	66	3	32	158	3
2 AVE	.258	102	299	33	77	12	1	9	41	2

CURRENT PLAYERS

RANDY MYERS

Position: Pitcher
Team: Chicago Cubs
Born: Sept. 19, 1962 Vancouver, WA
Height: 6'1" **Weight:** 210 lbs.
Bats: left **Throws:** left
Acquired: Signed as a free agent, 12/92

Player Summary	
Fantasy Value	$30 to $35
Card Value	6¢ to 10¢
Will	stifle left-handers
Can't	recapture old form
Expect	late-inning success
Don't Expect	top control

Myers is beginning to make concessions to age. No longer able to muster his old velocity on a consistent basis, he now mixes his low-90s fastball with a slider and a recently added curveball. He still overpowers left-handed hitters. Sometimes, however, he has trouble with righties—especially when his control is off. That happened a lot last year, when he averaged more than four walks per nine innings. The resulting ratio of strikeouts to walks was far below the form Myers had shown while saving an NL-record 53 games in 1993. Perhaps the heavy workloads are catching up to him. The three-time All-Star helps himself by stranding most inherited runners, keeping the ball in the park, and slamming the door on potential basestealers. That helps, since Myers is no help at all with his fielding because he falls off the mound in an awkward position.

Major League Pitching Register

	W	L	ERA	G	S	IP	H	ER	BB	SO
85 NL	0	0	0.00	1	0	2.0	0	0	1	2
86 NL	0	0	4.22	10	0	10.2	11	5	9	13
87 NL	3	6	3.96	54	6	75.0	61	33	30	92
88 NL	7	3	1.72	55	26	68.0	45	13	17	69
89 NL	7	4	2.35	65	24	84.1	62	22	40	88
90 NL	4	6	2.08	66	31	86.2	59	20	38	98
91 NL	6	13	3.55	58	6	132.0	116	52	80	108
92 NL	3	6	4.29	66	38	79.2	84	38	34	66
93 NL	2	4	3.11	73	53	75.1	65	26	26	86
94 NL	1	5	3.79	38	21	40.1	40	17	16	32
95 NL	1	2	3.88	57	38	55.2	49	24	28	59
Life	34	49	3.17	543	243	709.2	592	250	319	713
3 AVE	2	4	3.56	64	42	64.2	59	26	27	66

TIM NAEHRING

Position: Third base
Team: Boston Red Sox
Born: Feb. 1, 1967 Cincinnati, OH
Height: 6'2" **Weight:** 190 lbs.
Bats: right **Throws:** right
Acquired: Eighth-round pick in 6/88 free-agent draft

Player Summary	
Fantasy Value	$8 to $10
Card Value	5¢ to 8¢
Will	get hits
Can't	run much
Expect	some pop
Don't Expect	weak arm

Naehring could always hit. But he couldn't stay healthy long enough to prove it. Disabled five times in five years before 1995, he missed time with back and shoulder surgery. He also had wrist, ankle, and hamstring problems. Playing in 235 of 763 games, he even considered quitting. The Red Sox are glad he didn't. Handed the third-base job after the Scott Cooper trade, Naehring picked up the slack when injuries sidelined Jose Canseco. A .261 career hitter before '95, Naehring was at .344, fourth in the league, when the 1995 All-Stars were announced—without his name on the list. His on-base percentage was even higher, since he walks more than he fans. He is a fastball hitter who uses all fields and shows power to the alleys. He also provides strong defense. The former Miami of Ohio shortstop, a four-position infielder in previous seasons, is best at third, where he shows quick reactions, good hands, and a strong arm. His lone weakness is an inability to run.

Major League Batting Register

	BA	G	AB	R	H	2B	3B	HR	RBI	SB
90 AL	.271	24	85	10	23	6	0	2	12	0
91 AL	.109	20	55	1	6	1	0	0	3	0
92 AL	.231	72	186	12	43	8	0	3	14	0
93 AL	.331	39	127	14	42	10	0	1	17	1
94 AL	.276	80	297	41	82	18	1	7	42	1
95 AL	.307	126	433	61	133	27	2	10	57	0
Life	.278	361	1183	139	329	70	3	23	145	2
2 AVE	.293	127	453	63	133	28	2	11	62	1

CURRENT PLAYERS

CHARLES NAGY

Position: Pitcher
Team: Cleveland Indians
Born: May 5, 1967 Bridgeport, CT
Height: 6'3" **Weight:** 200 lbs.
Bats: left **Throws:** right
Acquired: First-round pick in 6/88 free-agent draft

Player Summary	
Fantasy Value	$13 to $16
Card Value	6¢ to 10¢
Will	post winning record
Can't	prevent home runs
Expect	numerous ground outs
Don't Expect	wildness

Nagy fits right in with a Cleveland rotation dominated by finesse pitchers with good control. Though he owns a diversified arsenal (a sinker, a forkball, a changeup, and a slurve), he favors ground outs over strikeouts as his means of survival. A survivor of 1993 shoulder surgery, Nagy has since won in double-digits twice. He is extremely effective against right-handed hitters. In 1995, he yielded less hits than innings, and fanned about seven and walked about three per game. His strikeout-to-walk ratio was an acceptable 2-to-1. Nagy's downfalls are the long ball and the running game. A former Olympian out of the University of Connecticut, Nagy hopes to recapture the form that made him a 17-game winner and All-Star for a lackluster Cleveland club in 1992. He completed 10 of 33 starts and threw three shutouts that summer. With his shoulder healthy and a strong team behind him, he should have no trouble posting winning logs in the years immediately ahead.

Major League Pitching Register

	W	L	ERA	G	CG	IP	H	ER	BB	SO
90 AL	2	4	5.91	9	0	45.2	58	30	21	26
91 AL	10	15	4.13	33	6	211.1	228	97	66	109
92 AL	17	10	2.96	33	10	252.0	245	83	57	169
93 AL	2	6	6.29	9	1	48.2	66	34	13	30
94 AL	10	8	3.45	23	3	169.1	175	65	48	108
95 AL	16	6	4.55	29	2	178.0	194	90	61	139
Life	57	49	3.97	136	22	905.0	966	399	266	581
2 AVE	16	9	3.95	33	3	219.1	232	96	68	154

JAIME NAVARRO

Position: Pitcher
Team: Chicago Cubs
Born: March 27, 1967 Bayamon, PR
Height: 6'4" **Weight:** 210 lbs.
Bats: right **Throws:** right
Acquired: Signed as a free agent, 4/95

Player Summary	
Fantasy Value	$8 to $10
Card Value	5¢ to 8¢
Will	show superb control
Can't	win fielding awards
Expect	righties to struggle
Don't Expect	frequent strikeouts

Navarro wasted little time justifying the free-agent spending of the Cubs. He won his first five NL decisions, resuming the form he had shown while winning 32 games in a two-year span with the Brewers. His last two Milwaukee years weren't so fortunate, however, with interference from shoulder, hamstring, and weight problems. He inadvertently helped opposing hitters by tipping his pitches. He didn't place his fastball, slider, and changeup with his usual precision location. But the Cubs were willing to bet Navarro could recapture his old form with a new start. With his control back in sync, he posted nine-inning averages of about five strikeouts, two and one-half walks, and eight and one-half hits. He kept the ball in the park—a tall order in Wrigley—and dominated right-handed batters. His biggest improvement over 1994 was his work against left-handed hitters. The Miami-Dade Community College product holds runners well but isn't much of a fielder.

Major League Pitching Register

	W	L	ERA	G	CG	IP	H	ER	BB	SO
89 AL	7	8	3.12	19	1	109.2	119	38	32	56
90 AL	8	7	4.46	32	3	149.1	176	74	41	75
91 AL	15	12	3.92	34	10	234.0	237	102	73	114
92 AL	17	11	3.33	34	5	246.0	224	91	64	100
93 AL	11	12	5.33	35	5	214.1	254	127	73	114
94 AL	4	9	6.62	29	0	89.2	115	66	35	65
95 NL	14	6	3.28	29	1	200.1	194	73	56	128
Life	76	65	4.13	212	25	1243.1	1319	571	374	652
3 AVE	11	10	4.80	36	2	188.2	211	101	62	117

CURRENT PLAYERS

DENNY NEAGLE

Position: Pitcher
Team: Pittsburgh Pirates
Born: Sept. 13, 1968 Prince Georges County, MD
Height: 6'4" **Weight:** 209 lbs.
Bats: left **Throws:** left
Acquired: Traded by Twins for John Smiley and Midre Cummings, 3/92

Player Summary	
Fantasy Value	$8 to $10
Card Value	6¢ to 10¢
Will	become big winner
Can't	get much velocity
Expect	help from hitting
Don't Expect	control to waver

Even though his Pirates team struggled at the start of the 1995 season, Neagle never looked back. He pitched into the sixth or beyond in 14 of his first 16 starts. In a 2-0 win over the Expos on June 23, he yielded only two bloop singles—both by David Segui. Neagle not only became a first-time All-Star but the first 10-game winner in the National League. He did it by blending the change with a high-80s fastball and a slider and curve that he uses only for show. He is a durable, intelligent pitcher who relies on exceptional control of his changeup. Everything works off the change, which bothers both righties and lefties because of its unique forkball-style drop. In 1995, he yielded about one hit per inning and less than two walks per game, and he kept the ball in the park. Neagle can bunt, field, and hold runners. He can also hit. He belted a home run in 1994 and a grand slam last year. The University of Minnesota product pitched for the Twins only briefly.

Major League Pitching Register

	W	L	ERA	G	CG	IP	H	ER	BB	SO
91 AL	0	1	4.05	7	0	20.0	28	9	7	14
92 NL	4	6	4.48	55	0	86.1	81	43	43	77
93 NL	3	5	5.31	50	0	81.1	82	48	37	73
94 NL	9	10	5.12	24	2	137.0	135	78	49	122
95 NL	13	8	3.43	31	5	209.2	221	80	45	150
Life	29	30	4.35	167	7	534.1	547	258	181	436
3 AVE	10	9	4.37	40	3	170.1	174	83	52	138

JEFF NELSON

Position: Pitcher
Team: New York Yankees
Born: Nov. 17, 1966 Baltimore, MD
Height: 6'8" **Weight:** 235 lbs.
Bats: right **Throws:** right
Acquired: Traded by Mariners with Jim Mecir and Tino Martinez for Sterling Hitchcock and Russ Davis, 12/95

Player Summary	
Fantasy Value	$4 to $6
Card Value	4¢ to 6¢
Will	assume heavy workload
Can't	freeze basestealers
Expect	more Ks than innings
Don't Expect	righties to hit

A rubber-armed reliever who ravages right-handed hitters, Nelson has been one of baseball's most anonymous performers since breaking in with the 1992 Mariners. He worked 66 games as a rookie and 71 times a year later, but he had trouble getting off the Seattle-Calgary shuttle. Last year, however, everything fell into place. Getting good location with his sinking fastball and hard slider in 1995, Nelson held hitters below the Mendoza Line and didn't let the long ball hurt him. He yielded five and one-half hits and three and one-half walks per nine innings, and stranded three-quarters of the baserunners he inherited. Nelson wasn't so fortunate with the running game, however. Baserunners' eyes lit up when they saw his slow delivery. Despite his size, he has no trouble fielding his position. He spent more than eight years in the minor leagues—several as a starter—before getting his first look at the majors. Now that he's there, Nelson intends to stay.

Major League Pitching Register

	W	L	ERA	G	S	IP	H	ER	BB	SO
92 AL	1	7	3.44	66	6	81.0	71	31	44	46
93 AL	5	3	4.35	71	1	60.0	57	29	34	61
94 AL	0	0	2.76	28	0	42.1	35	13	20	44
95 AL	7	3	2.17	62	2	78.2	58	19	27	96
Life	13	13	3.16	227	9	262.0	221	92	125	247
3 AVE	4	2	2.97	60	1	69.1	57	23	31	77

CURRENT PLAYERS

ROBB NEN

Position: Pitcher
Team: Florida Marlins
Born: Nov. 28, 1969 San Pedro, CA
Height: 6'4" **Weight:** 200 lbs.
Bats: right **Throws:** right
Acquired: Traded by Rangers with Kurt Miller for Cris Carpenter, 7/93

Player Summary	
Fantasy Value	$20 to $25
Card Value	5¢ to 8¢
Will	strand runners
Can't	improve control
Expect	last-inning heat
Don't Expect	gopher problems

A power-pitching closer whose control sometimes betrays him, Nen endured a mysterious slump last summer before returning to form. When he's on, few hitters can touch him. He converted all 15 of his save opportunities as Bryan Harvey's emergency replacement in 1994 and 12 of his first 16 in 1995. Nen complements a high-90s fastball with a slider and a curve, though he sometimes seems to survive with sheer heat. He strands inherited runners, keeps the ball in the park, and dominates right-handed hitters. He does his best work with runners in scoring position. When he's on, Nen averages one strikeout per inning and gets most other hitters to ground out. In 1995, he yielded less hits than innings and an average of three-plus walks per nine innings. Nen has some trouble holding runners close but few runners reach when he starts an inning. His fielding is fine. Originally property of the Rangers, Nen began his pro career in 1987. Robb is the son of former NL first baseman Dick Nen.

Major League Pitching Register

	W	L	ERA	G	S	IP	H	ER	BB	SO
93 AL	1	1	6.35	9	0	22.2	28	16	26	12
93 NL	1	0	7.02	15	0	33.1	35	26	20	27
94 NL	5	5	2.95	44	15	58.0	46	19	17	60
95 NL	0	7	3.29	62	23	65.2	62	24	23	68
Life	7	13	4.26	130	38	179.2	171	85	86	167
3 AVE	3	5	4.07	52	16	70.2	66	32	32	67

PHIL NEVIN

Position: Third base
Team: Detroit Tigers
Born: Jan. 19, 1971 Fullerton, CA
Height: 6'2" **Weight:** 180 lbs.
Bats: right **Throws:** right
Acquired: Traded by Astros for Mike Henneman, 8/95

Player Summary	
Fantasy Value	$3 to $5
Card Value	8¢ to 12¢
Will	hit line drives
Can't	hold his temper
Expect	strong fielding
Don't Expect	homer barrage

A glittering résumé is no guarantee of a good job. Neither is a temper tantrum directed at a new boss. No one could quarrel with Nevin's credentials. The former All-American from Cal State Fullerton not only played for the 1992 U.S. Olympic team but also won the Golden Spikes Award, given annually to the nation's top amateur. Then he was the nation's first pick in the 1992 amateur draft. Nevin went on to knock in 210 runs in 294 games at Triple-A Tucson in two and one-half years. Hitting .298 when promoted last year, Nevin suffered his first big setback. He flubbed an 18-game Houston trial, hitting .117 with no homers and a single RBI. He then compounded the agony by cursing out manager Terry Collins the day he left. Nevin apologized, but the Astros dumped him. He is better off doing damage with his bat. A line-drive hitter with some patience at the plate, he is also a fine fielder. He has good instincts, fine range, and superior throwing ability. He led Pacific Coast League third basemen in double plays and fielding percentage. Nevin needs to cut down his strikeouts and make better contact.

Major League Batting Register

	BA	G	AB	R	H	2B	3B	HR	RBI	SB
95 NL	.117	18	60	4	7	1	0	0	1	1
95 AL	.219	29	96	9	21	3	1	2	12	0
Life	.179	47	156	13	28	4	1	2	13	1

CURRENT PLAYERS

MARC NEWFIELD

Position: Outfield
Team: San Diego Padres
Born: Oct. 19, 1972 Sacramento, CA
Height: 6'4" **Weight:** 205 lbs.
Bats: right **Throws:** right
Acquired: Traded by Mariners with Ron Villone for Andy Benes and Greg Keagle, 7/95

Player Summary	
Fantasy Value	$4 to $6
Card Value	10¢ to 15¢
Will	play left
Can't	worry about Seattle
Expect	power
Don't Expect	top glove

Unable to find a home in the Mariner outfield, Newfield was sent to San Diego when the Mariners acquired Andy Benes for their successful playoff run last year. The Padres inserted Newfield in left field, and the big, strong power hitter looked like he was at home. He had a .491 slugging average, and he batted .417 against left-handed pitchers. A first-round pick in the 1990 free-agent draft, Newfield has shown big pop throughout his pro career. In 1994 at Triple-A Calgary, he put up 19 homers and a .593 slugging percentage. He also had a .413 on-base average with only 58 strikeouts, and he was named the No. 6 prospect in the Pacific Coast League by *Baseball America*. Newfield put his talent on display in his first pro game, hitting a 500-foot home run. He was later named to the Arizona League All-Star team. He also made the All-Star squad in 1991, this time in the Cal League. Newfield encountered foot problems and underwent surgery in 1992. A fast start in Double-A in 1993 earned him a call-up to the majors.

Major League Batting Register

	BA	G	AB	R	H	2B	3B	HR	RBI	SB
93 AL	.227	22	66	5	15	3	0	1	7	0
94 AL	.184	12	38	3	7	1	0	1	4	0
95 AL	.188	24	85	7	16	3	0	3	14	0
95 NL	.309	21	55	6	17	5	1	1	7	0
Life	.225	79	244	21	55	12	1	6	32	0

WARREN NEWSON

Position: Outfield
Team: Cleveland Indians
Born: July 3, 1964 Newnan, GA
Height: 5'7" **Weight:** 202 lbs.
Bats: left **Throws:** left
Acquired: Signed as a free agent, 12/95

Player Summary	
Fantasy Value	$1
Card Value	4¢ to 6¢
Will	hit to all fields
Can't	find former power
Expect	great batting eye
Don't Expect	daily spot

Body by Puckett doesn't guarantee skills like Puckett. Although he shares the squat physique of long-time All-Star Kirby Puckett, Newson has yet to make a major impression. Yet the potential is there. Blessed with a short, compact stroke and worlds of patience, Newson walks about as much as he strikes out—giving him a solid on-base percentage. He slaps hits to all fields, flashes some power, and even steals a few bases. If he ever reverts to the 22-homer, 36-steal form he showed as a minor leaguer in 1988, Newson should realize the full-time job he covets. Once he got to Seattle, he was placed in a left-field platoon with righty-hitting Rich Amaral. That lasted until the mid-August acquisition of Vince Coleman. A product of Middle Georgia College, Newson twice topped 100 walks in the minors. He also had 15 outfield assists one year, though he doesn't have a great reputation for defensive skills. Originally the property of the Padres, Newson was drafted in 1986.

Major League Batting Register

	BA	G	AB	R	H	2B	3B	HR	RBI	SB
91 AL	.295	71	132	20	39	5	0	4	25	2
92 AL	.221	63	136	19	30	3	0	1	11	3
93 AL	.300	26	40	9	12	0	0	2	6	0
94 AL	.255	63	102	16	26	5	0	2	7	1
95 AL	.261	84	157	34	41	2	2	5	15	2
Life	.261	307	567	98	148	15	2	14	64	8

CURRENT PLAYERS

DAVID NIED

Position: Pitcher
Team: Colorado Rockies
Born: Dec. 22, 1968 Dallas, TX
Height: 6'2" **Weight:** 185 lbs.
Bats: right **Throws:** right
Acquired: First-round pick from Braves in 11/92 expansion draft

Player Summary	
Fantasy Value	$0
Card Value	5¢ to 8¢
Will	win if healthy
Can't	halt injury hex
Expect	superb control
Don't Expect	hitting to help

For the second time in three big-league seasons, elbow problems kept Nied sidelined for months at a time. The inactivity gnawed at the young right-hander, who is still trying to justify his status as the first player chosen in the 1992 expansion draft. He also has had shoulder problems since reaching the majors. Nied shows signs of becoming a fine pitcher, nonetheless. Before throwing the first shutout in the history of the Rockies, he led the International League in wins, complete games, and strikeouts. He then helped pitch the Braves to a divisional title. A sinkerballer who also throws a cut fastball, a curve, and a changeup, Nied, a control artist, is more effective against right-handers and away from the hitters' haven in Denver. Even in other parks, he tends to surrender numerous home runs, because he's always around the plate. Nied can bunt and field, but he's not much of a hitter. Nor is he adept at holding runners on. He should improve with more experience. But Nied has to stay healthy.

Major League Pitching Register

	W	L	ERA	G	CG	IP	H	ER	BB	SO
92 NL	3	0	1.17	6	0	23.0	10	3	5	19
93 NL	5	9	5.17	16	1	87.0	99	50	42	46
94 NL	9	7	4.80	22	2	122.0	137	65	47	74
95 NL	0	0	20.77	2	0	4.1	11	10	3	3
Life	17	16	4.87	46	3	236.1	257	128	97	142
2 AVE	9	9	4.92	23	2	129.0	146	71	54	75

MELVIN NIEVES

Position: Outfield; first base
Team: San Diego Padres
Born: Dec. 28, 1971 San Juan, PR
Height: 6'2" **Weight:** 215 lbs.
Bats: right **Throws:** right
Acquired: Traded by Braves with Donnie Elliott and Vince Moore for Fred McGriff, 7/93

Player Summary	
Fantasy Value	$5 to $7
Card Value	5¢ to 8¢
Will	hit the long ball
Can't	stop striking out
Expect	pinch hits vs. lefties
Don't Expect	high batting mark

Because he's a low-average, high-power hitter who doesn't play the outfield very well, Nieves spent most of last summer as a pinch hitter against left-handed pitching. Although he got a few starts in the outfield corners (especially in left), he fared so poorly against lefties that he had trouble lifting his overall average above the dreaded Mendoza Line. The Padres had hoped for better things, since Nieves did produce three .300 seasons in the minors. In 1994, for example, he hit .308 with 25 homers and 92 RBI in 111 games at Triple-A Las Vegas. The switch-hitting slugger often delivers when he connects. One of his pinch hits was a two-run, 10th-inning homer that beat the Marlins, 7-4, in Miami. Whenever his statistics sag, it usually has something to do with his impatience at the plate. His approximately 5-1 ratio of strikeouts to walks would be good only if the belonged to a pitcher. For a hitter, it's totally unacceptable. Signed by the Braves at age 16, Nieves was the key player in the 1993 Fred McGriff trade.

Major League Batting Register

	BA	G	AB	R	H	2B	3B	HR	RBI	SB
92 NL	.211	12	19	0	4	1	0	0	1	0
93 NL	.191	19	47	4	9	0	0	2	3	0
94 NL	.263	10	19	2	5	1	0	1	4	0
95 NL	.205	98	234	32	48	6	1	14	38	2
Life	.207	139	319	38	66	8	1	17	46	2

CURRENT PLAYERS

DAVID NILSSON

Position: Outfield
Team: Milwaukee Brewers
Born: Dec. 14, 1969 Brisbane, Australia
Height: 6'3" **Weight:** 231 lbs.
Bats: left **Throws:** right
Acquired: Signed as a free agent, 2/87

Player Summary	
Fantasy Value	$10 to $13
Card Value	4¢ to 6¢
Will	hit line drives
Can't	add defense
Expect	a full season
Don't Expect	many strikeouts

As if the work stoppage didn't shave enough time off of the 1995 season, Nilsson also had to deal with Ross-River Fever, a mosquito bite-induced illness that stiffens the joints and muscles. He came to spring training suffering from the virus and ended up sidelined until June 24. Luckily for the Brewers, Nilsson hadn't lost anything at the plate in his time off. He rarely plays against left-handers, but he has always hit right-handers well. He adds line-drive power and makes pretty good contact (fanning 41 times in 1995), but he rarely walks. AL pitchers surrendered Nilsson just 24 free passes last year, leading to a fair .337 on-base percentage. Nilsson played five positions last year (catcher, first base, left field, right field, and DH)—but he is below average at all of them. He is especially scary in right field. His arm isn't great; as a catcher, he threw out just two baserunners in 47 innings. However, Nilsson didn't squawk about being moved around, did everything he was asked, and hit well enough.

Major League Batting Register

	BA	G	AB	R	H	2B	3B	HR	RBI	SB
92 AL	.232	51	164	15	38	8	0	4	25	2
93 AL	.257	100	296	35	76	10	2	7	40	3
94 AL	.275	109	397	51	109	28	3	12	69	1
95 AL	.278	81	263	41	73	12	1	12	53	2
Life	.264	341	1120	142	296	58	6	35	187	8
3 AVE	.271	115	384	51	104	21	2	12	66	2

C.J. NITKOWSKI

Position: Pitcher
Team: Detroit Tigers
Born: March 9, 1973 Suffern, NY
Height: 6'2" **Weight:** 185 lbs.
Bats: left **Throws:** left
Acquired: Traded by Reds with Dave Tuttle and Mark Lewis for David Wells, 7/95

Player Summary	
Fantasy Value	$4 to $6
Card Value	10¢ to 15¢
Will	struggle against righties
Can't	blow anybody away
Expect	good repertoire
Don't Expect	immediate success

Nitkowski was a star at St. John's University before becoming the Reds' first-round draft choice in 1994. He was drafted that high because of his assortment of pitches and the feeling that he was close to pitching in the majors. Nitkowski lacks an overpowering fastball, but he keeps hitters off balance with several off-speed pitches, including a baffling knuckle-curve. In his pro debut in 1994, Nitkowski walked 40 in 75 innings at Double-A, but he was 6-3 with a 3.50 ERA. Nitkowski began the 1995 year in Cincinnati. He allowed just one earned run in his first 12 innings, but soon he began to struggle when hitters stopped swinging at his pitches. Most of his deliveries wind up off the plate, and he had to come in with fastballs to avoid walking everybody. The Reds hated to part with Nitkowski, but they needed a veteran starter for the stretch run. Unfortunately, Tiger Stadium was the wrong place for Nitkowski to develop. While he is certainly capable of pitching in the majors, he may need a full season at Triple-A.

Major League Pitching Register

	W	L	ERA	G	CG	IP	H	ER	BB	SO
95 NL	1	3	6.12	9	0	32.1	41	22	15	18
95 AL	1	4	7.09	11	0	39.1	53	31	20	13
Life	2	7	6.66	20	0	71.2	94	53	35	31

CURRENT PLAYERS

OTIS NIXON

Position: Outfield
Team: Toronto Blue Jays
Born: Jan. 9, 1959 Evergreen, NC
Height: 6'2" **Weight:** 180 lbs.
Bats: both **Throws:** right
Acquired: Signed as a free agent, 12/95

Player Summary
Fantasy Value	$25 to $30
Card Value	6¢ to 10¢
Will	run often
Can't	keep runners honest
Expect	plenty of singles
Don't Expect	many errors

In his first season with Texas, Nixon provided the Rangers with something they have lacked lately—decent leadoff skills. He finished tied for second in the league in stolen bases and tied for his second-highest ever seasonal total despite playing a shortened season. Nixon led the Rangers in runs scored and hits. He also drew 58 walks and notched a .357 on-base percentage. On the down side, he struck out 85 times, far too many for a leadoff hitter. He is still fooled by off-speed pitches and doesn't bunt enough. Last year, he was caught stealing 21 times, the highest total in the AL. But he is still a fine baserunner. In the outfield, Nixon has top range and doesn't make fielding errors, but he owns a weak arm that runners test at will.

Major League Batting Register

	BA	G	AB	R	H	2B	3B	HR	RBI	SB
83 AL	.143	13	14	2	2	0	0	0	0	2
84 AL	.154	49	91	16	14	0	0	0	1	12
85 AL	.235	104	162	34	38	4	0	3	9	20
86 AL	.263	105	95	33	25	4	1	0	8	23
87 AL	.059	19	17	2	1	0	0	0	1	2
88 NL	.244	90	271	47	66	8	2	0	15	46
89 NL	.217	126	258	41	56	7	2	0	21	37
90 NL	.251	119	231	46	58	6	2	1	20	50
91 NL	.297	124	401	81	119	10	1	0	26	72
92 NL	.294	120	456	79	134	14	2	2	22	41
93 NL	.269	134	461	77	124	12	3	1	24	47
94 AL	.274	103	398	60	109	15	1	0	25	42
95 AL	.295	139	589	87	174	21	2	0	45	50
Life	.267	1245	3444	605	920	101	16	7	217	444
3 AVE	.281	145	561	86	158	19	2	0	37	54

HIDEO NOMO

Position: Pitcher
Team: Los Angeles Dodgers
Born: Aug. 31, 1968 Osaka, Japan
Height: 6'2" **Weight:** 180 lbs.
Bats: right **Throws:** right
Acquired: Signed as a free agent, 2/95

Player Summary
Fantasy Value	$15 to $20
Card Value	50¢ to 75¢
Will	baffle with windup
Can't	show perfect control
Expect	plenty of whiffs
Don't Expect	many homers

The sensational freshman campaign enjoyed by Nomo helped breathe life into baseball in 1995. An All-Star in Japan, Nomo came to America hoping to stick in Los Angeles' starting rotation and ended up pacing the club's pennant drive. His baffling motion and devastating split-finger pitch helped him pace the league in strikeouts, finishing ahead of second-place John Smoltz by 43 whiffs. Nomo led the Dodgers in ERA and had a terrific record despite receiving under four and one-half runs of support per game from his teammates. However, he did have some problems, the least of which was an exhausting amount of media attention. Tommy Lasorda works his starting pitchers hard, and Nomo was worn out when October rolled around. While he doesn't allow many homers, he led baseball with 19 wild pitches thrown, allowed plenty of walks, and had problems cutting off the running game due to his elaborate delivery—29 of 34 would-be base thieves were successful. Hitters can adjust to Nomo if they stop swinging at him; most of his splitters end up out of the strike zone. Nomo should continue to be an excellent pitcher for several years.

Major League Pitching Register

	W	L	ERA	G	CG	IP	H	ER	BB	SO
95 NL	13	6	2.54	28	4	191.1	124	54	78	236
Life	13	6	2.54	28	4	191.1	124	54	78	236

CURRENT PLAYERS

JON NUNNALLY

Position: Outfield
Team: Kansas City Royals
Born: Nov. 9, 1971 Pelham, NC
Height: 5'10" **Weight:** 190 lbs.
Bats: left **Throws:** right
Acquired: Rule 5 draft pick from Indians, 12/94

Player Summary	
Fantasy Value	$4 to $6
Card Value	8¢ to 12¢
Will	hit for power
Can't	curb strikeouts
Expect	defensive skill
Don't Expect	a trade

Few observers expected Nunnally to stick with the Royals after Kansas City plucked him off Cleveland's roster last winter. However, the young outfielder with only three years' pro experience (and none above high Class-A) provided a critical bat to the attack all season long. He homered in his first big-league at bat, becoming the first Royal ever to do so. At year's end, Nunnally was second on the club. As the season began, he was an unknown quantity. But despite a penchant for strikeouts, he had major-league talent. His 51 walks are an outstanding total for a first-year player, and his .357 on-base percentage is well above average. In terms of tools, Nunnally is the real thing: He can hit, hit for power, run, and throw. He hit just .162 against left-handers in 1995 and was caught stealing too much despite good speed. He has outstanding range and has the arm strength to play right field, although his accuracy is below average. It is uncertain whether he will begin the 1996 season at Triple-A, but Kansas City could do worse than continue to let Nunnally learn from his mistakes in the majors.

Major League Batting Register

	BA	G	AB	R	H	2B	3B	HR	RBI	SB
95 AL	.244	119	303	51	74	15	6	14	42	6
Life	.244	119	303	51	74	15	6	14	42	6

CHARLIE O'BRIEN

Position: Catcher
Team: Atlanta Braves
Born: May 1, 1961 Tulsa, OK
Height: 6'2" **Weight:** 205 lbs.
Bats: right **Throws:** right
Acquired: Signed as a free agent, 12/93

Player Summary	
Fantasy Value	$0
Card Value	4¢ to 6¢
Will	show agility
Can't	nail baserunners
Expect	power and walks
Don't Expect	stolen bases

Greg Maddux's personal catcher, Charlie O'Brien had another good season in 1995 and has cemented a reputation as a solid backup receiver. He has always had plenty of power and good defensive skills. However, O'Brien has never been able to win a starting post in the bigs due to a sagging bat. However, in 1995 he reached career bests in home runs and walks. His 29 free passes last season led to a good .343 on-base percentage despite a poor batting average. Anything O'Brien kicks in at the plate is a bonus, for he's most needed for what he does behind it. Throwing is not his strength; O'Brien tossed out just 20 of 91 runners trying to steal against him. In his defense, he catches perhaps the least able staff in the majors at holding runners on base. O'Brien calls a good game, blocks pitches well, and is rock-solid on home plate plays.

Major League Batting Register

	BA	G	AB	R	H	2B	3B	HR	RBI	SB
85 AL	.273	16	11	3	3	1	0	0	1	0
87 AL	.200	10	35	2	7	3	1	0	0	0
88 AL	.220	40	118	12	26	6	0	2	9	0
89 AL	.234	62	188	22	44	10	0	6	35	0
90 AL	.186	46	145	11	27	7	2	0	11	0
90 NL	.162	28	68	6	11	3	0	0	9	0
91 NL	.185	69	168	16	31	6	0	2	14	0
92 NL	.212	68	156	15	33	12	0	2	13	0
93 NL	.255	67	188	15	48	11	0	4	23	1
94 NL	.243	51	152	24	37	11	0	8	28	0
95 NL	.227	67	198	18	45	7	0	9	23	0
Life	.219	524	1427	144	312	77	3	33	166	1
3 AVE	.241	71	208	23	50	11	0	8	29	0

CURRENT PLAYERS

JOSE OFFERMAN

Position: Shortstop
Team: Los Angeles Dodgers
Born: Nov. 8, 1968 San Pedro de Macoris, Dominican Republic
Height: 6′ **Weight:** 160 lbs.
Bats: both **Throws:** right
Acquired: Signed as a free agent, 7/86

Player Summary	
Fantasy Value	$4 to $6
Card Value	4¢ to 6¢
Will	draw walks
Can't	wipe out errors
Expect	line drives
Don't Expect	top baserunning

It's pretty hard to fall much further than Offerman did in 1995. He made the All-Star team in July, but he was on the bench by August, replaced by a rookie during the stretch drive and playoffs. Despite his outstanding on-base skills, shaky defense drove him from the lineup in favor of Chad Fonville. Batting second in the Los Angeles lineup, Offerman drew 69 walks and had a fine .389 on-base percentage. He batted .301 against left-handers. He was caught stealing seven times last year, however, and that was nothing compared to his trouble in the field. Most of Offerman's 35 errors were easy ground balls that he simply couldn't handle. Much of his problems are blamed on poor concentration and sloppy mechanics. He is incredibly gifted, with a quick first step and a strong arm. Offerman can't ride his physical tools to work anymore unless he produces. He's still young enough to restart his career and be an All-Star several more times if he can get his game together.

Major League Batting Register

	BA	G	AB	R	H	2B	3B	HR	RBI	SB
90 NL	.155	29	58	7	9	0	0	1	7	1
91 NL	.195	52	113	10	22	2	0	0	3	3
92 NL	.260	149	534	67	139	20	8	1	30	23
93 NL	.269	158	590	77	159	21	6	1	62	30
94 NL	.210	72	243	27	51	8	4	1	25	2
95 NL	.287	119	429	69	123	14	6	4	33	2
Life	.256	579	1967	257	503	65	24	8	160	61
3 AVE	.261	131	472	64	123	16	6	2	45	12

CHAD OGEA

Position: Pitcher
Team: Cleveland Indians
Born: Nov. 9, 1970 Lake Charles, LA
Height: 6′2″ **Weight:** 200 lbs.
Bats: left **Throws:** right
Acquired: Third-round pick in 6/91 free-agent draft

Player Summary	
Fantasy Value	$8 to $12
Card Value	10¢ to 20¢
Will	rely on control
Can't	rely on Ks
Expect	a starting job
Don't Expect	little support

Ogea provided a quality No. 5 starter to the Indians for much of the 1995 season, at least until Ken Hill was acquired for the stretch run. Ogea still turned in a respectable ERA (the best among the Tribe starters last season) and a fine record. He enjoyed plenty of support: His teammates gave him an average of more than five and one-half runs per start. Another key to his success was his outstanding control, allowing only about two and one-half walks per nine innings last year. He has a good fastball, but he hasn't mastered the art of striking out major-league players yet. That should come, however. Ogea was third in the Cleveland organization in strikeouts in 1993 (135) and finished second in 1994 (163) while in the minors. He did have problems holding baserunners and fielding. He led Louisiana State to a National Championship in 1991 and was named second-team All-American that year. Ogea is just one of many young pitchers the Cleveland organization has stockpiled to replace veterans such as Orel Hershiser and Dennis Martinez as leaders of the rotation.

Major League Pitching Register

	W	L	ERA	G	CG	IP	H	ER	BB	SO
94 AL	0	1	6.06	4	0	16.1	21	11	10	11
95 AL	8	3	3.05	20	1	106.1	95	36	29	57
Life	8	4	3.45	24	1	122.2	116	47	39	68

CURRENT PLAYERS

TROY O'LEARY

Position: Outfield
Team: Boston Red Sox
Born: Aug. 4, 1969 Compton, CA
Height: 6′ **Weight:** 196 lbs.
Bats: left **Throws:** left
Acquired: Claimed from Brewers on waivers, 4/95

Player Summary
Fantasy Value.............$4 to $6
Card Value ....8¢ to 12¢
Will......................swing power bat
Can't ....show rifle arm
Expect ....success against righties
Don't Expect ....many steals

Milwaukee made a poor personnel decision in 1995, deciding that since O'Leary wasn't superstar material, he couldn't help the team. Boston, on the other hand, was happy to have a left-handed-hitting outfielder with some power and some speed, and grabbed him off the waiver wire. For much of the season, he ranked in the top three in the AL batting race. When O'Leary cooled down, the Red Sox simply sat him against most left-handers. At year's end, he had a team-leading 31 doubles, a .320 average against right-handed pitching, and had shown that he could play all three outfield positions adequately despite a mediocre arm. O'Leary runs well, but is not much of a basestealer. However, he puts himself in scoring position often due to his power. He took 29 walks and fanned 64 times in 1995, leading to a .355 on-base percentage. O'Leary has drawn as many as 73 walks in the minor leagues. If he can show a little more patience, he could become an ideal No. 2 hitter. As it is, O'Leary should develop into a fine platoon player.

Major League Batting Register

	BA	G	AB	R	H	2B	3B	HR	RBI	SB
93 AL	.293	19	41	3	12	3	0	0	3	0
94 AL	.273	27	66	9	18	1	1	2	7	1
95 AL	.308	112	399	60	123	31	6	10	49	5
Life	.302	158	506	72	153	35	7	12	59	6

JOHN OLERUD

Position: First base
Team: Toronto Blue Jays
Born: Aug. 5, 1968 Seattle, WA
Height: 6′5″ **Weight:** 205 lbs.
Bats: left **Throws:** left
Acquired: Third-round pick in 6/89 free-agent draft

Player Summary
Fantasy Value..............$17 to $20
Card Value ....12¢ to 15¢
Will......................make contact
Can't....................wow with power
Expect.....................production
Don't Expect ....great range

Olerud batted in his lifetime range for the second straight season last year. So maybe it is time to quit expecting him to put up Tony Gwynn-type batting averages. Olerud's .363 batting average in 1993 might have been entirely out of character. It is tempting to think that he could challenge for the batting crown every year when you watch his swing, one of the best in the game. Even if he is a .290 hitter, he has many other things going for him. Olerud posts outstanding on-base averages, takes many walks, and keeps his strikeouts to a minimum. He is especially effective against right-handed pitchers. He sprays hits to all fields and has the ability to drive the ball in the gaps. Olerud didn't drive the ball over the fence much in 1995, however. He is an effective fielder around first base, with fine concentration, good hands, and a strong arm. His range is average, and he isn't the fastest player around. Olerud should continue to provide a steady hand at first base.

Major League Batting Register

	BA	G	AB	R	H	2B	3B	HR	RBI	SB
89 AL	.375	6	8	2	3	0	0	0	0	0
90 AL	.265	111	358	43	95	15	1	14	48	0
91 AL	.256	139	454	64	116	30	1	17	68	0
92 AL	.284	138	458	68	130	28	0	16	66	1
93 AL	.363	158	551	109	200	54	2	24	107	0
94 AL	.297	108	384	47	114	29	2	12	67	1
95 AL	.291	135	492	72	143	32	0	8	54	0
Life	.296	795	2705	405	801	188	6	91	410	2
3 AVE	.317	154	548	85	174	44	2	17	87	0

CURRENT PLAYERS

JOSE OLIVA

Position: Third base
Team: St. Louis Cardinals
Born: March 3, 1971 San Pedro de Macoris, Dominican Republic
Height: 6'3" **Weight:** 215 lbs.
Bats: right **Throws:** right
Acquired: Traded by Braves for Anton French, 8/95

Player Summary
Fantasy Value	$1
Card Value	5¢ to 8¢
Will	bounce back
Can't	contact hit
Expect	some pop
Don't Expect	consistency

Oliva went from being the possible successor to Terry Pendleton in Atlanta to trade fodder for a minor leaguer in one awful season. Shut out of the Braves' third base job by Chipper Jones, Oliva complained that he didn't receive a fair shot. He was then jettisoned to the Cards, where he finished the year with a .142 batting average. Originally the property of the Rangers, Oliva has shown the ability to hit in the past. He had back-to-back 20-homer years in Triple-A in 1993 and 1994. He doesn't hit for average, but he did bat .253 in Triple-A in 1994. He also had a .493 slugging percentage that year, and *Baseball America* named him the No. 4 prospect in the International League. He is a power hitter who can drive in runs, but much of his inconsistency can be blamed on strikeouts. During his career he has fanned more than three times as often as he has walked. Oliva can also flash the leather. He was named best defensive third baseman in the Double-A Texas League in 1992. Oliva was signed by the Texas organization in 1987.

Major League Batting Register
	BA	G	AB	R	H	2B	3B	HR	RBI	SB
94 NL	.288	19	59	9	17	5	0	6	11	0
95 NL	.142	70	183	15	26	5	0	7	20	0
Life	.178	89	242	24	43	10	0	13	31	0

JOE OLIVER

Position: Catcher
Team: Milwaukee Brewers
Born: July 24, 1965 Memphis, TN
Height: 6'3" **Weight:** 220 lbs.
Bats: right **Throws:** right
Acquired: Signed as a free agent, 4/95

Player Summary
Fantasy Value	$4 to $6
Card Value	4¢ to 6¢
Will	show some pop
Can't	show speed
Expect	good defense
Don't Expect	a .270 average

After losing almost all of the 1994 season, Oliver returned last year to his place as one of the better catchers in major-league baseball, for the Brewers. He showed that his power remained, garnering a slugging percentage above the .425 mark. He also posted the top batting average of his career. While he likes to pull inside fastballs and yank them to the wall, he has learned to go with outside pitches. This enables him to utilize more of the field. With the glove on, Oliver is really valuable. He is a fine game-caller and handler of pitchers. He blocks balls in the dirt, shows fine mobility, and unleashes superb throws. His lack of a top success rate in throwing out basestealers last season was more a function of Brewers pitchers not holding runners on as well as they should have. He can't run a lick. Oliver's big challenge for 1996 is staying healthy; he missed most of 1994 with a bad ankle, and he broke a bone in his wrist in 1995.

Major League Batting Register
	BA	G	AB	R	H	2B	3B	HR	RBI	SB
89 NL	.272	49	151	13	41	8	0	3	23	0
90 NL	.231	121	364	34	84	23	0	8	52	1
91 NL	.216	94	269	21	58	11	0	11	41	0
92 NL	.270	143	485	42	131	25	1	10	57	2
93 NL	.239	139	482	40	115	28	0	14	75	0
94 NL	.211	6	19	1	4	0	0	1	5	0
95 AL	.273	97	337	43	92	20	0	12	51	2
Life	.249	649	2107	194	525	115	1	59	304	5
2 AVE	.254	124	431	44	109	25	0	14	66	1

CURRENT PLAYERS

PAUL O'NEILL

Position: Outfield
Team: New York Yankees
Born: Feb. 25, 1963 Columbus, OH
Height: 6'4" **Weight:** 215 lbs.
Bats: left **Throws:** left
Acquired: Traded by Reds with Joe DeBerry for Roberto Kelly, 10/92

Player Summary	
Fantasy Value	$20 to $24
Card Value	8¢ to 12¢
Will	mash righties
Can't	burn up the basepaths
Expect	patience at bat
Don't Expect	a Gold Glove

O'Neill had another terrific season in 1995, hitting .324 against right-handed pitching and continuing to hang in against left-handers (.259). He was probably the Yankees' best and most consistent offensive player in 1995. He combines average hitting ability, patience at bat, and power. He paced the team in home runs and finished first in slugging percentage and third in on-base percentage. Pitchers walked him 71 times last year, and could only fan him 76 times; this is a very good ratio for a power hitter. But that is part of O'Neill's consistent pattern of making good contact. He is a competent outfielder and rarely makes errors, but has mediocre range and doesn't throw well. He has a strong arm, but accuracy has been a problem. O'Neill registered only two assists last year. He does not run well and rarely attempts to steal bases.

Major League Batting Register

	BA	G	AB	R	H	2B	3B	HR	RBI	SB
85 NL	.333	5	12	1	4	1	0	0	1	0
86 NL	.000	3	2	0	0	0	0	0	0	0
87 NL	.256	84	160	24	41	14	1	7	28	2
88 NL	.252	145	485	58	122	25	3	16	73	8
89 NL	.276	117	428	49	118	24	2	15	74	20
90 NL	.270	145	503	59	136	28	0	16	78	13
91 NL	.256	152	532	71	136	36	0	28	91	12
92 NL	.246	148	496	59	122	19	1	14	66	6
93 AL	.311	141	498	71	155	34	1	20	75	2
94 AL	.359	103	368	68	132	25	1	21	83	5
95 AL	.300	127	460	82	138	30	4	22	96	1
Life	.280	1170	3944	542	1104	236	13	159	665	69
3 AVE	.323	143	511	86	165	34	2	25	100	3

STEVE ONTIVEROS

Position: Pitcher
Team: Oakland Athletics
Born: March 5, 1961 Tularosa, NM
Height: 6' **Weight:** 190 lbs.
Bats: right **Throws:** right
Acquired: Signed as a free agent, 1/94

Player Summary	
Fantasy Value	$10 to $13
Card Value	6¢ to 8¢
Will	pitch well if able
Can't	bank on health
Expect	some home runs
Don't Expect	many walks

Ontiveros continued to pitch well in 1995, earning a spot as the Athletics' lone All-Star. However, the home run ball he served up to Florida's Jeff Conine made Ontiveros the game's losing pitcher. Aside from that ignominy, he enjoyed some good times last season. He is still very stingy with baserunners, finishing high on the leader boards in both earned run average and fewest walks per nine innings. Since he rarely walks anybody, opponents must string together several hits to rally against him. Using his mix of sinking fastballs and confusing off-speed deliveries, he allowed over seven homers in 80 frames in 1995 after giving up just seven all season in '94; he was still well below the league average in that category. Often plagued by serious shoulder and elbow problems, he missed several weeks last year with bone spurs in his pitching arm that required surgery. However, he has shown the ability to recuperate.

Major League Pitching Register

	W	L	ERA	G	CG	IP	H	ER	BB	SO
85 AL	1	3	1.93	39	0	74.2	45	16	19	36
86 AL	2	2	4.71	46	0	72.2	72	38	25	54
87 AL	10	8	4.00	35	2	150.2	141	67	50	97
88 AL	3	4	4.61	10	0	54.2	57	28	21	30
89 NL	2	1	3.82	6	0	30.2	34	13	15	12
90 NL	0	0	2.70	5	0	10.0	9	3	3	6
93 AL	0	2	1.00	14	0	18.0	18	2	6	13
94 AL	6	4	2.65	27	2	115.1	93	34	26	56
95 AL	9	6	4.37	22	2	129.2	144	63	38	77
Life	33	30	3.62	204	6	656.1	613	264	203	381
2 AVE	9	6	3.47	31	3	154.2	147	59	40	83

CURRENT PLAYERS

JOSE OQUENDO

Position: Second base
Team: St. Louis Cardinals
Born: July 4, 1963 Rio Piedras, PR
Height: 5'10" **Weight:** 160 lbs.
Bats: both **Throws:** right
Acquired: Traded by Mets with Mark Davis for Argenis Salazar and John Young, 4/85

Player Summary	
Fantasy Value	$1 to $3
Card Value	5¢ to 7¢
Will	get on base
Can't	be a starter
Expect	strong glovework
Don't Expect	extra-base hits

Injuries to infielders Geronimo Pena and Ozzie Smith gave Oquendo a surprising amount of playing time in 1995. The veteran Redbird, completing his 11th straight season in St. Louis, performed adequately. He is still an excellent defensive second baseman and can get by at shortstop, his original position. He lacks speed but has sure hands, an accurate arm, and good lateral movement. In his seasons as an everyday player, he twice led the NL in chances per game. At the plate, he is still disciplined and will take a walk, and as a result he compiled an on-base percentage about 100 points higher than his batting average. However, walks are the sum total of his offensive value, since he doesn't hit for power or steal bases. As a utility man, he's fine; but frequent starts for Oquendo mean his team is in trouble.

Major League Batting Register

	BA	G	AB	R	H	2B	3B	HR	RBI	SB
83 NL	.213	120	328	29	70	7	0	1	17	8
84 NL	.222	81	189	23	42	5	0	0	10	10
86 NL	.297	76	138	20	41	4	1	0	13	2
87 NL	.286	116	248	43	71	9	0	1	24	4
88 NL	.277	148	451	36	125	10	1	7	46	4
89 NL	.291	163	556	59	162	28	7	1	48	3
90 NL	.252	156	469	38	118	17	5	1	37	1
91 NL	.240	127	366	37	88	11	4	1	26	1
92 NL	.257	14	35	3	9	3	1	0	3	0
93 NL	.205	46	73	7	15	0	0	0	4	0
94 NL	.264	55	129	13	34	2	2	0	9	1
95 NL	.209	88	220	31	46	8	3	2	17	1
Life	.256	1190	3202	339	821	104	24	14	254	35

JOE ORSULAK

Position: Outfield
Team: Florida Marlins
Born: May 31, 1962 Glen Ridge, NJ
Height: 6'1" **Weight:** 196 lbs.
Bats: left **Throws:** left
Acquired: Signed as a free agent, 12/95

Player Summary	
Fantasy Value	$4 to $6
Card Value	5¢ to 7¢
Will	find a way to play
Can't	get much respect
Expect	balanced offense
Don't Expect	stolen bases

Mets outfielders come and go, but it was Orsulak who always seems to be in the lineup. He began the 1995 season on the bench while others, young and old, played ahead of him. But the hard-nosed, hustling fly chaser got plenty of at bats as his competition wilted. Formerly a speedy center fielder in his Pittsburgh days, Orsulak has settled into the role of a good defensive player with a strong arm who can still patrol center in a pinch. Dallas Green often used Orsulak, who makes good contact, in the No. 2 and No. 5 spots, although he lacks the impact to fill such critical offensive roles. He has insufficient patience to wait for walks, little ability against left-handers, inadequate basestealing speed, and negligible extra-base power. He usually hits right-handers well, plays hard, and is durable, however.

Major League Batting Register

	BA	G	AB	R	H	2B	3B	HR	RBI	SB
83 NL	.182	7	11	0	2	0	0	0	1	0
84 NL	.254	32	67	12	17	1	2	0	3	0
85 NL	.300	121	397	54	119	14	6	0	21	24
86 NL	.249	138	401	60	100	19	6	2	19	24
88 AL	.288	125	379	48	109	21	3	8	27	9
89 AL	.285	123	390	59	111	22	5	7	55	5
90 AL	.269	124	413	49	111	14	3	11	57	6
91 AL	.278	143	486	57	135	22	1	5	43	6
92 AL	.289	117	391	45	113	18	3	4	39	5
93 NL	.284	134	409	59	116	15	4	8	35	5
94 NL	.260	96	292	39	76	3	0	8	42	4
95 NL	.283	108	290	41	82	19	2	1	37	1
Life	.278	1268	3926	523	1091	168	35	54	379	92
3 AVE	.275	130	382	53	105	14	2	7	45	4

CURRENT PLAYERS

DONOVAN OSBORNE

Position: Pitcher
Team: St. Louis Cardinals
Born: June 21, 1969 Roseville, CA
Height: 6'2" **Weight:** 195 lbs.
Bats: both **Throws:** left
Acquired: First-round pick in 6/90 free-agent draft

Player Summary	
Fantasy Value	$0
Card Value	4¢ to 6¢
Will	rehabilitate
Can't	blow away hitters
Expect	good control
Don't Expect	heavy workload

Recovering from serious shoulder surgery that wiped out his entire 1994 season, Osborne returned in 1995 and struggled to regain effectiveness—when he could pitch at all. In his first four starts, he allowed just five walks in 22 innings. But he got little support, and he had just an 0-1 record when he was disabled on May 15. This time, it was his elbow that hurt, and Osborne didn't work again until July 16. When he returned, Osborne pitched gamely but had big problems with left-handers. It was a disappointing year for Osborne on a Cardinals team full of disappointing performances, but at least he did some things right. He didn't walk many hitters, and he certainly would have had a better year if the Cardinals had averaged more than about three runs per game of support for him. He never won with velocity; but even so, he can't afford to give up homers at the rate he did in 1995. He needs to build up more arm strength to survive. He was an All-America pitcher at UNLV in 1989. Osborne should get another shot at the rotation this spring.

Major League Pitching Register

	W	L	ERA	G	CG	IP	H	ER	BB	SO
92 NL	11	9	3.77	34	0	179.0	193	75	38	104
93 NL	10	7	3.76	26	1	155.2	153	65	47	83
95 NL	4	6	3.81	19	0	113.1	112	48	34	82
Life	25	22	3.78	79	1	448.0	458	188	119	269
2 AVE	7	7	3.78	24	1	141.2	140	60	43	88

SPIKE OWEN

Position: Infield
Team: California Angels
Born: April 19, 1961 Cleburne, TX
Height: 5'10" **Weight:** 170 lbs.
Bats: both **Throws:** right
Acquired: Traded by Yankees for Jose Musset, 10/93

Player Summary	
Fantasy Value	$1 to $3
Card Value	5¢ to 7¢
Will	show steady glove
Can't	get regular duty
Expect	continued employment
Don't Expect	offensive flash

Despite a surprising .310 season in 1994, Owen had no place to start for California last year. The Angels slotted Damion Easley at second base, and Tony Phillips cut into Owen's time as a multiposition player. Of course, Owen did not help himself by slumping at the plate in 1995. A shoulder injury suffered last July cut into his playing time as well. Even when healthy, he lacks strong throwing skills at any infield position, but he has a reliable glove and positions himself well. He has always been a Punch-and-Judy hitter with strike-zone judgement but little power. His on-base average stayed over .300 for most of the season last year. Not blessed with much speed, he is a smart baserunner. He's not going to be a regular again, but should continue to find work coming off the pine.

Major League Batting Register

	BA	G	AB	R	H	2B	3B	HR	RBI	SB
83 AL	.196	80	306	36	60	11	3	2	21	10
84 AL	.245	152	530	67	130	18	8	3	43	16
85 AL	.259	118	352	41	91	10	6	6	37	11
86 AL	.231	154	528	67	122	24	7	1	45	4
87 AL	.259	132	437	50	113	17	7	2	48	11
88 AL	.249	89	257	40	64	14	1	5	18	0
89 NL	.233	142	437	52	102	17	4	6	41	3
90 NL	.234	149	453	55	106	24	5	5	35	8
91 NL	.255	139	424	39	108	22	8	3	26	2
92 NL	.269	122	386	52	104	16	3	7	40	9
93 AL	.234	103	334	41	78	16	2	2	20	3
94 AL	.310	82	268	30	83	17	2	3	37	2
95 AL	.229	82	218	17	50	9	3	1	28	3
Life	.246	1544	4930	587	1211	215	59	46	439	82
3 AVE	.263	104	319	34	84	17	3	2	35	3

CURRENT PLAYERS

MIKE PAGLIARULO

Position: Third base
Team: Texas Rangers
Born: March 15, 1960 Medford, MA
Height: 6'2" **Weight:** 201 lbs.
Bats: left **Throws:** right
Acquired: Signed as a free agent, 3/95

Player Summary	
Fantasy Value	$1
Card Value	5¢ to 7¢
Will	show good arm
Can't	find old power
Expect	plenty of whiffs
Don't Expect	regular duty

Fate plays strange games. Pagliarulo had spent 1994 with Japan's Seibu Lions, where he batted .263 with seven homers and 47 RBI in 285 at bats. Texas invited him to spring training last year, and he made the team as a bench player, occasional DH, and pinch hitter. When Rangers third sacker Dean Palmer suffered a season-ending torn biceps tendon on June 3, Pagliarulo was put at the hot corner. He contributed little offense. He struck out with his usual frequency and provided no power. For most of the season, Pagliarulo maintained an on-base percentage under the .300 level, and right-handers (who he is supposed to be able to hit) held him to an average under .250. Pagliarulo's throwing arm is strong and he's sure-handed, but his defense won't keep him around if he doesn't hit.

Major League Batting Register

	BA	G	AB	R	H	2B	3B	HR	RBI	SB
84 AL	.239	67	201	24	48	15	3	7	34	0
85 AL	.239	138	380	55	91	16	2	19	62	0
86 AL	.238	149	504	71	120	24	3	28	71	4
87 AL	.234	150	522	76	122	26	3	32	87	1
88 AL	.216	125	444	46	96	20	1	15	67	1
89 AL	.197	74	223	19	44	10	0	4	16	1
89 NL	.196	50	148	12	29	7	0	3	14	2
90 NL	.254	128	398	29	101	23	2	7	38	1
91 AL	.279	121	365	38	102	20	0	6	36	1
92 AL	.200	42	105	10	21	4	0	0	9	1
93 AL	.303	116	370	55	112	25	4	9	44	6
95 AL	.232	86	241	27	56	16	0	4	27	0
Life	.241	1246	3901	462	942	206	18	134	505	18
2 AVE	.273	106	321	43	88	22	2	7	37	3

TOM PAGNOZZI

Position: Catcher
Team: St. Louis Cardinals
Born: July 30, 1962 Tucson, AZ
Height: 6'1" **Weight:** 190 lbs.
Bats: right **Throws:** right
Acquired: Eighth-round pick in 6/83 free-agent draft

Player Summary	
Fantasy Value	$4 to $6
Card Value	5¢ to 7¢
Will	rehabilitate, again
Can't	win homer crown
Expect	decent average
Don't Expect	defensive troubles

Many players went sour on the 1995 Cardinals, but Pagnozzi was one of the more obvious cases. Usually a consistent hitter, he could not get untracked and failed to provide even his normal, average level of punch last year. He slugged in the .300 range for much of the season and had a substandard on-base percentage in the .250 range. He runs well for a catcher and makes good contact. Unfortunately, injuries have dogged the Gold Glove receiver for most of his career, and last year continued the pattern. A July 17 home plate collision with Montreal's Dave Silvestri proved disastrous for Pagnozzi, who wound up with a torn tendon in his left knee. When physically able, Pagnozzi displays defensive skills on par with any other catcher, including a quick release, a strong arm, and a celebrated ability to handle pitchers.

Major League Batting Register

	BA	G	AB	R	H	2B	3B	HR	RBI	SB
87 NL	.188	27	48	8	9	1	0	2	9	1
88 NL	.282	81	195	17	55	9	0	0	15	0
89 NL	.150	52	80	3	12	2	0	0	3	0
90 NL	.277	69	220	20	61	15	0	2	23	1
91 NL	.264	140	459	38	121	24	5	2	57	9
92 NL	.249	139	485	33	121	26	3	7	44	2
93 NL	.258	92	330	31	85	15	1	7	41	1
94 NL	.272	70	243	21	66	12	1	7	40	0
95 NL	.215	62	219	17	47	14	1	2	15	0
Life	.253	732	2279	188	577	118	11	29	247	14
3 AVE	.251	87	306	27	77	16	1	6	38	0

CURRENT PLAYERS

RAFAEL PALMEIRO

Position: First base
Team: Baltimore Orioles
Born: Sept. 24, 1964 Havana, Cuba
Height: 6′ **Weight:** 180 lbs.
Bats: left **Throws:** left
Acquired: Signed as a free agent, 12/93

Player Summary	
Fantasy Value	$25 to $30
Card Value	12¢ to 17¢
Will	provide offense
Can't	run like a deer
Expect	line drives
Don't Expect	much attention

Despite providing outstanding production for several seasons, Palmeiro simply hasn't attracted the kind of media acclaim that his talents warrant. Perhaps it's his slightly quiet nature, or perhaps it's because he shared a clubhouse with media darling Cal Ripken Jr. last year. Whatever the cause, Palmeiro just keeps hitting, but doesn't get many headlines. A very intelligent hitter, he works the strike zone until he gets a pitch he likes. If he doesn't see one, Palmeiro will just take the walk. He makes good contact and now hits left-handers as well as he does righties. He is a smart if not swift baserunner. At one time a left field prospect with the Cubs, Palmeiro's skills on defense rank with the best first sackers in the AL. He is a remarkably consistent hitter, and he also is arguably one of the five best first basemen in baseball.

Major League Batting Register

	BA	G	AB	R	H	2B	3B	HR	RBI	SB
86 NL	.247	22	73	9	18	4	0	3	12	1
87 NL	.276	84	221	32	61	15	1	14	30	2
88 NL	.307	152	580	75	178	41	5	8	53	12
89 AL	.275	156	559	76	154	23	4	8	64	4
90 AL	.319	154	598	72	191	35	6	14	89	3
91 AL	.322	159	631	115	203	49	3	26	88	4
92 AL	.268	159	608	84	163	27	4	22	85	2
93 AL	.295	160	597	124	176	40	2	37	105	22
94 AL	.319	111	436	82	139	32	0	23	76	7
95 AL	.310	143	554	89	172	30	2	39	104	3
Life	.300	1300	4857	758	1455	296	27	194	706	60
3 AVE	.308	159	611	113	188	40	1	38	110	12

DEAN PALMER

Position: Third base
Team: Texas Rangers
Born: Dec. 27, 1968 Tallahassee, FL
Height: 6′1″ **Weight:** 190 lbs.
Bats: right **Throws:** right
Acquired: Third-round pick in 6/86 free-agent draft

Player Summary	
Fantasy Value	$12 to $15
Card Value	7¢ to 10¢
Will	swing for fences
Can't	add stolen bases
Expect	defensive inconsistency
Don't Expect	a batting crown

The always-promising but frequently disappointing Palmer was enjoying a monster season in 1995 before a freak injury sidelined him for the year. On June 3, batting against Minnesota's Kevin Tapani, Palmer swung hard at a changeup and, in the process, ruptured the biceps tendon in his left arm. The tendon actually rolled up his arm towards his shoulder, and Palmer required surgery to reattach it to the elbow. Before disaster struck, the strapping third sacker was slugging at a .623 clip and was pacing his team in home runs and RBI; he had hit three homers in his last 12 at bats. He has had trouble mastering the strike zone in his career, but in 1995 drew 21 walks and fanned just 21 times (by far his best rate ever) until the injury. His on-base percentage was an outstanding .450. If he really has learned to lay off bad pitches, and can still swing, he could be a terrific hitter. Palmer's glovework at third could improve, but he throws well and always hustles.

Major League Batting Register

	BA	G	AB	R	H	2B	3B	HR	RBI	SB
89 AL	.105	16	19	0	2	2	0	0	1	0
91 AL	.187	81	268	38	50	9	2	15	37	0
92 AL	.229	152	541	74	124	25	0	26	72	10
93 AL	.245	148	519	88	127	31	2	33	96	11
94 AL	.246	93	342	50	84	14	2	19	59	3
95 AL	.336	36	119	30	40	6	0	9	24	1
Life	.236	526	1808	280	427	87	6	102	289	25
2 AVE	.245	140	500	79	123	25	2	30	90	8

CURRENT PLAYERS

CRAIG PAQUETTE

Position: Third base
Team: Oakland Athletics
Born: March 28, 1969 Long Beach, CA
Height: 6' **Weight:** 190 lbs.
Bats: right **Throws:** right
Acquired: Eighth-round pick in 6/89 free-agent draft

Player Summary	
Fantasy Value	$2 to $4
Card Value	5¢ to 7¢
Will	show power
Can't	lay off bad pitches
Expect	utility duty
Don't Expect	much speed

Paquette climbed steadily up the Athletics' minor-league ladder, hitting for power at every stop and impressing on defense. Unfortunately, even in the bushes he whiffed like crazy, and big-league pitchers have exploited the many holes in his swing. Last season, he struck out about five times as much as he walked, numbers that were just a slight improvement on his previous major-league 8-1 strikeout-to-walk ratio. Obviously, with such a problem making contact and a miserable on-base percentage (which hovered at about .250), he didn't stay in the lineup despite his ability to pop frequent home runs. The Athletics' supply of good minor-league prospects at third base meant Paquette needed to hone his utility skills to ensure himself a spot in the future. He saw action in the outfield and at shortstop last year as well as at the hot corner. A former college star at Golden West Junior College, Paquette is a plus defensively at every position due to his strong arm and good reflexes, which could ensure his major-league future.

Major League Batting Register

	BA	G	AB	R	H	2B	3B	HR	RBI	SB
93 AL	.219	105	393	35	86	20	4	12	46	4
94 AL	.143	14	49	0	7	2	0	0	0	1
95 AL	.226	105	283	42	64	13	1	13	49	5
Life	.217	224	725	77	157	35	5	25	95	10
2 AVE	.222	112	356	41	79	17	3	13	51	5

MARK PARENT

Position: Catcher
Team: Chicago Cubs
Born: Sept. 16, 1961 Ashford, OR
Height: 6'5" **Weight:** 240 lbs.
Bats: right **Throws:** right
Acquired: Claimed from Pirates on waivers, 9/95

Player Summary	
Fantasy Value	$0
Card Value	5¢ to 7¢
Will	fill in capably
Can't	outrun a snail
Expect	good throwing
Don't Expect	20 homers

The well-traveled Parent finally got a full season's worth of playing time in 1994, providing good production for the Cubs in a reserve role. However, Chicago cut him loose anyway. The Pirates quickly snapped up the veteran, and he played in Pittsburgh for most of the season. Given a chance at regular duty when Don Slaught went down early in 1995 with a hamstring injury, Parent responded with a power surge that surprised the entire league. By June, he had already cleared his previous major-league high in home runs. He hit well against both lefties and righties, and he had an on-base average at about .330 for much of the season. Of course, at his age, he is no coming star. He strikes out often and is slow, but he provides capable play at bat and in the field. He has a good arm, tossing out about one-third of runners trying to steal last year. The Cubs reclaimed him late in the season.

Major League Batting Register

	BA	G	AB	R	H	2B	3B	HR	RBI	SB
86 NL	.143	8	14	1	2	0	0	0	0	0
87 NL	.080	12	25	0	2	0	0	0	2	0
88 NL	.195	41	118	9	23	3	0	6	15	0
89 NL	.191	52	141	12	27	4	0	7	21	1
90 NL	.222	65	189	13	42	11	0	3	16	1
91 NL	.000	3	1	0	0	0	0	0	0	0
92 NL	.235	17	34	4	8	1	0	2	4	0
93 NL	.259	22	54	7	14	2	0	4	12	0
94 NL	.263	44	99	8	26	4	0	3	16	0
95 NL	.234	81	265	30	62	11	0	18	38	0
Life	.219	345	940	84	206	36	0	43	124	2

CURRENT PLAYERS

JEFF PARRETT

Position: Pitcher
Team: St. Louis Cardinals
Born: Aug. 26, 1961 Indianapolis, IN
Height: 6'3" **Weight:** 205 lbs.
Bats: right **Throws:** right
Acquired: Signed as a minor-league free agent, 4/95

Player Summary
Fantasy Value $1
Card Value . . . . 4¢ to 6¢
Will . . . . work often
Can't . . . . show pinpoint control
Expect . . . . strikeouts
Don't Expect . . . . marquee role

Parrett enjoyed a good comeback season in 1995. Recovering from a detached elbow ligament that sidelined him for much of the 1994 season, Parrett worked in the middle for St. Louis. He showed that he hadn't lost his good stuff. He finished the year with almost one strikeout per inning—one of the best ratios on the Cardinals staff. He notched his Ks using a good fastball and curve. Although Parrett has above-average stuff, he has never been able to break out of the middle relief role. In 1995, he allowed too many home runs and gave up too many wild pitches. Parrett didn't work that much with runners on; instead he was getting work in full innings, often with the Cardinals trailing. He has a decent pickoff move and is a good fielder, even though he is a bit awkward off the mound. Parrett was a ninth-round pick by the Brewers out of the University of Kentucky.

Major League Pitching Register

	W	L	ERA	G	CG	IP	H	ER	BB	SO
86 NL	0	1	4.87	12	0	20.1	19	11	13	21
87 NL	7	6	4.21	45	6	62.0	53	29	30	56
88 NL	12	4	2.65	61	6	91.2	66	27	45	62
89 NL	12	6	2.98	72	6	105.2	90	35	44	98
90 NL	5	10	4.64	67	2	108.2	119	56	55	86
91 NL	1	2	6.33	18	1	21.1	31	15	12	14
92 AL	9	1	3.02	66	0	98.1	81	33	42	78
93 NL	3	3	5.38	40	1	73.2	78	44	45	66
95 NL	4	7	3.64	59	0	76.2	71	31	28	71
Life	53	40	3.84	440	22	658.1	608	281	314	552
2 AVE	4	5	4.44	53	1	79.2	79	39	38	73

LANCE PARRISH

Position: Catcher
Team: Toronto Blue Jays
Born: June 15, 1956 Clarion, PA
Height: 6'3" **Weight:** 224 lbs.
Bats: right **Throws:** right
Acquired: Signed as a free agent, 4/95

Player Summary
Fantasy Value $0
Card Value . . . . 4¢ to 6¢
Will . . . . try to hang on
Can't . . . . get starting duty
Expect . . . . Cooperstown consideration
Don't Expect . . . . much offense

Parrish found another new home in 1995 with the Blue Jays. Toronto was left desperate for catching help by the departure of Pat Borders, Carlos Delgado's defensive problems, and Randy Knorr's injury. Parrish got plenty of playing time, but unfortunately contributed little to the Toronto attack. He has lost a great deal of bat speed and fanned too much. The great power he showed in his glory days with the Tigers is largely gone. Behind the plate, Parrish showed his cannon arm. One of the slowest baserunners in recent memory, he is no longer agile. But like most veteran catchers, he calls a decent game. He can still fill the backup role.

Major League Batting Register

	BA	G	AB	R	H	2B	3B	HR	RBI	SB
77 AL	.196	12	46	10	9	2	0	3	7	0
78 AL	.219	85	288	37	63	11	3	14	41	0
79 AL	.276	143	493	65	136	26	3	19	65	6
80 AL	.286	144	553	79	158	34	6	24	82	6
81 AL	.244	96	348	39	85	18	2	10	46	2
82 AL	.284	133	486	75	138	19	2	32	87	3
83 AL	.269	155	605	80	163	42	3	27	114	1
84 AL	.237	147	578	75	137	16	2	33	98	2
85 AL	.273	140	549	64	150	27	1	28	98	2
86 AL	.257	91	327	53	84	6	1	22	62	0
87 NL	.245	130	466	42	114	21	0	17	67	0
88 NL	.215	123	424	44	91	17	2	15	60	0
89 AL	.238	124	433	48	103	12	1	17	50	1
90 AL	.268	133	470	54	126	14	0	24	70	2
91 AL	.216	119	402	38	87	12	0	19	51	0
92 AL	.233	93	275	26	64	13	1	12	32	1
93 AL	.200	10	20	2	4	1	0	1	2	1
94 NL	.270	40	126	10	34	5	0	3	16	1
95 AL	.202	70	178	15	36	9	0	4	22	0
Life	.252	1988	7067	856	1782	305	27	324	1070	28

CURRENT PLAYERS

BOB PATTERSON

Position: Pitcher
Team: California Angels
Born: May 16, 1959 Jacksonville, FL
Height: 6'2" **Weight:** 192 lbs.
Bats: right **Throws:** left
Acquired: Signed as a free agent, 4/95

Player Summary	
Fantasy Value	$0
Card Value	5¢ to 7¢
Will	get work
Can't	impress with heater
Expect	dependable control
Don't Expect	many strikeouts

Patterson spent much of the year as the sole left-hander in the California bullpen. He pitched effectively in a very well-defined late-inning role, rarely facing tough right-handed hitters and seldom pitching more than one inning at a time. He held fellow lefties to a batting average under the .150 mark for much of the season last year, and his stinginess with walks makes Patterson valuable. At one time a starting pitcher with Pittsburgh, he bombed out in that role and had to go to the minors to reestablish himself. He got back to the majors by improving his command of a variety of off-speed pitches. His fastball is just average, but his control and variety of deliveries are good enough to keep him around. He generally gets ground balls, rarely getting any pitches high in the strike zone or giving up home runs. But still, he is highly unlikely to get many save opportunities.

Major League Pitching Register

	W	L	ERA	G	S	IP	H	ER	BB	SO
85 NL	0	0	24.75	3	0	4.0	13	11	3	1
86 NL	2	3	4.95	11	0	36.1	49	20	5	20
87 NL	1	4	6.70	15	0	43.0	49	32	22	27
89 NL	4	3	4.05	12	1	26.2	23	12	8	20
90 NL	8	5	2.95	55	0	94.2	88	31	21	70
91 NL	2	3	4.11	54	2	65.2	67	30	15	57
92 NL	6	3	2.92	60	9	64.2	59	21	23	43
93 AL	2	4	4.78	52	1	52.2	59	28	11	46
94 AL	2	3	4.07	47	1	42.0	35	19	15	30
95 AL	2	2	3.04	62	0	53.1	48	18	13	41
Life	34	30	4.14	371	19	483.0	490	222	136	355
3 AVE	3	3	3.93	63	1	57.1	54	25	16	45

JOHN PATTERSON

Position: Second base
Team: San Francisco Giants
Born: Feb. 11, 1967 Key West, FL
Height: 5'9" **Weight:** 168 lbs.
Bats: both **Throws:** right
Acquired: 23rd-round pick in 6/88 free-agent draft

Player Summary	
Fantasy Value	$1
Card Value	7¢ to 10¢
Will	show good speed
Can't	hit lefties
Expect	strong defense
Don't Expect	regular duty

Robby Thompson's injury problems have given Patterson plenty of chances to establish himself as a major-league hitter, but he has not taken advantage of the opportunity. Again in 1995, Patterson showed an inability to make consistent contact, middling power, and poor on-base skills. He fanned almost four times as much as he walked, and his on-base percentage was below .275 for much of the year. While he is fast and is an excellent baserunner, he doesn't reach base often enough to make use of his speed. Although he is a switch-hitter, Patterson has batted well under .200 against left-handers for his career. Despite his troubles at bat, Patterson continues to show good defensive skills at second base. He has fine range, turns the double play well, and rarely makes errors. A botched conversion to center field several years ago left him with a surgically repaired shoulder, but at least his throws are accurate if not strong. He should remain a useful major-league reserve due to his speed and defense for several more seasons.

Major League Batting Register

	BA	G	AB	R	H	2B	3B	HR	RBI	SB
92 NL	.184	32	103	10	19	1	1	0	4	5
93 NL	.188	16	16	1	3	0	0	1	2	0
94 NL	.237	85	240	36	57	10	1	3	32	13
95 NL	.205	95	205	27	42	5	3	1	14	4
Life	.215	228	564	74	121	16	5	5	52	22
2 AVE	.224	113	284	41	64	10	2	3	30	11

CURRENT PLAYERS

ROGER PAVLIK

Position: Pitcher
Team: Texas Rangers
Born: Oct. 4, 1967 Houston, TX
Height: 6'3" **Weight:** 220 lbs.
Bats: right **Throws:** right
Acquired: Second-round pick in 2/86 free-agent draft

Player Summary	
Fantasy Value	$4 to $6
Card Value	6¢ to 8¢
Will	keep hitters off balance
Can't	throw blazing fastball
Expect	plenty of chances
Don't Expect	a strikeout crown

After missing much of the 1994 season due to recurring shoulder problems, Pavlik returned physically sound last season. Despite numerous opportunities, however, he failed to establish himself in the Rangers rotation. He had just an average fastball following rotator cuff surgery, and too often he could not get his baffling curve and slider over for strikes. He worked behind in the count too often for comfort. Fellow right-handers batted over .300 against him for much of the season, and he allowed too many home runs. Despite these problems, he has shown that he can be a gifted pitcher who can mow down hitters. In many of his 1995 starts, Pavlik would dominate the opposition through three or four innings but fall apart quickly. This trait, and his penchant for getting ground balls, have led many to believe he would be best suited for relief work. However, he doesn't help himself much as a fielder and lacks a strong pickoff move; two things that would work against him as a reliever.

STEVE PEGUES

Position: Outfield
Team: Pittsburgh Pirates
Born: May 21, 1968 Pontotoc, MS
Height: 6'2" **Weight:** 190 lbs.
Bats: right **Throws:** right
Acquired: Claimed from Reds on waivers, 7/94

Player Summary	
Fantasy Value	$1
Card Value	6¢ to 8¢
Will	swing at anything
Can't	win regular job
Expect	decent power
Don't Expect	high on-base mark

A first-round pick of the Tigers in 1987, Pegues has speed and line-drive power. He can also throw, racking up 24 assists in the Triple-A Pacific Coast League in 1992. Unfortunately, he has watched his career stall due to an inability to master the strike zone. In the minors, he generally fanned seven to eight times as often as he took a walk. After the Tigers gave up on him, Pegues drifted to the Padres organization and got a few at bats with the 1994 Reds before the talent-thin Pirates inked him later that summer. Given a chance to assume a reserve role with occasional platoon duty in 1995, he hit about .290 with power against left-handers for much of the season and played fairly well in both right field and left field. Unfortunately, he also struck out about nine times more than he walked, leading to a poor on-base percentage. Due to his trouble with right-handers and his overaggressiveness at the plate, Pegues won't be a starter in the major leagues despite his tools and good pedigree. However, if he can hit .270 steadily, he'll hang around on somebody's bench.

Major League Pitching Register

	W	L	ERA	G	CG	IP	H	ER	BB	SO
92 AL	4	4	4.21	13	1	62.0	66	29	34	45
93 AL	12	6	3.41	26	2	166.1	151	63	80	131
94 AL	2	5	7.69	11	0	50.1	61	43	30	31
95 AL	10	10	4.37	31	2	191.2	174	93	90	149
Life	28	25	4.36	81	5	470.1	452	228	234	356
2 AVE	12	9	3.95	30	2	190.2	173	84	91	149

Major League Batting Register

	BA	G	AB	R	H	2B	3B	HR	RBI	SB
94 NL	.361	18	36	2	13	2	0	0	2	1
95 NL	.246	82	171	17	42	8	0	6	16	1
Life	.266	100	207	19	55	10	0	6	18	2

CURRENT PLAYERS

GERONIMO PENA

Position: Second base
Team: St. Louis Cardinals
Born: March 29, 1967 Distrito Nacional, Dominican Republic
Height: 6'1" **Weight:** 170 lbs.
Bats: both **Throws:** right
Acquired: Signed as a free agent, 12/84

Player Summary	
Fantasy Value	$6 to $9
Card Value	5¢ to 7¢
Will	have aches
Can't	afford strikeouts
Expect	balanced offense
Don't Expect	a Gold Glove

If Pena could just keep out of the doctor's office, he might become one of baseball's better second basemen. Unfortunately, he loses significant time to injuries every season. In 1995, it was a broken bone in his left leg that shelved him for a month, and a pulled hamstring kept him out of action for two weeks in June. The injury was all the more annoying because he had finally won St. Louis' second-base job outright when Luis Alicea was traded to Boston. When he did play, Pena had trouble making contact, averaging about one strikeout for every three at bats for much of the season. However, he was often used in the leadoff role last year, and he had an on-base percentage over the .350 mark. He has good baserunning speed but doesn't steal bases often. He has also shown flashes of power in the major leagues. Defensively, he's not the answer to a manager's prayers, but he's not a nightmare, either. Pena has good range and fair hands, and he is satisfactory turning the double play.

Major League Batting Register

	BA	G	AB	R	H	2B	3B	HR	RBI	SB
90 NL	.244	18	45	5	11	2	0	0	2	1
91 NL	.243	104	185	38	45	8	3	5	17	15
92 NL	.305	62	203	31	62	12	1	7	31	13
93 NL	.256	74	254	34	65	19	2	5	30	13
94 NL	.254	83	213	33	54	13	1	11	34	9
95 NL	.267	32	101	20	27	6	1	1	8	3
Life	.264	373	1001	161	264	60	8	29	122	54
2 AVE	.255	95	277	40	71	19	2	10	39	13

TONY PENA

Position: Catcher
Team: Cleveland Indians
Born: June 4, 1957 Monte Cristi, Dominican Republic
Height: 6' **Weight:** 185 lbs.
Bats: right **Throws:** right.
Acquired: Signed as a minor-league free agent, 2/94

Player Summary	
Fantasy Value	$1
Card Value	5¢ to 7¢
Will	block pitches well
Can't	hit right-handers
Expect	another year
Don't Expect	defensive lapses

Pena continues to hang on due to his catching savvy and line-drive bat. A Sandy Alomar injury gave Pena plenty of playing time early in 1995, and although the veteran didn't show much with a bat, he wasn't horrible. He continued to display good skills behind the dish. The longtime star knows AL hitters inside and out, calls pitches well, and is extremely agile. He doesn't throw like he once did, tossing out about 20 percent of baserunners in 1995. Never a patient hitter, Pena had some trouble making contact. He batted about .280 against lefties in 1995. He has played in five All-Star Games.

Major League Batting Register

	BA	G	AB	R	H	2B	3B	HR	RBI	SB
80 NL	.429	8	21	1	9	1	0	0	0	0
81 NL	.300	66	210	16	63	9	1	2	17	1
82 NL	.296	138	497	53	147	28	4	11	63	2
83 NL	.301	151	542	51	163	22	3	15	70	6
84 NL	.286	147	546	77	156	27	2	15	78	12
85 NL	.249	147	546	53	136	27	2	10	59	12
86 NL	.288	144	510	56	147	26	2	10	52	9
87 NL	.214	116	384	40	82	13	4	5	44	6
88 NL	.263	149	505	55	133	23	1	10	51	6
89 NL	.259	141	424	36	110	17	2	4	37	5
90 AL	.263	143	491	62	129	19	1	7	56	8
91 AL	.231	141	464	45	107	23	2	5	48	8
92 AL	.241	133	410	39	99	21	1	1	38	3
93 AL	.181	126	304	20	55	11	0	4	19	1
94 AL	.295	40	112	18	33	8	1	2	10	0
95 AL	.262	91	263	25	69	15	0	5	28	1
Life	.263	1881	6229	647	1638	290	27	106	671	80
2 AVE	.221	114	300	24	66	14	0	5	25	1

CURRENT PLAYERS

TERRY PENDLETON

Position: Third base
Team: Florida Marlins
Born: July 16, 1960 Los Angeles, CA
Height: 5'9" **Weight:** 195 lbs.
Bats: both **Throws:** right
Acquired: Signed as a free agent, 4/95

Player Summary	
Fantasy Value	$8 to $10
Card Value	8¢ to 12¢
Will	hit line drives
Can't	run like he used to
Expect	good defense
Don't Expect	another MVP year

Signed with little fanfare over the winter by the undermanned Marlins, Pendleton came to spring training in 1995 with a regular job virtually assured, even after his substandard plate performance of the previous two years. He acclimated well to his new surroundings. In Joe Robbie Stadium, his new home park, he batted nearly 100 points better than he did in road games. The 1991 NL MVP, Pendleton enjoyed a good comeback season, hitting both right-handers and left-handers, displaying medium-range power, and knocking in some runs. After numerous knee problems, he can no longer steal bases as he used to. He remains an aggressive hitter who rarely walks. Much of his value throughout his career has been defensive, and he remains a hustling third baseman with a good arm. However, he lacks his old outstanding range.

Major League Batting Register

	BA	G	AB	R	H	2B	3B	HR	RBI	SB
84 NL	.324	67	262	37	85	16	3	1	33	20
85 NL	.240	149	559	56	134	16	3	5	69	17
86 NL	.239	159	578	56	138	26	5	1	59	24
87 NL	.286	159	583	82	167	29	4	12	96	19
88 NL	.253	110	391	44	99	20	2	6	53	3
89 NL	.264	162	613	83	162	28	5	13	74	9
90 NL	.230	121	447	46	103	20	2	6	58	7
91 NL	.319	153	586	94	187	34	8	22	86	10
92 NL	.311	160	640	98	199	39	1	21	105	5
93 NL	.272	161	633	81	172	33	1	17	84	5
94 NL	.252	77	309	25	78	18	3	7	30	2
95 NL	.290	133	513	70	149	32	1	14	78	1
Life	.274	1611	6114	772	1673	311	38	125	825	122
3 AVE	.273	140	548	65	150	31	2	14	71	3

TROY PERCIVAL

Position: Pitcher
Team: California Angels
Born: Aug. 9, 1969 Fontana, CA
Height: 6'3" **Weight:** 200 lbs.
Bats: right **Throws:** right
Acquired: Sixth-round pick in 6/90 free-agent draft

Player Summary	
Fantasy Value	$1 to $3
Card Value	10¢ to 15¢
Will	graduate to closing
Can't	bank on health
Expect	many strikeouts
Don't Expect	control troubles

The Angels originally signed Percival to catch. However, his weak bat and strong arm convinced California's management to shift the big right-hander to mound duty. While he showed great potential in the minors, the hard-throwing Percival also had injury problems, and eventually needed surgery to clear debris from his pitching elbow. Questions as to whether he could recover the bite on his pitches have been answered. His fastball, which approaches 100 mph, is a dominating strikeout pitch; he also sports a good changeup. Most surprisingly, he has dramatically improved his control since his elbow problems subsided. Opponents compiled a batting average under the .175 mark against him for much of the season in 1995. He is clearly being groomed for future closing duties, and he performed extremely well as Lee Smith's setup man in his rookie campaign. Percival had 15 saves in Triple-A in 1994 and 12 saves in 1991 during his first year as a pitcher. He could use some work on his move to first, as baserunners ran wild last season. However, that is minor if his elbow stays healthy.

Major League Pitching Register

	W	L	ERA	G	S	IP	H	ER	BB	SO
95 AL	3	2	1.95	62	3	74.0	37	16	26	94
Life	3	2	1.95	62	3	74.0	37	16	26	94

CURRENT PLAYERS

CARLOS PEREZ

Position: Pitcher
Team: Montreal Expos
Born: Jan. 14, 1971 Nigua, Dominican Republic
Height: 6'3" **Weight:** 195 lbs.
Bats: left **Throws:** left
Acquired: Signed as a free agent, 7/88

Player Summary	
Fantasy Value	$10 to $12
Card Value	35¢ to 50¢
Will	amaze with antics
Can't	run on him
Expect	strikeouts
Don't Expect	a dull performance

When the little brother of Pascual, Yorkis, and Melido Perez debuted with the Expos early in the 1995 season, it soon became apparent that fans were in for something special. A favorite of Felipe Alou's, Carlos showed an excellent fastball (especially for a lefty) and an outstanding forkball. He was a crowd pleaser as well by punctuating his strikeouts (and successful pickoff throws) with a pump of the fist. He also runs off the field at full speed (seemingly a Perez family trait), and—just to make the picture complete—pitched well enough as a rookie to be Montreal's representative on the NL All-Star squad. Perez began in relief but quickly graduated to a starting role when other Expo hurlers proved inconsistent. Despite getting beaned by a foul ball in the dugout during a June game in Montreal, he seemingly enjoyed nearly every minute of his debut season. With better velocity than most left-handers, a fine pickoff move, a strikeout arsenal, and charisma, Perez looks to rival the greatest successes of his brothers, and quite possibly surpass them.

EDUARDO PEREZ

Position: Third base
Team: California Angels
Born: Sept. 11, 1969 Cincinnati, OH
Height: 6'4" **Weight:** 215 lbs.
Bats: right **Throws:** right
Acquired: First-round pick in 6/91 free-agent draft

Player Summary	
Fantasy Value	$1
Card Value	4¢ to 6¢
Will	get another shot
Can't	continue like this
Expect	a struggle
Don't Expect	infinite patience

Perez seems to have all of the tools necessary to be a big-league starter, but he just has not been able to put his game together at the major-league level. As a result, time is running out. When Garret Anderson took over in left field for the Angels last year, Tony Phillips played third base almost exclusively. With J.T. Snow doing an outstanding job at first, there was nowhere for Perez to go. At Triple-A Vancouver last year, he batted .325 with six homers, 37 RBI, a .504 slugging percentage, and a .386 on-base average. Still, he has fallen far from two years ago. He began 1994 as California's starting first baseman. However, he didn't add much offensively or defensively and was replaced. He batted .297 with seven homers, 38 RBI, 34 walks, and 53 strikeouts in 219 at bats at Vancouver in 1994. Perez is a below-average fielder at third. He doesn't have very good range, and his arm is not all that strong. His best position is probably first base—like his father, Tony, who was the first baseman for the Big Red Machine in the 1970s.

Major League Pitching Register

	W	L	ERA	G	CG	IP	H	ER	BB	SO
95 NL	10	8	3.69	28	2	141.1	142	58	28	106
Life	10	8	3.69	28	2	141.1	142	58	28	106

Major League Batting Register

	BA	G	AB	R	H	2B	3B	HR	RBI	SB
93 AL	.250	52	180	16	45	6	2	4	30	5
94 AL	.209	38	129	10	27	7	0	5	16	3
95 AL	.169	29	71	9	12	4	1	1	7	0
Life	.221	119	380	35	84	17	3	10	53	8

CURRENT PLAYERS

MELIDO PEREZ

Position: Pitcher
Team: New York Yankees
Born: Feb. 15, 1966 San Cristobal, Dominican Republic
Height: 6'4" **Weight:** 210 lbs.
Bats: right **Throws:** right
Acquired: Traded by White Sox with Domingo Jean and Bob Wickman for Steve Sax, 1/92

Player Summary
Fantasy Value	$6 to $8
Card Value	4¢ to 6¢
Will	return to rotation
Can't	count on health
Expect	good stuff
Don't Expect	consistency

For several years, Perez has been a good pitcher with occasional streaks of greatness. His control has always been here and there, but he has the best split-finger fastball in baseball and can throw it at several different speeds. In 1995, he never really got untracked due to a sore pitching shoulder. Almost from the start, he didn't have the bite on his pitches that he usually possesses, and he lacked any kind of location. In his 12 starts, he completed just one. Despite a couple of good games, Perez had a 5.66 ERA before the Yankees disabled him in early July. Opponents were hitting just .261 against him, but a combination of poor fastball velocity and some hanging splitters led to 10 homers and 31 walks in just 68 innings. When he was finally activated on Sept. 8, he languished on the bench. Perez, if healthy, is a No. 3 starter.

Major League Pitching Register
	W	L	ERA	G	CG	IP	H	ER	BB	SO
87 AL	1	1	7.84	3	0	10.1	18	9	5	5
88 AL	12	10	3.79	32	3	197.0	186	83	72	138
89 AL	11	14	5.01	31	2	183.1	187	102	90	141
90 AL	13	14	4.61	35	3	197.0	177	101	86	161
91 AL	8	7	3.12	49	0	135.2	111	47	52	128
92 AL	13	16	2.87	33	10	247.2	212	79	93	218
93 AL	6	14	5.19	25	0	163.0	173	94	64	148
94 AL	9	4	4.10	22	1	151.1	134	69	58	109
95 AL	5	5	5.58	13	1	69.1	70	43	31	44
Life	78	85	4.17	243	20	1354.2	1268	627	551	1092
3 AVE	8	8	4.75	24	1	151.1	147	80	60	117

MIKE PEREZ

Position: Pitcher
Team: Chicago Cubs
Born: Oct. 19, 1964 Yauco, PR
Height: 6' **Weight:** 187 lbs.
Bats: right **Throws:** right
Acquired: Signed as a minor-league free agent, 4/95

Player Summary
Fantasy Value	$1 to $3
Card Value	5¢ to 7¢
Will	throw sinkers
Can't	rack up saves
Expect	frequent innings
Don't Expect	many strikeouts

Used as a closer working his way through the Cardinals' system, Perez led three minor leagues in saves before he was called to the majors in 1990. He had success in middle relief for two years in St. Louis before serious shoulder troubles sidelined him in 1994. The Cubs signed him for 1995 and gave him plenty of work, but the recuperating righty showed that neither his velocity nor, surprisingly, his location, were equal to what he showed in 1992 and '93. Like most of the Cubs middle relievers, Perez started the season well. He became inconsistent with his breaking pitches, and he lost Cubs manager Jim Riggleman's confidence by mid-July. Although Perez did make an impressive recovery from his injury, he can't hang around long unless he can keep his sinking fastball low and avoid gopher balls. In 1995, he gave up far too many home runs for a pitcher without strikeout stuff. He has work to do to regain his claim to late-inning work in the big leagues.

Major League Pitching Register
	W	L	ERA	G	S	IP	H	ER	BB	SO
90 NL	1	0	3.95	13	1	13.2	12	6	3	5
91 NL	0	2	5.82	14	0	17.0	19	11	7	7
92 NL	9	3	1.84	77	0	93.0	70	19	32	46
93 NL	7	2	2.48	65	7	72.2	65	20	20	58
94 NL	2	3	8.71	36	12	31.0	52	30	10	20
95 NL	2	6	3.66	68	2	71.1	72	29	27	49
Life	21	16	3.47	273	22	298.2	290	115	99	185
3 AVE	4	4	4.34	64	9	65.1	73	32	21	47

YORKIS PEREZ

Position: Pitcher
Team: Florida Marlins
Born: Sept. 30, 1967 Bajos de Haina, Dominican Republic
Height: 6′ **Weight:** 180 lbs.
Bats: left **Throws:** left
Acquired: Signed as a minor-league free agent, 12/93

Player Summary
Fantasy Value	$1 to $3
Card Value	5¢ to 8¢
Will	face tough lefties
Can't	win closer's job
Expect	plenty of whiffs
Don't Expect	a trade

Working as the Marlins' top left-handed reliever, Perez topped the staff in appearances last summer, setting a career high for himself in the process. He didn't enjoy the unqualified success of his 1994 rookie campaign, however. Although Perez has a good fastball and curve, his control is suspect. Too often he pitches from behind in the count, allowing his share of walks and extra-base hits. Perez generally kept the ball low and allowed few homers in 1995. He has strikeout ability, fanning more than one man per inning last season. Even as other Marlin relievers suffered inconsistency, Florida manager Marcel Lachemann did not convert Perez to closing duties, realizing that the team needed Perez in the lefty short man role. Many times Perez entered to face just one or two hitters, and finished the season with fewer than one inning pitched per appearance. True to his role, he allowed left-handers to bat just .157. If he can continue to do that, Perez will stick around.

Major League Pitching Register
	W	L	ERA	G	S	IP	H	ER	BB	SO
91 NL	1	0	2.08	3	0	4.1	2	1	2	3
94 NL	3	0	3.54	44	0	40.2	33	16	14	41
95 NL	2	6	5.21	69	1	46.2	35	27	28	47
Life	6	6	4.32	116	1	91.2	70	44	44	91
2 AVE	3	3	4.34	70	1	54.3	43	26	26	55

HERB PERRY

Position: First base
Team: Cleveland Indians
Born: Sept. 15, 1969 Mayo, FL
Height: 6'2″ **Weight:** 210 lbs.
Bats: right **Throws:** right
Acquired: Second-round pick in 6/91 free-agent draft

Player Summary
Fantasy Value	$2 to $4
Card Value	15¢ to 20¢
Will	lash line shots
Can't	claim job yet
Expect	impressive numbers
Don't Expect	defensive wizardry

Despite his tremendous average-hitting and power potential, Perry is struggling to find at bats with the Tribe. Blocked from duty by switch-hitting Eddie Murray and lefty Paul Sorrento, Perry fought to get at bats when Dave Winfield was disabled. Even then Perry didn't get enough time to establish himself. He is a decent defensive first sacker, and he can also play third base if needed. He should hit enough to be a quality designated hitter if asked to fill that role. Not only does he have good extra-base sock, but he also hit about .300 against right-handers in 1995. He had a fine on-base percentage, a result of his high average and numerous walks. Perry's problems, besides being low on the depth chart, are that he is not above average with a glove anywhere, he is fairly slow, and he strikes out often. However, it's likely that he will inherit playing time in the near future when Murray slows down. Perry may even get a full-time slot. He is an exciting offensive player—just what Indians' opponents don't want to see in the pipeline.

Major League Batting Register
	BA	G	AB	R	H	2B	3B	HR	RBI	SB
94 AL	.111	4	9	1	1	0	0	0	1	0
95 AL	.315	52	162	23	51	13	1	3	23	1
Life	.304	56	171	24	52	13	1	3	24	1

CURRENT PLAYERS

ROBERTO PETAGINE

Position: First base
Team: San Diego Padres
Born: June 7, 1971 Nueva Esparita, Venezuela
Height: 6'1" **Weight:** 172 lbs.
Bats: left **Throws:** left
Acquired: Traded by Astros with Ken Caminiti, Andujar Cedeno, Steve Finley, Brian Williams, and a player to be named later for Derek Bell, Doug Brocail, Ricky Gutierrez, Pedro Martinez, Craig Shipley, and Phil Plantier, 12/94

Player Summary
Fantasy Value	$1
Card Value	8¢ to 12¢
Will	show patience
Can't	hit 25 homers
Expect	platoon duty
Don't Expect	stolen bases

Petagine was stuck behind Jeff Bagwell in the Astros system and was assuredly glad that San Diego liberated him last winter. Petagine made the Padres squad out of spring training, and he was used at first base, in left field, and as a pinch hitter. However, the young lefty didn't get regular playing time and failed to hit enough to push his way into further duty. A patient line-drive hitter with little speed or defensive value, Petagine does have fine potential. He was a .300 hitter several times in the minor leagues. At Double-A Jackson in 1993, he led the Texas League with a .334 batting average, 36 doubles, and 84 bases on balls. He was named the circuit's Player of the Year that season. His minor-league numbers project out to about 25 doubles and 80 walks in a full major-league season. In 1995, he took 26 free passes with the Padres, but due to his mediocre batting average, he posted a low on-base percentage. He is a fine fielder.

Major League Batting Register
	BA	G	AB	R	H	2B	3B	HR	RBI	SB
94 NL	.000	8	7	0	0	0	0	0	0	0
95 NL	.234	89	124	15	29	8	0	3	17	0
Life	.221	97	131	15	29	8	0	3	17	0

ANDY PETTITTE

Position: Pitcher
Team: New York Yankees
Born: June 15, 1972 Baton Rouge, LA
Height: 6'5" **Weight:** 220 lbs.
Bats: left **Throws:** left
Acquired: Signed as a free agent, 5/91

Player Summary
Fantasy Value	$9 to $11
Card Value	20¢ to 30¢
Will	move the ball around
Can't	dominate with heat
Expect	frequent starts
Don't Expect	many homers

One of the several new members of the Yankees rotation last season, Pettitte showed enough to hang around for further duty. He doesn't have an outstanding fastball, but he moves his pitches around the strike zone and possesses a battling attitude. Pettitte has a fine curveball, as well as a changeup. He moved into the Yankees starting rotation in June following injuries to Melido Perez and Scott Kamieniecki. Pettitte acquitted himself well in his first big-league season. In 1995, Pettitte held fellow left-handers to a microscopic batting average, and he did a reasonable job on righties. He was also able to keep the ball in the ballpark. He has a good pickoff move and is agile off the mound. Most importantly for a pitcher with just-above-average talent, Pettitte believes in himself. There are some things he needs to work on to guarantee future success. Since Pettitte does not strike out many hitters, he must keep the ball down consistently and cut down on walks. In 1994, he was 14-4 in the minor leagues. Pettitte has been a much-sought-after player in trade talks.

Major League Pitching Register
	W	L	ERA	G	CG	IP	H	ER	BB	SO
95 AL	12	9	4.17	31	3	175.0	183	81	63	114
Life	12	9	4.17	31	3	175.0	183	81	63	114

CURRENT PLAYERS

J.R. PHILLIPS

Position: First base
Team: San Francisco Giants
Born: April 29, 1970 West Covina, CA
Height: 6'1" **Weight:** 185 lbs.
Bats: left **Throws:** left
Acquired: Claimed from Angels on waivers, 12/92

Player Summary
Fantasy Value	$0
Card Value	5¢ to 7¢
Will	swing for fences
Can't	make contact
Expect	decent glovework
Don't Expect	many more chances

Charles Dickens could have written some of his classic novels about J.R. Phillips. The Giants have had Great Expectations of him for several years now, but A Tale of Two Cities is obvious: Phillips has hit very well at Triple-A Phoenix but can't seem to do anything right in San Francisco, where he has had nothing but Hard Times. He became the starting first sacker out of spring training, and he saw his position solidified when the Giants released Todd Benzinger in May. However, Phillips never came close to producing much at bat, striking out frequently, showing little power, and failing even to keep his average over .200 through much of the season. The offense he showed in the minors—including two straight 27-homer seasons in Triple-A in 1993 and 1994—has not surfaced in the show, largely due to his trouble with breaking pitches. He did sock a game-winning, 14th-inning home run against Houston July 16, but moments of joy were few. While he has worked hard to become a good defensive player, this alone won't keep him out of Bleak House.

Major League Batting Register
	BA	G	AB	R	H	2B	3B	HR	RBI	SB
93 NL	.313	11	16	1	5	1	1	1	4	0
94 NL	.132	15	38	1	5	0	0	1	3	1
95 NL	.195	92	231	27	45	9	0	9	28	1
Life	.193	118	285	29	55	10	1	11	35	2

TONY PHILLIPS

Position: Third base; outfield
Team: California Angels
Born: April 15, 1959 Atlanta, GA
Height: 5'10" **Weight:** 175 lbs.
Bats: both **Throws:** right
Acquired: Traded by Tigers for Chad Curtis, 4/95

Player Summary
Fantasy Value	$14 to $18
Card Value	5¢ to 7¢
Will	score runs
Can't	uncork strong throws
Expect	high on-base mark
Don't Expect	quiet demeanor

Phillips has developed into one of the AL's best players, annually finishing among the league leaders in walks and runs scored, adding extra-base power, and playing a variety of positions. Traded to California in the spring, he was a key component in the Angels surprising performance. Contributing leadoff skills and competitive fire, Phillips sported an outstanding on-base percentage that was above the .400 mark for much of the season. He rarely backs away from any player or umpire and was suspended for three games in 1995 for his part in a brawl with the Red Sox. Usually used in a utility role, Phillips provides steady, although unspectacular, defense. Although he no longer has outstanding speed, he is a smart baserunner.

Major League Batting Register
	BA	G	AB	R	H	2B	3B	HR	RBI	SB
82 AL	.210	40	81	11	17	2	2	0	8	2
83 AL	.248	148	412	54	102	12	3	4	35	16
84 AL	.266	154	451	62	120	24	3	4	37	10
85 AL	.280	42	161	23	45	12	2	4	17	3
86 AL	.256	118	441	76	113	14	5	5	52	15
87 AL	.240	111	379	48	91	20	0	10	46	7
88 AL	.203	79	212	32	43	8	4	2	17	0
89 AL	.262	143	451	48	118	15	6	4	47	3
90 AL	.251	152	573	97	144	23	5	8	55	19
91 AL	.284	146	564	87	160	28	4	17	72	10
92 AL	.276	159	606	114	167	32	3	10	64	12
93 AL	.313	151	566	113	177	27	0	7	57	16
94 AL	.281	114	438	91	123	19	3	19	61	13
95 AL	.261	139	525	119	137	21	1	27	61	13
Life	.266	1696	5860	975	1557	257	41	121	629	139
3 AVE	.284	156	591	125	168	26	2	21	71	16

CURRENT PLAYERS

MIKE PIAZZA

Position: Catcher
Team: Los Angeles Dodgers
Born: Sept. 4, 1968 Norristown, PA
Height: 6'3" **Weight:** 197 lbs.
Bats: right **Throws:** right
Acquired: 62nd-round pick in 6/88 free-agent draft

Player Summary	
Fantasy Value	$30 to $35
Card Value	80¢ to $1.50
Will	bomb homers
Can't	win a Gold Glove
Expect	an MVP Award
Don't Expect	basepath brilliance

Piazza's storybook career keeps getting better. The 1995 chapter included a mammoth home run to straightaway center field at the All-Star Game at Texas, a great slugging percentage, and another .300-plus average. He led the Dodgers to a surprising finish and emerged as an MVP candidate. Piazza used his quick swing and strong power to hit very well against left-handers in 1995. He held his own against right-handers as well. The low-round draft pick continues to hit better than anyone ever thought he would. His season totals are even more impressive when one considers he missed nearly a month of playing time in May because of a wrist injury. Although he's improving at all facets of his game behind the plate, Piazza is not likely to ever be a defensive standout. He has a strong throwing arm, but he lacks good footwork and does not yet show the ability to call a strong game. However, he is a battler and doesn't slack off behind the dish. He is one of the best players in baseball.

HIPOLITO PICHARDO

Position: Pitcher
Team: Kansas City Royals
Born: Aug. 22, 1969 Jicome Esperanza, Dominican Republic
Height: 6'1" **Weight:** 185 lbs.
Bats: right **Throws:** right
Acquired: Signed as a free agent, 12/87

Player Summary	
Fantasy Value	$1 to $3
Card Value	4¢ to 6¢
Will	throw splitters
Can't	make the headlines
Expect	frequent appearances
Don't Expect	many homers

Formerly a starter with the Royals, Pichardo has found his niche in middle relief. Used in the seventh and eighth innings by Royals manager Bob Boone in 1995, Pichardo was able to throw his sinking fastball and split-finger pitch for short periods nearly every other day. Although he doesn't strike out many hitters, he throws hard, and his offerings move around enough to induce hitters to beat the ball into the ground. Occasionally, Pichardo suffers from control problems. When he gets pitches high, he's hittable. Luckily for the Royals, that didn't happen often in 1995; he was able to pitch effectively to right-handers, and he didn't surrender too many home runs. It's unlikely that Pichardo will ever expand his role, but he's got a live arm and good action on his pitches. He hit the disabled list for a couple of weeks with a sore right elbow, but the injury is not believed to have any lasting effect. Kansas City's good defensive infield helped him last year.

Major League Batting Register

	BA	G	AB	R	H	2B	3B	HR	RBI	SB
92 NL	.232	21	69	5	16	3	0	1	7	0
93 NL	.318	149	547	81	174	24	2	35	112	3
94 NL	.319	107	405	64	129	18	0	24	92	1
95 NL	.346	112	434	82	150	17	0	32	93	1
Life	.322	389	1455	232	469	62	2	92	304	5
3 AVE	.327	142	535	88	175	23	1	35	115	2

Major League Pitching Register

	W	L	ERA	G	S	IP	H	ER	BB	SO
92 AL	9	6	3.95	31	0	143.2	148	63	49	59
93 AL	7	8	4.04	30	0	165.0	183	74	53	70
94 AL	5	3	4.92	45	3	67.2	82	37	24	36
95 AL	8	4	4.36	44	1	64.0	66	31	30	43
Life	29	21	4.19	150	4	440.1	479	205	156	208
3 AVE	8	6	4.36	48	2	110.1	124	54	40	56

CURRENT PLAYERS

GREG PIRKL

Position: First base
Team: Seattle Mariners
Born: Aug. 7, 1970 Long Beach, CA
Height: 6'5" **Weight:** 240 lbs.
Bats: right **Throws:** right
Acquired: Second-round pick in 6/88 free-agent draft

Player Summary	
Fantasy Value	$2 to $4
Card Value	6¢ to 10¢
Will	show power
Can't	overshadow Tino
Expect	a long shot
Don't Expect	top defense

With first baseman Tino Martinez out of the picture, Pirkl should get a chance to show what he can do for an extended time in spring training. He has been in Triple-A for three seasons now and has shown the ability to hit the ball. Pirkl batted in the .300 range with 15 homers for Tacoma in the Triple-A Pacific Coast League last year before being called up to the bigs. In 1994, the big first baseman batted .317 with 22 homers and 72 RBI for Calgary. For somebody who hits the ball hard and a long way, he doesn't have too many strikeouts. He notched only 58 Ks in 1994 at Calgary in 353 at bats; Pirkl was patient enough to wait for 24 bases on balls. He was drafted as a catcher out of Los Alamitos High School in California in 1988, where he was named High School Player of the Year by two area newspapers. He made the move to first base in 1991 in Class-A ball. He presents a big target at the initial sack. Pirkl doesn't have the best range around, but he does have a pretty good arm; he has played some third base in the minors. Don't look for him to steal many bases, however.

Major League Batting Register

	BA	G	AB	R	H	2B	3B	HR	RBI	SB
93 AL	.174	7	23	1	4	0	0	1	4	0
94 AL	.264	19	53	7	14	3	0	6	11	0
95 AL	.235	10	17	2	4	0	0	0	0	0
Life	.237	36	93	10	22	3	0	7	15	0

PHIL PLANTIER

Position: Outfield
Team: Detroit Tigers
Born: Jan. 27, 1969 Manchester, NH
Height: 5'11" **Weight:** 195 lbs.
Bats: left **Throws:** right
Acquired: Signed as a free agent, 12/95

Player Summary	
Fantasy Value	$4 to $6
Card Value	5¢ to 8¢
Will	try to stay put
Can't	dazzle with defense
Expect	homers and walks
Don't Expect	many steals

Even though he was viewed as a principal in the massive Padres-Astros trade last winter, Plantier never seemed to fit in with Houston. The Astros at one time in 1995 had three left-handed-hitting left fielders on their roster. Eventually, Plantier returned to his adopted hometown of San Diego and settled into everyday duty. He hit for a fine average and added his customary power and walks as well. Despite some career impediments due to injury, trade, and poor defense, Plantier is still a fine hitter with tremendous power and good strike-zone judgement. He knows how to wait for walks and total a fine on-base percentage. Oddly, he's been traded three times in the last couple of seasons despite strong power and a reputation as a good guy. Most of the reasons Plantier has been viewed as expendable probably stem from his non-hitting skills. He is a slow runner, doesn't throw particularly well, and has never shown much range in the outfield.

Major League Batting Register

	BA	G	AB	R	H	2B	3B	HR	RBI	SB
90 AL	.133	14	15	1	2	1	0	0	3	0
91 AL	.331	53	148	27	49	7	1	11	35	1
92 AL	.246	108	349	46	86	19	0	7	30	2
93 NL	.240	138	462	67	111	20	1	34	100	4
94 NL	.220	96	341	44	75	21	0	18	41	3
95 NL	.255	76	216	33	55	6	0	9	34	1
Life	.247	485	1531	218	378	74	2	79	243	11
3 AVE	.235	120	395	55	93	19	0	23	65	3

CURRENT PLAYERS

DAN PLESAC

Position: Pitcher
Team: Pittsburgh Pirates
Born: Feb. 4, 1962 Gary, IN
Height: 6'5" **Weight:** 215 lbs.
Bats: left **Throws:** left
Acquired: Signed as a free agent, 11/94

Player Summary	
Fantasy Value	$1 to $3
Card Value	4¢ to 6¢
Will	remain employed
Can't	blow hitters away
Expect	frequent use
Don't Expect	closing duties

After several rigorous years of closer duty with the Brewers, Plesac lost effectiveness, and his oft-used left arm appeared dead. However, he worked hard in two seasons with the Cubs to regain his strength, and he pitched well in 1994. The Cubs declined to re-ink him, though, and he joined former battery mate Mark Parent in Pittsburgh for 1995. Plesac prefers the middle role to closing now, since he enjoys pitching often. His skills against left-handers and his ability to keep the ball in the park make him useful in both late-inning spots and long work. Although he still has fair velocity on his fastball, the pitch doesn't move much. His best offering is a hard curve that freezes both lefty and righty hitters. He suffers occasionally from bouts of poor control, especially with the curve, but Plesac has a good attitude and will pitch as often as asked.

Major League Pitching Register

	W	L	ERA	G	S	IP	H	ER	BB	SO
86 AL	10	7	2.97	51	14	91.0	81	30	29	75
87 AL	5	6	2.61	57	23	79.1	63	23	23	89
88 AL	1	2	2.41	50	30	52.1	46	14	12	52
89 AL	3	4	2.35	52	33	61.1	47	16	17	52
90 AL	3	7	4.43	66	24	69.0	67	34	31	65
91 AL	2	7	4.29	45	8	92.1	92	44	39	61
92 AL	5	4	2.96	44	1	79.0	64	26	35	54
93 NL	2	1	4.74	57	0	62.2	74	33	21	47
94 NL	2	3	4.61	54	1	54.2	61	28	13	53
95 NL	4	4	3.58	58	3	60.1	53	24	27	57
Life	37	45	3.49	534	137	702.0	648	272	247	605
3 AVE	3	3	4.31	66	2	69.2	73	33	23	62

ERIC PLUNK

Position: Pitcher
Team: Cleveland Indians
Born: Sept. 3, 1963 Wilmington, CA
Height: 6'6" **Weight:** 220 lbs.
Bats: right **Throws:** right
Acquired: Signed as a free agent, 4/92

Player Summary	
Fantasy Value	$4 to $6
Card Value	4¢ to 6¢
Will	work in middle
Can't	notch many saves
Expect	plenty of strikeouts
Don't Expect	wildness of old

With his role as a setup man well-defined, Plunk had another outstanding season in the Cleveland bullpen. He fanned over one man per inning with far better control than he had shown in earlier seasons. Used primarily to get the ball to Jose Mesa, Plunk nailed right-handers to the wall. Left-handers managed to bat only a little better against the bespectacled righty. Plunk still throws very hard and keeps the ball low. In 1995, he allowed just five homers and about 20 percent of inherited runners to score. Despite an August slump in which he allowed 10 runs in five innings, he had a tremendous year. He cemented his reputation as a key member of the Indians pen. Plunk has gotten it together, and he looks nothing like the potentially good but completely out-of-control pitcher that used to work for the Yankees and Athletics.

Major League Pitching Register

	W	L	ERA	G	S	IP	H	ER	BB	SO
86 AL	4	7	5.31	26	0	120.1	91	71	102	98
87 AL	4	6	4.74	32	2	95.0	91	50	62	90
88 AL	7	2	3.00	49	5	78.0	62	26	39	79
89 AL	8	6	3.28	50	1	104.1	82	38	64	85
90 AL	6	3	2.72	47	0	72.2	58	22	43	67
91 AL	2	5	4.76	43	0	111.2	128	59	62	103
92 AL	9	6	3.64	58	4	71.2	61	29	38	50
93 AL	4	5	2.79	70	15	71.0	61	22	30	77
94 AL	7	2	2.54	41	3	71.0	61	20	37	73
95 AL	6	2	2.67	56	2	64.0	48	19	27	71
Life	57	44	3.73	472	32	859.2	743	356	504	793
3 AVE	7	3	2.65	64	7	81.0	67	24	37	87

CURRENT PLAYERS

LUIS POLONIA

Position: Outfield
Team: Atlanta Braves
Born: Oct. 12, 1964 Santiago City, Dominican Republic
Height: 5'8" **Weight:** 150 lbs.
Bats: left **Throws:** left
Acquired: Traded by Yankees for Troy Hughes, 8/95

Player Summary	
Fantasy Value	$5 to $7
Card Value	4¢ to 6¢
Will	hit singles
Can't	count on regular duty
Expect	some speed
Don't Expect	skilled glovework

After several seasons of decent play, Polonia finally ran out of luck in New York. The midsummer acquisition of Darryl Strawberry greased the skids for Polonia, who was dealt to the Braves in August. Reduced to a platoon role with the Yankees and unhappy with his lack of everyday playing time, Polonia continued to struggle in the leadoff spot, offering little on-base ability and reduced basestealing speed. He drew an inadequate total of walks for a top-of-the-order hitter with declining speed and no power. Polonia does make good contact and can still stretch singles into doubles. As a left fielder, he is barely adequate. He runs very well, but he has poor range. Although his arm is reasonably strong, he has poor accuracy and often heaves wild, unnecessary throws to the wrong base.

Major League Batting Register

	BA	G	AB	R	H	2B	3B	HR	RBI	SB
87 AL	.287	125	435	78	125	16	10	4	49	29
88 AL	.292	84	288	51	84	11	4	2	27	24
89 AL	.286	59	206	31	59	6	4	1	17	13
89 AL	.313	66	227	39	71	11	2	2	29	9
90 AL	.335	120	403	52	135	7	9	2	35	21
91 AL	.296	150	604	92	179	28	8	2	50	48
92 AL	.286	149	577	83	165	17	4	0	35	51
93 AL	.271	152	576	75	156	17	6	1	32	55
94 AL	.311	95	350	62	109	21	6	1	36	20
95 AL	.261	67	238	37	62	9	3	2	15	10
95 NL	.264	28	53	6	14	7	0	0	2	3
Life	.293	1095	3957	606	1159	150	56	17	327	283
3 AVE	.283	131	465	70	132	22	6	2	34	33

MARK PORTUGAL

Position: Pitcher
Team: Cincinnati Reds
Born: Oct. 30, 1962 Los Angeles, CA
Height: 6' **Weight:** 190 lbs.
Bats: right **Throws:** right
Acquired: Traded by Giants with Darren Lewis and Dave Burba for Deion Sanders, John Roper, Scott Service, Dave McCarty, and Ricky Pickett, 7/95

Player Summary	
Fantasy Value	$6 to $8
Card Value	5¢ to 8¢
Will	throw the curve
Can't	carry a staff
Expect	six-inning starts
Don't Expect	a strikeout crown

A late-season knee injury suffered in 1994 doesn't appear to have slowed the unspectacular but effective Portugal down. He is a dependable pitcher, with good control and an excellent assortment of off-speed stuff. He usually keeps the ball low in the strike zone. After arriving in a midseason trade, he ended up, at times, the only right-handed starter on the Reds staff, after Jose Rijo and Dave Burba went out with injuries. When Portugal got harmed last year, it was because of poor control and gophers. Opponents hit .262 against Portugal in 1995, with lefties and righties doing equally well. He is a fine hitting pitcher with a good pick-off move. Portugal has suffered serious knee, elbow, and shoulder problems in the last few years.

Major League Pitching Register

	W	L	ERA	G	CG	IP	H	ER	BB	SO
85 AL	1	3	5.55	6	0	24.1	24	15	14	12
86 AL	6	10	4.31	27	3	112.2	112	54	50	67
87 AL	1	3	7.77	13	0	44.0	58	38	24	28
88 AL	3	3	4.53	26	0	57.2	60	29	17	31
89 NL	7	1	2.75	20	2	108.0	91	33	37	86
90 NL	11	10	3.62	32	1	196.2	187	79	67	136
91 NL	10	12	4.49	32	1	168.1	163	84	59	120
92 NL	6	3	2.66	18	1	101.1	76	30	41	62
93 NL	18	4	2.77	33	1	208.0	194	64	77	131
94 NL	10	8	3.93	21	1	137.1	135	60	45	87
95 NL	11	10	4.01	31	1	181.2	185	81	56	96
Life	84	67	3.81	259	11	1340.0	1285	567	487	856
3 AVE	15	9	3.56	32	1	202.1	197	80	68	121

CURRENT PLAYERS

KIRBY PUCKETT

Position: Outfield
Team: Minnesota Twins
Born: March 14, 1961 Chicago, IL
Height: 5'9" **Weight:** 220 lbs.
Bats: right **Throws:** right
Acquired: First-round pick in 6/82 free-agent draft

Player Summary	
Fantasy Value	$20 to $25
Card Value	70¢ to $1.25
Will	hit, hit, hit
Can't	show old speed
Expect	leadership
Don't Expect	center field

After a spectacular 1994 campaign, Puckett cooled off a little last season. However, he still provided significant punch on an anemic Minnesota squad. He batted over .300 against both right-handers and left-handers, added his usual power, and hit for a higher average in the "Homerdome." He doesn't steal bases the way he once did, but he also doesn't strike out as often as he used to. Although he's never been a particularly patient hitter, he took 56 walks, giving him a fine .379 on-base percentage. Rich Becker's arrival has shifted Puckett permanently to right field, although the veteran still sees occasional action in center (as well as getting the odd start at designated hitter). Puckett's range has diminished over the years, but he still has a good arm and runs hard. He is a real team leader.

Major League Batting Register

	BA	G	AB	R	H	2B	3B	HR	RBI	SB
84 AL	.296	128	557	63	165	12	5	0	31	14
85 AL	.288	161	691	80	199	29	13	4	74	21
86 AL	.328	161	680	119	223	37	6	31	96	20
87 AL	.332	157	624	96	207	32	5	28	99	12
88 AL	.356	158	657	109	234	42	5	24	121	6
89 AL	.339	159	635	75	215	45	4	9	85	11
90 AL	.298	146	551	82	164	40	3	12	80	5
91 AL	.319	152	611	92	195	29	6	15	89	11
92 AL	.329	160	639	104	210	38	4	19	110	17
93 AL	.296	156	622	89	.184	39	3	22	89	8
94 AL	.317	108	439	79	139	32	3	20	112	6
95 AL	.314	137	538	83	169	39	0	23	99	3
Life	.318	1783	7244	1071	2304	414	57	207	1085	134
3 AVE	.309	154	615	98	190	43	2	25	119	7

TIM PUGH

Position: Pitcher
Team: Cincinnati Reds
Born: Jan. 26, 1967 Lake Tahoe, CA
Height: 6'6" **Weight:** 230 lbs.
Bats: right **Throws:** right
Acquired: Sixth-round pick in 6/89 free-agent draft

Player Summary	
Fantasy Value	$1 to $3
Card Value	4¢ to 6¢
Will	search for role
Can't	win with strikeouts
Expect	decent control
Don't Expect	runaway success

Pugh worked in both starting and long relief roles for the Reds last year, and made some real, although inconsistent, contributions. He began the year with the club and in the rotation, but he pitched poorly before going back to Triple-A to work on mechanics and control. However, even with injuries to Jose Rijo and the ineffectiveness of Kevin Jarvis and Frank Viola, Pugh couldn't crack the rotation when he came back. He did add some value by eating innings in middle relief. All in all, he had a decent season. Most of Pugh's problems came in the extra-base variety, allowing too many doubles and home runs in 1995. Pugh will never win with blazing fastballs and strikeouts, so he must instead refine his control and get ground balls in order to be effective. That was a real problem last season. He did hold lefties to a puny .203 mark in 1995, but, oddly, struggled with righties. He has work to do on both his pickoff move and fielding. He also doesn't add much with the bat. Pugh is at the point in his career that he needs to fulfill his early promise.

Major League Pitching Register

	W	L	ERA	G	CG	IP	H	ER	BB	SO
92 NL	4	2	2.58	7	0	45.1	47	13	13	18
93 NL	10	15	5.26	31	3	164.1	200	96	59	94
94 NL	3	3	6.04	10	1	47.2	60	32	26	24
95 NL	6	5	3.84	28	0	98.1	100	42	32	38
Life	23	25	4.63	76	4	355.2	407	183	130	174
2 AVE	8	10	4.69	31	2	137.1	156	72	48	68

CURRENT PLAYERS

BILL PULSIPHER

Position: Pitcher
Team: New York Mets
Born: Oct. 9, 1973 Fort Benning, GA
Height: 6'4" **Weight:** 195 lbs.
Bats: left **Throws:** left
Acquired: First-round pick in 6/91 free-agent draft

Player Summary	
Fantasy Value	$7 to $9
Card Value	15¢ to 20¢
Will	throw hard
Can't	show perfect control
Expect	seven-inning starts
Don't Expect	strikeout crown

After starting the 1995 season 6-4 with a 3.14 ERA at Triple-A Tidewater, the much-ballyhooed Pulsipher brought his bulldog attitude and impressive pitching arsenal to New York in mid-June. Immediately joining the Mets rotation, he showed a competitive spirit to go along with an explosive fastball and a sharp-dipping slider. A traditional power pitcher, Pulsipher should increase his strikeout rate with experience. He had periodic trouble with control, and had to come in occasionally with "get me over" fastballs. As a result he allowed a few too many home runs. Pulsipher has a good pickoff move and gets the ball to the plate in a hurry; few potential basestealers were successful while he was on the mound. A tough-minded hard-rock fan, Pulsipher was overpowering on many occasions. He's got the chance to be a dominating starting pitcher for many years, with the caveat that he has thrown a fairly high number of innings for a youngster. A 1994 Eastern League All-Star, he won 14 games with a 3.22 ERA and 171 strikeouts in 201 innings pitched that year.

Major League Pitching Register

	W	L	ERA	G	CG	IP	H	ER	BB	SO
95 NL	5	7	3.98	17	2	126.2	122	56	45	81
Life	5	7	3.98	17	2	126.2	122	56	45	81

PAUL QUANTRILL

Position: Pitcher
Team: Toronto Blue Jays
Born: Nov. 3, 1968 London, Ontario
Height: 6'1" **Weight:** 185 lbs.
Bats: left **Throws:** right
Acquired: Traded by Phillies for Howard Battle and Ricardo Jordan, 12/95

Player Summary	
Fantasy Value	$1 to $3
Card Value	4¢ to 6¢
Will	make his starts
Can't	hold runners
Expect	good control
Don't Expect	15 wins

If any baseball prognosticator had said that the Phillies' 1995 leader in starts and victories at season's end would be Paul Quantrill, he might have been checked for a virus. Sick or not, Quantrill was a lifesaver, pitching better last year than anyone could have predicted. When he worked in Boston, Quantrill was used mostly in relief, but the Phillies' injury-prone mound corps was so thin that he was pressed into service as a starter last summer. Despite a midseason slump, he was generally dependable and stayed healthy. He doesn't walk many hitters and lives on getting ground balls. While he does have good movement on his fastball, it's below-average in velocity, and his mistakes are hit hard. He allowed too many homers last year. Quantrill wins when he moves the ball around and gets one strike over the plate. He didn't throw a wild pitch in 1995, but Quantrill has a deliberate delivery and poor pickoff move.

Major League Pitching Register

	W	L	ERA	G	CG	IP	H	ER	BB	SO
92 AL	2	3	2.19	27	0	49.1	55	12	15	24
93 AL	6	12	3.91	49	1	138.0	151	60	44	66
94 AL	1	1	3.52	17	0	23.0	25	9	5	15
94 NL	2	2	6.00	18	0	30.0	39	20	10	13
95 NL	11	12	4.67	33	0	179.1	212	93	44	103
Life	22	30	4.16	144	1	419.2	482	194	118	221
3 AVE	8	10	4.46	45	0	138.0	160	68	38	74

CURRENT PLAYERS

SCOTT RADINSKY

Position: Pitcher
Team: Chicago White Sox
Born: March 3, 1968 Glendale, CA
Height: 6'3" **Weight:** 204 lbs.
Bats: left **Throws:** left
Acquired: Third-round pick in 6/86 free-agent draft

Player Summary	
Fantasy Value	$0
Card Value	4¢ to 6¢
Will	face lefties
Can't	afford control woes
Expect	a rebound
Don't Expect	many saves

Radinsky missed all of 1994 after being diagnosed with Hodgkin's disease. Happily, successful chemotherapy treatments have sent the disease into remission, and he was able to pitch in 1995. Unfortunately for Chicago, his year-long layoff manifested itself in rustiness and an inability for Radinsky to find the strike zone. He appeared to have lost a significant amount of velocity and a lot of location. Consequently, Radinsky was hit hard. Right-handers teed off at about a .300 clip, and fellow lefties, who Radinsky had always stifled, also batted around .300. He often faced just one or two hitters at a time, but even in a spot role, he still surrendered too many homers. A few years ago, Radinsky seemed likely to assume a closer role with Chicago. But even with the troubles experienced by other members of the White Sox pen in 1995, he couldn't get many save chances. With proper time to regain his groove, Radinsky should again be effective.

Major League Pitching Register

	W	L	ERA	G	S	IP	H	ER	BB	SO
90 AL	6	1	4.82	62	4	52.1	47	28	36	46
91 AL	5	5	2.02	67	8	71.1	53	16	23	49
92 AL	3	7	2.73	68	15	59.1	54	18	34	48
93 AL	8	2	4.28	73	4	54.2	61	26	19	44
95 AL	2	1	5.45	46	1	38.0	46	23	17	14
Life	24	16	3.62	316	32	275.2	261	111	129	201
2 AVE	5	2	4.79	62	3	48.1	56	26	19	30

BRAD RADKE

Position: Pitcher
Team: Minnesota Twins
Born: Oct. 27, 1972 Eau Claire, WI
Height: 6'2" **Weight:** 180 lbs.
Bats: right **Throws:** right
Acquired: Eighth-round pick in 6/91 free-agent draft

Player Summary	
Fantasy Value	$3 to $5
Card Value	20¢ to 30¢
Will	be in rotation
Can't	overpower with heat
Expect	ground ball outs
Don't Expect	many strikeouts

In spring training, he was just a raw rookie hoping for a bullpen job. By late season, Radke served as the Twins' unquestioned ace starting pitcher. He was a 1994 Double-A Southern League All-Star, going 12-9 with a 2.66 ERA. He skipped Triple-A on his way to the majors. After making his big-league debut out of the bullpen, the rest of his 1995 appearances were as a starter. First used as the fifth member of the rotation, Radke showed durability and decent control. As other Twins starters were traded or fell by the wayside, Radke moved up. He easily led the Minnesota staff in wins, starts, and innings pitched, as well as in a few not-so-good categories. Radke allowed a monstrous number of doubles and homers, largely because when he made mistakes high in the strike zone, hitters could easily tee off. Radke has just a mediocre fastball, but uses a sinker as well as a good curveball and changeup to induce ground balls. He took some lumps last year, but hung in and pitched pretty well, averaging well over six innings per start. Radke will make fewer mistakes as he collects more experience.

Major League Pitching Register

	W	L	ERA	G	CG	IP	H	ER	BB	SO
95 AL	11	14	5.32	29	2	181.0	195	107	47	75
Life	11	14	5.32	29	2	181.0	195	107	47	75

CURRENT PLAYERS

TIM RAINES

Position: Outfield
Team: Chicago White Sox
Born: Sept. 16, 1959 Sanford, FL
Height: 5'8" **Weight:** 186 lbs.
Bats: both **Throws:** right
Acquired: Traded by Expos with Jeff Carter and Mario Brito for Barry Jones and Ivan Calderon, 12/90

Player Summary
Fantasy Value	$7 to $9
Card Value	10¢ to 15¢
Will	hit for power
Can't	regain old speed
Expect	good on-base skills
Don't Expect	basepath mistakes

Last year, Raines underwent a transition in his role. Although he does all the things a successful leadoff man should do—get on base, steal, and hit for some power—the Sox decided that the speed of Ray Durham and Lance Johnson was more important. Raines hit No. 2 and had another good season. He posted a .374 on-base percentage and a .422 slugging mark. He doesn't hit left-handers as well as he once did. He now holds the AL record for consecutive stolen bases with 40. He still has decent range and speed in left field, but he does not throw well. Raines continues to steam toward the Hall of Fame.

Major League Batting Register

	BA	G	AB	R	H	2B	3B	HR	RBI	SB
79 NL	.000	6	0	0	0	0	0	0	0	2
80 NL	.050	15	20	5	1	0	0	0	0	5
81 NL	.304	88	313	61	95	13	7	5	37	71
82 NL	.277	156	647	90	179	32	8	4	43	78
83 NL	.298	156	615	133	183	32	8	11	71	90
84 NL	.309	160	622	106	192	38	9	8	60	75
85 NL	.320	150	575	115	184	30	13	11	41	70
86 NL	.334	151	580	91	194	35	10	9	62	70
87 NL	.330	139	530	123	175	34	8	18	68	50
88 NL	.270	109	429	66	116	19	7	12	48	33
89 NL	.286	145	517	76	148	29	6	9	60	41
90 NL	.287	130	457	65	131	11	5	9	62	49
91 AL	.268	155	609	102	163	20	6	5	50	51
92 AL	.294	144	551	102	162	22	9	7	54	45
93 AL	.306	115	415	75	127	16	4	16	54	21
94 AL	.266	101	384	80	102	15	5	10	52	13
95 AL	.285	133	502	81	143	25	4	12	67	13
Life	.296	2053	7766	1374	2295	371	109	146	829	777
3 AVE	.284	136	507	93	144	22	5	15	68	18

MANNY RAMIREZ

Position: Outfield
Team: Cleveland Indians
Born: May 30, 1972 Santo Domingo, Dominican Republic
Height: 6' **Weight:** 190 lbs.
Bats: right **Throws:** right
Acquired: First-round pick in 6/91 free-agent draft

Player Summary
Fantasy Value	$25 to $30
Card Value	50¢ to $1.00
Will	show strong arm
Can't	impress with speed
Expect	superior offense
Don't Expect	trouble with lefties

Moving quickly from the streets of New York to the bright lights of the AL's ballparks, Ramirez is an awesome young hitter. He has tremendous power, a quick bat, and a good idea of the strike zone. He is still fairly streaky, but he has shown that his excellent rookie campaign of 1994 was no fluke. Last summer, he racked up RBI batting sixth in the Cleveland lineup. He collected enough extra-base hits and got on base enough to score plenty of runs. Ramirez drew enough walks last season to compile a fine on-base percentage. It was one of the better marks on a team full of on-base threats. He does much of his damage against left-handed pitchers. From right field, Ramirez used his powerful arm to cut down baserunners, but he lacks outstanding range. He does not go back on balls well, and he has average speed at best, both in the field and on the basepaths. He's not going to be a stolen-base threat, but the Indians don't care about that at all. Ramirez is going to be a terrific hitter for many years to come.

Major League Batting Register

	BA	G	AB	R	H	2B	3B	HR	RBI	SB
93 AL	.170	22	53	5	9	1	0	2	5	0
94 AL	.269	91	290	51	78	22	0	17	60	4
95 AL	.308	137	484	85	149	26	1	31	107	6
Life	.285	250	827	141	236	49	1	50	172	10
2 AVE	.291	141	477	84	139	30	1	29	102	6

CURRENT PLAYERS

PAT RAPP

Position: Pitcher
Team: Florida Marlins
Born: July 13, 1967 Jennings, LA
Height: 6'3" **Weight:** 205 lbs.
Bats: right **Throws:** right
Acquired: First-round pick from Giants in 11/92 expansion draft

Player Summary	
Fantasy Value	$7 to $9
Card Value	8¢ to 12¢
Will	be in rotation
Can't	afford walks
Expect	ground balls
Don't Expect	runners to steal

The live-armed but heretofore inconsistent Rapp enjoyed a totally unexpected hot streak in 1995, winning eight in a row down the stretch. He put the exclamation mark on his streak with a stunning one-hitter, shutting down the vaunted Rockies offense 17-0 on Sept. 17 at Coors Field. Only a misplayed bloop single kept Rapp from joining baseball's record books. His big season was one reason the Marlins finally began to enjoy respectability in 1995. The one-time Giant hurler, who used a hard sinkerball to induce ground balls, held right-handed hitters to a minuscule average and kept the ball down more, giving up only 10 home runs. When he makes a mistake up in the zone, it goes a long way the other way. Left-handers continued to hit him well, and the number of walks he gives up is still a problem. Luckily, Rapp's pickoff move is strong, and his delivery is deceptive. If he can continue to locate his pitches effectively and keep off the injured list, Rapp could be a rotation anchor.

Major League Pitching Register

	W	L	ERA	G	CG	IP	H	ER	BB	SO
92 NL	0	2	7.20	3	0	10.0	8	8	6	3
93 NL	4	6	4.02	16	1	94.0	101	42	39	57
94 NL	7	8	3.85	24	2	133.1	132	57	69	75
95 NL	14	7	3.44	28	3	167.1	158	64	76	102
Life	25	23	3.80	71	6	404.2	399	171	190	237
3 AVE	10	8	3.72	27	2	156.1	155	65	74	92

JEFF REBOULET

Position: Infield
Team: Minnesota Twins
Born: April 30, 1964 Dayton, OH
Height: 6' **Weight:** 169 lbs.
Bats: right **Throws:** right
Acquired: 10th-round pick in 6/86 free-agent draft

Player Summary	
Fantasy Value	$1
Card Value	4¢ to 6¢
Will	show surprising bat
Can't	crack the lineup
Expect	versatility in field
Don't Expect	stolen bases

Reboulet, who is known as "The Inspector," continued his mission effectively in 1995, filling in anywhere the Twins needed him to. He generally sees most of his action at shortstop, but also played third and second and made several starts at first. He even appeared in one game as a catcher in 1995. Although Reboulet won't win any batting titles soon, he is a much improved hitter from his early form. He does enough things with the bat to be dangerous in some ways. Possessing a very good idea of the strike zone, Reboulet was patient at the plate, and he took enough walks to post a decent on-base percentage. He has line-drive power, and, although he isn't fast, Reboulet is a smart baserunner. Perhaps his most important attribute is his versatility. He can play any defensive position competently, and he has a good throwing arm. He's especially good on the left side of the infield. The mentality that allows him to come off the bench whenever needed has helped Reboulet survive.

Major League Batting Register

	BA	G	AB	R	H	2B	3B	HR	RBI	SB
92 AL	.190	73	137	15	26	7	1	1	16	3
93 AL	.258	109	240	33	62	8	0	1	15	5
94 AL	.259	74	189	28	49	11	1	3	23	0
95 AL	.292	87	216	39	63	11	0	4	23	1
Life	.256	343	782	115	200	37	2	9	77	9
3 AVE	.269	104	250	39	67	12	0	3	24	2

CURRENT PLAYERS

JEFF REED

Position: Catcher
Team: San Francisco Giants
Born: Nov. 12, 1962 Joliet, IL
Height: 6'2" **Weight:** 190 lbs.
Bats: left **Throws:** right
Acquired: Signed as a free agent, 1/93

Player Summary	
Fantasy Value	$0
Card Value	4¢ to 6¢
Will	show patience
Can't	count on a job
Expect	strong throwing
Don't Expect	much power

A former first-round pick and minor-league All-Star, Reed has never panned out as an everyday player. Now, however, he has settled into reserve duty. Last season, he rebounded from a weak 1994 campaign by hitting for a decent average and notching an excellent on-base percentage. However, Reed adds almost no power. He rarely bats against left-handers, and lost some at bats last year to fellow lefty reserve catcher Tom Lampkin. Reed has never had much speed, and he is rarely called on to run the bases. He is often replaced with pinch runners. Behind the dish, Reed is still valuable. He calls a good game, is reasonably good at blocking pitches, and threw out nearly 50 percent of the runners trying to steal against him in 1995. He has plied his trade for four major-league clubs, but only with the Reds did Reed ever get his chance to play regularly.

Major League Batting Register

	BA	G	AB	R	H	2B	3B	HR	RBI	SB
84 AL	.143	18	21	3	3	3	0	0	1	0
85 AL	.200	7	10	2	2	0	0	0	0	0
86 AL	.236	68	165	13	39	6	1	0	9	1
87 NL	.213	75	207	15	44	11	0	1	21	0
88 NL	.226	92	265	20	60	9	2	1	16	1
89 NL	.223	102	287	16	64	11	0	3	23	0
90 NL	.251	72	175	12	44	8	1	3	16	0
91 NL	.267	91	270	20	72	15	2	3	31	0
92 NL	.160	15	25	2	4	0	0	0	2	0
93 NL	.261	66	119	10	31	3	0	6	12	0
94 NL	.175	50	103	11	18	3	0	1	7	0
95 NL	.265	66	113	12	30	2	0	0	9	0
Life	.234	722	1760	136	411	71	6	20	147	2

JODY REED

Position: Second base
Team: San Diego Padres
Born: July 26, 1962 Tampa, FL
Height: 5'9" **Weight:** 165 lbs.
Bats: right **Throws:** right
Acquired: Signed as a free agent, 4/95

Player Summary	
Fantasy Value	$3 to $5
Card Value	4¢ to 6¢
Will	show defense
Can't	hit for power
Expect	a starting job
Don't Expect	many strikeouts

Reed has spent the last three years as an itinerant second baseman, finding a different home each season. In 1995, it was the Padres who came calling, and Reed performed very dependably. He has range as good as any second sacker in baseball, turns the double play well, and rarely makes errors. A weak throwing arm is Reed's only defensive shortcoming. For a Padres team used to Bip Roberts's fielding foibles, mediocre throwing was a fair price to pay for otherwise competent defense. At the dish, Reed is much more of an acquired taste. He has little extra-base power (since he can no longer deposit doubles off the short left-field wall at Fenway), doesn't hit for a high average, and doesn't steal bases. Reed takes his share of walks and gets on base a reasonable amount. He hits right-handers well, and he is a good bat handler and bunter. These attributes, plus his defense, make him a valuable player.

Major League Batting Register

	BA	G	AB	R	H	2B	3B	HR	RBI	SB
87 AL	.300	9	30	4	9	1	1	0	8	1
88 AL	.293	109	338	60	99	23	1	1	28	1
89 AL	.288	146	524	76	151	42	2	3	40	4
90 AL	.289	155	598	70	173	45	0	5	51	4
91 AL	.283	153	618	87	175	42	2	5	60	6
92 AL	.247	143	550	64	136	27	1	3	40	7
93 NL	.276	132	445	48	123	21	2	2	31	1
94 AL	.271	108	399	48	108	22	0	2	37	5
95 NL	.256	131	445	58	114	18	1	4	40	6
Life	.276	1086	3947	515	1088	241	10	25	335	35
3 AVE	.268	144	503	60	134	24	1	3	43	5

CURRENT PLAYERS

STEVE REED

Position: Pitcher
Team: Colorado Rockies
Born: March 11, 1966 Los Angeles, CA
Height: 6'2" **Weight:** 202 lbs.
Bats: right **Throws:** right
Acquired: Third-round pick from Giants in 11/92 expansion draft

Player Summary	
Fantasy Value	$2 to $4
Card Value	4¢ to 6¢
Will	freeze right-handers
Can't	dominate with heat
Expect	many innings
Don't Expect	many saves

Despite some mediocre statistics in the past, Reed has always been appreciated by Colorado manager Don Baylor. The Rockies, knowing exactly how good Reed is, turned away several trade offers for him. Finally, in 1995, Reed posted numbers worthy of his talent. His home ERA in Mile High Stadium during the 1993 and 1994 seasons was around three runs higher than his mark on the road. In neutral parks, Reed has always allowed little more than one run per nine innings. A submarine pitcher with pinpoint control and good sinking action on his fastball, he can pitch often with little discomfort and doesn't walk many hitters. Left-handers have always been a problem for Reed, but he held them to just a .218 mark in 1995. Last year, opponents socked eight homers off him. Reed lacks top velocity, but he can move the ball around enough to get punchouts when necessary. A former standout in the Giants system, he couldn't get a shot at big-league saves because of his short fastball.

Major League Pitching Register

	W	L	ERA	G	S	IP	H	ER	BB	SO
92 NL	1	0	2.30	18	0	15.2	13	4	3	11
93 NL	9	5	4.48	64	3	84.1	80	42	30	51
94 NL	3	2	3.94	61	3	64.0	79	28	26	51
95 NL	5	2	2.14	71	3	84.0	61	20	21	79
Life	18	9	3.41	214	9	248.0	233	94	80	192
3 AVE	6	3	3.48	77	4	90.0	87	35	30	71

CARLOS REYES

Position: Pitcher
Team: Oakland Athletics
Born: April 4, 1969 Miami, FL
Height: 6'1" **Weight:** 190 lbs.
Bats: both **Throws:** right
Acquired: Rule 5 draft pick from Braves, 12/93

Player Summary	
Fantasy Value	$2 to $4
Card Value	4¢ to 6¢
Will	mix his pitches
Can't	assume a key role
Expect	time on the farm
Don't Expect	great control

The Athletics used a Rule 5 pick on Reyes, kept him in the majors for all of 1994, and then retained him at the big-league level in 1995. But they don't seem to have much confidence in him and haven't given him much work. Used almost exclusively as a reliever in noncritical situations (he did make a few starts), Reyes used a moving fastball and his assortment of off-speed pitches and curves to hold opponents to a .264 average. He especially kept right-handers at bay. Unfortunately for Reyes, he continues to have trouble putting the ball over the plate consistently. Walks were a problem, and pitching behind in the count led to too many homers. His fastball is just average in velocity, but he does move it around the strike zone. Reyes's pickoff move and delivery are nothing special, and by all accounts the former Atlanta farmhand needs time to polish his game. He doesn't look ready to contribute in a significant role right now. Reyes is in danger of being pushed back to Triple-A without noticeable improvement in his control.

Major League Pitching Register

	W	L	ERA	G	S	IP	H	ER	BB	SO
94 AL	0	3	4.15	27	1	78.0	71	36	44	57
95 AL	4	6	5.09	40	0	69.0	71	39	28	48
Life	4	9	4.59	67	1	147.0	142	75	72	105
2 AVE	2	5	4.54	42	1	94.0	90	47	47	67

CURRENT PLAYERS

SHANE REYNOLDS

Position: Pitcher
Team: Houston Astros
Born: March 26, 1968 Bastrop, LA
Height: 6'3" **Weight:** 210 lbs.
Bats: right **Throws:** right
Acquired: Third-round pick in 6/89 free-agent draft

Player Summary	
Fantasy Value	$10 to $13
Card Value	6¢ to 10¢
Will	get strikeouts
Can't	carry team himself
Expect	great control
Don't Expect	many headlines

The talented but still-unheralded Reynolds wrapped up another fine season last fall, following up his impressive 1994 rookie year nicely. A star at the University of Texas, Reynolds was left off the 1989 College World Series roster. He has had to earn his respect. After finally convincing the Astros he could be a starter, he stepped up his game in 1994. He became perhaps the Astros' most dependable starter during their playoff chase in 1995. He employed an impressive array of pitches and most of all, superior control to confound opponents. Reynolds not only allowed fewer walks per game than any other NL starting pitcher, he also fanned nearly one man per inning, led Houston in strikeouts, and posted the best ERA of the starting staff. He improved dramatically against left-handers, but he had some trouble with righties. This may be explained by Reynolds's tendency to jam left-handers and work right-handers away. Unusually consistent in his two years at Triple-A (1992 and 1993), Reynolds has continued to pitch a steady brand of ball.

Major League Pitching Register

	W	L	ERA	G	S	IP	H	ER	BB	SO
92 NL	1	3	7.11	8	0	25.1	42	20	6	10
93 NL	0	0	0.82	5	0	11.0	11	1	6	10
94 NL	8	5	3.05	33	0	124.0	128	42	21	110
95 NL	10	11	3.47	30	3	189.1	196	73	37	175
Life	19	19	3.50	76	4	349.2	377	136	70	305
2 AVE	11	10	3.28	40	2	194.1	200	71	36	176

ARMANDO REYNOSO

Position: Pitcher
Team: Colorado Rockies
Born: May 1, 1966 San Luis Potosi, Mexico
Height: 6' **Weight:** 186 lbs.
Bats: right **Throws:** right
Acquired: Third-round pick from Braves in 11/92 expansion draft

Player Summary	
Fantasy Value	$1 to $3
Card Value	5¢ to 8¢
Will	battle hitters
Can't	win with strikeouts
Expect	decent control
Don't Expect	perfect health

In the Rockies' 1993 inaugural season, Reynoso was the team's most successful starting pitcher. The following year, he suffered severe ligament damage in his pitching elbow. When Reynoso returned after a rehabilitation assignment in the minors, he had lost some of the velocity on his fastball. However, he still had good control, decent sinking action on his pitches, and, most importantly, a battling attitude that has marked his career. Since escaping the crowded Braves farm system, Reynoso has shown that despite a lack of overpowering stuff, he is capable of pitching in the majors. Nevertheless, he is going to need to rehabilitate and restrengthen his elbow. He enjoys most of his success by getting ground balls and cannot afford to lose any of the bite on his slider and sinker. Last season, he left a few too many pitches high in the strike zone, allowing 10 home runs. Reynoso's outlook is still cloudy due to his injury. Some pitchers recover from elbow damage; some don't.

Major League Pitching Register

	W	L	ERA	G	CG	IP	H	ER	BB	SO
91 NL	2	1	6.17	6	0	23.1	26	16	10	10
92 NL	1	0	4.70	3	0	7.2	11	4	2	2
93 NL	12	11	4.00	30	4	189.0	206	84	63	117
94 NL	3	4	4.82	9	1	52.1	54	28	22	25
95 NL	7	7	5.32	20	0	93.0	116	55	36	40
Life	25	23	4.61	68	5	365.1	413	187	133	194
2 AVE	10	9	4.47	26	2	147.0	168	73	52	81

CURRENT PLAYERS

ARTHUR RHODES

Position: Pitcher
Team: Baltimore Orioles
Born: Oct. 24, 1969 Waco, TX
Height: 6'2" **Weight:** 206 lbs.
Bats: left **Throws:** left
Acquired: Second-round pick in 6/88 free-agent draft

Player Summary
Fantasy Value $1
Card Value . . . . 6¢ to 10¢
Will . . . . confound and confuse
Can't . . . . count out his arm
Expect . . . . strikeouts, walks
Don't Expect . . . . consistency

For what seems like the ten-millionth time to Orioles fans, Rhodes again failed to meet his impressive potential in 1995. The Orioles have tried him in the starting rotation, long relief, and even in short relief, but they haven't been able to find the best place for the talented but erratic left-hander. He has bouts of wildness that come at unexpected and inopportune times, and he often gives up home runs when forced to come in with below-average fastballs. Rhodes still throws with excellent velocity and has a terrific curve, but he can't seem to get into a consistent rhythm. His best outings in 1995 came when used in long relief situations, where the Orioles were well out of the game. Confidence and concentration may be the keys to Rhodes's troubles. There are many in the major leagues who believe that he should remain a starter, feeling that only long stretches of work will solve his problems. Again in 1995, he dominated as a starter at Triple-A before coming to the majors.

Major League Pitching Register

	W	L	ERA	G	CG	IP	H	ER	BB	SO
91 AL	0	3	8.00	8	0	36.0	47	32	23	23
92 AL	7	5	3.63	15	2	94.1	87	38	38	77
93 AL	5	6	6.51	17	0	85.2	91	62	49	49
94 AL	3	5	5.81	10	3	52.2	51	34	30	47
95 AL	2	5	6.21	19	0	75.1	68	52	48	77
Life	17	24	5.70	69	5	344.0	344	218	188	273
2 AVE	4	6	6.36	19	0	85.2	84	60	52	68

JOSE RIJO

Position: Pitcher
Team: Cincinnati Reds
Born: May 13, 1965 San Cristobal, Dominican Republic
Height: 6'2" **Weight:** 210 lbs.
Bats: right **Throws:** right
Acquired: Traded by Athletics with Tim Birtsas for Dave Parker, 12/87

Player Summary
Fantasy Value. . . . . $5 to $7
Card Value . . . . 15¢ to 20¢
Will . . . . rehabilitate
Can't . . . . be counted on
Expect . . . . return to duty
Don't Expect . . . . stuff of old

Prior to 1995, Rijo had been the second-best pitcher in the NL over the last five seasons. Now, all of that is up in the air. Last July, he went on the DL with elbow problems that did not respond to rest or cortisone shots. Surgery was deemed necessary, and the procedure ended Rijo's season. He is questionable for Opening Day 1996. Even if his elbow is ready to go, whether he can recapture past glory is in doubt. Rijo's best offering is a slider (felt by most to be the best in baseball), a pitch that puts heavy pressure on the elbow. His fastball also depends on the elbow for its sink. He is a dominating strikeout pitcher with good control, even with his aching elbow. He allowed lefty hitters an uncharacteristic .328 average.

Major League Pitching Register

	W	L	ERA	G	CG	IP	H	ER	BB	SO
84 AL	2	8	4.76	24	0	62.1	74	33	33	47
85 AL	6	4	3.53	12	0	63.2	57	25	28	65
86 AL	9	11	4.65	39	4	193.2	172	100	108	176
87 AL	2	7	5.90	21	1	82.1	106	54	41	67
88 NL	13	8	2.39	49	0	162.0	120	43	63	160
89 NL	7	6	2.84	19	1	111.0	101	35	48	86
90 NL	14	8	2.70	29	7	197.0	151	59	78	152
91 NL	15	6	2.51	30	3	204.1	165	57	55	172
92 NL	15	10	2.56	33	2	211.0	185	60	44	171
93 NL	14	9	2.48	36	2	257.1	218	71	62	227
94 NL	9	6	3.08	26	2	172.1	177	59	52	171
95 NL	5	4	4.17	14	0	69.0	76	32	22	62
Life	111	87	3.16	332	22	1786.0	1602	628	634	1556
3 AVE	11	7	2.96	29	2	192.1	184	63	53	179

CURRENT PLAYERS

CAL RIPKEN

Position: Shortstop
Team: Baltimore Orioles
Born: Aug. 24, 1960 Havre de Grace, MD
Height: 6'4" **Weight:** 220 lbs.
Bats: right **Throws:** right
Acquired: Second-round pick in 6/78 free-agent draft

Player Summary
Fantasy Value	$11 to $14
Card Value	$2.00 to $3.00
Will	provide some stick
Can't	show old mobility
Expect	a full schedule
Don't Expect	stolen bases

The new Iron Man of baseball broke Lou Gehrig's consecutive-game streak, playing in his 2,131st straight contest in Baltimore Sept. 6 before a capacity crowd and a national TV audience. Despite the media attention, Ripken performed well all season, continuing his tenure as one of the game's better shortstops. He still has good power, slugging .422 in 1995, and makes good contact. However, he doesn't get around quickly on as many pitches. Once one of baseball's star defensive shortstops, Ripken is now above average. He is sure-handed and throws well, but he lacks outstanding range. Steadiness and dependability are his game; flash and glitz have never been.

Major League Pitching Register
	BA	G	AB	R	H	2B	3B	HR	RBI	SB
81 AL	.128	23	39	1	5	0	0	0	0	0
82 AL	.264	160	598	90	158	32	5	28	93	3
83 AL	.318	162	663	121	211	47	2	27	102	0
84 AL	.304	162	641	103	195	37	7	27	86	2
85 AL	.282	161	642	116	181	32	5	26	110	2
86 AL	.282	162	627	98	177	35	1	25	81	4
87 AL	.252	162	624	97	157	28	3	27	98	3
88 AL	.264	161	575	87	152	25	1	23	81	2
89 AL	.257	162	646	80	166	30	0	21	93	3
90 AL	.250	161	600	78	150	28	4	21	84	3
91 AL	.323	162	650	99	210	46	5	34	114	6
92 AL	.251	162	637	73	160	29	1	14	72	4
93 AL	.257	162	641	87	165	26	3	24	90	1
94 AL	.315	112	444	71	140	19	3	13	75	1
95 AL	.262	144	550	71	144	33	2	17	88	0
Life	.276	2218	8577	1272	2371	447	42	327	1267	34
3 AVE	.278	161	628	89	175	30	3	20	98	1

BILL RISLEY

Position: Pitcher
Team: Seattle Mariners
Born: May 29, 1967 Chicago, IL
Height: 6'2" **Weight:** 215 lbs.
Bats: right **Throws:** right
Acquired: Claimed on waivers from Expos, 3/94

Player Summary
Fantasy Value	$4 to $6
Card Value	5¢ to 8¢
Will	work often
Can't	grab closing job
Expect	strikeouts
Don't Expect	control problems

Last season, Risley proved that his impressive 1994 rookie campaign was no fluke. Once again, he struck out more than one man per inning, hardly walked anybody, and served as a terrific set-up man to closer Bobby Ayala. Working in the late innings, Risley held opponents to a paltry on-base percentage in 1995 and shut down left-handed hitters. He uses a good fastball and curve to keep hitters off stride, and he is difficult to run on. However, Risley did have a few problems last year. Given a few chances to hold leads late in games, he blew six save opportunities and allowed nearly half of his inherited runners to score. The Mariners have a deep bullpen, luckily, and can afford to spot Risley effectively to make the best use of his talents. The Chicago native never got a chance with his former organizations, Cincinnati and Montreal (earning the nickname "Wild Bill" due to control troubles). But Risley's live arm is sure to keep him around for many years if he stays off the injured list.

Major League Pitching Register
	W	L	ERA	G	S	IP	H	ER	BB	SO
92 NL	1	0	1.80	3	0	5.0	4	1	1	2
93 NL	0	0	6.00	2	0	3.0	2	2	2	2
94 AL	9	6	3.44	37	0	52.1	31	20	19	61
95 AL	2	1	3.13	45	1	60.1	55	21	18	65
Life	12	7	3.28	85	1	120.2	92	44	40	130
2 AVE	7	5	3.29	51	1	70.1	53	26	24	80

CURRENT PLAYERS

KEVIN RITZ

Position: Pitcher
Team: Colorado Rockies
Born: June 8, 1965 Eatontown, NJ
Height: 6'4" **Weight:** 220 lbs.
Bats: right **Throws:** right
Acquired: Second-round pick from Tigers in 11/92 expansion draft

Player Summary	
Fantasy Value	$4 to $6
Card Value	5¢ to 8¢
Will	provide innings
Can't	dominate a game
Expect	trouble with lefties
Don't Expect	20-win season

Ritz was one of the NL's plainly average pitchers in 1995. His record hovered around the .500 mark all year, his ERA was almost identical to the run support he received from his Rockies teammates, and his strikeout-to-walk numbers were typical of the average NL pitcher. However, several factors elevate him from this mundane state. Pitching half of the games in homer-happy Denver means that a pitcher with an average ERA is actually pitching good baseball. In addition, he has made an impressive recovery from elbow injuries. He led the Rockies staff in innings pitched in 1995. He survives by moving his pitches around in the strike zone, keeping the ball low whenever possible. Ritz doesn't have the pure fastball to win with high strikes, and he gets beaten if his pitches rise. Ritz lacks a strong pickoff move and has a long delivery. A record of inconsistency and serious injuries mean that Ritz won't ever be a sure thing, but the Rockies were happy this average guy showed up in 1995.

Major League Pitching Register

	W	L	ERA	G	CG	IP	H	ER	BB	SO
89 AL	4	6	4.38	12	1	74.0	75	36	44	56
90 AL	0	4	11.05	4	0	7.1	14	9	14	3
91 AL	0	3	11.74	11	0	15.1	17	20	22	9
92 AL	2	5	5.60	23	0	80.1	88	50	44	57
94 NL	5	6	5.62	15	0	73.2	88	46	35	53
95 NL	11	11	4.21	31	0	173.1	171	81	65	120
Life	22	35	5.14	96	1	424.0	453	242	224	298
2 AVE	10	10	4.70	28	0	149.2	158	78	61	105

SID ROBERSON

Position: Pitcher
Team: Milwaukee Brewers
Born: Sept. 7, 1971 Jacksonville, FL
Height: 5'9" **Weight:** 170 lbs.
Bats: left **Throws:** left
Acquired: 29th-round pick in 6/92 free-agent draft

Player Summary	
Fantasy Value	$0
Card Value	10¢ to 15¢
Will	search for consistency
Can't	afford walks
Expect	relief work
Don't Expect	many strikeouts

Roberson lacks a power fastball, but he won in the minors using a deceptive crossfire delivery. He also pitched with the toughness prized by Milwaukee manager Phil Garner. When the Brewers called Roberson up last year, he joined what was, for a time, a four-rookie in five-pitchers starting rotation. He fared well for his first few starts, but soon hitters began to wait Roberson out and tee off on his assortment of off-speed deliveries. After just 13 starts, the Brewers had seen enough. Roberson made a return trip to Triple-A New Orleans before returning as a reliever in September. The smallish lefty doesn't have much strikeout ability. He didn't rack up big K totals even in the minors, and he can't afford lapses of control if he's going to win in the big leagues. AL hitters walked as often as they struck out against him. They also smacked an eye-popping 16 homers off Roberson in 1995. Lefties more than hung in against him, though he should be able to set them down. It's likely Roberson will start in Triple-A again in 1996 for continued work on refining his control.

Major League Pitching Register

	W	L	ERA	G	CG	IP	H	ER	BB	SO
95 AL	6	4	5.76	26	0	84.1	102	54	37	40
Life	6	4	5.76	26	0	84.1	102	54	37	40

CURRENT PLAYERS

BIP ROBERTS

Position: Second base; outfield
Team: San Diego Padres
Born: Oct. 27, 1963 Berkeley, CA
Height: 5'7" **Weight:** 165 lbs.
Bats: both **Throws:** right
Acquired: Signed as a free agent, 1/94

Player Summary	
Fantasy Value	$10 to $13
Card Value	6¢ to 10¢
Will	show leadoff skills
Can't	find a position
Expect	smart baserunning
Don't Expect	durability

Roberts enjoyed a good 1995 season at the plate, but his year ended prematurely when he suffered one of the strangest injuries in recent memory. While standing in the Padres bullpen in early September acting as a "dummy" hitter as Andy Ashby warmed up, Roberts turned to respond to a question and was hit in the leg by an errant Ashby fastball. A bone in the leg was fractured, and Roberts did not play afterward. The injury came at a tough time as the Padres were fighting for the playoffs. When healthy, Roberts spent most of his time in left field, shifting to occasional time at second base when Phil Plantier was reacquired and, finally, shortstop when Andjuar Cedeno slumped. Roberts isn't a Gold Glove candidate at any position, but his offensive skills make him a pretty good leadoff man. However, he took just 17 walks last year for a .346 on-base percentage. He must get on base more this season.

Major League Batting Register

	BA	G	AB	R	H	2B	3B	HR	RBI	SB
86 NL	.253	101	241	34	61	5	2	1	12	14
88 NL	.333	5	9	1	3	0	0	0	0	0
89 NL	.301	117	329	81	99	15	8	3	25	21
90 NL	.309	149	556	104	172	36	3	9	44	46
91 NL	.281	117	424	66	119	13	3	3	32	26
92 NL	.323	147	532	92	172	34	6	4	45	44
93 NL	.240	83	292	46	70	13	0	1	18	26
94 NL	.320	105	403	52	129	15	5	2	31	21
95 NL	.304	73	296	40	90	14	0	2	25	20
Life	.297	897	3082	516	915	145	27	25	232	218
3 AVE	.296	104	398	55	118	17	2	2	30	26

FRANK RODRIGUEZ

Position: Pitcher
Team: Minnesota Twins
Born: Dec. 11, 1972 Brooklyn, NY
Height: 6' **Weight:** 175 lbs.
Bats: right **Throws:** right
Acquired: Traded by Red Sox with J.J. Johnson for Rick Aguilera, 7/95

Player Summary	
Fantasy Value	$1
Card Value	8¢ to 10¢
Will	be in rotation
Can't	afford walks
Expect	a learning process
Don't Expect	another trade

For two years, the Red Sox regarded Rodriguez as the prize of their farm system. However, the chance to win the AL East in 1995 forced Boston's hand. A weakness in short relief led the BoSox to deal for Rick Aguilera, surrendering Rodriguez as the booty. After the initial shock of losing their closer, Minnesota players were happy to welcome Rodriguez. Kirby Puckett went so far as to predict future All-Star status for the green right-hander. Rodriguez is an excellent athlete who can hit, run, and field his position. He began his career at shortstop and did not pitch professionally until 1992, his second pro season. He is still learning how to work on the mound. After the trade, Minnesota manager Tom Kelly stuck Rodriguez into the rotation immediately, and he enjoyed sporadic success. Rodriguez has four pitches, with his best being a fine curve and a hard, rising fastball that has overpowering velocity. Control is still a problem. It will take time for Rodriguez to iron out the lumps in his game. At Triple-A in 1994, he was 8-13, but he turned in a 3.92 ERA and 160 strikeouts in 186 innings.

Major League Pitching Register

	W	L	ERA	G	CG	IP	H	ER	BB	SO
95 AL	5	8	6.13	25	0	105.2	114	72	57	59
Life	5	8	6.13	25	0	105.2	114	72	57	59

CURRENT PLAYERS

HENRY RODRIGUEZ

Position: Outfield; first base
Team: Montreal Expos
Born: Nov. 8, 1967 Santo Domingo, Dominican Republic
Height: 6'1" **Weight:** 210 lbs.
Bats: left **Throws:** left
Acquired: Traded by Dodgers with Jeff Treadway for Joey Eischen and Roberto Kelly, 5/95

Player Summary	
Fantasy Value	$3 to $5
Card Value	4¢ to 6¢
Will	battle for at bats
Can't	hit left-handers
Expect	defensive struggles
Don't Expect	many walks

Almost immediately after moving to the Expos, in a trade of disappointing left fielders, Rodriguez fractured his leg and missed three months. He returned in September and appeared healthy. He has played as a first baseman and, occasionally, in the outfield. Very early in his career, Rodriguez was typecast as a platoon player, and he still has few career at bats against lefties. His power is apparent, since even in Dodger Stadium he turned in decent home run totals coming off the bench. However, Rodriguez is still not a finished product. He swings at nearly everything pitchers throw to him, thus decreasing the number of good pitches he will actually get. Last season, Rodriguez fanned 29 times and took only 11 walks. His on-base percentage was just .293. Rodriguez wasn't fast before the broken leg. In the outfield, he's a left fielder due to poor range and a mediocre arm. He's got to provide more power to keep a job at the big-league level.

Major League Batting Register

	BA	G	AB	R	H	2B	3B	HR	RBI	SB
92 NL	.219	53	146	11	32	7	0	3	14	0
93 NL	.222	76	176	20	39	10	0	8	23	1
94 NL	.268	104	306	33	82	14	2	8	49	0
95 NL	.239	45	138	13	45	4	1	2	15	1
Life	.243	278	766	77	186	35	3	21	101	1
2 AVE	.255	111	304	33	77	15	1	10	46	1

IVAN RODRIGUEZ

Position: Catcher
Team: Texas Rangers
Born: Nov. 30, 1971 Vega Baja, PR
Height: 5'9" **Weight:** 205 lbs.
Bats: right **Throws:** right
Acquired: Signed as a free agent, 7/88

Player Summary	
Fantasy Value	$14 to $17
Card Value	12¢ to 20¢
Will	lash line drives
Can't	show great patience
Expect	good contact
Don't Expect	25 homers

Another year, another All-Star selection for Rodriguez. This time, he played the midsummer classic in his home stadium to wild cheers from a sellout crowd. In 1995, he was one of the few Rangers to hit consistently from wire to wire. He posted yet another fine batting average and added some extra-base hits. However, he didn't show the power production he had in 1994, and drew relatively fewer walks. His on-base percentage was just fair. "Little Pudge" makes good contact and is good on the hit-and-run. The Rangers used Rodriguez in the second, fifth, sixth, and seventh spots last season. He is productive in any of them. Rodriguez pounded left-handers clip and batted over .300 both at home and on the road. Defensively, there is no question: He is probably the best all-around defender in the AL. Rodriguez gunned down nearly half the runners who tried to steal on him last year, blocked pitches with his usual aplomb, and won some respect for his game-calling ability.

Major League Batting Register

	BA	G	AB	R	H	2B	3B	HR	RBI	SB
91 AL	.264	88	280	24	74	16	0	3	27	0
92 AL	.260	123	420	39	109	16	1	8	37	0
93 AL	.273	137	473	56	129	28	4	10	66	8
94 AL	.298	99	363	56	108	19	1	16	57	6
95 AL	.303	130	492	56	149	32	2	12	67	0
Life	.281	577	2028	231	569	111	8	49	254	14
3 AVE	.292	141	513	66	150	30	3	15	74	5

CURRENT PLAYERS

KENNY ROGERS

Position: Pitcher
Team: Texas Rangers
Born: Nov. 10, 1964 Savannah, GA
Height: 6'1" **Weight:** 205 lbs.
Bats: left **Throws:** left
Acquired: 39th-round pick in 6/82 free-agent draft

Player Summary	
Fantasy Value	$13 to $16
Card Value	10¢ to 15¢
Will	locate ball
Can't	dominate with Ks
Expect	some homers
Don't Expect	20 wins

Following up a 1994 season that included a perfect game is a tall order, but "the Gambler" did his best in 1995. Elevated to the role of staff ace, Rogers was named Texas' Opening Day starter and began the season well. However, he endured a poor two-month period, racking up a 5.10 mark in 14 starts. Then, in late August, he rebounded and virtually carried the Rangers rotation down the stretch. He finished the year pacing the staff in almost every category. Although Rogers doesn't have a power fastball, he has a nasty curve and decent velocity. Location is occasionally a problem for him; he pays the price for his mistakes by watching the baseball clear the fences. Rogers stymied left-handers last year, and his excellent pickoff move (and the arm of Ivan Rodriguez) led to about half of potential basestealers being caught. Rogers has become a very good pitcher, though he would likely benefit from being allowed to assume a No. 2 role.

Major League Pitching Register

	W	L	ERA	G	CG	IP	H	ER	BB	SO
89 AL	3	4	2.93	73	0	73.2	60	24	42	63
90 AL	10	6	3.13	69	0	97.2	93	34	42	74
91 AL	10	10	5.42	63	0	109.2	121	66	61	73
92 AL	3	6	3.09	81	0	78.2	80	27	26	70
93 AL	16	10	4.10	35	5	208.1	210	95	71	140
94 AL	11	8	4.46	24	6	167.1	169	83	52	120
95 AL	17	7	3.38	31	3	208.0	192	78	76	140
Life	70	51	3.88	376	14	943.1	925	407	370	680
3 AVE	17	10	3.98	35	6	226.1	221	100	77	156

MEL ROJAS

Position: Pitcher
Team: Montreal Expos
Born: Dec. 10, 1966 Haina, Dominican Republic
Height: 5'11" **Weight:** 185 lbs.
Bats: right **Throws:** right
Acquired: Signed as a free agent, 11/85

Player Summary	
Fantasy Value	$20 to $25
Card Value	5¢ to 8¢
Will	be a closer
Can't	hold runners
Expect	a rebound
Don't Expect	home runs

For years, Rojas has lobbied for full-time closer duty, but when John Wetteland went to New York, the results weren't good for the Expos. Rojas pitched poorly when entrusted with leads in 1995, blowing nine save chances. What's worse, he didn't appear to take much responsibility for his problems, leading Montreal's manager Felipe Alou (Mel's uncle) and GM Kevin Malone to dub their troubled reliever "the excuse man." Last season, Rojas allowed opponents about a .350 on-base mark courtesy of a fairly high walk total. Rojas also unleashed six wild pitches on the year. He has a poor pickoff move and a long windup. Location appeared to be his problem in 1995, since his velocity is still above average. While Rojas suffered a poor season in 1995, he's still got more raw ability than most closers. He keeps the ball low and in the park. If he is used judiciously, Rojas may ultimately excel in the closer's role he so obviously feels he can fill.

Major League Pitching Register

	W	L	ERA	G	S	IP	H	ER	BB	SO
90 NL	3	1	3.60	23	1	40.0	34	16	24	26
91 NL	3	3	3.75	37	6	48.0	42	20	13	37
92 NL	7	1	1.43	68	10	100.2	71	16	34	70
93 NL	5	8	2.95	66	10	88.1	80	29	30	48
94 NL	3	2	3.32	58	16	84.0	71	31	21	84
95 NL	4	4	4.12	59	30	67.2	69	31	29	61
Life	22	19	3.00	311	73	428.2	367	143	151	326
3 AVE	3	5	3.42	71	22	94.1	86	36	31	78

CURRENT PLAYERS

JOHN ROPER

Position: Pitcher
Team: San Francisco Giants
Born: Nov. 21, 1971 Moore County, NC
Height: 6' **Weight:** 170 lbs.
Bats: right **Throws:** right
Acquired: Traded by Reds with Deion Sanders, Scott Service, Dave McCarty, and Ricky Pickett for Mark Portugal, Dave Burba, and Darren Lewis, 7/95

Player Summary
Fantasy Value.................$2 to $4
Card Value ....6¢ to 10¢
Will........................sit righties down
Can't.........................rely on Ks
Expect..........................pressure
Don't Expect................top control

For the Giants, even though they received a prime-time player, the big key to the July trade with the Reds was John Roper. The Reds hated to give him up. Roper has struggled with injuries the past couple of years, but he has shown quite a bit of potential. He just hasn't been able to put it together in the big leagues. He relies on a knuckle-curve that, when it is working, is a devestating pitch. He doesn't have a very good fastball, and even at his best he usuallly doesn't strike many hitters out. He has trouble with left-handed hitters and he gives up too many round-trippers. In 1994, Roper held right-handed hitters to a minuscule .201 average while at Cincinnati. He was 7-0 with a 2.17 ERA at Triple-A Indianapolis before his call-up to the Reds, but even at Triple-A he fanned just 33 in 58 innings. He hasn't yet mastered his control and is very easy to run on. If he can get his pitches to move in on lefties, Roper has a chance to be a productive starter.

Major League Pitching Register

	W	L	ERA	G	CG	IP	H	ER	BB	SO
93 NL	2	5	5.63	16	0	80.0	92	50	36	54
94 NL	6	2	4.50	16	0	92.0	90	46	30	51
95 NL	0	0	16.88	3	0	8.0	15	11	6	6
Life	8	7	5.35	35	0	180.0	197	107	72	111
2 AVE	5	4	4.93	19	0	105.0	109	57	39	63

SCOTT RUFFCORN

Position: Pitcher
Team: Chicago White Sox
Born: Dec. 29, 1969 New Braunfels, TX
Height: 6'4" **Weight:** 210 lbs.
Bats: right **Throws:** right
Acquired: First-round pick in 6/91 free-agent draft

Player Summary
Fantasy Value.................$2 to $4
Card Value ....8¢ to 12¢
Will..............................get a shot
Can't.............worry about injuries
Expect............good heat if healthy
Don't Expect..............another 1995

Ouch. Ruffcorn had an awful season in 1995, though at the beginning he was supposed to challenge James Baldwin for a starting spot in the White Sox rotation. Ruffcorn went from being one of the most highly rated young hurlers in baseball to almost an afterthought for Chicago. Of course, injuries took their toll. When given the chance to pitch, however, Ruffcorn did not do well. He posted a 108 earned run average at Triple-A Nashville, giving up four earned runs in one-third of an inning. This was a complete 180-degree turnaround from 1994. That year, he was named the No. 3 prospect in the Triple-A American Association, according to a poll in *Baseball America*. He showed fine control with his fastball and curve. His out pitch was a slurve—a combination of a slider and a curve—and it was impressive. Ruffcorn was the 25th overall selection in the draft after a 7-1 campaign in his junior year at Baylor. He had been the team's MVP as a sophomore. In his second year as a pro, he blossomed, winning the MVP at Sarasota of the Class-A Florida State League.

Major League Pitching Register

	W	L	ERA	G	CG	IP	H	ER	BB	SO
93 AL	0	2	8.10	3	0	10.0	9	9	10	2
94 AL	0	2	12.79	2	0	6.1	15	9	5	3
95 AL	0	0	7.87	4	0	8.0	10	7	13	5
Life	0	4	9.25	9	0	24.1	34	25	28	10

CURRENT PLAYERS

BRUCE RUFFIN

Position: Pitcher
Team: Colorado Rockies
Born: Oct. 4, 1963 Lubbock, TX
Height: 6'2" **Weight:** 213 lbs.
Bats: both **Throws:** left
Acquired: Signed as a free agent, 12/92

Player Summary	
Fantasy Value	$7 to $9
Card Value	4¢ to 6¢
Will	get ground balls
Can't	afford injury
Expect	good stuff
Don't Expect	20 saves

It appeared for several years that although Ruffin had major-league velocity in his live left arm, he was never going to gain enough command to win in the bigs. He drifted from Philadelphia to Milwaukee without showing much, either as a starter or a reliever. Suddenly, when the fledgling Rockies inked him, Ruffin responded to the challenge of pitching in the thin air by getting—and keeping—the ball down in the strike zone. Walks have always been a problem for the hard-throwing left-hander, but Ruffin has cut down on his free passes in the last few seasons. He has spent well-earned time closing games for Colorado. Last year, however, an elbow injury shelved him for two months. When healthy, he held left-handers to a minuscule average. He blew few save chances and allowed few home runs. Ruffin should receive some late-inning work this year due to his previous performance.

Major League Pitching Register

	W	L	ERA	G	S	IP	H	ER	BB	SO
86 NL	9	4	2.46	21	0	146.1	138	40	44	70
87 NL	11	14	4.35	35	0	204.2	236	99	73	93
38 NL	6	10	4.43	55	3	144.1	151	71	80	82
89 NL	6	10	4.44	24	0	125.2	152	62	62	70
90 NL	6	13	5.38	32	0	149.0	178	89	62	79
91 NL	4	7	3.78	31	0	119.0	125	50	38	85
92 AL	1	6	6.67	25	0	58.0	66	43	41	45
93 NL	6	5	3.87	59	2	139.2	145	60	69	126
94 NL	4	5	4.04	56	16	55.2	55	25	30	65
95 NL	0	1	2.12	37	11	34.0	26	8	19	23
Life	53	75	4.19	375	32	1176.1	1272	547	518	738
3 AVE	4	4	3.66	60	12	85.2	84	35	44	81

JEFF RUSSELL

Position: Pitcher
Team: Texas Rangers
Born: Sept. 2, 1961 Cincinnati, OH
Height: 6'3" **Weight:** 205 lbs.
Bats: right **Throws:** right
Acquired: Signed as a free agent, 4/95

Player Summary	
Fantasy Value	$12 to $15
Card Value	5¢ to 8¢
Will	mix his pitches
Can't	show old fastball
Expect	one-inning appearances
Don't Expect	many walks

Injuries had Russell considering retirement after a frustrating 1994 season, but he elected to sign with the Rangers. Texas' inexperienced and inconsistent bullpen promised plenty of save chances. Russell got them, and he converted them. Used sparingly but well by Rangers skipper Johnny Oates, Russell fashioned a fine overall year. Opponents batted only .277 against the veteran right-hander, and he kept the ball in the park. The question one must ask of Russell, however, is what role does he play? Age and elbow problems simply will not allow him to assume his old workload. Someone else has to assume some of his critical late-inning chores. He does not throw with his old velocity, but Russell's curve moves well, and he has both good control and strikeout ability. He will be helpful if spotted effectively.

Major League Pitching Register

	W	L	ERA	G	S	IP	H	ER	BB	SO
83 NL	4	5	3.03	10	0	68.1	58	23	22	40
84 NL	6	18	4.26	33	0	181.2	186	86	65	101
85 AL	3	6	7.55	13	0	62.0	85	52	27	44
86 AL	5	2	3.40	37	2	82.0	74	31	31	54
87 AL	5	4	4.44	52	3	97.1	109	48	52	56
88 AL	10	9	3.82	34	0	188.2	183	80	66	88
89 AL	6	4	1.98	71	38	72.2	45	16	24	77
90 AL	1	5	4.26	27	10	25.1	23	12	16	16
91 AL	6	4	3.29	68	30	79.1	71	29	26	52
92 AL	4	3	1.63	59	30	66.1	55	12	25	48
93 AL	1	4	2.70	51	33	46.2	39	14	14	45
94 AL	1	6	5.09	42	17	40.2	43	23	16	28
95 AL	1	0	3.03	37	20	32.2	36	11	9	21
Life	53	70	3.77	534	183	1043.2	1007	437	393	670
3 AVE	1	4	3.76	51	26	46.2	47	20	16	36

CURRENT PLAYERS

KEN RYAN

Position: Pitcher
Team: Boston Red Sox
Born: Oct. 24, 1968 Pawtucket, RI
Height: 6'3" **Weight:** 200 lbs.
Bats: right **Throws:** right
Acquired: Signed as a free agent, 6/86

Player Summary	
Fantasy Value	$2 to $4
Card Value	4¢ to 6¢
Will	try to start over
Can't	afford walks
Expect	good fastball
Don't Expect	30 saves

The Red Sox had been grooming Ryan as a closer for two years and gave him the job in 1995. Unfortunately, a string of miserable outings shot Ryan right back to Double-A. Boston was forced to pull the trigger on the Rick Aguilera deal. Ryan appeared to have been making progress learning how to pitch in the majors, but he simply could not get the ball where he wanted it last season. He depends on keeping the ball low and inside, which he could not do consistently. He blew three of 10 save chances, and even when he got his saves, he did not pitch well. Opponents hit .284 against him and took plenty of walks. More importantly, Ryan did not seem to have much confidence that he could turn it around. The Red Sox thought it was best just to get him back to the minors. Unfortunately, he allowed 19 runs in 28 frames split between Double-A and Triple-A, leading the Red Sox to wonder if an injury was to blame. Whether he will get another shot at late relief is anyone's guess, but Ryan still has the same talent he did a year ago.

Major League Pitching Register

	W	L	ERA	G	S	IP	H	ER	BB	SO
92 AL	0	0	6.43	7	1	7.0	4	5	5	5
93 AL	7	2	3.60	47	1	50.0	43	20	29	49
94 AL	2	3	2.44	42	13	48.0	46	13	17	32
95 AL	0	4	4.96	28	7	32.2	34	18	24	34
Life	9	9	3.66	124	22	137.2	127	56	75	120
3 AVE	3	4	3.41	46	9	51.1	49	20	27	44

BRET SABERHAGEN

Position: Pitcher
Team: Colorado Rockies
Born: April 11, 1964 Chicago Heights, IL
Height: 6'1" **Weight:** 190 lbs.
Bats: right **Throws:** right
Acquired: Traded by Mets with a player to be named later for Arnold Gooch and Juan Acevedo, 7/95

Player Summary	
Fantasy Value	$8 to $10
Card Value	10¢ to 15¢
Will	pitch well if able
Can't	bank on health
Expect	spectacular control
Don't Expect	high ERA

Now that Saberhagen has disposed of that tired "even years-odd years" stuff, it's obvious that simple wear and tear on his slender figure is the key reason for his inconsistency. Last season, he pitched well when physically able, but shoulder aches made his active time considerably shorter than the Rockies would have hoped. In his first three starts in Colorado, he averaged over 120 pitches and, consequently, began to experience shoulder pain almost immediately. The low point came when he was the starter (and loser) in the 26-7 drubbing the Cubs gave Colorado at Mile High in August. Soon afterward, he began missing starts. When he is healthy, he has superior control, excellent velocity, and one of the most biting hard sliders anyone has seen.

Major League Pitching Register

	W	L	ERA	G	CG	IP	H	ER	BB	SO
84 AL	10	11	3.48	38	2	157.2	138	61	36	73
85 AL	20	6	2.87	32	10	235.1	211	75	38	158
86 AL	7	12	4.15	30	4	156.0	165	72	29	112
87 AL	18	10	3.36	33	15	257.0	246	96	53	163
88 AL	14	16	3.80	35	9	260.2	271	110	59	171
89 AL	23	6	2.16	36	12	262.1	209	63	43	193
90 AL	5	9	3.27	20	5	135.0	146	49	28	87
91 AL	13	8	3.07	28	7	196.1	165	67	45	136
92 NL	3	5	3.50	17	1	97.2	84	38	27	81
93 NL	7	7	3.29	19	4	139.1	131	51	17	93
94 NL	14	4	2.74	24	4	177.1	169	54	13	143
95 NL	7	6	4.18	25	3	153.0	165	71	33	100
Life	141	100	3.26	337	76	2227.2	2100	807	421	1510
3 AVE	12	6	3.32	27	4	187.1	185	69	24	136

CURRENT PLAYERS

TIM SALMON

Position: Outfield
Team: California Angels
Born: Aug. 24, 1968 Long Beach, CA
Height: 6'3" **Weight:** 220 lbs.
Bats: right **Throws:** right
Acquired: Third-round pick in 6/89 free-agent draft

Player Summary	
Fantasy Value	$30 to $35
Card Value	20¢ to 35¢
Will	show strong arm
Can't	provide speed
Expect	consistent offense
Don't Expect	a power outage

Young, handsome, and talented, Salmon seemed to have it all last summer. A key player for baseball's hottest team, he was inspiring some discussion as a possible MVP candidate by knocking out homers at a league-leading pace. Unfortunately, the Angels went into the tank in September, but it was no fault of Salmon's. He continued to show that he was a prime-time player at the plate. Overall, he enjoyed his greatest season yet in Angels garb. He compiled a superior .429 on-base percentage on the strength of his great batting average and ability to wait for bases on balls. He fanned 111 times, a good number considering his walks and power. Salmon had a tremendous season against left-handed pitchers. The Angels' right fielder is more than adequate defensively, although he lacks great speed. He has decent range, sure hands, and a good arm. He's not a threat to steal bases, but is a good enough baserunner to avoid mistakes. Salmon is as dependable a player as you can hope for.

Major League Batting Register

	BA	G	AB	R	H	2B	3B	HR	RBI	SB
92 AL	.177	23	79	8	14	1	0	2	6	1
93 AL	.283	142	515	93	146	35	1	31	95	5
94 AL	.287	100	373	67	107	18	2	23	70	1
95 AL	.330	143	537	111	177	34	3	34	105	5
Life	.295	408	1504	279	444	88	6	90	276	12
3 AVE	.302	148	548	104	165	33	2	34	104	4

JUAN SAMUEL

Position: Infield
Team: Kansas City Royals
Born: Dec. 9, 1960 San Pedro de Macoris, Dominican Republic
Height: 5'11" **Weight:** 170 lbs.
Bats: right **Throws:** right
Acquired: Traded by Tigers for Phil Hiatt, 9/95

Player Summary	
Fantasy Value	$2 to $4
Card Value	4¢ to 6¢
Will	try to hang on
Can't	be a starter
Expect	versatile offense
Don't Expect	good defense

Tiger manager Sparky Anderson literally brought the career of Juan Samuel back from the dead. Just two years ago, Samuel's future looked dim as he had bounced from club to club without helping anybody win. However, used carefully by Anderson in a reserve role, Samuel played well in limited duty. In his younger days he looked to be a coming star, but Samuel failed to master the strike zone. He also squandered his enormous physical talent with undisciplined play at bat, on the bases, and in the field. Late in his career, he has gotten smarter, and he adapted to his utility role. Joining the Royals for the second time in September, he got some time in at DH. He had mostly played first base and left field for the Tigers.

Major League Batting Register

	BA	G	AB	R	H	2B	3B	HR	RBI	SB
83 NL	.277	18	65	14	18	1	2	2	5	3
84 NL	.272	160	701	105	191	36	19	15	69	72
85 NL	.264	161	663	101	175	31	13	19	74	53
86 NL	.266	145	591	90	157	36	12	16	78	42
87 NL	.272	160	655	113	178	37	15	28	100	35
88 NL	.243	157	629	68	153	32	9	12	67	33
89 NL	.235	137	532	69	125	16	2	11	48	42
90 NL	.242	143	492	62	119	24	3	13	52	38
91 NL	.271	153	594	74	161	22	6	12	58	23
92 NL	.262	47	122	7	32	3	1	0	15	2
92 AL	.284	29	102	15	29	5	3	0	8	6
93 NL	.230	103	261	31	60	10	4	4	26	9
94 AL	.309	59	136	32	42	9	5	5	21	5
95 AL	.263	91	205	31	54	10	1	12	39	6
Life	.260	1563	5748	812	1494	272	95	149	660	369
2 AVE	.246	103	246	33	60	11	3	9	35	8

CURRENT PLAYERS

REY SANCHEZ

Position: Infield
Team: Chicago Cubs
Born: Oct. 15, 1967 Rio Piedras, PR
Height: 5'9" **Weight:** 170 lbs.
Bats: right **Throws:** right
Acquired: Traded by Rangers for Bryan House, 1/90

Player Summary
Fantasy Value	$4 to $6
Card Value	5¢ to 8¢
Will	show good glove
Can't	steal bases
Expect	.290 average
Don't Expect	many walks

In some ways, Sanchez was more valuable to the Cubs in 1995 than the numbers on the bottom of this page show; in some ways, he could have contributed more. He was hitting over .300 for much of the season, but he slumped in August and September due to a broken bone in his hand that hampered his swing. Some days, it simply hurt too much for Sanchez to play, but the scrappy second baseman refused to go on the disabled list. Even though his offense sagged, Sanchez's superior defense made him valuable. His range is as good as that of any second baseman in baseball. He doesn't make many errors and turns the double play very well. If he could add a few more pieces to his game, Sanchez could be an All-Star. Unfortunately, he has little power, is very aggressive at bat, and doesn't run well. The Cubs were not happy with Sanchez's on-base average, poor bunting, and unwillingness to take pitches while hitting in the No. 2 hole. Last year, Sanchez was demoted to the eighth slot.

Major League Batting Register
	BA	G	AB	R	H	2B	3B	HR	RBI	SB
91 NL	.261	13	23	1	6	0	0	0	2	0
92 NL	.251	74	255	24	64	14	3	1	19	2
93 NL	.282	105	344	35	97	11	2	0	28	1
94 NL	.285	96	291	26	83	13	1	0	24	2
95 NL	.278	114	428	57	119	22	2	3	27	6
Life	.275	402	1341	143	369	60	8	4	100	11
3 AVE	.282	123	412	45	116	18	2	1	31	4

RYNE SANDBERG

Position: Second base; third base
Team: Chicago Cubs
Born: Sept. 18, 1959 Spokane, WA
Height: 6'2" **Weight:** 190 lbs.
Bats: right **Throws:** right
Acquired: Traded by Phillies with Larry Bowa for Ivan DeJesus, 1/82

Player Summary
Fantasy Value	$8 to $12
Card Value	15¢ to 20¢
Will	solidify lineup
Can't	show old speed
Expect	shift to third
Don't Expect	MVP year

When Sandberg announced his return last year, it was as shocking as his departure on June 13, 1994. The 1984 NL MVP and nine-time Gold Glove winner was in the second year of a four-year contract when he quit for personal reasons, giving up $17 million in salary. But Sandberg says he's happier than he has been in a long time. In addition, he's pleased that the Cubs have restructured the front office. A healthy, happy Sandberg could help the Cubs reach postseason play for the first time since 1989. A 10-time All-Star, he is closing in on Joe Morgan's record of 266 home runs by a second baseman. Sandberg may shift to third, his original position with the Cubs, however. He was a brilliant fielder who led the league in assists seven times.

Major League Batting Register
	BA	G	AB	R	H	2B	3B	HR	RBI	SB
81 NL	.167	13	6	2	1	0	0	0	0	0
82 NL	.271	156	635	103	172	33	5	7	54	32
83 NL	.261	158	633	94	165	25	4	8	48	37
84 NL	.314	156	636	114	200	36	19	19	84	32
85 NL	.305	153	609	113	186	31	6	26	83	54
86 NL	.284	154	627	68	178	28	5	14	76	34
87 NL	.294	132	523	81	154	25	2	16	59	21
88 NL	.264	155	618	77	163	23	8	19	69	25
89 NL	.290	157	606	104	176	25	5	30	76	15
90 NL	.306	155	615	116	188	30	3	40	100	25
91 NL	.291	158	585	104	170	32	2	26	100	22
92 NL	.304	158	612	100	186	32	8	26	87	17
93 NL	.309	117	456	67	141	20	0	9	45	9
94 NL	.238	57	223	36	53	9	5	5	24	2
Life	.289	1879	7384	1179	2133	349	72	245	905	325

CURRENT PLAYERS

DEION SANDERS

Position: Outfield
Team: San Francisco Giants
Born: Aug. 9, 1967 Fort Myers, FL
Height: 6'1" **Weight:** 195 lbs.
Bats: left **Throws:** left
Acquired: Traded by Reds with John Roper, Scott Service, Dave McCarty, and Ricky Pickett for Mark Portugal, Dave Burba, and Darren Lewis, 7/95

Player Summary	
Fantasy Value	$10 to $13
Card Value	25¢ to 50¢
Will	add great speed
Can't	get on base consistently
Expect	interceptions
Don't Expect	long baseball career

Will he or won't he? The is-he-going-to-quit-baseball-for-football controversy surrounding Sanders overshadowed most of what he did on the diamond last year—which wasn't very much anyway. Always a purveyor of style more than substance, Sanders is a tremendous athlete who hasn't quite learned how to play baseball yet. Speed is his biggest asset on offense. Sanders can easily take the extra base on balls he hits, and is an aggressive baserunner who can create opportunities for his team. Unfortunately, he's just a mediocre basestealer. Sanders doesn't have much raw power and walks far too seldom for a leadoff man. His .327 on-base percentage is not adequate. In the field, he has impressive range but often breaks the wrong way on fly balls. He does not throw well.

Major League Batting Register

	BA	G	AB	R	H	2B	3B	HR	RBI	SB
89 AL	.234	14	47	7	11	2	0	2	7	1
90 AL	.158	57	133	24	21	2	2	3	9	8
91 NL	.191	54	110	16	21	1	2	4	13	11
92 NL	.304	97	303	54	92	6	14	8	28	26
93 NL	.276	95	272	42	75	18	6	6	28	19
94 NL	.283	92	375	58	106	17	4	4	28	38
95 NL	.268	85	343	48	92	11	8	6	28	24
Life	.264	494	1583	249	418	57	36	33	141	127
3 AVE	.276	107	395	59	109	18	7	6	33	33

REGGIE SANDERS

Position: Outfield
Team: Cincinnati Reds
Born: Dec. 1, 1967 Florence, SC
Height: 6'1" **Weight:** 180 lbs.
Bats: right **Throws:** right
Acquired: Seventh-round pick in 6/87 free-agent draft

Player Summary	
Fantasy Value	$25 to $30
Card Value	30¢ to 60¢
Will	show fine speed
Can't	win a Gold Glove
Expect	four-category offense
Don't Expect	great contact hitting

Sanders began the year as the Reds' fifth-place hitter, playing right field. However, injuries to both Ron Gant and Deion Sanders moved Reggie into the cleanup spot and into center field for a time in midseason. That Sanders could handle the load both offensively and defensively spoke of the strides he made in 1995. He emerged as a bona fide MVP candidate and one of the key players on a championship team. Sanders, a dynamic blend of power and speed, stole at a plus 75 percent success rate last year and reached a career high in homers, RBI, and average. He took 69 walks for a fine .397 on-base percentage. Sanders ranked among the league leaders in outfield assists and showed good range at two outfield spots. While Sanders had always shown five-tool potential in the past, last year was the first season he produced the kind of offense expected of him. He still has things to iron out, however, fanning too much and experiencing some awful slumps—especially in the postseason.

Major League Batting Register

	BA	G	AB	R	H	2B	3B	HR	RBI	SB
91 NL	.200	9	40	6	8	.0	0	.1	3	1
92 NL	.270	116	385	62	104	26	6	12	36	16
93 NL	.274	138	496	90	136	16	4	20	83	27
94 NL	.262	107	400	66	105	20	8	17	62	21
95 NL	.306	133	484	91	148	36	6	28	99	36
Life	.278	503	1805	315	501	98	24	78	283	101
3 AVE	.281	146	535	95	150	28	7	25	94	32

CURRENT PLAYERS

SCOTT SANDERS

Position: Pitcher
Team: San Diego Padres
Born: March 25, 1969 Hannibal, MO
Height: 6'4" **Weight:** 210 lbs.
Bats: right **Throws:** right
Acquired: Second-round pick in 6/90 free-agent draft

Player Summary
Fantasy Value	$4 to $6
Card Value	5¢ to 8¢
Will	be in the rotation
Can't	afford homers
Expect	strikeouts
Don't Expect	top velocity

Sanders has appeared to be on his way to becoming one of the NL's best young starters. At times, he has shown the ability to dominate a game. But further progress will come slowly. He had an on-again, off-again 1995 for reasons that became clear in July—Sanders was suffering from a strained ligament in his pitching elbow. He went on the disabled list July 21 and did not appear again until early September. Two relief outings later, Sanders's elbow hurt so much that he simply shut down for the year. Control continued to be his bugaboo. He has an outstanding fastball and changeup, but he is still learning how to use them in critical spots against major-league hitters. Despite allowing opponents just a .228 batting average, Sanders totaled a high ERA due to six wild pitches, 17 doubles, and a high 14 homers. His strikeout and walk numbers were excellent, as was the weak .198 mark that right-handers totaled against Sanders. His arm and potential mean that he will get every chance to come back in 1996.

Major League Pitching Register
	W	L	ERA	G	CG	IP	H	ER	BB	SO
93 NL	3	3	4.13	9	0	52.1	54	24	23	37
94 NL	4	8	4.78	23	0	111.0	103	59	48	109
95 NL	5	5	4.30	17	1	90.0	79	43	31	88
Life	12	16	4.48	49	1	253.1	236	126	102	234
2 AVE	6	8	4.59	26	1	129.0	117	66	51	126

BENITO SANTIAGO

Position: Catcher
Team: Cincinnati Reds
Born: March 9, 1965 Ponce, PR
Height: 6'1" **Weight:** 185 lbs.
Bats: right **Throws:** right
Acquired: Signed as a free agent, 4/95

Player Summary
Fantasy Value	$7 to $9
Card Value	5¢ to 8¢
Will	provide defense
Can't	show patience at bat
Expect	platoon duty
Don't Expect	20 homers

Following the 1994 season, it seemed that Santiago's career was in jeopardy. He had played two below-average years with the Marlins, showing decreased offensive ability, proneness to injuries, and some uncharacteristic defensive lapses. He wasn't offered a contract by Florida. However, the Reds came calling and gave him a reasonable role. His slugging percentage was a good .481, and he batted well against left-handers. During his career, he has always been a wild swinger. Santiago's on-base percentage was a decent .351, however. Santiago tossed out only about 25 percent of the runners trying to steal on him, an especially poor number considering the amount of left-handers pitching in Cincinnati. He blocks pitches well and has good hands behind the plate, though his overall mechanics are still poor. It's clear that Santiago still has a few years left.

Major League Batting Register
	BA	G	AB	R	H	2B	3B	HR	RBI	SB
86 NL	.290	17	62	10	18	2	0	3	6	0
87 NL	.300	146	546	64	164	33	2	18	79	21
88 NL	.248	139	492	49	122	22	2	10	46	15
89 NL	.236	129	462	50	109	16	3	16	62	11
90 NL	.270	100	344	42	93	8	5	11	53	5
91 NL	.267	152	580	60	155	22	3	17	87	8
92 NL	.251	106	386	37	97	21	0	10	42	2
93 NL	.230	139	469	49	108	19	6	13	50	10
94 NL	.273	101	337	35	92	14	2	11	41	1
95 NL	.286	81	266	40	76	20	0	11	44	2
Life	.262	1110	3944	436	1034	177	23	120	510	75
3 AVE	.260	124	414	48	108	20	3	14	52	5

CURRENT PLAYERS

STEVE SCARSONE

Position: Infield
Team: San Francisco Giants
Born: April 11, 1966 Anaheim, CA
Height: 6'2" **Weight:** 195 lbs.
Bats: right **Throws:** right
Acquired: Traded by Orioles for Mark Leonard, 3/93

Player Summary

Fantasy Value	$1 to $3
Card Value	4¢ to 6¢
Will	fill in everywhere
Can't	provide speed
Expect	some power
Don't Expect	top on-base mark

Matt Williams's broken foot proved to be a bonanza for Scarsone in 1995. He hit with unexpected power after taking over the third base job. He also showed an adequate glove. Left-handers hold no mystery for the versatile Scarsone. He was more than .300 against them last season, and his .400-plus slugging percentage overall was one of the best on the Giants. He still strikes out way too much and doesn't work the count well. Scarsone drew just 18 bases on balls last season, and his .333 on-base percentage wasn't good. He doesn't run well, but he doesn't make many mistakes on the bases. Defensively, Scarsone's versatility is his best marker. He doesn't have great skills at any position, but he can play third, second, first, and even the outfield. Following his good performance, Scarsone hit the bench after Williams returned to the lineup, batting only a handful of times over the last two months. His role is always uncertain. But injuries to both Williams and Robbie Thompson has made plenty of insurance necessary.

Major League Batting Register

	BA	G	AB	R	H	2B	3B	HR	RBI	SB
92 NL	.154	7	13	1	2	0	0	0	0	0
92 AL	.176	11	17	2	3	0	0	0	0	0
93 NL	.252	44	103	16	26	9	0	2	15	0
94 NL	.272	52	103	21	28	8	0	2	13	0
95 NL	.266	80	233	33	62	10	3	11	29	3
Life	.258	194	469	73	121	27	3	15	57	3

CURT SCHILLING

Position: Pitcher
Team: Philadelphia Phillies
Born: Nov. 14, 1966 Anchorage, AK
Height: 6'4" **Weight:** 215 lbs.
Bats: right **Throws:** right
Acquired: Traded by Astros for Jason Grimsley, 4/92

Player Summary

Fantasy Value	$10 to $13
Card Value	5¢ to 8¢
Will	win if able
Can't	count out injury
Expect	fine control
Don't Expect	blazing fastball

Injuries again diminished the performance and impact of Schilling in 1995. He pitched with excellent control as he paced the 1995 Phillies staff in strikeouts. That feat is truly surprising considering that he didn't appear after July 19 due to surgery to remove a bone spur from his ailing right shoulder. The injury was not initially believed to be serious, but the shoulder didn't respond to treatment. When healthy, Schilling held opponents to a minuscule .220 average and allowed just over two walks per game. Schilling's pickoff move isn't good, and his protracted delivery allowed 11 of 13 baserunners to steal successfully against him. However, his most serious problem is health. Elbow and shoulder ailments have now gutted most of his last two seasons, and those are the two most serious injuries a pitcher can face. While Schilling never lived on pure velocity, he can't afford to lose much bite on his fastball.

Major League Pitching Register

	W	L	ERA	G	CG	IP	H	ER	BB	SO
88 AL	0	3	9.82	4	0	14.2	22	16	10	4
89 AL	0	1	6.23	5	0	8.2	10	6	3	6
90 AL	1	2	2.54	35	0	46.0	38	13	19	32
91 NL	3	5	3.81	56	0	75.2	79	32	39	71
92 NL	14	11	2.35	42	10	226.1	165	59	59	147
93 NL	16	7	4.02	34	7	235.1	234	105	57	186
94 NL	2	8	4.48	13	1	82.1	87	41	28	58
95 NL	7	5	3.57	17	1	116.0	96	46	26	114
Life	43	42	3.56	206	19	805.0	731	318	241	618
3 AVE	9	8	4.01	24	3	160.1	155	72	42	132

CURRENT PLAYERS

PETE SCHOUREK

Position: Pitcher
Team: Cincinnati Reds
Born: May 10, 1969 Austin, TX
Height: 6'5" **Weight:** 205 lbs.
Bats: left **Throws:** left
Acquired: Claimed on waivers from Mets, 4/94

Player Summary
Fantasy Value	$10 to $13
Card Value	10¢ to 15¢
Will	try to follow up
Can't	add anything at bat
Expect	good stuff
Don't Expect	recognition

In a short time, Schourek has moved from the doghouse to the penthouse. His unlikely rise to fame has left most baseball experts flabbergasted. Before wearing out his welcome in New York, the lanky left-hander hadn't shown much velocity or good location. Being left-handed seemed to be his only marker. However, the Reds obviously saw something they liked, and when Dave Johnson got his hands on Schourek, everything changed. The Reds convinced him to make adjustments that added around 5 mph to his pitches, and suddenly everything fell into place. He blossomed into a surprise Cy Young candidate in 1995, assuming the role of staff ace when Jose Rijo went down with elbow problems. Schourek's win total ranked second in the league. He finished near the top of the loop in ERA and whiffs, with his totals in all three categories leading the Reds. He halted right-handers to about a .220 clip. Schourek doesn't run well, can't hit or bunt much, and is an average fielder. His pickoff move is weak for a left-hander, but is improving.

Major League Pitching Register

	W	L	ERA	G	S	IP	H	ER	BB	SO
91 NL	5	4	4.27	35	2	86.1	82	41	43	67
92 NL	6	8	3.64	22	0	136.0	137	55	44	60
93 NL	5	12	5.96	41	0	128.1	168	85	45	72
94 NL	7	2	4.09	22	0	81.1	90	37	29	69
95 NL	18	7	3.22	29	2	190.1	158	68	45	160
Life	41	33	4.14	149	3	622.1	635	286	206	428
3 AVE	12	8	4.21	35	1	152.1	158	71	45	116

TIM SCOTT

Position: Pitcher
Team: Montreal Expos
Born: Nov. 16, 1966 Hanford, CA
Height: 6'2" **Weight:** 205 lbs.
Bats: right **Throws:** right
Acquired: Traded by Padres for Archi Cianfrocco, 6/93

Player Summary
Fantasy Value	$1 to $3
Card Value	4¢ to 6¢
Will	appear often
Can't	hold runners
Expect	frequent duty
Don't Expect	an expanded role

Scott paced the busy Expos bullpen in appearances. He doesn't have an overpowering pitch, but he is durable and moves the ball around the strike zone. The former Dodger farmhand and Padre reliever has found a home with Montreal, working early and often in long, middle, and even short relief. However, he's in no danger of having to buy "I'm a closer" T-shirts. He blew too many save chances in 1995. Nevertheless, he does have value. When he entered a runners-on situation, Scott pitched well, allowing just 7 of 45 inherited baserunners to cross the plate, an excellent ratio. He did not pitch as well when starting an inning. Opponents batted about .220 overall against him. He allowed NL hitters six homers last year after giving up none in 1994. A key problem for the veteran righty is a flock of very comfortable baserunners. Between his poor pickoff move and Darrin Fletcher's poor throwing, enemies ran at will against Scott in 1995. He may want to pitch from the stretch all the time.

Major League Pitching Register

	W	L	ERA	G	S	IP	H	ER	BB	SO
91 NL	0	0	9.00	2	0	1.0	2	1	0	1
92 NL	4	1	5.26	34	0	37.2	39	22	21	30
93 NL	2	2	3.01	56	1	71.2	69	24	34	65
94 NL	5	2	2.70	40	1	53.1	51	16	18	37
95 NL	2	0	3.98	62	2	63.1	52	28	23	57
Life	18	5	3.61	194	6	227.0	213	91	96	190
3 AVE	5	2	3.22	61	2	72.2	66	26	28	60

CURRENT PLAYERS

DAVID SEGUI

Position: First base
Team: Montreal Expos
Born: July 19, 1966 Kansas City, KS
Height: 6'1" **Weight:** 202 lbs.
Bats: both **Throws:** left
Acquired: Traded by Mets for Reid Cornelius, 6/95

Player Summary	
Fantasy Value	$8 to $10
Card Value	5¢ to 8¢
Will	field his position
Can't	run much
Expect	decent average
Don't Expect	much power

After an injury to first baseman Cliff Floyd, the Expos felt it necessary to deal for a first sacker who could at least provide top defense. Segui had fallen into spot duty with the Mets due to a weak bat. With Montreal, however, he provided a fine glove and, as a bonus, had his best offensive season in the majors. He led the Expos in RBI and finished second on the club in average. Segui didn't play often against lefties, but hit about .300 in his few at bats, a big improvement from past seasons. He fanned only 47 times. However, his value at bat shouldn't be overstated. He rarely walks, and he provided below-average power numbers for a first baseman. Segui saw some time in left field last year, but he doesn't hit enough to play there, either. Fortunately, he is a good defensive player at both positions due to a sure glove and a strong arm. He is slow and lacks outstanding range in the pasture. He is fine as a fill-in player due to his glovework and ability to make contact.

Major League Batting Register

	BA	G	AB	R	H	2B	3B	HR	RBI	SB
90 AL	.244	40	123	14	30	7	0	2	15	0
91 AL	.278	86	212	15	59	7	0	2	22	1
92 AL	.233	115	189	21	44	9	0	1	17	1
93 AL	.273	146	450	54	123	27	0	10	60	2
94 NL	.241	92	336	46	81	17	1	10	43	0
95 NL	.309	130	456	68	141	25	4	12	68	2
Life	.271	609	1766	218	478	92	5	37	225	6
3 AVE	.276	141	479	65	132	26	2	13	66	1

KEVIN SEITZER

Position: Infield
Team: Milwaukee Brewers
Born: March 26, 1962 Springfield, IL
Height: 5'11" **Weight:** 180 lbs.
Bats: right **Throws:** right
Acquired: Signed as a free agent, 7/93

Player Summary	
Fantasy Value	$6 to $8
Card Value	4¢ to 6¢
Will	get on base
Can't	run very well
Expect	defensive problems
Don't Expect	much power

Seitzer has revitalized his career in Milwaukee. The lone consistent bat in the lineup, he finished second on the Brewers in average and on-base percentage in 1995. He has always been a disciplined hitter, and took more walks last season than strikeouts. While Seitzer has never smacked out many extra-base hits, he does make a good No. 2 hitter due to his patience and ability to make contact. Unfortunately, the understocked Brewers were often forced to use him in the No. 3 spot. Oddly, Seitzer hit an outstanding .331 against right-handers in 1995, while hitting scarcely over .200 against lefties. In the field, he isn't all you might wish for. He can't run and has little range at any position. He plays third because Milwaukee needs a third baseman. His arm is slightly above average, and he hustles, but he doesn't add anything at the position.

Major League Batting Register

	BA	G	AB	R	H	2B	3B	HR	RBI	SB
86 AL	.323	28	96	16	31	4	1	2	11	0
87 AL	.323	161	641	105	207	33	8	15	83	12
88 AL	.304	149	559	90	170	32	5	5	60	10
89 AL	.281	160	597	78	168	17	2	4	48	17
90 AL	.275	158	622	91	171	31	5	6	38	7
91 AL	.265	85	234	28	62	11	3	1	25	4
92 AL	.270	148	540	74	146	35	1	5	71	13
93 AL	.269	120	417	45	112	16	2	11	57	7
94 AL	.314	80	309	44	97	24	2	5	49	2
95 AL	.311	132	492	56	153	33	3	5	69	2
Life	.292	1221	4507	627	1317	236	32	59	511	74
3 AVE	.299	127	469	57	140	29	3	8	68	4

284

CURRENT PLAYERS

AARON SELE

Position: Pitcher
Team: Boston Red Sox
Born: June 25, 1970 Golden Valley, MN
Height: 6'5" **Weight:** 205 lbs.
Bats: right **Throws:** right
Acquired: First-round pick in 6/91 free-agent draft

Player Summary	
Fantasy Value	$15 to $18
Card Value	10¢ to 15¢
Will	recuperate
Can't	show perfect control
Expect	some home runs
Don't Expect	heavy workload

Count on Sele to assume 30 to 35 starts this year and continue his big-league apprenticeship. He has the raw stuff and good mechanics necessary to be a staff ace; or at least he did before shoulder problems cropped up last spring. The shoulder began bothering Sele after just a couple of games, and the young righty didn't pitch after mid-May. Sele's injury never got past being diagnosed as "tendinitis." He did not have surgery, but instead rested for the summer and is expected back in 1995. The injury is considered serious; he has not pitched all that many innings in the major leagues, and overwork cannot be blamed. Shoulder injuries usually affect velocity, and his best pitch was a moving fastball. He has had some control problems typical of young pitchers and does give up the home run. In his six starts last year, he surrendered three round-trippers, a decent ratio. Opponents hit .252 against Sele, who will get every chance to assume a role this year but will be brought back slowly.

SCOTT SERVAIS

Position: Catcher
Team: Chicago Cubs
Born: June 4, 1967 LaCrosse, WI
Height: 6'2" **Weight:** 195 lbs.
Bats: right **Throws:** right
Acquired: Traded by Astros with Luis Gonzalez for Rick Wilkins, 6/95

Player Summary	
Fantasy Value	$2 to $4
Card Value	4¢ to 6¢
Will	play hurt
Can't	contribute speed
Expect	plenty of strikeouts
Don't Expect	25 homers

The gutty and talented Servais was a different ballplayer after coming to Chicago in a trade. He missed several weeks with badly strained knee cartilage sustained in a home-plate collision with baserunner Darren Daulton—a play many felt was a dubious slide by the Philadelphia catcher. Despite that, Servais played hard and hit well, averaging nearly .300 in Cub pinstripes. He added a few home runs, finding the short fences and warm breezes of Wrigley Field much to his liking. He even took 32 walks in 1995, and ended up with a good .348 on-base percentage. However, Servais still has offensive weaknesses; he strikes out a lot and adds nothing on the bases. He had never been a good hitter before last season. Servais blocks pitches well but throws poorly. He calls a good game, and he has the respect of his teammates for playing hurt. The trade worked out very well for the Cubs in 1995, but the jury is out as to whether pitchers will regain their mastery over Servais.

Major League Pitching Register

	W	L	ERA	G	CG	IP	H	ER	BB	SO
93 AL	7	2	2.74	18	0	111.2	100	34	48	93
94 AL	8	7	3.83	22	2	143.1	140	61	60	105
95 AL	3	1	3.06	6	0	32.1	32	11	14	21
Life	18	10	3.32	46	2	287.1	272	106	122	219
2 AVE	9	6	3.44	24	1	156.2	149	60	66	120

Major League Batting Register

	BA	G	AB	R	H	2B	3B	HR	RBI	SB
91 NL	.162	16	37	0	6	3	0	0	6	0
92 NL	.239	77	205	12	49	9	0	0	15	0
93 NL	.244	85	258	24	63	11	0	11	32	0
94 NL	.195	78	251	27	49	15	1	9	41	0
95 NL	.265	80	264	38	70	22	0	13	47	2
Life	.233	336	1015	101	237	60	1	33	141	2
3 AVE	.232	95	303	35	70	19	0	13	48	1

CURRENT PLAYERS

JEFF SHAW

Position: Pitcher
Team: Chicago White Sox
Born: July 7, 1966 Washington Courthouse, OH
Height: 6'2" **Weight:** 200 lbs.
Bats: right **Throws:** right
Acquired: Traded by Expos for Jose DeLeon, 7/95

Player Summary
Fantasy Value $0
Card Value . . . . 4¢ to 6¢
Will . . . . allow gopher balls
Can't . . . . count on employment
Expect . . . . decent stuff
Don't Expect . . . . a key role

Shaw has gone from being a starter in the Cleveland system to a middle-relief role. He is blessed with both a good slider and a good forkball. He spent a couple of strong seasons in the Expos bullpen as a 10th man. Used intelligently in a protected role by Montreal manager Felipe Alou, Shaw was able to mask his sometimes erratic control and lack of velocity and provide value. In 1995, however, he just didn't get the job done. Part of a much-maligned and ineffective bullpen crew, Shaw racked up a very poor record in Montreal. He allowed opponents to bat just .250, but he gave up plenty of walks. Shaw didn't improve much when sent to Chicago in the summer, giving up too many gophers. He has improved his pickoff move and quickened his delivery, which means he holds runners better but may take something off his already mediocre fastball. He is also a good fielder.

Major League Pitching Register

	W	L	ERA	G	S	IP	H	ER	BB	SO
90 AL	3	4	6.66	12	0	48.2	73	36	20	25
91 AL	0	5	3.36	29	1	72.1	72	27	27	31
92 AL	0	1	8.22	2	0	7.2	7	7	4	3
93 NL	2	7	4.14	55	0	95.2	91	44	32	50
94 NL	5	2	3.88	46	1	67.1	67	29	15	47
95 NL	1	6	4.62	50	3	62.1	58	32	26	45
95 AL	0	0	6.52	9	0	9.2	12	7	1	6
Life	11	25	4.50	203	5	363.2	380	182	125	207
3 AVE	3	6	4.27	62	2	90.2	88	43	28	58

DANNY SHEAFFER

Position: Catcher
Team: St. Louis Cardinals
Born: Aug. 2, 1961 Jacksonville, FL
Height: 6' **Weight:** 190 lbs.
Bats: right **Throws:** right
Acquired: Signed as a minor-league free agent, 12/94

Player Summary
Fantasy Value $0
Card Value . . . . 4¢ to 6¢
Will . . . . hang around
Can't . . . . show any speed
Expect . . . . some power
Don't Expect . . . . everyday duty

Frequent injuries to Tom Pagnozzi gave Sheaffer a chance at extensive duty in 1995, and he responded with some of the best numbers of his career in terms of home runs and RBI. The former Rockie came to St. Louis with little fanfare this past winter, but he stepped in and performed well at bat and in the field. Sheaffer didn't hit for much of an average, but did take quite a few walks and turned in an above-average on-base percentage. The high point of his season was August 26, when he smacked a game-winning grand slam homer against his old Colorado teammates at Coors Field. Defensively, Sheaffer is agile behind the plate but doesn't throw very well. A high percentage of basestealers were successful with Sheaffer behind the dish in 1995. In addition to playing a career-high games at catcher, Sheaffer also played one game at third base. He probably won't be a utility player, but a team could do much worse at back-up catcher than Sheaffer.

Major League Batting Register

	BA	G	AB	R	H	2B	3B	HR	RBI	SB
87 AL	.121	25	66	5	8	1	0	1	5	0
89 AL	.063	7	16	1	1	0	0	0	0	0
93 NL	.278	82	216	26	60	9	1	4	32	2
94 NL	.218	44	110	11	24	4	0	1	12	0
95 NL	.231	76	208	24	48	10	1	5	30	0
Life	.229	234	616	67	141	24	2	11	79	2
2 AVE	.253	84	225	27	57	10	1	5	33	1

286

CURRENT PLAYERS

GARY SHEFFIELD

Position: Outfield
Team: Florida Marlins
Born: Nov. 18, 1968 Tampa, FL
Height: 5'11" **Weight:** 190 lbs.
Bats: right **Throws:** right
Acquired: Traded by Padres with Rich Rodriguez for Trevor Hoffman, Andres Berumen, and Jose Martinez, 6/93

Player Summary	
Fantasy Value	$15 to $20
Card Value	8¢ to 12¢
Will	show power
Can't	win a Gold Glove
Expect	health struggles
Don't Expect	low average

For the second straight season, Sheffield hit the tar out of the ball when he was healthy. But he wasn't very healthy. Sheffield has proven capable of an MVP performance over a full season. After missing much of 1994 with shoulder injuries, he began the 1995 season hitting .315 in his first 41 games with six homers, 14 steals, and 35 walks. However, he tore ligaments in his left thumb in late May and hit the 60-day disabled list. When Sheffield finally did return to the ballpark, he hadn't lost his stroke. He helped to key the Marlins' second-half surge. For the year, he drew 55 walks and fanned just 45 times. His offense is good enough to balance out his unsteady play in right field. His throwing is average, and his range and hands are just fair. Sheffield still runs well enough to chase down fly balls. However, injuries have kept him from being the player he should be.

Major League Batting Register

	BA	G	AB	R	H	2B	3B	HR	RBI	SB
88 AL	.237	24	80	12	19	1	0	4	12	3
89 AL	.247	95	368	34	91	18	0	5	32	10
90 AL	.294	125	487	67	143	30	1	10	67	25
91 AL	.194	50	175	25	34	12	2	2	22	5
92 NL	.330	146	557	87	184	34	3	33	100	5
93 NL	.294	140	494	67	145	20	5	20	73	17
94 NL	.276	87	322	61	89	16	1	27	78	12
95 NL	.324	63	213	46	69	8	0	16	46	19
Life	.287	730	2696	399	774	139	12	117	430	96
3 AVE	.293	111	396	68	116	17	2	25	78	18

CRAIG SHIPLEY

Position: Infield
Team: Houston Astros
Born: Jan. 7, 1963 Sydney, Australia
Height: 6'1" **Weight:** 190 lbs.
Bats: right **Throws:** right
Acquired: Traded by Padres with Derek Bell, Doug Brocail, Ricky Gutierrez, Pedro Martinez, and Phil Plantier for Ken Caminiti, Andujar Cedeno, Steve Finley, Brian Williams, Roberto Petagine, and a player to be named later, 12/94

Player Summary	
Fantasy Value	$1 to $3
Card Value	4¢ to 6¢
Will	hit left-handers
Can't	produce as a regular
Expect	decent defense
Don't Expect	top on-base mark

Shipley's 1994 season was a total surprise, but his 1995 campaign was more in line with reasonable expectations. Splitting the third base duty for the Astros with Dave Magadan, Shipley showed his usual range of skills. He can hit for a decent average, especially against left-handers (batting in the .280 range against them in 1995). He can fill in at several spots. In fact, Shipley played every infield position last season, and he can play the outfield. However, he doesn't have the power needed at a corner position and rarely walks, lowering his on-base percentage. Shipley came up as a shortstop, but he is probably best at third base, considering his average range. His throwing arm is average in both strength and accuracy, but he has good hands.

Major League Batting Register

	BA	G	AB	R	H	2B	3B	HR	RBI	SB
86 NL	.111	12	27	3	3	1	0	0	4	0
87 NL	.257	26	35	3	9	1	0	0	2	0
89 NL	.143	4	7	3	1	0	0	0	0	0
91 NL	.275	37	91	6	25	3	0	1	6	0
92 NL	.248	52	105	7	26	6	0	0	7	1
93 NL	.235	105	230	25	54	9	0	4	22	12
94 NL	.333	81	240	32	80	14	4	4	30	6
95 NL	.263	92	232	23	61	8	1	3	24	6
Life	.268	409	967	102	259	42	5	12	95	25
3 AVE	.284	108	276	32	78	13	2	4	30	9

CURRENT PLAYERS

RUBEN SIERRA

Position: Outfield
Team: New York Yankees
Born: Oct. 6, 1965 Rio Piedras, PR
Height: 6'1" **Weight:** 200 lbs.
Bats: both **Throws:** right
Acquired: Traded by Athletics with Jason Beverlin for Danny Tartabull, 7/95

Player Summary	
Fantasy Value	$10 to $15
Card Value	6¢ to 10¢
Will	hit with power
Can't	recapture lost time
Expect	aggressive swinging
Don't Expect	sharp defense

The trade of Sierra to New York wasn't a question of "what," it was only a matter of "when." After another disappointing half-year with the Athletics, in which he hit just .265, the talented but erratic Sierra was sent to the Bronx July 28. His overaggressive approach has resulted in diminishing power numbers and very low on-base percentages. In 1995, he drew 46 walks, a high total for him but low for most anybody else, and had a mediocre on-base percentage. He did bat .291 against lefties and socked a few home runs. However, he no longer has the speed he once did and is an inconsistent right fielder. To recapture the ability that once made him an MVP candidate, he will have to hit with power and cut down on his ever-expanding strike zone. If he doesn't, Sierra will be just another good player who could have been more.

Major League Batting Register

	BA	G	AB	R	H	2B	3B	HR	RBI	SB
86 AL	.264	113	382	50	101	13	10	16	55	7
87 AL	.263	158	643	97	169	35	4	30	109	16
88 AL	.254	156	615	77	156	32	2	23	91	18
89 AL	.306	162	634	101	194	35	14	29	119	8
90 AL	.280	159	608	70	170	37	2	16	96	9
91 AL	.307	161	661	110	203	44	5	25	116	16
92 AL	.278	151	601	83	167	34	7	17	87	14
93 AL	.233	158	630	77	147	23	5	22	101	25
94 AL	.268	110	426	71	114	21	1	23	92	8
95 AL	.263	126	479	73	126	32	0	19	86	5
Life	.272	1454	5679	809	1547	306	50	220	952	126
3 AVE	.254	152	590	86	150	30	2	25	109	14

MIKE SIMMS

Position: First base; outfield
Team: Houston Astros
Born: Jan. 12, 1967 Orange, CA
Height: 6'4" **Weight:** 185 lbs.
Bats: right **Throws:** right
Acquired: Signed as a minor-league free agent, 5/94

Player Summary	
Fantasy Value	$1 to $3
Card Value	5¢ to 8¢
Will	hit fly balls
Can't	steal bases
Expect	pinch-hitting duty
Don't Expect	defensive wizardry

Simms is a minor-league veteran with good batting records in the bushes. The long-time Houston farmhand assumed Jeff Bagwell's job after Bagwell's wrist was broken on July 30. Simms hit with power and batted nearly .300 against left-handers in his tour of duty with the Astros. He filled in as a left fielder on occasion when Bagwell returned from the disabled list. Simms showed quite a bit of pop in his bat and totaled a terrific .512 slugging percentage. He also had a fairly patient approach at bat, and he took 13 walks last year and had a .341 on-base percentage. Strikeouts have been a problem for him—he fanned 24 times in 1995. However, the performance Simms turned in 1995 may have earned him a job this season. He doesn't have any speed, doesn't do much against right-handers, and is nothing special in the pasture. So his future is going to rest on his ability to swing the lumber. Simms has had 182 round-trippers in the minor leagues, so he's proven that his power is no fluke.

Major League Batting Register

	BA	G	AB	R	H	2B	3B	HR	RBI	SB
90 NL	.308	12	13	3	4	1	0	1	2	0
91 NL	.203	49	123	18	25	5	0	3	16	1
92 NL	.250	15	24	1	6	1	0	1	3	0
94 NL	.083	6	12	1	1	1	0	0	0	1
95 NL	.256	50	121	14	31	4	0	9	24	1
Life	.229	132	293	37	67	12	0	14	45	3

CURRENT PLAYERS

DON SLAUGHT

Position: Catcher
Team: Pittsburgh Pirates
Born: Sept. 11, 1958 Long Beach, CA
Height: 6'1" **Weight:** 190 lbs.
Bats: right **Throws:** right
Acquired: Traded by Yankees for Willie Smith and Jeff Robinson, 12/89

Player Summary
Fantasy Value $1
Card Value . . . . 4¢ to 6¢
Will . . . . see spot duty
Can't . . . . show great arm
Expect . . . . plenty of singles
Don't Expect . . . . walks or strikeouts

Slaught's body may be slowing down, but his bat isn't. The veteran receiver strained his right hamstring in late April, and he didn't return to Pittsburgh until early July. In that time, Mark Parent took over the everyday job, and later, after Parent's trade, Angelo Encarnacion assumed the starting role. Slaught's at bats have decreased over the last two years. Through that, he hit for his typical high average when he did play, hitting over .300 against both righties and lefties. An aggressive hitter who makes excellent contact, Slaught fanned a minuscule number of times in 1995. He also notched a .361 on-base percentage. He has no power, doesn't throw well, and is one of baseball's slowest players. However, he calls games well and can lash line drives.

Major League Batting Register

	BA	G	AB	R	H	2B	3B	HR	RBI	SB
82 AL	.278	43	115	14	32	6	0	3	8	0
83 AL	.312	83	276	21	86	13	4	0	28	3
84 AL	.264	124	409	48	108	27	4	4	42	0
85 AL	.280	102	343	34	96	17	4	8	35	5
86 AL	.264	95	314	39	83	17	1	13	46	3
87 AL	.224	95	237	25	53	15	2	8	16	0
88 AL	.283	97	322	33	91	25	1	9	43	1
89 AL	.251	117	350	34	88	21	3	5	38	1
90 NL	.300	84	230	27	69	18	3	4	29	0
91 NL	.295	77	220	19	65	17	1	1	29	1
92 NL	.345	87	255	26	88	17	3	4	37	2
93 NL	.300	116	377	34	113	19	2	10	55	2
94 NL	.287	76	240	21	69	7	0	2	21	0
95 NL	.304	35	112	13	34	6	0	0	13	0
Life	.283	1231	3800	388	1075	225	28	71	440	18
AVE	.294	112	358	32	105	14	1	6	42	1

HEATHCLIFF SLOCUMB

Position: Pitcher
Team: Philadelphia Phillies
Born: June 7, 1966 Jamaica, NY
Height: 6'3" **Weight:** 220 lbs.
Bats: right **Throws:** right
Acquired: Traded by Indians for Ruben Amaro, 11/93

Player Summary
Fantasy Value . . . . $18 to $22
Card Value . . . . 6¢ to 8¢
Will . . . . throw low smoke
Can't . . . . save games
Expect . . . . relief duty
Don't Expect . . . . perfect control

The Phillies gave Slocumb a chance to be their closer in 1995, and he didn't disappoint—at least in the first half. Keying Philadelphia's unlikely rush to the top of the NL East, he was simply awesome in the first half. Through July 2, he had converted 20 saves in 22 chances, fanned 24 men in 30 innings, allowed just one extra-base hit, and fashioned a terrific 0.91 ERA. From that point, however, both his and the Phillies' seasons began to go down the drain. Walks and home runs began to come with alarming frequencies, as did blown saves; he ended up kicking away six of them in 1995. Still, even with his late-season struggles, Slocumb has proven he can close in the big leagues. Left-handers batted .220 against Slocumb. He tossed just three wild pitches in 1995, but needs to have more confidence in his pitches so he can chop his walks. It was the type of performance the Indians and Cubs, his former employers, had previously hoped Slocumb would be capable of.

Major League Pitching Register

	W	L	ERA	G	S	IP	H	ER	BB	SO
91 NL	2	1	3.45	52	1	62.2	53	24	30	34
92 NL	0	3	6.50	30	1	36.0	52	26	21	27
93 NL	1	0	3.38	10	0	10.2	7	4	4	4
93 AL	3	1	4.28	20	0	27.1	28	13	16	18
94 NL	5	1	2.86	52	0	72.1	75	23	28	58
95 NL	5	6	2.89	61	32	65.1	64	21	35	63
Life	16	12	3.64	225	34	274.1	279	111	134	204
3 AVE	6	3	3.08	57	12	71.2	71	24	33	58

CURRENT PLAYERS

JOHN SMILEY

Position: Pitcher
Team: Cincinnati Reds
Born: March 17, 1965 Phoenixville, PA
Height: 6'4" **Weight:** 215 lbs.
Bats: left **Throws:** left
Acquired: Signed as a free agent, 11/92

Player Summary	
Fantasy Value	$10 to $13
Card Value	4¢ to 6¢
Will	retire left-handers
Can't	complete games
Expect	curveballs
Don't Expect	many walks

Two years after surgery to remove a bone spur from his left elbow, Smiley has pitched well. Using his arsenal of sinkers, change-ups, and especially curves, he puts in a good six or seven innings nearly every time. He doesn't have the durability to finish. But he doesn't walk many hitters, has a good pickoff move to first base, and has cut down on his home runs. He gave up just 11 long balls last year. Left-handers haven't got a hope against him, batting just .225 in 1995, and overall, opponents could manage just a paltry .306 on-base percentage against Smiley. He was a big part of the Reds' title drive. Smiley has come back strong from injury and looks fully recovered. However, two serious elbow surgeries in anybody's career isn't great news. Smiley has been helped by the short seasons in 1994 and 1995. He probably shouldn't make more than 30 starts a year.

Major League Pitching Register

	W	L	ERA	G	CG	IP	H	ER	BB	SO
86 NL	1	0	3.86	12	0	11.2	4	5	4	9
87 NL	5	5	5.76	63	0	75.0	69	48	50	58
88 NL	13	11	3.25	34	5	205.0	185	74	46	129
89 NL	12	8	2.81	28	8	205.1	174	64	49	123
90 NL	9	10	4.64	26	2	149.1	161	77	36	86
91 NL	20	8	3.08	33	2	207.2	194	71	44	129
92 AL	16	9	3.21	34	5	241.0	205	86	65	163
93 NL	3	9	5.62	18	2	105.2	117	66	31	60
94 NL	11	10	3.86	24	1	158.2	169	68	37	112
95 NL	12	5	3.46	28	1	176.2	173	68	39	124
Life	102	75	3.67	300	26	1536.0	1451	627	401	993
3 AVE	11	10	4.06	28	2	175.2	183	79	42	119

DWIGHT SMITH

Position: Outfield
Team: Atlanta Braves
Born: Nov. 8, 1963 Tallahassee, FL
Height: 5'11" **Weight:** 175 lbs.
Bats: left **Throws:** right
Acquired: Signed as a free agent, 4/95

Player Summary	
Fantasy Value	$2 to $4
Card Value	4¢ to 6¢
Will	come off the bench
Can't	shine on defense
Expect	line drives
Don't Expect	stolen bases

Smith had another fine season in 1995. He spent the summer as an itinerant emergency player for the Braves, his fourth club in three years. His left-handed bat, great outlook, and ability to stay sharp while not playing every day make him extremely valuable as a reserve. He lacks the all-around ability to play regularly. Smith doesn't have much speed left and is a poor defensive outfielder with a weak arm. However, he can just plain smoke the ball. He came up with his share of big hits, as his RBI count will testify to. Smith doesn't often bat against left-handers, but he does just fine against lefties when asked. In the minors, Smith walked often; but in the majors he just takes an average amount of bases on balls. Coming off the bench productively is an extremely hard job, and Smith has proven he can do it well. His outstanding attitude is just another bonus in his favor, and he can even sing the National Anthem before games.

Major League Batting Register

	BA	G	AB	R	H	2B	3B	HR	RBI	SB
89 NL	.324	109	343	52	111	19	6	9	52	9
90 NL	.262	117	290	34	76	15	0	6	27	11
91 NL	.228	90	167	16	38	7	2	3	21	2
92 NL	.276	109	217	28	60	10	3	3	24	9
93 NL	.300	111	310	51	93	17	5	11	35	8
94 AL	.281	73	196	31	55	7	2	8	30	2
95 NL	.252	103	131	16	33	8	2	3	21	0
Life	.282	712	1654	228	466	83	20	43	210	41
2 AVE	.291	107	293	47	85	13	4	11	39	5

CURRENT PLAYERS

LEE SMITH

Position: Pitcher
Team: California Angels
Born: Dec. 4, 1957 Jamestown, LA
Height: 6'6" **Weight:** 269 lbs.
Bats: right **Throws:** right
Acquired: Signed as a free agent, 12/94

Player Summary	
Fantasy Value	$18 to $22
Card Value	10¢ to 15¢
Will	throw off-speed stuff
Can't	afford walks
Expect	another season
Don't Expect	30 saves

For the second straight time, Smith began the year unhittable and ended it mortal. His 1994 year with Baltimore was good on the whole, but after the All-Star break that season he didn't pitch well. Last season, he was a key player in the Angels' early push. Through June 25, he hadn't allowed an earned run through 20 games. But from that point on, he struggled. "Big Lee" can no longer throw with his old velocity, relying instead on changeups and breaking pitches. He generally keeps the ball low, whereas in his glory days, he was able to blow away any hitter with a high fastball. Smith is still good but is no longer capable of shouldering his old role.

Major League Pitching Register

	W	L	ERA	G	S	IP	H	ER	BB	SO
80 NL	2	0	2.91	18	0	21.2	21	7	14	17
81 NL	3	6	3.51	40	1	66.2	57	26	31	50
82 NL	2	5	2.69	72	17	117.0	105	35	37	99
83 NL	4	10	1.65	66	29	103.1	70	19	41	91
84 NL	9	7	3.65	69	33	101.0	98	41	35	86
85 NL	7	4	3.04	65	33	97.2	87	33	32	112
86 NL	9	9	3.09	66	31	90.1	69	31	42	93
87 NL	4	10	3.12	62	36	83.2	84	29	32	96
88 AL	4	5	2.80	64	29	83.2	72	26	37	96
89 AL	6	1	3.57	64	25	70.2	53	28	33	96
90 AL	2	1	1.88	11	4	14.1	13	3	9	17
90 NL	3	4	2.10	53	27	68.2	58	16	20	70
91 NL	6	3	2.34	67	47	73.0	70	19	13	67
92 NL	4	9	3.12	70	43	75.0	62	26	20	60
93 NL	2	4	4.50	55	43	50.0	49	25	9	49
93 AL	0	0	0.00	8	3	8.0	4	0	5	11
94 AL	1	4	3.29	41	33	38.1	34	14	11	42
95 AL	0	5	3.47	52	37	49.1	42	19	25	43
Life	68	87	2.95	943	471	1212.1	1048	397	452	1195
3 AVE	1	5	3.55	60	45	56.1	49	22	19	56

MARK SMITH

Position: Outfield
Team: Baltimore Orioles
Born: May 7, 1970 Pasedena, CA
Height: 6'4" **Weight:** 195 lbs.
Bats: right **Throws:** right
Acquired: First-round pick in 6/91 free-agent draft

Player Summary	
Fantasy Value	$2 to $4
Card Value	8¢ to 12¢
Will	show some pop
Can't	hit righties
Expect	more at bats
Don't Expect	an instant star

With Jeffrey Hammonds experiencing injury woes, Smith stepped in to play right field and left field for the O's. He showed some of the power that he displayed for several years in the minors. He also showed that he could hit left-handers. Smith batted .300 against southpaws last year. If he learns to hit right-handers, he could find a place in a starting outfield. Smith was able to bat only .188 against righties last year. He had 12 bases on balls, which helped him garner a .314 on-base percentage last year. He struck out only 22 times, not bad for a rookie who can hit the ball hard. A .277 batter at Triple-A Rochester in 1995, Smith belted 12 home runs and had 66 RBI in 364 at bats. It was the third straight season that he had one dozen or more homers at Rochester. He batted .247 with 19 home runs and 66 RBI there in 1994, and he had 12 homers, 68 RBI, and a .280 average in 1993. There was concern at Rochester that Smith was trying too hard to hit homers without getting quality at bats. In the field, Smith has enough arm to play right field, though he is probably better off in left.

Major League Batting Register

	BA	G	AB	R	H	2B	3B	HR	RBI	SB
94 AL	.143	3	7	0	1	0	0	0	2	0
95 AL	.231	37	104	11	24	5	0	3	15	3
Life	.225	40	111	11	25	5	0	3	17	3

CURRENT PLAYERS

OZZIE SMITH

Position: Shortstop
Team: St. Louis Cardinals
Born: Dec. 26, 1954 Mobile, AL
Height: 5'10" **Weight:** 168 lbs.
Bats: both **Throws:** right
Acquired: Traded by Padres for Garry Templeton, 2/82

Player Summary	
Fantasy Value	$2 to $4
Card Value	20¢ to 30¢
Will	try again
Can't	run like he used to
Expect	him to make contact
Don't Expect	140 games

Ozzie was hampered by injuries for most of 1995. He missed 77 games after undergoing arthroscopic shoulder surgery on May 31, and even when he returned, he had problems with the shoulder that kept him out of action for much of September. He did set a new record for double plays by a shortstop on Sept. 15, breaking Luis Aparicio's old mark. Smith still fields his position well; he knows NL hitters as well as anybody, and positions himself well. He turns the double play smoothly and doesn't make many fielding errors. At bat, Smith can't add power, but he puts the bat on the ball and will take a walk. He is a Hall of Famer.

Major League Batting Register

	BA	G	AB	R	H	2B	3B	HR	RBI	SB
78 NL	.258	159	590	69	152	17	6	1	46	40
79 NL	.211	156	587	77	124	18	6	0	27	28
80 NL	.230	158	609	67	140	18	5	0	35	57
81 NL	.222	110	450	53	100	11	2	0	21	22
82 NL	.248	140	488	58	121	24	1	2	43	25
83 NL	.243	159	552	69	134	30	6	3	50	34
84 NL	.257	124	412	53	106	20	5	1	44	35
85 NL	.276	158	537	70	148	22	3	6	54	31
86 NL	.280	153	514	67	144	19	4	0	54	31
87 NL	.303	158	600	104	182	40	4	0	75	43
88 NL	.270	153	575	80	155	27	1	3	51	57
89 NL	.273	155	593	82	162	30	8	2	50	29
90 NL	.254	143	512	61	130	21	1	1	50	32
91 NL	.285	150	550	96	157	30	3	3	50	35
92 NL	.295	132	518	73	153	20	2	0	31	43
93 NL	.288	141	545	75	157	22	6	1	53	21
94 NL	.262	98	381	51	100	18	3	3	30	6
95 NL	.199	44	156	16	31	5	1	0	11	4
Life	.261	2491	9169	1221	2396	392	67	26	775	573
3 AVE	.265	110	419	55	111	18	4	2	36	11

ZANE SMITH

Position: Pitcher
Team: Boston Red Sox
Born: Dec. 28, 1960 Madison, WI
Height: 6'1" **Weight:** 207 lbs.
Bats: left **Throws:** left
Acquired: Signed as a free agent, 4/95

Player Summary	
Fantasy Value	$5 to $7
Card Value	4¢ to 6¢
Will	get ground balls
Can't	afford wildness
Expect	20 starts
Don't Expect	strikeouts

Smith served as the Red Sox' fourth starter in 1995, and he pitched well enough down the stretch that he kept his spot in the postseason. However, it wasn't a good season. His strikeout per inning totals are around the lowest in the majors every year. Therefore, he lives on a sinkerball that starts out hard and, when it's working, burrows into the dirt as it approaches the plate and induces hitters to pound ground balls to infielders. When Smith's control isn't good, his pitches are as hittable as anybody's in the majors. He doesn't give up that many home runs or walks, but he allowed nearly 30 doubles last year and gave up well over 12 hits per nine innings. Left-handed hitters, who usually struggle against Smith, batted well against him. Shoulder and elbow surgeries have sapped him of some of his stuff and durability over the years.

Major League Pitching Register

	W	L	ERA	G	CG	IP	H	ER	BB	SO
84 NL	1	0	2.25	3	0	20.0	16	5	13	16
85 NL	9	10	3.80	42	2	147.0	135	62	80	85
86 NL	8	16	4.05	38	3	204.2	209	92	105	139
87 NL	15	10	4.09	36	9	242.0	245	110	91	130
88 NL	5	10	4.30	23	3	140.1	159	67	44	59
89 NL	1	13	3.49	48	0	147.0	141	57	52	93
90 NL	12	9	2.55	33	4	215.1	196	61	50	130
91 NL	16	10	3.20	35	6	228.0	234	81	29	120
92 NL	8	8	3.06	23	4	141.0	138	48	19	56
93 NL	3	7	4.55	14	1	83.0	97	42	22	32
94 NL	10	8	3.27	25	2	157.0	162	57	34	57
95 AL	8	8	5.61	24	0	110.2	144	69	23	47
Life	96	109	3.68	344	34	1836.0	1876	751	562	964
3 AVE	9	9	4.20	25	1	143.1	162	67	32	55

292

CURRENT PLAYERS

JOHN SMOLTZ

Position: Pitcher
Team: Atlanta Braves
Born: May 15, 1967 Detroit, MI
Height: 6'3" **Weight:** 185 lbs.
Bats: right **Throws:** right
Acquired: Traded by Tigers for Doyle Alexander, 8/87

Player Summary	
Fantasy Value	$10 to $14
Card Value	8¢ to 12¢
Will	shut down righties
Can't	surpass Maddux
Expect	plenty of strikeouts
Don't Expect	perfect control

Smoltz's struggles, with his own psyche and with his control on the mound, are legendary. He has been consulting with a sports psychologist for several years, with seemingly good results. He has gradually improved and is clearly one of the league's best right-handers. Late in 1994, he underwent surgery to remove a bone spur from his pitching elbow and spent much of last winter rehabilitating. He came back successfully. He served as the Braves' third starter and finished second in the NL in strikeouts to Hideo Nomo. Smoltz has a superior fastball that ranks as one of the best in the league, a good curve, and a sharp slider. Occasional bouts of wildness are his only problem. Smoltz tossed 13 wild pitches, the third-highest total in the league, and his walk total ranked in the top ten. However, these problems were less important than they might be as he held right-handers to a puny .206 average.

Major League Pitching Register

	W	L	ERA	G	CG	IP	H	ER	BB	SO
88 NL	2	7	5.48	12	0	64.0	74	39	33	37
89 NL	12	11	2.94	29	5	208.0	160	68	72	168
90 NL	14	11	3.85	34	6	231.1	206	99	90	170
91 NL	14	13	3.80	36	5	229.2	206	97	77	148
92 NL	15	12	2.85	35	9	246.2	206	78	80	215
93 NL	15	11	3.62	35	3	243.2	208	98	100	208
94 NL	6	10	4.14	21	1	134.2	120	62	48	113
95 NL	12	7	3.18	29	2	192.2	166	68	72	193
Life	90	82	3.53	231	31	1550.2	1346	609	572	1252
3 AVE	12	11	3.62	32	2	216.2	188	87	83	195

J.T. SNOW

Position: First base
Team: California Angels
Born: Feb. 26, 1968 Long Beach, CA
Height: 6'2" **Weight:** 202 lbs.
Bats: both **Throws:** left
Acquired: Traded by Yankees with Jerry Nielsen and Russ Springer for Jim Abbott, 12/92

Player Summary	
Fantasy Value	$12 to $15
Card Value	8¢ to 12¢
Will	try to repeat
Can't	add speed
Expect	top on-base mark
Don't Expect	batting title

The previously disappointing Snow performed very well in 1995, playing Gold Glove-caliber defense and chipping in strongly with the bat. As is his usual pattern, he hit much better early on than in the later months, slumping noticeably in August and September. All in all, however, he had a good year. Snow has line-drive power that should deliver 25 to 30 home runs a year as his career proceeds. He will take a walk, drawing 52 last year and notching a good .355 on-base percentage. But he will likely be hard-pressed to keep his average around .300 in the coming years. The key to his 1995 bat improvement was an unexpected .272 average against left-handers. He is one of the AL's better defensive first basemen, showing decent range to his right, a fine throwing arm, and good hands. Snow made just four errors last season. The former Yankee still has some convincing to do, however. He must prove in 1996 that his new level of performance is sustainable and not just a one-time deal.

Major League Batting Register

	BA	G	AB	R	H	2B	3B	HR	RBI	SB
92 AL	.143	7	14	1	2	1	0	0	2	0
93 AL	.241	129	419	60	101	18	2	16	57	3
94 AL	.220	61	223	22	49	4	0	8	30	0
95 AL	.289	143	544	80	157	22	1	24	102	2
Life	.257	340	1200	163	309	45	3	48	191	5
3 AVE	.258	125	448	60	116	16	1	18	71	2

CURRENT PLAYERS

LUIS SOJO

Position: Shortstop
Team: Seattle Mariners
Born: Jan. 3, 1966 Barquisimeto, Venezuela
Height: 5'11" **Weight:** 175 lbs.
Bats: right **Throws:** right
Acquired: Signed as a minor-league free agent, 1/94

Player Summary	
Fantasy Value	$2 to $4
Card Value	4¢ to 6¢
Will	make contact
Can't	steal bases
Expect	platoon duty
Don't Expect	defensive wizardry

The Mariners' complicated middle-infield picture allowed plenty of room for Sojo in 1995. He played 79 games at shortstop and 19 at second base, as Seattle manager Lou Piniella worked four different players in among the two positions. Sojo also saw action six times in left field. He is blessed with some pop in his bat. He chipped in some big extra-base hits last year, including a game-breaking three-run double in the Oct. 2 division tie-breaker against California. Sojo batted .352 against left-handers and hit .327 in road games. He adds little on the bases (some in Seattle refer to him as "so slow") and rarely walks. He took just 23 passes last year and totalled a .332 on-base percentage. Sojo doesn't often strike out, either, fanning only 19 times in 1995. His defense isn't all that you'd hope for. Although Sojo has good hands and stands in on the double play, he lacks range and doesn't impress with his arm. He is a consistent player at a middling level.

Major League Batting Register

	BA	G	AB	R	H	2B	3B	HR	RBI	SB
90 AL	.225	33	80	14	18	3	0	1	9	1
91 AL	.258	113	364	38	94	14	1	3	20	4
92 AL	.272	106	368	37	100	12	3	7	43	7
93 AL	.170	19	47	5	8	2	0	0	6	0
94 AL	.277	63	213	32	59	9	2	6	22	2
95 AL	.289	102	339	50	98	18	2	7	39	4
Life	.267	436	1411	176	377	58	8	24	139	18
2 AVE	.284	102	341	51	97	16	3	8	37	4

PAUL SORRENTO

Position: First base
Team: Cleveland Indians
Born: Nov. 17, 1965 Somerville, MA
Height: 6'2" **Weight:** 220 lbs.
Bats: left **Throws:** right
Acquired: Traded by Twins for Oscar Munoz and Curt Leskanic, 3/92

Player Summary	
Fantasy Value	$5 to $10
Card Value	4¢ to 6¢
Will	slug home runs
Can't	add speed
Expect	platoon duty
Don't Expect	contact hitting

It was a year of extremes for Sorrento. His club did extremely well. He hit for extreme power. An untimely injury was extremely frustrating. He reached a career high in home runs and slugged .511 despite getting a relatively low number of at bats. He also struck out a high 71 times, but drew 51 walks and had a decent .336 on-base percentage. He doesn't get very much playing time against left-handers, who give him extreme headaches (a .163 average in 1995). But against righties, Sorrento does well. A low doubles total caused some worry that he is becoming an all-or-nothing hitter. The one-time Twin is extremely slow and suffered in comparison to defense to Herb Perry. However, if he keeps socking home runs, Sorrento is going to be employable at least as a platoon player for several more years. He was hampered for several weeks late in the season by an extremely painful strain of his right hamstring, but he recovered by the playoffs.

Major League Batting Register

	BA	G	AB	R	H	2B	3B	HR	RBI	SB
89 AL	.238	14	21	2	5	0	0	0	1	0
90 AL	.207	41	121	11	25	4	1	5	13	1
91 AL	.255	26	47	6	12	2	0	4	13	0
92 AL	.269	140	458	52	123	24	1	18	60	0
93 AL	.257	148	463	75	119	26	1	18	65	3
94 AL	.280	95	322	43	90	14	0	14	62	0
95 AL	.235	104	323	50	76	14	0	25	79	1
Life	.256	568	1755	239	450	84	3	84	293	5
3 AVE	.259	133	427	64	110	20	0	22	80	1

CURRENT PLAYERS

SAMMY SOSA

Position: Outfield
Team: Chicago Cubs
Born: Oct. 10, 1968 San Pedro de Macoris, Dominican Republic
Height: 6' **Weight:** 175 lbs.
Bats: right **Throws:** right
Acquired: Traded by White Sox with Ken Patterson for George Bell, 3/92

Player Summary	
Fantasy Value	$30 to $35
Card Value	10¢ to 15¢
Will	show great tools
Can't	master strike zone
Expect	30 homers
Don't Expect	sharp fielding

Will historians look back on 1995 as "The Year Sosa Broke Through," or will they just see that it was his best season? A gifted hitter with quick wrists and tremendous power, Sosa worked harder last year to take outside pitches the other way, cut down on his swing, and try to make more consistent contact. He also drew a career-high 58 walks. His 134 strikeouts were around his usual total. Sosa provided a big power bat for the Cubs, although he continued to show a streaky nature. In one 19-game stretch in August, he hit 10 homers. Showing his excellent speed, he became a 30-30 member for the second time in 1995 as well. While Sosa has outstanding tools defensively, he does not make good use of them. He has trouble hitting the cutoff man and often misplays routine base hits. If he improved on the fundamentals, he could be a center fielder. As it is, right field is a challenge. His tremendous talent makes Sosa's inconsistency more unpalatable.

Major League Batting Register

	BA	G	AB	R	H	2B	3B	HR	RBI	SB
89 AL	.257	58	183	27	47	8	0	4	13	7
90 AL	.233	153	532	72	124	26	10	15	70	32
91 AL	.203	116	316	39	64	10	1	10	33	13
92 NL	.260	67	262	41	68	7	2	8	25	15
93 NL	.261	159	598	92	156	25	5	33	93	36
94 NL	.300	105	426	59	128	17	6	25	70	22
95 NL	.268	144	564	89	151	17	3	36	119	34
Life	.256	802	2881	419	738	110	27	131	423	159
3 AVE	.276	156	611	92	169	23	6	36	108	35

STEVE SPARKS

Position: Pitcher
Team: Milwaukee Brewers
Born: July 2, 1965 Tulsa, OK
Height: 6' **Weight:** 180 lbs.
Bats: right **Throws:** right
Acquired: Fifth-round pick in 6/87 free-agent draft

Player Summary	
Fantasy Value	$2 to $4
Card Value	10¢ to 15¢
Will	get his innings
Can't	impress with fastball
Expect	plenty of walks
Don't Expect	a Cy Young

The first exposure most baseball fans had to Sparks was during spring training 1994, when he dislocated his shoulder trying to tear a phone book in half after witnessing a motivational speech. That episode, and the natural stigma of his knuckleball, made him an oddity to many people. But the desperate Brewers came to see Sparks as very valuable in 1995. Offering a good performance for a mound staff filled with rookies, he was arguably the club's best starting pitcher. He began the season in the bullpen, but he ended up second on the club with 27 starts and led the Brewers in innings pitched. He finished nearly .500 despite getting the worst offensive support of anyone in Milwaukee's rotation. Like many knuckleball pitchers, Sparks had serious problems with walks, and he allowed opponents to bat .274. A big windup and a slow pitch allowed 16 of 23 runners to steal against Sparks. He has a fair pickoff move and doesn't field his position especially well. Sparks did a creditable job for the Brewers last year, but he needs to improve. Refinement of location is critical to Sparks's career, but control of the knuckleball is almost an oxymoron.

Major League Pitching Register

	W	L	ERA	G	CG	IP	H	ER	BB	SO
95 AL	9	11	4.63	33	3	202.0	210	104	86	96
Life	9	11	4.63	33	3	202.0	210	104	86	96

CURRENT PLAYERS

ED SPRAGUE

Position: Third base
Team: Toronto Blue Jays
Born: July 25, 1967 Castro Valley, CA
Height: 6'2" **Weight:** 215 lbs.
Bats: right **Throws:** right
Acquired: First-round pick in 6/88 free-agent draft

Player Summary	
Fantasy Value	$6 to $8
Card Value	4¢ to 6¢
Will	show some power
Can't	outrun molasses
Expect	strikeouts
Don't Expect	a Gold Glove

Sprague's poor 1995 performance was just another part of Toronto's disastrous season-long slide. He delivered adequate power numbers, finishing second on the club in home runs and RBI, but did little else. His batting average was poor, and in drawing 58 walks (not many, but a career high) he accumulated just a .333 on-base percentage. AL pitchers fanned him 96 times. Sprague hit just .222 against left-handed pitching last summer and batted below .250 both at home and on the road. He has no speed. In the field, he is mediocre. Sprague chases pop flies well and has a strong arm, but he often makes wild throws and doesn't have very good hands. His range is poor, and his 17 errors were the third-highest total in the league. Sprague began his career as a utility player, and, after some World Series heroics in 1992, has had several seasons to prove that he belongs in an everyday role. He is the son of Ed Sprague, a former major leaguer and a current scout.

Major League Batting Register

	BA	G	AB	R	H	2B	3B	HR	RBI	SB
91 AL	.275	61	160	17	44	7	0	4	20	0
92 AL	.234	22	47	6	11	2	0	1	7	0
93 AL	.260	150	546	50	142	31	1	12	73	1
94 AL	.240	109	405	38	97	19	1	11	44	1
95 AL	.244	144	521	77	127	27	2	18	74	0
Life	.251	486	1679	188	421	86	4	46	218	2
3 AVE	.248	155	568	63	141	29	2	16	73	1

SCOTT STAHOVIAK

Position: First base
Team: Minnesota Twins
Born: March 6, 1970 Waukegan, IL
Height: 6'5" **Weight:** 222 lbs.
Bats: left **Throws:** right
Acquired: First-round pick in 6/91 free-agent draft

Player Summary	
Fantasy Value	$4 to $6
Card Value	15¢ to 20¢
Will	be a starter
Can't	show much power
Expect	strikeout struggles
Don't Expect	great defense

The big, burly Stahoviak doesn't yet hit with the power one expects from a corner infielder. Future extra-base pop will likely be the determining factor in whether his career in the majors is long or short. He showed in 1995 that he can play a good first base and fill in at third if necessary. He also showed an aptitude for hitting for a decent average. Stahoviak's ability to make contact could use some serious work, as he whiffed 61 times in his rookie campaign. However, he did draw 30 walks, and he totaled a decent .341 on-base percentage. He rarely faced a left-hander and hit .077 in his handful of at bats. He totalled 13 and 12 home runs in 1993 and 1994, respectively, in the minors. He should be able to drive the ball a little better. Stahoviak played 69 times at first base in 1995 and in 22 games at third. While he's not fast, he stole five bases in six tries in his rookie campaign. His arm is thought to be too weak for third base, and his range is probably best suited for first as well. If he's healthy, Stahoviak will get another chance this summer to prove that he is a major-league player.

Major League Batting Register

	BA	G	AB	R	H	2B	3B	HR	RBI	SB
93 AL	.193	20	57	1	11	4	0	0	1	0
95 AL	.266	94	263	28	70	19	0	3	23	5
Life	.253	114	320	29	81	23	0	3	24	5

CURRENT PLAYERS

MIKE STANLEY

Position: Catcher
Team: New York Yankees
Born: June 25, 1963 Fort Lauderdale, FL
Height: 6' **Weight:** 190 lbs.
Bats: right **Throws:** right
Acquired: Signed as a free agent, 1/92

Player Summary	
Fantasy Value	$10 to $12
Card Value	4¢ to 6¢
Will	batter left-handers
Can't	throw out runners
Expect	strikeouts, walks
Don't Expect	a fast start

Stanley enjoyed another strong campaign in 1995, rebounding again from an early slump to help lead the Yankees into the postseason. Although he threw out just 29 percent of enemy basestealers last year, Stanley is valued behind the plate because of his game-calling skills. He is also adept at blocking pitches, and he has a great attitude as well. Stanley has real pop, posting a fine .481 slugging percentage in 1995. He gets aboard often, taking 57 walks and notching a .360 on-base percentage. He has shown a tendency toward hitting better in the second half of the year. That may explain why he fizzled with the Rangers, who rarely played him after his early slumps. He always hits left-handers well, batting .281 with good power against them last season. Stanley does tend to whiff often. He can't run well, but he rarely tries to do more than he's capable of.

Major League Batting Register

	BA	G	AB	R	H	2B	3B	HR	RBI	SB
86 AL	.333	15	30	4	10	3	0	1	1	1
87 AL	.273	78	216	34	59	8	1	6	37	3
88 AL	.229	94	249	21	57	8	0	3	27	0
89 AL	.246	67	122	9	30	3	1	1	11	1
90 AL	.249	103	189	21	47	8	1	2	19	1
91 AL	.249	95	181	25	45	13	1	3	25	0
92 AL	.249	68	173	24	43	7	0	8	27	0
93 AL	.305	130	423	70	129	17	1	26	84	1
94 AL	.300	82	290	54	87	20	0	17	57	0
95 AL	.268	118	399	63	107	29	1	18	83	1
Life	.270	850	2272	325	614	116	6	85	371	8
3 AVE	.290	126	427	72	124	26	1	23	86	1

TERRY STEINBACH

Position: Catcher
Team: Oakland Athletics
Born: March 2, 1962 New Ulm, MN
Height: 6'1" **Weight:** 195 lbs.
Bats: right **Throws:** right
Acquired: Ninth-round pick in 6/83 free-agent draft

Player Summary	
Fantasy Value	$8 to $10
Card Value	4¢ to 6¢
Will	swing the bat
Can't	do it himself
Expect	little speed
Don't Expect	many walks

Steinbach played well again in 1995, holding together a patchy pitching corps and kicking in at the plate. He is a very consistent hitter, batting around .280 with some home runs every season. Left-handers rarely give him any problems, and could hold him to only a .301 mark last year. Steinbach does have some weak spots on offense; he fans often and struck out 75 times last year. He rarely walks, and last summer took just 25 free passes. His below-average .322 on-base percentage is around his career norm. However, he's still one of baseball's best offensive receivers. His defensive skills make him a fine all-around player. Steinbach threw out nearly 40 percent of runners trying to steal against him, one of his best totals ever. He also showed good pitch-blocking and pitch-calling skills. Nagging injuries kept Steinbach out of some games last year.

Major League Batting Register

	BA	G	AB	R	H	2B	3B	HR	RBI	SB
86 AL	.333	6	15	3	5	0	0	2	4	0
87 AL	.284	122	391	66	111	16	3	16	56	1
88 AL	.265	104	351	42	93	19	1	9	51	3
89 AL	.273	130	454	37	124	13	1	7	42	1
90 AL	.251	114	379	32	95	15	2	9	57	0
91 AL	.274	129	456	50	125	31	1	6	67	2
92 AL	.279	128	438	48	122	20	1	12	53	2
93 AL	.285	104	389	47	111	19	1	10	43	3
94 AL	.285	103	369	51	105	21	2	11	57	2
95 AL	.278	114	406	43	113	26	1	15	65	1
Life	.275	1054	3648	419	1004	180	13	97	495	15
3 AVE	.283	126	455	56	129	26	2	14	65	2

CURRENT PLAYERS

DAVE STEVENS

Position: Pitcher
Team: Minnesota Twins
Born: March 4, 1970 Fullerton, CA
Height: 6'3" **Weight:** 210 lbs.
Bats: right **Throws:** right
Acquired: Traded by Cubs with Matt Walbeck for Willie Banks, 11/93

Player Summary
Fantasy Value................ $8 to $12
Card Value .... 6¢ to 8¢
Will .... throw hard
Can't .... keep ball in park
Expect .... save opportunities
Don't Expect .... great control

The hard-throwing Stevens finally got his shot at closing last year with the Twins. Results were mixed. Although he blew just two saves in 12 chances, the 5.07 ERA that he turned in doesn't lie. He had all kinds of problems getting the ball over the plate, and he was buffeted when forced to throw "get me over" fastballs. Batters rocked Stevens for 14 homers in 1995 and batted .285 against him. He didn't pitch inside often, and he paid the price; left-handers leaned out over the plate to get his fastball, and stroked .315 against him. Stevens certainly has strikeout ability, with a fine fastball and a good curve that he has problems controlling. But his pitches need refinement. Stevens should get some chances during the 1996 season in late relief. He's got the pure stuff to do the job, but his control certainly needs work. If he can't handle closing out games, he would best be used in middle relief. About 30 percent of inherited runners scored against Stevens in 1995, which is not that bad of a number for a set-up man.

KELLY STINNETT

Position: Catcher
Team: New York Mets
Born: Feb. 14, 1970 Lawton, OK
Height: 5'11" **Weight:** 195 lbs.
Bats: right **Throws:** right
Acquired: Rule 5 draft pick from Indians, 12/93

Player Summary
Fantasy Value...................... $1
Card Value .... 6¢ to 8¢
Will .... play with grit
Can't .... make contact
Expect .... reserve duty
Don't Expect .... home runs

Todd Hundley's injury problems gave Stinnett a chance at regular duty in 1995. Unfortunately, Stinnett proved that as of now, he makes a fine reserve. He just doesn't hit anything, as evidenced by a terribly high 65 strikeouts in just 196 at bats. He has good bat speed, but he is fooled by breaking pitches. He lacks power. Stinnett runs very well for a catcher and took 29 walks last year. His .338 on-base percentage wasn't bad. He still doesn't have that much professional experience, and he has lots of learning to do about hitting. Defensively, he is about average. He won Mets manager Dallas Green's favor in 1994 with his hard-nosed play and take-charge attitude. But Stinnett allowed over 80 percent of baserunners to steal on him last year. His throwing mechanics are still unpolished, although he has a strong arm and should improve. He blocks pitches well and, despite his lack of speed, is agile behind the dish. Used in a proper role, he could be a good backup catcher. In order to be a regular, Stinnett needs to refine every facet of his game.

Major League Pitching Register

	W	L	ERA	G	S	IP	H	ER	BB	SO
94 AL	5	2	6.80	24	0	45.0	55	34	23	24
95 AL	5	4	5.07	56	10	65.2	74	37	32	47
Life	10	6	5.77	80	10	110.2	129	71	55	71
2 AVE	6	4	5.87	48	6	68.1	80	45	34	43

Major League Batting Register

	BA	AB	R	H	2B	3B	HR	RBI	SB
94 NL	.253	47	150	20	38	6	2	2	14	2
95 NL	.219	77	196	23	43	8	1	4	18	2
Life	.234	124	346	43	81	14	3	6	32	4
2 AVE	.236	76	216	27	51	9	2	4	20	3

CURRENT PLAYERS

KEVIN STOCKER

Position: Shortstop
Team: Philadelphia Phillies
Born: Feb. 13, 1970 Spokane, WA
Height: 6'1" **Weight:** 178 lbs.
Bats: both **Throws:** right
Acquired: Second-round pick in 6/91 free-agent draft

Player Summary	
Fantasy Value	$4 to $6
Card Value	6¢ to 8¢
Will	try to hang on
Can't	hit for power
Expect	some steals
Don't Expect	a .300 season

Stocker's complete offensive collapse left the Phillies puzzled and frustrated. Not many expected Stocker to recapture the blazing performance level of his 1993 rookie season, but even fewer thought that he'd be anywhere near as bad as a .218 batter. He was bad in every situation, hitting under .220 against both left-handers and right-handers, batting .196 on the road, and stroking just .241 in Veterans Stadium. Stocker has mediocre bat speed and no power, so he generates few extra-base hits. He fanned 75 times last year—far too often for the 43 walks he took. His on-base percentage, high in the past, was a very poor .304 in 1995. Whether Stocker will ever come back with the stick is a fair question. He came out of nowhere two years ago with a checkered minor-league record, and he has declined at the plate steadily. If he could dazzle with the glove, Stocker could probably hold off the critics, but he continues to make mistakes on routine throws and boots his share of balls. He does have range up the middle and arm strength.

Major League Batting Register

	BA	G	AB	R	H	2B	3B	HR	RBI	SB
93 NL	.324	70	259	46	84	12	3	2	31	5
94 NL	.273	82	271	38	74	11	2	2	28	2
95 NL	.218	125	412	42	90	14	3	1	32	6
Life	.263	277	942	126	248	37	8	5	91	13
3 AVE	.262	109	368	49	96	14	3	2	35	5

TODD STOTTLEMYRE

Position: Pitcher
Team: Oakland Athletics
Born: May 20, 1965 Yakima, WA
Height: 6'3" **Weight:** 200 lbs.
Bats: left **Throws:** right
Acquired: Signed as a free agent, 4/95

Player Summary	
Fantasy Value	$4 to $6
Card Value	4¢ to 6¢
Will	get his strikeouts
Can't	control his temper
Expect	35 starts
Don't Expect	a Cy Young

Stottlemyre finally wore out his welcome with the Blue Jays and inked with the pitching-thin Athletics for 1995. Assuming the role of staff ace, the intense right-hander posted fine categories across the board in an impressive comeback season. He paced Oakland in nearly every category. Stottlemyre is durable and cuts off the running game quite well with a good pickoff move. It would be helpful if he wouldn't allow so many runners in the first place; the league on-base percentage against him was .343 last year. Right-handed batters teed off at an even .300 against Stottlemyre. His 26 home runs allowed ranked near the top of the American League leaders. Among AL pitchers, he ranked second (a distant second) in strikeouts to Randy Johnson. Perhaps the biggest reason for Stottlemyre's good 1995 won-lost mark was the nearly six and one-half runs per game his teammates scored for him.

Major League Pitching Register

	W	L	ERA	G	CG	IP	H	ER	BB	SO
88 AL	4	8	5.69	28	0	98.0	109	62	46	67
89 AL	7	7	3.88	27	0	127.2	137	55	44	63
90 AL	13	17	4.34	33	4	203.0	214	98	69	115
91 AL	15	8	3.78	34	1	219.0	194	92	75	116
92 AL	12	11	4.50	28	6	174.0	175	87	63	98
93 AL	11	12	4.84	30	1	176.2	204	95	69	98
94 AL	7	7	4.22	26	3	140.2	149	66	48	105
95 AL	14	7	4.55	31	2	209.2	228	106	80	205
Life	83	77	4.41	237	17	1348.2	1410	661	494	867
3 AVE	12	10	4.53	34	2	203.2	223	102	76	159

CURRENT PLAYERS

DOUG STRANGE

Position: Third base
Team: Seattle Mariners
Born: April 13, 1964 Greenville, SC
Height: 6'2" **Weight:** 170 lbs.
Bats: both **Throws:** right
Acquired: Signed as a free agent, 3/95

Player Summary
Fantasy Value	$1
Card Value	4¢ to 6¢
Will	play several spots
Can't	produce much power
Expect	decent contact
Don't Expect	hits versus lefties

A switch-hitter who's more potent from the left side, Strange spent the 1995 season sharing Seattle's third-base spot with righty-hitting slugger Mike Blowers. Strange also spent some time playing second base and left field. A singles hitter, Strange can bunt, execute the hit-and-run, and move runners along. His patience at the plate paid off in the eighth inning of the Division Series finale, when he drew a bases-loaded walk off David Cone to force home the tying run of a game the M's eventually won. Although Strange makes good contact, he is not usually known for his patience. He walked 10 times in 1995. A product of North Carolina State, Strange started his pro career in 1985, but spent most of the next eight years in the minors. Not known for power or speed, his versatility and switch-hitting skills have given him some job security. Although he had three .300 years in the minors, he will never be confused with Wade Boggs. Strange's hands, arm, and range rate no better than average.

Major League Batting Register
	BA	G	AB	R	H	2B	3B	HR	RBI	SB
89 AL	.214	64	196	16	42	4	1	1	14	3
91 NL	.444	3	9	0	4	1	0	0	1	1
92 NL	.160	52	94	7	15	1	0	1	5	1
93 AL	.256	145	484	58	124	29	0	7	60	6
94 AL	.212	73	226	26	48	12	1	5	26	1
95 AL	.271	74	155	19	42	9	2	2	21	0
Life	.236	411	1164	126	275	56	4	16	127	12
3 AVE	.245	110	326	39	80	19	1	5	40	2

DARRYL STRAWBERRY

Position: Outfield
Team: New York Yankees
Born: March 12, 1962 Los Angeles, CA
Height: 6'6" **Weight:** 215 lbs.
Bats: left **Throws:** left
Acquired: Signed as a free agent, 6/95

Player Summary
Fantasy Value	$3 to $5
Card Value	8¢ to 12¢
Will	fill DH vacancy
Can't	hit left-handers
Expect	one last chance
Don't Expect	return to 30-30

Strawberry's reign as one of baseball's premier sluggers probably ended in 1991. Since that time, he's had several suspensions for substance abuse, problems with the IRS, plus a variety of injuries that have greatly restricted his playing time. Both the Dodgers and Giants released the eight-time All-Star, and his career appeared to be over. But that was before George Steinbrenner decided Strawberry still had a big name in New York. His performance as a Yankee, however, did not justify the hype that preceded his signing. Strawberry's weaknesses were all too apparent: total futility against left-handed pitchers, a penchant for frequent strikeouts, and incompetence in the field. With Dion James and Ruben Sierra ranked ahead of him as designated hitters, Strawberry spent most of the summer sitting.

Major League Batting Register
	BA	G	AB	R	H	2B	3B	HR	RBI	SB
83 NL	.257	122	420	63	108	15	7	26	74	19
84 NL	.251	147	522	75	131	27	4	26	97	27
85 NL	.277	111	393	78	109	15	4	29	79	26
86 NL	.259	136	475	76	123	27	5	27	93	28
87 NL	.284	154	532	108	151	32	5	39	104	36
88 NL	.269	153	543	101	146	27	3	39	101	29
89 NL	.225	134	476	69	107	26	1	29	77	11
90 NL	.277	152	542	92	150	18	1	37	108	15
91 NL	.265	139	505	86	134	22	4	28	99	10
92 NL	.237	43	156	20	37	8	0	5	25	3
93 NL	.140	32	100	12	14	2	0	5	12	1
94 NL	.239	29	92	13	22	3	1	4	17	0
95 AL	.276	32	87	15	24	4	1	3	13	0
Life	.259	1384	4843	808	1256	226	36	297	899	205

CURRENT PLAYERS

FRANKLIN STUBBS

Position: First base; outfield
Team: Detroit Tigers
Born: Oct. 21, 1960 Laurinburg, NC
Height: 6'2" **Weight:** 209 lbs.
Bats: left **Throws:** left
Acquired: Signed as a free agent, 12/94

Player Summary	
Fantasy Value	$0
Card Value	4¢ to 6¢
Will	try to hang on
Can't	find old power
Expect	back-up service
Don't Expect	dynamic defense

Detroit's decision to sign Stubbs was a major mystery. He'd been out of the majors three years and wasn't about to displace Cecil Fielder as the Tigers first baseman. Moreover, Stubbs's presence would delay the team's youth movement. But someone must have remembered that Stubbs twice topped 20 homers in a big-league season, and figured he'd do even better with the cozy dimensions of Tiger Stadium. They were wrong. Given limited playing time, he collected only two home runs and 19 RBI. Stubbs split his time evenly between first base (when Fielder was a DH) and left field, getting into 20 games at each spot. That performance shouldn't have been surprising, since Stubbs has not had a solid season in the majors since 1990. He fans far too frequently, doesn't provide good defense, and adds only a modicum of speed. The former Virginia Tech All-American is probably washed-up.

Major League Batting Register

	BA	G	AB	R	H	2B	3B	HR	RBI	SB
84 NL	.194	87	217	22	42	2	3	8	17	2
85 NL	.222	10	9	0	2	0	0	0	2	0
86 NL	.226	132	420	55	95	11	1	23	58	7
87 NL	.233	129	386	48	90	16	3	16	52	8
88 NL	.223	115	242	30	54	13	0	8	34	11
89 NL	.291	69	103	11	30	6	0	4	15	3
90 NL	.261	146	448	59	117	23	2	23	71	19
91 AL	.213	103	362	48	77	16	2	11	38	13
92 AL	.229	92	288	37	66	11	1	9	42	11
95 AL	.250	62	116	13	29	11	0	2	19	0
Life	.232	945	2591	323	602	109	12	104	348	74

B.J. SURHOFF

Position: Outfield; first base; catcher
Team: Milwaukee Brewers
Born: Aug. 4, 1964 Bronx, NY
Height: 6'1" **Weight:** 200 lbs.
Bats: left **Throws:** right
Acquired: First-round pick in 6/85 free-agent draft

Player Summary	
Fantasy Value	$12 to $15
Card Value	6¢ to 12¢
Will	make good contact
Can't	find regular spot
Expect	line-drive stroke
Don't Expect	award for defense

Surhoff's .320 batting average ranked sixth in the American League last year. It was also a surprise, since he had averaged only .268 during eight previous seasons in the majors. But a solid performance against left-handed pitchers (.367) helped. A contact hitter who walks almost as often as he fans, Surhoff also supplies some power and speed. He had a career-best 13 homers last year and swiped seven bases in 10 tries. Surhoff's strong start last year tarnished his reputation as a second-half hitter. But he managed to stay strong all season. Valuable because of his versatility, he shared first base with righty-hitting John Jaha last year. The former Olympian, an All-American who was College Player of the Year at North Carolina, also caught 18 games and played all three outfield positions. Surhoff is decent enough to play all those positions, plus third.

Major League Batting Register

	BA	G	AB	R	H	2B	3B	HR	RBI	SB
87 AL	.299	115	395	50	118	22	3	7	68	11
88 AL	.245	139	493	47	121	21	0	5	38	21
89 AL	.248	126	436	42	108	17	4	5	55	14
90 AL	.276	135	474	55	131	21	4	6	59	18
91 AL	.289	143	505	57	146	19	4	5	68	5
92 AL	.252	139	480	63	121	19	1	4	62	14
93 AL	.274	148	552	66	151	38	3	7	79	12
94 AL	.261	40	134	20	35	11	2	5	22	0
95 AL	.320	117	415	72	133	26	3	13	73	7
Life	.274	1102	3884	472	1064	194	24	57	524	102
2 AVE	.295	140	509	74	150	34	3	11	81	10

301

CURRENT PLAYERS

BILL SWIFT

Position: Pitcher
Team: Colorado Rockies
Born: Oct. 27, 1961 South Portland, ME
Height: 6′ **Weight:** 180 lbs.
Bats: right **Throws:** right
Acquired: Signed as a free agent, 4/95

Player Summary	
Fantasy Value	$3 to $5
Card Value	5¢ to 8¢
Will	remain staff ace
Can't	quiet lefty bats
Expect	many ground outs
Don't Expect	injury-free year

Chronic shoulder problems almost stopped Swift from becoming the ace of the Colorado staff last summer. Landing on the DL twice, he was not able to work more than six innings in any of his last six starts. Though arthroscopic surgery has repaired the frayed labrum in his right shoulder, Swift's medical history reads like a wall chart from an ER. He's been disabled seven times since 1989. A sinkerballer who also throws a slider, a curve, and a changeup, Swift succeeds when he keeps the ball down and lets his defense do the work. He usually gets lots of ground outs. When his sinker didn't sink in Denver's alpine air, it often sailed. The University of Maine product threw a dozen gopher balls and let lefties rip him at a .312 clip. On the plus side, the former U.S. Olympian helps himself with his bat and glove. Swift can hit, bunt, and field. Few runners test him and less than half succeed.

Major League Pitching Register

	W	L	ERA	G	CG	IP	H	ER	BB	SO
85 AL	6	10	4.77	23	0	120.2	131	64	48	55
86 AL	2	9	5.46	29	1	115.1	148	70	55	55
88 AL	8	12	4.59	38	6	174.2	199	89	65	47
89 AL	7	3	4.43	37	0	130.0	140	64	38	45
90 AL	6	4	2.39	55	0	128.0	135	34	21	42
91 AL	1	2	1.99	71	0	90.1	74	20	26	48
92 NL	10	4	2.08	30	3	164.2	144	38	43	77
93 NL	21	8	2.82	34	1	232.2	195	73	55	157
94 NL	8	7	3.38	17	0	109.1	109	41	31	62
95 NL	9	3	4.94	19	0	105.2	122	58	43	68
Life	78	62	3.62	353	11	1371.1	1397	551	425	656
3 AVE	14	7	3.49	26	0	168.2	162	65	49	107

GREG SWINDELL

Position: Pitcher
Team: Houston Astros
Born: Jan. 2, 1965 Fort Worth, TX
Height: 6′3″ **Weight:** 225 lbs.
Bats: both **Throws:** left
Acquired: Signed as a free agent, 12/92

Player Summary	
Fantasy Value	$2 to $4
Card Value	5¢ to 8¢
Will	stop lefty batters
Can't	avoid gopher balls
Expect	very good control
Don't Expect	increased velocity

When Cleveland was bad, Swindell was good. He enjoyed his finest year as ace of the 1988 Indian team that finished next-to-last in the AL East with a 78-84 record. Swindell has since had to battle his weight, the pressure of pitching on his home turf, and a need to justify the huge free-agent contract Houston squandered on him in a fruitless effort to win its first pennant. Swindell was so erratic last year that he made seven relief appearances—the most of his major-league career. Though he held left-handers to a .234 average and showed fine overall control (2.29 walks per nine innings), Swindell struggled to win 10 games. The former All-American from the University of Texas throws a fastball, a slider, a curveball, and two types of changeups. But the velocity of the former power pitcher has declined sharply in recent seasons. Swindell has a good bat and a good pickoff move.

Major League Pitching Register

	W	L	ERA	G	CG	IP	H	ER	BB	SO
86 AL	5	2	4.23	9	1	61.2	57	29	15	46
87 AL	3	8	5.10	16	4	102.1	112	58	37	97
88 AL	18	14	3.20	33	12	242.0	234	86	45	180
89 AL	13	6	3.37	28	5	184.1	170	69	51	129
90 AL	12	9	4.40	34	3	214.2	245	105	47	135
91 AL	9	16	3.48	33	7	238.0	241	92	31	169
92 NL	12	8	2.70	31	5	213.2	210	64	41	138
93 NL	12	13	4.16	31	1	190.1	215	88	40	124
94 NL	8	9	4.37	24	1	148.1	175	72	26	74
95 NL	10	9	4.47	33	1	153.0	180	76	39	96
Life	102	94	3.80	272	40	1748.1	1839	739	372	1188
3 AVE	12	12	4.33	34	1	190.1	221	92	40	112

CURRENT PLAYERS

JEFF TABAKA

Position: Pitcher
Team: Houston Astros
Born: Jan. 17, 1964 Barberton, OH
Height: 6'2" **Weight:** 195 lbs.
Bats: right **Throws:** left
Acquired: Traded by Padres with Rich Loiselle for Phil Plantier, 7/95

Player Summary	
Fantasy Value	$1
Card Value	5¢ to 8¢
Will	calm lefty bats
Can't	find home plate
Expect	OK pickoff move
Don't Expect	chance to start

When used strictly against left-handed hitters, Tabaka is an effective relief pitcher. He limited southpaws to a .190 mark last year but managed only a .275 mark against righties. A sinker-slider pitcher who also throws a curve and a changeup, Tabaka yields less hits than innings, and averages more than seven strikeouts per nine innings. But he often has control problems (an average of just under five walks per game in 1995). The Kent State product keeps the ball in the park and retires most of the runners he inherits. Tabaka began his minor-league tenure as a starter in 1986 but became a big-league prospect after he switched to relief six years later. He's not much of a fielder but he has a fine pickoff move. Tabaka was originally drafted by the Montreal Expos in 1986. He later belonged to the Phillies, Brewers, Marlins, Pirates, and Padres. Tabaka would have reached the majors sooner if not for his inability to throw strikes. In two different seasons, he walked more men than he fanned.

Major League Pitching Register

	W	L	ERA	G	S	IP	H	ER	BB	SO
94 NL	3	1	5.27	39	1	41.0	32	24	27	32
95 NL	1	0	3.23	34	0	30.2	27	11	17	25
Life	4	1	4.40	73	1	71.2	59	35	44	57
2 AVE	3	1	4.51	47	1	46.1	38	23	29	37

KEVIN TAPANI

Position: Pitcher
Team: Los Angeles Dodgers
Born: Feb. 18, 1964 Des Moines, IA
Height: 6' **Weight:** 180 lbs.
Bats: right **Throws:** right
Acquired: Traded by Twins with Mark Guthrie for Ron Coomer, Jose Parra, and Greg Hansell, 7/95

Player Summary	
Fantasy Value	$5 to $7
Card Value	6¢ to 10¢
Will	throw strikes
Can't	stop home runs
Expect	ERA to improve
Don't Expect	a skipped turn

One of baseball's most consistent starting pitchers, Tapani has finished with double figures in victories six years in a row. He has not missed a start with an injury since August 1990. A control artist who lets his defense do the work, Tapani is a sinker-slider pitcher who also throws a forkball and a changeup. Though he always has a fine ratio of strikeouts to walks, he is not regarded as a power pitcher. Tapani depends upon keeping the ball down. When his sinker doesn't sink, he often gives up extra-base hits. That happened too often in the last two years, when Tapani's ERA soared out of the respectable range. Lefties were the chief problem for the Central Michigan product last year; they hit him at a .327 clip. Tapani has improved his pickoff move but is still no better than average. His fielding is in the same category.

Major League Pitching Register

	W	L	ERA	G	CG	IP	H	ER	BB	SO
89 NL	0	0	3.68	3	0	7.1	5	3	4	2
89 AL	2	2	3.86	5	0	32.2	34	14	8	21
90 AL	12	8	4.07	28	1	159.1	164	72	29	101
91 AL	16	9	2.99	34	4	244.0	225	81	40	135
92 AL	16	11	3.97	34	4	220.0	226	97	48	138
93 AL	12	15	4.43	36	3	225.2	243	111	57	150
94 AL	11	7	4.62	24	4	156.0	181	80	39	91
95 AL	6	11	4.92	20	3	133.2	155	73	34	88
95 NL	4	2	5.05	13	0	57.0	72	32	14	43
Life	79	65	4.10	197	19	1235.2	1305	563	273	769
3 AVE	13	13	4.66	36	4	220.1	251	114	55	142

CURRENT PLAYERS

TONY TARASCO

Position: Outfield
Team: Montreal Expos
Born: Dec. 9, 1970 New York, NY
Height: 6'1" **Weight:** 205 lbs.
Bats: left **Throws:** right
Acquired: Traded by Braves with Roberto Kelly and Esteban Yan for Marquis Grissom, 4/95

Player Summary	
Fantasy Value	$14 to $17
Card Value	10¢ to 15¢
Will	play good defense
Can't	practice patience
Expect	speed on the bases
Don't Expect	malaise to linger

Given a chance to play regularly for the first time last year, Tarasco got off to a hot start, then faded badly. He failed to show the same stroke that had produced a pair of .300 seasons in the minors and wound up sharing right field with Henry Rodriguez, Yamil Benitez, and F.P. Santangelo. Tarasco's biggest asset was his speed: He swiped 24 bases in 27 tries. He has definite 20-20 club potential but will have to make better contact—especially against right-handed pitchers (.249 in 1995). A low fastball hitter with an uppercut swing, Tarasco would be more productive if he were more selective at the plate. He often swings at pitches outside the strike zone, negating the possibility of a walk-and-steal situation. He'd also increase his value if he pulled less and used the whole field more. Tarasco's speed helps him in the outfield, where he has the range for center and the arm for right. He makes strong, accurate throws and catches everything he reaches. His best years should still be ahead of him.

Major League Batting Register

	BA	G	AB	R	H	2B	3B	HR	RBI	SB
93 NL	.229	24	35	6	8	2	0	0	2	0
94 NL	.273	87	132	16	36	6	0	5	19	5
95 NL	.249	126	438	64	109	18	4	14	40	24
Life	.253	237	605	86	153	26	4	19	61	29

DANNY TARTABULL

Position: Designated hitter; outfield
Team: Oakland Athletics
Born: Oct. 30, 1962 San Juan, PR
Height: 6'1" **Weight:** 205 lbs.
Bats: right **Throws:** right
Acquired: Traded by Yankees for Ruben Sierra and Jason Beverlin, 7/95

Player Summary	
Fantasy Value	$9 to $11
Card Value	6¢ to 10¢
Will	hit with power
Can't	reduce K ratio
Expect	DH duty
Don't Expect	speed on bases

During his 12-year career in the majors, Tartabull has topped 30 homers three times and 100 RBI four times. He's been such a bust over the past two seasons, however, that he's no longer regarded as one of the premier power threats in the game. Although his .335 on-base percentage was 99 points higher than his batting mark in '95, Tartabull wore out his welcome with the Yankees. He hit .195 in his first 26 games and .136 with 13 strikeouts in his final 12 games in pinstripes. In fairness to Tartabull, he has spent most of his career playing in ballparks that are not considered hitter-friendly to right-handed power hitters. If Tartabull connected more often, he'd have better results. But he's reached triple-digits in strikeouts eight times in his career. He's not much of a basestealer and a definite defensive liability.

Major League Batting Register

	BA	G	AB	R	H	2B	3B	HR	RBI	SB
84 AL	.300	10	20	3	6	1	0	2	7	0
85 AL	.328	19	61	8	20	7	1	1	7	1
86 AL	.270	137	511	76	138	25	6	25	96	4
87 AL	.309	158	582	95	180	27	3	34	101	9
88 AL	.274	146	507	80	139	38	3	26	102	8
89 AL	.268	133	441	54	118	22	0	18	62	4
90 AL	.268	88	313	41	84	19	0	15	60	1
91 AL	.316	132	484	78	153	35	3	31	100	6
92 AL	.266	123	421	72	112	19	0	25	85	2
93 AL	.250	138	513	87	128	33	2	31	102	0
94 AL	.256	104	399	68	102	24	1	19	67	1
95 AL	.236	83	280	34	66	16	0	8	35	0
Life	.275	1271	4532	696	1246	266	19	235	824	36
3 AVE	.249	126	463	74	115	28	1	22	79	0

CURRENT PLAYERS

ED TAUBENSEE

Position: Catcher
Team: Cincinnati Reds
Born: Oct. 31, 1968 Beeville, TX
Height: 6'4" **Weight:** 205 lbs.
Bats: left **Throws:** right
Acquired: Traded by Astros for Ross Powell and Marty Lister, 4/94

Player Summary
Fantasy Value	$6 to $8
Card Value	4¢ to 6¢
Will	show some power
Can't	nail baserunners
Expect	extra-base hits
Don't Expect	very much speed

Because of his ability to hit right-handed pitching, Taubensee is a good platoon catcher. He hit .291 against righties last year, but is not an automatic out against lefties either. His pinch homer off Atlanta's Pedro Borbon on June 22 capped a five-run rally in a 9-8 victory. Though he fanned more than twice for every walk, Taubensee got extra bases on 40 percent of his hits last year. He knocked in as many runs—in fewer at bats—than Benito Santiago, Cincinnati's No. 1 catcher, but did not provide the same defense. Taubensee negates his strong arm with a slow release, letting runners get the better of him 80 percent of the time. He calls a good game, however, and handles pitchers well. Taubensee is also adept at preventing wild pitches and blocking the plate. He can fill in at first base on occasion. Originally signed by the Reds, Taubensee drifted to Oakland in the Rule 5 draft before he was claimed on waivers by Cleveland.

Major League Batting Register

	BA	G	AB	R	H	2B	3B	HR	RBI	SB
91 AL	.242	26	66	5	16	2	1	0	8	0
92 NL	.222	104	297	23	66	15	0	5	28	2
93 NL	.250	94	288	26	72	11	1	9	42	1
94 NL	.283	66	187	29	53	8	2	8	21	2
95 NL	.284	80	218	32	62	14	2	9	44	2
Life	.255	370	1056	115	269	50	6	31	143	7
3 AVE	.272	92	266	34	72	13	2	10	40	2

JULIAN TAVAREZ

Position: Pitcher
Team: Cleveland Indians
Born: May 22, 1973 Santiago, Dominican Republic
Height: 6'2" **Weight:** 165 lbs.
Bats: right **Throws:** right
Acquired: Signed as a nondrafted free agent, 3/90

Player Summary
Fantasy Value	$7 to $9
Card Value	20¢ to 30¢
Will	show good control
Can't	crack the rotation
Expect	fine breaking ball
Don't Expect	runners to steal

After tying for the International League lead with 15 wins in 1994, Tavarez made a smooth transition to the Cleveland bullpen. Working as a set-up man for Jose Mesa, Tavarez led the league with 10 relief wins, tied for third with 85 relief innings, and held hitters to a .211 average with men in scoring position. His ERA at Jacobs Field, where he won six of seven decisions, was 1.72. Tavarez blends an above-average fastball with a breaking ball that managers rated tops in the International League two years ago. His nine-inning averages were outstanding: two-plus walks and seven-plus Ks. Tavarez held right-handed hitters to a .206 mark, stranded 81 percent of the runners he inherited, and controlled the running game so well that only five runners tried to steal against him (two succeeded). Cleveland went 43-14 in his 57 appearances. He worked in five of the six World Series games against Atlanta without yielding an earned run. With a year of experience under his belt, Tavarez will be first in line to succeed starter Dennis Martinez.

Major League Pitching Register

	W	L	ERA	G	S	IP	H	ER	BB	SO
93 AL	2	2	6.57	8	0	37.0	53	27	13	19
94 AL	0	1	21.60	1	0	1.2	6	4	1	0
95 AL	10	2	2.44	57	0	85.0	76	23	21	68
Life	12	5	3.93	66	0	123.2	135	54	35	87

CURRENT PLAYERS

MICKEY TETTLETON

Position: Outfield; first base; catcher
Team: Texas Rangers
Born: Sept. 19, 1960 Oklahoma City, OK
Height: 6'2" **Weight:** 212 lbs.
Bats: both **Throws:** right
Acquired: Signed as a free agent, 4/95

Player Summary	
Fantasy Value	$10 to $13
Card Value	8¢ to 12¢
Will	show great power
Can't	stop striking out
Expect	enormous patience
Don't Expect	sterling defense

Strange stats. There's no other way to explain Tettleton's first season in Texas last summer. With a final-week outburst that included a .556 average, five homers, and 11 RBI, he topped 30 homers for the fourth time in the last five seasons. He also finished with 107 walks, fourth in the league, and 110 strikeouts, just shy of the dubious Top 10. A switch-hitter who's better against righties, Tettleton likes high fastballs while batting right-handed and low fastballs when batting left-handed. His patience helps: Tettleton's .396 on-base percentage was one of the league's best. Since he has little speed or range, plus an arm that is neither accurate nor powerful, it's surprising that Tettleton spent most of his Texas time in right field. He also appeared as a catcher, first baseman, left fielder, and DH.

Major League Batting Register

	BA	G	AB	R	H	2B	3B	HR	RBI	SB
84 AL	.263	33	76	10	20	2	1	1	5	0
85 AL	.251	78	211	23	53	12	0	3	15	2
86 AL	.204	90	211	26	43	9	0	10	35	7
87 AL	.194	82	211	19	41	3	0	8	26	1
88 AL	.261	86	283	31	74	11	1	11	37	0
89 AL	.258	117	411	72	106	21	2	26	65	3
90 AL	.223	135	444	68	99	21	2	15	51	2
91 AL	.263	154	501	85	132	17	2	31	89	3
92 AL	.238	157	525	82	125	25	0	32	83	0
93 AL	.245	152	522	79	128	25	4	32	110	3
94 AL	.248	107	339	57	84	18	2	17	51	0
95 AL	.238	134	429	76	102	19	1	32	78	0
Life	.242	1325	4163	628	1007	183	15	218	645	21
3 AVE	.244	151	494	82	120	24	3	31	90	1

BOB TEWKSBURY

Position: Pitcher
Team: Texas Rangers
Born: Nov. 30, 1960 Concord, NH
Height: 6'4" **Weight:** 208 lbs.
Bats: right **Throws:** right
Acquired: Signed as a free agent, 4/95

Player Summary	
Fantasy Value	$4 to $6
Card Value	5¢ to 8¢
Will	keep ball down
Can't	strike men out
Expect	more victories
Don't Expect	gopher trouble

One of the best control pitchers in baseball, Tewksbury averaged only 1.39 walks per nine innings with the Rangers last year. Being around the plate was not always helpful, however, as hitters ripped him at a .319 clip. A finesse pitcher who relies on location, Tewksbury throws the same pitches that helped him win 33 games over a two-year span for St. Louis (1992 and 1993). His repertoire includes a mediocre fastball, a sharp curve, and two types of sliders—including one he uses as a changeup. The change may be his best pitch. Few batters fan against Tewksbury (three and one-half per nine innings last year). An accomplished artist off the field, he also tries to paint pictures with his pitches. He lets his defense do the work by keeping the ball down. When he doesn't, he gets ripped. Tewksbury keeps the ball in the park, holds runners well, and fields his position well.

Major League Pitching Register

	W	L	ERA	G	CG	IP	H	ER	BB	SO
86 AL	9	5	3.31	23	2	130.1	144	48	31	49
87 AL	1	4	6.75	8	0	33.1	47	25	7	12
87 NL	0	4	6.50	7	0	18.0	32	13	13	10
88 NL	0	0	8.10	1	0	3.1	6	3	2	1
89 NL	1	0	3.30	7	1	30.0	25	11	10	17
90 NL	10	9	3.47	28	3	145.1	151	56	15	50
91 NL	11	12	3.25	30	3	191.0	206	69	38	75
92 NL	16	5	2.16	33	5	233.0	217	56	20	91
93 NL	17	10	3.83	32	2	213.2	258	91	20	97
94 NL	12	10	5.32	24	4	155.2	190	92	22	79
95 AL	8	7	4.58	21	4	129.2	169	66	20	53
Life	85	66	3.72	214	24	1283.1	1445	530	198	534
3 AVE	14	11	4.58	30	4	192.2	239	98	24	89

CURRENT PLAYERS

FRANK THOMAS

Position: First base
Team: Chicago White Sox
Born: May 27, 1968 Columbus, GA
Height: 6'5" **Weight:** 257 lbs.
Bats: right **Throws:** right
Acquired: First-round pick in 6/89 free-agent draft

Player Summary

Fantasy Value	$35 to $40
Card Value	$2.00 to $3.00
Will	post MVP stats
Can't	steal too often
Expect	great patience
Don't Expect	strong defense

Pitchers are afraid to pitch to Frank Thomas. He led the majors last year with 136 bases on balls and wasn't happy about it. The former Auburn All-American likes to swing the bat. The reasons are obvious: Last year, Thomas became the first man in baseball history to record five straight seasons with at least a .300 average, 20 homers, 100 walks, 100 RBI, and 100 runs scored. He had shared the four-year record with Ted Williams and Lou Gehrig—not bad company. Thomas has an explosive swing and power to all fields. Had the White Sox been in contention last year, he almost certainly would have won his third consecutive MVP Award. Thomas was second in on-base percentage (.454), tied for second in homers (40), third in slugging (.606), and fifth in RBI (111). His patience at the plate and ability to make contact are amazing for a slugger: Thomas had 136 walks and 74 strikeouts, a ratio of nearly 2-to-1. His .389 batting average against left-handed pitchers wasn't too shabby either.

Major League Batting Register

	BA	G	AB	R	H	2B	3B	HR	RBI	SB
90 AL	.330	60	191	39	63	11	3	7	31	0
91 AL	.318	158	559	104	178	31	2	32	109	1
92 AL	.323	160	573	108	185	46	2	24	115	6
93 AL	.317	153	549	106	174	36	0	41	128	4
94 AL	.353	113	399	106	141	34	1	38	101	2
95 AL	.308	145	493	102	152	27	0	40	111	3
Life	.323	789	2764	565	893	185	8	182	595	16
3 AVE	.326	158	555	123	181	38	0	47	132	3

JIM THOME

Position: Third base
Team: Cleveland Indians
Born: Aug. 27, 1970 Peoria, IL
Height: 6'4" **Weight:** 220 lbs.
Bats: left **Throws:** right
Acquired: 13th-round pick in 6/89 free-agent draft

Player Summary

Fantasy Value	$20 to $25
Card Value	15¢ to 20¢
Will	hit the long ball
Can't	stop striking out
Expect	high on-base mark
Don't Expect	shift to new spot

Thome's terrific batting eye enabled him to finish third in the league last year with a .438 on-base percentage. When he wasn't drawing one of his 97 walks (fifth in the league), he was producing career highs in homers, hits, RBI, and runs scored. Though he hit 22 of his 25 homers against righties, he was no longer a liability against lefties. He raised his average against southpaws from .167 in 1994 to .275 last year. A low-ball hitter with power to all fields, Thome hit three home runs in a game two years ago. His two-out homer off Brad Clontz in the eighth inning of World Series game five gave Cleveland a much-needed insurance run as Atlanta scored twice in the ninth to make the final score 5-4. Thome has made dramatic strides on defense. Once so bad that the Indians thought about shifting him to first base, Thome has quick reactions, good hands, and a strong arm. Accuracy has been a problem, however. He was the International League Player of the Year in 1993.

Major League Batting Register

	BA	G	AB	R	H	2B	3B	HR	RBI	SB
91 AL	.255	27	98	7	25	4	2	1	9	1
92 AL	.205	40	117	8	24	3	1	2	12	2
93 AL	.266	47	154	28	41	11	0	7	22	2
94 AL	.268	98	321	58	86	20	1	20	52	3
95 AL	.314	137	452	92	142	29	3	25	73	4
Life	.278	349	1142	193	318	67	7	55	168	12
3 AVE	.289	113	372	71	107	24	2	21	59	4

CURRENT PLAYERS

MILT THOMPSON

Position: Outfield; first base
Team: Houston Astros
Born: Jan. 5, 1959 Washington, DC
Height: 5'11" **Weight:** 190 lbs.
Bats: left **Throws:** right
Acquired: Traded by Phillies for Tom Edens, 7/94

Player Summary
Fantasy Value $0
Card Value .... 4¢ to 6¢
Will .... see back-up duty
Can't .... hit the ball out
Expect .... decent fielding
Don't Expect .... patience at bat

A good hitter and speedy outfielder who had five years as an NL regular, Thompson has become a spare part now that he's reached the twilight of his career. A left-handed pinch hitter and late-inning defensive specialist, he can bunt, work the hit-and-run, and move runners along. But he's not likely to hit the ball out of the park. Thompson is no longer the burner who stole 47 bases for the 1987 Phillies, but he's still capable of getting down the line in a hurry. An impatient hitter, he fans nearly three times per walk—negating his speed potential. Thompson is mostly a slap hitter who uses all fields but will collect a double on occasion. His best position is left field but he also spent time in right last year. Thompson still has quick reactions and good range but his arm isn't the best. He can also fill in at first base.

Major League Batting Register

	BA	G	AB	R	H	2B	3B	HR	RBI	SB
84 NL	.303	25	99	16	30	1	0	2	4	14
85 NL	.302	73	182	17	55	7	2	0	6	9
86 NL	.251	96	299	38	75	7	1	6	23	19
87 NL	.302	150	527	86	159	26	9	7	43	46
88 NL	.288	122	378	53	109	16	2	2	33	17
89 NL	.290	155	545	60	158	28	8	4	68	27
90 NL	.218	135	418	42	91	14	7	6	30	25
91 NL	.307	115	326	55	100	16	5	6	34	16
92 NL	.293	109	208	31	61	9	1	4	17	18
93 NL	.262	129	340	42	89	14	2	4	44	9
94 NL	.274	96	241	34	66	7	0	4	33	9
95 NL	.220	92	132	14	29	9	0	2	19	4
Life	.277	1297	3695	488	1022	154	37	47	354	213
2 AVE	.268	132	340	45	91	12	1	5	45	11

ROBBY THOMPSON

Position: Second base
Team: San Francisco Giants
Born: May 10, 1962 West Palm Beach, FL
Height: 5'11" **Weight:** 173 lbs.
Bats: right **Throws:** right
Acquired: First-round pick in secondary phase of 6/83 free-agent draft

Player Summary
Fantasy Value .... $6 to $8
Card Value .... 5¢ to 8¢
Will .... try comeback trail
Can't .... solve right-handers
Expect .... Gold Glove defense
Don't Expect .... durability citation

After missing most of the 1994 campaign with a damaged shoulder, Thompson hoped to restore his reputation as one of baseball's top players at his position. But he failed to hit—especially against right-handers—and wound up sharing time with John Patterson, Steve Scarsone, and Mike Benjamin. Thompson was anemic against right-handed pitching (.216). Though he fans a bit too often for the job, Thompson has hit second in the order. He's a good hit-and-run man who can also drop a sacrifice to move runners up. When he reaches, Thompson has enough speed to reach double figures in stolen bases. His best asset is his glove, however. The University of Florida product has quick reactions, great range, and a fine arm. He turns the double play better than many of his NL colleagues.

Major League Batting Register

	BA	G	AB	R	H	2B	3B	HR	RBI	SB
86 NL	.271	149	549	73	149	27	3	7	47	12
87 NL	.262	132	420	62	110	26	5	10	44	16
88 NL	.264	138	477	66	126	24	6	7	48	14
89 NL	.241	148	547	91	132	26	11	13	50	12
90 NL	.245	144	498	67	122	22	3	15	56	14
91 NL	.262	144	492	74	129	24	5	19	48	14
92 NL	.260	128	443	54	115	25	1	14	49	5
93 NL	.312	128	494	85	154	30	2	19	65	10
94 NL	.209	35	129	13	27	8	2	2	7	3
95 NL	.223	95	336	51	75	15	0	8	23	1
Life	.260	1241	4385	636	1139	227	38	114	437	101
2 AVE	.273	117	436	71	119	23	1	14	45	6

CURRENT PLAYERS

RYAN THOMPSON

Position: Outfield
Team: New York Mets
Born: Nov. 4, 1967 Chestertown, MD
Height: 6'3" **Weight:** 200 lbs.
Bats: right **Throws:** right
Acquired: Traded by Blue Jays with Jeff Kent for David Cone, 8/92

Player Summary	
Fantasy Value	$6 to $8
Card Value	5¢ to 8¢
Will	seek regular job
Can't	avoid strikeouts
Expect	some long balls
Don't Expect	powerful throws

Thompson remains an enigma. He has a quick bat and good power, but he also has a penchant for strikeouts and a reputation for braggadocio that drives coaches crazy. Tried at all three outfield positions last year, Thompson didn't excel at any. In addition, he maintained his average of about four strikeouts per walk—negating much of his power. By the end of the season, Carl Everett and Alex Ochoa had stepped ahead of Thompson in Mets manager Dallas Green's pecking order. Once regarded as a hot-shot Toronto prospect, Thompson has seen his fortunes fall over the last two seasons. He hit only .237 against righties last year and failed to produce anything near his 18-homer performance of 1994. A dead fastball hitter who likes the ball high in the strike zone, Thompson is bamboozled by low breaking balls. A few attempts to bunt for infield hits would rattle opponents and hike Thompson's average. His speed serves him well in the outfield, where he has range and hands. But Thompson's arm isn't strong enough for right.

Major League Batting Register

	BA	G	AB	R	H	2B	3B	HR	RBI	SB
92 NL	.222	30	108	15	24	7	1	3	10	2
93 NL	.250	80	288	34	72	19	2	11	26	2
94 NL	.225	98	334	39	75	14	1	18	59	1
95 NL	.251	75	267	39	67	13	0	7	31	3
Life	.239	283	997	127	238	53	4	39	126	8
3 AVE	.239	101	353	44	84	18	1	15	48	2

MIKE TIMLIN

Position: Pitcher
Team: Toronto Blue Jays
Born: March 10, 1966 Midland, TX
Height: 6'4" **Weight:** 210 lbs.
Bats: right **Throws:** right
Acquired: Fifth-round pick in 6/87 free-agent draft

Player Summary	
Fantasy Value	$9 to $11
Card Value	4¢ to 6¢
Will	baffle right-handers
Can't	win without sinker
Expect	frequent outings
Don't Expect	ball to leave field

Elbow problems interfered with Timlin's 1995 season. Though he was extremely effective in limited action, the Southwestern University product would have seen more service if healthy. He is a sinkerballer who also throws a hard slider, a straight change, and a four-seam fastball. Timlin delivers from a three-quarters motion that is especially deceptive to right-handed hitters. They managed only a .159 batting average against him last year. Lefties, however, lit him up at a .298 clip. Timlin averages nearly eight strikeouts per nine innings, getting the rest of his outs on ground balls. He also allows nine-inning averages of about eight hits and three and one-half walks. His biggest asset is an uncanny ability to keep the ball down, and in the park. Timlin threw only one gopher ball in 1995. Signed as a starter in 1987, Timlin became a full-time reliever three years later. He had 22 saves and a 1.43 ERA in his only season as a minor-league closer. He's been a set-up man since reaching the majors in 1991.

Major League Pitching Register

	W	L	ERA	G	S	IP	H	ER	BB	SO
91 AL	11	6	3.16	63	3	108.1	94	38	50	85
92 AL	0	2	4.12	26	1	43.2	45	20	20	35
93 AL	4	2	4.69	54	1	55.2	63	29	27	49
94 AL	0	1	5.17	34	2	40.0	41	23	20	38
95 AL	4	3	2.14	31	5	42.0	38	10	17	36
Life	19	14	3.73	208	12	289.2	281	120	134	243
3 AVE	3	2	4.11	46	3	53.1	55	24	25	48

CURRENT PLAYERS

OZZIE TIMMONS

Position: Outfield
Team: Chicago Cubs
Born: Sept. 18, 1970 Tampa, FL
Height: 6'2" **Weight:** 205 lbs.
Bats: right **Throws:** right
Acquired: Fifth-round pick in 6/91 free-agent draft

Player Summary	
Fantasy Value	$4 to $6
Card Value	8¢ to 12¢
Will	seek regular spot
Can't	hit right-handers
Expect	pretty good power
Don't Expect	spectacular glove

After hitting 22 home runs at Triple-A Iowa in 1994, Timmons was handed a piece of the Cubs' left-field job last spring. After spending half the season in a right-left platoon with Scott Bullett, however, the team decided to scrap the experiment. Luis Gonzalez, acquired from Houston in midseason, became the full-time occupant of the position. Timmons was not a total washout; his .315 batting average against left-handed pitching was good enough to get another look. But he'll have to improve against righties (.203) if he wants to be anything more than a right-handed pinch hitter or platoon man. Timmons has good power: 42 percent of his hits last year went for extra bases. His problem is making contact. Timmons fanned nearly three times more than he walked. As a result, he does not have a good on-base percentage. Timmons doesn't steal many bases or add much defense to the lineup. In fact, his arm is too weak to allow him to play anywhere but left field. The University of Tampa product is in the big leagues strictly because of his bat. Timmons launched his pro career at Geneva, New York, in 1991.

Major League Batting Register

	BA	G	AB	R	H	2B	3B	HR	RBI	SB
95 NL	.263	77	171	30	45	10	1	8	28	3
Life	.263	77	171	30	45	10	1	8	28	3

LEE TINSLEY

Position: Outfield
Team: Boston Red Sox
Born: March 4, 1969 Shelbyville, KY
Height: 5'10" **Weight:** 185 lbs.
Bats: both **Throws:** right
Acquired: Traded by Mariners for Jim Smith, 3/94

Player Summary	
Fantasy Value	$7 to $9
Card Value	8¢ to 12¢
Will	use speed better
Can't	hit lefties hard
Expect	more playing time
Don't Expect	Rickey Henderson

Once called "little Rickey" because he's a speedy leadoff type who plays the outfield, Tinsley showed only flashes of Henderson's abilities last season. A better hitter against righties (.296) than lefties (.250), the switch-hitting Tinsley wound up sharing center field with Troy O'Leary, Willie McGee, and Dwayne Hosey. Tinsley's 2-1 ratio of strikeouts to walks did not earn him many points as a leadoff man. He did, however, hit the team's first leadoff homer since 1993 and produce a pair of four-hit games. Basically a slap hitter who specializes in singles, he gets an occasional extra-base hit. However, Oakland's former first-round draft choice still needs to better make use of his speed. Though he stole 18 bases, second on the Red Sox last season, he was also thrown out eight times. Tinsley's speed gives him good range in center but his arm is weak. The jury is still out about his bat. Tinsley hit .407 during a season-opening, 14-game hitting streak last year but then cooled sharply. With runners in scoring position, his career mark is .301.

Major League Batting Register

	BA	G	AB	R	H	2B	3B	HR	RBI	SB
93 AL	.158	11	19	2	3	1	0	1	2	0
94 AL	.222	78	144	27	32	4	0	2	14	13
95 AL	.284	100	341	61	97	17	1	7	41	18
Life	.262	189	504	90	132	22	1	10	57	31

CURRENT PLAYERS

SALOMON TORRES

Position: Pitcher
Team: Seattle Mariners
Born: March 11, 1972 San Pedro de Macoris, Dominican Republic
Height: 5'11" **Weight:** 165 lbs.
Bats: right **Throws:** right
Acquired: Traded by Giants for Shawn Estes and Wilson Delgado, 5/95

Player Summary	
Fantasy Value	$0
Card Value	5¢ to 8¢
Will	calm righty bats
Can't	find strike zone
Expect	another audition
Don't Expect	high whiff count

The tarnish is gathering around the Torres star. A once-brilliant prospect in the San Francisco system, he was traumatized by his forced entry into the 1993 NL West pennant chase. His misfortune at suffering all four losses during the club's 14-4 streak, left the team with 103 victories and one game behind Atlanta. Torres hasn't been the same since. His ERA has risen three years in a row, and one team has already thrown in the towel. Since he's just 24 years old, Torres could resurrect his fortunes, or he could join the long list of "can't miss" products who did. He throws a fastball, a slider, a curve, and a changeup, but he doesn't always show good control. Though he held righties to a .232 average last year, he threw one dozen gopher balls in 72 innings and wound up with a bloated ERA. Torres has learned to get help from his defense. But his inability to hit the right spots has sabotaged those efforts. Torres is a decent fielder but needs to work on holding runners.

Major League Pitching Register

	W	L	ERA	G	CG	IP	H	ER	BB	SO
93 NL	3	5	4.03	8	0	44.2	37	20	27	23
94 NL	2	8	5.44	16	1	84.1	95	51	34	42
95 NL	0	1	9.00	4	0	8.0	13	8	7	2
95 AL	3	8	6.00	16	1	72.0	87	48	42	45
Life	8	22	5.47	44	2	209.0	232	127	110	112
2 AVE	3	11	5.81	23	1	104.1	123	67	52	56

STEVE TRACHSEL

Position: Pitcher
Team: Chicago Cubs
Born: Oct. 31, 1970 Oxnard, CA
Height: 6'4" **Weight:** 205 lbs.
Bats: right **Throws:** right
Acquired: Eighth-round pick in 6/91 free-agent draft

Player Summary	
Fantasy Value	$6 to $8
Card Value	8¢ to 12¢
Will	seek '94 form
Can't	win home games
Expect	help from bat
Don't Expect	great control

The promise of Trachsel's rookie year disappeared overnight. He worked five or less innings in 13 of his 29 starts and threw 25 home run balls, second most in the National League. His best games were a 6-1 three-hitter at San Francisco on May 15, and a 1-0 loss to San Diego on June 21. Trachsel's inability to win at home has been a major mystery. His career mark at Wrigley Field now stands at 3-16. Trachsel throws a fastball, a big-breaking curve, and a forkball that he uses as a changeup. But he doesn't always throw them for strikes. His nine-inning average of four-plus walks last year was the worst among the Cubs' five starters. Trachsel also has trouble with right-handed hitters (.299) and with base-stealers (20 out of 26 made it). The Long Beach State product isn't much of a fielder but often helps himself with his hitting. His 13-for-49 effort last year produced a .265 average and included two doubles, four RBI, and six sacrifice bunts. He had two doubles in a game Aug. 4. He pitched a minor-league no-hitter in 1991.

Major League Pitching Register

	W	L	ERA	G	CG	IP	H	ER	BB	SO
93 NL	0	2	4.58	3	0	19.2	16	10	3	14
94 NL	9	7	3.21	22	1	146.0	133	52	54	108
95 NL	7	13	5.15	30	2	160.2	174	92	76	117
Life	16	22	4.25	55	3	326.1	323	154	133	239
2 AVE	10	12	4.12	32	2	193.1	192	88	81	142

CURRENT PLAYERS

ALAN TRAMMELL

Position: Shortstop
Team: Detroit Tigers
Born: Feb. 21, 1958 Garden Grove, CA
Height: 6′ **Weight:** 185 lbs.
Bats: right **Throws:** right
Acquired: Second-round pick in 6/76 free-agent draft

Player Summary	
Fantasy Value	$1 to $3
Card Value	10¢ to 15¢
Will	make choice
Can't	dazzle with glove
Expect	Hall of Fame notice
Don't Expect	easy retirement

Last year, Trammell and second baseman Lou Whitaker appeared for the 1,918 time, an AL record for teammates and a major-league record for a double-play combination. The Tigers held a retirement party for Trammell, but he didn't say that he was going to hang up his spikes. At the end of the season, he said he would see whether he was coming back to the Tigers. He really didn't have bad numbers in 1995. Trammell was one of the best shortstops of the 1980s. Is he a Hall of Famer? He has made six All-Star teams, won four Gold Gloves, and was named the 1984 World Series MVP.

Major League Batting Register

	BA	G	AB	R	H	2B	3B	HR	RBI	SB
77 AL	.186	19	43	6	8	0	0	0	0	0
78 AL	.268	139	448	49	120	14	6	2	34	3
79 AL	.276	142	460	68	127	11	4	6	50	17
80 AL	.300	146	560	107	168	21	5	9	65	12
81 AL	.258	105	392	52	101	15	3	2	31	10
82 AL	.258	157	489	66	126	34	3	9	57	19
83 AL	.319	142	505	83	161	31	2	14	66	30
84 AL	.314	139	555	85	174	34	5	14	69	19
85 AL	.258	149	605	79	156	21	7	13	57	14
86 AL	.277	151	574	107	159	33	7	21	75	25
87 AL	.343	151	597	109	205	34	3	28	105	21
88 AL	.311	128	466	73	145	24	1	15	69	7
89 AL	.243	121	449	54	109	20	3	5	43	10
90 AL	.304	146	559	71	170	37	1	14	89	12
91 AL	.248	101	375	57	93	20	0	9	55	11
92 AL	.275	29	102	11	28	7	1	1	11	2
93 AL	.329	112	401	72	132	25	3	12	60	12
94 AL	.267	76	292	38	78	17	1	8	28	3
95 AL	.269	74	223	28	60	12	0	2	23	3
Life	.287	2227	8095	1215	2320	410	55	184	987	220
3 AVE	.291	101	354	52	103	21	1	9	42	7

MIKE TROMBLEY

Position: Pitcher
Team: Minnesota Twins
Born: April 14, 1967 Springfield, MA
Height: 6′2″ **Weight:** 208 lbs.
Bats: right **Throws:** right
Acquired: 14th-round pick in 6/89 free-agent draft

Player Summary	
Fantasy Value	$0
Card Value	4¢ to 6¢
Will	get another chance
Can't	avoid gopher balls
Expect	trouble vs. lefties
Don't Expect	double-digit wins

During four stints with the Twins, Trombley has emitted mixed signals. He's been good at times, bad at others. Effective as a rookie starter in 1992, he had less success as a swingman a year later. He was abysmal as a reliever in '94 and not much better as a starter last year. Trombley features a fastball, a curve, and a changeup but doesn't always throw them for strikes (almost four walks per nine innings last year, opposed to six-plus strikeouts per game). Effective against right-handed hitters (.243), Trombley has trouble with southpaws (.297). When he doesn't keep his pitches down, he also has problems preventing the long ball (18 in 97⅔ innings). The former Duke standout yields just over one hit per inning. But his lack of success against southpaws, plus his penchant for throwing a fat pitch at the wrong time, has resulted in an inferior win-loss record. A big winner and two-time strikeout king in the minors, Trombley still has potential. He pitched a minor-league no-hitter in 1991.

Major League Pitching Register

	W	L	ERA	CG	S	IP	H	ER	BB	SO
92 AL	3	2	3.30	10	0	46.1	43	17	17	38
93 AL	6	6	4.88	44	0	114.1	131	62	41	85
94 AL	2	0	6.33	24	0	48.1	56	34	18	32
95 AL	4	8	5.62	20	0	97.2	107	61	42	68
Life	15	16	5.11	98	0	306.2	337	174	118	223
3 AVE	4	5	5.50	33	0	97.2	110	60	38	69

CURRENT PLAYERS

TOM URBANI

Position: Pitcher
Team: St. Louis Cardinals
Born: Jan. 21, 1968 Santa Cruz, CA
Height: 6'1" **Weight:** 190 lbs.
Bats: left **Throws:** left
Acquired: 13th-round pick in 6/90 free-agent draft

Player Summary	
Fantasy Value	$1
Card Value	5¢ to 8¢
Will	keep swing spot
Can't	retire righties
Expect	lots of finesse
Don't Expect	many strikeouts

During his three years in the big leagues, Urbani has been used as a swingman—starting against Atlanta and teams top-heavy with left-handed hitters, but otherwise pitching out of the bullpen. A control artist from Long Beach State, Urbani made 13 starts and 11 relief outings last year, with decidedly mixed results. Though he threw 11 home run balls in 82⅔ innings and yielded a nine-inning average of 10.78 hits, he emerged with a respectable ERA of 3.70. He is a sinker-slider pitcher who relies on deception and location; he throws more like Lyndon Johnson than Randy Johnson. In 1995, Urbani averaged five and one-half strikeouts per nine innings, giving him a 2-1 ratio of strikeouts to walks. He held left-handers to a .243 average. Since righties lit him up at a .323 clip, Urbani probably falls into the Paul Assenmacher category: a good guy to try when the team needs to retire one or two left-handed hitters. Urbani helps himself with a fine pickoff move, good fielding skills, and an ability to swing the bat.

ISMAEL VALDES

Position: Pitcher
Team: Los Angeles Dodgers
Born: Aug. 21, 1973 Victoria, Mexico
Height: 6'3" **Weight:** 183 lbs.
Bats: right **Throws:** right
Acquired: Signed as a free agent, 6/91

Player Summary	
Fantasy Value	$14 to $17
Card Value	6¢ to 10¢
Will	show improvement
Can't	hold baserunners
Expect	few walks
Don't Expect	erratic control

After opening the 1995 season in the bullpen, Valdes became a regular starter May 16 and responded with a strong season. He finished second on the Dodgers to Hideo Nomo in ERA and tied Nomo for second to Ramon Martinez in victories. Valdes not only reached the eighth inning in 14 of his 27 starts but went on to lead the Dodgers with six complete games. Two of them were shutouts. A good control pitcher, he walked two batters or less in 23 of his 33 appearances. He fanned a career-peak 11 batters in a game on Aug. 16, and he pitched 16 straight scoreless innings, also a career high, in September. He is a sinker-slider pitcher who also throws a forkball and a curveball. Valdes shows unusual poise for a man of such limited experience. He yields less hits than innings, maintains a 3-1 ratio of strikeouts to walks, and is equally effective against righties and lefties (both hit .228 against him last year). A power pitcher who's prone to hot and cold streaks, Valdes has trouble holding runners close. He's competent in the field and not too shabby at the plate.

Major League Pitching Register

	W	L	ERA	G	S	IP	H	ER	BB	SO
93 NL	1	3	4.65	18	0	62.0	73	32	26	33
94 NL	3	7	5.15	20	0	80.1	98	46	21	43
95 NL	3	5	3.70	24	0	82.2	99	34	21	52
Life	7	15	4.48	62	0	225.0	270	112	68	128
3 AVE	3	6	4.53	24	0	89.1	107	45	26	51

Major League Pitching Register

	W	L	ERA	G	CG	IP	H	ER	BB	SO
94 NL	3	1	3.18	21	0	28.1	21	10	10	28
95 NL	13	11	3.05	33	6	197.2	168	67	51	150
Life	16	12	3.07	54	6	226.0	189	77	61	178

CURRENT PLAYERS

JOHN VALENTIN

Position: Shortstop
Team: Boston Red Sox
Born: Feb. 18, 1967 Mineola, NY
Height: 6' **Weight:** 170 lbs.
Bats: right **Throws:** right
Acquired: Fifth-round pick in 6/88 free-agent draft

Player Summary	
Fantasy Value	$19 to $22
Card Value	10¢ to 15¢
Will	get on
Can't	make perfect throws
Expect	speed, power
Don't Expect	weak clutch bat

Suddenly last summer, Valentin became the best all-around shortstop in the AL. He finished with career highs in home runs, RBI, runs scored, hits, walks, total bases, and stolen bases. On the way, he became the fourth 20-20 player in Red Sox history. The former Team USA star also became the fifth shortstop in big-league history to hit three home runs in a game (June 2 vs. Seattle). His single and double that same day gave him a 5-for-5 performance and 15 total bases, most by any shortstop. Valentin began August with a six-RBI game at Detroit and finished it with a .319 average for the month. A great clutch hitter, Valentin tied the game or put the Bosox ahead with 27 of his RBI. Because he makes contact and walks, Valentin is a good No. 2 hitter. His .399 on-base percentage was second to Tim Naehring's .415 among the Red Sox regulars. Valentin has quick reactions, good range, and a strong—though not always accurate—throwing arm. A third-team All-American at Seton Hall, Valentin was a college teammate of Mo Vaughn.

Major League Batting Register

	BA	G	AB	R	H	2B	3B	HR	RBI	SB
92 AL	.276	58	185	21	51	13	0	5	25	1
93 AL	.278	144	468	50	130	40	3	11	66	3
94 AL	.316	84	301	53	95	26	2	9	49	3
95 AL	.298	135	520	108	155	37	2	27	102	20
Life	.292	421	1474	232	431	116	7	52	242	27
3 AVE	.297	138	492	82	146	39	3	18	83	10

JOSE VALENTIN

Position: Shortstop
Team: Milwaukee Brewers
Born: Oct. 12, 1969 Manati, PR
Height: 5'10" **Weight:** 175 lbs.
Bats: both **Throws:** right
Acquired: Traded by Padres with Ricky Bones and Matt Mieske for Gary Sheffield and Geoff Kellogg, 3/92

Player Summary	
Fantasy Value	$8 to $10
Card Value	5¢ to 8¢
Will	make great plays
Can't	hit left-handers
Expect	surprising power
Don't Expect	patient at bats

The results of the last two seasons should convince Valentin that he's not cut out for switch-hitting. He hit .135 against lefties in 1994 and .133 last year. No wonder he wound up sharing the shortstop job with Pat Listach and rookie Mark Loretta. For a guy with a little strike zone, Valentin needs to work more walks. If he stops lunging at bad pitches, his average will increase, and he could make better use of his baserunning ability. Valentin led the Brewers with 16 steals last year but can do much better. He has some power too—primarily right-handed pitching. Exactly half of his hits last season—37 out of 74—went for extra bases. A pull hitter against lefties, Valentin is much more successful when he uses all fields, his game-plan against righties. But his forte is fielding. Valentin led several leagues in chances, putouts, assists, and double plays. He has good instincts, exceptional range, soft hands, and a reliable throwing arm. He's widely considered one of the league's better defensive shortstops.

Major League Batting Register

	BA	G	AB	R	H	2B	3B	HR	RBI	SB
92 AL	.000	4	3	1	0	0	0	0	1	0
93 AL	.245	19	53	10	13	1	2	1	7	1
94 AL	.239	97	285	47	68	19	0	11	46	12
95 AL	.219	112	338	62	74	23	3	11	49	16
Life	.228	232	679	120	155	43	5	23	103	29
2 AVE	.229	131	391	68	90	26	2	14	60	17

CURRENT PLAYERS

FERNANDO VALENZUELA

Position: Pitcher
Team: San Diego Padres
Born: Nov. 1, 1960 Navojoa, Mexico
Height: 5'11" **Weight:** 202 lbs.
Bats: left **Throws:** left
Acquired: Signed as a free agent, 4/95

Player Summary	
Fantasy Value	$0
Card Value	4¢ to 6¢
Will	show good control
Can't	find old fastball
Expect	berth in rotation
Don't Expect	high whiff totals

After bouncing between the majors, the minors, and the Mexican League for four seasons, Valenzuela regained his foothold in the big leagues last summer. Signed by San Diego, he finished with the best winning percentage on the staff. Though he yielded more hits and homers than management would like, Valenzuela showed good control and kept the running game in check. By the end of the year, Valenzuela was San Diego's most consistent starter. A screwball specialist who also throws a sinker, a curve, and a change, Valenzuela has made a smooth transition from power to finesse. He helps his own cause with good defensive skills and an ability to hit. He won the Cy Young Award and Rookie of the Year Award in the same season (1981).

Major League Pitching Register

	W	L	ERA	G	CG	IP	H	ER	BB	SO
80 NL	2	0	0.00	10	0	17.2	8	0	5	16
81 NL	13	7	2.48	25	11	192.1	140	53	61	180
82 NL	19	13	2.87	37	18	285.0	247	91	83	199
83 NL	15	10	3.75	35	9	257.0	245	107	99	189
84 NL	12	17	3.03	34	12	261.0	218	88	106	240
85 NL	17	10	2.45	35	14	272.1	211	74	101	208
86 NL	21	11	3.14	34	20	269.1	226	94	85	242
87 NL	14	14	3.98	34	12	251.0	254	111	124	190
88 NL	5	8	4.24	23	3	142.1	142	67	76	64
89 NL	10	13	3.43	31	3	196.2	185	75	98	116
90 NL	13	13	4.59	33	5	204.0	223	104	77	115
91 AL	0	2	12.15	2	0	6.2	14	9	3	5
93 AL	8	10	4.94	32	5	178.2	179	98	79	78
94 NL	1	2	3.00	8	0	45.0	42	15	7	19
95 NL	8	3	4.98	29	0	90.1	101	50	34	57
Life	158	133	3.49	402	112	2669.1	2435	1036	1038	1918
2 AVE	9	7	4.95	32	3	140.2	146	77	59	71

DAVE VALLE

Position: Catcher
Team: Texas Rangers
Born: Oct. 30, 1960 Bayside, NY
Height: 6'2" **Weight:** 220 lbs.
Bats: right **Throws:** right
Acquired: Signed as a free agent, 12/94

Player Summary	
Fantasy Value	$0
Card Value	4¢ to 6¢
Will	supply strong defense
Can't	boost batting average
Expect	some power
Don't Expect	a regular job

Though he excels on defense, Valle has had more valleys than peaks as a hitter. He carried a batting average of .235 into 1995 and hit only five points higher. But he failed to homer in 75 at bats after reaching double-digits in three previous seasons. Granted, he saw limited playing time behind Pudge Rodriguez, but Valle also failed miserably against left-handers, sinking to .188 one year after stroking southpaws at a .265 clip. His usual patience was missing last year, when he fanned three times more than he walked. Valle's glove remains his main calling card. He nailed 33 percent of would-be basestealers last season and has led the AL in putouts, fielding percentage, and double plays by a catcher. He calls a good game, handles pitchers well, prevents wild pitches, and guards the plate against incoming runners.

Major League Batting Register

	BA	G	AB	R	H	2B	3B	HR	RBI	SB
84 AL	.296	13	27	4	8	1	0	1	4	0
85 AL	.157	31	70	2	11	1	0	0	4	0
86 AL	.340	22	53	10	18	3	0	5	15	0
87 AL	.256	95	324	40	83	16	3	12	53	2
88 AL	.231	93	290	29	67	15	2	10	50	0
89 AL	.237	94	316	32	75	10	3	7	34	0
90 AL	.214	107	308	37	66	15	0	7	33	1
91 AL	.194	132	324	38	63	8	1	8	32	0
92 AL	.240	124	367	39	88	16	1	9	30	0
93 AL	.258	135	423	48	109	19	0	13	63	1
94 AL	.232	46	112	14	26	8	1	2	10	0
95 AL	.240	36	75	7	18	3	0	0	5	1
Life	.235	928	2689	300	632	115	11	74	333	5

CURRENT PLAYERS

JOHN VANDER WAL

Position: Outfield; first base
Team: Colorado Rockies
Born: April 29, 1966 Grand Rapids, MI
Height: 6'2" **Weight:** 190 lbs.
Bats: left **Throws:** left
Acquired: Purchased from Expos, 3/94

Player Summary	
Fantasy Value	$1 to $3
Card Value	4¢ to 6¢
Will	deliver in clutch
Can't	excel on defense
Expect	pinch-hit success
Don't Expect	much work vs. lefties

Vander Wal had three ordinary seasons as a backup outfielder and reserve first baseman before blossoming into baseball's best pinch hitter last summer. He banged 28 pinch hits, three more than the 1976 major-league record of Jose Morales, while providing serious power off the bench. Forty percent of Vander Wal's hits went for extra bases, and he finished with .400 averages at home and against left-handed pitchers. Vander Wal's .344 average against righties wasn't too shabby either, especially since he was most often used against right-handers. Vander Wal was consistent all year. At one point, he even produced pinch hits in four consecutive appearances. A low-ball hitter with a good eye, Vander Wal has led the majors in pinch hits and pinch at bats two years in a row. He's not much of a basestealer but moves well enough to cover some ground in the outfield. He's best in left because his arm strength and accuracy are only average. First base is his best position because of his good hands.

Major League Batting Register

	BA	G	AB	R	H	2B	3B	HR	RBI	SB
91 NL	.213	21	61	4	13	4	1	1	8	0
92 NL	.239	105	213	21	51	8	2	4	20	3
93 NL	.233	106	215	34	50	7	4	5	30	6
94 NL	.245	91	110	12	27	3	1	5	15	2
95 NL	.347	105	101	15	35	8	1	5	21	1
Life	.251	428	700	86	176	30	9	20	94	12

WILLIAM VanLANDINGHAM

Position: Pitcher
Team: San Francisco Giants
Born: July 16, 1970 Columbia, TN
Height: 6'2" **Weight:** 210 lbs.
Bats: right **Throws:** right
Acquired: Fifth-round pick in 6/91 free-agent draft

Player Summary	
Fantasy Value	$8 to $10
Card Value	10¢ to 15¢
Will	win when healthy
Can't	hold baserunners
Expect	superb curveball
Don't Expect	hits by righties

Although he avoided the sophomore jinx, VanLandingham did not avoid the injury jinx that struck the San Francisco pitching staff last summer. In 18 starts, the former minor-league strikeout king showed he was the most effective member of the rotation (his 3.67 ERA led the ballclub). The hard-throwing VanLandingham allowed one hit per inning, seven strikeouts per nine innings, and less than three walks over the same span. A sinker-slider pitcher whose best pitch is an overhand curve, VanLandingham rattles right-handed hitters (.230 last year) but has trouble with lefties (.304). Occasional gopher balls and would-be basestealers also pose problems for him. All but four of the 17 runners who challenged him last year were successful. The one-time University of Kentucky standout is a competent defensive player otherwise. He's not much of a hitter, however. A lifelong starter, VanLandingham has made only two relief outings in a pro career that started in the Northwest League in 1991. Three years later, he won eight of his first 10 big-league decisions.

Major League Pitching Register

	W	L	ERA	G	CG	IP	H	ER	BB	SO
94 NL	8	2	3.54	16	0	84.0	70	33	43	56
95 NL	6	3	3.67	18	1	122.2	124	50	40	95
Life	14	5	3.61	34	1	206.2	194	83	83	151
2 AVE	9	3	3.61	21	1	128.1	119	51	53	93

CURRENT PLAYERS

TODD VAN POPPEL

Position: Pitcher
Team: Oakland Athletics
Born: Dec. 9, 1971 Hinsdale, IL
Height: 6'5" **Weight:** 210 lbs.
Bats: right **Throws:** right
Acquired: First-round pick in 6/90 free-agent draft

Player Summary
Fantasy Value	$4 to $6
Card Value	5¢ to 8¢
Will	realize promise
Can't	prevent gophers
Expect	improved record
Don't Expect	refined control

Van Poppel is still undergoing on-the-job training. He's been a starter, reliever, and starter again, but he has been betrayed by lack of control. The 14th player selected in the 1990 free-agent draft, Van Poppel held AL hitters to a .244 average last summer. But he has made only minor inroads toward solving his gopher problems. At least he has improved his strikeout-to-walk ratio to better than 2-to-1. His ratio of walks per nine innings also fell. A power pitcher who fanned nearly eight batters per nine innings, Van Poppel throws a fastball and a curve, and a change with a three-quarters motion that suggests Rick Sutcliffe. But Van Poppel is far from achieving Sutcliffe's results. Van Poppel's fielding and pickoff move are average, and his pitching is well below that. But there are some signs of improvement. Van Poppel hasn't been as successful as Chipper Jones—the player the Braves drafted when their first choice, Van Poppel, assured them he would opt for college over pro ball.

Major League Pitching Register
	W	L	ERA	G	CG	IP	H	ER	BB	SO
91 AL	0	0	9.64	1	0	4.2	7	5	2	6
93 AL	6	6	5.04	16	0	84.0	76	47	62	47
94 AL	7	10	6.09	23	0	116.2	108	79	89	83
95 AL	4	8	4.88	36	1	138.1	125	75	56	122
Life	17	24	5.39	76	1	343.2	316	206	209	258
3 AVE	7	10	5.41	30	0	134.1	123	81	83	100

ANDY VAN SLYKE

Position: Outfield
Team: Philadelphia Phillies
Born: Dec. 21, 1960 Utica, NY
Height: 6'2" **Weight:** 198 lbs.
Bats: left **Throws:** right
Acquired: Traded by Orioles for Gene Harris, 7/95

Player Summary
Fantasy Value	$1
Card Value	6¢ to 10¢
Will	play solid defense
Can't	recapture old form
Expect	patience at plate
Don't Expect	bat to catch fire

Age and injuries have taken their toll on Van Slyke. Plagued by a bad back, the three-time All-Star and five-time Gold Glove winner is no longer the player who reached double-digits in doubles, triples, and homers in 1988. Even at his peak, Van Slyke had trouble hitting lefties. Last year, when he hit .200 against NL southpaws in limited action, was no exception. His good eye helps to compensate; Van Slyke draws enough walks to push his on-base percentage nearly 100 points higher than his batting average. His power and speed are both on the decline, however. Van Slyke never has that problem while wearing a glove. He's lost a step but still reacts well, makes difficult catches look easy, and makes strong throws.

Major League Batting Register
	BA	G	AB	R	H	2B	3B	HR	RBI	SB
83 NL	.262	101	309	51	81	15	5	8	38	21
84 NL	.244	137	361	45	88	16	4	7	50	28
85 NL	.259	146	424	61	110	25	6	13	55	34
86 NL	.270	137	418	48	113	23	7	13	61	21
87 NL	.293	157	564	93	165	36	11	21	82	34
88 NL	.288	154	587	101	169	23	15	25	100	30
89 NL	.237	130	476	64	113	18	9	9	53	16
90 NL	.284	136	493	67	140	26	6	17	77	14
91 NL	.265	138	491	87	130	24	7	17	83	10
92 NL	.324	154	614	103	199	45	12	14	89	12
93 NL	.310	83	323	42	100	13	4	8	50	11
94 NL	.246	105	374	41	92	18	3	6	30	7
95 AL	.159	17	63	6	10	1	0	3	8	0
95 NL	.243	63	214	26	52	10	2	3	16	7
Life	.274	1658	5711	835	1562	293	91	164	792	245
3 AVE	.258	107	387	45	100	17	3	8	40	10

CURRENT PLAYERS

GREG VAUGHN

Position: Outfield
Team: Milwaukee Brewers
Born: July 3, 1965 Sacramento, CA
Height: 6′ **Weight:** 205 lbs.
Bats: right **Throws:** right
Acquired: Fourth-round pick in 6/86 free-agent draft

Player Summary	
Fantasy Value	$14 to $17
Card Value	5¢ to 8¢
Will	try to shake slump
Can't	reduce strikeouts
Expect	better homer total
Don't Expect	return to outfield

Vaughn's home run total and batting average continued their downward spiral in 1995 for the third straight season. Last year, he fell victim to a season-long slump that included a second-half benching for a solid week. It didn't help. Right-handers overpowered him all year, holding him to a .215 average, and he hit only .187 on the road. Recent shoulder surgery may have sapped Vaughn's strength; after hitting a career-best 30 homers in 1993, he slipped to 19 a year later and 17 last year. The surgery also prevented him from taking his usual station in left field. All of his 104 appearances last year were in the DH spot. Vaughn would be more valuable if he made more contact. He's topped 110 strikeouts in a season three times and would have made it last year too if he saw more action. At least he draws enough walks to boost his on-base percentage almost 100 points higher than his batting average. His return to the field is dubious but that's no loss.

Major League Batting Register

	BA	G	AB	R	H	2B	3B	HR	RBI	SB
89 AL	.265	38	113	18	30	3	0	5	23	4
90 AL	.220	120	382	51	84	26	2	17	61	7
91 AL	.244	145	542	81	132	24	5	27	98	2
92 AL	.228	141	501	77	114	18	2	23	78	15
93 AL	.267	154	569	97	152	28	2	30	97	10
94 AL	.254	95	370	59	94	24	1	19	55	9
95 AL	.224	108	392	67	88	19	1	17	59	10
Life	.242	801	2869	450	694	142	13	138	471	57
3 AVE	.250	136	510	85	128	28	2	25	80	11

MO VAUGHN

Position: First base
Team: Boston Red Sox
Born: Dec. 15, 1967 Norwalk, CT
Height: 6′1″ **Weight:** 230 lbs.
Bats: left **Throws:** right
Acquired: First-round pick in 6/89 free-agent draft

Player Summary	
Fantasy Value	$35 to $40
Card Value	15¢ to 25¢
Will	bury right-handers
Can't	avoid strikeouts
Expect	excitement
Don't Expect	stalwart defense

After watching his 1995 performance, it's hard to believe 22 players were selected ahead of Mo Vaughn in the 1989 amateur draft. The three-time Seton Hall All-American knocked in 126 runs, tied for first in the AL and the most by a Boston player since Jim Rice had 130 in 1979. Vaughn's 39 homers (three of them grand slams) tied for fourth in the league, his 315 total bases ranked fifth, and his 98 runs scored tied for 10th. No wonder he was voted the loop's MVP. Though Vaughn led the majors with 150 strikeouts, he hit when it counted: He batted .338 with runners in scoring position and .600 (9-for-15) with the bases loaded. Thirty-two of his RBI tied the score or put the Red Sox ahead. Vaughn is most dangerous when the opposing pitcher is right-handed (.322, 33 homers, 95 RBI). Vaughn had two homers in a game four times last year. No longer trying to pull every pitch, Vaughn hits with power to all fields. His mobility, footwork, and fielding at first base are often faulty.

Major League Batting Register

	BA	G	AB	R	H	2B	3B	HR	RBI	SB
91 AL	.260	74	219	21	57	12	0	4	32	2
92 AL	.234	113	355	42	83	16	2	13	57	3
93 AL	.297	152	539	86	160	34	1	29	101	4
94 AL	.310	111	394	65	122	25	1	26	82	4
95 AL	.300	140	550	98	165	28	3	39	126	11
Life	.285	590	2057	312	587	115	7	111	398	24
3 AVE	.302	155	571	96	172	34	2	37	119	7

CURRENT PLAYERS

RANDY VELARDE

Position: Infield; outfield
Team: California Angels
Born: Nov. 24, 1962 Midland, TX
Height: 6' **Weight:** 192 lbs.
Bats: right **Throws:** right
Acquired: Signed as a free agent, 11/95

Player Summary	
Fantasy Value	$6 to $8
Card Value	4¢ to 6¢
Will	fill a few holes
Can't	steal many bases
Expect	extra-base hits
Don't Expect	weak bat vs. lefties

One of baseball's most versatile players, Velarde made 53 starts at second, 24 at short, 13 at third, 14 in left field, and one in right last year. Yet he did not make an error in 40 games after Aug. 15. Velarde hit safely in 40 of his last 42 games, a .291 pace, and finished the year by slugging home runs for his final two hits. Velarde's value extends far beyond his versatility. He's a pesky little hitter who draws an enormous number of walks. A high-ball hitter who loves left-handers, Velarde delivers a surprising number of extra-base hits. That production, plus his good eye, helped him compile a .375 on-base percentage. Velarde moves well enough in the field at second, short, third, and the outfield. He also has quick reactions, good hands, and an adequate arm. He has played every position but catcher and pitcher.

Major League Batting Register

	BA	G	AB	R	H	2B	3B	HR	RBI	SB
87 AL	.182	8	22	1	4	0	0	0	1	0
88 AL	.174	48	115	18	20	6	0	5	12	1
89 AL	.340	33	100	12	34	4	2	2	11	0
90 AL	.210	95	229	21	48	6	2	5	19	0
91 AL	.245	80	184	19	45	11	1	1	15	3
92 AL	.272	121	412	57	112	24	1	7	46	7
93 AL	.301	85	226	28	68	13	2	7	24	2
94 AL	.279	77	280	47	78	16	1	9	34	4
95 AL	.278	111	367	60	102	19	1	7	46	5
Life	.264	658	1935	263	511	99	10	43	208	22
3 AVE	.283	106	344	54	98	19	2	9	41	4

ROBIN VENTURA

Position: Third base
Team: Chicago White Sox
Born: July 14, 1967 Santa Maria, CA
Height: 6'1" **Weight:** 198 lbs.
Bats: left **Throws:** right
Acquired: First-round pick in 6/88 free-agent draft

Player Summary	
Fantasy Value	$19 to $22
Card Value	10¢ to 15¢
Will	hit righties hard
Can't	steal bases often
Expect	patience at plate
Don't Expect	slumps on defense

Ventura's most recent season was the strangest of his career. The three-time Gold Glove winner began by making so many errors that the White Sox considered shifting him to first base. He ended by becoming the eighth player to connect for two grand slams in a single game (at Texas on Sept. 4). He finished with career highs in batting, home runs, RBI, and strikeouts. A former Oklahoma State All-American, Golden Spikes Award winner, and U.S. Olympian, Ventura has always been a selective hitter. He's had at least 90 walks four times in his six-year career. Ventura likes to take his whacks at low, inside fastballs but is also a team player who will sacrifice or work the hit-and-run to move runners along. A solid .300 hitter against right-handed pitching, Ventura has improved his work against southpaws in recent seasons. In the field, Ventura has quick reactions, soft hands, and a strong arm.

Major League Batting Register

	BA	G	AB	R	H	2B	3B	HR	RBI	SB
89 AL	.178	16	45	5	8	3	0	0	7	0
90 AL	.249	150	493	48	123	17	1	5	54	1
91 AL	.284	157	606	92	172	25	1	23	100	2
92 AL	.282	157	592	85	167	38	1	16	93	2
93 AL	.262	157	554	85	145	27	1	22	94	1
94 AL	.282	109	401	57	113	15	1	18	78	3
95 AL	.295	135	492	79	145	22	0	26	93	4
Life	.274	881	3183	451	873	147	5	110	519	13
3 AVE	.279	154	557	85	156	24	1	26	103	3

CURRENT PLAYERS

QUILVIO VERAS

Position: Second base
Team: Florida Marlins
Born: April 3, 1971 Santo Domingo, Dominican Republic
Height: 5'9" **Weight:** 166 lbs.
Bats: both **Throws:** right
Acquired: Traded by Mets for Carl Everett, 11/94

Player Summary	
Fantasy Value	$11 to $14
Card Value	12¢ to 20¢
Will	run like a deer
Can't	hit many homers
Expect	top leadoff job
Don't Expect	flawless defense

Though it drew yawns at the time, the deal that made Veras a Marlin truly helped both teams. While the diminutive second baseman led the NL in stolen bases, fellow freshman Carl Everett made an impression with the Mets. A switch-hitter who's better against right-handers, Veras is a good leadoff man because he's willing to wait for walks. He had 80 walks and 68 strikeouts last year, helping him build a .384 on-base percentage, second only to Gary Sheffield among the Marlins. Veras can fly, and he's a real nuisance when he gets on base. He filled the void created by Chuck Carr's inability to perform the same catalyst role with any consistency. Veras is still learning to read big-league pitchers and could become even more of a basestealing threat in the near future. Veras was nailed 21 times last year and would like to boost his 1995 success ratio of 73 percent. He's not much of a slugger, but he did manage extra bases on 28 percent of his hits (many of them singles he stretched). Veras has good range and makes the double-play pivot but makes more errors than the average second baseman.

Major League Batting Register

	BA	G	AB	R	H	2B	3B	HR	RBI	SB
95 NL	.261	124	440	86	115	20	7	5	32	56
Life	.261	124	440	86	115	20	7	5	32	56

DAVE VERES

Position: Pitcher
Team: Houston Astros
Born: Oct. 19, 1966 Montgomery, AL
Height: 6'2" **Weight:** 195 lbs.
Bats: right **Throws:** right
Acquired: Signed as a minor-league free agent, 5/92

Player Summary	
Fantasy Value	$4 to $6
Card Value	4¢ to 6¢
Will	show great control
Can't	strand all runners
Expect	multi-inning stints
Don't Expect	gopher-ball trouble

Veres became a bullpen workhorse in his sophomore season. He worked a career-high 72 games, tops among the Astros, with impressive results. He threw only five home run balls and held basestealers at bay. He notched almost eight hits allowed, two and one-half walks, and eight strikeouts per nine innings last year. He retired 66 percent of the runners he inherited—a figure he would like to improve. Still, he had a terrific year. None of this was expected from Veres, who had spent eight years in the minors. A sinkerballer who also throws a forkball and a slider, he pitched brilliantly as a set-up man for Todd Jones after incumbent closer John Hudek was sidelined by injury. Veres helps his own cause with a fine pickoff move and some success on the rare occasions he comes to plate. Veres can bunt and has even been known to deliver a base hit. He started his pro career in the Oakland system in 1986 but didn't become a full-time relief pitcher until six years later. He is a product of Mount Hood Community College in Oregon.

Major League Pitching Register

	W	L	ERA	G	S	IP	H	ER	BB	SO
94 NL	3	3	2.41	32	1	41.0	39	11	7	28
95 NL	5	1	2.26	72	1	103.1	89	26	30	94
Life	8	4	2.31	104	2	144.1	128	37	37	122
2 AVE	5	3	2.31	63	1	87.1	78	22	22	73

CURRENT PLAYERS

RANDY VERES

Position: Pitcher
Team: Florida Marlins
Born: Nov. 25, 1965 San Francisco, CA
Height: 6'3" **Weight:** 210 lbs.
Bats: right **Throws:** right
Acquired: Signed as a free agent, 4/95

Player Summary
```
Fantasy Value ..................... $0
Card Value ................... 4¢ to 6¢
Will................. stay in the bullpen
Can't............. keep control steady
Expect ..................... ground outs
Don't Expect ........ frequent strikeouts
```

After failing to distinguish himself in three previous big-league trials, Veres succeeded with the Marlins last summer. Though slowed by an attack of kidney stones, he worked a career-best 47 times, yielded less hits than innings pitched, and held right-handed hitters to a .246 batting average. Veres stranded 64 percent of the runners he inherited, picked up his second major-league save, and posted numbers that were good enough to merit a return invitation. If he can harness his control, his stock would improve. Veres walked more than four batters per nine innings last year. Since he's not a power pitcher—notching about five and one-half Ks per nine innings—putting extra runners on base does not help his cause. Veres does throw occasional gopher balls (six in 48⅔ innings), and that can be a fatal flaw for a relief pitcher. He also needs work holding runners; five of the six who tested him last year succeeded.

RON VILLONE

Position: Pitcher
Team: San Diego Padres
Born: Jan. 16, 1970 Englewood, NJ
Height: 6'3" **Weight:** 235 lbs.
Bats: left **Throws:** left
Acquired: Traded by Mariners with Marc Newfield for Andy Benes and Greg Keagle, 7/95

Player Summary
```
Fantasy Value ................. $1 to $3
Card Value ................. 6¢ to 10¢
Will................... throw late heat
Can't................. stop gopher balls
Expect ..................... a live arm
Don't Expect ............. a rotation role
```

No one doubts that Villone is a power pitcher. He averaged 12.97 strikeouts per nine innings in 19 games with the Padres last summer, one year after leading the Double-A Southern League with an 11.80 ratio. The former Olympian from the University of Massachusetts has an exceptional arm and a fastball to match. Used as a starter during his first pro season in 1993, he switched to relief the next year. After he held Double-A hitters to a .173 batting average, Villone was deemed ready for big-league competition. Though he was one of Seattle's top prospects, he was included in the Andy Benes swap only at the insistence of San Diego. Villone is projected as a top late-inning closer from the left side. Rookie jitters may have contributed to the gopher-ball problems Villone experienced last year. He also had first-batter troubles, leading to a poor percentage of inherited runners left stranded—almost 42 percent. But he yielded less hits than innings and showed enough control to whet San Diego's appetite. Villone was a first-round selection in 1992—the 14th player taken overall.

Major League Pitching Register

	W	L	ERA	G	S	IP	H	ER	BB	SO
89 AL	0	1	4.32	3	0	8.1	9	4	4	8
90 AL	0	3	3.67	26	1	41.2	38	17	16	16
94 NL	1	1	5.59	10	0	9.2	12	6	2	5
95 NL	4	4	3.88	47	1	48.2	46	21	22	31
Life	5	9	3.99	86	2	108.1	105	48	44	60

Major League Pitching Register

	W	L	ERA	G	S	IP	H	ER	BB	SO
95 AL	0	2	7.91	19	0	19.1	20	17	23	26
95 NL	2	1	4.21	19	1	25.2	24	12	11	37
Life	2	3	5.80	38	1	45.0	44	29	34	63

CURRENT PLAYERS

FERNANDO VINA

Position: Second base
Team: Milwaukee Brewers
Born: April 16, 1969 Sacramento, CA
Height: 5'9" **Weight:** 170 lbs.
Bats: left **Throws:** right
Acquired: Traded by Mets with Javier Gonzalez for Doug Henry, 12/94

Player Summary	
Fantasy Value	$2 to $4
Card Value	6¢ to 10¢
Will	try to win spot
Can't	practice patience
Expect	more stolen bases
Don't Expect	any kind of power

A little guy who makes good contact, Vina got the most at bats of his brief big-league career last year and made the most of the opportunity. Though he also appeared at short and third, he played more often at second base (99 games) than any other Brewer in 1995. His on-base percentage was 70 points higher than his batting average. It would be much higher if Vina showed any patience at the plate. Despite his tiny strike zone, he walks less than he fans (22 walks and 28 Ks last year). A slap hitter who stands close to the plate, Vina often reaches as a hit batsman. He can motor around the bases but hasn't been a basestealer in recent seasons. That's a surprise, since he twice topped 30 steals in the minors. He hasn't lost much speed but also hasn't played enough to get a good read on the moves of opposing pitchers. Vina doesn't hit the long ball or make many miscues in the field. But he's not about to win a Gold Glove either. If he wants to win a regular job, he'll have to earn it with his fast feet.

Major League Batting Register

	BA	G	AB	R	H	2B	3B	HR	RBI	SB
93 AL	.222	24	45	5	10	2	0	0	2	6
94 NL	.250	79	124	20	31	6	0	0	6	3
95 AL	.257	113	288	46	74	7	7	3	29	6
Life	.252	216	457	71	115	15	7	3	37	15

JOSE VIZCAINO

Position: Shortstop; second base
Team: New York Mets
Born: March 26, 1968 San Cristobal, Dominican Republic
Height: 6'1" **Weight:** 180 lbs.
Bats: both **Throws:** right
Acquired: Traded by Cubs for Anthony Young and Ottis Smith, 3/94

Player Summary	
Fantasy Value	$3 to $5
Card Value	4¢ to 6¢
Will	hit left-handers
Can't	show much power
Expect	strong fielding
Don't Expect	patient at bats

Vizcaino's 5-for-5 game at Florida Sept. 23 was the highlight of a late hot streak that pushed his average to .287, tying his 1993 career high. Hitting only .232 by June 5, the switch-hitting shortstop embarked on a roll that never stopped. He hit .346 against left-handed pitchers, helping him compile a career-best 56 RBI. Vizcaino still fans more than twice per walk but has enough bat control to drop sacrifice bunts or work the hit-and-run. He's an opposite-field hitter against lefties but goes up the middle against righties. He batted second for the Mets most of last season. Though he had 21 doubles last year, he's not a power hitter by any stretch of the imagination. But Vizcaino will single opponents to death. He runs well but is not much of a basestealer. He saves his speed for the field, where he charges well, ranges far to his right and left, and shows an accurate arm.

Major League Batting Register

	BA	G	AB	R	H	2B	3B	HR	RBI	SB
89 NL	.200	7	10	2	2	0	0	0	0	0
90 NL	.275	37	51	3	14	1	1	0	2	1
91 NL	.262	93	145	7	38	5	0	0	10	2
92 NL	.225	86	285	25	64	10	4	1	17	3
93 NL	.287	151	551	74	158	19	4	4	54	12
94 NL	.256	103	410	47	105	13	3	3	33	1
95 NL	.287	135	509	66	146	21	5	3	56	8
Life	.269	612	1961	224	527	69	17	11	172	27
3 AVE	.276	149	567	71	157	20	5	4	54	7

CURRENT PLAYERS

OMAR VIZQUEL

Position: Shortstop
Team: Cleveland Indians
Born: April 24, 1967 Caracas, Venezuela
Height: 5'9" **Weight:** 165 lbs.
Bats: both **Throws:** right
Acquired: Traded by Mariners for Felix Fermin, Reggie Jefferson, and cash, 12/93

Player Summary	
Fantasy Value	$7 to $9
Card Value	5¢ to 8¢
Will	bunt, run, steal
Can't	clear the fences
Expect	Gold Glove bid
Don't Expect	high on-base mark

Vizquel is a bastion of speed and defense in Cleveland's sea of sluggers. Though Cal Ripken and Gary DiSarcina topped Vizquel's .986 fielding percentage last year, Vizquel displayed acrobatics, range, and a great arm at shortstop. He made only nine errors in 624 regular-season chances, then again starred with the leather during post-season play. Vizquel had a 47-game error-less streak between June 12 and Aug. 4. By season's end, he had career highs in homers, RBI, and stolen bases. A good bunter and hit-and-run man who hit second in the high-powered Cleveland lineup all year, Vizquel topped the team with 10 sacrifice bunts (tied for fifth in the AL). Only Brady Anderson was more difficult to double; Vizquel rapped into double plays only four times. He makes good contact and walks as much as he fans. When he reaches, Vizquel often runs. Vizquel's reactions, range, and hands make him the AL's best-fielding shortstop.

Major League Batting Register

	BA	G	AB	R	H	2B	3B	HR	RBI	SB
89 AL	.220	143	387	45	85	7	3	1	20	1
90 AL	.247	81	255	19	63	3	2	2	18	4
91 AL	.230	142	426	42	98	16	4	1	41	7
92 AL	.294	136	483	49	142	20	4	0	21	15
93 AL	.255	158	560	68	143	14	2	2	31	12
94 AL	.273	69	286	39	78	10	1	1	33	13
95 AL	.266	136	542	87	144	28	0	6	56	29
Life	.256	865	2939	349	753	98	16	13	220	81
3 AVE	.264	136	524	74	138	20	1	3	47	21

PAUL WAGNER

Position: Pitcher
Team: Pittsburgh Pirates
Born: Nov. 14, 1967 Milwaukee, WI
Height: 6'1" **Weight:** 202 lbs.
Bats: right **Throws:** right
Acquired: 12th-round pick in 6/89 free-agent draft

Player Summary	
Fantasy Value	$1
Card Value	5¢ to 8¢
Will	win with support
Can't	always throw strikes
Expect	flashes of brilliance
Don't Expect	lopsided record

Wagner remains a true baseball enigma. He not only has a tremendous arm but mixes a live fastball with a biting slider. When he throws both pitches for strikes, Wagner is almost unbeatable. On Aug. 29, he came within one out of pitching a no-hitter against the Colorado Rockies, the NL's best-hitting team. He fanned 11, yielding only an infield single by Andres Galarraga in the ninth. Unfortunately for Wagner, that game was a lonely beacon in the fog last year. He led the majors in losses—the first time a Pirate has done that since Jose DeLeon went 2-19 in 1985. Poor run support was part of the problem, but Wagner also contributed. He walked nearly four batters per game, allowed more than one hit per inning, and failed to hold runners close. He yielded 25 steals in 30 chances. Wagner's work against lefties was better than in the past but the league still batted a solid .273 against him. He helps himself with his fielding and, occasionally, with his bat. His bunting needs work, however.

Major League Pitching Register

	W	L	ERA	G	CG	IP	H	ER	BB	SO
92 NL	2	0	0.69	6	0	13.0	9	1	5	5
93 NL	8	8	4.27	44	1	141.1	143	67	42	114
94 NL	7	8	4.59	29	1	119.2	136	61	50	86
95 NL	5	16	4.80	33	3	165.0	174	88	72	120
Life	22	32	4.45	112	5	439.0	462	217	169	325
3 AVE	8	12	4.58	41	2	165.1	177	84	64	123

CURRENT PLAYERS

TIM WAKEFIELD

Position: Pitcher
Team: Boston Red Sox
Born: Aug. 2, 1966 Melbourne, FL
Height: 6'2" **Weight:** 204 lbs.
Bats: right **Throws:** right
Acquired: Signed as a free agent, 4/95

Player Summary	
Fantasy Value	$9 to $11
Card Value	6¢ to 10¢
Will	baffle most batters
Can't	prevent gopher balls
Expect	many wins
Don't Expect	problems to return

Wakefield resurrected his career last year after the Red Sox commissioned ex-knuckleballers Phil and Joe Niekro to provide private coaching. Pittsburgh's postseason hero of 1992, Wakefield had lost his confidence and control. He was even a bust in the minors, convincing the frustrated Pirates to cut him. Whatever the Niekros said must have worked; in his first 17 games, Wakefield went 14-1 with a league-low 1.65 ERA. By winning 10 straight starts between June 29 and Aug. 13, Wakefield even became a candidate for the AL's Cy Young Award—not to mention Comeback Player of the Year. Twice, he took no-hitters into the eighth inning. Though he lost seven of his last nine, plus a start in the Division Series, Wakefield still held hitters to a .227 average, showed a solid pickoff move, and was second in the AL with a 2.95 ERA. In the eight games he started after a Bosox loss, Wakefield was 7-0 with a 1.32 ERA. He doesn't fan many (five and one-half per nine innings), but controls the knuckler well enough to keep walks down (three a game).

MATT WALBECK

Position: Catcher
Team: Minnesota Twins
Born: Oct. 2, 1969 Sacramento, CA
Height: 5'11" **Weight:** 190 lbs.
Bats: both **Throws:** right
Acquired: Traded by Cubs with Dave Stevens for Willie Banks, 11/93

Player Summary	
Fantasy Value	$1 to $3
Card Value	4¢ to 6¢
Will	play good defense
Can't	hit the long ball
Expect	solid bat vs. lefties
Don't Expect	high on-base mark

Walbeck has never been able to fill the shoes of Brian Harper, the hard-hitting veteran he succeeded as Minnesota's No. 1 catcher. The good-field, no-hit tag fits Walbeck better than his catcher's mitt. He hit .204 as a 1994 rookie, then lifted his mark to .257 last year—thanks to a .308 average against left-handed pitching. That's hardly surprising, since Walbeck is a natural right-handed batter who didn't even switch-hit from 1987 to 1989. He has no power, little speed, and extremely limited patience at the plate. Walbeck fanned three times more than he walked last year—a contrast from the year before, when he made better contact. His calling card is his defense, which ranks among the league's best. After nailing 40 percent of would-be basestealers in 1994, Walbeck slipped to 24 percent last year when his inexperienced pitching staff had trouble holding runners. But his game-calling, plate-blocking, and ability to prevent wild pitches were unscathed. Walbeck began his pro career in the Cub system in 1987.

Major League Pitching Register

	W	L	ERA	G	CG	IP	H	ER	BB	SO
92 NL	8	1	2.15	13	4	92.0	76	22	35	51
93 NL	6	11	5.61	24	3	128.1	145	80	75	59
95 AL	16	8	2.95	27	6	195.1	163	64	68	119
Life	30	20	3.59	64	13	415.2	384	166	178	229
2 AVE	12	10	3.93	27	5	174.1	164	76	75	96

Major League Batting Register

	BA	G	AB	R	H	2B	3B	HR	RBI	SB
93 NL	.200	11	30	2	6	2	0	1	6	0
94 AL	.204	97	338	31	69	12	0	5	35	1
95 AL	.257	115	393	40	101	18	1	1	44	3
Life	.231	223	761	73	176	32	1	7	85	4
2 AVE	.230	133	459	44	105	19	1	4	49	2

LARRY WALKER

Position: Outfield
Team: Colorado Rockies
Born: Dec. 1, 1966 Maple Ridge, British Columbia
Height: 6'3" **Weight:** 215 lbs.
Bats: left **Throws:** right
Acquired: Signed as a free agent, 4/95

Player Summary	
Fantasy Value	$30 to $35
Card Value	20¢ to 30¢
Will	hit long ball
Can't	get attention
Expect	great defense
Don't Expect	extended skid

The addition of Walker's left-handed power and howitzer of a throwing arm was the major factor in Colorado's postseason appearance last year. His 36 homers, 101 RBI, and .607 slugging percentage were career highs. Those marks left him among the NL leaders (second in slugging, tied for second in homers, and seventh in RBI). In addition, he tied Raul Mondesi and Sammy Sosa for the league lead with 13 outfield assists. Walker justified Don Baylor's decision to make him Colorado's cleanup man. Walker even wallops left-handed pitchers. For the second straight year, he had a better average against lefties than he did against righties. Walker also runs well; he swiped 16 bases in 19 tries last year. That speed helps him in right field. His great jumps, good range, and spectacular arm make him a formidable defensive player, challenged only by foolish runners. He's even thrown hitters out at first on potential base hits.

Major League Batting Register

	BA	G	AB	R	H	2B	3B	HR	RBI	SB
89 NL	.170	20	47	4	8	0	0	0	4	1
90 NL	.241	133	419	59	101	18	3	19	51	21
91 NL	.290	137	487	59	141	30	2	16	64	14
92 NL	.301	143	528	85	159	31	4	23	93	18
93 NL	.265	138	490	85	130	24	5	22	86	29
94 NL	.322	103	395	76	127	44	2	19	86	15
95 NL	.306	131	494	96	151	31	5	36	101	16
Life	.286	805	2860	464	817	178	21	135	485	114
3 AVE	.299	143	534	100	160	40	4	30	107	23

TIM WALLACH

Position: Third base
Team: California Angels
Born: Sept. 14, 1957 Huntington Park, CA
Height: 6'3" **Weight:** 202 lbs.
Bats: right **Throws:** right
Acquired: Signed as a free agent, 12/95

Player Summary	
Fantasy Value	$3 to $5
Card Value	5¢ to 8¢
Will	try to hang on
Can't	show old power
Expect	reduced action
Don't Expect	new Gold Glove

Injuries interfered with Wallach's season last year. Disabled in April with a bulging disc in his lower back, he later tore a posterior cruciate ligament in his left leg. Though troubled by recurring back pain, he hit .325 in May and .305 in August. But Wallach did not have the same stroke that he had in 1994. Wallach just can't get the bat around the way he once did. He's not quick in the field either, though he has three Gold Gloves on his trophy shelf. He still has good hands, but his arm, accuracy, and range are no better than average. He is a former All-American, Golden Spikes Award winner, and College Player of the Year at Cal State Fullerton.

Major League Batting Register

	BA	G	AB	R	H	2B	3B	HR	RBI	SB
80 NL	.182	5	11	1	2	0	0	1	2	0
81 NL	.236	71	212	19	50	9	1	4	13	0
82 NL	.268	158	596	89	160	31	3	28	97	6
83 NL	.269	156	581	54	156	33	3	19	70	0
84 NL	.246	160	582	55	143	25	4	18	72	3
85 NL	.260	155	569	70	148	36	3	22	81	9
86 NL	.233	134	480	50	112	22	1	18	71	8
87 NL	.298	153	593	89	177	42	4	26	123	9
88 NL	.257	159	592	52	152	32	5	12	69	2
89 NL	.277	154	573	76	159	42	0	13	77	3
90 NL	.296	161	626	69	185	37	5	21	98	6
91 NL	.225	151	577	60	130	22	1	13	73	2
92 NL	.223	150	537	53	120	29	1	9	59	2
93 NL	.222	133	477	42	106	19	1	12	62	0
94 NL	.280	113	414	68	116	21	1	23	78	0
95 NL	.266	97	327	24	87	22	2	9	38	0
Life	.259	2110	7747	871	2003	422	35	248	1083	50
3 AVE	.257	134	476	55	122	24	2	18	72	0

CURRENT PLAYERS

JEROME WALTON

Position: Outfield
Team: Cincinnati Reds
Born: July 8, 1965 Newnan, GA
Height: 6'1" **Weight:** 175 lbs.
Bats: right **Throws:** right
Acquired: Signed as a free agent, 11/93

Player Summary	
Fantasy Value	$1
Card Value	5¢ to 8¢
Will	play good defense
Can't	make strong throws
Expect	best bat vs. lefties
Don't Expect	many stolen bases

Resurrecting his career, Walton did a good job sharing the leadoff spot and center field job with lefty-hitting Thomas Howard last year. Playing ahead of light-hitting Darren Lewis, Walton hit .438 when leading off the first inning, hit .306 against lefties, and hit a career-peak eight home runs. One of them was a two-run game-winner in the bottom of the ninth against the Mets on May 6. Another was the Reds' first pinch homer of the 1995 season, 10 days later. Though not considered a slugger, Walton gets extra bases on 45 percent of his hits. He also walks often enough to produce a healthy on-base percentage (.368 last year). He moves well enough to do a good job in center and also fills in at first base. His throwing arm is nothing to write home about, however. Walton catches everything he can reach and rarely makes an error (two last year). Walton won NL Rookie of the Year honors with the Cubs in 1989.

DUANE WARD

Position: Pitcher
Team: Toronto Blue Jays
Born: May 28, 1964 Parkview, NM
Height: 6'4" **Weight:** 215 lbs.
Bats: right **Throws:** right
Acquired: Traded by Braves for Doyle Alexander, 7/86

Player Summary	
Fantasy Value	$4 to $6
Card Value	5¢ to 8¢
Will	seek big comeback
Can't	always find plate
Expect	tryout as closer
Don't Expect	pinpoint control

After leading the American League with 45 saves for Toronto in 1993, Ward has missed virtually two years while recuperating from a torn rotator cuff that had to be surgically repaired. Others have returned from such surgery, but few power pitchers in that situation have been able to recapture 100 percent of their former skills. And a two-year layoff can have devastating effects. Even before he got hurt, for example, Ward had occasional bouts of control trouble. He had more strikeouts than innings pitched four times, however, and could thrive if used properly. He pitched more than 60 games and 100 innings five years in a row from 1988 to 1992. He topped 70 appearances four straight years. That's a lot for any closer. A sinker-slider pitcher who dominated right-handed batters, Ward was known for getting his outs on strikeouts and ground balls.

Major League Batting Register

	BA	G	AB	R	H	2B	3B	HR	RBI	SB
89 NL	.293	116	475	64	139	23	3	5	46	24
90 NL	.263	101	392	63	103	16	2	2	21	14
91 NL	.219	123	270	42	59	13	1	5	17	7
92 NL	.127	30	55	7	7	0	1	0	1	1
93 AL	.000	5	2	2	0	0	0	0	0	1
94 NL	.309	46	68	10	21	4	0	1	9	1
95 NL	.290	102	162	32	47	12	1	8	22	10
Life	.264	523	1424	220	376	68	8	21	116	58

Major League Pitching Register

	W	L	ERA	G	S	IP	H	ER	BB	SO
86 NL	0	1	7.31	10	0	16.0	22	13	8	8
86 AL	0	1	13.50	2	0	2.0	3	3	4	1
87 AL	1	0	6.94	12	0	11.2	14	9	12	10
88 AL	9	3	3.30	64	15	111.2	101	41	60	91
89 AL	4	10	3.77	66	15	114.2	94	48	58	122
90 AL	2	8	3.45	73	11	127.2	101	49	42	112
91 AL	7	6	2.77	81	23	107.1	80	33	33	132
92 AL	7	4	1.95	79	12	101.1	76	22	39	103
93 AL	2	3	2.13	71	45	71.2	49	17	25	97
95 AL	0	1	27.00	4	0	2.2	11	8	5	3
Life	32	37	3.28	462	121	666.2	551	243	286	679

CURRENT PLAYERS

TURNER WARD

Position: Outfield
Team: Milwaukee Brewers
Born: April 11, 1965 Orlando, FL
Height: 6'2" **Weight:** 185 lbs.
Bats: both **Throws:** right
Acquired: Claimed from Blue Jays on waivers, 11/93

Player Summary	
Fantasy Value	$1
Card Value	4¢ to 6¢
Will	carry good glove
Can't	hit the long one
Expect	best bat vs. righties
Don't Expect	regular exposure

Although he's never hit much, Ward is a useful backup who can play all three outfield positions well. He has quick instincts, great range, soft hands, and a strong, accurate arm. Ward makes a surprising number of assists considering his playing time is so limited. A better left-handed batter, Ward is a singles hitter who sprays hits to all fields. He's hit as many as 10 homers only once in a pro career that started in 1986. He has a good eye and is willing to wait for walks. As a left-handed hitter, he prefers low fastballs, though high heat is his preference from the other side. Pitchers had his number in 1994, when they cooled him down quickly after a hot start. Ward's biggest asset as a hitter is his finely tuned batting eye, which helps him boost his on-base percentage nearly 100 points above his lowly batting average. Ward could improve his value by running more when he reaches. He missed most of last season with a severely strained hamstring.

Major League Batting Register

	BA	G	AB	R	H	2B	3B	HR	RBI	SB
90 AL	.348	14	46	10	16	2	1	1	10	3
91 AL	.239	48	113	12	27	7	0	0	7	0
92 AL	.345	18	29	7	10	3	0	1	3	0
93 AL	.192	72	167	20	32	4	2	4	28	3
94 AL	.232	102	367	55	85	15	2	9	45	6
95 AL	.264	44	129	19	34	3	1	4	16	6
Life	.240	298	851	123	204	34	6	19	109	18
2 AVE	.222	108	342	49	76	13	2	8	46	6

ALLEN WATSON

Position: Pitcher
Team: St. Louis Cardinals
Born: Nov. 18, 1970 Jamaica, NY
Height: 6'3" **Weight:** 190 lbs.
Bats: left **Throws:** left
Acquired: First-round pick in 6/91 free-agent draft

Player Summary	
Fantasy Value	$2 to $4
Card Value	5¢ to 8¢
Will	swing strong bat
Can't	get righties out
Expect	few walks
Don't Expect	trial in bullpen

Maybe they should try him at another position. Watson led NL pitchers with a .417 batting average last year but had a 4.96 ERA that ranked last in the St. Louis rotation. He has good control of his fastball, slider, and changeup and has no trouble with left-handed hitters (.200 last year). But righties lit him up at a .302 pace, and rival hitters treated him like a batting-practice pitcher in Home Run Derby (17 homers in 114⅓ innings). It was hardly surprising that Watson, who had split 24 previous decisions in the majors, couldn't finish on the sunny side of .500. Lack of run support worked against him, but he remained his own worst enemy. He yielded nearly 10 hits per nine innings and fanned less than four hitters over the same period—a miserable mark for a man regarded as a power pitcher. The Cardinals, trying shock treatment, even exiled him to the minors for a brief time last summer. Watson's fielding, hitting, and bunting give him an advantage over opponents. He's also improved his pickoff move.

Major League Pitching Register

	W	L	ERA	G	CG	IP	H	ER	BB	SO
93 NL	6	7	4.60	16	0	86.0	90	44	28	49
94 NL	6	5	5.52	22	0	115.2	130	71	53	74
95 NL	7	9	4.96	21	0	114.1	126	63	41	49
Life	19	21	5.07	59	0	316.0	346	178	122	172
3 AVE	7	8	5.12	24	0	125.1	138	72	50	69

CURRENT PLAYERS

DAVID WEATHERS

Position: Pitcher
Team: Florida Marlins
Born: Sept. 25, 1969 Lawrenceburg, TN
Height: 6'3" **Weight:** 205 lbs.
Bats: right **Throws:** right
Acquired: Second-round pick from Blue Jays in 11/92 expansion draft

Player Summary	
Fantasy Value	$1 to $3
Card Value	5¢ to 8¢
Will	try to hang on
Can't	deflate his ERA
Expect	erratic control
Don't Expect	huge Ks

Seldom has a season looked so much like a last chance. But that's the way Weathers has to look at 1996. His ERA has hovered above five for all three of his Florida seasons and his nine-inning average of bases on balls matched that figure last summer. Though he keeps the ball in the park, Weathers yields too many hits—especially against lefties who lit him up at a .315 clip last year. He should be able to weather that, but he has trouble controlling the running game, doesn't field his position well, and is a terrible hitter. He does run well for a big man, however, and he has appeared several times as a pinch runner. Weathers throws a fastball, a slider, and a changeup from a three-quarters delivery that doesn't deceive anybody. Toronto's third-round draft choice in June 1988, he had four seasons with double-digit victories. Weathers is still young enough to turn his career around—but he had better hurry.

LENNY WEBSTER

Position: Catcher
Team: Philadelphia Phillies
Born: Feb. 10, 1965 New Orleans, LA
Height: 5'9" **Weight:** 195 lbs.
Bats: right **Throws:** right
Acquired: Signed as a free agent, 4/95

Player Summary	
Fantasy Value	$1
Card Value	4¢ to 6¢
Will	retain caddie role
Can't	display any speed
Expect	best bat vs. lefties
Don't Expect	runners to be out

In five big-league seasons, Webster has never been anything more than a backup catcher. But he was valuable to the Phillies last year after All-Star Darren Daulton was shelved by injury. Although Webster is hardly a great hitter, he gets extra bases on nearly one-third of his hits. He's also a capable pinch hitter; in 1992, he went 5-for-6 in that role for Minnesota. A high fastball hitter who's vulnerable against breaking balls, Webster usually hits much better against left-handed pitching. That was not the case last year, however. He draws enough walks to post an on-base percentage 70 points higher than his batting average. That doesn't help him advance on the bases, however, since he has catcher's speed. The Grambling State product calls a good game, handles his pitchers well, prevents potential wild pitches, and knows how to block the plate. Webster's weakness is throwing: His arm is neither quick nor powerful.

Major League Pitching Register

	W	L	ERA	G	CG	IP	H	ER	BB	SO
91 AL	1	0	4.91	15	0	14.2	15	8	17	13
92 AL	0	0	8.10	2	0	3.1	5	3	2	3
93 NL	2	3	5.12	14	0	45.2	57	26	13	34
94 NL	8	12	5.27	24	0	135.0	166	79	59	72
95 NL	4	5	5.98	28	0	90.1	104	60	52	60
Life	15	20	5.48	83	0	289.0	347	176	143	182
2 AVE	8	11	5.51	33	0	146.1	175	89	71	84

Major League Batting Register

	BA	G	AB	R	H	2B	3B	HR	RBI	SB
89 AL	.300	14	20	3	6	2	0	0	1	0
90 AL	.333	2	6	1	2	1	0	0	0	0
91 AL	.294	18	34	7	10	1	0	3	8	0
92 AL	.280	53	118	10	33	10	1	1	13	0
93 AL	.198	49	106	14	21	2	0	1	8	1
94 NL	.273	57	143	13	39	10	0	5	23	0
94 NL	.273	57	143	13	39	10	0	5	23	0
95 NL	.267	49	150	18	40	9	0	4	14	0
Life	.262	242	577	66	151	35	1	14	67	1

CURRENT PLAYERS

BILL WEGMAN

Position: Pitcher
Team: Milwaukee Brewers
Born: Dec. 19, 1962 Cincinnati, OH
Height: 6'5" **Weight:** 220 lbs.
Bats: right **Throws:** right
Acquired: Fifth-round pick in 6/81 free-agent draft

Player Summary	
Fantasy Value	$0
Card Value	4¢ to 6¢
Will	pursue starter job
Can't	keep ball in park
Expect	excellent control
Don't Expect	double-digit wins

Although he's a finesse pitcher with good control, Wegman has suffered so many injuries in recent seasons that his once-promising career has come to a crossroads. He's won at least a dozen games in full separate seasons but has also succumbed to serious shoulder and elbow problems, plus assorted other ailments. A sinker-slider pitcher who also throws a curveball and a changeup, Wegman needs to keep the ball down. When he doesn't, it sails out of the park with alarming frequency. His ERA has risen, eventually costing him a spot in the Milwaukee rotation. Only four of his 37 appearances last season were starts. In addition, he doesn't seem to have a clue about how to retire left-handed hitters. Wegman helps his own cause by holding runners close but is otherwise only average in the field.

Major League Pitching Register

	W	L	ERA	G	CG	IP	H	ER	BB	SO
85 AL	2	0	3.57	3	0	17.2	17	7	3	6
86 AL	5	12	5.13	35	2	198.1	217	113	43	82
87 AL	12	11	4.24	34	7	225.0	229	106	53	102
88 AL	13	13	4.12	32	4	199.0	207	91	50	84
89 AL	2	6	6.71	11	0	51.0	69	38	21	27
90 AL	2	2	4.85	8	1	29.2	37	16	6	20
91 AL	15	7	2.84	28	7	193.1	176	61	40	89
92 AL	13	14	3.20	35	7	261.2	251	93	55	127
93 AL	4	14	4.48	20	5	120.2	135	60	34	50
94 AL	8	4	4.51	19	0	115.2	140	58	26	59
95 AL	5	7	5.35	37	0	70.2	89	42	21	50
Life	81	90	4.16	262	33	1482.2	1567	685	352	696
3 AVE	7	9	4.68	29	2	120.2	144	63	31	63

WALT WEISS

Position: Shortstop
Team: Colorado Rockies
Born: Nov. 28, 1963 Tuxedo, NY
Height: 6' **Weight:** 175 lbs.
Bats: both **Throws:** right
Acquired: Signed as a free agent, 1/94

Player Summary	
Fantasy Value	$5 to $7
Card Value	5¢ to 8¢
Will	play good defense
Can't	hike batting mark
Expect	great batting eye
Don't Expect	any kind of power

Though best-known for his sterling defense, Weiss has one of the most amazing batting eyes in the big leagues. Refusing to swing at anything outside the strike zone, he walks so frequently that his on-base percentage always ranks among the league leaders. Weiss was second in the National League with 98 walks and fourth with a .403 on-base percentage. Batting eighth—with the pitcher up next—accounts for some of the walks. He doesn't make enough contact for a Punch-and-Judy hitter, though he's a good bunter and competent hit-and-run man. Weiss stole a career-best 15 bases last year and was nailed only three times. His speed helps him in the field. He gobbles up everything hit his way. He has quick reactions, soft hands, and a reliable though not powerful arm. Weiss also turns the double play well. Once regarded as brittle, Weiss has been healthy the last three years.

Major League Batting Register

	BA	G	AB	R	H	2B	3B	HR	RBI	SB
87 AL	.462	16	26	3	12	4	0	0	1	1
88 AL	.250	147	452	44	113	17	3	3	39	4
89 AL	.233	84	236	30	55	11	0	3	21	6
90 AL	.265	138	445	50	118	17	1	2	35	9
91 AL	.226	40	133	15	30	6	1	0	13	6
92 AL	.212	103	316	36	67	5	2	0	21	6
93 NL	.266	158	500	50	133	14	2	1	39	7
94 NL	.251	110	423	58	106	11	4	1	32	12
95 NL	.260	137	427	65	111	17	3	1	25	15
Life	.252	933	2958	351	745	102	16	11	226	66
3 AVE	.258	156	525	68	136	16	4	1	37	14

CURRENT PLAYERS

DAVID WELLS

Position: Pitcher
Team: Cincinnati Reds
Born: May 20, 1963 Torrance, CA
Height: 6'4" **Weight:** 225 lbs.
Bats: left **Throws:** left
Acquired: Traded by Tigers for C.J. Nitkowski, Mark Lewis, and Dave Tuttle, 7/95

Player Summary	
Fantasy Value	$11 to $14
Card Value	5¢ to 8¢
Will	show good control
Can't	stop all righties
Expect	lefties to cringe
Don't Expect	control problems

Wells had a combined 16-8 record and 3.24 ERA while splitting the 1995 season between Detroit and Cincinnati. With a 9-0 mark in his last 15 starts for the Tigers, Wells made the All-Star Team for the first time. But the Reds acquired him on July 31. A control artist with a reputation for throwing first-pitch strikes, Wells was Detroit's staff ace before his trade. But the Tigers, rebuilding with youth, decided they couldn't afford the former Toronto standout. Wells is a power pitcher who throws a fastball, a curveball, and a changeup. He dominates left-handed hitters and keeps the ball in the park. His control helps Wells move his pitches around in the strike zone. He's also adept at changing speeds on his curve. Though his motion leaves him in poor fielding position, Wells manages to make most of the required plays. He's good at keeping runners close.

Major League Pitching Register

	W	L	ERA	G	CG	IP	H	ER	BB	SO
87 AL	4	3	3.99	18	0	29.1	37	13	12	32
88 AL	3	5	4.62	41	0	64.1	65	33	31	56
89 AL	7	4	2.40	54	0	86.1	66	23	28	78
90 AL	11	6	3.14	43	0	189.0	165	66	45	115
91 AL	15	10	3.72	40	2	198.1	188	82	49	106
92 AL	7	9	5.40	41	0	120.0	138	72	36	62
93 AL	11	9	4.19	32	0	187.0	183	87	42	139
94 AL	5	7	3.96	16	5	111.1	113	49	24	71
95 AL	10	3	3.04	18	3	130.1	120	44	37	83
95 NL	6	5	3.59	11	3	72.2	74	29	16	50
Life	79	61	3.77	314	13	1188.2	1149	498	320	792
3 AVE	12	9	3.75	29	5	190.2	187	79	45	130

DAVID WEST

Position: Pitcher
Team: Philadelphia Phillies
Born: Sept. 1, 1964 Memphis, TN
Height: 6'6" **Weight:** 230 lbs.
Bats: left **Throws:** left
Acquired: Traded by Twins for Mike Hartley, 12/92

Player Summary	
Fantasy Value	$1
Card Value	4¢ to 6¢
Will	show four pitches
Can't	always throw strikes
Expect	starting berth
Don't Expect	lefties to hit him

After winning a starter's job by default in 1994, West was expected to take a regular turn in the 1995 Philadelphia rotation. He made only eight starts, however, before being sidelined for the rest of the year with shoulder problems. A sinker-slider pitcher, West also throws a curveball and a changeup—all with a deceiving, three-quarters motion. He's especially tough on left-handed hitters, who can't even reach the Mendoza Line against him. A towering left-hander who has fought the Battle of the Bulge throughout his career, West was once a minor-league phenom in the Mets system. He pitched for the Mets and Twins before joining the Phils. West was at his best in 1993, when he made a career-high 76 appearances, all in relief, while posting a 2.92 ERA as a set-up man for Mitch Williams. West doesn't help himself with his defense or pickoff move but he gets occasional hits when not ordered to bunt.

Major League Pitching Register

	W	L	ERA	G	S	IP	H	ER	BB	SO
88 NL	1	0	3.00	2	0	6.0	6	2	3	3
89 NL	0	2	7.40	11	0	24.1	25	20	14	19
89 AL	3	2	6.41	10	0	39.1	48	28	19	31
90 AL	7	9	5.10	29	0	146.1	142	83	78	92
91 AL	4	4	4.54	15	0	71.1	66	36	28	52
92 AL	1	3	6.99	9	0	28.1	32	22	20	19
93 NL	6	4	2.92	76	3	86.1	60	28	51	87
94 NL	4	10	3.55	31	0	99.0	74	39	61	83
95 NL	3	2	3.79	8	0	38.0	34	16	19	25
Life	29	36	4.58	191	6	539.0	487	274	293	411
2 AVE	6	9	3.31	60	2	113.1	82	41	68	102

CURRENT PLAYERS

JOHN WETTELAND

Position: Pitcher
Team: New York Yankees
Born: Aug. 21, 1968 San Mateo, CA
Height: 6'2" **Weight:** 195 lbs.
Bats: right **Throws:** right
Acquired: Signed as a free agent, 4/95

Player Summary	
Fantasy Value	$30 to $35
Card Value	6¢ to 10¢
Will	convert most saves
Can't	stop basestealers
Expect	frequent strikeouts
Don't Expect	control to be shaky

Changing leagues didn't diminish Wetteland's value as a late-inning reliever. He held AL hitters to a .185 average, converted 31 saves in 37 chances, and stranded 69.6 percent of the runners he inherited. In his last seven appearances, Wetteland retired all 21 batters he faced (12 via strikeout) and earned a save each time. A power pitcher who averages more strikeouts than innings pitched, Wetteland also has exceptional control of his fastball and curveball. His two-walks-per-nine innings average was one of the AL's best. Wetteland throws both rising and sinking fastballs plus sharp-breaking curves from a three-quarters windup. Because he's always around the plate, he yields a few home runs but usually with no one on base. Wetteland has trouble holding runners but few reach against him. He helps himself in the field. Signed as a starter out of the College of San Mateo, he switched to relief with the Dodgers in 1989.

Major League Pitching Register

	W	L	ERA	G	S	IP	H	ER	BB	SO
89 NL	5	8	3.77	31	1	102.2	81	43	34	96
90 NL	2	4	4.81	22	0	43.0	44	23	17	36
91 NL	1	0	0.00	6	0	9.0	5	0	3	9
92 NL	4	4	2.92	67	37	83.1	64	27	36	99
93 NL	9	3	1.37	70	43	85.1	58	13	28	113
94 NL	4	6	2.83	52	25	63.2	46	20	21	68
95 AL	1	5	2.93	60	31	61.1	40	20	14	66
Life	26	30	2.93	308	137	448.1	338	146	153	487
3 AVE	5	6	2.35	70	38	81.2	56	21	24	94

LOU WHITAKER

Position: Second base
Team: Detroit Tigers
Born: May 12, 1957 Brooklyn, NY
Height: 5'11" **Weight:** 185 lbs.
Bats: left **Throws:** right
Acquired: Fifth-round pick in 6/75 free-agent draft

Player Summary	
Fantasy Value	$0
Card Value	5¢ to 8¢
Will	play 20th season
Can't	steal many bases
Expect	occasional power
Don't Expect	a heavy workload

Last year, Whitaker teamed with double-play partner Alan Trammell for their 1,918th joint appearance, an AL record for teammates and a major-league record for a double-play combination. Only Al Kaline and Ty Cobb have played more games for Detroit than Whitaker. He started last season on the disabled list with a strained right shoulder. Whitaker actually hit better against lefties (.308) than he did against righties (.291). He had an on-base mark of .372. He now has 244 homers, fifth on the Tiger career list. The five-time All-Star has lost a step in the field but still has good hands.

Major League Batting Register

	BA	G	AB	R	H	2B	3B	HR	RBI	SB
77 AL	.250	11	32	5	8	1	0	0	2	2
78 AL	.285	139	484	71	138	12	7	3	58	7
79 AL	.286	127	423	75	121	14	8	3	42	20
80 AL	.233	145	477	68	111	19	1	1	45	8
81 AL	.263	109	335	48	88	14	4	5	36	5
82 AL	.286	152	560	76	160	22	8	15	65	11
83 AL	.320	161	643	94	206	40	6	12	72	17
84 AL	.289	143	558	90	161	25	1	13	56	6
85 AL	.279	152	609	102	170	29	8	21	73	6
86 AL	.269	144	584	95	157	26	6	20	73	13
87 AL	.265	149	604	110	160	38	6	16	59	13
88 AL	.275	115	403	54	111	18	2	12	55	2
89 AL	.251	148	509	77	128	21	1	28	85	6
90 AL	.237	132	472	75	112	22	2	18	60	8
91 AL	.279	138	470	94	131	26	2	23	78	4
92 AL	.278	130	453	77	126	26	0	19	71	6
93 AL	.290	119	383	72	111	32	1	9	67	3
94 AL	.301	92	322	67	97	21	2	12	43	2
95 AL	.293	84	249	36	73	14	0	14	44	4
Life	.276	2390	8570	1386	2369	420	65	244	1084	143
3 AVE	.295	114	372	69	110	26	1	14	59	3

CURRENT PLAYERS

DEVON WHITE

Position: Outfield
Team: Florida Marlins
Born: Dec. 29, 1962 Kingston, Jamaica
Height: 6'2" **Weight:** 178 lbs.
Bats: both **Throws:** right
Acquired: Signed as a free agent, 11/95

Player Summary	
Fantasy Value	$13 to $16
Card Value	6¢ to 10¢
Will	show two-sided power
Can't	curb strikeout habit
Expect	great defense
Don't Expect	patience at the plate

Blinding speed and uncanny instincts have helped White win a half-dozen Gold Gloves, top 30 steals five times, and make the All-Star Team twice. He's even had a 20-20 season. But he has been a flop in the leadoff spot because of his tendency to fan too frequently (97 times in 427 at bats last year for the Jays). Though he's homered from both sides of the plate in more than one game, White hit .230 against lefties in 1995, after hitting .306 against southpaws in 1994. White hits to all fields against both righties and lefties, probably because he chases pitches anywhere. White walked only 29 times last year. He has a .392 career batting average in the LCS—a record for anyone with a minimum 50 at bats. White has led the AL in chances, putouts, and fielding percentage. He has outstanding range and a terrific throwing arm.

Major League Batting Register

	BA	G	AB	R	H	2B	3B	HR	RBI	SB
85 AL	.143	21	7	7	1	0	0	0	0	3
86 AL	.235	29	51	8	12	1	1	1	3	6
87 AL	.263	159	639	103	168	33	5	24	87	32
88 AL	.259	122	455	76	118	22	2	11	51	17
89 AL	.245	156	636	86	156	18	13	12	56	44
90 AL	.217	125	443	57	96	17	3	11	44	21
91 AL	.282	156	642	110	181	40	10	17	60	33
92 AL	.248	153	641	98	159	26	7	17	60	37
93 AL	.273	146	598	116	163	42	6	15	52	34
94 AL	.270	100	403	67	109	24	6	13	49	11
95 AL	.283	101	427	61	121	23	5	10	53	11
Life	.260	1268	4942	769	1284	246	58	131	515	249
3 AVE	.275	133	549	93	151	34	7	15	60	21

RICK WHITE

Position: Pitcher
Team: Pittsburgh Pirates
Born: Dec. 23, 1968 Springfield, OH
Height: 6'4" **Weight:** 215 lbs.
Bats: right **Throws:** right
Acquired: 15th-round pick in 6/90 free-agent draft

Player Summary	
Fantasy Value	$0
Card Value	5¢ to 8¢
Will	find a spot
Can't	fan many hitters
Expect	lively fastball
Don't Expect	runners to steal

White has the heat for relief and the repertoire for the rotation. But shuttling back and forth has hurt him the last two years. He began last year on the disabled list with a sprained right elbow, then he returned to start against Los Angeles on May 17. Little more than a month later, however, he was sent to Triple-A Calgary because of his erratic performance. After winning five of his last six starts in Calgary, he returned to Pittsburgh Sept. 1. While White's 92 mph fastball makes him valuable as a potential closer, his curve is a better pitch. He also throws a slider and a changeup, averaging less than three walks per nine innings. White is also good at keeping the ball in the park (three homers in 55 innings). He yields too many hits, however (nearly 11 per nine innings). Unless he lowers the league's .299 average against him last year, his job will be in jeopardy. White doesn't field or hit very well but is exceptional at holding runners on base. For that reason, White may be best-suited to putting out late-inning fires.

Major League Pitching Register

	W	L	ERA	G	S	IP	H	ER	BB	SO
94 NL	4	5	3.82	43	6	75.1	79	32	17	38
95 NL	2	3	4.75	15	0	55.0	66	29	18	29
Life	6	8	4.21	58	6	130.1	145	61	35	67

CURRENT PLAYERS

RONDELL WHITE

Position: Outfield
Team: Montreal Expos
Born: Feb. 23, 1972 Milledgeville, GA
Height: 6'1" **Weight:** 205 lbs.
Bats: right **Throws:** right
Acquired: First-round pick in 6/90 free-agent draft

Player Summary
Fantasy Value	$20 to $25
Card Value	10¢ to 15¢
Will	batter left-handers
Can't	reach often enough
Expect	20-20 performance
Don't Expect	defensive problems

Though he had Marquis Grissom's shoes to fill, White did a fine job for Montreal. In fact, he finished with more home runs and higher batting and on-base percentages than Grissom did in his first year with Atlanta. Given a chance to play, White showed the same speed-plus-power package he had showcased in the minors. He swiped 25 bases in 30 tries, smacked 13 homers, and delivered a sizzling .377 average against left-handed pitchers. His .356 on-base percentage will improve when White learns to show more patience at the plate. He had more than two strikeouts per walk last year. Such impatience negates the value of his speed. Squeezing more power out of his line-drive stroke is also a White priority. White's only weakness in the field is a mediocre throwing arm. But he compensates by cutting off balls hit into the gaps, charging balls hit in front of him, and making difficult grabs. White has a brilliant career ahead of him. He began as a compensation pick for California's signing of Mark Langston.

Major League Batting Register
	BA	G	AB	R	H	2B	3B	HR	RBI	SB
93 NL	.260	23	73	9	19	3	1	2	15	1
94 NL	.278	40	97	16	27	10	1	2	13	1
95 NL	.295	130	474	87	140	33	4	13	57	25
Life	.289	193	644	112	186	46	6	17	85	27

MARK WHITEN

Position: Outfield
Team: Philadelphia Phillies
Born: Nov. 25, 1966 Pensacola, FL
Height: 6'3" **Weight:** 215 lbs.
Bats: both **Throws:** right
Acquired: Traded by Red Sox for Dave Hollins, 7/95

Player Summary
Fantasy Value	$10 to $13
Card Value	5¢ to 8¢
Will	provide solid power
Can't	end streaky pattern
Expect	howitzer for an arm
Don't Expect	selective hitting

He can hit, he can run, he can throw. He bats from both sides of the plate. So why isn't Whiten an annual All-Star selection? Part of the problem may be consistency—or lack of it. He hit four home runs in a game on Sept. 7, 1993, and tied Jim Bottomley's one-game record of 12 RBI. But Whiten was a washout with the Blue Jays, Indians, Cards, and Red Sox before the Phils decided to take a chance. They knew what they were getting: a streaky power hitter prone to slumps and impatience at the plate. Whiten whiffed twice per walk last year but still posted an on-base percentage 100 points above his batting average. More than anything, Whiten likes to swing. He can carry a club when he's hot. A high fastball hitter as a righty, the left-handed Whiten likes the ball low. Because of his strong, accurate arm, few runners challenge him. His speed helps, but he sometimes makes mistakes in judgment.

Major League Batting Register
	BA	G	AB	R	H	2B	3B	HR	RBI	SB
90 AL	.273	33	88	12	24	1	1	2	7	2
91 AL	.243	116	407	46	99	18	7	9	45	4
92 AL	.254	148	508	73	129	19	4	9	43	16
93 NL	.253	152	562	81	142	13	4	25	99	15
94 NL	.293	92	334	57	98	18	2	14	53	10
95 AL	.185	32	108	13	20	3	0	1	10	1
95 NL	.269	60	212	38	57	10	1	11	37	7
Life	.256	633	2219	320	569	82	19	71	294	55
3 AVE	.263	128	464	73	122	18	3	19	76	13

CURRENT PLAYERS

MATT WHITESIDE

Position: Pitcher
Team: Texas Rangers
Born: Aug. 8, 1967 Charleston, MO
Height: 6′ **Weight:** 195 lbs.
Bats: right **Throws:** right
Acquired: 25th-round pick in 6/90 free-agent draft

Player Summary	
Fantasy Value	$1
Card Value	5¢ to 8¢
Will	strand inherited runners
Can't	throw fat first pitches
Expect	more set-up assignments
Don't Expect	basestealers to succeed

Whiteside solidified his grip on a big-league job with a solid showing as a Texas set-up man last summer. He yielded less hits than innings, held hitters to a .242 batting average, and allowed only one stolen base in 53 innings pitched. The rubber-armed righty made at least 40 appearances for the third year in a row while lowering his ERA by nearly one full run over its 1994 level. The Arkansas State physical education graduate throws strikes with three pitches: a fastball, a slider, and a changeup. Anxious to get ahead in the count, Whiteside often makes his first pitches too fat. Fastballs down the middle often come rocketing back in the opposite direction. Still, he managed to strand a fine 80 percent of the runners he inherited. When he's on, Whiteside gets most of his outs on ground balls and pop-ups. His quick delivery keeps runners at bay and his agility around the mound helps on balls hit back to the box. He converted three of four save chances last year and could see more last-inning duty.

Major League Pitching Register

	W	L	ERA	G	S	IP	H	ER	BB	SO
92 AL	1	1	1.93	20	4	28.0	26	6	11	13
93 AL	2	1	4.32	60	1	73.0	78	35	23	39
94 AL	2	2	5.02	47	1	61.0	68	34	28	37
95 AL	5	4	4.08	40	3	53.0	48	24	19	46
Life	10	8	4.14	167	9	215.0	220	99	81	135
3 AVE	3	3	4.53	57	2	73.0	76	37	28	48

DARRELL WHITMORE

Position: Outfield
Team: Florida Marlins
Born: Nov. 18, 1968 Front Royal, VA
Height: 6′1″ **Weight:** 210 lbs.
Bats: left **Throws:** right
Acquired: First-round pick from Indians in 11/92 expansion draft

Player Summary	
Fantasy Value	$0
Card Value	4¢ to 6¢
Will	add power, defense
Can't	rely on experience
Expect	use of speed
Don't Expect	hits vs. lefties

Injuries interfered with Whitmore's attempt to crack the Florida outfield last summer. A five-tools player whose game is built around speed and power, Whitmore also throws well enough to play right field in the majors. He is the last survivor of a once-heralded future Florida outfield that also included Nigel Wilson and Carl Everett. Whitmore was a mess at the plate during a 76-game stint with the Marlins in '93, their first season. But he had a banner year at Triple-A Edmonton a year later, working his way back to the big leagues. Speed could become his main calling card. The West Virginia University product has reached double-digits in steals three times in the minors. That speed gives him enough range to play center; he also has a wonderful throwing arm. Whitmore hammered 20 homers in 115 Triple-A Pacific Coast League games two years ago, and he may be able to be counted on for such production as soon as he learns the tendencies of big-league pitchers. He was the 16th overall selection in the 1992 expansion draft.

Major League Batting Register

	BA	G	AB	R	H	2B	3B	HR	RBI	SB
93 NL	.204	76	250	24	51	8	2	4	19	4
94 NL	.227	9	22	1	5	1	0	0	0	0
95 NL	.190	27	58	6	11	2	0	1	2	0
Life	.203	112	330	31	67	11	2	5	21	4

CURRENT PLAYERS

BOB WICKMAN

Position: Pitcher
Team: New York Yankees
Born: Feb. 6, 1969 Green Bay, WI
Height: 6'1" **Weight:** 212 lbs.
Bats: right **Throws:** right
Acquired: Traded by White Sox with Melido Perez and Domingo Jean for Steve Sax, 1/92

Player Summary	
Fantasy Value	$5 to $7
Card Value	5¢ to 8¢
Will	work often
Can't	hold runners
Expect	set-up work
Don't Expect	strikeouts

A former starter who switched to relief in 1994, Wickman made a career-high 63 appearances, including one start, last year. Used primarily as a set-up man for John Wetteland, Wickman held right-handed hitters to a .216 average and yielded less hits than innings. He is a sinkerballer who also throws a cut fastball, a slider, and a changeup. He depends upon his defense to retire opposing hitters. He averaged over five and one-half strikeouts per nine innings last year. Wickman tries to keep his pitches down but does not always succeed. He yielded less than four walks per nine innings and threw six home run balls in 80 innings. Wickman's natural sinker is the result of an unnatural accident: The University of Wisconsin product lost the tip of the index finger on his right hand in a farm machinery accident during his youth. The injury does not interfere with Wickman's fielding, which is average, or his ability to hold runners, which has improved from atrocious to below-average.

Major League Pitching Register

	W	L	ERA	G	S	IP	H	ER	BB	SO
92 AL	6	1	4.11	8	0	50.1	51	23	20	21
93 AL	14	4	4.63	41	4	140.0	156	72	69	70
94 AL	5	4	3.09	53	6	70.0	54	24	27	56
95 AL	2	4	4.05	63	1	80.0	77	36	33	51
Life	27	13	4.10	165	11	340.1	338	155	149	198
3 AVE	8	5	4.01	62	5	110.0	106	49	48	69

RICK WILKINS

Position: Catcher
Team: Houston Astros
Born: July 4, 1967 Jacksonville, FL
Height: 6'2" **Weight:** 210 lbs.
Bats: left **Throws:** right
Acquired: Traded by Cubs for Luis Gonzalez and Scott Servais, 6/95

Player Summary	
Fantasy Value	$7 to $9
Card Value	5¢ to 8¢
Will	lift average
Can't	hit southpaws
Expect	strong throws
Don't Expect	30 home runs

That big "30" under the home run column in Wilkins's career record sticks out like a sore thumb. Yes, he hit 30 home runs for the Cubs in 1993, but the wind at Wrigley Field must have been blowing out more often than not. Wilkins never hit more than 17 in any minor-league season or even reached double-digits in the majors. He has been anemic against left-handed pitchers (.154 and .158 averages) in the last two seasons and fans far too frequently (99 times in '93). A low fastball hitter, Wilkins has trouble with good breaking stuff. He steals a handful of bases a year but is more adept at stopping others. Though he spent long stretches of 1995 on the disabled list, Wilkins nailed 34 percent of the runners who challenged him. He's a good basic receiver whose lone weakness is preventing wild pitches. Wilkins calls a good game, handles his pitchers well, and has a strong, accurate arm. He's led several leagues in putouts, assists, double plays, and fielding percentage.

Major League Batting Register

	BA	G	AB	R	H	2B	3B	HR	RBI	SB
91 NL	.222	86	203	21	45	9	0	6	22	3
92 NL	.270	83	244	20	66	9	1	8	22	0
93 NL	.303	136	446	78	135	23	1	30	73	2
94 NL	.227	100	313	44	71	25	2	7	39	4
95 NL	.203	65	202	30	41	3	0	7	19	0
Life	.254	470	1408	193	358	69	4	58	175	9
3 AVE	.252	117	371	58	94	21	1	16	50	3

CURRENT PLAYERS

BERNIE WILLIAMS

Position: Outfield
Team: New York Yankees
Born: Sept. 13, 1968 San Juan, PR
Height: 6'2" **Weight:** 200 lbs.
Bats: both **Throws:** right
Acquired: Signed as a free agent, 9/85

Player Summary
Fantasy Value	$20 to $25
Card Value	8¢ to 12¢
Will	rip line drives
Can't	thrive in cold
Expect	extra-base hits
Don't Expect	low on-base mark

Williams reached career highs in average, triples, homers, and RBI in 1995. From Sept. 15 to the end of the season, his .364 mark helped the Yankees cement the AL's wild-card berth. His .392 on-base percentage ranked second to Wade Boggs among the Yankees. Williams had 49 multihit games to lead the team. He hit the fourth leadoff homer of his career on Aug. 6. His 46 hits in August tied Mike Piazza for the big-league lead. That wasn't surprising, since Williams usually warms with the weather. Once a wild swinger, he's improved his average in each of the last three seasons by showing more selectivity at the plate. He's now a solid .300 hitter from both sides of the plate. He's also a fine center fielder. He has quick reactions, soft hands, and a strong (though not always accurate) throwing arm. Williams had only one assist last year but seven the year before. Though he hasn't been a big basestealer in the majors, he can run. Williams has started 204 of the Yankees' last 206 games.

Major League Batting Register
	BA	G	AB	R	H	2B	3B	HR	RBI	SB
91 AL	.237	85	320	43	76	19	4	3	34	10
92 AL	.280	62	261	39	73	14	2	5	26	7
93 AL	.268	139	567	67	152	31	4	12	68	9
94 AL	.289	108	408	80	118	29	1	12	57	16
95 AL	.307	144	563	93	173	29	9	18	82	8
Life	.279	538	2119	322	592	122	20	50	267	50
3 AVE	.289	151	592	95	171	35	5	16	80	14

BRIAN WILLIAMS

Position: Pitcher
Team: San Diego Padres
Born: Feb. 15, 1969 Lancaster, SC
Height: 6'2" **Weight:** 195 lbs.
Bats: right **Throws:** right
Acquired: Traded by Astros with Andujar Cedeno, Ken Caminiti, Steve Finley, Roberto Petagine, and a player to be named later for Derek Bell, Doug Brocail, Ricky Gutierrez, Phil Plantier, and Craig Shipley, 12/94

Player Summary
Fantasy Value	$0
Card Value	4¢ to 6¢
Will	seek new start
Can't	throw strikes
Expect	swingman role
Don't Expect	the long ball

The jury is still out on Brian Williams. After a strong rookie showing as a Houston starter in 1992, he's had three mediocre years as a swingman. All that moving back and forth may have hurt, since his ERA has become more bloated in each succeeding season. His best stat was home runs allowed: three in 72 innings. A hard thrower who blends a fastball, a curveball, a slider, and a circle change, Williams averages more strikeouts than innings pitched and yields just over one hit per inning. But oh, those bases on balls! His nine-inning average of nearly five walks per game just doesn't cut it in the majors. He also needs to reduce an opponents' batting average of .279. Williams does help his own cause with good defensive skills, including a polished pickoff move that holds the running game in check. Only two of the four runners who challenged him last year made it.

Major League Pitching Register
	W	L	ERA	G	S	IP	H	ER	BB	SO
91 NL	0	1	3.75	2	0	12.0	11	5	4	4
92 NL	7	6	3.92	16	0	96.1	92	42	42	54
93 NL	4	4	4.83	42	3	82.0	76	44	38	56
94 NL	6	5	5.74	20	0	78.1	112	50	41	49
95 NL	3	10	6.00	44	0	72.0	79	48	38	75
Life	20	26	4.99	124	3	340.2	370	189	163	238
3 AVE	5	7	5.55	40	1	91.0	108	56	46	70

CURRENT PLAYERS

EDDIE WILLIAMS

Position: First base
Team: San Diego Padres
Born: Nov. 1, 1964 Shreveport, LA
Height: 6' **Weight:** 210 lbs.
Bats: right **Throws:** right
Acquired: Signed as a minor-league free agent, 12/93

Player Summary	
Fantasy Value	$3 to $5
Card Value	4¢ to 6¢
Will	show some power
Can't	steal any bases
Expect	good bat vs. lefties
Don't Expect	dazzling defense

After his strong finish in 1994, Williams was counted on to supply plenty of punch for the Padres last year. It didn't happen. Hamstring, knee, and shoulder injuries limited his mobility and cut into his production. For most of last season, Williams led the National League in banging into double plays. A better hitter against left-handed pitchers, Williams spent most of 1995 sharing his position with lefty-hitting first sackers Scott Livingstone and Roberto Petagine. Though Williams showed some power with 12 homers in 296 trips, his ratio was better in 1994. Williams makes fairly good contact but doesn't walk enough to build a high on-base percentage. He never steals bases and is somewhat of a liability as a baserunner. Never a defensive standout at third, his original position, Williams is equally inadequate at first. He has good hands but his range, arm, accuracy, and footwork are slightly below the big-league average.

Major League Batting Register

	BA	G	AB	R	H	2B	3B	HR	RBI	SB
86 AL	.143	5	7	2	1	0	0	0	1	0
87 AL	.172	22	64	9	11	4	0	1	4	0
88 AL	.190	10	21	3	4	0	0	0	1	0
89 AL	.274	66	201	25	55	8	0	3	10	1
90 NL	.286	14	42	5	12	3	0	3	4	0
94 NL	.331	49	175	32	58	11	1	11	42	0
95 NL	.260	97	296	35	77	11	1	12	47	0
Life	.270	263	806	111	218	37	2	30	109	1
2 AVE	.290	89	290	42	84	14	1	14	56	0

GERALD WILLIAMS

Position: Outfield
Team: New York Yankees
Born: Aug. 10, 1966 New Orleans, LA
Height: 6'2" **Weight:** 190 lbs.
Bats: right **Throws:** right
Acquired: 14th-round pick in 6/87 free-agent draft

Player Summary	
Fantasy Value	$1
Card Value	5¢ to 8¢
Will	play good defense
Can't	hit right-handers
Expect	more playing time
Don't Expect	consistent power

A fine fourth outfielder, Williams started 47 games for the Yankees last summer. Though his six homers and 28 RBI were career bests, he batted only .179 against right-handed pitching. His stock fell following a late-summer slump. Williams hit only .181 with no homers over his final 43 games. On the other hand, he made better contact than he had in the past. He drew enough walks to post an on-base percentage 80 points higher than his batting average. At 29, Williams worries about his chances of becoming an everyday player. He showed good speed and some power during his days in the minors. But he reached triple figures in games played only once in the big leagues. That happened in 1995, when he appeared 100 times, many of them as a pinch hitter or pinch runner. Because of his speed, Williams has good range in the outfield, where he played all three positions last summer. His arm isn't strong enough for right field, but Williams compensates with quick reactions and accurate throws.

Major League Batting Register

	BA	G	AB	R	H	2B	3B	HR	RBI	SB
92 AL	.296	15	27	7	8	2	0	3	6	2
93 AL	.149	42	67	11	10	2	3	0	6	2
94 AL	.291	57	86	19	25	8	0	4	13	1
95 AL	.247	100	182	33	45	18	2	6	28	4
Life	.243	214	362	70	88	30	5	13	53	9

CURRENT PLAYERS

MATT WILLIAMS

Position: Third base
Team: San Francisco Giants
Born: Nov. 28, 1965 Bishop, CA
Height: 6'2" **Weight:** 216 lbs.
Bats: right **Throws:** right
Acquired: First-round pick in 6/86 free-agent draft

Player Summary	
Fantasy Value	$30 to $35
Card Value	25¢ to 40¢
Will	burn left-handers
Can't	steal many bases
Expect	tremendous power
Don't Expect	defensive lapses

Twice in two years, Williams showed he could challenge Roger Maris's 1961 record of 61 home runs in a season. In 1994, he had 43 homers when the strike cut seven weeks off the schedule. When he hit his eighth homer of the 1995 season May 12, it gave Williams 62 taters in the course of his previous 162 games—the length of the schedule when Maris made his record run. Later that month, Williams broke his foot with a foul ball, idling him for three months. Giants hitting coach Bobby Bonds has helped Williams make better contact, lowering his strikeout total and raising his average without losing power. He hit .377 against lefties and .326 against righties last season; his .399 on-base mark was among the NL's best. A terrific fielder, the former UNLV All-American has led the NL in chances, putouts, assists, and double plays. He won his third Gold Glove in 1994.

Major League Batting Register

	BA	G	AB	R	H	2B	3B	HR	RBI	SB
87 NL	.188	84	245	28	46	9	2	8	21	4
88 NL	.205	52	156	17	32	6	1	8	19	0
89 NL	.202	84	292	31	59	18	1	18	50	1
90 NL	.277	159	617	87	171	27	2	33	122	7
91 NL	.268	157	589	72	158	24	5	34	98	5
92 NL	.227	146	529	58	120	13	5	20	66	7
93 NL	.294	145	579	105	170	33	4	38	110	1
94 NL	.267	112	445	74	119	16	3	43	96	1
95 NL	.336	76	283	53	95	17	1	23	65	2
Life	.260	1015	3735	525	970	163	24	225	647	28
3 AVE	.292	129	508	90	148	25	3	41	106	2

DAN WILSON

Position: Catcher
Team: Seattle Mariners
Born: March 25, 1969 Arlington Heights, IL
Height: 6'3" **Weight:** 190 lbs.
Bats: right **Throws:** right
Acquired: Traded by Reds with Bobby Ayala for Erik Hanson and Bret Boone, 11/93

Player Summary	
Fantasy Value	$4 to $6
Card Value	5¢ to 8¢
Will	show good glove
Can't	hit left-handers
Expect	All-Star future
Don't Expect	power explosion

Wilson has finally shaken the good-field, no-hit tag that has dogged him during his career. Strong at the start and finish, he had a .301 batting average on June 1 and a .300 mark over the final two months. Wilson's average of .278 was the best ever recorded by a Seattle backstop. He also had career highs in games, hits, doubles, triples, homers, and RBI. The former first-round draft choice (Cincinnati, June 1990) had a 10-game hitting streak, also a career best, in August, and knocked in eight runs over that span. Wilson homered in three straight games Sept. 10 to 12 and had a game-winning homer against the White Sox six days later. If he improves his work against left-handed pitching (.240 last year), he could become an All-Star. Wilson nailed 34 percent of the runners who tried to steal against him and led AL receivers in putouts and chances. During a game on Sept. 15, the University of Minnesota product nailed Tim Raines trying to steal—only the second time in 43 tries Raines was caught.

Major League Batting Register

	BA	G	AB	R	H	2B	3B	HR	RBI	SB
92 NL	.360	12	25	2	9	1	0	0	3	0
93 NL	.224	36	76	6	17	3	0	0	8	0
94 AL	.216	91	282	24	61	14	2	3	27	1
95 AL	.278	119	399	40	111	22	3	9	51	2
Life	.253	258	782	72	198	40	5	12	89	3
2 AVE	.249	131	423	39	105	22	3	7	48	2

CURRENT PLAYERS

TREVOR WILSON

Position: Pitcher
Team: San Francisco Giants
Born: June 7, 1966 Torrance, CA
Height: 6' **Weight:** 204 lbs.
Bats: left **Throws:** left
Acquired: Eighth-round pick in 6/85 free-agent draft

Player Summary
Fantasy Value	$1
Card Value	4¢ to 6¢
Will	test shoulder again
Can't	rack up strikeouts
Expect	frequent ground outs
Don't Expect	lefties to hit him

On the rare occasions when his shoulder is sound, Wilson is one of the game's better starters. Beyond his brilliant performances of 1991 and 1993, however, Wilson has battled severe shoulder problems that have once again clouded his future. He won only three of his 17 starts last year before returning to the disabled list. When right, the Oregon State southpaw is especially effective against left-handed hitters. They managed only a .179 mark against him in 1993, for example. Wilson's best pitch is a sweeping curve that he blends with a fastball and a slider to keep hitters guessing. Even before his latest physical problems, Wilson was not considered a power pitcher. Instead of shooting for strikeouts, he tries to keep the ball down, hoping his defense will gobble up ground balls for outs. Wilson's control doesn't always cooperate either. He is a competent fielder who keeps close tabs on the running game. Wilson sometimes helps himself with a bunt or a base hit.

Major League Pitching Register
	W	L	ERA	G	CG	IP	H	ER	BB	SO
88 NL	0	2	4.09	4	0	22.0	25	10	8	15
89 NL	2	3	4.35	14	0	39.1	28	19	24	22
90 NL	8	7	4.00	27	3	110.1	87	49	49	66
91 NL	13	11	3.56	44	2	202.0	173	80	77	139
92 NL	8	14	4.21	26	1	154.0	152	72	64	88
93 NL	7	5	3.60	22	1	110.0	110	44	40	57
95 NL	3	4	3.92	17	0	82.2	82	36	38	38
Life	41	46	3.87	154	7	720.1	657	310	300	425
2 AVE	5	5	3.75	21	1	101.1	101	42	44	50

DAVE WINFIELD

Position: Designated hitter
Team: Cleveland Indians
Born: Oct. 3, 1951 St. Paul, MN
Height: 6'6" **Weight:** 245 lbs.
Bats: right **Throws:** right
Acquired: Traded by Twins for Russ Swan, 8/94

Player Summary
Fantasy Value	$1
Card Value	20¢ to 30¢
Will	show leadership
Can't	use glove
Expect	some power
Don't Expect	many at bats

With an average under the Mendoza Line, Winfield didn't add much to the Indians attack last season. He was hurt during some of the season, and he was ineffective when he was playing. A future Hall of Famer, Winfield looks to be playing for his 500th home run. He has to hit 35 homers for No. 500, which appears to be at least two seasons away. He already achieved his dream of winning a World Series with the 1992 Blue Jays. When he retires, Winfield will go to Cooperstown.

Major League Batting Register
	BA	G	AB	R	H	2B	3B	HR	RBI	SB
73 NL	.277	56	141	9	39	4	1	3	12	0
74 NL	.265	145	498	57	132	18	4	20	75	9
75 NL	.267	143	509	74	136	20	2	15	76	23
76 NL	.283	137	492	81	139	26	4	13	69	26
77 NL	.275	157	615	104	169	29	7	25	92	16
78 NL	.308	158	587	88	181	30	5	24	97	21
79 NL	.308	159	597	97	184	27	10	34	118	15
80 NL	.276	162	558	89	154	25	6	20	87	23
81 AL	.294	105	388	52	114	25	1	13	68	11
82 AL	.280	140	539	84	151	24	8	37	106	5
83 AL	.283	152	598	99	169	26	8	32	116	15
84 AL	.340	141	567	106	193	34	4	19	100	6
85 AL	.275	155	633	105	174	34	6	26	114	19
86 AL	.262	154	565	90	148	31	5	24	104	6
87 AL	.275	156	575	83	158	22	1	27	97	5
88 AL	.322	149	559	96	180	37	2	25	107	9
90 AL	.267	132	475	70	127	21	2	21	78	0
91 AL	.262	150	568	75	149	27	4	28	86	7
92 AL	.290	156	583	92	169	33	3	26	108	2
93 AL	.271	143	547	72	148	27	2	21	76	2
94 AL	.252	77	294	35	74	15	3	10	43	2
95 AL	.191	46	115	11	22	5	0	2	4	1
Life	.283	2973	11003	1669	3110	540	88	465	1833	223
2 AVE	.262	126	481	61	126	24	3	18	68	2

CURRENT PLAYERS

BOBBY WITT

Position: Pitcher
Team: Texas Rangers
Born: May 11, 1964 Arlington, VA
Height: 6'2" **Weight:** 205 lbs.
Bats: right **Throws:** right
Acquired: Traded by Marlins for Wilson Heredia and Scott Podsednik, 8/95

Player Summary
Fantasy Value	$4 to $6
Card Value	4¢ to 6¢
Will	bank on his heat
Can't	find strike zone
Expect	hits from lefties
Don't Expect	reduction of ERA

The Rangers were at wit's end in an effort to land midseason pitching help. When the Marlins made Witt available, the Rangers remembered what he had done for them in 1990: a 17-10 record and a 3.36 ERA. The righty's return, however, was hardly triumphant. In 1995, Texas lost seven of his 10 starts, AL lefties lit him up at a .349 clip. Ironically, Witt did the one thing he wasn't expected to do: show decent control. Throughout his career, throwing strikes has been his bugaboo. A fastball-slider pitcher who also throws a curve and a cut fastball, Witt can still turn up the heat. When he loses concentration, he also loses the proper release point and his pitches flatten out. Witt's pickoff move isn't much and his fielding is only adequate. The former Oklahoma All-American and U.S. Olympian was a first-round draft choice in 1985.

Major League Pitching Register

	W	L	ERA	G	CG	IP	H	ER	BB	SO
86 AL	11	9	5.48	31	0	157.2	130	96	143	174
87 AL	8	10	4.91	26	1	143.0	114	78	140	160
88 AL	8	10	3.92	22	13	174.1	134	76	101	148
89 AL	12	13	5.14	31	5	194.1	182	111	114	166
90 AL	17	10	3.36	33	7	222.0	197	83	110	221
91 AL	3	7	6.09	17	1	88.2	84	60	74	82
92 AL	10	14	4.29	31	0	193.0	183	92	114	125
93 AL	14	13	4.21	35	5	220.0	226	103	91	131
94 AL	8	10	5.04	24	5	135.2	151	76	70	111
95 NL	2	7	3.90	19	1	110.2	104	48	47	95
95 AL	3	4	4.55	10	1	61.1	81	31	21	46
Life	96	107	4.52	279	39	1700.2	1586	854	1025	1459
3 AVE	10	13	4.45	34	5	201.2	216	100	89	149

MARK WOHLERS

Position: Pitcher
Team: Atlanta Braves
Born: Jan. 23, 1970 Holyoke, MA
Height: 6'4" **Weight:** 207 lbs.
Bats: right **Throws:** right
Acquired: Eighth-round pick in 6/88 free-agent draft

Player Summary
Fantasy Value	$30 to $35
Card Value	8¢ to 12¢
Will	mow batters down
Can't	hold runners on
Expect	microscopic ERA
Don't Expect	erratic control

Waiting for Wohlers went from agony to ecstasy last summer. In four previous seasons, the Braves wondered whether the hard-throwing reliever would ever show enough control to take command of the closer role. Throwing a fastball often timed in excess of 100 mph, Wohlers saved 21 straight games, a club record, between May 15 and Sept. 3. In 57 appearances after May 14, he had a 7-2 record, 1.37 ERA, and 84 strikeouts in 59⅔ innings. For the season, he held first batters to an .097 average (6-for-62) and right-handed hitters to a .191 mark. He finished with a nine-inning average of 12.53 strikeouts. One of his two World Series saves came when he pitched a perfect ninth in Tom Glavine's 1-0 win in the decisive game six. When he's on, Wohlers is unhittable. The NL's most intimidating closer blends his fastball with a slider, a forkball, and a newly perfected changeup. He's not much of a fielder or pickoff artist, but his pitching is so overpowering that it seldom matters.

Major League Pitching Register

	W	L	ERA	G	S	IP	H	ER	BB	SO
91 NL	3	1	3.20	17	2	19.2	17	7	13	13
92 NL	1	2	2.55	32	4	35.1	28	10	14	17
93 NL	6	2	4.50	46	0	48.0	37	24	22	45
94 NL	7	2	4.59	51	1	51.0	51	26	33	58
95 NL	7	3	2.09	65	25	64.2	51	15	24	90
Life	24	10	3.38	211	32	218.2	184	82	106	223
3 AVE	8	3	3.62	64	10	64.1	55	26	32	76

CURRENT PLAYERS

BRAD WOODALL

Position: Pitcher
Team: Atlanta Braves
Born: June 25, 1969 Atlanta, GA
Height: 6′ **Weight:** 175 lbs.
Bats: both **Throws:** left
Acquired: Signed as a nondrafted free agent, 6/91

Player Summary	
Fantasy Value	$0
Card Value	8¢ to 12¢
Will	seek starter job
Can't	throw ball hard
Expect	pinpoint control
Don't Expect	Glavine's double

More than any other pitcher in the minors last year, Woodall was considered a Tom Glavine clone. A crafty left-hander who relies on control and location, Woodall pitched his way to the brink of the majors in 1994 by posting a 15-6 record and league-best 2.38 ERA for Richmond, winning International League Pitcher of the Year honors. He even pitched the game that won the league championship for the Triple-A club. Woodall opened last year on Atlanta's 28-man roster, but lack of work forced his return to Richmond a month later. Then injuries set in. He missed two months with a painful cyst between the third and fourth toes on his left foot. Recovered from its surgical removal, Woodall then pulled a rib-cage muscle. He pitched well in limited action after his late-summer return. Woodall's fastball isn't much (about 84 mph), but he has good command of his curveball and changeup, knows how to change speeds, and spots his pitches well. He needs to stay healthy, however. In addition to last year's medical problems, Woodall has also had elbow woes.

Major League Pitching Register

	W	L	ERA	G	S	IP	H	ER	BB	SO
94 NL	0	1	4.50	1	0	6.0	5	3	2	2
95 NL	1	1	6.10	9	0	10.1	13	7	8	5
Life	1	2	5.51	10	0	16.1	18	10	10	7

TODD WORRELL

Position: Pitcher
Team: Los Angeles Dodgers
Born: Sept. 28, 1959 Arcadia, CA
Height: 6′5″ **Weight:** 222 lbs.
Bats: right **Throws:** right
Acquired: Signed as a free agent, 12/92

Player Summary	
Fantasy Value	$20 to $25
Card Value	5¢ to 8¢
Will	nail down games
Can't	hold runners on
Expect	frequent whiffs
Don't Expect	control trouble

Worrell saved a club-record 32 games for the Dodgers last season. He had topped 30 saves in each of his first three big-league seasons, for the 1986 to 1988 Cardinals, but he spent almost all of the time since recuperating from serious elbow and shoulder injuries. Worrell got off to a great start in 1995 by not allowing an earned run in his first 25 games. He converted all 12 save chances over that stretch. The result was his selection to the NL All-Star Team for the second time in his career. Worrell has good control of his sinking fastball, hard slider, and straight change. His three-quarters delivery confuses hitters, who managed a .221 mark against him. Worrell was most effective against first batters, who went 8-for-59 (.136) with 18 strikeouts. He allowed one hit or less in 42 of his 58 appearances. Though Worrell is a decent fielder, holding runners is not his forte.

Major League Pitching Register

	W	L	ERA	G	S	IP	H	ER	BB	SO
85 NL	3	0	2.91	17	5	21.2	17	7	7	17
86 NL	9	10	2.08	74	36	103.2	86	24	41	73
87 NL	8	6	2.66	75	33	94.2	86	28	34	92
88 NL	5	9	3.00	68	32	90.0	69	30	34	78
89 NL	3	5	2.96	47	20	51.2	42	17	26	41
92 NL	5	3	2.11	67	3	64.0	45	15	25	64
93 NL	1	1	6.05	35	5	38.2	46	26	11	31
94 NL	6	5	4.29	38	11	42.0	37	20	12	44
95 NL	4	1	2.02	59	32	62.1	50	14	19	61
Life	44	40	2.86	480	177	568.2	478	181	209	501
3 AVE	5	3	3.75	52	19	56.1	51	23	16	54

CURRENT PLAYERS

ANTHONY YOUNG

Position: Pitcher
Team: Chicago Cubs
Born: Jan. 19, 1966 Houston, TX
Height: 6'2" **Weight:** 215 lbs.
Bats: right **Throws:** right
Acquired: Traded by Mets with Ottis Smith for Jose Vizcaino, 3/94

Player Summary
Fantasy Value	$1
Card Value	4¢ to 6¢
Will	keep ball down
Can't	strike men out
Expect	set-up chores
Don't Expect	long bad spell

Young overcame serious elbow problems to claim a spot as a set-up man in the Cubs bullpen last summer. He is a sinker-slider pitcher who also throws a curve and a changeup. He showed good control but proved no mystery to NL batters, who hit him at a .288 clip. Since he also threw five home run balls in 41⅓ innings, Young's 3.70 ERA is miraculous. Once compared to Dwight Gooden (perhaps because they were on the same team), Young depends upon location and defense rather than power. Because he's good at keeping the ball down, he coaxes double plays—a big plus for a pitcher who often enters with men on base. He also helps himself with his bunting, hitting, fielding, and ability to hold baserunners. A converted starter, Young has made his mark in big-league history: He had the dubious distinction of losing 27 games in a row over two seasons (1992 and '93). Those days are long gone, though it's doubtful Young will ever realize the potential he showed as a Mets' farmhand.

ERIC YOUNG

Position: Second base; outfield
Team: Colorado Rockies
Born: May 18, 1967 New Brunswick, NJ
Height: 5'9" **Weight:** 180 lbs.
Bats: right **Throws:** right
Acquired: First-round pick from Dodgers in 11/92 expansion draft

Player Summary
Fantasy Value	$14 to $17
Card Value	4¢ to 6¢
Will	show great speed
Can't	carry good glove
Expect	top leadoff work
Don't Expect	home run barrage

Young was the late-summer catalyst of Colorado's successful drive to a berth in postseason play. He raised his average from .149 on July 1 to .317 and finished with a fine .404 on-base percentage. Both career-high marks would have ranked among the league leaders if Young had enough at bats to qualify. A contact hitter with a compact strike zone, Young walks far more often than he strikes out (49 walks, 29 Ks last year). He then tries to steal his way into scoring position (his 35 steals ranked sixth in the NL). He ripped lefties at a .400 clip last year but was no slouch against right-handers either (.274). In addition, Young provided unusual power for a leadoff hitter. Nearly one-third of his hits went for extra bases. The former Rutgers standout has enough speed to lead the league in steals but still gets thrown out too often. His speed gives him good range in the outfield, but Young's hands, arm, and inability to make the double-play pivot make him a liability in the infield.

Major League Pitching Register
	W	L	ERA	G	S	IP	H	ER	BB	SO
91 NL	2	5	3.10	10	0	49.1	48	17	12	20
92 NL	2	14	4.17	52	15	121.0	134	56	31	64
93 NL	1	16	3.77	39	3	100.1	103	42	42	62
94 NL	4	6	3.92	20	0	114.2	103	50	46	65
95 NL	3	4	3.70	32	2	41.1	47	17	14	15
Life	12	45	3.84	153	20	426.2	435	182	145	226
3 AVE	3	10	3.84	34	2	102.2	100	44	41	57

Major League Batting Register
	BA	G	AB	R	H	2B	3B	HR	RBI	SB
92 NL	.258	49	132	9	34	1	0	1	11	6
93 NL	.269	144	490	82	132	16	8	3	42	42
94 NL	.272	90	228	37	62	13	1	7	30	18
95 NL	.317	120	366	68	116	21	9	6	36	35
Life	.283	403	1216	196	344	51	18	17	119	101
3 AVE	.286	135	408	70	117	19	7	7	42	36

CURRENT PLAYERS

KEVIN YOUNG

Position: First base; third base
Team: Pittsburgh Pirates
Born: June 16, 1969 Alpena, MI
Height: 6'2" **Weight:** 219 lbs.
Bats: right **Throws:** right
Acquired: Seventh-round pick in 6/90 free-agent draft

Player Summary	
Fantasy Value	$1 to $3
Card Value	6¢ to 10¢
Will	get another look
Can't	stop striking out
Expect	increasing power
Don't Expect	strong fielding

Although he had a career-best five RBI against the Expos July 21, Young's hitting improved after he changed his batting stance three weeks later. He went 3-for-6 on Aug. 18, the night he changed his stance, and homered in the next two games. He went on to hit .308 for the month (20-for-65 in 18 games). That was good news for the Pirates, who had expected big things from Young after three .300 seasons in the minors. But his failures in 1993 and 1994 landed him back at Triple-A Calgary. In 1995, Young hit for the cycle on June 13 and had a .356 batting average at the time of his promotion. Despite his size, Young has never reached double-digits in homers in a pro career that began in 1990. He's not much of a basestealer either. A long swing and short patience at the plate work against him. Young fans nearly seven times per walk, often lunging at pitches well out of the strike zone. He's best at first but did tie an NL record when he made 11 assists from third base at Montreal on June 25.

Major League Batting Register

	BA	G	AB	R	H	2B	3B	HR	RBI	SB
92 NL	.571	10	7	2	4	0	0	0	4	1
93 NL	.236	141	449	38	106	24	3	6	47	2
94 NL	.205	59	122	15	25	7	2	1	11	0
95 NL	.232	56	181	13	42	9	0	6	22	1
Life	.233	266	759	68	177	40	5	13	84	4
2 AVE	.235	102	326	26	77	17	2	6	36	2

TODD ZEILE

Position: Third base
Team: Chicago Cubs
Born: Sept. 9, 1965 Van Nuys, CA
Height: 6'1" **Weight:** 190 lbs.
Bats: right **Throws:** right
Acquired: Traded by Cardinals for Mike Morgan, Paul Torres, and Francisco Morales, 6/95

Player Summary	
Fantasy Value	$10 to $13
Card Value	6¢ to 10¢
Will	show some pop
Can't	find old form
Expect	more patience
Don't Expect	fielding award

When Zeile knocked in 103 runs for the 1993 Cardinals, he hit lefties far better than he did last year. Though southpaws should be his country cousins, Zeile failed to hit his weight against them last year. After hitting .299 against lefties in 1994, he managed a meager .170 mark last year. That was a disappointment to the Cubs, who had thought his right-handed power would be well-matched with the friendly confines of Wrigley Field. Instead, he finished with his worst home run and RBI totals since 1992. Instead of showing his usual patience at the plate, Zeile lunged after anything near the zone. The result was a ratio of more than two strikeouts per walk, far from his 1-1 mark of the year before. His defense isn't great either. Last year, he was so erratic at third that he was moved to first for 35 games and even played left field twice. Zeile's speed translates into good range, but that's his only defensive asset.

Major League Batting Register

	BA	G	AB	R	H	2B	3B	HR	RBI	SB
89 NL	.256	28	82	7	21	3	1	1	8	0
90 NL	.244	144	495	62	121	25	3	15	57	2
91 NL	.280	155	565	76	158	36	3	11	81	17
92 NL	.257	126	439	51	113	18	4	7	48	7
93 NL	.277	157	571	82	158	36	1	17	103	5
94 NL	.267	113	415	62	111	25	1	19	75	1
95 NL	.246	113	426	50	105	22	0	14	52	1
Life	.263	836	2993	390	787	165	13	84	424	33
3 AVE	.265	148	545	75	144	32	1	20	89	3

ROOKIE PROSPECTS

JEFF ABBOTT

Position: Outfield
Team: Chicago White Sox
Born: Aug. 17, 1972 Atlanta, GA
Height: 6'2" **Weight:** 190 lbs.
Bats: right **Throws:** left
Acquired: Fourth-round pick in 6/94 free-agent draft

Player Summary
Fantasy Value $0
Card Value . . . . N/A
Will . . . . stay on fast track
Can't . . . . watch college stats
Expect . . . . majors by '96
Don't Expect. . . . . big hits

The White Sox liked Abbott so much that they drafted him twice—once in 1993 and again in 1994—and he has quickly justified this high opinion. In fact, few players from the Class of 1994 are on as fast a track to the major leagues as is Abbott. Last year, he blazed through the Class-A Carolina League with such ferocity that the White Sox gave him a midseason promotion to Double-A ball. A product of the University of Kentucky, Abbott was an outfielder on *Baseball America*'s 1994 All-America second team, mostly for batting .445. Despite missing most of the 1993 season with mononucleosis, he set a school record for runs in a career with 182. He hit 23 home runs and posted an .882 slugging percentage as a junior, garnering several honors. Upon reaching pro ball, Abbott spent most of the 1994 campaign with Hickory of the Class-A South Atlantic League, where he was named player of the month for August. He later attended the Fall Instructional League. Abbott has posted about a .500 slugging percentage thus far in his minor-league career.

Professional Batting Register

	BA	G	AB	R	H	2B	3B	HR	RBI	SB
94 R	.467	4	15	4	7	1	0	1	3	2
94 A	.393	63	224	47	88	16	6	6	48	2
95 A	.348	70	264	41	92	16	0	4	47	7
95 AA	.320	55	197	25	63	11	1	3	28	1

BOB ABREU

Position: Outfield
Team: Houston Astros
Born: March 11, 1974 Aragua, Venezuela
Height: 6' **Weight:** 160 lbs.
Bats: left **Throws:** right
Acquired: Signed as a nondrafted free agent 8/90

Player Summary
Fantasy Value $0
Card Value . . . . 25¢ to 40¢
Will. . . . . drive in runs
Can't . . . . pile up whiffs
Expect . . . . a promotion
Don't Expect . . . . a fence-buster

Abreu first appeared on this list after he posted two fine seasons as a 17-year-old and an 18-year-old phenom. Now, after a steady climb through the system, he seems ready for a major-league job, and he's still just 22. He has kept his batting average near or above .300 at all levels of pro ball, and he seems to get better as he moves higher. He even appeared to be gaining power in 1994 when, as the Double-A Texas League's second-youngest position player, he led the loop with a .530 slugging percentage and finished among the leaders in home run frequency. That trend fell off last year, when Abreu failed to hit the long ball in the Triple-A Pacific Coast League, a circuit that usually boosts home run totals. Considering his slender build, it's not all too surprising that he is not projecting as a major home run hitter at the present. Still, Abreu has a chance to deliver bona fide extra-base pop at the big-league level. He notched a .515 slugging percentage last season. He also possesses enough speed to stretch hits and steal bases.

Professional Batting Register

	BA	G	AB	R	H	2B	3B	HR	RBI	SB
91 R	.301	56	183	21	55	7	3	0	20	10
92 A	.292	135	480	81	140	21	4	8	48	15
93 A	.283	129	474	62	134	21	17	5	55	10
94 AA	.303	118	400	61	121	25	9	16	73	12
95 AAA	.304	114	415	72	126	24	17	10	75	16

ROOKIE PROSPECTS

WILLIE ADAMS

Position: Pitcher
Team: Oakland Athletics
Born: Oct. 8, 1972 Gallup, NM
Height: 6'7" **Weight:** 215 lbs.
Bats: right **Throws:** right
Acquired: Second-round pick in 6/93 free-agent draft

Player Summary	
Fantasy Value	$0
Card Value	10¢ to 15¢
Will	throw strikes
Can't	make 'em too fat
Expect	a craftsman
Don't Expect	long counts

Considering his size, you might expect Adams to throw with the velocity associated with a power pitcher. However, that's not the case. He can throw a fastball, but it won't necessarily put up exclamation points on the radar gun. If anything, his game depends on an uncanny ability to throw strikes. Last year, when he got off to a slow start, you couldn't blame it on a lack of control: He walked only 14 in his first 60 innings. Just as importantly, his game got straightened out. Adams put together a winning streak that spanned through June and July, and one of his victories came against Knoxville when he struck out 10. Later, Adams had some rough times at Triple-A Edmonton in the Pacific Coast League. He came to the A's via the 36th overall pick of the 1993 draft, with a selection Oakland earned through the loss of free agent Dave Stewart. Adams's ratio of strikeouts to innings has been impressive for most of his pro career, and he has a chance to see the big leagues this year if he keeps throwing strikes.

GEORGE ARIAS

Position: Third base
Team: California Angels
Born: March 12, 1972 Tucson, AZ
Height: 5'11" **Weight:** 190 lbs.
Bats: right **Throws:** right
Acquired: Seventh-round pick in 6/93 free-agent draft

Player Summary	
Fantasy Value	$0
Card Value	50¢ to $1.00
Will	hit 'em out
Can't	be overlooked anymore
Expect	decent contact
Don't Expect	many 0-fers

Last year, Arias was one of the outstanding players in all of the minor leagues, even though entering the season he was not one of the more ballyhooed Angel prospects. Playing for Midland of the Double-A Texas League, he put up big power numbers. He and teammate Todd Greene combined for 50 home runs before Greene was promoted to Triple-A ball. Arias, a third baseman, was selected as a Double-A All-Star, and he went 0-for-3 in the game. But that was an exception; he didn't take a lot of 0-fers during the season. He was able to deliver power without sacrificing average. His home field at Midland was not appreciably smaller than other parks, so his numbers aren't an example of inflated stats that can come out of some Texas League parks. Instead, you've got to give Arias credit for improving at every level and forcing himself into view. A project with the glove on at this point, Arias had 32 errors in 1994; he needs to cut down on his unforced mistakes. Nevertheless, soon he may present the Angels with the pleasant duty of finding a place for him in their lineup.

Professional Pitching Register

	W	L	ERA	G	CG	IP	H	ER	BB	SO
93 A	0	2	3.38	5	0	18.2	21	7	8	22
94 A	7	1	3.38	11	0	45.1	41	17	10	42
94 AA	4	3	4.30	10	0	60.2	58	29	23	33
95 AA	6	5	3.01	13	0	80.2	75	27	17	72
95 AAA	2	5	4.37	11	1	68.0	73	33	15	40

Professional Batting Register

	BA	G	AB	R	H	2B	3B	HR	RBI	SB
93 A	.217	74	253	55	13	3	9	41	6	
94 A	.280	134	514	89	144	28	3	23	80	6
95 AA	.279	134	520	91	145	19	10	30	104	3

ROOKIE PROSPECTS

KYM ASHWORTH

Position: Pitcher
Team: Los Angeles Dodgers
Born: July 31, 1976 Millicent, South Australia
Height: 6'2" **Weight:** 175 lbs.
Bats: left **Throws:** left
Acquired: Signed as a nondrafted free agent, 12/92

Player Summary
Fantasy Value	$0
Card Value	15¢ to 25¢
Will	hold his own
Can't	stay in Class-A
Expect	mound poise
Don't Expect	pinpoint control

Ashworth may never create the sensation that Hideo Nomo did for the Dodgers last year. But Ashworth nevertheless represents another example of what Los Angeles is doing on the international scene. On Opening Day of 1994, this Aussie was the youngest player on a full-season roster. Still, he managed to do quite well, making 24 starts and turning one of them into a July 4 no-hitter. He even received a brief call-up to Double-A, though he lasted only four innings in that start. Ashworth was only 16 years old when he broke into North American pro ball, and he still posted the second-lowest ERA in the rookie Pioneer League. He was considered among the top prospects in each of his first two seasons. In 1995, he put in more time in Class-A, though this time the Dodgers moved him from the California League to the Florida State League, a very good test for a prospect. He did well, holding league batters to a .253 batting average. His control will have to improve if he wants to advance; he had 64 walks and 24 wild pitches in 120 innings.

Professional Pitching Register
	W	L	ERA	G	CG	IP	H	ER	BB	SO
93 R	3	3	2.44	11	0	59.0	43	16	14	52
94 A	6	7	3.95	24	1	127.2	112	56	69	109
94 AA	0	1	4.50	1	0	4.0	5	2	0	6
95 A	7	4	3.53	24	1	120.0	111	47	64	97

JAMES BALDWIN

Position: Pitcher
Team: Chicago White Sox
Born: July 15, 1971 Southern Pines, NC
Height: 6'3" **Weight:** 210 lbs.
Bats: right **Throws:** right
Acquired: Fourth-round pick in 6/90 free-agent draft

Player Summary
Fantasy Value	$0
Card Value	10¢ to 15¢
Will	get another chance
Can't	let hitters lock in
Expect	a power pitcher
Don't Expect	great command

Some people are already writing off Baldwin because he failed in his first shot at the majors. That would be a mistake. He retains the same tools that got him there, and there's no reason why his next chance can't be successful. He needs to change speeds a little more—to keep batters from locking on to his power stuff. Of his arm, there can be little doubt. Even last year, while pitching for Nashville of the Triple-A American Association, Baldwin averaged around one strikeout per inning. The year before, he led the league with 156 strikeouts, and he ranked third with an opponents' batting average of .235. Baldwin entered the 1995 season having struck out 603 batters in 635 innings, an average of about eight and one-half per nine innings. Baldwin's strength is shown by the fact he was sought by many schools as a fullback. He also played baseball and basketball in high school, and he pitched against prospect John Roper.

Professional Pitching Register
	W	L	ERA	G	CG	IP	H	ER	BB	SO
90 R	1	6	4.10	9	0	37.1	32	17	18	32
91 R	3	1	2.12	6	0	34.0	16	8	16	48
91 A	1	4	5.30	7	1	37.1	40	22	27	23
92 A	10	7	2.52	27	2	175.1	149	49	52	176
93 AA	8	5	2.25	17	4	120.0	94	30	43	107
93 AAA	5	4	2.61	10	1	69.0	43	20	36	61
94 AAA	12	6	3.72	26	2	162.0	144	67	83	156
95 AAA	5	9	5.85	18	0	95.1	120	62	44	89
95 AL	0	1	12.89	6	0	14.2	32	21	9	10

ROOKIE PROSPECTS

MICHAEL BARRETT

Position: Infield
Team: Montreal Expos
Born: Oct. 22, 1976 Atlanta, GA
Height: 6'3" **Weight:** 185 lbs.
Bats: right **Throws:** right
Acquired: First-round pick in 6/95 free-agent draft

Player Summary
Fantasy Value	$0
Card Value	N/A
Will	drive in runs
Can't	play short
Expect	extra bases
Don't Expect	Wil Cordero

Their exceptional 1994 season meant that the Expos had to wait around until the 28th overall pick in the 1995 draft. When they finally got a chance, the Expos used it for this shortstop out of Pace Academy in Atlanta. Barrett became one of the earliest first-round signees, and he was assigned to the Expos rookie club in the Gulf Coast League. There he endured an inauspicious debut, going 0-for-4 with two strikeouts and one error. But he regrouped and owned six hits in his first 20 at bats. As the season wore on, he settled in nicely, even showing some of the extra-base pop he had demonstrated in high school. He had a .426 slugging percentage in the Gulf Coast League last year. With Wil Cordero still a youngster and entrenched as shortstop, the Expos might not be needing Barrett—or anyone else—to play shortstop for years. Besides, like other prospects, he may move around until the team finds the right position for him. It's still too early to tell if he will be able to handle the fielding aspects of shortstop. So the best thing for Barrett is just to play, produce, and develop.

Professional Batting Register
	BA	G	AB	R	H	2B	3B	HR	RBI	SB
95 R	.311	50	183	22	57	13	4	0	19	7
95 A	.100	3	10	0	1	0	0	0	1	0

TONY BATISTA

Position: Shortstop; infield
Team: Oakland Athletics
Born: Dec. 9, 1973 Puerto Plata, Dominican Republic
Height: 6' **Weight:** 165 lbs.
Bats: right **Throws:** right
Acquired: Signed as a nondrafted free agent, 6/92

Player Summary
Fantasy Value	$0
Card Value	15¢ to 25¢
Will	show strong arm
Can't	worry about others
Expect	good glove
Don't Expect	big power

His name is Leocadio Francisco Batista, but you can call him Tony. And you can keep an eye on his progress, too. Last year, he didn't hit much, but he was just 21 years old and playing in Double-A ball. Signed by Juan Marichal, Batista made the California League All-Star team in 1994 at the age of 20. He was recognized as one of the top defensive shortstops in the league, with an arm to go with it. He also showed an ability to hit the ball out of the park. That is quite a feat for someone who was listed at 145 pounds not long ago. He has already begun putting on some pounds, and it has translated into some long-ball power. Batista played ball in his native Dominican Republic in 1991, then in Arizona for two seasons. He got a brief look at the Triple-A Pacific Coast League in 1993, an indication the A's think well of him. He played well for Huntsville of the Double-A Southern League, especially considering his youth. He must sharpen his contact and cut down on his strikeouts.

Professional Batting Register
	BA	G	AB	R	H	2B	3B	HR	RBI	SB
92 R	.246	45	167	32	41	6	2	0	22	1
93 R	.327	24	104	21	34	6	2	2	17	6
93 AAA	.167	4	12	1	2	1	0	0	1	0
94 A	.281	119	466	91	131	26	3	17	68	7
95 AA	.255	120	419	55	107	23	1	16	61	7

ROOKIE PROSPECTS

HOWARD BATTLE

Position: Third base; infield
Team: Philadelphia Phillies
Born: March 25, 1972 Biloxi, MS
Height: 6' **Weight:** 197 lbs.
Bats: right **Throws:** right
Acquired: Traded by Blue Jays with Ricardo Jordan for Paul Quantrill, 12/95

Player Summary	
Fantasy Value	$0
Card Value	10¢ to 15¢
Will	steal a base
Can't	afford power loss
Expect	steady bat
Don't Expect	big-league star

Battle's march to the major leagues stalled a bit last year, as he repeated Triple-A and suffered a loss of power. However, this third baseman kept his batting average in the .250 range. His steady, if not spectacular, bat could get him some time in the majors. His ability to run won't hurt, either. He stole 26 times in the International League in 1994, being caught just twice. That ratio suffered last year, as he was caught stealing 11 times. Battle has now played six full seasons of pro ball, remarkable considering that he only turns 24 this season. He has made an impact at virtually every stop, putting up at least one stat that gains attention. In 1991, he did better than that, winning the team MVP award while playing for Myrtle Beach of the Class-A South Atlantic League. A year later, while playing in Dunedin, Battle was a member of the Class-A Florida State League All-Star squad. But those achievements won't mean much unless he takes the final step.

Professional Batting Register

	BA	G	AB	R	H	2B	3B	HR	RBI	SB
90 R	.266	61	233	25	62	17	1	5	32	5
91 A	.279	138	520	82	145	33	4	20	87	15
92 A	.254	136	520	76	132	27	3	17	85	6
93 AA	.278	141	521	66	145	21	5	7	70	12
94 AAA	.277	139	517	72	143	26	8	14	75	26
95 AAA	.251	118	443	43	111	17	4	8	48	10
95 AL	.200	9	15	3	3	0	0	0	0	1

TREY BEAMON

Position: Outfield
Team: Pittsburgh Pirates
Born: Feb. 11, 1974 Dallas, TX
Height: 6'3" **Weight:** 195 lbs.
Bats: left **Throws:** right
Acquired: Second-round pick in 6/92 free-agent draft

Player Summary	
Fantasy Value	$3 to $5
Card Value	20¢ to 35¢
Will	hit for average
Can't	play center or right
Expect	doubles
Don't Expect	homer power

Beamon would seem to be ready for a major-league job after an apprenticeship that began when he became the 61st overall pick in 1992. He played in the Triple-A Pacific Coast League last year and hit for average. That season followed one in which he led the Double-A Southern League in batting and helped carry the Carolina Mudcats to the final round of the playoffs. Beamon is a pure hitter, one who neither walks nor strikes out a great deal. As years go by, it is becoming increasingly apparent that his bat is his ticket to the majors. His arm is not among the best you'll ever see. He also didn't steal many bases last year, after a career-high 24 the previous season. Despite his size, he hasn't yet hit for power, and the fact that he didn't do so in the PCL suggests that he may not do it anywhere. He shapes up as a Gregg Jefferies type who will hit the gaps. On the artificial turf in Pittsburgh, that could translate into a nice slugging percentage. Beamon had a .454 slugging percentage last year, and he also had a pretty good-looking .387 on-base average.

Professional Batting Register

	BA	G	AB	R	H	2B	3B	HR	RBI	SB
92 R	.308	13	39	9	12	1	0	1	6	0
92 A	.290	19	69	15	20	5	0	3	9	4
93 A	.271	104	373	64	101	18	6	0	45	19
94 AA	.323	112	434	69	140	18	9	5	47	24
95 AAA	.334	118	452	74	151	29	5	5	62	18

ROOKIE PROSPECTS

DAVID BELL

Position: Second base; third base
Team: St. Louis Cardinals
Born: Sept. 14, 1972 Cincinnati, OH
Height: 5'10" **Weight:** 175 lbs.
Bats: right **Throws:** right
Acquired: Traded by Indians with Rick Heiserman and Pepe McNeal for Ken Hill, 7/95

Player Summary
Fantasy Value	$3 to $5
Card Value	10¢ to 15¢
Will	hit the ball
Can't	miss this chance
Expect	versatile fielder
Don't Expect	blue chipper

They say that timing is everything in life, and last year Bell's timing went from bad to good in a single day. One moment, he was enduring a mediocre year in the minors, with a ton of talent blocking his way to Cleveland. The next, he was heading for St. Louis as part of the Ken Hill deal with a chance to get a fresh start. Bell is still only 23 years old, but the question remains: Did he top out in 1994, when he hit 18 homers with 88 RBI at Triple-A Charlotte? Or can he battle back and still get a shot at the big leagues? Until last season, Bell's batting average had increased for three straight seasons, and his home run total had gone up four times in a row. Then he flattened out. His versatility may come in handy, as he can play second as well as third. But at least now he won't be lost in the crowd. The grandson of Gus Bell, the son of Buddy Bell, and the brother of Mike Bell, David did show that he could hit big-league pitching last year—at least at a .250 level.

Professional Batting Register
	BA	G	AB	R	H	2B	3B	HR	RBI	SB
90 R	.235	42	153	22	36	6	2	0	15	3
91 A	.230	136	491	47	113	24	1	5	63	3
92 A	.252	123	464	52	117	17	2	6	47	2
93 AA	.292	129	483	69	141	20	2	9	60	3
94 AAA	.293	134	481	66	141	17	4	18	88	2
95 AAA	.273	88	330	43	90	14	2	9	43	4
95 AL	.000	2	2	0	0	0	0	0	0	0
95 NL	.250	39	144	13	36	7	2	2	19	1

MIKE BELL

Position: Third base
Team: Texas Rangers
Born: Dec. 7, 1974 Cincinnati, OH
Height: 6'2" **Weight:** 185 lbs.
Bats: right **Throws:** right
Acquired: Sandwich second-round pick in 6/93 free-agent draft

Player Summary
Fantasy Value	$0
Card Value	10¢ to 15¢
Will	collect doubles
Can't	be a DH
Expect	some pop
Don't Expect	a Gold Glover

Mike is the latest product of a family tree that has already yielded his grandfather Gus, his father Buddy, and his brother David. Mike came to Texas as the 30th overall pick in the draft, and he has moved through the lower levels of the Texas organization. However, further progress will depend in large measure on his skill with the glove. In 1994, while playing in the Double-A South Atlantic League, Bell made 35 errors in only 121 games, second among all minor leaguers. However, no such doubts have surfaced about his bat. In his first two pro seasons, Bell averaged .281 with a total of 56 extra-base hits, while making the All-Star Team both times. In fact, he delivered an RBI double in the Sally League All-Star Game. Last year, in the faster competition of the Class-A Florida State League, Bell held his own at the plate. He had a .338 slugging average and a .327 on-base percentage—numbers that are not an embarrassment in the FSL, which is considered a tough loop to hit in. But if he doesn't catch the ball, neither bat nor bloodlines will get Bell to the majors.

Professional Batting Register
	BA	G	AB	R	H	2B	3B	HR	RBI	SB
93 R	.317	60	230	48	73	13	6	3	34	9
94 A	.263	120	475	58	125	22	6	6	58	16
95 A	.260	129	470	49	122	20	1	5	52	9

ROOKIE PROSPECTS

ALAN BENES

Position: Pitcher
Team: St. Louis Cardinals
Born: Jan. 21, 1972 Evansville, IN
Height: 6'5" **Weight:** 215 lbs.
Bats: right **Throws:** right
Acquired: First-round pick in 6/93 free-agent draft

Player Summary
Fantasy Value	$3 to $5
Card Value	20¢ to 40¢
Will	equal Andy
Can't	make it with injury
Expect	a quick arrival
Don't Expect	100 mph

Benes seemed to be a phone call away from a spot in the St. Louis rotation, until problems in his wing cost him most of the 1995 campaign. The injury was especially disappointing because he was off to an outstanding start last year with Louisville of the Triple-A American Association. He came to the Cardinals with the 16th overall pick in the draft, arriving without the hype that had accompanied his brother Andy a few years earlier. But chances are that Alan—even without the 100-mph fastball that Andy was said to have had when he was drafted—could make as big an impact. A look at his rapid rise through the minors indicates that Alan has quickly outgrown the competition at most levels. In 1994, he brushed aside the hitters in the Class-A South Atlantic League and Florida State League, eventually was boosted to Double-A, and even got a start in Triple-A. Out of Creighton University, Benes offers a fastball, a breaking ball, and a changeup, and he can throw all for strikes.

Professional Pitching Register

	W	L	ERA	G	CG	IP	H	ER	BB	SO
93 A	0	4	3.65	7	0	37.0	39	15	14	29
94 A	9	1	1.58	15	0	102.2	76	18	22	93
94 AA	7	2	2.98	13	1	87.2	58	29	26	75
94 AAA	1	0	2.93	2	1	15.1	10	5	4	16
95 AAA	4	2	2.41	11	2	56.0	37	15	14	54
95 NL	1	2	8.44	3	0	16.0	24	15	4	20

YAMIL BENITEZ

Position: Outfield
Team: Montreal Expos
Born: May 10, 1972 San Juan, PR
Height: 6'2" **Weight:** 190 lbs.
Bats: right **Throws:** right
Acquired: Signed as a nondrafted free agent, 10/89

Player Summary
Fantasy Value	$0
Card Value	10¢ to 20¢
Will	produce runs
Can't	give up at bats
Expect	extra-base pop
Don't Expect	patience at plate

Benitez seems to have done a nice job of getting overlooked when top prospects are mentioned. Maybe that's because of the path he has worn by walking back to the dugouts after his strikeouts. And there's no doubt that Benitez must improve his selectivity at the plate to address an imbalance between his walks and strikeouts—he had 128 Ks at Triple-A Ottawa and 44 bases on balls. But it's equally evident that Benitez can offer something in the way of production. Last year, playing in the Triple-A International League didn't exactly intimidate him. Throughout most of the season, not one of his teammates had more doubles, triples, or home runs than Benitez, and only one had more RBI. He'll even steal a base or two, but that won't be his ticket to the majors. Instead, his impact will come at bat. But he's got to learn to swing at strikes, or else he'll never get anything good to hit. And Benitez needs to hit to take the final step that would put him in the Montreal outfield.

Professional Batting Register

	BA	G	AB	R	H	2B	3B	HR	RBI	SB
90 R	.229	22	83	6	19	1	0	1	5	0
91 R	.239	54	197	20	47	9	5	5	38	10
92 A	.237	67	241	30	57	9	8	4	29	19
93 A	.273	111	411	70	112	21	5	15	61	18
94 AA	.259	126	475	58	123	18	4	17	91	18
95 AAA	.259	127	474	66	123	24	6	18	69	14
95 NL	.385	14	39	8	15	2	1	2	7	0

ROOKIE PROSPECTS

JAIME BLUMA

Position: Pitcher
Team: Kansas City Royals
Born: May 18, 1972 Beaufort, SC
Height: 5'11" **Weight:** 195 lbs.
Bats: right **Throws:** right
Acquired: Third-round pick in 6/94 free-agent draft

Player Summary
Fantasy Value $0
Card Value . . . . 10¢ to 20¢
Will . . . . get the ball
Can't. . . . . grow any taller
Expect . . . . a bullpen specialist
Don't Expect . . . . domination

It hasn't taken Bluma very long to bloom. Only one year out of college, he was a Double-A Texas League sensation. He led the Kansas City organization in saves, giving every indication he might step into a major-league job. As a closer, Bluma enjoyed a fine career at Wichita State, making three appearances in the College World Series. He wound up as the school's career leader with 34 saves and 114 games pitched. He earned first-team Missouri Valley Conference laurels in 1993 and 1994, and he finished with a 16-5 record and a 2.35 ERA. In 11 postseason games, he went 3-0 with an 0.48 ERA. But upon leaving college, Bluma kept up the success in pro ball, something not everyone does. He pitched at rookie and regular Class-A ball in 1994 without flinching at either one. In fact, he was named the Class-A Carolina League Pitcher of the Week for Aug. 21 to 27. He made it to Triple-A Omaha last year, posting numbers about as good as on the Double-A level. Bluma's size is a bit on the slight side for a right-hander, but you've got to watch him until he finds a level he can't handle.

Professional Pitching Register

	W	L	ERA	G	S	IP	H	ER	BB	SO
94 A	6	1	0.98	33	14	46.0	26	5	6	40
95 AA	4	3	3.09	42	22	55.1	38	19	9	31
95 AAA	0	0	3.04	18	4	23.2	21	8	14	12

HIRAM BOCACHICA

Position: Outfield
Team: Montreal Expos
Born: March 4, 1976 Ponce, PR
Height: 5'11" **Weight:** 170 lbs.
Bats: right **Throws:** right
Acquired: First-round pick in 6/94 free-agent draft

Player Summary
Fantasy Value $0
Card Value . . . . 15¢ to 30¢
Will . . . . hit for average
Can't . . . . regain lost time
Expect. . . . . a touch of power
Don't Expect . . . . a loss of speed

In 1995, his first full year, Bocachica was not able to play a full season of pro ball. He opened the season with Albany of the Class-A South Atlantic League and promptly suffered an ankle injury that kept him out for several weeks. Such a setback could naturally raise some concern when it involves a player whose game depends on quickness and range. But Bocachica showed that he could overcome an injury. All you have to do is look at his stolen-base total to see that the foot speed is still there. Bocachica also pretty much lived up to his advance billing as a fine fielder through his two seasons in pro ball. He wound up with a solid average last year, and he even threw in some extra-base hits. He showed a great deal of patience at the dish, taking 52 bases on balls and notching a .381 on-base percentage. Bocachica did not hit with a great deal of power, but that isn't all that unusual for a young prospect getting his first extended look at pro ball. A shortstop, he was the 21st overall pick in 1994. Bocachica need not worry about making the big leagues quickly. His best approach is to keep getting on base and then using his wheels.

Professional Batting Register

	BA	G	AB	R	H	2B	3B	HR	RBI	SB
94 R	.280	43	168	31	47	9	0	5	16	11
95 A	.284	96	380	65	108	20	10	2	30	47

ROOKIE PROSPECTS

JIM BONNICI

Position: First base
Team: Seattle Mariners
Born: Jan. 21, 1972 Omaha, NE
Height: 6'4" **Weight:** 200 lbs.
Bats: right **Throws:** right
Acquired: 58th-round pick in 6/90 free-agent draft

Player Summary	
Fantasy Value	$0
Card Value	N/A
Will	drive in runs
Can't	burn the basepaths
Expect	a good eye
Don't Expect	return to catching

One question for the Mariners is which is the real Bonnici—the first half version or the one they saw after the All-Star break? Through the end of May, Bonnici, playing for Port City of the Southern League, led all Seattle farmhands in the three Triple Crown categories. He was pacing the league in hits, RBI, doubles, on-base percentage, and slugging percentage. He even made the Double-A All-Star Game and scored a run for the American League farmhands. However, no one can keep up that pace, and Bonnici didn't either. After the break, he slumped until his average was down in the .270 range. Even so, he wound up with good numbers. He had a .484 slugging average and a .384 on-base percentage. A former catcher, he has benefited from a switch to first, especially when considering his power totals. It is good news that he no longer has Tino Martinez blocking his way at the big-league level. But the more immediate question is whether Bonnici can resume hitting the way he did early last year.

Professional Batting Register

	BA	G	AB	R	H	2B	3B	HR	RBI	SB
91 R	.331	51	178	36	59	2	4	0	38	8
92 A	.262	53	168	13	44	6	1	4	20	5
93 A	.307	104	375	69	115	21	1	9	58	0
94 A	.280	113	397	71	111	23	3	10	71	1
95 AA	.283	138	508	75	144	36	3	20	91	2

AARON BOONE

Position: Third base
Team: Cincinnati Reds
Born: March 9, 1973 La Mesa, CA
Height: 6'2" **Weight:** 190 lbs.
Bats: right **Throws:** right
Acquired: Third-round pick in 6/94 free-agent draft

Player Summary	
Fantasy Value	$0
Card Value	30¢ to 60¢
Will	bounce back
Can't	rely on name
Expect	good instincts
Don't Expect	a top arm

Sometimes you've got to take a step backward in order to go forward. That's what happened to Boone last year. He opened the season playing third base for Chattanooga of the Double-A Southern League, but within weeks he was demoted to Winston-Salem of the Class-A Carolina League. There he fit in a bit more comfortably, and began working toward the majors. No one should doubt that Boone retains an excellent chance to make the show. The grandson of Ray Boone, the son of Bob Boone, and the brother of Bret Boone, Aaron has an advantage and it goes beyond the fact that his name might open some doors. His background gives him an acute sense of what it takes to reach the majors, and, after all, the mental aspect is what separates major leaguers from minor leaguers. While in the Carolina League, Boone hit .317 over a 12-game stretch spanning late June and early July. He is considered a fine defender, though his arm is not exceptional. He showed signs of hitting with third-base power, notching a .420 slugging percentage at Winston-Salem.

Professional Batting Register

	BA	G	AB	R	H	2B	3B	HR	RBI	SB
94 R	.273	67	256	48	70	15	5	7	55	6
95 A	.261	108	395	61	103	19	1	14	50	11
95 AA	.227	23	66	6	15	3	0	0	3	2

ROOKIE PROSPECTS

STEVE BOURGEOIS

Position: Pitcher
Team: San Francisco Giants
Born: Aug. 4, 1972 Lutcher, LA
Height: 6'1" **Weight:** 220 lbs.
Bats: right **Throws:** right
Acquired: 21st-round pick in 6/93 free-agent draft

Player Summary	
Fantasy Value	$0
Card Value	N/A
Will	bring adequate stuff
Can't	pitch behind
Expect	three walks per game
Don't Expect	a reliever

Bourgeois, who comes from a family of 11, is emerging from a crowd in a bid to play for the Giants. They took him in the lower rounds of the draft, and so far he has done nothing but win. Last year, facing his most challenging competition to date, Bourgeois made it to the Double-A All-Star Game, where he hurled a scoreless inning. He came out of Northeast Louisiana State University and has moved swiftly through the system, always in a starting role. One cautionary note concerns his control. Over his first two pro seasons, covering three levels of ball, he averaged more than one base on balls per two innings. His strikeout-to-walk ratio is less than 2-to-1. That would not be good enough to keep him on track for San Francisco. He began to sharpen the ratio last year, getting it closer to one walk every three innings. On April 24 of last year, he struck out 10 in just five and two-thirds innings against Arkansas. On May 15, he allowed only four hits in a 1-0 victory. Bourgeois eventually got a call-up to Triple-A Phoenix.

MARK BRANDENBURG

Position: Pitcher
Team: Texas Rangers
Born: July 14, 1970 Houston, TX
Height: 6' **Weight:** 180 lbs.
Bats: right **Throws:** right
Acquired: 26th-round pick in 6/92 free-agent draft

Player Summary	
Fantasy Value	$0
Card Value	N/A
Will	pitch middle relief
Can't	start or close
Expect	a sidearmer
Don't Expect	nasty stuff

Brandenburg got the call to the majors late last July, when the Rangers were trying to work their way out of what would become a 10-game slump. The timing probably was not the best for Brandenburg, whose stuff is not of stopper quality. Indeed, he gave up three runs in four innings and took the loss. Still, he has done enough so that he merits a look. In 1994, in a stretch that spanned Class-A and Double-A, he amassed a 41-inning scoreless streak, second longest in the minors that year. A relief specialist for virtually his entire pro career, he throws sidearm; and he doesn't bring it particularly hard. Brandenburg doesn't walk many, which no doubt accounts for a great deal of his success. Triple-A batters last year compiled a .243 batting average against him, and he had a better than 3-1 strikeout-to-walk ratio. He was a member of an All-Star team that played in the World Port Tournament in 1993. He comes out of Texas Tech University, where he was a third-team All-American in 1991. Brandenburg has also worked as a substitute school teacher.

Professional Pitching Register

	W	L	ERA	G	CG	IP	H	ER	BB	SO
93 A	5	3	4.21	15	0	77.0	62	36	44	77
94 A	12	5	4.22	27	0	143.0	137	65	76	115
95 AA	12	3	2.85	22	2	145.1	140	46	53	91
95 AAA	1	1	3.38	6	0	34.2	38	13	13	23

Professional Pitching Register

	W	L	ERA	G	S	IP	H	ER	BB	SO
92 R	7	1	4.06	24	2	62.0	70	28	14	78
93 A	6	3	1.46	44	4	80.0	62	13	22	67
94 A	0	2	0.87	25	5	41.1	23	4	15	44
94 AA	5	4	1.74	37	8	62.0	50	12	12	63
95 AAA	0	5	2.02	35	2	58.0	52	13	15	51
95 AL	0	1	5.93	11	0	27.1	36	18	7	21

ROOKIE PROSPECTS

JAMIE BREWINGTON

Position: Pitcher
Team: San Francisco Giants
Born: Sept. 28, 1971 Greenville, NC
Height: 6'4" **Weight:** 190 lbs.
Bats: right **Throws:** right
Acquired: 10th-round pick in 6/92 free-agent draft

Player Summary	
Fantasy Value	$2 to $4
Card Value	N/A
Will	throw in 90s
Can't	fall behind
Expect	sliders
Don't Expect	complete games

Brewington made his major-league debut last July in the wake of the eight-man trade that created some openings on the San Francisco staff. He probably would have fought his way to the majors anyway, but if the trade cleared the way for him to emerge, then so much the better. Brewington was enjoying a fine season with Shreveport of the Double-A Texas League, in his first work above the Class-A level. He has the look of a power pitcher with a fastball, a slider, and a changeup. But he must watch his walks. He did not have a 2-1 strikeout-to-walk ratio in Double-A ball last season. Brewington made a big impression in his first year in pro ball, winning the Bill Parese Award for spirit, work ethic, and pride among first-year San Francisco system players. In 1993, he led Clinton to the Class-A Midwest League playoffs. A year later, he made a midseason jump to the California League. Brewington's first big-league start was something of an exception because he went seven innings; his pattern is to last into the sixth.

Professional Pitching Register

	W	L	ERA	G	CG	IP	H	ER	BB	SO
92 A	5	2	4.33	15	1	68.2	65	33	47	63
93 A	13	5	4.78	26	1	133.2	126	71	61	111
94 A	9	7	3.91	23	0	129.0	107	56	49	127
95 AA	8	3	3.06	16	1	88.1	72	30	55	74
95 NL	6	4	4.54	13	0	75.1	68	38	45	45

JIM BROWER

Position: Pitcher
Team: Texas Rangers
Born: Dec. 29, 1972 Edina, MN
Height: 6'2" **Weight:** 200 lbs.
Bats: right **Throws:** right
Acquired: Seventh-round pick in 6/94 free-agent draft

Player Summary	
Fantasy Value	$0
Card Value	N/A
Will	throw a slider
Can't	be rushed
Expect	a 90s fastball
Don't Expect	a polished change

The Rangers turned to a land of ice and snow and picked up someone who can deal a bit of heat. Brower, from the University of Minnesota, was one of the top strikeout artists in the Texas organization last year, just one season after being drafted. He pitched in the high Class-A Florida State League, and he was one of Charlotte's top two starters. He allowed about one hit per inning, but Florida State League batters notched a .256 batting average against him. He needs to cut down on his walks, as he didn't notch a strikeout-to-walk ratio of 2-1. Brower became a sensation after the draft in 1994, quickly pitching his way through the New York-Penn League and moving up to the South Atlantic League. There he won two Pitcher of the Week Awards, one for a 16-strikeout performance against Capital City and another for a no-hitter against Columbia. Sally League hitters batted only .186 against Brower. A fine all-around athlete, he played football and basketball in addition to baseball in high school. So far the Rangers seem to have resisted the temptation to rush him, and so he should be at the Double-A level in 1996.

Professional Pitching Register

	W	L	ERA	G	CG	IP	H	ER	BB	SO
94 A	9	4	2.01	16	4	98.1	66	22	32	99
95 A	7	10	3.89	27	2	173.2	170	75	62	110

ROOKIE PROSPECTS

KEVIN BROWN

Position: Catcher
Team: Texas Rangers
Born: April 21, 1973 Valparaiso, IN
Height: 6'2" **Weight:** 205 lbs.
Bats: right **Throws:** right
Acquired: Second-round pick in 6/94 free-agent draft

Player Summary	
Fantasy Value	$0
Card Value	10¢ to 20¢
Will	hit doubles
Can't	swing at balls
Expect	power hitting
Don't Expect	Rodriguez's arm

Brown has a chance to become one of the game's next power-hitting catchers, and he has a chance to do it quickly. Last year, he amassed what seems to be a modest home run total, but he did so in the Class-A Florida State League, which gives up homers grudgingly. To judge his bat speed, it might be more instructive to examine Brown's extra-base totals in his first two years of pro ball. He notched a .434 slugging average last season, and he had a .414 slugging percentage in his first pro year in 1994. He comes out of the University of Southern Indiana, where he was a two-time All-American. He hit .396 with 27 homers in his college career and capped it by being named Great Lakes Valley Conference Player of the Year in 1994. He broke into pro ball in 1994 with Hudson Valley of the New York-Penn League, and threw out 29.8 percent of would-be basestealers. Like many young power hitters, Brown strikes out a lot, though he cut down on his whiffs last year. No matter where the Rangers assign him in 1996, he seems headed for the majors some day soon.

JOHN BURKE

Position: Pitcher
Team: Colorado Rockies
Born: Feb. 9, 1970 Durango, CO
Height: 6'4" **Weight:** 215 lbs.
Bats: both **Throws:** right
Acquired: First-round pick in 6/92 free-agent draft

Player Summary	
Fantasy Value	$0
Card Value	N/A
Will	bring a curve
Can't	stay a prospect
Expect	wildness
Don't Expect	Denver in spring

The Rockies have sentimental, as well as practical, reasons for wanting Burke to succeed. Not only is he a home-state product, but he was also the first-ever amateur draft selection made by the franchise. And sometime very soon, the Rockies will see where this pick stands. Burke is now 26 years old, and he has completed his fourth year in pro ball. That certainly means that he quickly is running out of time for prospect status. He is trying to recover from a disastrous 1994 season in which he suffered from a mysterious loss of control. He also developed shoulder tendinitis and wound up working just 28 innings all year long, walking 27. Last year he bounced back, and was one of the top starters at Colorado Springs of the Triple-A Pacific Coast League. But he still has bouts of wildness, something the Rockies can't afford when the ball flies out of the park the way it does in Denver. Unless Burke can regain command of the zone, he will have no future in the bigs.

Professional Pitching Register

	W	L	ERA	G	CG	IP	H	ER	BB	SO
92 A	2	0	2.41	10	0	41.0	38	11	18	32
93 A	7	8	3.18	20	2	119.0	104	42	64	114
93 AAA	3	2	3.14	8	0	48.2	44	17	23	38
94 A	0	1	1.06	4	0	17.0	5	2	5	16
94 AAA	0	0	19.64	8	0	11.0	16	24	22	6
95 AAA	7	1	4.55	19	0	87.0	79	44	48	65

Professional Batting Register

	BA	G	AB	R	H	2B	3B	HR	RBI	SB
94 A	.246	68	232	33	57	19	1	6	32	0
95 A	.265	107	355	48	94	25	1	11	57	2
95 AAA	.400	3	10	1	4	1	0	0	0	0

ROOKIE PROSPECTS

HOMER BUSH

Position: Second base
Team: San Diego Padres
Born: Nov. 12, 1972 Miami, FL
Height: 5'11" **Weight:** 180 lbs.
Bats: right **Throws:** right
Acquired: Eighth-round pick in 6/91 free-agent draft

Player Summary	
Fantasy Value	$0
Card Value	N/A
Will	hit singles
Can't	get on base
Expect	speed
Don't Expect	walks

When you look at Bush's stolen base totals over the years, you suspect he might make a good leadoff man in the majors. Only one trouble: Judging by his base on balls totals, he'll have to hit his way on base. Last year in the Double-A Texas League, for instance, he drew just 15 bases on balls despite 432 official at bats, while striking out 83 times. He accumulated a .307 on-base average, and that just won't get it done. Fortunately for Bush, he has shown the ability to hit for average. While playing for Waterloo in 1993, he led the Class-A Midwest League with a .322 average and was named Player of the Year in the Padres organization. Only once in his first five pro seasons has he hit poorly. Still, you wonder why someone with Bush's speed doesn't take more pitches and try to increase his on-base percentage, especially when there is virtually no power to his game. A second baseman, Bush could make the jump to the majors as soon as this year, because the Padres have need at that spot.

Professional Batting Register

	BA	G	AB	R	H	2B	3B	HR	RBI	SB
91 R	.323	32	127	16	41	3	2	0	16	11
92 A	.234	108	367	37	86	10	5	0	18	14
93 A	.322	130	472	63	152	19	3	5	51	39
94 A	.335	39	161	37	54	10	3	0	16	9
94 AA	.298	59	245	35	73	11	4	3	14	20
95 AA	.280	108	432	53	121	12	5	5	37	34

JAY CANIZARO

Position: Second base
Team: San Francisco Giants
Born: July 4, 1973 Beaumont, TX
Height: 5'10" **Weight:** 175 lbs.
Bats: right **Throws:** right
Acquired: Fourth-round pick in 6/93 free-agent draft

Player Summary	
Fantasy Value	$0
Card Value	N/A
Will	get extra bases
Can't	swing for fences
Expect	decent speed
Don't Expect	a shortstop

With Robby Thompson on the down side of a fine career, second base could soon be there for the taking. That means good news for Canizaro, who is only a rung or two away from a job with the Giants. Last year, while playing for Shreveport of the Double-A Texas League, he showed a nice all-around game that could make him a useful big-league player. Through mid-August, he was leading his team in extra-base hits and home runs, and he trailed only Calvin Murray in stolen bases. Canizaro compiled a .464 slugging percentage. He also had 58 walks and notched a fine .379 on-base percentage. Canizaro's arm is more than adequate for second base, and he has shown enough range to play some shortstop in the pros. He comes out of Blinn Junior College in Texas, where he was named top junior college prospect by *Baseball America* in 1992. He also attended Oklahoma State. Upon being drafted, Canizaro began an efficient move through the San Francisco system. This year he should begin the season at the Pacific Coast League, where he could be a factor.

Professional Batting Register

	BA	G	AB	R	H	2B	3B	HR	RBI	SB
93 R	.261	49	180	34	47	10	6	3	41	12
94 A	.252	126	464	77	117	16	2	15	69	12
95 AA	.293	126	440	83	129	25	7	12	60	16

ROOKIE PROSPECTS

RAUL CASANOVA

Position: Catcher
Team: San Diego Padres
Born: Aug. 23, 1972 Humacao, PR
Height: 5'11" **Weight:** 200 lbs.
Bats: both **Throws:** right
Acquired: Traded by Mets with Wally Whitehurst and D.J. Dozier for Tony Fernandez, 12/92

Player Summary
Fantasy Value $0
Card Value .... 15¢ to 40¢
Will...................... hit with power
Can't..................... lose at bats
Expect .... injuries
Don't Expect............. another 1994

Casanova has learned a lot about baseball's ups and downs in the last two years. In 1994, he experienced a dream season, coming close to the Triple Crown in the Class-A California League. But last year, he ran into adversity in climbing a rung to the Double-A Southern League. Casanova came out of spring training late, then he had his season interrupted by ankle problems. Upon his return, he homered in three straight games in early June, but that kind of production was the exception. Casanova often struggled to find the zone he had experienced in 1994. He ended the season with a .448 slugging average. Casanova had experienced ankle trouble in 1993, and he went on the disabled list with a bad wrist in 1994. Perhaps his biggest challenge will be to remain healthy. Casanova was drafted by the Mets in the eighth round of the 1990 draft, and he was sent to San Diego as part of a deal that brought Tony Fernandez to New York.

Professional Batting Register

	BA	G	AB	R	H	2B	3B	HR	RBI	SB
90 R	.077	23	65	4	5	0	0	0	1	0
91 R	.217	37	129	19	28	4	2	0	9	3
92 R	.270	42	137	25	37	9	1	4	27	3
92 A	.167	5	18	2	3	0	0	0	1	0
93 A	.256	76	227	32	58	12	0	6	30	0
94 A	.340	123	471	83	160	27	2	23	120	1
95 AA	.271	89	306	42	83	18	0	12	44	4

LUIS CASTILLO

Position: Second base
Team: Florida Marlins
Born: Sept. 12, 1975 San Pedro de Macoris, Dominican Republic
Height: 5'11" **Weight:** 150 lbs.
Bats: right **Throws:** right
Acquired: Signed as a nondrafted free agent 8/92

Player Summary
Fantasy Value $0
Card Value........................ N/A
Will.................... get on base
Can't .... drive in runs
Expect .... nice hands
Don't Expect .... a shortstop

Castillo is another infielder out of the Dominican Republic's famed Home of Shortstops but, unlike so many other products of that community, he is ticketed for second base. Last year, he played at Kane County of the Class-A Midwest League, and he may have been as good a player as there was in the circuit. He hit .471 over a 12-game stretch that spanned June and July. At the All-Star break, he led the league with 54 runs and was tied with 30 stolen bases. As the season wound down, he was competing for best average and most steals in the Marlins' minor-league system. Castillo's slight build makes contact hitting a must, because he won't hit many home runs. His strikeout-to-walk ratio indicates an ability to get on base. He had 55 bases on balls last year and 50 strikeouts. Scouted and signed by Julian Camilo, Castillo went to school at Colegio San Benito Abad. Next year he should move up at least to high Class-A ball but, even if he doesn't, there is time, because Castillo is still just 20 years old.

Professional Batting Register

	BA	G	AB	R	H	2B	3B	HR	RBI	SB
94 R	.264	57	216	49	57	8	0	0	16	31
95 A	.326	89	340	71	111	4	4	0	23	41

ROOKIE PROSPECTS

RAMON CASTRO

Position: Catcher
Team: Houston Astros
Born: March 1, 1976 Vega Baja, PR
Height: 6'3" **Weight:** 195 lbs.
Bats: right **Throws:** right
Acquired: First-round pick in 6/94 free-agent draft

Player Summary	
Fantasy Value	$0
Card Value	N/A
Will	show strong arm
Can't	worry about demotion
Expect	a slow process
Don't Expect	Ivan Rodriguez

All first-round picks face a certain measure of expectations, but you couldn't blame Castro if he felt them more acutely than other players might. Not only did he become the first player from Puerto Rico to be picked in the first round of the June draft, he also comes out of the same town that produced Juan Gonzalez and Ivan Rodriguez. Scouted by Frankie Thon out of Lino P. Rivera High School, Castro became the 17th overall selection. Upon signing, he went to the rookie Gulf Coast League, where he tied for the club lead with three home runs. Last year the Astros tried to accelerate him into the high Class-A Florida State League, where he was the Opening Day catcher. But he started poorly and eventually found himself in short-season ball with Auburn of the New York-Penn League. There he batted .299 with nine homers and 49 RBI. He also had a .496 slugging percentage. The setback to short-season Class-A should be nothing to cause concern, as Castro will only be 20 years old when the 1996 season begins. He certainly has ample time for development.

Professional Batting Register

	BA	G	AB	R	H	2B	3B	HR	RBI	SB
94 R	.276	37	123	17	34	7	0	3	14	5
95 A	.276	99	334	46	92	22	0	9	57	0

ROGER CEDENO

Position: Outfield
Team: Los Angeles Dodgers
Born: Aug. 16, 1974 Valencia, Venezuela
Height: 6'1" **Weight:** 165 lbs.
Bats: both **Throws:** right
Acquired: Signed as a nondrafted free agent, 3/91

Player Summary	
Fantasy Value	$2 to $4
Card Value	15¢ to 25¢
Will	switch-hit
Can't	show top speed
Expect	good range
Don't Expect	162 games

The Dodgers, who have produced more Rookies of the Year than any other organization, have likely come up with another can't-miss prospect in Cedeno. Still just 21 years old, he has excelled at the highest levels of the minor leagues, and he should be stepping into the Dodgers lineup as early as this season. He is a speedy player who will hit for average, draw walks, steal bases, and score runs. He had 53 walks and a .393 on-base average last year in Triple-A. Signed by Camilo Pascual at the age of 17, Cedeno began his pro career in the Dominican Republic. At 18, he was named to the rookie Pioneer League All-Star team. In 1993, he became the youngest man to play in the Double-A Texas League since Bobby Tolan in 1964. Cedeno spent the entire 1994 campaign in Albuquerque of the Triple-A Pacific Coast League, at one point reaching base in 25 straight games. A center fielder, he has earned plaudits for his glove. He has experienced some hamstring problems, which is not good for a speed player.

Professional Batting Register

	BA	G	AB	R	H	2B	3B	HR	RBI	SB
92 R	.316	69	256	60	81	6	5	2	27	40
93 AA	.288	122	465	70	134	12	8	4	30	28
93 AAA	.222	6	18	1	4	1	0	0	3	0
94 AAA	.321	104	383	84	123	18	5	4	49	30
95 AAA	.305	99	367	67	112	19	9	2	44	23
95 NL	.238	40	42	4	10	2	0	0	3	1

ROOKIE PROSPECTS

BOBBY CHOUINARD

Position: Pitcher
Team: Oakland Athletics
Born: May 1, 1972 Manila, Philippines
Height: 6'1" **Weight:** 188 lbs.
Bats: right **Throws:** right
Acquired: Traded by Orioles with Allen Plaster for Harold Baines, 1/93

Player Summary	
Fantasy Value	$0
Card Value	N/A
Will	keep developing
Can't	be the ace
Expect	complete games
Don't Expect	Harold Baines

Chouinard has spent so much time in pro ball that it's hard to believe he is still just 23 years old. But all the time in development may prove worth it. He finally appears to be taking the strides that will bring him to the big leagues. Last year, in his first look at Double-A ball, he made the All-Star team and pitched a scoreless inning in the game. He proved to be one of the top starting pitchers for Oakland's Southern League team. He held Southern League hitters to a .246 batting average. A member of the 1989 Forest Grove, Oregon, Babe Ruth team that won a world title, Chouinard was selected by the Orioles in the fifth round of the 1990 draft. He spent three years in Birds' organization, with a distinct lack of success. However, he experienced a breakthrough season with Kane County in 1992, leading the Class-A Midwest League in ERA. That caught the eye of the A's, who got him in a deal that sent slugger Harold Baines to the Orioles. Project Chouinard as a third or fourth starter.

Professional Pitching Register

	W	L	ERA	G	CG	IP	H	ER	BB	SO
90 R	2	5	3.70	10	2	56.0	61	23	14	30
91 R	5	1	3.48	6	0	33.2	44	13	11	31
91 A	2	4	4.64	6	1	33.0	45	17	5	17
92 A	10	14	2.08	26	9	181.2	151	42	38	112
93 A	8	10	4.26	24	1	145.2	154	69	56	82
94 A	12	5	2.59	29	0	145.2	147	42	32	74
95 AA	14	8	3.62	29	1	166.2	155	67	50	106

McKAY CHRISTENSEN

Position: Outfield
Team: Chicago White Sox
Born: Aug. 14, 1975 Upland, CA
Height: 5'11" **Weight:** 180 lbs.
Bats: left **Throws:** left
Acquired: Traded by Angels with Andrew Lorraine, Bill Simas, and John Snyder for Jim Abbott and Tim Fortugno, 7/95

Player Summary	
Fantasy Value	$0
Card Value	N/A
Will	begin career
Can't	make up time
Expect	a strong makeup
Don't Expect	a quick trip

Christensen rates as one of the most unusual stories in all of baseball. Drafted in the first round by the Angels in 1994, he was traded to the White Sox without ever playing in the Angels organization. That's because he was in the midst of a two-year Mormon mission in Japan. He will not be available to play ball until sometime this year. Even so, the White Sox were adamant about acquiring Christensen when they were sending Jim Abbott to California for last year's stretch drive. The fact that both teams went out and got Christensen despite the circumstances tells you all you need to know about his talent. He comes out of Clovis High School in California, and he was among the fastest runners in the draft. He is probably the center fielder of the future for the Pale Hose. The down side for the White Sox is that Christensen is missing valuable time to learn how to use that speed. And there have been other "tools" prospects to come along who haven't been able to adjust to professional baseball. But if his principles are strong enough to commit to the mission, perhaps he will have the mental strength needed to make it in pro ball.

No minor-league experience

ROOKIE PROSPECTS

TONY CLARK

Position: First base; designated hitter
Team: Detroit Tigers
Born: June 15, 1972 Newton, KS
Height: 6'7" **Weight:** 240 lbs.
Bats: both **Throws:** right
Acquired: First-round pick in 6/90 free-agent draft

Player Summary	
Fantasy Value	$5 to $7
Card Value	10¢ to 20¢
Will	lose baseballs
Can't	star defensively
Expect	wild swings
Don't Expect	an outfielder

Clark leveled off in his first full season at Triple-A last year, dampening some of the expectations that arose from his outstanding 1994 campaign. But experiencing bumps in the road is part of the development process, particularly when injuries and other circumstances are part of the picture. The second overall pick in the 1990 draft, Clark arrived in pro baseball with more of a basketball background. He played at the University of Arizona and San Diego State University. He then had trouble getting the baseball experience that he needed. He missed the entire 1991 campaign with injury and played in only 88 games in his first three seasons. Then came Clark's breakthrough year with Trenton of the Double-A Eastern League in 1994, when he hit 21 homers with 86 RBI. He remains a tremendous power prospect, with the hefty K totals to prove it—he had 129 at Toledo last season. Clark could serve as DH or a first sacker this year.

Professional Batting Register

	BA	G	AB	R	H	2B	3B	HR	RBI	SB
90 R	.164	25	73	2	12	2	0	1	8	0
92 A	.306	27	85	12	26	9	0	5	17	1
93 A	.265	36	117	14	31	4	1	1	22	0
94 AA	.279	107	394	50	110	25	0	21	86	0
94 AAA	.261	25	92	10	24	4	0	2	13	2
95 AAA	.242	110	405	50	98	17	2	14	63	1
95 AL	.238	27	101	10	24	5	1	3	11	0

BARTOLO COLON

Position: Pitcher
Team: Cleveland Indians
Born: May 24, 1975 Altamira, Dominican Republic
Height: 6' **Weight:** 185 lbs.
Bats: right **Throws:** right
Acquired: Signed as a nondrafted free agent, 6/93

Player Summary	
Fantasy Value	$0
Card Value	N/A
Will	blow hitters away
Can't	gamble with elbow
Expect	a staff ace
Don't Expect	complete games

It seems hard to believe that not so long ago, Cleveland never seemed to have any pitching. Now the arms seem to be plentiful, with Colon as a prime example. He was one of the top pitchers in all of Class-A ball last year, starring in the Carolina League. By mid-July, he was tied for the organization lead with 12 wins, 141 strikeouts, and a 1.84 ERA. His season was filled with highlights: On April 15, he allowed one hit over seven innings to beat Lynchburg. In his next start, he fanned 13 in a 6-2 triumph over Salem. On July 14, he struck out 10 in a 5-2 victory. He held Carolina League hitters to a .202 batting average, and he struck out three and one-half batters for every walk. It was a sensational performance for a man who turned only 20 years old during the season. He was shut down in the second half with a problem in his elbow, but it did not appear to be serious. Colon spent 1993 in the Dominican League, finishing second in the Cibao Division with a 2.59 ERA. In the rookie Appalachian League in 1994, Colon allowed opponents only a .192 average.

Professional Pitching Register

	W	L	ERA	G	CG	IP	H	ER	BB	SO
94 R	7	4	3.14	12	0	66.0	46	23	44	84
95 A	13	3	1.96	21	0	128.2	91	28	39	152

ROOKIE PROSPECTS

ROCKY COPPINGER

Position: Pitcher
Team: Baltimore Orioles
Born: March 19, 1974 El Paso, TX
Height: 6'7" **Weight:** 240 lbs.
Bats: right **Throws:** right
Acquired: 19th-round pick in 6/93 free-agent draft

Player Summary	
Fantasy Value	$0
Card Value	N/A
Will	be a starter
Can't	change nickname
Expect	quality starts
Don't Expect	much Double-A

The Orioles must wince when they think about how close they came to losing Coppinger. He signed with the team just hours before the deadline for inking 1993 draftees. By then, he had missed a year of pro ball, but he had pitched for Hill Junior College, where he went 11-1 with a 2.90 ERA. He was an All-Region V pitcher and was named to the National Junior College All-Star team. Coppinger in 1994 spent his first pro season with Bluefield of the rookie Appalachian League, where he ranked seventh with a 2.45 ERA. This fast-developing prospect accelerated his climb last year, starting with Frederick of the Class-A Carolina League. At one point, he won four consecutive starts and allowed only 15 hits in 26⅔ innings, while striking out 32. When promoted to Double-A at the end of May, Coppinger led the minors with 91 strikeouts. He was successful at all three levels last year, holding Class-A, Double-A, and Triple-A hitters to batting averages under the Mendoza Line. Coppinger received his nickname at birth, when his dad said he looked like boxer Rocky Marciano.

Professional Pitching Register

	W	L	ERA	G	CG	IP	H	ER	BB	SO
94 R	4	3	2.45	14	0	73.1	51	20	40	88
95 A	7	1	1.57	11	2	68.2	46	12	24	91
95 AA	6	2	2.69	13	2	83.2	58	25	43	62
95 AAA	3	0	1.04	5	0	34.2	23	4	17	19

STEVE COX

Position: First base
Team: Oakland Athletics
Born: Oct. 31, 1974 Strathmore, CA
Height: 6'4" **Weight:** 225 lbs.
Bats: left **Throws:** left
Acquired: Fifth-round pick in 6/92 free-agent draft

Player Summary	
Fantasy Value	$0
Card Value	N/A
Will	draw a walk
Can't	go backward
Expect	production
Don't Expect	too many Ks

If you need to know the definition of a breakthrough season, just look at Cox's 1995 campaign. After three nondescript years in pro ball, he blossomed into one of the game's top power-hitting prospects last year. He rampaged through the Class-A California League, and he was among the top home run and RBI producers in the Oakland organization. Cox notched a .557 slugging percentage. He did all of this without a heavy strikeout toll. He notched 88 Ks last season, down from 95 in 1994. He also increased his bases on balls from 41 in '94 to 84 last year, giving him a .409 on-base average. Cox has all the appearance of the classic first baseman. He's left-handed with power, and he has the height to present a nice target for his fellow infielders. He's also still young, having accomplished his breakthrough season at the age of 20. He is not yet advanced enough to take advantage of Mark McGwire's injury problems, but the A's can enjoy the fact that Cox is in the pipeline. Expect Cox to get a shot at Double-A ball in 1996, and if he can hit in the Southern League, look out.

Professional Batting Register

	BA	G	AB	R	H	2B	3B	HR	RBI	SB
92 R	.234	52	184	30	43	4	1	1	35	1
93 A	.316	15	57	10	18	4	1	2	16	0
94 A	.241	99	311	37	75	19	2	6	32	2
95 A	.298	132	483	95	144	29	3	30	110	6

ROOKIE PROSPECTS

JACOB CRUZ

Position: Outfield
Team: San Francisco Giants
Born: Jan. 28, 1973 Oxnard, CA
Height: 6'1" **Weight:** 175 lbs.
Bats: left **Throws:** left
Acquired: Compensation second-round pick in 6/94 free-agent draft

Player Summary	
Fantasy Value	$0
Card Value	N/A
Will	fill out
Can't	win Triple Crown
Expect	a No. 2 hitter
Don't Expect	Clark's power

The Giants lost one of the game's better players when Will Clark walked away as a free agent after the 1993 season. Things could work out if Cruz keeps developing, however. He came to the Giants as the 32nd overall pick, the one awarded for the loss of Clark. Cruz has the look of a prospect who could come quickly. After a get-acquainted year at Class-A San Jose in the California League in 1994, Cruz moved to the Double-A Texas League last year and enjoyed success. He made the Double-A All-Star team and ranked among the top run-producers in the San Francisco organization. He showed some home run power, after showing none in his first season, and that potential could grow as he learns the pro game. He also had a .459 slugging percentage. Cruz, who attended Channel Islands High School, played for the gold medal-winning West squad at the Junior Olympic Festival. He attended Arizona State, where he hit .361 with 25 homers and 130 RBI. In his senior year, Cruz was named Pac 10 South Player of the Year, barely missing the Triple Crown.

Professional Batting Register

	BA	G	AB	R	H	2B	3B	HR	RBI	SB
94 A	.246	31	118	14	29	7	0	0	12	0
95 AA	.297	127	458	88	136	33	1	13	77	9

JOSE CRUZ JR.

Position: Outfield
Team: Seattle Mariners
Born: April 19, 1974 Arroyo, PR
Height: 6' **Weight:** 190 lbs.
Bats: both **Throws:** right
Acquired: First-round pick in 6/95 free-agent draft

Player Summary	
Fantasy Value	$0
Card Value	N/A
Will	bring bloodlines
Can't	Cruz on name
Expect	impact
Don't Expect	a flop

If Cruz can hit line drives all day long, no one should be surprised. He gets it from his father, who enjoyed a 19-year run in the big leagues, most of them with the Astros. The younger Cruz brings the potential to do as much damage as his daddy did. If anything, because of his heftier build, the younger Cruz promises more power. He also offers the ability to switch-hit, while his father was a lefty swinger. Cruz was taken with the third overall pick, and his high-level college experience could get him to the big leagues quickly. Cruz played at Rice, where he was a durable run producer. He was twice named a first-team All-American by *Baseball America*. Cruz remained unsigned for several weeks after the draft, but he eventually went to Everett of the Northwest League. He soon earned a promotion to Riverside of the Class-A California League, and hit a pair of home runs and drove in five runs in an Aug. 5 game against Modesto. He notched a .465 slugging percentage in the California League. Look for Cruz in Double-A in 1996.

Professional Batting Register

	BA	G	AB	R	H	2B	3B	HR	RBI	SB
95 A	.271	38	155	40	42	7	1	7	31	4

ROOKIE PROSPECTS

WILL CUNNANE

Position: Pitcher
Team: Florida Marlins
Born: April 24, 1974 Suffern, NY
Height: 6'2" **Weight:** 175 lbs.
Bats: right **Throws:** right
Acquired: Signed as a nondrafted free agent 8/92

Player Summary
Fantasy Value	$0
Card Value	15¢ to 25¢
Will	throw strikes
Can't	count on health
Expect	more Double-A
Don't Expect	1994's ERA

Cunnane's case illustrates the extraordinary difficulty in developing a player for the majors, particularly from the lower levels of the system. In 1994, he was something of a sensation, leading the minor leagues with a 1.43 ERA. But last year, after a promotion to Double-A Portland, he came down with a sore shoulder that landed him on the disabled list. After returning, he was not as dominant as he had been. No conclusions should be drawn from that, however. Some pitchers can put arm trouble behind them quickly, some can't. Only Cunnane himself can answer that question. Meantime, keep in mind the skill that enabled him to make so much progress in the first place. While pitching in the rookie Gulf Coast League in 1993, he allowed only eight walks in 66⅔ innings. In 1994, he gave up 23 free passes in 138⅔ innings while leading the league with four shutouts. One of the differences between 1994 and last year is that while both walk totals were impressive, Cunnane allowed hitters to bat .217 in 1994 as opposed to .264 last year. How far he goes in 1996 depends in part on the strength of Cunnane's wing.

Professional Pitching Register
	W	L	ERA	G	CG	IP	H	ER	BB	SO
93 R	3	3	2.70	16	0	66.2	75	20	8	64
94 A	11	3	1.43	32	5	138.2	110	22	23	106
95 AA	9	2	3.67	21	1	117.2	120	48	34	83

JEFF D'AMICO

Position: Pitcher
Team: Milwaukee Brewers
Born: Dec. 27, 1975 St. Petersburg, FL
Height: 6'7" **Weight:** 250 lbs.
Bats: right **Throws:** right
Acquired: First-round pick in 6/93 free-agent draft

Player Summary
Fantasy Value	$0
Card Value	15¢ to 20¢
Will	bring it
Can't	assume good health
Expect	a top curve
Don't Expect	a rush job

You couldn't have blamed the Brewers if they were holding their breath on D'Amico. They had drafted him 23rd overall in 1993 but watched as injuries kept him from ever appearing in a game. They had to wonder if he would be a first-rounder gone bust. Instead, they scarcely could have imagined a better scenario: When D'Amico finally did get back on the mound, he appeared to be every bit the dominating factor that they had hoped for. Last year, finally pitching in the Brewers' system, he turned in an All-Star season for Beloit of the Class-A Midwest League. Through mid-July, he led all Milwaukee farmhands in ERA and ranked near the top in strikeouts and victories also. He impressed the staff in Beloit, and why not? He averaged nearly one strikeout per inning. He also had a strikeout-to-walk ratio that approached 4-to-1. He held league batters to a composite .211 batting average. With a basic repertoire that includes a top-notch fastball, D'Amico definitely rates as a power prospect. If he can stay healthy, he will probably move to high Class-A.

Professional Pitching Register
	W	L	ERA	G	CG	IP	H	ER	BB	SO
95 A	13	3	2.39	21	3	132.0	102	35	31	119

ROOKIE PROSPECTS

JOHNNY DAMON

Position: Outfield
Team: Kansas City Royals
Born: Nov. 5, 1973 Fort Riley, KS
Height: 6′ **Weight:** 175 lbs.
Bats: left **Throws:** left
Acquired: Sandwich second-round pick in 6/92 free-agent draft

Player Summary	
Fantasy Value	$14 to $17
Card Value	40¢ to 80¢
Will	hit triples
Can't	go for homers
Expect	speed
Don't Expect	a high-strung star

If you drew up a list of the top 10 prospects in all of baseball, Damon would have to be on it. He is a mixture of speed and line-drive power that could terrorize pitchers for years to come. If anything, he seems to be getting better. He played at Double-A last year and added a component that hadn't emerged in his first three pro seasons—double-digit home run power. He made the Double-A All-Star team, played center field, and led off for the AL farmhands. Damon could well have been the top overall pick in the 1992 draft, but a subpar senior year dropped him down to where the Royals grabbed him as the 35th overall pick. Even so, he made *USA Today*'s High School All-America team. Ever since then, he has looked like a No. 1. Kansas City fans loved the excitement he created with his knack for hitting triples. They saw it in the second half last season, when he came up and made an impact. He was not overmatched during his first look at big-league pitching. Damon had a .441 slugging percentage, 12 walks, and zero caught-stealing attempts.

Professional Batting Register

	BA	G	AB	R	H	2B	3B	HR	RBI	SB
92 R	.349	50	192	58	67	12	9	4	24	23
92 A	.000	1	1	0	0	0	0	0	0	0
93 A	.290	127	511	82	148	25	13	5	50	59
94 A	.316	119	472	96	149	25	13	6	75	44
95 AA	.343	111	423	83	145	15	9	16	54	26
95 AL	.282	47	188	32	53	11	5	3	23	7

BEN DAVIS

Position: Catcher
Team: San Diego Padres
Born: March 10, 1977 Chester, PA
Height: 6′4″ **Weight:** 195 lbs.
Bats: both **Throws:** right
Acquired: First-round pick in 6/95 free-agent draft

Player Summary	
Fantasy Value	$0
Card Value	N/A
Will	hit extra bases
Can't	judge him yet
Expect	strong throws
Don't Expect	weak hits

The Padres know all about catching phenoms. At one time in the late 1980s, they had both Benito Santiago and Sandy Alomar in their organization. Now they hope that Davis can be in a class with those two. Davis was a member of *Baseball America*'s High School All-America team, and he was the publication's high school player of the year. The Padres made him the second overall pick in the draft, signed him, and assigned him to rookie ball. Playing for Idaho Falls of the rookie Pioneer League, Davis provided some eye-opening performances. Over one 15-game stretch, he hit .364 with 18 RBI. He ended the season drawing an impressive 17 walks and turning in a .426 slugging percentage. A switch-hitter, Davis was a big run producer in high school. Nearly half of his base hits in senior year went for extra bases. His high draft position should tell you what the Padres think of his arm. He comes out of Malvern Prep in Pennsylvania, not far from Philadelphia. With Davis's tools, the hometown fans could soon be coming out to the Vet to watch him in the bigs.

Professional Batting Register

	BA	G	AB	R	H	2B	3B	HR	RBI	SB
95 R	.279	52	197	36	55	8	3	5	46	0

ROOKIE PROSPECTS

JEFF DAVIS

Position: Pitcher
Team: Texas Rangers
Born: Aug. 20, 1972 Fall River, MA
Height: 6′ **Weight:** 170 lbs.
Bats: right **Throws:** right
Acquired: 28th-round pick in 6/93 free-agent draft

Player Summary	
Fantasy Value	$0
Card Value	N/A
Will	need a role
Can't	maintain K pace
Expect	strikes
Don't Expect	a closer

The Rangers opened themselves to a second guess in 1995, taking one of the best relievers in the minors and turning him into a starting pitcher. So far, Davis has made the move look like a work of genius. Last year, working in the Class-A Florida State League, he ranked as one of the Rangers' top farmhands. Though he did not strike out batters at the same rate as he did in the South Atlantic League, he still pitched well enough to show up among the leaders in victories. The experiment worked virtually from the start. Davis went seven scoreless innings on April 22, then went 4-0 in six May starts. He finished the year with a strikeout-to-walk ratio approaching 3-to-1. Out of Massasoit Community College in Brockton, Massachusetts, Davis moved into pro ball with a flourish. He led Erie of the New York-Penn League with 13 saves in 1993. He paced the entire Ranger organization with 19 saves in 1994. In his first two years of pro ball, Davis had more saves (32) than walks. If he falters as a starter, Davis can fall back on his experience in the bullpen.

TOMMY DAVIS

Position: Third base
Team: Baltimore Orioles
Born: May 21, 1973 Mobile, AL
Height: 6′1″ **Weight:** 195 lbs.
Bats: right **Throws:** right
Acquired: Second-round pick in 6/94 free-agent draft

Player Summary	
Fantasy Value	$0
Card Value	25¢ to 50¢
Will	provide power
Can't	linger at Class-A
Expect	more RBI
Don't Expect	Brooks Robinson

Davis was the first choice the Orioles made in the 1994 draft, arriving in the second round as the 54th overall selection. But so far, he has shown the same promise as virtually any first-rounder. He projects as a power-hitting third baseman, always a valuable commodity. He had 18 homers last year in his two stops, and he slugged .423 for Frederick of the Class-A Carolina League. In his first year of full-season pro ball, Davis played in the Class-A South Atlantic League, establishing himself as a home run hitter. His RBI total was a little on the low side, but learning to hit with men on base can take some time. Then again, sometimes hitting the ball, period, has been a bit of a problem; Davis will strike out a lot. He had 105 at Class-A last year. He comes out of the University of Mississippi, where he hit .409 as a junior and was named a first-team All-American by *Baseball America*. He played in the Cape Cod League in 1993, hitting .343 with a .500 slugging average. Davis turns 23 years old this May, which gives him limited time as a prospect.

Professional Pitching Register

	W	L	ERA	G	CG	IP	H	ER	BB	SO
93 A	0	5	3.65	27	0	37.0	32	15	10	41
94 A	2	3	3.99	45	0	49.2	53	22	11	72
95 A	12	7	2.89	26	0	165.1	159	53	37	105
95 AA	1	0	0.00	1	0	7.0	2	0	1	4

Professional Batting Register

	BA	G	AB	R	H	2B	3B	HR	RBI	SB
94 A	.273	61	216	35	59	10	1	5	35	2
95 A	.268	130	496	62	133	26	3	15	57	7
95 AA	.313	9	32	5	10	3	0	3	10	0

ROOKIE PROSPECTS

EDWIN DIAZ

Position: Second base
Team: Texas Rangers
Born: Jan. 15, 1975 Bayamon, PR
Height: 5'11" **Weight:** 172 lbs.
Bats: right **Throws:** right
Acquired: Second-round pick in 6/93 free-agent draft

Player Summary	
Fantasy Value	$0
Card Value	10¢ to 20¢
Will	cover ground
Can't	give up at bats
Expect	gradual promotions
Don't Expect	great glove

If you judged by the 1995 season's early days, you might have thought Diaz was overmatched at the high Class-A level. Playing for Charlotte of the Florida State League, he went through a 1-for-19 slump that included seven strikeouts. But he bounced back and began showing the bat he had wielded in his first two pro seasons. Not long after that slump, Diaz was named the league's Player of the Week, hitting .600 over five games with five doubles. His ninth-inning RBI single on May 21 beat Vero Beach. By June 7, Diaz had raised his average to .313, and *USA Today Baseball Weekly* tabbed him as a prospect to follow. He had a .418 slugging percentage last year, as well as a .341 on-base average. On a more discouraging note, Diaz does not seem to be cutting down on his strikeouts. After fanning more than one time per every four official trips to the plate in 1994, he shaved that only slightly last year. He doesn't walk very much, either. A second baseman, Diaz will cover ground, and he has an adequate arm. He may even steal a base or two.

Professional Batting Register

	BA	G	AB	R	H	2B	3B	HR	RBI	SB
93 R	.305	43	154	27	47	10	5	1	23	12
94 A	.264	122	413	52	109	22	7	11	60	11
95 A	.284	115	450	48	128	26	5	8	56	8

DAVID DOSTER

Position: Second base
Team: Philadelphia Phillies
Born: Oct. 8, 1970 Fort Wayne, IN
Height: 5'10" **Weight:** 185 lbs.
Bats: right **Throws:** right
Acquired: 27th-round pick in 6/93 free-agent draft

Player Summary	
Fantasy Value	$0
Card Value	N/A
Will	reach the gaps
Can't	play short
Expect	solid play
Don't Expect	fanfare

Lower-round draft picks often must force their way into the fore, because teams have less invested in them and tend to concentrate on developing high-profile selections. But Doster is making it impossible for the Phillies to overlook him. Through steady and sometimes spectacular work, he is emerging as a force in the Philadelphia farm system. He is a second baseman who plays a reliable game in the field and makes a big contribution at the plate. Playing for Clearwater in 1994, he was named the Phils' Player of the Month for May. He wound up leading the Class-A Florida State League with 42 doubles and made the All-Star Team. Doster kept up the good work when promoted to the Double-A Eastern League last year, ranking with the best offensive performers in the system. He had almost as many bases on balls (51) as strikeouts (61) last year, and that makes his production look so much the better. Doster is also a fine defensive asset. At one point, he went 36 games without an error. A mid-summer report in *USA Today Baseball Weekly* identified Doster as a prospect to watch.

Professional Batting Register

	BA	G	AB	R	H	2B	3B	HR	RBI	SB
93 A	.283	69	251	38	71	18	1	3	22	1
94 A	.281	131	480	76	135	42	4	13	74	12
95 AA	.265	139	551	84	146	39	3	21	79	11

ROOKIE PROSPECTS

MATT DREWS

Position: Pitcher
Team: New York Yankees
Born: Aug. 29, 1974 Sarasota, FL
Height: 6'8" **Weight:** 230 lbs.
Bats: right **Throws:** right
Acquired: First-round pick in 6/93 free-agent draft

Player Summary	
Fantasy Value	$0
Card Value	30¢ to 50¢
Will	be a starter
Can't	hide big numbers
Expect	velocity
Don't Expect	top breaking ball

When trade talk began in earnest for the 1995 stretch run, Drews attracted a lot of attention from teams willing to give the Yankees a veteran pitcher in return for prospects. The Yankees said no to any offer that would have included this imposing specimen. He enjoyed a fine season in the Class-A Florida State League last year. Playing in Tampa, not far from his home, Drews put up big numbers. He held FSL hitters to a .214 batting average and struck out almost seven batters per nine innings. He also had almost two and one-half strikeouts for every base on balls that he allowed last year. His grandfather, Karl, spent time with the Yankees during the 1940s, and Matt could be following in those footsteps within a year or two. Drews was an outstanding high school athlete who was widely recruited to play football and basketball. However, picking 13th in the draft, the Yankees made Drews the second high school pitcher taken in 1993. He was a nonroster invitee to major-league camp in 1994, and spent that season with Oneonta of the New York-Penn League.

Professional Pitching Register

	W	L	ERA	G	CG	IP	H	ER	BB	SO
94 A	7	6	2.10	14	1	90.0	76	21	19	69
95 A	15	7	2.27	28	3	182.0	142	46	58	140

MIKE DRUMRIGHT

Position: Pitcher
Team: Detroit Tigers
Born: April 14, 1974 Salina, KS
Height: 6'3" **Weight:** 210 lbs.
Bats: left **Throws:** right
Acquired: First-round pick in 6/95 free-agent draft

Player Summary	
Fantasy Value	$0
Card Value	N/A
Will	throw heavy ball
Can't	rely on change
Expect	decent breaking stuff
Don't Expect	a thrower

The Tigers need pitching. They approached draft day with that in mind in 1995. Using the 11th overall selection, they made Drumright the cornerstone of a draft that emphasized arms. Apparently the Tigers liked his arm more than most, and they couldn't have been too unhappy with his size, either. Drumright comes out of Wichita State University, a high-profile program, where he received exposure and solid competition. In fact, the Tigers no doubt had that in mind when they assigned him to Lakeland of the Class-A Florida State League. Drumright made his pro debut against Daytona on July 18, going three innings and allowing two runs while gaining no decision. Through his five outings, he averaged nearly one K per inning. He also held FSL hitters to a .247 batting average. Promoted to Jacksonville in the Double-A Southern League, Drumright actually pitched better; he had more Ks than innings. With the Tigers' decision to trade David Wells last summer, opportunities abound for a starting pitcher, and Drumright could take advantage.

Professional Pitching Register

	W	L	ERA	G	CG	IP	H	ER	BB	SO
95 A	1	1	4.29	5	0	21.0	19	10	9	19
95 AA	0	1	3.69	5	0	31.2	30	13	15	34

ROOKIE PROSPECTS

JERMAINE DYE

Position: Outfield
Team: Atlanta Braves
Born: Jan. 28, 1974 Oakland, CA
Height: 6′ **Weight:** 195 lbs.
Bats: right **Throws:** right
Acquired: 17th-round pick in 6/93 free-agent draft

Player Summary	
Fantasy Value	$0
Card Value	40¢ to 70¢
Will	add power
Can't	be run on
Expect	hits
Don't Expect	a center fielder

The Atlanta organization rightly enjoys an outstanding reputation for developing and maintaining pitchers. But that doesn't mean it neglects other areas, as its surplus of young outfielders will attest. Dye is just one of the fine young prospects who could be patrolling the pastures in Atlanta very soon. Double-A Southern League managers must think so, because he was named the league's top offensive prospect and best outfield arm in a *Baseball America* poll last year. Playing for Greenville, Dye showed power and an ability to hit for average. Early in the season, he captured a Player of the Week award. As the year went on, he ranked with the top Atlanta farmhands in batting average. He has shown some power, and could deliver even more as he fills out. He had a career-best .481 slugging average last year. For some reason, his basestealing totals showed a drop last year. So did his doubles; but that's understandable, since he collected 41 the previous year. Dye has an outstanding outfield arm; he led Class-A South Atlantic League outfielders with 21 assists and six double plays.

Professional Batting Register

	BA	G	AB	R	H	2B	3B	HR	RBI	SB
93 R	.347	56	218	23	69	20	1	2	39	9
94 A	.298	135	506	73	151	41	1	15	98	19
95 AA	.285	104	403	50	115	26	4	15	71	4

SCOTT ELARTON

Position: Pitcher
Team: Houston Astros
Born: Feb. 23, 1976 Lamar, CO
Height: 6′8″ **Weight:** 225 lbs.
Bats: right **Throws:** right
Acquired: First-round pick in 6/94 free-agent draft

Player Summary	
Fantasy Value	$0
Card Value	35¢ to 70¢
Will	bring IQ
Can't	master his control
Expect	a live arm
Don't Expect	extended slumps

Sometimes the sophomore jinx can strike in the minors as well as in the majors. Such may have been the case for Elarton, who slumped in his second pro season, just one year after breaking in with an 8-1 record. Assigned to Quad City of the Class-A Midwest League last year, he experienced problems in the early going before asserting himself. In Elarton's first five starts of 1995, he went 2-2 with a 7.11 ERA. His difficulties could be traced to the 21 walks he issued in just 25⅓ innings. That was almost as many bases on balls as he allowed in his first year of pro ball, covering 14 starts. However, he won three straight starts from May 6 to May 19. He tossed seven innings of scoreless ball on July 3, giving him a streak of 27 innings in which he allowed only four earned runs. He finished the season with a 4.45 ERA, but he had some pretty good stats. He needs to really cut down on the number of free passes he allows. Valedictorian of Lamar High School, Elarton can use that intelligence to make the inevitable adjustments. In fact, he may have already done so last year.

Professional Pitching Register

	W	L	ERA	G	CG	IP	H	ER	BB	SO
94 R	4	0	0.00	5	0	28.0	9	0	5	28
94 A	4	1	3.29	9	0	54.2	42	20	18	42
95 A	13	7	4.45	26	0	149.2	149	74	71	112

ROOKIE PROSPECTS

DARIN ERSTAD

Position: Outfield
Team: California Angels
Born: June 4, 1974 Jamestown, ND
Height: 6'2" **Weight:** 195 lbs.
Bats: left **Throws:** left
Acquired: First-round pick in 6/95 free-agent draft

Player Summary	
Fantasy Value	$0
Card Value	N/A
Will	hit for power
Can't	play center
Expect	attention
Don't Expect	a quick arrival

History tells us that a range of fates can befall first-round picks. Depending on what the player does with his tools, he can grow to major-league stardom or never get to the big leagues at all. That's the challenge facing Erstad, because he's now on center stage. Opposing pitchers will bear down on him, and his teammates will be watching closely to see what all the fuss is about. At least he seems to own the tools that could enable him to prosper amid all this. A top athlete who also was a kicker on Nebraska's football team, Erstad was the MVP in the Cape Cod League in 1994. He then hit .410 with 19 home runs for Nebraska in 1995. The Angels would seem to have no immediate need for Erstad, considering the fact that they just brought along some superb prospects. The early returns on Erstad's pro career were encouraging, as he quickly hit his way out of the rookie Arizona League and advanced to the Class-A California League. He had a .611 slugging average in 25 games in the Cal League. Erstad's first area of improvement needs to be to cut down his 3-1 ratio of strikeouts to walks.

Professional Batting Register

	BA	G	AB	R	H	2B	3B	HR	RBI	SB
95 R	.556	4	18	2	10	1	0	0	1	1
95 A	.363	25	113	24	41	7	3	5	24	3

RAMON FERMIN

Position: Pitcher
Team: Oakland Athletics
Born: Nov. 25, 1972 San Pedro de Macoris, Dominican Republic
Height: 6'3" **Weight:** 180 lbs.
Bats: right **Throws:** right
Acquired: Signed as a nondrafted free agent, 12/89

Player Summary	
Fantasy Value	$0
Card Value	N/A
Will	find a role
Can't	predict his track
Expect	some wildness
Don't Expect	authority

Fermin underwent a change in roles last year, moving from the end of the game to the beginning. Acting as a closer for Huntsville of the Double-A Southern League, he picked up seven saves. But then he was moved into the starting rotation. He thus returned to the niche he occupied in the Class-A Midwest League in 1992, when he went 5-5 with a 2.43 ERA while used exclusively as a starter. The fact, however, is that for most of his pro career, Fermin has been used both as a starter and a reliever. That reflects both his particular blend of skills and Oakland's needs at the big-league level. At any rate, his repertoire includes a healthy fastball, and that will serve him well wherever he pitches. Not long after joining the rotation, he delivered a seven-inning, two-hit outing against Knoxville on July 6, earning him the league's Pitcher of the Week honors. He does need to improve his strikeout-to-walk ratio. Fermin made the California League All-Star team in 1994.

Professional Pitching Register

	W	L	ERA	G	CG	IP	H	ER	BB	SO
91 R	3	0	2.13	7	1	25.1	20	6	4	11
91 A	1	0	4.38	3	0	12.1	16	6	3	5
92 A	7	8	3.59	28	1	120.1	116	48	54	55
93 A	4	6	6.15	31	0	67.1	78	46	37	47
94 A	9	6	3.59	29	0	133.0	129	53	42	120
95 AA	6	7	3.86	32	0	100.1	105	43	45	58
95 AL	0	0	13.50	1	0	1.1	4	2	1	0

ROOKIE PROSPECTS

JOE FONTENOT

Position: Pitcher
Team: San Francisco Giants
Born: March 20, 1977 Scott, LA
Height: 6'2" **Weight:** 180 lbs.
Bats: right **Throws:** right
Acquired: First-round pick in 6/95 free-agent draft

Player Summary	
Fantasy Value	$0
Card Value	N/A
Will	show control
Can't	improve on debut
Expect	a top fastball
Don't Expect	a lollipop curve

The Giants had not taken a high school pitcher with their first pick in over a decade, and Fontenot made them wait just a little while longer before they got his name on the dotted line. Taken with the 16th overall pick of the 1995 draft, Fontenot did not sign until at least half the other first-rounders were sewn up. But when he finally did get to work, it was something special to watch. The Giants assigned him to Bellingham of the Class-A Northwest League, where they eased him into pro ball. In his first two starts, covering four innings, Fontenot allowed two walks and no hits. Through his first 10⅓ pro innings, he allowed only two runs. Loop hitters were able to compile only a .209 batting average against him. Fontenot comes out of the bayou country, having done his scholastic pitching in Lafayette, Louisiana. He was easily the highest-rated high school pitcher in the state, striking out nearly five times as many batters as he walked. His impressive pro debut aside, Fontenot will probably get a ticket to low Class-A ball in 1996.

Professional Pitching Register

	W	L	ERA	G	CG	IP	H	ER	BB	SO
95 A	0	3	1.93	6	0	18.2	14	4	10	14

TOM FORDHAM

Position: Pitcher
Team: Chicago White Sox
Born: Feb. 20, 1974 El Cajon, CA
Height: 6'2" **Weight:** 210 lbs.
Bats: left **Throws:** left
Acquired: 11th-round pick in 6/93 free-agent draft

Player Summary	
Fantasy Value	$0
Card Value	N/A
Will	stick around
Can't	overpower you
Expect	quality starts
Don't Expect	complete games

Fordham is a big left-hander who throws the ball over the plate, and anyone who fits that description has a chance to reach the major leagues and stay there. Last year, the formula worked beautifully. He was one of the best pitchers in the minor leagues, particularly in the first half when he was in the Class-A Carolina League. He leveled off when he got to Double-A Birmingham, but he was due for some losses anyway. Still, he ranked among the win, ERA, and strikeout leaders in Chicago's farm system last year. He held hitters to a composite .220 batting average in the Carolina League, while Double-A hitters batted .250 against him last year. He came right out of Grossmont Junior College and has held his own no matter where he has pitched. A starter for most of his pro career, Fordham doesn't go the distance very often. He only completed one of his first nine Double-A starts. This might suggest a role in the bullpen as a middle reliever somewhere down the line. But if he keeps winning, there's no reason Fordham can't be a big-league starter.

Professional Pitching Register

	W	L	ERA	G	CG	IP	H	ER	BB	SO
93 R	1	1	1.80	3	0	10.0	9	2	3	12
93 A	4	3	3.52	10	1	53.2	39	21	24	43
94 A	14	9	3.63	28	2	183.2	183	74	44	169
95 A	9	0	2.04	13	1	84.0	66	19	35	78
95 AA	6	3	3.38	14	2	82.2	79	31	28	61

ROOKIE PROSPECTS

TIM FORKNER

Position: Third base
Team: Houston Astros
Born: March 28, 1973 Montrose, CO
Height: 5'11" **Weight:** 185 lbs.
Bats: left **Throws:** right
Acquired: 14th-round pick in 6/93 free-agent draft

Player Summary
Fantasy Value $0
Card Value. . . . . N/A
Will . . . . work deep counts
Can't . . . . fit expectations
Expect. . . . . three-baggers
Don't Expect . . . . many homers

If it's a power-hitting third baseman you want, then you'll have to find someone besides Forkner. He hit only one home run in his first two pro seasons, and he did not appreciably add to that total last year. But he has come up with other ways to grab attention—like make All-Star teams. He's now done it twice in a row, first in the Class-A Midwest League in 1994, and then last year in the Class-A Florida State League. In fact, he was named MVP of the FSL All-Star Game. He comes out of Seward County Community College and brings a couple of nice facets to his game. For one, he has a nice eye at the plate, which twice in the last three years has given him more walks than strikeouts. He had 60 bases on balls in the FSL last year (for a .408 on-base percentage), as opposed to 40 strikeouts. He also has a knack for doubles and triples, having led his team in three-baggers in his first pro season. He got a promotion to the Double-A Texas League last year, which is good because he'll be playing this season at 23 years of age. If he continues along the same career path, Forkner may be able to make the Texas League All-Stars.

Professional Batting Register

	BA	G	AB	R	H	2B	3B	HR	RBI	SB
93 A	.285	72	267	32	76	14	9	0	39	3
94 A	.298	124	429	57	128	23	4	6	57	6
95 A	.284	89	296	42	84	20	4	1	34	2
95 AA	.269	35	119	19	32	11	0	3	23	1

BRAD FULLMER

Position: Infield
Team: Montreal Expos
Born: Jan. 17, 1975 Los Angeles, CA
Height: 6'1" **Weight:** 185 lbs.
Bats: left **Throws:** right
Acquired: Second-round pick in 6/93 free-agent draft

Player Summary
Fantasy Value $0
Card Value. . . . . N/A
Will . . . . hit for average
Can't . . . . lose more time
Expect . . . . aggressiveness
Don't Expect . . . . a third sacker

Fullmer was the third player drafted by the Expos in 1993, behind first-rounders Chris Schwab and Josue Estrada, both of whom have had problems in pro ball. Fullmer outshone them both while in Albany of the South Atlantic League last year. Then again, he outshone a lot of people. Finally getting in the lineup after a late signing and shoulder surgery, Fullmer was one of the top hitters in the league. As the end of the year approached, he was battling fellow prospect Vlad Guerrero for the team batting lead. Fullmer ranked with the top RBI men in the Montreal farm system, and he collected more than 30 doubles. He looks like one of those lefties who can hit line drives all day. He also impressed with more walks (36) than strikeouts (33). The Expos will be anxious to see if he can do it at a higher level. He may have to hit, because defense does not seem to be his strongest suit. Perhaps it's the shoulder, but he made his share of errors at third last year. He served much of the year as a designated hitter. Maybe this year Fullmer will use the leather more.

Professional Batting Register

	BA	G	AB	R	H	2B	3B	HR	RBI	SB
95 A	.323	123	468	69	151	38	4	8	67	10

ROOKIE PROSPECTS

KARIM GARCIA

Position: Outfield
Team: Los Angeles Dodgers
Born: Oct. 29, 1975 Ciudad Obregon, Mexico
Height: 6' **Weight:** 172 lbs.
Bats: left **Throws:** left
Acquired: Signed as a nondrafted free agent, 7/92

Player Summary	
Fantasy Value	$2 to $4
Card Value	20¢ to 40¢
Will	hit for power
Can't	play center
Expect	a great arm
Don't Expect	hype

Veteran fans will remember the sensation that Fernando Valenzuela created en route to becoming the NL Rookie of the Year in 1981. Garcia has a chance to bring that same kind of excitement. He brings an element that can bring fans to the ballpark and pull them out of their seats—the ability to hit the ball far, and do it often. Garcia did not even turn 20 until last October, yet he has excelled at the highest levels of the minor leagues. Last year, he played for Albuquerque in the Triple-A Pacific Coast League. He hit for power and was named to the All-Star Team. Some Dodger prospects had been over-hyped in the past, their numbers inflated by the PCL's high altitudes. That is something of which to beware. But the fact remains that Garcia led the Florida State League in homers at age 18, and no one thinks the FSL will blow up power numbers. And, at age 19, he compiled a .542 slugging percentage and a .369 on-base percentage against Triple-A pitchers—impressive no matter what league. Garcia could play in Los Angeles this year.

Professional Batting Register

	BA	G	AB	R	H	2B	3B	HR	RBI	SB
93 A	.241	123	460	61	111	20	9	19	54	5
94 A	.265	121	452	72	120	28	10	21	84	8
95 AAA	.319	124	474	88	151	26	10	20	91	12
95 NL	.200	13	20	1	4	0	0	0	0	0

OMAR GARCIA

Position: First base
Team: New York Mets
Born: Nov. 16, 1971 Rio Pedras, PR
Height: 6' **Weight:** 187 lbs.
Bats: right **Throws:** right
Acquired: 18th-round pick in 6/89 free-agent draft

Player Summary	
Fantasy Value	$0
Card Value	N/A
Will	hit line drives
Can't	hit for power
Expect	a role player
Don't Expect	RBI

While the young pitchers in the Mets organization have received most of the attention, there are more than a couple of position players worth keeping in mind. One of them is Garcia, who has made a habit of hitting for a high average, no matter what the level. Last year it was at Triple-A Norfolk, where he ranked as one of the International League's top hitters for much of the season. He played first base for the NL farmhands in the Triple-A All-Star Game. Problem is, Garcia is only a singles hitter, which is a bit of a puzzle considering his build. You would think that by hitting the ball so often, he would have some homers just by accident. Instead, he doesn't even go for extra bases that often. Of his first 117 hits last year, only 26 took him past first base. That seemed to rule out a challenge to first baseman Rico Brogna last season. But Garcia might have a role as a platoon player or one who can come off the bench and get a big hit.

Professional Batting Register

	BA	G	AB	R	H	2B	3B	HR	RBI	SB
89 R	.255	32	98	15	25	3	1	0	8	6
90 R	.333	67	246	42	82	15	2	6	36	12
91 A	.251	108	394	63	99	11	4	4	50	12
92 A	.290	126	469	66	136	18	5	3	70	35
93 A	.322	129	485	73	156	17	7	3	76	25
94 AA	.358	64	246	38	88	14	4	5	42	3
94 AAA	.242	67	227	28	55	9	2	0	28	7
95 AA	.526	5	19	4	10	1	1	0	1	1
95 AAA	.309	115	430	55	133	21	7	3	64	3

ROOKIE PROSPECTS

NOMAR GARCIAPARRA

Position: Shortstop
Team: Boston Red Sox
Born: July 23, 1973 Whittier, CA
Height: 6′ **Weight:** 165 lbs.
Bats: right **Throws:** right
Acquired: First-round pick in 6/94 free-agent draft

Player Summary
Fantasy Value	$0
Card Value	30¢ to 60¢
Will	notch swipes
Can't	slay Green Monster
Expect	great range
Don't Expect	only a glove

With the small dimensions created by the Green Monster at Fenway Park, Garciaparra may soon be playing shortstop and left field at the same time. That's a bit of an overstatement, but it makes a point about the range that Garciaparra brings to shortstop. You hear stories of him ranging into left field to catch fly balls there. And there's more to Garciaparra's game than just a glove. He can run and hit, giving the Red Sox that kind of all-around player they have lacked all too often in their history. Originally drafted by Milwaukee in 1991, he instead went to Georgia Tech, where he majored in management—and starred in baseball. He batted .372 in his three-year college career, and he led his team to the Midwest II Region title in 1994. He played in the Arizona Fall League in 1994, making a favorable impression there. Last year he played in Double-A ball, where he impressed everyone. Especially impressive was his 50 bases on balls as opposed to his 42 strikeouts. Garciaparra may get a full season at Triple-A before joining the Red Sox in '97.

Professional Batting Register
	BA	G	AB	R	H	2B	3B	HR	RBI	SB
94 A	.295	28	105	20	31	8	1	1	16	5
95 AA	.267	125	513	77	137	20	8	8	47	35

JASON GIAMBI

Position: Third base
Team: Oakland Athletics
Born: Jan. 8, 1971 West Covina, CA
Height: 6′2″ **Weight:** 200 lbs.
Bats: left **Throws:** right
Acquired: Second-round pick in 6/92 free-agent draft

Player Summary
Fantasy Value	$5 to $7
Card Value	20¢ to 40¢
Will	stick in bigs
Can't	stay on farm
Expect	versatile play
Don't Expect	McGwire's power

Giambi got to the big leagues last summer and showed some versatility, delivering pop from both infield corners and also filling in at DH. Then again, moving around is nothing new to Giambi. His remarkable baseball résumé includes time with Kauai of the Hawaiian League, Fairbanks of the Alaska League, the U.S. team in the 1991 Pan Am Games in Cuba, and the U.S. Olympic team in Barcelona in 1992. That doesn't even count the trip he took to the College World Series with Long Beach State in 1991. Giambi has now spent four years in pro ball, but he has never put in enough time with any club to provide a sample of full-season numbers. But he has thrown out some impressive hints. In 1993, he hit 12 homers in the Class-A California League even though he missed nearly a month with thumb problems. He could hit 15 to 20 home runs in the majors, and draw 75 walks. He had a .537 slugging average last year in Triple-A. Giambi gives Oakland a valuable option if Mark McGwire's injury problems persist.

Professional Batting Register
	BA	G	AB	R	H	2B	3B	HR	RBI	SB
92 A	.317	13	41	9	13	3	0	3	13	1
93 A	.291	89	313	72	91	16	2	12	60	2
94 AA	.223	56	193	31	43	9	0	6	30	0
94 AAA	.318	52	176	28	56	20	0	4	38	1
95 AAA	.342	55	190	34	65	26	1	3	41	0
95 AL	.256	54	176	27	45	7	0	6	25	2

ROOKIE PROSPECTS

STEVE GIBRALTER

Position: Outfield
Team: Cincinnati Reds
Born: Oct. 9, 1972 Dallas, TX
Height: 6' **Weight:** 190 lbs.
Bats: right **Throws:** right
Acquired: Sixth-round pick in 6/90 free-agent draft

Player Summary
Fantasy Value	$0
Card Value	15¢ to 25¢
Will	strike out
Can't	assume recovery
Expect	occasional swipes
Don't Expect	singles hitter

Gibralter appeared to be on the verge of making a trip to Cincinnati last summer when a torn ligament in his thumb took a piece out of his season. Until the injury, he had rated as one of Cincinnati's top prospects. So productive was his season that long after his injury, he remained among the top Reds farmhands in all three Triple Crown categories. He was also able to turn in a .616 slugging percentage in half of a season last year. If you're with Reds management, you must wonder if the thumb damage will set back a long development project that had seemed to be producing a star. Gibralter began to take on the look of something special as far back as 1991, when he was named to the Class-A South Atlantic League's postseason All-Star Team. A year later, he led the Class-A Midwest League with home runs and RBI. A rise to Double-A seemed to set Gibralter back a little bit, and he needed two years at that level.

Professional Batting Register
	BA	G	AB	R	H	2B	3B	HR	RBI	SB
90 R	.259	52	174	26	45	11	3	4	27	9
91 A	.267	140	544	72	145	36	7	6	71	11
92 A	.306	137	529	92	162	32	3	19	99	12
93 AA	.237	132	477	65	113	25	3	11	47	7
94 AA	.270	133	460	71	124	28	3	14	63	10
95 AAA	.316	79	263	49	83	19	3	18	63	0
95 NL	.333	4	3	0	1	0	0	0	0	0

DERRICK GIBSON

Position: Outfield
Team: Colorado Rockies
Born: Feb. 5, 1975 Winter Haven, FL
Height: 6'2" **Weight:** 228 lbs.
Bats: right **Throws:** right
Acquired: 13th-round pick in 6/93 free-agent draft

Player Summary
Fantasy Value	$0
Card Value	40¢ to 70¢
Will	show speed
Can't	notch walks
Expect	average fielding
Don't Expect	consistent contact

Gibson is emerging as an exceptional power prospect who makes you wonder what he could accomplish if he ever could hit in Coors Field. He played for Asheville of the Class-A South Atlantic League last year and showed an exciting blend of speed and power. As the end of the campaign approached, he was leading the league in RBI, and he was battling Macon's Ron Wright for the home run championship. Even more impressive, Gibson was a 30-30 man. Not bad for someone just 20 years old. He turned in a .553 slugging percentage, and he has about a .490 slugging percentage thus far in his minor-league career. On the negative side, Gibson is a bit of an all-or-nothing hitter whose home run total exceeded the combined number of his doubles and triples. He also strikes out with the frequency you might expect from a young, raw slugger. He had 136 Ks last year in 506 at bats, and he will be challenged to cut that number as he moves up the ladder. Gibson walks infrequently; he had 29 last year. The same speed that serves him well on the bases should help him get to lots of balls in the outfield.

Professional Batting Register
	BA	G	AB	R	H	2B	3B	HR	RBI	SB
93 R	.151	34	119	13	18	2	2	0	10	3
94 A	.264	73	284	47	75	19	5	12	57	14
95 A	.292	135	506	91	148	16	10	32	115	31

ROOKIE PROSPECTS

ED GIOVANOLA

Position: Infield
Team: Atlanta Braves
Born: March 4, 1969 Los Gatos, CA
Height: 5'10" **Weight:** 170 lbs.
Bats: left **Throws:** right
Acquired: Sixth-round pick in 6/90 free-agent draft

Player Summary	
Fantasy Value	$0
Card Value	N/A
Will	get a shot
Can't	lose time
Expect	versatility
Don't Expect	everyday play

At 27 years of age, Giovanola is a little older than the classic prospect. He's trying to find his way in an organization that's loaded with talent. Despite these odds, it may be hard to ignore a player who can play more than one position and make a pitcher work hard. Giovanola has climbed through the Atlanta organization step by step, helping his ballclubs all along the way. Listed as a third baseman in the Atlanta press guide, he can also play shortstop. With the exception of 1994, when he hit 10 homers between Double-A and Triple-A ball, Giovanola has never been a power hitter. Then again, if he makes the Braves he won't need to be. He can concentrate on hitting for average, putting his bat on the ball, and drawing walks. He will steal the occasional base, nothing more. He projects as a utility player. He might even handle a regular job if given a chance. If he proves that he can handle the fielding tasks, Giovanola might give second base a try.

Professional Batting Register

	BA	G	AB	R	H	2B	3B	HR	RBI	SB
90 R	.388	25	98	25	38	6	0	0	13	6
90 A	.244	35	119	20	29	4	0	0	8	8
91 A	.254	101	299	50	76	9	0	6	27	18
92 AA	.267	75	270	39	72	5	0	5	30	4
93 AA	.281	120	384	70	108	21	5	5	43	6
94 AA	.238	25	84	13	20	6	1	4	16	2
94 AAA	.282	98	344	48	97	16	2	6	30	7
95 AAA	.321	99	321	45	103	18	2	4	36	8
95 NL	.071	13	14	2	1	0	0	0	0	0

WAYNE GOMES

Position: Pitcher
Team: Philadelphia Phillies
Born: Jan. 15, 1973 Hampton, VA
Height: 6'2" **Weight:** 205 lbs.
Bats: right **Throws:** right
Acquired: First-round pick in 6/93 free-agent draft

Player Summary	
Fantasy Value	$0
Card Value	10¢ to 15¢
Will	bring it
Can't	rule out closing
Expect	full counts
Don't Expect	a big winner

Just like the players on the field, people in the front office must sometimes make adjustments. Gomes's case provides an example. He may have been miscast as a closer when he was taken with the fourth overall pick in the draft. Gomes showed the necessary power for such a role in 1993, striking out 24 and allowing only five hits in 15 innings, but he didn't throw enough strikes. In fact, Gomes walked more than one batter per inning, and the last thing you want from a closer is to put extra men on base. So in 1994, Gomes became a starter and, though he continued to experience control problems, at least got the necessary work to develop his craft. Last year, while pitching in Double-A, he kept emerging. He won a league Pitcher of the Week award in early summer, and he threw an occasional sparkler. With his fastball and hard slider, he is able to sit batters down when he has to. He held Eastern League hitters to a .230 batting average last year. Gomes has the tools to pitch in the majors. But he won't if he doesn't throw strikes.

Professional Pitching Register

	W	L	ERA	G	S	IP	H	ER	BB	SO
93 A	1	0	1.20	14	4	15.0	5	2	17	24
94 A	6	8	4.74	23	1	104.1	85	55	82	102
95 AA	7	4	3.96	22	1	104.2	89	46	70	102

ROOKIE PROSPECTS

TODD GREENE

Position: Catcher
Team: California Angels
Born: May 8, 1971 Augusta, GA
Height: 5'9" **Weight:** 195 lbs.
Bats: right **Throws:** right
Acquired: 12th-round pick in 6/93 free-agent draft

Player Summary
Fantasy Value	$3 to $5
Card Value	60¢ to $1.25
Will	be a force
Can't	stop him
Expect	a decent eye
Don't Expect	a Gold Glove

When opponents think of the way the Angels hit the ball last year, they can only cringe to think that the Halos have another bona fide slugger on the way. Greene has become one of the top power prospects in the game, and not even steady promotions have cut into his ability to lose baseballs. In fact, his only competition for the Angels' minor-league home run crown came from Midland teammate George Arias. No one else was even close. Greene received a midsummer promotion to the Pacific Coast League, and he went only 3-for-16 in his first five games. However, he soon began doing what he had done at other stops, much to pitchers' chagrin. He turned in a .638 slugging percentage in Double-A and a .530 slugging percentage in Triple-A. Despite his hitting feats, or because of them, Greene represents a problem for the Angels. His hitting is well ahead of his glove, so the Angels may have to keep him on the farm well after his bat is ready for the majors. Or, they could bring Greene to the majors as a designated hitter and work on his glove there.

Professional Batting Register
	BA	G	AB	R	H	2B	3B	HR	RBI	SB
93 A	.269	76	305	55	82	15	3	15	71	4
94 A	.302	133	524	98	158	39	2	35	124	10
95 AA	.327	82	318	59	104	19	1	26	57	3
95 AAA	.250	43	168	28	42	3	1	14	35	1

BEN GRIEVE

Position: Outfield
Team: Oakland Athletics
Born: May 4, 1976 Arlington, TX
Height: 6'4" **Weight:** 200 lbs.
Bats: left **Throws:** right
Acquired: First-round pick in 6/94 free-agent draft

Player Summary
Fantasy Value	$0
Card Value	$1.00 to $2.00
Will	keep getting better
Can't	make it on name
Expect	a right fielder
Don't Expect	speed

If you judged by last year's home run totals alone, you'd wonder if Grieve was on track to fulfill the expectations that came with being the second overall pick in the 1994 draft. It might be better to put the home runs aside for a moment and judge him on the runs he drove in, and the fact that he received a late-summer promotion to the high Class-A California League. And it might be better still to keep in mind that this happened when he was just 19 years old. Grieve is the son of former major-league player and general manager Tom Grieve, and they form the first father-son combo to have been selected in the first round. Of course, the name alone won't bring the younger Grieve to the majors. But performances like his pro debut, when he made the Northwest League's postseason All-Star team, will help. Ben batted .261 in the Midwest League last year, with four homers and 62 RBI in 102 games. He also notched 60 walks for a .371 on-base average. He likely will spend more time in the Cal League, and one thing to watch in 1996 is whether he starts delivering the expected long ball.

Professional Batting Register
	BA	G	AB	R	H	2B	3B	HR	RBI	SB
94 A	.329	72	252	49	83	13	0	7	50	2
95 A	.261	130	478	70	125	21	1	6	76	13

ROOKIE PROSPECTS

VLADIMIR GUERRERO

Position: Outfield
Team: Montreal Expos
Born: Feb. 9, 1976 Nizao Bani, Dominican Republic
Height: 6'2" **Weight:** 170 lbs.
Bats: right **Throws:** right
Acquired: Signed as a nondrafted free agent, 3/93

Player Summary
Fantasy Value	$0
Card Value	N/A
Will	throw out runners
Can't	be out-tooled
Expect	power, speed
Don't Expect	a left fielder

Guerrero enjoyed nothing less than a spectacular season in his first extended look at the North American pros, assembling one of the best all-around games in the Class-A South Atlantic League last year. Throughout most of the season, he led Albany in runs, triples, homers, and RBI. Even amid these offensive credentials, his outfield throwing arm may be the best part of Guerrero's repertoire. He began the year by hitting in seven of his first eight games for a .407 average, and never let the pitchers get too far ahead of him. He batted .328 in a 16-game stretch that spanned June and July. *USA Today Baseball Weekly* tabbed him as a prospect to watch in its midsummer look at the farm systems. As the season headed toward its conclusion, Guerrero ranked among the top Montreal farmhands in all three Triple Crown categories. He had 30 walks and a .383 on-base percentage last year. He also turned in a .544 slugging average. He stole in double figures, and it will be interesting to see his limit in that category. He was caught stealing seven times. Look for Guerrero in either center field or right.

Professional Batting Register
	BA	G	AB	R	H	2B	3B	HR	RBI	SB
94 R	.314	37	137	24	43	13	3	5	25	0
95 A	.333	110	421	77	140	21	10	16	63	12

WILTON GUERRERO

Position: Shortstop
Team: Los Angeles Dodgers
Born: Oct. 24, 1974 Don Gregorio, Dominican Republic
Height: 5'11" **Weight:** 145 lbs.
Bats: right **Throws:** right
Acquired: Signed as a free agent, 10/91

Player Summary
Fantasy Value	$0
Card Value	N/A
Will	hit for average
Can't	hit for power
Expect	more seasoning
Don't Expect	stolen bases

Guerrero was quite simply one of the top hitters in all of the minor leagues last year. Playing for San Antonio of the Double-A Texas League, he made the All-Star team even though he was one of the youngest players in the circuit. It was not the first time that Guerrero has made an impression. In 1993, he was one of the top prospects in the rookie Pioneer League. In 1994, at the age of 19, Guerrero finished with the fifth-highest batting average in the high Class-A Florida State League. Last year, *USA Today Baseball Weekly* named him as one of its prospects to watch. As the season wound down, he hit .382 over a 17-game stretch. However, his game contains little power. He also turns in a weak strikeout-to-walk ratio, including 63 Ks and 26 bases on balls last year in Double-A. He was caught stealing 22 times in Double-A last year and 20 times in 1994. What you see from him is a lot of singles. Furthermore, the Dodgers already have shortstops who can hit. What the organization is looking for is defense, so Guerrero's road to Dodger Stadium could be paved with leather.

Professional Batting Register
	BA	G	AB	R	H	2B	3B	HR	RBI	SB
93 R	.297	66	256	44	76	5	1	0	21	20
94 A	.294	110	402	55	118	11	4	1	32	23
95 AA	.348	95	382	53	133	13	6	0	26	21
95 AAA	.327	14	49	10	16	1	1	0	2	2

ROOKIE PROSPECTS

JOSE GUILLEN

Position: Outfield
Team: Pittsburgh Pirates
Born: May 17, 1976 San Cristobal, Dominican Republic
Height: 5'11" **Weight:** 165 lbs.
Bats: right **Throws:** right
Acquired: Signed as a nondrafted free agent, 9/92

Player Summary
Fantasy Value	$0
Card Value	N/A
Will	keep developing
Can't	steal bases
Expect	great arm
Don't Expect	a quick arrival

Pittsburgh fans have seen some lean times in the last few years, but Guillen is just another reason to believe that things may be changing for the better. He has created excitement in the Pittsburgh organization for his power and for an arm that has been compared to some of the best in the majors. Last year, in his third year in the Pirates system, he also demonstrated the ability to hit for average. Playing for Erie in the Class-A New York-Penn League, he embarked on a late-season tear over which he hit .418 with five homers in 14 games. He was not bashful at the plate, walking only nine times in his first 194 official at bats. He compiled a .527 slugging average while in the New York-Penn League. He also played 10 games and had 34 at bats at Augusta in the Class-A South Atlantic League last year. Guillen began his career in the Dominican Summer League, playing when he was just 17 years old. He got a taste of rookie ball in the Gulf Coast League in 1994, and last year he showed the best results yet. However, the Pirates have brought him along slowly, and this year comes a new phase: full-season ball.

Professional Batting Register
	BA	G	AB	R	H	2B	3B	HR	RBI	SB
94 R	.264	30	110	17	29	4	1	4	11	2
95 A	.305	76	292	47	89	18	2	14	52	1

MIKE GULAN

Position: Third base
Team: St. Louis Cardinals
Born: Dec. 18, 1970 Steubenville, Ohio
Height: 6'1" **Weight:** 192 lbs.
Bats: right **Throws:** right
Acquired: Second-round pick in 6/92 free-agent draft

Player Summary
Fantasy Value	$0
Card Value	N/A
Will	produce extra bases
Can't	get on base
Expect	wild swings
Don't Expect	Gold Gloves

Gulan represents one of baseball's most prized packages—a third baseman who can hit for power. And he might be coming along at just the right time, with Busch Stadium expected to go to regular grass for 1996. That move will change the Cardinals' emphasis from speed to muscle. Gulan showed his power while with Springfield of the Class-A Midwest League in 1993, when nearly half of his 118 hits went for extra bases, 23 of them home runs. He hit eight homers for St. Petersburg in 1994, a decent total considering the difficulty of leaving the yard in the Class-A Florida State League. Last year at Arkansas in the Double-A Texas League, he homered in both games of an April 29 doubleheader. He homered twice against Tulsa June 6 as part of a stretch in which he delivered 14 RBI in 15 games. He had a .554 slugging percentage for Arkansas. The product of Kent State University was named to the Double-A All-Star Game and was promoted to Triple-A. Expect a lot of all-or-nothing at bats, because Gulan strikes out a lot and doesn't walk much.

Professional Batting Register
	BA	G	AB	R	H	2B	3B	HR	RBI	SB
92 A	.273	62	242	33	66	8	4	7	36	12
93 A	.259	132	455	81	118	28	4	23	76	8
94 A	.242	120	466	39	113	30	2	8	56	2
95 AA	.314	64	242	47	76	16	3	12	48	4
95 AAA	.236	58	195	21	46	10	4	5	27	2

ROOKIE PROSPECTS

ROY HALLADAY

Position: Pitcher
Team: Toronto Blue Jays
Born: May 14, 1977 Denver, CO
Height: 6'5" **Weight:** 200 lbs.
Bats: right **Throws:** right
Acquired: First-round pick in 6/95 free-agent draft

Player Summary	
Fantasy Value	$0
Card Value	N/A
Will	bring the tools
Can't	use two pitches
Expect	nice size
Don't Expect	quick arrival

For the second time in three years, the Blue Jays have made a tall, right-handed pitcher out of high school their first pick in the June draft. Back in 1993, it was Chris Carpenter, who is doing a nice job of making his way through the farm system. The Blue Jays are hoping for similar things from Halladay, who could be something special if he develops power to go along with his size. Probably the best prospect in the state of Colorado, Halladay was a dominant pitcher at West High School near Denver, allowing only one hit per three innings. He was taken with the 17th overall pick, signed, and assigned to the Gulf Coast League. There he went 3-5 with a 3.40 ERA in his 10 pro appearances, averaging just under one strikeout per inning and notching a strikeout-to-walk ratio of 3-to-1. He also held loop hitters to a composite .190 batting average. Blue Jays fans who endured the major-league club's worst season in several years should expect no quick help from Halladay. He won't arrive in the big leagues until around the turn of the century.

Professional Pitching Register

	W	L	ERA	G	CG	IP	H	ER	BB	SO
95 R	3	5	3.40	10	0	50.1	35	19	16	48

RYAN HANCOCK

Position: Pitcher
Team: California Angels
Born: Nov. 11, 1971 Santa Clara, CA
Height: 6'2" **Weight:** 215 lbs.
Bats: right **Throws:** right
Acquired: Second-round pick in 6/93 free-agent draft

Player Summary	
Fantasy Value	$0
Card Value	N/A
Will	give innings
Can't	afford knee trouble
Expect	hits
Don't Expect	a rush job

Hancock has battled back from a major knee injury to become one of the more intriguing pitching prospects in the California organization. He pitched for Midland of the Double-A Texas League last season and sent out two strong, opposite signals. On the one hand, he was hit hard, as his ERA and hits-to-innings ratio will attest. On the other, he was a durable pitcher, leading the team in innings and decisions. That's excellent news in light of concerns about his knee. However, the question involves Hancock's next step. Presumably, it would be the Triple-A Pacific Coast League. But, if he was hit that hard in Double-A, what might happen in the homer-happy PCL? At least Hancock helps himself by keeping the walks to a minimum. He allowed just under two and one-half walks per nine innings last year. The Angels have been rooting extra hard for Hancock since last July 27, when they dispatched two of their other pitching prospects—Bill Simas and Andrew Lorraine—to the White Sox in order to obtain Jim Abbott.

Professional Pitching Register

	W	L	ERA	G	CG	IP	H	ER	BB	SO
93 A	1	0	3.31	3	0	16.1	14	6	8	18
94 A	9	6	3.79	18	3	116.1	113	49	36	95
94 AA	3	4	5.81	8	0	48.0	63	31	11	35
95 AA	12	9	4.56	28	5	175.2	222	89	45	79

ROOKIE PROSPECTS

LaTROY HAWKINS

Position: Pitcher
Team: Minnesota Twins
Born: Dec. 21, 1972 Gary, IN
Height: 6'5" **Weight:** 193 lbs.
Bats: right **Throws:** right
Acquired: Seventh-round pick in 6/91 free-agent draft

Player Summary
Fantasy Value	$0
Card Value	15¢ to 25¢
Will	utilize a slider
Can't	give up on him
Expect	a top repertoire
Don't Expect	1994

After a meteoric climb through the minors, Hawkins got a chance to pitch in the majors last spring when rosters were expanded in the wake of the strike. He failed to take full advantage of the opportunity, allowing seven runs on seven hits in one and two-thirds innings in his first big-league start. He also dropped his next two starts, though he did show some improvement. Maybe it was time for Hawkins to step back after he climbed seven rungs in just over three years. Hawkins made his most dramatic climb in 1994, when he opened the season in high Class-A ball, proceeded to a dominating stint in Double-A, and finished by handling himself well at Triple-A. He is still so young that his ill-fated trip to the majors should not bother anyone. In 1994, Hawkins became the first two-time winner of the Twins' Sherry Robertson Award, given to the organization's top minor-league player. This year he should again challenge for a job in the Minnesota starting rotation.

Professional Pitching Register
	W	L	ERA	G	CG	IP	H	ER	BB	SO
91 R	4	3	4.75	11	0	55.0	62	29	26	47
92 R	3	3	3.29	11	2	63.0	57	23	21	71
93 A	15	5	2.06	26	4	157.1	110	36	41	179
94 A	4	0	2.33	6	1	38.2	32	10	6	36
94 AA	9	2	2.33	11	1	73.1	50	19	28	53
94 AAA	5	4	4.08	12	1	81.2	92	37	33	37
95 AAA	9	7	3.55	22	4	144.1	150	57	40	74
95 AL	2	3	8.67	6	1	27.0	39	26	12	9

JIMMY HAYNES

Position: Pitcher
Team: Baltimore Orioles
Born: Sept. 5, 1972 LaGrange, GA
Height: 6'4" **Weight:** 185 lbs.
Bats: right **Throws:** right
Acquired: Seventh-round pick in 6/91 free-agent draft

Player Summary
Fantasy Value	$2 to $4
Card Value	10¢ to 20¢
Will	get a chance
Can't	continue K rate
Expect	innings
Don't Expect	grand slams

No matter which end of a pitch he happens to be on, Haynes owns a gift for the spectacular. In his last high school game, he hit a grand slam. And since then, he has been grand in his pitching. He has finished among league leaders in several categories, has won awards, and has been chosen for All-Star teams wherever he has played. Haynes has been a strikeout artist for most of his minor-league career, overwhelming batters with a fastball, a curveball, and a changeup. For his first three years in pro ball, he averaged more than one strikeout per inning. He leveled off slightly in that department last year, but he still was sufficiently effective to lead the Triple-A International League with 140 strikeouts. Haynes showed good control, had a decent hits-to-innings ratio, and ranked among the top strikeout pitchers in the Baltimore organization. This year, Haynes should get a full opportunity to join a rotation that was not deep enough to sustain the Orioles in last year's pennant race.

Professional Pitching Register
	W	L	ERA	G	CG	IP	H	ER	BB	SO
91 R	3	2	1.60	14	1	62.0	44	11	21	67
92 A	7	11	2.56	24	4	144.0	131	41	45	141
93 A	12	8	3.03	27	2	172.1	139	58	61	174
94 AA	13	8	2.90	25	5	173.2	154	56	46	177
94 AAA	1	0	6.75	3	0	13.1	20	10	6	14
95 AAA	12	8	3.29	26	3	167.0	162	61	49	140
95 AL	2	1	2.25	4	0	24.0	11	6	12	22

ROOKIE PROSPECTS

RODNEY HENDERSON

Position: Pitcher
Team: Montreal Expos
Born: March 11, 1971 Greensburg, KY
Height: 6'4" **Weight:** 193 lbs.
Bats: right **Throws:** right
Acquired: Second-round pick in 6/92 free-agent draft

Player Summary	
Fantasy Value	$0
Card Value	N/A
Will	throw four pitches
Can't	hang in Double-A
Expect	a starter
Don't Expect	top health

Making the big leagues is tough enough when you're healthy, but Henderson has been trying to overcome big-time health problems. Last year, he made only 12 appearances for Harrisburg of the Double-A Eastern League before being shut down with a bad wing. That came just as he was trying to duplicate his fine 1994 season, when he started in Double-A and eventually climbed to the majors. In the big leagues, he made one effective relief appearance and two poor starts. Actually, it's remarkable that Henderson was pitching at all, since an auto crash nearly ended his career just as it was beginning. It took place in June 1992, just after Henderson was drafted, and the accident resulted in two fractured vertebrae and a broken pitching wrist. Despite that, he was promoted to high Class-A the next season and finished second among Florida State League starters in opponents' batting average. Now health, and not pitching ability, looms as the issue with Henderson.

Professional Pitching Register

	W	L	ERA	G	CG	IP	H	ER	BB	SO
92 A	0	0	6.00	1	0	3.0	2	2	5	2
93 A	12	7	2.90	22	1	143.0	110	46	44	127
93 AA	5	0	1.82	5	0	29.2	20	6	15	25
94 AA	2	0	1.50	2	0	12.0	5	2	4	16
94 AAA	6	9	4.62	23	0	122.2	123	63	67	100
94 NL	0	1	9.45	3	0	6.2	9	7	7	3
95 AA	3	6	4.31	12	0	56.1	51	27	18	53

CHAD HERMANSEN

Position: Shortstop
Team: Pittsburgh Pirates
Born: Sept. 10, 1977 Salt Lake City, UT
Height: 6'2" **Weight:** 175 lbs.
Bats: right **Throws:** right
Acquired: First-round pick in 6/95 free-agent draft

Player Summary	
Fantasy Value	$0
Card Value	N/A
Will	bring power
Can't	show big range
Expect	extra bases
Don't Expect	a shortstop

Despite the realities of being a small-market club, the Pirates went after Hermansen with gusto. The Bucs made him the 10th overall pick in the draft, then parted with enough money to complete a quick signing. He reported to the rookie Gulf Coast League and immediately began to validate their judgment. After just 92 pro at bats, Hermansen was hitting .304, and 14 of his 28 hits went for extra bases. He received a promotion to the New York-Penn League, where he continued to slug, notching 17 extra-base hits in 45 safeties. Hermansen had 27 bases on balls last year. He notched slugging percentages of .533 in rookie ball and .467 in Class-A. He also has shown that he knows how to knock in a run. That's the kind of power you might expect from someone with his build, and it continues the pattern of his career at Green Valley High School in Nevada, where he was in double figures in doubles and homers his senior year. There's a long way to go, but Hermansen couldn't have done more than he did in his debut. Hermansen's quick signing reflects a healthy hunger.

Professional Batting Register

	BA	G	AB	R	H	2B	3B	HR	RBI	SB
95 R	.304	24	92	14	28	10	1	3	17	0
95 A	.273	44	165	30	45	8	3	6	25	4

ROOKIE PROSPECTS

DUSTIN HERMANSON

Position: Pitcher
Team: San Diego Padres
Born: Dec. 21, 1972 Springfield, OH
Height: 6'2" **Weight:** 195 lbs.
Bats: right **Throws:** right
Acquired: First-round pick in 6/94 free-agent draft

Player Summary	
Fantasy Value	$1 to $3
Card Value	10¢ to 25¢
Will	get it done
Can't	let attitude slip
Expect	a closer
Don't Expect	the low minors

Baseball can make you humble in a hurry, and Hermanson might tell you that, because he found out about the game's ups and downs in the span of one year. In 1994, he became an immediate sensation after becoming the third overall pick in the draft. He posted an 0.43 ERA in 16 appearances at Double-A Wichita in the Texas League and earned a promotion to Triple-A. He even got some time in the majors early last year. But things went wrong, and the Padres sent Hermanson deep into their system to work out the kinks. When he did get back to Triple-A, Hermanson earned saves in four consecutive games, indicating that he was back on track. But his control still leaves a lot to be desired. Pacific Coast League batters hit .245 against him last year, while big-league batters hit .280. Hermanson pitched for the U.S. National Team in 1993, collecting seven saves with an 0.81 ERA. A finalist for the 1994 Golden Spikes Award, given to the top college player, he also was named first-team Academic All-Mid-American Conference in his senior year at Kent University.

RICHARD HIDALGO

Position: Outfield
Team: Houston Astros
Born: July 2, 1975 Caracas, Venezuela
Height: 6'2" **Weight:** 175 lbs.
Bats: right **Throws:** right
Acquired: Signed as a nondrafted free agent, 7/91

Player Summary	
Fantasy Value	$0
Card Value	30¢ to 50¢
Will	hit for average
Can't	play center
Expect	doubles
Don't Expect	a burner

Hidalgo was signed to his first pro contract the day he turned 16, reflecting Houston's enthusiasm over his ability. He has responded with a productive minor-league career which he has produced as he has progressed. Fans are not likely to forget him in the Class-A Midwest League, where he set a record with 47 doubles in 1994. He also led the league with 65 extra-base hits while making the All-Star team. Last year he made the jump to the Double-A Texas League. He ranked among the top San Diego farmhands in home runs while continuing to show his knack for hitting doubles. Hidalgo will probably fill out just a bit more and when he does, he might be even more likely to hit the ball over the wall. He has earned plaudits for his glove and his arm, and he could do well at either of the outfield corners. It wouldn't hurt him to draw a few more walks. He had 32 bases on balls last year as opposed to 76 strikeouts. But considering what he can do with the bat, Hidalgo would be well advised to remain aggressive.

Professional Pitching Register

	W	L	ERA	G	S	IP	H	ER	BB	SO
94 AA	1	0	0.43	16	8	21.0	13	1	6	30
94 AAA	0	0	6.14	7	3	7.1	6	5	5	6
95 AAA	0	1	3.50	31	11	36.0	35	14	29	42
95 NL	3	1	6.82	26	0	31.2	35	24	22	19

Professional Batting Register

	BA	G	AB	R	H	2B	3B	HR	RBI	SB
92 R	.310	51	184	20	57	7	3	1	27	14
93 A	.270	111	403	49	109	23	3	10	55	21
94 A	.292	124	476	68	139	47	6	12	76	12
95 AA	.266	133	489	59	130	28	6	14	59	8

ROOKIE PROSPECTS

AARON HOLBERT

Position: Shortstop
Team: St. Louis Cardinals
Born: Jan. 9, 1973 Torrance, CA
Height: 6′ **Weight:** 160 lbs.
Bats: right **Throws:** right
Acquired: First-round pick in 6/90 free-agent draft

Player Summary	
Fantasy Value	$0
Card Value	10¢ to 15¢
Will	run less
Can't	stay healthy
Expect	a punch hitter
Don't Expect	Smith's range

Holbert was a prime candidate for the unenviable task of following Ozzie Smith at shortstop. Holbert still could do it, but injuries have already robbed him of valuable development time. Last year he went on the disabled list with a hamstring pull, marking the second straight season he missed a significant stretch. The year before that, it was a knee problem; and back in 1991, he suffered a broken ankle. Not only do these setbacks raise the possibility that Holbert is injury-prone, but together they could be robbing him of the quickness and range he'll need at shortstop. Holbert did steal more than 100 bases over a two-year span in Class-A, but those days are likely over. He won't hit for much power, but he might put together some extra-base hits while hitting for a decent average. He had a .384 slugging percentage last year at Triple-A Louisville. However, that could all become secondary if he doesn't find a way to stay healthy. Already, Holbert has left open the door for someone to pass him.

Professional Batting Register

	BA	G	AB	R	H	2B	3B	HR	RBI	SB
90 R	.172	54	174	27	30	4	1	1	18	4
91 A	.223	59	215	22	48	5	1	1	24	5
92 A	.267	119	438	53	117	17	4	1	34	62
93 A	.265	121	457	60	121	18	3	2	31	45
94 AA	.296	59	233	41	69	10	6	2	19	9
94 R	.167	5	12	3	2	0	0	0	0	2
95 AAA	.257	112	401	57	103	16	4	9	40	14

DAMON HOLLINS

Position: Outfield
Team: Atlanta Braves
Born: June 12, 1974 Fairfield, CA
Height: 5′11″ **Weight:** 180 lbs.
Bats: right **Throws:** left
Acquired: Fourth-round pick in 6/92 free-agent draft

Player Summary	
Fantasy Value	$0
Card Value	N/A
Will	play anywhere
Can't	stop producing
Expect	strikeouts
Don't Expect	Justice's power

Hollins is one of the young talents who may soon be forcing the Braves to make some difficult decisions. He has moved smartly through the minor-league system, emerging as one of the top prospects in the rookie Appalachian League in 1993 and the Class-A Carolina League in 1994. Last year, he got his toughest test to date, and responded with a productive season in the Double-A Southern League. He is shaping up as a comer who can punish the ball. He probably won't hit with the same power as David Justice can, but Hollins certainly did his share for Greenville last year. Hollins finished fifth in Atlanta's system with 77 RBI, amassing more than any Atlanta minor leaguer above the Class-A level. His ninth-inning homer on May 12 beat Knoxville 4-3. That was the start of a 19-game stretch over which he hit .359. On June 17, he beat Knoxville again, this time with an eighth-inning grand slam. Hollins could play at either Double-A or Triple-A this season, working on his contact. He had 44 bases on balls last season, with 120 strikeouts.

Professional Batting Register

	BA	G	AB	R	H	2B	3B	HR	RBI	SB
92 R	.229	49	179	35	41	12	1	1	15	15
93 R	.321	62	240	37	77	15	2	7	51	10
94 A	.270	131	485	76	131	28	0	23	88	12
95 AA	.247	129	466	64	115	26	2	18	77	6

ROOKIE PROSPECTS

JOHN HOPE

Position: Pitcher
Team: Pittsburgh Pirates
Born: Dec. 12, 1970 Ft. Lauderdale, FL
Height: 6'3" **Weight:** 205 lbs.
Bats: right **Throws:** right
Acquired: Second-round pick in 6/89 free-agent draft

Player Summary	
Fantasy Value	$0
Card Value	N/A
Will	be on the cusp
Can't	change in majors
Expect	good control
Don't Expect	an eternal prospect

Hope compiled some fine statistics last year, but you can't help but wonder what is keeping him from doing it in the majors. After all, he was 24 years old and was spending his sixth year in pro ball. He had enjoyed a couple of cups of coffee in the majors in 1993 and 1994. But even with all that, in a season when the Pirates needed lots of help, he spent much of the season in the minors. When he finally managed to get into a big-league game, on July 1 against Houston, he walked three and allowed two hits and four earned runs without getting anyone out. In his next outing, five days later, he went one-third of an inning and permitted two runs. He enjoyed far greater success with Calgary of the Triple-A Pacific Coast League. But so far, Hope hasn't been able to do it in the bigs. This year will be the one where he either breaks through or is defined as just a Triple-A pitcher.

Professional Pitching Register

	W	L	ERA	G	CG	IP	H	ER	BB	SO
89 R	0	1	4.80	4	0	15.0	15	8	6	14
91 A	8	4	3.76	16	0	91.0	79	38	26	70
92 A	11	8	3.47	27	4	176.1	169	68	46	106
93 AA	9	4	4.37	21	0	111.1	123	54	29	66
93 AAA	2	1	6.33	4	0	21.1	30	15	2	6
93 NL	0	2	4.03	7	0	38.0	40	17	8	8
94 AAA	4	9	3.87	18	0	100.0	98	43	23	54
94 NL	0	0	5.79	9	0	14.0	18	9	4	6
95 AAA	7	1	2.79	13	3	80.2	76	25	11	41
95 NL	0	0	30.86	3	0	2.1	8	8	4	2

MIKE HUBBARD

Position: Catcher
Team: Chicago Cubs
Born: Feb. 16, 1971 Lynchburg, VA
Height: 6'1" **Weight:** 180 lbs.
Bats: right **Throws:** right
Acquired: Seventh-round pick in 6/92 free-agent draft

Player Summary	
Fantasy Value	$0
Card Value	N/A
Will	bring some speed
Can't	swing for fences
Expect	trouble with runners
Don't Expect	a quick arrival

Hubbard made his major-league debut last season when Scott Servais was injured, and Hubbard could be the Cubs' regular catcher as early as this year. He brings power potential that would fit nicely with the left field wall in Wrigley Field, and his catching is better than average. He also has a bit of speed, which would help on the league's artificial surfaces. Hubbard comes out of James Madison University in Virginia, where he majored in sports management. Upon turning pro, he had a get-acquainted season with Geneva of the rookie New York-Penn League. He blossomed in the Class-A Florida State League in 1993, making the All-Star Team. He cut down 41.4 percent of the runners trying to steal, and nearly batted .300. He spent the 1994 season with Orlando of the Double-A Southern League, again making the All-Star Team. He assembled a 19-game hitting streak in April and May. However, Hubbard only threw out 36 percent of runners. Some hard work and experience should be able to increase that number.

Professional Batting Register

	BA	G	AB	R	H	2B	3B	HR	RBI	SB
92 A	.240	50	183	25	44	4	4	3	25	6
93 A	.294	68	245	25	72	10	3	1	20	10
94 AA	.286	104	357	52	102	13	3	11	39	7
95 AAA	.260	75	254	28	66	6	3	5	23	6
95 NL	.174	15	23	2	4	0	0	0	1	0

ROOKIE PROSPECTS

SCOTT HUNTER

Position: Outfield
Team: New York Mets
Born: Dec. 17, 1975 Philadelphia, PA
Height: 6'2" **Weight:** 195 lbs.
Bats: right **Throws:** right
Acquired: Traded by Dodgers with Dwight Maness for Brett Butler, 8/95

Player Summary
Fantasy Value $0
Card Value. . . . . N/A
Will . . . . face competition
Can't. . . . . match Butler's contact
Expect . . . . a center fielder
Don't Expect . . . . refined talent

Hunter came to New York as part of a mid-August package that returned veteran center fielder Brett Butler to the Dodgers. Hunter thus left one team that is loaded with outfield prospects in favor of another club in the same situation. The upside is that Hunter need not worry about the logjam at the major-league level, because he's not ready to challenge for it yet. Even the Mets admit he is still a raw talent, which is why they assigned him to their low Class-A club in the South Atlantic League after the trade. He had been playing in the Class-A California League, where he had shown power and speed. He had a .438 slugging average and a .355 on-base average in the Cal League last year. He also had 36 bases on balls and 83 strikeouts. A center fielder, he is not at all built in the Brett Butler mold. Hunter is bigger and will hit for more power, but he will not make as much consistent contact. Drafted in the fifth round by the Dodgers in 1993, Hunter did not turn pro until 1994. Just 20 years old, he might get a test at New York's high Class-A club in the Florida State League this season.

EDWIN HURTADO

Position: Pitcher
Team: Toronto Blue Jays
Born: Feb. 1, 1970 Barquisimeto, Venezuela
Height: 6'3" **Weight:** 208 lbs.
Bats: right **Throws:** right
Acquired: Signed as a nondrafted free agent, 12/90

Player Summary
Fantasy Value $0
Card Value. . . . . N/A
Will . . . . get lefties out
Can't . . . . allow gophers
Expect . . . . a starter
Don't Expect . . . . awesome stats

After spending four seasons on the lowest levels of pro ball, Hurtado leaped to the majors last year, taking advantage of pitching woes in Toronto. At first, he served as a reliever, then he earned himself his first major-league start, going seven innings for a victory against Seattle on July 21. Hurtado broke into pro ball with two dominating seasons in the Dominican League. He went 18-1 over that span, competing for the league lead in several departments. That earned him a trip to the Class-A New York-Penn League for 1993, where he finished in the top 10 in shutouts, starts, wins, and ERA. A boost to the Class-A South Atlantic League did nothing to slow Hurtado, as he averaged nearly one strikeout per inning. A starting pitcher in the lower minors, Hurtado has shown he can excel either in the bullpen or starting rotation. Given that Toronto dealt David Cone last year, an opportunity presents itself. Hurtado will have to watch the gopher balls, as he allowed seven homers in Double-A Knoxville and 11 in the big leagues.

Professional Batting Register

	BA	G	AB	R	H	2B	3B	HR	RBI	SB
94 R	.316	64	237	45	75	12	4	2	28	5
95 A	.282	125	419	70	118	19	3	11	60	29

Professional Pitching Register

	W	L	ERA	G	CG	IP	H	ER	BB	SO
93 A	10	2	2.50	15	3	101.0	69	28	34	87
94 A	11	2	2.95	33	1	134.1	118	44	46	121
95 AA	2	4	4.45	11	0	54.2	54	27	25	38
95 AL	5	2	5.45	14	1	77.2	81	11	40	33

ROOKIE PROSPECTS

JESSE IBARRA

Position: First base
Team: San Francisco Giants
Born: July 12, 1972 Los Angeles, CA
Height: 6'3" **Weight:** 195 lbs.
Bats: both **Throws:** right
Acquired: Sixth-round pick in 6/94 free-agent draft

Player Summary	
Fantasy Value	$0
Card Value	N/A
Will	be fun to watch
Can't	put ceiling on him
Expect	homers in bunches
Don't Expect	return to catching

Not everyone who stars in the middle levels of the minors will make it all the way to the majors. However, when someone puts up the numbers that Ibarra did last year, you have to watch him and see how far the road will go. Ibarra smashed his way through the Class-A Midwest League, pacing Giants farmhands in all three Triple Crown categories. He hit more than twice as many homers as any other San Francisco minor leaguer, and he batted about 30 points higher than his nearest pursuer. He struck out 94 times, which is an acceptable number for a power hitter, and received 77 free passes. Ibarra comes out of John Bosco Tech in El Monte, California, and attended Loyola Marymount. In his first year of pro ball, he averaged approximately one homer for every 25 at bats, an eye-opening total for someone just getting started. Last year, he went on a tear late in the season, hitting 11 homers in a 20-game span. He was listed in the Giants media guide as a catcher, but Ibarra played first base last year and will stay there as long as he hits.

Professional Batting Register

	BA	G	AB	R	H	2B	3B	HR	RBI	SB
94 A	.226	67	252	32	57	15	1	10	37	0
95 A	.330	131	446	73	147	32	1	34	100	1

JASON ISRINGHAUSEN

Position: Pitcher
Team: New York Mets
Born: Sept. 7, 1972 Brighton, IL
Height: 6'3" **Weight:** 188 lbs.
Bats: right **Throws:** right
Acquired: 44th-round pick in 6/91 free-agent draft

Player Summary	
Fantasy Value	$10 to $13
Card Value	40¢ to 80¢
Will	show savage curve
Can't	ignore changeup
Expect	premier power
Don't Expect	dawdling

Isringhausen was one of two youngsters—the other being Bill Pulsipher—who arrived last summer to bring cheer to an otherwise dreary Mets season. Isringhausen made his major-league debut on July 17 against the Cubs, and he went seven impressive innings. He retired the side in order six times and fanned Mark Grace twice. With that game taking place in his home state, Isringhausen enjoyed the added thrill of performing in front of family and friends. He throws a plus fastball, a sharp curveball, and the makings of a changeup. He is also not afraid to bust batters inside, a quality that is guaranteed to endear him to big-league managers. Furthermore, Isringhausen likes to work fast, which will get him the best possible defensive support. Despite not playing pro ball the year he was drafted, Isringhausen made a spectacular move through the farm system. He was spectacular last year, holding Triple-A hitters to a .203 batting average. It's not impossible to see "Izzy" as a dominant starter for many years to come.

Professional Pitching Register

	W	L	ERA	G	CG	IP	H	ER	BB	SO
92 R	6	5	3.74	13	1	65.0	58	27	29	49
93 A	7	4	3.29	15	2	90.1	68	33	28	104
94 A	6	4	2.23	14	6	101.0	76	25	27	59
94 AA	5	4	3.02	14	2	92.1	78	31	23	69
95 AA	2	1	2.85	6	1	41.0	26	13	12	59
95 AAA	9	1	1.55	12	3	87.0	64	15	24	75
95 NL	9	2	2.81	14	1	93.0	88	29	31	55

ROOKIE PROSPECTS

DAMIAN JACKSON

Position: Shortstop
Team: Cleveland Indians
Born: Aug. 16, 1973 Los Angeles, CA
Height: 5'10" **Weight:** 160 lbs.
Bats: right **Throws:** right
Acquired: 44th-round pick in 6/91 free-agent draft

Player Summary	
Fantasy Value	$0
Card Value	N/A
Will	be deep in count
Can't	win Gold Glove
Expect	good speed
Don't Expect	power

You wonder what scouts were overlooking when they let Jackson remain untouched until late in the draft. On speed alone he would seem to deserve a higher nod. But all that matters to Cleveland now is that he is developing in the farm system. Jackson spent a second straight year with Canton-Akron of the Double-A Eastern League, trying to iron out the defensive problems he experienced in 1994. Jackson had 54 errors that year. He turned only 22 years old last year, so some of his miscues can be chalked up to inexperience. As for his offense, Jackson shapes up as an ignitor who can hit .250, work out some walks, steal bases, and score runs. Never in a four-year pro career has he stolen fewer than 26 bases, and he has averaged over 30 thefts per season. He has shown a tendency to strike out, not a good pattern for someone who doesn't show much power. He had 103 punchouts last year and 65 bases on balls. The earliest days of the 1996 season should tell a lot about Jackson. If he goes to another year of Double-A, he'll be stalled.

Professional Batting Register

	BA	G	AB	R	H	2B	3B	HR	RBI	SB
92 R	.248	62	226	32	56	12	1	0	23	29
93 A	.269	108	350	70	94	19	3	6	45	26
94 AA	.269	138	531	85	143	29	5	5	46	37
95 AA	.248	131	484	67	120	20	2	3	34	40

RYAN JACKSON

Position: Outfield
Team: Florida Marlins
Born: Nov. 15, 1971 Orlando, FL
Height: 6'3" **Weight:** 195 lbs.
Bats: left **Throws:** left
Acquired: Seventh-round pick in 6/94 free-agent draft

Player Summary	
Fantasy Value	$0
Card Value	N/A
Will	score runs
Can't	cool him
Expect	top on-base mark
Don't Expect	dominance

On a team loaded with stars, Jackson combined power and average about as well as any of his mates last year. Playing for Kane County, he flirted with .300, led the Class-A Midwest League in doubles, reached double figures in home runs, and produced more than 80 RBI. For much of the season, he ranked among the top Marlins minor leaguers in all three Triple Crown categories. The fact that he fell short at the end in no way diminishes his season. It was the second time in as many years of pro ball that Jackson emerged as one of the top offensive forces on his team. A year earlier, he led Elmira of the Class-A New York-Penn League in runs, hits, doubles, and homers. He puts the ball in play well for a power hitter, and he will draw enough walks to make him a very difficult out. He had 67 free passes last year, and turned in a .382 on-base percentage. Jackson may have been a little too mature for some of his competition, so it will be especially interesting to see how he fares at a higher level, either high Class-A or Double-A.

Professional Batting Register

	BA	G	AB	R	H	2B	3B	HR	RBI	SB
94 A	.290	72	276	46	80	18	1	6	41	4
95 A	.293	132	471	78	138	39	6	10	82	13

ROOKIE PROSPECTS

MARTY JANZEN

Position: Pitcher
Team: Toronto Blue Jays
Born: May 31, 1973 Miami, FL
Height: 6'2" **Weight:** 185 lbs.
Bats: right **Throws:** right
Acquired: Traded by Yankees with Jason Jarvis and Mike Gordon for David Cone, 7/95

Player Summary	
Fantasy Value	$0
Card Value	N/A
Will	be heard from
Can't	be Dave Cone
Expect	a reliable starter
Don't Expect	New York

Janzen would love nothing better than to be another prospect who blossoms after leaving the Yankees. He went from New York to the Blue Jays down the stretch of last year's pennant chase as part of the deal that brought David Cone to Yankee Stadium. At the time, people said the Yankees had given up relatively little to get a player of Cone's stature. Now Janzen, considered the key to the deal, has the chance to prove them wrong. Signed by the Yankees as a nondrafted free agent in August 1991, Janzen had not appeared above low Class-A ball until last year. But he opened the season in the Florida State League and dominated. He held FSL hitters to a .241 batting average. He worked his way up to Double-A ball. Just before the trade, he ranked among the top Yankee farmhands in wins, ERA, and strikeouts. *USA Today Baseball Weekly* had tabbed him a prospect to watch. Upon being traded, Janzen reported to Toronto's Double-A team in Knoxville and won his Southern League debut.

Professional Pitching Register

	W	L	ERA	G	CG	IP	H	ER	BB	SO
92 R	7	2	2.36	12	0	68.2	55	18	15	73
92 A	0	0	3.60	2	0	5.0	5	2	1	5
93 R	0	1	1.21	5	0	22.1	20	3	3	19
94 A	3	7	3.89	17	0	104.0	98	45	25	92
95 AA	6	3	3.31	10	2	68.0	52	25	21	60
95 A	10	3	2.61	18	1	113.2	102	33	30	104

RYAN JARONCYK

Position: Shortstop
Team: New York Mets
Born: March 26, 1977 Escondido, CA
Height: 6' **Weight:** 170 lbs.
Bats: both **Throws:** right
Acquired: First-round pick in 6/95 free-agent draft

Player Summary	
Fantasy Value	$0
Card Value	N/A
Will	leg out hits
Can't	rule out pop
Expect	a long project
Don't Expect	Ordonez's glove

In rebuilding their club, the Mets first stockpiled pitchers, then outfielders, and now, apparently, shortstops. Not only did they have Jose Vizcaino in the majors and outstanding fielder Rey Ordonez at Triple-A last year, but they also made Jaroncyk the 18th overall pick in the draft. He comes out of Orange Glen High School in California, where he showed speed and an ability to hit for average. His switch-hitting provides an extra dimension, and the Mets love his potential in the field. So far, Jaroncyk hasn't shown much power, but with his size, you can't rule out an occasional long ball. After signing Jaroncyk, the Mets assigned him to their club in the rookie Gulf Coast League. There he got off to a solid start, collecting 24 hits in his first 94 pro at bats. All but three were singles. Later, he began to add some punch. He ended his time there with a .329 slugging average. Expect Jaroncyk to be brought along very slowly; you may find him in short-season ball or low Class-A in 1996.

Professional Batting Register

	BA	G	AB	R	H	2B	3B	HR	RBI	SB
95 R	.276	44	174	31	48	5	3	0	14	7
95 A	.231	4	13	5	3	0	0	0	0	5

ROOKIE PROSPECTS

COREY JENKINS

Position: Outfield
Team: Boston Red Sox
Born: Aug. 25, 1976 Columbia, SC
Height: 6'2" **Weight:** 195 lbs.
Bats: right **Throws:** right
Acquired: First-round pick in 6/95 free-agent draft

Player Summary	
Fantasy Value	$0
Card Value	N/A
Will	adjust to wood
Can't	hide speed
Expect	an athlete
Don't Expect	Jim Rice

Jenkins was the second of two selections that the Red Sox enjoyed in the first round. After they addressed their pitching concerns by taking Andy Yount with the 15th overall pick, they tabbed Jenkins with the 24th. Jenkins has the physique and raw talent to make the Red Sox feel he could eventually have some fun with the left field wall in Fenway Park. But he is not in the mold of players who too often have been part of the Red Sox strategy. He looks like more than a one-dimensional basher who will play station-to-station ball and fare poorly the minute he leaves the shadow of the Green Monster. A product of Dreher High School in Columbia, South Carolina, Jenkins was a quick sign. He was dispatched to the Gulf Coast League, where he went 2-for-7 in his first two games. But after that he went into a tailspin, hitting .061 in 13 games from July 25 to Aug. 11. The Red Sox will have to be patient while he learns to make better contact. Jenkins had 11 walks and 43 strikeouts last year. He may be headed back to rookie level ball next year.

GEOFF JENKINS

Position: Outfield
Team: Milwaukee Brewers
Born: July 21, 1974 Olympia, WA
Height: 6'1" **Weight:** 200 lbs.
Bats: left **Throws:** right
Acquired: First-round pick in 6/95 free-agent draft

Player Summary	
Fantasy Value	$1
Card Value	N/A
Will	adjust in count
Can't	watch college stats
Expect	potent batting
Don't Expect	a flop

If you're a major-league scouting director, few feelings can match the one you get when you can quickly promote a recently drafted player. Even better is when the young man succeeds at the new level and you can do it again. That's what happened to the Brewers last year when their ninth overall pick enjoyed a spectacular pro debut. Jenkins, a star from the University of Southern California, succeeded at every level from college through Double-A in '95. A *Baseball America* first team All-American, Jenkins put on a show in the College World Series with his home run swing. Upon signing, he got his feet wet with Helena of the rookie Pioneer League, then got a promotion to Stockton of the Class-A California League. Back in his home state, his power showed in a hurry, and he hit his first pro home run July 26. He notched a .489 slugging percentage in 13 Cal League games. Still another promotion followed—this one to Double-A El Paso. In his second Double-A game, Jenkins went 4-for-4 with two triples. He could be in Milwaukee as early as this summer.

Professional Batting Register

	BA	G	AB	R	H	2B	3B	HR	RBI	SB
95 R	.321	7	28	2	9	0	1	0	9	0
95 A	.255	13	47	13	12	2	0	3	12	2
95 AA	.278	21	79	12	22	4	2	1	13	3

Professional Batting Register

	BA	G	AB	R	H	2B	3B	HR	RBI	SB
95 R	.145	35	124	12	18	1	0	1	6	5

ROOKIE PROSPECTS

ROBIN JENNINGS

Position: Outfield
Team: Chicago Cubs
Born: April 11, 1972 Singapore
Height: 6'2" **Weight:** 200 lbs.
Bats: left **Throws:** left
Acquired: 32nd-round pick in 6/91 free-agent draft

Player Summary	
Fantasy Value	$0
Card Value	N/A
Will	throw well
Can't	match Kieschnick
Expect	line drives
Don't Expect	a homer fest

Every club needs a lefty swinger who can hit line drives all day long, and Jennings could be filling that role for the Cubs before very long. He has now spent four years in pro ball, developing an impressive profile. He'll hit for average, show a bit of power, drive in some runs, and even help a bit on the basepaths. As an outfielder, he'll have to compete with higher-profile athletes like Brooks Kieschnick; but the only thing Jennings can do about that is produce. Originally drafted by the Orioles in 1990, Jennings broke into pro ball in 1992 and made the Class-A New York-Penn League All-Star Team. In the Class-A Midwest League in 1993, he finished second in hitting and led all outfielders with 20 assists. He advanced to the Class-A Florida State League in 1994 and struck out only once every 9.87 plate appearances. Last year, he showed his most power to date, notching a .484 slugging percentage. Whether that will translate to the deep right field wall at Wrigley Field is a question. But Jennings has talent.

Professional Batting Register

	BA	G	AB	R	H	2B	3B	HR	RBI	SB
92 A	.298	72	275	39	82	12	2	7	47	10
93 A	.308	132	474	64	146	29	5	3	65	11
94 A	.279	128	476	54	133	24	5	8	60	2
95 AA	.296	132	490	71	145	27	7	17	79	7

DEREK JETER

Position: Shortstop
Team: New York Yankees
Born: June 26, 1974 Pequannock, NJ
Height: 6'3" **Weight:** 185 lbs.
Bats: right **Throws:** right
Acquired: First-round pick in 6/92 free-agent draft

Player Summary	
Fantasy Value	$5 to $7
Card Value	50¢ to $1.00
Will	score runs
Can't	afford another demotion
Expect	New York in '96
Don't Expect	many homers

Jeter spent some time with the Yankees last year, but the ballclub eventually decided it wanted to go with veteran Tony Fernandez. That left Jeter in Triple-A for just a little more seasoning. This year—and perhaps for years to come—he should be the Yankee shortstop. Taken as the sixth overall pick in 1992, Jeter has won several awards, particularly in 1994 when he was named top minor leaguer by *Baseball America*, *The Sporting News*, *USA Today Baseball Weekly*, and Topps. A year earlier, he had been named to the Class-A South Atlantic League's All-Star team. In four years in pro ball, Jeter has shown the ability to hit for average, steal bases, get on base, and score. After striking out 95 times in 1993, he has improved his contact, and last year with Triple-A Columbus he walked more than he struck out. In the field, he has done a good job of improving his footwork, and his overall speed should give Jeter the range that is necessary.

Professional Batting Register

	BA	G	AB	R	H	2B	3B	HR	RBI	SB
92 R	.202	47	173	19	35	9	1	3	25	2
92 A	.243	11	37	4	9	0	0	1	4	0
93 A	.295	128	515	85	152	14	11	5	71	18
94 A	.329	69	292	61	96	13	8	0	39	28
94 AA	.377	34	122	17	46	7	2	2	13	12
94 AAA	.349	35	126	25	44	7	1	3	16	10
95 AAA	.317	123	486	96	154	27	9	2	45	20
95 AL	.250	15	48	5	12	4	1	0	7	0

ROOKIE PROSPECTS

JONATHAN JOHNSON

Position: Pitcher
Team: Texas Rangers
Born: July 16, 1974 Ocala, FL
Height: 6′ **Weight:** 180 lbs.
Bats: right **Throws:** right
Acquired: First-round pick in 6/95 free-agent draft

Player Summary
Fantasy Value	$0
Card Value	10¢ to 20¢
Will	throw tough curves
Can't	rely on heat
Expect	a fast track
Don't Expect	retreat

One of the chief qualities that separates a major-league player from a minor-league player is the desire to compete and excel against the best. With that in mind, you have to love what happened last year in the College World Series, when Johnson prevailed against Oklahoma's Mark Redman in what proved to be an epic meeting of first-rounders. It was the only game Florida State won in Omaha. No wonder the Rangers took Johnson with the seventh overall selection, making him the first college pitcher tabbed in the draft. Johnson, who performed for Team USA in 1994, also was a first-teamer on *Baseball America*'s All-America squad. Some scouts might say his height leaves him a little short for a right-hander, but smaller pitchers have done well in the majors. Johnson experienced some rough going in his early days as a pro, losing his first four decisions in the Class-A Florida State League. But he didn't pitch all that badly in the FSL, holding loop hitters to a .214 batting average. Johnson might be back in the Florida State League to start this season.

ANDRUW JONES

Position: Outfield
Team: Atlanta Braves
Born: April 23, 1977 Curacao
Height: 6′1″ **Weight:** 170 lbs.
Bats: right **Throws:** right
Acquired: Signed as a nondrafted free agent, 7/93

Player Summary
Fantasy Value	$0
Card Value	10¢ to 20¢
Will	tear up basepaths
Can't	run on him
Expect	big hits
Don't Expect	a quick trip

Jones was one of the most electrifying talents in the minor leagues last season, showing power and speed as he mashed his way through the Class-A South Atlantic League at the age of 18. He is being called a true five-tool player, meaning he can hit, hit for power, run, throw, and play defense. He was named Minor-League Player of the Month for April, hitting .341 with nine homers, including three in one game. By midseason, *USA Today Baseball Weekly* listed him as a prospect to watch, and *USA Today* named him as the Minor-League Player of the Year by the end of the season. He stole 10 bases over a seven-game stretch in mid-July. Obviously, no player can sustain those kinds of streaks, and the way Jones handles the inevitable valleys will determine how quickly he advances in the system. Remember, he doesn't turn 19 years old until late April, and Atlanta's abundance of talent means the Braves can afford to give prospects the time they need to bloom. That makes an assignment to high Class-A the most likely scenario for Jones. Of course, he could change that plan with a great spring training.

Professional Pitching Register
	W	L	ERA	G	CG	IP	H	ER	BB	SO
95 A	1	5	2.70	8	1	43.1	34	2	16	25

Professional Batting Register
	BA	G	AB	R	H	2B	3B	HR	RBI	SB
94 R	.290	63	238	42	69	14	3	3	26	21
95 A	.277	139	537	104	149	41	5	25	100	56

ROOKIE PROSPECTS

JAIME JONES

Position: Outfield
Team: Florida Marlins
Born: Aug. 2, 1976 San Diego, CA
Height: 6'4" **Weight:** 190 lbs.
Bats: left **Throws:** left
Acquired: First-round pick in 6/95 free-agent draft

Player Summary	
Fantasy Value	$0
Card Value	N/A
Will	show smooth swing
Can't	rule out right field
Expect	power
Don't Expect	blazing speed

Jones helped to enliven what was often a dreary season for Elmira, which finished with the worst record in the Class-A New York-Penn League last year. The sixth overall pick in the draft, Jones hit .328 in a 17-game stretch from mid-August to late August. Included in the hot spell were back-to-back games against Watertown in which Jones hit two home runs with three RBI. It was just a taste of what the Marlins hoped they were getting when they tabbed this young man out of Rancho Bernardo High School in San Diego. Like many other first-rounders, he is a fine all-around athlete, with a good arm and wheels. But it's his swing that has attracted raves from many of those who have witnessed it. At Elmira, Jones was a teammate of 1994 first-rounder Josh Booty, who has experienced a slow start to his career. This year, they both figure to be promoted and may play on the same team when they get a look at full-season ball.

JASON KENDALL

Position: Catcher
Team: Pittsburgh Pirates
Born: June 26, 1974 San Diego, CA
Height: 6' **Weight:** 181 lbs.
Bats: right **Throws:** right
Acquired: First-round pick in 6/92 free-agent draft

Player Summary	
Fantasy Value	$1 to $3
Card Value	25¢ to 50¢
Will	handle pitchers
Can't	show power
Expect	top contact
Don't Expect	bigs in spring

Kendall remains a fine defensive catcher who has probably exceeded expectations with the bat. It's possible that he will never be more than a singles hitter, but he is a tenacious batter who will drive in some runs and stay away from rally-stalling strikeouts. Few people ever expected him to contend for a batting title in the pros, but that's what he did last year in the Double-A Southern League. He had a .448 slugging percentage and a .414 on-base average, to boot. He is the son of former major-league catcher Fred Kendall, and Jason's acquaintance with the game is obvious. The younger Kendall made a name for himself at Torrance High School in California by hitting in 43 straight games, tying a national high school record. In 1994, he was named to the Carolina League All-Star Team. The only downer from his point of view is the emergence of Angelo Encarnacion, a 22-year-old who fared well in Pittsburgh last year. So unless Kendall blows the Pirates away in the spring, he might be at Triple-A in 1996.

Professional Batting Register

	BA	G	AB	R	H	2B	3B	HR	RBI	SB
95 R	.222	5	18	2	4	0	0	0	3	0
95 A	.284	31	116	21	33	6	2	4	11	5

Professional Batting Register

	BA	G	AB	R	H	2B	3B	HR	RBI	SB
92 R	.252	34	111	7	28	2	0	0	10	2
93 A	.276	102	366	43	101	17	4	1	40	8
94 A	.318	101	371	68	118	19	2	7	66	14
94 AA	.234	13	47	6	11	2	0	0	6	0
95 AA	.326	117	429	87	140	26	1	8	71	10

ROOKIE PROSPECTS

BROOKS KIESCHNICK

Position: Outfield
Team: Chicago Cubs
Born: June 6, 1972 Robstown, TX
Height: 6'4" **Weight:** 228 lbs.
Bats: left **Throws:** right
Acquired: First-round pick in 6/93 free-agent draft

Player Summary	
Fantasy Value	$2 to $4
Card Value	40¢ to 80¢
Will	hit some shots
Can't	play center
Expect	big slugging
Don't Expect	speed

Kieschnick was a pitcher and batter of note while playing for the University of Texas. These days, however, his only contact with pitching comes when he pummels it. Last year, in his third year as a pro, he moved up to Iowa of the Triple-A American Association, where he was one of the top power hitters in the circuit. He had a .495 slugging percentage and a .370 on-base average. A three-time All-American, Kieschnick led Texas to a pair of appearances in the College World Series. He was the Southwest Conference's outstanding player in 1992 with a .345 average. In 1993, he repeated as the conference's top performer, going 16-4 on the mound while fashioning a .374 batting average. His defensive game is not up to his bat, and he could wind up either at first base or left field. In his first year of pro ball, he was promoted two rungs during the season, and homered in his first Double-A game. Last year, he led all Cub farmhands in homers, and it's probably time to see if Kieschnick can reach Wrigley's right field wall.

Professional Batting Register

	BA	G	AB	R	H	2B	3B	HR	RBI	SB
93 R	.222	3	9	0	2	1	0	0	0	0
93 A	.182	6	22	1	4	2	0	0	2	0
93 AA	.341	25	91	12	31	8	0	2	10	1
94 AA	.282	126	468	57	132	25	3	14	55	3
95 AAA	.295	138	505	61	149	30	1	23	73	2

PAUL KONERKO

Position: Catcher
Team: Los Angeles Dodgers
Born: March 5, 1976 Providence, RI
Height: 6'3" **Weight:** 205 lbs.
Bats: right **Throws:** right
Acquired: First-round pick in 6/94 free-agent draft

Player Summary	
Fantasy Value	$0
Card Value	30¢ to 50¢
Will	hit for power
Can't	worry about Piazza
Expect	great command
Don't Expect	speed

While some teams search years in vain for a power-hitting catcher, the Dodgers are working on a surplus. Not only do they boast Mike Piazza in the majors, but they have Konerko in the pipeline. The fact that reservations have surfaced about Piazza's pitch-calling, and the possibility that he could be moved to another position, can only help Konerko. He enjoyed his second outstanding year in as many pro seasons in 1995 when he handled Class-A California League pitching at the age of 19. He had a .455 slugging percentage and a .362 on-base average last year. One year earlier, just out of high school, he led the Class-A Northwest League with 58 RBI and was selected for the All-Star Team. He was named Player of the Week for July 31 to Aug. 6. Konerko's rapid development increases the onus on 1992 first-rounder Ryan Luzinski, whose movement through the system has been sluggish. There's a good chance that one of them will be the catcher at Double-A San Antonio in 1996, and right now Konerko seems to have passed Luzinski.

Professional Batting Register

	BA	G	AB	R	H	2B	3B	HR	RBI	SB
94 A	.288	67	257	25	74	15	2	6	58	1
95 A	.277	118	448	77	124	21	1	19	77	3

ROOKIE PROSPECTS

MARC KROON

Position: Pitcher
Team: San Diego Padres
Born: April 2, 1973 Bronx, NY
Height: 6'2" **Weight:** 195 lbs.
Bats: right **Throws:** right
Acquired: Traded by Mets with Randy Curtis for Tracy Sanders, Frank Seminara, and Pablo Martinez, 12/93

Player Summary
Fantasy Value	$0
Card Value	N/A
Will	fall behind
Can't	coast on heat
Expect	3-2 pitches
Don't Expect	complete games

Kroon may turn out to be the key to a five-player deal that brought Frank Seminara to New York. Kroon seemed to prosper the moment he got to the West Coast, winning more games in his first Class-A California League season in 1994 than he had in his three previous campaigns. He developed further last year in his first look at Double-A ball. He improved his hits-to-innings ratio and lowered his ERA. He held Southern League hitters to a .211 batting average. He even got a taste of the big leagues. However, he continued to have trouble throwing strikes. Kroon is a power pitcher who has averaged about one strikeout per inning over the course of his five-year pro career. The walks and strikeouts take their toll late in the game; through late last season he had thrown only one complete game in his entire career. That pattern might take him to the bullpen, where his job would be to throw as hard as he can for as long as he can. Even as a reliever, however, Kroon needs some refining.

Professional Pitching Register
	W	L	ERA	G	CG	IP	H	ER	BB	SO
91 R	2	3	4.53	12	1	47.2	39	24	22	39
92 R	3	5	4.10	12	0	68.0	52	31	57	60
93 A	2	11	3.99	29	0	124.1	123	48	70	122
94 A	11	6	4.83	26	0	143.1	143	77	81	153
95 AA	7	5	3.51	22	0	115.1	90	45	61	123
95 NL	0	1	10.80	2	0	1.2	1	2	2	2

TODD LANDRY

Position: First base
Team: Milwaukee Brewers
Born: Aug. 21, 1972 Baton Rouge, LA
Height: 6'4" **Weight:** 215 lbs.
Bats: right **Throws:** right
Acquired: 31st-round pick in 6/93 free-agent draft

Player Summary
Fantasy Value	$0
Card Value	N/A
Will	go to Triple-A
Can't	play Tulsa every day
Expect	doubles
Don't Expect	El Paso stats

Landry is a big physical specimen who has given indications he can be a power-hitting first baseman on the major-league level. Playing in Double-A for the first time last year, he emerged with his best pro season to date, ranking among the top Milwaukee farmhands in both home runs and RBI. He was tabbed a prospect to watch by USA Today Baseball Weekly. He hit an inside-the-park grand slam against Tulsa on May 15. Nine days later, Landry victimized Tulsa again, this time by going 5-for-6 with a homer and four RBI. Unbelievably, Tulsa was on the receiving end a third time May 27 when Landry hit a three-run homer and a grand slam. He collected a Texas League Player of the Week award for his trouble. Landry wound up leading the El Paso club in home runs and battling for the RBI lead. He had a .466 slugging percentage. His doubles total stamps him as a bona fide power hitter. Unfortunately, so do his strikeouts. He had 100 strikeouts last year and only 33 walks. Landry can work on that this year in Triple-A.

Professional Batting Register
	BA	G	AB	R	H	2B	3B	HR	RBI	SB
93 R	.315	29	124	27	39	10	1	5	24	4
93 A	.302	38	149	26	45	6	0	4	24	4
94 A	.267	105	356	55	95	12	6	8	49	4
95 AA	.292	132	511	76	149	33	4	16	79	9

ROOKIE PROSPECTS

CHRIS LATHAM

Position: Outfield
Team: Los Angeles Dodgers
Born: May 26, 1973 Coeur d'Alene, Idaho
Height: 5'11" **Weight:** 174 lbs.
Bats: both **Throws:** right
Acquired: 11th-round pick in 6/91 free-agent draft

Player Summary	
Fantasy Value	$0
Card Value	N/A
Will	show speed
Can't	break into outfield
Expect	Triple-A
Don't Expect	Roger Cedeno

After winning the Class-A Northwest League batting title in 1994, Latham began last season as if he would dominate the Class-A Florida State League to the same extent. And in a way, he did. In mid-May, he led the league with 23 steals, 35 runs, and 32 walks. A 13-game hitting streak from May 31 to June 14 put his average at .309. All this earned him a promotion to the Double-A Texas League, where he opened with a 6-for-13 stretch. From July 11 to Aug. 2, Latham hit .373 with 10 extra-base hits. Eventually, he went to Triple-A. A switch-hitter with dominating speed, Latham has been in the Los Angeles system for several years now. It took him a long time to put low Class-A ball behind him, and 1995 marked the first time he adjusted to a higher league. Now he must contend with Roger Cedeno, Todd Hollandsworth, and Karim Garcia ahead of him in the system. But if last year is any indication, Latham established himself at a higher level, which gives the Dodgers great depth in the system.

Professional Batting Register
	BA	G	AB	R	H	2B	3B	HR	RBI	SB
91 R	.239	43	109	17	26	2	1	0	11	14
92 R	.271	31	85	12	23	4	0	0	5	3
93 A	.251	60	219	47	55	3	6	4	20	27
94 A	.300	123	479	98	189	24	10	7	47	61
95 A	.286	71	259	53	74	13	4	6	39	42
95 AA	.299	58	214	38	64	14	5	9	37	11
95 AAA	.167	5	18	2	3	0	1	0	3	1

JUAN LeBRON

Position: Outfield
Team: Kansas City Royals
Born: June 7, 1977 Arroyo, PR
Height: 6'4" **Weight:** 195 lbs.
Bats: right **Throws:** right
Acquired: First-round pick in 6/95 free-agent draft

Player Summary	
Fantasy Value	$0
Card Value	N/A
Will	play left or right
Can't	expand strike zone
Expect	long balls
Don't Expect	a center fielder

The Royals will be drafting differently now that they have substantially changed the look of their ballpark. Not only did they switch the playing surface from artificial turf to regular grass, but they also brought in the fences and lowered them. This lessens the emphasis on speed and increases the value of power, all of which play to the strength of last year's 19th overall pick in the draft. LeBron is a power prospect with a nice frame that can accommodate even more muscle as he matures. Upon signing, LeBron reported to Kansas City's club in the rookie Gulf Coast League. His debut was anything but auspicious, as he went 0-for-4 with three strikeouts and one error. Through his first 81 pro at bats, LeBron had walked only three times while fanning 28. He hit .162 over the first full month in pro ball. He will have to work on making contact, but that goes with the territory with young power hitters. LeBron may start in short-season Class-A this season.

Professional Batting Register
	BA	G	AB	R	H	2B	3B	HR	RBI	SB
95 R	.177	47	147	17	26	5	2	2	13	0

ROOKIE PROSPECTS

DERREK LEE

Position: First base
Team: San Diego Padres
Born: Sept. 6, 1975 Sacramento, CA
Height: 6'5" **Weight:** 205 lbs.
Bats: right **Throws:** right
Acquired: First-round pick in 6/93 free-agent draft

Player Summary

Fantasy Value	$0
Card Value	30¢ to 60¢
Will	pile up numbers
Can't	be Fred McGriff
Expect	strikeouts
Don't Expect	polish around bag

The Padres, who had Fred McGriff on their roster for more than two years, could be grooming someone in that mold. Lee is a power-hitting first baseman who really blossomed last year in the Class-A California League, producing more homers and RBI than he had in his two previous seasons combined. Not bad for someone who only turned 20 years old as the season came to an end. He is the son of Leon Lee, who was drafted by the Cardinals and worked his way to Triple-A before embarking on a career in Japan. Derrek is also the nephew of Leron Lee, a former San Diego outfielder. Last year Derrek was the Padres' top power prospect. He won the league's Topps Player of the Month award for June, and received mention in *USA Today Baseball Weekly*'s look at top prospects. Lee endured a tough July in which he hit only .206, but he still wound up with impressive numbers. He ended the year with a .496 slugging percentage. He faces a test this year in Double-A, but the Padres are moving him at the right pace.

Professional Batting Register

	BA	G	AB	R	H	2B	3B	HR	RBI	SB
93 R	.327	15	52	11	17	1	1	2	5	4
93 A	.274	20	73	13	20	5	1	1	10	0
94 A	.267	126	442	66	118	19	2	8	53	18
95 A	.301	128	502	82	151	25	2	23	95	14
95 AA	.111	2	9	0	1	0	0	0	1	0

JEFF LIEFER

Position: Third base
Team: Chicago White Sox
Born: Aug. 17, 1974 Upland, CA
Height: 6'3" **Weight:** 185 lbs.
Bats: left **Throws:** right
Acquired: First-round pick in 6/95 free-agent draft

Player Summary

Fantasy Value	$0
Card Value	N/A
Will	play the corners
Can't	replace Ventura
Expect	a solid frame
Don't Expect	a top defender

In terms of power at the corners, the White Sox were about as well-equipped as any team in baseball last year, with Frank Thomas at first and Robin Ventura at third. In a few years, we will see if the ballclub's instincts were right when it went after another player in that mold with the 25th overall pick in last year's draft. Like Ventura, Liefer is a lefty-swinging third baseman who was taken in the first round out of college. He comes out of Long Beach State, where he put together a nice all-around season in 1995. The White Sox must be hoping that he develops more quickly than he signed; he proved to be one of the more difficult first-round negotiations. It was the second time a team had experienced difficulty getting Liefer's name on the dotted line. He was originally selected by Cleveland in the sixth round in 1992, but he spurned the offer and instead chose to go to college. The Sox will likely start Liefer in full-season Class-A ball.

No minor-league experience

ROOKIE PROSPECTS

CARLTON LOEWER

Position: Pitcher
Team: Philadelphia Phillies
Born: Sept. 24, 1973 Lafayette, LA
Height: 6'6" **Weight:** 220 lbs.
Bats: both **Throws:** right
Acquired: First-round pick in 6/94 free-agent draft

Player Summary	
Fantasy Value	$0
Card Value	15¢ to 25¢
Will	show a fastball
Can't	make up lost time
Expect	ups and downs
Don't Expect	low-hit games

Loewer made his pro debut in 1995, about 10 months after he was drafted. A long negotiation accounted for the delay, and Loewer apparently came very close to returning to Mississippi State. But the important thing for the Phillies is that he now is in the pipeline, and only time will tell if his considerable talents can bring him to the bigs. His stats last year with Clearwater of the Class-A Florida State League were solid, though not overwhelming. He ranked fourth among Philadelphia farmhands in ERA. He could use some work on his hits-to-innings ratio, but if he improves his control, he should be fine. He was less than formidable in a couple of early-season starts; he allowed seven runs to Charlotte in three innings on April 22, and nine runs in three and one-third innings on May 7 against St. Lucie. After that, he turned in one of his top stretches, posting a 2.01 ERA over seven starts. Loewer clearly had his problems; Florida State League hitters batted .274 against him. He also saw some time in Double-A Reading, and more Double-A beckons.

Professional Pitching Register

	W	L	ERA	G	CG	IP	H	ER	BB	SO
95 A	7	5	3.30	20	1	114.2	124	42	36	83
95 AA	4	1	2.16	8	0	50.0	42	12	32	35

MARK LORETTA

Position: Shortstop
Team: Milwaukee Brewers
Born: Aug. 14, 1971 Santa Monica, CA
Height: 6' **Weight:** 175 lbs.
Bats: right **Throws:** right
Acquired: Seventh-round pick in 6/93 free-agent draft

Player Summary	
Fantasy Value	$1
Card Value	N/A
Will	give honest at bats
Can't	hit for power
Expect	alert play
Don't Expect	dazzling range

Loretta offers the potential to bring reliable defensive and offensive work to the Brewers. A shortstop, he was leading the Triple-A American Association in RBI through early August, and he finished second in the loop with 79. He also tied for second in base hits. Though not a home run hitter, Loretta can deliver consistent and effective contact, having averaged roughly .300 over three years of pro ball. As the RBI total suggests, he tends to make the base hits count, and even when he doesn't hit safely, he might move runners because he doesn't strike out much. He had only 47 Ks last year in Triple-A. Loretta made a favorable impression right out of the draft, moving swiftly through rookie ball and into the Class-A California League, where he drove in 31 runs in 201 at bats. That earned him a trip to Double-A in 1994, where he made the All-Star Team. His first stint at Triple-A ball was not successful, but he atoned in 1995. Loretta has probably accomplished all he can at the Triple-A level.

Professional Batting Register

	BA	G	AB	R	H	2B	3B	HR	RBI	SB
93 R	.321	6	28	5	9	1	0	1	8	0
93 A	.363	53	201	36	73	4	1	4	31	8
94 AA	.315	77	302	50	95	13	6	0	38	8
94 AAA	.210	43	138	16	29	7	0	1	14	2
95 AAA	.286	127	479	48	137	22	5	7	79	8
95 AL	.260	19	50	13	13	3	0	1	3	1

ROOKIE PROSPECTS

ANDREW LORRAINE

Position: Pitcher
Team: Chicago White Sox
Born: Aug. 11, 1972 Los Angeles, CA
Height: 6'3" **Weight:** 195 lbs.
Bats: left **Throws:** left
Acquired: Traded by Angels with McKay Christensen, Bill Simas, and John Snyder for Jim Abbott and Tim Fortugno, 7/95

Player Summary	
Fantasy Value	$0
Card Value	10¢ to 20¢
Will	give up homers
Can't	work above belt
Expect	intelligence
Don't Expect	deep counts

Lorraine came to the White Sox as part of the package the Angels assembled to get Jim Abbott for the stretch drive last year. Lorraine is an intriguing prospect who played ball at Stanford, in the Cape Cod League, and in the international arena before turning pro. He was a fourth-round draft pick of the Angels in 1993, and he needed less than two years to rocket all the way to the majors in 1994. His first four games with the Angels produced an 0-2 record with a 10.61 ERA. Among Lorraine's lowlights were back-to-back homers issued to Ivan Rodriguez and Jose Canseco in a game against Texas. It was just a matter of Lorraine needing a little more seasoning, and that's what he got last year before the trade. His 1995 numbers at Triple-A weren't all that impressive, but some of that can be attributed to the Triple-A Pacific Coast League's parks and altitudes. Of greater importance is Lorraine's stingy walk total. Lefties who throw strikes usually fare very well.

Professional Pitching Register

	W	L	ERA	G	CG	IP	H	ER	BB	SO
93 A	4	1	1.29	6	3	42.0	33	6	6	39
94 AAA	12	4	3.42	22	4	142.0	156	54	34	90
94 AL	0	2	10.61	4	0	18.2	30	22	11	10
95 AAA	10	7	4.54	25	4	136.2	156	69	42	77
95 AL	0	0	3.38	5	0	8.0	3	3	2	5

FAUSTO MACEY

Position: Pitcher
Team: San Francisco Giants
Born: Oct. 9, 1975 Santo Domingo, Dominican Republic
Height: 6'4" **Weight:** 185 lbs.
Bats: right **Throws:** right
Acquired: Signed as a free agent, 5/93

Player Summary	
Fantasy Value	$0
Card Value	N/A
Will	have ups and downs
Can't	easily go home
Expect	a nice repertoire
Don't Expect	a quick rise

Macey was only one of three workhorse starters at San Francisco's Class-A club in the California League last year, but his work stands out a bit more because he was doing it at a younger age than the others. His stats won't dazzle anybody, and he went through the highs and lows you might expect of a 19-year-old pitching in a high Class-A circuit. For instance, Macey allowed at least five runs in three consecutive starts spanning May and June. But he assembled his best streak of the season, registering four consecutive winning starts from June 13 to July 1, including seven shutout innings against Modesto June 18. Cal League hitters batted .261 against him last year, which is not all that bad considering his age. Signed by Luis Rosa, Macey appeared in the Dominican Summer League in 1993. He then moved to the States in 1994, splitting time between the rookie Arizona League and the Class-A Northwest League. So far in his pro career, Macey has thrown strikes, and he has made the adjustment of living and pitching so far away from home, a factor that should not be minimized.

Professional Pitching Register

	W	L	ERA	G	CG	IP	H	ER	BB	SO
94 R	2	2	2.16	9	0	50.0	37	12	8	26
94 A	2	1	3.58	5	0	27.2	30	11	8	22
95 A	8	9	3.89	28	1	171.0	167	74	50	94

ROOKIE PROSPECTS

DWIGHT MANESS

Position: Outfield
Team: New York Mets
Born: April 3, 1974 Chester, PA
Height: 6'3" **Weight:** 180 lbs.
Bats: right **Throws:** right
Acquired: Traded by Dodgers with Scott Hunter for Brett Butler, 8/95

Player Summary	
Fantasy Value	$0
Card Value	N/A
Will	bring tools
Can't	keep striking out
Expect	a fresh start
Don't Expect	a top basestealer

Maness came to the Mets as part of the package that brought center fielder Brett Butler back to Los Angeles for last year's stretch run. The deal could be the change of scenery that Maness needs, because he had been floundering in the Dodgers system. The Mets think he may have been brought along too soon, and the organization will handle him accordingly. Out of William Penn High School in Delaware, Maness came to the Dodgers in the third round of the 1992 draft. He struck out 36 times in his first 139 official at bats in the pros, a preview of his problems in making contact. He has shown an ability to steal a base, but his success rate has never been strong; in half a season at Double-A in 1994, he was caught more often than he made it. Last year, he improved a bit in successfully swiping bases. Maness enjoyed his best pro season in 1993 with Vero Beach of the Class-A Florida State League, collecting 31 extra-base hits. But two years later, he was back in Vero Beach, where the Mets took a gamble on his raw talent.

Professional Batting Register

	BA	G	AB	R	H	2B	3B	HR	RBI	SB
92 R	.252	44	139	24	35	6	3	0	12	18
93 A	.259	118	409	57	106	21	4	6	42	22
94 A	.250	74	248	38	62	13	1	3	26	21
94 AA	.219	57	215	32	47	5	5	5	20	15
95 A	.225	57	187	20	42	7	0	3	28	14
95 AA	.223	57	179	29	40	2	3	5	24	4

FELIX MARTINEZ

Position: Shortstop
Team: Kansas City Royals
Born: May 18, 1974 Nagua, Dominican Republic
Height: 6' **Weight:** 170 lbs.
Bats: both **Throws:** right
Acquired: Purchased from Hiroshima, 3/93

Player Summary	
Fantasy Value	$0
Card Value	N/A
Will	make contact
Can't	pile up errors
Expect	some steals
Don't Expect	Gagne's glove

Like many other organizations, the Royals are on a youth movement, and Martinez might soon be ready to take his place in it. A shortstop with quickness and arm strength, Martinez played for Wichita of the Double-A Texas League last year. There he refined his offensive game, leading the league with a career-high in steals. He also upgraded his contact, a must for someone who doesn't figure to hit many home runs. He had a .321 on-base percentage last season, garnering 31 bases on balls. He also will have to improve his defensive play if he hopes to succeed the sure-handed Greg Gagne at shortstop. Martinez committed 20 errors over his first 45 games last year, including three in one game on May 16 against Jackson, and eight over a five-game span. Martinez offers an impressive arm, which, combined with his footspeed and ability to switch-hit, makes him an interesting package. But he'll have to catch the ball consistently to help the Royals—or anyone—at shortstop.

Professional Batting Register

	BA	G	AB	R	H	2B	3B	HR	RBI	SB
93 R	.255	57	165	23	42	5	1	0	12	22
94 A	.268	117	400	65	107	16	4	2	43	19
95 AA	.263	127	426	53	112	15	3	3	30	44

ROOKIE PROSPECTS

DAVID McCARTY

Position: First base
Team: San Francisco Giants
Born: Nov. 23, 1969 Houston, TX
Height: 6'5" **Weight:** 213 lbs.
Bats: right **Throws:** left
Acquired: Traded by Reds with Deion Sanders, John Roper, Scott Service, and Ricky Pickett for Mark Portugal, Dave Burba, and Darren Lewis, 7/95

Player Summary
Fantasy Value	$2 to $4
Card Value	8¢ to 12¢
Will	get a fresh start
Can't	match Will Clark
Expect	flashes of power
Don't Expect	many more chances

McCarty is now in a no-man's land between prospect and journeyman, but he's included in this list because he may be in just the right situation. He was part of three organizations last summer. The Twins gave up on him in an early-June deal in which they sent him to Cincinnati for pitcher John Courtright. Several weeks later, the Reds shipped him to San Francisco as part of the transaction that brought pitchers Mark Portugal and Dave Burba to Cincinnati. This may represent the last chance for McCarty, a power-hitting first baseman who never made things happen the way the Twins hoped when they made him a first-round pick in the 1991 June draft. With the Giants, though, he has a chance to fill the hole left by Will Clark's exit. However, it's also possible that McCarty's 18-homer season with Double-A Orlando in 1992 was a fluke.

Professional Batting Register
	BA	G	AB	R	H	2B	3B	HR	RBI	SB
91 A	.380	15	50	16	19	3	0	3	8	3
91 AA	.261	28	88	18	23	4	0	3	11	0
92 AA	.272	129	456	75	124	16	2	18	79	6
92 AAA	.500	7	26	7	13	2	0	1	8	1
93 AAA	.385	40	143	42	55	11	0	8	31	5
93 AL	.214	98	350	36	75	15	2	2	21	2
94 AAA	.253	55	186	32	47	9	3	3	19	1
94 AL	.260	44	131	21	34	8	2	1	12	2
95 AAA	.345	74	291	62	100	29	3	12	51	1
95 AL	.218	25	55	10	12	3	1	0	4	0
95 NL	.250	12	20	1	5	1	0	0	2	1

QUINTON McCRACKEN

Position: Outfield
Team: Colorado Rockies
Born: March 16, 1970 Wilmington, NC
Height: 5'7" **Weight:** 170 lbs.
Bats: both **Throws:** right
Acquired: 25th-round pick in 6/92 free-agent draft

Player Summary
Fantasy Value	$1
Card Value	N/A
Will	make things happen
Can't	swing for fences
Expect	distracted pitchers
Don't Expect	a basher

Can a small, swift center fielder fit in on a team known for home runs? The answer is: Why not? Most clubs would be happy to have a player who can do what McCracken can, namely, to reach base and cause a distraction. He did it better than ever last year, posting a career high in batting average and piling up the stolen bases while playing in Double-A and Triple-A. He won't hit many home runs, not even in cozy Coors Field; but he can do his thing and leave the power to others. The 711th player selected in 1992, McCracken truly emerged as a player to watch a year later, when he stole 60 bases in 79 attempts. He posted on-base averages of .419 in Double-A and .418 in Triple-A. He was named the Rockies' minor-league player of the year. McCracken attended Duke University, where he became a two-sport man playing defensive back and second base. He majored in political science and history. Now "Q" would like to become part of the Rockies' history, and there's no reason to think that he can't.

Professional Batting Register
	BA	G	AB	R	H	2B	3B	HR	RBI	SB
92 A	.280	67	232	37	65	13	2	0	27	18
93 A	.292	127	483	94	141	17	7	2	58	60
94 AA	.278	136	544	94	151	27	4	5	39	36
95 AA	.357	55	221	33	79	11	4	1	26	26
95 AAA	.361	61	244	55	88	14	6	3	28	17
95 NL	.000	3	1	0	0	0	0	0	0	0

ROOKIE PROSPECTS

JASON McDONALD

Position: Infield
Team: Oakland Athletics
Born: March 20, 1972 Modesto, CA
Height: 5'8" **Weight:** 175 lbs.
Bats: both **Throws:** right
Acquired: Fourth-round pick in 6/93 free-agent draft

Player Summary	
Fantasy Value	$0
Card Value	N/A
Will	get to second
Can't	show huge power
Expect	range
Don't Expect	a first-ball hitter

To keep McDonald from reaching second base, you'd have to lock the doors of the ballpark. Well, maybe not, but it's close. With his exceptional speed, McDonald terrorized catchers in the Class-A California League last year soaring over the 60-steal mark by early August and leading the minors with 70. He also hit for a respectable average and piled up the extra-base hits. McDonald didn't need a base hit to do his damage, either. He drew almost as many walks as he had base hits, meaning that pitchers often went into deep counts against him, a factor that produces wear and tear and helps other hitters in the lineup. He had 110 bases on balls last year, after garnering 81 walks in 1994. He had a .401 on-base average in 1995. McDonald was named Cal League Player of the Week ending April 22 after stealing six bases and registering four straight three-hit games. A graduate of Elk Grove High School in California in 1990, McDonald attended the University of Houston. His quickness can only help him at short, and his switch-hitting is still another dimension.

Professional Batting Register

	BA	G	AB	R	H	2B	3B	HR	RBI	SB
93 A	.295	35	112	26	33	5	2	0	8	22
94 A	.238	116	404	67	96	11	9	2	31	52
95 A	.262	133	493	109	129	25	7	6	50	70

RYAN McGUIRE

Position: First base
Team: Boston Red Sox
Born: Nov. 23, 1971 Wilson, NC
Height: 6'2" **Weight:** 210 lbs.
Bats: left **Throws:** left
Acquired: Third-round pick in 6/93 free-agent draft

Player Summary	
Fantasy Value	$0
Card Value	N/A
Will	hit for average
Can't	overtake Vaughn
Expect	durable play
Don't Expect	big power

McGuire has at least a couple of things going against him at this stage of his career. First, he doesn't quite fit the popular image of a power-hitting first baseman, especially for someone with his great physical stature. Second, as a first baseman in the Boston organization, he is staring up at Mo Vaughn. Still, McGuire forces you to notice him. After all, anyone who finishes second in batting and third in on-base percentage in the Double-A Eastern League, as McGuire did last year, must have something to offer. He also had 58 walks and notched a .414 on-base percentage. He comes out of UCLA, where he led the NCAA Division I with 26 homers. After becoming the 79th player taken in the draft, he spent some time in the Class-A Florida State League, where he hit for average. A year later, he moved to the Class-A Carolina League, where he led the circuit in chances, putouts, and assists by a first baseman. McGuire also paced his club in runs, hits, doubles, RBI, and walks. McGuire will have to keep hitting and await his chance.

Professional Batting Register

	BA	G	AB	R	H	2B	3B	HR	RBI	SB
93 A	.324	58	213	23	69	12	2	4	38	2
94 A	.272	137	489	70	133	29	0	10	73	10
95 AA	.333	109	414	59	138	29	1	7	59	11

ROOKIE PROSPECTS

TONY McKNIGHT

Position: Pitcher
Team: Houston Astros
Born: June 29, 1977 Texarkana, AR
Height: 6'5" **Weight:** 210 lbs.
Bats: right **Throws:** right
Acquired: First-round pick in 6/95 free-agent draft

Player Summary	
Fantasy Value	$0
Card Value	N/A
Will	get ahead of hitters
Can't	be rushed
Expect	curveballs
Don't Expect	polished changeups

For the third straight year, the Astros grabbed a high school pitcher in the first round of the draft. For the second consecutive time, they chose a big right-hander. McKnight doesn't offer quite the same size as 6'7" Scott Elarton, the second of their first-rounders in 1994, but McKnight will be plenty big enough when he starts unleashing his fastball. McKnight comes from Arkansas High School in Arkansas, where he struck out eight times as many batters as he walked. Those are good stats no matter where you're playing, and the Astros were impressed enough to make McKnight the 22nd overall pick. Upon signing, he reported to Houston's club in the rookie Gulf Coast League, where he threw strikes and went 1-1 in his first three games. However, McKnight probably won't take the fast track like Billy Wagner, the high schooler taken in 1993 by the Astros. McKnight will likely begin this season in a short-season league or low Class-A ball. He has plenty of time to learn how to become a professional pitcher.

Professional Pitching Register

	W	L	ERA	G	CG	IP	H	ER	BB	SO
95 R	1	1	3.86	3	0	11.2	14	5	2	8

BILLY McMILLON

Position: Outfield
Team: Florida Marlins
Born: Nov. 17, 1971 Otero, NM
Height: 5'11" **Weight:** 172 lbs.
Bats: left **Throws:** left
Acquired: Eighth-round pick in 6/93 free-agent draft

Player Summary	
Fantasy Value	$0
Card Value	10¢ to 20¢
Will	put up numbers
Can't	hit 30 homers
Expect	a good eye
Don't Expect	glamour

The Marlins drafted a left-handed bat in the first round last year because of a perceived need for that commodity. But it's possible that they already had the answer right there in the system. McMillon is not what you'd call a high-profile pick, having arrived in the eighth round in 1993. At 5'11", he won't knock you out with his size. All he does is put numbers on the board. Last year while playing in the Double-A Eastern League—often described as a testing ground for hitters—McMillon hit for average and power. His home run totals were not eye-popping, but he compensated with doubles and a high on-base percentage. He notched a .423 on-base mark last year, and he helped himself by taking 96 bases on balls. He comes out of Clemson University, where he finished as the career leader with a .382 average. He also tied for fifth with 55 doubles. In his first pro season, McMillon finished fourth in the Class-A New York-Penn League with a .398 on-base percentage. In 1994, McMillon led the Class-A Midwest League and set a team record with 101 RBI.

Professional Batting Register

	BA	G	AB	R	H	2B	3B	HR	RBI	SB
93 A	.305	57	226	38	69	14	2	6	35	5
94 A	.252	137	496	88	125	25	3	17	101	7
95 AA	.313	141	518	92	162	29	3	14	93	15

ROOKIE PROSPECTS

PEPE McNEAL

Position: Catcher
Team: St. Louis Cardinals
Born: Aug. 11, 1975 Tampa, FL
Height: 6'3" **Weight:** 205 lbs.
Bats: right **Throws:** right
Acquired: Traded by Indians with David Bell and Rick Heiserman for Ken Hill, 7/95

Player Summary
Fantasy Value $0
Card Value. . . . . N/A
Will . . . . take slow track
Can't. . . . . reach Hill's stature
Expect . . . . work on throwing
Don't Expect . . . . hype

McNeal's career took a change of course in last year's flag chase when the Cleveland Indians put him in a package they assembled to bring in pitcher Ken Hill to bolster their chances. At the time, McNeal was playing for Burlington of the rookie Appalachian League and putting together some modest stats. He comes out of Armwood High School in Florida, where he played football and baseball. Cleveland made him its fifth pick in the 1994 draft, and he has not really been the center of much hype. In his first look at pro ball, McNeal collected only 13 singles in 99 trips to the plate, while throwing out just 21.5 percent of runners trying to steal. However, McNeal must have been doing something right because he caught the eye of the Cardinals. After the trade, he continued his modest work in the Appy League. He had a slugging average of just .301 last year, and he struck out 48 times opposed to 19 walks. While it's certainly hard not to like his size, he will have to learn the strike zone a little better. McNeal, whose middle name is Chevalier, figures to head for a low Class-A assignment this summer.

RAFAEL MEDINA

Position: Pitcher
Team: New York Yankees
Born: Feb. 15, 1975 Panama City, Panama
Height: 6'3" **Weight:** 194 lbs.
Bats: right **Throws:** right
Acquired: Signed as a free agent, 9/92

Player Summary
Fantasy Value $0
Card Value. . . . . N/A
Will . . . . be a starter
Can't . . . . pile up wins
Expect . . . . innings
Don't Expect . . . . the Triple Crown

Medina is a burly figure who has a presence on the mound and who gives the impression he could be a workhorse starter. That's just what he was in the Yankee organization last year, making 19 starts at Greensboro in the Class-A South Atlantic League before receiving a promotion to Tampa in the Class-A Florida State League. He was one of the top strikeout pitchers in the Yankee system, and collected 10 whiffs in a no-decision against Charleston, West Virginia, on July 3. Upon his promotion to the Florida State League, Medina hurled 13 scoreless innings in his first two starts. Despite all his impressive numbers, Medina had some trouble winning games. Through mid-August, he had won only five of 21 starts, a fact that could be chalked up to his youth. Medina played on the Panama Metro team, where he won the Triple Crown and was named top pitcher in the 1992 National Championship games. He has a brother, Ricardo, playing in the Cubs organization. Figure Rafael to start in the FSL in 1996.

Professional Batting Register

	BA	G	AB	R	H	2B	3B	HR	RBI	SB
94 R	.131	31	99	8	13	0	0	0	3	2
95 R	.205	54	185	13	42	8	0	2	27	4

Professional Pitching Register

	W	L	ERA	G	CG	IP	H	ER	BB	SO
93 R	2	0	0.66	5	0	27.1	16	2	12	21
94 A	3	7	4.66	14	1	73.1	67	38	35	59
95 A	6	6	3.63	25	1	129.0	115	52	50	133

ROOKIE PROSPECTS

DAVID MILLER

Position: Infield
Team: Cleveland Indians
Born: Dec. 9, 1973 Philadelphia, PA
Height: 6'4" **Weight:** 200 lbs.
Bats: left **Throws:** left
Acquired: First-round pick in 6/95 free-agent draft

Player Summary	
Fantasy Value	$0
Card Value	N/A
Will	hit with heft
Can't	make up holdout
Expect	some outfield play
Don't Expect	a singles hitter

Considering the muscle that Cleveland showed last year, you'd think the last thing this team would covet in the draft would be power. Then again, Miller has more to offer than just heft; he can run well, too. No wonder the front office liked Miller enough to call his name when the 23rd overall pick came along. A first baseman, he has some daunting competition above him in the organization. Last year, the Indians had both Paul Sorrento and Herbert Perry in the majors and super prospect Richie Sexson in the minors. However, the improvement Miller showed last year at Clemson University indicates he can do well. After hitting just one home run in 1994, he came close to reaching double figures in doubles, triples, homers, and steals last year. The trouble for Cleveland—which had very few rough spots in an otherwise sterling season—was that he was such a late sign that you won't find his name on the 1995 stat sheets. Miller should be ready to go this summer, and he may start in high Class-A or even Double-A.

No minor-league experience

TRAVIS MILLER

Position: Pitcher
Team: Minnesota Twins
Born: Nov. 2, 1972 Dayton, OH
Height: 6'3" **Weight:** 200 lbs.
Bats: right **Throws:** left
Acquired: Sandwich second-round pick in 6/94 free-agent draft

Player Summary	
Fantasy Value	$0
Card Value	N/A
Will	be a starter
Can't	walk batters
Expect	Triple-A in 1996
Don't Expect	strikeouts

Miller came into the Twins organization as the 34th overall pick in the draft, compensation for the team's having not signed first-round selection Jason Varitek the previous season. Miller comes out of National Trail High School in Paris, Ohio, where he played basketball and football in addition to baseball. Miller went on to Kent State University, where he threw a no-hitter against Wright State as a sophomore and went 9-0 as a junior. He made his professional debut about a month after the draft, coming out of the bullpen for Ft. Wayne of the Class-A Midwest League. He quickly joined the starting rotation and owned a 4-1 mark when he was promoted to the Double-A Southern League. Last year, Miller pitched in the Double-A Eastern League and finished second in strikeouts. However, his win-loss totals there won't awe anyone. He had more trouble throwing strikes than he did in 1994, and had 65 walks last year as opposed to 151 Ks. EL hitters compiled a .267 batting average against him. Miller must learn that strikes work wherever you pitch.

Professional Pitching Register

	W	L	ERA	G	CG	IP	H	ER	BB	SO
94 A	4	1	2.60	11	1	55.1	52	16	12	50
94 AA	0	0	2.84	1	0	6.1	3	2	2	4
95 AA	7	9	4.37	28	1	162.2	172	79	65	151

ROOKIE PROSPECTS

RALPH MILLIARD

Position: Second base
Team: Florida Marlins
Born: Dec. 30, 1973 Willemstad, Curacao
Height: 5'11" **Weight:** 170 lbs.
Bats: right **Throws:** right
Acquired: Signed as a nondrafted free agent, 8/93

Player Summary
Fantasy Value $0
Card Value .... N/A
Will .... score runs
Can't .... play short
Expect .... good makeup
Don't Expect .... a natural

Milliard is entering his fourth pro season in 1996, but that doesn't adequately describe the depth of his experience. He was a member of the Netherlands junior national team in 1989 and 1990, and he played for the national squad in 1991. So Milliard has been around the game for a while. After being signed by Tim Schmidt on Aug. 1, 1993, Milliard reported to the rookie Gulf Coast League, where he impressed on both sides of the ball. He struck out only once every 13.5 plate appearances, second-best in the league. He led the circuit's second basemen with 111 putouts and 257 chances. In 1994, he led the Class-A Midwest League with 97 runs, was third with 34 doubles, and made the midseason All-Star Team. Last year with Portland of the Double-A Eastern League, Milliard assembled a 19-game hitting streak in May, and once again excelled at scoring runs, leading the league with 104. He also had a .393 on-base average, in large part because of his 85 walks. It wouldn't be surprising to see Milliard go to Triple-A, and maybe the bigs, this year.

DOUG MILLION

Position: Pitcher
Team: Colorado Rockies
Born: Jan. 13, 1975 Ft. Thomas, KY
Height: 6'4" **Weight:** 205 lbs.
Bats: left **Throws:** left
Acquired: First-round pick in 6/94 free-agent draft

Player Summary
Fantasy Value $0
Card Value .... 30¢ to 50¢
Will .... keep advancing
Can't .... let adversity win
Expect .... better things
Don't Expect .... Denver in '96

After a hugely successful season in rookie ball, Million stepped up to high Class-A last year and learned a bit more about the long road to the majors. Pitching for Salem of the Carolina League, he opened the season with a three-inning stint in which he walked four batters. Then he suffered shoulder problems and wound up on the disabled list. Upon his return, he was 0-3 through June 3. At one point approaching midseason, he owned a 1-3 mark, and he had walked 33 in 40 innings. When you consider those kind of numbers, his final totals don't look all that bad. Another stat to consider is that Carolina League hitters compiled a .266 batting average against Million last year. Adversity is part of the game, and ballclubs watch to see how prospects handle it. The fact that Million was able to right himself is a good sign. Out of Sarasota High School in Florida, Million was the seventh overall pick in 1994. He was selected High School Player of the Year by *Baseball America*. Maybe the Rockies will repeat him in the Carolina League in '96.

Professional Batting Register

	BA	G	AB	R	H	2B	3B	HR	RBI	SB
93 R	.234	53	192	35	45	15	0	0	25	11
94 A	.297	133	515	97	153	34	2	8	67	10
95 AA	.267	128	464	104	124	22	3	11	40	22

Professional Pitching Register

	W	L	ERA	G	CG	IP	H	ER	BB	SO
94 R	1	0	1.50	3	0	12.0	8	2	3	19
94 A	5	3	2.34	10	0	57.2	50	15	21	75
95 A	5	7	4.62	24	0	111.0	111	57	79	85

ROOKIE PROSPECTS

SHEA MORENZ

Position: Outfield
Team: New York Yankees
Born: Jan. 22, 1974 Danville, NJ
Height: 6'2" **Weight:** 205 lbs.
Bats: left **Throws:** right
Acquired: First-round pick in 6/95 free-agent draft

Player Summary
Fantasy Value	$0
Card Value	N/A
Will	bring tools
Can't	advance quickly
Expect	long home runs
Don't Expect	Howie's fame

Morenz has long intrigued major-league ballclubs with his size and athletic ability, but he enjoyed football, too. He was talented enough to play quarterback for the University of Texas, which should tell you all you need to know about his agility and arm strength. So there's no question the Yankees got a nice physical specimen when they picked Morenz 27th overall in last June's draft. Trouble is, baseball requires a lot of time for skill development, and Morenz is getting a late start. Upon signing last year, he was assigned to Oneonta of the Class-A New York-Penn League, where he experienced the predictable growing pains. However, he gave a hint of his abilities in a 13-game span from Aug. 12 to 24, going 15-for-44 and driving in 18 runs. He showed some power with a .397 slugging average, and a lot of patience with a .370 on-base average. A relative of hockey Hall of Famer Howie Morenz, Shea could use some time in winter ball or the instructional league to get some at bats. Then it's a long climb to reach the outfield in New York.

Professional Batting Register
	BA	G	AB	R	H	2B	3B	HR	RBI	SB
95 A	.276	33	116	11	32	5	3	1	20	1

MATT MORRIS

Position: Pitcher
Team: St. Louis Cardinals
Born: Aug. 9, 1974 Middletown, NY
Height: 6'5" **Weight:** 210 lbs.
Bats: right **Throws:** right
Acquired: First-round pick in 6/95 free-agent draft

Player Summary
Fantasy Value	$0
Card Value	N/A
Will	bring it
Can't	jump too quickly
Expect	another Seton winner
Don't Expect	perfect control

Not much went right for the Cardinals last year, but one day they may be able to look back and say that things began to turn around the moment they selected this power pitcher. Morris comes out of New Jersey's Seton Hall University, a fertile program that has recently produced the likes of Mo Vaughn, John Valentin, and Kevin Morton. Morris arrived with the 12th overall pick, and he quickly got a chance to pitch before the hometown fans when the Cards sent him to New Jersey of the Class-A New York-Penn League. There he picked up a victory in his debut, going five scoreless innings and striking out six. It only took him another start to outgrow that competition, and he fast-tracked his way to St. Petersburg of the Class-A Florida State League. There things were a little bumpier at the beginning, but he handled the competition fairly uniformly. Morris probably could use an extended stay at high Class-A ball to help him smooth out his control, but of his arm there can be no doubts at all.

Professional Pitching Register
	W	L	ERA	G	CG	IP	H	ER	BB	SO
95 A	5	2	2.19	8	1	45.0	34	11	14	44

ROOKIE PROSPECTS

DAMIAN MOSS

Position: Pitcher
Team: Atlanta Braves
Born: Nov. 24, 1976 Darlinghurst, Australia
Height: 6' **Weight:** 187 lbs.
Bats: right **Throws:** left
Acquired: Signed as a free agent, 7/93

Player Summary	
Fantasy Value	$0
Card Value	20¢ to 40¢
Will	throw a curve
Can't	get home often
Expect	a strikeout king
Don't Expect	a rush job

This Australian import has fared well in two years of North American ball. Blessed with a live arm, Moss led the Atlanta farm system in strikeouts by a wide margin while playing for Macon of the Class-A South Atlantic League last year. And if you want to quibble and say that his K victims were inexperienced players, you're right. But it's also true that he was younger than most of them, because he didn't turn 19 years old until November. He also did a nice job of straightening himself out after a rocky start. Moss went 0-3 to open his Sally League career, then won six consecutive starts from early May through early June. At one point, he allowed only two earned runs over 32 innings while striking out 41. He wound up tied for the league lead in Ks with 177. Moss also held Sally League hitters to a .236 batting average. You can expect to see him in high Class-A this year, because it wouldn't make much sense to speed Moss along, especially with there being no need for a starter at the major-league level.

CHAD MOTTOLA

Position: Outfield
Team: Cincinnati Reds
Born: Oct. 15, 1971 Augusta, GA
Height: 6'3" **Weight:** 220 lbs.
Bats: right **Throws:** right
Acquired: First-round pick in 6/92 free-agent draft

Player Summary	
Fantasy Value	$0
Card Value	20¢ to 30¢
Will	field well
Can't	duplicate 1993
Expect	an offensive force
Don't Expect	a basestealer

After a four-year apprenticeship in the minors, Mottola seems on the verge of justifying the Reds' judgment when they made him their first pick in 1992. He jumped from the Double-A Southern League to the Triple-A American Association last season and wound up tied for fourth in the Reds farm system with 76 RBI. He also notched a .541 slugging percentage in the Southern League. That kind of production may have been a relief to the Reds, who watched Mottola slump back in 1994, when he first saw Double-A pitching. Originally drafted by the Orioles in the 10th round in 1989, Mottola instead attended the University of Central Florida, where he was named an All-American in 1992. He broke into pro ball later that year, helping Billings take the rookie Pioneer League championship. Then came a season to remember, as Mottola led the Class-A Carolina League with 91 RBI. The next season did not go quite that well, and Mottola owned only one home run by the All-Star break. But he has proven he can rebound, and now he awaits the call.

Professional Batting Register

	BA	G	AB	R	H	2B	3B	HR	RBI	SB
92 R	.286	57	213	53	61	8	3	12	37	12
93 A	.280	137	493	76	138	25	3	21	91	13
94 AA	.241	118	402	44	97	19	1	7	41	9
95 AA	.293	51	181	32	53	13	1	10	39	1
95 AAA	.259	69	239	40	62	11	1	8	37	8

Professional Pitching Register

	W	L	ERA	G	CG	IP	H	ER	BB	SO
94 R	2	5	3.58	12	1	60.1	30	24	55	77
95 A	9	10	3.56	27	0	149.1	134	59	70	177

ROOKIE PROSPECTS

TONY MOUNCE

Position: Pitcher
Team: Houston Astros
Born: Feb. 8, 1975 Sacramento, CA
Height: 6'2" **Weight:** 185 lbs.
Bats: left **Throws:** left
Acquired: Seventh-round pick in 6/94 free-agent draft

Player Summary
Fantasy Value $0
Card Value. . . . . N/A
Will . . . . strike people out
Can't. . . . . have long counts
Expect . . . . some complete games
Don't Expect. . . . . big rallies

Though taken one year later and six rounds lower than Billy Wagner, Mounce has started to rival his fellow Houston farmhand as a strikeout artist. Mounce stepped into pro ball in 1994 and promptly led the rookie Gulf Coast League with 72 strikeouts. Last year, he battled Wagner for the most strikeouts among Houston hopefuls. The fact that Wagner has done it against a higher level of competition should in no way detract from what Mounce has accomplished so far. He pitched in the Class-A Midwest League last year and dominated, leading the circuit in wins and finishing second in Ks. He was named Midwest League Player of the Week after hurling 13 scoreless innings in his first two starts. He fanned 12 at West Michigan on April 21, allowing no hits through six innings. His ratio of hits to innings was very good but, like many young lefties, he'll have to throw strikes more consistently. He held Midwest League hitters to a .205 batting average. Expect Mounce at high Class-A or possibly Double-A this season.

HEATH MURRAY

Position: Pitcher
Team: San Diego Padres
Born: April 19, 1973 Troy, OH
Height: 6'4" **Weight:** 205 lbs.
Bats: left **Throws:** left
Acquired: Third-round pick in 6/94 free-agent draft

Player Summary
Fantasy Value $0
Card Value. . . . . N/A
Will . . . . get complete games
Can't. . . . . order up runs
Expect. . . . . nice control
Don't Expect. . . . . first-round hype

Murray was overshadowed by first-round pick Dustin Hermanson coming out of the draft, but Murray's long-range impact may go beyond Hermanson's. Murray pitched in Class-A and Double-A ball last year, emerging as one of the top prospects in the San Diego system. He was tops in the San Diego farm system in victories, second in strikeouts, and tied for third in ERA. He held Class-A California League hitters to a .240 batting average last year, while Double-A Southern League hitters batted .267. Murray comes out of the University of Michigan, where he led the Wolverines to the 1994 Big 10 Title. Out of the draft, he enjoyed a solid first year in pro ball. He led the Class-A Northwest League in innings and allowed only 1.63 walks per nine innings, the best ratio in the league. In August, Murray went 3-2 with a 2.42 ERA. He was named Pitcher of the Week for Aug. 27, 1994. He also had some outings where he was victimized by poor run support. However, learning to deal with all kinds of circumstances is part of development, and Murray did an overall good job last year.

Professional Pitching Register

	W	L	ERA	G	CG	IP	H	ER	BB	SO
94 R	4	2	2.72	11	0	59.2	56	18	18	72
95 A	16	8	2.43	25	3	159.0	118	43	57	143

Professional Pitching Register

	W	L	ERA	G	CG	IP	H	ER	BB	SO
94 A	5	6	2.90	15	2	99.1	101	32	18	78
95 A	9	4	3.12	14	4	92.1	80	32	38	81
95 AA	5	4	3.38	14	0	77.1	83	29	42	71

ROOKIE PROSPECTS

MATT MURRAY

Position: Pitcher
Team: Boston Red Sox
Born: Sept. 26, 1970 Boston, MA
Height: 6'6" **Weight:** 235 lbs.
Bats: left **Throws:** right
Acquired: Traded by Braves with Mike Stanton for Marc Lewis and Mike Jacobs, 8/95

Player Summary	
Fantasy Value	$0
Card Value	N/A
Will	hang in there
Can't	make up time
Expect	a swingman
Don't Expect	his old stuff

Murray now has a chance to play in his hometown, but the road that took him there has been interesting to say the least. He was acquired from Atlanta last Aug. 31 for two minor-leaguers in a transaction that completed the trade that sent Mike Stanton to Boston. Murray had turned in an exceptional season that took him from Double-A all the way to the majors. Taken in the second round of the 1988 draft, after Steve Avery was chosen in the first, Murray seemed to be on a sure track to the majors when he went 11-7 for Burlington in 1990. But arm trouble intervened, wrecking virtually all of his 1991 and 1992 campaigns. Murray resumed pitching in 1993, and did well enough. But in 1994, there were times, particularly at Double-A Greenville, when he looked like anything but a prospect. A starter, Murray will likely get a chance to make the Boston rotation.

Professional Pitching Register

	W	L	ERA	G	CG	IP	H	ER	BB	SO
88 R	2	4	4.17	13	0	54.0	48	25	26	76
89 R	1	0	0.00	2	0	7.0	3	0	0	10
89 A	3	5	4.33	12	0	72.2	62	35	22	69
90 A	11	7	3.26	26	6	163.0	139	59	61	134
91 A	1	0	1.29	2	0	7.0	5	1	0	7
93 A	7	3	1.83	15	3	83.2	70	17	27	77
94 A	6	7	3.79	15	1	97.1	93	20	22	76
94 AA	3	4	5.08	12	0	67.1	89	38	31	48
95 AAA	14	3	2.54	24	0	152.1	128	43	42	103
95 AL	0	1	18.90	2	0	3.1	11	7	3	1
95 NL	0	2	6.75	4	0	10.2	10	8	5	3

CLEMENTE NUNEZ

Position: Pitcher
Team: Florida Marlins
Born: Feb. 10, 1975 Bonao, Dominican Republic
Height: 5'11" **Weight:** 180 lbs.
Bats: right **Throws:** right
Acquired: Signed as a nondrafted free agent, 12/91

Player Summary	
Fantasy Value	$0
Card Value	15¢ to 20¢
Will	advance in '96
Can't	lose second half
Expect	sentimental favorite
Don't Expect	another no-hitter

Nothing in gardening matches the feeling of watching a plant grow from seed to bloom, and that helps explain why Nunez is something special to the Marlins. He was the first player they ever signed, when he was 16 years old. Now, five years later, he is moving closer to the majors, looking better all the time. Last year he pitched for their affiliate in the Class-A Florida State League and turned in encouraging results. He finished fourth in the league in ERA and led the Marlins' farm system by a half-run more than anyone else. He was also tied for most wins in the chain. During one stretch Nunez won three straight starts, allowing 10 hits over a span of 21 innings. On May 28, he fired a no-hitter against West Palm Beach, striking out the first six hitters and finishing with 11 whiffs. Nunez led the league with 10 wins and four complete games in the first half, but fell off in the second. He allowed FSL hitters to compile a .216 batting average last year. He may need to work on his endurance.

Professional Pitching Register

	W	L	ERA	G	CG	IP	H	ER	BB	SO
92 R	5	5	2.78	12	3	71.1	55	22	25	26
93 A	4	3	3.98	14	0	63.1	66	28	17	34
94 A	6	5	3.10	19	2	98.2	86	34	24	66
95 A	12	6	2.48	19	4	123.1	99	34	22	79

SERGIO NUNEZ

Position: Second base
Team: Kansas City Royals
Born: Jan. 3, 1975 Santo Domingo, Dominican Republic
Height: 5'11" **Weight:** 155 lbs.
Bats: right **Throws:** right
Acquired: Signed as a nondrafted free agent, 11/91

Player Summary	
Fantasy Value	$0
Card Value	15¢ to 25¢
Will	get on base
Can't	drive in runs
Expect	singles hitter
Don't Expect	repeat of '94

Nunez created a sensation in 1994 when he led the rookie Gulf Coast League with a .397 average in his first season in North America. He won the batting title, made the All-Star Team, and was named the league's Topps Player of the Month for July and August. He also made the Short Season Rookie All-Star Team. He entered the final game of the season hitting .402, but he went 0-for-2 with a walk to finish at .397. In short, Nunez forced the Royals to jump him to the Class-A Carolina League last year. There he went 5-for-16 in his first four games, but he later fought a stomach ailment that dropped his average into the low .200s. He bounced back by going 9-for-14 in the games of June 26 to 29, winning Player of the Week honors. He took 51 walks last year, helping him to register a .317 on-base average. A second baseman, Nunez figures to have little power, but he can be a useful player in the lineup if he makes contact, gets on base, and uses his speed to steal bases. Nunez may start this year back in the Carolina League.

RYAN NYE

Position: Pitcher
Team: Philadelphia Phillies
Born: June 24, 1973 Biloxi, MS
Height: 6'2" **Weight:** 195 lbs.
Bats: right **Throws:** right
Acquired: Second-round pick in 6/94 free-agent draft

Player Summary	
Fantasy Value	$0
Card Value	N/A
Will	keep ball in play
Can't	steal Loewer's ink
Expect	lots of innings
Don't Expect	fancy stuff

Nye was the second pitcher the Phillies selected in the 1994 draft, with only first-rounder Carlton Loewer ahead of him. Since then, Nye has made above-average progress with average tools. Like Bob Tewksbury, Nye can serve as an example of what can happen if a pitcher consistently throws strikes. Pitching in the Class-A Florida State League last year, Nye allowed more hits than innings through his first 25 starts. But he was able to win more than he lost because he permitted just 30 walks over that span. Nye finished third in the Phils' farm system with 12 wins, boosting the pitching staff by providing innings, and he can give that increasingly lost art—a complete game. Nye authored Clearwater's first route-going performance of 1995, beating St. Petersburg 2-1. He slumped in May, going 0-3 in five starts, but rebounded. He allowed FSL hitters to compile a .259 batting average against him last year. Out of Texas Tech via Westark Community College, Nye figures to go to Double-A ball in 1996.

Professional Batting Register

	BA	G	AB	R	H	2B	3B	HR	RBI	SB
94 R	.397	59	232	64	92	9	7	5	24	37
95 A	.237	124	460	63	109	10	2	4	25	4

Professional Pitching Register

	W	L	ERA	G	CG	IP	H	ER	BB	SO
94 A	7	2	2.64	13	1	71.2	64	21	15	71
95 A	12	7	3.40	27	5	167.0	164	63	33	116

ROOKIE PROSPECTS

ALEX OCHOA

Position: Outfield
Team: New York Mets
Born: March 29, 1972 Miami Lakes, FL
Height: 6' **Weight:** 185 lbs.
Bats: right **Throws:** right
Acquired: Traded from Orioles with Damon Buford for Bobby Bonilla and Jimmy Williams, 7/95

Player Summary
Fantasy Value . . . . $5 to $7
Card Value . . . . 10¢ to 20¢
Will . . . . arrive this year
Can't . . . . hit 25 homers
Expect . . . . lots of tools
Don't Expect . . . . top steal mark

The Mets acquired Ochoa as part of the deal that sent Bobby Bonilla to Baltimore for last year's stretch drive, and they received praise around baseball for having pulled off quite a coup. Ochoa is viewed in some quarters as being a five-tool player—a top-level prospect. There's some question whether he will ever hit for big-time power, but he doesn't have to do that to make an impact. For one thing, he has the kind of arm that can dominate the base-paths from right field. He has stolen at least 28 bases three times in his minor-league career, though his percentage could use some improvement. He has delivered 20 or more doubles in four consecutive seasons. He compiled a .411 slugging percentage and a .328 on-base average playing for Rochester in the Triple-A International League. Ochoa was Baltimore's third pick in the 1991 draft. Out of Hialeah-Miami Lakes High School, he was born shortly after his parents emigrated from Cuba.

Professional Batting Register

	BA	G	AB	R	H	2B	3B	HR	RBI	SB
91 R	.307	53	179	26	55	8	3	1	30	11
92 A	.295	133	499	65	147	22	7	1	59	31
93 A	.276	137	532	84	147	29	5	13	90	34
94 AA	.301	134	519	77	156	25	2	14	82	28
95 AAA	.283	125	459	58	130	24	4	10	61	24
95 NL	.297	11	37	7	11	1	0	0	0	1

REY ORDONEZ

Position: Shortstop
Team: New York Mets
Born: Jan. 11, 1972 Havana, Cuba
Height: 5'10" **Weight:** 170 lbs.
Bats: both **Throws:** right
Acquired: Drafted from St. Paul, 10/93

Player Summary
Fantasy Value $0
Card Value . . . . 10¢ to 15¢
Will . . . . cover ground
Can't . . . . squander chance
Expect . . . . spectacular glove
Don't Expect . . . . punch

Ordonez is at a critical stage in his baseball career, having gone from prospect to suspect in a short time. At times last year, the prevailing notion held that he would be the Mets shortstop this year. But then grave doubts developed over his bat, making him seem like less than a sure thing. If it was just a matter of his glove, Ordonez might have won the job by now. He is a geniune, bona fide whiz in the field, reminding some people of Ozzie Smith. Ordonez throws well and has good footwork that enables him to cover territory. But late last season, he was still hitting in the .210 to .220 range with very little power. He's the classic example of a player who must do the little things like sacrifice and keep the ball out of the air. He had only a .261 on-base percentage last year, notching 27 bases on balls. Ordonez defected from the Cuban national team while in Buffalo in 1993 and went to play for St. Paul of the independent Northern League. The Mets won his rights in a lottery, and it seemed like quite a catch. This year, we'll see if it really was.

Professional Batting Register

	BA	G	AB	R	H	2B	3B	HR	RBI	SB
93 I	.283	15	60	10	17	4	0	0	7	3
94 A	.309	79	314	47	97	21	2	2	40	11
94 AA	.262	48	191	22	50	10	2	1	20	4
95 AAA	.214	125	439	49	94	21	4	2	50	11

ROOKIE PROSPECTS

RAFAEL ORELLANO

Position: Pitcher
Team: Boston Red Sox
Born: April 28, 1973 Humacao, PR
Height: 6'2" **Weight:** 160 lbs.
Bats: left **Throws:** left
Acquired: Signed as a nondrafted free agent, 11/92

Player Summary	
Fantasy Value	$0
Card Value	N/A
Will	minimize hits
Can't	burn out arm
Expect	a stringbean
Don't Expect	more Double-A

The dimensions of Fenway Park are always leading the Red Sox to seek special left-handed pitchers, and they may have found one in Orellano. Last summer, he delivered his second straight outstanding season, this time in the Double-A Eastern League. He led the Red Sox system in strikeouts and put together a fine hits-to-innings ratio. On Aug. 21, he notched his 11th victory, going seven shutout innings. At that point, he had assembled a 1.65 ERA over six starts. He held Eastern League hitters to a .213 batting average last year. Orellano blossomed in just his second year of pro ball, allowing Class-A Florida State League batters to hit just .197 against him in 1994. In one game, he struck out 10 of the first 11 batters he faced. He allowed only four earned runs in 41⅔ innings in August, earning Minor League Pitcher of the Month honors from the Red Sox. Orellano tends toward a high pitch count because of all the walks and Ks, and he needs some one- or two-pitch outs to avoid a recurrence of the tendinitis that shelved him in 1994.

Professional Pitching Register

	W	L	ERA	G	CG	IP	H	ER	BB	SO
93 A	1	2	5.79	11	0	18.2	22	12	7	13
94 R	1	0	2.03	4	0	13.1	6	3	4	10
94 A	11	3	2.40	16	2	97.1	68	26	25	103
95 AA	11	7	3.09	27	2	186.2	146	64	72	160

JAY PAYTON

Position: Outfield
Team: New York Mets
Born: Nov. 22, 1972 Zanesville, OH
Height: 5'11" **Weight:** 193 lbs.
Bats: right **Throws:** right
Acquired: Supplemental second-round pick in 6/94 free-agent draft

Player Summary	
Fantasy Value	$5 to $7
Card Value	$1.00 to $2.00
Will	be a force
Can't	play right
Expect	a high ceiling
Don't Expect	a free swinger

Payton came to New York as the 29th overall pick in the 1994 draft, as compensation for the loss of free agent Sid Fernandez. Payton could wind up having as much impact as anyone else in the grab bag, and that includes the first overall pick—pitcher Paul Wilson, who also went to the Mets. Payton is an outfielder who will probably play left field and hit for average, drive in runs, and perhaps hit 20 homers a year. He began his pro career with Pittsfield of the Class-A New York-Penn League, and he was promoted to Double-A just in time to help Binghamton win the Eastern League title. He returned to the Eastern League last year and was promoted to Triple-A, but not before he had accumulated enough stats to win the batting title and be named the EL's Player of the Year. He had a .535 slugging average and a .395 on-base percentage last season. On the downside, Payton had to undergo reconstructive surgery to a torn ligament in his elbow, and he may not be ready for the start of spring training. The Mets have their fingers crossed.

Professional Batting Register

	BA	G	AB	R	H	2B	3B	HR	RBI	SB
94 A	.365	58	219	47	80	16	2	3	37	10
94 AA	.280	8	25	3	7	1	0	0	1	1
95 AA	.345	85	357	59	123	20	3	14	54	16
95 AAA	.240	50	196	33	47	11	4	4	30	11

ROOKIE PROSPECTS

NEIFI PEREZ

Position: Shortstop
Team: Colorado Rockies
Born: Feb. 2, 1975 Villa Mella, Dominican Republic
Height: 6' **Weight:** 173 lbs.
Bats: both **Throws:** right
Acquired: Signed as a nondrafted free agent, 11/92

Player Summary
Fantasy Value $0
Card Value . . . . 15¢ to 25¢
Will. . . . . play in Colorado
Can't. . . . . overpower the ball
Expect . . . . great attitude
Don't Expect. . . . . bland style

The Rockies have concentrated heavily on signing and developing pitching prospects, but they have also managed to come up with some position hopefuls of note. One of them is Perez, a highly coveted shortstop who figures to be playing somewhere in Colorado this year—either at Triple-A Colorado Springs or with the big club in Denver. Either way, he has the look of a keeper. The Rockies have reportedly already turned down offers for him. Perez began last season as the starting shortstop for the Rockies' Triple-A club, even though he was just 20 years old. After a brief stretch in Colorado Springs, he was dropped a level to Double-A. But any way you look at it, he made progress. Perez is a switch-hitter who will catch the ball and hold his own at the plate. He doesn't project as a big power hitter, but he has decent size and might prosper in a park where the ball flies. He has done a good job of improving his contact-hitting skills. Perez had 24 bases on balls last year at Double-A, and he notched a .295 on-base average. That will have to increase.

Professional Batting Register

	BA	G	AB	R	H	2B	3B	HR	RBI	SB
93 A	.260	75	296	35	77	11	4	3	32	19
94 A	.239	134	506	64	121	16	7	1	35	9
95 AA	.253	116	427	59	108	28	3	5	43	5
95 AAA	.278	11	36	4	10	4	0	0	2	1

CHARLES PETERSON

Position: Outfield
Team: Pittsburgh Pirates
Born: May 8, 1974 Laurens, SC
Height: 6'3" **Weight:** 203 lbs.
Bats: right **Throws:** right
Acquired: First-round pick in 6/93 free-agent draft

Player Summary
Fantasy Value $0
Card Value . . . . 15¢ to 25¢
Will. . . . . bring speed
Can't. . . . . rule out power
Expect . . . . skills
Don't Expect . . . . 162-game player

The whole idea of drafting is to spot raw talent and try to develop it. That's exactly what seems to be happening with Peterson, a high school football star who is learning the game of baseball. He has now spent three years in pro baseball and even though he has run into injury problems, he keeps getting better. Last year he played in the Class-A Carolina League, and was off to a good start with a .327 average and six steals when he twisted an ankle. Still, he set career highs in homers, runs, RBI, walks, and stolen bases. He had a .345 on-base average in Class-A, which is good because the more he gets on base, the more he can dominate with his speed. Peterson was also singled out as a prospect to watch by *USA Today Baseball Weekly*. He received a late-season promotion to the Double-A Southern League and embarked on a hitting streak. Peterson spent the 1994 campaign in the Class-A South Atlantic League, where he missed 26 games due to injury. Still, he was named the team's Player of the Month for July. Peterson's biggest challenge now is to stay healthy.

Professional Batting Register

	BA	G	AB	R	H	2B	3B	HR	RBI	SB
93 R	.303	49	188	28	57	11	3	1	23	8
94 A	.255	108	415	55	106	14	6	4	40	27
95 A	.274	107	391	61	107	9	4	7	51	31
95 AA	.329	20	70	13	23	3	1	0	7	2

ROOKIE PROSPECTS

JOSE PETT

Position: Pitcher
Team: Toronto Blue Jays
Born: Jan. 8, 1976 Sao Paulo, Brazil
Height: 6'6" **Weight:** 210 lbs.
Bats: right **Throws:** right
Acquired: Signed as a nondrafted free agent, 7/92

Player Summary	
Fantasy Value	$0
Card Value	15¢ to 40¢
Will	stand out
Can't	pitch with tendinitis
Expect	continued adjustments
Don't Expect	perfect control

This young man from Brazil attracted considerable interest from major-league clubs before the Blue Jays prevailed and got his name on the dotted line. Pett stands out among prospects for several reasons, including his size, his native country, and his pitching ability. Last year he pitched in the Double-A Southern League and performed extremely well considering he was only 19 years old. He held Southern League hitters to a .244 batting average. *USA Today Baseball Weekly* identified him as a prospect to watch. Before playing pro ball, Pett was a member of a Brazil team that took part in the World Junior Championships in Monterrey, Mexico. In his first exposure to Toronto's farm system, Pett went 1-1 in four starts in the rookie Gulf Coast League in 1993, but he missed most of the campaign with shoulder tendinitis. Graduating to the Class-A Florida State League in 1994, Pett had his difficulties but enjoyed one stretch over which he went 2-1 with a 2.00 ERA. This year, Pett will probably be found in Double-A or Triple-A.

Professional Pitching Register

	W	L	ERA	G	CG	IP	H	ER	BB	SO
93 R	1	1	3.60	4	0	10.0	10	4	3	7
94 A	4	8	3.77	15	1	90.2	103	38	20	49
95 AA	8	9	4.26	26	1	141.2	132	67	48	89

JORGE POSADA

Position: Catcher; infield
Team: New York Yankees
Born: Aug. 17, 1971 Santurce, PR
Height: 6'2" **Weight:** 205 lbs.
Bats: both **Throws:** right
Acquired: Signed as a free agent, 5/91

Player Summary	
Fantasy Value	$0
Card Value	N/A
Will	move around
Can't	keep running to backstop
Expect	occasional power
Don't Expect	intimidated runners

Posada could well be the Yankees' catcher of the future, but don't be surprised if you occasionally see him at second base or at third. Those are all positions he has played while making the trip through New York's farm system. He arrived in pro ball as a second baseman and led the Class-A New York-Penn League with 42 double plays turned. Advancing to the Class-A South Atlantic League in 1992, Posada began seeing more action behind the plate and also put in some time at third. He made the Class-A Carolina League All-Star squad in 1993, even though he led the loop with 38 passed balls. His defensive problems continued in 1994 in the Triple-A International League, when he made 11 errors and allowed 65 steals in 83 attempts. He also suffered a fractured fibula and a dislocated ankle in a home plate collision. He hit well last year, notching a .435 slugging average and a .350 on-base percentage—thanks to 54 bases on balls. In spite of everything, the Yankees liked him enough to bring him for a peek at the majors last summer. Posada's versatility should serve him well.

Professional Batting Register

	BA	G	AB	R	H	2B	3B	HR	RBI	SB
91 A	.235	71	217	34	51	5	4	4	33	6
92 A	.277	101	339	60	94	22	4	12	58	11
93 A	.259	118	410	71	106	27	2	17	61	17
93 AA	.280	7	25	3	7	0	0	0	0	0
94 AAA	.240	92	313	46	75	13	3	11	48	5
95 AAA	.255	108	368	60	94	32	5	8	51	4

ROOKIE PROSPECTS

DANTE POWELL

Position: Outfield
Team: San Francisco Giants
Born: Aug. 25, 1973 Long Beach, CA
Height: 6'2" **Weight:** 185 lbs.
Bats: right **Throws:** right
Acquired: First-round pick in 6/94 free-agent draft

Player Summary	
Fantasy Value	$0
Card Value	N/A
Will	run the bases
Can't	play right field
Expect	occasional power
Don't Expect	consistent contact

Powell seems to be just a year or two away from giving the Giants a nice mixture of power and speed. He'll offer more quickness than slugging power, but he's hit enough in the low minors to suggest he could get his share of extra-base hits. Last year he played in the Class-A California League and ranked among team leaders in home runs, RBI, and steals. He turned in a .384 slugging percentage, though his game is speed. He disappointed with a .312 on-base average and 131 strikeouts; Powell should work on his contact-hitting skills. He came out of Millikan High School in California and went on to play for Cal State-Fullerton. He batted .315 with 109 stolen bases in his college career, and he helped his team to the 1994 College World Series. He also played for the U.S. National Team in 1994. When the Giants tabbed him as the 22nd overall pick in 1994, it marked the second time he had been a high-round pick. In 1991, he had been taken with a supplemental pick by Toronto. Powell made a nice impression after being drafted, going to the Northwest League and making the All-Star Team.

Professional Batting Register

	BA	G	AB	R	H	2B	3B	HR	RBI	SB
94 A	.314	42	169	31	53	15	2	5	25	27
95 A	.248	135	505	74	125	23	8	10	70	43

JAY POWELL

Position: Pitcher
Team: Florida Marlins
Born: Jan. 9, 1972 Meridian, MS
Height: 6'4" **Weight:** 221 lbs.
Bats: right **Throws:** right
Acquired: Traded by Orioles for Bret Barberie, 12/94

Player Summary	
Fantasy Value	$0
Card Value	N/A
Will	close
Can't	always find plate
Expect	Birds to lament
Don't Expect	return to rotation

Powell found himself in a new organization and a new role last year, and the results were spectacular. Acquired from the Orioles in the trade that sent second baseman Bret Barberie to Baltimore, Powell was switched to the bullpen and proceeded to lead the Florida system in saves by a wide margin. Pitching for Portland of the Double-A Eastern League, Powell was virtually unhittable for extended periods. Early in the season, he put together a stretch of two wins and seven saves that ended on an unearned run. In eight games spanning May and June, he allowed no runs until blowing a save June 7 against Norwich. For a month beginning July 20, he allowed no runs over 11 games, picking up seven saves. Powell notched three and one-half strikeouts per walk allowed last year, and he had one K per inning. He held EL hitters to a paltry .219 batting average. Clearly, he was more comfortable in the closer's role than he had been as a starter in 1994. Powell comes out of Mississippi State and can throw in the 90s. Based on last year, his future is in the pen.

Professional Pitching Register

	W	L	ERA	G	S	IP	H	ER	BB	SO
93 A	0	2	4.55	6	0	27.2	29	14	13	29
94 A	7	7	4.96	26	1	123.1	132	68	54	87
95 AA	5	4	1.87	50	24	53.0	42	11	15	53
95 NL	0	0	1.08	9	0	8.1	7	1	6	4

ROOKIE PROSPECTS

ARQUIMEDEZ POZO

Position: Second base
Team: Seattle Mariners
Born: Aug. 24, 1973 Santo Domingo, Dominican Republic
Height: 5'10" **Weight:** 160 lbs.
Bats: right **Throws:** right
Acquired: Signed as a nondrafted free agent, 8/90

Player Summary
Fantasy Value	$0
Card Value	10¢ to 20¢
Will	be in mix
Can't	duplicate 44 doubles
Expect	solid average
Don't Expect	an easy out

Pozo looks like he can soon be part of a trivia question—after all, how many major leaguers have the letter "Z" in both their first and last names? More importantly, Pozo represents some of the infield strength that the Mariners have assembled over the last few years. He could be battling it out with Desi Relaford for the second base job in Seattle as early as this year. Pozo blossomed in the Class-A California League in 1993, tying for the minor-league lead with 44 doubles and being named the Mariners' minor league Player of the Year. In 1994, he was promoted to Double-A and hit 14 homers, even though he spent a week on the disabled list with a strained right quadricep. He also fashioned the fourth-lowest strikeout ratio in the Southern League. Last year, Pozo played in the Triple-A Pacific Coast League and hit for average, but his doubles total did not come close to what it had been in the California League. However, he did have a .340 on-base average. Pozo has shown the ability with the wood and the leather.

ARIEL PRIETO

Position: Pitcher
Team: Oakland Athletics
Born: Oct. 22, 1966 Mariano, Cuba
Height: 6'3" **Weight:** 220 lbs.
Bats: right **Throws:** right
Acquired: First-round pick in 6/95 free-agent draft

Player Summary
Fantasy Value	$1
Card Value	N/A
Will	throw 94 mph
Can't	win without runs
Expect	hard slider
Don't Expect	a bust

Prieto was one of the intriguing international stories in the major leagues last year, joining Hideo Nomo of the Dodgers in the spotlight. Prieto arrived from Cuba, where he had been a star on that country's renowned national team. He pitched in an independent league and drew enough attention that the A's drafted him fifth overall. Upon being selected, he got thrown into a pennant race with the A's almost immediately. He didn't look out of place, but he suffered an injury that cost him some time. Prieto throws a fastball that gets well into the 90s. He also brings poise, confidence, experience, and presence. He got rave reviews for the speed with which he got to know the hitters. In his first two games, Prieto pitched well, but Oakland scored only two runs to support him. He ended up with a mediocre strikeout-to-walk ratio, and AL hitters had a .264 batting average against him last year. It should be very interesting to see what Prieto can do once he can spend an off-season and training camp preparing for the major-league grind.

Professional Batting Register
	BA	G	AB	R	H	2B	3B	HR	RBI	SB
92 A	.261	93	348	70	100	20	4	10	40	22
93 A	.342	127	515	98	176	44	6	13	83	10
94 AA	.289	119	447	70	129	31	1	14	54	11
95 AAA	.300	122	450	57	135	19	6	10	62	3
95 AL	.000	1	1	0	0	0	0	0	0	0

Professional Pitching Register
	W	L	ERA	G	CG	IP	H	ER	BB	SO
95 I	4	0	0.97	6	1	37.0	23	4	7	48
95 AL	2	6	4.97	14	1	58.0	57	32	32	37

ROOKIE PROSPECTS

STEVE RAIN

Position: Pitcher
Team: Chicago Cubs
Born: June 2, 1975 Los Angeles, CA
Height: 6'6" **Weight:** 225 lbs.
Bats: right **Throws:** right
Acquired: 12th-round pick in 6/93 free-agent draft

Player Summary	
Fantasy Value	$0
Card Value	N/A
Will	get the ball
Can't	rule out middle relief
Expect	presence
Don't Expect	rotation return

You can be sure that when the late innings arrived, hitters in the Class-A Midwest League were checking for signs of Rain. That's because this young prospect emerged as one of the top closers in the league, if not in the entire Chicago farm system. Converted from a starter, Rain seemed to thrive in his new role and gave himself another avenue through which to travel to the majors. He held Midwest League hitters to a .186 batting average and turned in a strikeout-to-walk ratio of almost 3-to-1. Rain came to pro ball straight out of Walnut High School in California, where he played baseball and helped win a title. Upon turning pro, he spent two years in the low minors, mostly as a starter. Significantly, he did not have one save in his first two years as a pro. However, that changed last year. He was one of two Rockford players selected to play in the Midwest League All-Star Game. *USA Today Baseball Weekly* touted him in its midseason report on prospects. A closer at lower levels doesn't always succeed when promoted, but Rain will get a chance.

Professional Pitching Register

	W	L	ERA	G	S	IP	H	ER	BB	SO
93 R	1	3	3.89	10	0	37.0	37	16	17	29
94 R	3	3	2.65	14	0	68.0	55	20	19	55
95 A	5	2	1.21	53	23	59.1	38	8	23	66

GARY RATH

Position: Pitcher
Team: Los Angeles Dodgers
Born: Jan. 10, 1973 Gulfport, MS
Height: 6'2" **Weight:** 185 lbs.
Bats: left **Throws:** left
Acquired: Second-round pick in 6/94 free-agent draft

Player Summary	
Fantasy Value	$0
Card Value	N/A
Will	vie for job
Can't	fall behind
Expect	competitor
Don't Expect	more Double-A

If this prospect keeps up the good work, then big-league hitters are soon going to be experiencing the Dodgers' Rath on a regular basis. Out of Mississippi State University, Rath has shot through the Los Angeles farm system and could be competing for a starting job as early as this summer. Last year, he was the winningest pitcher in the Dodger organization, with most of his victories coming with Double-A San Antonio. He held Texas League hitters to a .225 batting average. Not even superlative achievements in college—including getting named as a *Baseball America* first-team All-American—could have prepared him for such a timetable. But a solid debut in the Class-A Florida State League in 1994, in which Rath allowed only 55 hits in 62⅔ innings, stamped him as a prospect to watch. Last year, he pitched a scoreless inning in the Double-A All-Star Game. *USA Today Baseball Weekly* included him in its midsummer look at prospects. He had some troubles when he was first promoted to Triple-A, but Rath eventually worked them out.

Professional Pitching Register

	W	L	ERA	G	CG	IP	H	ER	BB	SO
94 A	5	6	2.73	13	0	62.2	55	19	23	50
95 AA	13	3	2.77	18	3	117.0	96	36	48	81
95 AAA	3	5	5.08	8	0	39.0	46	22	20	23

ROOKIE PROSPECTS

MARK REDMAN

Position: Pitcher
Team: Minnesota Twins
Born: Jan. 5, 1974 San Diego, CA
Height: 6'5" **Weight:** 210 lbs.
Bats: left **Throws:** left
Acquired: First-round pick in 6/95 free-agent draft

Player Summary	
Fantasy Value	$0
Card Value	N/A
Will	use his pitches
Can't	rule out ace role
Expect	changeup
Don't Expect	big adjustment

Nearly a decade ago, the Twins won the World Series with a rotation that featured an ace left-hander drafted out of college, Frank Viola. The Twins would be pleased if Redman could have anywhere near the same effect. He comes out of the University of Oklahoma, where he pitched with enough distinction to be named a first-team All-American by *Baseball America*. Redman led the Sooners into the College World Series, where he pitched well but lost. Minnesota made him the 13th overall pick, and he was the sixth pitcher selected. After signing, Redman broke into pro ball on July 25 with Fort Myers of the Class-A Florida State League and made quite an impression. He faced six St. Lucie batters and retired them all, three on strikeouts. On Aug. 4, he pitched four scoreless innings of relief against St. Petersburg. In his next two outings, he raised his scoreless innings streak to 14. He held FSL hitters to a .239 batting average. Redman's strong start may push him past high Class-A ball on the way to Double-A ball this year.

BRANDON REED

Position: Pitcher
Team: Detroit Tigers
Born: Dec. 18, 1974 Flint, MI
Height: 6'3" **Weight:** 165 lbs.
Bats: right **Throws:** right
Acquired: 45th-round pick in 6/94 free-agent draft

Player Summary	
Fantasy Value	$0
Card Value	N/A
Will	advance
Can't	make it as starter
Expect	game pitcher
Don't Expect	more Sally League

The Tigers may have come up with something special right in their backyard. Picking in the late rounds in 1994, they tabbed Reed, who became a sensation in the Class-A South Atlantic League last year. This right-hander had been exclusively a starter in his first year of pro ball, but he went to the Fayetteville bullpen, where something immediately clicked. He wound up leading the entire minor leagues with 41 saves. Reed struck out four and one-third batters for every free pass he allowed. He went to school at Lapeer High School in Michigan and, upon turning pro, turned in a so-so year for Bristol of the rookie Appalachian League. But last year, Reed was virtually untouchable. He owned 18 saves at midseason, and *USA Today Baseball Weekly* gave him a nod as a prospect to watch. Reed still faces long odds of ever having the same impact in the majors as he did last year in the Sally League, but it's important to remember he need not be a closer to help. Reed could succeed as a setup man as well.

Professional Pitching Register

	W	L	ERA	G	CG	IP	H	ER	BB	SO
95 A	2	1	2.76	8	0	32.2	28	10	13	26

Professional Pitching Register

	W	L	ERA	G	S	IP	H	ER	BB	SO
94 R	3	5	3.58	13	0	78.0	82	31	10	68
95 A	3	0	0.97	55	41	64.2	40	7	18	78

ROOKIE PROSPECTS

POKEY REESE

Position: Shortstop
Team: Cincinnati Reds
Born: June 10, 1973 Columbia, SC
Height: 5'11" **Weight:** 180 lbs.
Bats: right **Throws:** right
Acquired: First-round pick in 6/91 free-agent draft

Player Summary	
Fantasy Value	$0
Card Value	10¢ to 15¢
Will	dazzle at short
Can't	match Larkin's bat
Expect	nice arm
Don't Expect	162 games

No one should be misled by Reese's nickname, because he is anything but pokey on the bases or at shortstop. And now he is hoping to be just as quick in making the final move from the minors to a regular job in the big leagues. He has been a highly rated pick ever since the day the Reds made him the 20th overall selection in 1991. *Baseball America* termed him the best defensive player in the draft that year, and since then, he has been the best defender in the Cincinnati system. In 1992, Reese graduated to the Class-A South Atlantic League, where he made the All-Star Team. After the season, he underwent elbow surgery and, in 1993, suffered a hand injury. Reese turned in his best season yet in 1994, where he led Double-A Southern League shortstops with 221 putouts. Last year, Reese played for Cincinnati's Triple-A team in Indianapolis. He had 81 strikeouts and 36 walks, so he had some work to do with the lumber. He does not project to be the offensive whiz that Barry Larkin is, but Reese might hit .250 with the occasional home run.

Professional Batting Register

	BA	G	AB	R	H	2B	3B	HR	RBI	SB
91 R	.238	62	231	30	55	8	3	3	27	10
92 A	.268	106	380	50	102	19	3	6	53	19
93 AA	.212	102	345	35	73	17	4	3	37	8
94 AA	.269	134	484	77	130	23	4	12	49	21
95 AAA	.239	89	343	51	82	21	1	10	46	8

BRYAN REKAR

Position: Pitcher
Team: Colorado Rockies
Born: June 3, 1972 Oaklawn, IL
Height: 6'3" **Weight:** 208 lbs.
Bats: right **Throws:** right
Acquired: Second-round pick in 6/93 free-agent draft

Player Summary	
Fantasy Value	$2 to $4
Card Value	N/A
Will	work inside corner
Can't	rely on fastball
Expect	wide repertoire
Don't Expect	many hits

Rekar made his major-league debut on July 19, 1995, earning a victory over the hard-hitting Phillies. His arrival completed a rapid rise through the Colorado system, as he came out of Bradley University and needed only about 26 months to get to the majors. Rekar has a wide repertoire that includes a fastball, a change of speed, and a couple of breaking pitches. He enhances this assortment by not being reluctant to work the inside corner. He also will throw his breaking ball when behind in the count. Rekar throws a curveball that will sneak under the hands of a left-handed batter. Last year, he allowed less than one hit per inning, and Double-A hitters had a composite .215 batting average. Rekar seemed to get better as he progressed through the organization. After making 13 starts in rookie ball in 1993, he lowered his ERA in the faster company of the Class-A California League in 1994. The fact that he blazed through the higher minors last year speaks for itself. He could be a member of the Colorado rotation for years to come.

Professional Pitching Register

	W	L	ERA	G	CG	IP	H	ER	BB	SO
93 A	3	5	4.08	13	1	75.0	81	34	18	59
94 A	6	6	3.48	22	0	111.1	120	43	31	91
95 AA	6	3	2.13	12	1	80.1	65	19	16	80
95 AAA	4	2	1.49	7	2	48.1	29	8	13	39
95 NL	4	6	4.98	15	1	85.0	95	47	24	60

ROOKIE PROSPECTS

DESI RELAFORD

Position: Infield
Team: Seattle Mariners
Born: Sept. 16, 1973 Valdosta, GA
Height: 5'8" **Weight:** 155 lbs.
Bats: both **Throws:** right
Acquired: Fourth-round pick in 6/91 free-agent draft

Player Summary	
Fantasy Value	$0
Card Value	15¢ to 25¢
Will	need more work
Can't	worry about spot
Expect	top on-base mark
Don't Expect	Rodriguez

Last year, Relaford opened at Double-A ball for the second straight year. This time, however, instead of being demoted, he was boosted up to the Triple-A Pacific Coast League by the end of the campaign. That suggests that Relaford has made some necessary adjustments at the plate and is ready for a call to Seattle. One question is what position he will be playing when he gets there. Relaford appeared in the Double-A All-Star Game as a shortstop, and he has performed with distinction at that spot. However, the Mariners have phenom Alex Rodriguez as their top prospect, perhaps closing off that avenue. Thus, he moved to second when he arrived in Triple-A Tacoma, with Arquimedez Pozo also in the mix. Relaford brings the potential to compile a top on-base average and to steal bases. He has swiped at least 25 in three of his five pro seasons. He notched a .365 on-base mark in Double-A last year. Relaford won't be much of a home run hitter, though the Kingdome could help his totals.

Professional Batting Register

	BA	G	AB	R	H	2B	3B	HR	RBI	SB
91 R	.270	46	163	36	44	7	3	0	18	17
92 A	.216	130	445	53	96	18	1	3	34	27
93 AA	.244	133	472	49	115	16	4	8	47	16
94 A	.310	99	374	95	116	27	5	5	59	27
94 AA	.203	37	143	24	29	7	3	3	11	10
95 AA	.287	90	352	51	101	11	2	7	27	25
95 AAA	.239	30	113	20	27	5	1	2	7	6

EDGAR RENTERIA

Position: Shortstop
Team: Florida Marlins
Born: Aug. 7, 1975 Barranquilla, Colombia
Height: 6'1" **Weight:** 172 lbs.
Bats: right **Throws:** right
Acquired: Signed as a nondrafted free agent, 1/92

Player Summary	
Fantasy Value	$0
Card Value	N/A
Will	run wild
Can't	hit flies
Expect	spotty contact
Don't Expect	steady fielding

Renteria has a chance to be among the first home-grown impact players in Marlins history. The brother of a longtime Houston farmhand, he was signed as a free agent by Levy Ochoa, and Renteria has made his way smartly through the system. Last year, he played for Portland in the Double-A Eastern League and became a force on the bases, finishing among the organization's leaders in steals. When he was thrown out June 8 against Norwich, it ended a string of 13 straight successful attempts. Late in the summer, Renteria went on a hitting tear that gave him Player of the Week honors. But he has a way to go at the plate, as he strikes out way too often for someone with no power. He sat down with 85 punchouts last year. He must make more consistent contact, keep the ball out of the air, and take more pitches, all with the aim of getting on base more and using his speed. Renteria had a .329 on-base average last year. He made 10 errors last June, more than any shortstop in the league. Renteria will have to get more consistent with his glovework.

Professional Batting Register

	BA	G	AB	R	H	2B	3B	HR	RBI	SB
92 R	.288	43	163	25	47	8	1	0	9	10
93 A	.203	116	384	40	78	8	0	1	35	7
94 A	.253	128	439	46	111	15	1	0	36	6
95 AA	.289	135	508	70	147	15	7	7	68	30

ROOKIE PROSPECTS

RAY RICKEN

Position: Pitcher
Team: New York Yankees
Born: Aug. 11, 1973 Detroit, MI
Height: 6'5" **Weight:** 225 lbs.
Bats: right **Throws:** right
Acquired: Fifth-round pick in 6/94 free-agent draft

Player Summary
Fantasy Value $0
Card Value .... 15¢ to 30¢
Will .... keep moving
Can't .... change his style
Expect .... strikeouts
Don't Expect .... one-pitch outs

Ricken has been in pro ball for two years, and he received an in-season promotion both times. Last year, his rise was especially impressive. He began the season with Greensboro of the Class-A South Atlantic League, advanced to Tampa of the Class-A Florida State League, then received a boost to Norwich of the Double-A Eastern League. This rapid progress has placed him within range of a job in New York in 1996. He still could use some more seasoning in the high minors, nevertheless. Last year, the burly right-hander led Yankee farmhands with 148 strikeouts, and he also was in the hunt for the organization's ERA title. He held Double-A hitters to a .232 batting average and Class-A hitters to about a .180 mark. Along the way, *USA Today Baseball Weekly* named him as a prospect to watch. He was tied for the Sally League lead in Ks when promoted. Ricken comes out of the University of Michigan, where he was an All-Big Ten selection. In his first stop in pro ball, Ricken ranked second among New York-Penn League starters with 9.84 strikeouts per nine innings.

Professional Pitching Register

	W	L	ERA	G	CG	IP	H	ER	BB	SO
94 A	3	5	3.94	15	0	75.1	72	33	29	74
95 A	6	6	2.19	21	1	140.0	89	34	43	135
95 AA	4	2	2.72	8	1	53.0	44	16	24	43

ADAM RIGGS

Position: Second base
Team: Los Angeles Dodgers
Born: Oct. 4, 1972 Steubenville, Ohio
Height: 5'11" **Weight:** 180 lbs.
Bats: right **Throws:** right
Acquired: 22nd-round pick in 6/94 free-agent draft

Player Summary
Fantasy Value $0
Card Value .... N/A
Will .... steal some bases
Can't .... let bat carry him
Expect .... solid hits
Don't Expect .... a Gold Glove

The Dodgers, who so often produce the National League Rookie of the Year, last year delivered one of the top sensations in all of the minors. One year removed from being taken midway through the draft, Riggs starred for San Bernardino of the Class-A California League. He was named the league's Player of the Month for July, hitting .381 with seven homers and 25 RBI. Chasing the Triple Crown, he had to settle for winning the batting title and finishing third in homers and RBI. Along the way, he became a 20-20 man. He turned in a whopping .585 slugging percentage. He also drew 59 walks and had a .431 on-base average. The only drawback, and it's a big one, would be defense. At the end of May, the South Carolina product led all second basemen in the minors with 18 errors. That kind of defense won't make his progress very easy. But scouts have a saying: "The better he hits, the better he fields." That's their way of saying you can overlook some glove problems if the hitting is strong enough. But there's a limit to that, so Riggs better improve with the glove.

Professional Batting Register

	BA	G	AB	R	H	2B	3B	HR	RBI	SB
94 R	.312	62	234	55	73	20	3	5	44	19
94 A	.286	4	7	1	2	1	0	0	0	0
95 A	.362	134	542	111	196	39	5	24	106	31

ROOKIE PROSPECTS

MARQUIS RILEY

Position: Outfield
Team: California Angels
Born: Dec. 27, 1970 Ashdown, AR
Height: 5'11" **Weight:** 170 lbs.
Bats: right **Throws:** right
Acquired: Second-round pick in 6/92 free-agent draft

Player Summary
Fantasy Value	$0
Card Value	N/A
Will	work deep counts
Can't	crack big outfield
Expect	a role player
Don't Expect	extra bases

Riley is just about ready to step into a job with the Angels. But the only problem is that there may not be a job available for him. After all, how does one crack an outfield of Garret Anderson, Jim Edmonds, and Tim Salmon? Nevertheless, Riley brings qualifications as an ignitor, a force who can get on base, steal, and generally be a distraction to pitchers. Last year, Riley played with Vancouver of the Triple-A Pacific Coast League, and he passed the 25-steal mark for the third straight season. He won't be stealing 69 bases, as he did during his dream 1993 season in the California League, but 30 is not an unrealistic total. Riley is almost exclusively a singles hitter, and not even exposure to the PCL could give him a semblance of extra-base punch; only 12 of his first 116 hits went for extra bases. He had a .300 slugging percentage last year, as opposed to a .330 on-base percentage. At age 25, he must quickly find a way to make an impact somewhere. With his speed and ability to make contact, Riley could be a fine role player.

Professional Batting Register
	BA	G	AB	R	H	2B	3B	HR	RBI	SB
92 A	.239	52	201	47	48	12	1	0	12	7
93 A	.264	130	508	93	134	10	2	1	42	69
94 AA	.286	93	374	68	107	12	4	1	29	32
94 AAA	.214	4	14	3	3	0	0	0	1	1
95 AAA	.262	120	477	70	125	6	6	0	43	29

ARMANDO RIOS

Position: Outfield
Team: San Francisco Giants
Born: Sept. 13, 1971 Santurce, PR
Height: 5'9" **Weight:** 185 lbs.
Bats: left **Throws:** left
Acquired: Signed as a nondrafted free agent, 1/94

Player Summary
Fantasy Value	$0
Card Value	N/A
Will	get attention
Can't	swing for fences
Expect	a tough out
Don't Expect	40 steals

Rios rates as one of the long shots on this list but, since he has come this far, why should he stop now? Just two seasons into a pro career, Rios starred in the Class-A California League last year, reaching the 50-steal plateau, finishing third in doubles, hitting for average, and driving in runs. True, he was older than many opponents, but he can't be faulted for doing well, especially when he was so short on pro experience. Rios graduated from Villa Fontana High School in Puerto Rico, and he played in the Connie Mack World Series. He attended Louisiana State University, going to the College World Series twice. He was named to the College World Series and the South Regional All-Star Teams in 1993. Rios enjoyed an exceptional July last year, hitting .419 with 15 doubles, four homers, and 22 RBI. He led his team in doubles and hits by a wide margin. He had a .424 slugging percentage and a .382 on-base average. If he gets to a higher level of pro ball, Rios will have to keep using his legs to create attention.

Professional Batting Register
	BA	G	AB	R	H	2B	3B	HR	RBI	SB
94 A	.295	119	407	67	120	23	4	8	60	16
95 A	.293	128	488	76	143	34	3	8	75	51

ROOKIE PROSPECTS

MARIANO RIVERA

Position: Pitcher
Team: New York Yankees
Born: Nov. 29, 1969 Panama City, Panama
Height: 6'2" **Weight:** 168 lbs.
Bats: right **Throws:** right
Acquired: Signed as a nondrafted free agent, 2/90

Player Summary	
Fantasy Value	$1 to $3
Card Value	N/A
Will	pitch in New York
Can't	be inconsistent
Expect	gopher balls
Don't Expect	old K ratio

Rivera has done a remarkable job of remaining a prospect considering some of the injury problems he has experienced. He was on the way to a first-class season with Fort Lauderdale of the Class-A Florida State League in 1992 when he underwent season-ending elbow surgery. His recovery limited him to just 12 appearances in 1993, but he was back a year later, posting a combined 10-2 record at three levels. He spent a stretch on the DL with a strained shoulder early in the season and was shelved with a strained left hamstring in August. Last year, Rivera shuttled between New York and Triple-A ball, getting a chance to pitch in some big games as the Yankees fought for a wild-card spot. He no longer puts up the awesome strikeout ratios that he did earlier in his career, and he's got to learn how to keep the ball in the park. Still, he has shown enough that there's a chance he could step into a bigger role in the rotation this year.

Professional Pitching Register

	W	L	ERA	G	CG	IP	H	ER	BB	SO
90 R	5	1	0.17	22	1	52.0	17	1	7	58
91 A	4	9	2.75	29	1	114.2	103	35	36	123
92 A	5	3	2.28	10	3	59.1	40	15	5	42
93 R	0	1	2.25	2	0	4.0	2	1	1	6
93 A	1	0	2.06	10	0	39.1	31	9	15	32
94 A	3	0	2.21	7	0	36.2	34	9	12	27
94 AA	3	0	2.27	9	0	63.1	58	16	8	39
94 AAA	4	2	5.81	6	1	31.0	34	20	10	23
95 AAA	2	2	2.10	7	1	30.0	25	7	3	30
95 AL	5	3	5.51	19	0	67.0	71	41	30	51

RUBEN RIVERA

Position: Outfield
Team: New York Yankees
Born: Nov. 14, 1973 Chorrera, Panama
Height: 6'3" **Weight:** 200 lbs.
Bats: right **Throws:** right
Acquired: Signed as a nondrafted free agent, 11/90

Player Summary	
Fantasy Value	$4 to $6
Card Value	$1.00 to $2.00
Will	excite the crowds
Can't	be starter right away
Expect	power and speed
Don't Expect	contact hitter

Rivera is one of the most electrifying prospects in the game, period. He can bring speed and power to a ballclub, as a string of honors will attest. He became the fourth minor-leaguer in 1995 to reach the 20-homer, 20-stolen base mark, despite a slow start in which he did not steal his first base until May 9. He notched slugging averages of .523 in Double-A and .598 in Triple-A last year. First cousin of fellow Yankee prospect Mariano Rivera, Ruben began to collect honors when he made the 1993 All-Star Team in the Class-A New York-Penn League. He then enjoyed a spectacular season in 1994, winning MVP honors in the Class-A South Atlantic League and tying the circuit's home run title. After the season, he continued to impress with his work in the Arizona Fall League. The Yankees added Rivera to their 40-man roster just four days after his 21st birthday, and they brought him up to the majors late in 1995. He could begin working his way into a role with the Yankees as early as this summer.

Professional Batting Register

	BA	G	AB	R	H	2B	3B	HR	RBI	SB
92 R	.273	53	194	37	53	10	3	1	20	21
93 A	.276	55	199	45	55	7	6	13	47	12
94 A	.281	139	534	101	150	28	6	33	101	48
95 AA	.293	71	256	49	75	16	8	9	39	16
95 AAA	.270	48	174	37	47	8	2	15	35	8
95 AL	.000	5	1	0	0	0	0	0	0	0

ROOKIE PROSPECTS

ALEX RODRIGUEZ

Position: Shortstop
Team: Seattle Mariners
Born: July 27, 1975 New York, NY
Height: 6'3" **Weight:** 190 lbs.
Bats: right **Throws:** right
Acquired: First-round pick in 6/93 free-agent draft

Player Summary	
Fantasy Value	$4 to $6
Card Value	50¢ to $1.00
Will	find his spot
Can't	worry about '95
Expect	a top player
Don't Expect	zero errors

Rodriguez was the first overall pick in the 1993 draft, and he was rushed through the Mariners system. Well, it showed. But he has since got his head squarely on his shoulders, and he should be the M's starting shortstop for many years to come. Rodriguez showed in 1995 that he can hit major-league pitching. He had an impressive .408 slugging percentage. There were down sides to his performance also. His .264 on-base average was not good, and he struck out seven times for every base on balls he took. Those numbers should improve next year, however. He is a great fielder for his age, and one shudders to think how much better he can be with the glove. In 1993, Rodriguez was a prep All-American at Westminster Christian High School in Miami, and he was a finalist for the Golden Spikes Award, given annually to the nation's top amateur player. That year, he was the first high school player ever invited to try out for the U.S. National Team. Now, all Rodriguez needs is time to develop his batting.

Professional Batting Register

	BA	G	AB	R	H	2B	3B	HR	RBI	SB
94 A	.319	65	248	49	79	17	6	14	55	16
94 AA	.288	17	59	7	17	4	1	1	8	2
94 AAA	.311	32	119	22	37	7	4	6	21	2
94 AL	.204	17	54	4	11	0	0	0	2	3
95 AAA	.360	54	214	37	77	12	3	15	45	2
95 AL	.232	48	142	15	33	6	2	5	19	4

FELIX RODRIGUEZ

Position: Pitcher
Team: Los Angeles Dodgers
Born: Dec. 5, 1972 Montecristi, Dominican Republic
Height: 6'1" **Weight:** 180 lbs.
Bats: right **Throws:** right
Acquired: Signed as a free agent, 10/89

Player Summary	
Fantasy Value	$0
Card Value	N/A
Will	be back
Can't	win without polish
Expect	exceptional arm
Don't Expect	much experience

Rodriguez got to the big leagues last year and performed without much distinction, but he still looms as a prospect because of his age and the peculiar circumstances of his career. Rodriguez has only been pitching for three years, and he still has quite a bit to learn about his new assignment. Drafted as a catcher, he spent three years as a position player. On March 20, 1993, Dodgers Manager Tommy Lasorda used Rodriguez as a pitcher in an exhibition game. He hurled a shutout inning, and soon after that was on the way to a new career. Assigned to the Class-A Florida State League, he split 16 decisions, and he hurled a no-hitter on Aug. 28. After the season, he traveled with the Dodgers to the Far East on a "Friendship Series." In 1994, Rodriguez held opposing batters to a .219 average, fourth-best among Double-A and Triple-A pitchers. Don't be surprised if Rodriguez comes back stronger this year and wins a spot in the rotation. Even so, he may be best suited to spot starting and long relief duty, which was the role that he filled last year for the Dodgers.

Professional Pitching Register

	W	L	ERA	G	CG	IP	H	ER	BB	SO
93 A	8	8	3.75	32	2	132.0	109	55	71	80
94 AA	6	8	4.03	26	0	136.1	106	61	88	126
95 AAA	3	2	4.24	14	0	51.0	52	24	26	46
95 NL	1	1	2.53	11	0	10.2	11	3	5	5

ROOKIE PROSPECTS

VICTOR RODRIGUEZ

Position: Shortstop
Team: Florida Marlins
Born: Oct. 25, 1976 Guayama, PR
Height: 6'1" **Weight:** 175 lbs.
Bats: right **Throws:** right
Acquired: Second-round pick in 6/94 free-agent draft

Player Summary	
Fantasy Value	$0
Card Value	N/A
Will	flash the leather
Can't	hit it out
Expect	utility player
Don't Expect	move to third

The Marlins liked Rodriguez enough to make him the 39th overall pick in the draft. They probably liked him even more when they saw what he did in the rookie Gulf Coast League in 1994, especially after he missed half the season with elbow surgery. Now they'll have to see if he can ever develop enough skill with the wood to let his leather reach the big leagues. Last year in the Class-A Midwest League—while admittedly very young—Rodriguez had trouble making noise at the plate. It wasn't so much his average as the fact that he collected only 10 extra-base hits in his first 449 official trips to the plate. He looked especially good in late April and early May, when he fashioned an 11-game hitting streak. However, he wrapped up the first half of the season in a 3-for-31 slide. He did take 40 bases on balls, which were almost as many as his 47 strikeouts, so he seems to know the strike zone. Unlike some young players, Rodriguez seems to have few options as to his position in the field. He doesn't have the power to move to third, and the Marlins are stocked at second. Rodriguez will probably stay in low Class-A, at least to start this season.

Professional Batting Register

	BA	G	AB	R	H	2B	3B	HR	RBI	SB
94 R	.323	24	96	13	31	2	0	0	17	2
95 A	.235	127	472	65	111	9	1	0	43	18

SCOTT ROLEN

Position: Third base
Team: Philadelphia Phillies
Born: April 4, 1975 Evansville, IN
Height: 6'4" **Weight:** 195 lbs.
Bats: right **Throws:** right
Acquired: Second-round pick in 6/93 free-agent draft

Player Summary	
Fantasy Value	$0
Card Value	15¢ to 30¢
Will	hit with power
Can't	steal bases
Expect	majors in '96
Don't Expect	more FSL

Rolen rebounded from a two-month stint on the disabled list to show why he is one of the top prospects in the Philadelphia system. Out of Jasper High School in Indiana, he is a power-hitting third baseman who will be entering his fourth year of pro ball. Playing in the Class-A Florida State League last season, he homered about once every 24 official trips to the plate, a notable total for that circuit, which has some of the hardest parks in which to hit homers in the minors. Shortly after returning from his injury, Rolen hit two home runs in a game on June 6. He homered in the 10th inning on June 21, providing a victory. Over a 17-game stretch lasting from July 19 to Aug. 6, Rolen batted .328. He hit a grand slam against Dunedin on Aug. 13. Rolen enjoyed a breakthrough season in 1994, leading Spartanburg in games and making the postseason All-Star team in the Class-A South Atlantic League. This year he likely will be appearing in Double-A, and if he hits there, a trip to the majors could eventually follow.

Professional Batting Register

	BA	G	AB	R	H	2B	3B	HR	RBI	SB
93 R	.313	25	80	8	25	5	0	0	12	3
94 A	.294	138	513	83	151	34	5	14	72	6
95 A	.290	66	238	45	69	13	2	10	39	4
95 AA	.289	20	76	16	22	3	0	3	15	1

ROOKIE PROSPECTS

JOE ROSSELLI

Position: Pitcher
Team: San Francisco Giants
Born: May 28, 1972 Burbank, CA
Height: 6'1" **Weight:** 170 lbs.
Bats: right **Throws:** left
Acquired: Fifth-round pick in 6/90 free-agent draft

Player Summary	
Fantasy Value	$0
Card Value	10¢ to 20¢
Will	get people out
Can't	stay healthy
Expect	work on mechanics
Don't Expect	lots of innings

Rosselli gets people out when he is on the mound. However, health is not always that simple. He has lost parts of two seasons to shoulder problems, and last year his absence may have been a factor in the NL West race. He comes out of Alemany High in California, where he was highly recruited as a quarterback. However, he signed with the Giants and began building an impressive résumé, with 23 wins in his first three seasons. He was named the Class-A California League Pitcher of the Year in 1992. Just as he had broken into Double-A ball, though, Rosselli felt tightness in his shoulder and eventually underwent surgery. Resuming his climb in 1994, Rosselli starred at Double-A Shreveport before being boosted to Triple-A, where he ran into elbow problems and was put on the disabled list. He was still having some problems last year when he split the season between Triple-A and the bigs. Arm permitting, Rosselli will be around in 1996.

Professional Pitching Register

	W	L	ERA	G	CG	IP	H	ER	BB	SO
90 A	4	4	4.71	15	0	78.1	87	41	29	90
91 A	8	7	3.10	22	2	153.2	144	53	49	127
92 A	11	4	2.41	22	4	149.2	145	40	46	111
93 AA	0	1	3.13	4	0	23.0	22	8	7	19
94 AA	7	2	1.89	14	2	90.2	67	19	17	54
94 AAA	1	8	4.94	13	0	74.2	96	41	15	35
95 AAA	3	4	4.99	13	1	79.1	94	44	12	34
95 NL	2	1	8.70	9	0	30.0	39	29	20	7

GLENDON RUSCH

Position: Pitcher
Team: Kansas City Royals
Born: Nov. 7, 1974 Seattle, WA
Height: 6'2" **Weight:** 170 lbs.
Bats: left **Throws:** left
Acquired: 17th-round pick in 6/93 free-agent draft

Player Summary	
Fantasy Value	$0
Card Value	10¢ to 15¢
Will	be a starter
Can't	live off no-no
Expect	great control
Don't Expect	more saves

For some pitchers, a no-hitter in the lower levels of the minors turns out to be the high point of a career. That's not the case for Rusch, who built on his 1994 masterpiece with a highly successful season in the Class-A Carolina League last year. Now he must be considered one of the top pitching prospects in the game. Out of Shorecrest High in Seattle, Rusch was only in his second pro season when he fired his gem against Kane County of the Class-A Midwest League. He faced only 28 batters, striking out 11 of them, and losing his perfect game on a two-out walk in the seventh. He went on to post the league's top ERA in August, a mere 0.93. Upon being promoted to the Carolina League last year, he became even more dominant, leading the circuit in wins and ERA and finishing second in strikeouts with 147. He held Carolina League hitters to a composite .188 batting average. Rusch was used both in the rotation and the bullpen in 1994, even picking up a save, but his future definitely seems to be as a starter.

Professional Pitching Register

	W	L	ERA	G	CG	IP	H	ER	BB	SO
93 R	4	2	1.60	11	0	62.0	43	11	11	48
93 A	0	1	3.38	2	0	8.0	10	3	7	8
94 A	8	5	4.66	28	1	114.0	111	59	34	122
95 A	14	6	1.74	26	1	165.2	110	32	34	147

ROOKIE PROSPECTS

JASON RYAN

Position: Pitcher
Team: Chicago Cubs
Born: Jan. 23, 1976 Long Branch, NJ
Height: 6'2" **Weight:** 180 lbs.
Bats: both **Throws:** right
Acquired: Ninth-round pick in 6/94 free-agent draft

Player Summary
Fantasy Value $0
Card Value .... 25¢ to 40¢
Will .... make his starts
Can't................... blow 'em away
Expect .... breeding
Don't Expect .... complete games

Ryan has some baseball in his past, and if he keeps pitching the way he did in 1994 and '95, he will have some in his future, too. Ryan is the nephew of Ed Madjeski, a catcher for the A's, White Sox, and Giants in the 1930s. And Ryan's brother Sean played in the Philadelphia organization from 1990 to 1993. Jason comes out of Immaculata High School in New Jersey, where he played baseball and basketball for four years. Shortly after being drafted, he zoomed through the lower levels of the Cub chain and reached Double-A in a single season. He fanned 11 in a five-inning rookie Gulf Coast League game. He pitched a one-hit shutout in a seven-inning Class-A Appalachian League contest, and later won Appy League Pitcher of the Week laurels for another seven-inning shutout. Upon being promoted to Double-A, Ryan won both his starts. Last year he spent the season in the Class-A Florida State League, where he was one of Daytona's top starters. He held FSL hitters to a composite .250 batting average. Ryan will see more of Double-A this year.

Professional Pitching Register

	W	L	ERA	G	CG	IP	H	ER	BB	SO
94 R	3	2	2.44	11	1	59.0	39	16	12	62
94 AA	2	0	2.45	2	0	11.0	6	3	6	12
95 A	11	5	3.48	26	0	134.2	128	52	54	98

BRIAN SACKINSKY

Position: Pitcher
Team: Baltimore Orioles
Born: June 22, 1971 Pittsburgh, PA
Height: 6'4" **Weight:** 220 lbs.
Bats: right **Throws:** right
Acquired: Second-round pick in 6/92 free-agent draft

Player Summary
Fantasy Value $0
Card Value .... N/A
Will........................... need time
Can't................... assume health
Expect .... some bullpen work
Don't Expect .... stolen bases

Sackinsky was one of the top pitchers in the Oriole organization entering last year, but elbow problems virtually wrecked the 1994 season for him. Early on, he looked as good or better than the man who finished 10th in ERA in the Double-A Eastern League in 1994. But his elbow woes took his performance downhill, and soon he was on the disabled list. He still managed to post a strikeout-to-walk ratio of better-than 4-to-1, however. Sackinsky was a four-sport letterman at South Park High School in Pennsylvania, playing basketball, baseball, football, and golf. He pitched for the U.S. Junior National Team in 1989. Drafted by the Orioles in the 39th round in 1989, he did not sign; instead he went to Stanford, where he played with Jeffrey Hammonds. He was named to the Freshman All-America team. He blossomed in 1994, his third year of pro ball, getting named Orioles Pitcher of the Month for May. He has a knack for holding runners on base; in 1994, while with Bowie, Sackinsky allowed only four stolen bases in 177 innings.

Professional Pitching Register

	W	L	ERA	G	CG	IP	H	ER	BB	SO
92 R	2	2	3.58	5	0	27.2	30	11	9	33
92 A	0	3	13.06	5	0	10.1	20	15	6	10
93 A	9	12	3.20	27	1	171.2	167	61	53	153
94 AA	11	7	3.36	28	4	177.0	165	66	39	145
95 AAA	3	3	4.60	14	0	62.2	70	32	10	42

ROOKIE PROSPECTS

DONNIE SADLER

Position: Shortstop
Team: Boston Red Sox
Born: June 17, 1975 Golhson, Texas
Height: 5'6" **Weight:** 165 lbs.
Bats: right **Throws:** right
Acquired: 11th-round pick in 6/94 free-agent draft

Player Summary
Fantasy Value	$0
Card Value	N/A
Will	stretch hits
Can't	pass Garciaparra
Expect	intimidating speed
Don't Expect	consistent power

Sadler is looking at some pretty long odds as he tries to reach the majors as a 5'6" player from the 11th round. He is behind one of the game's top shortstop prospects in Nomar Garciaparra, who appears to have what it takes to stay around a long time. But like other prospects, Sadler shouldn't worry about things he can't control. Instead, he can go out and do what he did last year for West Michigan of the Class-A Midwest League. He was impressive enough that he made you remember him. Sadler led the Red Sox farm system with 41 stolen bases, and he compiled a high .397 on-base percentage. He also put up more than respectable power numbers. He had a .438 slugging percentage, surprising for a 165-pound player. Sadler attended Valley Mills in Texas, where he participated in football, basketball, track and baseball. He signed shortly after the draft and was assigned to the rookie Gulf Coast League, where he led the team in steals, runs, triples and walks. Anyone who can run like he can will be a prospect.

JULIO SANTANA

Position: Pitcher
Team: Texas Rangers
Born: Jan. 20, 1973, San Pedro de Macoris, Dominican Republic
Height: 6' **Weight:** 175 lbs.
Bats: right **Throws:** right
Acquired: Signed as a nondrafted free agent, 2/90

Player Summary
Fantasy Value	$0
Card Value	15¢ to 25¢
Will	get another look
Can't	return to short
Expect	better adjustment
Don't Expect	mound savvy

Santana endured a rough campaign last season for the first time since he converted from shortstop to pitcher. Working at the Triple-A level for the first time, he fared so poorly that he was demoted to the low minors. He eventually forced his way back to Double-A Tulsa in the Texas League, and he turned in some good outings. On July 6, he fired a two-hitter against Jackson. Eleven days later, he pitched eight impressive innings against San Antonio. He held TL hitters to a .239 batting average in 1995, a step back from the .205 batting average TL hitters accumulated in 1994 against him. Santana comes out of that famous Dominican town that has produced so many shortstops, but he was not destined to be in that mold. In three seasons in the Dominican League, he never hit with much power or got his average above .261. Upon becoming a full-time pitcher in 1993, he led the rookie Gulf Coast League with 26 outings, all in relief. In 1994, he became a starter and zoomed through Class-A up to Tulsa.

Professional Batting Register
	BA	G	AB	R	H	2B	3B	HR	RBI	SB
94 R	.272	53	206	52	56	8	6	1	16	32
95 A	.283	118	438	103	124	25	8	9	55	41

Professional Pitching Register
	W	L	ERA	G	CG	IP	H	ER	BB	SO
93 R	4	1	1.38	26	0	39.0	31	6	7	50
94 A	6	7	2.46	16	0	91.1	65	25	44	103
94 AA	7	2	2.90	11	2	71.1	50	23	41	45
95 A	0	3	3.73	5	1	31.1	32	13	16	27
95 AA	6	4	3.23	15	3	103.0	91	37	52	71
95 AAA	0	2	39.00	2	0	3.0	9	13	7	6

ROOKIE PROSPECTS

JASON SCHMIDT

Position: Pitcher
Team: Atlanta Braves
Born: Jan. 29, 1973 Kelso, WA
Height: 6'5" **Weight:** 185 lbs.
Bats: right **Throws:** right
Acquired: Eighth-round pick in 6/91 free-agent draft

Player Summary
Fantasy Value $0
Card Value .... N/A
Will .... challenge for rotation
Can't .... keep up whiff ratio
Expect .... baserunners
Don't Expect .... complete games

Schmidt is a big right-hander who had a big year last year. He may have an even bigger future. He led the Triple-A International League with a 2.25 ERA before being summoned to Atlanta, where he made a favorable impression late in the season. A career-long starting pitcher, he might challenge for a job in the Atlanta rotation, especially considering Steve Avery's struggles last season. Schmidt, Player of the Year in Washington state out of Kelso High School, led his rookie Gulf Coast League team in strikeouts in 1991. That marked the beginning of a pattern in which Schmidt would pile up whiffs at the rate of about one per inning. Indeed, last year he fanned 12 in his first 15 major-league innings. In 1994, he struck out eight and one-third batters per nine innings, second-best ratio among Double-A Southern League starters. That year he made one playoff start and won it, allowing one run in seven and two-thirds innings. With Atlanta, Schmidt can expect to see more postseason action.

Professional Pitching Register

	W	L	ERA	G	CG	IP	H	ER	BB	SO
91 R	3	4	2.38	11	0	45.1	32	12	23	44
92 A	0	3	4.01	7	0	24.2	31	11	19	33
92 R	3	4	4.01	11	0	58.1	55	26	31	56
93 A	7	11	4.94	22	0	116.2	128	64	47	110
94 AA	8	7	3.65	24	1	140.2	135	57	54	131
95 AAA	8	6	2.25	19	0	116.0	97	29	48	95
95 NL	2	2	5.76	9	0	25.0	27	16	18	19

DAN SERAFINI

Position: Pitcher
Team: Minnesota Twins
Born: Jan. 25, 1974 San Francisco, CA
Height: 6'1" **Weight:** 180 lbs.
Bats: both **Throws:** left
Acquired: First-round pick in 6/92 free-agent draft

Player Summary
Fantasy Value $0
Card Value .... 10¢ to 20¢
Will .... throw pitches galore
Can't .... always find zone
Expect .... busy relievers
Don't Expect .... consistency

The Twins drafted Serafini about eight months after they wrapped up a World Series title, and they're hoping he can help them rebuild toward another crown. He maintained a steady pace in his development last year, tying for third in the Double-A Eastern League with 12 wins. Among them was a two-hit shutout of Norwich on May 23, which gave him three straight wins and lowered his ERA to 1.88. Hot again in late June and early July, Serafini threw seven innings of two-hit ball against New Haven on July 5, at which point he had allowed one earned run over three starts. Seven days later, he fired eight scoreless innings against Portland. He allowed Double-A hitters to compile a .258 batting average against him last year. Serafini usually throws a lot of pitches, owing to a high ratio of walks and strikeouts per nine innings. That helps explain why he hurled only one complete game in his 28 starts last year. But a lack of route-going ability is not considered a flaw nowadays, so Serafini has a chance.

Professional Pitching Register

	W	L	ERA	G	CG	IP	H	ER	BB	SO
92 R	0	3	3.64	8	0	29.2	27	12	15	33
93 A	10	8	3.65	27	0	140.2	117	57	83	147
94 A	9	9	4.61	23	2	136.2	149	70	57	130
95 AAA	0	0	6.75	1	0	4.0	4	3	1	4
95 AA	12	9	3.38	27	1	162.2	155	61	72	123

ROOKIE PROSPECTS

RICHIE SEXSON

Position: First base
Team: Cleveland Indians
Born: Dec. 29, 1974 Portland, OR
Height: 6'6" **Weight:** 206 lbs.
Bats: right **Throws:** right
Acquired: 24th-round pick in 6/93 free-agent draft

Player Summary	
Fantasy Value	$0
Card Value	N/A
Will	flash the leather
Can't	stay in Class-A
Expect	Triple Crown run
Don't Expect	lumbering giant

Sexson has now spent three years in pro ball, and in the last two he has improved over the previous season. In fact, the way he dominated in the Class-A Carolina League in 1995, you have to think that Cleveland has another star on the way. He made a spirited, though unsuccessful, bid to win the Triple Crown, leading the circuit in hits, doubles, and RBI, while finishing second in the batting race and fourth in homers. He turned in a .508 slugging percentage and a .368 on-base average. In *Baseball America*'s annual rating of tools, Sexson was named the top batting prospect, the top power prospect, and best defensive first baseman in the Carolina League. An all-state player at Prairie High School, in the state of Washington, Sexson broke into pro ball with Burlington of the rookie Appalachian League in 1993, homering only once in 97 at bats. The next season, however, he led the Cleveland farm system with 88 runs and paced Class-A South Atlantic League first basemen with 62 assists. Sexson also assembled a 19-game hitting streak.

Professional Batting Register

	BA	G	AB	R	H	2B	3B	HR	RBI	SB
93 R	.186	40	97	11	18	3	0	1	5	1
94 A	.273	130	488	88	133	25	2	14	77	7
95 A	.306	131	494	80	151	34	0	22	85	4

ALVIE SHEPHERD

Position: Pitcher
Team: Baltimore Orioles
Born: May 12, 1974 Berwyn, IL
Height: 6'7" **Weight:** 215 lbs.
Bats: left **Throws:** right
Acquired: First-round pick in 6/95 free-agent draft

Player Summary	
Fantasy Value	$0
Card Value	N/A
Will	get chance
Can't	hit like Erstad
Expect	imposing size
Don't Expect	polished product

Few clubs had more trouble with the closer position, or received a worse win-loss record from its relievers, than Baltimore did last year. The Orioles are hoping that Shepherd can help to remedy that. Coincidentally or not, he was drafted in the same year that highly regarded prospect Armando Benitez failed to seize the closer role that had been envisioned for him. But even if Benitez—at 6'4" and 220 pounds—did not work out, the Orioles apparently believe the concept of physically big closers can. Picked 21st overall, Shepherd comes out of the University of Nebraska, where he was a teammate of first overall selection Darin Erstad. Shepherd throws about as hard as his imposing size might suggest. In fact, he was rated by *Baseball America* as having the best velocity among college pitchers before the draft. Shepherd was a late sign, and so the Orioles will have to wait until this year to get a look at him as a pro. But his stats and demeanor in college suggest that he has at least all of the tools for the job.

No minor-league experience

ROOKIE PROSPECTS

BILL SIMAS

Position: Pitcher
Team: Chicago White Sox
Born: Nov. 21, 1971 Hanford, CA
Height: 6'3" **Weight:** 225 lbs.
Bats: left **Throws:** right
Acquired: Traded by Angels with McKay Christensen, Andrew Lorraine, and John Snyder for Jim Abbott and Tim Fortugno, 7/95

Player Summary	
Fantasy Value	$0
Card Value	N/A
Will	be in bullpen
Can't	close in majors
Expect	role player
Don't Expect	gopher balls

Simas came to the White Sox organization as part of the package that California sent in order to acquire Jim Abbott for the stretch run. Simas made his major-league debut against the Angels on Aug. 15, hurling a perfect inning. A starter when he began his pro career in 1992, Simas is now looking at a job in middle relief. He is a product of Fresno City College in California. He broke in with Boise of the Class-A Northwest League, going the entire season without allowing a home run. Moving on to Cedar Rapids of the Class-A Midwest League in 1993, Simas finished second on the club in saves. A year later, he split the season between Class-A and Double-A, and he was especially impressive at Midland of the Texas League. He permitted only one run in 13 appearances and opponents batted only .100 against him. After the season, he underwent arthroscopic surgery to clean out his pitching elbow. Simas looked as good as new last year.

Professional Pitching Register

	W	L	ERA	G	S	IP	H	ER	BB	SO
92 A	6	5	3.95	14	1	70.2	82	31	29	39
93 A	8	4	4.95	35	6	80.0	93	44	36	62
94 A	5	2	2.11	37	13	47.0	44	11	10	34
94 AA	2	0	0.59	13	6	15.1	5	1	2	12
95 AL	1	1	2.57	14	0	14.0	15	4	10	16
95 AAA	7	4	3.62	37	6	49.2	56	20	17	56

MIKE SIROTKA

Position: Pitcher
Team: Chicago White Sox
Born: May 13, 1971 Chicago, IL
Height: 6'1" **Weight:** 200 lbs.
Bats: left **Throws:** left
Acquired: 15th-round pick in 6/93 free-agent draft

Player Summary	
Fantasy Value	$0
Card Value	N/A
Will	give you innings
Can't	feel he's made it
Expect	strikeouts
Don't Expect	more Midwest League

Sirotka got his first taste of the majors last July, when he made a start for a White Sox staff that had been thinned by injury. He came up from Double-A ball and gave a credible start, though he wound up taking the loss. With Chicago out of the race and no pennant pressure on him, Sirotka had an ideal chance to show the stuff that took him quickly through the farm system. He didn't produce great stats, but he didn't look all that bad, either. He emerged in 1994, making 27 starts and leading the Class-A Midwest League with eight complete games. He made the league's midseason and postseason All-Star squads. He led the White Sox organization in strikeouts that year, and was also named the left-handed pitcher on the Topps/National Association Class-A All-Star Team. One year earlier, Sirotka had helped to pitch Louisiana State University to the national title. He went 2-1 during the College World Series after posting a 2-0 mark in the NCAA South Regional. Now, Sirotka looks like a contender for a spot in the White Sox rotation in 1996.

Professional Pitching Register

	W	L	ERA	G	CG	IP	H	ER	BB	SO
93 R	0	0	0.00	3	0	5.0	4	0	2	8
93 A	0	1	6.10	7	0	10.1	12	7	6	12
94 A	12	9	3.07	27	8	196.2	183	67	58	173
95 AA	7	6	3.20	16	1	101.1	95	36	22	79
95 AAA	1	5	2.83	8	0	54.0	51	17	13	41
95 AL	1	2	4.19	6	0	34.1	39	16	17	19

ROOKIE PROSPECTS

STEVE SODERSTROM

Position: Pitcher
Team: San Francisco Giants
Born: April 3, 1972 Turlock, CA
Height: 6'3" **Weight:** 205 lbs.
Bats: right **Throws:** right
Acquired: First-round pick in 6/93 free-agent draft

Player Summary	
Fantasy Value	$0
Card Value	10¢ to 15¢
Will	get better
Can't	pitch with arm trouble
Expect	success in Triple-A
Don't Expect	overuse

Soderstrom seemed to get his career firmly on track last year after being slowed by contract and injury problems. Pitching in the Double-A Texas League, he was a member of Shreveport's starting rotation and posted numbers that indicated he was healthy after arm surgery. He finished among the top San Francisco farmhands in ERA, pointing him straight toward a stop at Triple-A ball this season. He also was able to hold Texas League hitters to a .241 batting average last year. Soderstrom was the sixth overall pick in the 1993 draft, but did not sign until July 28. An inflamed elbow kept him out until late August, when he began to throw on the side. He eventually worked out with the Giants in San Francisco. Shoulder and elbow ailments shadowed him in 1994, limiting him to just eight starts. He underwent surgery to remove blood clots from his right arm, then he began his rehab with 10 outings in the Arizona Fall League. Soderstrom became the highest baseball draft pick in Fresno State University history in 1993.

Professional Pitching Register

	W	L	ERA	G	CG	IP	H	ER	BB	SO
94 A	2	3	4.20	8	0	40.2	34	19	26	40
95 AA	9	5	3.41	22	0	116.0	106	44	51	91

CLINT SODOWSKY

Position: Pitcher
Team: Detroit Tigers
Born: July 13, 1972 Ponca City, OK
Height: 6'3" **Weight:** 180 lbs.
Bats: left **Throws:** right
Acquired: 11th-round pick in 6/91 free-agent draft

Player Summary	
Fantasy Value	$0
Card Value	N/A
Will	compete
Can't	rule out rotation
Expect	occasional shutout
Don't Expect	tidy pitching lines

Sodowsky knows how to make up for lost time. After needing four seasons to get through the lower levels of the Detroit farm system, he rocketed through the final three rungs in one satisfying campaign last year. He pitched well enough at the Double-A Southern League to be named to the All-Star Team. Next he was promoted to the Triple-A International League, where he survived some wildness to win five of six decisions. Finally summoned to Detroit, he won his major-league debut by going five innings against Cleveland. Out of Connors Junior College in Oklahoma, Sodowsky showed a knack for victory in the Class-A South Atlantic League in 1993, leading Fayetteville with 14 wins even though his ERA was over 5.00. Last year, he worked a perfect inning in the Double-A All-Star Game. He finished second in the Southern League in ERA and held SL hitters to a .233 batting average. At midseason, Sodowsky was leading the league with three shutouts before he was promoted.

Professional Pitching Register

	W	L	ERA	G	CG	IP	H	ER	BB	SO
91 R	0	5	3.76	14	0	55.0	49	23	34	44
92 R	2	2	3.54	15	0	56.0	46	22	29	48
93 A	14	10	5.09	27	1	155.2	177	88	51	80
94 A	6	3	3.83	19	1	110.1	111	47	34	73
95 AA	5	5	2.55	19	5	123.2	102	35	50	77
95 AAA	5	1	2.85	9	1	60.0	47	19	30	32
95 AL	2	2	5.01	6	0	23.1	24	13	18	14

ROOKIE PROSPECTS

SCOTT SPIEZIO

Position: Third base
Team: Oakland Athletics
Born: Sept. 21, 1972 Joliet, IL
Height: 6'2" **Weight:** 195 lbs.
Bats: both **Throws:** right
Acquired: Sixth-round pick in 6/93 free-agent draft

Player Summary
Fantasy Value $0
Card Value .... 10¢ to 20¢
Will .... collect doubles
Can't .... rule out A's
Expect .... solid at bats
Don't Expect .... 30 homers

The A's have developed quite a pipeline as far as power-hitting infielders are concerned. Last year, the farm system produced Jason Giambi, who can play both first and third. Next in line may be Spiezio, who delivered a season of note in the Double-A Southern League. Spiezio proved to be an impressive slugger, leading Huntsville in doubles, triples, walks, and RBI. He finished fourth overall in the Oakland farm system in RBI, and owned more than any Oakland prospect above Class-A. Signed by Marty Miller, Spiezio comes out of Morris High School, and he attended the University of Illinois. After a get-acquainted season in which he split time between rookie and Class-A ball, Spiezio spent a full year in the Class-A California League and was voted the All-Star Game MVP. Last year, he went on a hot streak from July 14 to 30, batting .403 with 15 extra-base hits and 17 RBI. He finished the season with a .449 slugging percentage. This year, Spiezio could enjoy a feast when he gets into the Pacific Coast League.

BRIAN STEPHENSON

Position: Pitcher
Team: Chicago Cubs
Born: July 17, 1973 Fullerton, CA
Height: 6'3" **Weight:** 205 lbs.
Bats: right **Throws:** right
Acquired: Second-round pick in 6/94 free-agent draft

Player Summary
Fantasy Value $0
Card Value .... N/A
Will .... take the ball
Can't .... afford a slow start
Expect .... average stats
Don't Expect .... a No. 1 spot

Stephenson has a chance to become a third-generation major leaguer. His grandfather Joe played for the Yankees, Cubs and White Sox in the 1940s, and his father, Jerry, pitched for the Red Sox, Seattle Pilots, and Dodgers. Brian comes out of Fullerton High School in California, by way of UCLA. Among his games at UCLA was a one-hit shutout against USC when the Trojans were ranked first in the nation. Signed by Spider Jorgenson, Stephenson has done all anyone could ask in his first two years in pro ball. Last year, he pitched in the fast-track Class-A Florida State League and survived a slow start to finish with a more than respectable season. He did not pick up his first victory of the season until May 10, when he beat Brevard County. That started him on a bit of a winning streak, but he still was only 4-7 with a 4.40 ERA near midseason. He finished the season allowing FSL hitters to compile a .256 batting average against him. His strong finish can only bode well for this year, when he will likely get a chance to show what he can do at Double-A.

Professional Batting Register

	BA	G	AB	R	H	2B	3B	HR	RBI	SB
93 A	.294	63	235	44	69	19	3	4	32	1
94 A	.280	127	453	84	127	32	5	14	68	5
95 AA	.282	141	528	78	149	33	8	13	86	10

Professional Pitching Register

	W	L	ERA	G	CG	IP	H	ER	BB	SO
94 A	3	3	3.52	11	2	61.1	58	24	10	42
95 A	10	9	3.96	26	0	150.0	145	66	58	109

ROOKIE PROSPECTS

SHANNON STEWART

Position: Outfield
Team: Toronto Blue Jays
Born: Feb. 25, 1974 Cincinnati, OH
Height: 6'1" **Weight:** 190 lbs.
Bats: right **Throws:** right
Acquired: First-round pick in 6/92 free-agent draft

Player Summary	
Fantasy Value	$2 to $4
Card Value	10¢ to 20¢
Will	get on base
Can't	copy White
Expect	lots of runs
Don't Expect	a slugger

Stewart may well be the successor to center fielder Devon White in the Toronto outfield. Admittedly, it won't be an easy act to follow, but Stewart had enough raw tools to be selected 19th overall in the 1992 draft. More evidence of his ability is the fact he starred in the baseball, football, and track programs while in high school. Stewart got his feet wet in the majors last season, completing an impressive comeback from a shoulder dislocation that ended his 1994 campaign after only 56 games. He had been selected to play in the Class-A South Atlantic League All-Star Game but was unable to participate. He spent most of last year at Double-A Knoxville, where he showed an ability to draw bases on balls and turn them into runs. He had 89 walks last year, with a .398 on-base average. He also finished among the Southern League leaders in stolen bases. Stewart could turn out to offer moderate power as his frame fills out and he learns to hit in the majors. But even without power, Stewart could help most clubs.

SCOTT SULLIVAN

Position: Pitcher
Team: Cincinnati Reds
Born: March 13, 1971 Tuscaloosa, AL
Height: 6'4" **Weight:** 210 lbs.
Bats: right **Throws:** right
Acquired: Second-round pick in 6/93 free-agent draft

Player Summary	
Fantasy Value	$0
Card Value	N/A
Will	work in bullpen
Can't	get hype
Expect	occasional save
Don't Expect	a closer

Sullivan is a relief specialist whose impact will probably outweigh his buildup. That's because middle relievers or setup men seldom receive the hype that starters and closers do. However, their job is an important one, and Sullivan has shown a talent for doing it well. He pitched in Triple-A ball last year, and specialized in brief appearances. In his 44 games, he collected only 59 innings. Meanwhile, he averaged nearly one strikeout per inning, keeping with the pattern he formed in his first two years of pro ball. He also held American Association hitters to a .232 batting average last season. Sullivan comes out of Auburn University, where he fanned 71 batters in 60⅓ innings as a senior. He also had the skills to play linebacker. Upon his entry into pro ball, Sullivan allowed only five and one-half hits per nine innings. He jumped all the way to Double-A in his second season, and at one point he recorded victories in five straight outings. In 37 innings over that streak, Sullivan allowed only 23 hits.

Professional Batting Register

	BA	G	AB	R	H	2B	3B	HR	RBI	SB
92 R	.233	50	172	44	40	1	0	1	11	32
93 A	.279	75	301	53	84	15	2	3	29	25
94 A	.324	56	225	39	73	10	5	4	25	39
95 AA	.287	138	498	89	143	24	6	5	55	42
95 AL	.211	12	38	2	8	0	0	0	1	2

Professional Pitching Register

	W	L	ERA	G	S	IP	H	ER	BB	SO
93 R	5	0	1.67	18	3	54.0	33	10	25	79
94 AA	11	7	3.41	34	7	121.1	101	46	40	111
95 AAA	4	3	3.53	44	1	58.2	51	32	24	54
95 NL	0	0	4.91	3	0	3.2	4	2	2	2

ROOKIE PROSPECTS

JEFF SUPPAN

Position: Pitcher
Team: Boston Red Sox
Born: Jan. 2, 1975 Oklahoma City, OK
Height: 6'2" **Weight:** 210 lbs.
Bats: right **Throws:** right
Acquired: Second-round pick in 6/93 free-agent draft

Player Summary	
Fantasy Value	$2 to $4
Card Value	15¢ to 25¢
Will	allow homers
Can't	pitch every day
Expect	toughness
Don't Expect	Clemens' velocity

Suppan will never forget the first batter he faced in his major-league debut. It was the Kansas City Royals' Keith Lockhart, who hit a home run on the night of July 17, 1995. Things figure to be much better than that for Suppan, who became the youngest man to start a game for the Red Sox in many years. He arrived in the majors just two years after being drafted, making the jump from the Double-A Eastern League, where he held loop hitters to a .232 batting average. Suppan also turned in a better-than 3-1 strikeout-to-walk ratio. He showed his mental toughness with Sarasota of the Class-A Florida State League in 1994, rebounding from a poor start to win 13 of his last 15 decisions. He also pitched eight scoreless innings to open the FSL's Western Division playoffs. In limited duty with the Red Sox last year, Suppan appeared both as a starter and in relief. He allowed four homers in his first 19⅔ innings, a weakness he will have to address. But he has shown enough to be considered for a spot on an improving Boston staff in 1996.

Professional Pitching Register

	W	L	ERA	G	CG	IP	H	ER	BB	SO
93 R	4	3	2.18	10	2	57.2	52	14	16	64
94 A	13	7	3.26	27	4	174.0	153	63	50	173
95 AA	6	2	2.36	15	1	99.0	86	26	26	88
95 AAA	2	3	5.32	7	0	45.2	50	27	9	32
95 AL	1	2	5.96	8	0	22.2	29	15	5	19

MIKE SWEENEY

Position: Catcher
Team: Kansas City Royals
Born: July 22, 1973 Orange, CA
Height: 6'1" **Weight:** 195 lbs.
Bats: right **Throws:** right
Acquired: 10th-round pick in 6/91 free-agent draft

Player Summary	
Fantasy Value	$0
Card Value	N/A
Will	need seasoning
Can't	bottle formula
Expect	high on-base mark
Don't Expect	leg hits

After Sweeney's first two years in pro ball, it might have taken a bit of optimism to see him taking his career much further. After all, he hit a combined .219 at the lowest levels of the minors. But Sweeney learned to hit. Not only has he advanced his career, but he even received a call-up to the bigs last year. The cup of coffee capped an outstanding season in which he hit for average and power while producing an outstanding on-base percentage in the Class-A Carolina League. Sweeney finished fourth in the Kansas City farm system in batting average, and he ranked third in homers. His ratio of strikeouts to walks—60 to 39—was a marvel. A lot of players would love the formula that turned his career around, but apparently he learned something when assigned to the Florida Instructional League after his second pro campaign. He finished the season with a .424 on-base average and a .548 slugging percentage. Sweeney no doubt could use some more seasoning, but don't rule out a job in Kansas City at some point during the '96 season.

Professional Batting Register

	BA	G	AB	R	H	2B	3B	HR	RBI	SB
91 R	.216	38	102	8	22	3	0	1	11	1
92 A	.221	59	199	17	44	12	1	4	28	3
93 A	.240	53	175	32	42	10	2	6	29	1
94 A	.301	86	276	47	83	20	3	10	52	0
95 A	.310	99	332	61	103	23	1	18	53	6
95 AL	.250	4	4	1	1	0	0	0	0	0

ROOKIE PROSPECTS

ANDY TAULBEE

Position: Pitcher
Team: San Francisco Giants
Born: Oct. 5, 1972 Atlanta, GA
Height: 6'4" **Weight:** 215 lbs.
Bats: right **Throws:** right
Acquired: Second-round pick in 6/94 free-agent draft

Player Summary	
Fantasy Value	$0
Card Value	N/A
Will	allow hits
Can't	forget debut
Expect	balls in play
Don't Expect	overpowering stuff

Taulbee will probably never forget his professional debut; his club was no-hit by Dodgers prospect Kym Ashworth. But if all goes well, Taulbee himself could be registering some memorable performances. He comes out of Clemson University, where he compiled a 27-8 mark over four years. He was a freshman on the 1991 team that went to the College World Series. As a sophomore, he was named to the ACC All-Tournament squad. After his junior year, he played in the Cape Cod League. Finally, in 1994, he went 12-4 with a 3.61 ERA, helping the Tigers to the ACC title. Taulbee broke into pro ball with San Jose of the Class-A California League in 1994, and was especially effective in late July, allowing only two earned runs over a span of three starts. Last year, he started with San Jose and was successful, holding California League hitters to a .226 batting average in 10 games. He was then promoted up to the Double-A Texas League, compiling the fifth-best ERA in the San Francisco chain. He'll likely start this season in Double-A, with hopes of a quick rise.

Professional Pitching Register

	W	L	ERA	G	CG	IP	H	ER	BB	SO
94 A	4	3	2.66	13	0	71.0	66	21	20	51
95 A	3	2	3.02	10	1	62.2	50	21	22	33
95 AA	4	5	3.95	14	1	86.2	107	38	27	38

REGGIE TAYLOR

Position: Outfield
Team: Philadelphia Phillies
Born: Jan. 12, 1977 Newberry, SC
Height: 6'1" **Weight:** 185 lbs.
Bats: left **Throws:** right
Acquired: First-round pick in 6/95 free-agent draft

Player Summary	
Fantasy Value	$0
Card Value	N/A
Will	bring tools
Can't	sit back
Expect	some brilliance
Don't Expect	quick rise

Out of Newberry High School in South Carolina, Taylor has the kind of tools that will impress any talent-hunter. He can run and throw, has nice size, and may even grow a bit more. In his scholastic career, Taylor showed both power and the ability to steal bases. The Phillies liked the total package so much that they called Taylor's name with the 14th overall pick. Assigned to the Phillies' rookie team in Martinsville of the Appalachian League, he got off to a slow start, hitting .180 in his first 12 games. But he eventually came around to show some of his ability. In 12 games from July 25 to Aug. 4, he hit .326. Taylor wound up leading the ballclub in triples and stolen bases, was second in RBI, and finished third in runs scored. On a less positive note, he led his team in whiffs, fanning about once every four official trips. He had 58 punchouts opposed to 23 bases on balls. The Phillies will most likely give Taylor a year of full-season ball at low Class-A, but his talent could take over very quickly.

Professional Batting Register

	BA	G	AB	R	H	2B	3B	HR	RBI	SB
95 R	.222	64	239	36	53	4	6	2	32	18

ROOKIE PROSPECTS

AMAURY TELEMACO

Position: Pitcher
Team: Chicago Cubs
Born: Jan. 19, 1974 Higuey, Dominican Republic
Height: 6'3" **Weight:** 210 lbs.
Bats: right **Throws:** right
Acquired: Signed as a nondrafted free agent, 5/91

Player Summary	
Fantasy Value	$0
Card Value	10¢ to 15¢
Will	be a starter
Can't	be inconsistent
Expect	strikeouts
Don't Expect	low pitch counts

Telemaco has been a member of the Cubs organization since he was 17 years old. After five years in the system, he could be ready to make a contribution at Wrigley Field. Last year he did his work at Orlando, where he collected 151 strikeouts, most in the chain and second in the Double-A Southern League. It was not the first time Telemaco had dominated the strikeout category. In his first year in North America, he paced the rookie Appalachian League with 93 in only 76 innings. In 1994, he was tied for the Class-A Florida State League lead in victories, and he was fourth in strikeouts when promoted to Double-A. Last year, Telemaco started well, picking up a Pitcher of the Week award in early July, but went 0-2 with a 6.30 ERA from July 31 to Aug. 15. He seemed to right himself near the end, if a four-hit shutout against Huntsville on Aug. 21 is any indication. If he can iron out some of his tendency toward inconsistency, Telemaco could be challenging for a job in Chicago later this summer.

Professional Pitching Register

	W	L	ERA	G	CG	IP	H	ER	BB	SO
92 R	3	5	4.01	12	2	76.1	71	34	17	93
92 A	0	1	7.94	2	0	5.2	9	5	5	5
93 A	8	11	3.45	23	3	143.2	129	55	54	133
94 A	7	3	3.40	11	2	76.2	62	29	23	59
94 AA	3	5	3.45	12	2	62.2	56	24	20	49
95 AA	8	8	3.29	22	3	147.2	112	54	42	151

JASON THOMPSON

Position: First base
Team: San Diego Padres
Born: June 13, 1971 Orlando, FL
Height: 6'4" **Weight:** 190 lbs.
Bats: left **Throws:** left
Acquired: Ninth-round pick in 6/93 free-agent draft

Player Summary	
Fantasy Value	$0
Card Value	30¢ to 50¢
Will	hit for extra bases
Can't	steal bases
Expect	some wild swings
Don't Expect	Pads in April

Thompson, like fellow farmhand Derrek Lee, is aiming to become San Diego's next first baseman. Thompson's first three years as a pro give every indication he can do it. He played in Double-A ball last season and tied for third in the Southern League with 20 home runs. A member of the All-Star Team, Thompson appeared in the Double-A midsummer classic and went 1-for-2 with an RBI. He also hit at least 20 doubles for the third time in as many pro seasons. He showed some patience at the dish, notching 62 bases on balls. Thompson comes out of Laguna Hills High School in California and attended the University of Arizona. He enjoyed an exceptional pro debut, leading the Class-A Northwest League with 25 doubles and finishing second with a .500 slugging percentage. In 1994, he split time between Class-A and Double-A ball, passing the 100-RBI plateau. Unfortunately, he also struck out 135 times in 468 official at bats. Thompson will have to keep working on that this year, probably at Triple-A, or maybe even in San Diego.

Professional Batting Register

	BA	G	AB	R	H	2B	3B	HR	RBI	SB
93 A	.300	66	240	36	72	25	1	7	38	3
94 A	.360	68	253	57	91	19	2	13	61	4
94 AA	.260	63	215	35	56	17	2	8	46	0
95 AA	.272	137	475	62	129	20	1	20	64	7

ROOKIE PROSPECTS

MICHAEL TUCKER

Position: Outfield
Team: Kansas City Royals
Born: June 25, 1971 South Boston, VA
Height: 6'2" **Weight:** 185 lbs.
Bats: left **Throws:** right
Acquired: First-round pick in 6/92 free-agent draft

Player Summary	
Fantasy Value	$3 to $5
Card Value	15¢ to 25¢
Will	need big year
Can't	play second
Expect	some pop
Don't Expect	many swipes

Tucker is facing a big year in 1996, after accomplishing all that he can on the minor-league level. He got a brief look at the majors last year in the heat of a wild-card race, but he was something less than a force. With other talents, such as Johnny Damon, ready to step in, the onus is on Tucker to show what he can do. Out of Longwood College, Tucker was a finalist for the Golden Spikes Award given to the nation's outstanding college baseball player. He performed for the 1992 U.S. Olympic Team, where he hit .291 and led the squad with 28 steals. Tucker broke into pro ball in 1993 with Wilmington of the Class-A Carolina League, and was promoted to Double-A on June 15. A nonroster invitee to spring training in 1994, he spent the year in Triple-A. There he made the transition from second base to the outfield. Tucker has shown some ability to hit for power, and may steal a base, but not at the rate he did in college or with the national team. He did have a .444 slugging percentage in Triple-A last year, and a .384 slugging mark in the majors.

Professional Batting Register

	BA	G	AB	R	H	2B	3B	HR	RBI	SB
93 A	.305	61	239	42	73	14	2	6	44	12
93 AA	.279	72	244	38	68	7	4	9	35	12
94 AAA	.276	132	489	75	134	16	7	21	77	11
95 AAA	.305	71	275	37	84	18	4	4	28	11
95 AL	.260	62	177	23	46	10	0	4	17	2

UGIE URBINA

Position: Pitcher
Team: Montreal Expos
Born: Feb. 15, 1974 Caracas, Venezuela
Height: 6'2" **Weight:** 185 lbs.
Bats: right **Throws:** right
Acquired: Signed as a nondrafted free agent, 11/90

Player Summary	
Fantasy Value	$1
Card Value	10¢ to 15¢
Will	get another chance
Can't	duplicate '93
Expect	knack for wins
Don't Expect	minor leagues

Urbina got his first look at the major leagues last year, and he wasn't quite ready. But that doesn't reflect poorly on his long-range chances. He's still only 22, and he pitched well in Triple-A last year. He held International League hitters to a .191 batting average. In 1994, he received the tragic news that his father had been shot to death during a robbery in his home in Caracas. After a three-week leave of absence, he returned to close out an impressive season in the Eastern League. With runners in scoring position, Urbina allowed opponents only a .163 batting average. A onetime member of Venezuela's junior national team, Urbina stamped himself as one of Montreal's top prospects when he went 10-1 in 16 starts in the Class-A Midwest League in 1993. Promoted to Harrisburg later that year, Urbina earned Eastern League Pitcher of the Week honors for July 5 to 11. Expect to see him contend for a job on the Montreal staff this season.

Professional Pitching Register

	W	L	ERA	G	CG	IP	H	ER	BB	SO
91 R	3	3	2.29	10	3	63.0	58	16	10	51
92 A	7	13	3.22	24	5	142.1	111	51	54	100
93 A	10	1	1.99	16	4	108.1	78	24	36	107
93 AA	4	5	3.99	11	3	70.0	63	31	32	45
94 AA	9	3	3.28	21	0	120.2	96	44	43	86
95 A	1	0	0.00	2	0	9.0	4	0	1	11
95 AAA	6	2	3.04	13	2	68.0	46	23	26	55
95 NL	2	2	6.17	7	0	23.1	26	16	14	15

ROOKIE PROSPECTS

PEDRO VALDES

Position: Outfield
Team: Chicago Cubs
Born: June 29, 1973 Fajardo, PR
Height: 6'1" **Weight:** 170 lbs.
Bats: left **Throws:** left
Acquired: 13th-round pick in 6/90 free-agent draft

Player Summary	
Fantasy Value	$0
Card Value	N/A
Will	be role player
Can't	stay in Double-A
Expect	outfield ability
Don't Expect	big power

Valdes does not project as a major-league star, but he could have a future as a useful role player. An outfielder, he can also fill in at first base, and he can hit for average from the left side of the plate. He doesn't figure to steal many bases or hit a bunch of home runs, but he can deliver a line drive in a key spot. Valdes attended Carlos Escober High School in Loiza, Puerto Rico, and pitched in the 1990 Connie Mack World Series. With Geneva of the Class-A New York-Penn League in 1992, he assembled an 11-game hitting streak. In the Class-A Midwest League a year later, Valdes set a Peoria team record by hitting in 18 consecutive games. He earned a promotion to the Class-A Florida State League that year. In 1994, Valdes got his first look at Double-A ball, and fit in nicely. He spent his second straight year in Double-A last season, and again he hit for average. He also had a .430 slugging average. But another year there would speak poorly for his chances. Valdes will have to break through to Triple-A.

Professional Batting Register

	BA	G	AB	R	H	2B	3B	HR	RBI	SB
91 R	.289	49	152	17	44	11	1	0	16	5
92 A	.260	99	366	35	95	17	0	5	44	4
93 A	.302	125	464	60	140	27	2	15	85	5
94 AA	.282	116	365	39	103	14	4	1	37	2
95 AA	.300	114	426	57	128	28	3	7	68	3

JASON VARITEK

Position: Catcher
Team: Seattle Mariners
Born: April 11, 1972 Rochester, MI
Height: 6'2" **Weight:** 210 lbs.
Bats: both **Throws:** right
Acquired: First-round pick in 6/94 free-agent draft

Player Summary	
Fantasy Value	$0
Card Value	30¢ to 50¢
Will	be in headlines
Can't	make up lost time
Expect	challenge from Widger
Don't Expect	another off-year

Varitek became a distinctive and somewhat controversial figure in 1993 when he declined to sign after the Minnesota Twins made him the 21st overall pick in the draft. He held out for a year, went back into the draft, and wound up as the Mariners' 14th overall pick in 1994. Even then, he wasn't an easy sign. When Varitek finally did put his name on the dotted line, some effects of the layoff really showed, as his statistics in the Double-A Southern League indicate. He had 61 bases on balls, with 125 strikeouts, and that gave him a .340 on-base average. He also had a .361 slugging percentage. All the evidence suggests that Varitek can enjoy a fine career in pro ball, getting to the majors rather quickly. As one reflection of his top prospect status, he was scheduled to take part in last year's Arizona Fall League. Despite the lofty regard in which he is held, however, Varitek faces competition from Chris Widger, a 24-year-old receiver who spent some time in the majors last year. It will be interesting to see how this battle winds up.

Professional Batting Register

	BA	G	AB	R	H	2B	3B	HR	RBI	SB
95 AA	.224	104	352	42	79	14	2	10	44	0

ROOKIE PROSPECTS

ANDREW VESSEL

Position: Outfield
Team: Texas Rangers
Born: March 11, 1975 Richmond, CA
Height: 6'3" **Weight:** 210 lbs.
Bats: right **Throws:** right
Acquired: Third-round pick in 6/93 free-agent draft

Player Summary	
Fantasy Value	$0
Card Value	N/A
Will	catch the ball
Can't	regain K habit
Expect	run producer
Don't Expect	top basestealer

Vessel proved to be quite a run-producer for a young man of 20 years old last year, finishing third in the fast-track Class-A Florida State League with 78 RBI. He also tied for second on the team in home runs and doubles. But the most hopeful sign in his development is the way in which he addressed the issue of making contact. In 1994, while in the Class-A South Atlantic League, Vessel struck out 102 times in 411 official trips to the plate. Last year, despite playing against tougher competition, he fanned only 75 times in almost 500 at bats, while walking slightly more often, 32 times. This adjustment, at such an early age, suggests a very high ceiling for Vessel. His biggest day of the year occurred on Aug. 5 at Tampa, when he went 5-for-6 with a grand slam. He finished with a .380 slugging percentage. Out of John F. Kennedy High School in Richmond, California, Vessel was a prep All-American in football and baseball. In his first full year of pros, he committed only one error in 111 games in the outfield.

Professional Batting Register

	BA	G	AB	R	H	2B	3B	HR	RBI	SB
93 R	.219	51	192	23	42	10	2	1	31	6
94 A	.241	114	411	40	99	23	2	8	55	7
95 A	.265	129	498	67	132	26	2	9	78	3

JOE VITIELLO

Position: Outfield; first base
Team: Kansas City Royals
Born: April 11, 1970 Cambridge, MA
Height: 6'2" **Weight:** 215 lbs.
Bats: right **Throws:** right
Acquired: First-round pick in 6/91 free-agent draft

Player Summary	
Fantasy Value	$5 to $7
Card Value	15¢ to 25¢
Will	show some power
Can't	worry about knee
Expect	improved contact
Don't Expect	a hint of speed

After leading the American Association with a .344 batting average and .440 on-base percentage in 1994, Vitiello spent most of his rookie season as a right-handed DH and reserve first baseman with the Royals. He showed good power but did not show the same patience at the plate that he had in the minors. The one-time University of Alabama star fanned three times per walk. He hit lefties well (.278) but struggled against right-handers (.224). A three-sport star in high school, Vitiello played the outfield in college before moving to first in the minors. After *Baseball America* named him the best power-hitting collegian available, he was the seventh overall pick in the amateur draft of June 1991. Vitiello attracted attention when he uncorked a 23-game hitting streak on the Triple-A level two years ago. He's always been considered a solid contact hitter. Because he lacks speed, Vitiello is better off as a first baseman or DH than he is as an outfielder. A 1994 knee injury limited his mobility even more.

Professional Batting Register

	BA	G	AB	R	H	2B	3B	HR	RBI	SB
91 A	.328	19	64	16	21	2	0	6	21	1
91 AA	.219	36	128	15	28	4	1	0	18	0
92 A	.285	115	400	52	114	16	1	8	65	0
93 AA	.288	117	413	62	119	25	2	15	66	2
94 AAA	.344	98	352	46	121	28	3	10	61	3
95 AL	.254	53	130	13	33	4	0	7	21	0
95 AAA	.279	59	229	33	64	14	2	12	42	0

ROOKIE PROSPECTS

TERRELL WADE

Position: Pitcher
Team: Atlanta Braves
Born: Jan. 25, 1973 Rembert, SC
Height: 6'3" **Weight:** 205 lbs.
Bats: left **Throws:** left
Acquired: Signed as a nondrafted free agent, 6/91

Player Summary	
Fantasy Value	$0
Card Value	20¢ to 30¢
Will	overpower people
Can't	succeed behind in count
Expect	toughness
Don't Expect	finesse

Wade leveled off last year, turning in only mediocre numbers after two dominating campaigns at the lower levels. He still has not learned how to throw strikes consistently, and it's hurting him more than it did against hitters in Class-A and Double-A. Also, Wade managed only one complete game in 23 starts in the Triple-A International League, a disappointingly low total even in an era when the complete game seems completely out of style. Still, at age 23, Wade remains an intriguing prospect who can give hitters a lot of trouble. In 1994, he earned honors as Pitcher of the Month for Double-A Greenville, going 3-1 en route to a berth on the All-Star team. When promoted to Triple-A Richmond, he held hitters to a .130 average when runners were in scoring position. In 1993, he earned the Phil Niekro Award as top minor-league pitcher in the organization. Wade is out of Hillcrest High School in South Carolina.

Professional Pitching Register

	W	L	ERA	G	CG	IP	H	ER	BB	SO
91 R	2	0	6.26	10	0	23.0	29	16	15	22
92 R	1	4	6.44	13	0	50.1	59	36	42	54
93 A	10	3	2.17	19	0	116.1	83	28	54	168
93 AA	1	1	3.21	8	1	42.0	32	15	29	40
94 AA	9	3	3.83	21	0	105.2	87	45	58	105
94 AAA	2	2	2.63	4	0	24.0	23	7	15	26
95 AAA	10	9	4.56	24	1	142.0	137	72	63	124
95 NL	0	1	4.50	3	0	4.0	3	2	4	3

BILLY WAGNER

Position: Pitcher
Team: Houston Astros
Born: June 25, 1971 Tannersville, VA
Height: 5'11" **Weight:** 180 lbs.
Bats: left **Throws:** left
Acquired: First-round pick in 6/93 free-agent draft

Player Summary	
Fantasy Value	$3 to $5
Card Value	30¢ to 40¢
Will	blow people away
Can't	match '94 stats
Expect	strikeouts
Don't Expect	a tall guy

Wagner made it to the big leagues last season, just a little over two years after becoming a first-rounder. He came into a game in New York and retired the only batter he faced. From that small beginning could come a career of note. Wagner rates as one of the game's top prospects, a hard thrower who in 1994 led all of professional baseball with 204 strikeouts. On seven different occasions, he fanned 11 or more. In one game, he sent 14 back to the dugout in just six innings against Springfield. Wagner struck out an average of 12 men per nine innings, allowing just under six hits, in being named to the Class-A Midwest League All-Star team. He comes out of Ferrum College, where he compiled a 17-3 mark over three seasons. He was named a 1993 All-American, and set an NCAA record for single-season strikeouts per nine innings. Last year, in the minors, he had a strikeout-to-walk ratio of exactly two and one-half to one. Wagner could challenge for a job in the Houston rotation this year, but he could also make the team in the bullpen.

Professional Pitching Register

	W	L	ERA	G	CG	IP	H	ER	BB	SO
93 A	1	3	4.08	7	0	28.2	25	13	25	31
94 A	8	9	3.29	26	2	153.0	99	56	91	204
95 AA	2	2	2.57	12	0	70.0	49	20	36	77
95 AAA	5	3	3.18	13	0	76.1	70	27	32	80
95 NL	0	0	0.00	1	0	0.1	0	0	0	0

ROOKIE PROSPECTS

BRET WAGNER

Position: Pitcher
Team: St. Louis Cardinals
Born: April 17, 1973 New Cumberland, PA
Height: 6′ **Weight:** 190 lbs.
Bats: left **Throws:** left
Acquired: First-round pick in 6/94 free-agent draft

Player Summary	
Fantasy Value	$0
Card Value	15¢ to 20¢
Will	allow few hits
Can't	win with soreness
Expect	ERA leader
Don't Expect	30 starts

In 1993, the Cardinals made a first-round pick of Alan Benes, a hard-throwing college pitcher who adapted quickly to pro ball and rose through the ranks. It's the Cardinals' good fortune that the same formula seems to be working in the case of Wagner. He pitched at two different levels last year and did reasonably well at both of them, even though he spent some time on the disabled list with shoulder trouble. His combined ERA of 2.42 placed him second among all Cardinal farmhands. He opened the season with St. Petersburg of the Class-A Florida State League, and he eventually was moved up to Double-A Arkansas. He gave an early-season hint of his stuff when he went seven innings against Kissimmee and faced only one batter over the minimum in a no-decision. After coming off the shelf, he registered five scoreless innings against Vero Beach. He held Florida State League hitters to a .228 batting average last year. This year, if his health permits, Wagner could blossom into a big winner.

Professional Pitching Register

	W	L	ERA	G	CG	IP	H	ER	BB	SO
94 A	4	2	2.09	10	0	56.1	37	13	10	53
95 A	5	4	2.12	17	1	93.1	77	22	28	59
95 AA	1	2	3.19	6	0	36.2	34	13	18	31

MATT WAGNER

Position: Pitcher
Team: Seattle Mariners
Born: April 4, 1972 Cedar Falls, IA
Height: 6′5″ **Weight:** 215 lbs.
Bats: right **Throws:** right
Acquired: Third-round pick in 6/94 free-agent draft

Player Summary	
Fantasy Value	$0
Card Value	N/A
Will	stay on fast track
Can't	worry about stats
Expect	Triple-A
Don't Expect	walks

When you look at the results of Wagner's first peek at Triple-A ball last year, you might wonder why he's included as a top prospect. But that would be the worst measuring stick to employ. First of all, the Pacific Coast League is a hitter's circuit. And second, Wagner was just a season removed from the draft, having zoomed from low Class-A to Double-A and finally to Triple-A. It's much better to focus on one stat in Wagner's 23 starts in the Double-A Southern League—he walked only 33 batters in 137 innings. That alone gives him a chance to win, once he gets fully acclimated to pro ball. He also held Double-A hitters to a .232 batting average. Another indication of his chances is the fact that Seattle used him in the Hall of Fame game in Cooperstown in 1994. He fired three innings of one-hit relief and picked up the victory. Wagner went to the University of Arkansas and Iowa State University, and picked up All-Big Eight honors in 1994. Upon turning pro, he had a 6-1 strikeout-to-walk ratio at Appleton in the Class-A Midwest League.

Professional Pitching Register

	W	L	ERA	G	CG	IP	H	ER	BB	SO
94 A	4	2	0.83	15	0	32.2	23	3	8	48
95 AA	5	8	2.82	23	0	137.0	121	43	33	111
95 AAA	1	5	6.27	6	1	33.0	43	23	17	33

ROOKIE PROSPECTS

TODD WALKER

Position: Infield
Team: Minnesota Twins
Born: May 25, 1973 Bakersfield, CA
Height: 6′ **Weight:** 170 lbs.
Bats: left **Throws:** right
Acquired: First-round pick in 6/94 free-agent draft

Player Summary
Fantasy Value	$4 to $6
Card Value	70¢ to $1.25
Will	hit with punch
Can't	win Triple Crown
Expect	20-20 man
Don't Expect	easy out

Few organizations had the quality of second basemen at the high levels that Minnesota did last year. In the majors, they wrote Chuck Knoblauch's name into the lineup card, while at Double-A, Walker was waiting for a shot. He made good use of his time in the Eastern League, hitting for average while becoming a 20-20 man in homers and stolen bases. He had a .478 slugging average, thanks to the extra bases he garnered on about 35 percent of his base hits last year. The eighth overall pick in 1994, Walker was all-state in soccer and the Louisiana Baseball Player of the Year in his senior season. He attended LSU, where he was a three-time All-American. He set a Southeastern Conference record in his sophomore year by hitting in 33 straight games. He narrowly missed the SEC Triple Crown, leading in homers and RBI and finishing second in batting. In his first pro season, Walker had 15 multihit games in just 46 contests, never going more than two games without a hit. He compiled a .532 slugging percentage and a .406 on-base average that year.

Professional Batting Register
	BA	G	AB	R	H	2B	3B	HR	RBI	SB
94 A	.304	46	171	29	52	5	2	10	34	6
95 AA	.290	137	513	83	149	27	3	21	85	23

DARYLE WARD

Position: First base
Team: Detroit Tigers
Born: June 27, 1975 Lynwood, CA
Height: 6′2″ **Weight:** 240 lbs.
Bats: left **Throws:** left
Acquired: 15th-round pick in 6/94 free-agent draft

Player Summary
Fantasy Value	$0
Card Value	15¢ to 20¢
Will	drive in runs
Can't	move to outfield
Expect	promotion in 1996
Don't Expect	wild swings

If Ward's first two years of pro ball are any indication, the Tigers are well insured against the day that Cecil Fielder is no longer the Detroit first baseman. Out of Rancho Santiago Junior College, Ward hit for power in rookie ball in 1994. Promoted to the Class-A South Atlantic League last year, he showed no signs of difficulty adjusting to the higher level. In fact, he became a sensation, leading the Tigers organization in RBI by a wide margin at midseason and finishing second in the league with 106 ribbies. Ward looks like he will be a run-producer first and a home run hitter second. Even better, he makes reasonable contact for a 20-year-old. Because of his great size, he is probably locked in at first base. He does seem to have enough talent with the leather to be an initial sacker. He will make it as a first baseman, or as a designated hitter, or not at all. He is looking at Tony Clark, another power-hitting first baseman, ahead of him in the Tigers' chain. But if Ward keeps producing runs, a spot will open for him.

Professional Batting Register
	BA	G	AB	R	H	2B	3B	HR	RBI	SB
94 R	.267	48	161	17	43	6	0	5	30	4
95 A	.284	137	524	75	149	32	0	14	106	1

ROOKIE PROSPECTS

JEFF WARE

Position: Pitcher
Team: Toronto Blue Jays
Born: Nov. 11, 1970 Norfolk, VA
Height: 6'3" **Weight:** 190 lbs.
Bats: right **Throws:** right
Acquired: Supplemental second-round pick in 6/91 free-agent draft

Player Summary
Fantasy Value	$0
Card Value	N/A
Will	compete for spot
Can't	afford more injuries
Expect	better things
Don't Expect	durability

Ware made it to the major leagues last year, completing a comeback from injuries that knocked him out for all of the 1993 season and parts of another. Unfortunately, he had about as much success in Toronto as most of the other Blue Jay pitchers did, which is to say not much at all. Over his first five big-league outings, all of them starts, he compiled an ERA over 5.00. He walked more batters than he struck out, and he allowed lefties to hit over .300 against him. Still, the Blue Jays hope to improve this year, with Ware being part of the recipe for success. The 35th overall selection in 1991, Ware attended Old Dominion, where he earned third-team All-America honors. He pitched for the United States in the 1991 Pan-Am Games. Ware turned pro with Dunedin of the Class-A Florida State League in 1992, going 4-1 with a 1.99 ERA in six May starts. Rehab for a sore shoulder put him out for 1993, and an elbow injury kept him out of the 1994 campaign until July 9. The Blue Jays were able to pick Ware as compensation for the White Sox signing George Bell.

Professional Pitching Register
	W	L	ERA	G	CG	IP	H	ER	BB	SO
92 A	5	3	2.63	12	1	75.1	64	22	30	49
94 AA	0	7	6.87	10	0	38.0	50	29	16	31
95 AAA	7	0	3.00	16	0	75.0	62	25	46	76
95 AL	2	1	5.47	5	0	26.1	28	16	21	18

JOHN WASDIN

Position: Pitcher
Team: Oakland Athletics
Born: Aug. 5, 1972 Fort Belvoir, VA
Height: 6'2" **Weight:** 190 lbs.
Bats: right **Throws:** right
Acquired: First-round pick in 6/93 free-agent draft

Player Summary
Fantasy Value	$0
Card Value	30¢ to 50¢
Will	put it over
Can't	worry about ERA
Expect	reliable starter
Don't Expect	complete games

You'd never know it to look at his ERA, but Wasdin enjoyed a pretty good year last season. And the fact that he reached the majors, and that he delivered some nice innings there, made his campaign all the more enjoyable. Working in Edmonton, Wasdin finished third in the Triple-A Pacific Coast League with 12 wins and 111 Ks. Only one A's farmhand, Bobby Chouinard, had more wins than did Wasdin. He flirted with a perfect game May 27, retiring the first 20 batters. In short, he came back nicely after being rocked for seven runs in three innings in his first Triple-A start. When promoted to the majors, Wasdin compiled a 2.51 ERA in his first four appearances before suffering an ineffective start against the Angels on the last weekend of the season. A graduate of Florida State who throws with nearly uncanny control, Wasdin had a fine campaign in 1994 in the Double-A Southern League. He was named that loop's No. 4 prospect by *Baseball America*. Wasdin could be competing for a job in Oakland's starting rotation in 1996.

Professional Pitching Register
	W	L	ERA	G	CG	IP	H	ER	BB	SO
93 R	0	0	3.00	1	0	3.0	3	1	0	1
93 A	2	6	2.37	12	0	64.2	49	17	13	51
94 A	3	1	1.69	6	0	26.2	17	5	5	30
94 AA	12	3	3.43	21	0	141.2	126	54	29	108
95 AAA	12	8	5.52	29	2	174.1	193	107	38	111
95 AL	1	1	4.67	5	0	17.1	14	9	3	6

ROOKIE PROSPECTS

PAT WATKINS

Position: Outfield
Team: Cincinnati Reds
Born: Sept. 2, 1972, Raleigh, NC
Height: 6'2" **Weight:** 185 lbs.
Bats: right **Throws:** right
Acquired: Supplemental second-round pick in 6/93 free-agent draft

Player Summary
Fantasy Value $0
Card Value .... 15¢ to 30¢
Will.................... hit with power
Can't .... crack Reds yet
Expect............. deliberate progress
Don't Expect .... another demotion

Watkins was drafted between the first and second rounds in 1993 with a pick awarded as compensation for the loss of free agent Greg Swindell. Watkins is a multitalented athlete whose skills were amply demonstrated when he narrowly missed being a 30-homer, 30-steal man in the Class-A Carolina League in 1994. He also showed enough ability in the outfield to be a center fielder. He didn't enjoy quite that amount of success last year, though on balance his season turned out well. Assigned to Double-A, Watkins began the season in Chattanooga's outfield, but slumped. Over one seven-game stretch in April, he hit .074 with eight strikeouts. He soon found himself back in Class-A, where he began to regain his stroke. Once again in Double-A, Watkins hit .400 over a 15-game stretch through June 18. He homered in three consecutive games July 22 to 24. That was part of a 16-game stretch over which he batted .367 with seven doubles and seven homers. The talent is still there, and Watkins's stumble shouldn't hurt at all.

Professional Batting Register

	BA	G	AB	R	H	2B	3B	HR	RBI	SB
93 R	.238	66	235	46	63	10	3	6	30	15
94 A	.290	132	524	107	152	24	5	27	83	31
95 A	.206	27	107	14	22	3	1	4	13	1
95 AA	.291	105	358	57	104	26	2	12	57	5

CHRIS WIDGER

Position: Catcher
Team: Seattle Mariners
Born: May 21, 1971 Wilmington, DE
Height: 6'3" **Weight:** 195 lbs.
Bats: right **Throws:** right
Acquired: Third-round pick in 6/92 free-agent draft

Player Summary
Fantasy Value $0
Card Value .... 15¢ to 30¢
Will .... hit home runs
Can't............ beat playoff experience
Expect .... versatility
Don't Expect............. strikeout king

Widger may be the Mariners' next catcher, and as early as this season. He received some important experience last year when he not only got his first chance to play in the big leagues, but also tasted life in the playoffs. He shows every sign of being a power-hitting receiver, especially in a park like the Kingdome. Strong—as shown by the fact he was a high school wrestler—Widger averaged roughly one homer per 20 official at bats while playing in Triple-A Tacoma. Widger began his pro career with Bellingham of the Northwest League, leading the circuit's receivers with a .987 fielding average. Promoted to Class-A in 1993, he batted .294 with five homers in four games during the California League playoffs. In 1994, Widger played for Jacksonville and was selected to play in the Double-A All-Star Game. He showed some versatility, playing first base and the outfield as well as catcher. That should give Widger an edge. Dan Wilson had a fine year as the Mariners catcher last year, but Widger could step in as Wilson's back-up.

Professional Batting Register

	BA	G	AB	R	H	2B	3B	HR	RBI	SB
92 A	.259	51	166	28	43	7	2	5	30	8
93 A	.264	97	360	44	95	28	2	9	58	5
94 AA	.260	116	388	58	101	15	3	16	59	8
95 AAA	.276	50	174	29	48	11	1	9	21	0
95 AL	.200	23	45	2	9	0	0	1	2	0

ROOKIE PROSPECTS

KEITH WILLIAMS

Position: Outfield
Team: San Francisco Giants
Born: April 21, 1972, Bedford, PA
Height: 6′ **Weight:** 190 lbs.
Bats: right **Throws:** right
Acquired: Seventh-round pick in 6/93 free-agent draft

Player Summary	
Fantasy Value	$0
Card Value	25¢ to 40¢
Will	hit for extra bases
Can't	supplant Bonds
Expect	occasional swipes
Don't Expect	weak average

Williams has now played at four different levels of the minor leagues, and he has batted at least .300 in all four of them. Last year, he also reached double figures in home runs and clobbered over 20 doubles, despite a limited number of at bats. Those numbers, combined with the fact he is coming off his first in-season promotion, make for a hopeful situation as Williams enters his fourth year of pro ball. He turns 24 years of age early this season, so this would probably be the time for a move to the majors. Williams comes out of Bedford High School in Pennsylvania and attended Clemson University. When he turned pro, he tore into Class-A Northwest League pitching, and he made the All-Star team. Upon his promotion to the Class-A California League, Williams launched 30 doubles in only 128 games, while coming within three RBI of 100. He is a fine fielder with the speed to run balls down in the gap and the arm to throw runners out. With his ability to hit for extra bases, Williams should be making noise in 1996—in Triple-A, in the majors, or in both.

Professional Batting Register

	BA	G	AB	R	H	2B	3B	HR	RBI	SB
93 A	.302	75	288	57	87	21	5	12	49	21
94 A	.300	128	504	91	151	30	8	21	97	4
95 AAA	.301	24	83	7	25	4	1	2	14	0
95 AA	.305	75	275	39	84	20	1	9	55	5

SHAD WILLIAMS

Position: Pitcher
Team: California Angels
Born: March 10, 1971 Fresno, CA
Height: 6′ **Weight:** 198 lbs.
Bats: right **Throws:** right
Acquired: 17th-round pick in 6/91 free-agent draft

Player Summary	
Fantasy Value	$0
Card Value	N/A
Will	need to move
Can't	hurt ankle again
Expect	a look in spring
Don't Expect	high winning mark

When a team suffers the excruciating disappointment that the Angels did last season, it can only look with hope to a better day. And perhaps Williams will be part of that better day. He spent the season in the Triple-A Pacific Coast League last season and put up respectable, though not outstanding, numbers. He led Vancouver's regular starters in ERA, and he was second to Keith Morrison in victories and starts. This came one season after a sprained right ankle knocked Williams out for more than a month. Even so, Williams can count 1994 as a triumph, because he received a promotion from Double-A to Triple-A. Before moving from Midland to Vancouver, he hurled a seven-inning no-hitter at Arkansas, with the lone baserunner reaching on a third-strike wild pitch. A baseball and basketball player in high school, Williams then moved on to Fresno City College. In 1992, he led the California farm system with 152 strikeouts. If Williams can show that kind of ability at a higher level early in 1996, he could be on the road to California.

Professional Pitching Register

	W	L	ERA	G	CG	IP	H	ER	BB	SO
92 A	13	11	3.26	27	7	179.1	161	65	55	152
93 AA	7	10	4.71	27	2	175.2	192	92	65	91
94 AA	3	0	1.11	5	1	32.1	13	4	4	29
94 AAA	4	6	4.60	16	1	86.0	100	44	30	42
95 AAA	9	7	3.37	25	3	149.2	142	56	48	114

ROOKIE PROSPECTS

ANTONE WILLIAMSON

Position: Third base
Team: Milwaukee Brewers
Born: July 18, 1973 Harbor, City, CA
Height: 6' **Weight:** 195 lbs.
Bats: left **Throws:** right
Acquired: First-round pick in 6/94 free-agent draft

Player Summary	
Fantasy Value	$1
Card Value	40¢ to 80¢
Will	hit
Can't	let hype distract him
Expect	RBI man
Don't Expect	home run power

This third baseman enjoyed a highly successful season in the Double-A Texas League last year, giving the Brewers some depth at a position where they already have emergent prospect Jeff Cirillo. Playing for El Paso, Williamson finished second in the league in RBI, and he ranked third on his club in doubles. No Milwaukee prospect at the upper levels drove in as many runs as Williamson did. He showed no signs of being intimidated when he got to Double-A, hitting safely in 22 straight games beginning on April 7. During the streak, he collected 14 extra-base hits and 28 RBI. Later, in one remarkable sequence, he collected hits in the 10th, 11th, and 13th innings against San Antonio. He then picked up three hits the next night, for six in a row. Williamson was drafted out of Arizona State, and *Baseball America* named him the second-best pure hitter in the college draft. He has not been a home run hitter in his two-year career, but with his build you can't rule out the chance he would develop into one. Williamson might soon be pushing Cirillo for a job.

Professional Batting Register

	BA	G	AB	R	H	2B	3B	HR	RBI	SB
94 R	.423	6	26	5	11	2	1	0	4	0
94 A	.224	23	85	6	19	4	0	3	13	0
94 AA	.250	14	48	8	12	3	0	1	9	0
95 AA	.309	104	392	62	121	30	6	7	90	3

ENRIQUE WILSON

Position: Shortstop
Team: Cleveland Indians
Born: July 27, 1975 Santo Domingo, Dominican Republic
Height: 5'11" **Weight:** 160 lbs.
Bats: both **Throws:** right
Acquired: Traded by Twins for Shawn Bryant, 2/94

Player Summary	
Fantasy Value	$0
Card Value	20¢ to 40¢
Will	surprise with power
Can't	worry about Jackson
Expect	useful at bats
Don't Expect	a homer leader

To get a sense of Wilson's talent, all you must do is examine the Opening Day roster for his Class-A Carolina League club last year. Wilson was the youngest man on the team, and he didn't turn 20 years old until well past the All-Star break. Still, he acquitted himself with distinction, making further promotion seem likely. He was acquired from Minnesota in a trade for left-handed pitcher Shawn Bryant in 1994. Wilson made an immediate impact on his new organization. He finished tied for second in the Class-A South Atlantic League with 12 triples, led the league's shortstops in games, chances, and assists, and made the postseason All-Star squad. He showed power by homering from both sides of the plate on July 15. Wilson was only 16 years old when he signed with the Twins and reported to their team in the Gulf Coast League. A year later, he was in the Appy League, where he led the club in homers and RBI. Wilson will continue to move as long as he continues to hit like he has and field like he has.

Professional Batting Register

	BA	G	AB	R	H	2B	3B	HR	RBI	SB
92 R	.341	13	44	12	15	1	0	0	8	3
93 R	.289	58	197	42	57	8	4	13	50	5
94 A	.279	133	512	82	143	28	12	10	72	21
95 A	.267	117	464	55	124	24	7	6	52	18

ROOKIE PROSPECTS

PAUL WILSON

Position: Pitcher
Team: New York Mets
Born: March 28, 1973 Orlando, FL
Height: 6'5" **Weight:** 217 lbs.
Bats: right **Throws:** right
Acquired: First-round pick in 6/94 free-agent draft

Player Summary	
Fantasy Value	$5 to $7
Card Value	40¢ to 80¢
Will	challenge for job
Can't	worry about attention
Expect	a power pitcher
Don't Expect	a miracle worker

No matter what the weather outside was like in New York this past winter, there was always some sunshine in the Mets offices. That's because the club was looking forward to having one of the top young pitching staffs in all of baseball, with Wilson expected to join Bill Pulsipher and Jason Isringhausen. Wilson starred in the Double-A Eastern League last year, winning the ERA title by more than half a run and being named the league's pitcher of the year. By then he was long since gone, having been promoted to Triple-A. Wilson comes out of Florida State, where he pitched the Seminoles into the College World Series. The Mets liked him so much that they made him the top overall pick in the draft. When he signed and got going in pro ball, he couldn't win a game, posting a combined 0-7 mark in rookie and Class-A ball. But even amid the defeats, you could see Wilson's stuff reflected in the strikeouts—one per inning. He has an explosive fastball, and he can bring an above-average slider and changeup to complement the heat.

Professional Pitching Register

	W	L	ERA	G	CG	IP	H	ER	BB	SO
94 R	0	2	3.00	3	0	12.0	8	4	4	13
94 A	0	5	5.06	8	0	37.1	32	21	17	37
95 AA	6	3	2.17	16	4	120.1	89	29	24	127
95 AAA	5	3	2.85	10	4	66.1	59	21	20	67

JAY WITASICK

Position: Pitcher
Team: St. Louis Cardinals
Born: Aug. 28, 1972 Baltimore, MD
Height: 6'4" **Weight:** 205 lbs.
Bats: right **Throws:** right
Acquired: Second-round pick in 6/93 free-agent draft

Player Summary	
Fantasy Value	$0
Card Value	N/A
Will	repeat Double-A
Can't	worry about back
Expect	K master
Don't Expect	nine innings

For the second straight year, Witasick experienced a rude jolt during the season. In 1994, it was injury; last year it was exposure to Double-A hitters. Witasick had been enjoying success in the Class-A Florida State League. He was tied for most wins in the farm system with seven, was leading with 109 strikeouts, and was fourth with a 2.74 ERA. He was also coming off a three-game stretch in which he allowed no earned runs in 21 innings while picking up three straight wins. Then he was promoted to Arkansas of the Double-A Texas League, where he won only two of seven starts while compiling an ERA near 7.00. Even so, he still managed to finish third in the St. Louis farm system with 135 strikeouts. In 1994, Witasick was 10-4 when a back injury cut his season short. In that sense, anything he accomplished last year was a plus, because he was able to make 25 starts. After an adjustment, Witasick should keep climbing the ladder. He certainly has shown that he has the ability to pitch—at least on the lower levels of professional baseball.

Professional Pitching Register

	W	L	ERA	G	CG	IP	H	ER	BB	SO
94 A	10	4	2.32	18	2	112.1	74	29	42	141
95 A	7	7	2.74	18	1	105.0	80	32	36	109
95 AA	2	4	6.88	7	0	34.0	46	26	16	26

ROOKIE PROSPECTS

BOB WOLCOTT

Position: Pitcher
Team: Seattle Mariners
Born: Sept. 8, 1973 Huntington Beach, CA
Height: 6′ **Weight:** 190 lbs.
Bats: right **Throws:** right
Acquired: Second-round pick in 6/92 free-agent draft

Player Summary	
Fantasy Value	$1 to $3
Card Value	15¢ to 25¢
Will	be major starter
Can't	expect a perfecto
Expect	ball in play
Don't Expect	deep counts

Wolcott not only made it to the majors last year, but he also helped the Mariners capture their first-ever divisional title. He also went against an overwhelming Indians lineup in the ALCS and won. He appeared in seven regular-season games for Seattle, winning three. That gave him a total of 16 victories on the season, achieved at three levels. He wound up second in the Seattle farm system with 13 wins, and he ranked second with a 3.10 ERA. In short, he is one of the top pitching prospects for a team that has finally put something together after nearly a generation of trying. Wolcott gave a hint of his future success when, as a 15-year-old, he hurled a perfect game for his Babe Ruth League team. All-State in baseball in high school, he passed up a chance to go to Stanford, instead signing with the Mariners. In his second season, he blossomed into a Northwest League All-Star, and Wolcott was on his way. In 1994, he made the Class-A California League All-Star Team, and he even received a one-game taste of life at Triple-A.

Professional Pitching Register

	W	L	ERA	G	CG	IP	H	ER	BB	SO
92 A	0	1	6.85	9	0	22.1	25	17	19	17
93 A	8	4	2.64	15	1	95.1	70	28	26	79
94 A	14	8	2.84	26	5	180.2	173	57	50	142
94 AAA	0	1	3.00	1	0	6.0	6	2	3	5
95 AA	7	3	2.20	12	2	86.0	60	21	13	53
95 AAA	6	3	4.08	13	2	79.1	94	36	16	43
95 AL	3	2	4.42	7	0	36.2	43	18	14	19

KERRY WOOD

Position: Pitcher
Team: Chicago Cubs
Born: June 16, 1977 Irving, TX
Height: 6′3″ **Weight:** 185 lbs.
Bats: right **Throws:** right
Acquired: First-round pick in 6/95 free-agent draft

Player Summary	
Fantasy Value	$0
Card Value	N/A
Will	break some bats
Can't	dwell on bad start
Expect	nice control
Don't Expect	a slow climb

If all goes the way the Cubs hope, hitters could be in for some rough days on the chilly spring days in Wrigley Field. With Wood on the mound throwing as hard as he does, the bees will be in the bat handle in a big way. Wood comes from Grand Prairie, Texas, not far from where the Rangers play. However, picking seventh overall in the draft, the Rangers never came close to getting the hometown boy. Instead, he went to the Cubs with the fourth pick. A late sign, Wood got very little experience in his first exposure to the pros. In his first start, he went three innings for Fort Myers of the rookie Gulf Coast League, allowing no hits and striking out two. He immediately was promoted to the Class-A New York-Penn League, where he had a poor start against Watertown, permitting eight runs in a third of an inning. But there should be plenty more chances for Wood. This year he likely will start at the lower levels, and if he pitches up to the ability level that he brings to the table, he has a chance to be promoted quickly.

Professional Pitching Register

	W	L	ERA	G	CG	IP	H	ER	BB	SO
95 R	0	0	0.00	1	0	3.0	0	0	1	2
95 A	0	0	10.38	2	0	4.1	5	5	5	5

ROOKIE PROSPECTS

JAMEY WRIGHT

Position: Pitcher
Team: Colorado Rockies
Born: Dec. 24, 1974 Oklahoma City, OK
Height: 6'5" **Weight:** 203 lbs.
Bats: right **Throws:** right
Acquired: First-round pick in 6/93 free-agent draft

Player Summary
Fantasy Value $0
Card Value . . . . 20¢ to 30¢
Will . . . . make adjustments
Can't. . . . . work behind
Expect . . . . Double-A
Don't Expect. . . . . missed starts

When you look at Wright's three-year career in pro ball, the first thing you notice is the durability. In each of the last two seasons, he made 27 starts, unlike some prospects who experience trouble with the pro routine when they come out of high school. Another thing that catches your eye is the improvement Wright made over his 1994 totals, when his ERA nearly hit 6.00. Last year he cut that by more than half, finishing fifth in the Class-A Carolina League. One item for concern involves control problems. If Wright walks people at the rate he did last year, he will have lots of problems pitching in Denver. In the Mile High air, each walk has the potential to become part of a three-run homer, and the hitters feast on pitchers who must work behind in the count. He does have plenty of time to work on his control. And he has shown the willingness to work. Wright, the 28th overall pick in 1993, is part of the Rockies strategy to concentrate on developing pitching from within.

JARET WRIGHT

Position: Pitcher
Team: Cleveland Indians
Born: Dec. 29, 1975 Anaheim, CA
Height: 6'2" **Weight:** 220 lbs.
Bats: right **Throws:** right
Acquired: First-round pick in 6/94 free-agent draft

Player Summary
Fantasy Value $0
Card Value . . . . 15¢ to 25¢
Will . . . . go to high Class-A
Can't. . . . . win with walks
Expect . . . . bloodlines
Don't Expect . . . . short games

Wright spent his first full season in pro ball last year, doing nothing to indicate that Cleveland made a mistake in tabbing him with the 10th overall pick in 1994. Pitching for Columbus of the Class-A South Atlantic League, Wright finished with the fourth-highest strikeout total in the Cleveland farm system. He only won five of 24 starts, but the important thing is that he was out there regularly and was very tough to hit. His base on ball totals are too high, and any future progress will depend on how he addresses the fundamental of pitching ahead and throwing strikes. Wright is the son of former major-leaguer Clyde Wright, who went 100-111 over a 10-year career with the Angels, Brewers, and Rangers. The younger Wright caught the eyes of the scouts during his senior year at Katella High. He went 8-2 and finished 10 of his 11 starts. That statistic did not translate to pro ball; he has yet to pitch a complete game. But *Baseball America* said that Wright had the best velocity of any high schooler in the '94 draft, and he can throw two different fastballs and a breaking pitch.

Professional Pitching Register

	W	L	ERA	G	CG	IP	H	ER	BB	SO
93 R	1	3	4.00	8	0	36.0	35	16	9	26
94 A	7	14	5.97	28	2	143.1	188	95	59	103
95 A	10	8	2.47	26	2	171.0	160	47	72	95
95 AA	0	1	9.00	1	0	3.0	6	3	3	0

Professional Pitching Register

	W	L	ERA	G	CG	IP	H	ER	BB	SO
94 R	0	1	5.40	4	0	13.1	13	8	9	16
95 A	5	6	3.00	24	0	129.0	93	43	79	113

ROOKIE PROSPECTS

DAVID YOCUM

Position: Pitcher
Team: Los Angeles Dodgers
Born: June 10, 1974 Miami, FL
Height: 6'1" **Weight:** 180 lbs.
Bats: left **Throws:** left
Acquired: First-round pick in 6/95 free-agent draft

Player Summary	
Fantasy Value	$0
Card Value	N/A
Will	come at batters
Can't	move too soon
Expect	a trip West
Don't Expect	slow progress

Yocum's experience at a high-level college program allowed the Dodgers to start him in the fast-track Class-A Florida State League. That assignment carried the advantage of letting him pitch not far from his Miami home. But if things go as hoped, every step up the ladder would take Yocum further from home: first to San Antonio, then to Albuquerque, and finally to Los Angeles. Taken with the 20th overall pick—13 notches behind Florida State teammate Jonathan Johnson—Yocum was the 10th pitcher selected. He also was the fifth from the college ranks. A left-hander, he helped the Seminoles to a berth in the College World Series. Though not a quick sign, Yocum did manage to make a deal in time to join the starting rotation for the Dodgers' FSL team in Vero Beach. In seven starts, he hardly looked out of place. He'll get a look in the spring as the Dodgers decide the best place for him to continue his trek westward.

ANDY YOUNT

Position: Pitcher
Team: Boston Red Sox
Born: Feb. 14, 1977 St. Louis, MO
Height: 6'2" **Weight:** 180 lbs.
Bats: right **Throws:** right
Acquired: First-round pick in 6/95 free-agent draft

Player Summary	
Fantasy Value	$0
Card Value	N/A
Will	throw low 90s
Can't	keep school pace
Expect	classic build
Don't Expect	another Clemens

After trying their luck with an outfielder (Trot Nixon in 1993) and a shortstop (Nomar Garciaparra in 1994), the Red Sox turned to a pitcher with their top selection in 1995. Yount was the first of two choices made by Boston in the initial round last year, coming nine notches before outfielder Corey Jenkins. The 15th overall selection, Yount was the second high schooler taken, trailing only fellow Texan Kerry Wood. The Red Sox are hoping that Yount's brand of Texas heat can lead them to some crisp Octobers and give them more success than they had in last year's postseason. He comes out of Kingwood High School, where he averaged more than one and one-half strikeouts per inning in his senior year, fanning four times as many batters as he walked. Assigned to Fort Myers of the rookie Gulf Coast League, Yount still averaged more than one strikeout per inning. The Red Sox must now decide whether to put him in short- or full-season Class-A ball.

Professional Pitching Register

	W	L	ERA	G	CG	IP	H	ER	BB	SO
95 A	2	1	2.96	8	0	27.1	22	9	12	20

Professional Pitching Register

	W	L	ERA	G	CG	IP	H	ER	BB	SO
95 R	0	1	2.76	5	0	16.1	13	5	6	17

Team Overviews

You'll find an overview of the 28 major-league organizations in this section. This section is arranged alphabetically, starting with the AL East, followed by the AL Central, the AL West, the NL East, the NL Central, and the NL West.

The teams are ordered as follows: Baltimore Orioles, Boston Red Sox, Detroit Tigers, New York Yankees, and Toronto Blue Jays in the AL East; Chicago White Sox, Cleveland Indians, Kansas City Royals, Milwaukee Brewers, and Minnesota Twins in the AL Central; California Angels, Oakland Athletics, Seattle Mariners, and Texas Rangers in the AL West; Atlanta Braves, Florida Marlins, Montreal Expos, New York Mets, and Philadelphia Phillies in the NL East; Chicago Cubs, Cincinnati Reds, Houston Astros, Pittsburgh Pirates, and St. Louis Cardinals in the NL Central; and Colorado Rockies, Los Angeles Dodgers, San Diego Padres, and San Francisco Giants in the NL West.

Each team overview begins with an analysis of that club's key players, as well as an examination of the team's 1995 season. The manager section includes the skipper's overall record, including each major-league ballclub he has managed, his overall record with his current team, and his record in 1995. The abbreviations for managers are: **W** = wins; **L** = losses; **PCT** = winning percentage. The executives listed make up the ownership and baseball structure for each organization.

The "Five-Year Finishes" show in what place each organization finished in its division in the last five years. If two or more clubs were tied for a position--such as the Baltimore Orioles and the Detroit Tigers, who tied for third in the 1993 AL East--each ballclub gets a "T" designation; the Orioles and the Tigers received a T3. Each team's overall five-year record is included; the "Rank" compares the five-year record against the other 28 major-league organizations. The ballparks that the franchise has occupied, plus the years that the organization was there, are shown. If more than one ballpark is listed for a given year, the franchise occupied both parks during that season. The seating capacity and the dimensions of the present ballpark are included, as is the team's address. A brief history of each organization is also presented.

AMERICAN LEAGUE EAST

BALTIMORE ORIOLES
71-73 .493 15 GB Manager: Phil Regan

Other baseball owners had to smile at the difficulties Orioles boss Peter Angelos had during the 1995 season. After refusing to use replacement players during spring training, Angelos went on to watch the real Orioles stumble through much of the season and finish well off the pace in the AL East. The finish doomed manager Phil Regan and GM Roland Hemond, each of whom were fired following the season. Davey Johnson replaced Regan but won't have the thrill of watching Cal Ripken break Lou Gehrig's consecutive-games played record. In a season filled with fan disenchantment for the game, Ripken's accomplishment stood out as an undeniable high point. The shortstop continued his high level of play (.262, 17 HR, 88 RBI) and remained one of the game's real heroes. Unfortunately for the Orioles, he could have used more help. Baltimore's offense was pretty good, thanks mostly to first baseman Rafael Palmeiro (.310, 39, 104), DH Harold Baines (.299, 24, 63), Ripken, and Brady Anderson (.262, 16, 64, 26 SBs), but the Oriole pitching staff had a desultory 4.31 ERA. Mike Mussina (19-9, 3.29 ERA, 158 Ks) was again the staff ace, and Kevin Brown (10-9, 3.60) had his moments, but Scott Erickson (13-10, 4.81) was erratic, Ben McDonald (3-6, 4.16) was hampered by injuries, and Jamie Moyer (8-6, 5.21) ran hot and cold. Doug Jones had 22 saves to lead a bullpen that received help from Jesse Orosco (2-4, 3.26).

Manager			
Davey Johnson	W	L	PCT
Major-league record	799	569	.584
with Orioles	0	0	.000
1995 record (with Reds)	85	59	.590
Coaches: Elrod Hendricks, Mike Flanagan, Lee May, Al Bumbry, Chuck Cottier, Steve Boros			

Five-Year Finishes

91	92	93	94	95
6	3	T3	2	3

Five-Year Record: 375-367; .505
Rank: 5th in AL; 9th in ML

Managing General Partner: Peter Angelos
Vice Chairman: Joseph Foss
GM: Pat Gillick
Director of Player Development: Syd Thrift
Assistant Director of Player Development: Don Buford
Scouting Director: Gary Nickels

Ballparks

Milwaukee: Lloyd Street Grounds 1901. St. Louis: Sportsman's Park 1902-1953. **Baltimore:** Memorial Stadium 1954-1991; Oriole Park at Camden Yards 1992-present
Capacity: 48,262

1995 Attendance: 3,098,475
Surface: natural grass
Left field fence: 333 feet
Center field fence: 400 feet
Right field fence: 318 feet
Left-center fence: 410 feet
Right-center fence: 373 feet

Address
Oriole Park at Camden Yards
333 West Camden Street
Baltimore, MD 21201

Team History

For nearly 45 years, futility in American League baseball had a home in St. Louis. The Browns, founded in 1902, wallowed at the bottom of the standings until 1944. Winning the pennant in 1944, they lost the Series to the crosstown Cardinals. The franchise began anew in 1954, moving to Baltimore. By developing a very productive farm system, the Orioles became pennant contenders by the 1960s. A first-ever World Series win came to the franchise in 1966, and the Orioles went on to become a force to be dealt with, challenging for the top honors for three consecutive years (1969 to '71). Boasting the talents of such players as Brooks and Frank Robinson, Boog Powell, Jim Palmer, and Cal Ripken Jr., as well as manager Earl Weaver, the franchise is noted for its unity and strong fundamentals. They have won seven division titles, six pennants, and three world titles (1966, 1970, and '83). They stumbled out of the blocks in 1984, but by 1989 they had recovered, going from last place to one game out of first.

AMERICAN LEAGUE EAST

BOSTON RED SOX
86-58 .597 0 GB Manager: Kevin Kennedy

After bumbling to a fourth-place finish in 1994, the Red Sox were not the favored pick for AL East champions in '95, particularly with the Yankees around. But Boston received contributions from familiar names and surprise players to roll to its first playoff since 1990. Boston made a good early charge and then held off the Yanks late in the year to grab the pennant under first-year manager Kevin Kennedy. The Sox were eliminated quickly in the playoffs by Cleveland, however. The clear leader of the '95 Sox was first baseman Mo Vaughn (.300, 39 HR, 126 RBI), who delivered key hits all year and led an offense that bashed 175 homers and scored 791 runs. Vaughn was a season-long catalyst who anchored the offense. He also received considerable help from Jose Canseco (.306, 24, 81). John Valentin (.298, 27, 102) became the first Boston shortstop to drive in 100 runs since Rico Petrocelli did it in 1970. Tim Naehring (.307, 10, 57) and Mike Greenwell (.297, 15, 76) added bats. While heat-hurling starter Roger Clemens (10-5, 4.18 ERA) still struggled to return to his form in the early 1990s, free-agent pick-up Tim Wakefield (16-8, 2.95) confounded opponents for much of the year with his dazzling knuckleball. Starter Eric Hanson (15-5, 4.24) was another key acquisition, while Rick Aguilera (3-3, 2.60, 32 saves) led a bullpen that was aided by Mike Maddux (4-1, 3.61).

Manager
Kevin Kennedy	W	L	PCT
Major-league record	224	196	.533
with Red Sox	86	58	.597
1995 record	86	58	.597

Coaches: Tim Johnson, Dave Oliver, Frank White, Dave Carlucci, John Cumberland, Jim Rice

Five-Year Finishes
91	92	93	94	95
T2	7	5	4	1

Five-Year Record: 377-368; .506
Rank: 4th in AL; 8th in ML

CEO: John Harrington
Executive VP, Baseball: Lou Gorman
GM: Dan Duquette
Assistant GM: Michael Port
Assistant GM: Elaine Steward
Director of Scouting: Wayne Britton
Director of Player Development: Edward Kenney

Address
Fenway Park
4 Yawkey Way
Boston, MA 02215

Ballparks

Huntington Avenue Grounds 1901-1911; Fenway Park 1912-present.
Capacity: 33,925
1995 Attendance: 2,164,378
Surface: natural grass

Left field fence: 315 feet
Center field fence: 390 feet
Right field fence: 302 feet
Left-center fence: 379 feet
Right-center fence: 380 feet

Team History

Long-suffering Beantown fans wish they could be transported back to the early 1900s, when the BoSox were winners—five pennants, four world titles. But after selling Babe Ruth to the Yankees in 1920, the franchise fell fast. The Sox rebounded in the 1940s and 1950s, but didn't bounce back quite enough, save a pennant in '46. The arrival of young blood in the 1960s helped elevate the team to a pennant in '67. Not until 1975, and the appearance of more youngsters, did the sagging Sox get another lift. They stretched out a run at a world championship in '75, only to lose to the Reds in game seven. Again in 1986, exceptional talent brought the BoSox a pennant, but not even the likes of Wade Boggs and Roger Clemens could overcome what seems to be the perpetual close-but-no-cigar syndrome. The Red Sox also won division championships in 1988 and '90, but failed to move past the Athletics in the LCS each time.

AMERICAN LEAGUE EAST

DETROIT TIGERS
60-84 .417 26 GB Manager: Sparky Anderson

If Lou Whitaker and Alan Trammell had not celebrated the fact that they were baseball history's longest-running double-play combination, the franchise may not have had anything to cheer about during the 1995 season. Not only did Detroit sink further from the contenders in the AL East, but it did so under the watchful eye of a manager, Sparky Anderson, who knew for much of the season that he was gone when the games ended. There was also the continued bickering between management and politicians about the future of Tiger Stadium. On the field, the Tigers had little reason for optimism. Their traditionally poor pitching staff was worse than usual, logging a 5.49 ERA and allowing opponents to hit .296. Detroit hitters would have loved to face those arms, since they managed just 654 runs and hit .247. Detroit traded its best pitcher, David Wells (10-3, 3.04 ERA) in midseason and was left with Felipe Lira (9-13, 4.31), Sean Bergman (7-10, 5.12), and Mike Moore (5-15, 7.53) as its primary starters. Mike Henneman (1.53, 18 saves) had a fair year as closer, considering he didn't have too many opportunities, but that was it for the bullpen. The offense was led by Travis Fryman (.275, 15 HR, 81 RBI) and Chad Curtis (.268, 21, 67), while Whitaker (.293, 14, 44) and Trammell (.269) had solid years playing part-time. Cecil Fielder (.243, 32, 82) was productive but not his usual awesome self.

Manager Buddy Bell	W	L	PCT
Major-league record	—	—	—
with Tigers	—	—	—
1995 record	—	—	—

Coaches: Glenn Ezell, Terry Francona, Fred Kendall, Jon Matlack, Ron Oester, Larry Herndon

Ballparks

Bennett Park 1901-1911; Tiger Stadium 1912-present.
Capacity: 52,416
1995 Attendance: 1,180,979
Surface: natural grass

Left field fence: 340 feet
Center field fence: 440 feet
Right field fence: 325 feet
Left-center fence: 365 feet
Right-center fence: 375 feet

Five-Year Finishes

91	92	93	94	95
T2	6	T3	5	4

Five-Year Record: 357-388; .479
Rank: 13th in AL; 23rd in ML

Chairman: Mike Ilitch
President/CEO: John McHale, Jr.
GM: Randy Smith
Assistant GM: Gary Vitto
Senior Director, Scouting: Joe Klein
Director, Minor League Operations: Dave Miller

Address
Tiger Stadium
Detroit, MI 48216

Team History

With a winning percentage of over .500, the Tigers have been perennial contenders since their inception in 1901. They have finished last only five times and have never had more than four consecutive losing seasons. The franchise has won 11 titles and brought world championships to the Motor City in 1935, 1945, 1968, and 1984. Then the Tigers brought a feisty manager on board in mid-1979. Sparky Anderson provided a mature, seasoned presence, shaping the Detroit club into a formidable force in less than five years. The Tigers were a mighty power in '84, boasting big arms on offense and defense. The next two years, however, they dipped down to third in their division. In 1987, they roared back to win the AL pennant, but could not grab the grand prize. In 1989, they bottomed out, finishing last in their division. The Tigers have found offense, but are still looking for pitching in the 1990s.

AMERICAN LEAGUE EAST

NEW YORK YANKEES
79-65 .549 7 GB Manager: Buck Showalter

Give Buck Showalter credit for one thing: He lasted longer than most of George Steinbrenner's other managers. After leading the Yankees to a wild-card berth in '95, Showalter decided not to accept the Boss' two-year contract offer when the season was over. After New York's strong showing in the strike-shortened '94 campaign, everyone thought the Yanks would win the AL East and head to the Series. But a runner-up finish wasn't good enough for Steinbrenner, and a first-round playoff loss to Seattle was particularly galling. Of course, his solution was to sign Darryl Strawberry at midseason and then former Met Doc Gooden after the campaign was over. First baseman Don Mattingly (.288, 7 HR, 49 RBI) ended his string of 1,785 games without a postseason appearance but was savaged by the media for much of the year for lack of run production. Plenty of other Yanks wielded big sticks in '95, including third baseman Wade Boggs (.324, 63 RBI), Bernie Williams (.307, 18, 82), Paul O'Neill (.300, 22, 96), Mike Stanley (.268, 18, 83), and Ruben Sierra (.263, 19, 86), a midseason acquisition from Oakland. The pitching situation was also pretty solid. The Yankees traded for David Cone (18-8, 3.57 ERA, 191 Ks) for the stretch run, and the move paid off. Other strong starters included Jack McDowell (15-10, 3.93, 157 Ks), Sterling Hitchcock (11-10, 4.70), and Andy Pettitte (12-9, 4.17). John Wetteland (31 saves) anchored the bullpen.

Manager Joe Torre	W	L	PCT
Major-league record	894	1003	.471
with Yankees	—	—	—
1995 record (with Cardinals)	20	27	.426

Coaches: Don Zimmer, Mel Stottlemyre, Chris Chambliss, Jose Cardenal, Willie Randolph, Tony Cloninger

Ballparks

American League Park 1901-1902; Hilltop Park 1903-1912; Polo Grounds 1913-1922; Shea Stadium 1974-1975; Yankee Stadium 1923-1973, 1976-present.
Capacity: 57,545
1995 Attendance: 1,705,257

Surface: natural grass
Left field fence: 318 feet
Center field fence: 408 feet
Right field fence: 314 feet
Left-center fence: 399 feet
Right-center fence: 385 feet

Five-Year Finishes

91	92	93	94	95
5	T4	2	1	2

Five-Year Record: 384-359; .517
Rank: 3rd in AL; 6th in ML

Principal Owner: George Steinbrenner
General Partner: Joseph Molloy
VP, GM: Bob Watson
VP, Player Development and Scouting: Bill Livesey
Assistant GM, Baseball Operations: Tim McCleary
Coordinator of Scouting: Kevin Elfering

Address
Yankee Stadium
Bronx, NY 10451

Team History

Easily baseball's showcase franchise, the Yankees have won a record 22 world championships and have fielded some of the game's greatest teams, players, and managers. The 1927 "Murderer's Row" unit featured immortals Babe Ruth and Lou Gehrig, while Hall of Famers like Joe DiMaggio, Yogi Berra, and Whitey Ford dotted the rosters in the 1930s, 1940s, and 1950s. The 1977 and '78 championship squads boasted Reggie Jackson and Catfish Hunter. The 1980s saw the Yankees twist in the wind. Owner George Steinbrenner had Billy Martin on a revolving door when it came to the skipper position. During Steinbrenner's 17 years as an owner, there were 17 different managers. By 1990, the Yankees were at the bottom of their division. In 1991 and '92, they had stepped up to fifth, and finished second in 1993. In 1994, the Bombers had the best record in the AL, and they were the first wild-card team in the AL in 1995.

AMERICAN LEAGUE EAST

TORONTO BLUE JAYS
56-88 .389 30 GB Manager: Cito Gaston

All those Blue Jays fans who hoped Toronto's mediocre 1994 finish was just a strike-induced aberration had to be distraught when the Jays sunk to fifth place in the AL East and tied Minnesota for the worst record in baseball. Although much of the same cast that won three-consecutive division titles in the early 1990s remained in place, Toronto proved inept at the plate and generous on the mound. The resulting 30-game gap between them and Boston (it would have been 44 had the Indians still been in the East) meant that the high times of world championships would end. The Jays need to rebuild, and that reconstruction must begin with the pitching staff. Toronto hurlers walked 654 hitters, a figure that shattered a club record that had been set during a 162-game schedule in 1980. Juan Guzman (4-14, 6.32 ERA) was unreliable, as was Pat Hentgen (10-14, 5.11), who had been a revelation during 1993 and '94. Al Leiter (11-11, 3.64) was average and rookie Edwin Hurtado (5-2, 5.45) showed promise, but that was about it for starting highlights. The bullpen was even worse and managed only 22 saves. Roberto Alomar (.300, 13 HR, 66 RBI) played well, while John Olerud (.291, 8, 54), rookie Shawn Green (.288, 15, 54) and Ed Sprague (.244, 18, 74) all produced. Devon White (.283, 10, 53), Paul Molitor (.270, 15, 60), and Joe Carter (.253, 25, 76) had off years.

Manager
Cito Gaston	W	L	PCT
Major-league record	529	457	.537
with Blue Jays	529	457	.537
1995 record	56	88	.389

Coaches: Bob Bailor, Larry Hisle, John Sullivan, Gene Tenace, Nick Leyva, Dennis Holmberg

Ballparks

Exhibition Stadium 1977-1989;
 SkyDome 1989-present
Capacity: 50,516
1995 Attendance: 2,826,483
Surface: artificial turf
Retractable Dome

Left field fence: 328 feet
Center field fence: 400 feet
Right field fence: 328 feet
Left-center fence: 375 feet
Right-center fence: 375 feet

Five-Year Finishes
91	92	93	94	95
1	1	1	3	5

Five-Year Record: 393-352; .528
Rank: 2nd in AL; 4th in ML

Chairman: P.N.T. Widdrington
President & CEO: Paul Beeston
GM: Gord Ash
VP, Baseball: Bob Mattick
VP, Baseball: Al LaMacchia
Director, Development: Mel Queen
Director, Scouting: Bob Engle

Address
1 Blue Jays Way
Suite 3200, SkyDome
Toronto, Ontario M5V 1J1

Team History

Unlike their 1977 expansion siblings, Seattle, the Blue Jays have enjoyed growing success over the years. Toronto asserted itself in the early 1980s and became a contender. The Jays won the 1985 AL East crown but choked away the '87 title, losing their last seven games. In 1989, the Blue Jays moved from Exhibition Stadium to the SkyDome. It was that same year that Cito Gaston took over as skipper. They rebounded to a division title again in '89, but that was as far as the Blue Jays progressed. The following season was disappointing for the Jays. After much effort, they failed to sew up their division in '90 on the final day of regular-season play. The team, developing a reputation for choking, put an end to that in 1992 by becoming world champions by winning in six games over Atlanta. The Blue Jays again took a trophy through customs in 1993 by beating the Phillies in six.

CHICAGO WHITE SOX

68-76 .472 32 GB Managers: Gene Lamont (11-20); Terry Bevington (57-56)

Those who expected the Sox to wage a season-long battle with Cleveland for Central supremacy were disappointed quickly. Chicago sunk to the bottom of the division early and spent the entire year taking on water. The awful start cost Gene Lamont his managerial job and left Terry Bevington with the unpleasant chore of watching the Indians dominate. After two straight pennants—one in the strike-shortened '94 campaign—the Sox looked quite ordinary. Even though they scored a decent amount of runs, their pitching was dreadful, and the team ERA of 4.85 was one of the worst in baseball. Frank Thomas (.308, 40 HR, 111 RBI, 102 runs, 136 BB) couldn't be blamed. He became the first player with five consecutive seasons of batting .300 with at least 20 homers, 100 RBI, 100 walks and 100 runs scored; quite a feat, considering two of the seasons were strike-abbreviated. Lance Johnson (.306, 10, 57, 40 SBs), Robin Ventura (.295, 26, 93), and Tim Raines (.285, 12, 67) were weapons as well. But the Sox lacked much power after Thomas and Ventura. Ozzie Guillen was again marvelous at shortstop, but even he couldn't get to all the balls opponents launched around Comiskey. Once the pride of the White Sox, the pitching staff faltered. Alex Fernandez (12-8, 3.80 ERA) was fair, and closer Roberto Hernandez (32 saves) was strong, but Wilson Alvarez (8-11, 4.32) was inconsistent and Jason Bere (8-15, 7.19) was awful.

Manager

Terry Bevington	W	L	PCT
Major-league record	57	56	.504
with White Sox	57	56	.504
1995 record	57	56	.504

Coaches: Jackie Brown, Doug Mansolino, Joe Nossek, Rick Peterson

Ballparks

South Side Park 1901-1910;
Comiskey Park 1910-1990;
Comiskey Park II 1991-present
Capacity: 44,321
1995 Attendance: 1,609,773

Surface: natural grass
Left field fence: 347 feet
Center field fence: 400 feet
Right field fence: 347 feet
Left-center fence: 375 feet
Right-center fence: 375 feet

Five-Year Finishes

91	92	93	94	95
2	3	1	1	3

Five-Year Record: 402-340; .542
Rank: 1st in AL; 2nd in ML

Chairman: Jerry Reinsdorf
Vice Chairman: Eddie Einhorn
Executive VP: Howard Pizer
Senior VP, Major League Operations: Ron Schueler
Director of Baseball Operations: Daniel Evans
Director of Scouting: Duane Shaffer

Address
Comiskey Park
333 W. 35th Street
Chicago, IL 60616

Team History

Although the Sox' 91-year history has been a roller coaster ride, no one could ever call it boring. They won the AL pennant in their first year (1901) and captured world championships in 1906 and 1917. Although baseball got a black eye when the infamous "Black Sox" scandal hit after the 1919 World Series, the Sox found themselves stripped of their stars. A drought began after this unfortunate event and the ChiSox didn't win another pennant for 40 years.

In 1959, under the ownership of Bill Veeck, the Sox experienced a resurgence and won their division title. The Sox also claimed AL West titles in 1983 and 1993. They had the best record in the new AL Central in 1994, and they finished second in their division in 1990 and 1991. The Sox also got a new home in 1991, located just across the street from where the old Comiskey stood.

AMERICAN LEAGUE CENTRAL

CLEVELAND INDIANS
100-44 .694 0 GB Manager: Mike Hargrove

In a season characterized in most cities by indifference, there was plenty to celebrate in Cleveland. After 41 years of futility, the Indians stampeded into the World Series. And though bounced by Atlanta, the Tribe and its fans will remember 1995 as a dream come true. Cleveland won 100 games last year, an accomplishment in 162 games but an amazing feat in 1995's 144-game format. Cleveland bolted out to an early lead and padded it to 30 games by the time the season ended. There was no shortage of heroes around Jacobs Field. Cleveland scored a major-league best 840 runs and hit .291 as a team. The Indians pitchers, meanwhile, had a combined 3.83 ERA and boasted four 10-plus game winners. Albert Belle (.317, 50 HR, 126 RBI) was the first player to hit 50 homers and 50 doubles in the same season. He also tied Babe Ruth's record of 17 homers in September. Eddie Murray (.323, 21, 82), Carlos Baerga (.314, 15, 90), Jim Thome (.314, 15, 90), Kenny Lofton (.310, 54 SBs), Manny Ramirez (.308, 31, 107), and Paul Sorrento (.235, 25, 79) helped form one of the most potent lineups in recent history, while Omar Vizquel (.266, 29 SBs) emerged as the best fielding shortstop in the AL. Ageless Dennis Martinez (12-5, 3.08 ERA) led a starting staff that included Orel Hershiser (16-6, 3.87) and Charles Nagy (16-6, 4.55), while Jose Mesa (3-0, 1.13) saved 46 games.

Manager Mike Hargrove	W	L	PCT
Major-league record	350	316	.526
with Indians	350	316	.526
1995 record	100	44	.694

Coaches: Luis Isaac, Charlie Manuel, Dave Nelson, Jeff Newman, Mark Wiley, Toby Harrah

Ballparks

League Park 1901-1946; Cleveland Stadium 1932-1993; Jacobs Field 1994-present
Capacity: 42,865
1995 Attendance: 2,842,725
Surface: natural grass

Left field fence: 325 feet
Center field fence: 405 feet
Right field fence: 325 feet
Left-center fence: 370 feet
Right-center fence: 375 feet

Five-Year Finishes

91	92	93	94	95
7	T4	6	2	1

Five-Year Record: 375-368; .505
Rank: 6th in AL; 10th in ML

Chairman of the Board & CEO: Richard E. Jacobs
VP, Baseball Operations: John Hart
Director of Baseball Operations & Asst. GM: Dan O'Dowd
Director, Scouting: Jay Robertson
Director Minor League Operations: Mark Shapiro

Address
2401 Ontario Street
Cleveland, OH 44115

Team History

Fans of the Indians finally got something to cheer about. In their earlier days, the Tribe was an AL power. Cleveland won the AL pennant in 1920 and again in '48, taking the world championship trophy both times. Six years later, they set a league record for wins (111), en route to the 1954 pennant. But from 1969 to 1992, the Tribe finished in last place in the AL East eight times and second to last 10 times. In 1990, Cleveland finished fourth in the AL East. Reality set in again in 1991, and the Indians plummeted to 105 losses. But a new regime took over, signing young stars to long-term contracts. The Indians moved into Jacobs Field in 1994 and finished second in the new AL Central. The Tribe almost realized its dream in 1995, winning 100 games and the AL pennant but losing the Series to the Braves.

AMERICAN LEAGUE CENTRAL

KANSAS CITY ROYALS
70-74 .486 30 GB Manager: Bob Boone

For a while there, it looked like the Royals had a real shot at the playoffs in Bob Boone's maiden season as manager, but a late-season slide that included losses in 11 of the last 13 games doomed the young Royals. The team searched all year for the right combination of talent. Kansas City used 51 players during the season, including 19 rookies, so finishing a few games off the wild-card pace wasn't all that bad. Still, the 30-game gap between the Royals and the Indians was the largest-ever between first and second-place clubs. Kansas City needs significant help on offense and some more pitching before KC be considered a real contender. However, there was still some excitement. Second-year outfielder Tom Goodwin (.288, 50 SBs) dueled with Cleveland's Kenny Lofton for the stolen-base title. Veterans Gary Gaetti (.261, 35 HR, 96 RBI) and Wally Joyner (.310, 12, 83) were the main power weapons on a team that could have used more. Bob Hamelin (.168, 7, 25), who had such a big year in '94 as a rookie, didn't produce. The Royals had a solid nucleus of starting pitching, with Kevin Appier (15-10, 3.89 ERA, 185 Ks), Mark Gubicza (12-14, 3.75), and Tom Gordon (12-12, 4.43) leading the way, but depth was a problem. Jeff Montgomery (2-3, 3.43, 31 saves) continued his strong pitching out of the bullpen, and Hipolito Pichardo (8-4, 4.36) was reliable.

Manager Bob Boone	W	L	PCT
Major-league record	70	74	.486
with Royals	70	74	.486
1995 record	70	74	.486

Coaches: Bruce Kison, Jamie Quirk, Greg Luzinski, Mitchell Page, Tim Foli, Guy Hansen

Ballparks

Municipal Stadium 1969-1972; Kauffman Stadium 1973-present
Capacity: 40,625
1995 Attendance: 1,232,969
Surface: natural grass

Left field fence: 330 feet
Center field fence: 400 feet
Right field fence: 330 feet
Left-center fence: 375 feet
Right-center fence: 375 feet

Five-Year Finishes

91	92	93	94	95
6	T5	3	3	2

Five-Year Record: 372-373; .499
Rank: 8th in AL; T14th in ML

CEO: David Glass
Executive VP & GM: Herk Robinson
VP, Baseball Operations: George Brett
Assistant GM: Jay Hinrichs
Director of Scouting: Art Stewart

Address
P.O. Box 419969
Kansas City, MO 64141-6969

Team History

The Kansas City Royals came into existence in 1968 to fill a void left by the departed A's. In no time at all, the Royals began to make themselves known. Moving quickly to the top of the AL West, they won divisional titles from 1976 through '78, led by George Brett. The team took its first pennant in 1980. In 1984, they took another AL West crown. They went on to win a world championship in 1985, overcoming 3-1 deficits in the playoffs and World Series. The Royals continued to show their strength from 1986 through '89 by remaining in second or third place in their division. In 1990, however, they plummeted to the sixth spot in the AL West. This fast, hard tumble came as a surprise to all, and the drought lasted a few years. The Royals have turned in solid seasons recently, however.

AMERICAN LEAGUE CENTRAL

MILWAUKEE BREWERS
65-79 .451 35 GB Manager: Phil Garner

Because the Brewers slid quickly to the depths of the AL Central, never to regain contact with the Cleveland Indians, fans who felt cheated by the 1994 strike and continued wrangling between players and management had to smile. Milwaukee's thorough failure meant that owner and ersatz commissioner Bud Selig didn't make that much money, and the grouchy Selig couldn't enjoy the season. What he will enjoy is the sight of a new convertible-roof stadium arising for the Brewers, thanks to a decision by the Wisconsin state assembly to help with the $250 million price tag. That should help bring the fans out to watch the Brewers, a good thing, since they had little reason to leave home during the '95 season. Milwaukee was so bad last year that several of the veterans on the team were designated for dismissal after the season. It's no wonder, since few Brewers had noteworthy performances, particularly on the mound. The team's 4.82 ERA was awful, and only two players, Ricky Bones (10-12, 4.63 ERA) and rookie Steve Sparks (9-11, 4.63), had more than six wins. And they weren't all that great. Mike Fetters (22 saves) was a solid reliever, and rookie Al Reyes (1-1, 2.43) was pretty reliable. B.J. Surhoff (.320, 13 HR, 73 RBI), Kevin Seitzer (.311), John Jaha (.313, 20, 65), and Jeff Cirillo (.277) led an offense that scored plenty of runs but didn't feature too much power.

Manager Phil Garner	W	L	PCT
Major-league record	279	304	.479
with Brewers	279	304	.479
1995 record	65	79	.451

Coaches: Bill Castro, Duffy Dyer, Tim Foli, Lamar Johnson, Don Rowe, Chris Bando

Five-Year Finishes

91	92	93	94	95
4	2	7	5	4

Five-Year Record: 362-383; .486
Rank: 11th in AL; 21st in ML

President, CEO: Bud Selig
Senior VP, Baseball Operations: Sal Bando
Scouting Director: Ken Califano
Director of Baseball Administration: Brian Small

Address
P.O. Box 3099
Milwaukee, WI 53201-3099

Ballparks

Seattle: Sicks Stadium 1969
Milwaukee: County Stadium 1970-present
Capacity: 53,192
1995 Attendance: 1,087,560
Surface: natural grass

Left field fence: 362 feet
Center field fence: 402 feet
Right field fence: 362 feet
Left-center fence: 392 feet
Right-center fence: 392 feet

Team History

After a one-year stint as the last-place, first-year Seattle Pilots, this franchise brought baseball back to Milwaukee in 1970. The Brewers floundered in the AL East for much of the next decade. By 1978, however, they posted their first winning season, finishing third. The Brew Crew really came alive in the early 1980s, due largely to the multitalented Robin Yount. The Brewers won the second-half crown in strike-shortened 1981. In 1982, they took their only AL pennant, not coincidentally during Yount's MVP, All-Star, and Gold Glove season, and took the Cardinals all the way to seven games in a futile bid for the world championship. The brightest moment for the franchise was their sprint out of the gate in 1987. The Brewers got off to a record-tying start of 13 consecutive wins. They hit the skids shortly thereafter, losing 12 games in a row. This decline has continued through much of the 1990s.

AMERICAN LEAGUE CENTRAL

MINNESOTA TWINS
56 88 .389 44 GB Manager: Tom Kelly

Perhaps the worst thing about the Twins' 1995 season was that manager Tom Kelly's career record evened out at .500. Only five years ago, Kelly had led the Twins to the World Series title and had established himself as an excellent leader. These days, it's all he can do to keep his job as the woefully undermanned Twins continue their slide. Last season, they tied Toronto for the worst record in baseball and showed few signs that prosperity was around the corner. Finishing 44 games behind the Indians, the Twins might need the rest of the decade to build another contender. Minnesota fielded a team with few established players on it and a pitching staff that could only be described as dreadful. With a team ERA of 5.76, it's no wonder the team averaged only 14,689 fans a game in '95, more than 9,000 off 1994's pace. Not even Twins star outfielder Kirby Puckett (.314, 23 HR, 99 RBI) was immune from the misery. First, his numbers weren't their usual glittering selves, and second, he sustained a broken jaw during the last week of the season when hit by a pitch. Puckett remained the main man on Minnesota, although second bagger Chuck Knoblauch (.333, 11, 63) and outfielders Pedro Munoz (.301, 18, 58) and Marty Cordova (.277, 24, 84) produced impressive numbers. The pitching staff had no heroes, although rookie Brad Radke (11-14, 5.32 ERA) showed some promise. The rest of the staff was wretched.

Manager
Tom Kelly	W	L	PCT
Major-league record	707	707	.500
with Twins	707	707	.500
1995 record	56	88	.389

Coaches: Terry Crowley, Ron Gardenhire, Rick Stelmaszek, Dick Such, Scott Ullger

Five-Year Finishes

91	92	93	94	95
1	2	T5	4	5

Five-Year Record: 364-380; .489
Rank: 10th in AL; 19th in ML

Owner: Carl R. Pohlad
Chairman of the Board: Howard T. Fox, Jr.
President: Jerry Bell
Executive VP, GM: Terry Ryan
VP, Asst. GM: Billy Smith
Director of Minor Leagues: Jim Rantz
Director of Scouting: Mike Radcliff

Address
501 Chicago Avenue South
Minneapolis, MN 55145

Ballparks

Washington: American League Park 1901-1910; Griffith Stadium 1911-1960 **Minnesota**: Metropolitan Stadium 1961-1981; Hubert H. Humphrey Metrodome 1982-present
Capacity: 56,783
1995 Attendance: 1,057,667

Surface: artificial turf
Stationary Dome
Left field fence: 343 feet
Center field fence: 408 feet
Right field fence: 327 feet
Left-center fence: 385 feet
Right-center fence: 367 feet

Team History

As the Washington Senators, this franchise mixed a few highs—three pennants and a 1924 world championship—with years of deep lows. After a move to the Twin Cities in 1960, the team won the 1965 pennant but slid out of contention for most of the next two decades. Perhaps all they needed was to be sheltered from the elements. The team moved indoors and captured the World Series in '87 with a young team of sluggers. In 1990, they finished last in their division. Then, as if a magic wand had been waved over the Metrodome, the Twins came back with a vengeance in '91. They posted a regular-season record of 95-67, won the pennant, and went seven games in the World Series, overcoming Atlanta for all the marbles. The Twins finished second in their division in 1992, then had a decline for the next few years.

AMERICAN LEAGUE WEST

CALIFORNIA ANGELS
78-67 .538 1 GB Manager: Marcel Lachemann

Although some of the Angels were able to derive some satisfaction about how the team fought back into a tie for the AL West title with Seattle during the last week of the season, they should consider how good things might have been if California hadn't blown a double-digit lead in the first place. For a while, the Angels were crafting a last-to-first drama that included amazing performances by veterans and rookies alike. Then came the collapse. California fell apart in all phases of the game, allowing the Mariners to catch them. And even though the Angels tied for the lead, they lost a one-game playoff for the division title. Their starting pitching triumvirate of Chuck Finley (15-12, 4.21 ERA), Jim Abbott (11-8, 3.70), and Mark Langston (15-6, 4.60) was as solid as any in the league. Closer Lee Smith (37 saves) continued his dominance, while rookie Troy Percival (3-2, 1.95) was a top set-up men. The Angels' offense was explosive and diverse. Tim Salmon (.332, 34 HR, 105 RBI) was an MVP candidate for much of the year, while rookie Garret Anderson (.323, 16, 69) was a revelation in the outfield. Chili Davis (.320, 20, 86) produced, while shortstop Gary DiSarcina (.309) played well and sparked the team before missing 42 games with a thumb injury. Jim Edmonds (.292, 33, 107) and J.T. Snow (.290, 24, 102) provided power, and Tony Phillips (.261, 26, 60) was a valuable utility man.

Manager Marcel Lachemann	W	L	PCT
Major-league record	109	112	.493
with Angels	109	112	.493
1995 record	78	67	.538

Coaches: Mick Billmeyer, Rod Carew, Chuck Hernandez, Bobby Knoop, Rick Burleson, Bill Lachemann, Joe Maddon

Ballparks

Los Angeles: Wrigley Field 1961; Dodger Stadium 1962-65 **Anaheim:** Anaheim Stadium 1966-present
Capacity: 64,593
1995 Attendance: 1,512,622

Surface: natural grass
Left field fence: 370 feet
Center field fence: 404 feet
Right field fence: 370 feet
Left-center fence: 386 feet
Right-center fence: 386 feet

Five-Year Finishes

91	92	93	94	95
7	T5	T5	4	2

Five-Year Record: 349-397; .468
Rank: 14th in AL; 24th in ML

Chairman of the Board: Gene Autry
President & CEO: Richard Brown
Executive VP: Jackie Autry
VP & GM: Bill Bavasi
Assistant GM: Tim Mead
Coordinator of Scouting Operations: Tim Kelly
Director, Player Development: Ken Forsch

Address
P.O. Box 2000
Anaheim, CA 92803

Team History

Cowboy singer Gene Autry gave birth to the Angels in Los Angeles in 1961. His Halos, however, have yet to ride off into the sunset with an AL pennant. Although they managed to finish third in 1964, they faltered for the next 14 years. They spent freely when the era of free-agency began in the mid-1970s. This strategy seemed to pay off for them a few years later. In 1979, they won a divisional title, using veteran free agents. The Angels did manage to repeat the feat in 1982 and '86. The loss in 1986 was perhaps the most painful of all as the California team was only one pitch away from clinching the pennant when fate stepped in. The Halos once again walked off empty handed, losing this time to Boston. In 1995, the Angels had a 10-game lead in the AL West in mid-August. They fell apart, tying the Mariners with a 78-66 record the last day of the season, and lost the one-game playoff.

AMERICAN LEAGUE WEST

OAKLAND ATHLETICS
67-77 .465 11 GB Manager: Tony LaRussa

You sure can't blame Tony La Russa for taking advantage of the two-week window to leave town after another poor season in Oakland. Even though La Russa is regarded as one of the most gifted managers in the American League, not even Merlin would have been able to take a team with this little pitching and offense to a title. The A's bashed a lot of homers, thanks mostly to slugging first baseman Mark McGwire, but they had only one double-figure winner among the hurlers; the Athletics' 4.93 ERA could hardly be considered close to what a contender should have. The A's sunk to last place in the AL West and finished out the season in typically indifferent fashion. McGwire (.274, 39 HR, 90 RBI) missed 40 games in '95, something that has become a common occurrence. Geronimo Berroa (.278, 22, 88) had a great year in the outfield and could be a future star, while catcher Terry Steinbach (.278, 15, 65), highly paid outfielder Rickey Henderson (.300, 32 SBs), and center fielder Stan Javier (.278, 36 SBs) were solid performers. Javier also was a standout in the field. Todd Stottlemyre (14-7, 4.55 ERA) led the weak pitching contingent with Steve Ontiveros (9-6, 4.37), the only other bankable performer on a staff that included disappointments like Ron Darling (4-7, 6.23) and Todd Van Poppel (4-8, 4.88). Dennis Eckersley saved 29 games to lead a shaky bullpen.

Manager Art Howe	W	L	PCT
Major-league record	392	418	.484
with Athletics	—	—	—
1995 record	—	—	—
Coaches: Bob Cluck			

Five-Year Finishes

91	92	93	94	95
4	1	7	2	4

Five-Year Record: 366-378; .492
Rank: 9th in AL; 18th in ML

Owner: Ken Hofmann
Owner: Steve Schott
Executive VP & GM: Sandy Alderson
Assistant GM: Billy Beane
Director of Player Development: Keith Lieppman
Director of Scouting: Grady Fuson

Address
Oakland-Alameda County Coliseum
Oakland, CA 94621

Ballparks

Philadelphia: Columbia Park 1901-1908; Shibe Park 1909-1954 **Kansas City:** Municipal Stadium 1955-1967 **Oakland:** Oakland-Alameda County Coliseum 1968-present
Capacity: 47,313

1995 Attendance: 1,174,310
Surface: natural grass
Left field fence: 330 feet
Center field fence: 400 feet
Right field fence: 330 feet
Left-center fence: 375 feet
Right-center fence: 375 feet

Team History

The Athletics have had a colorful existence. Formed in 1901 in Philadelphia, the A's captured world championships in 1910, 1911, '13, '29, and '30, before embarking on a dismal period that saw the franchise move to Kansas City. Then in 1968, Charlie Finley had a plan. He wanted to move his team to Oakland, make them a success, and sell lots of tickets. His Oakland team became a reality and the winning began—just not in front of as large an audience as had been anticipated. Three straight world titles came from 1972 to '74. After winning the division championship in the strike-affected '81 season, area businesses took over the reins. Packing the team with power and talent, the A's won pennants from 1988 to '90, with a world championship in 1989. Topping their division again in '92, Oakland went from first to worst in 1993.

AMERICAN LEAGUE WEST

SEATTLE MARINERS
79-66 .545 0 GB Manager: Lou Piniella

The Mariners refused to lose, staging an incredible late-season comeback and making it to the postseason for the first time in the team's 19-year history. Left for dead as California opened a double-digit lead in the AL West, the Mariners rallied to tie the Angels on the season's last day and then defeated the Halos in a one-game playoff to clinch the division title. Seattle then dispatched New York in the first round of the playoffs and scared the Indians in the ALCS before folding in six games. Seattle had a great offense, but the driving force behind the team was pitcher Randy Johnson (17-2, 2.54 ERA, 282 Ks). The Big Unit won big game after big game, capturing the nation's imagination. The pitching staff fortified by the late-season acquisition of Andy Benes (7-2, 5.86) and the contributions of Chris Bosio (10-8, 4.92) and Tim Belcher (10-12, 4.52). Norm Charlton (2-1, 1.51, 14 saves) and Bobby Ayala (6-5, 4.44, 19 saves) led the bullpen. Even though Ken Griffey (.261, 17 HR, 42 RBI) missed much of the season with a broken wrist, the Mariners still scored plenty of runs. Edgar Martinez (.354, 29, 113) won his second batting championship, while Tino Martinez (.292, 31, 110), Jay Buhner (.262, 40, 121), and Mike Blowers (.255, 23, 96) provided power. Joey Cora (.296), Vince Coleman (.343, 42 SBs) and Rich Amaral (.282, 21 SBs) added a speed component, making the Seattle Mariners even more dangerous.

Manager Lou Piniella	W	L	PCT
Major-league record	689	633	.521
with Mariners	210	209	.501
1995 record	79	66	.545

Coaches: Lee Elia, Bobby Cuellar, Matt Sinatro, John McLaren, Sam Mejias, Sam Perlozzo

Five-Year Finishes

91	92	93	94	95
5	7	4	3	1

Five-Year Record: 359-386; .482
Rank: 12th in AL; 22nd in ML

Ballpark

Kingdome 1977-present
Capacity: 59,166
1995 Attendance: 1,640,992
Surface: artificial turf
Stationary Dome

Left field fence: 331 feet
Center field fence: 405 feet
Right field fence: 312 feet
Left-center fence: 389 feet
Right-center fence: 380 feet

CEO: John Ellis
President & COO: Chuck Armstrong
VP, Baseball Operations: Woody Woodward
VP, Scouting & Player Development: Roge Jongewaard
Director, Baseball Administration: Lee Pelekoudas
Director, Player Development: Jim Beattie

Address
P.O. Box 4100
Seattle, WA 98104

Team History

When the Seattle Pilots flew out of the Pacific Northwest, Seattle was a little more than miffed to be stranded. Demanding a team to call their own, they were awarded the 1977 expansion team, the Seattle Mariners. Before 1995, the Mariners were dismal, only placing fourth in the AL West three times—1982, 1987, and 1993. In 1989, they claimed their first All-Star selection, Ken Griffey Jr. The Mariners posted their first winning season in 1991. But in 1993, manager Sweet Lou Piniella arrived to much fanfare, and he delivered in 1995. The "Refuse to Lose" Mariners came back from a 10-game deficit in mid-August to tie the Angels on the last day of the season. M's beat the Halos in a one-game playoff, then Seattle dropped two to the Yankees before winning three to win the divisional playoffs. The Mariners dream season was stopped by the Tribe in the ALCS.

AMERICAN LEAGUE WEST

TEXAS RANGERS
74-70 .514 4 GB Manager: Johnny Oates

After stumbling into first place last season with a below-.500 record in the strike-shortened AL West race, Texas should have been pleased with a 74-70 record in 1995. The Rangers, however, would much rather have 1994's finish than last year's record, because their improvement in winning percentage didn't correspond with a playoff berth. Believe it or not, the culprit for the Rangers last year wasn't pitching. Texas wasn't overpowering on the mound, but it wasn't its usual generous self. The Rangers finished fourth from the bottom in runs scored (690) in '95, quite a change from the high-powered offensive units that used to bash homers by the bushel. Texas still featured a few sluggers, but it didn't have the same pop throughout the lineup.

Juan Gonzalez (.295, 27 HR, 82 RBI) missed 54 games due to injury. Will Clark (.302, 16, 92) played most of the year, but he didn't hit as many homers as usual. Mickey Tettleton (.238, 32, 78) did his job well but still struck out 110 times. Ivan Rodriguez (.303, 12, 67) had another strong year behind the plate, and Otis Nixon (.295, 50 SBs) was a great leadoff man. The pitching staff was led by Kenny Rogers (17-7, 3.38, 140 Ks), while Roger Pavlik (10-10, 4.37) and Kevin Gross (9-15, 5.54) were somewhat erratic. Jeff Russell saved 20 games to lead a bullpen that got fine performances from Roger McDowell, Matt Whiteside, and Darren Oliver.

Manager
Johnny Oates	W	L	PCT
Major-league record	365	340	.518
with Rangers	74	70	.514
1995 record	74	70	.514

Coaches: Dick Bosman, Larry Hardy, Jerry Narron, Rudy Jaramillo, Bucky Dent, Ed Napoleon

Five-Year Finishes
91	92	93	94	95
3	4	2	1	3

Five-Year Record: 374-370; .503
Rank: 7th in AL; 11th in ML

Ballparks

Washington: Griffith Stadium 1961; Robert F. Kennedy Stadium 1962-1971 **Texas:** Arlington Stadium 1972-1993; The Ballpark in Arlington 1994-present
Capacity: 49,292

1995 Attendance: 1,985,910
Surface: natural grass
Left field fence: 332 feet
Center field fence: 400 feet
Right field fence: 325 feet
Left-center fence: 390 feet
Right-center fence: 379 feet

General Partner: Rusty Rose
President: Tom Schieffer
GM: Doug Melvin
Assistant GM, Personnel: Sandy Johnson

Address
P.O. Box 90111
Arlington, TX 76004

Team History

What can you expect from a team that began as the reincarnation of the Washington Senators? In the three decades since its inception in 1961 in the nation's capital, this franchise has won no titles and has rarely managed to sneak above .500. They circled the wagons in 1972 and headed west for Arlington. Racked by instability, the Rangers have become an exercise in futility. Billy Martin, taking a stab at making something happen, took the team as far as second place in 1974. The team had been worked so hard, though, that by mid-1975 they fizzled out. In 1977, four different managers attempted to take over the helm. The fourth one, Billy Hunter, drove the team to a club-record 94 wins. Since the move in '72 until 1993, the team reached second place in the AL West six times. Looking to build a strong tradition in their new stadium, the Rangers had the best record in the AL West in 1994.

NATIONAL LEAGUE EAST

ATLANTA BRAVES
90-54 .625 0 GB Manager: Bobby Cox

After five years of postseason frustration and failure, the Braves finally chopped their way to the World Series championship in '95, riding the best pitching staff in baseball and a lineup packed with clutch hitters at every position. Atlanta subdued Cleveland in six games to win the title that had eluded the Braves on several different occasions during the 1990s. It capped a fabulous job of rebuilding a franchise that had been woeful during the last part of the 1980s. It gave the long-suffering Atlanta fans their first title in any major sport. There was no way to exaggerate the value of the best pitching rotation in baseball. Greg Maddux (19-2, 1.63 ERA, 181 Ks) was once again a dominant force. He teamed with Tom Glavine (16-7, 3.08) and John Smoltz (12-7, 3.18) to form a troika that tormented opponents. Even though Steve Avery (7-13, 4.67) slipped in '95, the Braves were still kings of the mound. The bullpen was pretty good, too, thanks to Mark Wohlers (7-3, 2.09, 25 saves), Greg McMichael (7-2, 2.79), and Pedro Borbon (2-2, 3.09). While not an offensive juggernaut, the Braves had plenty of lumber. Youngsters Javier Lopez (.315, 14 HR, 51 RBI), Ryan Klesko (.310, 23, 70), and Chipper Jones (.265, 23, 86) performed all year, while vets Fred McGriff (.280, 27, 93), Marquis Grissom (.258, 29 SBs), and David Justice (.253, 24, 78) were other big producers.

Manager Bobby Cox	W	L	PCT
Major-league record	1115	962	.537
with Braves	760	670	.531
1995 record	90	54	.625

Coaches: Jim Beauchamp, Pat Corrales, Clarence Jones, Ned Yost, Leo Mazzone, Jimy Williams

Ballparks

Boston: South End Grounds 1871-1914; Braves Field 1914-1952 **Milwaukee:** County Stadium 1953-1965 **Atlanta:** Fulton County Stadium 1966-present
Capacity: 52,710

1995 Attendance: 2,561,831
Surface: natural grass
Left field fence: 330 feet
Center field fence: 402 feet
Right field fence: 330 feet
Left-center fence: 385 feet
Right-center fence: 385 feet

Five-Year Finishes

91	92	93	94	95
1	1	1	2	1

Five-Year Record: 454-290; .610
Rank: 1st in NL; 1st in ML

Owner: Ted Turner
Senior VP & Assistant to the President: Henry Aaron
Executive VP & GM: John Schuerholz
Assistant GM: Dean Taylor
Assistant GM/Player Personnel: Chuck LaMar

Address
P.O. Box 4064
Atlanta, GA 30302

Team History

The Braves began in the National Association in 1871 as the Boston Red Stockings. After winning four NA pennants and joining the National League in 1876, the Braves flourished and dominated the NL in the 1890s (winning five pennants). Money woes caused five decades of misery to follow, broken only by the "Miracle Braves" of 1914 and the pennant winners of 1948. Boston loved the Red Sox, so the Braves moved to Milwaukee in 1953. The Spahn- and Aaron-led club won a world championship in '57 and a pennant in '58. The Braves were the first club to shift twice, moving to Atlanta in 1966. The Braves won NL West titles in 1969 and 1982. The worst club in the league in 1990, the Braves won three straight NL West pennants. The team won NLCS in 1991 and 1992 but lost in the Series. Finally, in 1995, the Braves took the title.

NATIONAL LEAGUE EAST

FLORIDA MARLINS
67-76 .469 22½ GB Manager: Rene Lachemann

It had to kill the Marlins to see the Colorado Rockies, their expansion brethren, dousing each other with champagne and celebrating qualification for the playoffs after only three seasons of existence. Meanwhile, in South Florida, the Marlins crept into fourth place and continued their slow, methodical improvement. That gradual progress didn't put them in the race for a wild-card spot in 1995. Though the Marlins continued to develop some young talent, they didn't have enough to get past New York or Philadelphia, much less mount a playoff charge. Jeff Conine (.302, 25 HR, 105 RBI) remained the main hitting star in Miami, and he set team records for RBI and extra-base hits (52) in '95. Meanwhile, a pitching ace emerged during the second half of last season by the name of Pat Rapp (14-7, 3.44 ERA), who was 11-2 with a 2.28 ERA after the All-Star break, including nine straight wins. The rest of the top hitters included outfielder Gary Sheffield (.324, 16, 46), who struggled much of the year with injuries; veteran third baseman Terry Pendleton (.290, 14, 78); young first baseman Greg Colbrunn (.277, 23, 89); and infielder Quilvio Veras (.261, 56 SBs), who flashed speed and a good glove. Rapp didn't have too much help in the starting pitching department. John Burkett (14-14, 4.30) and Chris Hammond (9-6, 3.80) formed the nucleus of a shaky rotation, while Robb Nen registered 23 saves but also had an 0-7 record.

Manager
Rene Lachemann

	W	L	PCT
Major-league record	389	512	.432
with Marlins	182	238	.433
1995 record	67	76	.469

Coaches: Rusty Kuntz, Larry Rothschild, Cookie Rojas, Jose Morales, Rick Williams

Three-Year Finishes

93	94	95
6	5	4

Three-Year Record: 182-238, .433
Rank: 14th in NL; 28th in ML

Chairman: H. Wayne Huizenga
Executive VP & GM: Dave Dombrowski
Assistant GM: Frank Wren
Director of Scouting: Gary Hughes
Director of Latin American Operations: Al Avila
Director of Player Development: John Boles

Address
Joe Robbie Stadium
2267 NW 199th Street
Miami, FL 33056

Ballpark

Joe Robbie Stadium 1993-present
Capacity: 47,226
1995 Attendance: 1,670,255
Surface: natural grass

Left field fence: 335 feet
Center field fence: 410 feet
Right field fence: 345 feet
Left-center fence: 380 feet
Right-center fence: 380 feet

Team History

In 1989, the NL started a search for two teams to increase the loop's number of franchises from 12 to 14, matching the AL. The next year, Blockbuster Video owner Wayne Huizenga purchased half of Joe Robbie Stadium, intending to fill the stadium with 82 baseball games a year. His ownership group was chosen over several others in the South Florida area, and on June 10, 1990, the Marlins along with the Rockies were chosen as the two new NL franchises to play in the 1993 year. Carl Berger and Dave Dombrowski were initially hired to start the organization, with Rene Lachemann as the first manager. By signing such high-priced veterans as Gary Sheffield, the Marlins have shown that they are not afraid to spend money. There is a natural rivalry with the Rockies, and it was with consternation that the Marlins watched playoff baseball in Colorado in 1995, after only three years.

NATIONAL LEAGUE EAST

MONTREAL EXPOS
66-78 .458 24 GB Manager: Felipe Alou

After spending three years building a young nucleus designed to contend and not break the bank, the Expos spent much of 1995 starting all over again and paid the ultimate price of a last-place finish. After spawning so much excitement with their Eastern Division title in the strike-aborted '94 campaign, Montreal lacked punch on offense and was unable to control opposing bats. The Expos slid backward quickly after a reasonably strong start. Montreal's biggest cost-cutting measure came before the season when it traded center fielder Marquis Grissom to Atlanta for prospects. It emphasized the team's eye on the bottom line and helped start general manager Kevin Malone on the road to resignation. Montreal wasn't without talent. Although a record eight Expos reached double figures in homers, Montreal still only hit 118 as a team and had no one with more than 15. David Segui (.309, 12 HR, 68 RBI), Sean Berry (.318, 14, 55), Rondell White (.295, 13, 57), Wilfredo Cordero (.286, 10, 49), Darrin Fletcher (.286, 11, 45), and Moises Alou (.273, 14, 58) all had good years, but none was the big run-producer the Expos needed. Butch Henry (7-9, 2.84 ERA) continued his fine work as a starter, although his record didn't indicate it, while Pedro Martinez (14-10, 3.47, 174 Ks), excitable Carlos Perez (10-8, 3.69), and Jeff Fassero (13-14, 4.33) also had solid years. Mel Rojas saved 30 games, but he suffered from bouts of inconsistency.

Manager
Felipe Alou

	W	L	PCT
Major-league record	304	261	.538
with Expos	304	261	.538
1995 record	66	78	.458

Coaches: Tommy Harper, Pierre Arsenault, Joe Kerrigan, Jerry Manuel, Jim Tracy

Ballparks

Jarry Park 1969-1976; Stade Olympique 1977-present
Capacity: 46,500
1995 Attendance: 1,292,764
Retractable Dome
Surface: artificial turf

Left field fence: 325 feet
Center field fence: 404 feet
Right field fence: 325 feet
Left-center fence: 375 feet
Right-center fence: 375 feet

Five-Year Finishes

91	92	93	94	95
6	2	2	1	5

Five-Year Record: 392-351; .528
Rank: 2nd in NL; 3rd in ML

President & General Partner: Claude Brochu
VP, Baseball Operations: Bill Stoneman
GM: Jim Beattie
Director, Scouting: Ed Creech
Director, Player Development: Bill Geivett
Director, International Operations: Fred Ferreira

Address
P.O. Box 500, Station M
Montreal, Quebec
H1V 3P2 Canada

Team History

Named for the city's world exposition in the late 1960s, the Expos have given fans few highlights until recently. Their humble beginnings in tiny Jarry Park were matched by modest performances. The Expos did not contend for the NL East title until 1973, when their fourth-place finish betrayed the fact that they were only three and one-half games out of first. The franchise did not come close again until 1979, finishing second by two games to the eventual world champion Pirates. The Expos captured the division crown in 1981. From 1982 through 1989, the Expos never went above the third rung in their division. By 1991, the Expos were last in the division. Montreal built a fine farm system and has leaned on youngsters to provide talent. In 1992 and '93, the team finished second in the NL East. In 1994, the Expos had the best record in baseball.

NATIONAL LEAGUE EAST

NEW YORK METS
69-75 .479 21 GB Manager: Dallas Green

Consider the 1995 season successful for the Mets, if only because it marked their highest finish in five years. By tying the Phillies for second place in the Eastern Division on the season's last day, the Mets were able to consider themselves runners-up. Of course, that distinction didn't mean too much, since the Mets were 21 games away from the Braves and light years from contention. However, there is reason for hope at Shea Stadium, largely because of a group of young starting pitchers that showed enormous potential. The whole package got manager Dallas Green a contract for the '96 season and gave Shea Stadium inhabitants hope for the future. The ace of the pitching staff was midseason call-up Jason Isringhausen (9-2, 2.81 ERA), who was dominant at times. Also impressive were Bill Pulsipher (5-7, 3.98), Dave Mlicki (9-7, 4.26), and Bobby Jones (10- 10, 4.19), all of whom figure to improve. The Mets hitters don't have quite the same reason for encouragement, but they weren't awful in '95. New York hit .267 as a team and scored a respectable 657 runs. Leading the way was young first baseman Rico Brogna (.289, 22 HR, 76 RBI), while outfielder Joe Orsulak (.283) and infielders Jose Vizcaino (.287), Ed Alfonzo (.278), and Jeff Kent (.278, 20, 65) weren't easy outs, either. John Franco had another good year in the bullpen, saving 29 games, while Doug Henry and Jerry DiPoto were solid middle relievers.

Manager: Dallas Green	W	L	PCT
Major-league record	395	406	.493
with Mets	170	211	.446
1995 record	69	75	.479

Coaches: Mike Cubbage, Tom McCraw, Frank Howard, Greg Pavlick, Steve Swisher, Bobby Wine

Ballparks

Polo Grounds 1962-63; Shea Stadium 1964-present
Capacity: 55,601
1995 Attendance: 1,254,307
Surface: natural grass

Left field fence: 338 feet
Center field fence: 410 feet
Right field fence: 338 feet
Left-center fence: 371 feet
Right-center fence: 371 feet

Five-Year Finishes

91	92	93	94	95
5	5	7	3	T2

Five-Year Record: 332-410; .447
Rank: 13th in NL; 27th in ML

Chairman of the Board: Nelson Doubleday
President & CEO: Fred Wilpon
Executive VP, Baseball Operations: Joe McIlvaine
Assistant VP, Baseball Operations: Gerald Hunsicker
Director of Scouting: John Barr
Director of Minor Leagues: Steve Phillips

Address
126th Street & Roosevelt Avenue
Flushing, NY 11368

Team History

The 30-year history of the Big Apple's "other" franchise has been filled with meteoric highs and laughable lows. New York debuted in 1962 and lost 120 games, but the Miracle Mets stunned the baseball world in 1969 with a storybook World Series title. New York won another pennant in 1973 but was inept until a mid-1980s renaissance. The Mets struggled through the first four years of the decade, finishing last or next to last. They became contenders in '84 under new manager Davey Johnson. Another second-place finish was in order in 1985, as they closed the gap, finishing only three games out of first. Adding clutch-hitting and a fine offensive lineup to their sterling pitching staff, the Mets won it all in '86, bringing home their second world championship trophy. Although they took another division title in 1988, they have yet to duplicate the success enjoyed in the mid-1980s.

NATIONAL LEAGUE EAST

PHILADELPHIA PHILLIES
69-75 .479 21 GB Manager: Jim Fregosi

For a while there, the '95 Phillies confounded everyone, bolting to an early lead over Atlanta in the NL East with solid starting pitching and clutch hitting. By summer, however, no one was confused about the Phils. They had begun a long, ugly slide below .500 and staggered home tied with the Mets for second. Injuries, poor performances by veterans, and little offensive pop doomed the Phillies. By season's end, catcher Darren Daulton (.249, 9 HR, 55 RBI) had undergone his eighth knee surgery, and center fielder Lenny Dykstra (.264) was sidelined with lingering injuries. Starting pitchers Curt Schilling (7-5, 3.57 ERA) and Tommy Greene (0-5, 8.29) were also stung by injuries. The Phillies hit only 94 homers all year, by far the worst in baseball, and received disappointing performances from Daulton, Dykstra, and shortstop Kevin Stocker (.218). Expensive free agent Gregg Jefferies (.306, 11, 56) didn't start producing until the pennant race was over. Outfielder Jim Eisenreich (.316, 11, 55) was again dependable, second baseman Mickey Morandini (.283) continued to show a little pop, and Charlie Hayes (.276, 11, 85) had a fine year at third. Midseason acquisition Mark Whiten (.269, 11 HR) provided a little power. The starting pitching situation was glum, with only midseason pick-up Sid Fernandez (6-1, 3.34) proving dependable, although youngsters Michael Mimbs (9-7, 4.15) and Mike Williams (3-3, 3.29) showed promise. Reliever Ricky Bottalico (5-3, 2.46) had a big year, and closer Heathcliff Slocumb had 32 saves.

Manager			
Jim Fregosi	W	L	PCT
Major-league record	818	842	.492
with Phillies	364	368	.497
1995 record	69	75	.479

Coaches: Larry Bowa, Denis Menke, Johnny Podres, Mel Roberts, Mike Ryan, John Vuckovich

Five-Year Finishes

91	92	93	94	95
T3	6	1	4	T2

Five-Year Record: 368-377; .494
Rank: 9th in NL; 17th in ML

President, CEO, and General Partner: Bill Giles
Executive VP and COO: David Montgomery
Senior VP, GM: Lee Thomas
Assistant GM: Ed Wade
Director, Scouting: Mike Arbuckle

Address
P.O. Box 7575
Philadelphia, PA 19101

Ballparks

Philadelphia Base Ball Grounds 1887-1894; Baker Bowl 1895-1938; Shibe Park/Connie Mack Stadium 1938-1970; Veterans Stadium 1971-present
Capacity: 62,136

1995 Attendance: 2,043,588
Surface: artificial turf
Left field fence: 330 feet
Center field fence: 408 feet
Right field fence: 330 feet
Left-center fence: 371 feet
Right-center fence: 371 feet

Team History

The Phillies waited a record 97 years as a franchise to gain their first world championship. The 1915 pennant winners lost in the Series to Boston, while the 1950 NL champion "Whiz Kids" were dropped by the Yankees. The Phils won the NL East from 1976 to '78 but didn't reach the Series again until 1980, when they finally won. They won the 1983 NL flag but took only one game against the Orioles in the Series. Only once in the 1980s did the Phils grab second place in the NL East (1986), and that year they were over 20 games behind the first-place Mets. Winding up the decade with two successive last-place finishes, the outlook was grim. In 1992, they finished in last place, but they turned it around and won the NL pennant in 1993 with a bunch of gruff, fun-loving ballplayers, only to lose to Toronto.

NATIONAL LEAGUE CENTRAL

CHICAGO CUBS
73-71 .507 12 GB Jim Riggleman

One can imagine 1995 was pretty pleasant for Cubs manager Jim Riggleman, who endured the on-field results of the Padres' cost-cutting before bolting for Chicago along with GM Ed Lynch. It turned out to be a pretty good move for both men. Though Wrigley Field's finest weren't much of a playoff threat throughout the season, and still have a long way to go before they can catch the Reds in the NL Central, the Cubs finished above .500 in '95 and demonstrated some pretty good offensive pop. The Cubs finished fourth in the league in runs scored with 693 and had a strong .265 team batting average. Unfortunately, the team's 4.12 ERA made such fireworks at the plate necessary. Though the Cubs did have four pretty fair starters, their bullpen was inconsistent. Other than closer Randy Myers (NL-leading 38 saves) and middle man Larry Casian (1.93 ERA), Riggleman couldn't count on too much in relief. Starters Jamie Navarro (14-6, 3.28), Frank Castillo (11-10, 3.21), Jim Bullinger (12-8, 4.14), and Kevin Foster (12-11, 4.51) kept the Cubs in most games. First baseman Mark Grace (.326, 16 HR, 92 RBI) and outfielder Sammy Sosa (.268, 36, 119) fortified the middle of the Cub lineup. Shortstop Shawon Dunston (.296, 14, 69) had a solid year in the field and at the plate, as did outfielder Brian McRae (.288, 27 SBs) and second baseman Rey Sanchez (.278).

Manager			
Jim Riggleman	W	L	PCT
Major-league record	185	250	.425
with Cubs	73	71	.507
1995 record	73	71	.507

Coaches: Tony Muser, Marv Foley, Billy Williams, Ferguson Jenkins, Dave Bialas, Dan Radison, Max Oliveras

Five-Year Finishes

91	92	93	94	95
T3	4	4	5	3

Five-Year Record: 361-380; .487
Rank: 10th in NL; 20th in ML

President and CEO: Andy McPhail
GM: Ed Lynch
Director, Scouting: Al Goldis
Director, Minor Leagues: Jim Hendry

Ballparks

Union Base-Ball Grounds, 23rd Street Grounds, LakeFront Park, South Side Park pre-1916; Wrigley Field 1916-present
Capacity: 38,765
1995 Attendance: 1,893,925

Surface: natural grass
Left field fence: 355 feet
Center field fence: 400 feet
Right field fence: 353 feet
Left-center fence: 368 feet
Right-center fence: 368 feet

Address
1060 W. Addison Street
Chicago, IL 60613-4397

Team History

The Cubs are notorious for having baseball's longest championship drought. Born the White Stockings in 1870, the franchise dominated NL play during the late 1800s. Chicago won the 1906 pennant and featured the likes of double-play combo Joe Tinker, Johnny Evers, and Frank Chance, as well as pitcher Three Finger Brown. They captured world championships in 1907 and 1908, beating the Tigers both times. Despite seven NL pennants from 1910 to '45, the Cubs couldn't win another Series. It was about this time that the Cubs began to acquire their reputation for being perpetual also-rans. There were only three seasons from 1940 through 1966 that were winning ones, and the Cubs finished dead last six times. Chicago never won another pennant, though they did take the NL East in 1984 and 1989. In the 1990s, the Cubs have been mostly mediocre.

NATIONAL LEAGUE CENTRAL

CINCINNATI REDS
85-59 .590 0 GB Manager: Davey Johnson

While the typical craziness characterized the Reds off the field, some excellent play occurred on it. Cincinnati rolled to the Central Division title and then whipped Los Angeles in three games in the first round of the playoffs. Cincinnati bolted out to a big early lead in the Central and was able to withstand a 13-16 record after Aug. 31 to win comfortably over Houston by nine games. Though the Reds fell in four to Atlanta in the NLCS, one could imagine that manager Davey Johnson might be in for a contract extension. Wrong. Eccentric owner Marge Schott determined before the season began that Johnson would be out following the '95 campaign, and replaced by coach Ray Knight. Give Johnson and his players credit for putting together an exciting season and a moderately successful playoff run, however. The Reds did it primarily with offense and received tremendous performances from 1995 NL MVP Barry Larkin (.319, 15 HR, 66 RBI, 51 SB), Reggie Sanders (.306, 28, 99, 36), and a revitalized Ron Gant (.276, 29, 88). Cincinnati also found a top second baseman in young Bret Boone (.267, 15, 68), and enjoyed a career year from outfielder Thomas Howard (.302). The starting pitching was pretty solid, with Pete Schourek (18-7, 3.22 ERA), David Wells (6-5, 3.59), and John Smiley (12-5, 3.46) leading the way. Jeff Brantley anchored the bullpen and amassed 28 saves, while Mike Jackson (6-1, 2.39) was a strong set-up man.

Manager Ray Knight	W	L	PCT
Major-league record	—	—	—
with Reds	—	—	—
1995 record	—	—	—

Coaches: Don Gullett, Grant Jackson, Joel Youngblood, Hal McRae

Ballparks

Lincoln Park Grounds 1876; Avenue Grounds 1876-1879; Bank Street Grounds 1880; League Park 1890-1901; Palace of the Fans 1902-1911; Crosley Field 1912-1970; Riverfront Stadium 1970-present

Capacity: 52,952
1995 Attendance: 1,843,649
Surface: artificial turf
Left field fence: 330 feet
Center field fence: 404 feet
Right field fence: 330 feet
Left-center fence: 375 feet
Right-center fence: 375 feet

Five-Year Finishes

91	92	93	94	95
5	2	5	1	1

Five-Year Record: 388-356; .522
Rank: 3rd in NL; 5th in ML

President & CEO: Marge Schott
GM: Jim Bowden
Director of Scouting: Julian Mock
Director of Player Development: Sheldon Bender
Special Assistant to the GM: Gene Bennett

Address
100 Riverfront Stadium
Cincinnati, OH 45202

Team History

Baseball's first professional team has enjoyed recent history much more than its earlier decades. The Reds won the tainted 1919 World Series but didn't top the baseball world again until 1939. A 1961 pennant was followed by the emergence of the "Big Red Machine." During the 1970s, this powerhouse organization finished in first place six times, won four National League pennants, and won the 1975 and '76 World Series, with stars such as Pete Rose, Johnny Bench, and Joe Morgan. But the 1980s were not as kind to the franchise. To add to Cincy's woes, manager Pete Rose was shrouded in controversy over alleged gambling. In 1990, the Reds put the scandal behind and bolted all the way to first. The Reds then swept the favored Oakland A's in the Series and brought another world championship crown to Cincinnati. The Reds finished first in the NL Central in 1994 and 1995.

NATIONAL LEAGUE CENTRAL

HOUSTON ASTROS
76-68 .528 9 GB Manager: Terry Collins

The Astros began the 1995 season as many experts' pick to grab a playoff spot, based largely on their 66-49 finish during the aborted 1994 campaign. Houston played solid baseball for much of the year but fell apart at the end, lost three consecutive extra-inning games in the last week of the season, and finished a game behind Colorado in the wild-card race. The 'Stros scored a bunch of runs (747), finishing third overall in the NL, and also had a respectable 4.06 team ERA. But Houston suffered from a lack of power and didn't have a first-rate closer. The Astros could have also used a full season out of Jeff Bagwell (.290, 21 HR, 87 RBI), who broke his hand again and missed 30 games. But Houston wasn't punchless without Bagwell. Outfielder Derek Bell (.334, 86 RBI, 27 SBs), acquired during the off-season in a huge trade with San Diego, was excellent, and third baseman Dave Magadan (.313, 51 RBI) was a surprise. Second baseman Craig Biggio (.302, 22, 77, 33 SBs) had his best season, and young catcher Tony Eusebio (.299, 58 RBI) made good on the promise he showed in '94. No one stood out on the Astros pitching staff, although Houston boasted three 10-game winners: Shane Reynolds, Greg Swindell, and Doug Drabek. Dave Veres (5-1, 2.26 ERA) had a good year in the bullpen, as did Todd Jones (6-5, 3.07), who led Houston with just 15 saves.

Manager Terry Collins	W	L	PCT
Major-league record	142	117	.548
with Astros	142	117	.548
1995 record	76	68	.528

Coaches: Matt Galante, Steve Henderson, Julio Linares, Brent Storm, Rick Sweet

Ballparks

Colt Stadium 1962-64; The Astrodome: 1965-present
Capacity: 54,350
1993 Attendance: 1,363,801
Surface: artificial turf
Stationary Dome

Left field fence: 325 feet
Center field fence: 400 feet
Right field fence: 325 feet
Left-center fence: 375 feet
Right-center fence: 375 feet

Five-Year Finishes

91	92	93	94	95
6	4	3	2	3

Five-Year Record: 373-372; .501
Rank: 6th in NL; 13th in ML

Chairman, CEO: Drayton McLane Jr.
President: Tal Smith
Director of Scouting: Dan O'Brien
Director of Player Development: Fred Nelson
Director of Baseball Administration: Barry Waters

Address
The Astrodome
P.O. Box 288
Houston, TX 77001-0288

Team History

Baseball purists may curse the arrival of baseball in Texas. After three years outdoors as the Colt .45s, the franchise became the first to play indoors. In an attempt to beat the heat, the Astrodome was built in 1965. However, growing real grass indoors presented a problem. AstroTurf arrived the next year. Houston's play, however, hasn't been nearly so innovative. Although they contended for most of the 1970s, the Astros did not win their first division title until 1980.

In strike-split '81, Houston won the second half of the season, but lost to the Dodgers in postseason play. The Astros didn't see another division title until 1986, and failed in the attempt for a pennant when the Mets prevailed four games to two. After finishing dead last in 1991, the Astros depended on such young players as Jeff Bagwell to rebound, contending during much of the early 1990s.

NATIONAL LEAGUE CENTRAL

PITTSBURGH PIRATES
58-86 .403 27 GB Manager: Jim Leyland

While the Pirates continued their free-fall from among the game's elite to a Central Division basement-dweller, their fans had more on their minds than the team's mounting loss total. The 1995 season was characterized by perpetual uncertainty about the team's future. Would it stay in Pittsburgh, the city that had hosted it for 104 years? Or would it pull up stakes with a new owner and head to Washington, D.C., or some other hungry city? Pittsburgh again played before sparse crowds, although few can be blamed from staying away. Pittsburgh hit just .259 as a team last year and had a dreadful 4.69 ERA, easily one of the worst in the league. Outfielder Orlando Merced (.300, 15 HR, 83 RBI) was one of the few highlights, with infielders Carlos Garcia (.294, 50 RBI) and Nelson Liriano (.286) fairly dependable contact hitters. Outfielder Al Martin (.282, 13, 41) continued his steady play, and third basemen Jeff King (.265, 18, 87) showed he could still produce some runs. Denny Neagle (13-8, 3.43 ERA, 150 Ks) had his best year in the majors, but he didn't have much help from the starting staff. Paul Wagner (5-16, 4.80) was a huge disappointment, and rookies Esteban Loaiza (8-9, 5.16) and John Ericks (3-9, 4.58) showed a little promise. Dan Micelli saved 21 games, not bad considering the Pirates only won 58 times, and veteran Dan Plesac (4-4, 3.58) adjusted fairly well to his set-up role.

Manager Jim Leyland	W	L	PCT
Major-league record	781	774	.502
with Pirates	781	774	.502
1995 record	58	86	.403

Coaches: Rich Donnelly, Milt May, Ray Miller, Tommy Sandt, Spin Williams, Gene Lamont

Ballparks

Exposition Park 1891-1909;
 Forbes Field 1909-1970;
 Three Rivers Stadium 1970-present
Capacity: 47,972
1995 Attendance: 905,517

Surface: artificial turf
Left field fence: 335 feet
Center field fence: 400 feet
Right field fence: 335 feet
Left-center fence: 375 feet
Right-center fence: 375 feet

Five-Year Finishes

91	92	93	94	95
1	1	5	3	5

Five-Year Record: 380-364; .511
Rank: 4th in NL; 7th in ML

President, CEO: Mark Sauer
Senior VP and GM: Cam Bonifay
Director of Baseball Administation: John Sirignano
Director of Minor League Operations: Chet Montgomery
Director of Scouting: Paul Tinnell

Address
P.O. Box 7000
Pittsburgh, PA 15212

Team History

Pittsburgh won five pennants from 1900 through '30 and two World Series (1909 and '25). After sagging throughout the 1940s and 1950s, the Bucs stunned the Yankees in the 1960 fall classic. The Pirates captured the 1971 and 1979 world championships. The 1970s were a joyous time to be a Pirate fan. The Bucs finished first or second in the NL East nine out of 10 years. As the 1980s unfolded, that joy turned to pain. Instead of being a perennial contender, the highest level of success the Pirates attained was two trips to second in the division and three consecutive years (1984 through '86) in dead last. The early 1990s were good, however. From 1990 through 1992, the Pirates won the division title every year, though they didn't win the NL pennant. By 1993, they experienced a talent drain, losing Barry Bonds, Bobby Bonilla, and others because of salaries.

NATIONAL LEAGUE CENTRAL

ST. LOUIS CARDINALS
62-81 .434 22½ GB Managers: Joe Torre (20-27), Mike Jorgensen (42-54)

Mike Jorgensen's final winning percentage was just .002 better than the manager he replaced, Joe Torre. Torre was fired after just 47 games of the 1995 season for compiling a 20-27 mark with the Cards, and Jorgensen managed a 42-54 record after moving down from the front office. Tony LaRussa will guide the Cards next year, and he'll have to hope his team can score more runs and find some starting pitchers who can win more than seven games. No manager should have to suffer through a season like 1995. Outside of ancient relief pitcher Tom Henke (1.82 ERA, 36 saves), there weren't too many highlights under the Gateway Arch in 1995. St. Louis was never in contention for the wild-card berth and was lucky that Pittsburgh was in its division. Otherwise, the Cards would have been in last place. The offense managed only 563 runs all year and had few heroes. Young John Mabry (.307) was one of them, and he teamed with usual producers Bernard Gilkey (.298, 17 HR, 69 RBI), Brian Jordan (.296, 22, 81), and Ray Lankford (.277, 25, 82). After that, things were pretty sad. Third baseman Scott Cooper was a huge bust, and no other Card drove in more than 40 runs. Henke led a solid bullpen that was the strength of the pitching staff and was called upon often to bail out the St. Louis starters. Mike Morgan (7-7, 3.56) was the Cardinal "ace," a telling classification.

Manager Tony LaRussa	W	L	PCT
Major-league record	1320	1183	.527
with Cardinals	—	—	—
1995 record (with Athletics)	67	77	.465

Coaches: Dave Duncan, Tommie Reynolds, Dave Duncan, George Hendrick, Mark DeJohn

Five-Year Finishes

91	92	93	94	95
2	3	3	4	4

Five-Year Record: 369-374; .497
Rank: 8th in NL; 16th in ML

Chairman of the Board: August Busch III
Vice Chairman: Fred Kuhlmann
President, CEO: Mark Lamping
VP, GM: Walt Jocketty
Director of Player Development: Mike Jorgensen
Director, Major League Personnel: Jerry Walker
Director of Scouting: Marty Maier

Address
250 Stadium Plaza
St. Louis, MO 63102

Ballparks

Robison Field 1893-1920; Sportsman's Park 1920-1966; Busch Stadium 1966-present
Capacity: 57,078
1995 Attendance: 1,727,536

Surface: artificial turf
Left field fence: 330 feet
Center field fence: 402 feet
Right field fence: 330 feet
Left-center fence: 365 feet
Right-center fence: 375 feet

Team History

Born the Browns in 1884, the St. Louis Cardinals won six world championships from 1926 through '46, thanks mostly to Branch Rickey's fine farm system. St. Louis was back on top in 1964 and '67. The 1970s were thin on excitement for Cardinal fans, but then the tide turned. In strike-split '81, the Cards had the best winning percentage overall, but did not get to progress into postseason play due to the method of determining regular-season winners. They continued on in earnest in '82, winning the division, the pennant, and then took the World Series trophy after emerging victorious over Milwaukee. The St. Louis team migrated to the lower half of the standings for the next few years, but got right back in the thick of things in '85. They won pennants in 1985 and again in 1987. During the 1990s, however, the Redbirds have not finished closer than 10 games out of first place.

NATIONAL LEAGUE WEST

COLORADO ROCKIES
77-67 .535 1 GB Manager: Don Baylor

It seemed fitting that the Rockies would qualify for the NL wild-card spot on the season's final day with a thrilling comeback after trailing by six runs to San Francisco, since Colorado provided the league's most impressive collection of offensive fireworks all season. In becoming the fastest expansion team ever to qualify for the playoffs, the Rockies bashed 200 homers and became the first team in 18 years to boast four players with 30 or more dingers. Although it fell quickly to the Braves in the first round of the playoffs, Colorado inaugurated Coors Field with an assault on the scoreboard with a team designed to outscore the opposition, a fact evidenced by its 4.96 team ERA. Leading the way was Dante Bichette (.340, 40 HR, 128 RBI), who put up remarkable numbers and came close to a Triple Crown. Joining him were Vinny Castilla (.309, 32, 90), Larry Walker (.306, 36, 101), and Andres Galarraga (.280, 31, 106). Those four weren't alone. John Vander Wal (.347) and Eric Young (.317) produced all year. The pitching staff couldn't be depended upon for the same output. Bret Saberhagen (7-6, 4.18 ERA) was the "ace" of a staff that included Kevin Ritz (11-11, 4.21), Bill Swift (9-3, 4.94) and Armando Reynoso (7-7, 5.32), all of whom battled within the hitter-friendly Coors Field confines. The bullpen quartet of Bruce Ruffin, Steve Reed, Darren Holmes, and Curt Leskanic combined for 38 saves and 17 wins.

Manager Don Baylor	W	L	PCT
Major-league record	197	226	.466
with Rockies	197	226	.466
1995 record	77	67	.535

Coaches: Larry Bearnarth, Ron Hassey, Rick Mathews, Jackie Moore, Ken Griffey Sr.

Three-Year Finishes

93	94	95
6	3	2

Three-Year Record: 197-226; .466
Rank: 11th in NL; 25th in ML

Chairman, CEO: Jerry McMorris
Senior VP, GM: Bob Gebhard
VP, Player Personnel: Dick Balderson
Assistant GM: Tony Siegle
Director of Scouting: Pat Daugherty

Ballpark

Mile High Stadium 1993-94; Coors Field 1995-present
Capacity: 50,000
1995 Attendance: 3,341,998
Surface: natural grass

Left field fence: 347 feet
Center field fence: 415 feet
Right field fence: 350 feet
Left-center fence: 390 feet
Right-center fence: 375 feet

Address
Coors Field
2001 Blake Street
Denver, CO 80205

Team History

It took the Colorado Rockies only three years to taste postseason action; free agency and 4 million fans can make a team grow up in a hurry. In 1990, the NL chose the Rockies (along with the Marlins) as the latest round of franchise. Before beginning play in 1993, the Rockies chose Bob Gebhard as the GM. He in turn chose former slugger and batting coach Don Baylor as the team's first manager. First baseman Andres Galarraga in 1993 became the first player in expansion history to win a batting title by hitting .370. A record 4,483,270 patrons watched the Rockies in their initial season. While the owners figured baseball would go over big, they had no idea how hungry area fans were. The Rockies improved substantially in 1994, and by 1995 they finished just one game behind the Dodgers for the NL West crown and became the league's first wild-card entry.

NATIONAL LEAGUE WEST

LOS ANGELES DODGERS
78-66 .542 0 GB Manager: Tommy Lasorda

The 1995 Dodgers sure didn't win the Western Division with defense or contact. Despite committing an atrocious 130 errors as a team, including 35 by shortstop Jose Offerman, and setting a team record with 1,023 strikeouts (batting, not pitching), LA was able to overcome a slow start to surpass Colorado for the pennant. The Dodgers didn't have the same success in the postseason and lost to Cincinnati in three games, but L.A.'s young nucleus delivered throughout most of the season. Of course, some of the achievements of such Dodgers as Mike Piazza, Eric Karros, and Raul Mondesi were overshadowed by the hysteria surrounding the arrival and subsequent play of Japanese pitcher Hideo Nomo (13-6, 2.54 ERA). He captured the imaginations of fans and journalists alike throughout the league, and led the league in strikeouts with 236. Joining Nomo in an effective rotation were Ramon Martinez (17-7, 3.66), Ismael Valdes (13-11, 3.05), and Tom Candiotti (7-14, 3.50), who could have sued his teammates for lack of support. That didn't happen too often, however, thanks to guys like Piazza (.346, 32 HR, 93 RBI), Karros (.298, 32, 105), and Mondesi (.285, 26, 88). Center fielder Brett Butler (.300, 32 SBs) proved to be a solid leadoff man, and Dave Hansen (.287) showed promise at third base. Young Chad Fonville won the shortstop job from Offerman and teamed with Delino DeShields (39 SBs) in a solid double-play combination. Todd Worrell (4-1, 2.02) accumulated 32 saves.

Manager Tommy Lasorda	W	L	PCT
Major-league record	1558	1404	.526
with Dodgers	1558	1404	.526
1995 record	78	66	.542

Coaches: Mark Cresse, Dave Wallace, Joe Amalfitano, Bill Russell, Reggie Smith

Five-Year Finishes

91	92	93	94	95
2	6	4	1	1

Five-Year Record: 373-371; .501
Rank: 5th in NL; 12th in ML

President: Peter O'Malley
Executive VP: Fred Claire
Director, Minor League Operations: Charlie Blaney
Director, Scouting: Terry Reynolds

Ballparks

Brooklyn: Union Grounds, 1876; Washington Park 1891-1897; Ebbets Field 1913-1957 **Los Angeles:** Memorial Coliseum 1958-1961; Dodger Stadium 1962-present
Capacity: 56,000

1995 Attendance: 2,766,251
Surface: natural grass
Left field fence: 330 feet
Center field fence: 395 feet
Right field fence: 330 feet
Left-center fence: 385 feet
Right-center fence: 385 feet

Address
1000 Elysian Park Avenue
Los Angeles, CA 90012

Team History

The National League's most successful franchise got its start in Brooklyn in 1884, named after the borough's Trolley Dodgers. Flatbush fans suffered until "next year" finally brought a world championship in 1955. They cried two years later when Walter O'Malley moved the team to LA, where the Dodgers won World Series in 1959, 1963, 1965, 1977, and 1988. In 1989, the team from tinseltown finished fourth in their division. They took some steps in the right direction during 1990, regaining second place in the division, but finishing five games behind the eventual world champion Reds that season. Spirits were high in '91, but the mighty Dodgers fell apart down the stretch. LA finished the '91 season only one game behind the Braves. After coming so close, the '92 season was an extra-painful reality, though the Dodgers rebounded in 1993. The Dodgers finished first in the NL West in both 1994 and 1995.

NATIONAL LEAGUE WEST

SAN DIEGO PADRES
70-74 .486 8 GB Manager: Bruce Bochy

All those who ripped the Padres for their house-cleaning back in 1993 kept quiet during the '95 season. The young, revamped Padres flirted with .500 most of the year and even spent a little time in the NL wild-card race. Not bad for a franchise that had been "ruined" by cost-conscious owners just two years before. San Diego has a solid young nucleus of talent that needs a little more pop at the plate and a pitching staff that has some strong young arms. And then there's Tony Gwynn. Gwynn hit .368 to win his sixth NL batting title and drove in a career-high 90 runs, not bad for a singles hitter in a 144-game season. Veteran Ken Caminiti (.302, 26 HR, 94 RBI) teamed with Gwynn in a solid run-producing tandem, while Steve Finley (.297, 104 runs, 36 SBs) and catcher Brad Ausmus (.293) were solid throughout the year. Melvin Nieves (14 HR) showed some power in the outfield but struck out way too often, and Andujar Cedeno was solid at short, although his hitting needs to improve. Andy Ashby (12-10, 2.94 ERA) became the team's ace, and Joey Hamilton (6-9, 3.08) did a good job. Scott Sanders (5-5, 4.30) and Willie Blair (7- 5, 4.34) were solid, and ageless Fernando Valenzuela (8-3, 4.98) proved he could still get people out. Closer Trevor Hoffman had a big year, posting a 7-4 record and saving 31 games.

Manager Bruce Bochy:	W	L	PCT
Major-league record	70	74	.486
with Padres	70	74	.486
1995 record	70	74	.486

Coaches: Rob Picciolo, Merv Rettenmund, Dan Warthen, Sonny Siebert, Graig Nettles, Davey Lopes, Ty Waller, Grady Little

Ballpark

Jack Murphy Stadium 1969-present
Capacity: 46,510
1995 Attendance: 1,019,728
Surface: natural grass

Left field fence: 327 feet
Center field fence: 405 feet
Right field fence: 327 feet
Left-center fence: 370 feet
Right-center fence: 370 feet

Five-Year Finishes

91	92	93	94	95
3	3	7	4	3

Five-Year Record: 344-403; .461
Rank: 12th in NL; 26th in ML

Chairman of the Board: John Moores
CEO: Larry Lucchino
President: Dick Freeman
GM: Kevin Towers
Assistant GM: Steve Lubartich

Address
P.O. Box 2000
San Deigo, CA 92112-2000

Team History

A product of the 1969 expansion with Montreal, the Padres struggled below .500 for their first 15 seasons. Their first winning year—1984— also brought home a pennant. Taking three out of five games in the NLCS, the Padres put away the Cubs and faced the formidable force that was the Tigers. Unfortunately, for San Diego fans, the dream season ended in short order with the Tigers snuffing out any championship hopes the Padres had in only five games. The rest of the 1980s featured middle-division finishes. One little glimmer came in 1989, when the Padres finished second in their division, just three games behind the eventual pennant-winning Giants. Injuries hit the San Diego team hard in 1990, and it was evidenced in their next-to-last-place finish. The Pads rebounded somewhat in 1991 and '92, but in 1993 fell to the bottom as the team unloaded its high-priced veterans.

NATIONAL LEAGUE WEST

SAN FRANCISCO GIANTS
67-77 .465 11 GB Manager: Dusty Baker

No matter what the Giants tried to do to dress up the 1995 season, they couldn't get around the fact that the team just wasn't all that good. San Francisco hoped fans would flock to see Deion Sanders, acquired in midseason from Cincinnati, but more attention was devoted to the Neon One's final football destination than to how much Sanders added to the Giants' lineup. San Francisco finished next-to-last in the National League in hitting and pitching, and showed exactly how far it had fallen from its 1993 pennant run by logging its second straight sub-.500 season. Injuries played a role in the Giants' misfortune. Slugging third baseman Matt Williams (.336, 23 HR, 65 RBI) played in only 76 games, and Sanders (.268, 24 SBs) limped home with a bum ankle that needed surgical repair before he could continue his football career. Barry Bonds (.294, 33, 104, 31 SBs) had a great year by everybody's standards but his own, fellow outfielder Mark Carreon (.301, 17, 65) surprised with his strong output, and Glenallen Hill (.264, 24, 86) posted career highs in homers and RBI. In pitching, no SF hurler had an ERA below 3.00 for the season, a big reason for the team's overall 4.86 ERA. Al Leiter (10-12, 3.82) was the "ace" of the staff, although young William VanLandingham (6-3, 3.67) continued to show promise. Rod Beck saved 33 games, but he wasn't his usual overpowering self.

Manager Dusty Baker	W	L	PCT
Major-league record	225	196	.534
with Giants	225	196	.534
1995 record	67	77	.465
Coaches: Bobby Bonds, Bob Brenly, Wendell Kim, Bob Lillis, Dick Pole, Denny Sommers			

Ballparks

New York: Polo Grounds 1883-1888, 1891-1957; St. George Cricket Grounds 1889-1890
San Francisco: Seals Stadium 1958-1959; 3Com Park 1960-present
Capacity: 63,000

1995 Attendance: 1,241,497
Surface: natural grass
Left field fence: 335 feet
Center field fence: 400 feet
Right field fence: 328 feet
Left-center fence: 365 feet
Right-center fence: 365 feet

Five-Year Finishes

91	92	93	94	95
4	5	2	2	4

Five-Year Record: 372-373; .499
Rank: 7th in NL; T14th in ML

Managing General Partner: Peter Magowan
Senior VP and GM: Bob Quinn
Executive VP: Larry Baer
VP, Scouting and Player Personnel: Brian Sabean
Director of Player Development: Jack Hiatt
Coordinator of Scouting: Bob Hartsfield

Address
3Com Park
San Francisco, CA 94124

Team History

Few dispute the economic reasons for moving this proud franchise west from New York, but many believe the Giants were never the same after coming to San Francisco. The Giants dominated the NL before 1900, and they won 15 pennants and five world championships from 1904 to '54. Led by Willie Mays, Willie McCovey, and Juan Marichal, the Giants enjoyed 14 consecutive winning seasons after their 1958 move, but won only two more pennants—1962 and 1989. In the latter World Series, they lost to the world-shaking Athletics. The Giants also won their division in 1987, but lost the pennant to the Cardinals. When the 1990s began, San Francisco fans had little to cheer about. After almost moving out of the Bay Area, the Giants in 1993 returned to lose by one game against the Braves in one of the greatest pennant battles of all time.

Hall of Fame

Profiles of the players, managers, umpires, and executives who have been inducted into the National Baseball Hall of Fame and Museum in Cooperstown, New York, comprise this section. The profiles are presented in alphabetical order. At the end of each profile is a date in parentheses; this is the year the member was enshrined into the Hall.

In preparation for baseball's centennial in 1939, a National Baseball Museum was proposed, first as a matter of civic pride, and later as a memorial for the greatest of those who have ever played the game.

While the rules governing election to the Hall of Fame have varied in specifics over the years, in general the criteria has remained the same. One must be named on 75 percent of ballots cast by members of the Baseball Writers' Association of America. To be eligible, players must have played for at least 10 years. The players have to be retired for at least five years but not more than 20 years. A player is eligible for 15 years in the BBWAA vote.

If the player is not named on 75 percent of the ballots in 15 years, his name becomes eligible for consideration by the Committee on Baseball Veterans. This committee also considers managers, umpires, and executives for induction to Cooperstown. The same 75 percent rule applies. Anyone on baseball's permanently ineligible list is excluded from consideration.

The Committee on the Negro Leagues was added to the selection process in 1971. This board considered players who had 10 years of service in the pre-1946 Negro Leagues, and also those who made the major leagues. The Negro League board dissolved into the Veterans' Committee in 1977.

HANK AARON
Outfielder (1954-1976) Aaron is baseball's all-time leader in home runs with 755 and in RBI with 2,297. During a 23-year career with the Braves and the Brewers, "Hammerin' Hank" stood out as one of the game's most complete and consistent performers. He was the NL MVP in 1957 when he hit .322 with 44 home runs and 132 RBI. Aaron hit 40 home runs or more eight times and totaled over 100 RBI 11 times. (1982)

GROVER ALEXANDER
Pitcher (1911-1930) Despite his battles against alcohol and epilepsy, Alexander's 373 wins are tied for the NL record. With Philadelphia in 1916, he recorded a major-league-record 16 shutouts on his way to a 33-12 record. "Pete" led the senior loop in wins six times, ERA five times, and shutouts seven times. His 90 shutouts are second on the all-time list. (1938)

WALTER ALSTON
Manager (1954-1976) In 23 years as manager of the Dodgers, all under one-year contracts, Alston led the club to seven pennants and four world championships. Under his patient leadership, the Dodgers made pitching and defense a winning combination. His career record is 2,040-1,613—a .558 winning percentage. (1983)

HALL OF FAME

CAP ANSON
First baseman (1871-1897); manager (1879-1898) A baseball pioneer, as player, manager, and part-owner of NL Chicago, "Pop" Anson was the game's most influential figure in the 19th century. He hit .300 or better in 20 consecutive seasons and won five pennants. However, in 1887, his racist views led him to intimidate organized baseball into banning blacks. (1939)

LUIS APARICIO
Shortstop (1956-1973) No man played more games at shortstop—2,581—than Aparicio. The swift, sure-handed infielder played a vital role in championship seasons for the White Sox in 1959 and the Orioles in 1966. The winner of nine Gold Gloves, Aparicio led the AL in stolen bases nine times en route to 506 career thefts. (1984)

RICHIE ASHBURN
Outfielder (1948-1962) A classic leadoff hitter for the Phillies, Ashburn led the NL in batting twice (.338 in 1955 and .350 in 1958), runs three times, and walks four times. He batted .308 for his career and was even more impressive in center field, where he recorded 6,089 putouts (fifth all time). Ashburn finished his career with the Cubs and Mets. (1995)

LUKE APPLING
Shortstop (1930-1943; 1945-1950) Known better for his bat than his glove, Appling nonetheless played shortstop for the White Sox for 20 seasons. "Old Aches and Pains" led the AL in batting twice, finishing with a .310 career average, 1,116 RBI, and 1,319 runs scored. In 1936, he hit .388 with 128 RBI, despite hitting only six home runs. (1964)

EARL AVERILL
Outfielder (1929-1941) The only outfielder selected to the first six All-Star Games, Averill didn't turn pro until age 23, and didn't make the major leagues, with Cleveland, until age 26. In his first 10 seasons he was one of the game's best sluggers. In a 1933 doubleheader, he hit four home runs, three consecutively. Averill had more than 90 RBI in nine seasons. A congenital back condition cut his career short. (1975)

FRANK BAKER
Third baseman (1908-1922) Despite never hitting more than 12 home runs in a season, Baker was a slugger supreme during baseball's dead-ball era. He led the AL in home runs from 1911 to 1914. Two 1911 World Series home runs earned him his "Home Run" nickname. In six World Series with the A's and Yankees, he hit .363. (1955)

DAVE BANCROFT
Shortstop (1915-1930) One of the best fielding shortstops of all time, Bancroft set a major-league record in 1922 when he handled 984 chances. A heady ballplayer, "Beauty" was named captain of the Giants in 1920 and led them to three straight pennants. He batted over .300 five times. (1971)

ERNIE BANKS
Shortstop; first baseman (1953-1971) Banks combined unbridled enthusiasm with remarkable talent to become one of the most popular players of his era. As a shortstop he won back-to-back NL MVP Awards in 1958 and 1959 and a Gold Glove in 1960, before switching to first base. Despite his 512 career home runs, the Cubs did not win a pennant during his tenure. "Mr. Cub" had 2,583 lifetime hits and 1,636 RBI. (1977)

AL BARLICK
Umpire (1940-1971) A respected arbiter, Barlick worked in Jackie Robinson's first

game. Barlick umpired in seven All-Star contests and in seven World Series. (1989)

ED BARROW
Executive In 1918, BoSox manager Barrow transferred Babe Ruth from the mound to the outfield. Barrow followed Ruth to the Yankees. "Cousin Ed" was in charge of the Bronx Bombers from 1920 to 1947. (1953)

JAKE BECKLEY
First baseman (1888-1907) Beckley played more games at first base than anyone else. He had 2,930 hits, 1,600 runs, and 1,575 RBI. His handlebar mustache made him a fan favorite. "St. Jacob's" 243 career triples are fourth all time. (1971)

COOL PAPA BELL
Outfielder (1922-1946) Perhaps the fastest man to ever play the game, Bell starred as an outfielder in the Negro Leagues for more than two decades. Satchel Paige claimed Bell was so fast he could switch off the light and leap into bed before the room got dark. Often credited with scoring from second on a sacrifice fly, Bell hit .392 against organized major-league competition. (1974)

JOHNNY BENCH
Catcher (1967-1983) Upon his arrival in the big leagues in 1967, Bench was heralded as baseball's best defensive catcher. After his NL MVP year in 1970 at age 22, with 45 home runs and 148 RBI, he was baseball's best catcher, period. He won his second MVP in 1972. With Bench behind the plate, the Reds won four pennants and two World Series. In the 1976 World Series, he hit .533. He had 389 homers and 1,376 RBI. (1989)

CHIEF BENDER
Pitcher (1903-1917; 1925) An alumnus of the Carlisle Indian School, the half-Chippewa Bender overcame bigotry to become one of the Philadelphia A's most valued members. He had a career 212-127 record, and he won six World Series games. He led the AL in winning percentage three times, including a 17-3 mark in 1914. (1953)

YOGI BERRA
Catcher (1946-1965) If championships are the best measure of success, then Berra stands second to no one. His 14 World Series appearances, 75 Series games played, and 71 Series hits are all records. A three-time MVP, the Yankee hit 20 homers in 10 consecutive seasons. Known as well for his way with words, Berra will be remembered for the oft-quoted "It's never over till it's over." He had 1,430 lifetime RBI to go with his 358 home runs. (1972)

JIM BOTTOMLEY
First baseman (1922-1937) One of the first products of the famous Cardinals farm system, Bottomley was named NL MVP in 1928 for hitting .325 with 31 homers and driving in 136 runs. On September 16, 1924, "Sunny Jim" knocked in 12 runs with six hits against Brooklyn. He batted .310 lifetime with 1,422 runs batted in. (1974)

LOU BOUDREAU
Shortstop (1938-1952); manager (1942-1950; 1952-1957; 1960) Boudreau was one of the game's great shortstops. He was named Cleveland's player-manager at age 24. In 1948, he led the club to the AL pennant, hitting .355, scoring 116 runs, and driving in 106, and capturing the AL MVP Award. He led AL shortstops in fielding eight times. As a manager, he won 1,162 games. (1970)

ROGER BRESNAHAN
Catcher (1897; 1900-1915) The first catcher elected to the Hall of Fame, Bres-

nahan is most famous for pioneering the use of shin guards and batting helmets. Bresnahan hit .350 and stole 34 bases with the Giants in 1903. (1945)

LOU BROCK
Outfielder (1961-1979) Brock's career totals of 938 stolen bases and 3,023 hits, coupled with a .293 batting average, gained him admittance to the Hall. In 1974, at age 35, he stole 118 bases. He excelled in three World Series for the Cardinals, hitting .391 and scoring 16 runs. Brock reached 200 hits four times. (1985)

DAN BROUTHERS
First baseman (1879-1896; 1904) Baseball's premier 19th-century slugger, Brouthers toiled for 11 different clubs, in three major leagues, for 19 seasons. He was the first man to win back-to-back batting titles, in 1882 and 1883. He batted over .300 in 16 consecutive seasons, reaching .374 in 1883. (1945)

THREE FINGER BROWN
Pitcher (1903-1916) A farm accident in a corn grinder mutilated Brown's right hand, severing most of his index finger, mangling his middle finger, and paralyzing his little finger. The injuries, however, gave his pitches a natural sink and curve. Pitching with the Cubs, between 1904 and 1910 Brown's highest ERA was 1.86, helping Chicago to four pennants. He had a career 239-129 record, with a 2.06 ERA and 55 shutouts. (1948)

MORGAN BULKELEY
NL President (1876) In 1876, Bulkeley was named the first president of the new National League. He served one year without distinction and resigned. (1937)

JESSE BURKETT
Outfielder (1890-1905) In the 1890s, the left-handed-hitting Burkett hit over .400 two times. A fine baserunner and bunter, the third-strike foul-bunt rule was created due to Burkett's prowess at the art. "Crab" won three batting titles. He scored 1,720 runs, drew 1,029 walks, and notched 2,850 base hits in his 16-year career. (1946)

ROY CAMPANELLA
Catcher (1948-1957) Campanella, one of the great athletes of his time, had a .312 average, 41 homers, 103 runs scored, and 142 RBI in 1953—amazing marks for a backstop. In 1951, 1953, and 1955 the Dodger catcher was named the National League's MVP. He led his team to five pennants in 10 years. A 1958 automobile accident left Campanella paralyzed, and his struggle to remain active served as an inspiration to baseball fans everywhere. (1969)

ROD CAREW
First baseman; second baseman (1967-1985) An infielder with Minnesota and California, Carew was one of baseball's premier singles hitters, notching 3,053 hits and a lifetime .328 batting average. He topped .300 in 15 consecutive seasons on his way to seven batting titles, a mark surpassed only by Ty Cobb's 10. Carew's 1977 Most Valuble Player year consisted of a .388 batting average, 239 hits, 128 runs scored, and 100 runs batted in. (1991)

MAX CAREY
Outfielder (1910-1929) A tremendous defensive center fielder, primarily with Pittsburgh, Carey swiped 738 bases. In 1925, despite two broken ribs, "Scoops" batted .458 in the World Series as the Pirates defeated Washington. In game seven, his four hits and three runs scored beat the great Walter Johnson. Carey scored 1,545 runs and had 2,665 base hits in his 20-year career. (1961)

HALL OF FAME

STEVE CARLTON
Pitcher (1965-1988) "Lefty" set a major-league record with four Cy Young Awards (1972, '77, '80, and '82), won 329 games with a career 3.22 ERA, and finished second to Nolan Ryan on the all-time strikeout list with 4,136. In 1972, Carlton went 27-10 for a Phillies team that won just 59 games, accounting for a modern record 45.8 percent of his club's wins. He was devout in his work habits and in his refusal to speak to the press. (1994)

ALEXANDER CARTWRIGHT
Executive On September 23, 1845, Alexander Cartwright formed the Knickerbocker Base Ball Club and formalized a set of 20 rules that gave baseball its basic shape. While Cartwright's involvement with the game lasted only a few years, he is the man most responsible for the game that is played today. (1938)

HENRY CHADWICK
Writer-Statistician While Alexander Cartwright is baseball's inventor, Chadwick is the first man to chronicle the game. The only sportswriter enshrined in the Hall itself, Chadwick published guides and instructional booklets that helped popularize the game, and his method of scoring led to the game's wealth of statistics. (1938)

FRANK CHANCE
First baseman (1898-1914) Anchor of the Cubs' "Tinker-to-Evers-to-Chance" double-play combo, Chance helped Chicago win four pennants. While he was hardly a dominant player, he nevertheless hit .296 during his career and hit .310 in Series play. Chance's career was cut short by repeated beanings that eventually left him deaf in one ear. "The Peerless Leader" managed the Cubs for seven years. (1946)

HAPPY CHANDLER
Commissioner (1945-1951) The former governor and U.S. senator from Kentucky, Chandler succeeded Judge Kenesaw Mountain Landis as the second commissioner of baseball. Despite the opposition of most baseball owners, Chandler backed Branch Rickey's signing of Jackie Robinson and prevented a player strike by threatening to ban any striking player for life. Preferring a "yes-man," the owners voted Chandler out in 1951. (1982)

OSCAR CHARLESTON
Outfielder (1915-1941) Blessed with speed and power in abundance, center fielder Charleston is thought by many to be the greatest of all Negro League players. Superb defensively, on offense he could both steal a base and hit a home run. In 1932, he became player-manager of the Pittsburgh Crawfords, whose lineup, including Charleston, featured five Hall of Famers. The team went 99-36 that year, and Charleston hit .363. (1976)

JACK CHESBRO
Pitcher (1899-1909) Chesbro's 41 victories in 454⅔ innings in 1904 stand as one of the game's more remarkable single-season achievements. A master of the spitball, his wild pitch in the next to the last game of the 1904 season against Boston, however, cost New York the AL pennant. "Happy Jack" led his league in winning percentage in three seasons. (1946)

FRED CLARKE
Outfielder (1894-1911; 1913-1915); manager (1897-1915) For 19 of his 21 big-league seasons, Clarke was a manager as well as a player for the NL Louisville-Pittsburgh franchise. As a player, he hit .312 with 2,672 base hits and 1,619 runs scored. As manager he won one World Series, in 1909, and four pennants, includ-

ing three in a row from 1901 to 1903. "Cap" was 1,602-1,881 as a manager. (1945)

JOHN CLARKSON
Pitcher (1882-1894) Clarkson excelled during the years when the pitching distance was 50 feet. Six times he hurled more than 400 innings, twice more than 600. In 1885 with the White Stockings, he went 53-16. With the Beaneaters in 1889, Clarkson's record was 49-19 in 73 appearances. Winner of 328 career games, he had 485 complete games and led the NL in strikeouts three times. (1963)

ROBERTO CLEMENTE
Outfielder (1955-1972) Clemente won four NL batting titles and also possessed one of the strongest outfield arms in baseball history. Intensely proud of his Puerto Rican heritage, it was not until the 1971 World Series, when Clemente led Pittsburgh to victory with a .414 average, that he began to receive his due. In 13 of his 18 seasons he hit .300 or better, topping the .350 mark three times. On New Year's Eve, 1972, Clemente died in a plane crash bringing supplies to earthquake-ravaged Nicaragua. Clemente was the first Hispanic elected to the Hall of Fame. (1973)

TY COBB
Outfielder (1905-1928) The first man elected to the Hall of Fame, Cobb received more votes than any of his counterparts. Intense beyond belief, the daring Cobb epitomized the "scientific" style of play that dominated baseball in the first quarter of the 20th century. In 22 of his 24 seasons Cobb hit over .320, and his lifetime .366 average is still the all-time best. He led the AL in batting average 10 seasons. The "Georgia Peach's" 2,246 runs scored are the most in history, while his 4,189 hits and 891 stolen bases rank second and fourth, respectively. (1936)

MICKEY COCHRANE
Catcher (1925-1937) An exceptional defensive catcher and dangerous hitter, Cochrane led the Athletics and Tigers to five pennants, including two as Detroit manager. "Black Mike" cracked the .300 mark in eight seasons, and his lifetime .320 batting average is the highest of any catcher. Mickey was twice AL MVP. In 1937, Cochrane was beaned by Yankee pitcher Bump Hadley and suffered a fractured skull, ending his career at the age of 34. (1947)

EDDIE COLLINS
Second baseman (1906-1930) As Connie Mack's on-field manager, Collins led the Athletics to four pennants in five years. Traded to the White Sox, he helped that club to two more. An accomplished all-around ballplayer, Collins smacked 3,312 hits for a career average of .333, yet led the AL in batting only once. A consummate basestealer, he ranks sixth on the all-time list with 744 career swipes. "Cocky" scored 1,821 runs and drove in 1,300 runs in his 25-year career. (1939)

JIMMY COLLINS
Third baseman (1895-1908) Collins revolutionized the third base position by moving around, charging in, and fielding bunts bare-handed. Playing primarily for both the Boston Beaneaters in the National League and the Boston Pilgrims in the AL, Collins hit a robust .294, topping the .300 mark five times and the 100 RBI mark twice. (1945)

EARLE COMBS
Outfielder (1924-1935) While Babe Ruth and Lou Gehrig cleaned up at the plate, Combs set the table. As the leadoff man and center fielder for the Yankees, Combs scored 100 or more runs in eight straight

seasons. "The Kentucky Colonel" had a lifetime .325 average and scored 1,186 runs. A collision with an outfield fence in 1934 forced his retirement a year later. (1970)

CHARLES COMISKEY
Executive Comiskey parlayed modest field success into managerial brilliance, later becoming the first former player to be sole owner of a major-league franchise, the White Sox. The "Old Roman" assisted Ban Johnson in the formation of the American League. Some historians feel that his parsimonious spending habits indirectly led to the 1919 "Black Sox" scandal. (1939)

JOCKO CONLAN
Umpire (1941-1964) Conlan started umpiring by accident. In a 1935 minor-league game, when one of the regular umpires was overcome by the heat, Conlan was rushed in to pinch-ump. He umpired in six World Series and six All-Star Games. (1974)

TOMMY CONNOLLY
Umpire (1898-1931) Connolly became an NL umpire in 1898. Frustrated with the circuit, he signed with the AL in 1901. Thirty years later he was named chief of AL umpires. Connolly and Bill Klem became the first umpires named to the Hall of Fame. Connolly umpired in eight World Series, including the first, in 1903. (1953)

ROGER CONNOR
First baseman (1880-1897) Until Babe Ruth broke the mark in 1921, Connor held the lifetime record for home runs with 138. A career .317 hitter, the Giant first baseman was a bona fide dead-ball era slugger, smacking 233 triples, fifth all time. In his first game with the Giants in 1883, he hit such an impressive shot that the fans passed the hat and bought him a gold watch. He scored 1,620 runs and had 1,322 RBI in his career. (1976)

STAN COVELESKI
Pitcher (1912; 1916-1928) A coal miner at age 13, Coveleski didn't reach the majors to stay until 1916, at age 27. The spitball artist had his best years with Cleveland from 1918 to 1921, winning 20 games or more each season. Coveleski won 215 games, while his brother Harry won 81. Stan lost only 142 games and retired with a lifetime 2.89 ERA. (1969)

SAM CRAWFORD
Outfielder (1899-1917) Crawford played outfield for Detroit alongside Ty Cobb. The powerful Crawford is baseball's all-time leader in triples with 309, having smashed at least 10 in every full season he played. A native of Wahoo, Nebraska, "Wahoo Sam" retired only 39 hits shy of 3,000. He hit .309 lifetime, with 1,391 runs scored and 1,525 RBI. He later returned to baseball as an umpire in the Pacific Coast League. (1957)

JOE CRONIN
Shortstop (1926-1945); manager (1933-1947); AL President (1959-1973) For 50 years, Cronin excelled as a player, manager, and executive. In 1934 the Red Sox purchased the hard-hitting shortstop from Washington for a record $225,000. Cronin was a .301 career batter, and he had 1,233 runs scored and 1,424 RBI to go with his 515 doubles. As a manager, Cronin led the Senators to a pennant in 1933 and the Red Sox to one in 1946. From 1959 to 1973, he served as AL president. (1956)

CANDY CUMMINGS
Pitcher (1872-1877) Baseball's legendary inventor of the curveball, Cummings allegedly discovered the pitch while tossing clam shells as a youngster. Despite

HALL OF FAME

standing 5'9" and never weighing more than 120 pounds, he won 146 games from 1872 to 1877. (1939)

KIKI CUYLER
Outfielder (1921-1938) Pronounced "Cuy-Cuy," Kiki Cuyler hit a robust .354 as a Pirate rookie in 1924 and was heralded as "the next Ty Cobb." Kiki hit over .300 10 times and topped the .350 mark four times. He accumulated 2,299 hits for a lifetime mark of .321. He had 1,295 runs, 1,065 RBI, and 328 stolen bases during his career. (1968)

RAY DANDRIDGE
Third baseman (1933-1950) Dandridge excelled at third base in the Negro and Mexican Leagues, hitting for power and average while fielding with precision. He accumulated a .347 average against white big-league pitching. In 1949, he signed with the Giants and tore apart the American Association for Minneapolis, but at age 36 never received a call to the majors. (1987)

LEON DAY
Pitcher; second baseman; outfielder (1934-1949) Using a no-windup delivery, Day was a star pitcher in the Negro Leagues. He defeated the legendary Satchel Paige three out of four times and once struck out 19 men in one game. Day also played the field and posted an unofficial lifetime mark of .288. He was named to the Hall of Fame a week before he died. (1995)

DIZZY DEAN
Pitcher (1930-1941; 1947) Baseball's most colorful pitcher, Dean threw smoke, spoke in homespun hyperbole, and by age 26 had won 134 games for the Cardinals. After breaking his toe in the 1937 All-Star Game, Dean altered his pitching motion, hurt his arm, and never approached his previous record. He had a 150-83 career record with a 3.02 ERA. Dizzy was the last NL pitcher to notch 30 wins in a season when he went 30-7 in 1934. (1953)

ED DELAHANTY
Outfielder (1888-1903) One of five brothers to play in the majors, Delahanty was perhaps baseball's premier hitter of the 1890s. He hit .400 three times, and his .346 career mark is fourth all time. He lived as hard as he played. In 1903, Delahanty was suspended for drinking. En route to his home, "Big Ed" (age 35) was kicked off a train, fell into the Niagara River, and was swept over the falls to his death. (1945)

BILL DICKEY
Catcher (1928-1943; 1946) Catcher of 100 or more games for 13 consecutive seasons, Dickey hit .362 in 1936, still a record for the position. He also accumulated a .313 batting average and 1,209 RBI in his career. During his 17 years, the Yankees won nine pennants and captured eight world championships. Dickey is also credited with developing the receiving skills of Yogi Berra. (1954)

MARTIN DIHIGO
Pitcher; infielder; outfielder (1923-1945) The first Cuban elected to the Hall, Dihigo starred as a pitcher, infielder, and outfielder in Negro and Caribbean baseball. Winner of more than 250 games from the mound, he hit over .400 three times. He was one of the most versatile players in the game's history; he was able to play all of the infield positions, as well as being one of the best hurlers in history. (1977)

JOE DiMAGGIO
Outfielder (1936-1942; 1946-1951) "Joltin' Joe" led the Yankees to nine pennants while making 13 All-Star Teams in 13 sea-

sons. A three-time MVP, the quiet, graceful center fielder is often credited with being the best player of his generation. In 1941, "The Yankee Clipper" hit in a record 56 consecutive games. He led the AL in batting average twice, slugging average twice, triples once, home runs twice, runs scored once, and RBI twice. He retired with a .325 batting average, 361 home runs, 1,390 runs scored, and 1,537 RBI. (1955)

BOBBY DOERR
Second baseman (1937-1944; 1946-1951) Doerr was known for his reliable defensive play and potent bat. For 14 seasons he was one of the best second basemen in baseball, spending his entire career with the Red Sox, and never playing a game at another position. In 1944, Doerr led the AL in slugging at .528. He had a career .288 average, 223 homers, and 1,247 RBI. (1986)

DON DRYSDALE
Pitcher (1956-1969) In the early 1960s, Drysdale and teammate Sandy Koufax gave the Dodgers baseball's best pitching tandem. The intimidating Drysdale led the NL in Ks three times. He won the Cy Young Award in 1962, going 25-9 with a 2.83 ERA and a league-best 232 strikeouts. In 1968, "Big D" hurled six shutouts in a row on his way to 58 consecutive scoreless innings. He was 209-166 with a 2.95 ERA and 2,486 strikeouts. (1984)

HUGH DUFFY
Outfielder (1888-1906) In 1894, the diminutive Duffy hit .440 for NL Boston, the highest mark ever recorded under current rules. He also captured the Triple Crown that year, with 18 homers and 145 RBI. He compiled a career .324 average, 1,551 runs, and 1,299 RBI. After his retirement, Duffy continued in baseball another 48 seasons. (1945)

LEO DUROCHER
Manager (1939-1946; 1948-1955; 1966-1973) A shortstop for 17 years in the bigs, "Leo the Lip" as manager compiled a 2,008-1,709 record and a .540 winning percentage. In 1951, he piloted the Giants to the "Miracle at Coogan's Bluff" and reached three World Series overall, winning the championship in 1954. In 1947, he was suspended for one year for conduct detrimental to baseball. (1994)

BILLY EVANS
Umpire (1906-1927) Evans was a sportswriter and then did what many writers thought they could do better—be an umpire. He was one of the best, working six Series. (1973)

JOHNNY EVERS
Second baseman (1902-1917; 1922; 1929) Perhaps the best of the "Tinker-to-Evers-to-Chance" double-play combination, second baseman Evers relied on a steady glove and just enough hitting to help lead his club to five pennants in 16 seasons. Although he played most of his career with the Cubs, in 1914 he was the NL MVP with the "Miracle" Boston Braves. "The Trojan" had 919 runs and 324 stolen bases. (1946)

BUCK EWING
Catcher (1880-1897) Connie Mack called Ewing "the greatest catcher of all time." He eclipsed the .300 mark in 10 seasons, including a string of eight straight times. Ewing had a lifetime .303 batting average and scored 1,129 runs. (1939)

RED FABER
Pitcher (1914-1933) One of the last spitball pitchers, Faber spent his entire 20-year career with the White Sox, posting a 254-213 record. An illness and injury in 1919 left him untouched by the "Black Sox" scandal. He led the AL in ERA and in

complete games twice. Faber posted a career 3.15 ERA in 4,086⅔ innings, with 273 complete games. (1964)

BOB FELLER
Pitcher (1936-1941; 1945-1956) Phenom Feller left the farm at age 17 and struck out 15 in his first official big-league appearance. Amazingly, he was signed by a Cleveland scout for one dollar and an autographed baseball. Feller's fastball, once timed at over 98 mph, may have been the fastest of all time. "Rapid Robert" led the AL seven times in strikeouts, six seasons in wins, and four times in shutouts. Feller won 266 games, all for Cleveland, with three no-hitters. (1962)

RICK FERRELL
Catcher (1929-1947) One of the few players inducted primarily for his defense, Ferrell nonetheless hit .300 four times. He was a career .281 hitter and drew 931 walks. For four seasons with the Red Sox, Ferrell teamed with brother Wes. (1984)

ROLLIE FINGERS
Pitcher (1968-1985) The earliest to be used in a "closer" role, Fingers was the first pitcher to reach 300 saves. He was the fireman for the champion Athletics in the early 1970s, then led the NL in saves with San Diego. In 1981 with the Brewers, he won the MVP and Cy Young Awards. He had 341 career saves. (1992)

ELMER FLICK
Outfielder (1898-1910) A speedy outfielder for the Phillies and Indians, in 1905 Flick won the AL batting crown with an average of .308. In the spring of 1907, Detroit thought so much of Flick it offered Ty Cobb in trade but was turned down. That season Flick hit .302 in his last full season, while Cobb hit .350 in his first. Flick had a .313 career batting average. (1963)

WHITEY FORD
Pitcher (1950; 1953-1967) Ford's winning percentage of .690 is the best of any 20th-century pitcher. The Yankee pitcher led the American League in wins three times and ERA twice. Ford holds eight World Series pitching records, including wins (10) and strikeouts (94). His 25-4 record in 1961 earned him the Cy Young Award. "The Chairman of the Board" was 236-106 lifetime with a 2.75 ERA and 156 complete games. (1974)

RUBE FOSTER
Executive; pitcher As a star pitcher for a number of early black teams, and later as the first president of the Negro National League, Foster earned the title "Father of Black Baseball." Foster's efforts in organizing the NNL gave black baseball stability. He in effect saved the Negro League and made it popular. (1981)

JIMMIE FOXX
First baseman (1925-1942; 1944-1945) For 12 consecutive seasons with the Athletics and Red Sox, Foxx slammed 30 or more home runs and knocked in more than 100 runs. In 1933, Foxx hit .356, swatted 48 homers, and knocked in 163 runs to win the Triple Crown. Winner of three MVP Awards, "Double X" had a lifetime slugging average of .609, fourth all time. Foxx had 534 career homers, 1,922 runs batted in, and a .325 batting average. (1951)

FORD FRICK
NL President (1934-1951); Commissioner (1951-1965) Frick was named NL president in 1934. In 1951, he was elected commissioner. He helped establish the Hall of Fame, supported Branch Rickey's signing of Jackie Robinson, and presided over baseball's busiest period of expansion. (1970)

FRANKIE FRISCH
Second baseman (1919-1937) A member of more NL pennant winners than any other player, Frisch played in four fall classics with the Giants and four with the Cardinals. He cracked the .300 mark 13 times, scored 100 runs seven times, and was the 1931 NL MVP. As player-manager, "The Fordham Flash" led the "Gashouse Gang" to the title in 1934. He scored 1,532 career runs and hit .316. (1947)

PUD GALVIN
Pitcher (1875; 1879-1892) Nicknamed "Pud" because he made pudding out of hitters, Galvin was pitcher supreme for NL Buffalo in the 1880s. On his way to 364 career victories, Galvin pitched more than 400 innings nine times and won 46 games in 1883 and '84. "Gentle Jeems" is tied for 10th on the all-time list with 58 shutouts and is second all time with 646 complete games and 6,000⅓ innings. (1965)

LOU GEHRIG
First baseman (1923-1939) "The Iron Horse," Gehrig played in 2,130 consecutive games for the Yankees. Gehrig knocked 46 home runs and set the AL record for RBI with 184 in 1931. He had more than 40 home runs in five seasons, more than 150 RBI in seven seasons, and a .600 slugging percentage in nine seasons. "Columbia Lou" had a .632 career slugging percentage, a .340 batting average, 493 home runs, 1,995 RBI, and 1,888 runs scored. Although fatally ill with amyotrophic lateral sclerosis, he bid farewell to 61,000 fans at Yankee Stadium in 1939 by saying, "Today I consider myself the luckiest man on the face of the Earth." The waiting period for the Hall was waived, and Gehrig was admitted. (1939)

CHARLIE GEHRINGER
Second baseman (1924-1942) His efficient play at second base for the Tigers earned Gehringer the appellation "The Mechanical Man." He regularly led the league in fielding and hit over .300 in 13 of 16 seasons. He logged over 100 RBI and had 200 or more hits in seven seasons. In 1937, his loop-high .371 average made him AL MVP. He had a career .320 batting average, 2,839 hits, 1,774 runs scored, and 1,427 RBI. (1949)

BOB GIBSON
Pitcher (1959-1975) In 1968, Gibson had the second-lowest ERA in modern NL history, a stingy 1.12, while winning both Cy Young and MVP honors. He also won the Cy Young Award in 1970. In the 1967 World Series, he led St. Louis to victory over Boston, winning three times while giving up only 14 hits. Gibson's speed and control resulted in 251 career wins. "Hoot" had a career 2.91 ERA, 3,117 Ks, and 255 complete games. (1981)

JOSH GIBSON
Catcher (1930-1946) For 16 seasons Gibson reigned as the Negro Leagues' supreme slugger, perhaps smacking nearly 1,000 home runs and as many as 90 in a single season. The powerful catcher was often called the black Babe Ruth; in another time, Ruth may have been referred to as the poor man's Josh Gibson. One of the most dedicated players ever, Gibson would play 200 games over a single year. In 1947, with Jackie Robinson on the verge of breaking the big-league color line, Gibson, only age 36, died of a brain hemorrhage. (1972)

WARREN GILES
NL President (1951-1969) Giles started as president of minor-league Moline in 1919 and ended 50 years later as president of the NL. During his tenure, he oversaw the transfer of the Giants and Dodgers to California, and the addition of four expansion franchises. (1979)

LEFTY GOMEZ
Pitcher (1930-1943) Gomez's sense of humor was matched only by his skill on the mound. A 20-game winner four times for the Yankees, Gomez went undefeated in six World Series decisions. He led the American League in strikeouts three times and in ERA twice. His secret to success? Quipped Lefty, "Clean living and a fast outfield." "Goofy" was 189-102 with a 3.34 ERA. (1972)

GOOSE GOSLIN
Outfielder (1921-1938) The best hitter ever to play for the Senators, Goslin led Washington to its only three appearances in the World Series. He slugged three home runs in both the 1924 and 1925 fall classics. Goose had 100 RBI or more and batted over .300 in 11 seasons. He had 1,609 RBI, 2,735 hits, and a .316 average. (1968)

HANK GREENBERG
First baseman (1930; 1933-1941; 1945-1947) Despite playing only nine full seasons, Greenberg smacked 331 home runs and captured AL MVP honors in 1935 and 1940 for the Tigers. He lost three years to World War II but came back in 1946 to lead the AL in homers and RBI. He had league- and career-high totals of 58 dingers (1938) and 183 RBI (1937). "Hammerin' Hank" had a career .313 batting average, a .605 slugging percentage, and 1,276 RBI. (1956)

CLARK GRIFFITH
Manager (1901-1920) A leading pitcher of the 1890s, Griffith won 20 games in six straight seasons. Over a 20-year period the cagey "Old Fox" managed the White Sox, Yankees, Reds, and Senators. He had a 1,491-1,367 record and won only one pennant. He was also president of the Senators from 1920 to 1955. (1946)

BURLEIGH GRIMES
Pitcher (1916-1934) In 1934, Grimes threw the last legal spitter in baseball history. Over the preceding 19 seasons, he won 270 games with seven teams. One of a handful of pitchers allowed to throw the spitter after its ban in 1920, Grimes was the most successful. "Ol' Stubblebeard" won more than 20 games five times. (1964)

LEFTY GROVE
Pitcher (1925-1941) In an era dominated by hitting, the left-handed Grove was almost unhittable, winning 20 games or more seven straight seasons with Connie Mack's Philadelphia A's, including a remarkable 31-4 mark in 1931. That year, "Mose" was the AL MVP. On his way to 300 wins, he led the AL in strikeouts seven times, ERA nine times, complete games three times, and winning percentage five times. (1947)

CHICK HAFEY
Outfielder (1924-1937) Hafey's misfortune was to play before the advent of the batting helmet. Several beanings and a chronic sinus condition affected his vision, forcing him to wear glasses in an effort to correct the damage. Nevertheless, Chick hit over .300 in nine seasons and captured the NL title in 1931 with a .349 mark. He was known for his rifle arm and his line drives. Ill health and vision problems, however, forced the career .317 batter to retire. (1971)

JESSE HAINES
Pitcher (1918; 1920-1937) Knuckleballer Haines didn't make the big leagues for good until he was 26 years old. However, he stuck around until he was 45, winning 20 games three times and finishing with 210 victories for the Cardinals, including a no-hitter against the Braves in 1924. In 1927, he racked up a 24-10 record, lead-

ing the NL with 25 complete games and six shutouts. "Pop" had 209 complete games. (1970)

BILLY HAMILTON
Outfielder (1888-1901) While playing with Philadelphia and Boston in the NL, "Sliding Billy" ran into the record books. He was credited with 912 stolen bases, although for most of his career a runner received credit for a base theft by advancing an extra base on a hit. He had a lifetime .344 batting average. In 1894, his ability on the bases let him score a record 196 times. (1961)

WILL HARRIDGE
AL President (1931-1959) Harridge stayed out of the limelight and quietly led the league. An early supporter of the All-Star Game and night baseball, Harridge insisted on order. (1972)

BUCKY HARRIS
Manager (1924-1943; 1947-1948; 1950-1956) An above-average second baseman for the Senators, Harris was a natural leader who had his greatest success as manager. In his first season as player-manager in 1924, he led the Senators to their only world championship. He went on to manage another 28 seasons with five other clubs, going 2,157-2,218. Harris was a respected strategist. (1975)

GABBY HARTNETT
Catcher (1922-1941) In his time, Hartnett was likely the NL's best catcher. A fine defensive catcher, his best season was 1930, when he hit .339 with 37 home runs and 122 RBI. He was an All-Star from 1933 through 1938. In the 1934 game, he was the backstop when Ruth, Gehrig, Foxx, Simmons, and Cronin were struck out in order. He hit .344 as the NL MVP in 1935. His late-season, ninth-inning "homer in the gloaming" against Pittsburgh won the 1938 pennant for the Cubs. He had a .297 career batting average, with 236 homers and 1,179 RBI. (1955)

HARRY HEILMANN
Outfielder (1914; 1916-1930; 1932) In the four seasons that Heilmann won the AL batting crown, his lowest average was .393. He batted over .300 in 12 seasons and hit an amazing .403 in 1923. Playing mostly for Detroit, the slow-footed outfielder (nicknamed "Slug") wielded a line-drive bat that resulted in 2,660 hits, including 542 doubles, for a .342 average. (1952)

BILLY HERMAN
Second baseman (1931-1943; 1946-1947) A 10-time All-Star, Herman's 227 hits and 57 doubles in 1935 were tops in the NL. The best defensive second baseman in the loop, he hit .300 or better eight times in his career. After playing most of his career for the Cubs, in 1941 he was traded to Brooklyn. Herman had a career .304 batting average and 486 doubles. (1975)

HARRY HOOPER
Outfielder (1909-1925) A right field star, Hooper's arm was legendary (he averaged 20 assists a year) as he teamed with Duffy Lewis and Tris Speaker to give the BoSox the best outfield of the era. A lifetime .281 hitter, Hooper scored 1,429 runs. (1971)

ROGERS HORNSBY
Second baseman (1915-1937) Perhaps the greatest right-handed hitter of all time, Hornsby's career .358 average is second only to Ty Cobb's .366. "Rajah's" .424 mark in 1924 is the best of the century. His greatest success came with the Cardinals; from 1920 to 1925 he collected six straight batting titles, as well as two Triple Crowns. Hornsby's fierce demeanor made

WAITE HOYT
Pitcher (1918-1938) The Yankee pitching ace of the 1920s, Hoyt won 20 games only twice but compiled a 6-4 record in the World Series with a 1.83 ERA. In 1927, "Schoolboy" led the AL in wins (22) and ERA (2.63). He won in double figures 12 seasons and had a career 237-182 record. He was one of the first ex-ballplayers to work in broadcasting. (1969)

CAL HUBBARD
Umpire (1936-1951; 1954-1962) Hubbard is the only man in the baseball, college football, and pro football Halls of Fame. When he retired from football he became an AL umpire. (1976)

CARL HUBBELL
Pitcher (1928-1943) Hubbell used the screwball to notch 253 career wins and a 2.98 ERA, all for the Giants. From 1933 to 1937, he posted five straight 20-win seasons, and was NL MVP in '33 and '36. "King Carl" led the NL in wins three times, ERA three times, and strikeouts once. In the 1934 All-Star Game, the left-handed "Meal Ticket" struck out five straight Hall of Famers—Babe Ruth, Lou Gehrig, Jimmie Foxx, Al Simmons, and Joe Cronin. (1947)

MILLER HUGGINS
Manager (1913-1929) Huggins was the Yankee manager of the 1920s. Standing only 5'6", he was the one man able to temper the boisterous Babe Ruth. "The Mighty Mite's" 1927 Yankees team is widely considered the best of all time. "Hug" was 1,413-1,134 in his career, including five seasons with mediocre Cardinal clubs. He won six pennants and three Series in his 12 years with the Yankees. (1964)

WILLIAM HULBERT
Executive Hulbert, an official in the poorly run National Association during the 1870s, spearheaded the formation of the National League in 1876. Becoming NL president in 1877, Hulbert successfully dealt with such league problems as gambling and loose organization and kept the league alive. He also owned the Chicago White Stockings, an NL dynasty in the 1880s. (1995)

CATFISH HUNTER
Pitcher (1965-1979) Given his nickname by A's owner Charlie Finley, Hunter went directly from high school to the major leagues. Beginning in 1971, Catfish won more than 20 games five straight seasons and earned the Cy Young Award in 1974 with a 25-12 record. After three A's world championships (1972 to 1974), Hunter signed with the Yankees for $3.75 million in 1975, then the biggest contract in baseball history. He had a 224-166 career record with a 3.26 ERA and 2,012 strikeouts. (1987)

MONTE IRVIN
Outfielder (Negro Leagues 1939-1943; 1945-1948; NL 1949-1956) Despite twice leading the Negro National League in hitting, the 30-year-old Irvin was not signed by the Giants until 1949. He began his Negro League career in 1939, and he also played in the Mexican League, where he won a Triple Crown in 1940. In eight NL seasons, he hit .293, leading the league in RBI with 121 in 1951. (1973)

REGGIE JACKSON
Outfielder (1967-1987) "The Straw that Stirs the Drink," Jackson was a publicity hog, a prolific slugger, a superior outfielder, and most of all, a big winner. He played on 11 division winners and five world champions. "Mr. October's" finest moment came in game six of the 1977

Series, when he smacked three homers. The four-time home run king had 563 homers and 1,702 RBI, but he also compiled more strikeouts (2,597) than any other player. (1993)

TRAVIS JACKSON
Shortstop (1922-1936) A solid defensive shortstop for the Giants of the 1920s and 1930s, Jackson helped the club to four pennants. "Stonewall" also batted over .300 in six seasons. He accumulated a career average of .291. (1982)

FERGUSON JENKINS
Pitcher (1965-1983) After being traded from the Phillies to the Cubs in early 1966, Jenkins embarked on a string of six consecutive 20-plus win seasons. He won only 14 games in 1973 and was traded to Texas, where he won the 1974 Cy Young Award with a 25-12 record. One of the game's most durable pitchers, Jenkins had a career 284-226 record, with a 3.34 ERA and 3,192 Ks. (1991)

HUGHIE JENNINGS
Shortstop (1891-1903; 1907; 1909; 1912; 1918); manager (1907-1920; 1924) From 1894 to 1897 as shortstop of NL Baltimore, Jennings led the club to pennants. In his five years with Baltimore, he never hit below .328 and was a lifetime .311 hitter. He was 1,163-984 as a manager. (1945)

BAN JOHNSON
AL President (1901-1927) The founder of the American League, Johnson was arguably the most powerful man in baseball during the first quarter of the 20th century. When the minor Western League folded in 1893, Johnson revived it. He put it on solid footing and made it a major league in 1901. The "Black Sox" scandal of 1920 undermined his power, however, and led to the commissioner system, ultimately leading to Johnson's retirement in 1927. (1937)

JUDY JOHNSON
Third baseman (1919-1936) The greatest third baseman in Negro League history, Johnson combined steady defensive play with stellar batting performances. A line-drive hitter, Johnson hit .390 and .406 in two of his seasons with the Philadelphia Hilldales, leading them to two black World Series appearances. In later years, Judy scouted for the A's and Phillies. (1975)

WALTER JOHNSON
Pitcher (1907-1927) One of the first five men elected to the Hall, Johnson's legendary fastball and pinpoint control enabled him to win 417 games (second on the all-time list) with the usually inferior Senators. In his 20-year career, "The Big Train" led the AL in strikeouts 12 times, shutouts seven times, and in victories six times. Johnson's 110 shutouts are the most in history. "Barney's" 2.17 career ERA is eighth lowest, his 531 complete games rank fourth, and his 5,915 innings pitched are the third most in baseball. (1936)

ADDIE JOSS
Pitcher (1902-1910) In only nine seasons with Cleveland, Joss won 160 games with a winning percentage of .623 and an ERA of 1.89 (second all time). He struck out 920 batters and walked only 364 in 2,327 innings pitched. In 1911, he died of tubercular meningitis at age 31. The Hall's usual 10-year career requirement was waived for Joss. (1978)

AL KALINE
Outfielder (1953-1974) As a 20-year-old outfielder with Detroit in 1955, Kaline won the batting title, with a .340 average, to become the youngest batting champion ever. Although he never duplicated that

figure, he played in 18 All-Star Games, won 11 Gold Gloves, and accumulated 3,007 hits. He also belted 498 doubles, 399 home runs, and 1,583 RBI, with 1,622 runs scored and 1,277 walks. (1980)

TIM KEEFE
Pitcher (1880-1893) In only 14 seasons, Keefe won 342 games, one of six 19th-century pitchers to top the 300 mark. Remarkably, after overhand pitching was legalized in 1884, Keefe continued to pitch—and win—underhanded. "Sir Timothy" pioneered the use of the changeup to notch a career 2.62 ERA with 554 complete games. (1964)

WEE WILLIE KEELER
Outfielder (1892-1910) Keeler said, "I hit 'em where they ain't." Utilizing his good speed and batting skills, he developed the "Baltimore chop" to bounce the ball over and between infielders. From 1894 to 1901, he collected a major-league-record 200 hits each season. He had 2,932 career hits, 1,719 runs, and a .341 batting average. In 1897, he hit in 44 consecutive games. That same year he notched a personal best .424 batting average. (1939)

GEORGE KELL
Third baseman (1943-1957) An excellent third baseman and career .306 hitter, Kell excelled for five different clubs in the 1940s and 1950s. In 1949, he edged out Ted Williams for his only batting crown, hitting .3429 to Williams's .3427. Kell scored a lifetime 881 runs and drove in 870 runs. (1983)

JOE KELLEY
Outfielder (1891-1906; 1908) Kelley played for the great Baltimore teams of the 1890s and later went on to star with Brooklyn and Cincinnati. He batted over .300 for 11 straight years. In 1894, he hit .393 and went 9-for-9 in a doubleheader. Kelley had a lifetime .317 batting average, with 194 triples, and 1,424 runs scored. (1971)

GEORGE KELLY
First baseman (1915-1917; 1919-1930; 1932) After failing in his first three seasons in the bigs, Kelly came into his own for the Giants in 1919. From 1921 to 1926, Kelly hit over .300 and averaged 108 RBI, helping the Giants capture four pennants. He was a .297 hitter and totaled 1,020 RBI. (1973)

KING KELLY
Outfielder; catcher (1878-1893) Baseball's first celebrity, Kelly was the subject of the popular song, "Slide, Kelly, Slide" and recited "Casey At The Bat" on stage. On the field, he perfected the hit-and-run and developed the hook and head-first slides. He hit .308 lifetime and scored 1,357 runs. (1945)

HARMON KILLEBREW
First baseman; third baseman (1954-1975) Killebrew hit 573 home runs; only Babe Ruth hit more in AL history. Killebrew led the league in homers six times, each time hitting more than 40. "Killer" had 40 or more homers in eight different seasons. The 1969 AL MVP also drove in more than 100 RBI in nine years, pacing the AL three times. He hit only .256 lifetime but had 1,559 bases on balls. (1984)

RALPH KINER
Outfielder (1946-1955) Joining Pittsburgh after World War II, Kiner led or tied for the NL lead in homers in his first seven seasons. He had 369 lifetime dingers, 1,015 RBI, and 1,011 bases on balls in 10 years. Kiner has enjoyed a second career as a broadcaster for the Mets. (1975)

CHUCK KLEIN
Outfielder (1928-1944) Playing five and one-half seasons in Philadelphia's cozy Baker Bowl, Klein led the NL in homers four times and never hit below .337. He was the 1932 NL MVP and won the Triple Crown in 1933 (.368 average, 28 homers, 120 RBI). Klein set an all-time record for outfield assists with 44 in 1930. He had a lifetime .320 batting average, 300 homers, and 1,201 RBI. (1980)

BILL KLEM
Umpire (1905-1941) Baseball's best-known umpire, Klem revolutionized the position and is credited with being the first to employ hand signals and don a chest protector. He worked a record 18 World Series, and he was the umpire at the first All-Star Game in 1933. (1953)

SANDY KOUFAX
Pitcher (1955-1966) Koufax had two careers. His best record in his first six years was an 11-11 mark. But between 1961 and 1966, the lefty led the NL in wins and shutouts three times each and Ks four times. Koufax paced the Dodgers to pennants in '63, '65, and '66 while winning the Cy Young Award each year. His 25-5 record in 1963 earned him the NL MVP Award. Pitching in excruciating pain due to arthritis, Koufax led the NL in ERA his final five seasons, culminating with a 1.73 mark while going 27-9 in '66. He had a 165-87 record with a 2.76 career ERA, 2,396 Ks, and only 817 walks. (1972)

NAP LAJOIE
Second baseman (1896-1916) One of the best righty batters in history, Lajoie was the best second baseman of his era and became the first man at his position to be elected to the Hall. A graceful fielder, he hit over .300 16 times in his career. He won the Triple Crown in 1901, the American League's debut season; he batted .426 with 14 homers and 125 RBI. His presence gave the AL respect. Lajoie had a career .338 average, 3,242 hits, and 657 doubles. (1937)

KENESAW MOUNTAIN LANDIS
Commissioner (1920-1944) Baseball's first commissioner, Landis left his job as a federal judge in 1920 to take complete control of the major leagues. In cleaning up the "Black Sox" scandal, he restored the public's confidence in the integrity of baseball. His rule was law, and nobody dared challenge his authority. A champion of player rights, he unsuccessfully tried to halt the farm system—one of the few battles he ever lost. (1944)

TONY LAZZERI
Second baseman (1926-1939) The second baseman on the "Murderer's Row" Yankee teams of the 1920s and '30s, Lazzeri combined power, high average, and slick fielding. A career .292 hitter who socked 178 homers, "Poosh 'Em Up" topped the .300 mark five times and hit .354 in 1929. (1991)

BOB LEMON
Pitcher (1941-1942; 1946-1958) Lemon made the big leagues as a third baseman, but he made the Hall of Fame as a pitcher. Switched to pitching during World War II, Lemon won 20 games for the Indians seven times from 1948 to 1956. He led the AL in wins three times and in complete games five times. He had a career 207-128 record for a .618 winning percentage. As manager, he led the Yankees to a championship in 1978. (1976)

BUCK LEONARD
First baseman (1934-1948) In the Negro Leagues, Walter Leonard played Lou Gehrig to teammate Josh Gibson's Babe Ruth. Leonard played for the Homestead

Grays and helped lead them to nine consecutive pennants. He was a left-handed power hitter and clutch RBI man who hit for a high average. He twice led the NNL in hitting, peaking at .410 in 1947. In 1952, at age 45, Leonard turned down an offer from Bill Veeck to play for the St. Louis Browns. (1972)

FREDDIE LINDSTROM
Third baseman (1924-1936) Lindstrom survived two bad-hop grounders in the '24 World Series and went on to top the .300 mark seven times, including a .379 average in 1930. A year later an injury led to a switch to the outfield. He batted .311 lifetime, with 301 doubles and 895 runs scored. (1976)

POP LLOYD
Shortstop (1905-1932) The finest shortstop in Negro baseball, Lloyd's stellar performance in a 1909 exhibition series against Ty Cobb's Tigers so embarrassed Cobb he vowed never to play blacks again. In 1928, despite being age 44, Lloyd led the Negro National League in batting with an eye-popping .564 average. From his time in Cuba, his nickname was *"El Cuchara,"* which means "scoop" in Spanish. (1977)

ERNIE LOMBARDI
Catcher (1931-1947) Called "Schnozz" because of his enormous nose, Lombardi was a slow, awkward-looking catcher who could hit a ton. He surpassed the .300 mark 10 times. In 1938, his league-leading .342 average with Cincinnati earned him the NL MVP Award. Five years later with the Braves, Lombardi again led the league with a .330 average, becoming the only catcher to do so twice. He hit .306 lifetime, with 990 RBI. (1986)

AL LOPEZ
Catcher (1928; 1930-1947); manager (1951-1965; 1968-1969) A workhorse behind the plate, Lopez held the major-league record for games caught until 1987. He turned manager in 1951, and in 1954 led Cleveland to 111 wins. In 1959, he won another pennant with the White Sox. He drove his 17 teams to a 1,410-1,004 record for a .584 winning percentage. Usually losing the pennant to the Yankees, Lopez's clubs finished second in the AL 10 times. (1977)

TED LYONS
Pitcher (1923-1942; 1946) Lyons had the misfortune of pitching for some bad White Sox teams. He won 260 games, with 356 complete games. He led the AL in shutouts twice and wins twice. In 1942, he led the AL with a 2.10 ERA. At age 42, he served three years in World War II, then returned to baseball for one last season. (1955)

CONNIE MACK
Manager (1894-1896; 1901-1950) As player, manager, and owner, Mack had a career that spanned an incredible eight decades. Manager of the Athletics from 1901 to 1950, Mack built then tore apart several championship clubs. His first dynasty was from 1910 to 1914, when the Athletics won four pennants and three world championships. He sold off many of those players and finished in last place from 1915 to 1921. His second dynasty was the 1929 to 1931 clubs—three pennants and two world champs. He compiled a 3,731-3,948 record in his 53 years as a manager. (1937)

LARRY MacPHAIL
Executive As an executive with the Reds, Dodgers, and Yankees, MacPhail played a part in virtually every baseball development between the wars. He brought air travel and lights to the major leagues in 1935, and radio broadcasts to Brooklyn in 1938. (1978)

HALL OF FAME

MICKEY MANTLE
Outfielder (1951-1968) Named after Mickey Cochrane, Mantle was taught to switch hit and became baseball's leading switch-hitter. Succeeding Joe DiMaggio as Yankee center fielder, all Mantle did was match Joe's three MVP Awards (1956, 1957, 1962). "The Commerce Comet" hit .353 with 52 homers and 130 RBI to win the Triple Crown in 1956. He led the AL in home runs four times, RBI once, runs scored six times, and walks five times. If not for a series of knee injuries, Mantle may have been the best of all time. He had the most all-time World Series homers, RBI, and runs. He possessed a .298 batting average, 536 homers, 1,509 RBI, 1,677 runs scored, and 1,733 walks. (1974)

HEINIE MANUSH
Outfielder (1923-1939) Often overlooked, Manush was one of the best hitters during his era. Topping the .300 mark 11 times, he compiled a career average of .330. Playing for the Tigers, Browns, Senators, Braves, Pirates, and Dodgers, he led his league in hits twice. Manush notched 1,183 career RBI and 1,287 runs. (1964)

RABBIT MARANVILLE
Shortstop (1912-1933; 1935) A top defensive shortstop and consummate showman, Maranville was the kind of player that did the little things to make his team better. A superior fielder, he ranks first among all shortstops in putouts (5,139). Maranville collected 2,605 hits and scored 1,255 runs. (1954)

JUAN MARICHAL
Pitcher (1960-1975) In the mid-1960s, the Giants' Marichal was one of the best and most consistent pitchers in the game. His patented high leg kick masked a multitude of pitches. A six-time 20-game winner, Marichal somehow failed to win the Cy Young Award. His 243 career wins more than made up for that omission. He led the league in shutouts and in complete games twice. "The Dominican Dandy" had a career 243-142 record, a 2.89 ERA, 2,303 Ks, and 52 shutouts. (1983)

RUBE MARQUARD
Pitcher (1908-1925) In 1912, Marquard won his first 19 decisions for the Giants on his way to a 26-11 record. Although he won 23 games the following season, he never again matched his earlier play. Marquard had a 201-177 career record with 197 complete games. (1971)

EDDIE MATHEWS
Third baseman (1952-1968) Mathews combined with Hank Aaron to form one of the best power combos ever. For 14 consecutive years, Mathews hit 23 or more home runs, hitting 40 or more four times. A steady defensive player, he was an All-Star nine times. He led the NL in bases on balls in four seasons to retire with a total of 1,444. He also tallied 512 career homers, 1,453 RBI, and 1,509 runs scored. (1978)

CHRISTY MATHEWSON
Pitcher (1900-1916) As the most popular player in his day, Mathewson dispelled the notion at the time that ballplayers need be crude and uneducated. "Big Six" was also perhaps the game's best pitcher. For 12 consecutive seasons he won 20 or more games for the Giants, as his trademark "fadeaway," a screwball, baffled a generation of batters. In the 1905 World Series, he hurled three shutouts in six days. He led the NL in ERA in five seasons, in Ks five times, and in shutouts four times. "Matty" had a 373-188 career record, with a 2.13 ERA and 79 shutouts. (1936)

WILLIE MAYS
Outfielder (1951-1952; 1954-1973) Mays could do everything: hit, field, and run.

While the Giant center fielder's 660 home runs rank third all time, his magnificent over-the-shoulder catch of Vic Wertz's blast to center field in the 1954 World Series has become the standard against which all other catches are compared. "The Say Hey Kid" led the NL in slugging percentage five times, homers and stolen bases four times, triples three times, and runs scored twice. He had 3,283 career hits, a .302 batting average, a .557 slugging percentage, 1,903 RBI, and 2,062 runs scored. (1979)

JOE McCARTHY
Manager (1926-1946; 1948-1950) In 24 years as manager, McCarthy collected seven world championships and nine pennants. His 2,125-1,333 record gives him an all-time-best .615 winning percentage. Most of his success came with the Yankees, where he won four straight World Series from 1936 to 1939. After winning the National League pennant with the Cubs in 1929, McCarthy piloted the Yankees to a pennant in 1932 to become the first manager to win a pennant in both leagues. (1957)

TOMMY McCARTHY
Outfielder (1884-1896) McCarthy made a lasting mark by perfecting the fly-ball trap in order to throw out the lead runner of a double play, leading to the infield fly rule. Although known for his defense, in 1890 he hit a robust .350. He was a career .292 hitter and topped .300 four times. (1946)

WILLIE McCOVEY
First baseman (1959-1980) Willie McCovey joined Giants teammate Willie Mays to give NL pitchers the willies. McCovey smashed 30 or more home runs seven times, leading the NL in dingers three times and in RBI twice. In 1969, "Stretch" was NL MVP with a .320 average, 45 homers, and 126 RBI. That same year he drew a record 45 intentional walks. In 1970, McCovey homered in all 12 parks, a rare feat. "Big Mac" notched 521 homers, 1,555 RBI, 1,229 runs scored, and 1,345 walks. (1986)

JOE McGINNITY
Pitcher (1899-1908) While McGinnity's nickname "Iron Man" was derived from his off-season occupation in a foundry, it well described his mound efforts. For nine consecutive years he pitched 300-plus innings, topping 400 innings twice and leading the league four times. He had a career 246-142 record with a 2.66 ERA and 314 complete games. He then pitched another 17 seasons in the minors. (1946)

BILL McGOWAN
Umpire (1925-1954) McGowan earned his "No. 1" nickname in the AL because of his renown for accuracy. Chosen to work in eight World Series, he also worked four All-Star Games, including the first in 1933. (1992)

JOHN McGRAW
Manager (1899; 1901-1932) As third baseman for Baltimore in the 1890s, McGraw was talented enough to make the Hall on his merits as a player. As the Giants manager from 1902 to 1932, he dominated baseball during its "scientific" era, and successfully made the transition to the power game of the 1920s. Despite capturing 10 pennants, "Little Napoleon" won the World Series only three times. A manager for 33 years, McGraw racked up 2,784 victories in 4,801 games, both second on the all-time list to Connie Mack. (1937)

BILL McKECHNIE
Manager (1915; 1922-1926; 1928-1946) McKechnie may have been the best-liked manager ever while winning pennants

with three different teams. "The Deacon's" best effort, though, might have been with the fifth-place 1937 Braves, enough to win the Manager of the Year award. He won two world championships and was 1,896-1,723 in 25 years. (1962)

JOE MEDWICK
Outfielder (1932-1948) Medwick provided the power to light up the 1930s Cardinals' "Gashouse Gang." He led the NL in RBI three consecutive years and in hits twice. In 1937, "Ducky" (a nickname he loathed) batted .374 with 31 homers and 154 RBI to capture the Triple Crown. "Muscles" was a brawler who had a career .324 average, 1,383 RBI, and 540 doubles. In the 1934 World Series against Detroit, he was ordered from the field for his own safety. (1968)

JOHNNY MIZE
First baseman (1936-1942; 1946-1953) Despite losing three prime years to World War II, Mize still connected for 359 home runs, primarily with the Cardinals and Giants. He led the NL in homers four times and RBI three times. Sold to the Yankees in 1949, Mize played in five World Series, hitting three home runs in the 1952 classic. "The Big Cat" batted .312 lifetime, slugged .562, and drove in 1,337 runs. (1981)

JOE MORGAN
Second baseman (1963-1984) Where Morgan played, championships followed. After leading Cincinnati's "Big Red Machine" of the mid-1970s to two World Series victories, Morgan led the 1980 Astros to a division title. He then helped Philadelphia capture the pennant in 1983. "Little Joe" won back-to-back NL MVP Awards in 1975 and '76. Only 5'7", he had 268 career homers, 689 stolen bases, 1,133 RBI, 1,650 runs, and 1,865 walks. (1990)

STAN MUSIAL
Outfielder; first baseman (1941-1944; 1946-1963) Originally signed as a pitcher, Musial hurt his arm and transferred to the outfield. Joining the Cardinals in 1941, Musial batted .426 in 12 games, and he went on to lead the NL seven times in batting average. NL MVP in 1943, '46, and '48, he used his "corkscrew" batting stance to hit over .310 for 16 seasons in a row. When he retired in 1963, "Stan the Man" held more than 50 major-league and NL records. He had a career .331 batting average, 3,630 base hits (fourth all time), 725 doubles (third), 475 home runs, 1,951 RBI, and 1,949 runs scored. (1969)

HAL NEWHOUSER
Pitcher (1939-1955) The only pitcher to win back-to-back MVP Awards (in 1944 and '45), Newhouser was a Detroit native who pitched 15 seasons for the Tigers. Slighted by some as a wartime wonder, he had 275 Ks and a 26-9 record in 1946, and a 21-12 record in 1948. He had 207 career wins. (1992)

KID NICHOLS
Pitcher (1890-1901; 1904-1906) Ranked sixth all time in wins with 361, Nichols starred in the 1890s for Boston, leading them to five NL pennants. Winner of 30 games seven times, Nichols finished what he started. In his 501 Boston starts, he was relieved only 25 times. He had a lifetime 361-208 record and a 2.95 ERA. (1949)

JIM O'ROURKE
Outfielder (1872-1893; 1904) In 1876, O'Rourke collected the first base hit in NL history, one of 2,304 he'd gather for his career. A lifetime .310 hitter, O'Rourke's manner of speaking earned him the nickname "Orator Jim." (1945)

MEL OTT
Outfielder (1926-1947) Despite his small stature (5'9", 170 pounds), this Giant outfielder stands as a colossus among the game's sluggers. Ott's unique leg kick enabled him to generate the power for 511 home runs, the first man in NL history to hit 500. He led the NL in homers six times, but in RBI only once. When he retired in 1947, he held the NL career mark for homers, runs scored (1,859), RBI (1,860), and walks (1,708). "Master Melvin" retired with a .304 batting average. (1951)

SATCHEL PAIGE
Pitcher (Negro Leagues 1926-1947; 1950; AL 1948-1949; 1951-1953; 1965) The first African American ever elected to the Hall of Fame, Paige was the Negro Leagues' greatest drawing card. He began pitching for the Birmingham Black Barons in 1926 at age 20. His blazing fastball and effervescent personality made him a legend by age 30. He made his greatest mark on the game by pitching for the Kansas City Monarchs in the 1940s. In 1948, at age 42, he made his major-league debut and helped Cleveland to the AL pennant. (1971)

JIM PALMER
Pitcher (1965-1967; 1969-1984) Ace of Baltimore's powerful teams of the 1970s, Palmer won 20 games eight times on his way to three Cy Young Awards and 268 career wins. He led the AL in ERA twice and in innings pitched four times. He had a career 2.86 ERA, 2,212 Ks, and 1,311 walks in 3,948 innings pitched. (1990)

HERB PENNOCK
Pitcher (1912-1917; 1919-1934) Pennock finessed his way through 22 seasons to earn 240 wins. He had his greatest success with the Yankees of the 1920s, for whom he went 5-0 in World Series play. "The Knight of Kennett Square" won in double figures for 13 seasons and completed 247 of his 420 career starts. (1948)

GAYLORD PERRY
Pitcher (1962-1983) Though he won 314 games, struck out 3,534 batters, and registered a 3.11 ERA during a 22-year career, Perry was best known for throwing—or not throwing—a spitball. He won 20 games five times in his career. He won the AL Cy Young in 1972 and the NL Cy Young in 1978, making him the only pitcher in history to have won the award in both leagues. (1991)

EDDIE PLANK
Pitcher (1901-1917) A late bloomer, Plank didn't reach Connie Mack's A's until age 26. No matter, the left-hander blossomed to win 326 games. He won at least 20 games in eight seasons, with four in a row from 1902 to 1905. "Gettysburg Eddie" compiled 69 career shutouts (fifth all time) and a 2.35 ERA. (1946)

OLD HOSS RADBOURN
Pitcher (1880-1891) In 1884, Radbourn won 59 games for NL Providence, still an all-time record, notching a 1.38 ERA and 679 innings pitched. In only 12 seasons he chalked up 309 wins and a 2.67 ERA. Old Hoss's 489 career complete games are eighth on the all-time list. (1939)

PEE WEE REESE
Shortstop (1940-1942; 1946-1958) Reese led the Dodgers to seven pennants between 1941 and 1956. One of the top fielding shortstops during the 1940s and 1950s, Pee Wee was an All-Star from 1947 to 1954. He scored 1,338 runs in his career, leading the NL in 1947 with 132. When Branch Rickey signed Jackie Robinson, it was Reese, a Southerner, who led the Dodgers to accept Robinson as a teammate. (1984)

SAM RICE
Outfielder (1915-1934) Rice, a fleet 150-pounder, smacked 2,987 hits on his way to a .322 career average for Washington. He led the AL in hits twice and had 200 or more base hits six times. He scored 1,514 career runs and stole 351 bases. A master of bat control, Rice struck out only nine times in 616 at bats in 1929. (1963)

BRANCH RICKEY
Executive Rickey invented the farm system and built NL dynasties in St. Louis and Brooklyn. When he joined the Cardinals in 1919 as president and field manager, the franchise could not compete with richer clubs. "The Mahatma" began to buy minor-league clubs from which the Cards could obtain talent. By 1941, St. Louis had 32 minor-league affiliates. Rickey moved to Brooklyn in 1942 and integrated the major leagues in 1947, winning his biggest fight when he signed Jackie Robinson. (1967)

EPPA RIXEY
Pitcher (1912-1917; 1919-1933) Rixey was a very good pitcher for some not very good teams, winning 266 games while losing 251. A master of control, Rixey won in double figures in 14 seasons and won 20 games four times. In 1922, he went a league-leading 25-13 for Cincinnati. (1963)

PHIL RIZZUTO
Shortstop (1941-1942; 1946-1956) "Scooter" played Yankee shortstop for 13 years and went to the World Series in nine of them. Just 5'6", he won the AL MVP Award in 1950 with a .324 average, 200 hits, and 125 runs scored. He was selected for the All-Star Game five times. He embarked on a long broadcasting career after his playing days. (1994)

ROBIN ROBERTS
Pitcher (1948-1966) Despite a penchant for throwing the gopher ball, Roberts won 20 games for six consecutive seasons from 1950 to 1955. He topped the NL in wins four straight years, and in innings and complete games five times each. He also led the NL two years in a row in Ks. In 1952, he went 28-7 for the Phillies. Roberts was 286-245 with a 3.41 ERA. (1976)

BROOKS ROBINSON
Third baseman (1955-1977) One of the greatest fielding third basemen ever, Robinson won the Gold Glove 16 times in 23 seasons. The AL MVP in 1964, Brooks turned in a .317 average, 28 homers, and a league-leading 118 RBI. He sparkled in postseason play, posting a .348 average in 18 ALCS games. In the 1970 World Series, he led the Orioles over the Reds, hitting .429 and turning in one spectacular fielding play after another, earning him MVP honors for the Series. "Hoover" had 268 career homers, 1,357 RBI, and 1,232 runs. (1983)

FRANK ROBINSON
Outfielder (1956-1976) Robinson was the first player to be selected MVP in both leagues. He was named NL Rookie of the Year in 1956 and the loop's MVP in 1961, when he paced the NL with a .611 slugging average and led the Reds to a pennant. Traded to Baltimore after the '65 season, Frank responded in '66 by hitting .316, slugging 49 home runs, and knocking in 122 runs to win the Triple Crown. He hit 30 homers in 11 seasons, and his 586 career homers rank fourth on the all-time list. He also had 1,812 career runs batted in and 1,829 runs scored. Named manager of the Indians in 1975, Robinson was the first African American to manage a major-league team. (1982)

JACKIE ROBINSON
Second baseman (1947-1956) The first African American to play major-league baseball since 1884, Robinson succeeded under almost unbearable pressure to secure the black player a permanent place in the game. He endured numerous racial slights, even from his own teammates, without yielding his dignity, while leading the Dodgers to six pennants. A tremendous athlete, Robinson was a four-sport star at UCLA and also served in the Army during World War II. As a 28-year-old rookie for Brooklyn in 1947, Robinson's aggressive base-running and hitting earned him Rookie of the Year honors. Two years later, in 1949, he led the NL with a .342 average and was named NL MVP. He had a career .311 batting average. (1962)

WILBERT ROBINSON
Manager (1902; 1914-1931) A catching star for Baltimore in the 1890s, Robinson coached under the Giants' John McGraw before becoming Brooklyn's manager in 1914. "Uncle Robbie" won pennants in 1916 and 1920 but never won a World Series. He had a career 1,399-1,398 record. (1945)

EDD ROUSH
Outfielder (1913-1929; 1931) One of the great defensive outfielders, Roush swung his 48-ounce bat with enough authority to attain two NL batting titles and a .323 lifetime average. In his 10 years in Cincinnati, he never hit lower than .321. He had 1,099 career runs and 981 RBI. Roush habitually held out of spring training. (1962)

RED RUFFING
Pitcher (1924-1942; 1945-1947) In six seasons with the Red Sox, Ruffing couldn't win, going 39-96 from 1924 to 1930 and leading the AL in losses twice. After he was traded to the Yankees, he couldn't lose, with a career 273-225 record and a 7-2 mark in 10 World Series games. He won 20 games each season from 1936 to 1939. (1967)

AMOS RUSIE
Pitcher (1889-1895; 1897-1898; 1901) Rusie's fastball forced the rule makers to move the mound from 45 feet to 60 feet 6 inches. From 1890 to 1895, the Giants pitcher led the NL in Ks five times, yet he had about one walk for every K. "The Hoosier Thunderbolt" had eight 20-win seasons and 245 career victories. (1977)

BABE RUTH
Outfielder; pitcher (1914-1935) George Herman Ruth is arguably the greatest player of all time. A man of gargantuan appetites and ability, the Babe's mystique has transcended the sport of baseball and has become ingrained in American mythology. Starting his career as a pitcher with Boston, he was one of the best in the AL. In 1916, the Babe led the AL with a 1.75 ERA while going 23-12. He had 24 wins in '17 with a loop-high 35 complete games. Converted to the outfield part-time in 1918, he led the AL in homers with 11. After he was sold to the Yankees in 1920, he became a full-time flycatcher, and all but invented the home run, slugging 714 for his career, including a then-record 60 in 1927. He led the AL in homers 12 seasons, RBI six seasons, slugging percentage 12 times, and bases on balls 11 times. He had a career .342 batting average, .690 slugging average (first all time), 506 doubles, 2,213 RBI (second all time), 2,174 runs (second all time), and 2,056 walks (first all time). (1936)

RAY SCHALK
Catcher (1912-1929) Although Schalk's career average was .253, few complained when he was elected to the Hall. A superb

catcher, Ray's game was defense. In 1920, he caught four 20-game winners for the White Sox, and he caught four no-hitters, more than any other catcher. He holds the AL record for assists by a catcher (1,811). (1955)

MIKE SCHMIDT
Third baseman (1972-1989) The leader of a Phillies team that finally won its first world championship in 1980, Schmidt is credited with being the greatest all-around third baseman in history. A fine power hitter, he was an eight-time NL home run leader, had more than 100 RBI in a season nine times, and retired with 548 homers and 1,595 RBI. Schmidt was the NL MVP in 1980, '81, and '86 and won 10 Gold Gloves. (1995)

RED SCHOENDIENST
Second baseman (1945-1963) Schoendienst teamed with shortstop Marty Marion to form one of baseball's best-ever double-play combinations. Red could also hit, reaching a career-high .342 average in 1953. He had 2,449 career hits and 1,223 runs scored. (1989)

TOM SEAVER
Pitcher (1967-1986) In 1992, Seaver was named on a record 98.8 percent of the ballots for enshrinement, indicating his stature among fans. A three-time Cy Young winner (1969, '73, and '75), he also finished second twice and third once. "Tom Terrific" led the Mets to a miracle world championship in 1969. He won 311 games and struck out 3,640 batters, and his .603 winning percentage was the best of any 300-game winner since Lefty Grove retired in 1941. (1992)

JOE SEWELL
Shortstop (1920-1933) Sewell replaced Ray Chapman in the Cleveland lineup following Chapman's tragic death in 1920. One of the game's best shortstops, Sewell struck out only 114 times in 7,132 at bats. He had 1,141 runs and 1,051 RBI. (1977)

AL SIMMONS
Outfielder (1924-1941; 1943-1944) An unlikely looking hitter due to his "foot in the bucket" batting stance, Simmons was a leading slugger of his era. From 1929 to 1931, he helped the Athletics to three consecutive pennants, winning batting titles in both 1930 and 1931 with averages of .381 and .390. "Bucketfoot Al" batted over .300 in the first 11 seasons of his career, racking up 2,927 hits and a career .334 batting average. (1953)

GEORGE SISLER
First baseman (1915-1922; 1924-1930) Like Babe Ruth, Sisler's hitting was too good to be on a pitcher's schedule. He was switched to first base full-time in 1916 for the Browns and became one of the best, defensively. At bat he was simply unbelievable, hitting .407, .371, and .420 from 1920 to 1922. In 1920, "Gorgeous George" collected 257 base hits, still the all-time record. A sinus infection that affected his vision sidelined him in 1923. He returned to play seven more seasons. (1939)

ENOS SLAUGHTER
Outfielder (1938-1942; 1946-1959) Slaughter would do anything in order to win, using hustle to make up for any shortcomings in talent. His mad dash from first to home on a double won the 1946 World Series for the Cardinals. "Country" led the NL in base hits in 1942 before going to war; he led the league in RBI when he came back. (1985)

DUKE SNIDER
Outfielder (1947-1964) Known as the "Duke of Flatbush" to his Brooklyn fans, Snider was one of a trio of Hall of Fame

center fielders in New York during the 1950s. The others were named Willie Mays and Mickey Mantle. Snider hit 40 homers from 1953 to 1957. He had 407 career homers, 1,333 RBI, and 1,259 runs scored. (1980)

WARREN SPAHN
Pitcher (1942; 1946-1965) Baseball's winningest left-hander, Spahn didn't even stick in the majors until age 25. With the Braves, he won 20 games or more in 13 seasons, tying the major-league record. He led the league in wins eight times, complete games nine times, and strikeouts four times. He won the Cy Young Award in 1957. Spahn retired with 363 wins (fifth all time), 245 losses, a 3.09 ERA, 382 complete games, and 63 shutouts (sixth all time) in 5,243⅔ innings pitched. (1973)

AL SPALDING
Pitcher (1871-1878); executive A star pitcher in the 1870s, Spalding started a sporting goods company and took over NL Chicago. As a pitcher, he had a .796 career winning percentage. He helped write the new NL's constitution and was inducted as an executive. (1939)

TRIS SPEAKER
Outfielder (1907-1928) The best center fielder of his time, Speaker played close enough to the infield to take pick-off throws at second. "The Grey Eagle" hit over .300 in 18 seasons and topped .375 six times on his way to a career .345 mark (fifth all time). Traded from Boston to Cleveland in 1916, he won his only batting title, at .386. "Spoke" had a record 792 career doubles and 3,514 hits (fifth all time). (1937)

WILLIE STARGELL
Outfielder; first baseman (1962-1982) One of the strongest players ever, Stargell made tape-measure homers common. He had 13 consecutive years of 20 or more home runs, pacing the NL in 1971 and 1973. He was named season, NLCS, and World Series MVP in 1979, when he led the world champion Bucs. He had 475 career homers and 1,540 RBI. (1988)

CASEY STENGEL
Manager (1934-1936; 1938-1943; 1949-1960; 1962-1965) As manager of Brooklyn and Boston, Stengel earned a reputation as an entertaining, if not very effective, skipper. His creative use of the language, dubbed "Stengelese," made him a fan favorite. Named Yankee manager in 1949, "The Old Professor" won 10 pennants in 12 years, plus seven world championships. He had a career 1,905-1,842 record. (1966)

BILL TERRY
First baseman (1923-1936) A career .341 hitter, Terry was the last National Leaguer to hit over .400, batting .401 in 1930 with 254 hits. "Memphis Bill" had more than 100 RBI from 1927 to 1932. Showing long-ball power when he wanted, Terry smashed 28 homers in 1932. Generally, though, his strengths were doubles and triples. He took over as Giant manager in 1932 and led the team to three pennants. (1954)

SAM THOMPSON
Outfielder (1885-1898; 1906) Thompson was a home run hitter in an era when the talent was not appreciated. He had his greatest success with the Phillies in the 1890s, where he hit .407 in 1894. "Big Sam" led the NL in hits three times, and in homers and RBI twice each. He had 127 career homers, with a .331 average and 1,299 RBI. (1974)

JOE TINKER
Shortstop (1902-1916) Interestingly, Tinker, Johnny Evers, and Frank Chance

were all elected to the Hall in the same year. Shortstop Tinker was a fielding whiz who keyed the success of that double-play combo. Although not a great hitter, he stole 336 career bases to augment his .263 average. (1946)

PIE TRAYNOR
Third baseman (1920-1935; 1937) Traynor earned his way into the Hall of Fame as the best fielding third baseman of his era. A career .320 hitter for Pittsburgh, he hit .300 or better 10 times and had more than 100 RBI seven times. Pie had 1,273 career RBI and 1,183 runs. (1948)

DAZZY VANCE
Pitcher (1915; 1918; 1922-1935) As a 31-year-old rookie with Brooklyn in 1922, Vance won 18 games. Two years later his mark of 28-6 earned him league MVP honors. Armed with an incredible fastball, he led the major leagues in Ks in each of his first seven seasons and paced the NL in ERA three times. Dazzy had a career 197-140 record. (1955)

ARKY VAUGHAN
Shortstop (1932-1943; 1947-1948) One of the game's best hitting shortstops, only twice in 14 seasons did Vaughan fail to hit .300. In 1935, his .385 average for Pittsburgh led the NL. Arky notched a career .406 on-base percentage, .318 batting average, 1,173 runs, and 926 RBI. He eventually became a top fielder, leading the NL in putouts and assists three times. (1985)

BILL VEECK
Executive One of baseball's most colorful showmen, Veeck integrated the AL by signing Larry Doby with the Indians. He owned three AL teams—Cleveland, St. Louis, and Chicago. He sent the 3'7" Eddie Gaedel up to bat for the Browns, and as the chief of the White Sox, introduced baseball's first exploding scoreboard. (1991)

RUBE WADDELL
Pitcher (1897; 1899-1910) Waddell threw hard and lived even harder. In the AL's first six seasons, Rube was the circuit's best left-hander, under the watchful eye of Connie Mack, winning 20 games four straight years and leading the league in Ks six consecutive years. The eccentric Waddell had a career 193-143 record with 2,316 Ks. (1946)

HONUS WAGNER
Shortstop (1897-1917) One of the game's first five inductees to the Hall of Fame, Wagner hit over .300 15 consecutive seasons. Bowlegged and awkward looking, Wagner possessed tremendous speed and range afield. For his 21-year career, he had 722 stolen bases and a .327 batting average, highest of any shortstop. Honus led the NL in batting eight times, slugging six times, RBI five times, runs scored twice, and doubles seven times. "The Flying Dutchman" had 3,415 career hits, 640 doubles, 252 triples, 1,732 RBI, 1,736 runs scored, and 963 walks. Some consider Wagner the greatest player of all time. (1936)

BOBBY WALLACE
Shortstop (1894-1918) The first AL shortstop elected to the Hall, Wallace made his mark with the glove, leading the league in putouts three times and assists four times. He had 6.1 chances per game lifetime. (1953)

ED WALSH
Pitcher (1904-1917) Perhaps no other pitcher threw the spitball as successfully as Walsh. While his arm gave out after only seven full seasons as a starter, he recorded nearly 170 of his career 195 wins during that span. In 1908, he pitched

464 innings for the White Sox on his way to 40 victories. He led the AL in games pitched five times, innings pitched four times, and strikeouts twice. "Big Ed" had a career 195-126 record with a 1.82 ERA, the lowest of all time. (1946)

LLOYD WANER
Outfielder (1927-1942; 1944-1945) "Little Poison," to older brother Paul's "Big Poison," Lloyd Waner used his speed to cover the vast Forbes Field outfield, leading the NL in putouts four times. In 1927, Waner's rookie year, the little lead-off man hit 198 one-baggers. Waner had a .316 career batting average, 2,459 hits, and 1,201 runs scored. (1967)

PAUL WANER
Outfielder (1926-1945) "Big Poison" didn't settle for hitting singles like his little brother; 905 of Paul Waner's 3,152 career hits were for extra bases. He led the NL in hitting four times, peaking at .380 in 1927, when he led Pittsburgh to the pennant and was named league MVP. Waner retired with a .333 batting average, 605 doubles, 1,627 runs scored, and 1,309 RBI. (1952)

MONTE WARD
Pitcher; shortstop (1878-1894) Perhaps no figure in baseball had distinguished himself in so many areas as did Ward. As a pitcher for Providence, he led the NL in ERA in 1878 and in wins in 1879. Switched to shortstop in 1885, he became the best in the league for New York. Unhappy with the reserve clause, in 1890 he helped form the Players' League. Becoming a manager, he led the Giants to a championship in 1894. (1964)

GEORGE WEISS
Executive As farm director and general manager of the Yankees from 1932 to 1960, Weiss deserves much of the credit for creating the Yankee dynasty. He built the farm system to 21 teams, then became general manager and dealt from strength, constantly picking up precisely the player the Yankees needed in exchange for prospects plucked from the system he created. (1971)

MICKEY WELCH
Pitcher (1880-1892) The third man to win 300 games, Welch starred in the 1880s for Troy and New York of the NL. In 1885 he won 17 consecutive decisions on his way to 44 wins for the year. "Smiling Mickey" won at least 20 games nine times, with four seasons of more than 30. He had a career 307-210 record with a 2.71 ERA. (1973)

ZACK WHEAT
Outfielder (1909-1927) The Dodgers' first star, Wheat played left field in Ebbets Field for 18 seasons. A line-drive hitter, he topped the .300 mark in 14 seasons, including an NL-best .335 in 1918. He had a career .317 average, 2,884 hits, 1,248 RBI, 1,289 runs scored, and 205 stolen bases. (1959)

HOYT WILHELM
Pitcher (1952-1972) Wilhelm was the first pitcher elected to the Hall solely on his merits as a reliever. A knuckleballer, he toiled for nine teams, pitching in a record 1,070 games and winning 124 in relief. He started only 52 games in his 21-year career, compiling 227 saves and a 2.52 ERA. "Snacks" pitched five consecutive seasons (1964 to 1968) with an ERA under 2.00. (1985)

BILLY WILLIAMS
Outfielder (1959-1976) Williams's much admired swing produced 426 career homers and a .290 batting average. The NL Rookie of the Year in 1961, he had at least 20 home runs and 84 RBI in 13 consecutive seasons. His two best seasons

were in 1970 and 1972. In 1970, Billy hit .322 with 42 homers, a league-best 137 runs scored, and 129 RBI. He led the NL with a .333 batting average and a .606 slugging average, with 37 homers and 122 RBI in 1972. Playing most of his career for the Cubs, between 1963 and 1970 Williams played in an NL-record 1,117 consecutive games. (1987)

TED WILLIAMS
Outfielder (1939-1942; 1946-1960)
Williams's one desire was to walk down the street and have people say, "There goes the greatest hitter that ever lived." Arguably, he was. Despite missing nearly five years to the military, the Red Sox left fielder won two MVP Awards, six batting and four home run titles, and two Triple Crowns. "The Splendid Splinter" batted over .316 in each of his 19 seasons except one. In 1941, "The Kid" hit a .406 mark. He's the last player to attain that plateau. He had 30 or more homers in eight seasons, 20 or more in 16 seasons. "Teddy Ballgame" has the sixth-highest career batting average (.344), the second-highest slugging average (.634), the second-most bases on balls (2,019), the 10th-most home runs (521), and the 11th-most RBI (1,839). (1966)

VIC WILLIS
Pitcher (1898-1910) A big right-hander with a wicked curveball, Willis gained a reputation for durability, winning at least 20 games eight times. He pitched for the Boston Beaneaters, Pittsburgh Pirates, and St. Louis Cardinals, fashioning a 249-205 record and a 2.63 ERA. (1995)

HACK WILSON
Outfielder (1923-1934) From 1926 to 1930, the muscular, squat Wilson was one of the game's greatest sluggers. In 1930, the Cub outfielder hit an NL-record 56 homers and knocked in a major-league-record 190 runs. He led the NL in homers four times and in RBI twice. Liquor, however, was Wilson's downfall, and by the end of 1934, he was out of baseball. (1979)

GEORGE WRIGHT
Shortstop (1871-1882) The star shortstop for the original Cincinnati Red Stockings team that went undefeated for the entire 1869 season, Wright played through the 1882 season. He then helped start the Union Association in 1884. Later in life he served on baseball's Centennial Commission, and was instrumental in the creation of the National Baseball Hall of Fame. (1937)

HARRY WRIGHT
Manager (1871-1893) Harry Wright, the older brother of George, was player-manager of the Cincinnati Red Stockings (the first overtly all-professional team), which Harry led to some 130 consecutive victories. He helped start the National Association in 1871, and later managed a number of NL teams, going 225-60 in the National Association and 1,000-825 in the National League. (1953)

EARLY WYNN
Pitcher (1939; 1941-1944; 1946-1963)
Wynn was traded to Cleveland in 1949 and became a big winner. He won 20 games for the Indians four times and had eight consecutive winning seasons. Traded to the White Sox after the '57 season, "Gus" led Chicago to the pennant in 1959 by winning 22 games, plus the Cy Young Award. He had a 300-244 career record and a 3.54 ERA. (1972)

CARL YASTRZEMSKI
Outfielder (1961-1983) Spending his entire 23-year career with the Red Sox, Yastrzemski was the first AL player to collect over 3,000 hits and 400 home runs.

"Yaz" will always be remembered for one remarkable season—1967, the year of The Impossible Dream. He won the Triple Crown, and during a most remarkable September that season, he single-handedly won the pennant for Boston. Taking over left field for Ted Williams, "Captain Carl" won batting titles in 1963, '67, and '68. He had 3,419 career hits, a .285 average, 646 doubles, 452 home runs, 1,844 RBI, 1,816 runs scored, and 1,845 walks. (1989)

TOM YAWKEY
Executive Yawkey is one of the few inducted to the Hall who neither played, coached, umpired, nor served as a general manager. In 1933, at age 30, he received his inheritance and bought the Red Sox for $1.5 million. Boston at that time was a doormat and Fenway Park was falling apart. Over the next 44 seasons he spent lavishly on the club and the stadium, doling out another $1.5 million for renovations alone. (1980)

CY YOUNG
Pitcher (1890-1911) Young won 511 games, which is 94 victories more than runner-up Walter Johnson. In a career that bridged three decades and several eras of play, Cy was consistently superb. Blessed with speed, control, stamina, and just about every quality a successful pitcher needs, Young won 20 or more games 15 times, including nine seasons in a row from 1891 to 1899. He led his league in victories four times, and in ERA, winning percentage, and strikeouts twice each. Cy is also first on the complete-game list with 749 and innings pitched list with 7,356⅔. When they decided to give an award to the season's top pitcher, they named it after Young. (1937)

ROSS YOUNGS
Outfielder (1917-1926) Youngs was a star on four straight pennant winners for John McGraw's Giants in the early 1920s. On the verge of greatness, Youngs's skills deserted him in 1925. Diagnosed with Bright's disease, a terminal kidney disorder, Youngs gamely played one more season and died in 1927. He had a .322 career batting average with 1,491 hits and 812 runs scored. (1972)

AWARDS AND HIGHLIGHTS

Awards and Highlights

Baseball's top achievements and tributes are listed in this section. The all-time career leaders in several batting and pitching categories are included (with players active in 1995 in **bold**), as well as the leaders among active players. The all-time single-season leaders are next. The Most Valuable Players, the Cy Young Award winners, and the Rookies of the Year follow. Fielding excellence is acknowledged with the Gold Glove Award winners. Finally, the winners and losers of the World Series, the National League and American League Championship Series, and the Division Series are listed.

ALL-TIME LEADERS

BATTING AVERAGE
1. Ty Cobb .... .366
2. Rogers Hornsby .... .358
3. Joe Jackson .... .356
4. Ed Delahanty .... .346
5. Tris Speaker .... .345
6. Ted Williams .... .344
7. Billy Hamilton .... .344
8. Dan Brouthers .... .342
9. Babe Ruth .... .342
10. Harry Heilmann .... .342
11. Pete Browning .... .341
12. Willie Keeler .... .341
13. Bill Terry .... .341
14. George Sisler .... .340
15. Lou Gehrig .... .340
16. Jesse Burkett .... .338
17. Nap Lajoie .... .338
18. **Tony Gwynn** .... **.336**
19. Riggs Stephenson .... .336
20. **Wade Boggs** .... **.334**

HITS
1. Pete Rose 4,256
2. Ty Cobb 4,189
3. Hank Aaron 3,771
4. Stan Musial 3,630
5. Tris Speaker 3,514
6. Carl Yastrzemski 3,419
7. Honus Wagner 3,415
   Cap Anson 3,415
9. Eddie Collins 3,312
10. Willie Mays 3,283
11. Nap Lajoie 3,242
12. George Brett 3,154
13. Paul Waner 3,152
14. Robin Yount 3,142
15. **Dave Winfield** **3,110**
16. **Eddie Murray** **3,071**

17. Rod Carew 3,053
18. Lou Brock 3,023
19. Al Kaline 3,007
20. Roberto Clemente ... 3,000

DOUBLES
1. Tris Speaker 792
2. Pete Rose 746
3. Stan Musial 725
4. Ty Cobb 724
5. George Brett 665
6. Nap Lajoie 657
7. Carl Yastrzemski 646
8. Honus Wagner 640
9. Hank Aaron 624
10. Paul Waner 605
11. Robin Yount 583
12. Cap Anson 582
13. Charlie Gehringer ... 574
14. Harry Heilmann 542
15. Rogers Hornsby 541
16. **Dave Winfield** **540**
    Joe Medwick 540
18. Al Simmons 539
19. Lou Gehrig 534
20. **Eddie Murray** **532**

TRIPLES
1. Sam Crawford 309
2. Ty Cobb 295
3. Honus Wagner 252
4. Jake Beckley 243
5. Roger Connor 233
6. Tris Speaker 222
7. Fred Clarke 220
8. Dan Brouthers 205
9. Joe Kelley 194
10. Paul Waner 191
11. Bid McPhee 188
12. Eddie Collins 186

13. Ed Delahanty 185
14. Sam Rice 184
15. Edd Roush 182
    Jesse Burkett 182
17. Ed Konetchy 181
18. Buck Ewing 178
19. Stan Musial 177
    Rabbit Maranville ... 177

HOME RUNS
1. Hank Aaron 755
2. Babe Ruth 714
3. Willie Mays 660
4. Frank Robinson 586
5. Harmon Killebrew 573
6. Reggie Jackson 563
7. Mike Schmidt 548
8. Mickey Mantle 536
9. Jimmie Foxx 534
10. Ted Williams 521
    Willie McCovey 521
12. Eddie Mathews 512
    Ernie Banks 512
14. Mel Ott 511
15. Lou Gehrig 493
16. **Eddie Murray** **479**
17. Willie Stargell 475
    Stan Musial 475
19. **Dave Winfield** ... **465**
20. Carl Yastrzemski 452

RUNS BATTED IN
1. Hank Aaron 2,297
2. Babe Ruth 2,213
3. Lou Gehrig 1,995
4. Cap Anson 1,981
5. Stan Musial 1,951
6. Ty Cobb 1,937
7. Jimmie Foxx 1,922
8. Willie Mays 1,903

AWARDS AND HIGHLIGHTS

9. Mel Ott 1,860
10. Carl Yastrzemski 1,844
11. Ted Williams 1,839
12. **Dave Winfield** **1,833**
13. Al Simmons 1,827
14. **Eddie Murray** **1,820**
15. Frank Robinson 1,812
16. Honus Wagner 1,732
17. Reggie Jackson 1,702
18. Tony Perez 1,652
19. Ernie Banks 1,636
20. Goose Goslin 1,609

SLUGGING AVERAGE

1. Babe Ruth .... .690
2. Ted Williams .... .634
3. Lou Gehrig .... .632
4. Jimmie Foxx .... .609
5. Hank Greenberg .... .605
6. Joe DiMaggio .... .579
7. Rogers Hornsby .... .577
8. Johnny Mize .... .562
9. Stan Musial .... .559
10. Willie Mays .... .557
11. Mickey Mantle .... .557
12. Hank Aaron .... .555
13. Ralph Kiner .... .548
14. Hack Wilson .... .545
15. Chuck Klein .... .543
16. **Barry Bonds** .... **.541**
17. Duke Snider .... .540
18. Frank Robinson .... .537
19. **Fred McGriff** .... **.535**
20. Al Simmons .... .535

ON-BASE PERCENTAGE

1. Ted Williams .... .483
2. Babe Ruth .... .474
3. John McGraw .... .466
4. Billy Hamilton .... .455
5. Lou Gehrig .... .447
6. Rogers Hornsby .... .434
7. Ty Cobb .... .433
8. Jimmie Foxx .... .428
9. Tris Speaker .... .428
10. **Wade Boggs** .... **.428**
11. Ferris Fain .... .425
12. Eddie Collins .... .424
13. Dan Brouthers .... .423
14. Joe Jackson .... .423
15. Max Bishop .... .423
16. Mickey Mantle .... .423
17. Mickey Cochrane ..... .419
18. Stan Musial .... .418
19. Cupid Childs .... .416
20. Jesse Burkett .... .415

STOLEN BASES

1. **Rickey Henderson** **.1,149**
2. Lou Brock 938
3. Billy Hamilton 912
4. Ty Cobb 892
5. **Tim Raines** **777**
6. Eddie Collins 744
7. **Vince Coleman** **740**
8. Arlie Latham 739
9. Max Carey 738
10. Honus Wagner 722
11. Joe Morgan 689
12. Willie Wilson 668
13. Tom Brown 657
14. Bert Campaneris 649
15. George Davis 616
16. Dummy Hoy 594
17. Maury Wills 586
18. George Van Haltren ... 583
19. Hugh Duffy 574
20. **Ozzie Smith** **573**

RUNS SCORED

1. Ty Cobb 2,246
2. Babe Ruth 2,174
   Hank Aaron 2,174
4. Pete Rose 2,165
5. Willie Mays 2,062
6. Cap Anson 1,996
7. Stan Musial 1,949
8. Lou Gehrig 1,888
9. Tris Speaker 1,882
10. Mel Ott 1,859
11. Frank Robinson 1,829
12. Eddie Collins 1,821
13. Carl Yastrzemski 1,816
14. Ted Williams 1,798
15. Charlie Gehringer ... 1,774
16. Jimmie Foxx 1,751
17. Honus Wagner 1,736
18. Jim O'Rourke 1,732
19. Jesse Burkett 1,720
20. Willie Keeler 1,719
    Rickey Henderson **.1,719**

BASES ON BALLS

1. Babe Ruth 2,056
2. Ted Williams 2,019
3. Joe Morgan 1,865
4. Carl Yastrzemski 1,845
5. Mickey Mantle 1,733
6. Mel Ott 1,708
7. Eddie Yost 1,614
8. Darrell Evans 1,605
9. Stan Musial 1,599
10. Pete Rose 1,566

11. Harmon Killebrew ... 1,559
12. **Rickey Henderson** **.1,550**
13. Lou Gehrig 1,508
14. Mike Schmidt 1,507
15. Eddie Collins 1,499

GAMES PLAYED

1. Pete Rose 3,562
2. Carl Yastrzemski 3,308
3. Hank Aaron 3,298
4. Ty Cobb 3,035
5. Stan Musial 3,026
6. Willie Mays 2,992
7. **Dave Winfield** **2,973**
8. Rusty Staub 2,951
9. Brooks Robinson 2,896
10. Robin Yount 2,856
11. Al Kaline 2,834
12. Eddie Collins 2,826
13. Reggie Jackson 2,820
14. **Eddie Murray** **2,819**
15. Frank Robinson 2,808
16. Honus Wagner 2,792
17. Tris Speaker 2,789
18. Tony Perez 2,777
19. Mel Ott 2,730
20. George Brett 2,707

WINS

1. Cy Young 511
2. Walter Johnson 417
3. Christy Mathewson 373
   Pete Alexander 373
5. Pud Galvin 364
6. Warren Spahn 363
7. Kid Nichols 361
8. Tim Keefe 342
9. Steve Carlton 329
10. John Clarkson 328
11. Eddie Plank 326
12. Don Sutton 324
    Nolan Ryan 324
14. Phil Niekro 318
15. Gaylord Perry 314
16. Tom Seaver 311
17. Charley Radbourn ... 309
18. Mickey Welch 307
19. Early Wynn 300
    Lefty Grove 300

WINNING PERCENTAGE

1. Al Spalding .... .796
2. Dave Foutz .... .690
3. Whitey Ford .... .690
4. Bob Caruthers .... .688
5. Lefty Grove .... .680

AWARDS AND HIGHLIGHTS

6. Vic Raschi .... .667
7. Larry Corcoran .... .665
8. Christy Mathewson ..... .665
9. Sam Leever .... .660
10. Sal Maglie .... .657
11. Dick McBride .... .656
12. Sandy Koufax .... .655
13. Johnny Allen .... .654
14. Ron Guidry .... .651
15. **Roger Clemens** .... **.650**
16. Lefty Gomez .... .649
17. Dwight Gooden .... .649
18. John Clarkson .... .648
19. Mordecai Brown .... .648
20. Dizzy Dean .... .644

EARNED RUN AVERAGE
1. Ed Walsh 1.82
2. Addie Joss 1.89
3. Mordecai Brown 2.06
4. John Ward 2.10
5. Christy Mathewson 2.13
6. Al Spalding 2.14
7. Rube Waddell 2.16
8. Walter Johnson 2.17
9. Orval Overall 2.23
10. Will White 2.28
11. Ed Reulbach 2.28
12. Jim Scott 2.30
13. Tommy Bond 2.31
14. Eddie Plank 2.35
15. Larry Corcoran 2.36
16. George McQuillan 2.38
17. Eddie Cicotte 2.38
18. Ed Killian 2.38
19. Doc White 2.39
20. George Bradley 2.42

STRIKEOUTS
1. Nolan Ryan 5,714
2. Steve Carlton 4,136
3. Bert Blyleven 3,701
4. Tom Seaver 3,640
5. Don Sutton 3,574
6. Gaylord Perry 3,534
7. Walter Johnson 3,509
8. Phil Niekro 3,342
9. Fergie Jenkins 3,192
10. Bob Gibson 3,117
11. Jim Bunning 2,855
12. Mickey Lolich 2,832
13. Cy Young 2,803
14. Frank Tanana 2,773
15. Warren Spahn 2,583
16. Bob Feller 2,581
17. Jerry Koosman 2,556

18. Tim Keefe 2,543
19. Christy Mathewson ... 2,502
20. Don Drysdale 2,486

SAVES
1. **Lee Smith** **471**
2. Jeff Reardon 367
3. Rollie Fingers 341
4. **Dennis Eckersley** **323**
5. **Tom Henke** **311**
6. Rich Gossage 310
7. Bruce Sutter 300
8. **John Franco** **295**
9. **Dave Righetti** **252**
10. Dan Quisenberry 244
11. **Randy Myers** **243**
12. **Doug Jones** **239**
13. Sparky Lyle 238
14. Hoyt Wilhelm 227
15. **Jeff Montgomery** **218**
    Gene Garber 218
17. Dave Smith 216
18. **Rick Aguilera** **211**
19. Bobby Thigpen 201
20. Roy Face 193

COMPLETE GAMES
1. Cy Young 749
2. Pud Galvin 646
3. Tim Keefe 554
4. Kid Nichols 531
   Walter Johnson 531
6. Mickey Welch 525
   Bobby Mathews 525
8. Charley Radbourn 489
9. John Clarkson 485
10. Tony Mullane 468
11. Jim McCormick 466
12. Gus Weyhing 448
13. Pete Alexander 437
14. Christy Mathewson .. 434
15. Jack Powell 422
16. Eddie Plank 410
17. Will White 394
18. Amos Rusie 392
19. Vic Willis 388
20. Tommy Bond 386

SHUTOUTS
1. Walter Johnson 110
2. Pete Alexander 90
3. Christy Mathewson .. 79
4. Cy Young 76
5. Eddie Plank 69
6. Warren Spahn 63
7. Tom Seaver 61

Nolan Ryan 61
9. Bert Blyleven 60
10. Don Sutton 58
    Pud Galvin 58
12. Ed Walsh 57
13. Bob Gibson 56
14. Steve Carlton 55
    Mordecai Brown 55
16. Gaylord Perry 53
    Jim Palmer 53
18. Juan Marichal 52
19. Vic Willis 50
    Rube Waddell 50

GAMES PITCHED
1. Hoyt Wilhelm 1,070
2. Kent Tekulve 1,050
3. Rich Gossage 1,002
4. Lindy McDaniel 987
5. Rollie Fingers 944
6. **Lee Smith** **943**
7. Gene Garber 931
8. Cy Young 906
9. **Dennis Eckersley** **901**
10. Sparky Lyle 899
11. Jim Kaat 898
12. Jeff Reardon 880
13. Don McMahon 874
14. Phil Niekro 864
15. Charlie Hough 858
16. Roy Face 848
17. Tug McGraw 824
18. **Jesse Orosco** **819**
19. Nolan Ryan 807
20. Walter Johnson 802

INNINGS PITCHED
1. Cy Young 7,356.2
2. Pud Galvin 6,003.1
3. Walter Johnson 5,914.2
4. Phil Niekro 5,404.1
5. Nolan Ryan 5,386.0
6. Gaylord Perry 5,350.1
7. Don Sutton 5,282.1
8. Warren Spahn 5,243.2
9. Steve Carlton 5,217.1
10. Pete Alexander 5,190.0
11. Kid Nichols 5,056.1
12. Tim Keefe 5,047.1
13. Bert Blyleven 4,970.0
14. Bobby Mathews ... 4,956.1
15. Mickey Welch 4,802.0
16. Tom Seaver 4,782.2
17. Christy Mathewson 4,780.2
18. Tommy John 4,710.1
19. Robin Roberts 4,688.2

AWARDS AND HIGHLIGHTS

GAMES STARTED
1. Cy Young 815
2. Nolan Ryan 773
3. Don Sutton 756
4. Phil Niekro 716
5. Steve Carlton 709
6. Tommy John 700
7. Gaylord Perry 690
8. Pud Galvin 689
9. Bert Blyleven 685
10. Walter Johnson 666
11. Warren Spahn 665
12. Tom Seaver 647
13. Jim Kaat 625
14. Frank Tanana 616
15. Early Wynn 612

RATIO OF BASERUNNERS
1. Addie Joss 8.71
2. Ed Walsh 9.00
3. John Ward 9.40
4. Christy Mathewson 9.53
5. Walter Johnson 9.55
6. Mordecai Brown 9.59
7. George Bradley 9.80
8. Babe Adams 9.83
9. Tommy Bond 9.83
10. Juan Marichal 9.91
11. Rube Waddell 9.92
12. Larry Corcoran 9.94
13. Deacon Phillippe 9.95
14. Sandy Koufax 9.96
15. Ed Morris 9.97
16. Will White 10.00
17. Chief Bender 10.01
18. Terry Larkin 10.05
19. Eddie Plank 10.07
20. Doc White 10.09

ACTIVE LEADERS

HITS
1. Dave Winfield 3,110
2. Eddie Murray 3,071
3. Paul Molitor 2,789
4. Andre Dawson 2,758
5. Wade Boggs 2,541
6. Tony Gwynn 2,401
7. Ozzie Smith 2,396
8. Cal Ripken 2,371
9. Lou Whitaker 2,369
10. Rickey Henderson .. 2,338

HOME RUNS
1. Eddie Murray 479
2. Dave Winfield 465
3. Andre Dawson 436
4. Cal Ripken 327
   Joe Carter 327
6. Lance Parrish 324
7. Harold Baines 301
8. Jose Canseco 300
9. Darryl Strawberry 297
10. Gary Gaetti 292
    Barry Bonds 292

RUNS BATTED IN
1. Dave Winfield 1,833
2. Eddie Murray 1,820
3. Andre Dawson 1,577
4. Cal Ripken 1,267
5. Harold Baines 1,261
6. Joe Carter 1,173
7. Chili Davis 1,100
8. Don Mattingly 1,099
9. Kirby Puckett 1,085
10. Lou Whitaker 1,084

GAMES PLAYED
1. Dave Winfield 2,973
2. Eddie Murray 2,819
3. Andre Dawson 2,585
4. Ozzie Smith 2,491
5. Lou Whitaker 2,390
6. Paul Molitor 2,261
7. Alan Trammell 2,227
8. Cal Ripken 2,218
9. Rickey Henderson .. 2,192
10. Harold Baines 2,183

WINS
1. Dennis Martinez 231
2. Dennis Eckersley 192
3. Roger Clemens 182
4. Frank Viola 175
5. Dave Stewart 168
6. Mark Langston 166
7. Scott Sanderson 163
8. Mike Moore 161
9. Fernando Valenzuela . 158
10. Jimmy Key 152

GAMES PITCHED
1. Lee Smith 943
2. Dennis Eckersley 901
3. Jesse Orosco 819
4. Rick Honeycutt 734
5. Steve Bedrosian 732
6. Dave Righetti 718
7. Greg Harris 703
8. Roger McDowell 682
9. John Franco 661
10. Tom Henke 642

STRIKEOUTS
1. Roger Clemens 2,333
2. Dennis Eckersley ... 2,285
3. Mark Langston 2,252
4. Dennis Martinez 2,022
5. F. Valenzuela 1,918
6. Frank Viola 1,826
7. Dave Stewart 1,741
   David Cone 1,741
9. Danny Darwin 1,673
10. Mike Moore 1,667

SAVES
1. Lee Smith 471
2. Dennis Eckersley 323
3. Tom Henke 311
4. John Franco 295
5. Dave Righetti 252
6. Randy Myers 243
7. Doug Jones 239
8. Jeff Montgomery 218
9. Rick Aguilera 211
10. Mitch Williams 192

SINGLE-SEASON LEADERS (SINCE 1900)

BATTING AVERAGE	BA	YEAR
1. Nap Lajoie PHI (AL)	.426	1901
2. Rogers Hornsby STL (NL)	.424	1924
3. George Sisler STL (AL)	.420	1922
4. Ty Cobb DET	.420	1911
5. Ty Cobb DET	.410	1912
6. Joe Jackson CLE	.408	1911
7. George Sisler STL (AL)	.407	1920
8. Ted Williams BOS (AL)	.406	1941
9. Rogers Hornsby STL (NL)	.403	1925
10. Harry Heilmann DET	.403	1923
11. Rogers Hornsby STL (NL)	.401	1922

AWARDS AND HIGHLIGHTS

12. Bill Terry NY (NL)	.401	1930
13. Ty Cobb DET	.401	1922
14. Lefty O'Doul PHI (NL)	.398	1929
15. Harry Heilmann DET	.398	1927
16. Rogers Hornsby STL (NL)	.397	1921
17. Joe Jackson CLE	.395	1912
18. Tony Gwynn SD	.394	1994
19. Harry Heilmann DET	.394	1921
20. Babe Ruth NY (AL)	.393	1923

HITS	H	YEAR
1. George Sisler STL (AL)	257	1920
2. Lefty O'Doul PHI (NL)	254	1929
Bill Terry NY (NL)	254	1930
4. Al Simmons PHI (AL)	253	1925
5. Rogers Hornsby STL (AL)	250	1922
Chuck Klein PHI (NL)	250	1930
7. Ty Cobb DET	248	1911
8. George Sisler STL (AL)	246	1922
9. Heinie Manush STL (AL)	241	1928
Babe Herman BKN	241	1930
11. Wade Boggs BOS	240	1985
12. Rod Carew MIN	239	1977
13. Don Mattingly NY (AL)	238	1986
14. Harry Heilmann DET	237	1921
Paul Waner PIT	237	1927
Joe Medwick STL (NL)	237	1937
17. Jack Tobin STL (AL)	236	1921
18. Rogers Hornsby STL (NL)	235	1921
19. Lloyd Waner PIT	234	1929
Kirby Puckett MIN	234	1988

DOUBLES	2B	YEAR
1. Earl Webb BOS (AL)	67	1931
2. George Burns CLE	64	1926
Joe Medwick STL (NL)	64	1936
4. Hank Greenberg DET	63	1934
5. Paul Waner PIT	62	1932
6. Charlie Gehringer DET	60	1936
7. Tris Speaker CLE	59	1923
Chuck Klein PHI (NL)	59	1930
9. Billy Herman CHI (NL)	57	1935
Billy Herman CHI (NL)	57	1936

TRIPLES	3B	YEAR
1. Owen Wilson PIT	36	1912
2. Joe Jackson CLE	26	1912
Sam Crawford DET	26	1914
Kiki Cuyler PIT	26	1925
5. Sam Crawford DET	25	1903
Larry Doyle NY (NL)	25	1911
Tommy Long STL (NL)	25	1915
8. Ty Cobb DET	24	1911
Ty Cobb DET	24	1917
10. Ty Cobb DET	23	1912
Sam Crawford DET	23	1913

Earle Combs NY (AL)	23	1927
Adam Comorosky PIT	23	1930
Dale Mitchell CLE	23	1949

HOME RUNS	HR	YEAR
1. Roger Maris NY (AL)	61	1961
2. Babe Ruth NY (AL)	60	1927
3. Babe Ruth NY (AL)	59	1921
4. Jimmie Foxx PHI (AL)	58	1932
Hank Greenberg DET	58	1938
6. Hack Wilson CHI (NL)	56	1930
7. Babe Ruth NY (AL)	54	1920
Babe Ruth NY (AL)	54	1928
Ralph Kiner PIT	54	1949
Mickey Mantle NY (AL)	54	1961
11. Mickey Mantle NY (AL)	52	1956
Willie Mays SF	52	1965
George Foster CIN	52	1977
14. Ralph Kiner PIT	51	1947
Johnny Mize NY (NL)	51	1947
Willie Mays NY (NL)	51	1955
Cecil Fielder DET	51	1990
18. Jimmie Foxx BOS (AL)	50	1938
Albert Belle CLE (AL)	50	1995
20. Babe Ruth NY (AL)	49	1930
Lou Gehrig NY (AL)	49	1934
Lou Gehrig NY (AL)	49	1936
Ted Kluszewski CIN	49	1954
Willie Mays SF	49	1962
Harmon Killebrew MIN	49	1964
Frank Robinson BAL	49	1966
Harmon Killebrew MIN	49	1969
Andre Dawson CHI (NL)	49	1987
Mark McGwire OAK	49	1987

HOME RUN PERCENTAGE	HR%	YEAR
1. Babe Ruth NY (AL)	11.8	1920
2. Babe Ruth NY (AL)	11.1	1927
3. Babe Ruth NY (AL)	10.9	1921
4. Mickey Mantle NY (AL)	10.5	1961
5. Hank Greenberg DET	10.4	1938
6. Roger Maris NY (AL)	10.3	1961
7. Babe Ruth NY (AL)	10.1	1928
8. Jimmie Foxx PHI (AL)	9.9	1932
9. Ralph Kiner PIT	9.8	1949
10. Mickey Mantle NY (AL)	9.8	1956
11. Jeff Bagwell HOU	9.8	1994
12. Kevin Mitchell CIN	9.7	1994
13. Matt Williams SF	9.7	1994
14. Hack Wilson CHI (NL)	9.6	1930
15. Frank Thomas CHI (AL)	9.6	1994
16. Babe Ruth NY (AL)	9.5	1926
Hank Aaron ATL	9.5	1971
18. Jim Gentile BAL	9.5	1961
19. Barry Bonds SF	9.5	1994
20. Babe Ruth NY (AL)	9.5	1930

AWARDS AND HIGHLIGHTS

RUNS BATTED IN	RBI	YEAR
1. Hack Wilson CHI (NL)	190	1930
2. Lou Gehrig NY (AL)	184	1931
3. Hank Greenberg DET	183	1937
4. Lou Gehrig NY (AL)	175	1927
Jimmie Foxx BOS (AL)	175	1938
6. Lou Gehrig NY (AL)	174	1930
7. Babe Ruth NY (AL)	171	1921
8. Chuck Klein PHI (NL)	170	1930
Hank Greenberg DET	170	1935
10. Jimmie Foxx PHI (AL)	169	1932
11. Joe DiMaggio NY (AL)	167	1937
12. Al Simmons PHI (AL)	165	1930
Lou Gehrig NY (AL)	165	1934
14. Babe Ruth NY (AL)	164	1927
15. Babe Ruth NY (AL)	163	1931
Jimmie Foxx PHI (AL)	163	1933
17. Hal Trosky CLE	162	1936
18. Hack Wilson CHI (NL)	159	1929
Lou Gehrig NY (AL)	159	1937
Vern Stephens BOS (AL)	159	1949
Ted Williams BOS (AL)	159	1949

SLUGGING AVERAGE	SA	YEAR
1. Babe Ruth NY (AL)	.847	1920
2. Babe Ruth NY (AL)	.846	1921
3. Babe Ruth NY (AL)	.772	1927
4. Lou Gehrig NY (AL)	.765	1927
5. Babe Ruth NY (AL)	.764	1923
6. Rogers Hornsby STL (NL)	.756	1925
7. Jeff Bagwell HOU	.750	1994
8. Jimmie Foxx PHI (AL)	.749	1932
9. Babe Ruth NY (AL)	.739	1924
10. Babe Ruth NY (AL)	.737	1926
11. Ted Williams BOS (AL)	.735	1941
12. Babe Ruth NY (AL)	.732	1930
13. Ted Williams BOS	.731	1957
14. Frank Thomas CHI (AL)	.729	1994
15. Hack Wilson CHI (NL)	.723	1930
16. Rogers Hornsby STL (NL)	.722	1922
17. Lou Gehrig NY (AL)	.721	1930
18. Albert Belle CLE	.714	1994
19. Babe Ruth NY (AL)	.709	1928
20. Al Simmons PHI (AL)	.708	1930

ON-BASE PERCENTAGE	OBP	YEAR
1. Ted Williams BOS (AL)	.551	1941
2. Babe Ruth NY (AL)	.545	1923
3. Babe Ruth NY (AL)	.530	1920
4. Ted Williams BOS (AL)	.528	1957
5. Ted Williams BOS (AL)	.516	1954
6. Babe Ruth NY (AL)	.516	1926
7. Mickey Mantle NY (AL)	.515	1957
8. Babe Ruth NY (AL)	.513	1924
9. Babe Ruth NY (AL)	.512	1921
10. Rogers Hornsby STL (NL)	.507	1924
11. John McGraw STL (NL)	.505	1900
12. Ted Williams BOS (AL)	.499	1942
13. Ted Williams BOS (AL)	.499	1947
14. Rogers Hornsby BOS (NL)	.498	1928
15. Ted Williams BOS (AL)	.497	1946
16. Ted Williams BOS (AL)	.497	1948
17. Babe Ruth NY (AL)	.495	1931
18. Frank Thomas CHI (AL)	.494	1994
19. Babe Ruth NY (AL)	.493	1930
20. Arky Vaughan PIT (NL)	.491	1935

TOTAL BASES	TB	YEAR
1. Babe Ruth NY (AL)	457	1921
2. Rogers Hornsby STL (NL)	450	1922
3. Lou Gehrig NY (AL)	447	1927
4. Chuck Klein PHI (NL)	445	1930
5. Jimmie Foxx PHI (AL)	438	1932
6. Stan Musial STL (NL)	429	1948
7. Hack Wilson CHI (NL)	423	1930
8. Chuck Klein PHI (NL)	420	1932
9. Lou Gehrig NY (AL)	419	1930
10. Joe DiMaggio NY (AL)	418	1937
11. Babe Ruth NY (AL)	417	1927
12. Babe Herman BKN	416	1930
13. Lou Gehrig NY (AL)	410	1931
14. Rogers Hornsby CHI (NL)	409	1929
Lou Gehrig NY (AL)	409	1934

BASES ON BALLS	BB	YEAR
1. Babe Ruth NY (AL)	170	1923
2. Ted Williams BOS (AL)	162	1947
Ted Williams BOS (AL)	162	1949
4. Ted Williams BOS (AL)	156	1946
5. Eddie Yost WAS	151	1956
6. Eddie Joost PHI (AL)	149	1949
7. Babe Ruth NY (AL)	148	1920
Eddie Stanky BKN	148	1945
Jimmy Wynn HOU	148	1969
10. Jimmy Sheckard CHI (AL)	147	1911
11. Mickey Mantle NY (AL)	146	1957
12. Ted Williams BOS (AL)	145	1941
Ted Williams BOS (AL)	145	1942
Harmon Killebrew MIN	145	1969

RUNS SCORED	RS	YEAR
1. Babe Ruth NY (AL)	177	1921
2. Lou Gehrig NY (AL)	167	1936
3. Babe Ruth NY (AL)	163	1928
Lou Gehrig NY (AL)	163	1931
5. Babe Ruth NY (AL)	158	1920
Babe Ruth NY (AL)	158	1927
Chuck Klein PHI (NL)	158	1930
8. Rogers Hornsby CHI (NL)	156	1929
9. Kiki Cuyler CHI (NL)	155	1930
10. Lefty O'Doul PHI (NL)	152	1929
Woody English CHI (NL)	152	1930

AWARDS AND HIGHLIGHTS

Al Simmons PHI (AL)	152	1930
Chuck Klein PHI (NL)	152	1932
14. Babe Ruth NY (AL)	151	1923
Jimmie Foxx PHI (AL)	151	1932
Joe DiMaggio NY (AL)	151	1937
17. Babe Ruth NY (AL)	150	1930
Ted Williams BOS (AL)	150	1949
19. Lou Gehrig NY (AL)	149	1927
Babe Ruth NY (AL)	149	1931

STOLEN BASES	SB	YEAR
1. Rickey Henderson OAK	130	1982
2. Lou Brock STL	118	1974
3. Vince Coleman STL	110	1985
4. Vince Coleman STL	109	1987
5. Rickey Henderson OAK	108	1983
6. Vince Coleman STL	107	1986
7. Maury Wills LA	104	1962
8. Rickey Henderson OAK	100	1980
9. Ron LeFlore MON	97	1980
10. Ty Cobb DET	96	1915
Omar Moreno PIT	96	1980
12. Maury Wills LA	94	1965
13. Rickey Henderson NY (AL)	93	1988
14. Tim Raines MON	90	1983
15. Clyde Milan WAS	88	1912
16. Rickey Henderson NY (AL)	87	1986
17. Ty Cobb DET	83	1911
Willie Wilson KC	83	1979
19. Eddie Collins PHI (AL)	81	1910
Bob Bescher CIN	81	1911
Vince Coleman STL	81	1988

WINS	W	YEAR
1. Jack Chesbro NY (NL)	41	1904
2. Ed Walsh CHI (AL)	40	1908
3. Christy Mathewson NY (NL)	37	1908
4. Walter Johnson WAS	36	1913
5. Joe McGinnity NY (NL)	35	1904
6. Smoky Joe Wood BOS (AL)	34	1912
7. Cy Young BOS (AL)	33	1901
Christy Mathewson NY (NL)	33	1904
Walter Johnson WAS	33	1912
Grover Alexander PHI (NL)	33	1916
11. Cy Young BOS (AL)	32	1902
12. Joe McGinnity NY (NL)	31	1903
Christy Mathewson NY (NL)	31	1905
Jack Coombs PHI (AL)	31	1910
Grover Alexander PHI (NL)	31	1915
Jim Bagby CLE	31	1920
Lefty Grove PHI (AL)	31	1931
Denny McLain DET	31	1968
19. Christy Mathewson NY (NL)	30	1903
Grover Alexander PHI (NL)	30	1917
Dizzy Dean STL (NL)	30	1934

WINNING PERCENTAGE	W%	YEAR
1. Roy Face PIT	.947	1959
2. Rick Sutcliffe CHI (NL)	.941	1984
3. Johnny Allen CLE	.938	1937
4. Greg Maddux ATL	.905	1995
5. Randy Johnson SEA	.900	1995
6. Ron Guidry NY (AL)	.893	1978
7. Freddie Fitzsimmons BKN	.889	1940
8. Lefty Grove PHI (AL)	.886	1931
9. Bob Stanley BOS	.882	1978
10. Preacher Roe BKN	.880	1951
11. Tom Seaver CIN	.875	1981
12. Smoky Joe Wood BOS (AL)	.872	1912
13. David Cone NY (NL)	.870	1988
14. Orel Hershiser LA	.864	1985
15. Wild Bill Donovan DET	.862	1907
Whitey Ford NY (AL)	.862	1961

EARNED RUN AVERAGE	ERA	YEAR
1. Dutch Leonard BOS (AL)	0.96	1914
2. Three Finger Brown CHI (NL)	1.04	1906
3. Bob Gibson STL	1.12	1968
4. Christy Mathewson NY (NL)	1.14	1909
5. Walter Johnson WAS	1.14	1913
6. Jack Pfiester CHI (NL)	1.15	1907
7. Addie Joss CLE	1.16	1908
8. Carl Lundgren CHI (NL)	1.17	1907
9. Grover Alexander PHI (NL)	1.22	1915
10. Cy Young BOS (AL)	1.26	1908
11. Ed Walsh CHI (AL)	1.27	1910
12. Walter Johnson WAS	1.27	1918
13. Christy Mathewson NY (NL)	1.28	1905
14. Jack Coombs PHI (AL)	1.30	1910
15. Three Finger Brown CHI (NL)	1.31	1909

STRIKEOUTS	SO	YEAR
1. Nolan Ryan CAL	383	1973
2. Sandy Koufax LA	382	1965
3. Nolan Ryan CAL	367	1974
4. Rube Waddell PHI (AL)	349	1904
5. Bob Feller CLE	348	1946
6. Nolan Ryan CAL	341	1977
7. Nolan Ryan CAL	329	1972
8. Nolan Ryan CAL	327	1976
9. Sam McDowell CLE	325	1965
10. Sandy Koufax LA	317	1966
11. Walter Johnson WAS	313	1910
J.R. Richard HOU	313	1979
13. Steve Carlton PHI	310	1972
14. Mickey Lolich DET	308	1971
Randy Johnson SEA	308	1993

SAVES	SV	YEAR
1. Bobby Thigpen CHI (AL)	57	1990
2. Randy Myers CHI (NL)	53	1993
3. Dennis Eckersley OAK	51	1992

517

AWARDS AND HIGHLIGHTS

4. Dennis Eckersley OAK	48	1990	
Rod Beck SF	48	1993	
6. Lee Smith STL	47	1991	
7. Dave Righetti NY (AL)	46	1986	
Bryan Harvey CAL	46	1991	
Jose Mesa CLE	46	1995	
10. Dan Quisenberry KC	45	1983	
Bruce Sutter STL	45	1984	
Dennis Eckersley OAK	45	1988	
Bryan Harvey FLA	45	1993	
Jeff Montgomery KC	45	1993	
Duane Ward TOR	45	1993	

SHUTOUTS	ShO	YEAR
1. Pete Alexander PHI (NL)	16	1916
2. Jack Coombs PHI (AL)	13	1910
Bob Gibson STL (NL)	13	1968
4. Pete Alexander PHI (NL)	12	1915
5. Christy Mathewson NY (NL)	11	1908
Ed Walsh CHI (AL)	11	1908
Walter Johnson WAS	11	1913
Sandy Koufax LA (NL)	11	1963
Dean Chance LA (AL)	11	1964
10. Cy Young BOS (AL)	10	1904
Ed Walsh CHI (AL)	10	1906
Smoky Joe Wood BOS (AL)	10	1912
Dave Davenport STL (FL)	10	1915
Carl Hubbell NY (NL)	10	1933
Mort Cooper STL (NL)	10	1942
Bob Feller CLE	10	1946
Bob Lemon CLE	10	1948
Juan Marichal SF	10	1965
Jim Palmer BAL	10	1975
John Tudor STL	10	1985

COMPLETE GAMES	CG	YEAR
1. Jack Chesbro NY (NL)	48	1904
2. Vic Willis BOS (NL)	45	1902
3. Joe McGinnity NY (NL)	44	1903
4. George Mullin DET	42	1904
Ed Walsh CHI (AL)	42	1908
6. Noodles Hahn CIN	41	1901
Cy Young BOS (AL)	41	1902
Irv Young BOS (NL)	41	1905
9. Cy Young BOS (AL)	40	1904
10. Joe McGinnity BAL	39	1901
Bill Dinneen BOS (AL)	39	1902
Jack Taylor STL (NL)	39	1904
Vic Willis BOS (NL)	39	1904
Rube Waddell PHI (AL)	39	1904

GAMES PITCHED	GP	YEAR
1. Mike Marshall LA	106	1974
2. Kent Tekulve PIT	94	1979
3. Mike Marshall MON	92	1973
4. Kent Tekulve PIT	91	1978
5. Wayne Granger CIN	90	1969
Mike Marshall MIN	90	1979
Kent Tekulve PHI	90	1987
8. Mark Eichhorn TOR	89	1987
9. Wilbur Wood CHI (AL)	88	1968
10. Rob Murphy CIN	87	1987

INNINGS PITCHED	IP	YEAR
1. Ed Walsh CHI (AL)	464.0	1908
2. Jack Chesbro NY (NL)	454.2	1904
3. Joe McGinnity NY (NL)	434.0	1903
4. Ed Walsh CHI (AL)	422.1	1907
5. Vic Willis BOS (NL)	410.0	1902
6. Joe McGinnity NY (NL)	408.0	1904
7. Ed Walsh CHI (AL)	393.0	1912
8. Dave Davenport STL (FL)	392.2	1915
9. Christy Mathewson NY (NL)	390.2	1908
10. Jack Powell NY (NL)	390.1	1904

MOST VALUABLE PLAYERS

NATIONAL LEAGUE

CHALMERS
1911 Wildfire Schulte CHI (OF)
1912 Larry Doyle NY (2B)
1913 Jake Daubert BKN (1B)
1914 Johnny Evers BOS (2B)
1915-21 No Selection

LEAGUE
1922-23 No Selection
1924 Dazzy Vance BKN (P)
1925 Rogers Hornsby STL (2B)
1926 Bob O'Farrell STL (C)
1927 Paul Waner PIT (OF)
1928 Jim Bottomley STL (1B)
1929 Rogers Hornsby CHI (2B)

1930 No Selection

BASEBALL WRITERS ASSOCIATION OF AMERICA
1931 Frankie Frisch STL (2B)
1932 Chuck Klein PHI (OF)
1933 Carl Hubbell NY (P)
1934 Dizzy Dean STL (P)
1935 Gabby Hartnett CHI (C)
1936 Carl Hubbell NY (P)
1937 Joe Medwick STL (OF)
1938 Ernie Lombardi CIN (C)
1939 Bucky Walters CIN (P)
1940 Frank McCormick CIN (1B)
1941 Dolph Camilli BKN (1B)

1942 Mort Cooper STL (P)
1943 Stan Musial STL (OF)
1944 Marty Marion STL (SS)
1945 Phil Cavarretta CHI (1B)
1946 Stan Musial STL (1B)
1947 Bob Elliott BOS (3B)
1948 Stan Musial STL (OF)
1949 Jackie Robinson BKN (2B)
1950 Jim Konstanty PHI (P)
1951 Roy Campanella BKN (C)
1952 Hank Sauer CHI (OF)
1953 Roy Campanella BKN (C)
1954 Willie Mays NY (OF)
1955 Roy Campanella BKN (C)
1956 Don Newcombe BKN (P)

AWARDS AND HIGHLIGHTS

1957 Hank Aaron MIL (OF)
1958 Ernie Banks CHI (SS)
1959 Ernie Banks CHI (SS)
1960 Dick Groat PIT (SS)
1961 Frank Robinson CIN (OF)
1962 Maury Wills LA (SS)
1963 Sandy Koufax LA (P)
1964 Ken Boyer STL (3B)
1965 Willie Mays SF (OF)
1966 Roberto Clemente PIT (OF)
1967 Orlando Cepeda STL (1B)
1968 Bob Gibson STL (P)
1969 Willie McCovey SF (1B)
1970 Johnny Bench CIN (C)
1971 Joe Torre STL (3B)
1972 Johnny Bench CIN (C)
1973 Pete Rose CIN (OF)
1974 Steve Garvey LA (1B)
1975 Joe Morgan CIN (2B)
1976 Joe Morgan CIN (2B)
1977 George Foster CIN (OF)
1978 Dave Parker PIT (OF)
1979 Keith Hernandez STL (1B)
    Willie Stargell PIT (1B)
1980 Mike Schmidt PHI (3B)
1981 Mike Schmidt PHI (3B)
1982 Dale Murphy ATL (OF)
1983 Dale Murphy ATL (OF)
1984 Ryne Sandberg CHI (2B)
1985 Willie McGee STL (OF)
1986 Mike Schmidt PHI (3B)
1987 Andre Dawson CHI (OF)
1988 Kirk Gibson LA (OF)
1989 Kevin Mitchell SF (OF)
1990 Barry Bonds PIT (OF)
1991 Terry Pendleton ATL (3B)
1992 Barry Bonds PIT (OF)
1993 Barry Bonds SF (OF)
1994 Jeff Bagwell HOU (1B)
1995 Barry Larkin CIN (SS)

AMERICAN LEAGUE

CHALMERS
1911 Ty Cobb DET (OF)

1912 Tris Speaker BOS (OF)
1913 Walter Johnson WAS (P)
1914 Eddie Collins PHI (2B)
1915-21 No Selection

LEAGUE
1922 George Sisler STL (1B)
1923 Babe Ruth NY (OF)
1924 Walter Johnson WAS (P)
1925 Roger Peckinpaugh WAS (SS)
1926 George Burns CLE (1B)
1927 Lou Gehrig NY (1B)
1928 Mickey Cochrane PHI (C)
1929-30 No Selection

BASEBALL WRITERS ASSOCIATION OF AMERICA
1931 Lefty Grove PHI (P)
1932 Jimmie Foxx PHI (1B)
1933 Jimmie Foxx PHI (1B)
1934 Mickey Cochrane DET (C)
1935 Hank Greenberg DET (1B)
1936 Lou Gehrig NY (1B)
1937 Charlie Gehringer DET (2B)
1938 Jimmie Foxx BOS (1B)
1939 Joe DiMaggio NY (OF)
1940 Hank Greenberg DET (1B)
1941 Joe DiMaggio NY (OF)
1942 Joe Gordon NY (2B)
1943 Spud Chandler NY (P)
1944 Hal Newhouser DET (P)
1945 Hal Newhouser DET (P)
1946 Ted Williams BOS (OF)
1947 Joe DiMaggio NY (OF)
1948 Lou Boudreau CLE (SS)
1949 Ted Williams BOS (OF)
1950 Phil Rizzuto NY (SS)
1951 Yogi Berra NY (C)
1952 Bobby Shantz PHI (P)
1953 Al Rosen CLE (3B)
1954 Yogi Berra NY (C)
1955 Yogi Berra NY (C)

1956 Mickey Mantle NY (OF)
1957 Mickey Mantle NY (OF)
1958 Jackie Jensen BOS (OF)
1959 Nellie Fox CHI (2B)
1960 Roger Maris NY (OF)
1961 Roger Maris NY (OF)
1962 Mickey Mantle NY (OF)
1963 Elston Howard NY (C)
1964 Brooks Robinson BAL (3B)
1965 Zoilo Versalles MIN (SS)
1966 Frank Robinson BAL (OF)
1967 Carl Yastrzemski BOS (OF)
1968 Denny McLain DET (P)
1969 Harmon Killebrew MIN (3B)
1970 Boog Powell BAL (1B)
1971 Vida Blue OAK (P)
1972 Richie Allen CHI (1B)
1973 Reggie Jackson OAK (OF)
1974 Jeff Burroughs TEX (OF)
1975 Fred Lynn BOS (OF)
1976 Thurman Munson NY (C)
1977 Rod Carew MIN (1B)
1978 Jim Rice BOS (OF)
1979 Don Baylor CAL (DH)
1980 George Brett KC (3B)
1981 Rollie Fingers MIL (P)
1982 Robin Yount MIL (SS)
1983 Cal Ripken BAL (SS)
1984 Willie Hernandez DET (P)
1985 Don Mattingly NY (1B)
1986 Roger Clemens BOS (P)
1987 George Bell TOR (OF)
1988 Jose Canseco OAK (OF)
1989 Robin Yount MIL (OF)
1990 Rickey Henderson OAK (OF)
1991 Cal Ripken BAL (SS)
1992 Dennis Eckersley OAK (P)
1993 Frank Thomas CHI (1B)
1994 Frank Thomas CHI (1B)
1995 Mo Vaughn BOS (1B)

CY YOUNG AWARD WINNERS (ONE SELECTION 1956-66)

NATIONAL LEAGUE
1956 Don Newcombe BKN (RH)
1957 Warren Spahn MIL (LH)
1960 Vern Law PIT (RH)
1962 Don Drysdale LA (RH)

1963 Sandy Koufax LA (LH)
1965 Sandy Koufax LA (LH)
1966 Sandy Koufax LA (LH)
1967 Mike McCormick SF (LH)
1968 Bob Gibson STL (RH)
1969 Tom Seaver NY (RH)

1970 Bob Gibson STL (RH)
1971 Ferguson Jenkins CHI (RH)
1972 Steve Carlton PHI (LH)
1973 Tom Seaver NY (RH)
1974 Mike Marshall LA (RH)

AWARDS AND HIGHLIGHTS

1975 Tom Seaver NY (RH)
1976 Randy Jones SD (LH)
1977 Steve Carlton PHI (LH)
1978 Gaylord Perry SD (RH)
1979 Bruce Sutter CHI (RH)
1980 Steve Carlton PHI (LH)
1981 Fernando Valenzuela LA (LH)
1982 Steve Carlton PHI (LH)
1983 John Denny PHI (RH)
1984 Rick Sutcliffe CHI (RH)
1985 Dwight Gooden NY (RH)
1986 Mike Scott HOU (RH)
1987 Steve Bedrosian PHI (RH)
1988 Orel Hershiser LA (RH)
1989 Mark Davis SD (LH)
1990 Doug Drabek PIT (RH)
1991 Tom Glavine ATL (LH)
1992 Greg Maddux CHI (RH)
1993 Greg Maddux ATL (RH)
1994 Greg Maddux ATL (RH)
1995 Greg Maddux ATL (RH)

AMERICAN LEAGUE
1958 Bob Turley NY (RH)
1959 Early Wynn CHI (RH)
1961 Whitey Ford NY (LH)
1964 Dean Chance LA (RH)
1967 Jim Lonborg BOS (RH)
1968 Denny McLain DET (RH)
1969 Mike Cuellar BAL (LH)
    Denny McLain DET (RH)
1970 Jim Perry MIN (RH)
1971 Vida Blue OAK (LH)
1972 Gaylord Perry CLE (RH)
1973 Jim Palmer BAL (RH)
1974 Jim (Catfish) Hunter OAK (RH)
1975 Jim Palmer BAL (RH)
1976 Jim Palmer BAL (RH)
1977 Sparky Lyle NY (LH)
1978 Ron Guidry NY (LH)
1979 Mike Flanagan BAL (LH)
1980 Steve Stone BAL (RH)
1981 Rollie Fingers MIL (RH)

1982 Pete Vuckovich MIL (RH)
1983 LaMarr Hoyt CHI (RH)
1984 Willie Hernandez DET (LH)
1985 Bret Saberhagen KC (RH)
1986 Roger Clemens BOS (RH)
1987 Roger Clemens BOS (RH)
1988 Frank Viola MIN (LH)
1989 Bret Saberhagen KC (RH)
1990 Bob Welch OAK (RH)
1991 Roger Clemens BOS (RH)
1992 Dennis Eckersley OAK (RH)
1993 Jack McDowell CHI (RH)
1994 David Cone KC (RH)
1995 Randy Johnson SEA (LH)

ROOKIES OF THE YEAR (ONE SELECTION 1947-48)

NATIONAL LEAGUE
1947 Jackie Robinson BKN (1B)
1948 Alvin Dark BOS (SS)
1949 Don Newcombe BKN (P)
1950 Sam Jethroe BOS (OF)
1951 Willie Mays NY (OF)
1952 Joe Black BKN (P)
1953 Junior Gilliam BKN (2B)
1954 Wally Moon STL (OF)
1955 Bill Virdon STL (OF)
1956 Frank Robinson CIN (OF)
1957 Jack Sanford PHI (P)
1958 Orlando Cepeda SF (1B)
1959 Willie McCovey SF (1B)
1960 Frank Howard LA (OF)
1961 Billy Williams CHI (OF)
1962 Ken Hubbs CHI (2B)
1963 Pete Rose CIN (2B)
1964 Richie Allen PHI (3B)
1965 Jim Lefebvre LA (2B)
1966 Tommy Helms CIN (2B)
1967 Tom Seaver NY (P)
1968 Johnny Bench CIN (C)
1969 Ted Sizemore LA (2B)
1970 Carl Morton MON (P)
1971 Earl Williams ATL (C)
1972 Jon Matlack NY (P)
1973 Gary Matthews SF (OF)
1974 Bake McBride STL (OF)
1975 Jon Montefusco SF (P)

1976 Pat Zachry CIN (P)
    Butch Metzger SD (P)
1977 Andre Dawson MON (OF)
1978 Bob Horner ATL (3B)
1979 Rick Sutcliffe LA (P)
1980 Steve Howe LA (P)
1981 Fernando Valenzuela LA (P)
1982 Steve Sax LA (2B)
1983 Darryl Strawberry NY (OF)
1984 Dwight Gooden NY (P)
1985 Vince Coleman STL (OF)
1986 Todd Worrell STL (P)
1987 Benito Santiago SD (C)
1988 Chris Sabo CIN (3B)
1989 Jerome Walton CHI (OF)
1990 Dave Justice ATL (OF)
1991 Jeff Bagwell HOU (1B)
1992 Eric Karros LA (1B)
1993 Mike Piazza LA (C)
1994 Raul Mondesi LA (OF)
1995 Hideo Nomo LA (P)

AMERICAN LEAGUE
1949 Roy Sievers STL (OF)
1950 Walt Dropo BOS (1B)
1951 Gil McDougald NY (3B)
1952 Harry Byrd PHI (P)
1953 Harvey Kuenn DET (SS)
1954 Bob Grim NY (P)
1955 Herb Score CLE (P)

1956 Luis Aparicio CHI (SS)
1957 Tony Kubek NY (SS)
1958 Albie Pearson WAS (OF)
1959 Bob Allison WAS (OF)
1960 Ron Hansen BAL (SS)
1961 Don Schwall BOS (P)
1962 Tom Tresh NY (SS)
1963 Gary Peters CHI (P)
1964 Tony Oliva MIN (OF)
1965 Curt Blefary BAL (OF)
1966 Tommie Agee CHI (OF)
1967 Rod Carew MIN (2B)
1968 Stan Bahnsen NY (P)
1969 Lou Piniella KC (OF)
1970 Thurman Munson NY (C)
1971 Chris Chambliss CLE (1B)
1972 Carlton Fisk BOS (C)
1973 Al Bumbry BAL (OF)
1974 Mike Hargrove TEX (1B)
1975 Fred Lynn BOS (OF)
1976 Mark Fidrych DET (P)
1977 Eddie Murray BAL (DH)
1978 Lou Whitaker DET (2B)
1979 Alfredo Griffin TOR (SS)
    John Castino MIN (3B)
1980 Joe Charboneau CLE (OF)
1981 Dave Righetti NY (P)
1982 Cal Ripken BAL (SS)
1983 Ron Kittle CHI (OF)
1984 Alvin Davis SEA (1B)

AWARDS AND HIGHLIGHTS

1985 Ozzie Guillen CHI (SS)
1986 Jose Canseco OAK (OF)
1987 Mark McGwire OAK (1B)
1988 Walt Weiss OAK (SS)
1989 Gregg Olson BAL (P)
1990 Sandy Alomar CLE (C)
1991 Chuck Knoblauch MIN (2B)
1992 Pat Listach MIL (SS)
1993 Tim Salmon CAL (OF)
1994 Bob Hamelin KC (DH)
1995 Marty Cordova MIN (OF)

GOLD GLOVE AWARD WINNERS

COMBINED SELECTION-1957

P Bobby Shantz NY (AL)
C Sherm Lollar CHI (AL)
1B Gil Hodges BKN
2B Nellie Fox CHI (AL)
3B Frank Malzone BOS
SS Roy McMillan CIN
LF Minnie Minoso CHI (AL)
CF Willie Mays NY (NL)
RF Al Kaline DET

Pitchers/NL

1958 Harvey Haddix CIN
1959-60 Harvey Haddix PIT
1961 Bobby Shantz PIT
1962-63 Bobby Shantz STL
1964 Bobby Shantz PHI
1965-73 Bob Gibson STL
1974-75 Andy Messersmith LA
1976-77 Jim Kaat PHI
1978-80 Phil Niekro ATL
1981 Steve Carlton PHI
1982-83 Phil Niekro ATL
1984 Joaquin Andujar STL
1985 Rick Reuschel PIT
1986 Fernando Valenzuela LA
1987 Rick Reuschel SF
1988 Orel Hershiser LA
1989 Ron Darling NY
1990-92 Greg Maddux CHI
1993-95 Greg Maddux ATL

Pitchers/AL

1958-60 Bobby Shantz NY
1961 Frank Lary DET
1962-72 Jim Kaat MIN
1973 Jim Kaat MIN, CHI
1974-75 Jim Kaat CHI
1976-79 Jim Palmer BAL
1980-81 Mike Norris OAK
1982-86 Ron Guidry NY
1987-88 Mark Langston SEA
1989 Bret Saberhagen KC
1990 Mike Boddicker BOS
1991-95 Mark Langston CAL

Catchers/NL

1958-60 Del Crandall MIL
1961 Johnny Roseboro LA
1962 Del Crandall MIL
1963-64 Johnny Edwards CIN
1965 Joe Torre MIL
1966 Johnny Roseboro LA
1967 Randy Hundley CHI
1968-77 Johnny Bench CIN
1978-79 Bob Boone PHI
1980-82 Gary Carter MON
1983-85 Tony Pena PIT
1986 Jody Davis CHI
1987 Mike LaValliere PIT
1988-90 Benito Santiago SD
1991-92 Tom Pagnozzi STL
1993 Kurt Manwaring SF
1994 Tom Pagnozzi STL
1995 Charles Johnson FLA

Catchers/AL

1958-59 Sherm Lollar CHI
1960 Earl Battey WAS
1961-62 Earl Battey MIN
1963-64 Elston Howard NY
1965-69 Bill Freehan DET
1970-71 Ray Fosse CLE
1972 Carlton Fisk BOS
1973-75 Thurman Munson NY
1976-81 Jim Sundberg TEX
1982 Bob Boone CAL
1983-85 Lance Parrish DET
1986-88 Bob Boone CAL
1989 Bob Boone KC
1990 Sandy Alomar CLE
1991 Tony Pena BOS
1992-95 Ivan Rodriguez TEX

First Basemen/NL

1958-59 Gil Hodges LA
1960-65 Bill White STL
1966 Bill White PHI
1967-72 Wes Parker LA
1973 Mike Jorgenson MON
1974-77 Steve Garvey LA
1978-82 Keith Hernandez STL
1983 Keith Hernandez STL, NY
1984-88 Keith Hernandez NY
1989-90 Andres Galarraga MON
1991 Will Clark SF
1992-93 Mark Grace CHI
1994 Jeff Bagwell HOU
1995 Mark Grace CHI

First Basemen/AL

1958-61 Vic Power CLE
1962-63 Vic Power MIN
1964 Vic Power LA
1965-66 Joe Pepitone NY
1967-68 George Scott BOS
1969 Joe Pepitone NY
1970 Jim Spencer CAL
1971 George Scott BOS
1972-76 George Scott MIL
1977 Jim Spencer CHI
1978 Chris Chambliss NY
1979-80 Cecil Cooper MIL
1981 Mike Squires CHI
1982-84 Eddie Murray BAL
1985-89 Don Mattingly NY
1990 Mark McGwire OAK
1991-94 Don Mattingly NY
1995 J.T. Snow CAL

Second Basemen/NL

1958 Bill Mazeroski PIT
1959 Charlie Neal LA
1960-61 Bill Mazeroski PIT
1962 Ken Hubbs CHI
1963-67 Bill Mazeroski PIT
1968 Glenn Beckert CHI
1969 Felix Millan ATL
1970-71 Tommy Helms CIN
1972 Felix Millan ATL
1973-77 Joe Morgan CIN
1978 Davey Lopes LA
1979 Manny Trillo PHI
1980 Doug Flynn NY
1981-82 Manny Trillo PHI
1983-91 Ryne Sandberg CHI
1992 Jose Lind PIT
1993 Robby Thompson SF
1994-95 Craig Biggio HOU

Second Basemen/AL

1958 Frank Bolling DET
1959-60 Nellie Fox CHI
1961-65 Bobby Richardson NY
1966-68 Bobby Knoop CAL
1969-71 Dave Johnson BAL
1972 Doug Griffin BOS
1973-76 Bobby Grich BAL
1977-82 Frank White KC
1983-85 Lou Whitaker DET

AWARDS AND HIGHLIGHTS

1986-87 Frank White KC
1988-90 Harold Reynolds SEA
1991-95 Roberto Alomar TOR

Third Basemen/NL
1958-61 Ken Boyer STL
1962 Jim Davenport SF
1963 Ken Boyer STL
1964-68 Ron Santo CHI
1969 Clete Boyer ATL
1970-74 Doug Rader HOU
1975 Ken Reitz STL
1976-84 Mike Schmidt PHI
1985 Tim Wallach MON
1986 Mike Schmidt PHI
1987 Terry Pendleton STL
1988 Tim Wallach MON
1989 Terry Pendleton STL
1990 Tim Wallach MON
1991 Matt Williams SF
1992 Terry Pendleton ATL
1993-94 Matt Williams SF
1995 Ken Caminiti SD

Third Basemen/AL
1958-59 Frank Malzone BOS
1960-75 Brooks Robinson BAL
1976 Aurelio Rodriguez DET
1977-78 Graig Nettles NY
1979-84 Buddy Bell TEX
1985 George Brett KC
1986-89 Gary Gaetti MIN
1990 Kelly Gruber TOR
1991-93 Robin Ventura CHI
1994-95 Wade Boggs NY

Shortstops/NL
1958-59 Roy McMillan CIN
1960 Ernie Banks CHI
1961-62 Maury Wills LA
1963 Bobby Wine PHI
1964 Ruben Amaro PHI
1965 Leo Cardenas CIN
1966-67 Gene Alley PIT
1968 Dal Maxvill STL
1969-70 Don Kessinger CHI
1971 Bud Harrelson NY
1972 Larry Bowa PHI
1973 Roger Metzger HOU
1974-77 Dave Concepcion CIN
1978 Larry Bowa PHI
1979 Dave Concepcion CIN
1980-81 Ozzie Smith SD
1982-92 Ozzie Smith STL
1993 Jay Bell PIT
1994-95 Barry Larkin CIN

Shortstops/AL
1958-62 Luis Aparicio CHI
1963 Zoilo Versalles MIN
1964 Luis Aparicio BAL
1965 Zoilo Versalles MIN
1966 Luis Aparicio BAL
1967 Jim Fregosi CAL
1968 Luis Aparicio CHI
1969 Mark Belanger BAL
1970 Luis Aparicio CHI
1971 Mark Belanger BAL
1972 Eddie Brinkman DET
1973-78 Mark Belanger BAL
1979 Rick Burleson BOS
1980-81 Alan Trammell DET
1982 Robin Yount MIL
1983-84 Alan Trammell DET
1985 Alfredo Griffin OAK
1986-89 Tony Fernandez TOR
1990 Ozzie Guillen CHI
1991-92 Cal Ripken BAL
1993 Omar Vizquel SEA
1994-95 Omar Vizquel CLE

Outfielders/NL
1958
Frank Robinson CIN (LF)
Willie Mays SF (CF)
Hank Aaron MIL (RF)

1959
Jackie Brant SF (LF)
Willie Mays SF (CF)
Hank Aaron MIL (RF)

1960
Wally Moon LA (LF)
Willie Mays SF (CF)
Hank Aaron MIL (RF)

1961
Willie Mays SF
Roberto Clemente PIT
Vada Pinson CIN

1962
Willie Mays SF
Roberto Clemente PIT
Bill Virdon PIT

1963-68
Willie Mays SF
Roberto Clemente PIT
Curt Flood STL

1969
Roberto Clemente PIT
Curt Flood STL
Pete Rose CIN

1970
Roberto Clemente PIT
Tommy Agee NY
Pete Rose CIN

1971
Roberto Clemente PIT
Bobby Bonds SF
Willie Davis LA

1972
Roberto Clemente PIT
Cesar Cedeno HOU
Willie Davis LA

1973
Bobby Bonds SF
Cesar Cedeno HOU
Willie Davis LA

1974
Cesar Cedeno HOU
Cesar Geronimo CIN
Bobby Bonds SF

1975-76
Cesar Cedeno HOU
Cesar Geronimo CIN
Garry Maddox PHI

1977
Cesar Geronimo CIN
Garry Maddox PHI
Dave Parker PIT

1978
Garry Maddox PHI
Dave Parker PIT
Ellis Valentine MON

1979
Garry Maddox PHI
Dave Parker PIT
Dave Winfield SD

1980
Andre Dawson MON
Garry Maddox PHI
Dave Winfield SD

1981
Andre Dawson MON
Garry Maddox PHI
Dusty Baker LA

1979
Garry Maddox PHI
Dave Parker PIT
Dave Winfield SD

522

AWARDS AND HIGHLIGHTS

1980
Andre Dawson MON
Garry Maddox PHI
Dave Winfield SD

1981
Andre Dawson MON
Garry Maddox PHI
Dusty Baker LA

1982
Andre Dawson MON
Dale Murphy ATL
Garry Maddox PHI

1983
Andre Dawson MON
Dale Murphy ATL
Willie McGee STL

1984
Dale Murphy ATL
Bob Dernier CHI
Andre Dawson MON

1985
Willie McGee STL
Andre Dawson MON
Dale Murphy ATL

1986
Dale Murphy ATL
Willie McGee STL
Tony Gwynn SD

1987
Eric Davis CIN
Tony Gwynn SD
Andre Dawson CHI

1988
Andre Dawson CHI
Eric Davis CIN
Andy Van Slyke PIT

1989
Eric Davis CIN
Tony Gwynn SD
Andy Van Slyke PIT

1990-91
Barry Bonds PIT
Tony Gwynn SD
Andy Van Slyke PIT

1992
Barry Bonds PIT
Larry Walker MON
Andy Van Slyke PIT

1993
Barry Bonds SF
Marquis Grissom MON
Larry Walker MON

1994
Barry Bonds SF
Marquis Grissom MON
Darren Lewis SF

1995
Steve Finley SD
Marquis Grissom ATL
Raul Mondesi LA

Outfielders/AL

1958
Norm Siebern NY (LF)
Jimmy Piersall BOS (CF)
Al Kaline DET (RF)

1959
Minnie Minoso CLE (LF)
Al Kaline DET (CF)
Jackie Jenson BOS (RF)

1960
Minnie Minoso CHI (LF)
Jim Landis CHI (CF)
Roger Maris NY (RF)

1961
Al Kaline DET
Jimmy Piersall CLE
Jim Landis CHI

1962
Jim Landis CHI
Mickey Mantle NY
Al Kaline DET

1963
Al Kaline DET
Carl Yastrzemski BOS
Jim Landis CHI

1964
Al Kaline DET
Jim Landis CHI
Vic Davalillo CLE

1965
Al Kaline DET
Tom Tresh NY
Carl Yastrzemski BOS

1966
Al Kaline DET
Tommy Agee CHI
Tony Oliva MIN

1967
Carl Yastrzemski BOS
Paul Blair BAL
Al Kaline DET

1968
Mickey Stanley DET
Carl Yastrzemski BOS
Reggie Smith BOS

1969
Paul Blair BAL
Mickey Stanley DET
Carl Yastrzemski BOS

1970
Mickey Stanley DET
Paul Blair BAL
Ken Berry CHI

1971
Paul Blair BAL
Amos Otis KC
Carl Yastrzemski BOS

1972
Paul Blair BAL
Bobby Murcer NY
Ken Berry CAL

1973
Paul Blair BAL
Amos Otis KC
Mickey Stanley DET

1974
Paul Blair BAL
Amos Otis KC
Joe Rudi OAK

1975
Paul Blair BAL
Joe Rudi OAK
Fred Lynn BOS

1976
Joe Rudi OAK
Dwight Evans BOS
Rick Manning CLE

1977
Juan Beniquez TEX
Carl Yastrzemski BOS
Al Cowens KC

1978
Fred Lynn BOS
Dwight Evans BOS
Rick Miller CAL

AWARDS AND HIGHLIGHTS

1979
Dwight Evans BOS
Sixto Lezcano MIL
Fred Lynn BOS

1980
Fred Lynn BOS
Dwayne Murphy OAK
Willie Wilson KC

1981
Dwayne Murphy OAK
Dwight Evans BOS
Rickey Henderson OAK

1982-84
Dwight Evans BOS
Dave Winfield NY
Dwayne Murphy OAK

1985
Gary Pettis CAL
Dave Winfield NY
Dwight Evans BOS
Dwayne Murphy OAK

1986
Jesse Barfield TOR
Kirby Puckett MIN
Gary Pettis CAL

1987
Jesse Barfield TOR
Kirby Puckett MIN
Dave Winfield NY

1988
Devon White CAL
Gary Pettis CAL
Kirby Puckett MIN

1989
Devon White CAL
Gary Pettis DET
Kirby Puckett MIN

1990
Ken Griffey Jr. SEA
Ellis Burks BOS
Gary Pettis TEX

1991-92
Ken Griffey Jr. SEA
Devon White TOR
Kirby Puckett MIN

1993-95
Ken Griffey Jr. SEA
Kenny Lofton CLE
Devon White TOR

THE WORLD SERIES 1903-95

YEAR	WINNER	SERIES	LOSER	YEAR	WINNER	SERIES	LOSER
1903	BOS Pilgrims	5-3	PIT Pirates (NL)	1940	CIN Reds (NL)	4-3	DET Tigers (AL)
1904	NO SERIES			1941	NY Yankees (AL)	4-1	BKN Dodgers (NL)
1905	NY Giants (NL)	4-1	PHI Athletics (AL)	1942	STL Cardinals (NL)	4-1	NY Yankees (AL)
1906	CHI White Sox (AL)	4-2	CHI Cubs (NL)	1943	NY Yankees (AL)	4-1	STL Cardinals (NL)
1907	CHI Cubs (NL)	4-0	DET Tigers (AL)	1944	STL Cardinals (NL)	4-2	STL Browns (AL)
1908	CHI Cubs (NL)	4-1	DET Tigers (AL)	1945	DET Tigers (AL)	4-3	CHI Cubs (NL)
1909	PIT Pirates (NL)	4-3	DET Tigers (AL)	1946	STL Cardinals (NL)	4-3	BOS Red Sox (AL)
1910	PHI Athletics (AL)	4-1	CHI Cubs (NL)	1947	NY Yankees (AL)	4-3	BKN Dodgers (NL)
1911	PHI Athletics (AL)	4-2	NY Giants (NL)	1948	CLE Indians (AL)	4-2	BOS Braves (NL)
1912	BOS Red Sox (AL)	4-3	NY Giants (NL)	1949	NY Yankees (AL)	4-1	BKN Dodgers (NL)
1913	PHI Athletics (AL)	4-1	NY Giants (NL)	1950	NY Yankees (AL)	4-0	PHI Phillies (NL)
1914	BOS Braves (NL)	4-0	PHI Athletics (AL)	1951	NY Yankees (AL)	4-2	NY Giants (NL)
1915	BOS Red Sox (AL)	4-1	PHI Phillies (NL)	1952	NY Yankees (AL)	4-3	BKN Dodgers (NL)
1916	BOS Red Sox (AL)	4-1	BKN Robins (NL)	1953	NY Yankees (AL)	4-2	BKN Dodgers (NL)
1917	CHI White Sox (AL)	4-2	NY Giants (NL)	1954	NY Giants (NL)	4-0	CLE Indians (AL)
1918	BOS Red Sox (AL)	4-2	CHI Cubs (NL)	1955	BKN Dodgers (NL)	4-3	NY Yankees (AL)
1919	CIN Reds (NL)	5-3	CHI White Sox (AL)	1956	NY Yankees (AL)	4-3	BKN Dodgers (NL)
1920	CLE Indians (AL)	5-2	BKN Robins (NL)	1957	MIL Braves (NL)	4-3	NY Yankees (AL)
1921	NY Giants (NL)	5-3	NY Yankees (AL)	1958	NY Yankees (AL)	4-3	MIL Braves (NL)
1922	NY Giants (NL)	4-0	NY Yankees (AL)	1959	LA Dodgers (NL)	4-2	CHI White Sox (AL)
1923	NY Yankees (AL)	4-2	NY Giants (NL)	1960	PIT Pirates (NL)	4-3	NY Yankees (AL)
1924	WAS Senators (AL)	4-3	NY Giants (NL)	1961	NY Yankees (AL)	4-1	CIN Reds (NL)
1925	PIT Pirates (NL)	4-3	WAS Senators (AL)	1962	NY Yankees (AL)	4-3	SF Giants (NL)
1926	STL Cardinals (NL)	4-3	NY Yankees (AL)	1963	LA Dodgers (NL)	4-0	NY Yankees (AL)
1927	NY Yankees (AL)	4-0	PIT Pirates (NL)	1964	STL Cardinals (NL)	4-3	NY Yankees (AL)
1928	NY Yankees (AL)	4-0	STL Cardinals (NL)	1965	LA Dodgers (NL)	4-3	MIN Twins (AL)
1929	PHI Athletics (AL)	4-1	CHI Cubs (NL)	1966	BAL Orioles (AL)	4-0	LA Dodgers (NL)
1930	PHI Athletics (AL)	4-2	STL Cardinals (NL)	1967	STL Cardinals (NL)	4-3	BOS Red Sox (AL)
1931	STL Cardinals (NL)	4-3	PHI Athletics (AL)	1968	DET Tigers (AL)	4-3	STL Cardinals (NL)
1932	NY Yankees (AL)	4-0	CHI Cubs (NL)	1969	NY Mets (NL)	4-1	BAL Orioles (AL)
1933	NY Giants (NL)	4-1	WAS Senators (AL)	1970	BAL Orioles (AL)	4-1	CIN Reds (NL)
1934	STL Cardinals (NL)	4-3	DET Tigers (AL)	1971	PIT Pirates (NL)	4-3	BAL Orioles (AL)
1935	DET Tigers (AL)	4-2	CHI Cubs (NL)	1972	OAK Athletics (AL)	4-3	CIN Reds (NL)
1936	NY Yankees (AL)	4-2	NY Giants (NL)	1973	OAK Athletics (AL)	4-3	NY Mets (NL)
1937	NY Yankees (AL)	4-1	NY Giants (NL)	1974	OAK Athletics (AL)	4-1	LA Dodgers (NL)
1938	NY Yankees (AL)	4-0	CHI Cubs (NL)	1975	CIN Reds (NL)	4-3	BOS Red Sox (AL)
1939	NY Yankees (AL)	4-0	CIN Reds (NL)	1976	CIN Reds (NL)	4-0	NY Yankees (AL)

AWARDS AND HIGHLIGHTS

1977	NY Yankees (AL)	4-2	LA Dodgers (NL)	1987	MIN Twins (AL)	4-3	STL Cardinals (NL)
1978	NY Yankees (AL)	4-2	LA Dodgers (NL)	1988	LA Dodgers (NL)	4-1	OAK Athletics (AL)
1979	PIT Pirates (NL)	4-3	BAL Orioles (AL)	1989	OAK Athletics (AL)	4-0	SF Giants (NL)
1980	PHI Phillies (NL)	4-2	KC Royals (AL)	1990	CIN Reds (NL)	4-0	OAK Athletics (AL)
1981	LA Dodgers (NL)	4-2	NY Yankees (AL)	1991	MIN Twins (AL)	4-3	ATL Braves (NL)
1982	STL Cardinals (NL)	4-3	MIL Brewers (AL)	1992	TOR Blue Jays (AL)	4-2	ATL Braves (NL)
1983	BAL Orioles (AL)	4-1	PHI Phillies (NL)	1993	TOR Blue Jays (AL)	4-2	PHI Phillies (NL)
1984	DET Tigers (AL)	4-1	SD Padres (NL)	1994	NO SERIES		
1985	KC Royals (AL)	4-3	STL Cardinals (NL)	1995	ATL Braves (NL)	4-2	CLE Indians (AL)
1986	NY Mets (NL)	4-3	BOS Red Sox (AL)				

LEAGUE CHAMPIONSHIP SERIES 1969-95

NLCS

YEAR	WINNER	SERIES	LOSER
1969	NY Mets (E)	3-0	ATL Braves (W)
1970	CIN Reds (W)	3-0	PIT Pirates (E)
1971	PIT Pirates (E)	3-1	SF Giants (W)
1972	CIN Reds (W)	3-2	PIT Pirates (E)
1973	NY Mets (E)	3-2	CIN Reds (W)
1974	LA Dodgers (W)	3-1	PIT Pirates (E)
1975	CIN Reds (W)	3-0	PIT Pirates (E)
1976	CIN Reds (W)	3-0	PHI Phillies (E)
1977	LA Dodgers (W)	3-1	PHI Phillies (E)
1978	LA Dodgers (W)	3-1	PHI Phillies (E)
1979	PIT Pirates (W)	3-0	CIN Reds (W)
1980	PHI Phillies (E)	3-2	HOU Astros (W)
1981	NL EAST PLAYOFF		
	MON Expos	3-2	PHI Phillies
	NL WEST PLAYOFF		
	LA Dodgers	3-2	HOU Astros
	LCS		
	LA Dodgers (W)	3-2	MON Expos (E)
1982	STL Cardinals (E)	3-0	ATL Braves (W)
1983	PHI Phillies (E)	3-1	LA Dodgers (W)
1984	SD Padres (W)	3-2	CHI Cubs (E)
1985	STL Cardinals (E)	4-2	LA Dodgers (W)
1986	NY Mets (E)	4-2	HOU Astros (W)
1987	STL Cardinals (E)	4-3	SF Giants (W)
1988	LA Dodgers (W)	4-3	NY Mets (E)
1989	SF Giants (W)	4-1	CHI Cubs (E)
1990	CIN Reds (W)	4-2	PIT Pirates (E)
1991	ATL Braves (W)	4-3	PIT Pirates (E)
1992	ATL Braves (W)	4-3	PIT Pirates (E)
1993	PHI Phillies (E)	4-2	ATL Braves (W)
1994	NO SERIES		
1995	ATL Braves (E)	4-0	CIN Reds (C)

ALCS

YEAR	WINNER	SERIES	LOSER
1969	BAL Orioles (E)	3-0	MIN Twins (W)
1970	BAL Orioles (E)	3-0	MIN Twins (W)
1971	BAL Orioles (E)	3-0	OAK Athletics (W)
1972	OAK Athletics (W)	3-2	DET Tigers (E)
1973	OAK Athletics (W)	3-2	BAL Orioles (E)
1974	OAK Athletics (W)	3-1	BAL Orioles (E)
1975	BOS Red Sox (E)	3-0	OAK Athletics (W)
1976	NY Yankees (E)	3-2	KC Royals (W)
1977	NY Yankees (E)	3-2	KC Royals (W)
1978	NY Yankees (E)	3-1	KC Royals (W)
1979	BAL Orioles (E)	3-1	CAL Angels (W)
1980	KC Royals (W)	3-0	NY Yankees (E)
1981	AL EAST PLAYOFF		
	NY Yankees	3-2	MIL Brewers
	AL WEST PLAYOFF		
	OAK Athletics	3-0	KC Royals
	LCS		
	NY Yankees (E)	3-0	OAK Athletics (W)
1982	MIL Brewers (E)	3-2	CAL Angels (W)
1983	BAL Orioles (E)	3-1	CHI White Sox (W)
1984	DET Tigers (E)	3-0	KC Royals (W)
1985	KC Royals (W)	4-3	TOR Blue Jays (E)
1986	BOS Red Sox (E)	4-3	CAL Angels (W)
1987	MIN Twins (W)	4-1	DET Tigers (E)
1988	OAK Athletics (W)	4-0	BOS Red Sox (E)
1989	OAK Athletics (W)	4-1	TOR Blue Jays (E)
1990	OAK Athletics (W)	4-0	BOS Red Sox (E)
1991	MIN Twins (W)	4-1	TOR Blue Jays (E)
1992	TOR Blue Jays (E)	4-2	OAK Athletics (W)
1993	TOR Blue Jays (E)	4-2	CHI White Sox (W)
1994	NO SERIES		
1995	CLE Indians (C)	4-2	SEA Mariners (W)

DIVISION SERIES 1995

NATIONAL LEAGUE

YEAR	WINNER	SERIES	LOSER
1995	ATL Braves (E)	3-1	COL Rockies (W)
	CIN Reds (C)	3-0	LA Dodgers (W)

AMERICAN LEAGUE

YEAR	WINNER	SERIES	LOSER
1995	CLE Indians (C)	3-0	BOS Red Sox (E)
	SEA Mariners (W)	3-2	NY Yankees (E)

Yearly Team and Individual Leaders

In this section, you will find how each National League and American League organization did in each season since 1900. Included also are each league's individual leaders in batting and pitching for each year.

W = wins; **L** = losses; **PCT** = winning percentage; **GB** = games the team finished behind the league winner or the division winner; **R** = runs scored by the team; **OR** = runs scored by the team's opponents; **BA** = team batting average; **FA** = team fielding average; **ERA** = team earned run average. The league's total runs, opponents runs, batting average, fielding average, and earned run average are shown totaled below the columns. The team that won the World Series received a star (★), the team that won the LCS but not the fall classic received a bullet (•).

The year's individual leaders in each league follow, beginning with hitters' categories—batting average, hits, doubles, triples, home runs, runs batted in, slugging average, stolen bases, and runs scored. Pitchers' categories follow—wins, winning percentage, earned run average, strikeouts, saves, complete games, shutouts, games pitched, and innings pitched. Most of these categories will have the top three leaders in the league. When two or more players tied for a position, it is indicated. If there are two who were far and away the leaders in any one category, and many who either tied or were among the ordinary, only two players are listed.

1900 NATIONAL LEAGUE STANDINGS

	W	L	PCT	GB	R	OR
BKN	82	54	.603	—	816	722
PIT	79	60	.568	4.5	733	612
PHI	75	63	.543	8	810	792
BOS	66	72	.478	17	778	739
CHI	65	75	.464	19	635	751
STL	65	75	.464	19	744	748
CIN	62	77	.446	21.5	703	745
NY	60	78	.435	23	713	823
					5932	5932

BATTING AVERAGE
Honus Wagner PIT .... .381
Elmer Flick PHI .... .367
Jesse Burkett STL .... .363

HITS
Willie Keeler BKN 204
Jesse Burkett STL 203
Honus Wagner PIT 201

DOUBLES
Honus Wagner PIT 45
Nap Lajoie PHI 33
two tied at 32

TRIPLES
Honus Wagner PIT 22

C. Hickman NY 17
Joe Kelley BKN 17

HOME RUNS
Herman Long BOS 12
Elmer Flick PHI 11
Mike Donlin STL 10

RUNS BATTED IN
Elmer Flick PHI 110
Ed Delahanty PHI 109
Honus Wagner PIT 100

STOLEN BASES
Patsy Donovan STL 45
Van Haltren NY 45
Jimmy Barrett CIN 44

RUNS SCORED
Roy Thomas PHI 132
Jimmy Slagle PHI 115
two tied at 114

WINS
Joe McGinnity BKN 28
four tied at 20

EARNED RUN AVERAGE
Rube Waddell PIT 2.37
Ned Garvin CHI 2.41
Jack Taylor CHI 2.55

STRIKEOUTS
Rube Waddell PIT 130
Noodles Hahn CIN 132
Cy Young STL 115

SAVES
Frank Kitson BKN 4

COMPLETE GAMES
Pink Hawley NY 34

SHUTOUTS
four tied at 4

INNINGS PITCHED
Joe McGinnity BKN 343

526

1901 AMERICAN LEAGUE STANDINGS

	W	L	PCT	GB	R	OR
PHI	83	53	.610	—	775	636
STL	78	58	.574	5	619	607
BOS	77	60	.562	6.5	664	600
CHI	74	60	.552	8	675	602
CLE	69	67	.507	14	686	667
WAS	61	75	.449	22	707	790
DET	52	83	.385	30.5	566	657
BAL	50	88	.362	34	715	848
					5407	5407

BATTING AVERAGE
N. Lajoie PHI, CLE .... .378
Ed Delahanty WAS .... .376
C. Hickman BOS, CLE .... .361

HITS
C. Hickman BOS, CLE 193
Lave Cross PHI 191
Bill Bradley CLE 187

DOUBLES
Ed Delahanty WAS 43
Harry Davis PHI 43
two tied at 39

TRIPLES
Jimmy Williams BAL 21

Buck Freeman BOS 19
two tied at 14

HOME RUNS
Socks Seybold PHI 16
three tied at 11

RUNS BATTED IN
Buck Freeman BOS 121
C. Hickman BOS, CLE 110
Lave Cross PHI 108

STOLEN BASES
Topsy Hartsel PHI 47
Sam Mertes CHI 46
Dave Fultz PHI 44

RUNS SCORED
Topsy Hartsel PHI 109
Dave Fultz PHI 109
Sammy Strang CHI 108

WINS
Cy Young BOS 32
Rube Waddell PHI 24
two tied at 22

EARNED RUN AVERAGE
Ed Siever DET 1.91
Rube Waddell PHI 2.05
B. Bernhard PHI, CLE 2.15

STRIKEOUTS
Rube Waddell PHI 210
Cy Young BOS 160
Jack Powell STL 137

SAVES
Jack Powell STL 2

COMPLETE GAMES
Cy Young BOS 41

SHUTOUTS
Addie Joss CLE 5

INNINGS PITCHED
Cy Young BOS 385

1901 NATIONAL LEAGUE STANDINGS

	W	L	PCT	GB	R	OR
PIT	90	49	.647	—	776	534
PHI	83	57	.593	7.5	668	543
BKN	79	57	.581	9.5	744	600
STL	76	64	.543	14.5	792	689
BOS	69	69	.500	20.5	531	556
CHI	53	86	.381	37	578	699
NY	52	85	.380	37	544	755
CIN	52	87	.374	38	561	818
					5194	5194

BATTING AVERAGE
Jesse Burkett STL .... .382
Ed Delahanty PHI .... .357
J. Sheckard BKN .... .354

HITS
Jesse Burkett STL 226
W. Keeler BKN 202
J. Sheckard BKN 196

DOUBLES
Ed Delahanty PHI 39
Tom Daly BKN 38
Honus Wagner PIT 37

TRIPLES
Jimmy Sheckard BKN 19

Elmer Flick PHI 17

HOME RUNS
Sam Crawford CIN 16
Jimmy Sheckard BKN 11
Jesse Burkett STL 10

RUNS BATTED IN
Honus Wagner PIT 126
Ed Delahanty PHI 108
two tied at 104

STOLEN BASES
Honus Wagner PIT 49
Topsy Hartsel CHI 41
Sammy Strang NY 40

RUNS SCORED
Jesse Burkett STL 142
W. Keeler BKN 123
G. Beaumont PIT 120

WINS
B. Donovan BKN 25
Jack Harper STL 23
two tied at 22

EARNED RUN AVERAGE
Jesse Tannehill PIT 2.18
D. Phillippe PIT 2.22
Al Orth PHI 2.27

STRIKEOUTS
Noodles Hahn CIN 239
B. Donovan BKN 226
T. Hughes CHI 225

SAVES
Jack Powell STL 3

COMPLETE GAMES
Noodles Hahn CIN 41

SHUTOUTS
three tied at 6

INNINGS PITCHED
Noodles Hahn CIN 375

1902 AMERICAN LEAGUE STANDINGS

	W	L	PCT	GB	R	OR
PHI	83	53	.610	—	775	636
STL	78	58	.574	5	619	607
BOS	77	60	.562	6.5	664	600
CHI	74	60	.552	8	675	602
CLE	69	67	.507	14	686	667
WAS	61	75	.449	22	707	790
DET	52	83	.385	30.5	566	657
BAL	50	88	.362	34	715	848
					5407	5407

BATTING AVERAGE
N. Lajoie PHI, CLE .... .378
Ed Delahanty WAS .... .376
C. Hickman BOS, CLE ..... .361

HITS
C. Hickman BOS, CLE 193
Lave Cross PHI 191
Bill Bradley CLE 187

DOUBLES
Ed Delahanty WAS 43
Harry Davis PHI 43
two tied at 39

TRIPLES
Jimmy Williams BAL 21

Buck Freeman BOS 19
two tied at 14

HOME RUNS
Socks Seybold PHI 16
three tied at 11

RUNS BATTED IN
Buck Freeman BOS 121
C. Hickman BOS, CLE 110
Lave Cross PHI 108

STOLEN BASES
Topsy Hartsel PHI 47
Sam Mertes CHI 46
Dave Fultz PHI 44

RUNS SCORED
Topsy Hartsel PHI 109
Dave Fultz PHI 109
Sammy Strang CHI 108

WINS
Cy Young BOS 32
Rube Waddell PHI 24
two tied at 22

EARNED RUN AVERAGE
Ed Siever DET 1.91
Rube Waddell PHI 2.05
Bill Bernhard PHI, CLE 2.15

STRIKEOUTS
Rube Waddell PHI 210
Cy Young BOS 160
Jack Powell STL 137

SAVES
Jack Powell STL 2

COMPLETE GAMES
Cy Young BOS 41

SHUTOUTS
Addie Joss CLE 5

INNINGS PITCHED
Cy Young BOS 385

1902 NATIONAL LEAGUE STANDINGS

	W	L	PCT	GB	R	OR
PIT	103	36	.741	—	775	440
BKN	75	63	.543	27.5	564	519
BOS	73	64	.533	29	572	516
CIN	70	70	.500	33.5	633	566
CHI	68	69	.496	34	530	501
STL	56	78	.418	44.5	517	695
PHI	56	81	.409	46	484	649
NY	48	88	.353	53.5	401	590
					4476	4476

BATTING AVERAGE
G. Beaumont PIT .... .357
Sam Crawford CIN .... .333
W. Keeler BKN .... .333

HITS
G. Beaumont PIT 193
W. Keeler BKN 186
Sam Crawford CIN 185

DOUBLES
Honus Wagner PIT 33
Fred Clarke PIT 27
Duff Cooley BOS 26

TRIPLES
Sam Crawford CIN 22

Tommy Leach PIT 22
Honus Wagner PIT 16

HOME RUNS
Tommy Leach PIT 6
Jake Beckley CIN 5
two tied at 4

RUNS BATTED IN
Honus Wagner PIT 91
Tommy Leach PIT 85
Sam Crawford CIN 78

STOLEN BASES
Honus Wagner PIT 42
Jimmy Slagle CHI 40
Patsy Donovan STL 34

RUNS SCORED
Honus Wagner PIT 105
Fred Clarke PIT 103
G. Beaumont PIT 100

WINS
Jack Chesbro PIT 28
Togie Pittinger BOS 27
Vic Willis BOS 27

EARNED RUN AVERAGE
Jack Taylor CHI 1.33
Noodles Hahn CIN 1.77
Jesse Tannehill PIT 1.95

STRIKEOUTS
Vic Willis BOS 225
Doc White PHI 185

SAVES
Vic Willis BOS 3

COMPLETE GAMES
Vic Willis BOS 45

SHUTOUTS
Christy Mathewson NY 8
Jack Chesbro PIT 8

INNINGS PITCHED
Vic Willis BOS 410

1903 AMERICAN LEAGUE STANDINGS

	W	L	PCT	GB	R	OR
★ BOS	91	47	.659	—	708	504
PHI	75	60	.556	14.5	597	519
CLE	77	63	.550	15	639	579
NY	72	62	.537	17	579	573
DET	65	71	.478	25	567	539
STL	65	74	.468	26.5	500	525
CHI	60	77	.438	30.5	516	613
WAS	43	94	.314	47.5	437	691
					4543	4543

BATTING AVERAGE
Nap Lajoie CLE .344
Sam Crawford DET .335
P. Dougherty BOS .331

HITS
P. Dougherty BOS 195
Sam Crawford DET 184
Freddie Parent BOS 170

DOUBLES
Socks Seybold PHI 45
Nap Lajoie CLE 41
Buck Freeman BOS 39

TRIPLES
Sam Crawford DET 25

Bill Bradley CLE 22
Buck Freeman BOS 20

HOME RUNS
Buck Freeman BOS 13
C. Hickman CLE 12
Hobe Ferris BOS 9

RUNS BATTED IN
Buck Freeman BOS 104
C. Hickman CLE 97
Nap Lajoie CLE 93

STOLEN BASES
Harry Bay CLE 45
Ollie Pickering PHI 40
two tied at 35

RUNS SCORED
P. Dougherty BOS 107
Bill Bradley CLE 101
two tied at 95

WINS
Cy Young BOS 28
Eddie Plank PHI 23
four tied at 21

EARNED RUN AVERAGE
Earl Moore CLE 1.77
Cy Young BOS 2.08
Bill Bernhard CLE 2.12

STRIKEOUTS
Rube Waddell PHI 302
Bill Donovan DET 187
two tied at 176

SAVES
five tied at 2

COMPLETE GAMES
three tied at 34

SHUTOUTS
Cy Young BOS 7

INNINGS PITCHED
Cy Young BOS 342

1903 NATIONAL LEAGUE STANDINGS

	W	L	PCT	GB	R	OR
PIT	91	49	.650	—	793	613
NY	84	55	.604	6.5	729	567
CHI	82	56	.594	8	695	599
CIN	74	65	.532	16.5	765	656
BKN	70	66	.515	19	667	682
BOS	58	80	.420	32	578	699
PHI	49	86	.363	39.5	617	738
STL	43	94	.314	46.5	505	795
					5349	5349

BATTING AVERAGE
Honus Wagner PIT .355
Fred Clarke PIT .351
Mike Donlin CIN .351

HITS
G. Beaumont PIT 209
Cy Seymour CIN 191
George Browne NY 185

DOUBLES
Sam Mertes NY 32
Harry Steinfeldt CIN 32
Fred Clarke PIT 32

TRIPLES
Honus Wagner PIT 19

Mike Donlin CIN 18
Tommy Leach PIT 17

HOME RUNS
Jimmy Sheckard BKN 9
six tied at 7

RUNS BATTED IN
Sam Mertes NY 104
Honus Wagner PIT 101
Jack Doyle BKN 91

STOLEN BASES
Jimmy Sheckard BKN 67
Frank Chance CHI 67
two tied at 46

RUNS SCORED
G. Beaumont PIT 137
Mike Donlin CIN 110
George Browne NY 105

WINS
Joe McGinnity NY 31
C. Mathewson NY 30
two tied at 25

EARNED RUN AVERAGE
Sam Leever PIT 2.06
C. Mathewson NY 2.26
Jake Weimer CHI 2.30

STRIKEOUTS
C. Mathewson NY 267
Joe McGinnity NY 171

SAVES
Carl Lundgren CHI 3
Roscoe Miller NY 3

COMPLETE GAMES
Joe McGinnity NY 44

SHUTOUTS
Sam Leever PIT 7

INNINGS PITCHED
Joe McGinnity NY 434

1904 AMERICAN LEAGUE STANDINGS

	W	L	PCT	GB	R	OR
BOS	95	59	.617	—	608	466
NY	92	59	.609	1.5	598	526
CHI	89	65	.578	6	600	482
CLE	86	65	.570	7.5	647	482
PHI	81	70	.536	12.5	557	503
STL	65	87	.428	29	481	604
DET	62	90	.408	32	505	627
WAS	38	113	.252	55.5	437	743
					4433	4433

BATTING AVERAGE
Nap Lajoie CLE .376
W. Keeler NY .343
Harry Davis PHI .309

HITS
Nap Lajoie CLE 208
W. Keeler NY 186
Bill Bradley CLE 183

DOUBLES
Nap Lajoie CLE 49
Jimmy Collins BOS 33
Bill Bradley CLE 32

TRIPLES
Joe Cassidy WAS 19
Buck Freeman BOS 19
Chick Stahl BOS 19

HOME RUNS
Harry Davis PHI 10
Buck Freeman BOS 7
Danny Murphy PHI 7

RUNS BATTED IN
Nap Lajoie CLE 102
Buck Freeman BOS 84
Bill Bradley CLE 83

STOLEN BASES
Elmer Flick CLE 38
Harry Bay CLE 38
Emmet Heidrick STL 35

RUNS SCORED
Dougherty BOS, NY 113
Elmer Flick CLE 97
Bill Bradley CLE 94

WINS
Jack Chesbro NY 41
Eddie Plank PHI 26
Cy Young BOS 26

EARNED RUN AVERAGE
Addie Joss CLE 1.59
Rube Waddell PHI 1.62
Doc White CHI 1.78

STRIKEOUTS
Rube Waddell PHI 349
Jack Chesbro NY 239
Jack Powell NY 202

SAVES
Casey Patten WAS 3

COMPLETE GAMES
Jack Chesbro NY 48

SHUTOUTS
Cy Young BOS 10

INNINGS PITCHED
Jack Chesbro NY 455

1904 NATIONAL LEAGUE STANDINGS

	W	L	PCT	GB	R	OR
★ NY	106	47	.693	—	744	476
CHI	93	60	.608	13	599	517
CIN	88	65	.575	18	695	547
PIT	87	66	.569	19	675	592
STL	75	79	.487	31.5	602	595
BKN	56	97	.366	50	497	614
BOS	55	98	.359	51	491	749
PHI	52	100	.342	53.5	571	784
					4874	4874

BATTING AVERAGE
Honus Wagner PIT .349
M. Donlin CIN, NY .329
Jake Beckley STL .325

HITS
G. Beaumont PIT 185
Jake Beckley STL 179
Honus Wagner PIT 171

DOUBLES
Honus Wagner PIT 44
Sam Mertes NY 28
Joe Delahanty BOS 27

TRIPLES
Harry Lumley BKN 18
Honus Wagner PIT 14
three tied at 13

HOME RUNS
Harry Lumley BKN 9
Dave Brain STL 7
four tied at 6

RUNS BATTED IN
Bill Dahlen NY 80
Sam Mertes NY 78
Harry Lumley BKN 78

STOLEN BASES
Honus Wagner PIT 53
Bill Dahlen NY 47
Sam Mertes NY 47

RUNS SCORED
George Browne NY 99
Honus Wagner PIT 97
Ginger Beaumont PIT 97

WINS
Joe McGinnity NY 35
C. Mathewson NY 33
Jack Harper CIN 23

EARNED RUN AVERAGE
Joe McGinnity NY 1.61
Ned Garvin BKN 1.68
T. Brown CHI 1.86

STRIKEOUTS
C. Mathewson NY 212
Vic Willis BOS 196

SAVES
Joe McGinnity NY 5

COMPLETE GAMES
Jack Taylor STL 39
Vic Willis BOS 39

SHUTOUTS
Joe McGinnity NY 9

INNINGS PITCHED
Joe McGinnity NY 408

1905 AMERICAN LEAGUE STANDINGS

	W	L	PCT	GB	R	OR
PHI	92	56	.622	—	623	492
CHI	92	60	.605	2	612	451
DET	79	74	.516	15.5	512	602
BOS	78	74	.513	16	579	564
CLE	76	78	.494	19	567	587
NY	71	78	.477	21.5	586	622
WAS	64	87	.424	29.5	559	623
STL	54	99	.353	40.5	511	608
					4549	4549

BATTING AVERAGE
Elmer Flick CLE .306
W. Keeler NY .302
Harry Bay CLE .301

HITS
George Stone STL 187
Harry Davis PHI 173
Sam Crawford DET 171

DOUBLES
Harry Davis PHI 47
Sam Crawford DET 38
two tied at 37

TRIPLES
Elmer Flick CLE 18
Hobe Ferris BOS 16
Terry Turner CLE 14

HOME RUNS
Harry Davis PHI 8
George Stone STL 7
five tied at 6

RUNS BATTED IN
Harry Davis PHI 83
Lave Cross PHI 77
Jiggs Donahue CHI 76

STOLEN BASES
Danny Hoffman PHI 46
Dave Fultz NY 44
Jake Stahl WAS 41

RUNS SCORED
Harry Davis PHI 93
Fielder Jones CHI 91
Harry Bay CLE 90

WINS
Rube Waddell PHI 27
Eddie Plank PHI 24
two tied at 23

EARNED RUN AVERAGE
Rube Waddell PHI 1.48
Doc White CHI 1.76
Cy Young BOS 1.82

STRIKEOUTS
Rube Waddell PHI 287
Eddie Plank PHI 210
Cy Young BOS 210

SAVES
Jim Buchanan STL 2

COMPLETE GAMES
three tied at 35

SHUTOUTS
Ed Killian DET 8

INNINGS PITCHED
George Mullin DET 348

1905 NATIONAL LEAGUE STANDINGS

	W	L	PCT	GB	R	OR
★ NY	105	48	.686	—	780	505
PIT	96	57	.627	9	692	570
CHI	92	61	.601	13	667	442
PHI	83	69	.546	21.5	708	602
CIN	79	74	.516	26	735	698
STL	58	96	.377	47.5	535	734
BOS	51	103	.331	54.5	468	733
BKN	48	104	.316	56.5	506	807
					5091	5091

BATTING AVERAGE
Cy Seymour CIN .377
Honus Wagner PIT .363
Mike Donlin NY .356

HITS
Cy Seymour CIN 219
Mike Donlin NY 216
Honus Wagner PIT 199

DOUBLES
Cy Seymour CIN 40
John Titus PHI 36
Honus Wagner PIT 32

TRIPLES
Cy Seymour CIN 21

Sam Mertes NY 17
Sherry Magee PHI 17

HOME RUNS
Fred Odwell CIN 9
Cy Seymour CIN 8
three tied at 7

RUNS BATTED IN
Cy Seymour CIN 121
Sam Mertes NY 108
Honus Wagner PIT 101

STOLEN BASES
Billy Maloney CHI 59
Art Devlin NY 59
Honus Wagner PIT 57

RUNS SCORED
Mike Donlin NY 124
Roy Thomas PHI 118
Miller Huggins CIN 117

WINS
C. Mathewson NY 31
Togie Pittinger PHI 23
Red Ames NY 22

EARNED RUN AVERAGE
C. Mathewson NY 1.28
Ed Reulbach CHI 1.42
Bob Wicker CHI 2.02

STRIKEOUTS
C. Mathewson NY 206
Red Ames NY 198
Orval Overall CIN 173

SAVES
Claude Elliott NY 6

COMPLETE GAMES
Irv Young BOS 41

SHUTOUTS
C. Mathewson NY 8

INNINGS PITCHED
Irv Young BOS 378

1906 AMERICAN LEAGUE STANDINGS

	W	L	PCT	GB	R	OR
★ CHI	93	58	.616	—	570	460
NY	90	61	.596	3	644	543
CLE	89	64	.582	5	663	482
PHI	78	67	.538	12	561	543
STL	76	73	.510	16	558	498
DET	71	78	.477	21	518	599
WAS	55	95	.367	37.5	518	664
BOS	49	105	.318	45.5	463	706
					4495	4495

BATTING AVERAGE
George Stone STL .358
Nap Lajoie CLE .355
Hal Chase NY .323

HITS
Nap Lajoie CLE 214
George Stone STL 208
Elmer Flick CLE 194

DOUBLES
Nap Lajoie CLE 48
Harry Davis PHI 42
Elmer Flick CLE 34

TRIPLES
Elmer Flick CLE 22
George Stone STL 20
Sam Crawford DET 16

HOME RUNS
Harry Davis PHI 12
C. Hickman WAS 9
George Stone STL 6

RUNS BATTED IN
Harry Davis PHI 96
Nap Lajoie CLE 91
George Davis CHI 80

STOLEN BASES
Elmer Flick CLE 39
John Anderson WAS 39
two tied at 37

RUNS SCORED
Elmer Flick CLE 98
Topsy Hartsel PHI 96
Wee Willie Keeler NY 96

WINS
Al Orth NY 27
Jack Chesbro NY 23
two tied at 22

EARNED RUN AVERAGE
Doc White CHI 1.52
Barney Pelty STL 1.59
Addie Joss CLE 1.72

STRIKEOUTS
Rube Waddell PHI 196
Cy Falkenberg WAS 178

SAVES
Otto Hess CLE 3
Chief Bender PHI 3

COMPLETE GAMES
Al Orth NY 36

SHUTOUTS
Ed Walsh CHI 10

INNINGS PITCHED
Al Orth NY 339

1906 NATIONAL LEAGUE STANDINGS

	W	L	PCT	GB	R	OR
CHI	116	36	.763	—	705	381
NY	96	56	.632	20	625	510
PIT	93	60	.608	23.5	623	470
PHI	71	82	.464	45.5	528	564
BKN	66	86	.434	50	496	625
CIN	64	87	.424	51.5	533	582
STL	52	98	.347	63	470	607
BOS	49	102	.325	66.5	408	649
					4388	4388

BATTING AVERAGE
Honus Wagner PIT .339
Harry Steinfeldt CHI .327
Harry Lumley BKN .324

HITS
Harry Steinfeldt CHI 176
Honus Wagner PIT 175
Seymour CIN, NY 165

DOUBLES
Honus Wagner PIT 38
Sherry Magee PHI 36
Kitty Bransfield PHI 28

TRIPLES
Wildfire Schulte CHI 13
Fred Clarke PIT 13
two tied at 12

HOME RUNS
Tim Jordan BKN 12
Harry Lumley BKN 9
Cy Seymour CIN, NY 8

RUNS BATTED IN
Jim Nealon PIT 83
Harry Steinfeldt CHI 83
Cy Seymour CIN, NY 80

STOLEN BASES
Frank Chance CHI 57
Sherry Magee PHI 55
Art Devlin NY 54

RUNS SCORED
Frank Chance CHI 103
Honus Wagner PIT 103
Jimmy Sheckard CHI 90

WINS
Joe McGinnity NY 27
T. Brown CHI 26
Vic Willis PIT 23

EARNED RUN AVERAGE
T. Brown CHI 1.04
Jack Pfiester CHI 1.51
Ed Reulbach CHI 1.65

STRIKEOUTS
F. Beebe CHI, STL 171
Big Jeff Pfeffer BOS 158
Red Ames NY 156

SAVES
George Ferguson NY 7

COMPLETE GAMES
Irv Young BOS 37

SHUTOUTS
T. Brown CHI 9

INNINGS PITCHED
Irv Young BOS 358

1907 AMERICAN LEAGUE STANDINGS

	W	L	PCT	GB	R	OR
DET	92	58	.613	—	694	532
PHI	88	57	.607	1.5	582	511
CHI	87	64	.576	5.5	588	474
CLE	85	67	.559	8	530	525
NY	70	78	.473	21	605	665
STL	69	83	.454	24	542	555
BOS	59	90	.396	32.5	464	558
WAS	49	102	.325	43.5	506	691
					4511	4511

BATTING AVERAGE
Ty Cobb DET .... .350
Sam Crawford DET .... .323
George Stone STL .... .320

HITS
Ty Cobb DET 212
George Stone STL 191
Sam Crawford DET 188

DOUBLES
Harry Davis PHI 37
Sam Crawford DET 34
two tied at 30

TRIPLES
Elmer Flick CLE 18

Sam Crawford DET 17
Ty Cobb DET 14

HOME RUNS
Harry Davis PHI 8
three tied at 5

RUNS BATTED IN
Ty Cobb DET 119
Socks Seybold PHI 92
Harry Davis PHI 87

STOLEN BASES
Ty Cobb DET 49
Wid Conroy NY 41
Elmer Flick CLE 41

RUNS SCORED
Sam Crawford DET 102
Davy Jones DET 101
Ty Cobb DET 97

WINS
Addie Joss CLE 27
Doc White CHI 27
two tied at 25

EARNED RUN AVERAGE
Ed Walsh CHI 1.60
Ed Killian DET 1.78
Addie Joss CLE 1.83

STRIKEOUTS
Rube Waddell PHI 232
Ed Walsh CHI 206
Eddie Plank PHI 183

SAVES
three tied at 4

COMPLETE GAMES
Ed Walsh CHI 37

SHUTOUTS
Eddie Plank PHI 8

INNINGS PITCHED
Ed Walsh CHI 422

1907 NATIONAL LEAGUE STANDINGS

	W	L	PCT	GB	R	OR
★ CHI	107	45	.704	—	574	390
PIT	91	63	.591	17	634	510
PHI	83	64	.565	21.5	512	476
NY	82	71	.536	25.5	574	5102
BKN	65	83	.439	40	446	522
CIN	66	87	.431	41.5	526	519
BOS	58	90	.392	47	502	652
STL	52	101	.340	55.5	419	608
					4187	4187

BATTING AVERAGE
Honus Wagner PIT .... .350
Sherry Magee PHI .... .328
G. Beaumont BOS .... .322

HITS
G. Beaumont BOS 187
Honus Wagner PIT 180
Tommy Leach PIT 166

DOUBLES
Honus Wagner PIT 38
Sherry Magee PHI 28
two tied at 25

TRIPLES
W. Alperman BKN 16

John Ganzel CIN 16
two tied at 14

HOME RUNS
Dave Brain BOS 10
Harry Lumley BKN 9
Red Murray STL 7

RUNS BATTED IN
Sherry Magee PHI 85
Honus Wagner PIT 82
Ed Abbaticchio PIT 82

STOLEN BASES
Honus Wagner PIT 61
Johnny Evers CHI 46
Sherry Magee PHI 46

RUNS SCORED
Spike Shannon NY 104
Tommy Leach PIT 102
Honus Wagner PIT 98

WINS
C. Mathewson NY 24
Orval Overall CHI 23
Tully Sparks PHI 22

EARNED RUN AVERAGE
Jack Pfiester CHI 1.15
Carl Lundgren CHI 1.17
T. Brown CHI 1.39

STRIKEOUTS
C. Mathewson NY 178
Buck Ewing CIN 147

SAVES
Joe McGinnity NY 4

COMPLETE GAMES
Stoney McGlynn STL 33

SHUTOUTS
Christy Mathewson NY 8
Orval Overall CHI 8

INNINGS PITCHED
S. McGlynn STL 352

1908 AMERICAN LEAGUE STANDINGS

	W	L	PCT	GB	R	OR
DET	90	63	.588	—	647	547
CLE	90	64	.584	.5	568	457
CHI	88	64	.579	1.5	537	470
STL	83	69	.546	6.5	544	483
BOS	75	79	.487	15.5	564	513
PHI	68	85	.444	22	486	562
WAS	67	85	.441	22.5	479	539
NY	51	103	.331	39.5	459	713
					4284	4284

BATTING AVERAGE
Ty Cobb DET .... .324
Sam Crawford DET .... .311
Doc Gessler BOS .... .308

HITS
Ty Cobb DET 188
Sam Crawford DET 184
two tied at 168

DOUBLES
Ty Cobb DET 36
Sam Crawford DET 33
C. Rossman DET 33

TRIPLES
Ty Cobb DET 20

Sam Crawford DET 16
Jake Stahl BOS, NY 16

HOME RUNS
Sam Crawford DET 7
Bill Hinchman CLE 6
three tied at 5

RUNS BATTED IN
Ty Cobb DET 108
Sam Crawford DET 80
two tied at 74

STOLEN BASES
Patsy Dougherty CHI 47
Charlie Hemphill NY 42
G. Schaefer DET 40

RUNS SCORED
Matty McIntyre DET 105
Sam Crawford DET 102
G. Schaefer DET 96

WINS
Ed Walsh CHI 40
Addie Joss CLE 24
Ed Summers DET 24

EARNED RUN AVERAGE
Addie Joss CLE 1.16
Cy Young BOS 1.26
Ed Walsh CHI 1.42

STRIKEOUTS
Ed Walsh CHI 269
Rube Waddell STL 232
Tom Hughes WAS 165

SAVES
Ed Walsh CHI 6

COMPLETE GAMES
Ed Walsh CHI 42

SHUTOUTS
Ed Walsh CHI 11

INNINGS PITCHED
Ed Walsh CHI 464

1908 NATIONAL LEAGUE STANDINGS

	W	L	PCT	GB	R	OR
★ CHI	99	55	.643	—	624	461
NY	98	56	.636	1	652	456
PIT	98	56	.636	1	585	469
PHI	83	71	.539	16	504	445
CIN	73	81	.474	26	489	544
BOS	63	91	.409	36	537	622
BKN	53	101	.344	46	377	516
STL	49	105	.318	50	371	626
					4139	4139

BATTING AVERAGE
Honus Wagner PIT .... .354
Mike Donlin NY .... .334
Larry Doyle NY .... .308

HITS
Honus Wagner PIT 201
Mike Donlin NY 198
two tied at 167

DOUBLES
Honus Wagner PIT 39
Sherry Magee PHI 30
Frank Chance CHI 27

TRIPLES
Honus Wagner PIT 19

Hans Lobert CIN 18
two tied at 16

HOME RUNS
Tim Jordan BKN 12
Honus Wagner PIT 10
Red Murray STL 7

RUNS BATTED IN
Honus Wagner PIT 109
Mike Donlin NY 106
Cy Seymour NY 92

STOLEN BASES
Honus Wagner PIT 53
Red Murray STL 48
Hans Lobert CIN 47

RUNS SCORED
Fred Tenney NY 101
Honus Wagner PIT 100
Tommy Leach PIT 93

WINS
C. Mathewson NY 37
T. Brown CHI 29
Ed Reulbach CHI 24

EARNED RUN AVERAGE
C. Mathewson NY 1.43
T. Brown CHI 1.47
G. McQuillan PHI 1.53

STRIKEOUTS
C. Mathewson NY 259
Nap Rucker BKN 199
Orval Overall CHI 167

SAVES
three tied at 5

COMPLETE GAMES
C. Mathewson NY 34

SHUTOUTS
C. Mathewson NY 11

INNINGS PITCHED
C. Mathewson NY 391

1909 AMERICAN LEAGUE STANDINGS

	W	L	PCT	GB	R	OR
DET	98	54	.645	—	666	493
PHI	95	58	.621	3.5	605	408
BOS	88	63	.583	9.5	597	550
CHI	78	74	.513	20	492	463
NY	74	77	.490	23.5	590	587
CLE	71	82	.464	27.5	493	532
STL	61	89	.407	36	441	575
WAS	42	110	.276	56	380	656
					4264	4264

BATTING AVERAGE
Ty Cobb DET .377
Eddie Collins PHI .346
Nap Lajoie CLE .324

HITS
Ty Cobb DET 216
Eddie Collins PHI 198
Sam Crawford DET 185

DOUBLES
Sam Crawford DET 35
Nap Lajoie CLE 33
Ty Cobb DET 33

TRIPLES
Frank Baker PHI 19
Danny Murphy PHI 14
Sam Crawford DET 14

HOME RUNS
Ty Cobb DET 9
Tris Speaker BOS 7
two tied at 6

RUNS BATTED IN
Ty Cobb DET 107
Sam Crawford DET 97
Frank Baker PHI 85

STOLEN BASES
Ty Cobb DET 76
Eddie Collins PHI 67
Donie Bush DET 53

RUNS SCORED
Ty Cobb DET 116
Donie Bush DET 114
Eddie Collins PHI 104

WINS
George Mullin DET 29
Frank Smith CHI 25
Ed Willett DET 21

EARNED RUN AVERAGE
Harry Krause PHI 1.39
Ed Walsh CHI 1.41
Chief Bender PHI 1.66

STRIKEOUTS
Frank Smith CHI 177
W. Johnson WAS 164
Heinie Berger CLE 162

SAVES
Frank Arellanes BOS 8

COMPLETE GAMES
Frank Smith CHI 37

SHUTOUTS
Ed Walsh CHI 8

INNINGS PITCHED
Frank Smith CHI 365

1909 NATIONAL LEAGUE STANDINGS

	W	L	PCT	GB	R	OR
★ PIT	110	42	.724	—	699	447
CHI	104	49	.680	6.5	635	390
NY	92	61	.601	18.5	623	546
CIN	77	76	.503	33.5	606	599
PHI	74	79	.484	36.5	516	518
BKN	55	98	.359	55.5	444	627
STL	54	98	.355	56	583	731
BOS	45	108	.294	65.5	435	683
					4541	4541

BATTING AVERAGE
Honus Wagner PIT .339
Mike Mitchell CIN .310
Dick Hoblitzell CIN .308

HITS
Larry Doyle NY 172
Eddie Grant PHI 170
Honus Wagner PIT 168

DOUBLES
Honus Wagner PIT 39
Sherry Magee PHI 33
Dots Miller PIT 31

TRIPLES
Mike Mitchell CIN 17
Sherry Magee PHI 14
Ed Konetchy STL 14

HOME RUNS
Red Murray NY 7
three tied at 6

RUNS BATTED IN
Honus Wagner PIT 100
Red Murray NY 91
Dots Miller PIT 87

STOLEN BASES
Bob Bescher CIN 54
Red Murray NY 48
Dick Egan CIN 39

RUNS SCORED
Tommy Leach PIT 126
Fred Clarke PIT 97
two tied at 92

WINS
T. Brown CHI 27
Howie Camnitz PIT 25
C. Mathewson NY 25

EARNED RUN AVERAGE
C. Mathewson NY 1.14
T. Brown CHI 1.31
Orval Overall CHI 1.42

STRIKEOUTS
Orval Overall CHI 205
Nap Rucker BKN 201
Earl Moore PHI 173

SAVES
T. Brown CHI 7

COMPLETE GAMES
T. Brown CHI 32

SHUTOUTS
Orval Overall CHI 9

INNINGS PITCHED
T. Brown CHI 343

1910 AMERICAN LEAGUE STANDINGS

	W	L	PCT	GB	R	OR
★ PHI	102	48	.680	—	673	441
NY	88	63	.583	14.5	626	557
DET	86	68	.558	18	679	582
BOS	81	72	.529	22.5	638	564
CLE	71	81	.467	32	548	657
CHI	68	85	.444	35.5	457	479
WAS	66	85	.437	36.5	501	550
STL	47	107	.305	57	451	743
					4573	4573

BATTING AVERAGE
Nap Lajoie CLE .... .384
Ty Cobb DET .... .383
Tris Speaker BOS .... .340

HITS
Nap Lajoie CLE 227
Ty Cobb DET 194
Eddie Collins PHI 188

DOUBLES
Nap Lajoie CLE 51
Ty Cobb DET 35
Duffy Lewis BOS 29

TRIPLES
Sam Crawford DET 19
Danny Murphy PHI 18
Bris Lord CLE, PHI 18

HOME RUNS
Jake Stahl BOS 10
Ty Cobb DET 8
Duffy Lewis BOS 8

RUNS BATTED IN
Sam Crawford DET 120
Ty Cobb DET 91
Eddie Collins PHI 81

STOLEN BASES
Eddie Collins PHI 81
Ty Cobb DET 65
two tied at 49

RUNS SCORED
Ty Cobb DET 106
Nap Lajoie CLE 94
Tris Speaker BOS 92

WINS
Jack Coombs PHI 31
Russ Ford NY 26
Walter Johnson WAS 25

EARNED RUN AVERAGE
Ed Walsh CHI 1.27
Jack Coombs PHI 1.30
W. Johnson WAS 1.36

STRIKEOUTS
W. Johnson WAS 313
Ed Walsh CHI 258
Jack Coombs PHI 224

SAVES
Ed Walsh CHI 5

COMPLETE GAMES
Walter Johnson WAS 38

SHUTOUTS
Jack Coombs PHI 13

INNINGS PITCHED
W. Johnson WAS 370

1910 NATIONAL LEAGUE STANDINGS

	W	L	PCT	GB	R	OR
CHI	104	50	.675	—	712	499
NY	91	63	.591	13	715	567
PIT	86	67	.562	17.5	655	576
PHI	78	75	.510	25.5	674	639
CIN	75	79	.487	29	620	684
BKN	64	90	.416	40	497	623
STL	63	90	.412	40.5	639	718
BOS	53	100	.346	50.5	495	701
					5007	5007

BATTING AVERAGE
Sherry Magee PHI .... .331
Vin Campbell PIT .... .326
Solly Hofman CHI .... .325

HITS
Bobby Byrne PIT 178
Honus Wagner PIT 178
two tied at 172

DOUBLES
Bobby Byrne PIT 43
Sherry Magee PHI 39
Zack Wheat BKN 36

TRIPLES
Mike Mitchell CIN 18
Sherry Magee PHI 17
two tied at 16

HOME RUNS
Fred Beck BOS 10
Wildfire Schulte CHI 10
two tied at 8

RUNS BATTED IN
Sherry Magee PHI 123
Mike Mitchell CIN 88
Red Murray NY 87

STOLEN BASES
Bob Bescher CIN 70
Red Murray NY 57
Dode Paskert CIN 51

RUNS SCORED
Sherry Magee PHI 110
Miller Huggins STL 101
Bobby Byrne PIT 101

WINS
C. Mathewson NY 27
T. Brown CHI 25
Earl Moore PHI 22

EARNED RUN AVERAGE
King Cole CHI 1.80
T. Brown CHI 1.86
C. Mathewson NY 1.89

STRIKEOUTS
Earl Moore PHI 185
C. Mathewson NY 184

SAVES
T. Brown CHI 7
Harry Gaspar CIN 7

COMPLETE GAMES
three tied at 27

SHUTOUTS
four tied at 6

INNINGS PITCHED
Nap Rucker BKN 320

1911 AMERICAN LEAGUE STANDINGS

	W	L	PCT	GB	R	OR
★ PHI	101	50	.669	—	861	601
DET	89	65	.578	13.5	831	776
CLE	80	73	.523	22	691	712
CHI	77	74	.510	24	719	624
BOS	78	75	.510	24	680	643
NY	76	76	.500	25.5	684	724
WAS	64	90	.416	38.5	625	766
STL	45	107	.296	56.5	567	812
					5658	5658

BATTING AVERAGE
Ty Cobb DET .... .420
Joe Jackson CLE .... .408
Sam Crawford DET .... .378

HITS
Ty Cobb DET 248
Joe Jackson CLE 233
Sam Crawford DET 217

DOUBLES
Ty Cobb DET 47
Joe Jackson CLE 45
Frank Baker PHI 42

TRIPLES
Ty Cobb DET 24
Birdie Cree NY 22
Joe Jackson CLE 19

HOME RUNS
Frank Baker PHI 11
Ty Cobb DET 8
Tris Speaker BOS 8

RUNS BATTED IN
Ty Cobb DET 127
Frank Baker PHI 115
Sam Crawford DET 115

STOLEN BASES
Ty Cobb DET 83
Clyde Milan WAS 58
Birdie Cree NY 48

RUNS SCORED
Ty Cobb DET 147
Joe Jackson CLE 126
Donie Bush DET 126

WINS
Jack Coombs PHI 28
Ed Walsh CHI 27
Walter Johnson WAS 25

EARNED RUN AVERAGE
Vean Gregg CLE 1.80
W. Johnson WAS 1.90
Joe Wood BOS 2.02

STRIKEOUTS
Ed Walsh CHI 255
Joe Wood BOS 231

SAVES
three tied at 4

COMPLETE GAMES
Walter Johnson WAS 36

SHUTOUTS
Eddie Plank PHI 6
Walter Johnson WAS 6

INNINGS PITCHED
Ed Walsh CHI 369

1911 NATIONAL LEAGUE STANDINGS

	W	L	PCT	GB	R	OR
NY	99	54	.647	—	756	542
CHI	92	62	.597	7.5	757	607
PIT	85	69	.552	14.5	744	557
PHI	79	73	.520	19.5	658	669
STL	75	74	.503	22	671	745
CIN	70	83	.458	29	682	706
BKN	64	86	.427	33.5	539	659
BOS	44	107	.291	54	699	1021
					5506	5506

BATTING AVERAGE
Honus Wagner PIT .... .334
Dots Miller BOS .... .333
Chief Meyers NY .... .332

HITS
Dots Miller BOS 192
Dick Hoblitzell CIN 180
Jake Daubert BKN 176

DOUBLES
Ed Konetchy STL 38
Dots Miller BOS 36
Owen Wilson PIT 34

TRIPLES
Larry Doyle NY 25
Mike Mitchell CIN 22
Wildfire Schulte CHI 21

HOME RUNS
Wildfire Schulte CHI 21
Fred Luderus PHI 16
Sherry Magee PHI 15

RUNS BATTED IN
Wildfire Schulte CHI 107
Owen Wilson PIT 107
Fred Luderus PHI 99

STOLEN BASES
Bob Bescher CIN 80
Josh Devore NY 61
Fred Snodgrass NY 51

RUNS SCORED
J. Sheckard CHI 121
Miller Huggins STL 106
Bob Bescher CIN 106

WINS
Grover Alexander PHI 28
C. Mathewson NY 26
Rube Marquard NY 24

EARNED RUN AVERAGE
C. Mathewson NY 1.99
Lew Richie CHI 2.31
Babe Adams PIT 2.33

STRIKEOUTS
Rube Marquard NY 237
G. Alexander PHI 227
Nap Rucker BKN 190

SAVES
T. Brown CHI 13

COMPLETE GAMES
Grover Alexander PHI 31

SHUTOUTS
Grover Alexander PHI 7

INNINGS PITCHED
G. Alexander PHI 367

1912 AMERICAN LEAGUE STANDINGS

	W	L	PCT	GB	R	OR
★ BOS	105	47	.691	—	799	544
WAS	91	61	.599	14	699	581
PHI	90	62	.592	15	779	658
CHI	78	76	.506	28	639	648
CLE	75	78	.490	30.5	677	681
DET	69	84	.451	36.5	720	777
STL	53	101	.344	53	552	764
NY	50	102	.329	55	630	842
					5495	5495

BATTING AVERAGE
Ty Cobb DET .... .409
Joe Jackson CLE .... .395
Tris Speaker BOS .... .383

HITS
Ty Cobb DET 226
Joe Jackson CLE 226
Tris Speaker BOS 222

DOUBLES
Tris Speaker BOS 53
Joe Jackson CLE 44
Frank Baker PHI 40

TRIPLES
Joe Jackson CLE 26
Ty Cobb DET 23
two tied at 21

HOME RUNS
Frank Baker PHI 10
Tris Speaker BOS 10
Ty Cobb DET 7

RUNS BATTED IN
Frank Baker PHI 130
Duffy Lewis BOS 109
Sam Crawford DET 109

STOLEN BASES
Clyde Milan WAS 88
Eddie Collins PHI 63
Ty Cobb DET 61

RUNS SCORED
Eddie Collins PHI 137
Tris Speaker BOS 136
Joe Jackson CLE 121

WINS
Joe Wood BOS 34
Walter Johnson WAS 33
Ed Walsh CHI 27

EARNED RUN AVERAGE
W. Johnson WAS 1.39
Joe Wood BOS 1.91
Ed Walsh CHI 2.15

STRIKEOUTS
W. Johnson WAS 303
Joe Wood BOS 258
Ed Walsh CHI 254

SAVES
Ed Walsh CHI 10

COMPLETE GAMES
Joe Wood BOS 35

SHUTOUTS
Joe Wood BOS 10

INNINGS PITCHED
Ed Walsh CHI 393

1912 NATIONAL LEAGUE STANDINGS

	W	L	PCT	GB	R	OR
NY	103	48	.682	—	823	571
PIT	93	58	.616	10	751	565
CHI	91	59	.607	11.5	756	668
CIN	75	78	.490	29	656	722
PHI	73	79	.480	30.5	670	688
STL	63	90	.412	41	659	830
BKN	58	95	.379	46	651	754
BOS	52	101	.340	52	693	861
					5659	5659

BATTING AVERAGE
H. Zimmerman CHI .... .372
Chief Meyers NY .... .358
Bill Sweeney BOS .... .344

HITS
H. Zimmerman CHI 207
Bill Sweeney BOS 204
Vin Campbell BOS 185

DOUBLES
H. Zimmerman CHI 41
Dode Paskert PHI 37
Honus Wagner PIT 35

TRIPLES
Owen Wilson PIT 36
Honus Wagner PIT 20
Red Murray NY 20

HOME RUNS
H. Zimmerman CHI 14
Wildfire Schulte CHI 12
three tied at 11

RUNS BATTED IN
Honus Wagner PIT 102
Bill Sweeney BOS 100
H. Zimmerman CHI 99

STOLEN BASES
Bob Bescher CIN 67
Max Carey PIT 45
Fred Snodgrass NY 43

RUNS SCORED
Bob Bescher CIN 120
Max Carey PIT 114
two tied at 102

WINS
Larry Cheney CHI 26
Rube Marquard NY 26
Claude Hendrix PIT 24

EARNED RUN AVERAGE
Jeff Tesreau NY 1.96
C. Mathewson NY 2.12
Nap Rucker BKN 2.21

STRIKEOUTS
G. Alexander PHI 195
Claude Hendrix PIT 176
Rube Marquard NY 175

SAVES
Slim Sallee STL 6

COMPLETE GAMES
Larry Cheney CHI 28

SHUTOUTS
Nap Rucker BKN 6

INNINGS PITCHED
G. Alexander PHI 310

1913 AMERICAN LEAGUE STANDINGS

	W	L	PCT	GB	R	OR
★ PHI	96	57	.627	—	794	592
WAS	90	64	.584	6.5	596	561
CLE	86	66	.566	9.5	633	536
BOS	79	71	.527	15.5	631	610
CHI	78	74	.513	17.5	488	498
DET	66	87	.431	30	624	716
NY	57	94	.377	38	529	668
STL	57	96	.373	39	528	642
					4823	4823

BATTING AVERAGE
Ty Cobb DET .390
Joe Jackson CLE .373
Tris Speaker BOS .363

HITS
Joe Jackson CLE 197
Sam Crawford DET 193
Frank Baker PHI 190

DOUBLES
Joe Jackson CLE 39
Tris Speaker BOS 35
Frank Baker PHI 34

TRIPLES
Sam Crawford DET 23
Tris Speaker BOS 22
Joe Jackson CLE 17

HOME RUNS
Frank Baker PHI 12
Sam Crawford DET 9
Ping Bodie CHI 8

RUNS BATTED IN
Frank Baker PHI 117
Duffy Lewis BOS 90
Stuffy McInnis PHI 90

STOLEN BASES
Clyde Milan WAS 75
Danny Moeller WAS 62
Eddie Collins PHI 55

RUNS SCORED
Eddie Collins PHI 125
Frank Baker PHI 116
Joe Jackson CLE 109

WINS
Walter Johnson WAS 36
Cy Falkenberg CLE 23
Reb Russell CHI 22

EARNED RUN AVERAGE
W. Johnson WAS 1.14
Eddie Cicotte CHI 1.58
Jim Scott CHI 1.90

STRIKEOUTS
W. Johnson WAS 243
Vean Gregg CLE 166
Cy Falkenberg CLE 166

SAVES
Chief Bender PHI 13

COMPLETE GAMES
W. Johnson WAS 29

SHUTOUTS
Walter Johnson WAS 11

INNINGS PITCHED
W. Johnson WAS 346

1913 NATIONAL LEAGUE STANDINGS

	W	L	PCT	GB	R	OR
NY	101	51	.664	—	684	515
PHI	88	63	.583	12.5	693	636
CHI	88	65	.575	13.5	720	630
PIT	78	71	.523	21.5	673	585
BOS	69	82	.457	31.5	641	690
BKN	65	84	.436	34.5	595	613
CIN	64	89	.418	37.5	607	717
STL	51	99	.340	49	528	755
					5141	5141

BATTING AVERAGE
Jake Daubert BKN .350
Gavvy Cravath PHI .341
Jim Viox PIT .317

HITS
Gavvy Cravath PHI 179
Jake Daubert BKN 178
George Burns NY 173

DOUBLES
Red Smith BKN 40
George Burns NY 37
Sherry Magee PHI 36

TRIPLES
Vic Saier CHI 21
Dots Miller PIT 20
Ed Konetchy STL 17

HOME RUNS
Gavvy Cravath PHI 19
Fred Luderus PHI 18
Vic Saier CHI 14

RUNS BATTED IN
Gavvy Cravath PHI 128
H. Zimmerman CHI 95
Vic Saier CHI 92

STOLEN BASES
Max Carey PIT 61
Hy Myers BOS 57
Hans Lobert PHI 41

RUNS SCORED
Max Carey PIT 99
Tommy Leach CHI 99
Hans Lobert PHI 98

WINS
Tom Seaton PHI 27
C. Mathewson NY 25
Rube Marquard NY 23

EARNED RUN AVERAGE
C. Mathewson NY 2.06
Babe Adams PIT 2.15
Jeff Tesreau NY 2.17

STRIKEOUTS
Tom Seaton PHI 168
Jeff Tesreau NY 167
G. Alexander PHI 159

SAVES
Larry Cheney CHI 11

COMPLETE GAMES
Lefty Tyler BOS 28

SHUTOUTS
Grover Alexander PHI 9

INNINGS PITCHED
Tom Seaton PHI 322

1914 AMERICAN LEAGUE STANDINGS

	W	L	PCT	GB	R	OR
PHI	99	53	.651	—	749	529
BOS	91	62	.595	8.5	589	510
WAS	81	73	.526	19	572	519
DET	80	73	.523	19.5	615	618
STL	71	82	.464	28.5	523	615
CHI	70	84	.455	30	487	560
NY	70	84	.455	30	537	550
CLE	51	102	.333	48.5	538	709
					4610	4610

BATTING AVERAGE
Ty Cobb DET .... .368
Eddie Collins PHI .... .344
Tris Speaker BOS .... .338

HITS
Tris Speaker BOS 193
Sam Crawford DET 183
Frank Baker PHI 182

DOUBLES
Tris Speaker BOS 46
Duffy Lewis BOS 37
two tied at 34

TRIPLES
Sam Crawford DET 26
Larry Gardner BOS 19
Tris Speaker BOS 18

HOME RUNS
Frank Baker PHI 9
Sam Crawford DET 8
two tied at 6

RUNS BATTED IN
Sam Crawford DET 104
Stuffy McInnis PHI 95
Tris Speaker BOS 90

STOLEN BASES
Fritz Maisel NY 74
Eddie Collins PHI 58
Tris Speaker BOS 42

RUNS SCORED
Eddie Collins PHI 122
Eddie Murphy PHI 101
Tris Speaker BOS 101

WINS
Walter Johnson WAS 28
Harry Coveleski DET 22
Ray Collins BOS 20

EARNED RUN AVERAGE
Dutch Leonard BOS 0.96
Rube Foster BOS 1.70
W. Johnson WAS 1.72

STRIKEOUTS
W. Johnson WAS 225
Willie Mitchell CLE 179
Dutch Leonard BOS 176

SAVES
five tied at 4

COMPLETE GAMES
W. Johnson WAS 33

SHUTOUTS
Walter Johnson WAS 9

INNINGS PITCHED
W. Johnson WAS 372

1914 NATIONAL LEAGUE STANDINGS

	W	L	PCT	GB	R	OR
★ BOS	94	59	.614	—	657	548
NY	84	70	.545	10.5	672	576
STL	81	72	.529	13	558	540
CHI	78	76	.506	16.5	605	638
BKN	75	79	.487	19.5	622	618
PHI	74	80	.481	20.5	651	687
PIT	69	85	.448	25.5	503	540
CIN	60	94	.390	34.5	530	651
					4798	4798

BATTING AVERAGE
Jake Daubert BKN .... .329
Beals Becker PHI .... .325
Jack Dalton BKN .... .319

HITS
Sherry Magee PHI 171
George Burns NY 170
Zack Wheat BKN 170

DOUBLES
Sherry Magee PHI 39
H. Zimmerman CHI 36
George Burns NY 35

TRIPLES
Max Carey PIT 17
three tied at 12

HOME RUNS
Gavvy Cravath PHI 19
Vic Saier CHI 18
Sherry Magee PHI 15

RUNS BATTED IN
Sherry Magee PHI 103
Gavvy Cravath PHI 100
Zack Wheat BKN 89

STOLEN BASES
George Burns NY 62
Buck Herzog CIN 46
Cozy Dolan STL 42

RUNS SCORED
George Burns NY 100
Sherry Magee PHI 96
Jake Daubert BKN 89

WINS
Dick Rudolph BOS 27
three tied at 26

EARNED RUN AVERAGE
Bill Doak STL 1.72
Bill James BOS 1.90
Jeff Pfeffer BKN 1.97

STRIKEOUTS
G. Alexander PHI 214
Jeff Tesreau NY 189
Hippo Vaughn CHI 165

SAVES
Red Ames CIN 6
Slim Sallee STL 6

COMPLETE GAMES
Grover Alexander PHI 32

SHUTOUTS
Jeff Tesreau NY 8

INNINGS PITCHED
G. Alexander PHI 355

1915 AMERICAN LEAGUE STANDINGS

	W	L	PCT	GB	R	OR
★ BOS	101	50	.669	—	669	499
DET	100	54	.649	2.5	778	597
CHI	93	61	.604	9.5	717	509
WAS	85	68	.556	17	569	491
NY	69	83	.454	32.5	584	588
STL	63	91	.409	39.5	521	680
CLE	57	95	.375	44.5	539	670
PHI	43	109	.283	58.5	545	888
					4922	4922

BATTING AVERAGE
Ty Cobb DET .... .369
Eddie Collins CHI .... .332
Jack Fournier CHI .... .322

HITS
Ty Cobb DET 208
Sam Crawford DET 183
Bobby Veach DET 178

DOUBLES
Bobby Veach DET 40
four tied at 31

TRIPLES
Sam Crawford DET 19
Jack Fournier CHI 18
three tied at 17

HOME RUNS
Braggo Roth CHI, CLE 7
Rube Oldring PHI 6
five tied at 5

RUNS BATTED IN
Bobby Veach DET 112
Sam Crawford DET 112
Ty Cobb DET 99

STOLEN BASES
Ty Cobb DET 96
Fritz Maisel NY 51
Eddie Collins CHI 46

RUNS SCORED
Ty Cobb DET 144
Eddie Collins CHI 118
Ossie Vitt DET 116

WINS
Walter Johnson WAS 28
three tied at 24

EARNED RUN AVERAGE
Joe Wood BOS 1.49
W. Johnson WAS 1.55
Ernie Shore BOS 1.64

STRIKEOUTS
W. Johnson WAS 203
Red Faber CHI 182
John Wyckoff PHI 157

SAVES
Carl Mays BOS 7

COMPLETE GAMES
W. Johnson WAS 35

SHUTOUTS
Walter Johnson WAS 7
Jim Scott CHI 7

INNINGS PITCHED
W. Johnson WAS 337

1915 NATIONAL LEAGUE STANDINGS

	W	L	PCT	GB	R	OR
PHI	90	62	.592	—	589	463
BOS	83	69	.546	7	582	545
BKN	80	72	.526	10	536	560
CHI	73	80	.477	17.5	570	620
PIT	73	81	.474	18	557	520
STL	72	81	.471	18.5	590	601
CIN	71	83	.461	20	516	585
NY	69	83	.454	21	582	628
					4522	4522

BATTING AVERAGE
Larry Doyle NY .... .320
Fred Luderus PHI .... .315
Tommy Griffith CIN .... .307

HITS
Larry Doyle NY 189
Tommy Griffith CIN 179
Bill Hinchman PIT 177

DOUBLES
Larry Doyle NY 40
Fred Luderus PHI 36
Vic Saier CHI 35

TRIPLES
Tommy Long STL 25

Honus Wagner PIT 17
Tommy Griffith CIN 16

HOME RUNS
Gavvy Cravath PHI 24
Cy Williams CHI 13
Wildfire Schulte CHI 12

RUNS BATTED IN
Gavvy Cravath PHI 115
Sherry Magee BOS 87
Tommy Griffith CIN 85

STOLEN BASES
Max Carey PIT 36
Buck Herzog CIN 35
two tied at 29

RUNS SCORED
Gavvy Cravath PHI 89
Larry Doyle NY 86
Dave Bancroft PHI 85

WINS
G. Alexander PHI 31
Dick Rudolph BOS 22
two tied at 21

EARNED RUN AVERAGE
G. Alexander PHI 1.22
Fred Toney CIN 1.58
Al Mamaux PIT 2.04

STRIKEOUTS
G. Alexander PHI 241
Jeff Tesreau NY 176
Tom Hughes BOS 171

SAVES
Tom Hughes BOS 9

COMPLETE GAMES
Grover Alexander PHI 36

SHUTOUTS
Grover Alexander PHI 12

INNINGS PITCHED
G. Alexander PHI 376

1916 AMERICAN LEAGUE STANDINGS

	W	L	PCT	GB	R	OR
★ BOS	91	63	.591	—	550	480
CHI	89	65	.578	2	601	497
DET	87	67	.565	4	670	595
NY	80	74	.519	11	577	561
STL	79	75	.513	12	588	545
CLE	77	77	.500	14	630	602
WAS	76	77	.497	14.5	536	543
PHI	36	117	.235	54.5	447	776
					4599	4599

RUNS SCORED
Ty Cobb DET 113
Jack Graney CLE 106
Tris Speaker CLE 102

WINS
Walter Johnson WAS 25
Bob Shawkey NY 24
Babe Ruth BOS 23

EARNED RUN AVERAGE
Babe Ruth BOS 1.75
Eddie Cicotte CHI 1.78
W. Johnson WAS 1.90

STRIKEOUTS
W. Johnson WAS 228
Elmer Myers PHI 182
Babe Ruth BOS 170

SAVES
Bob Shawkey NY 8

COMPLETE GAMES
W. Johnson WAS 36

SHUTOUTS
Babe Ruth BOS 9

INNINGS PITCHED
W. Johnson WAS 370

BATTING AVERAGE
Tris Speaker CLE .... .386
Ty Cobb DET .... .371
Joe Jackson CHI .... .341

HITS
Tris Speaker CLE 211
Joe Jackson CHI 202
Ty Cobb DET 201

DOUBLES
Jack Graney CLE 41
Tris Speaker CLE 41
Joe Jackson CHI 40

TRIPLES
Joe Jackson CHI 21

Eddie Collins CHI 17
two tied at 15

HOME RUNS
Wally Pipp NY 12
Frank Baker NY 10
two tied at 7

RUNS BATTED IN
Del Pratt STL 103
Wally Pipp NY 93
Bobby Veach DET 91

STOLEN BASES
Ty Cobb DET 68
A. Marsans STL 46
Burt Shotton STL 41

1916 NATIONAL LEAGUE STANDINGS

	W	L	PCT	GB	R	OR
BKN	94	60	.610	—	585	471
PHI	91	62	.595	2.5	581	489
BOS	89	63	.586	4	542	453
NY	86	66	.566	7	597	504
CHI	67	86	.438	26.5	520	541
PIT	65	89	.422	29	484	586
CIN	60	93	.392	33.5	505	617
STL	60	93	.392	33.5	476	629
					4290	4290

RUNS SCORED
George Burns NY 105
Max Carey PIT 90
Dave Robertson NY 88

WINS
Grover Alexander PHI 33
Jeff Pfeffer BKN 25
Eppa Rixey PHI 22

EARNED RUN AVERAGE
G. Alexander PHI 1.55
R. Marquard BKN 1.58
Eppa Rixey PHI 1.85

STRIKEOUTS
G. Alexander PHI 167
Larry Cheney BKN 166
Al Mamaux PIT 163

SAVES
Red Ames STL 8

COMPLETE GAMES
G. Alexander PHI 38

SHUTOUTS
Grover Alexander PHI 16

INNINGS PITCHED
G. Alexander PHI 389

BATTING AVERAGE
Hal Chase CIN .... .339
Jake Daubert BKN .... .316
Bill Hinchman PIT .... .315

HITS
Hal Chase CIN 184
Dave Robertson NY 180
Zack Wheat BKN 177

DOUBLES
Bert Niehoff PHI 42
Zack Wheat BKN 32
Dode Paskert PHI 30

TRIPLES
Bill Hinchman PIT 16

three tied at 15

HOME RUNS
Dave Robertson NY 12
Cy Williams CHI 12
Gavvy Cravath PHI 11

RUNS BATTED IN
H. Zimmerman CHI, NY 83
Hal Chase CIN 82
Bill Hinchman PIT 76

STOLEN BASES
Max Carey PIT 63
Benny Kauff NY 40
Bob Bescher STL 39

1917 AMERICAN LEAGUE STANDINGS

	W	L	PCT	GB	R	OR
★ CHI	100	54	.649	—	656	464
BOS	90	62	.592	9	555	454
CLE	88	66	.571	12	584	543
DET	78	75	.510	21.5	639	577
WAS	74	79	.484	25.5	543	566
NY	71	82	.464	28.5	524	558
STL	57	97	.370	43	510	687
PHI	55	98	.359	44.5	529	691
					4540	4540

BATTING AVERAGE
Ty Cobb DET .... .383
George Sisler STL .... .353
Tris Speaker CLE .... .352

HITS
Ty Cobb DET 225
George Sisler STL 190
Tris Speaker CLE 184

DOUBLES
Ty Cobb DET 44
Tris Speaker CLE 42
Bobby Veach DET 31

TRIPLES
Ty Cobb DET 24
Joe Jackson CHI 17
Joe Judge WAS 15

HOME RUNS
Wally Pipp NY 9
Bobby Veach DET 8
Ping Bodie PHI 7

RUNS BATTED IN
Bobby Veach DET 103
Ty Cobb DET 102
Happy Felsch CHI 102

STOLEN BASES
Ty Cobb DET 55
Eddie Collins CHI 53
Ray Chapman CLE 52

RUNS SCORED
Donie Bush DET 112
Ty Cobb DET 107
Ray Chapman CLE 98

WINS
Eddie Cicotte CHI 28
Babe Ruth BOS 24
two tied at 23

EARNED RUN AVERAGE
Eddie Cicotte CHI 1.53
Carl Mays BOS 1.74
Stan Coveleski CLE 1.81

STRIKEOUTS
W. Johnson WAS 188
Eddie Cicotte CHI 150
Dutch Leonard BOS 144

SAVES
Dave Danforth CHI 9

COMPLETE GAMES
Babe Ruth BOS 35

SHUTOUTS
Stan Coveleski CLE 9

INNINGS PITCHED
Eddie Cicotte CHI 347

1917 NATIONAL LEAGUE STANDINGS

	W	L	PCT	GB	R	OR
NY	98	56	.636	—	635	457
PHI	87	65	.572	10	578	500
STL	82	70	.539	15	531	567
CIN	78	76	.506	20	601	611
CHI	74	80	.481	24	552	567
BOS	72	81	.471	25.5	536	552
BKN	70	81	.464	26.5	511	559
PIT	51	103	.331	47	464	595
					4408	4408

BATTING AVERAGE
Edd Roush CIN .... .341
R. Hornsby STL .... .327
Zack Wheat BKN .... .312

HITS
Heinie Groh CIN 182
George Burns NY 180
Edd Roush CIN 178

DOUBLES
Heinie Groh CIN 39
F. Merkle BKN, CHI 31
Red Smith BOS 31

TRIPLES
Rogers Hornsby STL 17

Gavvy Cravath PHI 16
Hal Chase CIN 15

HOME RUNS
Dave Robertson NY 12
Gavvy Cravath PHI 12
Rogers Hornsby STL 8

RUNS BATTED IN
H. Zimmerman NY 102
Hal Chase CIN 86
Gavvy Cravath PHI 83

STOLEN BASES
Max Carey PIT 46
George Burns NY 40
Benny Kauff NY 30

RUNS SCORED
George Burns NY 103
Heinie Groh CIN 91
Benny Kauff NY 89

WINS
Grover Alexander PHI 30
Fred Toney CIN 24
Hippo Vaughn CHI 23

EARNED RUN AVERAGE
F. Anderson NY 1.44
G. Alexander PHI 1.83
Pol Perritt NY 1.88

STRIKEOUTS
G. Alexander PHI 200
Hippo Vaughn CHI 195
Phil Douglas CHI 151

SAVES
Slim Sallee NY 4

COMPLETE GAMES
Grover Alexander PHI 34

SHUTOUTS
Grover Alexander PHI 8

INNINGS PITCHED
G. Alexander PHI 388

1918 AMERICAN LEAGUE STANDINGS

	W	L	PCT	GB	R	OR
★ BOS	75	51	.595	—	474	380
CLE	73	54	.575	2.5	504	447
WAS	72	56	.563	4	461	412
NY	60	63	.488	13.5	493	475
STL	58	64	.475	15	426	448
CHI	57	67	.460	17	457	446
DET	55	71	.437	20	476	557
PHI	52	76	.406	24	412	538
					3703	3703

BATTING AVERAGE
Ty Cobb DET .382
George Burns PHI .352
George Sisler STL .341

HITS
George Burns PHI 178
Ty Cobb DET 161
two tied at 154

DOUBLES
Tris Speaker CLE 33
Harry Hooper BOS 26
Babe Ruth BOS 26

TRIPLES
Ty Cobb DET 14
Harry Hooper BOS 13
Bobby Veach DET 13

HOME RUNS
Tilly Walker PHI 11
Babe Ruth BOS 11
two tied at 6

RUNS BATTED IN
Bobby Veach DET 78
George Burns PHI 70
two tied at 66

STOLEN BASES
George Sisler STL 45
Braggo Roth CLE 35
Ty Cobb DET 34

RUNS SCORED
Ray Chapman CLE 84
Ty Cobb DET 83
Harry Hooper BOS 81

WINS
Walter Johnson WAS 23
Stan Coveleski CLE 22
Carl Mays BOS 21

EARNED RUN AVERAGE
W. Johnson WAS 1.27
Stan Coveleski CLE 1.82

STRIKEOUTS
W. Johnson WAS 162
Jim Shaw WAS 129

SAVES
George Mogridge NY 7

COMPLETE GAMES
Carl Mays BOS 30
Scott Perry PHI 30

SHUTOUTS
Carl Mays BOS 8
Walter Johnson WAS 8

INNINGS PITCHED
Scott Perry PHI 332

1918 NATIONAL LEAGUE STANDINGS

	W	L	PCT	GB	R	OR
CHI	84	45	.651	—	538	393
NY	71	53	.573	10.5	480	415
CIN	68	60	.531	15.5	530	496
PIT	65	60	.520	17	466	412
BKN	57	69	.452	25.5	360	463
PHI	55	68	.447	26	430	507
BOS	53	71	.427	28.5	424	469
STL	51	78	.395	33	454	527
					3682	3682

BATTING AVERAGE
Zack Wheat BKN .335
Edd Roush CIN .333
Heinie Groh CIN .320

HITS
C. Hollocher CHI 161
Heinie Groh CIN 158
Edd Roush CIN 145

DOUBLES
Heinie Groh CIN 28
Les Mann CHI 27
Gavvy Cravath PHI 27

TRIPLES
Jake Daubert BKN 15

three tied at 13

HOME RUNS
Gavvy Cravath PHI 8
Walt Cruise STL 6
Cy Williams PHI 6

RUNS BATTED IN
Sherry Magee CIN 76
George Cutshaw PIT 68
Fred Luderus PHI 67

STOLEN BASES
Max Carey PIT 58
George Burns NY 40
Charlie Hollocher CHI 26

RUNS SCORED
Heinie Groh CIN 88
George Burns NY 80
Max Flack CHI 74

WINS
Hippo Vaughn CHI 22
Claude Hendrix CHI 20
three tied at 19

EARNED RUN AVERAGE
Hippo Vaughn CHI 1.74
Lefty Tyler CHI 2.00
Wilbur Cooper PIT 2.11

STRIKEOUTS
Hippo Vaughn CHI 148
Wilbur Cooper PIT 117
B. Grimes BKN 113

SAVES
four tied at 3

COMPLETE GAMES
Art Nehf BOS 28

SHUTOUTS
Hippo Vaughn CHI 8

INNINGS PITCHED
Hippo Vaughn CHI 290

1919 AMERICAN LEAGUE STANDINGS

	W	L	PCT	GB	R	OR
CHI	88	52	.629	—	667	534
CLE	84	55	.604	3.5	636	537
NY	80	59	.576	7.5	578	506
DET	80	60	.571	8	618	578
STL	67	72	.482	20.5	533	567
BOS	66	71	.482	20.5	564	552
WAS	56	84	.400	32	533	570
PHI	36	104	.257	52	457	742
					4586	4586

BATTING AVERAGE
Ty Cobb DET .... .384
Bobby Veach DET .... .355
George Sisler STL .... .352

HITS
Bobby Veach DET 191
Ty Cobb DET 191
Joe Jackson CHI 181

DOUBLES
Bobby Veach DET 45
Tris Speaker CLE 38
Ty Cobb DET 36

TRIPLES
Bobby Veach DET 17
George Sisler STL 15
Harry Heilmann DET 15

HOME RUNS
Babe Ruth BOS 29
three tied at 10

RUNS BATTED IN
Babe Ruth BOS 114
Bobby Veach DET 101
Joe Jackson CHI 96

STOLEN BASES
Eddie Collins CHI 33
George Sisler STL 28
Ty Cobb DET 28

RUNS SCORED
Babe Ruth BOS 103
George Sisler STL 96
Ty Cobb DET 92

WINS
Eddie Cicotte CHI 29
Stan Coveleski CLE 24
Lefty Williams CHI 23

EARNED RUN AVERAGE
W. Johnson WAS 1.49
Eddie Cicotte CHI 1.82
Carl Weilman STL 2.07

STRIKEOUTS
W. Johnson WAS 147
Jim Shaw WAS 128

SAVES
three tied at 5

COMPLETE GAMES
Eddie Cicotte CHI 30

SHUTOUTS
Walter Johnson WAS 7

INNINGS PITCHED
Eddie Cicotte CHI 307
Jim Shaw WAS 307

1919 NATIONAL LEAGUE STANDINGS

	W	L	PCT	GB	R	OR
★ CIN	96	44	.686	—	577	401
NY	87	53	.621	9	605	470
CHI	75	65	.536	21	454	407
PIT	71	68	.511	24.5	472	466
BKN	69	71	.493	27	525	513
BOS	57	82	.410	38.5	465	563
STL	54	83	.394	40.5	463	552
PHI	47	90	.343	47.5	510	699
					4071	4071

BATTING AVERAGE
Gavvy Cravath PHI .... .341
Edd Roush CIN .... .321
R. Hornsby STL .... .318

HITS
Ivy Olsen BKN 164
R. Hornsby STL 163
two tied at 162

DOUBLES
Ross Youngs NY 31
George Burns NY 30
Fred Luderus PHI 30

TRIPLES
Billy Southworth PIT 14

Hy Myers BKN 14

HOME RUNS
Gavvy Cravath PHI 12
Benny Kauff NY 10
Cy Williams PHI 9

RUNS BATTED IN
Hy Myers BKN 73
Edd Roush CIN 71
Rogers Hornsby STL 71

STOLEN BASES
George Burns NY 40
George Cutshaw PIT 36
Carson Bigbee PIT 31

RUNS SCORED
George Burns NY 86
Jake Daubert CIN 79
Heinie Groh CIN 79

WINS
Jesse Barnes NY 25
Slim Sallee CIN 21
Hippo Vaughn CHI 21

EARNED RUN AVERAGE
G. Alexander CHI 1.72
Hippo Vaughn CHI 1.79
Dutch Ruether CIN 1.82

STRIKEOUTS
Hippo Vaughn CHI 141
Hod Eller CIN 137
G. Alexander CHI 121

SAVES
Oscar Tuero STL 4

COMPLETE GAMES
Wilbur Cooper PIT 27

SHUTOUTS
Grover Alexander CHI 9

INNINGS PITCHED
Hippo Vaughn CHI 307

1920 AMERICAN LEAGUE STANDINGS

	W	L	PCT	GB	R	OR
★ CLE	98	56	.636	—	857	642
CHI	96	58	.623	2	794	665
NY	95	59	.617	3	838	629
STL	76	77	.497	21.5	797	766
BOS	72	81	.471	25.5	650	698
WAS	68	84	.447	29	723	802
DET	61	93	.396	37	652	833
PHI	48	106	.312	50	558	834
					5869	5869

BATTING AVERAGE
George Sisler STL .... .407
Tris Speaker CLE .... .388
Joe Jackson CHI .... .382

HITS
George Sisler STL 257
Eddie Collins CHI 224
Joe Jackson CHI 218

DOUBLES
Tris Speaker CLE 50
George Sisler STL 49
Joe Jackson CHI 42

TRIPLES
Joe Jackson CHI 20
George Sisler STL 18
Harry Hooper BOS 17

HOME RUNS
Babe Ruth NY 54
George Sisler STL 19
Tilly Walker PHI 17

RUNS BATTED IN
Babe Ruth NY 137
B. Jacobson STL 122
George Sisler STL 122

STOLEN BASES
Sam Rice WAS 63
George Sisler STL 42
Braggo Roth WAS 24

RUNS SCORED
Babe Ruth NY 158
George Sisler STL 137
Tris Speaker CLE 137

WINS
Jim Bagby CLE 31
Carl Mays NY 26
Stan Coveleski CLE 24

EARNED RUN AVERAGE
Bob Shawkey NY 2.45
Stan Coveleski CLE 2.49
Urban Shocker STL 2.71

STRIKEOUTS
Stan Coveleski CLE 133
Lefty Williams CHI 128

SAVES
Dickie Kerr CHI 5
Urban Shocker STL 5

COMPLETE GAMES
Jim Bagby CLE 30

SHUTOUTS
Carl Mays NY 6

INNINGS PITCHED
Jim Bagby CLE 340

1920 NATIONAL LEAGUE STANDINGS

	W	L	PCT	GB	R	OR
BKN	93	61	.604	—	660	528
NY	86	68	.558	7	682	543
CIN	82	71	.536	10.5	639	569
PIT	79	75	.513	14	530	552
CHI	75	79	.487	18	619	635
STL	75	79	.487	18	675	682
BOS	62	90	.408	30	523	670
PHI	62	91	.405	30.5	565	714
					4893	4893

BATTING AVERAGE
R. Hornsby STL .... .370
Fred Nicholson PIT .... .360
Ross Youngs NY .... .351

HITS
R. Hornsby STL 218
Milt Stock STL 204
Ross Youngs NY 204

DOUBLES
Rogers Hornsby STL 44
three tied at 36

TRIPLES
Hy Myers BKN 22
Rogers Hornsby STL 20

(cont.)
Edd Roush CIN 16

HOME RUNS
Cy Williams PHI 15
Irish Meusel PHI 14
George Kelly NY 11

RUNS BATTED IN
George Kelly NY 94
Rogers Hornsby STL 94
Edd Roush CIN 90

STOLEN BASES
Max Carey PIT 52
Edd Roush CIN 36
Frankie Frisch NY 34

RUNS SCORED
George Burns NY 115
D. Bancroft PHI, NY 102
Jake Daubert CIN 97

WINS
G. Alexander CHI 27
Wilbur Cooper PIT 24
Burleigh Grimes BKN 23

EARNED RUN AVERAGE
G. Alexander CHI 1.91
Babe Adams PIT 2.16
B. Grimes BKN 2.22

STRIKEOUTS
G. Alexander CHI 173
Hippo Vaughn CHI 131
B. Grimes BKN 131

SAVES
Bill Sherdel STL 6

COMPLETE GAMES
G. Alexander CHI 33

SHUTOUTS
Babe Adams PIT 8

INNINGS PITCHED
G. Alexander CHI 363

1921 AMERICAN LEAGUE STANDINGS

	W	L	PCT	GB	R	OR
NY	98	55	.641	—	948	708
CLE	94	60	.610	4.5	925	712
STL	81	73	.526	17.5	835	845
WAS	80	73	.523	18	704	738
BOS	75	79	.487	23.5	668	696
DET	71	82	.464	27	883	852
CHI	62	92	.403	36.5	683	858
PHI	53	100	.346	45	657	894
					6303	6303

BATTING AVERAGE
Harry Heilmann DET .... .394
Ty Cobb DET .... .389
Babe Ruth NY .... .378

HITS
Harry Heilmann DET 237
Jack Tobin STL 236
George Sisler STL 216

DOUBLES
Tris Speaker CLE 52
Babe Ruth NY 44
two tied at 43

TRIPLES
Howard Shanks WAS 18
Jack Tobin STL 18
George Sisler STL 18

HOME RUNS
Babe Ruth NY 59
Ken Williams STL 24
Bob Meusel NY 24

RUNS BATTED IN
Babe Ruth NY 171
Harry Heilmann DET 139
Bob Meusel NY 135

STOLEN BASES
George Sisler STL 35
Bucky Harris WAS 29
Sam Rice WAS 26

RUNS SCORED
Babe Ruth NY 177
Jack Tobin STL 132
R. Peckinpaugh NY 128

WINS
Carl Mays NY 27
Urban Shocker STL 27
Red Faber CHI 25

EARNED RUN AVERAGE
Red Faber CHI 2.48
G. Mogridge WAS 3.00
Carl Mays NY 3.05

STRIKEOUTS
W. Johnson WAS 143
Urban Shocker STL 132

SAVES
Jim Middleton DET 7
Carl Mays NY 7

COMPLETE GAMES
Red Faber CHI 32

SHUTOUTS
Sad Sam Jones BOS 5

INNINGS PITCHED
Carl Mays NY 337

1921 NATIONAL LEAGUE STANDINGS

	W	L	PCT	GB	R	OR
★ NY	94	59	.614	—	840	637
PIT	90	63	.588	4	692	595
STL	87	66	.569	7	809	681
BOS	79	74	.516	15	721	697
BKN	77	75	.507	16.5	667	681
CIN	70	83	.458	24	618	649
CHI	64	89	.418	30	668	773
PHI	51	103	.331	43.5	617	919
					5632	5632

BATTING AVERAGE
R. Hornsby STL .... .397
Edd Roush CIN .... .352
Austin McHenry STL .... .350

HITS
R. Hornsby STL 235
Frankie Frisch NY 211
Carson Bigbee PIT 204

DOUBLES
Rogers Hornsby STL 44
George Kelly NY 42
Jimmy Johnston BKN 41

TRIPLES
Rogers Hornsby STL 18

Ray Powell BOS 18
three tied at 17

HOME RUNS
George Kelly NY 23
Rogers Hornsby STL 21
Cy Williams PHI 18

RUNS BATTED IN
R. Hornsby STL 126
George Kelly NY 122
two tied at 102

STOLEN BASES
Frankie Frisch NY 49
Max Carey PIT 37
Jimmy Johnston BKN 28

RUNS SCORED
R. Hornsby STL 131
Frankie Frisch NY 121
Dave Bancroft NY 121

WINS
Burleigh Grimes BKN 22
Wilbur Cooper PIT 22
two tied at 20

EARNED RUN AVERAGE
Bill Doak STL 2.59
Babe Adams PIT 2.64
Whitey Glazner PIT 2.77

STRIKEOUTS
B. Grimes BKN 136
Wilbur Cooper PIT 134
Dolf Luque CIN 102

SAVES
Lou North STL 7

COMPLETE GAMES
Burleigh Grimes BKN 30

SHUTOUTS
eight tied at 3

INNINGS PITCHED
Wilbur Cooper PIT 327

1922 AMERICAN LEAGUE STANDINGS

	W	L	PCT	GB	R	OR
NY	94	60	.610	—	758	618
STL	93	61	.604	1	867	643
DET	79	75	.513	15	828	791
CLE	78	76	.506	16	768	817
CHI	77	77	.500	17	691	691
WAS	69	85	.448	25	650	706
PHI	65	89	.422	29	705	830
BOS	61	93	.396	33	598	769
					5865	5865

BATTING AVERAGE
George Sisler STL .... .420
Ty Cobb DET .... .401
Tris Speaker CLE .... .378

HITS
George Sisler STL 246
Ty Cobb DET 211
Jack Tobin STL 207

DOUBLES
Tris Speaker CLE 48
Del Pratt BOS 44
two tied at 42

TRIPLES
George Sisler STL 18

Ty Cobb DET 16
B. Jacobson STL 16

HOME RUNS
Ken Williams STL 39
Tilly Walker PHI 37
Babe Ruth NY 35

RUNS BATTED IN
Ken Williams STL 155
Bobby Veach DET 126
Marty McManus STL 109

STOLEN BASES
George Sisler STL 51
Ken Williams STL 37
Bucky Harris WAS 25

RUNS SCORED
George Sisler STL 134
Lu Blue DET 131
Ken Williams STL 128

WINS
Eddie Rommel PHI 27
Joe Bush NY 26
Urban Shocker STL 24

EARNED RUN AVERAGE
Red Faber CHI 2.81
H. Philette DET 2.85
Bob Shawkey NY 2.91

STRIKEOUTS
Urban Shocker STL 149
Red Faber CHI 148
Bob Shawkey NY 130

SAVES
Sad Sam Jones NY 8

COMPLETE GAMES
Red Faber CHI 31

SHUTOUTS
George Uhle CLE 5

INNINGS PITCHED
Red Faber CHI 352

1922 NATIONAL LEAGUE STANDINGS

	W	L	PCT	GB	R	OR
★ NY	93	61	.604	—	852	658
CIN	86	68	.558	7	766	677
PIT	85	69	.552	8	865	736
STL	85	69	.552	8	863	819
CHI	80	74	.519	13	771	808
BKN	76	78	.494	17	743	754
PHI	57	96	.373	35.5	738	920
BOS	53	100	.346	39.5	596	822
					6194	6194

BATTING AVERAGE
R. Hornsby STL .... .401
Ray Grimes CHI .... .354
Hack Miller CHI .... .352

HITS
R. Hornsby STL 250
Carson Bigbee PIT 215
Dave Bancroft NY 209

DOUBLES
Rogers Hornsby STL 46
Ray Grimes CHI 45
Pat Duncan CIN 44

TRIPLES
Jake Daubert CIN 22

Irish Meusel NY 17
two tied at 15

HOME RUNS
R. Hornsby STL 42
Cy Williams PHI 26
two tied at 17

RUNS BATTED IN
R. Hornsby STL 152
Irish Meusel NY 132
Zack Wheat BKN 112

STOLEN BASES
Max Carey PIT 51
Frankie Frisch NY 31
George Burns CIN 30

RUNS SCORED
R. Hornsby STL 141
Max Carey PIT 140
two tied at 117

WINS
Eppa Rixey CIN 25
Wilbur Cooper PIT 23
Dutch Ruether BKN 21

EARNED RUN AVERAGE
P. Douglas NY 2.63
Rosy Ryan NY 3.01
Pete Donohue CIN 3.12

STRIKEOUTS
Dazzy Vance BKN 134
Wilbur Cooper PIT 129
Jimmy Ring PHI 116

SAVES
Claude Jonnard NY 5

COMPLETE GAMES
Wilbur Cooper PIT 27

SHUTOUTS
two tied at 5

INNINGS PITCHED
Eppa Rixey CIN 313

1923 AMERICAN LEAGUE STANDINGS

	W	L	PCT	GB	R	OR
★ NY	98	54	.645	—	823	622
DET	83	71	.539	16	831	741
CLE	82	71	.536	16.5	888	746
WAS	75	78	.490	23.5	720	747
STL	74	78	.487	24	688	720
PHI	69	83	.454	29	661	761
CHI	69	85	.448	30	692	741
BOS	61	91	.401	37	584	809
					5887	5887

BATTING AVERAGE
H. Heilmann DET .... .403
Babe Ruth NY .... .393
Tris Speaker CLE .... .380

HITS
C. Jamieson CLE 222
Tris Speaker CLE 218
Harry Heilmann DET 211

DOUBLES
Tris Speaker CLE 59
George Burns BOS 47
Babe Ruth NY 45

TRIPLES
Goose Goslin WAS 18
Sam Rice WAS 18
two tied at 15

HOME RUNS
Babe Ruth NY 41
Ken Williams STL 29
Harry Heilmann DET 18

RUNS BATTED IN
Babe Ruth NY 131
Tris Speaker CLE 130
Harry Heilmann DET 115

STOLEN BASES
Eddie Collins CHI 47
Johnny Mostil CHI 41
Bucky Harris WAS 23

RUNS SCORED
Babe Ruth NY 151
Tris Speaker CLE 133
C. Jamieson CLE 130

WINS
George Uhle CLE 26
Sad Sam Jones NY 21
Hooks Dauss DET 21

EARNED RUN AVERAGE
Stan Coveleski CLE 2.76
Waite Hoyt NY 3.02
Allan Russell WAS 3.03

STRIKEOUTS
W. Johnson WAS 130
Joe Bush NY 125
Bob Shawkey NY 125

SAVES
Allan Russell WAS 9

COMPLETE GAMES
George Uhle CLE 29

SHUTOUTS
Stan Coveleski CLE 5

INNINGS PITCHED
George Uhle CLE 358

1923 NATIONAL LEAGUE STANDINGS

	W	L	PCT	GB	R	OR
NY	95	58	.621	—	854	679
CIN	91	63	.591	4.5	708	629
PIT	87	67	.565	8.5	786	696
CHI	83	71	.539	12.5	756	704
STL	79	74	.516	16	746	732
BKN	76	78	.494	19.5	753	741
BOS	54	100	.351	41.5	636	798
PHI	50	104	.325	45.5	748	1008
					5987	5987

BATTING AVERAGE
R. Hornsby STL .... .384
Zack Wheat BKN .... .375
Jim Bottomley STL .... .371

HITS
Frankie Frisch NY 223
Jigger Statz CHI 209
Pie Traynor PIT 208

DOUBLES
Edd Roush CIN 41
G. Grantham CHI 36
C. Tierney PIT, PHI 36

TRIPLES
Pie Traynor PIT 19

Max Carey PIT 19
Edd Roush CIN 18

HOME RUNS
Cy Williams PHI 41
Jack Fournier BKN 22
Hack Miller CHI 20

RUNS BATTED IN
Irish Meusel NY 125
Cy Williams PHI 114
Frankie Frisch NY 111

STOLEN BASES
Max Carey PIT 51
G. Grantham CHI 43
two tied at 32

RUNS SCORED
Ross Youngs NY 121
Max Carey PIT 120
Frankie Frisch NY 116

WINS
Dolf Luque CIN 27
Johnny Morrison PIT 25
G. Alexander CHI 22

EARNED RUN AVERAGE
Dolf Luque CIN 1.93
Eppa Rixey CIN 2.80
Vic Keen CHI 3.00

STRIKEOUTS
Dazzy Vance BKN 197
Dolf Luque CIN 151
B. Grimes BKN 119

SAVES
Claude Jonnard NY 5

COMPLETE GAMES
Burleigh Grimes BKN 33

SHUTOUTS
Dolf Luque CIN 6

INNINGS PITCHED
B. Grimes BKN 327

1924 AMERICAN LEAGUE STANDINGS

	W	L	PCT	GB	R	OR
★ WAS	92	62	.597	—	755	613
NY	89	63	.586	2	798	667
DET	86	68	.558	6	849	796
STL	74	78	.487	17	769	809
PHI	71	81	.467	20	685	778
CLE	67	86	.438	24.5	755	814
BOS	67	87	.435	25	737	806
CHI	66	87	.431	25.5	793	858
					6141	6141

BATTING AVERAGE
Babe Ruth NY.................. .378
C. Jamieson CLE............. .359
Bibb Falk CHI................... .352

HITS
Sam Rice WAS.................. 216
C. Jamieson CLE.............. 213
Ty Cobb DET..................... 211

DOUBLES
Harry Heilmann DET........ 45
Joe Sewell CLE................. 45
two tied at........................ 41

TRIPLES
Wally Pipp NY................... 19
Goose Goslin WAS........... 17
Harry Heilmann DET........ 16

HOME RUNS
Babe Ruth NY.................... 46
Joe Hauser PHI.................. 27
B. Jacobson STL............... 19

RUNS BATTED IN
Goose Goslin WAS........... 129
Babe Ruth NY.................... 121
Bob Meusel NY................. 120

STOLEN BASES
Eddie Collins CHI.............. 42
Bob Meusel NY................. 26
Sam Rice WAS.................. 24

RUNS SCORED
Babe Ruth NY.................... 143
Ty Cobb DET..................... 115
Eddie Collins CHI.............. 108

WINS
Walter Johnson WAS........ 23
Herb Pennock NY............. 21
two tied at........................ 20

EARNED RUN AVERAGE
W. Johnson WAS.............. 2.72
Tom Zachary WAS............ 2.75
Herb Pennock NY............. 2.83

STRIKEOUTS
W. Johnson WAS.............. 158
Howard Ehmke BOS......... 119
Bob Shawkey NY.............. 114

SAVES
Firpo Marberry WAS......... 15

COMPLETE GAMES
Sloppy Thurston CHI........ 28

SHUTOUTS
Walter Johnson WAS........ 6

INNINGS PITCHED
Howard Ehmke BOS......... 315

1924 NATIONAL LEAGUE STANDINGS

	W	L	PCT	GB	R	OR
NY	93	60	.608	—	857	641
BKN	92	62	.597	1.5	717	675
PIT	90	63	.588	3	724	588
CIN	83	70	.542	10	649	579
CHI	81	72	.529	12	698	699
STL	65	89	.422	28.5	740	750
PHI	55	96	.364	37	676	849
BOS	53	100	.346	40	520	800
					5581	5581

BATTING AVERAGE
R. Hornsby STL................ .424
Zack Wheat BKN.............. .375
Ross Youngs NY............... .356

HITS
R. Hornsby STL................ 227
Zack Wheat BKN.............. 212
Frankie Frisch NY............. 198

DOUBLES
R. Hornsby STL................ 43
Zack Wheat BKN.............. 41
George Kelly NY............... 37

TRIPLES
Edd Roush CIN................. 21
Rabbit Maranville PIT....... 20
Glenn Wright PIT.............. 18

HOME RUNS
Jack Fournier BKN............ 27
Rogers Hornsby STL........ 25
Cy Williams PHI................ 24

RUNS BATTED IN
George Kelly NY............... 136
Jack Fournier BKN............ 116
two tied at........................ 111

STOLEN BASES
Max Carey PIT.................. 49
Kiki Cuyler PIT.................. 32
Cliff Heathcote CHI........... 26

RUNS SCORED
Frankie Frisch NY............. 121
R. Hornsby STL................ 121
Max Carey PIT.................. 113

WINS
Dazzy Vance BKN............. 28
Burleigh Grimes BKN....... 22
two tied at........................ 20

EARNED RUN AVERAGE
Dazzy Vance BKN............. 2.16
Hugh McQuillan NY.......... 2.69
Eppa Rixey CIN................. 2.76

STRIKEOUTS
Dazzy Vance BKN............. 262
B. Grimes BKN................. 135

SAVES
Jackie May Cin.................. 6

COMPLETE GAMES
Dazzy Vance BKN............. 30
Burleigh Grimes BKN....... 30

SHUTOUTS
six tied at........................... 4

INNINGS PITCHED
B. Grimes BKN................. 311

1925 AMERICAN LEAGUE STANDINGS

	W	L	PCT	GB	R	OR
WAS	96	55	.636	—	829	670
PHI	88	64	.579	8.5	831	713
STL	82	71	.536	15	900	906
DET	81	73	.526	16.5	903	829
CHI	79	75	.513	18.5	811	770
CLE	70	84	.455	27.5	782	817
NY	69	85	.448	28.5	706	774
BOS	47	105	.309	49.5	639	922
					6401	6401

BATTING AVERAGE
H. Heilmann DET .... .393
Tris Speaker CLE .... .389
Al Simmons PHI .... .387

HITS
Al Simmons PHI 253
Sam Rice WAS 227
Harry Heilmann DET 225

DOUBLES
Marty McManus STL 44
Earl Sheely CHI 43
Al Simmons PHI 43

TRIPLES
Goose Goslin WAS 20
Johnny Mostil CHI 16
George Sisler STL 15

HOME RUNS
Bob Meusel NY 33
Ken Williams STL 25
Babe Ruth NY 25

RUNS BATTED IN
Bob Meusel NY 138
Harry Heilmann DET 134
Al Simmons PHI 129

STOLEN BASES
Johnny Mostil CHI 43
Goose Goslin WAS 27
Sam Rice WAS 26

RUNS SCORED
Johnny Mostil CHI 135
Al Simmons PHI 122
Earle Combs NY 117

WINS
Eddie Rommel PHI 21
Ted Lyons CHI 21
two tied at 20

EARNED RUN AVERAGE
S. Coveleski WAS 2.84
Herb Pennock NY 2.96
Ted Blankenship CHI 3.03

STRIKEOUTS
Lefty Grove PHI 116
W. Johnson WAS 108

SAVES
Firpo Marberry WAS 15

COMPLETE GAMES
Sherry Smith CLE 22
Howard Ehmke BOS 22

SHUTOUTS
Ted Lyons CHI 5

INNINGS PITCHED
Herb Pennock NY 277

1925 NATIONAL LEAGUE STANDINGS

	W	L	PCT	GB	R	OR
★ PIT	95	58	.621	—	912	715
NY	86	66	.566	8.5	736	702
CIN	80	73	.523	15	690	643
STL	77	76	.503	18	828	764
BOS	70	83	.458	25	708	802
BKN	68	85	.444	27	786	866
PHI	68	85	.444	27	812	930
CHI	68	86	.442	27.5	723	773
					6195	6195

BATTING AVERAGE
R. Hornsby STL .... .403
Jim Bottomley STL .... .367
Zack Wheat BKN .... .359

HITS
Jim Bottomley STL 227
Zack Wheat BKN 221
Kiki Cuyler PIT 220

DOUBLES
Jim Bottomley STL 44
Kiki Cuyler PIT 43
Zack Wheat BKN 42

TRIPLES
Kiki Cuyler PIT 26
three tied at 16

HOME RUNS
Rogers Hornsby STL 39
Gabby Hartnett CHI 24
Jack Fournier BKN 22

RUNS BATTED IN
R. Hornsby STL 143
Jack Fournier BKN 130
Jim Bottomley STL 128

STOLEN BASES
Max Carey PIT 46
Kiki Cuyler PIT 41
Sparky Adams CHI 26

RUNS SCORED
Kiki Cuyler PIT 144
R. Hornsby STL 133
Zack Wheat BKN 125

WINS
Dazzy Vance BKN 22
Eppa Rixey CIN 21
Pete Donohue CIN 21

EARNED RUN AVERAGE
Dolf Luque CIN 2.63
Eppa Rixey CIN 2.88
Pete Donohue CIN 3.08

STRIKEOUTS
Dazzy Vance BKN 221
Dolf Luque CIN 140

SAVES
Johnny Morrison PIT 4
Guy Bush CHI 4

COMPLETE GAMES
Pete Donohue CIN 27

SHUTOUTS
three tied at 4

INNINGS PITCHED
Pete Donohue CIN 301

1926 AMERICAN LEAGUE STANDINGS

	W	L	PCT	GB	R	OR
NY	91	63	.591	—	847	713
CLE	88	66	.571	3	738	612
PHI	83	67	.553	6	677	570
WAS	81	69	.540	8	802	761
CHI	81	72	.529	9.5	730	665
DET	79	75	.513	12	793	830
STL	62	92	.403	29	682	845
BOS	46	107	.301	44.5	562	835
					5831	5831

BATTING AVERAGE
Heinie Manush DET .... .378
Babe Ruth NY .... .372
two tied at .... .367

HITS
Sam Rice WAS 216
George Burns CLE 216
Goose Goslin WAS 201

DOUBLES
George Burns CLE 64
Al Simmons PHI 53
Tris Speaker CLE 52

TRIPLES
Lou Gehrig NY 20

C. Gehringer DET 17
two tied at 15

HOME RUNS
Babe Ruth NY 47
Al Simmons PHI 19
Tony Lazzeri NY 18

RUNS BATTED IN
Babe Ruth NY 146
George Burns CLE 114
Tony Lazzeri NY 114

STOLEN BASES
Johnny Mostil CHI 35
Sam Rice WAS 24
Bill Hunnefield CHI 24

RUNS SCORED
Babe Ruth NY 139
Lou Gehrig NY 135
Johnny Mostil CHI 120

WINS
George Uhle CLE 27
Herb Pennock NY 23
Urban Shocker NY 19

EARNED RUN AVERAGE
Lefty Grove PHI 2.51
George Uhle CLE 2.83
Ted Lyons CHI 3.01

STRIKEOUTS
Lefty Grove PHI 194
George Uhle CLE 159

SAVES
Firpo Marberry WAS 22

COMPLETE GAMES
George Uhle CLE 32

SHUTOUTS
Ed Wells DET 4

INNINGS PITCHED
George Uhle CLE 318

1926 NATIONAL LEAGUE STANDINGS

	W	L	PCT	GB	R	OR
★ STL	89	65	.578	—	817	678
CIN	87	67	.565	2	747	651
PIT	84	69	.549	4.5	769	689
CHI	82	72	.532	7	682	602
NY	74	77	.490	13.5	663	668
BKN	71	82	.464	17.5	623	705
BOS	66	86	.434	22	624	719
PHI	58	93	.384	29.5	687	900
					5612	5612

BATTING AVERAGE
B. Hargrave CIN .... .353
C. Christenson CIN .... .350
Earl Smith PIT .... .346

HITS
Eddie Brown BOS 201
Kiki Cuyler PIT 197
Sparky Adams CHI 193

DOUBLES
Jim Bottomley STL 40
Edd Roush CIN 37
Hack Wilson CHI 36

TRIPLES
Paul Waner PIT 22

Curt Walker CIN 20
Pie Traynor PIT 17

HOME RUNS
Hack Wilson CHI 21
Jim Bottomley STL 19
Cy Williams PHI 18

RUNS BATTED IN
Jim Bottomley STL 120
Hack Wilson CHI 109
Les Bell STL 100

STOLEN BASES
Kiki Cuyler PIT 35
Sparky Adams CHI 27
two tied at 23

RUNS SCORED
Kiki Cuyler PIT 113
Paul Waner PIT 101
two tied at 99

WINS
four tied at 20

EARNED RUN AVERAGE
Ray Kremer PIT 2.61
Charlie Root CHI 2.82
Jesse Petty BKN 2.84

STRIKEOUTS
Dazzy Vance BKN 140
Charlie Root CHI 127
two tied at 103

SAVES
Chick Davies NY 6

COMPLETE GAMES
Carl Mays CIN 24

SHUTOUTS
Pete Donohue CIN 5

INNINGS PITCHED
Pete Donohue CIN 286

1927 AMERICAN LEAGUE STANDINGS

	W	L	PCT	GB	R	OR
★ NY	110	44	.714	—	975	599
PHI	91	63	.591	19	841	726
WAS	85	69	.552	25	782	730
DET	82	71	.536	27.5	845	805
CHI	70	83	.458	39.5	662	708
CLE	66	87	.431	43.5	668	766
STL	59	94	.386	50.5	724	904
BOS	51	103	.331	59	597	856
					6094	6094

BATTING AVERAGE
H. Heilmann DET .... .398
Al Simmons PHI .... .392
Lou Gehrig NY .... .373

HITS
Earle Combs NY 231
Lou Gehrig NY 218
two tied at 201

DOUBLES
Lou Gehrig NY 52
George Burns CLE 51
Harry Heilmann DET 50

TRIPLES
Earle Combs NY 23

Heinie Manush DET 18
Lou Gehrig NY 18

HOME RUNS
Babe Ruth NY 60
Lou Gehrig NY 47
Tony Lazzeri NY 18

RUNS BATTED IN
Lou Gehrig NY 175
Babe Ruth NY 164
two tied at 120

STOLEN BASES
George Sisler STL 27
Bob Meusel NY 24
three tied at 22

RUNS SCORED
Babe Ruth NY 158
Lou Gehrig NY 149
Earle Combs NY 137

WINS
Waite Hoyt NY 22
Ted Lyons CHI 22
Lefty Grove PHI 20

EARNED RUN AVERAGE
Wilcy Moore NY 2.28
Waite Hoyt NY 2.63

STRIKEOUTS
Lefty Grove PHI 174
Rube Walberg PHI 136

SAVES
G. Braxton WAS 13
Wilcy Moore NY 13

COMPLETE GAMES
Ted Lyons CHI 30

SHUTOUTS
Hod Lisenbee WAS 4

INNINGS PITCHED
Tommy Thomas CHI 308
Ted Lyons CHI 308

1927 NATIONAL LEAGUE STANDINGS

	W	L	PCT	GB	R	OR
PIT	94	60	.610	—	817	659
STL	92	61	.601	1.5	754	665
NY	92	62	.597	2	817	720
CHI	85	68	.556	8.5	750	661
CIN	75	78	.490	18.5	643	653
BKN	65	88	.425	28.5	541	619
BOS	60	94	.390	34	651	771
PHI	51	103	.331	43	678	903
					5651	5651

BATTING AVERAGE
Paul Waner PIT .... .380
Rogers Hornsby NY .... .361
Lloyd Waner PIT .... .355

HITS
Paul Waner PIT 237
Lloyd Waner PIT 223
Frankie Frisch STL 208

DOUBLES
R. Stephenson CHI 46
Paul Waner PIT 42
two tied at 36

TRIPLES
Paul Waner PIT 18

Jim Bottomley STL 15
F. Thompson PHI 14

HOME RUNS
Hack Wilson CHI 30
Cy Williams PHI 30
Rogers Hornsby NY 26

RUNS BATTED IN
Paul Waner PIT 131
Hack Wilson CHI 129
Rogers Hornsby NY 125

STOLEN BASES
Frankie Frisch STL 48
Max Carey BKN 32
Harvey Hendrick BKN 29

RUNS SCORED
Lloyd Waner PIT 133
Rogers Hornsby NY 133
Hack Wilson CHI 119

WINS
Charlie Root CHI 26
Jesse Haines STL 24
Carmen Hill PIT 22

EARNED RUN AVERAGE
Ray Kremer PIT 2.47
G. Alexander STL 2.52
Dazzy Vance BKN 2.70

STRIKEOUTS
Dazzy Vance BKN 184
Charlie Root CHI 145
Jackie May CIN 121

SAVES
Bill Sherdel STL 6

COMPLETE GAMES
three tied at 25

SHUTOUTS
Jesse Haines STL 6

INNINGS PITCHED
Charlie Root CHI 309

1928 AMERICAN LEAGUE STANDINGS

	W	L	PCT	GB	R	OR
★ NY	101	53	.656	—	894	685
PHI	98	55	.641	2.5	829	615
STL	82	72	.532	19	772	742
WAS	75	79	.487	26	718	705
CHI	72	82	.468	29	656	725
DET	68	86	.442	33	744	804
CLE	62	92	.403	39	674	830
BOS	57	96	.373	43.5	589	770
					5876	5876

BATTING AVERAGE
Goose Goslin WAS .... .379
Heinie Manush STL .... .378
Lou Gehrig NY .... .374

HITS
Heinie Manush STL 241
Lou Gehrig NY 210
Sam Rice WAS 202

DOUBLES
Lou Gehrig NY 47
Heinie Manush STL 47
Bob Meusel NY 45

TRIPLES
Earle Combs NY 21
Heinie Manush STL 20
C. Gehringer DET 16

HOME RUNS
Babe Ruth NY 54
Lou Gehrig NY 27
Goose Goslin WAS 17

RUNS BATTED IN
Lou Gehrig NY 142
Babe Ruth NY 142
Bob Meusel NY 113

STOLEN BASES
Buddy Myer BOS 30
Johnny Mostil CHI 23
Harry Rice DET 20

RUNS SCORED
Babe Ruth NY 163
Lou Gehrig NY 139
Earle Combs NY 118

WINS
Lefty Grove PHI 24
George Pipgras NY 24
Waite Hoyt NY 23

EARNED RUN AVERAGE
G. Braxton WAS 2.51
Herb Pennock NY 2.56
Lefty Grove PHI 2.58

STRIKEOUTS
Lefty Grove PHI 183
George Pipgras NY 139
Tommy Thomas CHI 129

SAVES
Waite Hoyt NY 8

COMPLETE GAMES
Red Ruffing BOS 25

SHUTOUTS
Herb Pennock NY 5

INNINGS PITCHED
George Pipgras NY 301

1928 NATIONAL LEAGUE STANDINGS

	W	L	PCT	GB	R	OR
STL	95	59	.617	—	807	636
NY	93	61	.604	2	807	653
CHI	91	63	.591	4	714	615
PIT	85	67	.559	9	837	704
CIN	78	74	.513	16	648	686
BKN	77	76	.503	17.5	665	640
BOS	50	103	.327	44.5	631	878
PHI	43	109	.283	51	660	957
					5769	5769

BATTING AVERAGE
R. Hornsby BOS .... .387
Paul Waner PIT .... .370
F. Lindstrom NY .... .358

HITS
F. Lindstrom NY 231
Paul Waner PIT 223
Lloyd Waner PIT 221

DOUBLES
Paul Waner PIT 50
Chick Hafey STL 46
two tied at 42

TRIPLES
Jim Bottomley STL 20
Paul Waner PIT 19
Lloyd Waner PIT 14

HOME RUNS
Hack Wilson CHI 31
Jim Bottomley STL 31
Chick Hafey STL 27

RUNS BATTED IN
Jim Bottomley STL 136
Pie Traynor PIT 124
Hack Wilson CHI 120

STOLEN BASES
Kiki Cuyler CHI 37
Frankie Frisch STL 29
two tied at 19

RUNS SCORED
Paul Waner PIT 142
Jim Bottomley STL 123
Lloyd Waner PIT 121

WINS
Larry Benton NY 25
Burleigh Grimes PIT 25
Dazzy Vance BKN 22

EARNED RUN AVERAGE
Dazzy Vance BKN 2.09
Sheriff Blake CHI 2.47

STRIKEOUTS
Dazzy Vance BKN 200
Pat Malone CHI 155

SAVES
Bill Sherdel STL 5
Hal Haid STL 5

COMPLETE GAMES
Burleigh Grimes PIT 28
Larry Benton NY 28

SHUTOUTS
five tied at 4

INNINGS PITCHED
Burleigh Grimes PIT 331

1929 AMERICAN LEAGUE STANDINGS

	W	L	PCT	GB	R	OR
★ PHI	104	46	.693	—	901	615
NY	88	66	.571	18	899	775
CLE	81	71	.533	24	717	736
STL	79	73	.520	26	733	713
WAS	71	81	.467	34	730	776
DET	70	84	.455	36	926	928
CHI	59	93	.388	46	627	792
BOS	58	96	.377	48	605	803
					6138	6138

BATTING AVERAGE
Lew Fonseca CLE .... .369
Al Simmons PHI .... .365
Heinie Manush STL .... .355

HITS
Dale Alexander DET 215
C. Gehringer DET 215
Al Simmons PHI 212

DOUBLES
Roy Johnson DET 45
C. Gehringer DET 45
Heinie Manush STL 45

TRIPLES
C. Gehringer DET 19

Russ Scarritt BOS 17
Bing Miller PHI 16

HOME RUNS
Babe Ruth NY 46
Lou Gehrig NY 35
Al Simmons PHI 34

RUNS BATTED IN
Al Simmons PHI 157
Babe Ruth NY 154
Dale Alexander DET 137

STOLEN BASES
C. Gehringer DET 27
Bill Cissell CHI 25
Bing Miller PHI 24

RUNS SCORED
C. Gehringer DET 131
Roy Johnson DET 128
Lou Gehrig NY 127

WINS
G. Earnshaw PHI 24
Wes Ferrell CLE 21
Lefty Grove PHI 20

EARNED RUN AVERAGE
Lefty Grove PHI 2.81
F. Marberry WAS 3.06
T. Thomas CHI 3.19

STRIKEOUTS
Lefty Grove PHI 170
G. Earnshaw PHI 149
George Pipgras NY 125

SAVES
Firpo Marberry WAS 11

COMPLETE GAMES
Tommy Thomas CHI 24

SHUTOUTS
four tied at 4

INNINGS PITCHED
Sam Gray STL 305

1929 NATIONAL LEAGUE STANDINGS

	W	L	PCT	GB	R	OR
CHI	98	54	.645	—	982	758
PIT	88	65	.575	10.5	904	780
NY	84	67	.556	13.5	897	709
STL	78	74	.513	20	831	806
PHI	71	82	.464	27.5	897	1032
BKN	70	83	.458	28.5	755	888
CIN	66	88	.429	33	686	760
BOS	56	98	.364	43	657	876
					6609	6609

BATTING AVERAGE
Lefty O'Doul PHI .... .398
Babe Herman BKN .... .381
R. Hornsby CHI .... .380

HITS
Lefty O'Doul PHI 254
Lloyd Waner PIT 234
Rogers Hornsby CHI 229

DOUBLES
J. Frederick BKN 52
Rogers Hornsby CHI 47
Chick Hafey STL 47

TRIPLES
Lloyd Waner PIT 20

Curt Walker CIN 15
Paul Waner PIT 15

HOME RUNS
Chuck Klein PHI 43
Mel Ott NY 42
two tied at 39

RUNS BATTED IN
Hack Wilson CHI 159
Mel Ott NY 151
Rogers Hornsby CHI 149

STOLEN BASES
Kiki Cuyler CHI 43
Evar Swanson CIN 33
Frankie Frisch STL 24

RUNS SCORED
Rogers Hornsby CHI 156
Lefty O'Doul PHI 152
Mel Ott NY 138

WINS
Pat Malone CHI 22
Red Lucas CIN 19
Charlie Root CHI 19

EARNED RUN AVERAGE
Bill Walker NY 3.09
B. Grimes PIT 3.13
Charlie Root CHI 3.47

STRIKEOUTS
Pat Malone CHI 166
Watty Clark BKN 140

SAVES
Johnny Morrison BKN 8
Guy Bush CHI 8

COMPLETE GAMES
Red Lucas CIN 28

SHUTOUTS
Pat Malone CHI 5

INNINGS PITCHED
Watty Clark BKN 279

1930 AMERICAN LEAGUE STANDINGS

	W	L	PCT	GB	R	OR
★ PHI	102	52	.662	—	951	751
WAS	94	60	.610	8	892	689
NY	86	68	.558	16	1062	898
CLE	81	73	.526	21	890	915
DET	75	79	.487	27	783	833
STL	64	90	.416	38	751	886
CHI	62	92	.403	40	729	884
BOS	52	102	.338	50	612	814
					6670	6670

BATTING AVERAGE
Al Simmons PHI .... .381
Lou Gehrig NY .... .379
Babe Ruth NY .... .359

HITS
Johnny Hodapp CLE 225
Lou Gehrig NY 220
Al Simmons PHI 211

DOUBLES
Johnny Hodapp CLE 51
Manush STL/WAS 49
two tied at 47

TRIPLES
Earle Combs NY 22
Carl Reynolds CHI 18
Lou Gehrig NY 17

HOME RUNS
Babe Ruth NY 49
Lou Gehrig NY 41
two tied at 37

RUNS BATTED IN
Lou Gehrig NY 174
Al Simmons PHI 165
Jimmie Foxx PHI 156

STOLEN BASES
Marty McManus DET 23
C. Gehringer DET 19
three tied at 17

RUNS SCORED
Al Simmons PHI 152
Babe Ruth NY 150
C. Gehringer DET 144

WINS
Lefty Grove PHI 28
Wes Ferrell CLE 25
two tied at 22

EARNED RUN AVERAGE
Lefty Grove PHI 2.54
Wes Ferrell CLE 3.31
Lefty Stewart STL 3.45

STRIKEOUTS
Lefty Grove PHI 209
G. Earnshaw PHI 193
Bump Hadley WAS 162

SAVES
Lefty Grove PHI 9

COMPLETE GAMES
Ted Lyons CHI 29

SHUTOUTS
three tied at 3

INNINGS PITCHED
Ted Lyons CHI 298

1930 NATIONAL LEAGUE STANDINGS

	W	L	PCT	GB	R	OR
STL	92	62	.597	—	1004	784
CHI	90	64	.584	2	998	870
NY	87	67	.565	5	959	814
BKN	86	68	.558	6	871	738
PIT	80	74	.519	12	891	928
BOS	70	84	.455	22	693	835
CIN	59	95	.383	33	665	857
PHI	52	102	.338	40	944	1199
					7025	7025

BATTING AVERAGE
Bill Terry NY .... .401
Babe Herman BKN .... .393
Chuck Klein PHI .... .386

HITS
Bill Terry NY 254
Chuck Klein PHI 250
Babe Herman BKN 241

DOUBLES
Chuck Klein PHI 59
Kiki Cuyler CHI 50
Babe Herman BKN 48

TRIPLES
Adam Comorosky PIT 23

Paul Waner PIT 18
two tied at 17

HOME RUNS
Hack Wilson CHI 56
Chuck Klein PHI 40
Wally Berger BOS 38

RUNS BATTED IN
Hack Wilson CHI 190
Chuck Klein PHI 170
Kiki Cuyler CHI 134

STOLEN BASES
Kiki Cuyler CHI 37
Babe Herman BKN 18
Paul Waner PIT 18

RUNS SCORED
Chuck Klein PHI 158
Kiki Cuyler CHI 155
Woody English CHI 152

WINS
Ray Kremer PIT 20
Pat Malone CHI 20
F. Fitzsimmons NY 19

EARNED RUN AVERAGE
Dazzy Vance BKN 2.61
Carl Hubbell NY 3.87

STRIKEOUTS
Bill Hallahan STL 177
Dazzy Vance BKN 173

SAVES
Hi Bell STL 8

COMPLETE GAMES
Erv Brame PIT 22
Pat Malone CHI 22

SHUTOUTS
Charlie Root CHI 4
Dazzy Vance BKN 4

INNINGS PITCHED
Ray Kremer PIT 276

1931 AMERICAN LEAGUE STANDINGS

	W	L	PCT	GB	R	OR
PHI	107	45	.704	—	858	626
NY	94	59	.614	13.5	1067	760
WAS	92	62	.597	16	843	691
CLE	78	76	.506	30	885	833
STL	63	91	.409	45	722	870
BOS	62	90	.408	45	625	800
DET	61	93	.396	47	651	836
CHI	56	97	.366	51.5	704	939
					6355	6355

BATTING AVERAGE
Al Simmons PHI .... .390
Babe Ruth NY .... .373
Ed Morgan CLE .... .351

HITS
Lou Gehrig NY 211
Earl Averill CLE 209
Al Simmons PHI 200

DOUBLES
Earl Webb BOS 67
Dale Alexander DET 47
Red Kress STL 46

TRIPLES
Roy Johnson DET 19

Lou Gehrig NY 15
Lu Blue CHI 15

HOME RUNS
Lou Gehrig NY 46
Babe Ruth NY 46
Earl Averill CLE 32

RUNS BATTED IN
Lou Gehrig NY 184
Babe Ruth NY 163
Earl Averill CLE 143

STOLEN BASES
Ben Chapman NY 61
Roy Johnson DET 33
Jack Burns STL 19

RUNS SCORED
Lou Gehrig NY 163
Babe Ruth NY 149
Earl Averill CLE 140

WINS
Lefty Grove PHI 31
Wes Ferrell CLE 22
two tied at 21

EARNED RUN AVERAGE
Lefty Grove PHI 2.06
Lefty Gomez NY 2.67
Bump Hadley WAS 3.06

STRIKEOUTS
Lefty Grove PHI 175
G. Earnshaw PHI 152

SAVES
Wilcy Moore BOS 10

COMPLETE GAMES
Lefty Grove PHI 27
Wes Ferrell CLE 27

SHUTOUTS
Lefty Grove PHI 4

INNINGS PITCHED
Rube Walberg PHI 291

1931 NATIONAL LEAGUE STANDINGS

	W	L	PCT	GB	R	OR
★ STL	101	53	.656	—	815	614
NY	87	65	.572	13	768	599
CHI	84	70	.545	17	828	710
BKN	79	73	.520	21	681	673
PIT	75	79	.487	26	636	691
PHI	66	88	.429	35	684	828
BOS	64	90	.416	37	533	680
CIN	58	96	.377	43	592	742
					5537	5537

BATTING AVERAGE
Chick Hafey STL .... .349
Bill Terry NY .... .349
Jim Bottomley STL .... .348

HITS
Lloyd Waner PIT 214
Bill Terry NY 213
two tied at 202

DOUBLES
Sparky Adams STL 46
Wally Berger BOS 44
three tied at 43

TRIPLES
Bill Terry NY 20

Babe Herman BKN 16
Pie Traynor PIT 15

HOME RUNS
Chuck Klein PHI 31
Mel Ott NY 29
Wally Berger BOS 19

RUNS BATTED IN
Chuck Klein PHI 121
Mel Ott NY 115
Bill Terry NY 112

STOLEN BASES
Frankie Frisch STL 28
Babe Herman BKN 17
two tied at 16

RUNS SCORED
Chuck Klein PHI 121
Bill Terry NY 121
Woody English CHI 117

WINS
Bill Hallahan STL 19
Heinie Meine PIT 19
Jumbo Elliott PHI 19

EARNED RUN AVERAGE
Bill Walker NY 2.26
Carl Hubbell NY 2.65
Ed Brandt BOS 2.92

STRIKEOUTS
Bill Hallahan STL 159
Carl Hubbell NY 155
Dazzy Vance BKN 150

SAVES
Jack Quinn BKN 15

COMPLETE GAMES
Red Lucas CIN 24

SHUTOUTS
Bill Walker NY 6

INNINGS PITCHED
Heinie Meine PIT 284

1932 AMERICAN LEAGUE STANDINGS

	W	L	PCT	GB	R	OR
★ NY	107	47	.695	—	1002	724
PHI	94	60	.610	13	981	752
WAS	93	61	.604	14	840	716
CLE	87	65	.572	19	845	747
DET	76	75	.503	29.5	799	787
STL	63	91	.409	44	736	898
CHI	49	102	.325	56.5	667	897
BOS	43	111	.279	64	566	915
					6436	6436

BATTING AVERAGE
D. Alexander DET, BOS .. .367
Jimmie Foxx PHI .... .364
Lou Gehrig NY .... .349

HITS
Al Simmons PHI 216
Heinie Manush WAS 214
Jimmie Foxx PHI 213

DOUBLES
Eric McNair PHI 47
C. Gehringer DET 44
Joe Cronin WAS 43

TRIPLES
Joe Cronin WAS 18
Tony Lazzeri NY 16
Buddy Myer WAS 16

HOME RUNS
Jimmie Foxx PHI 58
Babe Ruth NY 41
Al Simmons PHI 35

RUNS BATTED IN
Jimmie Foxx PHI 169
Lou Gehrig NY 151
Al Simmons PHI 151

STOLEN BASES
Ben Chapman NY 38
Gee Walker DET 30
R. Johnson DET, BOS 20

RUNS SCORED
Jimmie Foxx PHI 151
Al Simmons PHI 144
Earle Combs NY 143

WINS
G. Crowder WAS 26
Lefty Grove PHI 25
Lefty Gomez NY 24

EARNED RUN AVERAGE
Lefty Grove PHI 2.84
Red Ruffing NY 3.09
Ted Lyons CHI 3.28

STRIKEOUTS
Red Ruffing NY 190
Lefty Grove PHI 188

SAVES
Firpo Marberry WAS 13

COMPLETE GAMES
Lefty Grove PHI 27

SHUTOUTS
Tommy Bridges DET 4
Lefty Grove PHI 4

INNINGS PITCHED
G. Crowder WAS 327

1932 NATIONAL LEAGUE STANDINGS

	W	L	PCT	GB	R	OR
CHI	90	64	.584	—	720	633
PIT	86	68	.558	4	701	711
BKN	81	73	.526	9	752	747
PHI	78	76	.506	12	844	796
BOS	77	77	.500	13	649	655
NY	72	82	.468	18	755	706
STL	72	82	.468	18	684	717
CIN	60	94	.390	30	575	715
					5680	5680

BATTING AVERAGE
Lefty O'Doul BKN .... .368
Bill Terry NY .... .350
Chuck Klein PHI .... .348

HITS
Chuck Klein PHI 226
Bill Terry NY 225
Lefty O'Doul BKN 219

DOUBLES
Paul Waner PIT 62
Chuck Klein PHI 50
R. Stephenson CHI 49

TRIPLES
Babe Herman CIN 19
Gus Suhr PIT 16
Chuck Klein PHI 15

HOME RUNS
Chuck Klein PHI 38
Mel Ott NY 38
Bill Terry NY 28

RUNS BATTED IN
Don Hurst PHI 143
Chuck Klein PHI 137
Pinky Whitney PHI 124

STOLEN BASES
Chuck Klein PHI 20
Tony Piet PIT 19
two tied at 18

RUNS SCORED
Chuck Klein PHI 152
Bill Terry NY 124
Lefty O'Doul BKN 120

WINS
Lon Warneke CHI 22
Watty Clark BKN 20
Guy Bush CHI 19

EARNED RUN AVERAGE
Lon Warneke CHI 2.37
Carl Hubbell NY 2.50
Huck Betts BOS 2.80

STRIKEOUTS
Dizzy Dean STL 191
Carl Hubbell NY 137
Pat Malone CHI 120

SAVES
Jack Quinn BKN 8

COMPLETE GAMES
Red Lucas CIN 28

SHUTOUTS
three tied at 4

INNINGS PITCHED
Dizzy Dean STL 286

1933 AMERICAN LEAGUE STANDINGS

	W	L	PCT	GB	R	OR
WAS	99	53	.651	—	850	665
NY	91	59	.607	7	927	768
PHI	79	72	.523	19.5	875	853
CLE	75	76	.497	23.5	654	669
DET	75	79	.487	25	722	733
CHI	67	83	.447	31	683	814
BOS	63	86	.423	34.5	700	758
STL	55	96	.364	43.5	669	820
					6080	6080

BATTING AVERAGE
Jimmie Foxx PHI .... .356
H. Manush WAS .... .336
Lou Gehrig NY .... .334

HITS
Heinie Manush WAS 221
C. Gehringer DET 204
Jimmie Foxx PHI 204

DOUBLES
Joe Cronin WAS 45
Bob Johnson PHI 44
Jack Burns STL 43

TRIPLES
Heinie Manush WAS 17
Earl Averill CLE 16
Earle Combs NY 16

HOME RUNS
Jimmie Foxx PHI 48
Babe Ruth NY 34
Lou Gehrig NY 32

RUNS BATTED IN
Jimmie Foxx PHI 163
Lou Gehrig NY 139
Al Simmons CHI 119

STOLEN BASES
Ben Chapman NY 27
Gee Walker DET 26
Evar Swanson CHI 19

RUNS SCORED
Lou Gehrig NY 138
Jimmie Foxx PHI 125
Heinie Manush WAS 115

WINS
Lefty Grove PHI 24
G. Crowder WAS 24
Earl Whitehill WAS 22

EARNED RUN AVERAGE
Mel Harder CLE 2.95
T. Bridges DET 3.09
Lefty Gomez NY 3.18

STRIKEOUTS
Lefty Gomez NY 163
Bump Hadley STL 149
Red Ruffing NY 122

SAVES
Jack Russell WAS 13

COMPLETE GAMES
Lefty Grove PHI 21

SHUTOUTS
Oral Hildebrand CLE 6

INNINGS PITCHED
Bump Hadley STL 317

1933 NATIONAL LEAGUE STANDINGS

	W	L	PCT	GB	R	OR
★ NY	91	61	.599	—	636	515
PIT	87	67	.565	5	667	619
CHI	86	68	.558	6	646	536
BOS	83	71	.539	9	552	531
STL	82	71	.536	9.5	687	609
BKN	65	88	.425	26.5	617	695
PHI	60	92	.395	31	607	760
CIN	58	94	.382	33	496	643
					4908	4908

BATTING AVERAGE
Chuck Klein PHI .... .368
Spud Davis PHI .... .349
R. Stephenson CHI .... .329

HITS
Chuck Klein PHI 223
Chick Fullis PHI 200
Paul Waner PIT 191

DOUBLES
Chuck Klein PHI 44
Joe Medwick STL 40
F. Lindstrom PIT 39

TRIPLES
Arky Vaughan PIT 19

Paul Waner PIT 16
two tied at 12

HOME RUNS
Chuck Klein PHI 28
Wally Berger BOS 27
Mel Ott NY 23

RUNS BATTED IN
Chuck Klein PHI 120
Wally Berger BOS 106
Mel Ott NY 103

STOLEN BASES
Pepper Martin STL 26
Chick Fullis PHI 18
Frankie Frisch STL 18

RUNS SCORED
Pepper Martin STL 122
Chuck Klein PHI 101
Paul Waner PIT 101

WINS
Carl Hubbell NY 23
three tied at 20

EARNED RUN AVERAGE
Carl Hubbell NY 1.66
Lon Warneke CHI 2.00
H. Schumacher NY 2.16

STRIKEOUTS
Dizzy Dean STL 199
Carl Hubbell NY 156
Tex Carleton STL 147

SAVES
Phil Collins PHI 6

COMPLETE GAMES
Dizzy Dean STL 26
Lon Warneke CHI 26

SHUTOUTS
Carl Hubbell NY 10

INNINGS PITCHED
Carl Hubbell NY 309

1934 AMERICAN LEAGUE STANDINGS

	W	L	PCT	GB	R	OR
DET	101	53	.656	—	958	708
NY	94	60	.610	7	842	669
CLE	85	69	.552	16	814	763
BOS	76	76	.500	24	820	775
PHI	68	82	.453	31	764	838
STL	67	85	.441	33	674	800
WAS	66	86	.434	34	729	806
CHI	53	99	.349	47	704	946
					6305	6305

BATTING AVERAGE
Lou Gehrig NY .... .363
C. Gehringer DET .... .356
H. Manush WAS .... .349

HITS
C. Gehringer DET 214
Lou Gehrig NY 210
Hal Trosky CLE 206

DOUBLES
Hank Greenberg DET 63
C. Gehringer DET 50
Earl Averill CLE 48

TRIPLES
Ben Chapman NY 13
Heinie Manush WAS 11

HOME RUNS
Lou Gehrig NY 49
Jimmie Foxx PHI 44
Hal Trosky CLE 35

RUNS BATTED IN
Lou Gehrig NY 165
Hal Trosky CLE 142
H. Greenberg DET 139

STOLEN BASES
Bill Werber BOS 40
Jo-Jo White DET 28
Ben Chapman NY 26

RUNS SCORED
C. Gehringer DET 134
Bill Werber BOS 129
two tied at 128

WINS
Lefty Gomez NY 26
S. Rowe DET 24
Tommy Bridges DET 22

EARNED RUN AVERAGE
Lefty Gomez NY 2.33
Mel Harder CLE 2.61
Johnny Murphy NY 3.12

STRIKEOUTS
Lefty Gomez NY 158
T. Bridges DET 151

SAVES
Jack Russell WAS 7

COMPLETE GAMES
Lefty Gomez NY 25

SHUTOUTS
Mel Harder CLE 6
Lefty Gomez NY 6

INNINGS PITCHED
Lefty Gomez NY 282

1934 NATIONAL LEAGUE STANDINGS

		W	L	PCT	GB	R	OR
★	STL	95	58	.621	—	799	656
	NY	93	60	.608	2	760	583
	CHI	86	65	.570	8	705	639
	BOS	78	73	.517	16	683	714
	PIT	74	76	.493	19.5	735	713
	BKN	71	81	.467	23.5	748	795
	PHI	56	93	.376	37	675	794
	CIN	52	99	.344	42	590	801
						5695	5695

BATTING AVERAGE
Paul Waner PIT .... .362
Bill Terry NY .... .354
Kiki Cuyler CHI .... .338

HITS
Paul Waner PIT 217
Bill Terry NY 213
Ripper Collins STL 200

DOUBLES
Kiki Cuyler CHI 42
Ethan Allen PHI 42
Arky Vaughan PIT 41

TRIPLES
Joe Medwick STL 18
Paul Waner PIT 16
Gus Suhr PIT 13

HOME RUNS
Mel Ott NY 35
Ripper Collins STL 35
Wally Berger BOS 34

RUNS BATTED IN
Mel Ott NY 135
Ripper Collins STL 128
Wally Berger BOS 121

STOLEN BASES
Pepper Martin STL 23
Kiki Cuyler CHI 15
Dick Bartell PHI 13

RUNS SCORED
Paul Waner PIT 122
Mel Ott NY 119
Ripper Collins STL 116

WINS
Dizzy Dean STL 30
Hal Schumacher NY 23
Lon Warneke CHI 22

EARNED RUN AVERAGE
Carl Hubbell NY 2.30
Dizzy Dean STL 2.66
Waite Hoyt NY 2.93

STRIKEOUTS
Dizzy Dean STL 195
Van Mungo BKN 184
Paul Dean STL 150

SAVES
Carl Hubbell NY 8

COMPLETE GAMES
Carl Hubbell NY 25

SHUTOUTS
Dizzy Dean STL 7

INNINGS PITCHED
Van Mungo BKN 315

1935 AMERICAN LEAGUE STANDINGS

	W	L	PCT	GB	R	OR
★ DET	93	58	.616	—	919	665
NY	89	60	.597	3	818	632
CLE	82	71	.536	12	776	739
BOS	78	75	.510	16	718	732
CHI	74	78	.487	19.5	738	750
WAS	67	86	.438	27	823	903
STL	65	87	.428	28.5	718	930
PHI	58	91	.389	34	710	869
					6220	6220

BATTING AVERAGE
Buddy Myer WAS .... .349
Joe Vosmik CLE .... .348
Jimmie Foxx PHI .... .346

HITS
Joe Vosmik CLE 216
Buddy Myer WAS 215
Doc Cramer PHI 214

DOUBLES
Joe Vosmik CLE 47
Hank Greenberg DET 46
M. Solters BOS, STL 45

TRIPLES
Joe Vosmik CLE 20
John Stone WAS 18
Hank Greenberg DET 16

HOME RUNS
Hank Greenberg DET 36
Jimmie Foxx PHI 36
Lou Gehrig NY 30

RUNS BATTED IN
H. Greenberg DET 170
Lou Gehrig NY 119
Jimmie Foxx PHI 115

STOLEN BASES
Bill Werber BOS 29
Lyn Lary WAS, STL 28
Mel Almada BOS 20

RUNS SCORED
Lou Gehrig NY 125
C. Gehringer DET 123
H. Greenberg DET 121

WINS
Wes Ferrell BOS 25
Mel Harder CLE 22
T. Bridges DET 21

EARNED RUN AVERAGE
Lefty Grove BOS 2.70
Ted Lyons CHI 3.02
Red Ruffing NY 3.12

STRIKEOUTS
T. Bridges DET 163
S. Rowe DET 140
Lefty Gomez NY 138

SAVES
Jack Knott STL 7

COMPLETE GAMES
Wes Ferrell BOS 31

SHUTOUTS
Schoolboy Rowe DET 6

INNINGS PITCHED
Wes Ferrell BOS 322

1935 NATIONAL LEAGUE STANDINGS

	W	L	PCT	GB	R	OR
CHI	100	54	.649	—	847	597
STL	96	58	.623	4	829	625
NY	91	62	.595	8.5	770	675
PIT	86	67	.562	13.5	743	647
BKN	70	83	.458	29.5	711	767
CIN	68	85	.444	31.5	646	772
PHI	64	89	.418	35.5	685	871
BOS	38	115	.248	61.5	575	852
					5806	5806

BATTING AVERAGE
Arky Vaughan PIT .... .385
Joe Medwick STL .... .353
Gabby Hartnett CHI .... .344

HITS
Billy Herman CHI 227
Joe Medwick STL 224
four tied at 203

DOUBLES
Billy Herman CHI 57
Ethan Allen PHI 46
Joe Medwick STL 46

TRIPLES
Ival Goodman CIN 18

Lloyd Waner PIT 14
Joe Medwick STL 13

HOME RUNS
Wally Berger BOS 34
Mel Ott NY 31
Dolf Camilli PHI 25

RUNS BATTED IN
Wally Berger BOS 130
Joe Medwick STL 126
Ripper Collins STL 122

STOLEN BASES
Augie Galan CHI 22
Pepper Martin STL 20
F. Bordagaray BKN 18

RUNS SCORED
Augie Galan CHI 133
Joe Medwick STL 132
Pepper Martin STL 121

WINS
Dizzy Dean STL 28
Carl Hubbell NY 23
Paul Derringer CIN 22

EARNED RUN AVERAGE
Cy Blanton PIT 2.58
Bill Swift PIT 2.70
H. Schumacher NY 2.89

STRIKEOUTS
Dizzy Dean STL 190
Carl Hubbell NY 150
two tied at 143

SAVES
Dutch Leonard BKN 8

COMPLETE GAMES
Dizzy Dean STL 29

SHUTOUTS
five tied at 4

INNINGS PITCHED
Dizzy Dean STL 325

1936 AMERICAN LEAGUE STANDINGS

	W	L	PCT	GB	R	OR
★ NY	102	51	.667	—	1065	731
DET	83	71	.539	19.5	921	871
CHI	81	70	.536	20	920	873
WAS	82	71	.536	20	889	799
CLE	80	74	.519	22.5	921	862
BOS	74	80	.481	28.5	775	764
STL	57	95	.375	44.5	804	1064
PHI	53	100	.346	49	714	1045
					7009	7009

BATTING AVERAGE
Luke Appling CHI .... .388
Earl Averill CLE .... .378
Bill Dickey NY .... .362

HITS
Earl Averill CLE 232
C. Gehringer DET 227
Hal Trosky CLE 216

DOUBLES
C. Gehringer DET 60
Gee Walker DET 55
two tied at 50

TRIPLES
Earl Averill CLE 15
Red Rolfe NY 15
Joe DiMaggio NY 15

HOME RUNS
Lou Gehrig NY 49
Hal Trosky CLE 42
Jimmie Foxx BOS 41

RUNS BATTED IN
Hal Trosky CLE 162
Lou Gehrig NY 152
Jimmie Foxx BOS 143

STOLEN BASES
Lyn Lary STL 37
J. Powell WAS, NY 26
Bill Werber BOS 23

RUNS SCORED
Lou Gehrig NY 167
Harlond Clift STL 145
C. Gehringer DET 144

WINS
Tommy Bridges DET 23
Vern Kennedy CHI 21
three tied at 20

EARNED RUN AVERAGE
Lefty Grove BOS 2.81
Johnny Allen CLE 3.44
Pete Appleton WAS 3.53

STRIKEOUTS
T. Bridges DET 175
Johnny Allen CLE 165
Bobo Newsom WAS 156

SAVES
Pat Malone NY 9

COMPLETE GAMES
Wes Ferrell BOS 28

SHUTOUTS
Lefty Grove BOS 6

INNINGS PITCHED
Wes Ferrell BOS 301

1936 NATIONAL LEAGUE STANDINGS

	W	L	PCT	GB	R	OR
NY	92	62	.597	—	742	621
CHI	87	67	.565	5	755	603
STL	87	67	.565	5	795	794
PIT	84	70	.545	8	804	718
CIN	74	80	.481	18	722	760
BOS	71	83	.461	21	631	715
BKN	67	87	.435	25	662	752
PHI	54	100	.351	38	726	874
					5837	5837

BATTING AVERAGE
Paul Waner PIT .... .373
Babe Phelps BKN .... .367
Joe Medwick STL .... .351

HITS
Joe Medwick STL 223
Paul Waner PIT 218
Frank Demaree CHI 212

DOUBLES
Joe Medwick STL 64
Billy Herman CHI 57
Paul Waner PIT 53

TRIPLES
Ival Goodman CIN 14

Dolf Camilli PHI 13
Joe Medwick STL 13

HOME RUNS
Mel Ott NY 33
Dolf Camilli PHI 28
two tied at 25

RUNS BATTED IN
Joe Medwick STL 138
Mel Ott NY 135
Gus Suhr PIT 118

STOLEN BASES
Pepper Martin STL 23
three tied at 17

RUNS SCORED
Arky Vaughan PIT 122
Pepper Martin STL 121
Mel Ott NY 120

WINS
Carl Hubbell NY 26
Dizzy Dean STL 24
Paul Derringer CIN 19

EARNED RUN AVERAGE
Carl Hubbell NY 2.31
D. MacFayden BOS 2.87
Frank Gabler NY 3.12

STRIKEOUTS
Van Mungo BKN 238
Dizzy Dean STL 195
Cy Blanton PIT 127

SAVES
Dizzy Dean STL 11

COMPLETE GAMES
Dizzy Dean STL 28

SHUTOUTS
seven tied at 4

INNINGS PITCHED
Dizzy Dean STL 315

1937 AMERICAN LEAGUE STANDINGS

	W	L	PCT	GB	R	OR
★ NY	102	52	.662	—	979	671
DET	89	65	.578	13	935	841
CHI	86	68	.558	16	780	730
CLE	83	71	.539	19	817	768
BOS	80	72	.526	21	821	775
WAS	73	80	.477	28.5	757	841
PHI	54	97	.358	46.5	699	854
STL	46	108	.299	56	715	1023
					6503	6503

BATTING AVERAGE
C. Gehringer DET .... .371
Lou Gehrig NY .... .351
Joe DiMaggio NY .... .346

HITS
Beau Bell STL 218
Joe DiMaggio NY 215
Gee Walker DET 213

DOUBLES
Beau Bell STL 51
Hank Greenberg DET 49
Wally Moses PHI 48

TRIPLES
Dixie Walker CHI 16
Mike Kreevich CHI 16
two tied at 15

HOME RUNS
Joe DiMaggio NY 46
Hank Greenberg DET 40
Lou Gehrig NY 37

RUNS BATTED IN
H. Greenberg DET 183
Joe DiMaggio NY 167
Lou Gehrig NY 159

STOLEN BASES
Chapman WAS, BOS 35
Bill Werber PHI 35
Gee Walker DET 23

RUNS SCORED
Joe DiMaggio NY 151
Red Rolfe NY 143
Lou Gehrig NY 138

WINS
Lefty Gomez NY 21
Red Ruffing NY 20
Roxie Lawson DET 18

EARNED RUN AVERAGE
Lefty Gomez NY 2.33
Monty Stratton CHI 2.40
Johnny Allen CLE 2.55

STRIKEOUTS
Lefty Gomez NY 194
Newsom WAS, BOS 166
Lefty Grove BOS 153

SAVES
Clint Brown CHI 18

COMPLETE GAMES
W. Ferrell BOS, WAS 26

SHUTOUTS
Lefty Gomez NY 6

INNINGS PITCHED
W. Ferrell BOS, WAS 281

1937 NATIONAL LEAGUE STANDINGS

	W	L	PCT	GB	R	OR
NY	95	57	.625	—	732	602
CHI	93	61	.604	3	811	682
PIT	86	68	.558	10	704	646
STL	81	73	.526	15	789	733
BOS	79	73	.520	16	579	556
BKN	62	91	.405	33.5	616	772
PHI	61	92	.399	34.5	724	869
CIN	56	98	.364	40	612	707
					5567	5567

BATTING AVERAGE
Joe Medwick STL .... .374
Johnny Mize STL .... .364
Gabby Hartnett CHI .... .354

HITS
Joe Medwick STL 237
Paul Waner PIT 219
Johnny Mize STL 204

DOUBLES
Joe Medwick STL 56
Johnny Mize STL 40
Dick Bartell NY 38

TRIPLES
Arky Vaughan PIT 17
Gus Suhr PIT 14
two tied at 12

HOME RUNS
Joe Medwick STL 31
Mel Ott NY 31
Dolf Camilli PHI 27

RUNS BATTED IN
Joe Medwick STL 154
Frank Demaree CHI 115
Johnny Mize STL 113

STOLEN BASES
Augie Galan CHI 23
Stan Hack CHI 16
four tied at 13

RUNS SCORED
Joe Medwick STL 111
Stan Hack CHI 106
Billy Herman CHI 106

WINS
Carl Hubbell NY 22
three tied at 20

EARNED RUN AVERAGE
Jim Turner BOS 2.38
Cliff Melton NY 2.61
Dizzy Dean STL 2.69

STRIKEOUTS
Carl Hubbell NY 159
Lee Grissom CIN 149
Cy Blanton PIT 143

SAVES
Mace Brown PIT 7
Cliff Melton NY 7

COMPLETE GAMES
Jim Turner BOS 24

SHUTOUTS
three tied at 5

INNINGS PITCHED
C. Passeau PHI 292

1938 AMERICAN LEAGUE STANDINGS

	W	L	PCT	GB	R	OR
★ NY	99	53	.651	—	966	710
BOS	88	61	.591	9.5	902	751
CLE	86	66	.566	13	847	782
DET	84	70	.545	16	862	795
WAS	75	76	.497	23.5	814	873
CHI	65	83	.439	32	709	752
STL	55	97	.362	44	755	962
PHI	53	99	.349	46	726	956
					6581	6581

BATTING AVERAGE
Jimmie Foxx BOS .... .349
Jeff Heath CLE .... .343
Ben Chapman BOS .... .340

HITS
Joe Vosmik BOS 201
Doc Cramer BOS............... 198
two tied at 197

DOUBLES
Joe Cronin BOS................... 51
George McQuinn STL......... 42
two tied at 40

TRIPLES
Jeff Heath CLE 18
Earl Averill CLE 15
Joe DiMaggio NY 13

HOME RUNS
Hank Greenberg DET 58
Jimmie Foxx BOS 50
Harlond Clift STL 34

RUNS BATTED IN
Jimmie Foxx BOS 175
H. Greenberg DET 146
Joe DiMaggio NY 140

STOLEN BASES
Frank Crosetti NY 27
Lyn Lary CLE 23
Bill Werber PHI 19

RUNS SCORED
H. Greenberg DET............ 144
Jimmie Foxx BOS............. 139
C. Gehringer DET............. 133

WINS
Red Ruffing NY................... 21
Bobo Newsom STL............ 20
Lefty Gomez NY 18

EARNED RUN AVERAGE
Lefty Grove BOS 3.08
Red Ruffing NY 3.31
Lefty Gomez NY 3.35

STRIKEOUTS
Bob Feller CLE 240
Bobo Newsom STL 226
Lefty Mills STL 134

SAVES
Johnny Murphy NY 11

COMPLETE GAMES
Bobo Newsom STL............ 31

SHUTOUTS
Lefty Gomez NY 4

INNINGS PITCHED
Bobo Newsom STL 330

1938 NATIONAL LEAGUE STANDINGS

	W	L	PCT	GB	R	OR
CHI	89	63	.586	—	713	598
PIT	86	64	.573	2	707	630
NY	83	67	.553	5	705	637
CIN	82	68	.547	6	723	634
BOS	77	75	.507	12	561	618
STL	71	80	.470	17.5	725	721
BKN	69	80	.463	18.5	704	710
PHI	45	105	.300	43	550	840
					5388	5388

BATTING AVERAGE
Ernie Lombardi CIN .... .342
Johnny Mize STL .... .337
F. McCormick CIN .... .327

HITS
F. McCormick CIN 209
Stan Hack CHI 195
Lloyd Waner PIT 194

DOUBLES
Joe Medwick STL 47
F. McCormick CIN 40
two tied at 36

TRIPLES
Johnny Mize STL 16
Don Gutteridge STL 15
Gus Suhr PIT 14

HOME RUNS
Mel Ott NY 36
Ival Goodman CIN 30
Johnny Mize STL 27

RUNS BATTED IN
Joe Medwick STL 122
Mel Ott NY 116
Johnny Rizzo PIT 111

STOLEN BASES
Stan Hack CHI 16
Ernie Koy BKN 15
C. Lavagetto BKN 15

RUNS SCORED
Mel Ott NY 116
Stan Hack CHI 109
Dolf Camilli BKN 106

WINS
Bill Lee CHI 22
Paul Derringer CIN 21
Clay Bryant CHI 19

EARNED RUN AVERAGE
Bill Lee CHI 2.66
Charlie Root CHI 2.86
Paul Derringer CIN 2.93

STRIKEOUTS
Clay Bryant CHI 135
Paul Derringer CIN 132
Vander Meer CIN 125

SAVES
Dick Coffman NY 12

COMPLETE GAMES
Paul Derringer CIN 26

SHUTOUTS
Bill Lee CHI 9

INNINGS PITCHED
Paul Derringer CIN 307

1939 AMERICAN LEAGUE STANDINGS

	W	L	PCT	GB	R	OR
★ NY	106	45	.702	—	967	556
BOS	89	62	.589	17	890	795
CLE	87	67	.565	20.5	797	700
CHI	85	69	.552	22.5	755	737
DET	81	73	.526	26.5	849	762
WAS	65	87	.428	41.5	702	797
PHI	55	97	.362	51.5	711	1022
STL	43	111	.279	64.5	733	1035
					6404	6404

BATTING AVERAGE
Joe DiMaggio NY.............. .381
Jimmie Foxx BOS.............. .360
Bob Johnson PHI.............. .338

HITS
Red Rolfe NY.............. 213
G. McQuinn STL.............. 195
Ken Keltner CLE.............. 191

DOUBLES
Red Rolfe NY.............. 46
Ted Williams BOS.............. 44
Hank Greenberg DET.............. 42

TRIPLES
Buddy Lewis WAS.............. 16
B. McCoskey DET.............. 14
two tied at.............. 13

HOME RUNS
Jimmie Foxx BOS.............. 35
Hank Greenberg DET.............. 33
Ted Williams BOS.............. 31

RUNS BATTED IN
Ted Williams BOS.............. 145
Joe DiMaggio NY.............. 126
Bob Johnson PHI.............. 114

STOLEN BASES
George Case WAS.............. 51
Mike Kreevich CHI.............. 23
Pete Fox DET.............. 23

RUNS SCORED
Red Rolfe NY.............. 139
Ted Williams BOS.............. 131
Jimmie Foxx BOS.............. 130

WINS
Bob Feller CLE.............. 24
Red Ruffing NY.............. 21
two tied at.............. 20

EARNED RUN AVERAGE
Lefty Grove BOS.............. 2.54
Ted Lyons CHI.............. 2.76
Bob Feller CLE.............. 2.85

STRIKEOUTS
Bob Feller CLE.............. 246
B. Newsom STL, DET.............. 192

SAVES
Johnny Murphy NY.............. 19

COMPLETE GAMES
B. Newsom STL, DET.............. 24
Bob Feller CLE.............. 24

SHUTOUTS
Red Ruffing NY.............. 5

INNINGS PITCHED
Bob Feller CLE.............. 297

1939 NATIONAL LEAGUE STANDINGS

	W	L	PCT	GB	R	OR
CIN	97	57	.630	—	767	595
STL	92	61	.601	4.5	779	633
BKN	84	69	.549	12.5	708	645
CHI	84	70	.545	13	724	678
NY	77	74	.510	18.5	703	685
PIT	68	85	.444	28.5	666	721
BOS	63	88	.417	32.5	572	659
PHI	45	106	.298	50.5	553	856
					5472	5472

BATTING AVERAGE
Don Padgett STL.............. .399
Johnny Mize STL.............. .349
F. McCormick CIN.............. .332

HITS
F. McCormick CIN.............. 209
Joe Medwick STL.............. 201
Johnny Mize STL.............. 197

DOUBLES
Enos Slaughter STL.............. 52
Joe Medwick STL.............. 48
Johnny Mize STL.............. 44

TRIPLES
Billy Herman CHI.............. 18
Ival Goodman CIN.............. 16
Johnny Mize STL.............. 14

HOME RUNS
Johnny Mize STL.............. 28
Mel Ott NY.............. 27
Dolf Camilli BKN.............. 26

RUNS BATTED IN
F. McCormick CIN.............. 128
Joe Medwick STL.............. 117
Johnny Mize STL.............. 108

STOLEN BASES
Lee Handley PIT.............. 17
Stan Hack CHI.............. 17
Bill Werber CIN.............. 15

RUNS SCORED
Bill Werber CIN.............. 115
Stan Hack CHI.............. 112
Billy Herman CHI.............. 111

WINS
Bucky Walters CIN.............. 27
Paul Derringer CIN.............. 25
Curt Davis STL.............. 22

EARNED RUN AVERAGE
Bucky Walters CIN.............. 2.29
Bob Bowman STL.............. 2.60
Carl Hubbell NY.............. 2.75

STRIKEOUTS
C. Passeau PHI, CHI.............. 137
Bucky Walters CIN.............. 137
Mort Cooper STL.............. 130

SAVES
two tied at.............. 9

COMPLETE GAMES
Bucky Walters CIN.............. 31

SHUTOUTS
Lou Fette BOS.............. 6

INNINGS PITCHED
Bucky Walters CIN.............. 319

1940 AMERICAN LEAGUE STANDINGS

	W	L	PCT	GB	R	OR
DET	90	64	.584	—	888	717
CLE	89	65	.578	1	710	637
NY	88	66	.571	2	817	671
BOS	82	72	.532	8	872	825
CHI	82	72	.532	8	735	672
STL	67	87	.435	23	757	882
WAS	64	90	.416	26	665	811
PHI	54	100	.351	36	703	932
					6147	6147

BATTING AVERAGE
Joe DiMaggio NY .... .352
Luke Appling CHI .... .348
Ted Williams BOS .... .344

HITS
Rip Radcliff STL 200
Doc Cramer BOS 200
B. McCoskey DET 200

DOUBLES
Hank Greenberg DET 50
Lou Boudreau CLE 46
Rudy York DET 46

TRIPLES
B. McCoskey DET 19
Lou Finney BOS 15
Charlie Keller NY 15

HOME RUNS
Hank Greenberg DET 41
Jimmie Foxx BOS 36
Rudy York DET 33

RUNS BATTED IN
H. Greenberg DET 150
Rudy York DET 134
Joe DiMaggio NY 133

STOLEN BASES
George Case WAS 35
Gee Walker WAS 21
Joe Gordon NY 18

RUNS SCORED
Ted Williams BOS 134
H. Greenberg DET 129
B. McCoskey DET 123

WINS
Bob Feller CLE 27
Bobo Newsom DET 21
Al Milnar CLE 18

EARNED RUN AVERAGE
Bob Feller CLE 2.61
Bobo Newsom DET 2.83
Johnny Rigney CHI 3.11

STRIKEOUTS
Bob Feller CLE 261
Bobo Newsom DET 164
Johnny Rigney CHI 141

SAVES
Al Benton DET 17

COMPLETE GAMES
Bob Feller CLE 31

SHUTOUTS
three tied at 4

INNINGS PITCHED
Bob Feller CLE 320

1940 NATIONAL LEAGUE STANDINGS

	W	L	PCT	GB	R	OR
★ CIN	100	53	.654	—	707	528
BKN	88	65	.575	12	697	621
STL	84	69	.549	16	747	699
PIT	78	76	.506	22.5	809	783
CHI	75	79	.487	25.5	681	636
NY	72	80	.474	27.5	663	659
BOS	65	87	.428	34.5	623	745
PHI	50	103	.327	50	494	750
					5421	5421

BATTING AVERAGE
Debs Garms PIT .... .355
Spud Davis PIT .... .326
Ernie Lombardi CIN .... .319

HITS
F. McCormick CIN 191
Stan Hack CHI 191
Johnny Mize STL 182

DOUBLES
F. McCormick CIN 44
Arky Vaughan PIT 40
Jim Gleeson CHI 39

TRIPLES
Arky Vaughan PIT 15
Chet Ross BOS 14
three tied at 13

HOME RUNS
Johnny Mize STL 43
Bill Nicholson CHI 25
J. Rizzo PIT, CIN, PHI 24

RUNS BATTED IN
Johnny Mize STL 137
F. McCormick CIN 127
M. Van Robays PIT 116

STOLEN BASES
Lonny Frey CIN 22
Stan Hack CHI 21
Terry Moore STL 18

RUNS SCORED
Arky Vaughan PIT 113
Johnny Mize STL 111
Bill Werber CIN 105

WINS
Bucky Walters CIN 22
Paul Derringer CIN 20
Claude Passeau CHI 20

EARNED RUN AVERAGE
Bucky Walters CIN 2.48
C. Passeau CHI 2.50

STRIKEOUTS
Kirby Higbe PHI 137
Whit Wyatt BKN 124
C. Passeau CHI 124

SAVES
three tied at 7

COMPLETE GAMES
Bucky Walters CIN 29

SHUTOUTS
Manny Salvo BOS 5
Whit Wyatt BKN 5

INNINGS PITCHED
Bucky Walters CIN 305

1941 AMERICAN LEAGUE STANDINGS

	W	L	PCT	GB	R	OR
★ NY	101	53	.656	—	830	631
BOS	84	70	.545	17	865	750
CHI	77	77	.500	24	638	649
CLE	75	79	.487	26	677	668
DET	75	79	.487	26	686	743
STL	70	84	.455	31	765	823
WAS	70	84	.455	31	728	798
PHI	64	90	.416	37	713	840
					5902	5902

BATTING AVERAGE
Ted Williams BOS .... .406
Cecil Travis WAS .... .359
Joe DiMaggio NY .... .357

HITS
Cecil Travis WAS 218
Jeff Heath CLE 199
Joe DiMaggio NY 193

DOUBLES
Lou Boudreau CLE 45
Joe DiMaggio NY 43
Walt Judnich STL 40

TRIPLES
Jeff Heath CLE 20

Cecil Travis WAS 19
Ken Keltner CLE 13

HOME RUNS
Ted Williams BOS 37
Charlie Keller NY 33
Tommy Henrich NY 31

RUNS BATTED IN
Joe DiMaggio NY 125
Jeff Heath CLE 123
Charlie Keller NY 122

STOLEN BASES
George Case WAS 33
Joe Kuhel CHI 20
Jeff Heath CLE 18

RUNS SCORED
Ted Williams BOS 135
Joe DiMaggio NY 122
Dom DiMaggio BOS 117

WINS
Bob Feller CLE 25
Thorton Lee CHI 22
Dick Newsome BOS 19

EARNED RUN AVERAGE
Thorton Lee CHI 2.37
Al Benton DET 2.97
C. Wagner BOS 3.07

STRIKEOUTS
Bob Feller CLE 260
Bobo Newsom DET 175
Thorton Lee CHI 130

SAVES
Johnny Murphy NY 15

COMPLETE GAMES
Thorton Lee CHI 30

SHUTOUTS
Bob Feller CLE 6

INNINGS PITCHED
Bob Feller CLE 343

1941 NATIONAL LEAGUE STANDINGS

	W	L	PCT	GB	R	OR
BKN	100	54	.649	—	800	581
STL	97	56	.634	2.5	734	589
CIN	88	66	.571	12	616	564
PIT	81	73	.526	19	690	643
NY	74	79	.484	25.5	667	706
CHI	70	84	.455	30	666	670
BOS	62	92	.403	38	592	720
PHI	43	111	.279	57	501	793
					5266	5266

BATTING AVERAGE
Pete Reiser BKN .... .343
J. Cooney BOS .... .319
Joe Medwick BKN .... .318

HITS
Stan Hack CHI 186
Pete Reiser BKN 184
Danny Litwhiler PHI 180

DOUBLES
Pete Reiser BKN 39
Johnny Mize STL 39
Johnny Rucker NY 38

TRIPLES
Pete Reiser BKN 17

Elbie Fletcher PIT 13
Johnny Hopp STL 11

HOME RUNS
Dolf Camilli BKN 34
Mel Ott NY 27
Bill Nicholson CHI 26

RUNS BATTED IN
Dolf Camilli BKN 120
Bobby Young NY 104
two tied at 100

STOLEN BASES
Danny Murtaugh PHI 18
Stan Benjamin PHI 17
two tied at 16

RUNS SCORED
Pete Reiser BKN 117
Stan Hack CHI 111
Joe Medwick BKN 100

WINS
Kirby Higbe BKN 22
Whit Wyatt BKN 22
two tied at 19

EARNED RUN AVERAGE
Elmer Riddle CIN 2.24
Whit Wyatt BKN 2.34
Ernie White STL 2.40

STRIKEOUTS
J. Vander Meer CIN 202
Whit Wyatt BKN 176
Bucky Walters CIN 129

SAVES
Jumbo Brown NY 8

COMPLETE GAMES
Bucky Walters CIN 27

SHUTOUTS
Whit Wyatt BKN 7

INNINGS PITCHED
Bucky Walters CIN 302

1942 AMERICAN LEAGUE STANDINGS

	W	L	PCT	GB	R	OR
NY	103	51	.669	—	801	507
BOS	93	59	.612	9	761	594
STL	82	69	.543	19.5	730	637
CLE	75	79	.487	28	590	659
DET	73	81	.474	30	589	587
CHI	66	82	.446	34	538	609
WAS	62	89	.411	39.5	653	817
PHI	55	99	.357	48	549	801
					5211	5211

BATTING AVERAGE
Ted Williams BOS .... .356
Johnny Pesky BOS........... .331
Stan Spence WAS .... .323

HITS
Johnny Pesky BOS............ 205
Stan Spence WAS 203
two tied at 186

DOUBLES
Don Kolloway CHI 40
Harlond Clift STL 39
Jeff Heath CLE 37

TRIPLES
Stan Spence WAS.............. 15
Jeff Heath CLE 13
Joe DiMaggio NY 13

HOME RUNS
Ted Williams BOS 36
Chet Laabs STL 27
Charlie Keller NY 26

RUNS BATTED IN
Ted Williams BOS 137
Joe DiMaggio NY 114
Charlie Keller NY 108

STOLEN BASES
George Case WAS 44
Mickey Vernon WAS........... 25
two tied at 22

RUNS SCORED
Ted Williams BOS 141
Joe DiMaggio NY.............. 123
Dom DiMaggio BOS 110

WINS
Tex Hughson BOS.............. 22
Ernie Bonham NY 21
two tied at 17

EARNED RUN AVERAGE
Ted Lyons CHI................ 2.10
Ernie Bonham NY............ 2.27
Spud Chandler NY.......... 2.38

STRIKEOUTS
Bobo Newsom WAS 113
Tex Hughson BOS............ 113

SAVES
Johnny Murphy NY 11

COMPLETE GAMES
Ernie Bonham NY 22
Tex Hughson BOS.............. 22

SHUTOUTS
Ernie Bonham NY 6

INNINGS PITCHED
Tex Hughson BOS............ 281

1942 NATIONAL LEAGUE STANDINGS

	W	L	PCT	GB	R	OR
★ STL	106	48	.688	—	755	482
BKN	104	50	.675	2	742	510
NY	85	67	.559	20	675	600
CIN	76	76	.500	29	527	545
PIT	66	81	.449	36.5	585	631
CHI	68	86	.442	38	591	665
BOS	59	89	.399	44	515	645
PHI	42	109	.278	62.5	394	706
					4784	4784

BATTING AVERAGE
Ernie Lombardi BOS........ .330
Enos Slaughter STL .... .318
Stan Musial STL .... .315

HITS
Enos Slaughter STL 188
Bill Nicholson CHI 173
three tied at...................... 166

DOUBLES
Marty Marion STL 38
Joe Medwick BKN 37
Stan Hack CHI 36

TRIPLES
Enos Slaughter STL 17
Bill Nicholson CHI 11
Stan Musial STL 10

HOME RUNS
Mel Ott NY 30
Johnny Mize NY 26
Dolf Camilli BKN 26

RUNS BATTED IN
Johnny Mize NY 110
Dolf Camilli BKN 109
Enos Slaughter STL 98

STOLEN BASES
Pete Reiser BKN 20
N. Fernandez BOS 15
Pee Wee Reese BKN 15

RUNS SCORED
Mel Ott NY 118
Enos Slaughter STL 100
Johnny Mize NY 97

WINS
Mort Cooper STL 22
Johnny Beazley STL 21
two tied at 19

EARNED RUN AVERAGE
Mort Cooper STL 1.78
J. Beazley STL 2.13
Curt Davis BKN 2.36

STRIKEOUTS
J. Vander Meer CIN 186
Mort Cooper STL 152
Kirby Higbe BKN 115

SAVES
Hugh Casey BKN 13

COMPLETE GAMES
Jim Tobin BOS 28

SHUTOUTS
Mort Cooper STL 10

INNINGS PITCHED
Jim Tobin BOS 288

1943 AMERICAN LEAGUE STANDINGS

	W	L	PCT	GB	R	OR
★ NY	98	56	.636	—	669	542
WAS	84	69	.549	13.5	666	595
CLE	82	71	.536	15.5	600	577
CHI	82	72	.532	16	573	594
DET	78	76	.506	20	632	560
STL	72	80	.474	25	596	604
BOS	68	84	.447	29	563	607
PHI	49	105	.318	49	497	717
					4796	4796

BATTING AVERAGE
Luke Appling CHI .... .328
Dick Wakefield DET .... .316
Ralph Hodgin CHI .... .314

HITS
Dick Wakefield DET 200
Luke Appling CHI 192
Doc Cramer DET 182

DOUBLES
Dick Wakefield DET 38
George Case WAS 36
two tied at 35

TRIPLES
Johnny Lindell NY 12

Wally Moses CHI 12
two tied at 11

HOME RUNS
Rudy York DET 34
Charlie Keller NY 31
Vern Stephens STL 22

RUNS BATTED IN
Rudy York DET 118
Nick Etten NY 107
Billy Johnson NY 94

STOLEN BASES
George Case WAS 61
Wally Moses CHI 56
Thurman Tucker CHI 29

RUNS SCORED
George Case WAS 102
Charlie Keller NY 97
Dick Wakefield DET 91

WINS
Spud Chandler NY 20
Dizzy Trout DET 20
Early Wynn WAS 18

EARNED RUN AVERAGE
Spud Chandler NY 1.64
Ernie Bonham NY 2.27

STRIKEOUTS
Allie Reynolds CLE 151
Hal Newhouser DET 144

SAVES
G. Maltzberger CHI 14

COMPLETE GAMES
Spud Chandler NY 20
Tex Hughson BOS 20

SHUTOUTS
Spud Chandler NY 5
Dizzy Trout DET 5

INNINGS PITCHED
Jim Bagby CLE 273

1943 NATIONAL LEAGUE STANDINGS

	W	L	PCT	GB	R	OR
STL	105	49	.682	—	679	475
CIN	87	67	.565	18	608	543
BKN	81	72	.529	23.5	716	674
PIT	80	74	.519	25	669	605
CHI	74	79	.484	30.5	632	600
BOS	68	85	.444	36.5	465	612
PHI	64	90	.416	41	571	676
NY	55	98	.359	49.5	558	713
					4898	4898

BATTING AVERAGE
Stan Musial STL .... .357
Billy Herman BKN .... .330
Walker Cooper STL .... .318

HITS
Stan Musial STL 220
Mickey Witek NY 195
Billy Herman BKN 193

DOUBLES
Stan Musial STL 48
Vince DiMaggio PIT 41
Billy Herman BKN 41

TRIPLES
Stan Musial STL 20

Lou Klein STL 14
two tied at 12

HOME RUNS
Bill Nicholson CHI 29
Mel Ott NY 18
Ron Northey PHI 16

RUNS BATTED IN
Bill Nicholson CHI 128
Bob Elliott PIT 101
Billy Herman BKN 100

STOLEN BASES
Arky Vaughan BKN 20
Peanuts Lowrey CHI 13
three tied at 12

RUNS SCORED
Arky Vaughan BKN 112
Stan Musial STL 108
Bill Nicholson CHI 95

WINS
Elmer Riddle CIN 21
Mort Cooper STL 21
Rip Sewell PIT 21

EARNED RUN AVERAGE
Max Lanier STL 1.90
Mort Cooper STL 2.30
Whit Wyatt BKN 2.49

STRIKEOUTS
J. Vander Meer CIN 174
Mort Cooper STL 141
Al Javery BOS 134

SAVES
Les Webber BKN 10

COMPLETE GAMES
Rip Sewell PIT 25

SHUTOUTS
Hi Bithorn CHI 7

INNINGS PITCHED
Al Javery BOS 303

1944 AMERICAN LEAGUE STANDINGS

	W	L	PCT	GB	R	OR
STL	89	65	.578	—	684	587
DET	88	66	.571	1	658	581
NY	83	71	.539	6	674	617
BOS	77	77	.500	12	739	676
CLE	72	82	.468	17	643	677
PHI	72	82	.468	17	525	594
CHI	71	83	.461	18	543	662
WAS	64	90	.416	25	592	664
					5058	5058

BATTING AVERAGE
Lou Boudreau CLE .... .327
Bobby Doerr BOS .... .325
Bob Johnson BOS .... .324

HITS
S. Stirnweiss NY 205
Lou Boudreau CLE 191
Stan Spence WAS 187

DOUBLES
Lou Boudreau CLE 45
Ken Keltner CLE 41
Bob Johnson BOS 40

TRIPLES
Johnny Lindell NY 16
Snuffy Stirnweiss NY 16
Don Gutteridge STL 11

HOME RUNS
Nick Etten NY 22
Vern Stephens STL 20
three tied at 18

RUNS BATTED IN
Vern Stephens STL 109
Bob Johnson BOS 106
Johnny Lindell NY 103

STOLEN BASES
Snuffy Stirnweiss NY 55
George Case WAS 49
Glenn Myatt WAS 26

RUNS SCORED
S. Stirnweiss NY 125
Bob Johnson BOS 106
Roy Cullenbine CLE 98

WINS
Hal Newhouser DET 29
Dizzy Trout DET 27
Nels Potter STL 19

EARNED RUN AVERAGE
Dizzy Trout DET 2.12
H. Newhouser DET 2.22
Tex Hughson BOS 2.26

STRIKEOUTS
Hal Newhouser DET 187
Dizzy Trout DET 144
Bobo Newsom PHI 142

SAVES
three tied at 12

COMPLETE GAMES
Dizzy Trout DET 33

SHUTOUTS
Dizzy Trout DET 7

INNINGS PITCHED
Dizzy Trout DET 352

1944 NATIONAL LEAGUE STANDINGS

	W	L	PCT	GB	R	OR
★ STL	105	49	.682	—	772	490
PIT	90	63	.588	14.5	744	662
CIN	89	65	.578	16	573	537
CHI	75	79	.487	30	702	669
NY	67	87	.435	38	682	773
BOS	65	89	.422	40	593	674
BKN	63	91	.409	42	690	832
PHI	61	92	.399	43.5	539	658
					5295	5295

BATTING AVERAGE
Dixie Walker BKN .... .357
Stan Musial STL .... .347
Joe Medwick NY .... .337

HITS
Phil Cavarretta CHI 197
Stan Musial STL 197
T. Holmes BOS 195

DOUBLES
Stan Musial STL 51
Augie Galan BKN 43
T. Holmes BOS 42

TRIPLES
Johnny Barrett PIT 19

Bob Elliott PIT 16
Phil Cavarretta CHI 15

HOME RUNS
Bill Nicholson CHI 33
Mel Ott NY 26
Ron Northey PHI 22

RUNS BATTED IN
Bill Nicholson CHI 122
Bob Elliott PIT 108
Ron Northey PHI 104

STOLEN BASES
Johnny Barrett PIT 28
Tony Lupien PHI 18
Roy Hughes CHI 16

RUNS SCORED
Bill Nicholson CHI 116
Stan Musial STL 112
Jim Russell PIT 109

WINS
Bucky Walters CIN 23
Mort Cooper STL 22
two tied at 21

EARNED RUN AVERAGE
Ed Heusser CIN 2.38
Bucky Walters CIN 2.40
Mort Cooper STL 2.46

STRIKEOUTS
Bill Voiselle NY 161
Max Lanier STL 141
Al Javery BOS 137

SAVES
Ace Adams NY 13

COMPLETE GAMES
Jim Tobin BOS 28

SHUTOUTS
Mort Cooper STL 7

INNINGS PITCHED
Bill Voiselle NY 313

1945 AMERICAN LEAGUE STANDINGS

	W	L	PCT	GB	R	OR
★ DET	88	65	.575	—	633	565
WAS	87	67	.565	1.5	622	562
STL	81	70	.536	6	597	548
NY	81	71	.533	6.5	676	606
CLE	73	72	.503	11	557	548
CHI	71	78	.477	15	596	633
BOS	71	83	.461	17.5	599	674
PHI	52	98	.347	34.5	494	638
					4774	4774

BATTING AVERAGE
S. Stirnweiss NY .... .309
T. Cuccinello CHI .... .308
J. Dickshot CHI .... .302

HITS
S. Stirnweiss NY 195
Wally Moses CHI 168
Vern Stephens STL 165

DOUBLES
Wally Moses CHI 35
Snuffy Stirnweiss NY 32
George Binks WAS 32

TRIPLES
Snuffy Stirnweiss NY 22

Wally Moses CHI 15
Joe Kuhel WAS 13

HOME RUNS
Vern Stephens STL 24
three tied at 18

RUNS BATTED IN
Nick Etten NY 111
Roy Cullenbine CLE, DET .. 93
Vern Stephens STL 89

STOLEN BASES
Snuffy Stirnweiss NY 33
George Case WAS 30
Glenn Myatt WAS 30

RUNS SCORED
S. Stirnweiss NY 107
Vern Stephens STL 90
Roy Cullenbine CLE, DET .. 83

WINS
Hal Newhouser DET 25
Boo Ferriss BOS 21
Roger Wolff WAS 20

EARNED RUN AVERAGE
H. Newhouser DET 1.81
Al Benton DET 2.02
Roger Wolff WAS 2.12

STRIKEOUTS
Hal Newhouser DET 212
Nels Potter STL 129
Bobo Newsom PHI 127

SAVES
Jim Turner NY 10

COMPLETE GAMES
Hal Newhouser DET 29

SHUTOUTS
Hal Newhouser DET 8

INNINGS PITCHED
Hal Newhouser DET 313

1945 NATIONAL LEAGUE STANDINGS

	W	L	PCT	GB	R	OR
CHI	98	56	.636	—	735	532
STL	95	59	.617	3	756	583
BKN	87	67	.565	11	795	724
PIT	82	72	.532	16	753	686
NY	78	74	.513	19	668	700
BOS	67	85	.441	30	721	728
CIN	61	93	.396	37	536	694
PHI	46	108	.299	52	548	865
					5512	5512

BATTING AVERAGE
Phil Cavarretta CHI .... .355
T. Holmes BOS .... .352
Goody Rosen BKN .... .325

HITS
T. Holmes BOS 224
Goody Rosen BKN 197
Stan Hack CHI 193

DOUBLES
Tommy Holmes BOS 47
Dixie Walker BKN 42
two tied at 36

TRIPLES
Luis Olmo BKN 13

Andy Pafko CHI 12
two tied at 11

HOME RUNS
Tommy Holmes BOS 28
Chuck Workman BOS 25
B. Adams PHI, STL 22

RUNS BATTED IN
Dixie Walker BKN 124
T. Holmes BOS 117
two tied at 110

STOLEN BASES
R. Schoendienst STL 26
Johnny Barrett PIT 25
Dain Clay CIN 19

RUNS SCORED
Eddie Stanky BKN 128
Goody Rosen BKN 126
T. Holmes BOS 125

WINS
R. Barrett BOS, STL 23
Hank Wyse CHI 22
two tied at 19

EARNED RUN AVERAGE
Ray Prim CHI 2.40
C. Passeau CHI 2.46
Harry Brecheen STL 2.52

STRIKEOUTS
Preacher Roe PIT 148
Hal Gregg BKN 139

SAVES
Ace Adams NY 15
Andy Karl PHI 15

COMPLETE GAMES
R. Barrett BOS, STL 24

SHUTOUTS
Claude Passeau CHI 5

INNINGS PITCHED
R. Barrett BOS, STL 285

AMERICAN LEAGUE STANDINGS

1946 AL

	W	L	PCT	GB	R	OR	BA	FA	ERA
BOSTON	104	50	.675	—	792	594	.271	.977	3.38
DETROIT	92	62	.597	12	704	567	.258	.974	3.22
NEW YORK	87	67	.565	17	684	547	.248	.975	3.13
WASHINGTON	76	78	.494	28	608	706	.260	.966	3.74
CHICAGO	74	80	.481	30	562	595	.257	.972	3.10
CLEVELAND	68	86	.442	36	537	638	.245	.975	3.62
ST. LOUIS	66	88	.429	38	621	710	.251	.974	3.95
PHILADELPHIA	49	105	.318	55	529	680	.253	.971	3.90
					5037	5037	.256	.973	3.50

BATTING AVERAGE
M. Vernon WAS......... .353
Ted Williams BOS...... .342
Johnny Pesky BOS.... .335

HITS
Johnny Pesky BOS..... 208
Mickey Vernon WAS... 207
Luke Appling CHI........ 180

DOUBLES
Mickey Vernon WAS..... 51
Stan Spence WAS........ 50
Johnny Pesky BOS....... 43

TRIPLES
Hank Edwards CLE 16
Buddy Lewis WAS 13
three tied at................... 10

HOME RUNS
Hank Greenberg DET... 44
Ted Williams BOS......... 38
Charlie Keller NY 30

RUNS BATTED IN
H. Greenberg DET...... 127
Ted Williams BOS...... 123
Rudy York BOS 119

SLUGGING AVERAGE
Ted Williams BOS...... .667
H. Greenberg DET..... .604
Charlie Keller NY .... .533

STOLEN BASES
George Case CLE 28
Snuffy Stirnweiss NY 18
Eddie Lake DET............ 15

RUNS SCORED
Ted Williams BOS....... 142
Johnny Pesky BOS..... 115
Eddie Lake DET.......... 105

WINS
Hal Newhouser DET..... 26
Bob Feller CLE 26
Boo Ferriss BOS........... 25

WINNING PERCENTAGE
Boo Ferriss BOS........ .806
H. Newhouser DET.... .743
Spud Chandler NY..... .714

EARNED RUN AVERAGE
H. Newhouser DET.... 1.94
Spud Chandler NY..... 2.10
Bob Feller CLE 2.18

STRIKEOUTS
Bob Feller CLE 348
Hal Newhouser DET ... 275
Tex Hughson BOS...... 172

SAVES
Bob Klinger BOS............. 9
Earl Caldwell CHI............ 8
Johnny Murphy NY 7

COMPLETE GAMES
Bob Feller CLE 36
Hal Newhouser DET..... 29
Boo Ferriss BOS........... 26

SHUTOUTS
Bob Feller CLE 10
four tied at....................... 6

GAMES PITCHED
Bob Feller CLE 48
Boo Ferriss BOS........... 40
Bob Savage PHI 40

INNINGS PITCHED
Bob Feller CLE 371
Hal Newhouser DET ... 292
Tex Hughson BOS...... 278

NATIONAL LEAGUE STANDINGS

1946 NL

	W	L	PCT	GB	R	OR	BA	FA	ERA
★ ST. LOUIS*	98	58	.628	—	712	545	.265	.980	3.01
BROOKLYN	96	60	.615	2	701	570	.260	.972	3.05
CHICAGO	82	71	.536	14.5	626	581	.254	.976	3.24
BOSTON	81	72	.529	15.5	630	592	.264	.972	3.35
PHILADELPHIA	69	85	.448	28	560	705	.258	.975	3.99
CINCINNATI	67	87	.435	30	523	570	.239	.975	3.08
PITTSBURGH	63	91	.409	34	552	668	.250	.970	3.72
NEW YORK	61	93	.396	36	612	685	.255	.973	3.92
					4916	4916	.256	.974	3.42

*Defeated Brooklyn in a playoff 2 games to 0

BATTING AVERAGE
Stan Musial STL .... .365
Johnny Hopp BOS ..... .333
Dixie Walker BKN .... .319

HITS
Stan Musial STL 228
Dixie Walker BKN 184
Enos Slaughter STL.... 183

DOUBLES
Stan Musial STL 50
Tommy Holmes BOS 35
Whitey Kurowski STL.... 32

TRIPLES
Stan Musial STL 20
Phil Cavarretta CHI....... 10
Pee Wee Reese BKN ... 10

HOME RUNS
Ralph Kiner PIT 23
Johnny Mize NY 22
Enos Slaughter STL...... 18

RUNS BATTED IN
Enos Slaughter STL.... 130
Dixie Walker BKN 116
Stan Musial STL 103

SLUGGING AVERAGE
Stan Musial STL .... .587
Del Ennis PHI .... .485
Enos Slaughter STL.... .465

STOLEN BASES
Pete Reiser BKN........... 34
Bert Haas CIN............... 22
Johnny Hopp BOS 21

RUNS SCORED
Stan Musial STL 124
Enos Slaughter STL.... 100
Eddie Stanky BKN 98

WINS
Howie Pollet STL 21
Johnny Sain BOS 20
Kirby Higbe BKN............ 17

WINNING PERCENTAGE
Murry Dickson STL .... .714
Kirby Higbe BKN......... .680
Howie Pollet STL .... .677

EARNED RUN AVERAGE
Howie Pollet STL 2.10
Johnny Sain BOS 2.21
Joe Beggs CIN............ 2.32

STRIKEOUTS
Johnny Schmitz CHI ... 135
Kirby Higbe BKN.......... 134
Johnny Sain BOS 129

SAVES
Ken Raffensberger PHI... 6
four tied at...................... 5

COMPLETE GAMES
Johnny Sain BOS 24
Howie Pollet STL 22
Dave Koslo NY 17

SHUTOUTS
Ewell Blackwell CIN......... 6
Harry Brecheen STL....... 5
three tied at..................... 4

GAMES PITCHED
Ken Trinkle NY............... 48
Murry Dickson STL 47
Hank Behrman BKN 47

INNINGS PITCHED
Howie Pollet STL 266
Dave Koslo NY 265
Johnny Sain BOS 265

AMERICAN LEAGUE STANDINGS

1947 AL

	W	L	PCT	GB	R	OR	BA	FA	ERA
★ NEW YORK	97	57	.630	—	794	568	.271	.981	3.39
DETROIT	85	69	.552	12	714	642	.258	.975	3.57
BOSTON	83	71	.539	14	720	669	.265	.977	3.81
CLEVELAND	80	74	.519	17	687	588	.259	.983	3.44
PHILADELPHIA	78	76	.506	19	633	614	.252	.976	3.51
CHICAGO	70	84	.455	27	553	661	.256	.975	3.64
WASHINGTON	64	90	.416	33	496	675	.241	.976	3.97
ST. LOUIS	59	95	.383	38	564	744	.241	.977	4.33
					5161	5161	.256	.977	3.71

BATTING AVERAGE
Ted Williams BOS...... .343
B. McCoskey PHI........ .328
Johnny Pesky BOS.... .324

HITS
Johnny Pesky BOS..... 207
George Kell DET......... 188
Ted Williams BOS....... 181

DOUBLES
Lou Boudreau CLE 45
Ted Williams BOS......... 40
Tommy Henrich NY 35

TRIPLES
Tommy Henrich NY 13
Mickey Vernon WAS.... 12
Dave Philley CHI........... 11

HOME RUNS
Ted Williams BOS....... 32
Joe Gordon CLE 29
Jeff Heath STL.............. 27

RUNS BATTED IN
Ted Williams BOS....... 114
Tommy Henrich NY 98
Joe DiMaggio NY.......... 97

SLUGGING AVERAGE
Ted Williams BOS...... .634
Joe DiMaggio NY....... .522
Joe Gordon CLE .... .496

STOLEN BASES
Bob Dillinger STL........... 34
Dave Philley CHI........... 21
two tied at 12

RUNS SCORED
Ted Williams BOS....... 125
Tommy Henrich NY 109
Johnny Pesky BOS..... 106

WINS
Bob Feller CLE 20
Allie Reynolds NY 19
Phil Marchildon PHI 19

WINNING PERCENTAGE
Allie Reynolds NY ...... .704
Joe Dobson BOS .... .692
Phil Marchildon PHI ... .679

EARNED RUN AVERAGE
Joe Haynes CHI.......... 2.42
Bob Feller CLE 2.68
Dick Fowler PHI 2.81

STRIKEOUTS
Bob Feller CLE 196
Hal Newhouser DET ... 176
W. Masterson WAS 135

SAVES
Joe Page NY.................. 17
Eddie Klieman CLE....... 17
Russ Christopher PHI... 12

COMPLETE GAMES
Hal Newhouser DET 24
Early Wynn WAS 22
Eddie Lopat CHI 22

SHUTOUTS
Bob Feller CLE 5
three tied at..................... 4

GAMES PITCHED
Eddie Klieman CLE........ 58
Joe Page NY.................. 56
Earl Johnson BOS 45

INNINGS PITCHED
Bob Feller CLE 299
Hal Newhouser DET ... 285
Phil Marchildon PHI 277

NATIONAL LEAGUE STANDINGS

1947 NL

	W	L	PCT	GB	R	OR	BA	FA	ERA
BROOKLYN	94	60	.610	—	774	668	.272	.978	3.82
ST. LOUIS	89	65	.578	5	780	634	.270	.979	3.53
BOSTON	86	68	.558	8	701	622	.275	.974	3.62
NEW YORK	81	73	.526	13	830	761	.271	.974	4.44
CINCINNATI	73	81	.474	21	681	755	.259	.977	4.41
CHICAGO	69	85	.448	25	567	722	.259	.975	4.04
PHILADELPHIA	62	92	.403	32	589	687	.258	.974	3.96
PITTSBURGH	62	92	.403	32	744	817	.261	.975	4.68
					5666	5666	.265	.976	4.06

BATTING AVERAGE
H. Walker STL, PHI ... .363
Bob Elliott BOS .... .317
Phil Cavarretta CHI ..... .314

HITS
T. Holmes BOS 191
H. Walker STL, PHI 186
two tied at 183

DOUBLES
Eddie Miller CIN 38
Bob Elliott BOS 35
two tied at 33

TRIPLES
H. Walker STL, PHI 16
Stan Musial STL 13
Enos Slaughter STL...... 13

HOME RUNS
Ralph Kiner PIT 51
Johnny Mize NY............ 51
Willard Marshall NY 36

RUNS BATTED IN
Johnny Mize NY.......... 138
Ralph Kiner PIT 127
Walker Cooper NY...... 122

SLUGGING AVERAGE
Ralph Kiner PIT .... .639
Johnny Mize NY.......... .614
Walker Cooper NY ..... .586

STOLEN BASES
Jackie Robinson BKN ... 29
Pete Reiser BKN............ 14
two tied at 13

RUNS SCORED
Johnny Mize NY.......... 137
J. Robinson BKN 125
Ralph Kiner PIT 118

WINS
Ewell Blackwell CIN 22
four tied at..................... 21

WINNING PERCENTAGE
Larry Jansen NY .... .808
G. Munger STL .... .762
Ewell Blackwell CIN ... .733

EARNED RUN AVERAGE
Warren Spahn BOS ... 2.33
Ewell Blackwell CIN ... 2.47
Ralph Branca BKN..... 2.67

STRIKEOUTS
Ewell Blackwell CIN 193
Ralph Branca BKN...... 148
Johnny Sain BOS 132

SAVES
Hugh Casey BKN........... 18
Harry Gumbert CIN....... 10
Ken Trinkle NY............... 10

COMPLETE GAMES
Ewell Blackwell CIN 23
Johnny Sain BOS 22
Warren Spahn BOS 22

SHUTOUTS
Warren Spahn BOS........ 7
George Munger STL 6
Ewell Blackwell CIN 6

GAMES PITCHED
Ken Trinkle NY............... 62
Kirby Higbe BKN, PIT ... 50
H. Behrman PIT, BKN... 50

INNINGS PITCHED
Warren Spahn BOS.... 290
Ralph Branca BKN...... 280
Ewell Blackwell CIN 273

AMERICAN LEAGUE STANDINGS

1948 AL

	W	L	PCT	GB	R	OR	BA	FA	ERA
★ CLEVELAND*	97	58	.626	—	840	568	.282	.982	3.22
BOSTON	96	59	.619	1	907	720	.274	.981	4.26
NEW YORK	94	60	.610	2.5	857	633	.278	.979	3.75
PHILADELPHIA	84	70	.545	12.5	729	735	.260	.981	4.43
DETROIT	78	76	.506	18.5	700	726	.267	.974	4.15
ST. LOUIS	59	94	.386	37	671	849	.271	.972	5.01
WASHINGTON	56	97	.366	40	578	796	.244	.974	4.65
CHICAGO	51	101	.336	44.5	559	814	.251	.974	4.89
					5841	5841	.266	.977	4.29

* Defeated Boston in a 1-game playoff

BATTING AVERAGE
Ted Williams BOS...... .369
Lou Boudreau CLE .... .355
Dale Mitchell CLE ...... .336

HITS
Bob Dillinger STL........ 207
Dale Mitchell CLE 204
Lou Boudreau CLE 199

DOUBLES
Ted Williams BOS........ 44
Tommy Henrich NY 42
Hank Majeski PHI 41

TRIPLES
Tommy Henrich NY 14
B. Stewart NY, WAS..... 13
three tied at.................. 11

HOME RUNS
Joe DiMaggio NY.......... 39
Joe Gordon CLE 32
Ken Keltner CLE 31

RUNS BATTED IN
Joe DiMaggio NY........ 155
Vern Stephens BOS ... 137
Ted Williams BOS....... 127

SLUGGING AVERAGE
Ted Williams BOS...... .615
Joe DiMaggio NY........ .598
Tommy Henrich NY ... .554

STOLEN BASES
Bob Dillinger STL........... 28
Gill Coan WAS.............. 23
Mickey Vernon WAS..... 15

RUNS SCORED
Tommy Henrich NY 138
Dom DiMaggio BOS ... 127
two tied at 124

WINS
Hal Newhouser DET..... 21
Gene Bearden CLE 20
Bob Lemon CLE 20

WINNING PERCENTAGE
Jack Kramer BOS ...... .783
Gene Bearden CLE ... .741
Vic Raschi NY............. .704

EARNED RUN AVERAGE
Gene Bearden CLE ... 2.43
R. Scarborough WAS. 2.82
Bob Lemon CLE 2.82

STRIKEOUTS
Bob Feller CLE 164
Bob Lemon CLE 147
Hal Newhouser DET ... 143

SAVES
R. Christopher CLE....... 17
Joe Page NY.................. 16
two tied at 10

COMPLETE GAMES
Bob Lemon CLE 20
Hal Newhouser DET..... 19
two tied at 18

SHUTOUTS
Bob Lemon CLE 10
Gene Bearden CLE 6
Vic Raschi NY................. 6

GAMES PITCHED
Joe Page NY.................. 55
Al Widmar STL............... 49
Frank Biscan STL 47

INNINGS PITCHED
Bob Lemon CLE 294
Bob Feller CLE 280
Hal Newhouser DET ... 272

NATIONAL LEAGUE STANDINGS

1948 NL

	W	L	PCT	GB	R	OR	BA	FA	ERA
BOSTON	91	62	.595	—	739	584	.275	.976	3.37
ST. LOUIS	85	69	.552	6.5	742	646	.263	.980	3.91
BROOKLYN	84	70	.545	7.5	744	667	.261	.973	3.75
PITTSBURGH	83	71	.539	8.5	706	699	.263	.977	4.15
NEW YORK	78	76	.506	13.5	780	704	.256	.974	3.93
PHILADELPHIA	66	88	.429	25.5	591	729	.259	.964	4.08
CINCINNATI	64	89	.418	27	588	752	.247	.973	4.47
CHICAGO	64	90	.416	27.5	597	706	.262	.972	4.00
					5487	5487	.261	.974	3.95

BATTING AVERAGE
Stan Musial STL .... .376
Richie Ashburn PHI .... .333
T. Holmes BOS .... .325

HITS
Stan Musial STL 230
T. Holmes BOS 190
Stan Rojek PIT............ 186

DOUBLES
Stan Musial STL 46
Del Ennis PHI 40
Alvin Dark BOS............. 39

TRIPLES
Stan Musial STL 18
Johnny Hopp PIT 12
Enos Slaughter STL...... 11

HOME RUNS
Johnny Mize NY............. 40
Ralph Kiner PIT 40
Stan Musial STL 39

RUNS BATTED IN
Stan Musial STL 131
Johnny Mize NY........... 125
Ralph Kiner PIT 123

SLUGGING AVERAGE
Stan Musial STL .... .702
Johnny Mize NY.......... .564
Sid Gordon NY............ .537

STOLEN BASES
Richie Ashburn PHI 32
Pee Wee Reese BKN ... 25
Stan Rojek PIT.............. 24

RUNS SCORED
Stan Musial STL 135
Whitey Lockman NY ... 117
Johnny Mize NY........... 110

WINS
Johnny Sain BOS 24
Harry Brecheen STL..... 20
two tied at 18

WINNING PERCENTAGE
H. Brecheen STL .... .741
Sheldon Jones NY ..... .667
Johnny Sain BOS .... .615

EARNED RUN AVERAGE
H. Brecheen STL 2.24
Dutch Leonard PHI 2.51
Johnny Sain BOS 2.60

STRIKEOUTS
Harry Brecheen STL... 149
Rex Barney BKN......... 138
Johnny Sain BOS 137

SAVES
Harry Gumbert CIN....... 17
Ted Wilks STL 13
Kirby Higbe PIT.............. 10

COMPLETE GAMES
Johnny Sain BOS 28
Harry Brecheen STL..... 21
Johnny Schmitz CHI 18

SHUTOUTS
Harry Brecheen STL........ 7
four tied at........................ 4

GAMES PITCHED
Harry Gumbert CIN....... 61
Ted Wilks STL 57
Kirby Higbe PIT.............. 56

INNINGS PITCHED
Johnny Sain BOS 315
Larry Jansen NY 277
Warren Spahn BOS.... 257

AMERICAN LEAGUE STANDINGS

1949 AL

	W	L	PCT	GB	R	OR	BA	FA	ERA
★ NEW YORK	97	57	.630	—	829	637	.269	.977	3.69
BOSTON	96	58	.623	1	896	667	.282	.980	3.97
CLEVELAND	89	65	.578	8	675	574	.260	.983	3.36
DETROIT	87	67	.565	10	751	655	.267	.978	3.77
PHILADELPHIA	81	73	.526	16	726	725	.260	.976	4.23
CHICAGO	63	91	.409	34	648	737	.257	.977	4.30
ST. LOUIS	53	101	.344	44	667	913	.254	.971	5.21
WASHINGTON	50	104	.325	47	584	868	.254	.973	5.10
					5776	5776	.263	.977	4.20

BATTING AVERAGE
George Kell DET......... .343
Ted Williams BOS...... .343
Bob Dillinger STL........ .324

HITS
Dale Mitchell CLE 203
Ted Williams BOS........ 194
Dom DiMaggio BOS ... 186

DOUBLES
Ted Williams BOS.......... 39
George Kell DET............ 38
Dom DiMaggio BOS 34

TRIPLES
Dale Mitchell CLE 23
Bob Dillinger STL........... 13
Elmer Valo PHI 12

HOME RUNS
Ted Williams BOS.......... 43
Vern Stephens BOS 39
four tied at..................... 24

RUNS BATTED IN
Vern Stephens BOS ... 159
Ted Williams BOS....... 159
Vic Wertz DET 133

SLUGGING AVERAGE
Ted Williams BOS....... .650
V. Stephens BOS........ .539
Tommy Henrich NY ... .526

STOLEN BASES
Bob Dillinger STL.......... 20
Phil Rizzuto NY 18
Elmer Valo PHI 14

RUNS SCORED
Ted Williams BOS....... 150
Eddie Joost PHI 128
Dom DiMaggio BOS ... 126

WINS
Mel Parnell BOS 25
Ellis Kinder BOS 23
Bob Lemon CLE 22

WINNING PERCENTAGE
Ellis Kinder BOS .... .793
Mel Parnell BOS .... .781
Allie Reynolds NY ...... .739

EARNED RUN AVERAGE
Mike Garcia CLE......... 2.36
Mel Parnell BOS 2.77
Virgil Trucks DET........ 2.81

STRIKEOUTS
Virgil Trucks DET......... 153
Hal Newhouser DET ... 144
two tied at 138

SAVES
Joe Page NY.................. 27
Al Benton CLE 10
Tom Ferrick STL 6

COMPLETE GAMES
Mel Parnell BOS 27
Bob Lemon CLE 22
Hal Newhouser DET 22

SHUTOUTS
Ellis Kinder BOS 6
Virgil Trucks DET............. 6
Mike Garcia CLE.............. 5

GAMES PITCHED
Joe Page NY.................. 60
Dick Welteroth WAS 52
Tom Ferrick STL 50

INNINGS PITCHED
Mel Parnell BOS 295
Hal Newhouser DET ... 292
Bob Lemon CLE 280

NATIONAL LEAGUE STANDINGS

1949 NL

	W	L	PCT	GB	R	OR	BA	FA	ERA
BROOKLYN	97	57	.630	—	879	651	.274	.980	3.80
ST. LOUIS	96	58	.623	1	766	616	.277	.976	3.44
PHILADELPHIA	81	73	.526	16	662	668	.254	.974	3.89
BOSTON	75	79	.487	22	706	719	.258	.976	3.99
NEW YORK	73	81	.474	24	736	693	.261	.973	3.82
PITTSBURGH	71	83	.461	26	681	760	.259	.978	4.57
CINCINNATI	62	92	.403	35	627	770	.260	.977	4.34
CHICAGO	61	93	.396	36	593	773	.256	.970	4.50
					5650	5650	.262	.975	4.04

BATTING AVERAGE
J. Robinson BKN .... .342
Stan Musial STL .... .338
Enos Slaughter STL... .336

HITS
Stan Musial STL 207
J. Robinson BKN 203
Bobby Thomson NY.... 198

DOUBLES
Stan Musial STL 41
Del Ennis PHI 39
two tied at 38

TRIPLES
Stan Musial STL 13
Enos Slaughter STL..... 13
Jackie Robinson BKN... 12

HOME RUNS
Ralph Kiner PIT 54
Stan Musial STL 36
Hank Sauer CIN, CHI ... 31

RUNS BATTED IN
Ralph Kiner PIT 127
J. Robinson BKN 124
Stan Musial STL 123

SLUGGING AVERAGE
Ralph Kiner PIT .... .658
Stan Musial STL .... .624
J. Robinson BKN .... .528

STOLEN BASES
Jackie Robinson BKN... 37
P. Reese BKN................ 26
four tied at..................... 12

RUNS SCORED
P. Reese BKN.............. 132
Stan Musial STL 128
J. Robinson BKN 122

WINS
Warren Spahn BOS...... 21
Howie Pollet STL 20
K. Raffensberger CIN ... 18

WINNING PERCENTAGE
Preacher Roe BKN .... .714
Howie Pollet STL .... .690
two tied at .... .680

EARNED RUN AVERAGE
Dave Koslo NY 2.50
Gerry Staley STL 2.73
Howie Pollet STL 2.77

STRIKEOUTS
Warren Spahn BOS.... 151
D. Newcombe BKN..... 149
Larry Jansen NY 113

SAVES
Ted Wilks STL 9
Jim Konstanty PHI 7
Nels Potter BOS 7

COMPLETE GAMES
Warren Spahn BOS...... 25
K. Raffensberger CIN ... 20
Don Newcombe BKN.... 19

SHUTOUTS
four tied at....................... 5

GAMES PITCHED
Ted Wilks STL 59
Jim Konstanty PHI 53
Erv Palica BKN 49

INNINGS PITCHED
Warren Spahn BOS.... 302
K. Raffensberger CIN . 284
Larry Jansen NY 260

AMERICAN LEAGUE STANDINGS

1950 AL

	W	L	PCT	GB	R	OR	BA	FA	ERA
★ NEW YORK	98	56	.636	—	914	691	.282	.980	4.15
DETROIT	95	59	.617	3	837	713	.282	.981	4.12
BOSTON	94	60	.610	4	1027	804	.302	.981	4.88
CLEVELAND	92	62	.597	6	806	654	.269	.978	3.75
WASHINGTON	67	87	.435	31	690	813	.260	.972	4.66
CHICAGO	60	94	.390	38	625	749	.260	.977	4.41
ST. LOUIS	58	96	.377	40	684	916	.246	.967	5.20
PHILADELPHIA	52	102	.338	46	670	913	.261	.974	5.49
					6253	6253	.271	.976	4.58

BATTING AVERAGE
Billy Goodman BOS ... .354
George Kell DET .... .340
Dom DiMaggio BOS .. .328

HITS
George Kell DET 218
Phil Rizzuto NY 200
Dom DiMaggio BOS ... 193

DOUBLES
George Kell DET 56
Vic Wertz DET 37
Phil Rizzuto NY 36

TRIPLES
Dom DiMaggio BOS 11
Bobby Doerr BOS 11
Hoot Evers DET 11

HOME RUNS
Al Rosen CLE 37
Walt Dropo BOS 34
Joe DiMaggio NY 32

RUNS BATTED IN
Vern Stephens BOS ... 144
Walt Dropo BOS 144
Yogi Berra NY 124

SLUGGING AVERAGE
Joe DiMaggio NY .... .585
Walt Dropo BOS .... .583
Hoot Evers DET .... .551

STOLEN BASES
Dom DiMaggio BOS 15
Elmer Valo PHI 12
Phil Rizzuto NY 12

RUNS SCORED
Dom DiMaggio BOS ... 131
Vern Stephens BOS ... 125
Phil Rizzuto NY 125

WINS
Bob Lemon CLE 23
Vic Raschi NY 21
Art Houtteman DET 19

WINNING PERCENTAGE
Vic Raschi NY .... .724
Eddie Lopat NY .... .692
Early Wynn CLE .... .692

EARNED RUN AVERAGE
Early Wynn CLE 3.20
Ned Garver STL 3.39
Bob Feller CLE 3.43

STRIKEOUTS
Bob Lemon CLE 170
Allie Reynolds NY 160
Vic Raschi NY 155

SAVES
Mickey Harris WAS 15
Joe Page NY 13
Tom Ferrick STL, NY 11

COMPLETE GAMES
Ned Garver STL 22
Bob Lemon CLE 22
two tied at 21

SHUTOUTS
Art Houtteman DET 4

GAMES PITCHED
Mickey Harris WAS 53
Ellis Kinder BOS 48
three tied at 46

INNINGS PITCHED
Bob Lemon CLE 288
Art Houtteman DET 275
Ned Garver STL 260

NATIONAL LEAGUE STANDINGS

1950 NL

	W	L	PCT	GB	R	OR	BA	FA	ERA
PHILADELPHIA	91	63	.591	—	722	624	.265	.975	3.50
BROOKLYN	89	65	.578	2	847	724	.272	.979	4.28
NEW YORK	86	68	.558	5	735	643	.258	.977	3.71
BOSTON	83	71	.539	8	785	736	.263	.970	4.14
ST. LOUIS	78	75	.510	12.5	693	670	.259	.978	3.97
CINCINNATI	66	87	.431	24.5	654	734	.260	.976	4.32
CHICAGO	64	89	.418	26.5	643	772	.248	.968	4.28
PITTSBURGH	57	96	.373	33.5	681	857	.264	.977	4.96
					5760	5760	.261	.975	4.14

BATTING AVERAGE
Stan Musial STL .... .346
J. Robinson BKN .... .328
Duke Snider BKN....... .321

HITS
Duke Snider BKN........ 199
Stan Musial STL 192
Carl Furillo BKN 189

DOUBLES
R. Schoendienst STL.... 43
Stan Musial STL 41
Jackie Robinson BKN ... 39

TRIPLES
Richie Ashburn PHI 14
Gus Bell PIT.................. 11
Duke Snider BKN.......... 10

HOME RUNS
Ralph Kiner PIT 47
Andy Pafko CHI 36
two tied at 32

RUNS BATTED IN
Del Ennis PHI 126
Ralph Kiner PIT 118
Gil Hodges BKN........... 113

SLUGGING AVERAGE
Stan Musial STL .... .596
Andy Pafko CHI .... .591
Ralph Kiner PIT .... .590

STOLEN BASES
Sam Jethroe BOS......... 35
Pee Wee Reese BKN ... 17
Duke Snider BKN.......... 16

RUNS SCORED
Earl Torgeson BOS..... 120
Eddie Stanky NY......... 115
Ralph Kiner PIT 112

WINS
Warren Spahn BOS...... 21
Robin Roberts PHI........ 20
Johnny Sain BOS 20

WINNING PERCENTAGE
Sal Maglie NY .... .818
Jim Konstanty PHI ...... .696
Curt Simmons PHI...... .680

EARNED RUN AVERAGE
Sal Maglie NY 2.71
Ewell Blackwell CIN 2.97
Larry Jansen NY 3.01

STRIKEOUTS
Warren Spahn BOS.... 191
Ewell Blackwell CIN.... 188
Larry Jansen NY 161

SAVES
Jim Konstanty PHI 22
Bill Werle PIT 8
two tied at 7

COMPLETE GAMES
Vern Bickford BOS......... 27
Warren Spahn BOS...... 25
Johnny Sain BOS 25

SHUTOUTS
four tied at........................ 5

GAMES PITCHED
Jim Konstanty PHI 74
Murry Dickson PIT 51
Bill Werle PIT 48

INNINGS PITCHED
Vern Bickford BOS....... 312
Robin Roberts PHI....... 304
Warren Spahn BOS.... 293

AMERICAN LEAGUE STANDINGS

1951 AL

	W	L	PCT	GB	R	OR	BA	FA	ERA
★ NEW YORK	98	56	.636	—	798	621	.269	.975	3.56
CLEVELAND	93	61	.604	5	696	594	.256	.978	3.38
BOSTON	87	67	.565	11	804	725	.266	.977	4.14
CHICAGO	81	73	.526	17	714	644	.270	.975	3.50
DETROIT	73	81	.474	25	685	741	.265	.973	4.29
PHILADELPHIA	70	84	.455	28	736	745	.262	.978	4.47
WASHINGTON	62	92	.403	36	672	764	.263	.973	4.49
ST. LOUIS	52	102	.338	46	611	882	.247	.971	5.18
					5716	5716	.262	.975	4.12

BATTING AVERAGE
Ferris Fain PHI............ .344
M. Minoso CLE, CHI .. .326
George Kell DET........ .319

HITS
George Kell DET......... 191
Dom DiMaggio BOS ... 189
Nellie Fox CHI.............. 189

DOUBLES
Sam Mele WAS 36
George Kell DET............ 36
Eddie Yost WAS 36

TRIPLES
M. Minoso CLE, CHI...... 14
Nellie Fox CHI................ 12
R. Coleman STL, CHI.... 12

HOME RUNS
Gus Zernial CHI, PHI.... 33
Ted Williams BOS......... 30
Eddie Robinson CHI 29

RUNS BATTED IN
G. Zernial CHI, PHI..... 129
Ted Williams BOS....... 126
Eddie Robinson CHI ... 117

SLUGGING AVERAGE
Ted Williams BOS...... .556
Larry Doby CLE .... .512
Gus Zernial CHI, PHI. .511

STOLEN BASES
M. Minoso CLE, CHI..... 31
Jim Busby CHI............... 26
Phil Rizzuto NY............. 18

RUNS SCORED
Dom DiMaggio BOS ... 113
M. Minoso CLE, CHI... 112
two tied at 109

WINS
Bob Feller CLE 22
Eddie Lopat NY............ 21
Vic Raschi NY............... 21

WINNING PERCENTAGE
Bob Feller CLE .... .733
Eddie Lopat NY.......... .700
Allie Reynolds NY...... .680

EARNED RUN AVERAGE
S. Rogovin DET, CHI. 2.78
Eddie Lopat NY.......... 2.91
Early Wynn CLE 3.02

STRIKEOUTS
Vic Raschi NY............. 164
Early Wynn CLE 133
Bob Lemon CLE 132

SAVES
Ellis Kinder BOS 14
Carl Scheib PHI 10
Lou Brissie PHI, CLE....... 9

COMPLETE GAMES
Ned Garver STL............. 24
Early Wynn CLE 21
Eddie Lopat NY............. 20

SHUTOUTS
Allie Reynolds NY 7
three tied at..................... 4

GAMES PITCHED
Ellis Kinder BOS 63
Lou Brissie PHI, CLE.... 56
Mike Garcia CLE............ 47

INNINGS PITCHED
Early Wynn CLE 274
Bob Lemon CLE 263
Vic Raschi NY.............. 258

NATIONAL LEAGUE STANDINGS

1951 NL

	W	L	PCT	GB	R	OR	BA	FA	ERA
NEW YORK*	98	59	.624	—	781	641	.260	.972	3.48
BROOKLYN	97	60	.618	1	855	672	.275	.979	3.88
ST. LOUIS	81	73	.526	15.5	683	671	.264	.980	3.95
BOSTON	76	78	.494	20.5	723	662	.262	.976	3.75
PHILADELPHIA	73	81	.474	23.5	648	644	.260	.977	3.81
CINCINNATI	68	86	.442	28.5	559	667	.248	.977	3.70
PITTSBURGH	64	90	.416	32.5	689	845	.258	.972	4.79
CHICAGO	62	92	.403	34.5	614	750	.250	.971	4.34
					5552	5552	.260	.975	3.96

*Defeated Brooklyn in a playoff 2 games to 1

BATTING AVERAGE
Stan Musial STL .... .355
Richie Ashburn PHI ... .344
J. Robinson BKN .... .338

HITS
Richie Ashburn PHI 221
Stan Musial STL 205
Carl Furillo BKN 197

DOUBLES
Alvin Dark NY 41
Ted Kluszewski CIN...... 35
two tied at 33

TRIPLES
Stan Musial STL 12
Gus Bell PIT.................. 12
Monte Irvin NY 11

HOME RUNS
Ralph Kiner PIT 42
Gil Hodges BKN............ 40
Roy Campanella BKN... 33

RUNS BATTED IN
Monte Irvin NY 121
Sid Gordon BOS 109
Ralph Kiner PIT 109

SLUGGING AVERAGE
Ralph Kiner PIT .... .627
Stan Musial STL .... .614
R. Campanella BKN.... .590

STOLEN BASES
Sam Jethroe BOS......... 35
Richie Ashburn PHI 29
Jackie Robinson BKN... 25

RUNS SCORED
Stan Musial STL 124
Ralph Kiner PIT 124
Gil Hodges BKN........... 118

WINS
Sal Maglie NY 23
Larry Jansen NY 23
two tied at 22

WINNING PERCENTAGE
Preacher Roe BKN .... .880
Sal Maglie NY .... .793
D. Newcombe BKN.... .690

EARNED RUN AVERAGE
Chet Nichols BOS...... 2.88
Sal Maglie NY 2.93
Warren Spahn BOS ... 2.98

STRIKEOUTS
Warren Spahn BOS 164
D. Newcombe BKN..... 164
Sal Maglie NY 146

SAVES
Ted Wilks STL, PIT........ 13
Frank Smith CIN 11
Jim Konstanty PHI 9

COMPLETE GAMES
Warren Spahn BOS 26
Robin Roberts PHI........ 22
Sal Maglie NY 22

SHUTOUTS
Warren Spahn BOS 7
Robin Roberts PHI.......... 6
K. Raffensberger CIN 5

GAMES PITCHED
Ted Wilks STL, PIT........ 65
Bill Werle PIT................. 59
Jim Konstanty PHI 58

INNINGS PITCHED
Robin Roberts PHI...... 315
Warren Spahn BOS.... 311
Sal Maglie NY 298

AMERICAN LEAGUE STANDINGS

1952 AL

	W	L	PCT	GB	R	OR	BA	FA	ERA
★ NEW YORK	95	59	.617	—	727	557	.267	.979	3.14
CLEVELAND	93	61	.604	2	763	606	.262	.975	3.32
CHICAGO	81	73	.526	14	610	568	.252	.980	3.25
PHILADELPHIA	79	75	.513	16	664	723	.253	.977	4.15
WASHINGTON	78	76	.506	17	598	608	.239	.978	3.37
BOSTON	76	78	.494	19	668	658	.255	.976	3.80
ST. LOUIS	64	90	.416	31	604	733	.250	.974	4.12
DETROIT	50	104	.325	45	557	738	.243	.975	4.25
					5191	5191	.253	.977	3.67

BATTING AVERAGE
Ferris Fain PHI............ .327
Dale Mitchell CLE ...... .323
Mickey Mantle NY...... .311

HITS
Nellie Fox CHI.............. 192
Bobby Avila CLE......... 179
two tied at 176

DOUBLES
Ferris Fain PHI............. 43
Mickey Mantle NY......... 37
two tied at 33

TRIPLES
Bobby Avila CLE............ 11
three tied at................... 10

HOME RUNS
Larry Doby CLE 32
Luke Easter CLE........... 31
Yogi Berra NY................ 30

RUNS BATTED IN
Al Rosen CLE 105
Eddie Robinson CHI ... 104
Larry Doby CLE 104

SLUGGING AVERAGE
Larry Doby CLE .... .541
Mickey Mantle NY...... .530
Al Rosen CLE .... .524

STOLEN BASES
Minnie Minoso CHI 22
Jim Rivera STL, CHI..... 21
J. Jensen NY, WAS 18

RUNS SCORED
Larry Doby CLE 104
Bobby Avila CLE.......... 102
Al Rosen CLE 101

WINS
Bobby Shantz PHI 24
Early Wynn CLE 23
two tied at 22

WINNING PERCENTAGE
Bobby Shantz PHI ..... .774
Vic Raschi NY............. .727
Allie Reynolds NY ...... .714

EARNED RUN AVERAGE
Allie Reynolds NY 2.06
Mike Garcia CLE........ 2.37
Bobby Shantz PHI 2.48

STRIKEOUTS
Allie Reynolds NY 160
Early Wynn CLE 153
Bobby Shantz PHI 152

SAVES
Harry Dorish CHI 11
Satchel Paige STL........ 10
Johnny Sain NY.............. 7

COMPLETE GAMES
Bob Lemon CLE 28
Bobby Shantz PHI 27
Allie Reynolds NY 24

SHUTOUTS
Allie Reynolds NY 6
Mike Garcia CLE............. 6
two tied at 5

GAMES PITCHED
Bill Kennedy CHI............ 47
Mike Garcia CLE............ 46
Satchel Paige STL......... 46

INNINGS PITCHED
Bob Lemon CLE 310
Mike Garcia CLE.......... 292
Early Wynn CLE 286

NATIONAL LEAGUE STANDINGS

1952 NL

	W	L	PCT	GB	R	OR	BA	FA	ERA
BROOKLYN	96	57	.627	—	775	603	.262	.982	3.53
NEW YORK	92	62	.597	4.5	722	639	.256	.974	3.59
ST. LOUIS	88	66	.571	8.5	677	630	.267	.977	3.66
PHILADELPHIA	87	67	.565	9.5	657	552	.260	.975	3.07
CHICAGO	77	77	.500	19.5	628	631	.264	.976	3.58
CINCINNATI	69	85	.448	27.5	615	659	.249	.982	4.01
BOSTON	64	89	.418	32	569	651	.233	.975	3.78
PITTSBURGH	42	112	.273	54.5	515	793	.231	.970	4.65
					5158	5158	.253	.976	3.73

BATTING AVERAGE
Stan Musial STL .... .336
F. Baumholtz CHI .... .325
Ted Kluszewski CIN ... .320

HITS
Stan Musial STL 194
R. Schoendienst STL.. 188
Bobby Adams CIN 180

DOUBLES
Stan Musial STL 42
R. Schoendienst STL...... 40
Roy McMillan CIN 32

TRIPLES
Bobby Thomson NY...... 14
Enos Slaughter STL...... 12
Ted Kluszewski CIN...... 11

HOME RUNS
Hank Sauer CHI............. 37
Ralph Kiner PIT............. 37
Gil Hodges BKN............. 32

RUNS BATTED IN
Hank Sauer CHI........... 121
Bobby Thomson NY.... 108
Del Ennis PHI 107

SLUGGING AVERAGE
Stan Musial STL .... .538
Hank Sauer CHI.......... .531
Ted Kluszewski CIN... .509

STOLEN BASES
Pee Wee Reese BKN ... 30
Sam Jethroe BOS......... 28
Jackie Robinson BKN... 24

RUNS SCORED
Stan Musial STL 105
Solly Hemus STL 105
J. Robinson BKN 104

WINS
Robin Roberts PHI........ 28
Sal Maglie NY 18
three tied at.................. 17

WINNING PERCENTAGE
Hoyt Wilhelm NY......... .833
Robin Roberts PHI...... .800
Joe Black BKN............ .789

EARNED RUN AVERAGE
Hoyt Wilhelm NY......... 2.43
Warren Hacker CHI ... 2.58
Robin Roberts PHI..... 2.59

STRIKEOUTS
Warren Spahn BOS.... 183
Bob Rush CHI.............. 157
Robin Roberts PHI...... 148

SAVES
Al Brazle STL................. 16
Joe Black BKN............... 15
two tied at 11

COMPLETE GAMES
Robin Roberts PHI........ 30
Murry Dickson PIT 21
Warren Spahn BOS...... 19

SHUTOUTS
Curt Simmons PHI.......... 6
K. Raffensberger CIN 6

GAMES PITCHED
Hoyt Wilhelm NY........... 71
Joe Black BKN.............. 56
Eddie Yuhas STL........... 54

INNINGS PITCHED
Robin Roberts PHI..... 330
Warren Spahn BOS.... 290
Murry Dickson PIT 278

AMERICAN LEAGUE STANDINGS

1953 AL

	W	L	PCT	GB	R	OR	BA	FA	ERA
★ NEW YORK	99	52	.656	—	801	547	.273	.979	3.20
CLEVELAND	92	62	.597	8.5	770	627	.270	.979	3.64
CHICAGO	89	65	.578	11.5	716	592	.258	.980	3.41
BOSTON	84	69	.549	16	656	632	.264	.975	3.58
WASHINGTON	76	76	.500	23.5	687	614	.263	.979	3.66
DETROIT	60	94	.390	40.5	695	923	.266	.978	5.25
PHILADELPHIA	59	95	.383	41.5	632	799	.256	.977	4.67
ST. LOUIS	54	100	.351	46.5	555	778	.249	.974	4.48
					5512	5512	.262	.978	3.99

BATTING AVERAGE
M. Vernon WAS .... .337
Al Rosen CLE .... .336
Billy Goodman BOS ... .313

HITS
Harvey Kuenn DET 209
Mickey Vernon WAS ... 205
Al Rosen CLE 201

DOUBLES
Mickey Vernon WAS 43
George Kell BOS 41
Sammy White BOS 34

TRIPLES
Jim Rivera CHI 16
Mickey Vernon WAS 11
two tied at 9

HOME RUNS
Al Rosen CLE 43
Gus Zernial PHI 42
Larry Doby CLE 29

RUNS BATTED IN
Al Rosen CLE 145
Mickey Vernon WAS ... 115
R. Boone CLE, DET 114

SLUGGING AVERAGE
Al Rosen CLE .... .613
Gus Zernial PHI .... .559
Yogi Berra NY .... .523

STOLEN BASES
Minnie Minoso CHI 25
Jim Rivera CHI 22
Jackie Jensen WAS 18

RUNS SCORED
Al Rosen CLE 115
Eddie Yost WAS 107
Mickey Mantle NY 105

WINS
Bob Porterfield WAS 22
Bob Lemon CLE 21
Mel Parnell BOS 21

WINNING PERCENTAGE
Eddie Lopat NY .... .800
Whitey Ford NY .... .750
Mel Parnell BOS .... .724

EARNED RUN AVERAGE
Eddie Lopat NY 2.42
Billy Pierce CHI 2.72
V. Trucks STL, CHI 2.93

STRIKEOUTS
Billy Pierce CHI 186
V. Trucks STL, CHI 149
Early Wynn CLE 138

SAVES
Ellis Kinder BOS 27
Harry Dorish CHI 18
Allie Reynolds NY 13

COMPLETE GAMES
Bob Porterfield WAS 24
Bob Lemon CLE 23
Mike Garcia CLE 21

SHUTOUTS
Bob Porterfield WAS 9
Billy Pierce CHI 7
three tied at 5

GAMES PITCHED
Ellis Kinder BOS 69
Marlan Stuart STL 60
Morrie Martin PHI 58

INNINGS PITCHED
Bob Lemon CLE 287
Mike Garcia CLE 272
Billy Pierce CHI 271

NATIONAL LEAGUE STANDINGS

1953 NL

	W	L	PCT	GB	R	OR	BA	FA	ERA
BROOKLYN	105	49	.682	—	955	689	.285	.980	4.10
MILWAUKEE	92	62	.597	13	738	589	.266	.976	3.30
PHILADELPHIA	83	71	.539	22	716	666	.265	.975	3.80
ST. LOUIS	83	71	.539	22	768	713	.273	.977	4.23
NEW YORK	70	84	.455	35	768	747	.271	.975	4.25
CINCINNATI	68	86	.442	37	714	788	.261	.978	4.64
CHICAGO	65	89	.422	40	633	835	.260	.967	4.79
PITTSBURGH	50	104	.325	55	622	887	.247	.973	5.22
					5914	5914	.266	.975	4.29

BATTING AVERAGE
Carl Furillo BKN .... .344
R. Schoendienst STL. .342
Stan Musial STL .... .337

HITS
Richie Ashburn PHI 205
Stan Musial STL 200
Duke Snider BKN......... 198

DOUBLES
Stan Musial STL 53
Alvin Dark NY 41
two tied at 38

TRIPLES
Jim Gilliam BKN............. 17
Bill Bruton MIL 14
two tied at 11

HOME RUNS
Eddie Mathews MIL 47
Duke Snider BKN........... 42
Roy Campanella BKN... 41

RUNS BATTED IN
R. Campanella BKN.... 142
Eddie Mathews MIL 135
Duke Snider BKN......... 126

SLUGGING AVERAGE
Duke Snider BKN........ .627
Eddie Mathews MIL ... .627
R. Campanella BKN... .611

STOLEN BASES
Bill Bruton MIL................ 26
Pee Wee Reese BKN ... 22
Jim Gilliam BKN............. 21

RUNS SCORED
Duke Snider BKN........ 132
Stan Musial STL 127
Alvin Dark NY 126

WINS
Warren Spahn MIL........ 23
Robin Roberts PHI........ 23
two tied at 20

WINNING PERCENTAGE
Carl Erskine BKN........ .769
Warren Spahn MIL...... .767
two tied at .... .750

EARNED RUN AVERAGE
Warren Spahn MIL..... 2.10
Robin Roberts PHI..... 2.75
Harvey Haddix STL.... 3.06

STRIKEOUTS
Robin Roberts PHI...... 198
Carl Erskine BKN........ 187
V. Mizell STL................ 173

SAVES
Al Brazle STL 18
Hoyt Wilhelm NY........... 15
Jim Hughes BKN 9

COMPLETE GAMES
Robin Roberts PHI........ 33
Warren Spahn MIL........ 24
two tied at 19

SHUTOUTS
Harvey Haddix STL......... 6
Robin Roberts PHI.......... 5
Warren Spahn MIL.......... 5

GAMES PITCHED
Hoyt Wilhelm NY........... 68
Al Brazle STL................. 60
Johnny Hetki PIT 54

INNINGS PITCHED
Robin Roberts PHI...... 347
Warren Spahn MIL...... 266
Harvey Haddix STL..... 253

AMERICAN LEAGUE STANDINGS

1954 AL

	W	L	PCT	GB	R	OR	BA	FA	ERA
CLEVELAND	111	43	.721	—	746	504	.262	.979	2.78
NEW YORK	103	51	.669	8	805	563	.268	.979	3.26
CHICAGO	94	60	.610	17	711	521	.267	.982	3.05
BOSTON	69	85	.448	42	700	728	.266	.972	4.01
DETROIT	68	86	.442	43	584	664	.258	.978	3.81
WASHINGTON	66	88	.429	45	632	680	.246	.977	3.84
BALTIMORE	54	100	.351	57	483	668	.251	.975	3.88
PHILADELPHIA	51	103	.331	60	542	875	.236	.972	5.18
					5203	5203	.257	.977	3.72

BATTING AVERAGE
Bobby Avila CLE .... .341
Minnie Minoso CHI .... .320
Irv Noren NY .... .319

HITS
Nellie Fox CHI 201
Harvey Kuenn DET 201
Bobby Avila CLE 189

DOUBLES
Mickey Vernon WAS 33
Minnie Minoso CHI 29
Al Smith CLE 29

TRIPLES
Minnie Minoso CHI 18
Pete Runnels WAS 15
Mickey Vernon WAS 14

HOME RUNS
Larry Doby CLE 32
Ted Williams BOS 29
Mickey Mantle NY 27

RUNS BATTED IN
Larry Doby CLE 126
Yogi Berra NY 125
Jackie Jensen BOS 117

SLUGGING AVERAGE
Minnie Minoso CHI .... .535
Mickey Mantle NY ...... .525
Al Rosen CLE .... .506

STOLEN BASES
Jackie Jensen BOS 22
Jim Rivera CHI 18
Minnie Minoso CHI 18

RUNS SCORED
Mickey Mantle NY 129
Minnie Minoso CHI 119
Bobby Avila CLE 112

WINS
Bob Lemon CLE 23
Early Wynn CLE 23
Bob Grim NY 20

WINNING PERCENTAGE
S. Consuegra CHI ...... .842
Bob Grim NY .... .769
Bob Lemon CLE .... .767

EARNED RUN AVERAGE
Mike Garcia CLE 2.64
Bob Lemon CLE 2.72
Early Wynn CLE 2.73

STRIKEOUTS
Bob Turley BAL 185
Early Wynn CLE 155
Virgil Trucks CHI 152

SAVES
Johnny Sain NY 22
Ellis Kinder BOS 15
Ray Narleski CLE 13

COMPLETE GAMES
Bob Porterfield WAS 21
Bob Lemon CLE 21
Early Wynn CLE 20

SHUTOUTS
Virgil Trucks CHI 5
Mike Garcia CLE 5

GAMES PITCHED
S. Dixon WAS, PHI 54
three tied at 48

INNINGS PITCHED
Early Wynn CLE 271
Virgil Trucks CHI 265
Mike Garcia CLE 259

NATIONAL LEAGUE STANDINGS

1954 NL

	W	L	PCT	GB	R	OR	BA	FA	ERA
★ NEW YORK	97	57	.630	—	732	550	.264	.975	3.09
BROOKLYN	92	62	.597	5	778	740	.270	.978	4.31
MILWAUKEE	89	65	.578	8	670	556	.265	.981	3.19
PHILADELPHIA	75	79	.487	22	659	614	.267	.975	3.59
CINCINNATI	74	80	.481	23	729	763	.262	.977	4.50
ST. LOUIS	72	82	.468	25	799	790	.281	.976	4.50
CHICAGO	64	90	.416	33	700	766	.263	.974	4.51
PITTSBURGH	53	101	.344	44	557	845	.248	.971	4.92
					5624	5624	.265	.976	4.07

BATTING AVERAGE
Willie Mays NY .... .345
Don Mueller NY .... .342
Duke Snider BKN .... .341

HITS
Don Mueller NY 212
Duke Snider BKN 199
two tied at 195

DOUBLES
Stan Musial STL 41
three tied at 39

TRIPLES
Willie Mays NY 13
Granny Hamner PHI 11
Duke Snider BKN 10

HOME RUNS
Ted Kluszewski CIN 49
Gil Hodges BKN 42
two tied at 41

RUNS BATTED IN
Ted Kluszewski CIN 141
Gil Hodges BKN 130
Duke Snider BKN 130

SLUGGING AVERAGE
Willie Mays NY .... .667
Duke Snider BKN .... .647
Ted Kluszewski CIN .. .642

STOLEN BASES
Bill Bruton MIL 34
Johnny Temple CIN 21
Dee Fondy CHI 20

RUNS SCORED
Duke Snider BKN 120
Stan Musial STL 120
Willie Mays NY 119

WINS
Robin Roberts PHI 23
Johnny Antonelli NY 21
Warren Spahn MIL 21

WINNING PERCENTAGE
Johnny Antonelli NY ... .750
B. Lawrence STL .... .714
Ruben Gomez NY ...... .654

EARNED RUN AVERAGE
J. Antonelli NY 2.30
Lew Burdette MIL 2.76
Curt Simmons PHI 2.81

STRIKEOUTS
Robin Roberts PHI 185
Harvey Haddix STL 184
Carl Erskine BKN 166

SAVES
Jim Hughes BKN 24
Frank Smith CIN 20
Marv Grissom NY 19

COMPLETE GAMES
Robin Roberts PHI 29
Warren Spahn MIL 23
Curt Simmons PHI 21

SHUTOUTS
Johnny Antonelli NY 6

GAMES PITCHED
Jim Hughes BKN 60
Al Brazle STL 58
Johnny Hetki PIT 58

INNINGS PITCHED
Robin Roberts PHI 337
Warren Spahn MIL 283
two tied at 260

AMERICAN LEAGUE STANDINGS

1955 AL

	W	L	PCT	GB	R	OR	BA	FA	ERA
NEW YORK	96	58	.623	—	762	569	.260	.978	3.23
CLEVELAND	93	61	.604	3	698	601	.257	.981	3.39
CHICAGO	91	63	.591	5	725	557	.268	.981	3.37
BOSTON	84	70	.545	12	755	652	.264	.977	3.72
DETROIT	79	75	.513	17	775	658	.266	.976	3.79
KANSAS CITY	63	91	.409	33	638	911	.261	.976	5.35
BALTIMORE	57	97	.370	39	540	754	.240	.972	4.21
WASHINGTON	53	101	.344	43	598	789	.248	.974	4.62
					5491	5491	.258	.977	3.96

BATTING AVERAGE
Al Kaline DET .... .340
Vic Power KC .... .319
George Kell CHI .... .312

HITS
Al Kaline DET 200
Nellie Fox CHI 198
two tied at 190

DOUBLES
Harvey Kuenn DET 38
Vic Power KC 34
Billy Goodman BOS 31

TRIPLES
Andy Carey NY 11
Mickey Mantle NY 11
Vic Power KC 10

HOME RUNS
Mickey Mantle NY 37
Gus Zernial KC 30
Ted Williams BOS 28

RUNS BATTED IN
Ray Boone DET 116
Jackie Jensen BOS 116
Yogi Berra NY 108

SLUGGING AVERAGE
Mickey Mantle NY ...... .611
Al Kaline DET .... .546
Gus Zernial KC .... .508

STOLEN BASES
Jim Rivera CHI 25
Minnie Minoso CHI 19
Jackie Jensen BOS 16

RUNS SCORED
Al Smith CLE 123
Al Kaline DET 121
Mickey Mantle NY 121

WINS
Whitey Ford NY 18
Bob Lemon CLE 18
Frank Sullivan BOS 18

WINNING PERCENTAGE
Tommy Byrne NY .... .762
Whitey Ford NY .... .720
Billy Hoeft DET .... .696

EARNED RUN AVERAGE
Billy Pierce CHI 1.97
Whitey Ford NY 2.63
Early Wynn CLE 2.82

STRIKEOUTS
Herb Score CLE 245
Bob Turley NY 210
Billy Pierce CHI 157

SAVES
Ray Narleski CLE 19
Tom Gorman KC 18
Ellis Kinder BOS 18

COMPLETE GAMES
Whitey Ford NY 18
Billy Hoeft DET 17

SHUTOUTS
Billy Hoeft DET 7
three tied at 6

GAMES PITCHED
Ray Narleski CLE 60
Don Mossi CLE 57
Tom Gorman KC 57

INNINGS PITCHED
Frank Sullivan BOS 260
Whitey Ford NY 254
Bob Turley NY 247

NATIONAL LEAGUE STANDINGS

1955 NL

	W	L	PCT	GB	R	OR	BA	FA	ERA
★ BROOKLYN	98	55	.641	—	857	650	.271	.978	3.68
MILWAUKEE	85	69	.552	13.5	743	668	.261	.975	3.85
NEW YORK	80	74	.519	18.5	702	673	.260	.976	3.77
PHILADELPHIA	77	77	.500	21.5	675	666	.255	.981	3.93
CINCINNATI	75	79	.487	23.5	761	684	.270	.977	3.95
CHICAGO	72	81	.471	26	626	713	.247	.975	4.17
ST. LOUIS	68	86	.442	30.5	654	757	.261	.975	4.56
PITTSBURGH	60	94	.390	38.5	560	767	.244	.972	4.39
					5578	5578	.259	.976	4.04

BATTING AVERAGE
Richie Ashburn PHI ... .338
Willie Mays NY .... .319
Stan Musial STL .... .319

HITS
Ted Kluszewski CIN.... 192
Hank Aaron MIL.......... 189
Gus Bell CIN 188

DOUBLES
Hank Aaron MIL........... 37
Johnny Logan MIL 37
Duke Snider BKN......... 34

TRIPLES
Willie Mays NY.............. 13
Dale Long PIT............... 13
Bill Bruton MIL 12

HOME RUNS
Willie Mays NY.............. 51
Ted Kluszewski CIN...... 47
Ernie Banks CHI 44

RUNS BATTED IN
Duke Snider BKN........ 136
Willie Mays NY............ 127
Del Ennis PHI 120

SLUGGING AVERAGE
Willie Mays NY............ .659
Duke Snider BKN....... .628
Eddie Mathews MIL ... .601

STOLEN BASES
Bill Bruton MIL 25
Willie Mays NY.............. 24
Ken Boyer STL 22

RUNS SCORED
Duke Snider BKN........ 126
Willie Mays NY............ 123
two tied at 116

WINS
Robin Roberts PHI........ 23
Don Newcombe BKN.... 20
two tied at 17

WINNING PERCENTAGE
D. Newcombe BKN.... .800
Robin Roberts PHI..... .622
Joe Nuxhall CIN.......... .586

EARNED RUN AVERAGE
Bob Friend PIT........... 2.83
D. Newcombe BKN.... 3.20
Bob Buhl MIL 3.21

STRIKEOUTS
Sam Jones CHI........... 198
Robin Roberts PHI...... 160
Harvey Haddix STL..... 150

SAVES
Jack Meyer PHI 16
Ed Roebuck BKN.......... 12
two tied at 11

COMPLETE GAMES
Robin Roberts PHI........ 26
Don Newcombe BKN.... 17
Warren Spahn MIL......... 16

SHUTOUTS
Joe Nuxhall CIN............. 5
Murry Dickson PHI.......... 4
Sam Jones CHI............... 4

GAMES PITCHED
Clem Labine BKN 60
Hoyt Wilhelm NY............ 59
Paul LaPalme STL......... 56

INNINGS PITCHED
Robin Roberts PHI...... 305
Joe Nuxhall CIN........... 257
Warren Spahn MIL....... 246

AMERICAN LEAGUE STANDINGS

1956 AL

	W	L	PCT	GB	R	OR	BA	FA	ERA
★ NEW YORK	97	57	.630	—	857	631	.270	.977	3.63
CLEVELAND	88	66	.571	9	712	581	.244	.978	3.32
CHICAGO	85	69	.552	12	776	634	.267	.979	3.73
BOSTON	84	70	.545	13	780	751	.275	.972	4.17
DETROIT	82	72	.532	15	789	699	.279	.976	4.06
BALTIMORE	69	85	.448	28	571	705	.244	.977	4.20
WASHINGTON	59	95	.383	38	652	924	.250	.972	5.33
KANSAS CITY	52	102	.338	45	619	831	.252	.973	4.86
					5756	5756	.260	.975	4.16

BATTING AVERAGE
Mickey Mantle NY ...... .353
Ted Williams BOS ...... .345
Harvey Kuenn DET ..... .332

HITS
Harvey Kuenn DET 196
Al Kaline DET 194
Nellie Fox CHI............. 192

DOUBLES
Jimmy Piersall BOS 40
Al Kaline DET 32
Harvey Kuenn DET....... 32

TRIPLES
four tied at..................... 11

HOME RUNS
Mickey Mantle NY 52
Vic Wertz CLE 32
Yogi Berra NY............... 30

RUNS BATTED IN
Mickey Mantle NY....... 130
Al Kaline DET 128
Vic Wertz CLE 106

SLUGGING AVERAGE
Mickey Mantle NY ...... .705
Ted Williams BOS ...... .605
Charlie Maxwell DET . .534

STOLEN BASES
Luis Aparicio CHI 21
Jim Rivera CHI............... 20
Bobby Avila CLE............ 17

RUNS SCORED
Mickey Mantle NY 132
Nellie Fox CHI............. 109
Minnie Minoso CHI 106

WINS
Frank Lary DET 21
five tied at 20

WINNING PERCENTAGE
Whitey Ford NY .... .760
three tied at................. .690

EARNED RUN AVERAGE
Whitey Ford NY 2.47
Herb Score CLE.......... 2.53
Early Wynn CLE 2.72

STRIKEOUTS
Herb Score CLE........... 263
Billy Pierce CHI............ 192
Paul Foytack DET........ 184

SAVES
George Zuverink BAL ... 16
Tom Morgan NY 11
Don Mossi CLE.............. 11

COMPLETE GAMES
Billy Pierce CHI.............. 21
Bob Lemon CLE 21
Frank Lary DET 20

SHUTOUTS
Herb Score CLE 5

GAMES PITCHED
George Zuverink BAL ... 62
Jack Crimian KC 54
Tom Gorman KC............ 52

INNINGS PITCHED
Frank Lary DET 294
Early Wynn CLE 278
Billy Pierce CHI............ 276

NATIONAL LEAGUE STANDINGS

1956 NL

	W	L	PCT	GB	R	OR	BA	FA	ERA
BROOKLYN	93	61	.604	—	720	601	.258	.981	3.57
MILWAUKEE	92	62	.597	1	709	569	.259	.979	3.11
CINCINNATI	91	63	.591	2	775	658	.266	.981	3.85
ST. LOUIS	76	78	.494	17	678	698	.268	.978	3.97
PHILADELPHIA	71	83	.461	22	668	738	.252	.975	4.20
NEW YORK	67	87	.435	26	540	650	.244	.976	3.78
PITTSBURGH	66	88	.429	27	588	653	.257	.973	3.74
CHICAGO	60	94	.390	33	597	708	.244	.976	3.96
					5275	5275	.256	.977	3.77

BATTING AVERAGE
Hank Aaron MIL......... .328
Bill Virdon STL, PIT ... .319
R. Clemente PIT .... .311

HITS
Hank Aaron MIL........... 200
Richie Ashburn PHI 190
Bill Virdon STL, PIT 185

DOUBLES
Hank Aaron MIL............. 34
three tied at.................. 33

TRIPLES
Bill Bruton MIL 15
Hank Aaron MIL............. 14
two tied at 11

HOME RUNS
Duke Snider BKN.......... 43
Frank Robinson CIN 38
Joe Adcock MIL 38

RUNS BATTED IN
Stan Musial STL 109
Joe Adcock MIL 103
Ted Kluszewski CIN.... 102

SLUGGING AVERAGE
Duke Snider BKN........ .598
Joe Adcock MIL........... .597
Hank Aaron MIL.......... .558

STOLEN BASES
Willie Mays NY.............. 40
Jim Gilliam BKN............. 21
Bill White NY 15

RUNS SCORED
Frank Robinson CIN ... 122
Duke Snider BKN........ 112
Hank Aaron MIL........... 106

WINS
Don Newcombe BKN.... 27
Warren Spahn MIL 20
Johnny Antonelli NY 20

WINNING PERCENTAGE
D. Newcombe BKN.... .794
Bob Buhl MIL .... .692
two tied at .... .655

EARNED RUN AVERAGE
Lew Burdette MIL....... 2.70
Warren Spahn MIL 2.78
J. Antonelli NY 2.86

STRIKEOUTS
Sam Jones CHI............ 176
H. Haddix STL, PHI 170
Bob Friend PIT............. 166

SAVES
Clem Labine BKN 19
Hersh Freeman CIN...... 18
Turk Lown CHI............... 13

COMPLETE GAMES
Robin Roberts PHI 22
Warren Spahn MIL........ 20
Bob Friend PIT.............. 19

SHUTOUTS
Lew Burdette MIL............ 6
Johnny Antonelli NY 5
Don Newcombe BKN...... 5

GAMES PITCHED
Roy Face PIT................. 68
Hersh Freeman CIN...... 64
Hoyt Wilhelm NY........... 64

INNINGS PITCHED
Bob Friend PIT............. 314
Robin Roberts PHI...... 297
Warren Spahn MIL...... 281

AMERICAN LEAGUE STANDINGS

1957 AL

	W	L	PCT	GB	R	OR	BA	FA	ERA
NEW YORK	98	56	.636	—	723	534	.268	.980	3.00
CHICAGO	90	64	.584	8	707	566	.260	.982	3.35
BOSTON	82	72	.532	16	721	668	.262	.976	3.88
DETROIT	78	76	.506	20	614	614	.257	.980	3.56
BALTIMORE	76	76	.500	21	597	588	.252	.981	3.46
CLEVELAND	76	77	.497	21.5	682	722	.252	.974	4.06
KANSAS CITY	59	94	.386	38.5	563	710	.244	.979	4.19
WASHINGTON	55	99	.357	43	603	808	.244	.979	4.85
					5210	5210	.255	.979	3.79

BATTING AVERAGE
Ted Williams BOS...... .388
Mickey Mantle NY...... .365
G. Woodling CLE....... .321

HITS
Nellie Fox CHI.............. 196
Frank Malzone BOS ... 185
Minnie Minoso CHI 176

DOUBLES
Billy Gardner BAL 36
Minnie Minoso CHI 36
Frank Malzone BOS 31

TRIPLES
Harry Simpson KC, NY ... 9
Gil McDougald NY 9
Hank Bauer NY 9

HOME RUNS
Roy Sievers WAS 42
Ted Williams BOS 38
Mickey Mantle NY 34

RUNS BATTED IN
Roy Sievers WAS 114
Vic Wertz CLE 105
three tied at................. 103

SLUGGING AVERAGE
Ted Williams BOS...... .731
Mickey Mantle NY...... .665
Roy Sievers WAS ...... .579

STOLEN BASES
Luis Aparicio CHI 28
Minnie Minoso CHI 18
Jim Rivera CHI.............. 18

RUNS SCORED
Mickey Mantle NY 121
Nellie Fox CHI.............. 110
Jimmy Piersall BOS.... 103

WINS
Jim Bunning DET 20
Billy Pierce CHI............. 20
three tied at.................. 16

WINNING PERCENTAGE
Dick Donovan CHI ..... .727
Tom Sturdivant NY .... .727
Jim Bunning DET....... .714

EARNED RUN AVERAGE
Bobby Shantz NY 2.45
Tom Sturdivant NY ... 2.54
Jim Bunning DET....... 2.69

STRIKEOUTS
Early Wynn CLE 184
Jim Bunning DET........ 182
C. Johnson BAL........... 177

SAVES
Bob Grim NY................. 19
Ray Narleski CLE 16
Ike Delock BOS 11

COMPLETE GAMES
Dick Donovan CHI 16
Billy Pierce CHI............. 16
Tom Brewer BOS.......... 15

SHUTOUTS
Jim Wilson CHI 5
Billy Pierce CHI............... 4
Bob Turley NY 4

GAMES PITCHED
George Zuverink BAL ... 56
Tex Clevenger WAS 52
Dick Hyde WAS 52

INNINGS PITCHED
Jim Bunning DET........ 267
Early Wynn CLE 263
Billy Pierce CHI............ 257

NATIONAL LEAGUE STANDINGS

1957 NL

	W	L	PCT	GB	R	OR	BA	FA	ERA
★ MILWAUKEE	95	59	.617	—	772	613	.269	.981	3.47
ST. LOUIS	87	67	.565	8	737	666	.274	.979	3.78
BROOKLYN	84	70	.545	11	690	591	.253	.979	3.35
CINCINNATI	80	74	.519	15	747	781	.269	.982	4.62
PHILADELPHIA	77	77	.500	18	623	656	.250	.976	3.79
NEW YORK	69	85	.448	26	643	701	.252	.974	4.01
CHICAGO	62	92	.403	33	628	722	.244	.975	4.13
PITTSBURGH	62	92	.403	33	586	696	.268	.972	3.88
					5426	5426	.260	.977	3.88

BATTING AVERAGE
Stan Musial STL .... .351
Willie Mays NY .... .333
Frank Robinson CIN .. .322

HITS
Schoendienst NY, MIL. 200
Hank Aaron MIL 198
Frank Robinson CIN ... 197

DOUBLES
Don Hoak CIN 39
Stan Musial STL 38
Ed Bouchee PHI 35

TRIPLES
Willie Mays NY 20
Bill Virdon PIT 11
two tied at 9

HOME RUNS
Hank Aaron MIL 44
Ernie Banks CHI 43
Duke Snider BKN 40

RUNS BATTED IN
Hank Aaron MIL 132
Del Ennis STL 105
two tied at 102

SLUGGING AVERAGE
Willie Mays NY .... .626
Stan Musial STL .... .612
Hank Aaron MIL .... .600

STOLEN BASES
Willie Mays NY 38
Jim Gilliam BKN 26
Don Blasingame STL 21

RUNS SCORED
Hank Aaron MIL 118
Ernie Banks CHI 113
Willie Mays NY 112

WINS
Warren Spahn MIL 21
Jack Sanford PHI 19
Bob Buhl MIL 18

WINNING PERCENTAGE
Bob Buhl MIL .... .720
Jack Sanford PHI .... .704
Warren Spahn MIL ..... .656

EARNED RUN AVERAGE
J. Podres BKN 2.66
Don Drysdale BKN 2.69
Warren Spahn MIL 2.69

STRIKEOUTS
Jack Sanford PHI 188
Dick Drott CHI 170
Moe Drabowsky CHI ... 170

SAVES
Clem Labine BKN 17
Marv Grissom NY 14
Turk Lown CHI 12

COMPLETE GAMES
Warren Spahn MIL 18
Bob Friend PIT 17
Ruben Gomez NY 16

SHUTOUTS
Johnny Podres BKN 6
three tied at 4

GAMES PITCHED
Turk Lown CHI 67
Roy Face PIT 59
Clem Labine BKN 58

INNINGS PITCHED
Bob Friend PIT 277
Warren Spahn MIL 271
Lew Burdette MIL 257

AMERICAN LEAGUE STANDINGS

1958 AL

	W	L	PCT	GB	R	OR	BA	FA	ERA
★ NEW YORK	92	62	.597	—	759	577	.268	.978	3.22
CHICAGO	82	72	.532	10	634	615	.257	.981	3.61
BOSTON	79	75	.513	13	697	691	.256	.976	3.92
CLEVELAND	77	76	.503	14.5	694	635	.258	.974	3.73
DETROIT	77	77	.500	15	659	606	.266	.982	3.59
BALTIMORE	74	79	.484	17.5	521	575	.241	.980	3.40
KANSAS CITY	73	81	.474	19	642	713	.247	.979	4.15
WASHINGTON	61	93	.396	31	553	747	.240	.980	4.53
					5159	5159	.254	.979	3.77

BATTING AVERAGE
Ted Williams BOS...... .328
Pete Runnels BOS..... .322
Harvey Kuenn DET.... .319

HITS
Nellie Fox CHI............. 187
Frank Malzone BOS ... 185
Vic Power KC, CLE.... 184

DOUBLES
Harvey Kuenn DET...... 39
Vic Power KC, CLE...... 37
Al Kaline DET 34

TRIPLES
Vic Power KC, CLE...... 10
three tied at..................... 9

HOME RUNS
Mickey Mantle NY......... 42
Rocky Colavito CLE...... 41
Roy Sievers WAS 39

RUNS BATTED IN
Jackie Jensen BOS 122
Rocky Colavito CLE.... 113
Roy Sievers WAS 108

SLUGGING AVERAGE
Rocky Colavito CLE... .620
Bob Cerv KC............... .592
Mickey Mantle NY...... .592

STOLEN BASES
Luis Aparicio CHI 29
Jim Rivera CHI.............. 21
Jim Landis CHI 19

RUNS SCORED
Mickey Mantle NY....... 127
Pete Runnels BOS...... 103
Vic Power KC, CLE....... 98

WINS
Bob Turley NY 21
Billy Pierce CHI............. 17
two tied at 16

WINNING PERCENTAGE
Bob Turley NY .... .750
Cal McLish CLE .... .667
Billy Pierce CHI........... .607

EARNED RUN AVERAGE
Whitey Ford NY 2.01
Billy Pierce CHI........... 2.68
J. Harshman BAL....... 2.89

STRIKEOUTS
Early Wynn CHI 179
Jim Bunning DET........ 177
Bob Turley NY 168

SAVES
Ryne Duren NY.............. 20
Dick Hyde WAS 18
Leo Kiely BOS 12

COMPLETE GAMES
Bob Turley NY 19
Billy Pierce CHI............. 19
Frank Lary DET 19

SHUTOUTS
Whitey Ford NY 7
Bob Turley NY 6
three tied at..................... 4

GAMES PITCHED
Tex Clevenger WAS 55
D. Tomanek CLE, KC ... 54
Dick Hyde WAS 53

INNINGS PITCHED
Frank Lary DET 260
Pedro Ramos WAS..... 259
Dick Donovan CHI 248

NATIONAL LEAGUE STANDINGS

1958 NL

	W	L	PCT	GB	R	OR	BA	FA	ERA
MILWAUKEE	92	62	.597	—	675	541	.266	.980	3.21
PITTSBURGH	84	70	.545	8	662	607	.264	.978	3.56
SAN FRANCISCO	80	74	.519	12	727	698	.263	.975	3.98
CINCINNATI	76	78	.494	16	695	621	.258	.983	3.73
CHICAGO	72	82	.468	20	709	725	.265	.975	4.22
ST. LOUIS	72	82	.468	20	619	704	.261	.974	4.12
LOS ANGELES	71	83	.461	21	668	761	.251	.975	4.47
PHILADELPHIA	69	85	.448	23	664	762	.266	.978	4.32
					5419	5419	.262	.977	3.95

BATTING AVERAGE
Richie Ashburn PHI ... .350
Willie Mays SF .... .347
Stan Musial STL .... .337

HITS
Richie Ashburn PHI 215
Willie Mays SF 208
Hank Aaron MIL 196

DOUBLES
Orlando Cepeda SF 38
Dick Groat PIT 36
Stan Musial STL 35

TRIPLES
Richie Ashburn PHI 13
three tied at 11

HOME RUNS
Ernie Banks CHI 47
Frank Thomas PIT 35
two tied at 31

RUNS BATTED IN
Ernie Banks CHI 129
Frank Thomas PIT 109
Harry Anderson PHI 97

SLUGGING AVERAGE
Ernie Banks CHI .... .614
Willie Mays SF .... .583
Hank Aaron MIL .... .546

STOLEN BASES
Willie Mays SF 31
Richie Ashburn PHI 30
Tony Taylor CHI 21

RUNS SCORED
Willie Mays SF 121
Ernie Banks CHI 119
Hank Aaron MIL 109

WINS
Bob Friend PIT 22
Warren Spahn MIL 22
Lew Burdette MIL 20

WINNING PERCENTAGE
Warren Spahn MIL ...... .667
Lew Burdette MIL .... .667
Bob Friend PIT .... .611

EARNED RUN AVERAGE
Stu Miller SF 2.47
Sam Jones STL 2.88
Lew Burdette MIL 2.91

STRIKEOUTS
Sam Jones STL 225
Warren Spahn MIL 150
two tied at 143

SAVES
Roy Face PIT 20
Clem Labine LA 14
Dick Farrell PHI 11

COMPLETE GAMES
Warren Spahn MIL 23
Robin Roberts PHI 21
Lew Burdette MIL 19

SHUTOUTS
Carl Willey MIL 4
four tied at 3

GAMES PITCHED
Don Elston CHI 69
J. Klippstein CIN, LA 57
Roy Face PIT 57

INNINGS PITCHED
Warren Spahn MIL 290
Lew Burdette MIL 275
Bob Friend PIT 274

AMERICAN LEAGUE STANDINGS

1959 AL

	W	L	PCT	GB	R	OR	BA	FA	ERA
CHICAGO	94	60	.610	—	669	588	.250	.979	3.29
CLEVELAND	89	65	.578	5	745	646	.263	.978	3.75
NEW YORK	79	75	.513	15	687	647	.260	.978	3.60
DETROIT	76	78	.494	18	713	732	.258	.978	4.20
BOSTON	75	79	.487	19	726	696	.256	.978	4.17
BALTIMORE	74	80	.481	20	551	621	.238	.976	3.56
KANSAS CITY	66	88	.429	28	681	760	.263	.973	4.35
WASHINGTON	63	91	.409	31	619	701	.237	.973	4.01
					5391	5391	.253	.977	3.86

BATTING AVERAGE
Harvey Kuenn DET .... .353
Al Kaline DET .... .327
Pete Runnels BOS ..... .314

HITS
Harvey Kuenn DET 198
Nellie Fox CHI 191
Pete Runnels BOS 176

DOUBLES
Harvey Kuenn DET 42
Frank Malzone BOS 34
Nellie Fox CHI 34

TRIPLES
Bob Allison WAS 9
Gil McDougald NY 8

HOME RUNS
Rocky Colavito CLE 42
H. Killebrew WAS 42
Jim Lemon WAS 33

RUNS BATTED IN
Jackie Jensen BOS 112
Rocky Colavito CLE 111
H. Killebrew WAS 105

SLUGGING AVERAGE
Al Kaline DET .... .530
H. Killebrew WAS ...... .516
Mickey Mantle NY ...... .514

STOLEN BASES
Luis Aparicio CHI 56
Mickey Mantle NY 21
two tied at 20

RUNS SCORED
Eddie Yost DET 115
Mickey Mantle NY 104
Vic Power CLE 102

WINS
Early Wynn CHI 22
Cal McLish CLE 19
Bob Shaw CHI 18

WINNING PERCENTAGE
Bob Shaw CHI .... .750
Cal McLish CLE .... .704
Early Wynn CHI .... .688

EARNED RUN AVERAGE
Hoyt Wilhelm BAL 2.19
C. Pascual WAS 2.64
Bob Shaw CHI 2.69

STRIKEOUTS
Jim Bunning DET 201
C. Pascual WAS 185
Early Wynn CHI 179

SAVES
Turk Lown CHI 15
three tied at 14

COMPLETE GAMES
Camilo Pascual WAS 17
Don Mossi DET 15
Milt Pappas BAL 15

SHUTOUTS
Camilo Pascual WAS 6
Early Wynn CHI 5
Milt Pappas BAL 4

GAMES PITCHED
George Staley CHI 67
Turk Lown CHI 60
Tex Clevenger WAS 50

INNINGS PITCHED
Early Wynn CHI 256
Jim Bunning DET 250
Paul Foytack DET 240

NATIONAL LEAGUE STANDINGS

1959 NL

	W	L	PCT	GB	R	OR	BA	FA	ERA
★ LOS ANGELES*	88	68	.564	—	705	670	.257	.981	3.79
MILWAUKEE	86	70	.551	2	724	623	.265	.979	3.51
SAN FRANCISCO	83	71	.539	4	705	613	.261	.974	3.47
PITTSBURGH	78	76	.506	9	651	680	.263	.975	3.90
CHICAGO	74	80	.481	13	673	688	.249	.977	4.01
CINCINNATI	74	80	.481	13	764	738	.274	.978	4.31
ST. LOUIS	71	83	.461	16	641	725	.269	.975	4.34
PHILADELPHIA	64	90	.416	23	599	725	.242	.973	4.27
					5462	5462	.260	.977	3.95

* Defeated Milwaukee in a playoff 2 games to 0

BATTING AVERAGE
Hank Aaron MIL.......... .355
J. Cunningham STL ... .345
Orlando Cepeda SF... .317

HITS
Hank Aaron MIL.......... 223
Vada Pinson CIN 205
Orlando Cepeda SF.... 192

DOUBLES
Vada Pinson CIN 47
Hank Aaron MIL............. 46
Willie Mays SF 43

TRIPLES
Charlie Neal LA............. 11
Wally Moon LA.............. 11
three tied at..................... 9

HOME RUNS
Eddie Mathews MIL ... 46
Ernie Banks CHI 45
Hank Aaron MIL............ 39

RUNS BATTED IN
Ernie Banks CHI 143
Frank Robinson CIN ... 125
Hank Aaron MIL.......... 123

SLUGGING AVERAGE
Hank Aaron MIL.......... .636
Ernie Banks CHI .... .596
Eddie Mathews MIL ... .593

STOLEN BASES
Willie Mays SF 27
three tied at.................... 23

RUNS SCORED
Vada Pinson CIN 131
Willie Mays SF 125
Eddie Mathews MIL ... 118

WINS
Lew Burdette MIL........... 21
Sam Jones SF 21
Warren Spahn MIL......... 21

WINNING PERCENTAGE
Roy Face PIT .... .947
Vern Law PIT .... .667
Johnny Antonelli SF... .655

EARNED RUN AVERAGE
Sam Jones SF 2.83
Stu Miller SF 2.84
Bill Buhl MIL................ 2.86

STRIKEOUTS
Don Drysdale LA......... 242
Sam Jones SF 209
Sandy Koufax LA........ 173

SAVES
Lindy McDaniel STL...... 15
Don McMahon MIL 15
Don Elston CHI 13

COMPLETE GAMES
Warren Spahn MIL........ 21
Vern Law PIT 20
Lew Burdette MIL.......... 20

SHUTOUTS
seven tied at 4

GAMES PITCHED
Bill Henry CHI 65
Don Elston CHI 65
Lindy McDaniel STL...... 62

INNINGS PITCHED
Warren Spahn MIL....... 292
Lew Burdette MIL........ 290
Johnny Antonelli SF.... 282

AMERICAN LEAGUE STANDINGS

1960 AL

	W	L	PCT	GB	R	OR	BA	FA	ERA
NEW YORK	97	57	.630	—	746	627	.260	.979	3.52
BALTIMORE	89	65	.578	8	682	606	.253	.982	3.52
CHICAGO	87	67	.565	10	741	617	.270	.982	3.60
CLEVELAND	76	78	.494	21	667	693	.267	.978	3.95
WASHINGTON	73	81	.474	24	672	696	.244	.973	3.77
DETROIT	71	83	.461	26	633	644	.239	.977	3.64
BOSTON	65	89	.422	32	658	775	.261	.976	4.62
KANSAS CITY	58	96	.377	39	615	756	.249	.979	4.38
					5414	5414	.255	.978	3.87

BATTING AVERAGE
Pete Runnels BOS..... .320
Al Smith CHI .... .315
Minnie Minoso CHI .... .311

HITS
Minnie Minoso CHI 184
Nellie Fox CHI............ 175
B. Robinson BAL 175

DOUBLES
Tito Francona CLE....... 36
Bill Skowron NY 34
two tied at 32

TRIPLES
Nellie Fox CHI............. 10
Brooks Robinson BAL.... 9

HOME RUNS
Mickey Mantle NY........ 40
Roger Maris NY 39
Jim Lemon WAS 38

RUNS BATTED IN
Roger Maris NY 112
Minnie Minoso CHI 105
Vic Wertz BOS............ 103

SLUGGING AVERAGE
Roger Maris NY .... .581
Mickey Mantle NY...... .558
H. Killebrew WAS ...... .534

STOLEN BASES
Luis Aparicio CHI 51
Jim Landis CHI 23
Lenny Green WAS....... 21

RUNS SCORED
Mickey Mantle NY...... 119
Roger Maris NY 98
two tied at 89

WINS
Jim Perry CLE.............. 18
Chuck Estrada BAL 18
Buddy Daley KC 16

WINNING PERCENTAGE
Jim Perry CLE............ .643
Art Ditmar NY............. .625
Chuck Estrada BAL ... .621

EARNED RUN AVERAGE
F. Baumann CHI........ 2.67
Jim Bunning DET....... 2.79
Hal Brown BAL 3.06

STRIKEOUTS
Jim Bunning DET........ 201
Pedro Ramos WAS..... 160
Early Wynn CHI 158

SAVES
Mike Fornieles BOS...... 14
J. Klippstein CLE 14
Ray Moore CHI, WAS... 13

COMPLETE GAMES
Frank Lary DET 15
Pedro Ramos WAS....... 14
Ray Herbert KC 14

SHUTOUTS
Jim Perry CLE................. 4
Whitey Ford NY 4
Early Wynn CHI 4

GAMES PITCHED
Mike Fornieles BOS 70
Gerry Staley CHI.......... 64
Tex Clevenger WAS 53

INNINGS PITCHED
Frank Lary DET 274
Pedro Ramos WAS..... 274
Jim Perry CLE............. 261

NATIONAL LEAGUE STANDINGS

1960 NL

	W	L	PCT	GB	R	OR	BA	FA	ERA
★ PITTSBURGH	95	59	.617	—	734	593	.276	.979	3.49
MILWAUKEE	88	66	.571	7	724	658	.265	.976	3.76
ST. LOUIS	86	68	.558	9	639	616	.254	.976	3.64
LOS ANGELES	82	72	.532	13	662	593	.255	.979	3.40
SAN FRANCISCO	79	75	.513	16	671	631	.255	.972	3.44
CINCINNATI	67	87	.435	28	640	692	.250	.979	4.00
CHICAGO	60	94	.390	35	634	776	.243	.977	4.35
PHILADELPHIA	59	95	.383	36	546	691	.239	.974	4.01
					5250	5250	.255	.977	3.76

BATTING AVERAGE
Dick Groat PIT .... .325
Norm Larker LA .... .323
Willie Mays SF .... .319

HITS
Willie Mays SF 190
Vada Pinson CIN 187
Dick Groat PIT 186

DOUBLES
Vada Pinson CIN 37
Orlando Cepeda SF 36
two tied at 33

TRIPLES
Bill Bruton MIL 13
Willie Mays SF 12
Vada Pinson CIN 12

HOME RUNS
Ernie Banks CHI 41
Hank Aaron MIL 40
Eddie Mathews MIL 39

RUNS BATTED IN
Hank Aaron MIL 126
Eddie Mathews MIL 124
Ernie Banks CHI 117

SLUGGING AVERAGE
F. Robinson CIN .... .595
Hank Aaron MIL .... .566
Ken Boyer STL .... .562

STOLEN BASES
Maury Wills LA 50
Vada Pinson CIN 32
Tony Taylor CHI, PHI 26

RUNS SCORED
Bill Bruton MIL 112
Eddie Mathews MIL 108
two tied at 107

WINS
Ernie Broglio STL 21
Warren Spahn MIL 21
Vern Law PIT 20

WINNING PERCENTAGE
Ernie Broglio STL .... .700
Vern Law PIT .... .690
Warren Spahn MIL ..... .677

EARNED RUN AVERAGE
Mike McCormick SF ... 2.70
Ernie Broglio STL 2.74
Don Drysdale LA 2.84

STRIKEOUTS
Don Drysdale LA 246
Sandy Koufax LA 197
Sam Jones SF 190

SAVES
Lindy McDaniel STL 26
Roy Face PIT 24
Bill Henry CIN 17

COMPLETE GAMES
Warren Spahn MIL 18
Vern Law PIT 18
Lew Burdette MIL 18

SHUTOUTS
Jack Sanford SF 6
Don Drysdale LA 5

GAMES PITCHED
Roy Face PIT 68
Lindy McDaniel STL 65
Don Elston CHI 60

INNINGS PITCHED
Larry Jackson STL 282
Lew Burdette MIL 276
Bob Friend PIT 276

AMERICAN LEAGUE STANDINGS

1961 AL

	W	L	PCT	GB	R	OR	BA	FA	ERA
★ NEW YORK	109	53	.673	—	827	612	.263	.980	3.46
DETROIT	101	61	.623	8	841	671	.266	.976	3.55
BALTIMORE	95	67	.586	14	691	588	.254	.980	3.22
CHICAGO	86	76	.531	23	765	726	.265	.980	4.06
CLEVELAND	78	83	.484	30.5	737	752	.266	.977	4.15
BOSTON	76	86	.469	33	729	792	.254	.977	4.29
MINNESOTA	70	90	.438	38	707	778	.250	.972	4.28
LOS ANGELES	70	91	.435	38.5	744	784	.245	.969	4.31
KANSAS CITY	61	100	.379	47.5	683	863	.247	.972	4.74
WASHINGTON	61	100	.379	47.5	618	776	.244	.975	4.23
					7342	7342	.256	.976	4.02

BATTING AVERAGE
Norm Cash DET .... .361
Al Kaline DET .... .324
Jimmy Piersall CLE .... .322

HITS
Norm Cash DET 193
B. Robinson BAL 192
Al Kaline DET 190

DOUBLES
Al Kaline DET 41
Tony Kubek NY............. 38
Brooks Robinson BAL... 38

TRIPLES
Jake Wood DET............ 14
Marty Keough WAS 9
Jerry Lumpe KC.............. 9

HOME RUNS
Roger Maris NY 61
Mickey Mantle NY......... 54
two tied at 46

RUNS BATTED IN
Roger Maris NY 142
Jim Gentile BAL 141
Rocky Colavito DET.... 140

SLUGGING AVERAGE
Mickey Mantle NY....... .687
Norm Cash DET .... .662
Jim Gentile BAL .... .646

STOLEN BASES
Luis Aparicio CHI 53
Dick Howser KC............ 37
Jake Wood DET............ 30

RUNS SCORED
Roger Maris NY 132
Mickey Mantle NY....... 132
Rocky Colavito DET.... 129

WINS
Whitey Ford NY 25
Frank Lary DET 23
Steve Barber BAL 18

WINNING PERCENTAGE
Whitey Ford NY .... .862
Ralph Terry NY .... .842
Luis Arroyo NY............ .750

EARNED RUN AVERAGE
Dick Donovan WAS ... 2.40
Bill Stafford NY 2.68
Don Mossi DET.......... 2.96

STRIKEOUTS
Camilo Pascual MIN ... 221
Whitey Ford NY 209
Jim Bunning DET........ 194

SAVES
Luis Arroyo NY.............. 29
Hoyt Wilhelm BAL......... 18
Mike Fornieles BOS...... 15

COMPLETE GAMES
Frank Lary DET 22
Camilo Pascual MIN 15
Steve Barber BAL.......... 14

SHUTOUTS
Camilo Pascual MIN 8
Steve Barber BAL........... 8
three tied at..................... 4

GAMES PITCHED
Luis Arroyo NY.............. 65
Tom Morgan LA 59
Turk Lown CHI............... 59

INNINGS PITCHED
Whitey Ford NY 283
Frank Lary DET 275
Jim Bunning DET........ 268

NATIONAL LEAGUE STANDINGS

1961 NL

	W	L	PCT	GB	R	OR	BA	FA	ERA
CINCINNATI	93	61	.604	—	710	653	.270	.977	3.78
LOS ANGELES	89	65	.578	4	735	697	.262	.975	4.04
SAN FRANCISCO	85	69	.552	8	773	655	.264	.977	3.77
MILWAUKEE	83	71	.539	10	712	656	.258	.982	3.89
ST. LOUIS	80	74	.519	13	703	668	.271	.972	3.74
PITTSBURGH	75	79	.487	18	694	675	.273	.975	3.92
CHICAGO	64	90	.416	29	689	800	.255	.970	4.48
PHILADELPHIA	47	107	.305	46	584	796	.243	.976	4.61
					5600	5600	.262	.976	4.03

BATTING AVERAGE
R. Clemente PIT .... .351
Vada Pinson CIN .... .343
Ken Boyer STL .... .329

HITS
Vada Pinson CIN 208
R. Clemente PIT 201
Hank Aaron MIL 197

DOUBLES
Hank Aaron MIL 39
Vada Pinson CIN 34
three tied at 32

TRIPLES
George Altman CHI 12
three tied at 11

HOME RUNS
Orlando Cepeda SF 46
Willie Mays SF 40
Frank Robinson CIN 37

RUNS BATTED IN
Orlando Cepeda SF 142
Frank Robinson CIN ... 124
Willie Mays SF 123

SLUGGING AVERAGE
F. Robinson CIN .... .611
Orlando Cepeda SF ... .609
Hank Aaron MIL .... .594

STOLEN BASES
Maury Wills LA 35
Vada Pinson CIN 23
Frank Robinson CIN 22

RUNS SCORED
Willie Mays SF 129
Frank Robinson CIN ... 117
Hank Aaron MIL 115

WINS
Joey Jay CIN 21
Warren Spahn MIL 21
Jim O'Toole CIN 19

WINNING PERCENTAGE
Johnny Podres LA ..... .783
Jim O'Toole CIN .... .679
Joey Jay CIN .... .677

EARNED RUN AVERAGE
Warren Spahn MIL 3.02
Jim O'Toole CIN 3.10
Curt Simmons STL 3.13

STRIKEOUTS
Sandy Koufax LA 269
Stan Williams LA 205
Don Drysdale LA 182

SAVES
Stu Miller SF 17
Roy Face PIT 17
two tied at 16

COMPLETE GAMES
Warren Spahn MIL 21
Sandy Koufax LA 15
two tied at 14

SHUTOUTS
Joey Jay CIN 4
Warren Spahn MIL 4

GAMES PITCHED
Jack Baldschun PHI 65
Stu Miller SF 63
Roy Face PIT 62

INNINGS PITCHED
Lew Burdette MIL 272
Warren Spahn MIL 263
Don Cardwell CHI 259

AMERICAN LEAGUE STANDINGS

1962 AL

	W	L	PCT	GB	R	OR	BA	FA	ERA
★ NEW YORK	96	66	.593	—	817	680	.267	.979	3.70
MINNESOTA	91	71	.562	5	798	713	.260	.979	3.89
LOS ANGELES	86	76	.531	10	718	706	.250	.973	3.70
DETROIT	85	76	.528	10.5	758	692	.248	.974	3.81
CHICAGO	85	77	.525	11	707	658	.257	.982	3.73
CLEVELAND	80	82	.494	16	682	745	.245	.978	4.14
BALTIMORE	77	85	.475	19	652	680	.248	.980	3.69
BOSTON	76	84	.475	19	707	756	.258	.979	4.22
KANSAS CITY	72	90	.444	24	745	837	.263	.979	4.79
WASHINGTON	60	101	.373	35.5	599	716	.250	.978	4.04
					7183	7183	.255	.978	3.97

BATTING AVERAGE
Pete Runnels BOS ..... .326
Mickey Mantle NY ...... .321
Floyd Robinson CHI ... .312

HITS
B. Richardson NY 209
Jerry Lumpe KC 193
B. Robinson BAL 192

DOUBLES
Floyd Robinson CHI...... 45
C. Yastrzemski BOS 43
Ed Bressoud BOS......... 40

TRIPLES
Gino Cimoli KC 15
three tied at................... 10

HOME RUNS
H. Killebrew MIN............ 48
Norm Cash DET 39
two tied at 37

RUNS BATTED IN
H. Killebrew MIN............ 126
Norm Siebern KC......... 117
Rocky Colavito DET.... 112

SLUGGING AVERAGE
Mickey Mantle NY .... .605
H. Killebrew MIN......... .545
Rocky Colavito DET.... .514

STOLEN BASES
Luis Aparicio CHI........... 31
Chuck Hinton WAS....... 28
Jake Wood DET............ 24

RUNS SCORED
Albie Pearson LA 115
Norm Siebern KC........ 114
Bob Allison MIN 102

WINS
Ralph Terry NY 23
three tied at................... 20

WINNING PERCENTAGE
Ray Herbert CHI .... .690
Whitey Ford NY .... .680
two tied at .... .667

EARNED RUN AVERAGE
Hank Aguirre DET...... 2.21
Robin Roberts BAL 2.78
Whitey Ford NY 2.90

STRIKEOUTS
Camilo Pascual MIN ... 206
Jim Bunning DET 184
Ralph Terry NY 176

SAVES
Dick Radatz BOS.......... 24
Marshall Bridges NY 18
Terry Fox DET 16

COMPLETE GAMES
Camilo Pascual MIN 18
Jim Kaat MIN 16
Dick Donovan CLE 16

SHUTOUTS
Camilo Pascual MIN 5
Dick Donovan CLE 5
Jim Kaat MIN 5

GAMES PITCHED
Dick Radatz BOS.......... 62
John Wyatt KC.............. 59

INNINGS PITCHED
Ralph Terry NY 299
Jim Kaat MIN 269
Jim Bunning DET........ 258

NATIONAL LEAGUE STANDINGS

1962 NL

	W	L	PCT	GB	R	OR	BA	FA	ERA
SAN FRANCISCO*	103	62	.624	—	878	690	.278	.977	3.79
LOS ANGELES	102	63	.618	1	842	697	.268	.970	3.62
CINCINNATI	98	64	.605	3.5	802	685	.270	.977	3.75
PITTSBURGH	93	68	.578	8	706	626	.268	.976	3.37
MILWAUKEE	86	76	.531	15.5	730	665	.252	.980	3.68
ST. LOUIS	84	78	.519	17.5	774	664	.271	.979	3.55
PHILADELPHIA	81	80	.503	20	705	759	.260	.977	4.28
HOUSTON	64	96	.400	36.5	592	717	.246	.973	3.83
CHICAGO	59	103	.364	42.5	632	827	.253	.977	4.54
NEW YORK	40	120	.250	60.5	617	948	.240	.967	5.04

*Defeated Los Angeles in a playoff 2 games to 1 — 7278 7278 .261 .975 3.94

BATTING AVERAGE
Tommy Davis LA .... .346
F. Robinson CIN .... .342
Stan Musial STL .... .330

HITS
Tommy Davis LA 230
Frank Robinson CIN ... 208
Maury Wills LA............ 208

DOUBLES
Frank Robinson CIN 51
Willie Mays SF 36
Dick Groat PIT 34

TRIPLES
four tied at..................... 10

HOME RUNS
Willie Mays SF.............. 49
Hank Aaron MIL............ 45
Frank Robinson CIN 39

RUNS BATTED IN
Tommy Davis LA 153
Willie Mays SF 141
Frank Robinson CIN ... 136

SLUGGING AVERAGE
F. Robinson CIN .... .624
Hank Aaron MIL.......... .618
Willie Mays SF .... .615

STOLEN BASES
Maury Wills LA............ 104
Willie Davis LA.............. 32
two tied at 26

RUNS SCORED
Frank Robinson CIN ... 134
Maury Wills LA............ 130
Willie Mays SF 130

WINS
Don Drysdale LA............ 25
Jack Sanford SF 24
Bob Purkey CIN 23

WINNING PERCENTAGE
Bob Purkey CIN .... .821
Jack Sanford SF .... .774
Don Drysdale LA......... .735

EARNED RUN AVERAGE
Sandy Koufax LA 2.54
Bob Shaw MIL 2.80
Bob Purkey CIN.......... 2.81

STRIKEOUTS
Don Drysdale LA......... 232
Sandy Koufax LA 216
Bob Gibson STL 208

SAVES
Roy Face PIT................ 28
Ron Perranoski LA........ 20
Stu Miller SF 19

COMPLETE GAMES
Warren Spahn MIL........ 22
Art Mahaffey PHI 20
Billy O'Dell SF................ 20

SHUTOUTS
Bob Gibson STL 5
Bob Friend PIT................ 5

GAMES PITCHED
Ron Perranoski LA........ 70
Jack Baldshun PHI 67
Ed Roebuck LA............. 64

INNINGS PITCHED
Don Drysdale LA......... 314
Bob Purkey CIN 288
Billy O'Dell SF............. 281

AMERICAN LEAGUE STANDINGS

1963 AL

	W	L	PCT	GB	R	OR	BA	FA	ERA
NEW YORK	104	57	.646	—	714	547	.252	.982	3.07
CHICAGO	94	68	.580	10.5	683	544	.250	.979	2.97
MINNESOTA	91	70	.565	13	767	602	.255	.976	3.28
BALTIMORE	86	76	.531	18.5	644	621	.249	.984	3.45
CLEVELAND	79	83	.488	25.5	635	702	.239	.977	3.79
DETROIT	79	83	.488	25.5	700	703	.252	.981	3.90
BOSTON	76	85	.472	28	666	704	.252	.978	3.97
KANSAS CITY	73	89	.451	31.5	615	704	.247	.980	3.92
LOS ANGELES	70	91	.435	34	597	660	.250	.974	3.52
WASHINGTON	56	106	.346	48.5	578	812	.227	.971	4.42
					6599	6599	.247	.978	3.63

BATTING AVERAGE
C. Yastrzemski BOS .. .321
Al Kaline DET .... .312
Rich Rollins MIN .... .307

HITS
C. Yastrzemski BOS ... 183
Pete Ward CHI............. 177
Albie Pearson LA 176

DOUBLES
C. Yastrzemski BOS 40
Pete Ward CHI............... 34
three tied at.................... 32

TRIPLES
Zoilo Versalles MIN....... 13
Jim Fregosi LA............... 12
Chuck Hinton WAS 12

HOME RUNS
H. Killebrew MIN 45
Dick Stuart BOS............. 42
Bob Allison MIN 35

RUNS BATTED IN
Dick Stuart BOS........... 118
Al Kaline DET 101
H. Killebrew MIN 96

SLUGGING AVERAGE
H. Killebrew MIN .... .555
Bob Allison MIN .... .533
Elston Howard NY ..... .528

STOLEN BASES
Luis Aparicio BAL 40
Chuck Hinton WAS 25
two tied at 18

RUNS SCORED
Bob Allison MIN 99
Albie Pearson LA 92
three tied at................... 91

WINS
Whitey Ford NY 24
Jim Bouton NY 21
Camilo Pascual MIN 21

WINNING PERCENTAGE
Whitey Ford NY .... .774
Jim Bouton NY .... .750
Dick Radatz BOS........ .714

EARNED RUN AVERAGE
Gary Peters CHI 2.33
Juan Pizarro CHI 2.39
C. Pascual MIN............ 2.46

STRIKEOUTS
Camilo Pascual MIN ... 202
Jim Bunning DET........ 196
Dick Stigman MIN 193

SAVES
Stu Miller BAL 27
Dick Radatz BOS........... 25
three tied at.................... 21

COMPLETE GAMES
Ralph Terry NY 18
Camilo Pascual MIN 18
Dick Stigman MIN 15

SHUTOUTS
Ray Herbert CHI 7
Jim Bouton NY................. 6

GAMES PITCHED
Stu Miller BAL................ 71
Dick Radatz BOS........... 66
Bill Dailey MIN 66

INNINGS PITCHED
Whitey Ford NY 269
Ralph Terry NY 268
Monbouquette BOS 267

NATIONAL LEAGUE STANDINGS

1963 NL

	W	L	PCT	GB	R	OR	BA	FA	ERA
★ LOS ANGELES	99	63	.611	—	640	550	.251	.975	2.85
ST. LOUIS	93	69	.574	6	747	628	.271	.976	3.32
SAN FRANCISCO	88	74	.543	11	725	641	.258	.975	3.35
PHILADELPHIA	87	75	.537	12	642	578	.252	.978	3.09
CINCINNATI	86	76	.531	13	648	594	.246	.978	3.29
MILWAUKEE	84	78	.519	15	677	603	.244	.980	3.27
CHICAGO	82	80	.506	17	570	578	.238	.976	3.08
PITTSBURGH	74	88	.457	25	567	595	.250	.972	3.10
HOUSTON	66	96	.407	33	464	640	.220	.974	3.44
NEW YORK	51	111	.315	48	501	774	.219	.967	4.12
					6181	6181	.245	.975	3.29

BATTING AVERAGE
Tommy Davis LA .... .326
R. Clemente PIT .... .320
two tied at .... .319

HITS
Vada Pinson CIN 204
Hank Aaron MIL 201
Dick Groat STL 201

DOUBLES
Dick Groat STL 43
Vada Pinson CIN 37
three tied at 36

TRIPLES
Vada Pinson CIN 14
Tony Gonzalez PHI 12
three tied at 11

HOME RUNS
Willie McCovey SF 44
Hank Aaron MIL 44
Willie Mays SF 38

RUNS BATTED IN
Hank Aaron MIL 130
Ken Boyer STL 111
Bill White STL 109

SLUGGING AVERAGE
Hank Aaron MIL .... .586
Willie Mays SF .... .582
Willie McCovey SF ..... .566

STOLEN BASES
Maury Wills LA 40
Hank Aaron MIL 31
Vada Pinson CIN 27

RUNS SCORED
Hank Aaron MIL 121
Willie Mays SF 115
Curt Flood STL 112

WINS
Sandy Koufax LA 25
Juan Marichal SF 25
two tied at 23

WINNING PERCENTAGE
Ron Perranoski LA ..... .842
Sandy Koufax LA .... .833
two tied at .... .767

EARNED RUN AVERAGE
Sandy Koufax LA 1.88
Dick Ellsworth CHI 2.11
Bob Friend PIT 2.34

STRIKEOUTS
Sandy Koufax LA 306
Jim Maloney CIN 265
Don Drysdale LA 251

SAVES
Lindy McDaniel CHI 22
Ron Perranoski LA 21
two tied at 16

COMPLETE GAMES
Warren Spahn MIL 22
Sandy Koufax LA 20
Dick Ellsworth CHI 19

SHUTOUTS
Sandy Koufax LA 11
Warren Spahn MIL 7
two tied at 6

GAMES PITCHED
Ron Perranoski LA 69
Jack Baldschun PHI 65
Larry Bearnarth NY 58

INNINGS PITCHED
Juan Marichal SF 321
Don Drysdale LA 315
Sandy Koufax LA 311

AMERICAN LEAGUE STANDINGS

1964 AL

	W	L	PCT	GB	R	OR	BA	FA	ERA
NEW YORK	99	63	.611	—	730	577	.253	.983	3.15
CHICAGO	98	64	.605	1	642	501	.247	.981	2.72
BALTIMORE	97	65	.599	2	679	567	.248	.985	3.16
DETROIT	85	77	.525	14	699	678	.253	.982	3.84
LOS ANGELES	82	80	.506	17	544	551	.242	.978	2.91
CLEVELAND	79	83	.488	20	689	693	.247	.981	3.75
MINNESOTA	79	83	.488	20	737	678	.252	.977	3.58
BOSTON	72	90	.444	27	688	793	.258	.977	4.50
WASHINGTON	62	100	.383	37	578	733	.231	.979	3.98
KANSAS CITY	57	105	.352	42	621	836	.239	.975	4.71
					6607	6607	.247	.980	3.63

BATTING AVERAGE
Tony Oliva MIN .... .323
B. Robinson BAL .... .317
Elston Howard NY ...... .313

HITS
Tony Oliva MIN 217
B. Robinson BAL 194
B. Richardson NY 181

DOUBLES
Tony Oliva MIN 43
Ed Bressoud BOS 41
Brooks Robinson BAL ... 35

TRIPLES
Rich Rollins MIN 10
Zoilo Versalles MIN 10
three tied at 9

HOME RUNS
H. Killebrew MIN 49
Boog Powell BAL 39
Mickey Mantle NY 35

RUNS BATTED IN
B. Robinson BAL 118
Dick Stuart BOS 114
two tied at 111

SLUGGING AVERAGE
Boog Powell BAL .... .606
Mickey Mantle NY ...... .591
Tony Oliva MIN .... .557

STOLEN BASES
Luis Aparicio BAL 57
Al Weis CHI 22
Vic Davalillo CLE 21

RUNS SCORED
Tony Oliva MIN 109
Dick Howser CLE 101
H. Killebrew MIN 95

WINS
Gary Peters CHI 20
Dean Chance LA 20
three tied at 19

WINNING PERCENTAGE
Wally Bunker BAL .... .792
Whitey Ford NY .... .739
Gary Peters CHI .... .714

EARNED RUN AVERAGE
Dean Chance LA 1.65
Joe Horlen CHI 1.88
Whitey Ford NY 2.13

STRIKEOUTS
Al Downing NY 217
Camilo Pascual MIN ... 213
Dean Chance LA 207

SAVES
Dick Radatz BOS 29
Hoyt Wilhelm CHI 27
Stu Miller BAL 23

COMPLETE GAMES
Dean Chance LA 15
Camilo Pascual MIN 14
three tied at 13

SHUTOUTS
Dean Chance LA 11
Whitey Ford NY 8
Milt Pappas BAL 7

GAMES PITCHED
John Wyatt KC 81
Dick Radatz BOS 79
Hoyt Wilhelm CHI 73

INNINGS PITCHED
Dean Chance LA 278
Gary Peters CHI 274
Jim Bouton NY 271

NATIONAL LEAGUE STANDINGS

1964 NL

	W	L	PCT	GB	R	OR	BA	FA	ERA
★ ST. LOUIS	93	69	.574	—	715	652	.272	.973	3.43
CINCINNATI	92	70	.568	1	660	566	.249	.979	3.07
PHILADELPHIA	92	70	.568	1	693	632	.258	.975	3.36
SAN FRANCISCO	90	72	.556	3	656	587	.246	.975	3.19
MILWAUKEE	88	74	.543	5	803	744	.272	.977	4.12
LOS ANGELES	80	82	.494	13	614	572	.250	.973	2.95
PITTSBURGH	80	82	.494	13	663	636	.264	.972	3.52
CHICAGO	76	86	.469	17	649	724	.251	.975	4.08
HOUSTON	66	96	.407	27	495	628	.229	.976	3.41
NEW YORK	53	109	.327	40	569	776	.246	.974	4.25
					6517	6517	.254	.975	3.54

BATTING AVERAGE
R. Clemente PIT .... .339
Rico Carty MIL .... .330
Hank Aaron MIL......... .328

HITS
Curt Flood STL 211
R. Clemente PIT 211
two tied at 201

DOUBLES
Lee Maye MIL 44
R. Clemente PIT 40
Billy Williams CHI........... 39

TRIPLES
Dick Allen PHI................ 13
Ron Santo CHI............... 13
two tied at 11

HOME RUNS
Willie Mays SF 47
Billy Williams CHI........... 33
three tied at................... 31

RUNS BATTED IN
Ken Boyer STL 119
Ron Santo CHI............. 114
Willie Mays SF 111

SLUGGING AVERAGE
Willie Mays SF .... .607
Ron Santo CHI........... .564
Dick Allen PHI............. .557

STOLEN BASES
Maury Wills LA............... 53
Lou Brock CHI, STL....... 43
Willie Davis LA............... 42

RUNS SCORED
Dick Allen PHI.............. 125
Willie Mays SF 121
Lou Brock CHI, STL.... 111

WINS
Larry Jackson CHI 24
Juan Marichal SF.......... 21
Ray Sadecki STL 20

WINNING PERCENTAGE
Sandy Koufax LA........ .792
Juan Marichal SF....... .724
Jim O'Toole CIN .... .708

EARNED RUN AVERAGE
Sandy Koufax LA........ 1.74
Don Drysdale LA........ 2.18
Chris Short PHI........... 2.20

STRIKEOUTS
Bob Veale PIT.............. 250
Bob Gibson STL 245
Don Drysdale LA......... 237

SAVES
Hal Woodeshick HOU... 23
Al McBean PIT 22
Jack Baldschun PHI...... 21

COMPLETE GAMES
Juan Marichal SF.......... 22
Don Drysdale LA........... 21
Larry Jackson CHI 19

SHUTOUTS
Sandy Koufax LA............. 7
four tied at....................... 5

GAMES PITCHED
Bob Miller LA 74
Ron Perranoski LA........ 72
Jack Baldschun PHI...... 71

INNINGS PITCHED
Don Drysdale LA.......... 321
Larry Jackson CHI 298
Bob Gibson STL 287

AMERICAN LEAGUE STANDINGS

1965 AL

	W	L	PCT	GB	R	OR	BA	FA	ERA
MINNESOTA	102	60	.630	—	774	600	.254	.973	3.14
CHICAGO	95	67	.586	7	647	555	.246	.980	2.99
BALTIMORE	94	68	.580	8	641	578	.238	.980	2.98
DETROIT	89	73	.549	13	680	602	.238	.981	3.35
CLEVELAND	87	75	.537	15	663	613	.250	.981	3.30
NEW YORK	77	85	.475	25	611	604	.235	.978	3.28
CALIFORNIA	75	87	.463	27	527	569	.239	.981	3.17
WASHINGTON	70	92	.432	32	591	721	.228	.977	3.93
BOSTON	62	100	.383	40	669	791	.251	.974	4.24
KANSAS CITY	59	103	.364	43	585	755	.240	.977	4.24
					6388	6388	.242	.978	3.46

BATTING AVERAGE
Tony Oliva MIN .... .321
C. Yastrzemski BOS .. .312
Vic Davalillo CLE .... .301

HITS
Tony Oliva MIN 185
Zoilo Versalles MIN 182
Rocky Colavito CLE 170

DOUBLES
C. Yastrzemski BOS 45
Zoilo Versalles MIN 45
Tony Oliva MIN 40

TRIPLES
Bert Campaneris KC 12
Zoilo Versalles MIN 12
Luis Aparicio BAL 10

HOME RUNS
Tony Conigliaro BOS 32
Norm Cash DET 30
Willie Horton DET 29

RUNS BATTED IN
Rocky Colavito CLE 108
Willie Horton DET 104
Tony Oliva MIN 98

SLUGGING AVERAGE
C. Yastrzemski BOS .. .536
T. Conigliaro BOS ...... .512
Norm Cash DET .... .512

STOLEN BASES
Bert Campaneris KC 51
Jose Cardenal CAL 37
Zoilo Versalles MIN 27

RUNS SCORED
Zoilo Versalles MIN 126
Tony Oliva MIN 107
Tom Tresh NY 94

WINS
Mudcat Grant MIN 21
Mel Stottlemyre NY 20
Jim Kaat MIN 18

WINNING PERCENTAGE
Mudcat Grant MIN ..... .750
Denny McLain DET .... .727
Mel Stottlemyre NY .... .690

EARNED RUN AVERAGE
Sam McDowell CLE 2.18
Eddie Fisher CHI 2.40
Sonny Siebert CLE 2.43

STRIKEOUTS
Sam McDowell CLE.... 325
Mickey Lolich DET 226
Denny McLain DET..... 192

SAVES
Ron Kline WAS 29
Eddie Fisher CHI 24
Stu Miller BAL 24

COMPLETE GAMES
Mel Stottlemyre NY 18
Mudcat Grant MIN 14
Sam McDowell CLE 14

SHUTOUTS
Mudcat Grant MIN 6
four tied at 4

GAMES PITCHED
Eddie Fisher CHI 82
Ron Kline WAS 74
Bob Lee CAL 69

INNINGS PITCHED
Mel Stottlemyre NY 291
Sam McDowell CLE.... 273
Mudcat Grant MIN 270

NATIONAL LEAGUE STANDINGS

1965 NL

	W	L	PCT	GB	R	OR	BA	FA	ERA
★ LOS ANGELES	97	65	.599	—	608	521	.245	.979	2.81
SAN FRANCISCO	95	67	.586	2	682	593	.252	.976	3.20
PITTSBURGH	90	72	.556	7	675	580	.265	.977	3.01
CINCINNATI	89	73	.549	8	825	704	.273	.981	3.88
MILWAUKEE	86	76	.531	11	708	633	.256	.978	3.52
PHILADELPHIA	85	76	.528	11.5	654	667	.250	.975	3.53
ST. LOUIS	80	81	.497	16.5	707	674	.254	.979	3.77
CHICAGO	72	90	.444	25	635	723	.238	.974	3.78
HOUSTON	65	97	.401	32	596	711	.237	.974	3.84
NEW YORK	50	112	.309	47	495	752	.221	.974	4.06
					6558	6558	.249	.977	3.54

BATTING AVERAGE
R. Clemente PIT .... .329
Hank Aaron MIL .... .318
Willie Mays SF .... .317

HITS
Pete Rose CIN 209
Vada Pinson CIN 204
Billy Williams CHI 203

DOUBLES
Hank Aaron MIL 40
Billy Williams CHI 39
two tied at 35

TRIPLES
Johnny Callison PHI 16
three tied at 14

HOME RUNS
Willie Mays SF 52
Willie McCovey SF 39
Billy Williams CHI 34

RUNS BATTED IN
Deron Johnson CIN 130
Frank Robinson CIN ... 113
Willie Mays SF 112

SLUGGING AVERAGE
Willie Mays SF .... .645
Hank Aaron MIL .... .560
Billy Williams CHI ...... .552

STOLEN BASES
Maury Wills LA 94
Lou Brock STL 63
Jimmy Wynn HOU 43

RUNS SCORED
Tommy Harper CIN 126
Willie Mays SF 118
Pete Rose CIN 117

WINS
Sandy Koufax LA 26
Tony Cloninger MIL 24
Don Drysdale LA 23

WINNING PERCENTAGE
Sandy Koufax LA .... .765
Jim Maloney CIN .... .690
Sammy Ellis CIN .... .688

EARNED RUN AVERAGE
Sandy Koufax LA 2.04
Juan Marichal SF 2.13
Vern Law PIT 2.15

STRIKEOUTS
Sandy Koufax LA 382
Bob Veale PIT 276
Bob Gibson STL 270

SAVES
Ted Abernathy CHI 31
Billy McCool CIN 21
Frank Linzy SF 21

COMPLETE GAMES
Sandy Koufax LA 27
Juan Marichal SF 24
two tied at 20

SHUTOUTS
Juan Marichal SF 10
Sandy Koufax LA 8
three tied at 7

GAMES PITCHED
Ted Abernathy CHI 84
Woodeshick HOU, STL.. 78
Lindy McDaniel CHI 71

INNINGS PITCHED
Sandy Koufax LA 336
Don Drysdale LA 308
Bob Gibson STL 299

AMERICAN LEAGUE STANDINGS

1966 AL

	W	L	PCT	GB	R	OR	BA	FA	ERA
★ BALTIMORE	97	63	.606	—	755	601	.258	.981	3.32
MINNESOTA	89	73	.549	9	663	581	.249	.977	3.13
DETROIT	88	74	.543	10	719	698	.251	.980	3.85
CHICAGO	83	79	.512	15	574	517	.231	.976	2.68
CLEVELAND	81	81	.500	17	574	586	.237	.978	3.23
CALIFORNIA	80	82	.494	18	604	643	.232	.979	3.56
KANSAS CITY	74	86	.463	23	564	648	.236	.977	3.56
WASHINGTON	71	88	.447	25.5	557	659	.234	.977	3.70
BOSTON	72	90	.444	26	655	731	.240	.975	3.92
NEW YORK	70	89	.440	26.5	611	612	.235	.977	3.41
					6276	6276	.240	.978	3.44

BATTING AVERAGE
F. Robinson BAL......... .316
Tony Oliva MIN .... .307
Al Kaline DET .... .288

HITS
Tony Oliva MIN 191
Frank Robinson BAL... 182
Luis Aparicio BAL 182

DOUBLES
C. Yastrzemski BOS 39
Brooks Robinson BAL... 35
Frank Robinson BAL... 34

TRIPLES
Bobby Knoop CAL 11
Bert Campaneris KC 10
Ed Brinkman WAS 9

HOME RUNS
Frank Robinson BAL.... 49
H. Killebrew MIN 39
Boog Powell BAL 34

RUNS BATTED IN
Frank Robinson BAL... 122
H. Killebrew MIN 110
Boog Powell BAL 109

SLUGGING AVERAGE
F. Robinson BAL......... .637
H. Killebrew MIN .... .538
Al Kaline DET .... .534

STOLEN BASES
Bert Campaneris KC ... 52
Don Buford CHI 51
Tommy Agee CHI 44

RUNS SCORED
Frank Robinson BAL... 122
Tony Oliva MIN 99
two tied at 98

WINS
Jim Kaat MIN 25
Denny McLain DET....... 20
E. Wilson BOS, DET..... 18

WINNING PERCENTAGE
Sonny Siebert CLE .... .667
Jim Kaat MIN .... .658
E. Wilson BOS, DET... .621

EARNED RUN AVERAGE
Gary Peters CHI 1.98
Joe Horlen CHI 2.43
Steve Hargan CLE..... 2.48

STRIKEOUTS
Sam McDowell CLE.... 225
Jim Kaat MIN 205
E. Wilson BOS, DET ... 200

SAVES
Jack Aker KC 32
Ron Kline WAS 23
Larry Sherry DET.......... 20

COMPLETE GAMES
Jim Kaat MIN 19
Denny McLain DET....... 14
E. Wilson BOS, DET..... 13

SHUTOUTS
Luis Tiant CLE 5
Sam McDowell CLE........ 5
Tommy John CHI............ 5

GAMES PITCHED
E. Fisher CHI, BAL 67
Casey Cox WAS 66
Jack Aker KC 66

INNINGS PITCHED
Jim Kaat MIN 305
Denny McLain DET..... 264
E. Wilson BOS, DET... 264

NATIONAL LEAGUE STANDINGS

1966 NL

	W	L	PCT	GB	R	OR	BA	FA	ERA
LOS ANGELES	95	67	.586	—	606	490	.256	.979	2.62
SAN FRANCISCO	93	68	.578	1.5	675	626	.248	.974	3.24
PITTSBURGH	92	70	.568	3	759	641	.279	.978	3.52
PHILADELPHIA	87	75	.537	8	696	640	.258	.982	3.57
ATLANTA	85	77	.525	10	782	683	.263	.976	3.68
ST. LOUIS	83	79	.512	12	571	577	.251	.977	3.11
CINCINNATI	76	84	.475	18	692	702	.260	.980	4.08
HOUSTON	72	90	.444	23	612	695	.255	.972	3.76
NEW YORK	66	95	.410	28.5	587	761	.239	.975	4.17
CHICAGO	59	103	.364	36	644	809	.254	.974	4.33
					6624	6624	.256	.977	3.61

BATTING AVERAGE
Matty Alou PIT .... .342
Felipe Alou ATL .... .327
Rico Carty ATL .... .326

HITS
Felipe Alou ATL 218
Pete Rose CIN 205
R. Clemente PIT 202

DOUBLES
Johnny Callison PHI 40
Pete Rose CIN 38
Vada Pinson CIN 35

TRIPLES
Tim McCarver STL 13
Lou Brock STL 12
R. Clemente PIT 11

HOME RUNS
Hank Aaron ATL 44
Dick Allen PHI 40
Willie Mays SF 37

RUNS BATTED IN
Hank Aaron ATL 127
R. Clemente PIT 119
Dick Allen PHI 110

SLUGGING AVERAGE
Dick Allen PHI .... .632
Willie McCovey SF .... .586
Willie Stargell PIT .... .581

STOLEN BASES
Lou Brock STL 74
Sonny Jackson HOU 49
Maury Wills LA 38

RUNS SCORED
Felipe Alou ATL 122
Hank Aaron ATL 117
Dick Allen PHI 112

WINS
Sandy Koufax LA 27
Juan Marichal SF 25
two tied at 21

WINNING PERCENTAGE
Juan Marichal SF .... .806
Sandy Koufax LA .... .750
Gaylord Perry SF .... .724

EARNED RUN AVERAGE
Sandy Koufax LA 1.73
Mike Cuellar HOU 2.22
Juan Marichal SF 2.23

STRIKEOUTS
Sandy Koufax LA 317
Jim Bunning PHI 252
Bob Veale PIT.............. 229

SAVES
Phil Regan LA 21
Billy McCool CIN 18
Roy Face PIT 18

COMPLETE GAMES
Sandy Koufax LA 27
Juan Marichal SF 25
Bob Gibson STL 20

SHUTOUTS
six tied at........................ 5

GAMES PITCHED
Clay Carroll ATL 73
Pete Mikkelsen PIT....... 71
Darold Knowles PHI...... 69

INNINGS PITCHED
Sandy Koufax LA 323
Jim Bunning PHI 314
Juan Marichal SF........ 307

AMERICAN LEAGUE STANDINGS

1967 AL

	W	L	PCT	GB	R	OR	BA	FA	ERA
BOSTON	92	70	.568	—	722	614	.255	.977	3.36
DETROIT	91	71	.562	1	683	587	.243	.978	3.32
MINNESOTA	91	71	.562	1	671	590	.240	.978	3.14
CHICAGO	89	73	.549	3	531	491	.225	.979	2.45
CALIFORNIA	84	77	.522	7.5	567	587	.238	.982	3.19
BALTIMORE	76	85	.472	15.5	654	592	.240	.980	3.32
WASHINGTON	76	85	.472	15.5	550	637	.223	.978	3.38
CLEVELAND	75	87	.463	17	559	613	.235	.981	3.25
NEW YORK	72	90	.444	20	522	621	.225	.976	3.24
KANSAS CITY	62	99	.385	29.5	533	660	.233	.978	3.68
					5992	5992	.236	.979	3.23

BATTING AVERAGE
C. Yastrzemski BOS .. .326
F. Robinson BAL .... .311
Al Kaline DET .... .308

HITS
C. Yastrzemski BOS ... 189
Cesar Tovar MIN 173
two tied at 171

DOUBLES
Tony Oliva MIN 34
Cesar Tovar MIN 32
C. Yastrzemski BOS 31

TRIPLES
Paul Blair BAL 12
Don Buford CHI 9

HOME RUNS
H. Killebrew MIN 44
C. Yastrzemski BOS 44
Frank Howard WAS 36

RUNS BATTED IN
C. Yastrzemski BOS ... 121
H. Killebrew MIN 113
Frank Robinson BAL 94

SLUGGING AVERAGE
C. Yastrzemski BOS .. .622
F. Robinson BAL .... .576
H. Killebrew MIL .... .558

STOLEN BASES
Bert Campaneris KC 55
Don Buford CHI 34
Tommy Agee CHI 28

RUNS SCORED
C. Yastrzemski BOS ... 112
H. Killebrew MIN 105
Cesar Tovar MIN 98

WINS
Jim Lonborg BOS 22
Earl Wilson DET 22
Dean Chance MIN 20

WINNING PERCENTAGE
Joe Horlen CHI .... .731
Jim Lonborg BOS .... .710
Earl Wilson DET .... .667

EARNED RUN AVERAGE
Joe Horlen CHI 2.06
Gary Peters CHI 2.28
Sonny Siebert CLE 2.38

STRIKEOUTS
Jim Lonborg BOS 246
Sam McDowell CLE.... 236
Dean Chance MIN 220

SAVES
Minnie Rojas CAL 27
John Wyatt BOS 20
Bob Locker CHI 20

COMPLETE GAMES
Dean Chance MIN 18
Jim Lonborg BOS 15
Steve Hargan CLE 15

SHUTOUTS
five tied at 6

GAMES PITCHED
Bob Locker CHI 77
Minnie Rojas CAL 72
Bill Kelso CAL 69

INNINGS PITCHED
Dean Chance MIN 284
Jim Lonborg BOS 273
Earl Wilson DET 264

NATIONAL LEAGUE STANDINGS

1967 NL

	W	L	PCT	GB	R	OR	BA	FA	ERA
★ ST. LOUIS	101	60	.627	—	695	557	.263	.978	3.05
SAN FRANCISCO	91	71	.562	10.5	652	551	.245	.979	2.92
CHICAGO	87	74	.540	14	702	624	.251	.981	3.48
CINCINNATI	87	75	.537	14.5	604	563	.248	.980	3.05
PHILADELPHIA	82	80	.506	19.5	612	581	.242	.978	3.10
PITTSBURGH	81	81	.500	20.5	679	693	.277	.978	3.74
ATLANTA	77	85	.475	24.5	631	640	.240	.978	3.47
LOS ANGELES	73	89	.451	28.5	519	595	.236	.975	3.21
HOUSTON	69	93	.426	32.5	626	742	.249	.974	4.03
NEW YORK	61	101	.377	40.5	498	672	.238	.975	3.73
					6218	6218	.249	.978	3.38

BATTING AVERAGE
R. Clemente PIT .... .357
Tony Gonzalez PHI .... .339
Matty Alou PIT .... .338

HITS
R. Clemente PIT 209
Lou Brock STL 206
Vada Pinson CIN 187

DOUBLES
Rusty Staub HOU 44
Orlando Cepeda STL 37
Hank Aaron ATL 37

TRIPLES
Vada Pinson CIN 13
Lou Brock STL 12
Billy Williams CHI 12

HOME RUNS
Hank Aaron ATL 39
Jimmy Wynn HOU 37
two tied at 31

RUNS BATTED IN
O. Cepeda STL 111
R. Clemente PIT 110
Hank Aaron ATL 109

SLUGGING AVERAGE
Hank Aaron ATL .... .573
Dick Allen PHI .... .566
R. Clemente PIT .... .554

STOLEN BASES
Lou Brock STL 52
Maury Wills PIT 29
Joe Morgan HOU 29

RUNS SCORED
Lou Brock STL 113
Hank Aaron ATL 113
Ron Santo CHI 107

WINS
Mike McCormick SF 22
F. Jenkins CHI 20
two tied at 17

WINNING PERCENTAGE
Dick Hughes STL .... .727
Mike McCormick SF ... .688
Bob Veale PIT .... .667

EARNED RUN AVERAGE
Phil Niekro ATL 1.87
Jim Bunning PHI 2.29
Chris Short PHI 2.39

STRIKEOUTS
Jim Bunning PHI 253
F. Jenkins CHI 236
Gaylord Perry SF 230

SAVES
Ted Abernathy CIN 28
Frank Linzy SF 17
Roy Face PIT 17

COMPLETE GAMES
F. Jenkins CHI 20
three tied at 18

SHUTOUTS
Jim Bunning PHI 6
three tied at 5

GAMES PITCHED
Ron Perranoski LA 70
Ted Abernathy CIN 70
Ron Willis STL 65

INNINGS PITCHED
Jim Bunning PHI 302
Gaylord Perry SF 293
F. Jenkins CHI 289

AMERICAN LEAGUE STANDINGS

1968 AL

	W	L	PCT	GB	R	OR	BA	FA	ERA
★ DETROIT	103	59	.636	—	671	492	.235	.983	2.71
BALTIMORE	91	71	.562	12	579	497	.225	.981	2.66
CLEVELAND	86	75	.534	16.5	516	504	.234	.979	2.66
BOSTON	86	76	.531	17	614	611	.236	.979	3.33
NEW YORK	83	79	.512	20	536	531	.214	.979	2.79
OAKLAND	82	80	.506	21	569	544	.240	.977	2.94
MINNESOTA	79	83	.488	24	562	546	.237	.973	2.89
CALIFORNIA	67	95	.414	36	498	615	.227	.977	3.43
CHICAGO	67	95	.414	36	463	527	.228	.977	2.75
WASHINGTON	65	96	.404	37.5	524	665	.224	.976	3.64
					5532	5532	.230	.978	2.98

BATTING AVERAGE
C. Yastrzemski BOS .. .301
Danny Cater OAK ...... .290
Tony Oliva MIN .... .289

HITS
B. Campaneris OAK ... 177
Cesar Tovar MIN 167
two tied at 164

DOUBLES
Reggie Smith BOS........ 37
Brooks Robinson BAL... 36
C. Yastrzemski BOS 32

TRIPLES
Jim Fregosi CAL 13
Tom McCraw CHI 12
two tied at 10

HOME RUNS
Frank Howard WAS 44
Willie Horton DET 36
Ken Harrelson BOS 35

RUNS BATTED IN
Ken Harrelson BOS 109
Frank Howard WAS.... 106
Jim Northrup DET 90

SLUGGING AVERAGE
Frank Howard WAS ... .552
Willie Horton DET ...... .543
Ken Harrelson BOS ... .518

STOLEN BASES
B. Campaneris OAK 62
Jose Cardenal CLE....... 40
Cesar Tovar MIN 35

RUNS SCORED
Dick McAuliffe DET....... 95
C. Yastrzemski BOS 90
two tied at 89

WINS
Denny McLain DET....... 31
Dave McNally BAL........ 22
two tied at 21

WINNING PERCENTAGE
Denny McLain DET.... .838
Ray Culp BOS .... .727
Luis Tiant CLE .... .700

EARNED RUN AVERAGE
Luis Tiant CLE 1.60
Sam McDowell CLE.... 1.81
Dave McNally BAL..... 1.95

STRIKEOUTS
Sam McDowell CLE.... 283
Denny McLain DET..... 280
Luis Tiant CLE 264

SAVES
Al Worthington MIN....... 18
Wilbur Wood CHI 16
Dennis Higgins WAS 13

COMPLETE GAMES
Denny McLain DET....... 28
Luis Tiant CLE 19
Mel Stottlemyre NY....... 19

SHUTOUTS
Luis Tiant CLE 9

GAMES PITCHED
Wilbur Wood CHI 88
Hoyt Wilhelm CHI 72
Bob Locker CHI 70

INNINGS PITCHED
Denny McLain DET..... 336
Dean Chance MIN 292
Mel Stottlemyre NY..... 279

NATIONAL LEAGUE STANDINGS

1968 NL

	W	L	PCT	GB	R	OR	BA	FA	ERA
ST. LOUIS	97	65	.599	—	583	472	.249	.978	2.49
SAN FRANCISCO	88	74	.543	9	599	529	.239	.975	2.71
CHICAGO	84	78	.519	13	612	611	.242	.981	3.41
CINCINNATI	83	79	.512	14	690	673	.273	.978	3.56
ATLANTA	81	81	.500	16	514	549	.252	.980	2.92
PITTSBURGH	80	82	.494	17	583	532	.252	.979	2.74
LOS ANGELES	76	86	.469	21	470	509	.230	.977	2.69
PHILADELPHIA	76	86	.469	21	543	615	.233	.980	3.36
NEW YORK	73	89	.451	24	473	499	.228	.979	2.72
HOUSTON	72	90	.444	25	510	588	.231	.975	3.26
					5577	5577	.243	.978	2.99

BATTING AVERAGE
Pete Rose CIN............ .335
Matty Alou PIT .... .332
Felipe Alou ATL .... .317

HITS
Pete Rose CIN............ 210
Felipe Alou ATL 210
Glenn Beckert CHI....... 189

DOUBLES
Lou Brock STL.............. 46
Pete Rose CIN.............. 42
Johnny Bench CIN........ 40

TRIPLES
Lou Brock STL.............. 14
R. Clemente PIT 12
Willie Davis LA.............. 10

HOME RUNS
Willie McCovey SF........ 36
Dick Allen PHI............... 33
Ernie Banks CHI 32

RUNS BATTED IN
Willie McCovey SF...... 105
Billy Williams CHI........... 98
Ron Santo CHI............... 98

SLUGGING AVERAGE
Willie McCovey SF..... .545
Dick Allen PHI............ .520
Billy Williams CHI....... .500

STOLEN BASES
Lou Brock STL.............. 62
Maury Wills PIT............. 52
Willie Davis LA.............. 36

RUNS SCORED
Glenn Beckert CHI........ 98
Pete Rose CIN.............. 94
Tony Perez CIN 93

WINS
Juan Marichal SF.......... 26
Bob Gibson STL 22
F. Jenkins CHI 20

WINNING PERCENTAGE
Steve Blass PIT .... .750
Juan Marichal SF........ .743
Bob Gibson STL .... .710

EARNED RUN AVERAGE
Bob Gibson STL 1.12
Bobby Bolin SF 1.99
Bob Veale PIT............. 2.05

STRIKEOUTS
Bob Gibson STL 268
F. Jenkins CHI 260
Bill Singer LA 227

SAVES
Phil Regan LA, CHI....... 25
Joe Hoerner STL 17
Clay Carroll ATL, CIN ... 17

COMPLETE GAMES
Juan Marichal SF.......... 30
Bob Gibson STL 28
F. Jenkins CHI 20

SHUTOUTS
Bob Gibson STL 13
Don Drysdale LA............. 8
two tied at 7

GAMES PITCHED
Ted Abernathy CIN 78
Phil Regan LA, CHI....... 73
Clay Carroll ATL, CIN ... 68

INNINGS PITCHED
Juan Marichal SF........ 326
F. Jenkins CHI 308
Bob Gibson STL 305

AMERICAN LEAGUE STANDINGS

1969 AL

EAST	W	L	PCT	GB	R	OR	BA	FA	ERA
• BALTIMORE	109	53	.673	—	779	517	.265	.984	2.83
DETROIT	90	72	.556	19	701	601	.242	.979	3.31
BOSTON	87	75	.537	22	743	736	.251	.975	3.92
WASHINGTON	86	76	.531	23	694	644	.251	.978	3.49
NEW YORK	80	81	.497	28.5	562	587	.235	.979	3.23
CLEVELAND	62	99	.385	46.5	573	717	.237	.976	3.94

WEST	W	L	PCT	GB	R	OR	BA	FA	ERA
MINNESOTA	97	65	.599	—	790	618	.268	.977	3.24
OAKLAND	88	74	.543	9	740	678	.249	.979	3.71
CALIFORNIA	71	91	.438	26	528	652	.230	.978	3.54
KANSAS CITY	69	93	.426	28	586	688	.240	.975	3.72
CHICAGO	68	94	.420	29	625	723	.247	.981	4.21
SEATTLE	64	98	.395	33	639	799	.234	.974	4.35
					7960	7960	.246	.978	3.62

BATTING AVERAGE
Rod Carew MIN .... .332
Reggie Smith BOS .... .309
Tony Oliva MIN .... .309

HITS
Tony Oliva MIN 197
Horace Clarke NY 183
Paul Blair BAL 178

DOUBLES
Tony Oliva MIN 39
Reggie Jackson OAK 36
Davey Johnson BAL 34

TRIPLES
Del Unser WAS 8
Horace Clarke NY 7
Reggie Smith BOS 7

HOME RUNS
Harmon Killebrew MIN 49
Frank Howard WAS 48
Reggie Jackson OAK 47

RUNS BATTED IN
Harmon Killebrew MIN 140
Boog Powell BAL 121
Reggie Jackson OAK 118

SLUGGING AVERAGE
Reggie Jackson OAK .... .608
Rico Petrocelli BOS .... .589
Harmon Killebrew MIN .... .584

STOLEN BASES
Tommy Harper SEA 73
Bert Campaneris OAK 62
Cesar Tovar MIN 45

RUNS SCORED
Reggie Jackson OAK 123
Frank Howard WAS 111
Frank Robinson BAL 111

WINS
Denny McLain DET 24
Mike Cuellar BAL 23
four tied at 20

WINNING PERCENTAGE
Jim Palmer BAL .... .800
Jim Perry MIN .... .769
Dave McNally BAL .... .741

EARNED RUN AVERAGE
Dick Bosman WAS 2.19
Jim Palmer BAL 2.34
Mike Cuellar BAL 2.38

STRIKEOUTS
Sam McDowell CLE 279
Mickey Lolich DET 271
Andy Messersmith CAL 211

SAVES
Ron Perranoski MIN 31
Ken Tatum CAL 22
Sparky Lyle BOS 17

COMPLETE GAMES
Mel Stottlemyre NY 24
Denny McLain DET 23
two tied at 18

SHUTOUTS
Denny McLain DET 9
Jim Palmer BAL 6
Mike Cuellar BAL 5

GAMES PITCHED
Wilbur Wood CHI 76
Ron Perranoski MIN 75
Sparky Lyle BOS 71

INNINGS PITCHED
Denny McLain DET 325
Mel Stottlemyre NY 303
Mike Cuellar BAL 291

NATIONAL LEAGUE STANDINGS

1969 NL

EAST	W	L	PCT	GB	R	OR	BA	FA	ERA
★ NEW YORK	100	62	.617	—	632	541	.242	.980	2.99
CHICAGO	92	70	.568	8	720	611	.253	.979	3.34
PITTSBURGH	88	74	.543	12	725	652	.277	.975	3.61
ST. LOUIS	87	75	.537	13	595	540	.253	.978	2.94
PHILADELPHIA	63	99	.389	37	645	745	.241	.978	4.14
MONTREAL	52	110	.321	48	582	791	.240	.971	4.33

WEST	W	L	PCT	GB	R	OR	BA	FA	ERA
ATLANTA	93	69	.574	—	691	631	.258	.981	3.53
SAN FRANCISCO	90	72	.556	3	713	636	.242	.974	3.26
CINCINNATI	89	73	.549	4	798	768	.277	.974	4.11
LOS ANGELES	85	77	.525	8	645	561	.254	.980	3.08
HOUSTON	81	81	.500	12	676	668	.240	.975	3.60
SAN DIEGO	52	110	.321	41	468	746	.225	.975	4.24
					7890	7890	.250	.977	3.59

BATTING AVERAGE
Pete Rose CIN .348
Roberto Clemente PIT .345
Cleon Jones NY .340

HITS
Matty Alou PIT 231
Pete Rose CIN 218
Lou Brock STL 195

DOUBLES
Matty Alou PIT 41
Don Kessinger CHI 38
three tied at 33

TRIPLES
Roberto Clemente PIT 12
Pete Rose CIN 11
three tied at 10

HOME RUNS
Willie McCovey SF 45
Hank Aaron ATL 44
Lee May CIN 38

RUNS BATTED IN
Willie McCovey SF 126
Ron Santo CHI 123
Tony Perez CIN 122

SLUGGING AVERAGE
Willie McCovey SF .656
Hank Aaron ATL .607
Dick Allen PHI .573

STOLEN BASES
Lou Brock STL 53
Joe Morgan HOU 49
Bobby Bonds SF 45

RUNS SCORED
Pete Rose CIN 120
Bobby Bonds SF 120
Jimmy Wynn HOU 113

WINS
Tom Seaver NY 25
Phil Niekro ATL 23
two tied at 21

WINNING PERCENTAGE
Tom Seaver NY .781
Juan Marichal SF .656
two tied at .654

EARNED RUN AVERAGE
Juan Marichal SF 2.10
Steve Carlton STL 2.17
Bob Gibson STL 2.18

STRIKEOUTS
Ferguson Jenkins CHI 273
Bob Gibson STL 269
Bill Singer LA 247

SAVES
Fred Gladding HOU 29
Wayne Granger CIN 27
Cecil Upshaw ATL 27

COMPLETE GAMES
Bob Gibson STL 28
Juan Marichal SF 27
Gaylord Perry SF 26

SHUTOUTS
Juan Marichal SF 8
Ferguson Jenkins CHI 7
Claude Osteen LA 7

GAMES PITCHED
Wayne Granger CIN 90
Dan McGinn MON 74
two tied at 71

INNINGS PITCHED
Gaylord Perry SF 325
Claude Osteen LA 321
Bill Singer LA 316

AMERICAN LEAGUE STANDINGS

1970 AL

EAST	W	L	PCT	GB	R	OR	BA	FA	ERA
★ BALTIMORE	108	54	.667	—	792	574	.257	.981	3.15
NEW YORK	93	69	.574	15	680	612	.251	.980	3.24
BOSTON	87	75	.537	21	786	722	.262	.974	3.87
DETROIT	79	83	.488	29	666	731	.238	.978	4.09
CLEVELAND	76	86	.469	32	649	675	.249	.979	3.91
WASHINGTON	70	92	.432	38	626	689	.238	.982	3.80

WEST	W	L	PCT	GB	R	OR	BA	FA	ERA
MINNESOTA	98	64	.605	—	744	605	.262	.980	3.23
OAKLAND	89	73	.549	9	678	593	.249	.977	3.30
CALIFORNIA	86	76	.531	12	631	630	.251	.980	3.48
KANSAS CITY	65	97	.401	33	611	705	.244	.976	3.78
MILWAUKEE	65	97	.401	33	613	751	.242	.978	4.21
CHICAGO	56	106	.346	42	633	822	.253	.975	4.54
					8109	8109	.250	.978	3.71

BATTING AVERAGE
- Alex Johnson CAL .... .329
- Carl Yastrzemski BOS ...... .329
- Tony Oliva MIN .... .325

HITS
- Tony Oliva MIN 204
- Alex Johnson CAL 202
- Cesar Tovar MIN 195

DOUBLES
- Cesar Tovar MIN 36
- Tony Oliva MIN 36
- Amos Otis KC 36

TRIPLES
- Cesar Tovar MIN 13
- Mickey Stanley DET 11
- Amos Otis KC 9

HOME RUNS
- Frank Howard WAS 44
- Harmon Killebrew MIN 41
- Carl Yastrzemski BOS 40

RUNS BATTED IN
- Frank Howard WAS 126
- Tony Conigliaro BOS 116
- Boog Powell BAL 114

SLUGGING AVERAGE
- Carl Yastrzemski BOS ...... .592
- Boog Powell BAL .... .549
- Harmon Killebrew MIN .... .546

STOLEN BASES
- Bert Campaneris OAK 42
- Tommy Harper MIL 38
- Sandy Alomar CAL 35

RUNS SCORED
- Carl Yastrzemski BOS 125
- Cesar Tovar MIN 120
- two tied at 109

WINS
- Dave McNally BAL 24
- Jim Perry MIN 24
- Mike Cuellar BAL 24

WINNING PERCENTAGE
- Mike Cuellar BAL .... .750
- Dave McNally BAL .... .727
- two tied at .... .667

EARNED RUN AVERAGE
- Diego Segui OAK 2.56
- Jim Palmer BAL 2.71
- Clyde Wright CAL 2.83

STRIKEOUTS
- Sam McDowell CLE 304
- Mickey Lolich DET 230
- Bob Johnson KC 206

SAVES
- Ron Perranoski MIN 34
- Lindy McDaniel NY 29
- two tied at 27

COMPLETE GAMES
- Mike Cuellar BAL 21
- Sam McDowell CLE 19
- Jim Palmer BAL 17

SHUTOUTS
- Jim Palmer BAL 5
- Chuck Dobson OAK 5
- three tied at 4

GAMES PITCHED
- Wilbur Wood CHI 77
- Mudcat Grant OAK 72
- Darold Knowles WAS 71

INNINGS PITCHED
- Sam McDowell CLE 305
- Jim Palmer BAL 305
- Mike Cuellar BAL 298

NATIONAL LEAGUE STANDINGS

1970 NL

EAST	W	L	PCT	GB	R	OR	BA	FA	ERA
PITTSBURGH	89	73	.549	—	729	664	.270	.979	3.70
CHICAGO	84	78	.519	5	806	679	.259	.978	3.76
NEW YORK	83	79	.512	6	695	630	.249	.979	3.45
ST. LOUIS	76	86	.469	13	744	747	.263	.977	4.06
PHILADELPHIA	73	88	.453	15.5	594	730	.238	.981	4.17
MONTREAL	73	89	.451	16	687	807	.237	.977	4.50

WEST	W	L	PCT	GB	R	OR	BA	FA	ERA
• CINCINNATI	102	60	.630	—	775	681	.270	.976	3.69
LOS ANGELES	87	74	.540	14.5	749	684	.270	.978	3.82
SAN FRANCISCO	86	76	.531	16	831	826	.262	.973	4.50
HOUSTON	79	83	.488	23	744	763	.259	.978	4.23
ATLANTA	76	86	.469	26	736	772	.270	.977	4.33
SAN DIEGO	63	99	.389	39	681	788	.246	.975	4.36
					8771	8771	.258	.977	4.05

BATTING AVERAGE
Rico Carty ATL .... .366
Joe Torre STL .... .325
Manny Sanguillen PIT ..... .325

HITS
Billy Williams CHI 205
Pete Rose CIN 205
Joe Torre STL 203

DOUBLES
Wes Parker LA 47
Willie McCovey SF 39
Pete Rose CIN 37

TRIPLES
Willie Davis LA 16
Don Kessinger CHI 14
two tied at 10

HOME RUNS
Johnny Bench CIN 45
Billy Williams CHI 42
Tony Perez CIN 40

RUNS BATTED IN
Johnny Bench CIN 148
Billy Williams CHI 129
Tony Perez CIN 129

SLUGGING AVERAGE
Willie McCovey SF .... .612
Tony Perez CIN .... .589
Johnny Bench CIN .... .587

STOLEN BASES
Bobby Tolan CIN 57
Lou Brock STL 51
Bobby Bonds SF 48

RUNS SCORED
Billy Williams CHI 137
Bobby Bonds SF 134
Pete Rose CIN 120

WINS
Gaylord Perry SF 23
Bob Gibson STL 23
Ferguson Jenkins CHI 22

WINNING PERCENTAGE
Bob Gibson STL .... .767
Gary Nolan CIN .... .720
Luke Walker PIT .... .714

EARNED RUN AVERAGE
Tom Seaver NY 2.82
Wayne Simpson CIN 3.02
Luke Walker PIT 3.04

STRIKEOUTS
Tom Seaver NY 283
Bob Gibson STL 274
Ferguson Jenkins CHI 274

SAVES
Wayne Granger CIN 35
Dave Giusti PIT 26
Jim Brewer LA 24

COMPLETE GAMES
Ferguson Jenkins CHI 24
Gaylord Perry SF 23
Bob Gibson STL 23

SHUTOUTS
Gaylord Perry SF 5
four tied at 4

GAMES PITCHED
Ron Herbel SD, NY 76
Dick Selma PHI 73
two tied at 67

INNINGS PITCHED
Gaylord Perry SF 329
Ferguson Jenkins CHI 313
Bob Gibson STL 294

AMERICAN LEAGUE STANDINGS

1971 AL

EAST	W	L	PCT	GB	R	OR	BA	FA	ERA
• BALTIMORE	101	57	.639	—	742	530	.261	.981	2.99
DETROIT	91	71	.562	12	701	645	.254	.983	3.63
BOSTON	85	77	.525	18	691	667	.252	.981	3.80
NEW YORK	82	80	.506	21	648	641	.254	.981	3.43
WASHINGTON	63	96	.396	38.5	537	660	.230	.977	3.70
CLEVELAND	60	102	.370	43	543	747	.238	.981	4.28

WEST	W	L	PCT	GB	R	OR	BA	FA	ERA
OAKLAND	101	60	.627	—	691	564	.252	.981	3.05
KANSAS CITY	85	76	.528	16	603	566	.250	.979	3.25
CHICAGO	79	83	.488	22.5	617	597	.250	.975	3.12
CALIFORNIA	76	86	.469	25.5	511	576	.231	.980	3.10
MINNESOTA	74	86	.463	26.5	654	670	.260	.980	3.81
MILWAUKEE	69	92	.429	32	534	609	.229	.977	3.38
					7472	7472	.247	.980	3.46

BATTING AVERAGE
Tony Oliva MIN .... .337
Bobby Murcer NY .... .331
Merv Rettenmund BAL .... .318

HITS
Cesar Tovar MIN 204
Sandy Alomar CAL 179
Rod Carew MIN 177

DOUBLES
Reggie Smith BOS 33
Paul Schaal KC 31
two tied at 30

TRIPLES
Freddie Patek KC 11
Rod Carew MIN 10
Paul Blair BAL 8

HOME RUNS
Bill Melton CHI 33
Norm Cash DET 32
Reggie Jackson OAK 32

RUNS BATTED IN
Harmon Killebrew MIN 119
Frank Robinson BAL 99
Reggie Smith BOS 96

SLUGGING AVERAGE
Tony Oliva MIN .... .546
Bobby Murcer NY .... .543
Norm Cash DET .... .531

STOLEN BASES
Amos Otis KC 52
Freddie Patek KC 49
Sandy Alomar CAL 39

RUNS SCORED
Don Buford BAL 99
Bobby Murcer NY 94
Cesar Tovar MIN 94

WINS
Mickey Lolich DET 25
Vida Blue OAK 24
Wilbur Wood CHI 22

WINNING PERCENTAGE
Dave McNally BAL .... .808
Vida Blue OAK .... .750
Chuck Dobson OAK .... .750

EARNED RUN AVERAGE
Vida Blue OAK 1.82
Wilbur Wood CHI 1.91
Jim Palmer BAL 2.68

STRIKEOUTS
Mickey Lolich DET 308
Vida Blue OAK 301
Joe Coleman DET 236

SAVES
Ken Sanders MIL 31
Ted Abernathy KC 23
Fred Scherman DET 20

COMPLETE GAMES
Mickey Lolich DET 29
Vida Blue OAK 24
Wilbur Wood CHI 22

SHUTOUTS
Vida Blue OAK 8
Mel Stottlemyre NY 7
Wilbur Wood CHI 7

GAMES PITCHED
Ken Sanders MIL 83
Fred Scherman DET 69
Tom Burgmeier KC 67

INNINGS PITCHED
Mickey Lolich DET 376
Wilbur Wood CHI 334
Vida Blue OAK 312

NATIONAL LEAGUE STANDINGS

1971 NL

EAST	W	L	PCT	GB	R	OR	BA	FA	ERA
★ PITTSBURGH	97	65	.599	—	788	599	.274	.979	3.31
ST. LOUIS	90	72	.556	7	739	699	.275	.978	3.85
CHICAGO	83	79	.512	14	637	648	.258	.980	3.61
NEW YORK	83	79	.512	14	588	550	.249	.981	2.99
MONTREAL	71	90	.441	25.5	622	729	.246	.976	4.12
PHILADELPHIA	67	95	.414	30	558	688	.233	.981	3.71

WEST	W	L	PCT	GB	R	OR	BA	FA	ERA
SAN FRANCISCO	90	72	.556	—	706	644	.247	.972	3.32
LOS ANGELES	89	73	.549	1	663	587	.266	.979	3.23
ATLANTA	82	80	.506	8	643	699	.257	.977	3.75
CINCINNATI	79	83	.488	11	586	581	.241	.984	3.35
HOUSTON	79	83	.488	11	585	567	.240	.983	3.13
SAN DIEGO	61	100	.379	28.5	486	610	.233	.974	3.22
					7601	7601	.252	.979	3.47

BATTING AVERAGE
Joe Torre STL .363
Ralph Garr ATL .343
Glenn Beckert CHI .342

HITS
Joe Torre STL 230
Ralph Garr ATL 219
Lou Brock STL 200

DOUBLES
Cesar Cedeno HOU 40
Lou Brock STL 37
two tied at 34

TRIPLES
Joe Morgan HOU 11
Roger Metzger HOU 11
Willie Davis LA 10

HOME RUNS
Willie Stargell PIT 48
Hank Aaron ATL 47
Lee May CIN 39

RUNS BATTED IN
Joe Torre STL 137
Willie Stargell PIT 125
Hank Aaron ATL 118

SLUGGING AVERAGE
Hank Aaron ATL .669
Willie Stargell PIT .628
Joe Torre STL .555

STOLEN BASES
Lou Brock STL 64
Joe Morgan HOU 40
Ralph Garr ATL 30

RUNS SCORED
Lou Brock STL 126
Bobby Bonds SF 110
Willie Stargell PIT 104

WINS
Ferguson Jenkins CHI 24
three tied at 20

WINNING PERCENTAGE
Don Gullett CIN .727
Steve Carlton STL .690
Al Downing LA .690

EARNED RUN AVERAGE
Tom Seaver NY 1.76
Dave Roberts SD 2.10
Don Wilson HOU 2.45

STRIKEOUTS
Tom Seaver NY 289
Ferguson Jenkins CHI 263
Bill Stoneman MON 251

SAVES
Dave Giusti PIT 30
Mike Marshall MON 23
Jim Brewer LA 22

COMPLETE GAMES
Ferguson Jenkins CHI 30
Tom Seaver NY 21
two tied at 20

SHUTOUTS
four tied at 5

GAMES PITCHED
Wayne Granger CIN 70
Jerry Johnson SF 67
Mike Marshall MON 66

INNINGS PITCHED
Ferguson Jenkins CHI 325
Bill Stoneman MON 295
Tom Seaver NY 286

AMERICAN LEAGUE STANDINGS

1972 AL

EAST	W	L	PCT	GB	R	OR	BA	FA	ERA
DETROIT	86	70	.551	—	558	514	.237	.984	2.96
BOSTON	85	70	.548	.5	640	620	.248	.978	3.47
BALTIMORE	80	74	.519	5	519	430	.229	.983	2.53
NEW YORK	79	76	.510	6.5	557	527	.249	.978	3.05
CLEVELAND	72	84	.462	14	472	519	.234	.981	2.92
MILWAUKEE	65	91	.417	21	493	595	.235	.977	3.45

WEST	W	L	PCT	GB	R	OR	BA	FA	ERA
★ OAKLAND	93	62	.600	—	604	457	.240	.979	2.58
CHICAGO	87	67	.565	5.5	566	538	.238	.977	3.12
MINNESOTA	77	77	.500	15.5	537	535	.244	.974	2.84
KANSAS CITY	76	78	.494	16.5	580	545	.255	.981	3.24
CALIFORNIA	75	80	.484	18	454	533	.242	.981	3.06
TEXAS	54	100	.351	38.5	461	628	.217	.972	3.53
					6441	6441	.239	.979	3.06

BATTING AVERAGE
Rod Carew MIN .... .318
Lou Piniella KC .... .312
Dick Allen CHI .... .308

HITS
Joe Rudi OAK 181
Lou Piniella KC 179
Bobby Murcer NY 171

DOUBLES
Lou Piniella KC 33
Joe Rudi OAK 32
Bobby Murcer NY 30

TRIPLES
Joe Rudi OAK 9
Carlton Fisk BOS 9
Paul Blair BAL 8

HOME RUNS
Dick Allen CHI 37
Bobby Murcer NY 33
two tied at 26

RUNS BATTED IN
Dick Allen CHI 113
John Mayberry KC 100
Bobby Murcer NY 96

SLUGGING AVERAGE
Dick Allen CHI .... .603
Carlton Fisk BOS .... .538
Bobby Murcer NY .... .537

STOLEN BASES
Bert Campaneris OAK 52
Dave Nelson TEX 51
Freddie Patek KC 33

RUNS SCORED
Bobby Murcer NY 102
Joe Rudi OAK 94
Tommy Harper BOS 92

WINS
Wilbur Wood CHI 24
Gaylord Perry CLE 24
Mickey Lolich DET 22

WINNING PERCENTAGE
Catfish Hunter OAK .... .750
Blue Moon Odom OAK ..... .714
Luis Tiant BOS .... .714

EARNED RUN AVERAGE
Luis Tiant BOS 1.91
Gaylord Perry CLE 1.92
Catfish Hunter OAK 2.04

STRIKEOUTS
Nolan Ryan CAL 329
Mickey Lolich DET 250
Gaylord Perry CLE 234

SAVES
Sparky Lyle NY 35
Terry Forster CHI 29
Rollie Fingers OAK 21

COMPLETE GAMES
Gaylord Perry CLE 29
Mickey Lolich DET 23
two tied at 20

SHUTOUTS
Nolan Ryan CAL 9
Wilbur Wood CHI 8
Mel Stottlemyre NY 7

GAMES PITCHED
Paul Lindblad TEX 66
Rollie Fingers OAK 65
Wayne Granger MIN 63

INNINGS PITCHED
Wilbur Wood CHI 377
Gaylord Perry CLE 343
Mickey Lolich DET 327

NATIONAL LEAGUE STANDINGS

1972 NL

EAST	W	L	PCT	GB	R	OR	BA	FA	ERA
PITTSBURGH	96	59	.619	—	691	512	.274	.978	2.81
CHICAGO	85	70	.548	11	685	567	.257	.979	3.22
NEW YORK	83	73	.532	13.5	528	578	.225	.980	3.26
ST. LOUIS	75	81	.481	21.5	568	600	.260	.977	3.42
MONTREAL	70	86	.449	26.5	513	609	.234	.978	3.59
PHILADELPHIA	59	97	.378	37.5	503	635	.236	.981	3.66

WEST	W	L	PCT	GB	R	OR	BA	FA	ERA
• CINCINNATI	95	59	.617	—	707	557	.251	.982	3.21
HOUSTON	84	69	.549	10.5	708	636	.258	.980	3.77
LOS ANGELES	85	70	.548	10.5	584	527	.256	.974	2.78
ATLANTA	70	84	.455	25	628	730	.258	.974	4.27
SAN FRANCISCO	69	86	.445	26.5	662	649	.244	.974	3.69
SAN DIEGO	58	95	.379	36.5	488	665	.227	.976	3.78
					7265	7265	.248	.978	3.45

BATTING AVERAGE
Billy Williams CHI .... .333
Ralph Garr ATL .... .325
Dusty Baker ATL .... .321

HITS
Pete Rose CIN 198
Lou Brock STL 193
Billy Williams CHI 191

DOUBLES
Cesar Cedeno HOU 39
Willie Montanez PHI 39
Ted Simmons STL 36

TRIPLES
Larry Bowa PHI 13
Pete Rose CIN 11
three tied at 8

HOME RUNS
Johnny Bench CIN 40
Nate Colbert SD 38
Billy Williams CHI 37

RUNS BATTED IN
Johnny Bench CIN 125
Billy Williams CHI 122
Willie Stargell PIT 112

SLUGGING AVERAGE
Billy Williams CHI .... .606
Willie Stargell PIT .... .558
Johnny Bench CIN .... .541

STOLEN BASES
Lou Brock STL 63
Joe Morgan CIN 58
Cesar Cedeno HOU 55

RUNS SCORED
Joe Morgan CIN 122
Bobby Bonds SF 118
Jimmy Wynn HOU 117

WINS
Steve Carlton PHI 27
Tom Seaver NY 21
two tied at 20

WINNING PERCENTAGE
Gary Nolan CIN .... .750
Steve Carlton PHI .... .730
Milt Pappas CHI .... .708

EARNED RUN AVERAGE
Steve Carlton PHI 1.97
Gary Nolan CIN 1.99
Don Sutton LA 2.08

STRIKEOUTS
Steve Carlton PHI 310
Tom Seaver NY 249
Bob Gibson STL 208

SAVES
Clay Carroll CIN 37
Tug McGraw NY 27
Dave Giusti PIT 22

COMPLETE GAMES
Steve Carlton PHI 30
Ferguson Jenkins CHI 23
Bob Gibson STL 23

SHUTOUTS
Don Sutton LA 9
Steve Carlton PHI 8
Fred Norman SD 6

GAMES PITCHED
Mike Marshall MON 65
Clay Carroll CIN 65
Pedro Borbon CIN 62

INNINGS PITCHED
Steve Carlton PHI 346
Ferguson Jenkins CHI 289
Phil Niekro ATL 282

AMERICAN LEAGUE STANDINGS

1973 AL

EAST	W	L	PCT	GB	R	OR	BA	FA	ERA
BALTIMORE	97	65	.599	—	754	561	.266	.981	3.07
BOSTON	89	73	.549	8	738	647	.267	.979	3.65
DETROIT	85	77	.525	12	642	674	.254	.982	3.90
NEW YORK	80	82	.494	17	641	610	.261	.976	3.34
MILWAUKEE	74	88	.457	23	708	731	.253	.977	3.98
CLEVELAND	71	91	.438	26	680	826	.256	.978	4.58

WEST	W	L	PCT	GB	R	OR	BA	FA	ERA
★ OAKLAND	94	68	.580	—	758	615	.260	.978	3.29
KANSAS CITY	88	74	.543	6	755	752	.261	.974	4.19
MINNESOTA	81	81	.500	13	738	692	.270	.978	3.77
CALIFORNIA	79	83	.488	15	629	657	.253	.975	3.53
CHICAGO	77	85	.475	17	652	705	.256	.977	3.86
TEXAS	57	105	.352	37	619	844	.255	.974	4.64
					8314	8314	.259	.977	3.82

BATTING AVERAGE
Rod Carew MIN .... .350
George Scott MIL .... .306
Tommy Davis BAL .... .306

HITS
Rod Carew MIN 203
Dave May MIL 189
Bobby Murcer NY 187

DOUBLES
Sal Bando OAK 32
Pedro Garcia MIL 32
three tied at 30

TRIPLES
Rod Carew MIN 11
Al Bumbry BAL 11
Jorge Orta CHI 10

HOME RUNS
Reggie Jackson OAK 32
Frank Robinson CAL 30
Jeff Burroughs TEX 30

RUNS BATTED IN
Reggie Jackson OAK 117
George Scott MIL 107
John Mayberry KC 100

SLUGGING AVERAGE
Reggie Jackson OAK ...... .531
Sal Bando OAK .... .498
Frank Robinson CAL ...... .489

STOLEN BASES
Tommy Harper BOS 54
Billy North OAK 53
Dave Nelson TEX 43

RUNS SCORED
Reggie Jackson OAK 99
three tied at 98

WINS
Wilbur Wood CHI 24
Joe Coleman DET 23
Jim Palmer BAL 22

WINNING PERCENTAGE
Catfish Hunter OAK .... .808
Jim Palmer BAL .... .710
Vida Blue OAK .... .690

EARNED RUN AVERAGE
Jim Palmer BAL 2.40
Bert Blyleven MIN 2.52
Bill Lee BOS 2.75

STRIKEOUTS
Nolan Ryan CAL 383
Bert Blyleven MIN 258
Bill Singer CAL 241

SAVES
John Hiller DET 38
Sparky Lyle NY 27
Rollie Fingers OAK 22

COMPLETE GAMES
Gaylord Perry CLE 29
Nolan Ryan CAL 26
Bert Blyleven MIN 25

SHUTOUTS
Bert Blyleven MIN 9
Gaylord Perry CLE 7
Jim Palmer BAL 6

GAMES PITCHED
John Hiller DET 65
Rollie Fingers OAK 62
Doug Bird KC 54

INNINGS PITCHED
Wilbur Wood CHI 359
Gaylord Perry CLE 344
Nolan Ryan CAL 326

NATIONAL LEAGUE STANDINGS

1973 NL

EAST	W	L	PCT	GB	R	OR	BA	FA	ERA
• NEW YORK	82	79	.509	—	608	588	.246	.980	3.26
ST. LOUIS	81	81	.500	1.5	643	603	.259	.975	3.25
PITTSBURGH	80	82	.494	2.5	704	693	.261	.976	3.73
MONTREAL	79	83	.488	3.5	668	702	.251	.974	3.71
CHICAGO	77	84	.478	5	614	655	.247	.975	3.66
PHILADELPHIA	71	91	.438	11.5	642	717	.249	.979	3.99

WEST	W	L	PCT	GB	R	OR	BA	FA	ERA
CINCINNATI	99	63	.611	—	741	621	.254	.982	3.40
LOS ANGELES	95	66	.590	3.5	675	565	.263	.981	3.00
SAN FRANCISCO	88	74	.543	11	739	702	.262	.974	3.79
HOUSTON	82	80	.506	17	681	672	.251	.981	3.75
ATLANTA	76	85	.472	22.5	799	774	.266	.974	4.25
SAN DIEGO	60	102	.370	39	548	770	.244	.973	4.16
					8062	8062	.254	.977	3.66

BATTING AVERAGE
Pete Rose CIN .... .338
Cesar Cedeno HOU .... .320
Garry Maddox SF .... .319

HITS
Pete Rose CIN 230
Ralph Garr ATL 200
Lou Brock STL 193

DOUBLES
Willie Stargell PIT 43
Al Oliver PIT 38
three tied at 36

TRIPLES
Roger Metzger HOU 14
Garry Maddox SF 10
Gary Matthews SF 10

HOME RUNS
Willie Stargell PIT 44
Davey Johnson ATL 43
Darrell Evans ATL 41

RUNS BATTED IN
Willie Stargell PIT 119
Lee May HOU 105
two tied at 104

SLUGGING AVERAGE
Willie Stargell PIT .... .646
Darrell Evans ATL .... .556
Davey Johnson ATL .... .546

STOLEN BASES
Lou Brock STL 70
Joe Morgan CIN 67
Cesar Cedeno HOU 56

RUNS SCORED
Bobby Bonds SF 131
Joe Morgan CIN 116
Pete Rose CIN 115

WINS
Ron Bryant SF 24
Tom Seaver NY 19
Jack Billingham CIN 19

WINNING PERCENTAGE
Tommy John LA .... .696
Don Gullett CIN .... .692
Ron Bryant SF .... .667

EARNED RUN AVERAGE
Tom Seaver NY 2.08
Don Sutton LA 2.42
Wayne Twitchell PHI 2.50

STRIKEOUTS
Tom Seaver NY 251
Steve Carlton PHI 223
Jon Matlack NY 205

SAVES
Mike Marshall MON 31
Tug McGraw NY 25
two tied at 20

COMPLETE GAMES
Tom Seaver NY 18
Steve Carlton PHI 18
Jack Billingham CIN 16

SHUTOUTS
Jack Billingham CIN 7
Dave Roberts HOU 6
two tied at 5

GAMES PITCHED
Mike Marshall MON 92
Pedro Borbon CIN 80
Elias Sosa SF 71

INNINGS PITCHED
Steve Carlton PHI 293
Jack Billingham CIN 293
Tom Seaver NY 290

AMERICAN LEAGUE STANDINGS

1974 AL

EAST	W	L	PCT	GB	R	OR	BA	FA	ERA
BALTIMORE	91	71	.562	—	659	612	.256	.980	3.27
NEW YORK	89	73	.549	2	671	623	.263	.977	3.31
BOSTON	84	78	.519	7	696	661	.264	.977	3.72
CLEVELAND	77	85	.475	14	662	694	.255	.977	3.80
MILWAUKEE	76	86	.469	15	647	660	.244	.980	3.76
DETROIT	72	90	.444	19	620	768	.247	.975	4.16

WEST	W	L	PCT	GB	R	OR	BA	FA	ERA
★ OAKLAND	90	72	.556	—	689	551	.247	.977	2.95
TEXAS	84	76	.525	5	690	698	.272	.974	3.82
MINNESOTA	82	80	.506	8	673	669	.272	.976	3.64
CHICAGO	80	80	.500	9	684	721	.268	.977	3.94
KANSAS CITY	77	85	.475	13	667	662	.259	.976	3.51
CALIFORNIA	68	94	.420	22	618	657	.254	.977	3.52
					7976	7976	.258	.977	3.62

BATTING AVERAGE
Rod Carew MIN .... .364
Jorge Orta CHI .... .316
Hal McRae KC .... .310

HITS
Rod Carew MIN 218
Tommy Davis BAL 181
Don Money MIL 178

DOUBLES
Joe Rudi OAK 39
George Scott MIL 36
Hal McRae KC 36

TRIPLES
Mickey Rivers CAL 11
Amos Otis KC 9

HOME RUNS
Dick Allen CHI 32
Reggie Jackson OAK 29
Gene Tenace OAK 26

RUNS BATTED IN
Jeff Burroughs TEX 118
Sal Bando OAK 103
Joe Rudi OAK 99

SLUGGING AVERAGE
Dick Allen CHI .... .563
Reggie Jackson OAK .... .514
Jeff Burroughs TEX .... .504

STOLEN BASES
Billy North OAK 54
Rod Carew MIN 38
John Lowenstein CLE 36

RUNS SCORED
Carl Yastrzemski BOS 93
Bobby Grich BAL 92
Reggie Jackson OAK 90

WINS
Catfish Hunter OAK 25
Ferguson Jenkins TEX 25
four tied at 22

WINNING PERCENTAGE
Mike Cuellar BAL .... .688
Catfish Hunter OAK .... .676
Ferguson Jenkins TEX ..... .676

EARNED RUN AVERAGE
Catfish Hunter OAK 2.49
Gaylord Perry CLE 2.51
Andy Hassler CAL 2.61

STRIKEOUTS
Nolan Ryan CAL 367
Bert Blyleven MIN 249
Ferguson Jenkins TEX 225

SAVES
Terry Forster CHI 24
Tom Murphy MIL 20
Bill Campbell MIN 19

COMPLETE GAMES
Ferguson Jenkins TEX 29
Gaylord Perry CLE 28
Mickey Lolich DET 27

SHUTOUTS
Luis Tiant BOS 7
Catfish Hunter OAK 6
Ferguson Jenkins TEX 6

GAMES PITCHED
Rollie Fingers OAK 76
Tom Murphy MIL 70
Steve Foucault TEX 69

INNINGS PITCHED
Nolan Ryan CAL 333
Ferguson Jenkins TEX 328
Gaylord Perry CLE 322

NATIONAL LEAGUE STANDINGS

1974 NL

EAST	W	L	PCT	GB	R	OR	BA	FA	ERA
PITTSBURGH	88	74	.543	—	751	657	.274	.975	3.49
ST. LOUIS	86	75	.534	1.5	677	643	.265	.977	3.48
PHILADELPHIA	80	82	.494	8	676	701	.261	.976	3.91
MONTREAL	79	82	.491	8.5	662	657	.254	.976	3.60
NEW YORK	71	91	.438	17	572	646	.235	.975	3.42
CHICAGO	66	96	.407	22	669	826	.251	.969	4.28

WEST	W	L	PCT	GB	R	OR	BA	FA	ERA
LOS ANGELES	102	60	.630	—	798	561	.272	.975	2.97
CINCINNATI	98	64	.605	4	776	631	.260	.979	3.41
ATLANTA	88	74	.543	14	661	563	.249	.979	3.05
HOUSTON	81	81	.500	21	653	632	.263	.982	3.46
SAN FRANCISCO	72	90	.444	30	634	723	.252	.972	3.78
SAN DIEGO	60	102	.370	42	541	830	.229	.973	4.58
					8070	8070	.255	.976	3.62

BATTING AVERAGE
Ralph Garr ATL .... .353
Al Oliver PIT .... .321
two tied at .... .314

HITS
Ralph Garr ATL 214
Dave Cash PHI 206
Steve Garvey LA 200

DOUBLES
Pete Rose CIN 45
Al Oliver PIT 38
Johnny Bench CIN 38

TRIPLES
Ralph Garr ATL 17
Al Oliver PIT 12
Dave Cash PHI 11

HOME RUNS
Mike Schmidt PHI 36
Johnny Bench CIN 33
Jimmy Wynn LA 32

RUNS BATTED IN
Johnny Bench CIN 129
Mike Schmidt PHI 116
Steve Garvey LA 111

SLUGGING AVERAGE
Mike Schmidt PHI .... .546
Willie Stargell PIT .... .537
Reggie Smith STL .... .528

STOLEN BASES
Lou Brock STL 118
Davey Lopes LA 59
Joe Morgan CIN 58

RUNS SCORED
Pete Rose CIN 110
Mike Schmidt PHI 108
Johnny Bench CIN 108

WINS
Phil Niekro ATL 20
Andy Messersmith LA 20
two tied at 19

WINNING PERCENTAGE
Andy Messersmith LA ...... .769
Don Sutton LA .... .679
Buzz Capra ATL .... .667

EARNED RUN AVERAGE
Buzz Capra ATL 2.28
Phil Niekro ATL 2.38
Jon Matlack NY 2.41

STRIKEOUTS
Steve Carlton PHI 240
Andy Messersmith LA 221
Tom Seaver NY 201

SAVES
Mike Marshall LA 21
Randy Moffitt SF 15
Pedro Borbon CIN 14

COMPLETE GAMES
Phil Niekro ATL 18
Steve Carlton PHI 17
Jim Lonborg PHI 16

SHUTOUTS
Jon Matlack NY 7
Phil Niekro ATL 6

GAMES PITCHED
Mike Marshall LA 106
Larry Hardy SD 76
Pedro Borbon CIN 73

INNINGS PITCHED
Phil Niekro ATL 302
Andy Messersmith LA 292
Steve Carlton PHI 291

AMERICAN LEAGUE STANDINGS

1975 AL

EAST	W	L	PCT	GB	R	OR	BA	FA	ERA
• BOSTON	95	65	.594	—	796	709	.275	.977	3.98
BALTIMORE	90	69	.566	4.5	682	553	.252	.983	3.17
NEW YORK	83	77	.519	12	681	588	.264	.978	3.29
CLEVELAND	79	80	.497	15.5	688	703	.261	.978	3.84
MILWAUKEE	68	94	.420	28	675	792	.250	.971	4.34
DETROIT	57	102	.358	37.5	570	786	.249	.972	4.27

WEST	W	L	PCT	GB	R	OR	BA	FA	ERA
OAKLAND	98	64	.605	—	758	606	.254	.977	3.27
KANSAS CITY	91	71	.562	7	710	649	.261	.976	3.47
TEXAS	79	83	.488	19	714	733	.256	.971	3.86
MINNESOTA	76	83	.478	20.5	724	736	.271	.973	4.05
CHICAGO	75	86	.466	22.5	655	703	.255	.978	3.93
CALIFORNIA	72	89	.447	25.5	628	723	.246	.971	3.89
					8281	8281	.258	.975	3.78

BATTING AVERAGE
Rod Carew MIN................ .359
Fred Lynn BOS................. .331
Thurman Munson NY....... .318

HITS
George Brett KC............... 195
Rod Carew MIN................ 192
Thurman Munson NY....... 190

DOUBLES
Fred Lynn BOS................. 47
Reggie Jackson OAK........ 39
three tied at 38

TRIPLES
Mickey Rivers CAL............ 13
George Brett KC............... 13
Jorge Orta CHI.................. 10

HOME RUNS
George Scott MIL.............. 36
Reggie Jackson OAK........ 36
John Mayberry KC............ 34

RUNS BATTED IN
George Scott MIL.............. 109
John Mayberry KC............ 106
Fred Lynn BOS................. 105

SLUGGING AVERAGE
Fred Lynn BOS................. .566
John Mayberry KC............ .547
Boog Powell CLE.............. .524

STOLEN BASES
Mickey Rivers CAL............ 70
C. Washington OAK.......... 40
Amos Otis KC................... 39

RUNS SCORED
Fred Lynn BOS................. 103
John Mayberry KC............ 95
Bobby Bonds NY............... 93

WINS
Jim Palmer BAL................ 23
Catfish Hunter NY............. 23
Vida Blue OAK.................. 22

WINNING PERCENTAGE
Mike Torrez BAL............... .690
Dennis Leonard KC.......... .682
Jim Palmer BAL................ .676

EARNED RUN AVERAGE
Jim Palmer BAL................ 2.09
Catfish Hunter NY............. 2.58
Dennis Eckersley CLE...... 2.60

STRIKEOUTS
Frank Tanana CAL............ 269
Bert Blyleven MIN............. 233
G. Perry CLE, TEX............ 233

SAVES
Goose Gossage CHI......... 26
Rollie Fingers OAK............ 24
Tom Murphy MIL............... 20

COMPLETE GAMES
Catfish Hunter NY............. 30
Jim Palmer BAL................ 25
Gaylord Perry CLE, TEX ... 25

SHUTOUTS
Jim Palmer BAL................ 10
Catfish Hunter NY............. 7

GAMES PITCHED
Rollie Fingers OAK............ 75
Paul Lindblad OAK............ 68
Goose Gossage CHI......... 62

INNINGS PITCHED
Catfish Hunter NY............. 328
Jim Palmer BAL................ 323
G. Perry CLE, TEX............ 306

NATIONAL LEAGUE STANDINGS

1975 NL

EAST	W	L	PCT	GB	R	OR	BA	FA	ERA
PITTSBURGH	92	69	.571	—	712	565	.263	.976	3.01
PHILADELPHIA	86	76	.531	6.5	735	694	.269	.976	3.82
NEW YORK	82	80	.506	10.5	646	625	.256	.976	3.39
ST. LOUIS	82	80	.506	10.5	662	689	.273	.973	3.57
CHICAGO	75	87	.463	17.5	712	827	.259	.972	4.49
MONTREAL	75	87	.463	17.5	601	690	.244	.973	3.72

WEST	W	L	PCT	GB	R	OR	BA	FA	ERA
★ CINCINNATI	108	54	.667	—	840	586	.271	.984	3.37
LOS ANGELES	88	74	.543	20	648	534	.248	.979	2.92
SAN FRANCISCO	80	81	.497	27.5	659	671	.259	.976	3.74
SAN DIEGO	71	91	.438	37	552	683	.244	.971	3.48
ATLANTA	67	94	.416	40.5	583	739	.244	.972	3.91
HOUSTON	64	97	.398	43.5	664	711	.254	.979	4.04
					8014	8014	.257	.976	3.62

BATTING AVERAGE
Bill Madlock CHI .... .354
Ted Simmons STL .... .332
Manny Sanguillen PIT ..... .328

HITS
Dave Cash PHI.................. 213
Steve Garvey LA 210
Pete Rose CIN 210

DOUBLES
Pete Rose CIN 47
Dave Cash PHI.................. 40
two tied at.......................... 39

TRIPLES
Ralph Garr ATL 11
four tied at 10

HOME RUNS
Mike Schmidt PHI............... 38
Dave Kingman NY.............. 36
Greg Luzinski PHI 34

RUNS BATTED IN
Greg Luzinski PHI 120
Johnny Bench CIN 110
Tony Perez CIN 109

SLUGGING AVERAGE
Dave Parker PIT .... .541
Greg Luzinski PHI .... .540
Mike Schmidt PHI............. .523

STOLEN BASES
Davey Lopes LA 77
Joe Morgan CIN 67
Lou Brock STL 56

RUNS SCORED
Pete Rose CIN 112
Dave Cash PHI................. 111
Davey Lopes LA 108

WINS
Tom Seaver NY 22
Randy Jones SD 20
Andy Messersmith LA 19

WINNING PERCENTAGE
Don Gullet CIN .... .789
Tom Seaver NY .... .710
Burt Hooton CHI, LA .... .667

EARNED RUN AVERAGE
Randy Jones SD 2.24
Andy Messersmith LA 2.29
Tom Seaver NY 2.38

STRIKEOUTS
Tom Seaver NY 243
John Montefusco SF 215
Andy Messersmith LA 213

SAVES
Rawley Eastwick CIN 22
Al Hrabosky STL 22
Dave Giusti PIT 17

COMPLETE GAMES
Andy Messersmith LA 19
Randy Jones SD 18
two tied at........................... 15

SHUTOUTS
Andy Messersmith LA 7
Randy Jones SD 6
Jerry Reuss PIT 6

GAMES PITCHED
Gene Garber PHI 71
Will McEnaney CIN 70
two tied at........................... 67

INNINGS PITCHED
Andy Messersmith LA 322
Randy Jones SD 285
Tom Seaver NY 280

AMERICAN LEAGUE STANDINGS

1976 AL

EAST	W	L	PCT	GB	R	OR	BA	FA	ERA
• NEW YORK	97	62	.610	—	730	575	.269	.980	3.19
BALTIMORE	88	74	.543	10.5	619	598	.243	.982	3.32
BOSTON	83	79	.512	15.5	716	660	.263	.978	3.52
CLEVELAND	81	78	.509	16	615	615	.263	.980	3.47
DETROIT	74	87	.460	24	609	709	.257	.974	3.87
MILWAUKEE	66	95	.410	32	570	655	.246	.975	3.64

WEST	W	L	PCT	GB	R	OR	BA	FA	ERA
KANSAS CITY	90	72	.556	—	713	611	.269	.978	3.21
OAKLAND	87	74	.540	2.5	686	598	.246	.977	3.26
MINNESOTA	85	77	.525	5	743	704	.274	.973	3.69
CALIFORNIA	76	86	.469	14	550	631	.235	.977	3.36
TEXAS	76	86	.469	14	616	652	.250	.976	3.45
CHICAGO	64	97	.398	25.5	586	745	.255	.979	4.25
					7753	7753	.256	.977	3.52

BATTING AVERAGE
George Brett KC .... .333
Hal McRae KC .... .332
Rod Carew MIN .... .331

HITS
George Brett KC 215
Rod Carew MIN 200
Chris Chambliss NY 188

DOUBLES
Amos Otis KC 40
four tied at 34

TRIPLES
George Brett KC 14
Phil Garner OAK 12
Rod Carew MIN 12

HOME RUNS
Graig Nettles NY 32
Sal Bando OAK 27
Reggie Jackson BAL 27

RUNS BATTED IN
Lee May BAL 109
Thurman Munson NY 105
Carl Yastrzemski BOS 102

SLUGGING AVERAGE
Reggie Jackson BAL .... .502
Jim Rice BOS .... .482
Graig Nettles NY .... .475

STOLEN BASES
Billy North OAK 75
Ron LeFlore DET 58
Bert Campaneris OAK 54

RUNS SCORED
Roy White NY 104
Rod Carew MIN 97
Mickey Rivers NY 95

WINS
Jim Palmer BAL 22
Luis Tiant BOS 21
Wayne Garland BAL 20

WINNING PERCENTAGE
Bill Campbell MIN .... .773
Wayne Garland BAL .... .741
Doc Ellis NY .... .680

EARNED RUN AVERAGE
Mark Fidrych DET 2.34
Vida Blue OAK 2.35
Frank Tanana CAL 2.44

STRIKEOUTS
Nolan Ryan CAL 327
Frank Tanana CAL 261
B. Blyleven MIN, TEX 219

SAVES
Sparky Lyle NY 23
Dave LaRoche CLE 21
two tied at 20

COMPLETE GAMES
Mark Fidrych DET 24
Frank Tanana CAL 23
Jim Palmer BAL 23

SHUTOUTS
Nolan Ryan CAL 7
three tied at 6

GAMES PITCHED
Bill Campbell MIN 78
Rollie Fingers OAK 70
Paul Lindblad OAK 65

INNINGS PITCHED
Jim Palmer BAL 315
Catfish Hunter NY 299
Vida Blue OAK 298

NATIONAL LEAGUE STANDINGS

1976 NL

EAST	W	L	PCT	GB	R	OR	BA	FA	ERA
PHILADELPHIA	101	61	.623	—	770	557	.272	.981	3.08
PITTSBURGH	92	70	.568	9	708	630	.267	.975	3.36
NEW YORK	86	76	.531	15	615	538	.246	.979	2.94
CHICAGO	75	87	.463	26	611	728	.251	.978	3.93
ST. LOUIS	72	90	.444	29	629	671	.260	.973	3.60
MONTREAL	55	107	.340	46	531	734	.235	.976	3.99

WEST	W	L	PCT	GB	R	OR	BA	FA	ERA
★ CINCINNATI	102	60	.630	—	857	633	.280	.984	3.51
LOS ANGELES	92	70	.568	10	608	543	.251	.980	3.02
HOUSTON	80	82	.494	22	625	657	.256	.978	3.56
SAN FRANCISCO	74	88	.457	28	595	686	.246	.971	3.53
SAN DIEGO	73	89	.451	29	570	662	.247	.978	3.65
ATLANTA	70	92	.432	32	620	700	.245	.973	3.86
					7739	7739	.255	.977	3.50

BATTING AVERAGE
Bill Madlock CHI .... .339
Ken Griffey CIN .... .336
Garry Maddox PHI .... .330

HITS
Pete Rose CIN 215
W. Montanez SF, ATL 206
Steve Garvey LA 200

DOUBLES
Pete Rose CIN 42
Jay Johnstone PHI 38
two tied at 37

TRIPLES
Dave Cash PHI.................. 12
Cesar Geronimo CIN.......... 11
two tied at 10

HOME RUNS
Mike Schmidt PHI 38
Dave Kingman NY 37
Rick Monday CHI 32

RUNS BATTED IN
George Foster CIN 121
Joe Morgan CIN 111
Mike Schmidt PHI 107

SLUGGING AVERAGE
Joe Morgan CIN .... .576
George Foster CIN .... .530
Mike Schmidt PHI............. .524

STOLEN BASES
Davey Lopes LA 63
Joe Morgan CIN 60
two tied at............................ 58

RUNS SCORED
Pete Rose CIN 130
Joe Morgan CIN 113
Mike Schmidt PHI 112

WINS
Randy Jones SD 22
Jerry Koosman NY 21
Don Sutton LA 21

WINNING PERCENTAGE
Steve Carlton PHI............. .741
John Candelaria PIT......... .696
two tied at......................... .677

EARNED RUN AVERAGE
John Denny STL 2.52
Doug Rau LA................... 2.57
Tom Seaver NY 2.59

STRIKEOUTS
Tom Seaver NY 235
J.R. Richard HOU.............. 214
Jerry Koosman NY 200

SAVES
Rawley Eastwick CIN 26
Skip Lockwood NY 19
Ken Forsch HOU................ 19

COMPLETE GAMES
Randy Jones SD 25
Jerry Koosman NY 17
Jon Matlack NY 16

SHUTOUTS
Jon Matlack NY 6
John Montefusco SF 6
two tied at............................. 5

GAMES PITCHED
Dale Murray MON 81
Charlie Hough LA 77
Butch Metzger SD 77

INNINGS PITCHED
Randy Jones SD 315
J.R. Richard HOU............. 291
two tied at......................... 271

633

AMERICAN LEAGUE STANDINGS

1977 AL

EAST	W	L	PCT	GB	R	OR	BA	FA	ERA
★ NEW YORK	100	62	.617	—	831	651	.281	.979	3.61
BALTIMORE	97	64	.602	2.5	719	653	.261	.983	3.74
BOSTON	97	64	.602	2.5	859	712	.281	.978	4.11
DETROIT	74	88	.457	26	714	751	.264	.978	4.13
CLEVELAND	71	90	.441	28.5	676	739	.269	.979	4.10
MILWAUKEE	67	95	.414	33	639	765	.258	.978	4.32
TORONTO	54	107	.335	45.5	605	882	.252	.974	4.57

WEST	W	L	PCT	GB	R	OR	BA	FA	ERA
KANSAS CITY	102	60	.630	—	822	651	.277	.978	3.52
TEXAS	94	68	.580	8	767	657	.270	.982	3.56
CHICAGO	90	72	.556	12	844	771	.278	.974	4.25
MINNESOTA	84	77	.522	17.5	867	776	.282	.978	4.36
CALIFORNIA	74	88	.457	28	675	695	.255	.976	3.72
SEATTLE	64	98	.395	38	624	855	.256	.976	4.83
OAKLAND	63	98	.391	38.5	605	749	.240	.970	4.04
					10247	10247	.266	.977	4.06

BATTING AVERAGE
Rod Carew MIN .... .388
Lyman Bostock MIN .... .336
Ken Singleton BAL .... .328

HITS
Rod Carew MIN 239
Ron LeFlore DET 212
Jim Rice BOS 206

DOUBLES
Hal McRae KC 54
Reggie Jackson NY 39
two tied at 38

TRIPLES
Rod Carew MIN 16
Jim Rice BOS 15
Al Cowens KC 14

HOME RUNS
Jim Rice BOS 39
Graig Nettles NY 37
Bobby Bonds CAL 37

RUNS BATTED IN
Larry Hisle MIN 119
Bobby Bonds CAL 115
Jim Rice BOS 114

SLUGGING AVERAGE
Jim Rice BOS .... .593
Rod Carew MIN .... .570
Reggie Jackson NY .... .550

STOLEN BASES
Freddie Patek KC 53
Mike Page OAK 42
two tied at 41

RUNS SCORED
Rod Carew MIN 128
Carlton Fisk BOS 106
George Brett KC 105

WINS
Jim Palmer BAL 20
Dave Goltz MIN 20
Dennis Leonard KC 20

WINNING PERCENTAGE
Paul Splittorff KC .... .727
Ron Guidry NY .... .696
Tom Johnson MIN .... .696

EARNED RUN AVERAGE
Frank Tanana CAL 2.54
Bert Blyleven TEX 2.72
Nolan Ryan CAL 2.77

STRIKEOUTS
Nolan Ryan CAL 341
Dennis Leonard KC 244
Frank Tanana CAL 205

SAVES
Bill Campbell BOS 31
Sparky Lyle NY 26
Lerrin LaGrow CHI 25

COMPLETE GAMES
Jim Palmer BAL 22
Nolan Ryan CAL 22
two tied at 21

SHUTOUTS
Frank Tanana CAL 7
three tied at 5

GAMES PITCHED
Sparky Lyle NY 72
Tom Johnson MIN 71
Bill Campbell BOS 69

INNINGS PITCHED
Jim Palmer BAL 319
Dave Goltz MIN 303
Nolan Ryan CAL 299

NATIONAL LEAGUE STANDINGS

1977 NL

EAST	W	L	PCT	GB	R	OR	BA	FA	ERA
PHILADELPHIA	101	61	.623	—	847	668	.279	.981	3.71
PITTSBURGH	96	66	.593	5	734	665	.274	.977	3.61
ST. LOUIS	83	79	.512	18	737	688	.270	.978	3.81
CHICAGO	81	81	.500	20	692	739	.266	.977	4.01
MONTREAL	75	87	.463	26	665	736	.260	.980	4.01
NEW YORK	64	98	.395	37	587	663	.244	.978	3.77

WEST	W	L	PCT	GB	R	OR	BA	FA	ERA
• LOS ANGELES	98	64	.605	—	769	582	.266	.981	3.22
CINCINNATI	88	74	.543	10	802	725	.274	.984	4.21
HOUSTON	81	81	.500	17	680	650	.254	.978	3.54
SAN FRANCISCO	75	87	.463	23	673	711	.253	.972	3.75
SAN DIEGO	69	93	.426	29	692	834	.249	.971	4.43
ATLANTA	61	101	.377	37	678	895	.254	.972	4.85
					8556	8556	.262	.977	3.91

BATTING AVERAGE
Dave Parker PIT .338
Garry Templeton STL .322
George Foster CIN .320

HITS
Dave Parker PIT 215
Pete Rose CIN 204
Garry Templeton STL 200

DOUBLES
Dave Parker PIT 44
Dave Cash MON 42
two tied at 41

TRIPLES
Garry Templeton STL 18
three tied at 11

HOME RUNS
George Foster CIN 52
Jeff Burroughs ATL 41
Greg Luzinski PHI 39

RUNS BATTED IN
George Foster CIN 149
Greg Luzinski PHI 130
Steve Garvey LA 115

SLUGGING AVERAGE
George Foster CIN .631
Greg Luzinski PHI .594
Reggie Smith LA .576

STOLEN BASES
Frank Taveras PIT 70
Cesar Cedeno HOU 61
Gene Richards SD 56

RUNS SCORED
George Foster CIN 124
Ken Griffey CIN 117
Mike Schmidt PHI 114

WINS
Steve Carlton PHI 23
Tom Seaver NY, CIN 21
four tied at 20

WINNING PERCENTAGE
John Candelaria PIT .800
Tom Seaver NY, CIN .778
Larry Christenson PHI .760

EARNED RUN AVERAGE
John Candelaria PIT 2.34
Tom Seaver NY, CIN 2.58
Burt Hooton LA 2.62

STRIKEOUTS
Phil Niekro ATL 262
J.R. Richard HOU 214
Steve Rogers MON 206

SAVES
Rollie Fingers SD 35
Bruce Sutter CHI 31
Goose Gossage PIT 26

COMPLETE GAMES
Phil Niekro ATL 20
Tom Seaver NY, CIN 19
two tied at 17

SHUTOUTS
Tom Seaver NY, CIN 7
Rick Reuschel CHI 4
Steve Rogers MON 4

GAMES PITCHED
Rollie Fingers SD 78
Dan Spillner SD 76
Dave Tomlin SD 76

INNINGS PITCHED
Phil Niekro ATL 330
Steve Rogers MON 302
Steve Carlton PHI 283

AMERICAN LEAGUE STANDINGS

1978 AL

EAST	W	L	PCT	GB	R	OR	BA	FA	ERA
★ NEW YORK*	100	63	.613	—	735	582	.267	.982	3.18
BOSTON	99	64	.607	1	796	657	.267	.977	3.54
MILWAUKEE	93	69	.574	6.5	804	650	.276	.977	3.65
BALTIMORE	90	71	.559	9	659	633	.258	.982	3.56
DETROIT	86	76	.531	13.5	714	653	.271	.981	3.64
CLEVELAND	69	90	.434	29	639	694	.261	.980	3.97
TORONTO	59	102	.366	40	590	775	.250	.979	4.54

WEST	W	L	PCT	GB	R	OR	BA	FA	ERA
KANSAS CITY	92	70	.568	—	743	634	.268	.976	3.44
CALIFORNIA	87	75	.537	5	691	666	.259	.978	3.65
TEXAS	87	75	.537	5	692	632	.253	.976	3.36
MINNESOTA	73	89	.451	19	666	678	.267	.977	3.69
CHICAGO	71	90	.441	20.5	634	731	.264	.977	4.21
OAKLAND	69	93	.426	23	532	690	.245	.971	3.62
SEATTLE	56	104	.350	35	614	834	.248	.978	4.67

* Defeated Boston in a 1-game playoff   9509 9509 .261 .978 3.76

BATTING AVERAGE
Rod Carew MIN .333
Al Oliver TEX .324
Jim Rice BOS .315

HITS
Jim Rice BOS 213
Ron LeFlore DET 198
Rod Carew MIN 188

DOUBLES
George Brett KC 45
Carlton Fisk BOS 39
Hal McRae KC 39

TRIPLES
Jim Rice BOS 15
Rod Carew MIN 10
Dan Ford MIN 10

HOME RUNS
Jim Rice BOS 46
Larry Hisle MIL 34
Don Baylor CAL 34

RUNS BATTED IN
Jim Rice BOS 139
Rusty Staub DET 121
Larry Hisle MIL 115

SLUGGING AVERAGE
Jim Rice BOS .600
Larry Hisle MIL .533
Doug DeCinces BAL .526

STOLEN BASES
Ron LeFlore DET 68
Julio Cruz SEA 59
Bump Wills TEX 52

RUNS SCORED
Ron LeFlore DET 126
Jim Rice BOS 121
Don Baylor CAL 103

WINS
Ron Guidry NY 25
Mike Caldwell MIL 22
two tied at 21

WINNING PERCENTAGE
Ron Guidry NY .893
Bob Stanley BOS .882
Larry Gura KC .800

EARNED RUN AVERAGE
Ron Guidry NY 1.74
Jon Matlack TEX 2.27
Mike Caldwell MIL 2.36

STRIKEOUTS
Nolan Ryan CAL 260
Ron Guidry NY 248
Dennis Leonard KC 183

SAVES
Goose Gossage NY 27
Dave LaRoche CAL 25
Don Stanhouse BAL 24

COMPLETE GAMES
Mike Caldwell MIL 23
Dennis Leonard KC 20
Jim Palmer BAL 19

SHUTOUTS
Ron Guidry NY 9
Mike Caldwell MIL 6
Jim Palmer BAL 6

GAMES PITCHED
Bob Lacey OAK 74
Dave Heaverlo OAK 69
Elias Sosa OAK 68

INNINGS PITCHED
Jim Palmer BAL 296
Dennis Leonard KC 295
Mike Caldwell MIL 293

NATIONAL LEAGUE STANDINGS

1978 NL

EAST	W	L	PCT	GB	R	OR	BA	FA	ERA
PHILADELPHIA	90	72	.556	—	708	586	.258	.983	3.33
PITTSBURGH	88	73	.547	1.5	684	637	.257	.973	3.41
CHICAGO	79	83	.488	11	664	724	.264	.978	4.05
MONTREAL	76	86	.469	14	633	611	.254	.979	3.42
ST. LOUIS	69	93	.426	21	600	657	.249	.978	3.58
NEW YORK	66	96	.407	24	607	690	.245	.979	3.87

WEST	W	L	PCT	GB	R	OR	BA	FA	ERA
• LOS ANGELES	95	67	.586	—	727	573	.264	.978	3.12
CINCINNATI	92	69	.571	2.5	710	688	.256	.978	3.81
SAN FRANCISCO	89	73	.549	6	613	594	.248	.977	3.30
SAN DIEGO	84	78	.519	11	591	598	.252	.975	3.28
HOUSTON	74	88	.457	21	605	634	.258	.978	3.63
ATLANTA	69	93	.426	26	600	750	.244	.975	4.08
					7742	7742	.254	.978	3.57

BATTING AVERAGE
Dave Parker PIT .334
Steve Garvey LA .316
Jose Cruz HOU .315

HITS
Steve Garvey LA 202
Pete Rose CIN 198
Enos Cabell HOU 195

DOUBLES
Pete Rose CIN 51
Jack Clark SF 46
Ted Simmons STL 40

TRIPLES
Garry Templeton STL 13
Dave Parker PIT 12
Gene Richards SD 12

HOME RUNS
George Foster CIN 40
Greg Luzinski PHI 35
Dave Parker PIT 30

RUNS BATTED IN
George Foster CIN 120
Dave Parker PIT 117
Steve Garvey LA 113

SLUGGING AVERAGE
Dave Parker PIT .585
Reggie Smith LA .559
George Foster CIN .546

STOLEN BASES
Omar Moreno PIT 71
Frank Taveras PIT 46
Davey Lopes LA 45

RUNS SCORED
Ivan DeJesus CHI 104
Pete Rose CIN 103
Dave Parker PIT 102

WINS
Gaylord Perry SD 21
Ross Grimsley MON 20
two tied at 19

WINNING PERCENTAGE
Gaylord Perry SD .778
Burt Hooton LA .655
Ross Grimsley MON .645

EARNED RUN AVERAGE
Craig Swan NY 2.43
Steve Rogers MON 2.47
Pete Vuckovich STL 2.54

STRIKEOUTS
J.R. Richard HOU 303
Phil Niekro ATL 248
Tom Seaver CIN 226

SAVES
Rollie Fingers SD 37
Kent Tekulve PIT 31
Doug Bair CIN 28

COMPLETE GAMES
Phil Niekro ATL 22
Ross Grimsley MON 19
two tied at 16

SHUTOUTS
Bob Knepper SF 6
four tied at 4

GAMES PITCHED
Kent Tekulve PIT 91
Mark Littell STL 72
Donnie Moore CHI 71

INNINGS PITCHED
Phil Niekro ATL 334
J.R. Richard HOU 275
Ross Grimsley MON 263

AMERICAN LEAGUE STANDINGS

1979 AL

EAST	W	L	PCT	GB	R	OR	BA	FA	ERA
• BALTIMORE	102	57	.642	—	757	582	.261	.980	3.26
MILWAUKEE	95	66	.590	8	807	722	.280	.980	4.03
BOSTON	91	69	.569	11.5	841	711	.283	.977	4.03
NEW YORK	89	71	.556	13.5	734	672	.266	.981	3.83
DETROIT	85	76	.528	18	770	738	.269	.981	4.27
CLEVELAND	81	80	.503	22	760	805	.258	.978	4.57
TORONTO	53	109	.327	50.5	613	862	.251	.975	4.82

WEST	W	L	PCT	GB	R	OR	BA	FA	ERA
CALIFORNIA	88	74	.543	—	866	768	.282	.978	4.34
KANSAS CITY	85	77	.525	3	851	816	.282	.977	4.45
TEXAS	83	79	.512	5	750	698	.278	.979	3.86
MINNESOTA	82	80	.506	6	764	725	.278	.979	4.13
CHICAGO	73	87	.456	14	730	748	.275	.972	4.10
SEATTLE	67	95	.414	21	711	820	.269	.978	4.58
OAKLAND	54	108	.333	34	573	860	.239	.972	4.75
					10527	10527	.270	.978	4.22

BATTING AVERAGE
Fred Lynn BOS .... .333
George Brett KC .... .329
Brian Downing CAL .... .326

HITS
George Brett KC 212
Jim Rice BOS 201
Buddy Bell TEX 200

DOUBLES
Cecil Cooper MIL 44
Chet Lemon CHI 44
three tied at 42

TRIPLES
George Brett KC 20
Paul Molitor MIL 16
two tied at 13

HOME RUNS
Gorman Thomas MIL 45
Fred Lynn BOS 39
Jim Rice BOS 39

RUNS BATTED IN
Don Baylor CAL 139
Jim Rice BOS 130
Gorman Thomas MIL 123

SLUGGING AVERAGE
Fred Lynn BOS .... .637
Jim Rice BOS .... .596
Sixto Lezcano MIL .... .573

STOLEN BASES
Willie Wilson KC 83
Ron LeFlore DET 78
Julio Cruz SEA 49

RUNS SCORED
Don Baylor CAL 120
George Brett KC 119
Jim Rice BOS 117

WINS
Mike Flanagan BAL 23
Tommy John NY 21
Jerry Koosman MIN 20

WINNING PERCENTAGE
Mike Caldwell MIL .... .727
Mike Flanagan BAL .... .719
Jack Morris DET .... .708

EARNED RUN AVERAGE
Ron Guidry NY 2.78
Tommy John NY 2.96
Dennis Eckersley BOS 2.99

STRIKEOUTS
Nolan Ryan CAL 223
Ron Guidry NY 201
Mike Flanagan BAL 190

SAVES
Mike Marshall MIN 32
Jim Kern TEX 29
two tied at 21

COMPLETE GAMES
Dennis Martinez BAL 18
three tied at 17

SHUTOUTS
Dennis Leonard KC 5
Mike Flanagan BAL 5
Nolan Ryan CAL 5

GAMES PITCHED
Mike Marshall MIN 90
Sid Monge CLE 76
Jim Kern TEX 71

INNINGS PITCHED
Dennis Martinez BAL 292
Tommy John NY 276
Mike Flanagan BAL 266

NATIONAL LEAGUE STANDINGS

1979 NL

EAST	W	L	PCT	GB	R	OR	BA	FA	ERA
★ PITTSBURGH	98	64	.605	—	775	643	.272	.979	3.41
MONTREAL	95	65	.594	2	701	581	.264	.979	3.14
ST. LOUIS	86	76	.531	12	731	693	.278	.980	3.72
PHILADELPHIA	84	78	.519	14	683	718	.266	.983	4.16
CHICAGO	80	82	.494	18	706	707	.269	.975	3.88
NEW YORK	63	99	.389	35	593	706	.250	.978	3.84

WEST	W	L	PCT	GB	R	OR	BA	FA	ERA
CINCINNATI	90	71	.559	—	731	644	.264	.980	3.58
HOUSTON	89	73	.549	1.5	583	582	.256	.978	3.20
LOS ANGELES	79	83	.488	11.5	739	717	.263	.981	3.83
SAN FRANCISCO	71	91	.438	19.5	672	751	.246	.974	4.16
SAN DIEGO	68	93	.422	22	603	681	.242	.978	3.69
ATLANTA	66	94	.413	23.5	669	763	.256	.970	4.18
					8186	8186	.261	.978	3.73

BATTING AVERAGE
Keith Hernandez STL ...... .344
Pete Rose PHI .... .331
Ray Knight CIN .... .318

HITS
Garry Templeton STL 211
Keith Hernandez STL 210
Pete Rose PHI 208

DOUBLES
Keith Hernandez STL 48
Warren Cromartie MON 46
Dave Parker PIT 45

TRIPLES
Garry Templeton STL 19
three tied at 12

HOME RUNS
Dave Kingman CHI 48
Mike Schmidt PHI 45
Dave Winfield SD 34

RUNS BATTED IN
Dave Winfield SD 118
Dave Kingman CHI 115
Mike Schmidt PHI 114

SLUGGING AVERAGE
Dave Kingman CHI .... .613
Mike Schmidt PHI .... .564
George Foster CIN .... .561

STOLEN BASES
Omar Moreno PIT 77
Billy North SF 58
two tied at 44

RUNS SCORED
Keith Hernandez STL 116
Omar Moreno PIT 110
three tied at 109

WINS
Phil Niekro ATL 21
Joe Niekro HOU 21
three tied at 18

WINNING PERCENTAGE
Tom Seaver CIN .... .727
Joe Niekro HOU .... .656
Silvio Martinez STL .... .652

EARNED RUN AVERAGE
J.R. Richard HOU 2.71
Tom Hume CIN 2.76
Dan Schatzeder MON 2.83

STRIKEOUTS
J.R. Richard HOU 313
Steve Carlton PHI 213
Phil Niekro ATL 208

SAVES
Bruce Sutter CHI 37
Kent Tekulve PIT 31
Gene Garber ATL 25

COMPLETE GAMES
Phil Niekro ATL 23
J.R. Richard HOU 19
two tied at 13

SHUTOUTS
Tom Seaver CIN 5
Steve Rogers MON 5
Joe Niekro HOU 5

GAMES PITCHED
Kent Tekulve PIT 94
Enrique Romo PIT 84
Grant Jackson PIT 72

INNINGS PITCHED
Phil Niekro ATL 342
J.R. Richard HOU 292
Joe Niekro HOU 264

AMERICAN LEAGUE STANDINGS

1980 AL

EAST	W	L	PCT	GB	R	OR	BA	FA	ERA
NEW YORK	103	59	.636	—	820	662	.267	.978	3.58
BALTIMORE	100	62	.617	3	805	640	.273	.985	3.64
MILWAUKEE	86	76	.531	17	811	682	.275	.977	3.71
BOSTON	83	77	.519	19	757	767	.283	.977	4.38
DETROIT	84	78	.519	19	830	757	.273	.979	4.25
CLEVELAND	79	81	.494	23	738	807	.277	.983	4.68
TORONTO	67	95	.414	36	624	762	.251	.979	4.19

WEST	W	L	PCT	GB	R	OR	BA	FA	ERA
• KANSAS CITY	97	65	.599	—	809	694	.286	.978	3.83
OAKLAND	83	79	.512	14	686	642	.259	.979	3.46
MINNESOTA	77	84	.478	19.5	670	724	.265	.977	3.93
TEXAS	76	85	.472	20.5	756	752	.284	.977	4.02
CHICAGO	70	90	.438	26	587	722	.259	.973	3.92
CALIFORNIA	65	95	.406	31	698	797	.265	.978	4.52
SEATTLE	59	103	.364	38	610	793	.248	.977	4.38
					10201	10201	.269	.978	4.03

BATTING AVERAGE
George Brett KC .... .390
Cecil Cooper MIL .... .352
Miguel Dilone CLE .... .341

HITS
Willie Wilson KC 230
Cecil Cooper MIL 219
Mickey Rivers TEX 210

DOUBLES
Robin Yount MIL 49
Al Oliver TEX 43
Jim Morrison CHI 40

TRIPLES
Willie Wilson KC 15
Alfredo Griffin TOR 15
two tied at 11

HOME RUNS
Reggie Jackson NY 41
Ben Oglivie MIL 41
Gorman Thomas MIL 38

RUNS BATTED IN
Cecil Cooper MIL 122
George Brett KC 118
Ben Oglivie MIL 118

SLUGGING AVERAGE
George Brett KC .... .664
Reggie Jackson NY .... .597
Ben Oglivie MIL .... .563

STOLEN BASES
R. Henderson OAK 100
Willie Wilson KC 79
Miguel Dilone CLE 61

RUNS SCORED
Willie Wilson KC 133
Robin Yount MIL 121
Al Bumbry BAL 118

WINS
Steve Stone BAL 25
Tommy John NY 22
Mike Norris OAK 22

WINNING PERCENTAGE
Steve Stone BAL .... .781
Rudy May NY .... .750
Scott McGregor BAL .... .714

EARNED RUN AVERAGE
Rudy May NY 2.46
Mike Norris OAK 2.53
Britt Burns CHI 2.84

STRIKEOUTS
Len Barker CLE 187
Mike Norris OAK 180
Ron Guidry NY 166

SAVES
Dan Quisenberry KC 33
Goose Gossage NY 33
Ed Farmer CHI 30

COMPLETE GAMES
Rick Langford OAK 28
Mike Norris OAK 24
Matt Keough OAK 20

SHUTOUTS
Tommy John NY 6
Geoff Zahn MIN 5
three tied at 4

GAMES PITCHED
Dan Quisenberry KC 75
Doug Corbett MIN 73
two tied at 67

INNINGS PITCHED
Rick Langford OAK 290
Mike Norris OAK 284
Larry Gura KC 283

NATIONAL LEAGUE STANDINGS

1980 NL

EAST	W	L	PCT	GB	R	OR	BA	FA	ERA
★ PHILADELPHIA	91	71	.562	—	728	639	.270	.979	3.43
MONTREAL	90	72	.556	1	694	629	.257	.977	3.48
PITTSBURGH	83	79	.512	8	666	646	.266	.978	3.58
ST. LOUIS	74	88	.457	17	738	710	.275	.981	3.93
NEW YORK	67	95	.414	24	611	702	.257	.975	3.85
CHICAGO	64	98	.395	27	614	728	.251	.974	3.89

WEST	W	L	PCT	GB	R	OR	BA	FA	ERA
HOUSTON*	93	70	.571	—	637	589	.261	.978	3.10
LOS ANGELES	92	71	.564	1	663	591	.263	.981	3.25
CINCINNATI	89	73	.549	3.5	707	670	.262	.983	3.85
ATLANTA	81	80	.503	11	630	660	.250	.975	3.77
SAN FRANCISCO	75	86	.466	17	573	634	.244	.975	3.46
SAN DIEGO	73	89	.451	19.5	591	654	.255	.980	3.65
					7852	7852	.259	.978	3.60

*Defeated Los Angeles in a 1-game playoff

BATTING AVERAGE
Bill Buckner CHI .... .324
Keith Hernandez STL ...... .321
Garry Templeton STL ...... .319

HITS
Steve Garvey LA 200
Gene Richards SD 193
Keith Hernandez STL 191

DOUBLES
Pete Rose PHI 42
Bill Buckner CHI 41
Andre Dawson MON 41

TRIPLES
Rodney Scott MON 13
Omar Moreno PIT 13
two tied at 11

HOME RUNS
Mike Schmidt PHI 48
Bob Horner ATL 35
Dale Murphy ATL 33

RUNS BATTED IN
Mike Schmidt PHI 121
George Hendrick STL 109
Steve Garvey LA 106

SLUGGING AVERAGE
Mike Schmidt PHI .... .624
Jack Clark SF .... .517
Dale Murphy ATL .... .510

STOLEN BASES
Ron LeFlore MON 97
Omar Moreno PIT 96
Dave Collins CIN 79

RUNS SCORED
Keith Hernandez STL 111
Mike Schmidt PHI 104
Dale Murphy ATL 98

WINS
Steve Carlton PHI 24
Joe Niekro HOU 20
Jim Bibby PIT 19

WINNING PERCENTAGE
Jim Bibby PIT .... .760
Jerry Reuss LA .... .750
Steve Carlton PHI .... .727

EARNED RUN AVERAGE
Don Sutton LA 2.20
Steve Carlton PHI 2.34
Jerry Reuss LA 2.51

STRIKEOUTS
Steve Carlton PHI 286
Nolan Ryan HOU 200
Mario Soto CIN 182

SAVES
Bruce Sutter CHI 28
Tom Hume CIN 25
Rollie Fingers SD 23

COMPLETE GAMES
Steve Rogers MON 14
Steve Carlton PHI 13
two tied at 11

SHUTOUTS
Jerry Reuss LA 6
J.R. Richard HOU 4
Steve Rogers MON 4

GAMES PITCHED
Dick Tidrow CHI 84
Tom Hume CIN 78
Kent Tekulve PIT 78

INNINGS PITCHED
Steve Carlton PHI 304
Steve Rogers MON 281
Phil Niekro ATL 275

AMERICAN LEAGUE STANDINGS

1981 AL

EAST	W	L	PCT	GB	R	OR	BA	FA	ERA
MILWAUKEE**	62	47	.569	—	493	459	.257	.982	3.91
BALTIMORE	59	46	.562	1	429	437	.251	.983	3.70
• NEW YORK*†	59	48	.551	2	421	343	.252	.982	2.90
DETROIT	60	49	.550	2	427	404	.256	.984	3.53
BOSTON	59	49	.546	2.5	519	481	.275	.979	3.81
CLEVELAND	52	51	.505	7	431	442	.263	.978	3.88
TORONTO	37	69	.349	23.5	329	466	.226	.975	3.81

WEST	W	L	PCT	GB	R	OR	BA	FA	ERA
OAKLAND*†	64	45	.587	—	458	403	.247	.980	3.30
TEXAS	57	48	.543	5	452	389	.270	.984	3.40
CHICAGO	54	52	.509	8.5	476	423	.272	.979	3.47
KANSAS CITY**	50	53	.485	11	397	405	.267	.982	3.56
CALIFORNIA	51	59	.464	13.5	476	453	.256	.977	3.70
SEATTLE	44	65	.404	20	426	521	.251	.979	4.23
MINNESOTA	41	68	.376	23	378	486	.240	.978	3.98
					6112	6112	.256	.980	3.66

BATTING AVERAGE
Carney Lansford BOS ..... .336
Tom Paciorek SEA .... .326
Cecil Cooper MIL .... .320

HITS
R. Henderson OAK 135
Carney Lansford BOS 134
two tied at 133

DOUBLES
Cecil Cooper MIL 35
Al Oliver TEX 29
Tom Paciorek SEA 28

TRIPLES
John Castino MIN 9
four tied at 7

HOME RUNS
four tied at 22

RUNS BATTED IN
Eddie Murray BAL 78
Tony Armas OAK 76
Ben Oglivie MIL 72

SLUGGING AVERAGE
Bobby Grich CAL .... .543
Eddie Murray BAL .... .534
Dwight Evans BOS .... .522

STOLEN BASES
Rickey Henderson OAK 56
Julio Cruz SEA 43
Ron LeFlore CHI 36

RUNS SCORED
Rickey Henderson OAK 89
Dwight Evans BOS 84
Cecil Cooper MIL 70

WINS
four tied at 14

WINNING PERCENTAGE
Pete Vuckovich MIL .... .778
Dennis Martinez BAL .... .737
Scott McGregor BAL .... .722

EARNED RUN AVERAGE
Dave Righetti NY 2.05
Sammy Stewart BAL 2.32
Steve McCatty OAK 2.33

STRIKEOUTS
Len Barker CLE 127
Britt Burns CHI 108
two tied at 107

SAVES
Rollie Fingers MIL 28
Goose Gossage NY 20
Dan Quisenberry KC 18

COMPLETE GAMES
Rick Langford OAK 18
Steve McCatty OAK 16
Jack Morris DET 15

SHUTOUTS
four tied at 4

GAMES PITCHED
Doug Corbett MIN 54
Rollie Fingers MIL 47
Shane Rawley SEA 46

INNINGS PITCHED
Dennis Leonard KC 202
Jack Morris DET 198
Rick Langford OAK 195

NATIONAL LEAGUE STANDINGS

1981 NL

EAST	W	L	PCT	GB	R	OR	BA	FA	ERA
ST. LOUIS	59	43	.578	—	464	417	.265	.981	3.63
MONTREAL**†	60	48	.556	2	443	394	.246	.980	3.30
PHILADELPHIA*	59	48	.551	2.5	491	472	.273	.980	4.05
PITTSBURGH	46	56	.451	13	407	425	.257	.979	3.56
NEW YORK	41	62	.398	18.5	348	432	.248	.968	3.55
CHICAGO	38	65	.369	21.5	370	483	.236	.974	4.01

WEST	W	L	PCT	GB	R	OR	BA	FA	ERA
CINCINNATI	66	42	.611	—	464	440	.267	.981	3.73
LOS ANGELES*†	63	47	.573	4	450	356	.262	.980	3.01
HOUSTON**	61	49	.555	6	394	331	.257	.980	2.66
SAN FRANCISCO	56	55	.505	11.5	427	414	.250	.977	3.28
ATLANTA	50	56	.472	15	395	416	.243	.976	3.45
SAN DIEGO	41	69	.373	26	382	455	.256	.977	3.72
					5035	5035	.255	.978	3.49

*Winner of first half **Winner of second half †Winner of playoff

BATTING AVERAGE
Bill Madlock PIT .... .341
Pete Rose PHI .... .325
Dusty Baker LA .... .320

HITS
Pete Rose PHI 140
Bill Buckner CHI 131
Dave Concepcion CIN 129

DOUBLES
Bill Buckner CHI 35
Ruppert Jones SD 34
Dave Concepcion CIN 28

TRIPLES
Craig Reynolds HOU 12
Gene Richards SD 12
Tommy Herr STL 9

HOME RUNS
Mike Schmidt PHI 31
Andre Dawson MON 24
two tied at 22

RUNS BATTED IN
Mike Schmidt PHI 91
George Foster CIN 90
Bill Buckner CHI 75

SLUGGING AVERAGE
Mike Schmidt PHI .... .644
Andre Dawson MON .... .553
George Foster CIN .... .519

STOLEN BASES
Tim Raines MON 71
Omar Moreno PIT 39
Rodney Scott MON 30

RUNS SCORED
Mike Schmidt PHI 78
Pete Rose PHI 73
Andre Dawson MON 71

WINS
Tom Seaver CIN 14
Steve Carlton PHI 13
F. Valenzuela LA 13

WINNING PERCENTAGE
Tom Seaver CIN .... .875
Steve Carlton PHI .... .765
Nolan Ryan HOU .... .688

EARNED RUN AVERAGE
Nolan Ryan HOU 1.69
Bob Knepper HOU 2.18
Burt Hooton LA 2.28

STRIKEOUTS
F. Valenzuela LA 180
Steve Carlton PHI 179
Mario Soto CIN 151

SAVES
Bruce Sutter STL 25
Greg Minton SF 21
Neil Allen NY 18

COMPLETE GAMES
F. Valenzuela LA 11
Mario Soto CIN 10
Steve Carlton PHI 10

SHUTOUTS
Fernando Valenzuela LA 8
Bob Knepper HOU 5
Burt Hooton LA 4

GAMES PITCHED
Gary Lucas SD 57
Greg Minton SF 55
two tied at 51

INNINGS PITCHED
F. Valenzuela LA 192
Steve Carlton PHI 190
Mario Soto CIN 175

AMERICAN LEAGUE STANDINGS

1982 AL

EAST	W	L	PCT	GB	R	OR	BA	FA	ERA
• MILWAUKEE	95	67	.586	—	891	717	.279	.980	3.98
BALTIMORE	94	68	.580	1	774	687	.266	.984	3.99
BOSTON	89	73	.549	6	753	713	.274	.981	4.03
DETROIT	83	79	.512	12	729	685	.266	.981	3.80
NEW YORK	79	83	.488	16	709	716	.256	.979	3.99
CLEVELAND	78	84	.481	17	683	748	.262	.980	4.11
TORONTO	78	84	.481	17	651	701	.262	.978	3.95

WEST	W	L	PCT	GB	R	OR	BA	FA	ERA
CALIFORNIA	93	69	.574	—	814	670	.274	.983	3.82
KANSAS CITY	90	72	.556	3	784	717	.285	.979	4.08
CHICAGO	87	75	.537	6	786	710	.273	.976	3.87
SEATTLE	76	86	.469	17	651	712	.254	.978	3.88
OAKLAND	68	94	.420	25	691	819	.236	.974	4.54
TEXAS	64	98	.395	29	590	749	.249	.981	4.28
MINNESOTA	60	102	.370	33	657	819	.257	.982	4.72
					10163	10163	.264	.980	4.07

BATTING AVERAGE
Willie Wilson KC .... .332
Robin Yount MIL .... .331
Rod Carew CAL .... .319

HITS
Robin Yount MIL 210
Cecil Cooper MIL 205
Paul Molitor MIL 201

DOUBLES
Robin Yount MIL 46
Hal McRae KC 46
Frank White KC 45

TRIPLES
Willie Wilson KC 15
Larry Herndon DET 13
Robin Yount MIL 12

HOME RUNS
Reggie Jackson CAL 39
Gorman Thomas MIL 39
Dave Winfield NY 37

RUNS BATTED IN
Hal McRae KC 133
Cecil Cooper MIL 121
Andre Thornton CLE 116

SLUGGING AVERAGE
Robin Yount MIL .... .578
Dave Murray NY .... .560
Eddie Murray BAL .... .549

STOLEN BASES
R. Henderson OAK 130
Damaso Garcia TOR 54
Julio Cruz SEA 46

RUNS SCORED
Paul Molitor MIL 136
Robin Yount MIL 129
Dwight Evans BOS 122

WINS
LaMarr Hoyt CHI 19
Jim Palmer BAL 18
three tied at 18

WINNING PERCENTAGE
Pete Vuckovich MIL .... .750
Jim Palmer BAL .... .750
Geoff Zahn CAL .... .692

EARNED RUN AVERAGE
Rick Sutcliffe CLE 2.96
Bob Stanley BOS 3.10
Jim Palmer BAL 3.13

STRIKEOUTS
Floyd Bannister SEA 209
Len Barker CLE 187
Dave Righetti NY 163

SAVES
Dan Quisenberry KC 35
Goose Gossage NY 30
Rollie Fingers MIL 29

COMPLETE GAMES
Dave Stieb TOR 19
Jack Morris DET 17
Rick Langford OAK 15

SHUTOUTS
Dave Stieb TOR 5
Geoff Zahn CAL 4
Ken Forsch CAL 4

GAMES PITCHED
Ed Vande Berg SEA 78
Tippy Martinez BAL 76
Dan Quisenberry KC 72

INNINGS PITCHED
Dave Stieb TOR 288
Jim Clancy TOR 267
Jack Morris DET 266

NATIONAL LEAGUE STANDINGS

1982 NL

EAST	W	L	PCT	GB	R	OR	BA	FA	ERA
★ ST. LOUIS	92	70	.568	—	685	609	.264	.981	3.37
PHILADELPHIA	89	73	.549	3	664	654	.260	.981	3.61
MONTREAL	86	76	.531	6	697	616	.262	.980	3.31
PITTSBURGH	84	78	.519	8	724	696	.273	.977	3.81
CHICAGO	73	89	.451	19	676	709	.260	.979	3.92
NEW YORK	65	97	.401	27	609	723	.247	.972	3.88

WEST	W	L	PCT	GB	R	OR	BA	FA	ERA
ATLANTA	89	73	.549	—	739	702	.256	.979	3.82
LOS ANGELES	88	74	.543	1	691	612	.264	.979	3.26
SAN FRANCISCO	87	75	.537	2	673	687	.253	.973	3.64
SAN DIEGO	81	81	.500	8	675	658	.257	.976	3.52
HOUSTON	77	85	.475	12	569	620	.247	.978	3.42
CINCINNATI	61	101	.377	28	545	661	.251	.980	3.66
					7947	7947	.258	.978	3.60

BATTING AVERAGE
Al Oliver MON .... .331
Bill Madlock PIT .... .319
Leon Durham CHI .... .312

HITS
Al Oliver MON 204
Bill Buckner CHI 201
Andre Dawson MON 183

DOUBLES
Al Oliver MON 43
Terry Kennedy SD 42
Andre Dawson MON 37

TRIPLES
Dickie Thon HOU 10
three tied at 9

HOME RUNS
Dave Kingman NY 37
Dale Murphy ATL 36
Mike Schmidt PHI 35

RUNS BATTED IN
Dale Murphy ATL 109
Al Oliver MON 109
Bill Buckner CHI 105

SLUGGING AVERAGE
Mike Schmidt PHI .... .547
Pedro Guerrero LA .... .536
Leon Durham CHI .... .521

STOLEN BASES
Tim Raines MON 78
Lonnie Smith STL 68
Omar Moreno PIT 60

RUNS SCORED
Lonnie Smith STL 120
Dale Murphy ATL 113
Mike Schmidt PHI 108

WINS
Steve Carlton PHI 23
Steve Rogers MON 19
F. Valenzuela LA 19

WINNING PERCENTAGE
Phil Niekro ATL .... .810
Steve Rogers MON .... .704
Steve Carlton PHI .... .676

EARNED RUN AVERAGE
Steve Rogers MON 2.40
Joe Niekro HOU 2.47
Joaquin Andujar STL 2.47

STRIKEOUTS
Steve Carlton PHI 286
Mario Soto CIN 274
Nolan Ryan HOU 245

SAVES
Bruce Sutter STL 36
Greg Minton SF 30
Gene Garber ATL 30

COMPLETE GAMES
Steve Carlton PHI 19
F. Valenzuela LA 18
Joe Niekro HOU 16

SHUTOUTS
Steve Carlton PHI 6
Joaquin Andujar STL 5
Joe Niekro HOU 5

GAMES PITCHED
Kent Tekulve PIT 85
Greg Minton SF 78
Rod Scurry PIT 76

INNINGS PITCHED
Steve Carlton PHI 296
F. Valenzuela LA 285
Steve Rogers MON 277

AMERICAN LEAGUE STANDINGS

1983 AL

EAST	W	L	PCT	GB	R	OR	BA	FA	ERA
★ BALTIMORE	98	64	.605	—	799	652	.269	.981	3.63
DETROIT	92	70	.568	6	789	679	.274	.980	3.80
NEW YORK	91	71	.562	7	770	703	.273	.978	3.86
TORONTO	89	73	.549	9	795	726	.277	.981	4.12
MILWAUKEE	87	75	.537	11	764	708	.277	.982	4.02
BOSTON	78	84	.481	20	724	775	.270	.979	4.34
CLEVELAND	70	92	.432	28	704	785	.265	.980	4.43

WEST	W	L	PCT	GB	R	OR	BA	FA	ERA
CHICAGO	99	63	.611	—	800	650	.262	.981	3.67
KANSAS CITY	79	83	.488	20	696	767	.271	.974	4.25
TEXAS	77	85	.475	22	639	609	.255	.982	3.31
OAKLAND	74	88	.457	25	708	782	.262	.974	4.34
CALIFORNIA	70	92	.432	29	722	779	.260	.977	4.31
MINNESOTA	70	92	.432	29	709	822	.261	.980	4.66
SEATTLE	60	102	.370	39	558	740	.240	.978	4.12
					10177	10177	.266	.979	4.06

BATTING AVERAGE
Wade Boggs BOS .... .361
Rod Carew CAL .... .339
Lou Whitaker DET .... .320

HITS
Cal Ripken BAL 211
Wade Boggs BOS 210
Lou Whitaker DET 206

DOUBLES
Cal Ripken BAL 47
Wade Boggs BOS 44
two tied at 42

TRIPLES
Robin Yount MIL 10
three tied at 9

HOME RUNS
Jim Rice BOS 39
Tony Armas BOS 36
Ron Kittle CHI 35

RUNS BATTED IN
Cecil Cooper MIL 126
Jim Rice BOS 126
Dave Winfield NY 116

SLUGGING AVERAGE
George Brett KC .... .563
Jim Rice BOS .... .550
Eddie Murray BAL .... .538

STOLEN BASES
R. Henderson OAK 108
Rudy Law CHI 77
Willie Wilson KC 59

RUNS SCORED
Cal Ripken BAL 121
Eddie Murray BAL 115
Cecil Cooper MIL 106

WINS
LaMarr Hoyt CHI 24
Rich Dotson CHI 22
Ron Guidry NY 21

WINNING PERCENTAGE
Rich Dotson CHI .... .759
Scott McGregor BAL .... .720
LaMarr Hoyt CHI .... .706

EARNED RUN AVERAGE
Rick Honeycutt TEX 2.42
Mike Boddicker BAL 2.77
Dave Stieb TOR 3.04

STRIKEOUTS
Jack Morris DET 232
Floyd Bannister CHI 193
Dave Stieb TOR 187

SAVES
Dan Quisenberry KC 45
Bob Stanley BOS 33
Ron Davis MIN 30

COMPLETE GAMES
Ron Guidry NY 21
Jack Morris DET 20
Dave Stieb TOR 14

SHUTOUTS
Mike Boddicker BAL 5
Britt Burns CHI 4
Dave Stieb TOR 4

GAMES PITCHED
Dan Quisenberry KC 69
Ed Vande Berg SEA 68
Ron Davis MIN 66

INNINGS PITCHED
Jack Morris DET 294
Dave Stieb TOR 278
Dan Petry DET 266

NATIONAL LEAGUE STANDINGS

1983 NL

EAST	W	L	PCT	GB	R	OR	BA	FA	ERA
• PHILADELPHIA	90	72	.556	—	696	635	.249	.976	3.34
PITTSBURGH	84	78	.519	6	659	648	.264	.982	3.55
MONTREAL	82	80	.506	8	677	646	.264	.981	3.58
ST. LOUIS	79	83	.488	11	679	710	.270	.976	3.79
CHICAGO	71	91	.438	19	701	719	.261	.982	4.08
NEW YORK	68	94	.420	22	575	680	.241	.976	3.68

WEST	W	L	PCT	GB	R	OR	BA	FA	ERA
LOS ANGELES	91	71	.562	—	654	609	.250	.974	3.10
ATLANTA	88	74	.543	3	746	640	.272	.978	3.67
HOUSTON	85	77	.525	6	643	646	.257	.977	3.45
SAN DIEGO	81	81	.500	10	653	653	.250	.979	3.62
SAN FRANCISCO	79	83	.488	12	687	697	.247	.973	3.70
CINCINNATI	74	88	.457	17	623	710	.239	.981	3.98
					7993	7993	.255	.978	3.63

BATTING AVERAGE
Bill Madlock PIT .... .323
Lonnie Smith STL .... .321
Jose Cruz HOU .... .318

HITS
Jose Cruz HOU 189
Andre Dawson MON 189
Rafael Ramirez ATL 185

DOUBLES
Al Oliver MON 38
Johnny Ray PIT 38
Bill Buckner CHI 38

TRIPLES
Brett Butler ATL 13
Omar Moreno HOU 11
two tied at 10

HOME RUNS
Mike Schmidt PHI 40
Dale Murphy ATL 36
two tied at 32

RUNS BATTED IN
Dale Murphy ATL 121
Andre Dawson MON 113
Mike Schmidt PHI 109

SLUGGING AVERAGE
Dale Murphy ATL .... .540
Andre Dawson MON .... .539
Pedro Guerrero LA .... .531

STOLEN BASES
Tim Raines MON 90
Alan Wiggins SD 66
Steve Sax LA 56

RUNS SCORED
Tim Raines MON 133
Dale Murphy ATL 131
two tied at 104

WINS
John Denny PHI 19
three tied at 17

WINNING PERCENTAGE
John Denny PHI .... .760
three tied at .... .652

EARNED RUN AVERAGE
Atlee Hammaker SF 2.25
John Denny PHI 2.37
Bob Welch LA 2.65

STRIKEOUTS
Steve Carlton PHI 275
Mario Soto CIN 242
Larry McWilliams PIT 199

SAVES
Lee Smith CHI 29
Al Holland PHI 25
Greg Minton SF 22

COMPLETE GAMES
Mario Soto CIN 18
Steve Rogers MON 13
Bill Gullickson MON 10

SHUTOUTS
Steve Rogers MON 5
three tied at 4

GAMES PITCHED
Bill Campbell CHI 82
Kent Tekulve PIT 76
G. Hernandez CHI, PHI 74

INNINGS PITCHED
Steve Carlton PHI 284
Mario Soto CIN 274
Steve Rogers MON 273

AMERICAN LEAGUE STANDINGS

1984 AL

EAST	W	L	PCT	GB	R	OR	BA	FA	ERA
★ DETROIT	104	58	.642	—	829	643	.271	.979	3.49
TORONTO	89	73	.549	15	750	696	.273	.980	3.86
NEW YORK	87	75	.537	17	758	679	.276	.977	3.78
BOSTON	86	76	.531	18	810	764	.283	.977	4.18
BALTIMORE	85	77	.525	19	681	667	.252	.981	3.71
CLEVELAND	75	87	.463	29	761	766	.265	.977	4.26
MILWAUKEE	67	94	.416	36.5	641	734	.262	.978	4.06

WEST	W	L	PCT	GB	R	OR	BA	FA	ERA
KANSAS CITY	84	78	.519	—	673	686	.268	.979	3.92
CALIFORNIA	81	81	.500	3	696	697	.249	.980	3.96
MINNESOTA	81	81	.500	3	673	675	.265	.980	3.85
OAKLAND	77	85	.475	7	738	796	.259	.975	4.48
CHICAGO	74	88	.457	10	679	736	.247	.981	4.13
SEATTLE	74	88	.457	10	682	774	.258	.979	4.31
TEXAS	69	92	.429	14.5	656	714	.261	.977	3.91
					10027	10027	.264	.979	3.99

BATTING AVERAGE
Don Mattingly NY .... .343
Dave Winfield NY .... .340
Wade Boggs BOS .... .325

HITS
Don Mattingly NY 207
Wade Boggs BOS 203
Cal Ripken BAL 195

DOUBLES
Don Mattingly NY 44
Larry Parrish TEX 42
George Bell TOR 39

TRIPLES
Dave Collins TOR 15
Lloyd Moseby TOR 15
two tied at 10

HOME RUNS
Tony Armas BOS 43
Dave Kingman OAK 35
three tied at 33

RUNS BATTED IN
Tony Armas BOS 123
Jim Rice BOS 122
Dave Kingman OAK 118

SLUGGING AVERAGE
Harold Baines CHI .... .541
Don Mattingly NY .... .537
Dwight Evans BOS .... .532

STOLEN BASES
Rickey Henderson OAK 66
Dave Collins TOR 60
Brett Butler CLE 52

RUNS SCORED
Dwight Evans BOS 121
R. Henderson OAK 113
Wade Boggs BOS 109

WINS
Mike Boddicker BAL 20
Bert Blyleven CLE 19
Jack Morris DET 19

WINNING PERCENTAGE
Doyle Alexander TOR .... .739
Bert Blyleven CLE .... .731
Dan Petry DET .... .692

EARNED RUN AVERAGE
Mike Boddicker BAL 2.79
Dave Stieb TOR 2.83
Bert Blyleven CLE 2.87

STRIKEOUTS
Mark Langston SEA 204
Dave Stieb TOR 198
Mike Witt CAL 196

SAVES
Dan Quisenberry KC 44
Bill Caudill OAK 36
G. Hernandez DET 32

COMPLETE GAMES
Charlie Hough TEX 17
Mike Boddicker BAL 16
Rich Dotson CHI 14

SHUTOUTS
Geoff Zahn CAL 5
Bob Ojeda BOS 5
two tied at 4

GAMES PITCHED
G. Hernandez DET 80
Dan Quisenberry KC 72
Aurelio Lopez DET 71

INNINGS PITCHED
Dave Stieb TOR 267
Charlie Hough TEX 266
Doyle Alexander TOR 262

NATIONAL LEAGUE STANDINGS

1984 NL

EAST	W	L	PCT	GB	R	OR	BA	FA	ERA
CHICAGO	96	65	.596	—	762	658	.260	.981	3.75
NEW YORK	90	72	.556	6.5	652	676	.257	.979	3.60
ST. LOUIS	84	78	.519	12.5	652	645	.252	.982	3.58
PHILADELPHIA	81	81	.500	15.5	720	690	.266	.975	3.62
MONTREAL	78	83	.484	18	593	585	.251	.978	3.31
PITTSBURGH	75	87	.463	21.5	615	567	.255	.980	3.11

WEST	W	L	PCT	GB	R	OR	BA	FA	ERA
• SAN DIEGO	92	70	.568	—	686	634	.259	.978	3.48
ATLANTA	80	82	.494	12	632	655	.247	.978	3.57
HOUSTON	80	82	.494	12	693	630	.264	.979	3.32
LOS ANGELES	79	83	.488	13	580	600	.244	.975	3.17
CINCINNATI	70	92	.432	22	627	747	.244	.977	4.16
SAN FRANCISCO	66	96	.407	26	682	807	.265	.973	4.39
					7894	7894	.255	.978	3.59

BATTING AVERAGE
Tony Gwynn SD .... .351
Lee Lacy PIT .... .321
Chili Davis SF .... .315

HITS
Tony Gwynn SD 213
Ryne Sandberg CHI 200
Tim Raines MON 192

DOUBLES
Johnny Ray PIT 38
Tim Raines MON 38
two tied at 36

TRIPLES
Juan Samuel PHI 19
Ryne Sandberg CHI 19
Jose Cruz HOU 13

HOME RUNS
Dale Murphy ATL 36
Mike Schmidt PHI 36
Gary Carter MON 27

RUNS BATTED IN
Gary Carter MON 106
Mike Schmidt PHI 106
Dale Murphy ATL 100

SLUGGING AVERAGE
Dale Murphy ATL .... .547
Mike Schmidt PHI .... .536
Ryne Sandberg CHI .... .520

STOLEN BASES
Tim Raines MON 75
Juan Samuel PHI 72
Alan Wiggins SD 70

RUNS SCORED
Ryne Sandberg CHI 114
Tim Raines MON 106
Alan Wiggins SD 106

WINS
Joaquin Andujar STL 20
Mario Soto CIN 18
Dwight Gooden NY 17

WINNING PERCENTAGE
Rick Sutcliffe CHI .... .941
Mario Soto CIN .... .720
Dwight Gooden NY .... .654

EARNED RUN AVERAGE
Alejandro Pena LA 2.48
Dwight Gooden NY 2.60
Orel Hershiser LA 2.66

STRIKEOUTS
Dwight Gooden NY 276
F. Valenzuela LA 240
Nolan Ryan HOU 197

SAVES
Bruce Sutter STL 45
Lee Smith CHI 33
Jesse Orosco NY 31

COMPLETE GAMES
Mario Soto CIN 13
F. Valenzuela LA 12
Joaquin Andujar STL 12

SHUTOUTS
Alejandro Pena LA 4
Joaquin Andujar STL 4
Orel Hershiser LA 4

GAMES PITCHED
Ted Power CIN 78
Gary Lavelle SF 77
Greg Minton SF 74

INNINGS PITCHED
Joaquin Andujar STL 261
F. Valenzuela LA 261
Joe Niekro HOU 248

AMERICAN LEAGUE STANDINGS

1985 AL

EAST	W	L	PCT	GB	R	OR	BA	FA	ERA
TORONTO	99	62	.615	—	759	588	.269	.980	3.31
NEW YORK	97	64	.602	2	839	660	.267	.979	3.69
DETROIT	84	77	.522	15	729	688	.253	.977	3.78
BALTIMORE	83	78	.516	16	818	764	.263	.979	4.38
BOSTON	81	81	.500	18.5	800	720	.282	.977	4.06
MILWAUKEE	71	90	.441	28	690	802	.263	.977	4.39
CLEVELAND	60	102	.370	39.5	729	861	.265	.977	4.91

WEST	W	L	PCT	GB	R	OR	BA	FA	ERA
★ KANSAS CITY	91	71	.562	—	687	639	.252	.980	3.49
CALIFORNIA	90	72	.556	1	732	703	.251	.982	3.91
CHICAGO	85	77	.525	6	736	720	.253	.982	4.07
MINNESOTA	77	85	.475	14	705	782	.264	.980	4.48
OAKLAND	77	85	.475	14	757	787	.264	.977	4.41
SEATTLE	74	88	.457	17	719	818	.255	.980	4.68
TEXAS	62	99	.385	28.5	617	785	.253	.980	4.56
					10317	10317	.261	.979	4.15

BATTING AVERAGE
Wade Boggs BOS .... .368
George Brett KC .... .335
Don Mattingly NY .... .324

HITS
Wade Boggs BOS 240
Don Mattingly NY 211
Bill Buckner BOS 201

DOUBLES
Don Mattingly NY 48
Bill Buckner BOS 46
Wade Boggs BOS 42

TRIPLES
Willie Wilson KC 21
Brett Butler CLE 14
Kirby Puckett MIN 13

HOME RUNS
Darrell Evans DET 40
Carlton Fisk CHI 37
Steve Balboni KC 36

RUNS BATTED IN
Don Mattingly NY 145
Eddie Murray BAL 124
Dave Winfield NY 114

SLUGGING AVERAGE
George Brett KC .... .585
Don Mattingly NY .... .567
Jesse Barfield TOR .... .536

STOLEN BASES
Rickey Henderson NY 80
Gary Pettis CAL 56
Brett Butler CLE 47

RUNS SCORED
Rickey Henderson NY 146
Cal Ripken BAL 116
Eddie Murray BAL 111

WINS
Ron Guidry NY 22
Bret Saberhagen KC 20
two tied at 18

WINNING PERCENTAGE
Ron Guidry NY .... .786
Bret Saberhagen KC .... .769
Charlie Leibrandt KC .... .654

EARNED RUN AVERAGE
Dave Stieb TOR 2.48
Charlie Leibrandt KC 2.69
Bret Saberhagen KC 2.87

STRIKEOUTS
B. Blyleven CLE, MIN 206
Floyd Bannister CHI 198
Jack Morris DET 191

SAVES
Dan Quisenberry KC 37
Bob James CHI 32
two tied at 31

COMPLETE GAMES
Bert Blyleven CLE, MIN ... 24
Charlie Hough TEX 14
Mike Moore SEA 14

SHUTOUTS
Bert Blyleven CLE, MIN ... 5
Jack Morris DET 4
Britt Burns CHI 4

GAMES PITCHED
Dan Quisenberry KC 84
Ed Vande Berg SEA 76
two tied at 74

INNINGS PITCHED
B. Blyleven CLE, MIN 294
Oil Can Boyd BOS 272
Dave Stieb TOR 265

NATIONAL LEAGUE STANDINGS

1985 NL

EAST	W	L	PCT	GB	R	OR	BA	FA	ERA
• ST. LOUIS	101	61	.623	—	747	572	.264	.983	3.10
NEW YORK	98	64	.605	3	695	568	.257	.982	3.11
MONTREAL	84	77	.522	16.5	633	636	.247	.981	3.55
CHICAGO	77	84	.478	23.5	686	729	.254	.979	4.16
PHILADELPHIA	75	87	.463	26	667	673	.245	.978	3.68
PITTSBURGH	57	104	.354	43.5	568	708	.247	.979	3.97

WEST	W	L	PCT	GB	R	OR	BA	FA	ERA
LOS ANGELES	95	67	.586	—	682	579	.261	.974	2.96
CINCINNATI	89	72	.553	5.5	677	666	.255	.980	3.71
HOUSTON	83	79	.512	12	706	691	.261	.976	3.66
SAN DIEGO	83	79	.512	12	650	622	.255	.980	3.40
ATLANTA	66	96	.407	29	632	781	.246	.976	4.19
SAN FRANCISCO	62	100	.383	33	556	674	.233	.976	3.61
					7899	7899	.252	.979	3.59

BATTING AVERAGE
Willie McGee STL .... .353
Pedro Guerrero LA .... .320
Tim Raines MON .... .320

HITS
Willie McGee STL 216
Dave Parker CIN 198
Tony Gwynn SD 197

DOUBLES
Dave Parker CIN 42
Glenn Wilson PHI 39
Tommy Herr STL 38

TRIPLES
Willie McGee STL 18
Juan Samuel PHI 13
Tim Raines MON 13

HOME RUNS
Dale Murphy ATL 37
Dave Parker CIN 34
two tied at 33

RUNS BATTED IN
Dave Parker CIN 125
Dale Murphy ATL 111
Tommy Herr STL 110

SLUGGING AVERAGE
Pedro Guerrero LA .... .577
Dave Parker CIN .... .551
Dale Murphy ATL .... .539

STOLEN BASES
Vince Coleman STL 110
Tim Raines MON 70
Willie McGee STL 56

RUNS SCORED
Dale Murphy ATL 118
Tim Raines MON 115
Willie McGee STL 114

WINS
Dwight Gooden NY 24
John Tudor STL 21
Joaquin Andujar STL 21

WINNING PERCENTAGE
Orel Hershiser LA .... .864
Dwight Gooden NY .... .857
Bryn Smith MON .... .783

EARNED RUN AVERAGE
Dwight Gooden NY 1.53
John Tudor STL 1.93
Orel Heshiser LA 2.03

STRIKEOUTS
Dwight Gooden NY 268
Mario Soto CIN 214
Nolan Ryan HOU 209

SAVES
Jeff Reardon MON 41
Lee Smith CHI 33
two tied at 27

COMPLETE GAMES
Dwight Gooden NY 16
F. Valenzuela LA 14
John Tucor STL 14

SHUTOUTS
John Tudor STL 10
Dwight Gooden NY 8
two tied at 5

GAMES PITCHED
Tim Burke MON 78
Mark Davis SF 77
Scott Garrelts SF 74

INNINGS PITCHED
Dwight Gooden NY 277
John Tudor STL 275
F. Valenzuela LA 272

AMERICAN LEAGUE STANDINGS

1986 AL

EAST	W	L	PCT	GB	R	OR	BA	FA	ERA
• BOSTON	95	66	.590	—	794	696	.271	.979	3.93
NEW YORK	90	72	.556	5.5	797	738	.271	.979	4.11
DETROIT	87	75	.537	8.5	798	714	.263	.982	4.02
TORONTO	86	76	.531	9.5	809	733	.269	.984	4.08
CLEVELAND	84	78	.519	11.5	831	841	.284	.975	4.57
MILWAUKEE	77	84	.478	18	667	734	.255	.976	4.01
BALTIMORE	73	89	.451	22.5	708	760	.258	.978	4.30

WEST	W	L	PCT	GB	R	OR	BA	FA	ERA
CALIFORNIA	92	70	.568	—	786	684	.255	.983	3.84
TEXAS	87	75	.537	5	771	743	.267	.980	4.11
KANSAS CITY	76	86	.469	16	654	673	.252	.980	3.82
OAKLAND	76	86	.469	16	731	760	.252	.978	4.31
CHICAGO	72	90	.444	20	644	699	.247	.981	3.93
MINNESOTA	71	91	.438	21	741	839	.261	.980	4.77
SEATTLE	67	95	.414	25	718	835	.253	.975	4.65
					10449	10449	.262	.979	4.18

BATTING AVERAGE
Wade Boggs BOS .... .357
Don Mattingly NY .... .352
Kirby Puckett MIN............ .328

HITS
Don Mattingly NY 238
Kirby Pucket MIN............ 223
Tony Fernandez TOR 213

DOUBLES
Don Mattingly NY 53
Wade Boggs BOS 47
three tied at 39

TRIPLES
Brett Butler CLE 14
Ruben Sierra TEX 10
two tied at............................. 9

HOME RUNS
Jesse Barfield TOR 40
Dave Kingman OAK 35
Gary Gaetti MIN 34

RUNS BATTED IN
Joe Carter CLE 121
Jose Canseco OAK 117
Don Mattingly NY 113

SLUGGING AVERAGE
Don Mattingly NY .... .573
Jesse Barfield TOR .... .559
Kirby Puckett MIN............ .537

STOLEN BASES
Rickey Henderson NY 87
Gary Pettis CAL 50
John Cangelosi CHI 50

RUNS SCORED
Rickey Henderson NY 130
Kirby Puckett MIN........... 119
Don Mattingly NY 117

WINS
Roger Clemens BOS.......... 24
Jack Morris DET 21
Ted Higuera MIL 20

WINNING PERCENTAGE
Roger Clemens BOS.......... .857
Dennis Rasmussen NY ... .750
Jack Morris DET .... .724

EARNED RUN AVERAGE
Roger Clemens BOS....... 2.48
Ted Higuera MIL 2.79
Mike Witt CAL 2.84

STRIKEOUTS
Mark Langston SEA 245
Roger Clemens BOS........ 238
Jack Morris DET................ 223

SAVES
Dave Righetti NY 46
Don Aase BAL.................... 34
Tom Henke TOR................. 27

COMPLETE GAMES
Tom Candiotti CLE 17
Bert Blyleven MIN 16
two tied at 15

SHUTOUTS
Jack Morris DET.................. 6
Bruce Hurst BOS................. 4
Ted Higuera MIL.................. 4

GAMES PITCHED
Mitch Williams TEX 80
Dave Righetti NY 74
Greg Harris TEX................. 73

INNINGS PITCHED
Bert Blyleven MIN 272
Mike Witt CAL 269
Jack Morris DET................ 267

NATIONAL LEAGUE STANDINGS

1986 NL

EAST	W	L	PCT	GB	R	OR	BA	FA	ERA
★ NEW YORK	108	54	.667	—	783	578	.263	.978	3.11
PHILADELPHIA	86	75	.534	21.5	739	713	.253	.978	3.85
ST. LOUIS	79	82	.491	28.5	601	611	.236	.981	3.37
MONTREAL	78	83	.484	29.5	637	688	.254	.979	3.78
CHICAGO	70	90	.438	37	680	781	.256	.980	4.49
PITTSBURGH	64	98	.395	44	663	700	.250	.978	3.90

WEST	W	L	PCT	GB	R	OR	BA	FA	ERA
HOUSTON	96	66	.593	—	654	569	.255	.979	3.15
CINCINNATI	86	76	.531	10	732	717	.254	.978	3.91
SAN FRANCISCO	83	79	.512	13	698	618	.253	.977	3.33
SAN DIEGO	74	88	.457	22	656	723	.261	.978	3.99
LOS ANGELES	73	89	.451	23	638	679	.251	.971	3.76
ATLANTA	72	89	.447	23.5	615	719	.250	.978	3.97
					8096	8096	.253	.978	3.72

BATTING AVERAGE
Tim Raines MON .... .334
Steve Sax LA .... .332
Tony Gwynn SD .... .329

HITS
Tony Gwynn SD 211
Steve Sax LA 210
Tim Raines MON 194

DOUBLES
Von Hayes PHI 46
Steve Sax LA 43
Sid Bream PIT 37

TRIPLES
Mitch Webster MON 13
Juan Samuel PHI 12
Tim Raines MON 10

HOME RUNS
Mike Schmidt PHI 37
Glenn Davis HOU 31
Dave Parker CIN 31

RUNS BATTED IN
Mike Schmidt PHI 119
Dave Parker CIN 116
Gary Carter NY 105

SLUGGING AVERAGE
Mike Schmidt PHI .... .547
Darryl Strawberry NY ...... .507
Kevin McReynolds SD .... .504

STOLEN BASES
Vince Coleman STL 107
Eric Davis CIN 80
Tim Raines MON 70

RUNS SCORED
Tony Gwynn SD 107
Von Hayes PHI 107
two tied at 97

WINS
F. Valenzuela LA 21
Mike Krukow SF 20
two tied at 18

WINNING PERCENTAGE
Bob Ojeda NY .... .783
Dwight Gooden NY .... .739
Sid Fernandez NY .... .727

EARNED RUN AVERAGE
Mike Scott HOU 2.22
Bob Ojeda NY 2.57
Ron Darling NY 2.81

STRIKEOUTS
Mike Scott HOU 306
F. Valenzuela LA 242
Floyd Youmans MON 202

SAVES
Todd Worrell STL 36
Jeff Reardon MON 35
Dave Smith HOU 33

COMPLETE GAMES
F. Valenzuela LA 20
Rick Rhoden PIT 12
Dwight Gooden NY 12

SHUTOUTS
Mike Scott HOU 5
Bob Knepper HOU 5
two tied at 3

GAMES PITCHED
Craig Lefferts SD 83
Roger McDowell NY 75
two tied at 74

INNINGS PITCHED
Mike Scott HOU 275
F. Valenzuela LA 269
Bob Knepper HOU 258

AMERICAN LEAGUE STANDINGS

1987 AL

EAST	W	L	PCT	GB	R	OR	BA	FA	ERA
DETROIT	98	64	.605	—	896	735	.272	.980	4.02
TORONTO	96	66	.593	2	845	655	.269	.982	3.74
MILWAUKEE	91	71	.562	7	862	817	.276	.976	4.62
NEW YORK	89	73	.549	9	788	758	.262	.983	4.36
BOSTON	78	84	.481	20	842	825	.278	.982	4.77
BALTIMORE	67	95	.414	31	729	880	.258	.982	5.01
CLEVELAND	61	101	.377	37	742	957	.263	.975	5.28

WEST	W	L	PCT	GB	R	OR	BA	FA	ERA
★ MINNESOTA	85	77	.525	—	786	806	.261	.984	4.63
KANSAS CITY	83	79	.512	2	715	691	.262	.979	3.86
OAKLAND	81	81	.500	4	806	789	.260	.977	4.32
SEATTLE	78	84	.481	7	760	801	.272	.980	4.49
CHICAGO	77	85	.475	8	748	746	.258	.981	4.30
CALIFORNIA	75	87	.463	10	770	803	.252	.981	4.38
TEXAS	75	87	.463	10	823	849	.266	.976	4.63
					11112	11112	.265	.980	4.46

BATTING AVERAGE
Wade Boggs BOS .... .363
Paul Molitor MIL .... .353
Alan Trammell DET .... .343

HITS
Kevin Seitzer KC 207
Kirby Puckett MIN 207
Alan Trammell DET 205

DOUBLES
Paul Molitor MIL 41
Wade Boggs BOS 40

TRIPLES
Willie Wilson KC 15
Luis Polonia OAK 10
Phil Bradley SEA 10

HOME RUNS
Mark McGwire OAK 49
George Bell TOR 47
four tied at 34

RUNS BATTED IN
George Bell TOR 134
Dwight Evans BOS 123
Mark McGwire OAK 118

SLUGGING AVERAGE
Mark McGwire OAK .... .618
George Bell TOR .... .605
Wade Boggs BOS .... .588

STOLEN BASES
Harold Reynolds SEA 60
Willie Wilson KC 59
Gary Redus CHI 52

RUNS SCORED
Paul Molitor MIL 114
George Bell TOR 111
two tied at 110

WINS
Roger Clemens BOS 20
Dave Stewart OAK 20
Mark Langston SEA 19

WINNING PERCENTAGE
Roger Clemens BOS .... .690
Jimmy Key TOR .... .680
two tied at .... .643

EARNED RUN AVERAGE
Jimmy Key TOR 2.76
Frank Viola MIN 2.90
Roger Clemens BOS 2.97

STRIKEOUTS
Mark Langston SEA 262
Roger Clemens BOS 256
Ted Higuera MIL 240

SAVES
Tom Henke TOR 34
Jeff Reardon MIN 31
Dave Righetti NY 31

COMPLETE GAMES
Roger Clemens BOS 18
Bruce Hurst BOS 15
Bret Saberhagen KC 15

SHUTOUTS
Roger Clemens BOS 7
Bret Saberhagen KC 4

GAMES PITCHED
Mark Eichhorn TOR 89
Mitch Williams TEX 85
Dale Mohorcic TEX 74

INNINGS PITCHED
Charlie Hough TEX 285
Roger Clemens BOS 282
Mark Langston SEA 272

NATIONAL LEAGUE STANDINGS

1987 NL

EAST	W	L	PCT	GB	R	OR	BA	FA	ERA
• ST. LOUIS	95	67	.586	—	798	693	.263	.982	3.91
NEW YORK	92	70	.568	3	823	698	.268	.978	3.84
MONTREAL	91	71	.562	4	741	720	.265	.976	3.92
PHILADELPHIA	80	82	.494	15	702	749	.254	.980	4.18
PITTSBURGH	80	82	.494	15	723	744	.264	.980	4.20
CHICAGO	76	85	.472	18.5	720	801	.264	.979	4.55

WEST	W	L	PCT	GB	R	OR	BA	FA	ERA
SAN FRANCISCO	90	72	.556	—	783	669	.260	.980	3.68
CINCINNATI	84	78	.519	6	783	752	.266	.979	4.24
HOUSTON	76	86	.469	14	648	678	.253	.981	3.84
LOS ANGELES	73	89	.451	17	635	675	.252	.975	3.72
ATLANTA	69	92	.429	20.5	747	829	.258	.982	4.63
SAN DIEGO	65	97	.401	25	668	763	.260	.976	4.27
					8771	8771	.261	.979	4.08

BATTING AVERAGE
Tony Gwynn SD .... .370
Pedro Guerrero LA .... .338
Tim Raines MON .... .330

HITS
Tony Gwynn SD 218
Pedro Guerrero LA 184
Ozzie Smith STL 182

DOUBLES
Tim Wallach MON 42
Ozzie Smith STL 40
Andres Galarraga MON 40

TRIPLES
Juan Samuel PHI 15
Tony Gwynn SD 13
two tied at 11

HOME RUNS
Andre Dawson CHI 49
Dale Murphy ATL 44
Darryl Strawberry NY 39

RUNS BATTED IN
Andre Dawson CHI 137
Tim Wallach MON 123
Mike Schmidt PHI 113

SLUGGING AVERAGE
Jack Clark STL .... .597
Eric Davis CIN .... .593
Darryl Strawberry NY ...... .583

STOLEN BASES
Vince Coleman STL 109
Tony Gwynn SD 56
Billy Hatcher HOU 53

RUNS SCORED
Tim Raines MON 123
Vince Coleman STL 121
Eric Davis CIN 120

WINS
Rick Sutcliffe CHI 18
Shane Rawley PHI 17
two tied at 16

WINNING PERCENTAGE
Dwight Gooden NY .... .682
Rick Sutcliffe CHI .... .643
Bob Welch LA .... .625

EARNED RUN AVERAGE
Nolan Ryan HOU 2.76
Mike Dunne PIT 3.03
Orel Hershiser LA 3.06

STRIKEOUTS
Nolan Ryan HOU 270
Mike Scott HOU 233
Bob Welch LA 196

SAVES
Steve Bedrosian PHI 40
Lee Smith CHI 36
Todd Worrell STL 33

COMPLETE GAMES
Rick Reuschel PIT, SF 12
F. Valenzuela LA 12
Orel Hershiser LA 10

SHUTOUTS
Rick Reuschel PIT, SF 4
Bob Welch LA 4

GAMES PITCHED
Kent Tekulve PHI 90
Rob Murphy CIN 87
Frank Williams CIN 85

INNINGS PITCHED
Orel Hershiser LA 265
Bob Welch LA 252
F. Valenzuela LA 251

AMERICAN LEAGUE STANDINGS

1988 AL

EAST	W	L	PCT	GB	R	OR	BA	FA	ERA
BOSTON	89	73	.549	—	813	689	.283	.984	3.97
DETROIT	88	74	.543	1	703	658	.250	.982	3.71
MILWAUKEE	87	75	.537	2	682	616	.257	.981	3.45
TORONTO	87	75	.537	2	763	680	.268	.982	3.60
NEW YORK	85	76	.528	3.5	772	748	.263	.978	4.26
CLEVELAND	78	84	.481	11	666	731	.261	.980	4.16
BALTIMORE	54	107	.335	34.5	550	789	.238	.980	4.54

WEST	W	L	PCT	GB	R	OR	BA	FA	ERA
OAKLAND	104	58	.642	—	800	620	.263	.983	3.44
MINNESOTA	91	71	.562	13	759	672	.274	.986	3.93
KANSAS CITY	84	77	.522	19.5	704	648	.259	.980	3.65
CALIFORNIA	75	87	.463	29	714	771	.261	.979	4.32
CHICAGO	71	90	.441	32.5	631	757	.244	.976	4.12
TEXAS	70	91	.435	33.5	637	735	.252	.979	4.05
SEATTLE	68	93	.422	35.5	664	744	.257	.980	4.15
					9858	9858	.259	.981	3.97

BATTING AVERAGE
Wade Boggs BOS .366
Kirby Puckett MIN .356
Mike Greenwell BOS .325

HITS
Kirby Puckett MIN 234
Wade Boggs BOS 214
Mike Greenwell BOS 192

DOUBLES
Wade Boggs BOS 45
three tied at 42

TRIPLES
Willie Wilson KC 11
Harold Reynolds SEA 11
Robin Yount MIL 11

HOME RUNS
Jose Canseco OAK 42
Fred McGriff TOR 34
Mark McGwire OAK 32

RUNS BATTED IN
Jose Canseco OAK 124
Kirby Puckett MIN 121
Mike Greenwell BOS 119

SLUGGING AVERAGE
Jose Canseco OAK .569
Fred McGriff TOR .552
Gary Gaetti MIN .551

STOLEN BASES
Rickey Henderson NY 93
Gary Pettis DET 44
Paul Molitor MIL 41

RUNS SCORED
Wade Boggs BOS 128
Jose Canseco OAK 120
Rickey Henderson NY 118

WINS
Frank Viola MIN 24
Dave Stewart OAK 21
Mark Gubicza KC 20

WINNING PERCENTAGE
Frank Viola MIN .774
Bruce Hurst BOS .750
Mark Gubicza KC .714

EARNED RUN AVERAGE
Allan Anderson MIN 2.45
Ted Higuera MIL 2.45
Frank Viola MIN 2.64

STRIKEOUTS
Roger Clemens BOS 291
Mark Langston SEA 235
Frank Viola MIN 193

SAVES
Dennis Eckersley OAK 45
Jeff Reardon MIN 42
Doug Jones CLE 37

COMPLETE GAMES
Roger Clemens BOS 14
Dave Stewart OAK 14
Bobby Witt TEX 13

SHUTOUTS
Roger Clemens BOS 8
three tied at 4

GAMES PITCHED
Chuck Crim MIL 70
Bobby Thigpen CHI 68
Mitch Williams TEX 67

INNINGS PITCHED
Dave Stewart OAK 276
Mark Gubicza KC 270
Roger Clemens BOS 264

NATIONAL LEAGUE STANDINGS

1988 NL

EAST	W	L	PCT	GB	R	OR	BA	FA	ERA
NEW YORK	100	60	.625	—	703	532	.256	.981	2.91
PITTSBURGH	85	75	.531	15	651	616	.247	.980	3.47
MONTREAL	81	81	.500	20	628	592	.251	.978	3.08
CHICAGO	77	85	.475	24	660	694	.261	.980	3.84
ST. LOUIS	76	86	.469	25	578	633	.249	.981	3.47
PHILADELPHIA	65	96	.404	35.5	597	734	.239	.976	4.14

WEST	W	L	PCT	GB	R	OR	BA	FA	ERA
★ LOS ANGELES	94	67	.584	—	628	544	.248	.977	2.96
CINCINNATI	87	74	.540	7	641	596	.246	.980	3.35
SAN DIEGO	83	78	.516	11	594	583	.247	.981	3.28
SAN FRANCISCO	83	79	.512	11.5	670	626	.248	.980	3.39
HOUSTON	82	80	.506	12.5	617	631	.244	.978	3.41
ATLANTA	54	106	.338	39.5	555	741	.242	.976	4.09
					7522	7522	.248	.979	3.45

BATTING AVERAGE
Tony Gwynn SD .... .313
Rafael Palmeiro CHI .... .307
Andre Dawson CHI .... .303

HITS
A. Galarraga MON 184
Andre Dawson CHI 179
Rafael Palmeiro CHI 178

DOUBLES
Andres Galarraga MON 42
Rafael Palmeiro CHI 41
Chris Sabo CIN 40

TRIPLES
Andy Van Slyke PIT 15
Vince Coleman STL 10
three tied at 9

HOME RUNS
Darryl Strawberry NY 39
Glenn Davis HOU 30
two tied at 29

RUNS BATTED IN
Will Clark SF 109
Darryl Strawberry NY 101
two tied at 100

SLUGGING AVERAGE
Darryl Strawberry NY ...... .545
A. Galarraga MON .... .540
Will Clark SF .... .508

STOLEN BASES
Vince Coleman STL 81
Gerald Young HOU 65
Ozzie Smith STL 57

RUNS SCORED
Brett Butler SF 109
Kirk Gibson LA 106
Will Clark SF 102

WINS
Orel Hershiser LA 23
Danny Jackson CIN 23
David Cone NY 20

WINNING PERCENTAGE
David Cone NY .... .870
Tom Browning CIN .... .783
two tied at .... .742

EARNED RUN AVERAGE
Joe Magrane STL 2.18
David Cone NY 2.22
Orel Hershiser LA 2.26

STRIKEOUTS
Nolan Ryan HOU 228
David Cone NY 213
Jose DeLeon STL 208

SAVES
John Franco CIN 39
Jim Gott PIT 34
Todd Worrell STL 32

COMPLETE GAMES
Orel Hershiser LA 15
Danny Jackson CIN 15
Eric Show SD 13

SHUTOUTS
Orel Hershiser LA 8
Tim Leary LA 6
Danny Jackson CIN 6

GAMES PITCHED
Rob Murphy CIN 76
Jeff Robinson PIT 75
Juan Agosto HOU 75

INNINGS PITCHED
Orel Hershiser LA 267
Danny Jackson CIN 261
Tom Browning CIN 251

AMERICAN LEAGUE STANDINGS

1989 AL

EAST	W	L	PCT	GB	R	OR	BA	FA	ERA
TORONTO	89	73	.549	—	731	651	.260	.980	3.58
BALTIMORE	87	75	.537	2	708	686	.252	.986	4.00
BOSTON	83	79	.512	6	774	735	.277	.980	4.01
MILWAUKEE	81	81	.500	8	707	679	.259	.975	3.80
NEW YORK	74	87	.460	14.5	698	792	.269	.980	4.50
CLEVELAND	73	89	.451	16	604	654	.245	.981	3.65
DETROIT	59	103	.364	30	617	816	.242	.979	4.53

WEST	W	L	PCT	GB	R	OR	BA	FA	ERA
★ OAKLAND	99	63	.611	—	712	576	.261	.979	3.09
KANSAS CITY	92	70	.568	7	690	635	.261	.982	3.55
CALIFORNIA	91	71	.562	8	669	578	.256	.985	3.28
TEXAS	83	79	.512	16	695	714	.263	.978	3.91
MINNESOTA	80	82	.494	19	740	738	.276	.982	4.28
SEATTLE	73	89	.451	26	694	728	.257	.977	4.00
CHICAGO	69	92	.429	29.5	693	750	.271	.975	4.23
					9732	9732	.261	.980	3.88

BATTING AVERAGE
Kirby Puckett MIN .... .339
Carney Lansford OAK ..... .336
Wade Boggs BOS .... .330

HITS
Kirby Puckett MIN 215
Wade Boggs BOS 205
Steve Sax NY 205

DOUBLES
Wade Boggs BOS 51
Kirby Puckett MIN 45
Jody Reed BOS 42

TRIPLES
Ruben Sierra TEX 14
Devon White CAL 13
Phil Bradley BAL 10

HOME RUNS
Fred McGriff TOR 36
Joe Carter CLE 35
Mark McGwire OAK 33

RUNS BATTED IN
Ruben Sierra TEX 119
Don Mattingly NY 113
Nick Esasky BOS 108

SLUGGING AVERAGE
Ruben Sierra TEX .... .543
Fred McGriff TOR .... .525
Robin Yount MIL .... .511

STOLEN BASES
R. Henderson NY, OAK 77
Cecil Espy TEX 45
Devon White CAL 44

RUNS SCORED
R. Henderson NY, OAK 113
Wade Boggs BOS 113
two tied at 101

WINS
Bret Saberhagen KC 23
Dave Stewart OAK 21
two tied at 19

WINNING PERCENTAGE
Bret Saberhagen KC .... .793
Bert Blyleven CAL .... .773
Storm Davis OAK .... .731

EARNED RUN AVERAGE
Bret Saberhagen KC 2.16
Chuck Finley CAL 2.57
Mike Moore OAK 2.61

STRIKEOUTS
Nolan Ryan TEX 301
Roger Clemens BOS 230
Bret Saberhagen KC 193

SAVES
Jeff Russell TEX 38
Bobby Thigpen CHI 34
three tied at 33

COMPLETE GAMES
Bret Saberhagen KC 12
Jack Morris DET 10
Chuck Finley CAL 9

SHUTOUTS
Bert Blyleven CAL 5
Kirk McCaskill CAL 4
Bret Saberhagen KC 4

GAMES PITCHED
Chuck Crim MIL 76
Rob Murphy BOS 74
Kenny Rogers TEX 73

INNINGS PITCHED
Bret Saberhagen KC 262
Dave Stewart OAK 258
Mark Gubicza KC 255

NATIONAL LEAGUE STANDINGS

1989 NL

EAST	W	L	PCT	GB	R	OR	BA	FA	ERA
CHICAGO	93	69	.574	—	702	623	.261	.980	3.43
NEW YORK	87	75	.537	6	683	595	.246	.976	3.29
ST. LOUIS	86	76	.531	7	632	608	.258	.982	3.36
MONTREAL	81	81	.500	12	632	630	.247	.979	3.48
PITTSBURGH	74	88	.457	19	637	680	.241	.975	3.64
PHILADELPHIA	67	95	.414	26	629	735	.243	.979	4.04

WEST	W	L	PCT	GB	R	OR	BA	FA	ERA
• SAN FRANCISCO	92	70	.568	—	699	600	.250	.982	3.30
SAN DIEGO	89	73	.549	3	642	626	.251	.976	3.38
HOUSTON	86	76	.531	6	647	669	.239	.977	3.64
LOS ANGELES	77	83	.481	14	554	536	.240	.981	2.95
CINCINNATI	75	87	.463	17	632	691	.247	.980	3.73
ATLANTA	63	97	.394	28	584	680	.234	.976	3.70
					7673	7673	.246	.978	3.49

BATTING AVERAGE
Tony Gwynn SD .... .336
Will Clark SF .... .333
Lonnie Smith ATL .... .315

HITS
Tony Gwynn SD 203
Will Clark SF 196
Roberto Alomar SD 184

DOUBLES
Pedro Guerrero STL 42
Tim Wallach MON 42
Howard Johnson NY 41

TRIPLES
Robby Thompson SF 11
Bobby Bonilla PIT 10
three tied at 9

HOME RUNS
Kevin Mitchell SF 47
Howard Johnson NY 36
two tied at 34

RUNS BATTED IN
Kevin Mitchell SF 125
Pedro Guerrero STL 117
Will Clark SF 111

SLUGGING AVERAGE
Kevin Mitchell SF .... .635
Howard Johnson NY .... .559
Will Clark SF .... .546

STOLEN BASES
Vince Coleman STL 65
Juan Samuel PHI, NY 42
Roberto Alomar SD 42

RUNS SCORED
Howard Johnson NY 104
Will Clark SF 104
Ryne Sandberg CHI 104

WINS
Mike Scott HOU 20
Greg Maddux CHI 19
two tied at 18

WINNING PERCENTAGE
Mike Bielecki CHI .... .720
D. Martinez MON .... .696
Rick Reuschel SF .... .680

EARNED RUN AVERAGE
Scott Garrelts SF 2.28
Orel Hershiser LA 2.31
Mark Langston MON 2.39

STRIKEOUTS
Jose DeLeon STL 201
Tim Belcher LA 200
Sid Fernandez NY 198

SAVES
Mark Davis SD 44
Mitch Williams CHI 36
John Franco CIN 32

COMPLETE GAMES
Tim Belcher LA 10
Bruce Hurst SD 10
three tied at 9

SHUTOUTS
Tim Belcher LA 8
Doug Drabek PIT 5
three tied at 4

GAMES PITCHED
Mitch Williams CHI 76
Rob Dibble CIN 74
Jeff Parrett PHI 72

INNINGS PITCHED
Orel Hershiser LA 257
Tom Browning CIN 250
two tied at 245

AMERICAN LEAGUE STANDINGS

1990 AL

EAST	W	L	PCT	GB	R	OR	BA	FA	ERA
BOSTON	88	74	.543	—	699	664	.272	.980	3.72
TORONTO	86	76	.531	2	767	661	.265	.986	3.84
DETROIT	79	83	.488	9	750	754	.259	.979	4.39
CLEVELAND	77	85	.475	11	732	737	.267	.981	4.26
BALTIMORE	76	85	.472	11.5	669	698	.245	.985	4.04
MILWAUKEE	74	88	.457	14	732	760	.256	.976	4.08
NEW YORK	67	95	.414	21	603	749	.241	.980	4.21

WEST	W	L	PCT	GB	R	OR	BA	FA	ERA
• OAKLAND	103	59	.636	—	733	570	.254	.986	3.18
CHICAGO	94	68	.580	9	682	633	.258	.980	3.61
TEXAS	83	79	.512	20	676	696	.259	.979	3.83
CALIFORNIA	80	82	.494	23	690	706	.260	.978	3.79
SEATTLE	77	85	.475	26	640	680	.259	.979	3.69
KANSAS CITY	75	86	.466	27.5	707	709	.267	.980	3.93
MINNESOTA	74	88	.457	29	666	729	.265	.983	4.12
					9746	9746	.259	.981	3.91

BATTING AVERAGE
George Brett KC .... .329
R. Henderson OAK .... .325
Rafael Palmeiro TEX .... .319

HITS
Rafael Palmeiro TEX 191
Wade Boggs BOS 187
Roberto Kelly NY 183

DOUBLES
George Brett KC 45
Jody Reed BOS 45
two tied at 44

TRIPLES
Tony Fernandez TOR 17
Sammy Sosa CHI 10
three tied at 9

HOME RUNS
Cecil Fielder DET 51
Mark McGwire OAK 39
Jose Canseco OAK 37

RUNS BATTED IN
Cecil Fielder DET 132
Kelly Gruber TOR 118
Mark McGwire OAK 108

SLUGGING AVERAGE
Cecil Fielder DET .... .592
R. Henderson OAK .... .577
Jose Canseco OAK .... .543

STOLEN BASES
R. Henderson OAK 65
Steve Sax NY 43
Roberto Kelly NY 42

RUNS SCORED
Rickey Henderson OAK ... 119
Cecil Fielder DET 104
Harold Reynolds SEA 100

WINS
Bob Welch OAK 27
Dave Stewart OAK 22
Roger Clemens BOS 21

WINNING PERCENTAGE
Bob Welch OAK .... .818
Roger Clemens BOS ...... .778
Dave Stieb TOR .... .750

EARNED RUN AVERAGE
Roger Clemens BOS 1.93
Chuck Finley CAL 2.40
Dave Stewart OAK 2.56

STRIKEOUTS
Nolan Ryan TEX 232
Bobby Witt TEX 221
Erik Hanson SEA 211

SAVES
Bobby Thigpen CHI 57
Dennis Eckersley OAK 48
Doug Jones CLE 43

COMPLETE GAMES
Jack Morris DET 11
Dave Stewart OAK 11
five tied at 7

SHUTOUTS
Roger Clemens BOS 4
Dave Stewart OAK 4
three tied at 3

GAMES PITCHED
Bobby Thigpen CHI 77
Jeff Montgomery KC 73
Duane Ward TOR 73

INNINGS PITCHED
Dave Stewart OAK 267
Jack Morris DET 250
Bob Welch OAK 238

NATIONAL LEAGUE STANDINGS

1990 NL

EAST	W	L	PCT	GB	R	OR	BA	FA	ERA
PITTSBURGH	95	67	.586	—	733	619	.259	.979	3.40
NEW YORK	91	71	.562	4	775	613	.256	.978	3.42
MONTREAL	85	77	.525	10	662	598	.250	.982	3.37
CHICAGO	77	85	.475	18	690	774	.263	.980	4.34
PHILADELPHIA	77	85	.475	18	646	729	.255	.981	4.07
ST. LOUIS	70	92	.432	25	599	698	.256	.979	3.87

WEST	W	L	PCT	GB	R	OR	BA	FA	ERA
★ CINCINNATI	91	71	.562	—	693	597	.265	.983	3.39
LOS ANGELES	86	76	.531	5	728	685	.262	.979	3.72
SAN FRANCISCO	85	77	.525	6	719	710	.262	.983	4.08
HOUSTON	75	87	.463	16	573	656	.242	.978	3.61
SAN DIEGO	75	87	.463	16	673	673	.257	.977	3.68
ATLANTA	65	97	.401	26	682	821	.250	.974	4.58
					8173	8173	.256	.980	3.79

BATTING AVERAGE
Willie McGee STL .... .335
Eddie Murray LA .... .330
Dave Magadan NY .... .328

HITS
Brett Butler SF 192
Lenny Dykstra PHI 192
Ryne Sandberg CHI 188

DOUBLES
Gregg Jefferies NY 40
Bobby Bonilla PIT 39
Chris Sabo CIN 38

TRIPLES
Mariano Duncan CIN 11
Tony Gwynn SD 10
three tied at 9

HOME RUNS
Ryne Sandberg CHI 40
Darryl Strawberry NY 37
Kevin Mitchell SF 35

RUNS BATTED IN
Matt Williams SF 122
Bobby Bonilla PIT 120
Joe Carter SD 115

SLUGGING AVERAGE
Barry Bonds PIT .... .565
Ryne Sandberg CHI .... .559
Kevin Mitchell SF .... .544

STOLEN BASES
Vince Coleman STL 77
Eric Yelding HOU 64
Barry Bonds PIT 52

RUNS SCORED
Ryne Sandberg CHI 116
Bobby Bonilla PIT 112
Brett Butler SF 108

WINS
Doug Drabek PIT 22
Ramon Martinez LA 20
Frank Viola NY 20

WINNING PERCENTAGE
Doug Drabek PIT .... .786
Ramon Martinez LA .... .769
Dwight Gooden NY .... .731

EARNED RUN AVERAGE
Danny Darwin HOU 2.21
Zane Smith MON, PIT 2.55
Ed Whitson SD 2.60

STRIKEOUTS
David Cone NY 233
Dwight Gooden NY 223
Ramon Martinez LA 223

SAVES
John Franco NY 33
Randy Myers CIN 31
Lee Smith STL 27

COMPLETE GAMES
Ramon Martinez LA 12
Doug Drabek PIT 9
Bruce Hurst SD 9

SHUTOUTS
Mike Morgan LA 4
Bruce Hurst SD 4

GAMES PITCHED
Juan Agosto HOU 82
Paul Assenmacher CHI 74
Greg Harris SD 73

INNINGS PITCHED
Frank Viola NY 250
Greg Maddux CHI 237
Ramon Martinez LA 234

AMERICAN LEAGUE STANDINGS

1991 AL

EAST	W	L	PCT	GB	R	OR	BA	FA	ERA
TORONTO	91	71	.562	—	684	622	.257	.980	3.50
BOSTON	84	78	.519	7	731	712	.269	.981	4.01
DETROIT	84	78	.519	7	817	794	.247	.983	4.51
MILWAUKEE	83	79	.512	8	799	744	.271	.981	4.14
NEW YORK	71	91	.438	20	674	777	.256	.979	4.42
BALTIMORE	67	95	.414	24	686	796	.254	.985	4.59
CLEVELAND	57	105	.352	34	576	759	.254	.976	4.23

WEST	W	L	PCT	GB	R	OR	BA	FA	ERA
★ MINNESOTA	95	67	.586	—	776	652	.280	.985	3.69
CHICAGO	87	75	.534	8	758	681	.262	.982	3.79
TEXAS	85	77	.525	10	829	814	.270	.979	4.47
OAKLAND	84	78	.519	11	760	776	.248	.982	4.57
SEATTLE	83	79	.512	12	702	674	.255	.983	3.79
KANSAS CITY	82	80	.506	13	727	722	.264	.980	3.92
CALIFORNIA	81	81	.500	14	653	649	.255	.984	3.69
					10172	10172	.260	.981	4.09

BATTING AVERAGE
Julio Franco TEX .... .341
Wade Boggs BOS .... .332
Willie Randolph MIL .... .327

HITS
Paul Molitor MIL 216
Cal Ripken BAL 210
two tied at 203

DOUBLES
Rafael Palmeiro TEX 49
Cal Ripken BAL 46
Ruben Sierra TEX 44

TRIPLES
Lance Johnson CHI 13
Paul Molitor MIL 13
Roberto Alomar TOR 11

HOME RUNS
Cecil Fielder DET 44
Jose Canseco OAK 44
Cal Ripken BAL 34

RUNS BATTED IN
Cecil Fielder DET 133
Jose Canseco OAK 122
Ruben Sierra TEX 116

SLUGGING AVERAGE
Danny Tartabull KC .... .593
Cal Ripken BAL .... .566
Jose Canseco OAK .... .556

STOLEN BASES
Rickey Henderson OAK 58
Roberto Alomar TOR 53
Tim Raines CHI 51

RUNS SCORED
Paul Molitor MIL 133
Jose Canseco OAK 115
Rafael Palmeiro TEX 115

WINS
Scott Erickson MIN 20
Bill Gullickson DET 20
Mark Langston CAL 19

WINNING PERCENTAGE
Scott Erickson MIN .... .714
Mark Langston CAL .... .704
Bill Gullickson DET .... .690

EARNED RUN AVERAGE
Roger Clemens BOS 2.62
T. Candiotti CLE,TOR 2.65
Bill Wegman MIL 2.84

STRIKEOUTS
Roger Clemens BOS 241
Randy Johnson SEA 228
Nolan Ryan TEX 203

SAVES
Bryan Harvey CAL 46
Dennis Eckersley OAK 43
Rick Aguilera MIN 42

COMPLETE GAMES
Jack McDowell CHI 15
Roger Clemens BOS 13
two tied at 10

SHUTOUTS
Roger Clemens BOS 4
four tied at 3

GAMES PITCHED
Duane Ward TOR 81
Mike Jackson SEA 72
Gregg Olson BAL 72

INNINGS PITCHED
Roger Clemens BOS 271
Jack McDowell CHI 254
Jack Morris MIN 247

NATIONAL LEAGUE STANDINGS

1991 NL

EAST	W	L	PCT	GB	R	OR	BA	FA	ERA
PITTSBURGH	98	64	.605	—	768	632	.263	.981	3.44
ST. LOUIS	84	78	.519	14	651	648	.255	.982	3.69
PHILADELPHIA	78	84	.481	20	629	680	.241	.981	3.86
CHICAGO	77	83	.481	20	695	734	.253	.982	4.03
NEW YORK	77	84	.478	20.5	640	646	.244	.977	3.56
MONTREAL	71	90	.441	26.5	579	655	.246	.979	3.64

WEST	W	L	PCT	GB	R	OR	BA	FA	ERA
• ATLANTA	94	68	.580	—	749	644	.258	.978	3.49
LOS ANGELES	93	69	.574	1	665	565	.253	.980	3.06
SAN DIEGO	84	78	.519	10	636	646	.244	.982	3.57
SAN FRANCISCO	75	87	.463	19	649	697	.246	.982	4.03
CINCINNATI	74	88	.457	20	689	691	.258	.979	3.83
HOUSTON	65	97	.401	29	605	717	.244	.974	4.00
					7955	7955	.250	.980	3.68

BATTING AVERAGE
Terry Pendleton ATL......... .319
Hal Morris CIN................. .318
Tony Gwynn SD .... .317

HITS
Terry Pendleton ATL......... 187
Brett Butler LA................. 182
Chris Sabo CIN 175

DOUBLES
Bobby Bonilla PIT.............. 44
Felix Jose STL 40
two tied at.......................... 36

TRIPLES
Ray Lankford STL 15
Tony Gwynn SD 11
Steve Finley HOU.............. 10

HOME RUNS
Howard Johnson NY 38
Matt Williams SF 34
Ron Gant ATL 32

RUNS BATTED IN
Howard Johnson NY 117
Barry Bonds PIT............... 116
Will Clark SF 116

SLUGGING AVERAGE
Will Clark SF .... .536
Howard Johnson NY .... .535
Terry Pendleton ATL........ .517

STOLEN BASES
Marquis Grissom MON....... 76
Otis Nixon ATL 72
Delino DeShields MON 56

RUNS SCORED
Brett Butler LA................. 112
Howard Johnson NY 108
Ryne Sandberg CHI 104

WINS
John Smiley PIT................. 20
Tom Glavine ATL 20
Steve Avery ATL 18

WINNING PERCENTAGE
Jose Rijo CIN .... .714
John Smiley PIT .... .714
Steve Avery ATL .... .692

EARNED RUN AVERAGE
Dennis Martinez MON..... 2.39
Jose Rijo CIN 2.51
Tom Glavine ATL 2.55

STRIKEOUTS
David Cone NY 241
Greg Maddux CHI 198
Tom Glavine ATL 192

SAVES
Lee Smith STL 47
Rob Dibble CIN 31
two tied at.......................... 30

COMPLETE GAMES
Tom Glavine ATL 9
Dennis Martinez MON......... 9
Terry Mulholland PHI........... 8

SHUTOUTS
Dennis Martinez MON......... 5
Ramon Martinez LA 4
three tied at 3

GAMES PITCHED
Barry Jones MON 77
Paul Assenmacher CHI...... 75
Mike Stanton ATL 74

INNINGS PITCHED
Greg Maddux CHI 263
Tom Glavine ATL 247
Mike Morgan LA 236

663

AMERICAN LEAGUE STANDINGS

1992 AL

EAST	W	L	PCT	GB	R	OR	BA	FA	ERA
★ TORONTO	96	66	.593	—	780	682	.263	.985	3.91
MILWAUKEE	92	70	.568	4	740	604	.268	.986	3.43
BALTIMORE	89	73	.549	7	705	656	.259	.985	3.79
CLEVELAND	76	86	.469	20	674	746	.266	.978	4.11
NEW YORK	76	86	.469	20	733	746	.261	.982	4.21
DETROIT	75	87	.463	21	791	794	.256	.981	4.60
BOSTON	73	89	.451	23	599	669	.246	.978	3.58

WEST	W	L	PCT	GB	R	OR	BA	FA	ERA
OAKLAND	96	66	.593	—	745	672	.258	.979	3.73
MINNESOTA	90	72	.556	6	747	653	.277	.985	3.70
CHICAGO	86	76	.531	10	738	690	.261	.979	3.82
TEXAS	77	85	.475	19	682	753	.250	.975	4.09
CALIFORNIA	72	90	.444	24	579	671	.243	.979	3.84
KANSAS CITY	72	90	.444	24	610	667	.256	.980	3.81
SEATTLE	64	98	.395	32	679	799	.263	.982	4.55
					9802	9802	.259	.981	3.94

BATTING AVERAGE
Edgar Martinez SEA .... .343
Kirby Puckett MIN............ .329
Frank Thomas CHI .... .323

HITS
Kirby Puckett MIN............ 210
Carlos Baerga CLE 205
Paul Molitor MIL 195

DOUBLES
Edgar Martinez SEA 46
Frank Thomas CHI 46
two tied at 40

TRIPLES
Lance Johnson CHI........... 12
Mike Devereaux BAL......... 11
Brady Anderson BAL......... 10

HOME RUNS
Juan Gonzalez TEX 43
Mark McGwire OAK 42
Cecil Fielder DET 35

RUNS BATTED IN
Cecil Fielder DET 124
Joe Carter TOR 119
Frank Thomas CHI 115

SLUGGING AVERAGE
Mark McGwire OAK .... .585
Edgar Martinez SEA .... .544
Frank Thomas CHI .... .536

STOLEN BASES
Kenny Lofton CLE 66
Pat Listach MIL.................. 54
Brady Anderson BAL......... 53

RUNS SCORED
Tony Phillips DET 114
Frank Thomas CHI 108
Roberto Alomar TOR 105

WINS
Kevin Brown TEX 21
Jack Morris TOR 21
Jack McDowell CHI 20

WINNING PERCENTAGE
Mike Mussina BAL .... .783
Jack Morris TOR .... .778
Juan Guzman TOR .... .762

EARNED RUN AVERAGE
Roger Clemens BOS........ 2.41
Kevin Appier KC 2.46
Mike Mussina BAL 2.54

STRIKEOUTS
Randy Johnson SEA 241
Melido Perez NY 218
Roger Clemens BOS......... 208

SAVES
Dennis Eckersley OAK 51
Rick Aguilera MIN 41
Jeff Montgomery KC 39

COMPLETE GAMES
Jack McDowell CHI 13
Roger Clemens BOS......... 11
Kevin Brown TEX 11

SHUTOUTS
Roger Clemens BOS......... 5
Mike Mussina BAL 4
Dave Fleming SEA 4

GAMES PITCHED
Kevin Rogers TEX 81
Duane Ward TOR 79
Steve Olin CLE 72

INNINGS PITCHED
Kevin Brown TEX 266
Bill Wegman MIL 262
Jack McDowell CHI 261

NATIONAL LEAGUE STANDINGS

1992 NL

EAST	W	L	PCT	GB	R	OR	BA	FA	ERA
PITTSBURGH	96	66	.593	—	693	595	.255	.984	3.35
MONTREAL	87	75	.537	9	648	581	.252	.980	3.25
ST. LOUIS	83	79	.512	13	631	604	.262	.985	3.38
CHICAGO	78	84	.481	18	593	624	.254	.982	3.39
NEW YORK	72	90	.444	24	599	653	.235	.981	3.66
PHILADELPHIA	70	92	.432	26	686	717	.253	.978	4.11

WEST	W	L	PCT	GB	R	OR	BA	FA	ERA
• ATLANTA	98	64	.605	—	682	569	.254	.982	3.14
CINCINNATI	90	72	.556	8	660	609	.260	.984	3.46
SAN DIEGO	82	80	.506	16	617	636	.255	.982	3.56
HOUSTON	81	81	.500	17	608	668	.246	.981	3.72
SAN FRANCISCO	72	90	.444	26	574	647	.244	.982	3.61
LOS ANGELES	63	99	.389	35	548	636	.248	.972	3.41
					7539	7539	.252	.981	3.50

BATTING AVERAGE
Gary Sheffield SD .... .330
Andy Van Slyke PIT .... .324
John Kruk PHI .... .323

HITS
Terry Pendleton ATL 199
Andy Van Slyke PIT 199
Ryne Sandberg CHI 186

DOUBLES
Andy Van Slyke PIT 45
three tied at 40

TRIPLES
Deion Sanders ATL 14
Steve Finley HOU 13
Andy Van Slyke PIT 12

HOME RUNS
Fred McGriff SD 35
Barry Bonds PIT 34
Gary Sheffield SD 33

RUNS BATTED IN
Darren Daulton PHI 109
Terry Pendleton ATL 105
Fred McGriff SD 104

SLUGGING AVERAGE
Barry Bonds PIT .... .624
Gary Sheffield SD .... .580
Fred McGriff SD .... .556

STOLEN BASES
Marquis Grissom MON 78
Delino DeShields MON 46
two tied at 44

RUNS SCORED
Barry Bonds PIT 109
Dave Hollins PHI 104
Andy Van Slyke PIT 103

WINS
Greg Maddux CHI 20
Tom Glavine ATL 20
four tied at 16

WINNING PERCENTAGE
Bob Tewksbury STL .... .762
Tom Glavine ATL .... .714
Charlie Liebrandt ATL ...... .682

EARNED RUN AVERAGE
Bill Swift SF 2.08
Bob Tewksbury STL 2.16
Greg Maddux CHI 2.18

STRIKEOUTS
John Smoltz ATL 215
David Cone NY 214
Greg Maddux CHI 199

SAVES
Lee Smith STL 43
Randy Myers SD 38
John Wetteland MON 37

COMPLETE GAMES
Terry Mulholland PHI 12
Doug Drabek PIT 10
Curt Schilling PHI 10

SHUTOUTS
David Cone NY 5
Tom Glavine ATL 5

GAMES PITCHED
Joe Boever HOU 81
Doug Jones HOU 80
two tied at 77

INNINGS PITCHED
Greg Maddux CHI 268
Doug Drabek PIT 257
John Smoltz ATL 247

665

AMERICAN LEAGUE STANDINGS

1993 AL

EAST	W	L	PCT	GB	R	OR	BA	FA	ERA
★ TORONTO	95	67	.586	—	847	742	.279	.982	4.21
NEW YORK	88	74	.543	7	821	761	.279	.983	4.35
BALTIMORE	85	77	.525	10	786	745	.267	.984	4.31
DETROIT	85	77	.525	10	899	837	.275	.979	4.65
BOSTON	80	82	.494	15	686	698	.264	.980	3.77
CLEVELAND	76	86	.469	19	790	813	.275	.976	4.58
MILWAUKEE	69	93	.426	26	733	792	.258	.979	4.45

WEST	W	L	PCT	GB	R	OR	BA	FA	ERA
CHICAGO	94	68	.580	—	776	664	.265	.982	3.70
TEXAS	86	76	.531	8	835	751	.267	.979	4.28
KANSAS CITY	84	78	.519	10	675	694	.263	.984	4.04
SEATTLE	82	80	.506	12	734	731	.260	.985	4.20
CALIFORNIA	71	91	.438	23	684	770	.260	.980	4.34
MINNESOTA	71	91	.438	23	693	830	.264	.984	4.71
OAKLAND	68	94	.420	26	715	846	.254	.982	4.90
					10674	10674	.267	.981	4.32

BATTING AVERAGE
John Olerud TOR .... .363
Paul Molitor TOR .... .332
Roberto Alomar TOR ...... .326

HITS
Paul Molitor TOR 211
Carlos Baerga CLE 200
John Olerud TOR 200

DOUBLES
John Olerud TOR 54
Devon White TOR 42
two tied at 40

TRIPLES
Lance Johnson CHI 14
Joey Cora CHI 13
David Hulse TEX 10

HOME RUNS
Juan Gonzalez TEX 46
Ken Griffey SEA 45
Frank Thomas CHI 41

RUNS BATTED IN
Albert Belle CLE 129
Frank Thomas CHI 128
Joe Carter TOR 121

SLUGGING AVERAGE
Juan Gonzalez TEX .... .632
Ken Griffey SEA .... .617
Frank Thomas CHI .... .607

STOLEN BASES
Kenny Lofton CLE 70
Roberto Alomar TOR 55
Luis Polonia CAL 55

RUNS SCORED
Rafael Palmeiro TEX 124
Paul Molitor TOR 121
two tied at 116

WINS
Jack McDowell CHI 22
Randy Johnson SEA 19
Pat Hentgen TOR 19

WINNING PERCENTAGE
Jimmy Key NY .... .750
Randy Johnson SEA .... .704
Kevin Appier KC .... .692

EARNED RUN AVERAGE
Kevin Appier KC 2.56
Wilson Alvarez CHI 2.95
Jimmy Key NY 3.00

STRIKEOUTS
Randy Johnson SEA 308
Mark Langston CAL 196
Juan Guzman TOR 194

SAVES
Jeff Montgomery KC 45
Duane Ward TOR 45
Tom Henke TEX 40

COMPLETE GAMES
Chuck Finley CAL 13
Kevin Brown TEX 12
two tied at 10

SHUTOUTS
Jack McDowell CHI 4
three tied at 3

GAMES PITCHED
Greg Harris BOS 80
Scott Radinsky CHI 73
three tied at 71

INNINGS PITCHED
Cal Eldred MIL 258
Jack McDowell CHI 257
Mark Langston CAL 256

666

NATIONAL LEAGUE STANDINGS

1993 NL

EAST	W	L	PCT	GB	R	OR	BA	FA	ERA
• PHILADELPHIA	97	65	.599	—	877	740	.274	.977	3.95
MONTREAL	94	68	.580	3	732	682	.257	.975	3.55
ST. LOUIS	87	75	.537	10	758	744	.272	.982	4.09
CHICAGO	84	78	.519	13	738	739	.270	.982	4.18
PITTSBURGH	75	87	.463	22	707	806	.267	.983	4.77
FLORIDA	64	98	.395	33	581	724	.248	.980	4.13
NEW YORK	59	103	.364	38	672	744	.248	.975	4.05

WEST	W	L	PCT	GB	R	OR	BA	FA	ERA
ATLANTA	104	58	.642	—	767	599	.262	.983	3.14
SAN FRANCISCO	103	59	.636	1	808	636	.276	.984	3.61
HOUSTON	85	77	.525	19	716	630	.267	.979	3.49
LOS ANGELES	81	81	.500	23	675	662	.261	.979	3.50
CINCINNATI	73	89	.451	31	722	785	.264	.980	4.51
COLORADO	67	95	.414	37	758	927	.273	.973	5.41
SAN DIEGO	61	101	.377	43	679	772	.252	.974	4.23
					10190	10190	.264	.978	4.04

BATTING AVERAGE
Andres Galarraga COL ... .370
Tony Gwynn SD .... .358
Gregg Jefferies STL .... .342

HITS
Lenny Dykstra PHI 194
Mark Grace CHI 193
Marquis Grissom MON..... 188

DOUBLES
Charlie Hayes COL 45
Lenny Dykstra PHI 44
Dante Bichette COL 43

TRIPLES
Steve Finley HOU 13
Brett Butler LA 10
two tied at 9

HOME RUNS
Barry Bonds SF 46
David Justice ATL 40
Matt Williams SF 38

RUNS BATTED IN
Barry Bonds SF 123
David Justice ATL............ 120
Ron Gant ATL................. 117

SLUGGING AVERAGE
Barry Bonds SF............... .677
Andres Galarraga COL ... .602
Matt Williams SF .... .561

STOLEN BASES
Chuck Carr FLA 58
Marquis Grissom MON...... 53
Otis Nixon ATL 47

RUNS SCORED
Lenny Dykstra PHI 143
Barry Bonds SF 129
Ron Gant ATL.................. 113

WINS
Tom Glavine ATL 22
John Burkett SF 22
Billy Swift SF 21

WINNING PERCENTAGE
Mark Portugal HOU......... .818
Tommy Greene PHI........ .800
Tom Glavine ATL .... .786

EARNED RUN AVERAGE
Greg Maddux ATL 2.36
Jose Rijo CIN 2.48
Mark Portugal HOU......... 2.77

STRIKEOUTS
Jose Rijo CIN 227
John Smoltz ATL 208
Greg Maddux ATL 197

SAVES
Randy Myers CHI 53
Rod Beck SF 48
Bryan Harvey FLA 45

COMPLETE GAMES
Greg Maddux ATL 8
five tied at 7

SHUTOUTS
Pete Harnisch HOU 4
Ramon Martinez LA 3

GAMES PITCHED
Mike Jackson SF 81
Rod Beck SF 76
David West PHI 76

INNINGS PITCHED
Greg Maddux ATL 267
Jose Rijo CIN 257
John Smoltz ATL 244

AMERICAN LEAGUE STANDINGS

1994 AL

EAST	W	L	PCT	GB	R	OR	BA	FA	ERA
NEW YORK	70	43	.619	—	670	534	.290	.982	4.34
BALTIMORE	63	49	.563	6.5	589	497	.272	.986	4.31
TORONTO	55	60	.478	16	566	579	.269	.981	4.70
BOSTON	54	61	.470	17	552	621	.263	.981	4.93
DETROIT	53	62	.465	18	652	671	.265	.981	5.38

CENTRAL	W	L	PCT	GB	R	OR	BA	FA	ERA
CHICAGO	67	46	.593	—	633	498	.287	.981	3.96
CLEVELAND	66	47	.584	1	679	562	.290	.980	4.36
KANSAS CITY	64	51	.557	4	574	532	.269	.982	4.23
MINNESOTA	53	60	.469	14	594	688	.276	.982	5.68
MILWAUKEE	53	62	.461	15	547	586	.263	.981	4.62

WEST	W	L	PCT	GB	R	OR	BA	FA	ERA
TEXAS	52	62	.456	—	613	697	.280	.976	5.45
OAKLAND	51	63	.447	1	549	589	.260	.979	4.80
SEATTLE	49	63	.438	2	569	616	.269	.977	4.99
CALIFORNIA	47	68	.409	5.5	543	660	.264	.983	5.42
					8330	8330	.273	.981	4.80

BATTING AVERAGE
Paul O'Neill NY .... .359
Albert Belle CLE .... .357
Frank Thomas CHI .... .353

HITS
Kenny Lofton CLE 160
Paul Molitor TOR 155
Albert Belle CLE 147

DOUBLES
Chuck Knoblauch MIN 45
Albert Belle CLE 35
two tied at 34

TRIPLES
Lance Johnson CHI 14
Vince Coleman KC 12
Kenny Lofton CLE 9

HOME RUNS
Ken Griffey Jr. SEA 40
Frank Thomas CHI 38
Albert Belle CLE 36

RUNS BATTED IN
Kirby Puckett MIN 112
Joe Carter TOR 103
two tied at 101

SLUGGING AVERAGE
Frank Thomas CHI .... .729
Albert Belle CLE .... .714
Ken Griffey Jr. SEA .... .674

STOLEN BASES
Kenny Lofton CLE 60
Vince Coleman KC 50
Otis Nixon BOS 42

RUNS SCORED
Frank Thomas CHI 106
Kenny Lofton CLE 105
Ken Griffey Jr. SEA 94

WINS
Jimmy Key NY 17
David Cone KC 16
Mike Mussina BAL 16

WINNING PERCENTAGE
Jason Bere CHI .... .857
Jimmy Key NY .... .810
Mark Clark CLE .... .786

EARNED RUN AVERAGE
Steve Ontiveros OAK 2.65
Roger Clemens BOS 2.85
David Cone KC 2.94

STRIKEOUTS
Randy Johnson SEA 204
Roger Clemens BOS 168
Chuck Finley CAL 148

SAVES
Lee Smith BAL 33
Jeff Montgomery KC 27
Rick Aguilera MIN 23

COMPLETE GAMES
Randy Johnson SEA 9
Chuck Finley CAL 7
Dennis Martinez CLE 7

SHUTOUTS
Randy Johnson SEA 4
five tied at 3

GAMES PITCHED
Bob Wickman NY 53
Jose Mesa CLE 51
two tied at 50

INNINGS PITCHED
Chuck Finley CAL 183
Jack McDowell CHI 181
Cal Eldred MIL 179

NATIONAL LEAGUE STANDINGS

1994 NL

EAST	W	L	PCT	GB	R	OR	BA	FA	ERA
MONTREAL	74	40	.649	—	585	454	.278	.979	3.56
ATLANTA	68	46	.596	6	542	448	.267	.982	3.57
NEW YORK	55	58	.487	18.5	506	526	.250	.980	4.13
PHILADELPHIA	54	61	.470	20.5	521	497	.262	.978	3.85
FLORIDA	51	64	.443	23.5	468	576	.266	.978	4.50

CENTRAL	W	L	PCT	GB	R	OR	BA	FA	ERA
CINCINNATI	66	48	.579	—	609	490	.286	.983	3.78
HOUSTON	66	49	.574	.5	602	503	.278	.983	3.97
PITTSBURGH	53	61	.465	13	466	580	.259	.980	4.64
ST. LOUIS	53	61	.465	13	535	621	.263	.982	5.14
CHICAGO	49	64	.434	16.5	500	549	.259	.982	4.47

WEST	W	L	PCT	GB	R	OR	BA	FA	ERA
LOS ANGELES	58	56	.509	—	532	509	.270	.980	4.17
SAN FRANCISCO	55	60	.478	3.5	504	500	.249	.985	3.99
COLORADO	53	64	.453	6.5	573	638	.274	.981	5.15
SAN DIEGO	47	70	.402	12.5	479	531	.275	.975	4.08
					7422	7422	.267	.980	4.21

BATTING AVERAGE
Tony Gwynn SD .... .394
Jeff Bagwell HOU .... .367
Moises Alou MON .... .339

HITS
Tony Gwynn SD 165
Jeff Bagwell HOU 147
Dante Bichette COL 147

DOUBLES
Craig Biggio HOU 44
Larry Walker MON 44
two tied at 35

TRIPLES
Darren Lewis SF 9
Brett Butler LA 9
three tied at 8

HOME RUNS
Matt Williams SF 43
Jeff Bagwell HOU 39
Barry Bonds SF 37

RUNS BATTED IN
Jeff Bagwell HOU 116
Matt Williams SF 96
Dante Bichette COL 95

SLUGGING AVERAGE
Jeff Bagwell HOU .... .750
Kevin Mitchell CIN .... .681
Barry Bonds SF .... .647

STOLEN BASES
Craig Biggio HOU 39
Deion Sanders ATL, CIN 38
Marquis Grissom MON 36

RUNS SCORED
Jeff Bagwell HOU 104
Marquis Grissom MON 96
two tied at 89

WINS
Ken Hill MON 16
Greg Maddux ATL 16
two tied at 14

WINNING PERCENTAGE
Marvin Freeman COL .... .833
Bret Saberhagen NY .... .778
Ken Hill MON .... .762

EARNED RUN AVERAGE
Greg Maddux ATL 1.56
Bret Saberhagen NY 2.74
Doug Drabek HOU 2.84

STRIKEOUTS
Andy Benes SD 189
Jose Rijo CIN 171
Greg Maddux ATL 156

SAVES
John Franco NY 30
Rod Beck SF 28
Doug Jones PHI 27

COMPLETE GAMES
Greg Maddux ATL 10
Doug Drabek HOU 6
Tom Candiotti LA 5

SHUTOUTS
Ramon Martinez LA 3
Greg Maddux ATL 3
two tied at 2

GAMES PITCHED
Steve Reed COL 61
Mel Rojas MON 58
Jose Bautista CHI 58

INNINGS PITCHED
Greg Maddux ATL 202
Danny Jackson PHI 179
Bret Saberhagen NY 177

AMERICAN LEAGUE STANDINGS

1995 AL

EAST	W	L	PCT	GB	R	OR	BA	FA	ERA
BOSTON	86	58	.597	—	791	698	.280	.978	4.39
NEW YORK	79	65	.549	7	749	688	.276	.986	4.56
BALTIMORE	71	73	.493	15	704	640	.262	.986	4.31
DETROIT	60	84	.417	26	654	844	.247	.981	5.49
TORONTO	56	88	.389	30	642	777	.260	.982	4.88

CENTRAL	W	L	PCT	GB	R	OR	BA	FA	ERA
• CLEVELAND	100	44	.694	—	840	607	.291	.982	3.83
KANSAS CITY	70	74	.486	30	629	691	.260	.984	4.49
CHICAGO	68	76	.472	32	755	758	.280	.980	4.85
MILWAUKEE	65	79	.451	35	740	747	.266	.981	4.82
MINNESOTA	56	88	.389	44	703	889	.279	.981	5.76

WEST	W	L	PCT	GB	R	OR	BA	FA	ERA
SEATTLE*	79	66	.545	—	796	708	.276	.980	4.50
CALIFORNIA	78	67	.538	1	801	697	.277	.982	4.52
TEXAS	74	70	.514	4.5	691	720	.265	.982	4.66
OAKLAND	67	77	.465	11.5	730	761	.264	.981	4.93
					10225	10225	.270	.982	4.71

*Defeated California in a 1-game playoff

TING AVERAGE
Edgar Martinez SEA .356
Chuck Knoblauch MIN .333
Tim Salmon CAL .330

HITS
Lance Johnson CHI 186
Edgar Martinez SEA 182
Chuck Knoblauch MIN 179

DOUBLES
Albert Belle CLE 52
Edgar Martinez SEA 52
Kirby Puckett MIN 39

TRIPLES
Kenny Lofton CLE 13
Lance Johnson CHI 12
Brady Anderson BAL 10

HOME RUNS
Albert Belle CLE 50
Jay Buhner SEA 40
Frank Thomas CHI 40

RUNS BATTED IN
Albert Belle CLE 126
Mo Vaughn BOS 126
Jay Buhner SEA 121

SLUGGING AVERAGE
Albert Belle CLE .690
Edgar Martinez SEA .628
Frank Thomas CHI .606

STOLEN BASES
Kenny Lofton CLE 54
Tom Goodwin KC 50
Otis Nixon TEX 50

RUNS SCORED
Albert Belle CLE 121
Edgar Martinez SEA 121
Jim Edmonds CAL 120

WINS
Mike Mussina BAL 19
David Cone TOR, NY 18
Randy Johnson SEA 18

WINNING PERCENTAGE
Randy Johnson SEA .900
Erik Hanson BOS .737
two tied at .727

EARNED RUN AVERAGE
Randy Johnson SEA 2.48
Tim Wakefield BOS 2.95
Dennis Martinez CLE 3.08

STRIKEOUTS
Randy Johnson SEA 294
Todd Stottlemyre OAK 205
Chuck Finley CAL 195

SAVES
Jose Mesa CLE 46
Lee Smith CAL 37
two tied at 32

COMPLETE GAMES
Jack McDowell NY 8
Scott Erickson MIN, BAL 7
Mike Mussina BAL 7

SHUTOUTS
Mike Mussina BAL 4
Randy Johnson SEA 3
six tied at 2

GAMES PITCHED
Jesse Orosco BAL 65
Roger McDowell TEX 64
three tied at 63

INNINGS PITCHED
David Cone TOR, NY 229
Mike Mussina BAL 222
Jack McDowell NY 218

NATIONAL LEAGUE STANDINGS

1995 NL

EAST	W	L	PCT	GB	R	OR	BA	FA	ERA
★ ATLANTA	90	54	.625	—	645	540	.250	.982	3.44
NEW YORK	69	75	.479	21	657	618	.267	.979	3.88
PHILADELPHIA	69	75	.479	21	615	658	.262	.982	4.21
FLORIDA	67	76	.469	22.5	673	673	.262	.979	4.27
MONTREAL	66	78	.458	24	621	638	.259	.980	4.11

CENTRAL	W	L	PCT	GB	R	OR	BA	FA	ERA
CINCINNATI	85	59	.590	—	747	623	.270	.986	4.03
HOUSTON	76	68	.528	9	747	674	.275	.979	4.06
CHICAGO	73	71	.507	12	693	671	.265	.979	4.13
ST. LOUIS	62	81	.434	22.5	563	658	.247	.980	4.09
PITTSBURGH	58	86	.403	27	629	736	.259	.978	4.70

WEST	W	L	PCT	GB	R	OR	BA	FA	ERA
LOS ANGELES	78	66	.542	—	634	609	.264	.976	3.66
COLORADO	77	67	.535	1	785	783	.282	.981	4.97
SAN DIEGO	70	74	.486	8	668	672	.272	.980	4.13
SAN FRANCISCO	67	77	.465	11	652	776	.253	.980	4.86
					9329	9329	.263	.980	4.18

BATTING AVERAGE
Tony Gwynn SD .... .368
Mike Piazza LA .... .346
Dante Bichette COL .... .340

HITS
Dante Bichette COL 197
Tony Gwynn SD 197
Mark Grace CHI 180

DOUBLES
Mark Grace CHI 51
Dante Bichette COL 38
Brian McRae CHI 38

TRIPLES
Brett Butler NY, LA 9
Eric Young COL 9
three tied at 8

HOME RUNS
Dante Bichette COL 40
Sammy Sosa CHI 36
Larry Walker COL 36

RUNS BATTED IN
Dante Bichette COL 128
Sammy Sosa CHI 119
Andres Galarraga COL 106

SLUGGING AVERAGE
Dante Bichette COL .... .620
Larry Walker COL .... .607
Mike Piazza LA .... .606

STOLEN BASES
Quilvio Veras FLA 56
Barry Larkin CIN 51
Delino DeShields LA 39

RUNS SCORED
Craig Biggio HOU 123
Barry Bonds SF 109
Steve Finley SD 104

WINS
Greg Maddux ATL 19
Pete Schourek CIN 18
Ramon Martinez LA 17

WINNING PERCENTAGE
Greg Maddux ATL .... .905
Pete Schourek CIN .... .720
Ramon Martinez LA .... .708

EARNED RUN AVERAGE
Greg Maddux ATL 1.63
Hideo Nomo LA 2.54
Andy Ashby SD 2.94

STRIKEOUTS
Hideo Nomo LA 236
John Smoltz ATL 193
Greg Maddux ATL 181

SAVES
Randy Myers CHI 38
Tom Henke STL 36
Rod Beck SF 33

COMPLETE GAMES
Greg Maddux ATL 10
Mark Leiter SF 7
Ismael Valdes LA 6

SHUTOUTS
Greg Maddux ATL 3
Hideo Nomo LA 3

GAMES PITCHED
Curt Leskanic COL 76
David Veres HOU 72
Steve Reed COL 71

INNINGS PITCHED
Greg Maddux ATL 210
Denny Neagle PIT 210
Ramon Martinez LA 206

1995 AWARDS

AL MOST VALUABLE PLAYER VOTING

PLAYER	1st	2nd	3rd	Tot
Mo Vaughn BOS	12	12	4	308
Albert Belle CLE	11	10	7	300
Edgar Martinez SEA	4	5	12	244
Jose Mesa CLE	1	-	1	130
Jay Buhner SEA	-	-	1	120
Randy Johnson SEA	-	1	2	111
Tim Salmon CAL	-	-	-	110
Frank Thomas CHI	-	-	-	86
John Valentin BOS	-	-	-	57
Gary Gaetti KC	-	-	-	45
Rafael Palmeiro BAL	-	-	-	34
Manny Ramirez CLE	-	-	-	30
Tim Wakefield BOS	-	-	-	20
Jim Edmonds CAL	-	-	-	18
Paul O'Neill NY	-	-	-	14
Mark McGwire OAK	-	-	-	7
Chuck Knoblauch MIN	-	-	-	5
Wade Boggs NY	-	-	-	5
Gary DiSarcina CAL	-	-	-	3
Cal Ripken BAL	-	-	-	3
Kirby Puckett MIN	-	-	-	2

AL CY YOUNG AWARD VOTING

PLAYER	1st	2nd	3rd	Tot
Randy Johnson SEA	26	2	-	136
Jose Mesa CLE	2	13	5	54
Tim Wakefield BOS	-	6	11	29
David Cone TOR, NY	-	5	3	18
Mike Mussina BAL	-	2	8	14
Charles Nagy CLE	-	-	1	1

AL ROOKIE OF THE YEAR VOTING

PLAYER	1st	2nd	3rd	Tot
Marty Cordova MIN	13	13	1	105
Garret Anderson CAL	13	10	4	99
Andy Pettitte NY	1	1	8	16
Troy Percival CAL	1	2	2	13
Shawn Green TOR	-	2	2	8
Ray Durham CHI	-	-	3	3
Julian Tavarez CLE	-	-	3	3
John Nunnally KC	-	-	2	2
Tom Goodwin KC	-	-	1	1
Brad Radke MIN	-	-	1	1
Steve Sparks MIL	-	-	1	1

NL MOST VALUABLE PLAYER VOTING

PLAYER	1st	2nd	3rd	Tot
Barry Larkin CIN	11	5	7	281
Dante Bichette COL	6	6	6	251
Greg Maddux ATL	7	8	5	249
Mike Piazza LA	3	7	6	214
Eric Karros LA	-	2	3	135
Reggie Sanders CIN	-	-	-	120
Larry Walker COL	-	-	1	88
Sammy Sosa CHI	-	-	-	81
Tony Gwynn SD	-	-	-	72
Craig Biggio HOU	-	-	-	58
Ron Gant CIN	-	-	-	31
Barry Bonds SF	-	-	-	21
Mark Grace CHI	-	-	-	14
Derek Bell HOU	-	-	-	12
Jeff Bagwell HOU	-	-	-	5
Charlie Hayes PHI	-	-	-	4
Andres Galarraga COL	-	-	-	4
Chipper Jones ATL	-	-	-	3
Vinny Castilla COL	-	-	-	3
Fred McGriff ATL	-	-	-	2
Pete Schourek CIN	-	-	-	2
Jeff Conine FLA	-	-	-	1
Tom Henke STL	-	-	-	1

NL CY YOUNG AWARD VOTING

PLAYER	1st	2nd	3rd	Tot
Greg Maddux ATL	28	-	-	140
Pete Schourek CIN	-	16	7	55
Tom Glavine ATL	-	6	12	30
Hideo Nomo LA	-	5	4	19
Ramon Martinez LA	-	1	5	8

NL ROOKIE OF THE YEAR VOTING

PLAYER	1st	2nd	3rd	Tot
Hideo Nomo LA	18	9	1	118
Chipper Jones ATL	10	18	-	104
Quilvio Veras FLA	-	1	11	14
Jason Isringhausen NY	-	-	4	4
John Mabry STL	-	-	4	4
Carlos Perez MON	-	-	4	4
Chad Fonville LA	-	-	1	1
Brian Hunter HOU	-	-	1	1
Charles Johnson FLA	-	-	1	1
Ismael Valdes LA	-	-	1	1